W9-CCM-739

ENCYCLOPEDIA OF **ADOLESCENCE**

Volume 1

Normative Processes in Development

ENCYCLOPEDIA OF ADOLESCENCE

EDITORS-IN-CHIEF

B. BRADFORD BROWN

University of Wisconsin-Madison

Madison, WI

USA

MITCHELL J. PRINSTEIN

University of North Carolina at Chapel Hill

Chapel Hill, NC

USA

VOLUME 1

NORMATIVE PROCESSES IN DEVELOPMENT

ELSEVIER

AMSTERDAM BOSTON HEIDELBERG LONDON NEW YORK OXFORD
PARIS SAN DIEGO SAN FRANCISCO SINGAPORE SYDNEY TOKYO
Academic Press is an imprint of Elsevier

ACADEMIC PRESS

Academic Press is an imprint of Elsevier
32 Jamestown Road, London NW1 7BY, UK
225 Wyman Street, Waltham, MA 02451, USA
525 B Street, Suite 1900, San Diego, CA 92101-4495, USA

British Library Cataloguing in Publication Data
A catalogue record for this book is available from the British Library

Library of Congress Catalog Number: 2011924972

ISBN (print): 978-0-12-373915-5

For information on all Elsevier publications
visit our website at books.elsevier.com

Printed and bound in Italy

11 10 9 8 7 6 5 4 3 2 1

Editorial: Sera Relton, Jason Mitchell, Joanne Collett
Production: Mike Nicholls

EDITOR BIOGRAPHIES

Dr B. Bradford Brown is Professor of Human Development and former Chair of the Department of Educational Psychology at the University of Wisconsin-Madison. He received an A.B. in sociology from Princeton University and a PhD in human development from the University of Chicago before joining the faculty of the University of Wisconsin in 1979. Dr Brown's research has focused on adolescent peer relations. He is especially well known for his work on teenage peer groups and peer pressure and their influence on school achievement, social interaction patterns, and social adjustment. He is the former Editor of the *Journal of Research on Adolescence* and a past member of the Executive Council of the Society for Research on Adolescence. He also chaired (2006–08) the SRA Study Group on Parental Involvement in Adolescent Peer Relations. He is the co-editor or co-author of 5 books, including *The Development of Romantic Relationships in Adolescence* (with Wyndol Furman and Candice Feiring), *The World's Youth: Adolescence in 8 Regions of the Globe* (with Reed Larson and T.S. Saraswathi), and *Linking Parents and Family to Adolescent Peer Relations: Ethnic and Cultural Considerations* (with Nina Mounts). Dr Brown has served as a consultant for numerous groups, including the Carnegie Council on Adolescent Development, the National Campaign to Prevent Teen Pregnancy, the National Academy of Sciences Board on Science Education as well as the Board on Children, Youth and Families, and the Blue Ribbons Schools program of the U.S. Department of Education.

Mitchell J. Prinstein, PhD is a Bowman and Gordon Gray Distinguished Term Professor and the Director of Clinical Psychology at the University of North Carolina at Chapel Hill. He received his PhD in clinical psychology from the University of Miami and completed his internship and postdoctoral fellowship at the Brown University Clinical Psychology Training Consortium. Professor Prinstein's research examines interpersonal models of internalizing symptoms and health risk behaviors among adolescents, with a specific focus on the unique role of peer relationships in the developmental psychopathology of depression and self-injury. He is the PI on several past and active grants from the National Institute of Mental Health, the National Institute of Child and Human Development, and several private foundations. He has served as an Associate Editor for the *Journal of Consulting and Clinical Psychology*, an editorial board member for several developmental psychopathology journals, and a member of the NIH Study Section on Psychosocial Development, Risk, and Prevention. Professor Prinstein has received several national and university-based awards recognizing his contributions to research (American Psychological Association Society of Clinical Psychology Theodore Blau Early Career Award, Columbia University/Brickell Award for research on suicidality, APA Fellow of the Society of Clinical Child and Adolescent Psychology), teaching (UNC Chapel Hill Tanner Award for Undergraduate Teaching), and professional development of graduate students (American Psychological Association of Graduate Students Raymond D. Fowler Award).

EDITORIAL ADVISORY BOARD

CONTRIBUTORS

B Amani
University of California, Los Angeles, CA, USA

S E A Anderson
Tufts University, Medford, MA, USA

K M Antshel
SUNY – Upstate Medical University, Syracuse, NY, USA

E Applegate
University of California, Los Angeles, CA, USA

S Arel
University of Michigan, Ann Arbor, MI, USA

E M Arnold
Wake Forest University School of Medicine, Winston-Salem, NC, USA

S R Asher
Duke University, Durham, NC, USA

S B Avny
Virginia Commonwealth University, Richmond, VA, USA

R A Barkley
Medical University of South Carolina, Charleston, SC, USA

S M Bascoe
University of Rochester, Rochester, NY, USA

C Beam
University of Virginia, Charlottesville, VA, USA

R S Beidas
Temple University, Philadelphia, PA, USA

V W Berninger
University of Washington, Seattle, WA, USA

L S Blackwell
University of Miami, Coral Gables, FL, USA

P S Bobkowski
University of North Carolina at Chapel Hill, Chapel Hill, NC, USA

B Bogin
Loughborough University, Loughborough, Leicestershire, UK

M J Boyd
Tufts University, Medford, MA, USA

R H Bradley
Arizona State University, Tempe, AZ, USA

M Braun
University of Wisconsin-Madison, Madison, WI, USA

D A Brent
Western Psychiatric Institute and Clinic, Pittsburgh, PA, USA

E C Briggs
Duke University Medical Center, Durham, NC, USA

B B Brown
University of Wisconsin-Madison, Madison, WI, USA

J D Brown
University of North Carolina at Chapel Hill, Chapel Hill, NC, USA

R C Brown
Virginia Commonwealth University, Richmond, VA, USA

R T Brown
Wayne State University, Detroit, MI, USA

M C Buchmann
University of Zurich, Zurich, Switzerland

S Burg
Columbia University, New York, NY, USA

J P Byrnes
Temple University, Philadelphia, PA, USA

L L Caldwell
Penn State University, University Park, PA, USA

C M Callahan
University of Virginia, Charlottesville, VA, USA

S E Carter
University of North Carolina at Chapel Hill, Chapel Hill, NC, USA

C B Cha
Harvard University, Cambridge, MA, USA

J Chuang
Columbia University, New York, NY, USA

T Chung
University of Pittsburgh Medical Center, Pittsburgh, PA, USA

A H N Cillessen
Radboud University, Nijmegen, The Netherlands

C E Clardy
Fuller Theological Seminary, Pasadena, CA, USA

W A Collins
University of Minnesota, Minneapolis, MN, USA

K J Conger
University of California, Davis, CA, USA

J Connolly
York University, Toronto, ON, Canada

N A Constantine
Public Health Institute, Oakland, CA, USA; University of California, Berkeley, CA, USA

K S Cortina
University of Michigan, Ann Arbor, MI, USA

M J Cox
University of North Carolina, Chapel Hill, NC, USA

S A Crawley
Temple University, Philadelphia, PA, USA

L J Crockett
University of Nebraska-Lincoln, Lincoln, NE, USA

S J Crowley
Rush University Medical Center, Chicago, IL, USA

I Cruz
University of Miami, Coral Gables, FL, USA

E A Daniels
University of Oregon, Bend, OR, USA

J Darrah
University of Alberta, Edmonton, AB, Canada

P Dashora
The Ohio State University, Columbus, OH, USA

P T Davies
University of Rochester, Rochester, NY, USA

T E Davison
Deakin University, Melbourne, VIC, Australia

K Deater-Deckard
Virginia Polytechnic Institute and State University, Blacksburg, VA, USA

D DeLay
Florida Atlantic University, Boca Raton, FL, USA

M Delsing
Nijmegen, The Netherlands

J J A Denissen
Humboldt University, Berlin, Germany

L M Diamond
University of Utah, Salt Lake City, UT, USA

D M Dick
Virginia Commonwealth University, Richmond, VA, USA

M J Dietz
Concordia University-Wisconsin, Mequon, WI, USA

J K Dijkstra
University of Groningen, Groningen, The Netherlands

O Doyle
Duke University School of Medicine, Durham, NC, USA

D A G Drabick
Temple University, Philadelphia, PA, USA

S R Driscoll
Cornell University, Ithaca, NY, USA

E F Dubow
Bowling Green State University, Bowling Green, OH, USA

W H Ducat
Griffith University and Griffith Health Institute, Gold Coast, QLD, Australia

S N Duffy
DePaul University, Chicago, IL, USA

V Dupéré
Tufts University, Medford, MA, USA

A C Edwards
Virginia Commonwealth University, Richmond, VA, USA

H Eidelman
Harvard Graduate School of Education, Cambridge, MA, USA

N Eisenberg
Arizona State University, Tempe, AZ, USA

R E Emery
University of Virginia, Charlottesville, VA, USA

R C M E Engels
Radboud University, Nijmegen, The Netherlands

F-A Esbensen
University of Missouri-St. Louis, St. Louis, MO, USA

G Espinoza
UCLA, Los Angeles, CA, USA

C Esposito-Smythers
George Mason University, Fairfax, VA, USA

D A Fedele
Oklahoma State University, Stillwater, OK, USA

L L Fermin
The New York Foundling, New York, NY, USA

M H Fisher
University of Massachusetts Boston, Boston, MA, USA

C Flanagan
University of Wisconsin-Madison, Madison, WI, USA

M Flynn
Temple University, Philadelphia, PA, USA

M E Ford
George Mason University, Fairfax, VA, USA

R G Fortgang
Cornell University, Ithaca, NY, USA

V A Foshee
University of North Carolina at Chapel Hill, Chapel Hill, NC, USA

A J Freeman
University of North Carolina at Chapel Hill, Chapel Hill, NC, USA

N L Galambos
University of Alberta, Edmonton, AB, Canada

A L Gaskin
University of North Carolina at Chapel Hill, Chapel Hill, NC, USA

A N Gilbert
Duke University, Durham, NC, USA

E S Goldfarb
Montclair State University, Montclair, NJ, USA

D B Goldston
Duke University School of Medicine, Durham, NC, USA

A Gonzalez
San Diego State University/University of California, San Diego, CA, USA

K E Grant
DePaul University, Chicago, IL, USA

P Greenfield
UCLA, Los Angeles, CA, USA

M M Griffin
Vanderbilt University, Nashville, TN, USA

M Griffiths
Nottingham Trent University, Nottingham, UK

H C Gustafsson
University of North Carolina, Chapel Hill, NC, USA

M Habib
North Shore University Hospital, Manhasset, NY, USA

S Hales
Medical University of South Carolina, Charleston, SC, USA

C T Halpern
University of North Carolina at Chapel Hill, Chapel Hill, NC, USA

B L Halpern-Felsher
University of California, San Francisco, CA, USA

J L Hanson
University of Wisconsin at Madison, Madison, WI, USA

J Harper
University of Southern California, Los Angeles, CA, USA

R D Harris
University of Arizona, Tucson, AZ, USA

S Harter
University of Denver, Denver, CO, USA

C M Hartung
University of Wyoming, Laramie, WY, USA

M Hasselhorn
German Institute for International Educational Research, Frankfurt am Main, Germany

A Haydon
University of North Carolina at Chapel Hill, Chapel Hill, NC, USA

R Hayes
University of Nebraska-Lincoln, Lincoln, NE, USA

N Heilbron
Duke University Medical Center, Durham, NC, USA

S W Henggeler
Medical University of South Carolina, Charleston, SC, USA

L M Hilt
University of Wisconsin at Madison, Madison, WI, USA

A N Ho
University of Maryland, College Park, MD, USA

R M Hodapp
Vanderbilt University, Nashville, TN, USA

N L Holt
University of Alberta, Edmonton, AB, Canada

B J Houltberg
Indiana University–Purdue University, Fort Wayne, IN, USA

A L Howard
University of North Carolina, Chapel Hill, NC, USA

R Hutteman
Humboldt University, Berlin, Germany

K M Jackson
Brown University, Providence, RI, USA

D C Jones
University of Washington, Seattle, WA, USA

S M Jones
Harvard Graduate School of Education, Cambridge, MA, USA

K Kao
Arizona State University, Tempe, AZ, USA

D P Keating
University of Michigan, Ann Arbor, MI, USA

P C Kendall
Temple University, Philadelphia, PA, USA

P K Kerig
University of Utah, Salt Lake City, UT, USA

M K Kiely
Tufts University, Medford, MA, USA

J Kim
Virginia Polytechnic Institute and State University, Blacksburg, VA, USA

C I Kimberg
University of Miami, Coral Gables, FL, USA

P E King
Fuller Theological Seminary, Pasadena, CA, USA

D Kirby
ETR Associates, Scotts Valley, CA, USA

M Kleinjan
Radboud University, Nijmegen, The Netherlands

C J Knight
University of Alberta, Edmonton, AB, Canada

A Knoverek
Chaddock, Quincy, IL, USA

R Kobak
University of Delaware, Newark, DE, USA

B Kracke
University of Erfurt, Erfurt, Germany

L Kramer
University of Illinois, Urbana, IL, USA

C N Kyriakos
College of the Holy Cross, Worcester, MA, USA

V Labruna
North Shore University Hospital, Manhasset, NY, USA

A S Labuhn
German Institute for International Educational Research, Frankfurt am Main, Germany

J E Lansford
Duke University, Durham, NC, USA

T A M Lansu
Radboud University, Nijmegen, The Netherlands

M K Larson
Emory University, Atlanta, GA, USA

B Laursen
Florida Atlantic University, Boca Raton, FL, USA

C Leaper
University of California, Santa Cruz, CA, USA

D B Lee
University of North Carolina at Chapel Hill, Chapel Hill, NC, USA

E K Lefler
University of Northern Iowa, Cedar Falls, IA, USA

R M Lerner
Tufts University, Medford, MA, USA

C M Lescano
Bradley/Hasbro Children's Research Center, Providence, RI, USA

T Leventhal
Tufts University, Medford, MA, USA

T D Little
University of Kansas, Lawrence, KS, USA

S R Lowe
University of Massachusetts Boston, Boston, MA, USA

J B Maas
Cornell University, Ithaca, NY, USA

J P MacEvoy
Boston College, Chestnut Hill, MA, USA

S D Madsen
McDaniel College, Westminster, MD, USA

J Magill-Evans
University of Alberta, Edmonton, AB, Canada

J L Mahoney
University of California, Irvine, CA, USA

A Maier
Michigan State University, East Lansing, MI, USA

T Malti
University of Toronto Mississauga, Mississauga, ON, Canada

C A Markstrom
West Virginia University, Morgantown, WV, USA

M J Martin
University of Rochester, Rochester, NY, USA

A Mason-Singh
University of Maryland, College Park, MD, USA

R A Mayers
Columbia University, New York, NY, USA

L Mayeux
University of Oklahoma, Norman, OK, USA

M P McCabe
Deakin University, Melbourne, VIC, Australia

M R McCart
Medical University of South Carolina, Charleston, SC, USA

C J McIsaac
Centre for Addiction and Mental Health, Toronto, ON, Canada

D McKay
Fordham University, Bronx, NY, USA

B D McLeod
Virginia Commonwealth University, Richmond, VA, USA

S D McMahon
DePaul University, Chicago, IL, USA

A-L McRee
University of North Carolina at Chapel Hill, Chapel Hill, NC, USA

N M Melhem
Western Psychiatric Institute and Clinic, Pittsburgh, PA, USA

E Mezzacappa
Children's Hospital Boston, Boston, MA, USA

N G Milburn
University of California, Los Angeles, CA, USA

A Miller
George Mason University, Fairfax, VA, USA

B Miller
Eunice Kennedy Shriver *National Institute of Child Health and Human Development, Rockville, MD, USA*

L J Miller
Columbia University, New York, NY, USA

T C Missett
University of Virginia, Charlottesville, VA, USA

L Mufson
Columbia University College of Physicians and Surgeons, New York, NY, USA

G C Nagayama Hall
University of Oregon, Eugene, OR, USA

C M Napolitano
Tufts University, Medford, MA, USA

E W Neblett Jr
University of North Carolina at Chapel Hill, Chapel Hill, NC, USA

S Nelemans
Utrecht University, Utrecht, The Netherlands

M P Neuenschwander
University of Applied Sciences Northwestern Switzerland, Solothurn, Switzerland

B M Newman
University of Rhode Island, Kingston, RI, USA

P R Newman
Wakefield, RI, USA

F Neziroglu
Bio-Behavioral Institute, Great Neck, NY, USA

J Ng
University of Oregon, Eugene, OR, USA

R S Niaura
The Schroeder Institute for Tobacco Research and Policy Studies at LEGACY, Washington, DC, USA

P Noack
University of Jena, Jena, Germany

M K Nock
Harvard University, Cambridge, MA, USA

C Ochner
Columbia University College of Physicians and Surgeons, New York, NY, USA

R K Parrila
University of Alberta, Edmonton, AB, Canada

R Patton
The Ohio State University, Columbus, OH, USA

S Perren
University of Zurich, Zurich, Switzerland

D Peterson
University at Albany, Albany, NY, USA

K V Petrides
University College London (UCL), London, UK

T F Piehler
Hennepin County Medical Center, Minneapolis, MN, USA

E E Pinderhughes
Tufts University, Medford/Somerville, MA, USA

S D Pollak
University of Wisconsin at Madison, Madison, WI, USA

A Poorthuis
Utrecht University, Utrecht, The Netherlands

H A Priess
University of Wisconsin–Madison, Madison, WI, USA

C M Puleo
Temple University, Philadelphia, PA, USA

A M Quinoy
Virginia Commonwealth University, Richmond, VA, USA

A L Quittner
University of Miami, Coral Gables, FL, USA

B Reichow
Yale Child Study Center, New Haven, CT, USA

M D Resnick
University of Minnesota, Minneapolis, MN, USA

H L M Reyes
University of North Carolina at Chapel Hill, Chapel Hill, NC, USA

B Reynolds
The Ohio State University, Columbus, OH, USA

J E Rhodes
University of Massachusetts Boston, Boston, MA, USA

D Riser
Virginia Polytechnic Institute and State University, Blacksburg, VA, USA

R S Robbins
Cornell University, Ithaca, NY, USA

S L Romero
University of Miami, Coral Gables, FL, USA

W M Rote
University of Rochester, Rochester, NY, USA

M J Rotheram-Borus
University of California, Los Angeles, CA, USA

J Rowen
University of Virginia, Charlottesville, VA, USA

M Rubinlicht
Bowling Green State University, Bowling Green, OH, USA

K D Rudolph
University of Illinois, Champaign, IL, USA

S T Russell
University of Arizona, Tucson, AZ, USA

K Salmela-Aro
University of Helsinki, Helsinki, Finland

J Santelli
Columbia University, New York, NY, USA

R C Savin-Williams
Cornell University, Ithaca, NY, USA

K L Schmid
Tufts University, Medford, MA, USA

B Schneider
Michigan State University, East Lansing, MI, USA

W Schneider
University of Würzburg, Würzburg, Germany

D Schwartz
University of Southern California, Los Angeles, CA, USA

S E O Schwartz
University of Massachusetts Boston, Boston, MA, USA

E K Seaton
University of North Carolina at Chapel Hill, Chapel Hill, NC, USA

C A Settipani
Temple University, Philadelphia, PA, USA

D I Shapiro
Emory University, Atlanta, GA, USA

H Shaw
Oregon Research Institute, Eugene, OR, USA

A Sheffield Morris
Oklahoma State University, Tulsa, OK, USA

J Shibley Hyde
University of Wisconsin–Madison, Madison, WI, USA

S Shulman
Bar Ilan University, Ramat Gan, Israel

R K Silbereisen
University of Jena, Jena, Germany

B Simons-Morton
DESPR, NICHD, National Institutes of Health, Bethesda, MD, USA

M M Sinton
Washington University School of Medicine, Saint Louis, MO, USA

N Slesnick
The Ohio State University, Columbus, OH, USA

D Šmahel
Masaryk University, Brno, Czech Republic

J G Smetana
University of Rochester, Rochester, NY, USA

P R Smith
Madison Learning, Seattle, WA, USA

L Smolak
Kenyon College, Gambier, OH, USA

S Soitos
Utrecht University, Utrecht, The Netherlands

K Soren
Columbia University, New York, NY, USA

M A Southam-Gerow
Virginia Commonwealth University, Richmond, VA, USA

L P Spear
Binghamton University, Binghamton, NY, USA

H Stack-Cutler
University of Alberta, Edmonton, AB, Canada

L Steinberg
Temple University, Philadelphia, PA, USA

E Stice
Oregon Research Institute, Eugene, OR, USA

J R Stone III
University of Louisville, Louisville, KY, USA

K Subrahmanyam
California State University, Los Angeles, CA, USA

D Swendeman
University of California, Los Angeles, CA, USA

L A Taliaferro
University of Minnesota, Minneapolis, MN, USA

J J Taylor
DePaul University, Chicago, IL, USA

T Ter Bogt
Utrecht University, Utrecht, The Netherlands

S Thomaes
Utrecht University, Utrecht, The Netherlands

E M Thompson
University of Arizona, Tucson, AZ, USA

R Thompson
Juvenile Protective Association, Chicago, IL, USA

M Tolou-Shams
Bradley/Hasbro Children's Research Center, Providence, RI, USA

M J Tomasik
University of Jena, Jena, Germany

E Trejos-Castillo
Texas Tech University, Lubbock, TX, USA

Y T Uhls
UCLA, Los Angeles, CA, USA

L Unwin
University of London, London, UK

M A G van Aken
Utrecht University, Utrecht, The Netherlands

A Van Meter
University of North Carolina at Chapel Hill, Chapel Hill, NC, USA

A T Vazsonyi
Auburn University, Auburn, AL, USA

R Veenstra
University of Groningen, Groningen, The Netherlands

D L Vietze
City University of New York, NY, USA

A C Villanti
Johns Hopkins Bloomberg School of Public Health, Baltimore, MD, USA

F R Volkmar
Yale Child Study Center, New Haven, CT, USA

E F Walker
Emory University, Atlanta, GA, USA

F Wang
University of North Carolina, Chapel Hill, NC, USA

M S Weeks
Duke University, Durham, NC, USA

V R Weersing
San Diego State University/University of California, San Diego, CA, USA

J Weiser
The Ohio State University, Columbus, OH, USA

J Weismoore
George Mason University, Fairfax, VA, USA

L A Wiesner
Yale Child Study Center, New Haven, CT, USA

A Wigfield
University of Maryland, College Park, MD, USA

D E Wilfley
Washington University School of Medicine, Saint Louis, MO, USA

H Winetrobe
University of California, Los Angeles, CA, USA

A R Wolfson
College of the Holy Cross, Worcester, MA, USA

C M Worthman
Emory University, Atlanta, GA, USA

L Wray-Lake
Claremont Graduate University, Claremont, CA, USA

W Wu
University of Kansas, Lawrence, KS, USA

J F Young
Rutgers University, New Brunswick, NJ, USA

E A Youngstrom
University of North Carolina at Chapel Hill, Chapel Hill, NC, USA

M Yudron
Harvard Graduate School of Education, Cambridge, MA, USA

N Zarrett
University of South Carolina, Columbia, SC, USA

M J Zimmer-Gembeck
Griffith University and Griffith Health Institute, Gold Coast, QLD, Australia

GUIDE TO USING THE ENCYCLOPEDIA

Structure of the Encyclopedia

The material in the encyclopedia is arranged as a series of articles in alphabetical order within each volume.

There are three features to help you easily find the topic you're interested in: an alphabetical contents list, cross-references to other relevant articles within each article, and a full subject index.

1. Alphabetical Contents List

The alphabetical contents list, which appears at the front of each volume, lists the entries in the order that they appear in the encyclopedia. It includes both the volume number and the page number of each entry.

2. Cross-references

All of the entries in the encyclopedia have been cross-referenced. The cross-references, which appear at the end of an entry as a See also list, serve three different functions:

i. To draw the readers' attention to related material in other entries
ii. To indicate material that broadens and extends the scope of the article
iii. To indicate material that covers a topic in more depth

Example

The following list of cross-references appears at the end of the entry 'Autonomy, Development of'.

See also: Adolescence, Theories of; Adolescent Decision-Making; Civic and Political Engagement; Cultural Influences on Adolescent Development; Family Relationships; Leisure; Metacognition and Self-regulated Learning; Out-of-School Activities; Parent–Child Relationship; Socialization.

3. Index

The index includes page numbers for quick reference to the information you're looking for. The index entries differentiate between references to a whole entry, a part of an entry, and a table or figure.

4. Contributors

At the start of each volume there is list of the authors who contributed to the encyclopedia.

PREFACE

Thirty years ago a prominent U.S. scholar spoke to a large audience at a major conference on child development, bemoaning our severely limited knowledge about the critical years of development between childhood and adulthood. In the three decades since that meeting, scientific research on adolescence has progressed dramatically, to the point that our knowledge can easily fill the three volumes of this encyclopedia. Addressing 125 major issues of adolescent development and behavior, the *Encyclopedia of Adolescence* documents the diverse and complex routes that young people take on their way to adulthood.

Our understanding of adolescence has progressed through the efforts of scholars in several academic disciplines, including psychology, sociology, anthropology, medicine, biology and neurology, cognitive science, psychiatry, education, epidemiology, public health, and economics. Their work has revealed similarities and contrasts in the nature of adolescence in different cultures, nations, and historical eras. Accordingly, the individuals whom we asked to contribute articles to the encyclopedia represent a panoply of academic disciplines and hail from several continents and many different countries. They include many of the most prominent and accomplished scholars in their respective fields. Readers are provided with insights from seasoned scholars with high levels of expertise on the topic they are describing in their article.

Each article provides a thorough review of the latest research on its focal topic. Articles introduce readers to important empirical findings as well as theories and concepts that form the foundation for work on the topic. Authors present this material in a way that is accessible to individuals who do not already have an extensive background in the topic, so the articles serve as an excellent introduction for undergraduate and graduate students, or even advanced secondary school students. Seasoned scholars in other research domains will find the articles to be an informative starting point for understanding an issue outside of their normal area of research expertise. Each article includes a glossary to help readers who are unfamiliar with common terms or constructs used in research on a given topic. Authors also include a set of suggested readings to guide individuals who want to pursue a more extensive and sophisticated understanding of the topic.

Unlike most encyclopedias, which contain short articles on very specific topics, the *Encyclopedia of Adolescence* features longer articles that provide a more comprehensive overview/analysis of a major aspect of adolescence. This gives readers a more sophisticated understanding of key issues and helps them to recognize the connections among different components of adolescent development and behavior. These comprehensive articles each offer a thorough understanding of developmental theories, a review of recent empirical findings that inform our current understanding of adolescents today, and a clear agenda for the future of empirical study on adolescence. Each author also refers readers to other, related articles in the encyclopedia, to help capture themes and interrelated issues throughout these volumes.

Each article has been carefully reviewed by members of an Editorial Board that includes some of the most prominent scholars of adolescence across Europe and North America. Their comments and suggestions, along with reviews by the Editors-in-Chief, have ensured that the articles address all important aspects of their focal topics and provide readers with a clear understanding of the issues attendant to these topics. Editorial Board members also helped to ensure that articles were international in scope and attended to factors creating individual variability in adolescent behavior and development.

We have assembled these articles into three separate volumes, each covering a different major segment of research on adolescence. Volume 1 addresses issues related to normative processes in development. Articles consider characteristics of biological, cognitive, intellectual, psychological, spiritual, moral, and vocational development. The volume also features articles reviewing major theories of adolescence and the history of this stage of life, along with overviews of substages within adolescence and processes of transition into and out of this period in the life span. Volume 2 underscores the fact that adolescents are heavily influenced by the social contexts in which they live. Key interpersonal relationships, social groups, and social or cultural institutions form the focus of many articles in this volume. Other contributions concern social roles and cultural or societal conditions that guide individuals' passage through adolescence. Volume 3 recognizes the challenges to healthy development that many young people encounter during adolescence. Articles detail different psychological disorders and problem behaviors that young people may manifest, as well as medical conditions and maltreatment by others that can hamper healthy functioning. Modes of prevention and intervention also are included in this volume.

Within each volume, articles are arranged alphabetically. A comprehensive index across all three volumes allows readers to easily locate commentary on specific facets of adolescence within particular articles. Because every aspect of adolescence is affected by multiple factors there is some overlap in content among articles, but this has been minimized so that each article provides distinctive insights on the nature of development and behavior during this stage of life.

We would like to dedicate the encyclopedia to the memory of Dr Stuart Hauser, who initially served as Co-Editor-in-Chief (with Bradford Brown) through the early stages of this project, until his untimely death in 2009. Stuart's insightful research on several aspects of adolescence, along with his leadership in the scientific community, inspired several generations of researchers, many of whose work is represented in various articles in each volume. Without Stuart's efforts, it is unlikely that this project ever would have come to fruition. His work and his spirit live on in the insights that readers take away from the articles in these volumes.

We also appreciate the extensive contributions of Mr Jason Mitchell and Ms Sera Relton, who served successively as managing editors through various stages of the encyclopedia. Our outstanding Editorial Board guided the selection of topics and contributors, then carefully reviewed each article to ensure that it was a comprehensive but accessible summary of what scientists have learned about each aspect of adolescent development and behavior. Editorial Board members include: Mara Brendgen, Jeanne Brooks-Gunn, Marlis Buchmann, Laurie Chassin, W. Andrew Collins, Felton Earls, Daniel Keating, Jari-Erik Nurmi, Alice Schlegel, and Rainer Silbereisen.

Our work on the encyclopedia has been a truly collaborative venture. Although we follow convention in listing our names alphabetically, our contributions have been equal, with Dr Brown taking primary responsibility for Volume 1, Dr Prinstein for Volume 3, and oversight of articles in Volume 2 split evenly between us.

The word, adolescence, has Latin roots that mean "to grow into maturity." Our knowledge about adolescence, itself, continues to mature. We hope that the information in these volumes will inspire readers to make their own contributions to our understanding of this stage of life or will help them to assist young people in making a healthy and successful journey into adulthood.

B. Bradford Brown
Mitchell J. Prinstein
Co-Editors-in-Chief

CONTENTS

VOLUME 3: PSYCHOPATHOLOGY AND NON-NORMATIVE PROCESSES

Academic Achievement

J P Byrnes, Temple University, Philadelphia, PA, USA

Glossary

Assessment: The use of tests and other forms of measurement to determine the extent of some trait or ability in an individual or groups of individuals.

Attentional control: The ability to intentionally focus and sustain one's attention on something (e.g., what one is reading).

Emergent literacy: The progressive attainment of precursor skills to reading such as the ability to hear sounds that two words have in common (e.g., rhymes) or know that text is read in a particular direction (e.g., left to right).

Meta-analysis: A kind of review article in which an author: (a) locates a number of studies, (b) computes effect sizes for group differences for each study, and (c) determines the average effect size across all studies.

Metacognition: The aspect of the mind referring to the ability to think about one's own thought processes, and to plan and monitor one's performance.

Socioeconomic status (SES): SES is an index of standard of living. It is a hybrid of family income and parent education. High SES families are more affluent than low SES families and parents in high SES families have more education than parents in low SES families.

Variance accounted for: Variance is a statistical construct that is an index of the extent to which individual scores on a test differ from one another. When everyone gets the same score, there is no variance. When people get many different scores, there is considerable variance. When differences in performance can be linked to some factor (e.g., high scorers had one type of instruction while low scorers had a different kind of instruction), we say that the factor 'accounts for' some portion of the variance.

Working memory: In contrast to permanent memory that refers to the mental storehouse of one's knowledge, working memory is more short-term and transient. When one tries to hold in mind some new item of information (e.g., the just-stated phone number of a new acquaintance), one uses working memory.

Introduction

Within policy-making circles and the scholarly literature on academic achievement, the guiding principles of children's education are often hotly debated. Should a math curriculum emphasize facts or concepts? Is it developmentally appropriate for children to learn academic skills in kindergarten? However, one guiding principle that seems to be accepted by all sides in educational debates is that children need to become proficient in a wide range of academic skills by the time they are young adults. The benefits of academic achievement are manifold. For example, consider the fact that average incomes in the United States increase by \$10 000 to \$20 000 with each increment in education level (e.g., \$21 000 for high school dropouts vs. \$31 000 and \$57 000 for those who have high school and college diplomas, respectively). In addition, studies in the United States and many other countries have shown that academic achievement is also associated with higher levels of physical health, mental health, and technological innovation; technological innovation, in turn, promotes greater national prosperity. It is understandable, then, that multiple constituencies (e.g., policy makers, educators, parents, etc.) have a vested interest in promoting academic achievement in children, adolescents, and young adults.

Measures of Academic Achievement: Strengths and Weaknesses

At its basis, governmental policy making is a form of problem solving. In particular, policies are created or revised to address perceived problems in society such as low levels of literacy or high levels of teenage pregnancy in specific subgroups of a population. One aspect of effective problem solving is the regular use of assessments and data collection to determine the existence or extent of some matter of concern. To illustrate, in 1967 the United States Congress passed a law to create the National Assessment of Educational Progress (NAEP) to serve as the 'Nation's Report Card.' The motivation for doing so was that Congress wanted to know whether American children were, in fact, acquiring the skills they would need to be productive members of the workforce. The law mandates that every few years, tests are to be given to national, representative samples of children in the fourth, eighth, and twelfth grades. Should the overall level of achievement in children be found to be too low, Congress would then enact policies to improve performance (e.g., the No Child Left Behind legislation). Local school districts in the United States have been assessing the performance of their students using a similar logic and approach, but often using various different standardized tests such as the Iowa Test of Basic Skills or Stanford Achievement Test. When NAEP is implemented every few years, in contrast, children in every state are given the same test. Teams of educational researchers, assessment specialists, and educators devise the content of NAEP. The use of assessments in this manner is wisespread throughout the world.

However, it is not enough that policy makers simply gather data. Rather, a key prerequisite of solving school-related problems effectively is the use of accurate assessments. Just as inaccurate medical tests can lead to faulty diagnoses and the implementation of the wrong medical treatments, inaccurate academic assessments can lead to faulty inferences about the nature of academic achievement (e.g., overall reading skills are thought to be too low when they are not) and the implementation of new instructional strategies based on this inference (e.g., abandoning the current reading approach in favor of another one). Experts in the area of assessment use the term 'validity' when issues of test accuracy arise. A valid test measures what it is designed to measure (e.g., reading skills for a standardized reading test) and should be relatively free from bias. Tests can be invalid for a specific population of students for various reasons, but one common problem arises when the topics that appear on the standardized test do not overlap with the topics that may be covered in the curriculum of a school system. Students are learning information, but not necessarily the information on the test. The school system then gets blamed for doing a poor job of educating children. Given the No Child Left Behind legislation in the United States that imposes penalties on schools when children do not show adequate yearly progress in their skill acquisition, many teachers understandably end up 'teaching to the test.' At the international level, assessments such as the Trends in International Mathematics and Science Study (TIMSS) show that coverage of topics is, not surprisingly, associated with higher scores on TIMSS.

There is no such thing as a perfectly valid test, however. As well designed as NAEP is, for example, each child is given a limited amount of time to respond to questions (e.g., 60 min for 45 math questions). In addition, some items are intentionally included on NAEP to prompt reforms; there is no expectation that the majority of children actually spend time learning these more advanced skills. Thus, national performance appears to be less advanced than if a typical standardized test were used. Regardless of the assessment in question, some argue that open-ended responses yield more accurate indices of skill than multiple-choice tests that often include options that are designed to seduce respondents to the wrong answer. When gender or ethnic differences arise on high stake tests, some have questioned the content of the test (e.g., it is biased toward males or affluent children) and, hence, argue that the results are not valid for these subgroups. When test results are dismissed for issues of timing or content reasons, they cannot obviously drive any reforms that may or may not be needed.

Age Trends in Achievement by Subject Area

Many standardized tests that are used at the local level in the United States focus primarily on achievement in reading and math, and more occasionally, in science. This pattern is common in Europe as well. Depending on the year, national tests such as the NAEP have focused on achievement in reading, math, science, writing, history, geography, and civics (though reading and math have been assessed more often than the others). Performance on local and national tests provides some insight into the average levels of skill in students at various ages. To illustrate some achievement results, age trends in four content areas are considered next.

Reading

If all goes well in a child's schooling, he or she will progress from (a) demonstrating a rudimentary set of emergent literacy skills during the preschool period (e.g., recognizing letters, identifying component sounds in words) to (b) the ability to decode and comprehend individual written words and full sentences during the first few grades of elementary school, to (c) the ability to comprehend paragraphs and book-length segments of text using a variety of reading strategies such as inference making, to finally (d) the ability to evaluate the quality of texts, understand the differences between higher-quality and lower-quality texts (e.g., what makes a book a 'classic'), and understand the different purposes served by different literary genres. In addition, skilled readers engage in comprehension processes in an automatic and rapid manner. To a greater or lesser degree, standardized tests attempt to capture some of these component abilities.

To illustrate, the NAEP for reading subdivides performance into three primary levels: basic, proficient, and advanced. The national goal is to have most children at each grade level performing at least at the proficient level. At the eighth grade, children are assigned to the basic level if their performance suggests that they understand the overall meaning of what they read, can make simple inferences, and can make connections between the content of what they read and aspects of their own lives. At the next higher level, proficient readers have all of the basic abilities but also show more skill at inference making. At the highest level, advanced readers have the added abilities of (a) understanding how authors use various literary devices and (b) critically evaluating texts. Advanced readers also provide more thorough and thoughtful responses than students in the other categories.

Results for the 2007 assessment showed that 27% of eighth graders performed below the basic level, while 43%, 27%, and 2% performed at the basic, proficient, and advanced levels, respectively. Thus, once again, most of these American students (70%) performed at or below the basic level.

For twelfth graders, the basic readers can once again understand the main idea of a passage that is appropriate for their age group, draw simple (obvious) inferences, make connections to their own lives, and identify certain elements of an author's style. Proficient readers, in contrast, can also draw more implicit inferences and can recognize an author's use of specific literary devices. At the highest level, advanced readers are able to recognize more advanced themes, analyze both the meaning and form of texts, and use examples of the text to back up their analyses. Once again, advanced readers provide responses that are thorough and thoughtful. Twelfth graders were not tested on the 2007 NAEP but were tested on the 2005 NAEP for reading. That assessment showed that 27% of twelfth graders scored below the basic level, while 38%, 30%, and 5% scored at the basic, proficient, and advanced levels, respectively.

Overall, then, these and other smaller-scale studies show that many children in the United States learn to decode and understand large segments of text via inference making and literal comprehension. Only a minority of even twelfth graders demonstrates the more sophisticated levels of strategic processing, criticism, and analysis required for an advanced technological society. These findings are generally consistent with those of the international study called Programme for International Student Assessment (PISA) that has been conducted several times in the 2000s. In the 2003 PISA, performance was subdivided into five levels that increase in sophistication with respect to skills in comprehension, inference making, and locating information. Fifteen-year-olds in Finland, Korea, Canada, Australia, New Zealand, Ireland, Liechtenstein, Sweden, The Netherlands, Hong Kong, and Belgium all performed one standard deviation about the international mean. Students in the United States performed near the mean. However, the majority of students in all countries performed in the middle levels of performance (i.e., Levels 2, 3, and 4). Thus, children around the world acquire a certain amount of reading proficiency, but the average child does not attain a sufficiently high level of skill to thrive in the modern world economy.

Mathematics

The goals of contemporary (i.e., reform) mathematics instruction are to:

1. instill in students the belief that mathematics is a meaningful, goal-directed activity that can help them solve a variety of real-world and theoretical problems;
2. foster students' learning the math facts, math concepts, computational skills, and strategies they need to solve a wide range of problems;
3. promote the acquisition of efficient and flexible approaches to problem solving; and
4. instill in students adaptive mathematical behaviors and beliefs (e.g., persisting in the face of failure on math problems).

Unfortunately, this reform characterization of mathematics achievement does not overlap entirely with the content of most local and national assessments in that the latter focus more on demonstrated (factual) knowledge and skill than on beliefs and motivational profiles. In addition, some of the more common local standardized tests primarily require computational skill mixed together with relatively unsophisticated problem-solving skill.

A variety of small-scale studies in the developmental literature on mathematics show that children progressively acquire a fair amount of factual knowledge (mainly in the form of answers to computational problems such as '$3 \times 7 = ?$') and computational proficiency in addition, subtraction, multiplication, and division by the time they enter high school. Some adolescent students in high school demonstrate facility in algebraic computations and geometric proofs as well, though the level of success is not especially impressive, at least in the United States. Due in part to the tendency of US high school students to avoid mathematics after a mandatory number of semesters, relatively few students gain proficiency in high level math such as trigonometry, precalculus, and calculus.

The primary deficiency at each grade level is in students' conceptual understanding of facts and procedures. In other words, even when students correctly perform computational algorithms and derive the correct answer to problems, they fail to understand why the answers are what they are (e.g., why the correct answer to '$-3 + 1$' is '-2') and why they have to employ specialized procedures in some cases (e.g., invert and multiply when dividing fractions). More often, the lack of conceptual understanding leads to mindless errors such as responding that the answer to '204 – 17' is '213.' In this example, students encounter the problem of trying to subtract 7 from 4 in the 'ones' column and 1 from 0 in the 'tens' column. Instead of regrouping, some students simply reverse the numbers (take 4 away from 7 and 0 away from 1). These children are not troubled by the fact that their answer is larger than the largest of the subtrahends. Small-scale studies have shown that it is possible to enhance procedural skill by promoting greater conceptual knowledge in students. Given that traditional classrooms emphasize factual knowledge and computational proficiency over conceptual understanding and problem solving, the results of small-scale studies are not surprising. Observational studies of reform classrooms in the United States and comparable classrooms in high-performing countries in Asia that emphasize concepts and problem solving show less mindless errors, but some computational problems persist.

To get a sense of national levels of performance, it is useful to once again consult the results of NAEP in which performance is categorized into the basic, proficient, and advanced levels for most subject areas. For eighth graders on the 2009 NAEP for math, children were assigned to the basic level when they can perform some basic computations with whole numbers, fractions, and decimals and can solve simple word problems. The proficient level was assigned when children could also estimate, show a conceptual understanding, judge the reasonableness of answers, solve problems, and explain their answers. The advanced level was assigned when they also perform complex, nonroutine problems and engage in sophisticated reasoning. The percentages were 27% below basic, 39% basic, 26% proficient, and 8% advanced. Although performance has improved over time since the 1990s, most (66%) children in the eighth grade perform at or below the basic level. Twelfth graders were not tested on NAEP in 2009 but were in 2005. Their percentages were 39% below basic, 38% basic, 21% proficient, and 2%

advanced. Thus, as the difficulty of math increases with age, the percentages of US students falling into the proficient and advanced levels falls from 34% to just 23%.

These findings for performance for children in the United States are comparable to those of international studies such as TIMSS or PISA. On the 2003 PISA, the focus was specifically on mathematics. The items were not designed to simply measure the ability to perform operations, but how well students could solve problems in the context of real-life situations ('mathematics literacy'). The topics centered on four areas of mathematics (space and shape, change and relationships, quantity, and uncertainty) and ranged in difficulty from simple reproduction of familiar computational algorithms to problems requiring more reflection and creative solutions. Scores on the 85 questions were constructed so that the mean was 500, and performance was categorized into six levels. Of the 40 countries participating, Norway's 15-year-olds performed at the middle (20th position) and those of the United States performed seven ranks below that (i.e., 27 countries performed better). The top five countries were Canada, Netherlands, Korea, Finland, and Hong Kong-China (first place). Students in the United States performed, on average, between levels 2 and 3 on the scale. At level 2, students can mainly perform basic algorithms for problems where little inference making is needed to know what to do. Level 3 students can perform multiple-step solutions, use simple problem-solving strategies, and draw straightforward conclusions from information. Once again, these results are not encouraging for many countries, including the United States.

Science

The goal of contemporary (reform) science instruction is to help all students develop some of the skills, beliefs, and attitudes of practicing scientists. In other words, students should gain the ability to use or at least appreciate the specialized procedures of science (e.g., well-designed experiments) to discern the underlying causal structure of factors operating in a specific situation. They should also be able to construct or recognize testable hypotheses that derive from the premises of theories and know what kinds of evidence support the hypotheses and what kinds disconfirm them. In addition, they should recognize the ever-evolving nature of science (e.g., that the facts and theories in texts are neither fixed nor final). Finally, they should recognize the universality of biases that keep scientists and nonscientists from recognizing or discovering evidence against a favored theory and work to guard against these biases from affecting conclusions they draw from their work or the work of others. The reason for hoping that all students gain such skills is that many contemporary definitions of higher-order thinking or high-quality thinking specify the very same skills. Students may not become practicing scientists themselves, but, as noted above, good policy making derives from, first, appealing to evidence rather than argument or speculation and, second, being able to judge the quality of evidence. Consider the contemporary debates about global warming or evolution in the United States. The key disagreement is the credibility of the evidence and how to interpret it.

In the United States, science instruction tries to foster increasingly sophisticated skills with age. In elementary schools, for example, children may primarily be asked to engage in skills such as collecting and classifying objects from nature (e.g., different kinds of leaves). Later, in the fifth and sixth grades, they may be asked to learn facts about physical science (e.g., fundamentals of plate tectonics). Finally, in high school, they are given introductory courses in earth science and biology, and college bound students may also take courses in chemistry and physics. In all these courses, the traditional approach (that is still prevalent in many classrooms) is a heavy emphasis on learning facts and laws over engaging in the inquiry and scientific investigation. Labs may or may not be directly tied to lectures and the focus is on proper procedures rather than understanding how to use the procedures to investigate scientific questions or test hypotheses. In reform classrooms, in contrast, there is a heavy emphasis on inquiry and investigation. Students may spend weeks gathering evidence about some phenomenon (e.g., the degree of pollution in neighboring streams) and learn content as needed in these investigations.

Given the gradual introduction of science and prevalence of traditional approaches in the United States, one would expect that the results of recent NAEPs for science would show little in the way of advanced scientific thinking even in twelfth graders. In fact, the results show just that. As is the norm on NAEP, performance is categorized into basic, proficient, and advanced levels. The higher levels correspond to the kinds of desired skills identified above. At the fourth grade, the percentages were 34% below basic, 39% basic, 25% proficient, and 2% advanced. For eighth graders, the percentages were 43%, 30%, 24%, and 3%; for twelfth graders, they were 40% below basic, 39% basic, 19% proficient, and 1% advanced. Thus, as was the case for mathematics, as the science content and skills required become more demanding with age, the percentages of US students who demonstrate the desired highest two levels drops from 27% to 20%. These findings are mirrored in a variety of small-scale studies that show most US high school and college students harbor many scientific misconceptions and they are not proficient in skills such as hypothesis testing and creating experiments to isolate the causes of outcomes.

At the international level, 15-year-olds from the United States performed in the middle of the distribution for the PISA science scale in 2003, scoring significantly worse than peers in 16 other countries but significantly better than peers in 13 countries. What US students could do was recall simple factual knowledge, use common scientific knowledge to draw conclusions, and recognize questions that can be answered with scientific explanations. What they could not do, on average, is create or use conceptual models to make predictions, analyze the methodology of scientific investigations, and compare data to evaluate alternative viewpoints. Their peers in countries such as Finland, Japan, Hong Kong-China, and Korea demonstrated some of the latter skills. In 2006, the PISA focus was primarily on science and was much more comprehensive than in 2003, which allowed for the categorization of responses into six levels. The content focused on physical systems (e.g., the structure of matter), living systems (e.g., cells), earth and space systems (e.g., atmosphere), and technology systems (e.g., the role of technology in solving problems). The skills included recognizing questions that could be answered scientifically, recognizing key features of scientific methodology, and providing scientific explanations of everyday situations.

Most students (72%) in the 57 participating countries performed at levels 2, 3, and 4, in which abilities ranged from being able to give possible scientific explanations of familiar situations and interpret texts literally (level 2) to making scientific inferences that link content to real life, integrating explanations, and communicating their thoughts effectively (level 4). This time, Lithuania performed in the middle of the 57 countries and the United States performed seven ranks below that. The top five countries were Finland, Estonia, Hong Kong-China, Canada, and Macao-China. These findings once again show that many high school students around the world are acquiring a certain amount of scientific literacy, but not at a level adequate to be successful in contemporary technological society that is wrought with environmental (e.g., global warming, depletion of natural resources, natural disasters), medical (e.g., AIDS), and economic problems (e.g., large disparities in national GDPs).

Social Studies

The social studies include domains such as history, civics, geography, and economics. The goals of contemporary social studies instruction include helping students (a) become knowledgeable and active citizens, (b) get in touch with their personal identities and values, and (c) develop a sensitivity to other cultures and values. When students see that cultural, economic, and governmental systems change over time within the same country and also differ across countries at the same point in history, they may be more likely to understand their place in time and in the world, less likely to assume that the current state of their country is the way it has always been and always will be, and less likely to develop ethnocentric beliefs. Social studies instruction done poorly creates students who can merely rattle off a large number of facts and dates. In the United States, social studies instruction tends to be somewhat cursory until children reach fifth grade, where they begin to examine key events in US history. Later in middle school they may begin to learn about other cultures in more depth. US and world history are covered once again in high school, and many school systems make courses in civics a requirement for graduation under the assumption that students need to understand the workings of their own government and their rights and responsibilities as citizens.

As was noted above for science, the gradual introduction of social studies topics in the curriculum and emphasis on memorization of facts tends to produce a citizenry that lacks depth in their understanding of cultures and history. The superficial understanding of US students is reflected in NAEPs that have been conducted for history, geography, and civics. Each of these assessments has shown that the majority of students score at the basic level or below basic level. These levels correspond to the appreciation of simple timelines, identification of key figures in US history (e.g., George Washington), and some appreciation of cultural differences. The ability to reason in a sophisticated way about social studies content is largely absent in student performance.

Overall, then, students around the world seem to acquire increased knowledge and skill with age in domains such as reading, mathematics, science, and social studies. However, the general trend is for the proportion of proficient and advanced levels to drop off as the intellectual demands of the content increases. Students in some countries fare better than students in the United States, but the general finding that students do not acquire the skills they need to be successful in contemporary society is unfortunately shared across many industrialized countries.

Factors Predictive of Achievement

So far, the preceding portrait of academic achievement has focused on average levels of performance or what is true of the typical student at various age levels. However, these averages are generally based on normal distributions of scores within domains, in which some students (about 16%) perform below average, some (about 68%) perform near the average level, and some (about 16%) perform above average. As noted earlier, there are many stakeholders who are keenly interested in raising the achievement level of all students given pressures such as No Child Left Behind legislation and economic competition among nations. The first step in knowing how to raise performance is to find answers to questions such as how do students who perform at the above average level differ from those who perform at the average level or below? What is true of high performers that could be modified in their lower-performing peers? When children are given achievement tests at the end of an academic year and differences arise in their scores, what antecedent factors can be used to explain who will do better than whom? In what follows, nine factors that predict end-of-year differences are briefly examined.

Prior Knowledge

The best predictor of knowledge growth across an academic year is the level of knowledge that students have on the first day of school. Existing knowledge in a student's mind serves as a foundation upon which later knowledge is built. Consider an analogy. If a large crystal and small crystal were both placed in a stream that contained dissolved salts, the large crystal would grow much larger, much faster than the small crystal. So, the best way to reduce differences in groups at the end of the year is to make sure that they all have the same knowledge on the first day of school. In statistical terms, prior knowledge often accounts for 50–65% of the variance in knowledge growth at all age levels.

Self-Regulation

Self-regulated students are in control of their own learning. They plan well, organize their time and study effectively, motivate themselves, regularly monitor how well they are doing, and find ways to avoid distractions and procrastination. When children are young and not self-regulated, they can still show solid growth across an academic year when teachers and parents regulate their learning for them. However, in middle school, high school, and college, students are increasingly expected to self-regulate. They may be only told once in a college course, for example, that a 15-page paper is due in 6 weeks. Students must use strategies to remember this deadline, plan out the paper, retrieve references, write drafts, and so on, all on their own.

In the later grades, students who get the best grades and show the highest achievement are self-regulated. Statistically, self-regulation has varied in the amount of variance it predicts depending on the way it has been measured. Some studies of older students suggest it can account for as much as 20% of the variance in end-of-year achievement. Studies of younger students have not been conducted because it is assumed they lack the self-regulatory skills described above.

Motivation

There are many aspects to motivation including interests (e.g., I love to read), goals (e.g., I plan on getting good grades this semester), values (e.g., it matters to me if I do poorly in school), self-efficacy (e.g., I feel that I have the ability to accomplish this task), attributing outcomes to specific causes (e.g., how hard I studied vs. how smart I am), and emotional reactions to outcomes (e.g., embarrassment vs. pride). Factors such as interest and self-efficacy have been found to predict 10–15% of the variance in end-of-year achievement. So, if two children start out an academic year with the same level of knowledge but one is much more interested, the more interested student will learn more. Strong interest only partially compensates, however, for lack of knowledge. Interest is uniformly high in young children and drops over time through adolescence. As such, interest accounts for less variance in achievement in young children than in adolescents.

Socioeconomic Status

It should be no surprise to learn that children demonstrate higher levels of achievement when they come from affluent homes with well-educated parents than if they come from disadvantaged homes with parents who have less education. On the 2005 NAEP for math, for example, scores increase with each level of parent education level: high school dropout (mean = 130), graduated high school (mean = 138), some education after high school (mean = 148), and graduated college (mean = 161). However, socioeconomic status (SES) does not predict as much as factors such as prior knowledge and self-efficacy. Comprehensive reviews suggest that, at all age levels, SES accounts for about 10% of the variance when other predictors are controlled. Thus, differences will be evident in end-of-year test scores between high SES and low SES students even when children in these groups enter a school with the same level of knowledge. However, the gap would be far larger if two students of the same SES background entered school with large differences in initial knowledge.

Peers, Families, and Neighborhood Factors

In contemporary ecological and stage-fit models, variables such as SES are part of interdependent socio-cultural systems in a child's life that are nested within each other. Children participate in family contexts, school contexts, and neighborhood contexts. The cultural values, beliefs, and behaviors of other actors in these contexts influence what children care about, what they believe about themselves and schooling, and how they behave. High-achieving children not only come from families in which both parents are well-educated and affluent (as noted above), but also live in neighborhoods where most other children come from similar families and attend schools where most other children are achievement oriented. For example, whereas the college attendance rate of US students in many low-income urban high schools may be 20–30%, nearly 100% of children attending high schools in many affluent neighborhoods attend college. Peer, family, and neighborhood factors have been found to predict achievement (and other outcomes such as social competence, or delinquency) even after controlling for prior achievement.

Intelligence

Students differ both in terms of the domain-specific knowledge they bring to the classroom (e.g., their math knowledge) and in terms of more domain-general abilities such as their intelligence. Theorists differ with respect to their definitions and measures of intelligence, but some influential theories have in common aspects such as speed of processing, working memory, use of strategies, metacognition, and attentional control. Students who score highly on measures of these aspects of intelligence show more learning in school settings. However, after controlling for domain specific knowledge and skills, general intelligence only accounts for about 8–10% of the variance in achievement.

Curriculum and Instruction

When questions arise about the impact of instruction on achievement, it is important to consider two aspects of instruction: the content that is covered and the way this material is taught. Children will obviously not perform well on end-of-year assessments if they have not been exposed to the content on these assessments. For example, if children in reform mathematics classrooms are not asked to memorize multiplication facts but timed end-of-year tests require this knowledge, these children will not perform as well as they could. As noted above, international studies such as TIMSS reveal that coverage is correlated with performance (countries that emphasize the content on TIMSS do better than countries that do not). Some longitudinal studies of US students show that course taking patterns (an index of content exposure) predicts around 10% of the variance after controlling for prior achievement.

But in addition to considering what is taught, the issue of how material is taught has been the subject of fierce debates for many years (e.g., the Whole Language vs. Phonics debate in reading). Firm estimates of the effects of method are difficult to determine because it is rare to find true experiments in the literature in which students are randomly assigned to different instructional approaches. Nonexperimental studies in which schools that adopted some curriculum package are compared to schools that adopted a different package are difficult to interpret. Teachers who voluntarily adopt reform approaches are very different from those who do not. In addition, it is possible that children could perform well regardless of the method, as long as a highly skilled teacher is involved. Further, if teachers could somehow vary what they do with individual children (e.g., teach one child using method X, another with method Y, and third with method Z, etc.), this variability across students could be large enough to be both detectable and influential on performance. Instead, however, a single teacher often broadcasts the same method to an entire room of students. Hence, there is little variance (and instruction can be considered nearly a constant). Perhaps for this reason, meta-analyses have suggested that characteristics of children (e.g., their initial skill level and SES) account for much more variance in outcomes than instructional methods. However, methodological limitations and problems with how techniques are measured in these studies could also explain the lack of strong effects. More research is needed to clarify the relative importance of method.

Learning Difficulties

Until the use of discrepancy criteria to assign children to diagnostic categories became questioned, a number of school districts in the United States defined a child with learning disabilities as one whose intelligence fell into the normal range (as measured by IQ tests) but who was at least 2 years behind in their academic achievement (as measured by standardized tests). This discrepancy alone explains the serious consequences of having a diagnosis of reading disability or math disability. On national tests such as the 2007 NAEP for reading, the average score for children diagnosed with a disability was 217 (out of 500) while the average score for children not so diagnosed was 266. The effect size for this 49-point difference is $d = 1.15$ and any effect size over 0.80 is considered large (see below). Even with prolonged tutoring and other interventions, a child who scores at the tenth percentile for core reading skills may only improve to the thirtieth percentile. Thus, learning difficulties have strong effects on achievement gains and are difficult to remediate. Many recent studies have attempted to identify the neurological basis of disorders such as reading disability and autism.

Gender, Racial, and Ethnic Differences in Achievement

Although the moniker of No Child Left Behind (NCLB) legislation suggests that individual children are of particular concern, in reality, NCLB is intended to eliminate performance gaps in specific demographic subgroups of the US population such as boys versus girls, or Caucasian and Asian versus African American, Hispanic, and Native American. How large are gender differences in the domains discussed earlier (i.e., reading, math, science, and social studies)? How large are racial and ethnic differences in these domains? Why do they occur and what can be done to eliminate them?

Gender Differences

Effect sizes are a useful and standardized way for determining the average size of group differences in performance such as gender differences. Effect sizes are computed by subtracting one group mean from another and dividing by the standard deviation of the combined distribution of scores. Doing so puts mean differences all on the same scale (i.e., standard deviation units) in the same way that the Euro puts various different European currencies on the same scale. Effect sizes of about 0.20 or less are considered small; those 0.80 or larger are considered large, and those in the middle (i.e., 0.50) are considered medium.

Large-scale studies (e.g., NAEP) and meta-analyses of many smaller studies with US students suggest that the average effect size for both younger (e.g., fourth grade) and older students (e.g., twelfth grade) in reading achievement is $d = -0.20$. This finding means that females do better than males but the difference is small. International studies such as PISA show that across the 27 participating countries, the effect size for 15-year-olds on the reading scale was $d = -0.34$, showing once again that females do better but this time the difference is small to medium. However, on PISA, countries varied in the size of the reading gap ranging from a high of $d = 0.59$ in Iceland to a low of $d = 0.20$ in Korea.

In the case of mathematics, the story is a bit more complicated. Overall many studies, measures, and age groups in the United States, the average effect size is $d = 0.20$, but this time favoring males. However, the gap does not really approach 0.20 until (a) comparisons are made between average (nongifted) 15-year-old males and females, (b) comparisons are made between gifted preteen males and females, (c) the measures require reasoning (e.g., the SAT), or (d) the measures focus on the highest level math (e.g., calculus). So the question becomes, why does the difference only become apparent in these situations? No differences emerge on tests of computational skill in algebra, for example, nor on other difficult tests such as NAEP ($d = 0.04$). On international tests such as the 2003 PISA that specifically focused on contextualized problem solving in mathematics, the effect size was just $d = 0.11$, which means males did better on average but the difference was small. The countries in which no significant difference emerged on PISA included Australia, Austria, Belgium, Japan, the Netherlands, Norway, and Poland. In Iceland, there was a significant difference favoring females.

In science, the differences for US students are even smaller than in math, with most effect sizes being less than 0.10 (favoring males). These findings are consistent with those of international studies such as TIMSS that also report effect sizes on the order of 0.10, and PISA in which the science results are reported to be among the smallest of all of the content areas tested.

In social studies, the effect sizes for gender differences on the NAEPs for civics, history, and geography are all less than 0.10 (favoring males). In sum, then, gender differences are apparent in some select subject areas but are generally small to nonexistent. The variation across countries and aspects of performance (e.g., the SAT vs. other kinds of tests) is still in need of a full accounting (though some reasonable approximations are provided later in this article).

Ethnic and Racial Differences

In contrast to the findings for gender differences in which differences are small and appear only for some aspects of some subjects, ethnic and racial differences in achievement are often medium and consistent across all subject areas. On the NAEP for reading, for example, White and Asian students perform considerably better than Black and Hispanic students (moderate effect sizes in the 0.30–0.40 range). On the verbal section of the SAT, the effect sizes are even larger (large effect sizes in the 0.60 to 1.0 range). The findings are comparable for other subject areas such as math and science. The especially large gap for the math SAT means that many minority students lack the scores they need to be admitted to the most selective universities in the United States.

European studies of ethnic and racial differences are less common in the achievement literature, presumably because of these countries are sometimes more ethnically and racially homogenous than the United States.

Explaining the Differences

Most theoretical accounts in the scholarly literature on gender and ethnic differences were developed to account for differences in a single content area (e.g., mathematics) and often appeal to a single explanatory factor (e.g., genetic differences). The shortcomings of such models become apparent when one tries to use them to explain the entire pattern of results where differences (a) are sometimes small, sometimes medium, and sometimes large within content area, and (b) change in size with age and across content areas. To explain such variations, a single factor explanation is not adequate because it could only deal with consistency. In addition, if an account holds for one domain (e.g., gender differences in mathematics are due to cultural beliefs suggesting it is a 'male' subject), it should also hold for other domains (e.g., history, science, reading, etc.). Some accounts lose their explanatory force when generalized in this manner. In the past 10 to 15 years, a growing number of authors have attempted to construct and test more comprehensive models and found increased explanatory success. The ecological model and stage-fit model described earlier are examples of these more comprehensive accounts.

One additional comprehensive model is the Opportunity-Propensity (O–P) account that was designed to find a way to integrate all of the findings regarding the factors that predict achievement described above (i.e., prior knowledge, motivation, etc.). The basic premise of the O–P framework is that learners are more likely to attain high levels of achievement within a particular domain (e.g., mathematics) if two necessary conditions are met: (a) they are given genuine opportunities to enhance their skills in the domain (the opportunity condition) and (b) they are willing and able to take advantage of these opportunities (the propensity condition). When individual or group differences are observed in achievement, the O-P framework suggests that one should try to account for this result by determining the extent to which the opportunity and propensity conditions had been fulfilled in individuals who performed poorly. (e.g., low performers were presented with fewer opportunities to learn than high performers; low performers were presented with as many opportunities as high performers but the former were unable to benefit from these opportunities due to lack of preparation).

Starting with this central premise, one then considers how each of the predictive factors might relate either to opportunities to learn or to the propensity to take advantage of opportunities to learn. In the model, opportunities to learn are culturally defined contexts in which an individual is presented with content to learn (e.g., by a teacher or parent, an author, etc.) or given opportunities to practice skills. Children would be expected to show higher achievement if they are taught by a skilled teacher who treats all children fairly and equitably and if they are adequately and systematically exposed to the content required on end-of-year assessments.

In contrast, propensity factors are any factors that relate to the ability or willingness to learn content once it has been exposed or presented in particular contexts. As such, factors such as preexisting knowledge, motivation, and self-regulation all pertain to the propensity component. That is, children would be more willing and able to take advantage of learning opportunities if they bring to these learning opportunities prerequisite skills, the desire to learn the content, and the spontaneous tendency to utilize effective strategies where appropriate.

With such a multifaceted model, the ability to explain the complex pattern of variable effect sizes described above becomes more possible. Several studies using large national databases on achievement showed that a combination of opportunity and propensity factors accounted for 50–80% of the variance in math and science achievement. Importantly, when factors such as prior knowledge, family SES, coursework, and student motivation are controlled, factors such as gender and ethnicity no longer explain variance in achievement. To illustrate these findings with a high school example, students who (a) come to high school with equivalent levels of prior knowledge, SES, and motivation and (b) take the same courses show identical levels of achievement at the end of high school.

Implications for Improving Achievement

The earlier section on achievement results for specific subject areas showed that students in various countries seem to acquire a certain amount of skill in reading, mathematics, science, and social studies but not enough to be successful in the contemporary global and technological economy. Thus, something has to change in the way children are educated to elevate the performance of all students. The section on gender and ethnic differences amplified this conclusion by showing how the average, mediocre level of performance obscures the fact that students in some demographic subgroups are more likely to perform below the average than students in other demographic subgroups (e.g., males in reading, Black students in math). In addition, there is considerable variation in overall levels of performance across countries. Comprehensive explanatory models bring some hope of providing insight as to how to both eliminate within- and between-country differences and elevate the performance of all students.

For example, if the Opportunity-Propensity model continues to receive empirical support and continues to evolve through the inclusion of more factors and more precise measurement, it suggests a two-step solution:

1. create interventions that promote comparable levels of knowledge, motivation, and self-regulation in children before they enter a particular level of schooling (e.g., between birth and age 5 in the case of first grade; during elementary and middle school for high school); and
2. ensure that all children in various demographic subgroups are exposed to the content they need from highly skilled teachers.

Interventions that only introduce a new curriculum into a school or only provide teacher training are essentially implementing the second step without also implementing the first step. The evidence suggests the two-step solution would be far more effective than the more common one-step solution. Even when instruction improves under the latter strategy, it will not eliminate preexisting group differences in knowledge, motivation, or self-regulation. Moreover, only the most knowledgeable, motivated, and self-regulated students will benefit.

See also: Achievement Motivation; Peer Influence.

Further Reading

Alexander PA and Winne PH (eds.) (2006) *Handbook of Educational Psychology*, 2nd edn. Mahwah, NJ: Lawrence Erlbaum Associates and Division 15 of the American Psychology Association.

Byrnes JP (2008) *Cognitive Development and Learning in Instructional Contexts*, 3rd edn. Boston, MA: Pearson/Allyn & Bacon Publishers.

Byrnes JP and Miller DC (2007) The relative importance of predictors of math and science achievement: An opportunity–propensity analysis. *Contemporary Educational Psychology* 32: 599–629.

Sirin SR (2005) Socioeconomic status and academic achievement: A meta-analytic review of research. *Review of Educational Research* 75: 417–453.

Relevant Websites

http://nces.ed.gov/nationsreportcard/ – For information and results of NAEP.

www.pisa.oecd.org/ – For information and results of PISA.

http://ed.gov/nclb/landing.jhtml – For information regarding No Child Left Behind Legislation and findings

Achievement Motivation

A Wigfield, A N Ho, and A Mason-Singh, University of Maryland, College Park, MD, USA

Glossary

Expectancy-value theory: A theory claiming that individuals' performance on different activities and choices of them will be influenced by what an individual expects to encounter in the setting and how much the individual values the things that are expected.

Learned helplessness: A condition in which a person has been conditioned or taught to believe that he or she has no control over a situation; so the person behaves as if he or she is helpless and dependent on others in that situation.

Self-determination theory: A theory describing how adolescents come to feel capable of making their own decisions and taking ownership of their actions without necessarily being separate or alienated from parents or other adults who may advise about decisions.

Introduction

The Latin root of 'motivation' means 'to move'; thus, fundamentally motivational psychologists study what moves people to act and why people think and do what they do. Motivation researchers study factors that influence individuals' choices about which tasks to do, the persistence with which they pursue those tasks, the intensity of their engagement in the tasks, their reflections about their performance, and their emotions about all these things. Achievement motivation is a type of motivation that is related to performance on tasks involving standards of excellence.

In this article, we discuss prominent current theoretical models of achievement motivation and research that supports them; how achievement motivation develops across the school years (focusing on the middle and high school years); and group differences in motivation. We then discuss parent, school, and peer influences on motivation during adolescence.

Current Achievement Motivation Theories and Constructs

Many current theories of motivation focus on individuals' beliefs, values, and goals as determining their motivation; these theories thus emphasize social-cognitive variables. There is an emerging focus in recent theoretical work on contextual influences on motivation, and how motivation is a joint product of the individual and the context.

Theories Focused on Competence and Control Beliefs

A number of motivation theories focus on students' beliefs about their ability and efficacy to perform achievement tasks as crucial motivational mediators of achievement behavior. Ability or competence beliefs are children's evaluations of their competence in different areas. Researchers have documented that children's and adolescents' ability beliefs relate to and predict their achievement performance in different achievement domains like math and reading, even when previous performance is controlled. Bandura's construct of self-efficacy also deals with individuals' sense of competence; however, Bandura defined self-efficacy as a generative capacity where different subskills are organized into courses of action. Research has shown that individuals' efficacy for different achievement tasks is a major determinant of activity choice, willingness to expend effort, and persistence in and out of school; individuals who have strong efficacy beliefs choose more difficult tasks, persist longer, and exert more effort on the tasks.

Locus of control refers to individuals' sense of what controls the outcomes they experience. Internal control means the individual believes that he or she controls the outcome; external control means the outcome is determined by other things. Internal locus of control beliefs correlate positively with achievement. Control beliefs also relate to competence beliefs: Children who believe they control their achievement outcomes feel more competent.

Attribution theorists built on the work on locus of control and competence beliefs in developing their theory of how individuals interpret, or make attributions for, their performance. The most common attributions are ability, effort, task difficulty, and luck. Research has shown that attributing success to ability and effort results in positive motivation and achievement. When individuals do poorly on a task, attributing their failure to lack of effort or poor strategy use leads to more positive motivation the next time they undertake a similar activity. Attributing failure to lack of ability is most debilitating to subsequent motivation, especially when individuals view their ability as something that is fixed.

Theories Dealing with Individuals' Intrinsic Motivation, Interests, Values, and Goals

Theories dealing with competence, expectancy, and control beliefs provide powerful explanations of individuals' performance on different kinds of achievement activities. However, these theories do not systematically address another important motivational question: Does the individual *want* to do the task? Even if people are certain they can do a task and think they can control the outcome, they may not want to engage in it. Once the decision is made to engage in a task or activity, there are different reasons for doing so. The theories and constructs discussed next focus on these aspects of motivation.

A basic theoretical distinction in the motivation literature is between intrinsic motivation and extrinsic motivation.

 doi:10.1016/B978-0-12-373915-5.00002-4

When individuals are intrinsically motivated, they do activities for their own sake and out of interest in the activity. When they are intrinsically motivated, individuals become deeply engaged in activities. Extrinsic motivation refers to doing an activity to receive a reward or for some other purpose. Self-determination theorists go beyond the extrinsic–intrinsic motivation dichotomy in their discussion of *internalization*, the process of transferring the regulation of behavior from outside to inside the individual. They defined several phases of motivation that are involved in the process of going from external to more internalized regulation. In this model, intrinsic motivation only occurs when the individual autonomously controls the behavior.

One important debate in the field has concerned whether the use of rewards in schools undermines intrinsic motivation. The use of rewards is ubiquitous in schools; yet, theorists who believe intrinsic motivation has many positive effects on students' learning have shown that under certain conditions, the use of such rewards can undermine students' sense of control and autonomy over their achievement outcomes and reduce their intrinsic motivation. This is particularly true when students already possess intrinsic motivation for the activity in question; research with children and adolescents has shown that this undermining indeed occurs. In addition, extrinsic rewards can change students' perception of control from the sense that they control their own achievement outcomes to the sense that the teacher is controlling them. In the 1990s, some behaviorally oriented researchers disputed these claims and conducted meta-analyses of the work in this area that led them to conclude that rewards overall did not undermine intrinsic motivation. A series of debates about this ensued in the literature. Although differences of opinion remained at the end of the debate, research has established that rewards can undermine intrinsic motivation under certain conditions, and so they should be used thoughtfully in school settings.

A construct closely related to intrinsic motivation is interest, and researchers studying interest distinguish between individual and situational interest. As the name implies, individual or personal interest is a characteristic of the individual, and is conceptualized either as a relatively stable disposition or as an active state. By contrast, situational interest stems from conditions in the environment. There are significant but moderate relations between interest and learning of different kinds. When students are interested in the material with which they are working, they process it more deeply and are more involved with it.

Expectancy-value theories include competence-related beliefs and also achievement values, which have to do with different incentives for doing activities. There are different aspects of achievement values. Attainment value refers to the importance of the activity to the individual. Intrinsic value is the enjoyment the individual gets from performing the activity, and so is conceptually linked to intrinsic motivation and interest. Utility value is determined by how well a task relates to current and future goals such as career goals. A task can have positive utility value to a person because it facilitates important future goals, even if he or she is not interested in task for its own sake. In this particular sense, utility value ties conceptually to extrinsic motivation. Finally, cost refers to what one has to give up to do something else; spending time on homework means less time for socializing with friends. Research has shown that children and adolescents' task values predict course plans and enrollment decisions in mathematics, physics, and English and involvement in sport activities even after controlling for prior performance levels.

Goals refer to the purposes individuals have for doing different activities. Proximal goals are short-term goals for specific activities, and distal goals are long-term goals such as planning to complete high school. Both kinds of goals are important for students' success in school. Researchers also have distinguished broader goal orientations students have toward their learning. Initially, three such goal orientations were distinguished. A mastery goal orientation refers to a focus on improving skills, mastering material, and learning new things (this orientation also has been called task involved or learning). A performance or ego orientation is a focus on maximizing favorable evaluations of competence and minimizing negative evaluations of competence. A work-avoidant goal orientation means that the child does not wish to engage in academic activities. This orientation has received less research attention compared to the others.

In the 1990s, researchers differentiated performance and mastery goal orientations into approach and avoid components. Performance-approach goals are students' desire to demonstrate competence and outperform others. Performance-avoid goals involve the desire to avoid looking incompetent. Mastery-approach means wanting to develop new skills and improve; mastery-avoid goals involve perfectionist tendencies. Researchers have demonstrated that mastery-approach goals relate to deep engagement in learning and intrinsic motivation. Performance-avoid goals relate to disengagement with achievement activities. Performance-approach goals are associated with higher GPAs in college students. There have been debates among researchers about the relative merits of performance-approach goals, however.

Situative and Contextual Theories

Motivation researchers increasingly are interested in how children's motivation is affected by the different educational contexts that they experience and acknowledge that motivation is not a stable individual characteristic that operates similarly in different settings. Instead, children and adolescents' motivation is situated in, and strongly influenced by, what occurs in classrooms. For example, the kinds of tasks and activities they experience in different subject areas, how teachers organize and structure these activities (and the classroom environment more generally), and students' relations and interactions with other students all impact motivation in fundamental ways.

Some of the researchers interested in context and motivation have developed sociocultural and situative theories of learning and motivation: these theories are based in part on Vygotsky's sociocultural theory that emphasizes the social nature of learning and development. These theorists posit that individuals' motivation reflects their engagement with the community of learners in their classrooms, and meaningful engagement is not possible by a given individual if the whole community is not engaged. This 'distributed' view of knowledge and motivation rests on different assumptions about the nature of motivation than the assumptions made by social-cognitive theorists about the importance of individual beliefs, values, goals, and other motivation-related constructs *residing in the individual* that are seen as determinants of motivation. The different theoretical traditions tend to employ different kinds of research methods as well; research grounded in social-cognitive theories relies on questionnaires and often treats the individual as the unit of analysis. Socioculturally based research utilizes interviews, observations, and other ways of capturing motivation in situ. This research also can emphasize the classroom or context rather than the individual as the unit of analysis.

Development of Achievement Motivation

Early Development of Achievement Motivation

Young children's reactions to success and failure likely provide the foundation for the development of the different motivational beliefs, values, and goals discussed in this article. Children between 2½ and 3½ years old start to show self-evaluative, nonverbal expressions following a successful or unsuccessful action. The earliest indicators of achievement motivation are facial expressions of joy after success and sadness after failure. The experience of success (around 30 months) precedes the experience of failure (around 36 months). Several months later, children show postural expressions of pride and shame following success and failure. When competing with others, 3- and 4-year-old children initially show joy after winning and sadness after losing. It is only when they look at their competitor that they express pride and shame.

Development of Achievement Motivation During Childhood and Adolescence

Children's motivation changes in a number of ways across the school years; the research documenting these changes has focused primarily on children's competence and efficacy beliefs, intrinsic motivation, and goal orientations. First, children's competence beliefs, achievement values, and intrinsic motivation are differentiated across different achievement domains quite early on. Evidence for this assertion comes from factor analytic studies of children's competence beliefs, values, and intrinsic motivation in different domains; the children included in these studies range in age from 5 to 18. These studies indicate that, for example, children's competence beliefs in reading, math, social studies, music, and so on form separate factors in children as young as age 5. Some developmental theorists proposed that children's characteristics such as motivation begin as fairly general or global constructs and become differentiated across age; the research just discussed indicates that this differentiation begins early in the school years. The implication of these findings is that children understand different subject areas or achievement domains early on, and likely differ in their motivation across them.

Second, the correlations of children's competence beliefs, values, and intrinsic motivation with a variety of outcome variables increase in strength over time. Outcomes assessed include children's grades; teacher and parent ratings of children's performance, competence, and valuing of different activities; children's choice of activities, and time spent on them. These findings indicate that children's motivation corresponds more closely to their achievement outcomes as they get older, that is, the two sets of variables are in greater synchrony with one another as children move through school. Longitudinal studies of the relations of beliefs, values, and intrinsic motivation to achievement outcomes show that these relations are reciprocal, that is, each influences the other over time. These reciprocal relations are especially apparent by early adolescence.

Third, the overall pattern of change in children's competence-related beliefs, values, and intrinsic motivation for different school activities is negative. This pattern has been shown in a variety of longitudinal studies spanning the elementary and secondary school years, and done in different countries around the world. Young children tend to be optimistic in their beliefs, values, and intrinsic motivation for achievement; older children are more realistic and sometimes pessimistic about their achievement. One particular illustration of this is a study that looked at how children in elementary school ranked themselves with respect to their ability in reading. In the first grade, most children said they were the best reader in their class. By the fourth grade, children's self-ratings were much more dispersed. The declines continue into middle and high school, although normative studies show some attenuation of the decline during high school. Other work shows that during secondary school, some children become quite apathetic about school and attempt to avoid school work when it is possible for them to do so. This pattern can result in students dropping out of school when that option becomes available for them. We return to the implications of these findings later.

There are two important exceptions to this general pattern. First, not all young children are overly optimistic about their competence in different areas; even in preschool, some children react quite negatively to failure and are pessimistic about their ability to accomplish different activities. These children may be more likely to display learned helplessness during the elementary school years, which means they believe they cannot succeed on challenging tasks and activities because they do not think they have the skills to do so. Second, although the overall pattern is one of decline, there are exceptions to this rule such that some children's motivation increases across the school years and others' motivation does not change greatly. The different patterns of change in motivation occur in students achieving at higher or lower levels. Although it is important to acknowledge these exceptions, the primary pattern is one of decline in competence beliefs, values, and intrinsic motivation across childhood and through the adolescent years, at least until the end of high school.

There have been fewer developmental studies of children's achievement goal orientations; these studies show that children focus more on performance rather than on mastery goals as they get older.

Fourth, children's competence beliefs, values, and intrinsic motivation become more stable over time. Longitudinal studies of relations over time in these variables show that as children get older, these correlations increase in strength, reaching 0.80 for competence beliefs, 0.74 for achievement values during middle school, and 0.86 for a composite of reading, social studies, and school intrinsic motivation in high school. These findings suggest that children's relative position in the distribution of scores for these different variables is consistent over time. That is, children who have positive competence beliefs maintain them, as do children who have negative competence beliefs. Putting these findings together with the findings about mean differences, as children's competence beliefs, values, and intrinsic motivation decline over time, their position relative to other children in their group stays consistent. This greater stability likely means that adolescents' competence beliefs, values, and intrinsic motivation are more difficult to change than during childhood.

The declines in children's beliefs and values, their stronger relations with outcomes, and increasing stability have been explained in two main ways. One explanation focuses on psychological processes within the child. As they go through school, children are evaluated more frequently and receive more and clearer feedback about their performance, which provides them with more information about their performance. They also spend more time with same-age peers and become adept at comparing themselves with other children. As a result, their self-evaluations often come to correspond more clearly with their own outcomes and reflect their judgments of how they are doing relative to others. With these changes, children's beliefs, values, and intrinsic motivation become more realistic and accurate (in the sense of correlating with outcomes), and stable.

The second explanation concerns changes in the school environments that children experience. As just noted, children are evaluated more frequently as they go through school, and with the current focus on accountability and performance standards in schools, these evaluations have increasingly high stakes for students and teachers, particularly during middle and high school. There often is more competition among students, and a focus on comparing oneself to others. School days become routinized and focus on producing various kinds of assignments and products that may not be of great interest to many students. As a result of these and other kinds of changes, children's competence beliefs, values, and intrinsic motivation for school decline. They focus more on performance outcomes rather than on improving their skills and learning for its own sake. We return to some of these points later.

Group Differences in Motivation

Researchers studying achievement motivation have found gender and ethnic differences in motivation in a variety of achievement domains, including reading, writing, math, and science. This section provides an overview of available findings related to gender differences in achievement motivation during adolescence and early adolescence, focusing on the major motivation constructs that have been discussed in this article.

Gender Differences

Studies have shown that gender differences in students' achievement motivation are age-specific, domain-specific, and culture-specific. Overall, boys and girls generally follow gender role stereotypes in their motivation-related beliefs and behaviors over time. Girls tend to report stronger interest and efficacy in language arts and the arts, whereas boys tend to have more interest and higher efficacy in mathematics and science. Additionally, research shows that gender differences in motivation are seen as early as the beginning of elementary school.

In the domain of reading, girls often report having higher motivation in reading than boys during early adolescence. In the domain of mathematics, girls are more likely to attribute their success to hard work and effort, whereas boys are more likely to attribute their success to ability. Similar patterns of gender differences are seen for attributions of success and failure within the domain of science.

Studies of efficacy and competence beliefs document that girls begin school with higher perceptions of abilities in reading than do boys; whereas boys' beliefs about math and science are more positive than girls' beliefs. During middle school, girls also report higher self-efficacy and self-concept beliefs in writing than do boys. However, in one study considering the extent to which students identified with statements stereotypically associated with male and female characteristics, results showed no gender differences, suggesting that a more feminine orientation may predict students' motivation and achievement in language arts better than the category of gender itself.

Patterns of development show that all children's competency beliefs decline throughout the school years, but there appear to be gender differences in the rate of change in different academic domains. For example, girls' mathematics competence beliefs show a slower decline than boys, suggesting that the gender differences gap in mathematics competence narrows over time. In language arts, boys and girls tend to have similar self-perceptions of their ability at the start of elementary school. However, as children go through their elementary schooling, boys' perceptions of their ability in language arts decline at a more rapid pace over time when compared to girls. By middle school and throughout high school, the gender differences developmental pattern shows that girls' competence beliefs in language arts continue to remain higher than boys, although the gender gap decreases in high school.

Studies done in the 1980s showed that boys and girls tend to follow gender stereotypic patterns in terms of their achievement values, with boys having more positive values in domains such as math and sports, and girls in reading/English and music. However, recent studies have found no gender differences in math value, or rate of change in valuing of mathematics, but have found gender differences in value for English (favoring girls) and sports value and competence beliefs favoring boys. Within the domain of writing, gender differences have been found in students' perceived value of writing. Between middle and high school, males generally rate themselves more highly on math talent, expectancies, and values than do females, and females generally follow similar patterns for English. During elementary school, girls' valuing of language arts declines more quickly than boys', but by high school, the pattern is reversed such that boys show more of a decline in value perceptions of language arts than girls.

Another area that has received some research attention is how the gender composition of groups in school influence students' learning. Learning groups containing more males than females can impede the girls' involvement in the group and their learning. Interestingly, similar findings occurred for groups containing more females than males, such that males were less involved in the group and their learning. Groups containing equal numbers of boys and girls were more likely to produce equal achievement and patterns of interactions for both boys and girls.

Ethnic Differences in Achievement Motivation

Past studies of youth in the United States have shown that ethnic variations exist in students' achievement motivation; it is important to understand that these differences often vary with socioeconomic status, gender, and school environments.

In the light of research findings regarding the achievement gap seen between African American and European American students, it has also been found that African American students have positive competence beliefs about different academic subjects, even when faced with failure, and, when compared to their European American peers, seem to have stronger self-competence beliefs in school even when they are doing less well in school. For example, one study found that African American students had higher reading self-efficacy beliefs than European American students. However, when students' self-efficacy was correlated with their reading achievement, statistically significant results were found only for European-American students. A different pattern was found in a study examining Hispanic- and European American students' self-efficacy in the domain of writing. Hispanic high school students had lower essay writing performance and writing efficacy, and higher writing apprehension than their European American peers. Within this study, self-efficacy had a direct effect on apprehension, which in turn, affected students' performance. Perhaps, the content within reading is based on knowledge and experiences that may be more reflective of the daily lives of European American students, thus requiring more effort and motivation among African American and Hispanic students to understand and comprehend the materials. It may be that lack of content familiarity and relatedness may also attribute to Hispanic students' lower efficacy and performance in writing.

African American students have reported higher preference for challenge and involvement (aspects of intrinsic motivation) in reading than European American children during early adolescence. However, some studies have shown that non-European American (African American, Asian, Hispanic Biracial, and Other) students report engaging in more avoidant behaviors in reading when compared to European American students, while other research has found no ethnic differences in reading avoidance. Within a sample of students from socioeconomically disadvantaged families, researchers found a decline in intrinsic motivation for reading during the transition to middle and high school for both Asian and Hispanic participants. Additionally, intrinsic motivation was positively associated with achievement for Asian American students, but the relations were nonsignificant for Hispanic American students.

Ethnic differences also have been found in students' academic attitudes and values during adolescence and early adolescence. One study found that Mexican American and Chinese American students reported having more positive attitudes and values than did European American students in high school. More specifically, the Mexican American and Chinese American students reported higher educational utility beliefs and values than did the European American students. Additionally, Chinese American students reported higher ratings of value for academic success than did their Mexican American and European American peers. These more positive attitudes and values existed even when Mexican American students had lower grades and Chinese American students had similar grades when compared to students of European backgrounds. Similar results were found in other studies examining ethnic minority students' academic values, such that African American students tended to have higher ratings of the importance of reading than did their European American peers.

Research on peers' valuing and devaluing of achievement has found ethnic by gender interactions in the way middle school students nominate their classmates when examining achievement values and motivation among adolescent and early adolescent peers. One study of students from monoethnic schools where the majority of students were from low socioeconomic status (SES) backgrounds found that both elementary and middle school aged African American and Latino girls tended to nominate same-gendered peers who were high or average achievers as classmates they respected, admired, and wanted to be like. However, a different pattern was seen for boys' peer nominations. During elementary school, African American and Latino boys showed a preference for nominating same-gendered high achieving classmates. By the seventh grade, both African American and Latino boys were more likely to nominate same-gendered classmates who were low achievers as peers they admired, respected, and wanted to be like.

In sum, researchers have found interesting gender and ethnic differences in achievement motivation. Explanations for these differences often focus on the different kinds of socialization practices girls and boys experience, and differences in broader cultural beliefs, cultural values, societal customs, and parental practices within specific ethnic groups in the United States. For example, one explanation put forth by researchers regarding the ethnic gap differences seen in students' achievement motivation is that involuntary ethnic minorities, such as African Americans, may adopt an oppositional identity by showing disdain or disregard toward achievement-related behaviors valued by the larger majority group as a way to protect their social identity within American society. Future studies seeking to investigate group differences in students' achievement motivation should carefully consider the interrelationships among ethnicity, gender, and socioeconomic status in order to capture how specific differences may exist within and across different groups.

Cultural Differences in Motivation

Researchers are examining the nature of adolescents' motivation in different countries in part to examine if the major current motivation theories and constructs pertain to different cultures; the list of suggested readings at the end of this article includes one book looking at current motivation theories in a cross-cultural perspective. Research has shown both similarities and differences in adolescents' motivation in different cultures. Studies based on self-determination theory have found that the basic needs postulated in that theory (autonomy, competence, and relatedness) are prevalent in a variety of cultures, even cultures identified as collectivist, and that when these needs are satisfied, individuals in many different cultures experience psychological well-being. However, the relative weighting of the needs in relation to well-being vary across cultures; for instance, in collectivist cultures, fulfilling the need for relatedness is especially important in this regard. Studies done in different countries have shown that students' ability beliefs, values, and interest predict achievement outcomes such as performance and choice in a manner similar to that found in studies done in North America and Australia. There is evidence that mean-level change in beliefs and values may vary across culture, however. A recent study of American and Chinese seventh and eighth grade students' valuing of academic achievement showed that (as found in the studies discussed earlier) American children's valuing of achievement declined. The Chinese children (who lived outside Beijing) maintained the same level of valuing of achievement across seventh and eighth grade. Research now is needed on the reasons for the different patterns of change in these (and other) countries. Studies of children and adolescents' attributions have found that students in Asian countries tend to attribute their successes more to effort than to ability relative to children and adolescents in the West, perhaps because they view achievement outcomes as more controllable. Finally, qualitative studies indicate that students in different countries may understand concepts such as 'ability' differently, with individuals in some cultures seeing it as a combination of ability and effort. Investigating cultural differences in motivation remains an important priority for future research, in order to determine the adequacy of current prevalent theories for explaining motivation in different cultural settings.

Parental Influences

In a 1966 study, school success was found to be predicted strongly by family background. Since this finding, achievement motivation researchers have been exploring how parental motivation, attitudes and beliefs influence their children's own motivational attitudes and beliefs and their academic performance. In the past, researchers predominantly focused on how general parent beliefs and parenting styles influence their adolescents' general achievement motivation. Recently, researchers have taken more interest in examining domain-specific parent beliefs and parenting philosophies and how these influence their adolescents' domain-specific achievement motivation.

Family Demographic Influences

Family demographic characteristics influence adolescents' motivation either directly or indirectly in several ways. Factors such as family structure, socioeconomic status, parent work demands, quality of neighborhood, and so on can all influence the ways parents interact with their adolescents and thus impact their motivation. As will be discussed later, adolescents' motivation is directly influenced by their parents' beliefs and behaviors. The extent of these influences can differ by family structure (i.e., single-parent family, two-parent family, extended family), demands on parents' time (e.g., having to work more than one job), and environmental opportunities (e.g., quality of schools, safety, and occupational availability). In addition, parents' cultural backgrounds and ethnicity can either directly or indirectly affect adolescents' motivation. For example, some researchers argue that parents value characteristics that they think will help their children succeed in their world. In the reading/language domain, some research has suggested that African American families value story-telling in their sons more than their reading ability (as in most European American families) because this skill will ensure the survival of cultural story-telling in these communities.

Adolescents can also be influenced indirectly by parents' own backgrounds and experiences. For example, some research has shown that rural adolescents may not be highly motivated to go to college if none of their close (in terms of physical distance) nuclear or extended family members has attended college. Although SES does predict parental involvement in children's school activities, SES is not related to parents' *personal* involvement (e.g., knowing adolescents' social networks) with their children or to their adolescent's academic motivation. However, parental involvement at *school* (e.g., going to parent–teacher conferences, being a member of the parent–teacher association) is positively related to economically disadvantaged children's academic motivation. Interestingly, there is no relation of these variables for nondisadvantaged children. Family configuration also seems to influence how involved parents are and in which domains (i.e., school, personal, and cognitive-intellectual). For example, single-parent families are less likely to be involved in school activities than two-parent families; however, no relationship has been found between family configuration, academic motivation, and *cognitive-intellectual* involvement (e.g., helping child with their algebra homework, teaching child how to think abstractly) or personal involvement.

In summary, although demographic factors are important in their own right, family demographic characteristics are often mediated by parents' beliefs and behaviors with their adolescents either positively or negatively. These psychological and social resources thus can exacerbate or ameliorate the effects of poverty and other demographic factors. We discuss these influences next.

Parental Beliefs and Behaviors

Parents' beliefs are related to parents' behaviors for their adolescents' domain-specific academic achievement. In addition, parent beliefs are consistently positively related to their adolescent's own self- and task-beliefs across various domains such as English, math, and sports. Parents seem to play a role in promoting involvement in these domains during the early elementary years, which leads to greater interest and motivation to continue these activities (or similar activities) into adolescence. Parents' domain-specific values even seem to influence an adolescent's domain-specific values and their occupational aspirations past adolescence. In this section, we discuss research on how parents' beliefs and behaviors relate to and influence their adolescent children's motivation.

Parental beliefs

Myriad studies have shown that parental beliefs about their children's abilities in academic (e.g., math and reading) and nonacademic (e.g., sports) domains predict children's own achievement motivation beliefs, performance, and affect.

Most notably, parents' beliefs are more strongly related to children's own beliefs than is children's actual academic performance. These relationships of parent–child beliefs have been found in multiple domains, including mathematics, English, athletics, educational attainment, and occupational aspirations. Parents seem to rely significantly on objective feedback such as grades when formulating perceptions of their children's ability beliefs, and so the relations of parent and child beliefs seem to be based on this performance information. If parents have positive beliefs about their children's competence with corresponding high expectations, provide adequate resources for feelings of connectedness, and allow children to experience autonomy, then children are likely to have competence beliefs and high motivation.

Parents' gender stereotypes have also been found to influence their children's ability perceptions and performance above and beyond that of students' previous performance across these domains. For example, mothers tend to attribute their son's successes in math and sports and their daughter's success in English to natural talent (as opposed to hard work). These gender stereotypes also seem to skew parents' ratings of their adolescents' own domain-specific abilities. In addition, parents seem to talk about academic domains differently with their sons and daughters, with fathers discussing physics with more conceptual language with their sons than when they discuss physics with their daughters.

Parental behaviors

Parents influence their children's motivation through the types of learning experiences and opportunities that they provide for their children, which can then influence children's interest and ability beliefs in these skills. Parents' abilities to manage their children's experiences and intellectual skills are strongly related to children's academic success (even in stressful economic situations). In adolescence this translates into active involvement and monitoring of adolescents' school work, which has been shown to be consistently associated with positive achievement motivation. More importantly, parents who support mastery goals (i.e., the goals to learn and improve) tend to have adolescents with higher grades than adolescents with parents who do not support mastery goals.

Parents' general parenting styles have been related to mastery and performance goals. Specifically, authoritative parenting styles (high demands and high responsiveness) are positively related to adolescents' mastery goals, academic performance, and school engagement; authoritarian parenting styles (high demands and low responsiveness) have been shown to be positively related to performance-approach goals; and permissive parenting styles (low demands and high responsiveness) have been shown to be related to low mastery goals and high performance goals. In addition, controlling parenting styles have been consistently related to performance goals in children and adolescents. The positive influences of authoritative parenting help maintain high levels of academic adjustment over adolescence, whereas neglectful (low demands and low responsiveness) parenting seems to propagate continually lower levels of academic adjustment across the adolescent years. It is important to note that parenting styles vary across different cultures; in some cultures, the authoritarian parenting style is associated with positive achievement outcomes.

Parents also can influence their adolescent's motivation through their supportive behaviors. For example, a longitudinal study found that high reading achievement does not seem to continue into adolescence void of social motivations supported by parents and teachers. Most intriguingly, 'anxious motivation' (i.e., concerns about parent and teacher reactions to performance) seemed to be one of the most influential motivators for high achievement in adolescence for these students.

Research has shown that the impact of socioeconomic factors on motivation and achievement are mediated by parent behaviors (e.g., autonomy support, structure, controlling behaviors). Additionally, gender differences have been found in how these processes work. Mothers have been found to be more significantly impacted by stressful life events (e.g., death of a relative, financial instability, poor work hours), which thereby negatively influenced mothers' autonomy support and structure for their children. Fathers, on the other hand, were not influenced by such stressful events. However, fathers' behaviors toward their children have been shown to be positively influenced by the amount of social support that fathers receive from their friends, family, and neighborhood.

Situational pressures, parental attitudes, and psychological processes (e.g., desire for the child to raise social status) can influence controlling parental behavior in mothers. For example, when mothers are placed in high-pressure performance conditions with their children, they tend to be more controlling than when placed in low-pressure conditions. As children get older, these maternal behavioral trends seem to continue. For example, when mothers perceive their adolescents' environments (both current and future) as more threatening, they tend to have more controlling behaviors and endorse controlling attitudes. This effect has not been found with fathers.

Generally speaking, the research conducted to date on how parent–child beliefs and behaviors promote adolescent achievement motivation proposes three main suggestions for parents:

1. create an appropriate structure of learning experiences,
2. provide consistent and supportive parenting (including emotional support), and
3. teach children through observational learning.

However, it is important to remember that these suggestions are all influenced by the adolescent's culture, age, individual characteristics, and family context.

Parent–Child Attachment During Adolescence

Parent–child attachment during adolescence is of increasing interest to researchers. Although traditionally only studied in young children and adults, current research is expanding this work to include the adolescent developmental period. Parent–child attachment security has been linked to many positive school outcomes (e.g., proper coping with anxiety, appropriate social skills, good grades) and parent–child attachment insecurity has been linked to a myriad of negative school outcomes (e.g., more cases of attention deficit hyperactivity disorder (ADHD), lower grades, poor emotion regulation, inadequate social skills). Despite assumptions that peer relations are more important to adolescents than relations with parents in many ways, attachment researchers have found that adolescents' and young adults' representations of relatedness (i.e., perceived closeness) to their parents seem to be more influential in predicting academic motivation than their representations of relatedness to their friends. These findings suggest that parents still play important roles in motivating their children into late adolescence and early adulthood than is commonly presumed.

New work seems to suggest that parent–child attachment may influence how children perceive all adult relationships. For example, children who thought that an unknown adult would be a more autonomy-supportive teacher *before* being taught a lesson reported higher levels of rapport with the unknown adult *after* meeting them. These findings suggest that parents may be important mediators for how children will perceive (and will continue to perceive) other adults, including teachers. As such, it is important for researchers to further examine these perceptions of adult relationships in childhood to determine whether children's adult perceptions can influence how they perceive adults (and presumed role models) into their adolescent years and how these perceptions may influence their academic motivation.

Future Directions

Fathers are rarely examined in much of the work on parental influence on academic motivation and thus deserve more consideration in future work. In addition, researchers are starting to examine how parent–child relationships differentially influence adolescents based on cultural backgrounds, but much more research on the specific ways in which such relationships differ across culture is needed. Parent–child attachment during adolescence is also starting to be examined in more detail, but more work on this construct is needed. Lastly, it is not clear whether a reciprocal relationship exists between parent beliefs and behaviors and adolescent motivation. As reported previously, most of this work only examines the influence that parental beliefs and behaviors have on adolescent motivation – not the other way around. Future work needs to examine this possibility.

School Influences

Children's experiences in school impact their motivation in a variety of positive and negative ways. We focus in this section on how different classroom practices at different levels influence adolescents' motivation, how teacher–student relations influence children's motivation, and what happens when students transition from one level of school to the next.

Classroom Practices and Adolescents' Motivation

Children's school experiences that impact their motivation can be thought of as occurring at different levels. There are specific tasks and activities that children do, relations between individual students and teachers, practices that impact entire classes of students, and organizational issues that impact all of the students attending a given school. With respect to classroom tasks and activities, research has shown that when tasks and assignments are meaningful to students, reasonably but not too challenging, and varied so that they do not get too repetitive, students are more motivated to engage in them. These motivationally boosting properties of tasks are enhanced when students' performance is evaluated on them with respect to their mastery of the material and improvement, rather than relative performance to others. Teachers support students' developing sense of competence best when they focus on the growth of student skills and mastery.

Another common classroom practice is the use of rewards. We discussed earlier how rewards sometimes undermine students' intrinsic motivation for activities they enjoy, particularly when those rewards are used to control students. Rewards and praise can be used effectively to increase students' motivation when all students see they have the chance to obtain them, the rewards provide information about how they are doing rather than being given solely for completion of activities or to control students, and they are based on mastery of material rather than relative performance.

One of the practices that has received a great deal of research attention is grouping students by their level of performance or ability. This practice impacts students in a given class and also can affect their experiences across the school day. There are two kinds of ability grouping: within a classroom (when students in a given class are separated into different groups for the purposes of instruction), and between class grouping or tracking (when entire classes are made up of students of a given ability or performance level; tracking becomes more prevalent in middle and high school). A major purpose of ability grouping is to help teachers cope with the challenge of having too wide a dispersion of ability in a given classroom; by grouping by ability teachers can focus their instruction. The effects of ability grouping on students' motivation are mixed and depend in part to which students compare themselves to. Students doing less well in school are able to maintain a stronger sense of competence when grouped with like-performing peers. By contrast, the competence beliefs of students performing well actually can suffer when they are ability-grouped because they only have other high-achieving students to whom they compare themselves. More broadly, students in the lower track are at risk of being labeled as being less competent, and such labels can negatively impact their self-esteem and sense that they will do well in school. Another challenge with ability grouping is that teachers assigned to teach the lower track classes often are less experienced and sometimes are the weaker teachers in the school. Schools that have done away with ability grouping often have higher achievers work with lower achievers, and research has shown that this has benefits for both groups. Decisions about whether to ability-group or not often are based on political and educational considerations, and many parents of high-achieving students strongly support its use. It therefore is a practice that likely will remain in place.

Another practice at the classroom level that has received a great deal of research attention is cooperative learning, or students working together in groups to complete different assignments. Cooperative learning has been shown to have positive effects on students' achievement, relations with other students, and motivation. One of the reasons it positively impacts motivation is that it capitalizes on students' interest in working with and socializing with their peers. Cooperative learning also can be effective with students of different achievement levels if the tasks and activities they do in groups are structured in ways that allow all members of the team to contribute. Indeed, for cooperative learning to be effective, teachers must carefully structure the groups and ensure that all students are accountable for the work produced by the group.

Teacher–Student Relations and Student Motivation

The ways in which teachers and students interact influence students' motivation in different ways. One way is how they support students' autonomy and control over their own learning. Research indicates that when students have some of this control they are more positively motivated to learn, and teachers have an important role in supporting that autonomy. Autonomy support becomes even more important during adolescence; one of the tasks of adolescents is to become more independent from the important adults in their lives. When teachers support students' autonomy over their learning, this process can be facilitated. Research has indicated that autonomy support does not mean complete independence and freedom to do anything they want; autonomy support is most effective when teachers continue to provide a structure for students.

The nature of the affective relationship between teachers and students also impacts students' motivation. When teachers care about students, show interest in their lives, and provide emotional support to them, students are more likely to engage in classroom activities, have more positive competence beliefs, and be motivated to achieve. Teachers' affective relations with students contribute to motivation in these ways even when the quality of parent and peer relations is controlled in statistical analyses of these relationships. The affective relations of teachers and students are of central importance during adolescence. Even as adolescents separate to a degree from the adults in their lives, the quality of their emotional relationships with teachers is key to their motivation and achievement.

School Transitions and Student Motivation

Most adolescents go through two school transitions, elementary to middle and middle to high school, and each can impact students' motivation and achievement. We noted earlier that children's academic motivation declines over age. These changes are particularly large for students who do poorly (either emotionally or academically) at school. Research has shown that the transition from elementary to middle school can accelerate these negative changes. Adolescents experience a variety of transitions along with school transitions (puberty, changing relations with parents, increasing cognitive maturity, increasing concern with identity, increasing sexuality and heterosociality, and increasing focus on peer relationships), and experiencing a number of transitions at the same time can be difficult. Moreover, there are important structural and organizational differences between secondary school and elementary school that can exacerbate the challenges associated with the transition. Most secondary schools are substantially larger than elementary schools because several elementary schools come together in one middle school. As a result, students' friendship networks often are disrupted as they attend classes with students from several different schools. Students have been found to feel more anonymous and alienated because of the larger size of many secondary schools. Rules for student conduct often become more severe because there are so many students with whom teachers and administrators have to monitor. Opportunities to participate in and play leadership roles in school activities often decline over these school transitions due to the limited number of slots in such niches and the increasing size of the student body. These kinds of changes affect the students' sense of belonging as well as their sense of social competence. Students typically have several teachers every day with little opportunity to interact with any one teacher on any deeper dimension beyond the academic content of what is being taught and disciplinary issues. As a result, the likelihood of students and teachers forming close, supportive bonds is less in secondary than in elementary schools. Researchers have argued that these structural changes result in a school environment that does not fit well with the developing adolescent. At a time when adolescents desire more social interaction, autonomy, and activity involvement, schools can have a difficult time providing such opportunities.

Research on the transition to high school suggests that similar changes occur at this transition. High schools are typically even larger and more bureaucratic than middle and junior high schools, which has been shown to undermine the sense of community among teachers and students. Such environments have been shown to undermine the motivation and involvement of students, especially those not doing particularly well academically, and those who are alienated from the values of the adults in the high school. These changes contribute to some adolescents' decisions, particularly those who are already on the margins of the school community, to withdraw from school prior to graduation.

Based in part on research on the impact of the transitions to middle and high school on students' motivation, different reform efforts have been undertaken to change the organization and structure of middle schools and some high schools in order to minimize the negative impact of the transition on adolescents' motivation, engagement, and achievement. These efforts focus on creating teams of students and teachers, smaller learning communities within the larger school, creating opportunities for teachers and students to interact outside of the content being taught, and providing more opportunities for student involvement. These and other reform efforts are designed to help students connect to the school and the staff there. Research on some of these efforts, particularly those having to do with the creation of small learning communities within the larger school structure, has found that the reforms have positive influences on adolescents' motivation and achievement.

School and Motivation in Different Cultures

The research on schooling and its effects on students' motivation summarized in this section was done primarily in the United States. Researchers are beginning to examine variations in school structure and classroom practices in different countries and how they may relate to students' motivation. We note two illustrative examples. In Germany, researchers have examined how schools in East Germany changed after the country reunified, and are looking at how students' performance was being affected by these changes. They are also examining student motivation in the three different tracks prevalent in many German schools. Research in Korea has shown that whole class instruction and strong teacher control over classrooms are prevalent in many schools: such practices go against recommendations by motivation theorists that students have greater control over their learning and instruction be differentiated for different students. Interestingly, Korean children perform well in the international studies of achievement such as TIMSS and PISA; however, it appears that many Korean children lack confidence in their abilities and express little interest in their school work. The complex relationships among school structure and teaching practices, student performance, and student motivation in different countries need further research attention, to provide us with a more complete picture of these relationships.

Peers and Motivation During Adolescence

Peer relations become increasingly important during adolescence, for a variety of reasons, and they influence adolescents' motivation in school. When children are socially supported and accepted by their peers, they have stronger motivation, better achievement outcomes, and are more engaged at school. Further, positive peer relations and social support can help ease school transitions. In contrast, socially rejected and highly aggressive children, and also those who are victimized by others, are at risk for poorer achievement and motivation.

The stereotypical view of 'peer influences' is that peers often exert negative influences on one another in different areas, such as the likelihood of engaging in risky behaviors, or other activities that parents and teachers find unacceptable. Peer influences on achievement motivation are not uniformly negative; peer groups at school can have either a positive or negative effect on motivation across various activity settings. Children who come together in peer groups often share similar motivational orientations and activity preferences, and such groupings reinforce and strengthen their existing motivational orientation and activity preferences over time. Whether such effects are positive or negative depends on the nature of the peer group's motivational orientation. High-achieving children who seek out other high achievers as friends develop even more positive academic motivation over time. Conversely, lower-achieving children with less positive academic motivation who form groups do even less well as a result of the group's influences.

Conclusion

Adolescence is a time of continued change in children's achievement motivation. Adolescents' beliefs, values, and goals that determine how they are motivated or not motivated to approach different activities become increasingly well-defined and stable over time, but are also highly responsive to the influence of parents, schools, and peers. We are learning more about the development of motivation in different cultures, but work on that topic remains a major priority for the future.

See also: Academic Achievement; Adolescent Decision-Making; Gender Issues; Gender Roles; Motivation; Parenting Practices and Styles; Peer Influence; Schools and Schooling; Self-Development During Adolescence; Self-Esteem; Socialization.

Further Reading

Eccles JS and Wigfield A (2002) Motivational beliefs, values, and goals. *Annual Review of Psychology* 53: 109–132.

Heckhausen J and Heckhausen H (2010) *Motivation and Action*, 2nd English Edition. Cambridge: Cambridge University Press.

McInerney DM and Van Etten S (2004) *Big Theories Revisited: Research on Sociocultural Influences on Motivation and Learning*, vol. 4. Greenwich, CT: Information Age Press.

Schunk DH, Pintrich PR, and Meece JL (2007) *Motivation in Education: Theory, Research, and Applications*, 3rd edn. Upper Saddle River, NJ: Prentice Hall.

Schunk DH and Zimmerman BJ (2008) *Motivation and Self-regulated Learning: Theory, Research, and Applications*. New York: Taylor Francis.

Urdan TC and Karabenick SA (2010) *The Decade Ahead: Theoretical Perspectives on Motivation and Achievement, Vol. 16A: Advances in Motivation and Achievement*. Bingley, UK: Emerald Group.

Weiner B (1992) *Human Motivation: Metaphors, Theories, and Research*. Newbury Park, CA: Sage Publications.

Wentzel KR and Wigfield A (eds.) (2009) *Handbook of Motivation at School*. Mahwah, NJ: Taylor-Frances.

Wigfield A, Byrnes JB, and Eccles JS (2006) Adolescent development. In: Alexander PA and Winne P (eds.) *Handbook of Educational Psychology*, 2nd edn., pp. 87–113. Mahwah, NJ: Erlbaum.

Wigfield A and Cambria J (2010) Students' achievement values, goal orientations, and interest: Definitions, development, and relations to achievement outcomes. *Developmental Review* 30: 1–35.

Wigfield A, Eccles JS, Schiefele U, Roeser R, and Davis-Kean P (2006) Development of achievement motivation. In: Damon W and Eisenberg N (eds.) *Handbook of Child Psychology*, 6th edn., vol. 3, pp. 933–1002. New York: Wiley.

Adolescence, Theories of

B M Newman, University of Rhode Island, Kingston, RI, USA
P R Newman, Wakefield, RI, USA

Glossary

Autonomy: Achieving a state of self-reliance and self-determination; not being dependent on others for emotional regulation or decision-making.
Drive: A Freudian term describing an unconscious force compelling some action to dispel the tension created by a biological or intrapsychic need within the organism.
Ego: A component of the Freudian psychic system that operates in both the unconscious and conscious realm, charged with gratifying drives without encountering recriminations from the world outside the unconscious self.
Equilibrium: A Piagetian term in which cognitive structures that represent reality symbolically "inside one's head" match the reality they are attempting to describe.
Ethologist: One who studies the relations between human (or animal) organisms and their environments.
Id: An unconscious component of the Freudian psychic system that is focused on gratifying all desires and needs of the organism.
Social role: A status or position within an organization or society with prescribed patterns of behavior.
Superego: An unconscious component of the Freudian psychic system representing the child's understanding of parental/societal rules and expectations; thus, a person's "moral compass."
Virtual community: A group of individuals who have relationships strictly through the electronic media, not face-to-face interaction.

Introduction

Adolescence is both universal and culturally constructed, resulting in diverse views about its defining characteristics. Across cultures, people experience a gradual physical transition from childhood status to adult status including changes in reproductive capacities, physical stature, body shape, strength, endurance, and the maturation of the brain. The period of pubertal development may begin as early as age 9 and continue into the 20s. Cultures vary widely, however, in how young people are treated including the timing of access to certain rights and privileges, entry into specific settings, and expectations for assuming adult roles and responsibilities. Social environments may accelerate the transition into adulthood or delay it.

A theory is a logical system of concepts that helps explain observations and contributes to the development of a body of knowledge. Theories of adolescence help to define the boundaries of the period by pointing to essential features of one or more aspects of adolescent functioning. Some theories provide a framework for distinguishing stages or phases within adolescence, offering concepts that differentiate the essential capacities that emerge over the years of pubertal maturation. Theories distinguish adolescence from childhood and early adulthood, placing this period into the context of the lifespan.

Theories of adolescence differ in their scope and range of applicability. Some theories, sometimes referred to as grand theories, offer concepts and hypotheses about multiple domains, usually over a long period of the lifespan, and are applicable across multiple contexts. Psychosexual theory is an example of a grand theory which encompasses ideas about the dynamics of mental life, sexual and aggressive drives, morality, family dynamics, personality, and psychopathology. The grand theories are often stimuli for more focused, mid-level theories that address a specific domain or process.

In other instances, mid-level theories stand alone as models for explaining particular aspects of behavior. For example, social network theory focuses on the way individuals become affiliated with one another, how allegiances are formed, and the links and influences that occur across members of various groups. This theory has relevance for understanding the social and interpersonal experiences of adolescents and the spread of antisocial or prosocial attitudes and behaviors in peer groups.

Finally, some theories are of emerging importance to the study of adolescence. For example, biosocial theory which has emerged from evolutionary theory, incorporates knowledge about brain functioning into social cognition, the interaction of emotion and cognition, and the impact of environmental conditions on the expression of genetic predispositions.

Families of Theories

The following sections provide an introduction to 10 families of theories that have guided scholarship in the field of adolescent development. Families are identified by their link to a shared intellectual tradition or theoretical foundation, and their contribution to the understanding of a common set of questions about adolescent development. For each family, we provide an overview of the scope of the theory, that is, a description of the theory's range of applicability. We also present basic assumptions about the nature of development, and contributions to the field of adolescent development and behavior.

Psychosexual Theories

Scope

Psychosexual theory is a grand theory that addresses the development of mental life and personality, including drives, emotions, memories, fantasies, dreams, logical and irrational thoughts.

 Encyclopedia of Adolescence, Volume 1 doi:10.1016/B978-0-12-373915-5.00003-6

The theory provides an analysis of the developmental origins of mental life, the role of early experiences in shaping later psychological functioning, the nature of inner conflicts, and the causes of symptoms associated with mental disorders.

Assumptions

Sexual and aggressive drives find unique modes of expression in the individual's psychological functioning through successive developmental stages. Childhood experiences have a continuing influence on adult thoughts and behavior. All behavior (except that resulting from fatigue) is motivated and has meaning.

Contributions of psychosexual theory for adolescence

Psychosexual theory views adolescence as the beginning of the final stage in the development of mental life and personality. During this period, the person develops sexual interests and seeks to find ways of satisfying sexual impulses in mature, dyadic relationships. The onset of puberty brings about a reawakening of Oedipal or Electra conflicts (in which individuals have a close, emotional, somewhat sexualized bond to the other-sex parent and a competitive feeling toward the same-sex parent) and a reworking of earlier childhood identifications.

Sigmund Freud introduced the concept of ego and its executive functions in managing the expression of impulses, negotiating between the id and the superego, striving to attain goals embedded in the ego ideal, and assessing reality. Building on this conceptualization, several mid-level theories emerged which highlight aspects of ego functioning and the nature of ego development from adolescence into adulthood.

Anna Freud outlined new ego capacities that emerge from infancy through adolescence. She highlighted the various threats that id poses to ego at each stage of development. and provided a classification of defense mechanisms that ego uses to protect itself from unruly and unacceptable impulses. She gave special attention to the period of adolescence as a time of increased sexual and aggressive energy which is linked to the biological changes of puberty. At this time, children are likely to be overwhelmed by libidinal energy and ego is more or less fighting for its life. Anger and aggression become more intense, sometimes to the point of getting out of hand. Appetites become enormous. Oral and anal interests resurface, expressed as pleasure in dirt and disorder, exhibitionistic tendencies, brutality, cruelty to animals, and enjoyment of various forms of vulgarity. Adolescents may vacillate in their behavior from loving to mean, compliant to rebellious, or self-centered to altruistic, as ego tries to assert itself in the midst of conflicting and newly energized libidinal forces.

Peter Blos expanded the concept of ego and the mechanisms of defense by theorizing about coping mechanisms that emerge in adolescence as young people find ways of adapting psychologically to the physical transitions of puberty. By the end of adolescence, ego conflicts present at the beginning of puberty are transformed into more manageable aspects of identity construction. Blos noted five major accomplishments of ego development for young people who navigate adolescence successfully:

1. Judgment, interests, intellect, and other ego functions emerge which are specific to the individual and very stable.
2. The conflict-free area of ego expands, allowing adolescents to find satisfaction in new relationships and experiences.
3. An irreversible sexual identity is formed.
4. The egocentrism of childhood is replaced by a balance between thoughts about oneself and thoughts about others.
5. A boundary between one's public and private selves is established.

A number of other scholars expanded the theoretical analysis of ego development, highlighting the creative and adaptive nature of ego functioning in adolescence and the ego's role in shaping individuality and identity.

Cognitive Developmental Theories

Scope

Cognition is the process of organizing and making meaning of experience. Cognitive developmental theory focuses on how knowing emerges and is transformed into logical, systematic capacities for reasoning and problem solving. Perhaps the most widely known and influential cognitive theorist is Jean Piaget.

Assumptions

Humans strive to achieve equilibrium, a balance of organized structures within motor, sensory, and cognitive domains. When structures are in equilibrium, they provide effective ways of interacting with the environment. Whenever changes in the person or in the environment require a revision of the basic structures, they are thrown into disequilibrium.

Contributions of cognitive developmental theory for adolescence

Cognitive developmental theory hypothesized a unique stage of thinking that emerges in adolescence, formal operational thought. According to Inhelder and Piaget, at this stage a person is able to conceptualize about many variables interacting simultaneously. Formal operational reasoning results in the creation of a system of logical principles that can be used for problem solving. Thought becomes reflective, so that adolescents can think about their thinking, evaluate logical inferences of their thoughts, and form hypotheses about the relationships among observations. Formal operational reasoning is propositional and probabilistic; the person can hypothesize about possible outcomes and evaluate the likelihood of one outcome over another. This is the kind of intelligence on which science and philosophy are built.

Theoretical work outlining stages of cognition and the processes that bring about changes in reasoning led others to explore whether this same quality of thought might apply in domains other than scientific reasoning. Two mid-level theories emerged, one focusing on moral development led by Lawrence Kohlberg, and one focusing on social cognition, with work by Robert Selman, William Damon, and others. These theories described qualitative shifts in reasoning from childhood to adolescence, hypothesizing about the ability of adolescents to step back from their own point of view, and to take multiple perspectives into account as they evaluate moral and social scenarios.

The theoretical characterization of formal operational thought led to extensive empirical investigation. Although research generally finds that adolescents are better able than younger children to solve problems involving multiple variables and problems in which they have to inhibit the impulse to reach an answer before processing all the information, these abilities are not universally well developed in adolescence. They are strongly influenced by culture and schooling, and they do not emerge as a clearly coordinated 'package' of new capacities at a specific time associated with puberty. As a result, recent theorists have focused on specific aspects of reasoning. This work is converging with studies in neuroscience on the maturation of the prefrontal cortex, and focuses on features of executive functioning and meaning making.

Work by scholars such as Deanna Kuhn and Paul Klaczynski point to the role of mental representations and the awareness of alternative interpretations in adolescents' ability to solve specific reasoning problems. Klaczynski identified two complementary processes that improve in adolescence. One results in increased speed of processing, automatic recognition of patterns that have been experienced in the past, and quick, well-rehearsed responses. The other increases a person's ability to allocate attention and manage the controlled execution of a task. Klaczynski argues that what develops in adolescents is a greater capacity to inhibit the reliance on first impressions, stereotypes, and overly simplistic solutions as they review and evaluate information. Kuhn suggests that the trajectory of cognitive development in adolescence is especially sensitive to the person's self-directed engagement with cognitive challenges. The range and diversity of cognitive abilities observed among adolescents are products of the differences in interest, motivation, and values that adolescents invest in specific types of problems and their solutions.

Identity Theories

Scope

Erik Erikson introduced psychosocial theory, which addresses patterned changes in self-understanding, identity formation, social relationships, and worldview across the lifespan. A major contribution of psychosocial theory is the identification of adolescence as the period of life when a person formulates a personal identity, a framework of values and commitments that guide major life choices in the transition to adulthood. The construct of personal identity has stimulated many theories that consider the process of identity formation and the relationship of identity to subsequent developmental goals, especially intimacy, academic attainment, career paths, and ideological commitments.

Assumptions

Development is a product of the ongoing interactions between individuals and their social environments. Societies, with their structures, laws, roles, rituals, and sanctions, are organized to guide individual growth toward a particular ideal of mature adulthood. However, every society faces problems in attempting to balance the needs of the individual with the needs of the group. All individuals face some strains as they seek to express their individuality while maintaining the support of their groups and attempting to fit into their society. Attaining maturity involves reduced reliance on the expectations and plans of others. These are replaced by new levels of self-determination and focus on one's own aspirations and goals.

Contributions of identity theory for adolescence

The psychosocial crisis of adolescence, personal identity versus identity confusion, highlights the need for individuals to find self-definition and a sense of meaning and purpose as they move into adulthood. The achievement of personal identity requires reworking the self concept, including an integration of past identifications, current talents and abilities, and a vision of oneself moving into the future. Identity formation is widely adopted as a central developmental challenge of adolescence. The concept captures the spirit of a push toward individuality, societal values of self-determination and agency, and expectations that young people will begin to take ownership of their path toward adulthood by making commitments to specific roles and values, and by rejecting others.

One of the most widely used frameworks for assessing identity status was devised by James Marcia. Erikson conceptualized identity as a tension between two states: identity achievement and identity confusion. In contrast, Marcia differentiated four states based on two criteria: crisis and commitment. Crisis consists of a period of role experimentation and active decision making among alternative choices. Commitment consists of demonstrations of personal involvement in occupational choice, religion, political ideology, and interpersonal relationships. Identity status is assessed as identity achievement, foreclosure, moratorium, or confusion. People who are classified as identity achieved have experienced a period of questioning and exploration, and have made occupational and ideological commitments. Those classified as foreclosed have not experienced a period of exploration, but demonstrate strong occupational and ideological commitments. Their occupational and ideological beliefs are often close to those of their parents. People classified as being in a state of psychosocial moratorium are involved in ongoing crisis and questioning. They have postponed their commitments, but are comfortable with experiencing a period of open exploration. Those classified as identity confused are unable to make commitments, and experience anxiety and distress about their uncertainty.

This framework of identity formation and identity status has led to mid-level theories about specific aspects of identity, including gender identity, career identity, ethnic identity, and multicultural identity. In each of these areas, scholars have recognized the dynamic interaction between personal qualities and the social roles, opportunities, and demands that may exist at the time.

Theorists such as Michael Berzonsky and Wim Meeus have provided micro theories to explore differences in how young people process identity-relevant information. For example, some adolescents are very close-minded, rejecting experiences that disconfirm their strongly held beliefs. Others are open to diverse experiences, seeking new ideas and information to widen their view of what might be possible in life. These theories focus on daily experiences that provide information which may confirm or modify the sense of identity.

Evolutionary And Biosocial Theories

Scope

Charles Darwin's theory of evolution explains how diverse and increasingly more complex life-forms come to exist.

Assumptions

Natural laws that apply to plant and animal life also apply to humans.

Contributions of evolutionary theory for adolescence

A major implication of evolutionary theory for adolescence is that the future of a species depends on the capacity of individuals to find a mate, reproduce, and rear their young. Factors that contribute to the health of individuals as they reach reproductive age, characteristics of environments that promote or discourage mate selection, and capacities of sexually mature partners to protect and rear their offspring are highlighted. Since adolescence is the period when mature sexual and reproductive capacities flourish, and when attitudes toward marriage and childbearing crystallize, the quality of life for adolescents has essential implications for the future of the species.

Ethologists ask about behavioral systems that serve adaptive functions. Among those, one of the most robust is the ability of infants to signal distress in order to engage caregiving behaviors, and the ability of caregivers to comfort, soothe, and protect their infants from harm. Attachment theory explores these abilities, suggesting that as result of sensitive, responsive caregiving, infants form mental representations of self and other, and an expectation about whether or not they can rely on their caregivers to provide safety and comfort. When caregiving is indifferent, harsh, or unpredicatable, infants form an insecure, anxious, or disorganized mental representation of their caregivers. These mental representations generalize to other significant close relationships, especially friendships, romantic relationships in adolescence, and parenting as adults. According to attachment theory, there is the possibility of continuity or revision of the attachment relationship in adolescence. Attachment to parents in later adolescence and adulthood has been characterized as reflecting one of three orientations:

1. autonomous, which is reflective of an open, confident narrative about parent–child relationships;
2. dismissive, which is reflective of minimizing the parent–child relationship, accompanied by an inability to recall many details of the relationship; or
3. preoccupied, which is reflective of continuing anger toward parents and a confused, vague, or passive narrative.

Older adolescents who have a secure relationship with their parents can begin to explore the ideological, occupational, and interpersonal alternatives that provide the content for their own identities. Those who are still emotionally dependent on their parents and require constant reassurance of their affection show a greater tendency to experience identity confusion.

Contemporary applications of evolutionary theory focus on the integration of biological and social forces to create a biosocial analysis of development. The concept of phenotype reflects this integration– the expression of genetic structure in a specific environment. The work of Jay Belsky and Lawrence Steinberg provide examples of this biosocial approach. Studies that combine biological mechanisms such as endocrinology, immunology, or genetics and behavior have contributed to our understanding of the establishment of gendered behavior, sexual interest, strategies of mate selection, and the relationship of harsh or rejecting parenting and the onset of puberty.

Family Theories

Scope

Family theories focus on the dynamic interactions among family members, describing changes in typical patterns of parent–child relationships, and the characteristics of family interactions that enhance or disrupt development. From an evolutionary perspective, families have evolved as the social context to support human development. Human infants have few innate reflexes, but they have a wealth of sensory and motor capacities to engage in social interactions, and an enormous capacity to learn. Families have evolved as contexts within which infants and children are protected from harm, nurtured, educated, and socialized into their cultures.

Assumptions

Development in families is reciprocal. The changing abilities, roles, and needs of each family member influence the development of other members of the family group, and the family's level of functioning has consequences for development of each individual member.

Contributions of family theories for adolescence

Introduced by Evelyn Duvall and Ruben Hill in the 1940s, family development theory offered a conceptualization of families changing in a systematic pattern from family formation to widowhood. In the most well-known version of family development theory, two stages are of particular relevance for adolescence, when children enter adolescence, and when the children are leaving the family, called the launching stage. In the first of these stages, parents need to find ways to help adolescent children establish their separate identities. Adolescents are thought to be able to contribute in new ways to the tasks of the family, and at the same time, parents are challenged to accommodate adolescents' desires for more space, resources, and personal freedom. Maintaining open communication during this period may be difficult due to the increased activity of adolescents coupled with the involvement of parents in the labor market. The second stage is the first phase of family contraction. As children leave home, families adapt by changing patterns of communication and reallocating resources. Relationships between children and their parents may become more ambiguous, and parents may be less clear about how to support their children who are striving to achieve a new level of self-sufficiency.

The concept of differentiation, which emerged from Murray Bowen's conceptualization of family systems theory, is associated with psychosocial maturity and a healthy emergence of individuality in adolescence. Within the family context, identity exploration is facilitated by an open exchange of ideas and a certain level of challenge. Adolescents require opportunities to express their separateness within the boundaries of the family. This takes place as parents encourage their children to express new ideas and differing points of view without making them feel guilty when they disagree. Ideally, individuality is achieved in a context of mutual caring and emotional support.

Olsen's circumplex model of family systems emphasizes the importance of a balance among three dimensions: cohesion, flexibility, and communication for preserving adaptive functioning in families. Adolescence presents new challenges in each of these domains as adolescents' efforts to establish an expanded voice in decision making and new levels of autonomy may disrupt earlier patterns of family interactions, boundaries, and rules.

Differentiation requires an age-appropriate balance between autonomy and connection. Laurence Steinberg has conceptualized the nature and development of autonomy. Autonomy is the ability to regulate one's behavior and to select and guide one's own decisions and actions without undue control from or dependence on one's parents. In optimal parent–child relationships, within the context of emerging autonomy, the sense of connection is still preserved. Built on a history of nurture and care, parents and children strive to preserve a continuing close, supportive relationship into adulthood. However, those bonds are reworked in later adolescence and early adulthood through a process of self-definition. Adolescents who achieve autonomy can recognize and accept both the similarities and the differences between themselves and their parents, while still feeling love, understanding, and connection with them. Adolescents who experience high levels of parental control and frequent exposure to parental conflict are likely to have difficulties in achieving a comfortable sense of autonomy.

Parenting practices are theorized to have a substantial impact on adolescents' behavior, including academic achievement, peer relationships, capacity for self-regulation, and emerging identity. The theoretical construct of parenting styles has been described in various ways by Baumrind, Hoffman, Darling and Steinberg, and Maccoby and Martin. Theories of parenting typically consider the ways that parents coordinate warmth and control, closeness and flexibility, reciprocity and bidirectional communication, and power. Parenting styles have been characterized as authoritarian (high control, low warmth), authoritative (high control, high warmth), permissive (low control, high warmth), and neglectful (low control, low warmth). Other theories of parenting use the term 'democratic parenting' to refer to the willingness to involve children in decision making while still communicating clear and high standards for behavior. Parenting styles that combine emotional warmth, high standards, and open communication are thought to be optimal for supporting emotional maturation and emerging identity in adolescence. Recent theories by Meeus, van Doorn, and Branje focus on the context of the adults' marital relationship as it impacts the parent–child relationship and the effectiveness of parenting practices. High levels of marital conflict and unresolved tensions in the marital dyad are transmitted to the adolescent–parent relationship and undermine the effectiveness of authoritative parenting.

Interpersonal Theories

Scope

Interpersonal theories highlight the social nature of humans and the central role of belonging, connection, and social or group identity for well-being in adolescence. George Herbert Mead and Charles Cooley provided a framework for thinking about the social construction of the self which takes shape as other people respond to our gestures and actions. With increasing maturity, one begins to anticipate the reactions of others, thereby forming a social self, a set of expectations about how one's behavior will evoke reactions in others. Family is considered the primary group in which face-to-face interactions are especially salient and have the greatest impact on shaping self-concept.

Assumptions

Interpersonal behavior has an evolutionary basis. Humans are social animals whose survival depends on integration into social groups. Thus, humans have strong needs for a sense of connection and belonging to social groups. Humans collaborate and communicate in complex ways to achieve shared goals. Humans have needs to be understood. The goal of communication is the coordination of understanding between two or more people around shared meaning. Communication is made possible when people engage in interactions that involve mutually shared symbols. Anxiety results from problems in interpersonal relationships. When people do not have shared symbols to express their emotions, fantasies, or thoughts, their mental lives become isolated.

Contributions of interpersonal theories for adolescence

In adolescence, the need for group belonging expands beyond the family to include other kinds of group affiliation. Two lines of theory have emerged within the interpersonal perspective, one focusing on the nature of close, dyadic friendships including popularity, loneliness, peer rejection, and best friends, and the other focusing on the nature of peer group structure, group affiliation, and peer group influences.

Harry Stack Sullivan, who influenced the former line of theory, identified adolescence as a time when the capacity for intimacy is emerging. He described three phases of adolescence:

1. preadolescence when children form close personal best friend relationships, typically with same-sex friends;
2. early adolescence when teens extend their friendships to include members of the other sex and begin to explore sexualized interactions; and
3. late adolescence, when a person discovers how to integrate sexual feelings and intimacy in a close relationship.

Work by Denise Kandel, Duane Burhmester, Willard Hartup, Thomas Berndt, Steven Asher, and Andrew Collins among many others have contributed to this line of theory about close relationships to develop a detailed picture of changing capacities for close friendships, increasing importance of friends in middle childhood and adolescence, the emergence of romantic relationships, and stability and change that characterize friendship relationships throughout adolescence.

Dexter Dunphy, who provided a framework for the second direction, described two patterns of peer group boundaries: cliques (small groups of about six members who enjoy frequent face-to-face interactions) and crowds (looser associations among several cliques). Cliques provide the immediate context for interpersonal interactions. Recent theories by Herman Schwendinger, Bradford Brown, and others view crowds in a different way, as prototypes for social identities. Crowds are usually recognized by a few predominant characteristics, such as their orientation toward academics, involvement in athletics, use of drugs, or involvement in deviant behavior. Crowds are more reputational than cliques, reflecting students' values and attitudes, preferred activities, and school and nonschool engagement. Phil and Barbara Newman's analysis of group identity versus alienation as the psychosocial crisis of early adolescence expanded on the salience of group identifications during this period of life. Group identity is a developmental precursor to personal identity. Chronic conflict about one's integration into meaningful groups and associated feelings of alienation can lead to lifelong difficulties in areas of personal health, work, and the formation of intimate family bonds.

An emerging focus is the use of network theory to examine the process through which adolescents become connected to one another. Some scholars have used this approach to link peer networks to adolescent drug use. This theory examines the likelihood that people will form networks, the stability of these networks, and patterns of influence within and among networks. Social network theory can be used to describe patterns of social support, social identity, peer influence, contagion of beliefs or risky behaviors, patterns of exchange of resources, or the flow of information. Social network theory provides a way of conceptualizing the value and meaning of virtual communities for adolescents such as those formed in the Internet, as well as ways that adolescents are linked across communities and countries.

Ecological Theories

Scope

Ecological theories focus on the interaction of persons and environments with particular attention to how the features of environments require unique adaptations, both physical and psychological.

Assumptions

The father of ecological theory as it applies to human behavior was Kurt Lewin who argued that all behavior must be understood in light of the field or context in which the behavior takes place.

Contributions of ecological theory for adolescence

Lewin saw the process of developmental change as a continuous modification of regions, needs, and forces that encourage or inhibit behavior. He viewed adolescence as an example of how field theory might be used to interpret complex life events. His primary analogy for adolescence was the image of the 'marginal man' straddling the boundary between two regions, childhood and adulthood. This marginality includes being scornful of the group one desires to leave and uncertain about or even rejected by the group one wishes to join. Three events occur during adolescence that explain many of the phenomena characteristic of the life stage.

1. During a period of movement from one region to another, the total lifespace is enlarged, bringing the young person into contact with more information about the environment and, presumably, about oneself.
2. A widening lifespace results in greater uncertainty about the nature of each new region.
3. Biological changes associated with puberty alter innerpersonal regions and perceptual-motor regions of the lifespace.

Rapid expansion of regions and uncertainty about both personal and environmental structures of the lifespace result in an emotional tension during adolescence. Characteristics of adolescent behavior including emotional instability, value conflicts, hostility toward group members, and radical changes in ideology are results of the dramatic changes and persistent instability in the adolescent's lifespace.

Lewin's field theory inspired two related but distinct theoretical elaborations: ecological theory, as formulated by Roger Barker, and ecological systems theory, as formulated by Urie Bronfenbrenner. Whereas Lewin concerned himself with the psychological representation of the environment, Barker studied the objective, measurable environment within which the person behaves. Barker and his colleagues studied how adolescents use and are influenced by the settings they encounter. One of the most influential studies to emerge from this perspective compared behavior settings in large enrollment and small enrollment high schools. Students at small schools felt greater pressure to participate in the life of the school. Students at large schools were more likely to become specialists in specific activities, whereas students at small schools were more likely to develop general, well-rounded participation and competences. These findings supported the theoretical proposition that development in adolescence is, in part, a product of the normative expectations and opportunities for participation in behavior settings of one's community.

Urie Bronfenbrenner expanded ecological theory to encompass the wider interlocking system of systems in which human behavior takes place. The study of development requires an analysis of changes that occur within systems, as well as changes that take place as a result of interactions among systems. Some changes are patterned, developmental transformations, such as change in a child's capacity for coordinated movement and voluntary, goal-directed action. Other changes are societal, such as a community decision to restructure a school system from an elementary (Grades K–6), junior high (Grades 7–9), and high school (Grades 10–12) system to an elementary (Grades K–5), middle school (Grades 6–8), and high school (Grades 9–12) system. Some changes reflect the decline or improvement of resources in a setting.

The concept of person–environment fit, a theoretical outgrowth of the ecological systems perspective, has been elaborated by Jacquelynne Eccles, who focused on the appropriateness of middle school environments in relation to the developmental needs of adolescents. She examined middle school at the classroom, school, and district levels, pointing out discrepancies between the desired directions for growth in early adolescence and the educational structure and opportunities typically provided for students in these schools. This approach highlights challenges to adaptation that occur when environments are poorly designed for the developmental competences of individuals who are required to function in them.

Social Role and Life Course Theories

Scope

Social roles serve as a bridge between individuals and their society. Every society has a range of roles, and individuals learn about the expectations associated with them. As people enter new roles, they modify their behavior to conform to role expectations. Each role is usually linked to one or more related or reciprocal roles such as student and teacher, or parent and child. Life course theory focuses on the integration and sequencing of roles and role transitions over time in historical context.

Assumptions

All cultures offer new roles that await individuals as they move from one stage of life to another. Development can be understood as a process of role gain and role loss over the life course.

Contributions of social role and life course theory for adolescence

Some roles are directly associated with age, such as the role of a high school student. Other roles may be accessible only to those of a certain age who demonstrate other relevant skills, traits, or personal preferences. In many elementary schools, for example, fifth-grade students serve in the role of crossing guards to help younger children cross the streets near the school. Families, organizations, and communities have implicit theories of development that determine what role positions open up for individuals in adolescence. Graduating from high school, getting a job, voting, or joining the military are examples of role transitions that bring new expectations during adolescence. The stress of adolescence can be explained in part by expectations for teens to be involved in many time-intensive, highly structured roles at the same time.

From the life course perspective, the person's identity is formed by the roles one enacts and by the timing of entry into or exit from salient roles in relation to one's peers and community. Glen Elder studied the impact of the Great Depression on children. He found that those who were adolescents during the depression coped more effectively than those who were young children. Under conditions of parental unemployment and economic hardship, adolescents were able to contribute to their family by earning a bit of money or taking on responsibilities for younger children while their parents looked for work. In contrast, young children felt more helpless in the face of their family's economic strain. In the transition into adulthood, adolescents in families with fewer economic resources are more likely to make early transitions into roles such as worker and parent, transitions that carry with them a sense of being older than their peers.

Each person's life course can be thought of as a pattern of adaptations to the configuration of cultural expectations, resources, and barriers experienced during a particular time. For example, Ingrid Schoon has focused on the transition from dependent childhood to productive adulthood in a changing sociohistorical context, and the intergenerational transmission of disadvantage. The impact of timing on role transitions has been a long-term interest in the study of the onset of puberty. Studies have focused on pubertal timing, especially early and late maturing. Early pubertal timing foreshortens the developmental phase of middle childhood and accelerates the young person's entry into social roles and related expectations that are usually delayed until an older chronological age.

Cultural Theories

Scope

Culture refers to systems of meanings and patterns of behaviors shared by a group of people and transmitted from one generation to the next. Physical culture encompasses the objects, technologies, structures, tools, and other artifacts of a group. Social culture consists of norms, roles, beliefs, values, rites, and customs.

Assumptions

Culture guides development through encounters with certain objects, roles, and settings, and also through the meanings linked to actions. There is a bidirectional influence between individuals and their cultures: individual development is shaped by culture, but individuals also create and modify cultures. Whereas the capacity to create culture is universal, generalizations about human development are limited by their cultural context.

Contributions of cultural theories for adolescence

The extent to which development is viewed as distinct stages of life depends on the degree to which socialization within a culture is characterized by continuity or discontinuity. Continuity is found when a child is given information and responsibilities that apply directly to his or her adult behavior. For example, Margaret Mead observed that in Samoan society, girls of 6 or 7 years of age commonly took care of their younger siblings. As they grew older, their involvement in caregiving increased; however, the behaviors that were expected of them were not substantially changed. When there is continuity, development is a gradual, fluid transformation, in which adult competencies are built directly on childhood accomplishments. Discontinuity is found when children are either barred from activities that are open only to adults or is expected to 'unlearn' information or behaviors that are accepted in children but considered inappropriate for adults. The change from expectations of virginity before marriage to expectations of sexual responsiveness after marriage is an example of discontinuity.

Culture interacts with biological development in determining whether development is perceived as stage-like and how each period of life is experienced. This concept is illustrated by the ways in which different cultures mark an adolescent girl's first menstruation. In some societies, people fear menstruation and treat girls as if they were dangerous to others. In other societies, girls are viewed as having powerful magic that will affect their own future and that of the tribe so they are treated with new reverence. In still others, the perceived shamefulness of sex requires that menstruation be kept as secret as possible. Cultures thus determine how a biological change is marked by others and how it is experienced by the person. The internalization of certain cultural values and beliefs can serve as impediments to achievement through mechanisms such as stereotype threat, as demonstrated in the work of John Ogbu or Claude Steele, or as buffers against stress, as illustrated in the writings of Bame Nsamenang about the convergence of traditional and modern approaches to education in Africa.

The dimensions of individualism and collectivism provide another cultural lens for understanding adolescent development. Adolescence is a particularly salient time for the development of ideology. Cultural socialization toward a more individualistic or collectivistic worldview is likely to be transformed from adherence to the values of parents and other community leaders into an internalized sense of personal beliefs and life goals. The formation of personal identity, including crystallization of a sense of oneself in the future, is shaped by the incorporation of an individualistic or collectivistic sense of adult responsibility and maturity. This has implications for a young person's orientation to work, family, citizenship, and moral obligations. Cigdem Kagitcibasi suggests that individualism and collectivism at the cultural level reflect needs for autonomy and relatedness at the individual level. Despite pressures from urbanization toward a more autonomous self-construal, the well-being of individuals requires an effective balance of these two sets of needs.

Dynamic Systems Theories

Scope

Systems theories describe characteristics of systems and the relationships among the component parts found within the system. In any system, the whole is more than the sum of its parts. Whether it is a cell, an organ, an individual, a family, or a corporation, a system is composed of interdependent elements that share some common goals, interrelated functions, boundaries, and an identity.

Assumptions

Systems change in the direction of adjusting to or incorporating more of the environment into themselves in order to prevent disorganization as a result of environmental fluctuations. The components and the whole are always in tension. What one understands and observes depends on where one stands in a complex set of interrelationships

Contributions of dynamic systems theories for adolescence

All living entities are both parts and wholes. An adolescent is a part of a family, a classroom or workgroup, a friendship group, and a society. An adolescent is also a whole – a coordinated, complex system composed of physical, cognitive, emotional, social, and self subsystems. Part of the story of development is told in an analysis of the adaptive regulation and organization of those subsystems. Simultaneously, the story is told in the way larger systems fluctuate and impinge on individuals, forcing adaptive regulation and reorganization as a means of achieving stability at higher levels of system organization.

Richard Lerner, who has advanced the study of adolescence through developmental systems theory, emphasizes the ongoing interaction and integration of the person across many levels from the genetic to the behavioral level, within the nested contexts of the person, family, community, and culture. Plasticity, the capacity for change, is at the heart of this approach. Both individuals and their contexts have potential for change, and for fostering or constraining change across boundaries. The magnitude of change that is possible varies across individuals and contexts, as well as within individuals over the lifespan. The person in the setting is the focus of analysis. The boundary between the person and the environment is fuzzy; as an open system, a person is continuously influenced by information and resources from the environment and, at the same time, creates or modifies the environment to preserve system functioning.

Isabela Granic and Gerald Patterson applied the dynamic systems theory perspective to an understanding of the etiology of antisocial behavior, providing new ideas about the establishment of antisocial behavior patterns. First, they explored the process through which daily interactions contribute to the emergence of more complex systems of behavior. They used the idea of attractors to characterize several types of stable patterns of parent–child interaction, and introduced the idea of cascading constraints. This term refers to the fact that once behaviors are organized as attractors, these attractors become structured and resist change. Therefore, they serve to constrain future behaviors. This idea captures the reality that an attractor is both the result of interactions that occur before the behavior has stabilized and the cause of behaviors that occur once the attractor has been formed.

Positive youth development is a strength-based perspective emerging from the convergence of several theoretical ideas: resilience, positive psychology, ecological theory, and developmental systems theory. Resilience is a term used to characterize individuals who exhibit positive outcomes in the face of threats to development such as prolonged, severe poverty, or a parent with a serious mental illness. Faced with these or other difficulties, resilient individuals show low levels of psychological symptoms and function effectively in the basic developmental tasks expected for their stage of life. Over time, they create lives that integrate their own personal strengths with the resources and opportunities of their community, meeting the community's expectations for maturity. Although the experience of resilience is highly individual, reflecting unique patterns of life challenges and coping strategies, the notion of resilience underscores a widely shared human capacity to recover from adversity. Theorists have identified a small number of factors that support resilience including relationships with high functioning, supportive adults in the family; intelligence; self-control; high self-esteem; and a strong desire to have a positive impact on their environment.

Positive psychology, advanced through the writings of Martin Seligman, views individuals as active agents who can enhance their lives and achieve new levels of happiness and fulfillment through the decisions they make. Hope and optimism are highlighted as ego strengths that counteract the negative impact of discouraging thoughts and experiences. Hopefulness is associated with higher goals, higher levels of confidence that the goal will be reached, and greater persistence in the face of barriers to goal attainment, thus leading to higher overall levels of performance. Because hopefulness combines a desire to achieve new goals and a belief that one will be able to find successful paths toward those goals, it is essential for behavior change. The application of positive psychology to adolescence has been advanced by William Damon who focused on the development of 'noble purpose.' Damon has identified ways that young people show evidence of positive development by making meaningful and sustained commitments to projects that benefit the larger community.

Peter Benson extended the application of resilience and positive psychology to an analysis of the relationship of optimal development to both internal and external assets. Internal assets are physical, intellectual, emotional, and social capacities. External assets are supports, expectations, and opportunities that are likely to enhance development. The premise of the assets perspective is that communities can enhance youth development by providing programs that include opportunities for youth to acquire or strengthen their assets. Positive development occurs when the strengths of youth are aligned with resources for growth in key contexts, especially home, school, and community.

Why So Many Theories?

The diversity of theories presented above reflects the multifaceted nature of adolescence as well as different ideas about factors that account for growth and the direction of maturity. Growth at puberty and the associated changes in physical stature and reproductive capacity are accompanied by important changes in cognitive capacities, interpersonal competence, and emotional life. In most societies, the adolescent years typically bring changes in social roles, access to new settings, and expectations for new levels of self-sufficiency, social engagement, and self-control. Adolescence is at once a time of intrapsychic and interpersonal transformation.

Theories of adolescence have played a key role in highlighting the complexity of this period of life, especially clarifying advances in reasoning, emotional expression, and the complexity of social roles and interpersonal relationships. Theory has led the way in focusing attention on the capacity of adolescents to direct the course of their development through the formation of a personal identity. Yet, no theory of development addresses all these domains.

The prominence of theories changes over time, influenced by other sectors in the study of development and other related disciplines. New evidence from cognitive neuroscience, genetic research, and the biological bases of behavior are informing the way we think about emotion and cognition, and the importance of social contexts for supporting cognition. The diversity of youth, including racial, ethnic, and cultural variations as well as international studies of youth, casts a new light on normative expectations about pathways from childhood to adulthood. The diversity of settings has also received new attention through the study of families, peer groups, schools, and communities, resulting in a new appreciation for the challenges adolescents face as they traverse multiple environments.

Evolving Need for New Theoretical Approaches That Address Emerging Knowledge and the Questions That Such Knowledge Inspire

New evidence and observations result in the expansion, revision, or rejection of aspects of earlier theories. Earlier theories that placed a strong emphasis on either biological maturation or environmental control are being replaced by theories that take a more probabilistic view of development as the changing person encounters multiple environments that are also changing.

As we review the focus and emphasis of current theories, several areas require new theoretical perspectives.

1. There is a need for more consideration of the bidirectional influence of adolescents and their parents, especially how parenting an adolescent may contribute to the emergence of a more generative capacity among adults and how adolescents who observe their parents enacting various life roles are influenced toward their own identity strivings.
2. Changes in the nature of later adolescence and the increasingly ambiguous trajectory into adulthood have implications for identity theory, family theory, and the notion of positive youth development. As cultural pathways toward adulthood change, we need new ways of conceptualizing psychosocial maturity in adolescence.
3. Relatively little theory is available to guide thinking about the nature of care and caregiving among adolescents, yet we know that in many cultures and in many families in the United States, adolescents provide important care for younger siblings and for aging grandparents.
4. The challenge to dynamic systems theory is to understand the reciprocal regulation of the person and the environment over time. How is the person shaped and defined by the contexts in which he or she functions? How does the person influence these contexts to foster more optimal environments for growth? The theory needs to be elaborated to consider the active role of adolescents in choosing settings, modifying the settings in which they engage, and determining the intensity of involvement in these settings/activities.
5. There has been a separation between theories that focus on logical thought or reasoning and theories that focus on other aspects of mental life, especially drives, emotions, and motivation. New research in neuroscience suggests that cognition and emotion work together in complex ways to evaluate situations and plan actions. New theories are needed to conceptualize the way that emotion and reason converge during adolescence to guide decision making. Current theories offer inadequate consideration of feelings of guilt, shame, pride, and joy in life as they influence mental life.
6. The evolutionary emphasis on the social nature of human beings leads to new attention to underlying needs to belong, motivation for connection, and the impact of social exclusion in adolescence. Theory is needed to guide thinking about how strivings toward belonging and strivings toward personal identity influence each other during adolescence.
7. As society changes, adolescents are on the forefront of adaptation to new technologies, family contexts, economic opportunities, and educational resources. Given the neural plasticity that is ongoing during adolescence, we assume that adolescents are adapting new cognitive structures that allow them to cope with the changing environment. Scholars need to pay closer attention to adolescents' ways of thinking, their patterns of behavior, and the nature of their relationships in order to gain greater insight about likely pathways into adulthood for the next generation. This will require an interdisciplinary, qualitative approach that will inform new theory.

See also: Attachment; Cognitive Development; Cultural Influences on Adolescent Development; Globalization and Adolescence; The History of the Study of Adolescence; Stages of Adolescence; Transitions into Adolescence; Transitions to Adulthood.

Further Reading

Brown B and Dietz EL (2009) Informal peer groups in middle childhood and adolescence. In: Rubin KH, Bukowski WM, and Laursen B (eds.) *Handbook of Peer Interaction, Relationships, and Groups*. New York: Guilford.

Collins WA and Steinberg L (2006) Adolescent development in interpersonal context. In: Damon W and Eisenberg N (eds.) *Handbook of Child Psychology, Vol. 4: Socioemotional Processes*, pp. 1003–1067. New York: Wiley

Eccles JS and Roeser RW (2009) Schools, academic motivation, and stage-environment fit. In: Lerner RM and Steinberg L (eds.) *Handbook of Adolescent Psychology*, 3rd edn., pp. 404–434. Hoboken, NJ: Wiley.

Granic I, Dishion TJ, and Hollenstein T (2005) The family ecology of adolescence: A dynamic systems perspective on normative development. In: Adams G and Berzonsky M (eds.) *Blackwell Handbook of Adolescence*. New York: Blackwell.

Kroger J (2007) *Identity Development: Adolescence Through Adulthood*, 2nd edn. Thousand Oaks, CA: Sage.

Kuhn D (2008) Formal operations from a 21st century perspective. *Human Development* 51: 48–55.

Masten AS (2001) Ordinary magic: Resilience processes in development. *American Psychologist* 56: 227–238.

Newman BM and Newman PR (2007) *Theories of Human Development*. New York: Psychology Press.

Repetti RL, Taylor SE, and Seeman TE (2002) Risky families: Family social environments and the mental and physical health of offspring. *Psychological Bulletin* 128: 330–366.

Romer D and Walker EF (2007) *Adolescent Psychopathology and the Developing Brain*. New York: Oxford University Press.

Silbereisen RK and Lerner RM (eds.) (2007) *Approaches to Positive Youth Development*. London: Sage.

Smith SR, Hamon RR, Ingoldsby BB, and Miller JE (2009) *Exploring Family Theories*. New York: Oxford University Press.

Relevant Websites

http://social.jrank.org/pages/16/Adolescence.html – Adolescence – grand theories of adolescent development, biological changes associated with puberty – social changes associated with adolescence in Western industrialized countries.

http://www.mentalhelp.net/poc/view_doc.php?type=doc&id=7924&cn=28 – Major child development theories and theorists.

http://psychology.about.com/od/developmentstudyguide/p/devtheories.htm – Theories of development.

http://classweb.gmu.edu/awinsler/ordp/theory.html – Theories of development.

Adolescent Decision-Making

B L Halpern-Felsher, University of California, San Francisco, CA, USA

Glossary

Dual-process models: These models argue that both intuitive and analytic processing are working in tandem, along two parallel paths. One important path reflects the more analytic, rational processing, and the second path represents the noncognitive components involved in decision-making.

Judgment of risk: Also referred to as risk perception or perceived risk. This is an individual's perceived chance that a risk would occur should one engage in a behavior or experience an event.

Normative decision-making: Deliberate, analytic process, following which yields the decision a rational individual would make.

Introduction

What should I wear to school today? Should I take the AP or regular biology class? What career path should I choose? Should I go out on that date? I don't have a condom, should I still have sex? All of my friends are drinking at the party, should I? Should I just try one cigarette? Can I participate in that research study? I'm thinking that I don't want to use that new acne medicine; do I have to?

These are just a few of the many decisions adolescents frequently face. Making these decisions occurs within a complicated, interrelated context of mixed cultural messages, adult monitoring, peer pressures, and policy and legal restrictions, as well as individual-level physical, cognitive, emotional, and psychosocial development. Compared to childhood, adolescents are provided greater opportunities to make these decisions in some areas such as friendship, class choices, and extracurricular activities. However, some opportunities for independence such as deciding on medical treatment, choosing whether or not to have an abortion, consenting for research participation, or using illicit substances are subject to restriction. Adults continually try to strike the difficult balance between allowing adolescents opportunities for autonomy and practice in decision-making and wanting to keep them safe. For adolescents, learning to make decisions, experience positive and negative consequences, derive insights from these outcomes, and navigate the multiple influences on their maturation constitute an important developmental task.

This article provides an overview of adolescent decision-making, including definitions of competent decision-making, descriptions of decision-making models, and the physical, cognitive, social, emotional, and contextual influences on adolescent decision-making. The article also discusses implications of adolescent decision-making that are relevant to health educators, healthcare providers, policy makers, and adolescent researchers.

What Is Competent Decision-Making?

Definitions of what constitutes a competent decision as well as the process of and mechanisms underlying decision-making vary widely. A common metric of adolescent decision-making competence is to use adults' decision-making strategies as the standard by which adolescents should be judged. For example, studies have compared adolescents and adults on their ability to judge risks, resist peer pressure, or seek advice from others. Using adults as the gold standard has been justified since adults are seen as fully competent within the law to make decisions. Other definitions compare individual decision-making against a model presumed to represent competent decision-making. For example, legal standards typically indicate that decisions must be made knowingly; that one must understand all procedures, related outcomes, and alternative courses of action; and that the choice must be made without substantial input or control from others. Other models include a more descriptive list of strategies that people should use to make competent decisions. More recently, the focus has shifted to identifying different pathways or processes that adolescents compared to adults utilize when making choices, and to understanding what influences those processes. I now turn to a discussion of two of the most common models of decision-making: Normative and dual-process models.

Normative Models of Decision-Making

Normative models are commonly used to describe decision-making. These models have been typically used to explain engagement in health-promoting behavior, such as using sunscreen, seeking medical treatment, or wearing seatbelts. They have also been used to describe health-compromising decisions such as using tobacco, drinking alcohol, engaging in risky sexual behavior, and so on.

Normative models describe a deliberate, analytic process of decision-making. Intentions to behave are the most proximal predictor of engagement or nonengagement in any given behavior. These intentions are determined by the following: First, people make an assessment concerning both the potential positive and negative consequences of the behavior such as getting pregnant from having sex, feeling more relaxed after drinking alcohol, winning the debate contest, or getting into trouble for smoking. Second, perceptions of vulnerability to those consequences, such as the likelihood of getting into an accident after driving drunk or the chance of peer recognition after trying out for the school play, help determine the ultimate decision made. Third, individuals consider the desire to engage in the behavior despite potential consequences (e.g., I know

 Encyclopedia of Adolescence, Volume 1 doi:10.1016/B978-0-12-373915-5.00010-3

that I can get an STD from having sex, but it is more important for me to keep my relationship partner happy). Finally, decision-making is determined in part by perceptions of the extent to which similar others are engaging in the behavior (e.g., most of my friends are smoking pot, so why shouldn't I? or Many of my friends are joining the club, so I'll give it a try).

Many theories of health behavior have incorporated elements of these normative decision-making models, including the Theory of Reasoned Action, Theory of Planned Behavior, and the Health Belief Model. While specific model components vary across theories, in general these theories postulate, and empirical evidence has supported the notion that adoption of health-promoting and health-compromising behaviors are the result of a deliberative, rational, and analytical process, with the outcome of this process leading to increased or decreased likelihood of performing the behavior. The behavior chosen is the one that will yield the greatest expected utility. The rational choice would be based on the components that are most valued by the individual. For example, social norms, or the perceived notion of the extent to which others are engaging in the behavior, might be the greatest influence on one person's decision, while perceived likelihood of getting into trouble might be the greatest determinant for another person's decision-making process.

According to these normative models, competent decision-making is defined by the *process* of how decisions are made. Competence is not determined by the actual decision, action, behavior, or outcome. In this case, for example, while adults might disagree with an adolescent's decisions to have sex, an adolescent can still demonstrate decision-making competence by showing that he or she has considered and weighed all of the options (e.g., have sex, not have sex, just kiss), potential risks (e.g., getting pregnant, feeling guilty) and benefits (e.g., pleasure), value of each outcome, and other key components involved in the decision-making process.

It is important to note that in this normative, rational decision-making process, individuals are expected to not only consider engaging in a particular action, but to also consider the consequences associated with *not* choosing an event or behavior. This is especially important for adolescents, for whom often the choice is between engaging or not engaging in a risky behavior, both of which have positive and negative outcomes for youth. For example, a recent study showed that in addition to reporting some positive outcomes such as feeling responsible for gaining a good reputation, adolescents who decided not to have sex or to postpone sex reported experiencing some negative consequences related to that decision (e.g., having a partner become angry), compared with adolescents who chose to have sex, and these negative experiences increased with age if the adolescent remained abstinent.

Use of and age differences in decision-making

There are surprisingly few studies that have incorporated the full normative decision-making process to examine whether the components of the model are utilized by adolescents, to compare adolescents' and adults' decision-making, or to examine age differences in decision-making competence within the adolescent years. A review of the small literature base paints a mixed picture regarding adolescent decision-making competency. Michels and colleagues conducted a qualitative study to examine the extent to which adolescents report considering the decision-making components when deciding whether or not to have sex. They found that despite presumptions about adolescents lacking a decision process, adolescents' sexual decision-making does involve consideration of contextual factors, future goals, risks, benefits, and partner relationships. Other qualitative research similarly indicates that adolescents consider risks, benefits, and the value of behavior-related outcomes just prior to deciding on a particular behavior.

The few quantitative studies examining age differences in usage of the normative components of decision-making have yielded mixed results. Some studies suggest no or few age differences between adolescents and adults in the decision-making process. Other studies have demonstrated significant age differences, with younger adolescents showing less competence in considering the decision-making elements in the normative models than older adolescents and/or adults. The age differences reported by these studies suggest that competence in spontaneously using the components of the rational decision-making models continues to increase throughout adolescence and into young adulthood. For example, research with adolescents in grades 6, 8, 10, and 12 as well as young adults asked participants to give advice to peers to solve three different hypothetical dilemmas: whether or not to seek cosmetic surgery (medical domain), whether or not to participate in an experimental study for the use of a new acne medicine (informed consent domain), and one concerning which parent to live with after divorce (family domain). With some differences by scenario, adults were more likely to spontaneously consider risks and benefits and to suggest seeking advice than were the adolescents.

Dual-Process Models of Decision-Making

The decision-making models discussed in the previous section have been extremely useful in predicting a number of behaviors, especially those involving decisions that are less emotionally charged. The application of these models is limited when used to explain behaviors involving more irrational, impulsive, socially undesirable, or emotionally charged behavior such as tobacco use, unsafe driving, or risky sex. Importantly, when placed within a developmental framework, decision-making must be defined as much more than a series of complex cognitive, analytic, and rational processes. Instead, for an adolescent, the process of decision-making needs to be immersed within the set of psychosocial, cognitive, emotional, experiential, and contextual changes that define adolescence. These rational decision-making models are also less applicable to adolescents and some young adults for whom the ability to analytically process information is not yet fully formed. To address the less deliberate and more social, emotional, and reactive process often employed by adolescents, theory and research support the adoption of dual-process models that reflect multiple paths to decision-making.

Dual-process models challenge the notion that decision-making competence only involves a deliberate, analytic process, or that decision-making involves a continuum from intuitive to analytic processing. Instead, these models argue that both intuitive and analytic processing are working in tandem, along two parallel paths. One important path reflects the more analytic, rational processing, as discussed previously with respect to the rational decision-making models. In this path, decision-making includes cognitive skills such as consideration of outcomes, perceptions of behavioral-linked risks and benefits, attitudes about the behaviors and related outcomes, and beliefs in what others expect them to do (i.e., social norms). These factors are expected to predict intentions to behave, with intentions being the most immediate predictor of actual behavior. Competent decision-making also dictates that the decision maker has the capacity to make autonomous decisions; is capable of finding, utilizing, and incorporating new information into the decision; can judge the value of advice from other sources; can implement the decision; obtains and utilizes feedback from the decision; makes decisions that are congruent with personal goals; and is ultimately satisfied with the decision.

The second path in the dual-process models represents the noncognitive components involved in decision-making. This is the less planned, heuristic, reactive, and affective path. This is the process often employed by adolescents. Gerrard and Gibbons have operationalized this second path, defining several constructs that are particularly relevant to adolescent decision-making. According to their Protype-Willingness Model, this second path includes descriptive social norms such as personal perceptions and misperceptions about the extent to which peers and other important groups are engaging in a behavior. Research has shown that adolescents are guided by perceived peer norms and peer acceptance of behavior to a much greater extent than are adults. This heuristic path also includes images or perceptions regarding others who have engaged or are engaging in a behavior. For example, adolescents are less likely to smoke if they hold negative images that smokers are dirty, wrinkled, and have yellow teeth. In contrast, adolescents who are exposed to positive images of smokers are more likely to view smoking favorably and therefore try smoking. Social norms and images are then expected to predict willingness to consider a behavior. Willingness to engage is differentiated from the planful notion of intentions. While adolescents may not have an active plan in mind to smoke, have unprotected sex, or engage in delinquent behavior, they often may find themselves in situations in which they would consider engaging in the behavior even though they were originally committed to avoiding it. This deflected trajectory in original intentions is thought to result in part from adolescents' psychosocial immaturity, including being more impulsive and more susceptible to peer pressure than adults. These maturity indices are discussed more in the following sections.

Emerging from the dual-process models and research on cognition, affect, and developmental processes involved in decision-making, Reyna and colleagues have proposed the Fuzzy Trace Theory in which they have operationalized two paths of reasoning. One form of reasoning, they argue, is gist-based, or rooted in the general meaning that the event or decision evokes for a particular individual. Reyna argues that gist-based reasoning derives from experience and knowledge accumulated over time. She argues that adults bring information to new contexts in the form of these gists, and that they tend to use these heuristics or intuition-based reasoning more than they rely on specific details. In contrast, less experienced decision makers rely more on verbatim reasoning, which are literal representations guiding decisions. These verbatim representations are more detailed, in which the decision maker focuses more on facts, details, and weighing of trade-offs to guide their choices. Given that adolescents have less experience than adults, adolescents are more likely to make decisions using verbatim processing. With age, adolescents will increase their use of gist-based reasoning. However, Reyna does note that adolescents tend to evoke both forms of reasoning, thus providing additional support for the dual process involved in adolescent decision-making.

Judgment and Decision-Making

While the entire decision-making process is critical for competent decision-making, a great deal of research and theory has focused predominately on individuals' judgments concerning behavioral outcomes, including both positive and negative consequences. As discussed earlier, theories of decision-making emphasize that decisions will largely be influenced by the extent to which individuals perceive that the risks and/or benefits will occur should they engage in a particular behavior. In the next section, we discuss these judgments, also known as perceptions or expectations, and how they relate to behavior.

Judgments of Risks

A great deal of theory and research has emphasized the importance of risk judgments on decision-making. The relationship between risk perceptions and risk behavior has been particularly applied to adolescents, as descriptions of risk taking often make reference to adolescents' beliefs that they are invulnerable to harm. The concept of adolescent 'invulnerability' is pervasive in both scientific and lay circles. The notion that adolescents believe they are invulnerable to harm can be traced to Elkind. Adopting and extending Piaget's developmental stages, Elkind proposed that during entry into formal operations, young adolescents are cognitively egocentric, focused mostly on themselves and their well-being. Consequently, the adolescent believes that he or she is unique and not susceptible to potential problems that others may face. It is believed that this 'personal fable' yields perceptions of invulnerability, thus explaining in part adolescents' engagement in risky behaviors. In this section, we describe some of the findings from the risk perception literature. In so doing, it is noted how the research on risk perceptions and especially age differences in risk perceptions as well as the relationship between perceptions and behavior varies depending on the methods used and operationalizations of risk perceptions.

Several investigators have compared individuals' perceived likelihood of harm against actual risk statistics. For example, studies have compared perceived chance of getting lung cancer from smoking cigarettes against actual odds of lung cancer among smokers. Others have examined adolescents' perceived chance of dying in the near future. These studies generally indicate that adolescents and adults overestimate their risk of experiencing a negative outcome, compared to actual statistics.

Other studies have focused on group differences in risk perceptions, comparing for example adolescents of different ages or adolescents and adults. Studies examining age differences in perceived risks within adolescent samples have yielded mixed results. Some studies show that perceived risks decrease over time throughout adolescence, with younger adolescents perceiving greater risks associated with various risk behaviors than do older adolescents. Other studies have demonstrated a curvilinear relationship with age, whereas another small set of research finds within adolescent age no differences in perceptions of behavior-related risks. Only a few studies have examined differences in perceived risks between adolescents and adults. In general, in contrast to theories that adolescents perceive themselves to be invulnerable to harm, these studies show that adolescents perceive greater risk than do adults.

Studies have also compared perceived risk between adolescents who have engaged in a risk behavior and those who have not, thus testing the theory that engagers hold lower perceptions of risk. These studies have yielded varied results, with some studies showing that adolescents who have engaged in a risk perceive lower chance of experiencing related negative outcomes, and other studies showing engagers perceiving less chance of risk. Explanations for these mixed results likely stems from the types of measures used. For the most part, the studies that have shown a positive relationship between perceptions of risk and greater likelihood of engagement in risky behaviors have elicited general judgments about the likelihood of a given outcome occurring without making the judgment conditional on a behavioral antecedent. For example, individuals have inquired about the chance of getting an STD without specifying the sexual act or whether protection was used. Thus, individuals who are engaging in a risk behavior are truly more likely to experience a negative outcome than are nonengagers. Conversely, nonengagers rate their risk of experiencing the negative outcome as lower than do engagers because they are not engaging in the risk behavior. Instead of using these unconditional risk assessments, it is important to use conditional risk assessments in which the behavior or event linked to the outcome is specified (e.g., "Imagine you drank two bottles of beer and then drove five miles. What is the percent chance that you would get into an accident?"). Conditional risk assessments are more closely related to factors incorporated in models of health behavior and have been better predictors of behavior than unconditional risk assessments.

Another explanation for these mixed findings likely stems from the fact that the majority of studies assessing the link between risk perceptions and behavior or decision-making have employed a cross-sectional design. Therefore, the direction of influence between behavior and risk perceptions is not discernible. Although perceptions of risk are theorized to motivate behavior, it is plausible to suggest that risk perceptions are reflective of behavioral experiences. Using longitudinal, prospective data in which perceptions of risk were assessed prior to the onset of risk behavior, Halpern-Felsher and colleagues examined whether perceptions of risk actually predict behavior. Results showed that adolescents who held the lowest perceptions of long-term smoking risks were almost four times more likely to start smoking than were adolescents with the highest perceptions of risk. Perceptions of short-term risks were also important, with adolescents holding the lowest perceptions of short-term smoking risks being nearly three times more likely to initiate smoking. Similarly, adolescents with the highest perceptions that second-hand smoke would harm others were least likely to begin smoking at subsequent data collection waves.

Further, the nature of the relationship between risk perceptions and behavior is likely to change over time, depending on factors such as experience, which are known to bias judgment. Studies have shown that risk perceptions are affected by experienced outcomes, whereby individuals who have personally experienced a negative outcome linked to an event or risk behavior perceive the same or similar outcome as more likely to happen than do individuals without such outcome experience (see below for more on the role of experience in risk judgments). Thus, when examining the role of behavioral experience on risk judgments, it is important to also examine the effects of outcome experience either statistically or by limiting the samples to those with or without such outcome experience.

Risk perceptions have also commonly been measured using the concept of optimistic bias, or the extent to which one believes they are at risk compared to others. Optimistic bias is an underestimation of the likelihood of personally experiencing negative events, or an overestimation of the likelihood of personally experiencing positive events. Optimistic bias is typically assessed by asking participants to compare their level of risk to others' levels, either directly (e.g., "Compared to another person my same age and gender, my risk of dying in a tornado is …") or indirectly (e.g., by comparing risk estimates for self and estimates for another person). The outcome is considered to be an optimistic bias if it is positive in value (i.e., if the risk judgment for others is greater than that for self). Optimistic bias measures are not directly comparable to risk judgments in that a person can be optimistically biased at any level of risk judgment. For instance, an individual can be biased even if he or she estimates the risks for both self and another as very low, or judges the risk for self and another as very high.

As with research using other measures of risk perceptions, studies examining optimism among adolescents show a mixed picture. Some studies show that adolescents exhibit a general tendency toward optimistic bias, whereas another study found that teenagers were less optimistically biased regarding negative future life events than were their parents.

Finally, risk perceptions have been measured using more general assessments, such as inquiring about the risk of being harmed in general versus the chance of a specific outcome occurring. These studies generally find that adolescents do acknowledge or are concerned about harm associated with risks. However, perceptions of general risk are less likely to yield reliable and valid results than are perceptions of specific negative outcomes such as getting pregnant, being caught, and so on.

Benefit Perceptions

As indicated earlier, decision-making involves consideration of both the risks and the benefits of engaging and not engaging in a given behavior. Nevertheless, studies have focused predominately on perceptions of risk. More recently, the importance of considering positive outcomes or benefits in adolescent decision-making has resurfaced, resulting in a surge of research on the role of benefit perceptions in adolescent decision-making. Benefit perceptions are likely to yield important information regarding what motivates adolescents to engage in or refrain from behavior, especially when they are well aware of the many risks inherent in risk behaviors but still choose to engage. Decisional Balance Inventory, a construct of the Transtheoretical Model created by Prokhorov and colleagues, incorporates a weighing of both the benefits (pros) and risks (cons) in predicting behavior and behavior change. The model encompasses three factors: social pros (e.g., kids who drink alcohol have more friends), coping pros (e.g., smoking relieves tension), and cons (e.g., marijuana smells). This construct includes a number of social and short-term outcomes rather than solely relying on long-term health outcomes that are less salient to adolescents and young adults. Decision-making among adolescents may hinge not only on their perceptions of risks (short-term and long-term) but on benefits as well. Using this inventory, research by Prokhorov found that scores on the smoking pros scale increased and con scores decreased as adolescents' susceptibility to smoking increased. Focusing just on perceptions of benefits, it has been shown that adolescents with the highest perceptions of smoking-related benefits were three times more likely to smoke cigarettes. Others have shown that adolescents value sexual benefits such as intimacy, sexual pleasure, and elevated social status, and adolescents expect that their sexual relationships will satisfy these goals. Reyna's Fuzzy Trace Theory similarly argues that adolescents consider and weigh benefits as well as risks in their decision-making process, with adolescents often putting greater weight on benefits than the risks.

Summary

Despite great variation in definitions and measures of risk and benefit judgments, it is clear that these perceptions play an important role in adolescents' decisions. Research suggests that in addition to health risks (e.g., lung cancer, pregnancy), adolescents view perceptions of and knowledge about social risks as critical in their decision-making. This is consistent with the research showing that adolescence is a time when peers and other social factors play a large role in adolescent development, and therefore their decisions. It also stands to reason that perceptions of benefits play an important role in adolescents' decision-making. Indeed, research shows that perceptions of social benefits outweigh the desire to avoid risks, especially for decisions involving social interactions (e.g., sexual behavior). Recognizing that some behaviors involve risks, but desiring to reach for the benefits, appears to also translate into the types of choices adolescents make. For example, being aware of the risks inherent in intercourse, recent research indicates that adolescents choose to have oral sex as a method of reducing their risk while reaping similar benefits of intimacy and pleasure. Research also demonstrates that adolescents will smoke light cigarettes in part because they believe, albeit incorrectly, that the risks are lower compared to regular cigarettes. These studies show that adolescents' choice of behaviors is in part due to their balancing of perceived risks and benefits.

Factors Influencing Adolescent Decision-Making

There are a number of individual and contextual factors influencing adolescent decision-making. Some of these factors, such as cognitive and psychosocial development, impact the timing and ability of decision-making competence, as well as the process by which decision-making occurs. Other factors, such as parent and peer influences, impact the process of decision-making as well as specific components of the decision process. Others (e.g., policies) influence age or circumstances under which decision-making can occur, or define circumstances in which adolescents are or are not culpable for their actions. These various factors are reviewed next.

Adolescent Development

Adolescence is a period of extreme and rapid cognitive, psychological, social, emotional, and physical changes that yield changes in decision-making capacities. Physical maturation, and particularly the development of secondary sexual characteristics, results in the adolescent having a more adult-like appearance, and thus seeming capable of performing adult-like decisions. Adolescents are also changing cognitively. Thinking becomes more abstract and less concrete, allowing adolescents to consider multiple aspects of their actions and decisions at one time, assess the potential consequences of a decision, consider possible outcomes associated with behavioral choices, and plan for the future. These cognitive changes are coupled with psychosocial development, including increased social and peer comparison, greater peer affiliation, and susceptibility to peer pressure. These adolescent changes typically translate into adolescents' desire to participate in, and eventually lead, their decisions. In the following sections, the components of adolescent development most influential on decision-making will be reviewed.

Psychosocial maturity

Literature from developmental and cognitive psychology point to specific psychosocial abilities that are needed for competent decision-making. These competencies include autonomy, resistance to undue influence from others, self-reliance, perspective taking, future time perspective, and impulse control. The ability to make one's own decisions is considered an essential component of decision-making competence by developmental psychologists and decision theorists. Legal standards for determining whether a health care decision is competent also stipulate that individuals must be able to make their own choice, based on their own determination and without substantial control by others. In order to make autonomous decisions, individuals must have the ability to resist undue pressure from others. Also needed is self-reliance, which refers to the absence of excessive reliance on others, to having a sense of control over life, and to taking the initiative. Self-reliance not only affords the decision maker the confidence to make decisions, it also allows people to move forward to actually make the decision. While autonomy is certainly important, it does not negate the need to understand the value of advice from others. Inherent in the ability to recognize and acknowledge when advice is needed involves social perspective taking, or the ability to recognize that other people may have different points of view or different knowledge sets from one's own. Future perspective taking, including the ability to project into the future, to consider possible positive and negative outcomes associated with choices, and to plan for the future are hallmarks of decision-making competence. Utilizing these capacities requires adolescents to be able to control their desire to act impulsively.

These key decision-making competencies are immature during adolescence, thus contributing to their more nascent decision-making abilities. Compared to adults, adolescents' actions are often impulsive rather than planned; they often do not recognize when advice is needed; typically do not have the ability to recognize that other people may have different points of view or sets of knowledge from their own; and do not have an adequate sense of the future or plan for the future. Of particular importance is that adolescents are significantly more susceptible to peer pressure than are adults. This explains largely why adolescents are much more likely to get into a vehicle crash when driving with their peers than when driving alone or with an adult, thus defending the graduated licensing laws restricting other adolescents as passengers during the first year of licensure. Research shows that perspective taking increases gradually until young adulthood. The ability to think about the future, have impulse control, and become self-reliant also continue to increase well into the late adolescent years. Thus, while older adolescents' (generally after age 16) and adults' cognitive capacities such as the ability to consider and judge risks and process information are similar, adolescents and adults differ substantially in their psychosocial maturity. These differing developmental trajectories support the value of the dual-process models discussed earlier.

Brain development

There are four lobes in the brain: parietal lobe, occipital lobe, temporal lobe, and the frontal lobe. The frontal lobe is the largest part of the brain, and contains the prefrontal cortex, which is located in front of the brain, behind the forehead. The prefrontal cortex is responsible for executive functions, including cognition, thought, imagination, abstract thinking, planning, and impulse control. In short, the prefrontal cortex oversees critical abilities for decision-making. Research has shown that during adolescence, gray matter, or the tissue in the frontal lobe responsible for our ability to think, is reduced or selectively 'pruned' during the adolescent and young adult years. Simultaneously, a process of myelination occurs, where the white matter in the brain matures to work more efficiently. These processes have been shown to continue through age 25. As such, the aspects of the brain responsible for decision-making, impulse control, peer susceptibility, and other aspects of psychosocial maturity are not fully developed until young adulthood, with males developing even more slowly than females.

The Role of Personal and Vicarious Experience

Adolescents have less personal and vicarious experience with making decisions than do adults. As such, adolescents have less opportunity to receive positive and negative feedback about the choices they have made, and fewer chances to obtain knowledge about available choices. Once learned, adolescents become increasingly capable of transferring the knowledge learned from one decision to other choices. Acquiring such knowledge further increases cognitive capacities such as the ability to reason better and process information faster and more efficiently. Through experience and practice, adolescents develop expertise that can be generalized to other behaviors. As has been repeatedly demonstrated in research, acquiring such knowledge and skills requires time, practice, and effort.

Experience with and knowledge about decisions and obtaining feedback from those decisions is especially important when one considers that perceptions of risks and benefits play a critical role in decision-making. Adolescents who engage in a behavior without experiencing negative consequences might believe that they are less likely to experience harm and therefore discount harm in the future. For example, despite tobacco prevention and intervention messages arguing that cigarettes are harmful, research suggests that just over half of adolescents report experiencing either a positive or negative consequence, and 45% report both positive and negative consequences. Importantly, social consequences such as getting into trouble or having friends upset were reported as or more often than the health consequences, adding further support to the view that experiences with social as well as health consequences are likely to play a role in decision-making. Adolescents also experience a number of social, emotional, and physical risks and benefits after first experiencing sex. Thus, research supports the notion that adolescents perceive less risk associated with many behaviors, and that such perceptions play a key role in their decision-making.

In addition to personal experiences with various decisions and related outcomes, research has demonstrated the importance of vicarious experience, or knowledge about behaviors and related positive and negative outcomes experienced by others. For example, research demonstrates that exposure to earthquakes results in increased perceived chance that an earthquake will occur. Similarly, knowledge about a peers' positive experience with risk behaviors has been associated with increased perceptions that a similar positive experience will occur.

These findings have important implications for current health messages trying to reduce adolescent risk. Typically, health educators attempt to deter adolescents from engaging in health risk behaviors by conveying messages about risks, with the hope that such information will inform their decision-making. However, such messages focus mostly on long-term health risks such as getting lung cancer from smoking. For an adolescent who is more concerned about peer acceptance and approval as well as with immediate gratification, a message focused on long-term negative consequences is less likely to deter behavior, especially when such negative consequences are rarely experienced by them or their friends. Instead, communicating more realistic messages about short-term health risks, demystifying benefits, and providing a better balanced message will have a greater impact on adolescents' behavioral decisions.

Gender Differences in Decision-Making

Adolescent boys and girls do differ in their perceptions of and concerns over health-related risks and benefits. Girls are generally more worried about risks than are boys. For example, girls are more likely to believe that they can get an STD from having unprotected sex, get lung cancer from smoking, and have an accident while driving drunk. In contrast, boys perceive that they are more likely to experience positive outcomes such as experiencing pleasure from sex. Despite these differences in perceptions, studies have not determined whether the actual decision-making process differs between adolescent boys and girls. The few studies that have examined gender differences in decision-making have generally found that the process is remarkably similar.

Cultural Variation in Decision-Making

Despite the numerous studies on decision-making, few have examined cultural variation in adolescent decision-making competence, risk perceptions, benefit perceptions, or psychosocial maturity. In this case, culture is defined broadly, to include race, ethnicity, country of origin, acculturation, language usage, and social class. The few studies relevant here have shown that there is racial, ethnic, and cultural variation in certain areas of psychosocial development known to influence decision-making capacities, such as autonomy, orientation to the future, and values for academic achievement. Research has also shown that approaches to decision-making itself vary. For example, while in the United States and many Northern European countries the decision-making process is relatively individualized, in some cultures such as some Native American tribes and Asian cultures, decision-making is a shared, group process with input from many stakeholders. Thus, the impact of the decision impacts on many more than just the individual.

There are also few studies on the role of culture in the link between perceptions and behavior. It is possible that the level of perceived risk (and benefit) may differ across groups of individuals, possibly as a factor of culture, socioeconomic status, or differences in exposure to behavior-related outcomes, for example. Alternatively, groups of adolescents or young adults might perceive the same level of risk or benefit, but these perceptions might have different implications for their smoking, in part due to differences in perceived control, risk-reducing strategies used, or value placed on the negative outcome (e.g., bad breath or trouble breathing) as compared to the value placed on the benefit (e.g., looking cool) of smoking. Significant cultural differences in sexual perceptions have been found, whereby Asian and at times Hispanic youth perceived greater risk and less benefits of sex than did their European American counterparts. However, the relationship between these perceptions and sexual behavior did not vary across racial groups. Clearly, much more research is needed on their role of culture in adolescent decision-making.

Summary and Implications

Understanding adolescent decision-making, including how and the extent to which adolescents make competent decisions, is of great importance to researchers and practitioners in many fields such as the behavioral sciences, medicine, social work, law, and social policy. Interest in adolescent decision-making stems largely from our desire to understand, predict, and ultimately mitigate negative consequences by preventing adolescents' engagement in risky and delinquent behavior. Understanding adolescents' competency to make decisions also has important implications for policies and laws concerning adolescents' ability to consent for research, consent for medical treatment, refuse medical treatment, and be tried as an adult after committing a violent crime.

Research on adolescent decision-making has focused on a number of different avenues. One segment of the literature has focused on models of decision-making, with findings addressing the process by which adolescents should and do make decisions. In general, these studies show that adolescents do indeed employ a rational, analytic process of decision-making; however, the exact components of the model used by adolescents as well as the weighing of certain components (e.g., benefits over risks) may not coincide with adult models of decision-making. Further, results suggest that adolescents are less likely to utilize or spontaneously consider ideal components of decision-making, compared to adults. Nevertheless, research clearly shows that adolescents' perceptions of low risk and high benefit predict their engagement in subsequent risk behaviors. There is also support that dual-process models that emphasize noncognitive components of decision-making are superior in explaining adolescent decision-making and predicting behavior compared to rational, analytic models of decision-making. These dual pathways are consistent with a large set of literature arguing that while by mid- to late adolescence most individuals have the cognitive abilities to understand and judge risks, adolescents lack the psychosocial maturity required to consistently make and act upon decisions. In particular, compared to adults, adolescents are impulsive and more susceptible to peer pressure.

The results from the numerous studies on adolescent decision making, cognitive and psychosocial maturity, and perceptions of risks and benefits have important implications. Research on the relationship between perceptions and behavior supports efforts to reduce adolescents' engagement in risk behaviors through providing them with information about risks. More recently, it has been recognized that rather than solely focus efforts on disseminating information about the health implications of risky behavior, we need to broaden our discussions to include aspects of decision-making most relevant and immediate to youth. For example, we need to acknowledge the potential benefits of various risky behaviors, and discuss safer ways of obtaining similar benefits or help adolescents learn how to delay the need or acknowledge and defer the desire for such benefits. We also need to include in the discussion social consequences that adolescents highly value in their decision-making process. For example, studies have shown that adolescents care greatly about whether they are popular or look more grown up, and such desires to gain positive social feedback and avoid negative social consequences influence their decisions. Program curricula have also focused on developing adolescents' skills such as skills to resist peer pressure.

In view of the literature demonstrating adolescents' relative lack of maturity, it stands to reason that federal, state, and local laws restrict adolescents' ability to make certain decisions such as consent for research. Similarly, research showing that adolescents' decision-making is less competent compared to adults or compared to standards set forth in normative decision-making models has led to justifying raising the age at which adolescents accused of violent crimes may be tried as adults. It is thus imperative that we protect adolescents from serious harm while simultaneously providing them with appropriate and safe opportunities to practice and grow their decision-making skills.

See also: Brain Development; Cognitive Development; Impulsivity and Adolescence; Risk-Taking Behavior; Risky Sexual Behavior.

Further Reading

Cauffman E and Steinberg L (2000) (Im)maturity of judgment in adolescence: Why adolescents may be less culpable than adults. *Behavioral Sciences & the Law* 18: 741–760.

Fischhoff B (2008) Assessing adolescent decision-making competence. *Developmental Review* 28(1): 12–28.

Gibbons FX, Houlihan AE, and Gerrard M (2009) Reason and reaction: The utility of a dual-focus, dual-processing perspective on promotion and prevention of adolescent health risk behavior. *British Journal of Health Psychology* 14(Pt 2): 231–248.

Giedd JN (2008) The teen brain: Insights from neuroimaging. *Journal of Adolescent Health* 42: 335–343.

Gittler J, Quigley-Rick M, and Saks MJ (1990) *Adolescent Health Care Decision Making: The Law and Public Policy.* Washington, DC: Carnegie Council on Adolescent Development.

Halpern-Felsher BL and Cauffman E (2001) Costs and benefits of a decision: Decision-making competence in adolescents and adults. *Journal of Applied Developmental Psychology* 22: 257–273.

Millstein SG and Halpern-Felsher BL (2002) Perceptions of risk and vulnerability. *Journal of Adolescent Health* 31S: 10–27.

Reyna VF and Farley F (2006) Risk and rationality in adolescent decision making. Implications for theory, practice, and public policy. *Psychological Science in the Public Interest* 7: 1–44.

Steinberg L, Cauffman E, Woolard J, Graham S, and Banich M (2009) Are adolescents less mature than adults? Minors' access to abortion, the juvenile death penalty, and the alleged APA 'flip-flop'. *American Psychologist* 64(7): 583–594.

Adolescent Driving Behavior: A Developmental Challenge

B Simons-Morton, DESPR, NICHD, National Institutes of Health, Bethesda, MD, USA

Glossary

Age-related safety gradient: The effect of those who are older at licensure to have lower crash rates that decline faster than those licensed at younger ages.
Distraction: Eyes off the forward roadway for 1 s or longer.
g-Force events: Elevated kinematic (gravitational) events measured by an accelerometer.
Graduated driver licensing: Three-stage license system used in many Western countries, involving (1) learner permit with a long period of supervised practice; (2) provisional license with some limits; and (3) unrestricted license.
Hazard anticipation: The ability to identify and react to potential road hazards.
Risky driving: Includes elevated rates of g-force events (usual driving performance), speeding, close following; drinking and driving, drowsy driving, and secondary task engagement and distraction.

Introduction

To adults, driving is largely a requirement of daily living. However, to many adolescents, driving is a rite of passage that provides new opportunities for independence and social engagement. Because driving first begins for most people during adolescence and because it is one of the most dangerous activities in which the vast majority of adolescents engage, it is both a developmental challenge and a public health problem. Like few other developmental challenges, driving poses a serious threat to life and health. While risk is somewhat inherent in the task, an understanding of the developmental aspects of adolescent driving behavior suggests effective solutions to the problem.

The purpose of this article is to describe adolescent driving as a developmental challenge for parents, policy makers, and adolescents themselves. The article takes a largely US-centric perspective, but seeks to demonstrate that the issues are similar in other developed countries where licensure occurs during adolescence and people commonly travel in personal vehicles. The article describes two stages of the young driver problem. Novice young drivers experience highly elevated crash risk for at least the first year of independent driving due mainly to inexperience. However, young drivers remain at high risk well into the twenties, particularly under certain driving conditions and due mainly to risky driving behavior and poor judgment. Finally, the article reviews the major prevention approaches and evaluates their actual and potential contributions to the resolution of the problem and facilitation of healthful development.

Adolescent Driving as a Public Health Problem

Adolescents are generally quite healthy, but have very high rates of injury and death due to motor vehicle crashes compared with other age groups. Teenage driving presents a classic tradeoff between mobility and safety. Getting a license dramatically increases adolescent mobility and independence from parental authority and also relieves parents from the burden of transporting their teenage children. However, the younger teenagers get licensed, the more they drive, the greater their exposure to crash risks. Crash risk among the youngest licensed drivers is high in all Western countries, relative to older drivers, but this is particularly the case in the United States, Canada, and Australia where teenagers can get licensed at relatively young ages. Licensure is legal at age 16 in most US states and Canadian provinces, 17 in Australia and England, and 18 in many European countries. However, in practice, most English and European adolescents do not actually get licensed for some time, often years, after they become eligible because the licensing processes are relatively difficult (much more difficult than in the United States) and public transportation is highly advanced, making driving less necessary for adolescents. About half of US teenagers get licensed by age 17 and the vast majority is licensed by age 18. Conversely, less than half of Europeans are licensed as teenagers. Driving-related problems in general and young driver problems, in particular, are particularly exacerbated in the United States, Canada, and Australia owing to their large geographic size, extreme reliance on motor vehicles, and poorly developed public transportation. Consequently, adolescents in these countries have much earlier and greater exposure than adolescents in Europe and elsewhere, driving and riding with other adolescent drivers at earlier ages, and for many more miles.

While early licensure exposes adolescents to the risks associated with driving, it should be recognized that crash rates for US adolescents begin a steep increase at age 14, when they start riding as passengers with teenage drivers (about 40% of adolescent crash fatalities are passengers), and remain higher for 16–19-year-olds than for any age group younger than 70, as shown in **Figure 1**. When assessed per 100 000 population, fatal crashes for 16–19-year-olds have declined somewhat over the past two decades, mainly because adolescents today get licensed at somewhat older ages, and also because fatal crash rates among all drivers have declined as vehicles and roadways have become safer. Nevertheless, in every Western country studied, newly licensed teenagers have the highest crash rates of any age group, except the very old. Crash rates are highest immediately after licensure, decline very rapidly for a period of months, and then decline slowly for a period of years before stabilizing at about age 30.

 Encyclopedia of Adolescence, Volume 1 doi:10.1016/B978-0-12-373915-5.00012-7

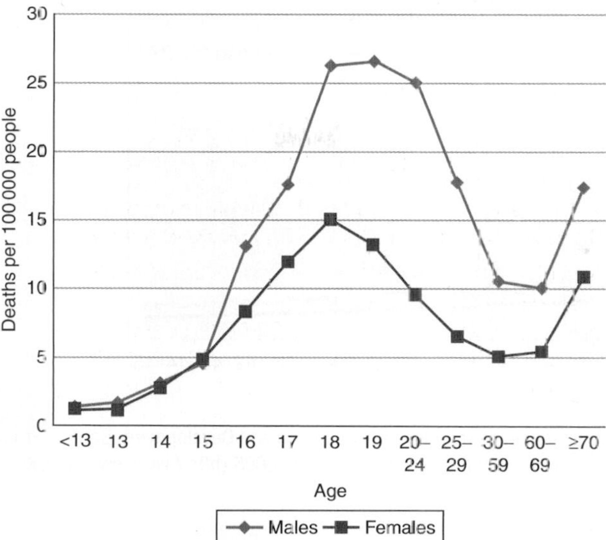

Figure 1 Deaths in passenger vehicles per 100 000 people by age and gender, 2008. Source: US Department of Transportation's Fatality Analysis Reporting System (FARS).

Rates of fatal crashes, which commonly involve high speeds, late night, multiple passengers, bad weather, unfamiliar roads, alcohol, or combinations of these risks, are notably higher for males than females, as shown in **Figure 1**. Also, compared with older, more experienced drivers, less experienced drivers are more likely to be at fault in crashes and to be involved in crashes that are speed-related and due to overcorrection errors, the types of crashes that are associated with going too fast for conditions, judgment errors, risky driving, and inattention. The phenomenon of highly elevated crash rates among adolescents is known in public health as the young driver problem. Not surprisingly, preventing motor vehicle crashes among adolescents is a prominent health objective in most developed and many developing countries.

Safe Driving as a Developmental Challenge

Driving is a developmental challenge because it is a complex and dangerous activity undertaken during adolescence. As with all developmental challenges, the hope is that the adolescent will learn from the experience and not suffer a lifelong setback, such as injury or death, cause an injury or death, or be charged with a driving-related crime such as drinking and driving or involuntary manslaughter. The role of parents and policy is to provide contexts within which the adolescent can meet the developmental challenge with minimum risk.

Like most developmental challenges, safe driving is learned through many hours of experience. Learning to drive safely is difficult at any age, but may be particularly difficult among adolescents because safe driving requires attention, self-control, and good judgment – general capabilities that are not fully developed among adolescents. Ultimately, nearly every driver develops a reasonable level of safety competence over time, as evidenced by the relatively low crash rates among adults, but safety competence develops gradually. There are two important stages in adolescent development of safe driving competence. The first stage, the novice driver stage, is defined by highly elevated crash rates at licensure that decline rapidly during the first year or so of licensure. The novice young driver problem is largely a matter of inexperience and the lengthy period of time required to learn how to drive safely. The second stage, the young driver stage, is defined by higher-than-average crash rates for young drivers relative to older, experienced adults. This part of the young driver problem is due greatly to the propensity of younger drivers to drive in a more risky fashion than older, more experienced drivers.

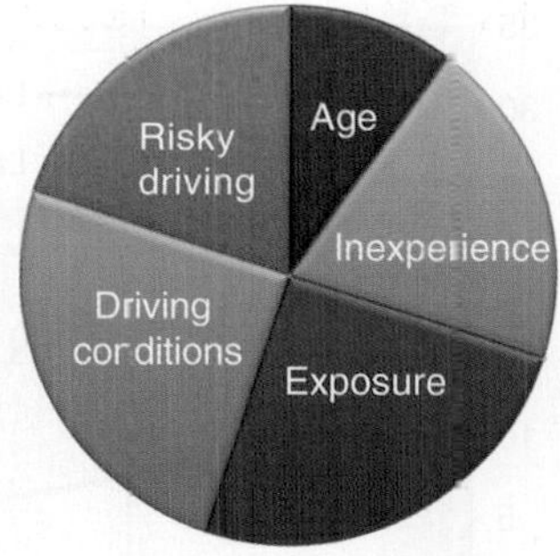

Figure 2 The causes of the young driver problem include inexperience, age, driving conditions, and risk taking, as shown in **Figure 1**.

Figure 2 shows a pie chart that presents the contributions of the most important factors in the developmental challenge of safe driving, which include young age inexperience, exposure, driving conditions, and risky behavior. Each slice and factor represents a reasonable estimate of the proportion of the safe driving challenge. However, keep in mind that the risk factors are highly interrelated and overlapping and vary in importance during the novice and young driver periods. Here, we discuss why and how each of these factors is important to the safe driving challenge.

Age

The first year of licensure is typified by extremely high crash rates immediately after licensure that decline rapidly for 6–12 months and then more slowly for years. It seems that novice drivers are not very good when first licensed. While this risk declines rapidly during the first year of licensure, it remains elevated for young drivers into the mid-twenties. There is very little evidence that training and prelicense practice is protective in this regard. The only prelicense factor that is known to influence crash rates during the first year of licensure is age.

Shown in **Figure 3** are crash rates for European drivers licensed at various ages, starting at age 18. As shown, younger age at licensure is a risk factor and older age at licensure is protective. While the first year of driving is more dangerous than any other year regardless of age at licensure, age is a significant modifying factor, as shown in **Figure 3**. Drivers who first get licensed in their twenties have a similar pattern of crash rates as those who get licensed at age 18, high at first and declining rapidly. However, the initial rate is higher for the younger drivers and declines somewhat more slowly. By the mid-twenties, crash rates are essentially identical,

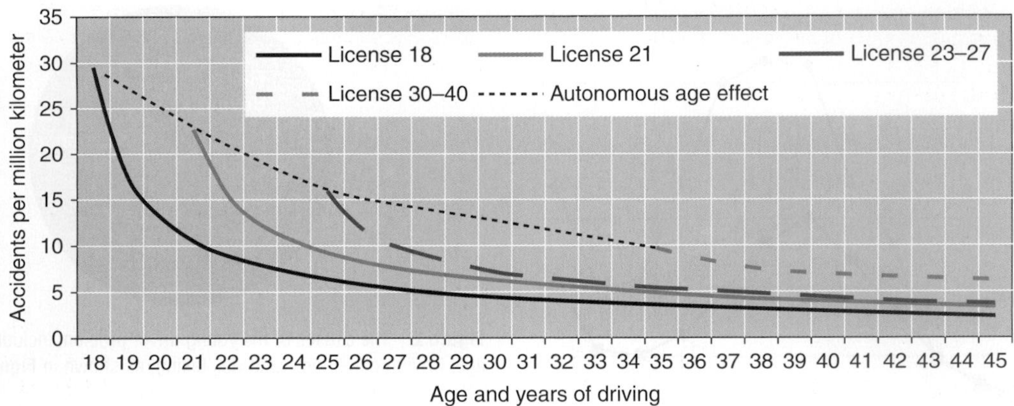

Figure 3 Crash rates by age of licensure among European members of the Organization of Economic Co-Operation and Development. Source: From Vlakveld WP. Jonge beginnende automobilisten, hun ongevalsrisico en maatregelen om dit terug te dringen. SWOV, 2005 (http://www.swov.nl/UK/Research/publicaties/inhoud/publicaties).

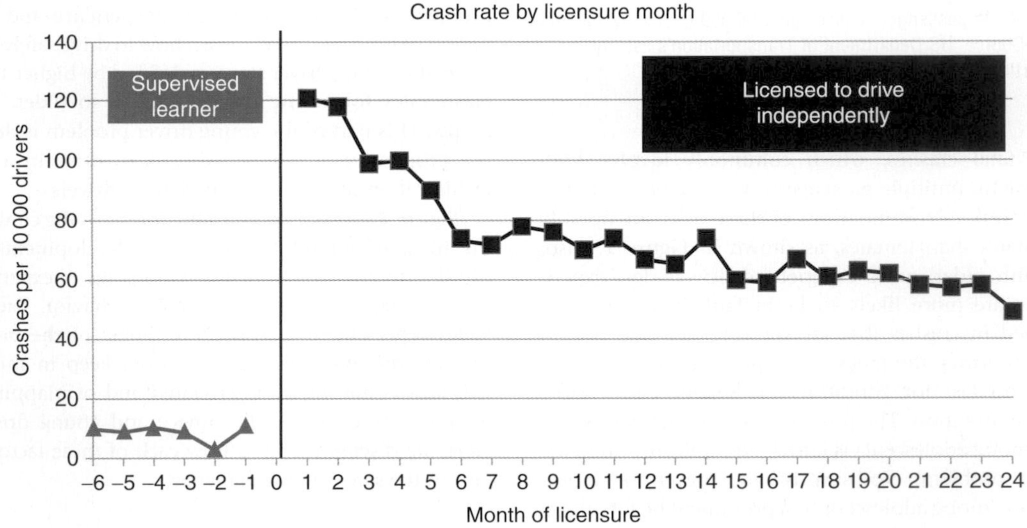

Figure 4 Crash rates based on motor vehicle office records for Nova Scotia, Canada. Source: Adapted from Mayhew DR, Simpson HM, and Pak A (2003) Changes in collision rates among novice drivers during the first months of driving. *Accident Analysis and Prevention* 35: 683–691.

regardless of the age at licensure. The dashed line in **Figure 3** shows the age-related safety gradient for older age at licensure. Note the lower crash rates for the first several years after licensure of 21-year-olds compared with 18-year-olds.

The very high crash rate for Canadian 16–19-year-olds during the first 2 years of licensure is shown in **Figure** 4. Note that the slope shown here is similar to the one shown in **Figure** 3, with highly elevated crash rates at licensure that decline rapidly during the first 6 months of licensure and then more slowly over the next year and a half. Similar data have been reported for novice young drivers in the United States, Australia, The Netherlands, and other countries, providing evidence that the novice young driver problem is universal.

Other evidence of the effect of young age is provided by the very high crash and injury rates among newly licensed drivers in Iowa, where adolescents can get special licenses to drive to school at age 14. In contrast, New Jersey, the only US state in which the age of licensure is 17, has the lowest crash and injury rates among 16-year-olds in the nation. Clearly, there is an age effect on crash rates. The lower the age at licensure, the higher the initial crash rate and the slower they decline.

The safety gradient for older age at licensure, or risk gradient for younger age at licensure, can be attributed to maturity, which of course is highly correlated with age. On average, by almost any measure, older adolescents are more mature than younger adolescents, and almost invariably, each adolescent is more mature at 17 than 16. Recent research shows that brain development continues into the twenties and incomplete brain development is a likely factor in the age gradient of risk. However, many other factors have important influences on maturity, including parenting and other socialization factors.

Adolescent females, of course, tend to be ahead of males in many areas of development, including self-control and judgment, and adolescent males are more aggressive and risk-taking. Not surprisingly, during adolescence (and at every age), males have higher fatal crash rates than females, but the differences between males and females in nonfatal crash rates are modest or nonexistent, particularly among adolescents during the first year of licensure, suggesting that the dangers inherent in learning to drive are similar for boys and girls, but girls may be better at managing the greatest risks. However, despite the importance of young age at licensure, driving inexperience is a much greater part of the problem.

Inexperience and the Learning Curve

The pattern of high crash rates during the first months of licensure followed by a rapid and then more gradual decline is consistent with the vast literature showing that the development of complex psycho-motor skills is prolonged. With driving, as with all complex activities, experience is the most important predictor of achievement. Every supervising parent quickly finds out that basic vehicle management can be learned in a matter of hours, even by the youngest and least coordinated adolescent. Most novices learn reasonably well how to maintain the vehicle within marked lanes, accelerate and brake smoothly, back up, turn, and park in no more than a half dozen lessons. In farming regions of the United States, it is common for early adolescents and even preadolescent children to drive tractors, pick up trucks, and other motorized equipment (effectively, if not necessarily safely) on private land where a license is not required. Certainly, as novices gain experience their vehicle management improves, but vehicle management is not much related to safety. Rarely does a crash occur because the driver simply loses control of the vehicle without some precipitating cause such as excessive speed or inattention (probably just as rarely as a crash is averted at the last moment because of skillful handling of the vehicle, although the myth that skillful avoidance maneuvering protects one from a crash remains popular. Race car drivers and police officers have advanced driving skills, but have higher than average off-duty crash rates). Being able to manage the vehicle is a necessary but not a sufficient requirement for safe driving, which requires constant attention and consistent exercise of good judgment, which develop slowly over a period of years.

Experience is a valuable teacher in a wide range of everyday activities and is a key element in the development of expertise. At the early stage of learning a new skill, error rates are very high but decline rapidly with experience. From a learning theory perspective, errors provide feedback, leading to improvements in performance. However, the rate of learning gradually slows as basic skills are mastered and the simplest errors are reduced, but errors remain fairly high for a long time as the learner encounters more difficult applications requiring nuanced expertise. Learning any new skill involves a certain amount of trial and error, and learning to drive is no exception.

Because cognitive demands are greater during periods of intense learning, novices may be particularly prone to driving errors. In part, this is because novices have not developed automatic driving responses. Research on skill development and the acquisition of expertise shows that people can deal with a task or problem either by relying on what they have done in similar situations in the past (automaticity) or work out a new situation then and there. The memory-based alternative is fast and effortless, while the creative approach is effortful and error-prone. Because novices have relatively few relevant memories to rely on, they tend to be inconsistent and error-prone.

In contrast to novices, experts in almost any area, for example, mathematics, chess, sports, and driving, are quickly able to allocate their attention to the important elements and patterns in structured and unstructured problems and have immediate access to a huge cognitive store of memorized and automated knowledge about problems and solutions. Similarly, driving competence can be expected to advance only through feedback from frequent experience with a wide variety of driving situations encountered over a long period of time. Safe driving requires the ability to maneuver in a variety of complex traffic conditions, identify and react to hazards, anticipate the actions of other vehicles, manage distractions, correctly signal intended actions, and otherwise drive in a manner that keeps the vehicle well separated in space and time from other vehicles and objects. The main way to avoid crashes is to pay attention to the roadway and adjust driving to minimize the vehicle's proximity in space and time to other vehicles and hazards. Inexperienced drivers in general are less able to recognize and anticipate potential hazards, prone to extended inattention at inopportune times, and drive generally too fast and too close for safety.

Exposure

The more a person drives, the greater the risk of a crash. Relative to low mileage drivers, high mileage drivers may have more total crashes but lower crash rates. This is consistent with the decline in crash rates by age (and experience) shown in **Figures 3** and **4**, which also shows that crash rates decline with years and miles of lifetime exposure. Exposure as a crash risk is most notable among the least experienced drivers, which poses the young driver dilemma, which is that driving performance improves only with driving experience, but the more novices drive the greater their risk of crashing. A partial solution to the dilemma will be discussed later in the article. Here, we emphasize that exposure increases crash risk among novices mainly because novices are not very good drivers and have little experience or context for dealing with novel events. Even experienced drivers perform badly when exposed to driving conditions with which they are not familiar. For example, residents in areas that get a lot of snow have lower snow-related crash rates than residents in areas that get snow only occasionally. Every driving condition is novel to novices, making their exposure relatively more dangerous than similar exposure for more experienced drivers.

In addition, relatively unfamiliar, nonroutine actions require greater cognitive executive function than routine actions, and their performance is conscious and controlled rather than automated and responsive. Managing complex tasks like those involved in driving requires a substantial proportion of available cognitive capacity, particularly during intense learning phases when very little of the driving process has been automated. For a novice, the various actions required to drive are relatively novel and complicated. However, with experience, driving tasks such as acceleration, braking, visual scan, shifting, and hazard detection become increasingly automated in the sense that performance does not require purposeful attention, imposes relatively modest cognitive demand, and is less susceptible to distraction.

Driving Conditions

Not all driving conditions are equally dangerous. Crashes are more likely for all drivers at night and under inclement, complex, and novel conditions (road construction is an example of a novel road condition that is dangerous because the barriers and detour signs are unfamiliar and disorienting and even experienced drivers do not always react in the safest manner). However, all of these driving conditions are novel and risky for novices and young drivers. For example, compared with driving during the day, driving at night is more dangerous on a per mile basis for younger than older drivers.

Teenage passengers also impose risk for teenage drivers. For older drivers, passengers pose little or no increase in crash risk and may even be protective. However, crash risk increases for teenage drivers with each additional passenger. Male teenage passengers, in particular, increase crash risks among teenage drivers, particularly for male drivers. Also, risky driving in general (increased speed and close following) among both male and female teenage drivers is elevated with male teenage passengers. These effects may be due to the tendency of teenage passengers to be distracting or of teenage drivers to be distracted by teenage passengers. Also, teenage drivers may be susceptible to perceived social norms (e.g., my passenger will think better of me if I drive faster or slower than usual) or alterations in the mood or social environment within the vehicle.

Driving conditions, age, and inexperience are thought to interact. Certain driving conditions impose risk in part because they are novel and therefore are particularly challenging to novice and relatively inexperienced young drivers. Other driving conditions, such as teenage passenger presence, may pose risk because they create a special social context that may influence teenage driving behavior. Moreover, younger drivers are thought to be less able than older drivers to correctly judge the complexity and inherent risks of various driving situations and therefore fail to adapt appropriately to driving conditions.

Risky Driving

Usual driving style

Teenage drivers not only have higher crash rates than experienced adults, they also drive in a more risky style. Recent 'naturalistic driving' research using sensitive instrumentation of study participants' own vehicles installed during the first 18 months of licensure, shows that teenagers relative to adults (mostly parents) on average drive faster, follow more closely, accelerate faster, brake harder, and turn more sharply. Hard braking is a good case in point. On average, novice adolescent drivers have about eight times the rate of hard braking events as experienced adults. Indeed, experienced drivers rarely brake so hard that passengers are made uncomfortable (−45 g-force or greater), but young drivers do this routinely. Mostly, hard braking is a matter of beginning to brake relatively late, due either to a failure to anticipate the need to stop or a style of driving where late braking is acceptable or preferred. The risk associated with late braking, of course, is that the margin for error is less. If the lead vehicle brakes suddenly, the trailing vehicle is more likely to crash if the driver waits until the last second to brake rather than anticipating this potential hazard and beginning to brake early. Hard turns provide another case in point. Experienced adults rarely exceed g-forces of +0.5 or greater in turns, but young drivers do routinely, placing themselves at increased risk for skidding, overcorrection, and losing control of the vehicle.

Curiously, when teenagers drive with their parents in the vehicle, their rate of elevated g-force events is almost identical to the rates of adults, suggesting that teens can drive in a smooth and careful manner, but they do not when their parents are present to witness it. Survey data also indicate that on average, young drivers drive in a more risky fashion than older drivers, tailgating, weaving through traffic, and speeding. Other survey data show that on average, teenagers assess their driving skills as being quite high even during the early months of licensure when they clearly are not very good, and self-assessment of risk is relatively stable over the first 18 months of driving. This is in contrast to the expectation that perceived skill would improve with experience and performance, as it typically does for other tasks. Teenage risky driving may be a matter of trial and error, purposeful testing of the limits of ability and technology, a high psychological threshold for risk taking, or a failure to perceive risky driving as such. For whatever reason, it seems that on average, younger drivers have a more risky style of driving than older drivers.

Impairment

Drinking and driving is relatively uncommon for young novices, but increases during adolescence, as shown in **Figure 5**. Drinking and driving among teenagers is a lethal combination. Indeed, it has been shown in controlled test track research that driving performance deteriorates more precipitously and at much lower blood alcohol levels for teenagers compared with experienced adults. Out on the highway, a much higher proportion of fatal crashes involve alcohol among younger relative to older drivers. This may be due more to the effects of alcohol on young drivers than to the prevalence of drinking and driving. The combination of being inexperienced at both drinking and driving may render adolescents particularly susceptible to crashes for the obvious reasons that inebriation affects both judgment and motor skills, and teenagers tend generally to drive in a relatively risky manner. Teenage drinking often occurs in association with driving because the vehicle is often the only environment available for this illegal activity and driving is part of the experience of drinking and being drunk. Therefore, drinking and driving often occurs late at night with multiple passengers in the vehicle. Under the influence of alcohol teenage drivers may become more susceptible to peer influence than they might be otherwise. All of these factors are likely to combine to increase risk dramatically for teenage drivers and passengers.

Driving under the influence of marijuana and other drugs almost certainly occurs more or less in proportion to the prevalence of their use in general. Marijuana, of course, is among the most prevalent drugs among adolescents in Western countries and the prevalence of driving while stoned is probably fairly high among young drivers. However, there are no reliable prevalence rates on driving while under the influence of marijuana or other drugs.

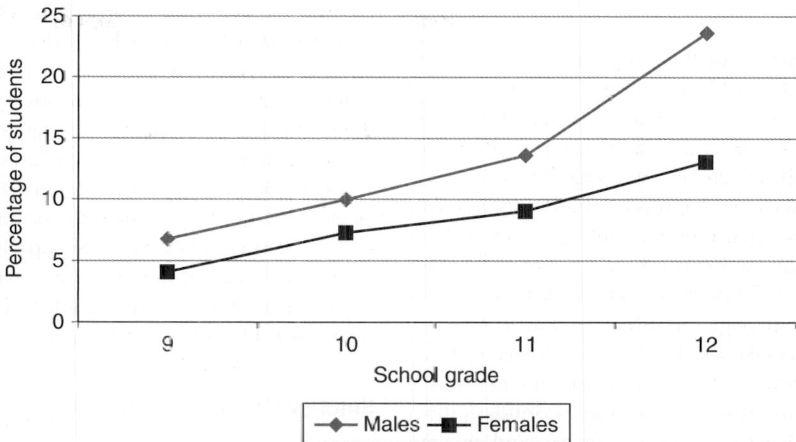

Figure 5 Percentage of students who drove a vehicle one or more times in the past 30 days when they had been drinking alcohol. Source: Youth Risk Behavior Survey, Centers for Disease Control (http://apps nccd.cdc.gov/yrbss/QuestYearTable).

Drowsiness is another important crash risk factor that may be relatively prevalent among young drivers and may be as big of a problem as any impairment other than drinking. Research in driving simulators has demonstrated that drowsiness can have effects on driving very similar to alcohol. No prevalence rates of drowsy driving among adolescents could be located, but it is thought to be a factor in up to 10% of crashes among drivers of all ages. Because many adolescents are sleep-deprived somewhat often, drowsy driving may be particularly important in this group, particularly in combination with driving inexperience.

Distraction and inattention due to secondary tasks

Most crashes are due to a combination of driver inattention and an unanticipated event. Driver inattention reduces the potential reaction time for braking and maneuvering, and in the vast majority of cases, these few seconds of potential reaction time are much more important in preventing a crash than any actual last-split-second avoidance maneuvering. Recent naturalistic driving studies in which the vehicles of drivers were instrumented with sophisticated equipment (including GPS, accelerometers, and cameras) have enabled assessment of driving performance and outcomes in drivers of various ages. Tiny cameras (usually mounted on the rear view mirror) aimed at the driver that record continuously have demonstrated that drivers engage in an astounding array and frequency of secondary tasks and this is particularly true for young drivers. From the moment they get licensed, teenagers drive and use cell phones, text message, deal with their music, and the like. This is not surprising, given the prevalence of electronic device use among adolescents generally. However, compared with adults, teenagers place relatively few restraints on their use of these devices. Cell phone use and text messaging are particularly important causes of driver distraction leading to crashes.

Distraction is usually measured by how long the driver's eyes are not looking at the forward roadway. These 'eye glance' analyses cannot determine what the driver is seeing but they can determine when and for how long the driver is incapable of seeing aspects of the roadway when they look away from the road and ignore vehicle mirrors. The longer the period of distraction, the greater is the risk. Long periods of distraction reduce the amount of time to react in the case of an unexpected event, such as a vehicle or pedestrian entering the roadway or the lead vehicle stopping suddenly. Invariably, the amount of time available to respond to a hazard is more important than the actual braking, turning, or other avoidance maneuver.

Long periods of distraction occur commonly when dialing, texting, and visually searching for music. Visual fixation on an external event is also common and problematic. While teens are generally facile with technology, novice teenage drivers are not good at dividing their attention. In a recent study, we recruited a sample of experienced and novice drivers to drive a vehicle on a test track that has an intersection with a lighted traffic signal. After a few practice passes through the intersection, as the vehicle approached the intersection (200′), we handed the drivers a cell phone and asked them to dial a number and obtain local traffic and weather information, and then turned the signal yellow. Older drivers tended to be clumsy with the phone, dialing a few digits before looking up, invariably seeing the yellow light and then stopping at the red light, seldom completing the cell phone task before stopping. Novice teenagers, on the other hand, were quite facile with the cell phone and obtained the information rapidly; however, a third of them failed to look up in time to stop at the red light. Six months later we tested them again with the identical result.

Novice teenage drivers may be particularly prone to distraction. Novice drivers tend to have poor scanning patterns in general, often fixating on a particular object for a long period, and sometimes look directly at a potential hazard without preparing or reacting. Perhaps more importantly, experienced drivers tend to become uncomfortable when they have their eyes off the frontal roadway for more than a second, but teenage drivers do not show this same reluctance. This may be a matter of the automaticity discussed earlier, where experienced drivers typically look back to the roadway after only a moment of distraction without consciously thinking about how long it has been since they looked away from the roadway, while novices have a less developed sense of this and are prone to protracted distraction.

High Risk Drivers

There is substantial variability in crash risk among young drivers, as there is among adult drivers. Over a third of novices report crashing at least once during the first year of driving (compared with about 1 out of 20 experienced adults who crash annually). A small percentage of drivers at every age, adolescents included, have a disproportionate number of crashes. Presumably, this variability in crash experience is due in part to driver attention, self control, and judgment. Most drivers, young and old, drive in accordance with their actual and perceived ability to manage the vehicle in traffic. Generally, less confident drivers take fewer risks, drive slower, follow at greater distances, require greater gaps in traffic before turning or merging, and so on. Alternatively, more confident drivers take more risk, drive faster, follow closely, and merge aggressively. In part, this explains the higher crash rates of males compared with females at every age. When the driver is a good judge of his or her own abilities and keeps driving risk within manageable limits, crash risk is minimized. However, it is easy to misjudge one's competence and novices in particular, given their lack of experience and maturity, tend to overestimate their ability, thereby creating or allowing risky driving situations. Many insurance companies provide a discount on premiums for teenager drivers who get good grades in school because they have lower crash rates than teenagers who do badly in school. The same characteristics that enable students to get good grades are probably responsible for their relatively better crash rates, mainly greater maturity in terms of self-control and judgment.

Surprisingly, few personality or temperament variables are associated with crash risks and none as important as inexperience. Sensation-seeking and the propensity for risk-taking are perhaps the only psychological factors consistently associated with crash experience. Adolescents with a pattern of risky behavior, substance use in particular, have higher crash risk. Adolescents who report low levels of parental monitoring and involvement are at elevated and persistent crash risk (more about this later in the article).

As noted, attention is one of the most important factors in safe driving. Attention while driving is likely to vary among adolescents due to maturity, experience, and possibly mood. Attention-deficit hyperactivity disorder (ADHD) adolescents provide an extreme example of a high-risk group, crashing at frighteningly high rates, presumably because they are easily distracted from the driving task. Apparently, a big part of the problem is that adolescents with ADHD do not consistently take their medicines due to the side effects or other reasons. They tend to drive better when medicated, but not so well when not. Of course, apart from ADHD, adolescents' capacities for maintaining attention to any activity vary, and those who are better able to concentrate their attention on the driving task should be at less risk than those who are easily distracted.

Laws of Accident Causation

A recent paper by Elvik described four laws of accident causation developed with experienced drivers in mind. However, it is uncanny how well they describe the young driver problem. The first law of accident causation is the universal law of learning, which is based on the premise that crash rates decrease the more miles one drives. The second law is that rare events increase the likelihood of a crash. The third law is that error rates are higher for relatively complex driving situations. The fourth law is that error increases when demands on cognitive capacity are high. These laws succinctly describe why young novice drivers have high rates. Basically, they have little experience, tend to mishandle novel and complex driving situations, and their cognitive capacity is challenged by the complexity of learning to drive safely, particularly while engaging routinely in secondary tasks and coping with the distraction and social influences of teenage passengers.

Solutions to the Problem

Everything that is done to improve the safety of drivers and vehicle occupants in general is important for teenage driving safety. Safe road designs, safe vehicles, safety devices, and programs and policies that discourage high risk, drowsy, drunk, and distracted driving, contribute to the safety of young drivers. However, there are no special and efficacious programs for preventing crashes among young drivers, but there are such programs for novices. Effective prevention of novice teenage driving problems is based on the understanding that teenagers are not safe when first licensed and particularly at risk under more complex driving situations. Therefore, it is protective to delay licensure as long as possible and then limit driving to less risky conditions, at least for a time, while novices gain experience and develop competence. The special programs and policies directed at young drivers are shown in **Table 1** and described here in terms of their purposes and safety effects.

Driver Education

Driver education generally achieves its primary goals of training novices in basic vehicle management skills and preparing them for licensure. Completing a driver education course certified by the state almost always leads to successful attainment of a license. These courses generally consist of a minimum of 6 h of classroom and 4–8 h of behind-the-wheel driving with an instructor. The classroom training is designed to prepare students to pass the licensing exam covering the 'rules of the road.' The on-road instruction is designed to prepare the student to pass the state driving test. Indeed, in many states these days, the driving school instructor actually conducts the driving test and grades the student. Driving tests in the United States, even those administered by the state department responsible for licensing, tend not to be discriminating. Many state road tests are actually conducted on an off-road track without any actual traffic. Because the driving portion of the licensing examination is expensive and time-consuming, there is substantial incentive for states to pass the vast majority of those who take the test and minimize the time and expense of retesting. Therefore, success rates are very high in most states. In contrast, road tests in England, some parts of Europe, Japan, and some other countries, are actually very demanding, with relatively high failure rates. The main effect of tough testing is that people do not take the test until they really need to drive. Actually, there is little or no evidence that road tests are associated with safe driving.

Table 1 Novice driver programs and the evidence of their safety effects

Safety approaches and goals	*Evidence of safety effects*
Driver education: Teach novice teenage drivers the rules of the road and train them to manage the vehicle well enough to pass the provisional licensing examination.	None. Driver education has a good record of achievement in preparing students for the licensing examinations. There is no evidence that driver education improves safety after licensure.
Supervised practice: Practice driving is designed to provide learners with experience managing the vehicle in a range of traffic conditions.	Limited. While the more practice driving a novice gets the better, the only safety effects are due to the delay in licensing that occurs due to additional hours of practice. There is little or no evidence that practice driving itself improves independent driving performance or safety.
Graduate Driver Licensing (GDL): Three-stage GDL licensing includes (1) a long period and many hours of practice driving; (2) provisional license allowing novices to drive unsupervised with restrictions on late night driving, alcohol, number of teenage passengers, etc.; and (3) unrestricted license, usually at age 18 only if novice had no GDL violations.	Strong. GDL has been well evaluated and found to reduce crash fatalities. Other research has shown that the stronger the GDL provisions, the better the effects on safety.
Parental management: The goal of parental management is to extend the GDL concept of limiting the driving conditions novices are exposed to while they gain driving experience.	Good. The Checkpoints Program has been evaluated in five randomized trials and shown to increase parent limit setting, adoption of a parent–teen driving agreement, and protect against risky driving, citations, and crashes.
Electronic feedback systems: The goal of these systems is to provide feedback to drivers when they exceed a g-force limit. This information can be stored and shared with parents.	Favorable. Several studies have shown that most teenagers reduce risky driving behavior when a devise is installed in their vehicle and the data are made available to the family. Participation rates have been low in most studies, limiting potential generalization.

These tests are designed to determine whether the driver can manage the vehicle reasonably well and possibly assess their ability to deal with moderately complex driving conditions, not to assess driving safety. As noted, safety is more a matter of attention and judgment than vehicle management.

While driver education is effective at preparing novices for the driver licensing examination, there is no evidence that driver education provides safety effects upon licensure. Indeed, substantial research in the United States has shown no safety effects of even the very best driver education programs. In Japan, Scandinavia, France, and other European countries where driver education often involves many hours of professional on-road instruction, there is little evidence that it has an effect on independent driving safety, except to the extent it delays licensure. There is great variability in emphases by various driving schools and driving instructors and no evidence-based standards linking skills typically taught by driving instructors and independent driving outcomes. Meanwhile, there is evidence that hazard anticipation skills are important in safe driving, but these skills are seldom taught in driver education. 'Advanced skills training' courses are now popular in many parts of the US. Basically, these programs teach novices how to get into and out of skids and the basics of avoiding a crash through last-second maneuvering. These programs have generally not been evaluated but one Swedish study showed that participants actually had higher crash rates following the course than the controls. To the extent these courses teach teenagers that crashes are a matter of maneuvering ability and not the prevention of the situations that require such maneuvering, they should be considered a threat to safety.

Supervised Practice Driving

In the United States, the minimum requirements for parental supervised driving have increased in recent years from a few hours to an average of about 50 h, similar to the amounts required and obtained in Australia and Canada. Many European countries require even more supervised practice driving than in the United States, and it is not uncommon for learners to complete over 100 h of supervised driving. The idea is that the more supervised practice driving novices get prior to licensure, the better they should be able to manage the vehicle, the more experience they should have under a wide range of driving conditions, and the more time parents would have to impress upon their children the importance of safe driving behavior. While supervised practice driving is undoubtedly a good thing, there is surprisingly little evidence that the amount of parent-supervised practice driving is associated with reduced post-licensure crash rates. None of the few US studies that have examined this question has shown effects. Similarly, no effect was found in a French study. A Swedish study of 18–20-year-old drivers reported effects from extensive supervised practice driving (mean of about 120 h). While more supervised practice driving is certainly better than less, the primary advantage of requirements for a high amount of supervised practice driving is that it delays the age at which adolescents get licensed and reduces (delays) their driving exposure.

As shown in **Figure 4**, prelicense supervised practice driving is very safe, but as soon as adolescents get licensed, their crash rates go way up. No matter how much supervised practice driving teenagers obtain or the quality of instruction parents provided to them, there are a number of reasons that the safety benefits of supervised practice driving are likely to be limited. When supervising novice teenage drivers, instructors and parents can be expected to maintain a high priority on safety, guiding teenagers through complex driving situations, anticipating and warning of hazards, keeping internal vehicle environment free from distraction, and otherwise codriving. Most supervised practice is routine, exposing novices to limited variety in driving. The lack of varied practice and codriving by parents could largely explain why parent-supervised practice driving is very safe relative to the early period of independent driving. Only with the onset of independent driving do teenagers begin to deal on their own with complex driving situations – some not encountered previously while supervised – often in the presence of teenage passengers.

Graduated Driver Licensing

Graduated Driver Licensing (GDL) is based on the recognition that newly licensed teenagers need independent driving experience to become better, but this early experience should be gained under the least dangerous driving conditions possible. GDL has gradually been adopted by all Australian and Canadian provinces and US states. GDL includes three stages: (1) the leaner permit, with a long period of required adult-supervised practice driving; (2) provisional license stage, with limits on late night driving, alcohol, and increasingly on the number of teen passengers and the use of electronic devices while driving; and (3) unrestricted license, usually after 12 months on a provisional license or at age 18 and only when no violations have occurred. GDL has been evaluated frequently and significant reductions in crashes and injuries have generally been reported. One of the effects of GDL is the requirement for about 50 h of supervised practice during the learner permit, which has had the effect of delaying licensure, thereby reducing exposure. It appears that GDL is generally enforced only when a teenager is stopped for another reason and is found by the police also to be in violation of GDL, for example, after midnight. However, GDL does appear to alter norms regarding in the safety of novice teenage driving and empowers parents to set limits on their newly licensed teenage children.

GDL is a developmentally appropriate approach to driving safety. It attempts to minimize the high risk of learning to drive by requiring lots of practice with supervising adults, presumably parents, so that teens gain experience and parents have ample opportunity to set standards and expectations. Then, adolescents are allowed to drive, but not under the most dangerous conditions, late at night, with multiple teenage passengers, while impaired. However, GDL is not really enforced and its main strength is that it empowers parents to manage the first year of driving.

Parental Management of Novice Teenage Driving

Parenting practices and modeling provide important influences on adolescent behaviors of all kinds, and driving is no exception. Modest associations have been shown between parent and teenage child driving records, crash experience, and risky driving behavior. Like GDL, a major goal of parental management is to limit the complexity of driving conditions for some months after licensure while newly licensed teenagers develop complex driving skills. There are two promising and complementary approaches to parental management of novice teenage driving. The first is parent limit setting and the second provides electronic feedback to novice teenagers and parents about the teen's driving behavior.

Parent limit setting

Nearly all parents set modest limits on their newly licensed teenagers. However, in general, these limits tend not to be strict, tend to focus on the details of the trip and not on safety, and quickly fade altogether in a matter of months. However, teenagers whose parents imposed more strict limits on teenage passengers and night driving reported less risky driving behavior and fewer traffic violations and crashes. The Checkpoints Program has been shown in several randomized trials to increase parental limit setting and improve safety outcomes by fostering the adoption of a parent–teen driving agreement that clarifies novice teenage driving limits and the requirements and timing for gaining additional driving privileges.

Electronic Feedback

Teenagers may not realize that their driving is risky and there is no way for parents to know how their teenagers drive because teenagers do not drive the same way on their own as they do when the parent is a passenger in the vehicle. Several recent studies have evaluated the effects of electronic devices installed in the vehicles of novice teenager drivers that provide visual feedback in the form of a blinking light each time the vehicle exceeds a set g-force limit (such as fast starts and hard braking and turning) assessed by an accelerometer. Some of these devices include cameras that record driver behavior and the forward roadway. The events are stored, downloaded, evaluated by remote staff, and made available every week for the teen and parent access on a password-protected website. Evaluations have shown that most teens reduce the number of triggered events within a few weeks after installation and maintain a low rate of events as long as their parents bother to review the weekly feedback. Unfortunately, only a very small percentage of families have been willing to use these devices. Reasons for this reluctance include the high cost of the devices and parents' trust in their teenagers and desire not to invade teenage privacy. Moreover, in two of the studies, many participating parents quickly lost interest and stopped reviewing the weekly reports regularly.

Summary

Driving is a dangerous activity, particularly for novice and young drivers. Young age, inexperience, exposure, driving conditions, and risky driving behavior contribute to the problem. The challenge is to moderate risk by limiting the complexity of early driving experience and altering norms associated with teenage driving. GDL and parental management are protective for novices, but no special programs protect older teenagers from risk other than road and traffic solutions that reduce risk among the general population.

See also: Adolescence, Theories of; Adolescent Sleep; Alcohol Use; Brain Development; Cognitive Development; Executive Function; Impulsivity and Adolescence; Risk-Taking Behavior; Sleep Patterns and Challenges.

Further Reading

Elvik R (2006) The laws of accident causation. *Accident Analysis and Prevention* 38: 742–747.

Evans L (2004) *Traffic Safety*. Bloomfield Hills, MI: Science Serving Society.

Groeger JA (2000) *Understanding Driving: Applying Cognitive Psychology to a Complex Everyday Task*. Hove, UK: Taylor and Francis Group, Psychology Press.

Mayhew DR, Simpson HM, and Pak A (2003) Changes in collision rates among novice drivers during the first months of driving. *Accident Analysis and Prevention* 35: 683–691.

Simons-Morton BG and Ouimet MC (2005) Parent involvement in novice teen driving: A review of the literature. *Injury Prevention* 12: 30–37.

Simons-Morton BG, Catalano R, and Ouimet MC (2008) Parenting and the young driver problem. *American Journal of Preventive Medicine* 35(3S): S294–S303.

Twisk Divera AM and Stacey C (2007) Trends in young driver risk and countermeasures in European countries. *Journal of Safety Research* 38: 245–257.

Vanderbilt T (2009) *Traffic: Why We Drive the Way We Do and What it Says About Us*. New York: First Vantage Books.

Williams AF (2003) Teenage drivers: Patterns of risk. *Journal of Safety Research* 34: 5–15.

Relevant Websites

http://www.aaafoundation.org/home/ – American Automobile Association Foundation.
http://www.cdc.gov/ – Centers for Disease Control and Prevention.
http://www.iihs.org/ – Insurance Institute for Highway Safety.
http://www.nhtsa.gov/ – National Highway Traffic Safety Administration.

Adolescent Moral Development

A Sheffield Morris, Oklahoma State University, Tulsa, OK, USA
N Eisenberg, Arizona State University, Tempe, AZ, USA
B J Houltberg, Indiana University–Purdue University, Fort Wayne, IN, USA

Glossary

Care-related moral reasoning: Moral reasoning based on the relationship of the self to others.
Empathy: An emotional reaction to another's emotional state or condition (e.g., poverty) that is highly similar to (or consistent with) the other person's state or condition. For example, if a girl sees another child who is sad or hurt and, as a consequence, feels sad herself, she is experiencing empathy.
Guilt: An emotion that is typically in response to a specific behavior or action. It involves a painful or agitated feeling concerning regret over a specific wrongdoing.
Justice moral reasoning: Moral reasoning about moral conflicts that involve issues of justice. Reasoning changes with age from that reflecting motivations based on self-concern to reasoning reflecting concern for community interests and justice.
Moral behavior: Voluntary behavior deemed by an individual or group as right or good. The 'right' or good can be defined in different ways, such as in terms of acting in ways that are just or promote the welfare of others; however, it can also be viewed as acting in a manner that complies with group standards about important issues of right and wrong such as religious practices. Some investigators differentiate moral behavior from social conventional behaviors that involve compliance with customs and regulations intended to ensure social coordination and social organization, such as choices about modes of dress, table manners, and forms of greeting (e.g., using 'Sir' when addressing a male teacher).
Moral identity: The individual's view of the self, or self-concept, based on content considered to be moral, such as moral values, moral behavior, and moral roles. Moral identity is believed to be an important source of moral motivation and there is individual variation in the extent to which identity is morally based.
Moral reasoning: The structure of an individual's reasoning about hypothetical or real-life moral dilemmas that may or may not include behaviors.
Prosocial behavior: Voluntary behavior intended to benefit another.
Prosocial moral reasoning: Reasoning about moral dilemmas in which one person's needs or desires conflict with those of others in a context in which the role of prohibitions, authorities' dictates, and formal obligation is minimal.
Shame: A negative evaluation of the self, rather than a focus on a particular wrongdoing (contrast with guilt), typically in response to an action, wrong doing, or others' focus on the self.
Sympathy: Feelings of concern for another in reaction to the other's emotional state or condition. Sympathy likely often, but not always, stems from empathy; it can also stem from retrieving cognitions about another's state or condition.

Introduction

Understanding the complexity of moral behavior, determining right from wrong, and developing one's own personal moral code are important components of adolescent development. Moral development during adolescence is facilitated by changes in social relationships, biological processes, cognitive abilities, and self-understanding. These changes provide a context that shapes the development of morality, prosocial behavior (e.g., voluntary behavior intended to benefit another such as comforting, sharing, and helping), and civic engagement. For example, in terms of social relationships, although families remain important during adolescence, peers are increasingly influential and parent–adolescent relationships change with increasing autonomy. Advances in executive functioning and regulatory control in the brain allow youth to think more abstractly and increasingly understand others' perspectives and societal views. Moreover, social problem solving and interpersonal negotiation skills advance, and this is accompanied by increased understanding of the psychological and moral self in relation to others. Based on such changes, adolescence is an important period for studying moral development. However, much of the research on adolescent moral development has focused on negative behaviors, such as aggression and delinquency, although there is a smaller body of research on adolescent moral reasoning, prosocial behavior, moral identity, and moral emotions. In this article, we draw on all of the aforementioned bodies of research, with a primary focus on adolescent moral reasoning, moral emotions, and positive behavior (i.e., prosocial behavior, empathy-related responding).

Theories of Moral Development

Justice Moral Reasoning

Lawrence Kohlberg's justice-oriented model of moral reasoning has received much attention in the moral development literature. Building on the work of Jean Piaget, Kohlberg viewed moral development as a continual process of moving through six stages (later reduced to five) throughout the life span. Early stages of Kohlberg's model are characterized as

Encyclopedia of Adolescence, Volume 1 doi:10.1016/B978-0-12-373915-5.00027-9

preconventional morality; it includes reasoning based on fixed rules and avoidance of punishment (stage 1) and judgment of actions based on one's own individual needs (stage 2). Preconventional moral reasoning is used predominately from early childhood to early adolescence, and conventional moral reasoning emerges around the age of 13 for most individuals. Most people operate within the conventional stage of moral reasoning which focuses on living up to social expectations and roles (stage 3) and maintaining law and order by following rules, duties, and respecting authority (stage 4). Although some adolescents are able to utilize stage 4 (social system and conscience) reasoning, stage 3 reasoning or 'being good' according to positive social expectations (trust, loyalty, respect, and gratitude) are more common among youth. Stage 4 reasoning increases with age and emphasizes fulfilling agreed upon responsibilities and laws unless in the extreme case that these duties violate a set social norm. Postconventional moral reasoning is centered on ideals: it focuses on moral principles. At Stage 5, right behavior involves upholding rules that are in the best interest of the group ('the greatest good'), are impartial, or were agreed upon by the group. Some values and rights, however, such as life and liberty, are universally viewed as right and must be upheld in any society, regardless of majority opinion. What is considered 'right' behavior at Stage 6 is commitment to self-chosen ethical principles reflecting universal principles of justice (e.g., equality of human rights for all, respect for the dignity of each human being). At this stage, when laws conflict with such principles, it is considered appropriate to act in accordance with the universal principles rather than the law.

Although some of the assumptions about the nature of justice-oriented approaches to moral reasoning have been challenged (e.g., that they emerge in a given order and that each stage is a totally new structure and replaces the prior one), there seems to be a transition during adolescence from individual-focused to other- and justice-oriented forms of reasoning. However, the emphasis on justice and the individualistic nature of people in this model have been challenged regarding its application to more collectivistic societies. Whether adolescent justice moral reasoning leads to increased moral behavior also has been questioned; the evidence in this regard is mixed.

Prosocial Moral Reasoning

Among others, Carol Gilligan argued that a justice-oriented approach does not take into account care-related moral thinking that may be more common among females. The focus of care-oriented reasoning is on relationships, with motivation for moral behavior stemming from care rather than justice concerns. Thus, care or prosocial moral reasoning is less about formal obligations or the need for justice but more concerned with conflicting needs or the desires of individuals in relation to others. The majority of evidence suggests that both males and females reason based on care *and* justice-oriented principles. In general, moral reasoning during the adolescent stage of development is characterized by moving from an emphasis on expected or normative behaviors to more self-reflective and internalized modes of moral reasoning. Research conducted by Nancy Eisenberg and colleagues indicates that there seems to be a gradual decrease with age in moral reasoning that focuses on conformity and individual self-interest accompanied by an increase in other-oriented motives and a concern for the welfare of both the self and others.

Social Domain Theory

Elliot Turiel's social domain theory distinguishes between the development of morality and other domains of social knowledge. The understanding of specific social domains stems from experiences with adults, peers, and siblings. Children develop by synthesizing experiences in the morality domain (e.g., the effects of harming another person) with experiences in the conventional domain, rules about behavior (e.g., displaying good manners). The conventional domain provides social order through agreed upon behaviors, whereas the morality domain focuses on social welfare and preventing harm. Thus, within this view, morality is organized around concepts of harm and fairness and convention is concerned with social organization. Research has confirmed such distinctions in a number of studies in the United States and across cultures. Turiel argued that morality and convention develop in parallel frameworks, and that younger children and individuals with lower levels of moral reasoning are likely to engage in moral behavior due to concerns about fairness and welfare rather than the overall level of moral reasoning ability. Moral development researchers (e.g., Judith Smetana and Larry Nucci) often include other social domains in their work such as the psychological domain, pertaining to the understanding of the self and the causes of one's behavior; the personal domain, pertaining to issues that concern individual choice and privacy; and the prudential domain, pertaining to issues of safety, comfort, and health. In this article, we focus primarily on the development of the moral domain and components of the psychological domain that are relevant to moral behavior and identity.

Social Cognitive Approach

The social cognitive theory of moral development stems from learning theory and argues that moral development occurs through observation, modeling, and resulting cognitions. There is an emphasis on distinguishing between moral competence (i.e., the ability to know right from wrong) and moral performance (i.e., following through on a moral behavior). As children develop, increased social experiences and resulting cognitions improve moral awareness and the ability to determine right from wrong. Moral performance is thought to be influenced more by rewards and incentives. Much of the work from this perspective has focused on moral behaviors such as resistance to temptation (mostly for younger children), prosocial behavior, and aggressive behavior. There is limited research on moral reasoning from this perspective, likely because it is more difficult to examine in terms of modeling. Albert Bandura is the theorist most commonly associated with this viewpoint, and there is less developmental research examining this perspective in adolescence compared to research examining theories about moral reasoning.

Researchers such as Gerald Patterson argue that the social environment of the child shapes the ability of children to demonstrate prosocial, moral behavior and avoid deviant behavior through positive or negative reinforcement. In some families, parents utilize ineffective and inconsistent punishment for deviant behaviors and permit daily interactions with family members where coercive child behaviors are reinforced. Coercive behaviors become functional and often escalate in intensity (e.g., physical attack) and are utilized in order to control other family members. This is coupled with a lack of reinforcing prosocial behavior. These patterns that are established during childhood carry into adolescence, and provide a foundation for later adjustment difficulties. During middle childhood, this learned behavior within the family extends outside of the family to interactions with peers and may cause academic failure, leading to associations with deviant peers and delinquent behavior during adolescence.

Moral Self/Identity

Theorists such as Agusto Blasi and Daniel Hart have attempted to understand individual behavior and moral motivation in terms of identity or self understanding. Moral motivation (the desire to do good) is thought to stem from the need for consistency between one's moral self and enacted behaviors. Thus, an individual's desire to be a 'moral person' may influence specific behaviors. With age, children develop increasing complex and differentiated views of themselves within contexts of development (e.g., moral, academic, social). Meaning and commitment to specific domains also increases with age, as self-conceptions are differentiated and then integrated throughout development. Research indicates that there are individual differences in the weight that people place in their moral identify. Some see morality as an essential component of their identity, whereas others see moral ideals and demands as fluctuating given a situation, or less in their control. Researchers such as Larry Nucci have argued for a more contextualized view of moral identity, corresponding to morality, conventional, and personal domains (see social domain theory), and that there is risk in viewing moral identity as fixed.

Moral Reasoning

Moral reasoning reflects how individuals justify moral decisions, and includes the structure and/or content of an individual's reasoning about real-life or hypothetical moral dilemmas. As mentioned previously, moral reasoning has been examined primarily in terms of justice moral reasoning and prosocial moral reasoning. Much of the early research on moral reasoning focused on preadolescent children and utilized hypothetical moral dilemmas. Research on adolescent moral reasoning has often utilized real-life dilemmas and includes an analysis of how events and responses are remembered.

In general, moral reasoning continues to mature during adolescence and into adulthood. A summary of research on Kohlberg's justice reasoning stages was discussed previously, and subsequent sections discuss links between moral reasoning and overall adjustment. Research on prosocial moral reasoning is illustrated by the work conducted by Nancy Eisenberg and colleagues. They followed children through adolescence into early adulthood in order to examine the development of prosocial moral reasoning. In general, they found that self-reflective and internalized modes of moral reasoning (e.g., reasoning about others' perspectives, feelings about the consequences of choices, internalized values) increased in use, whereas stereotypic reasoning (expected normative behavior, e.g., 'it is nice to help') decreased in use from childhood until the late teens. Although there is some support for this trend holding in diverse cultures, there is a need for more research to examine cultural relevance and potential differences. Further, there is some evidence that gender differences do exist among adolescents, as adolescent and adult females tend to express more care-oriented reasoning and self-attributions than do adolescent males. However, in general, moral reasoning and attributions regarding motives for prosocial behavior tend to stabilize and become more other-oriented with age during the adolescent years. Moreover, as adolescents move into adulthood, they tend to focus increasingly (but seldom solely) on moral ideals and principles.

Prosocial Behavior and Volunteering

Prosocial behavior is defined as voluntary behavior intended to benefit another. Typically, adolescent prosocial behavior is examined with questionnaires, but some researchers have utilized observational methods. Theoretically, prosocial behavior reflects one's own moral value system rather a motivation of self-interest or social desirability. However, it is difficult to determine the motivation for prosocial behavior, which complicates establishing the empirical link between moral reasoning and prosocial behavior. Questionnaires have typically been utilized to examine constructs related to moral behavior such as empathy, sympathy, and aggression (discussed subsequently).

Prosocial behavior has been positively associated with academic (grades, motivation, aspirations) and socioemotional (empathy-related responding, social competence), and sociocognitive (level of social cognition, prosocial moral reasoning) outcomes in youth, and negatively associated with aggression and delinquency. One might expect that displays of prosocial behavior would follow the same pattern as the increase in moral reasoning during adolescence. However, although adolescents do tend to display more prosocial behavior than do children, in general, there does not appear to be a gradual increase in prosocial behavior during adolescence and young adulthood. There is some evidence that girls are (or view themselves as) more prosocial than boys and this may be more important to their self-image and values. This gender difference in prosocial behavior may be in part due to the type of behaviors (masculine vs. feminine tasks) measured in adolescence. It also may be that boys and girls equally operate from a moral value system, but it may be more culturally appropriate to demonstrate prosocial behaviors for girls compared to boys.

An important venue for engaging in prosocial behavior is volunteering and community service. Adolescence is an opportune time to engage in such activities. In general, adolescent volunteers tend to be more extraverted, committed to others, and are more likely to continue to volunteer into adulthood. Differences in parenting are associated with adolescent volunteering such that parents who are warm and demanding are more likely to have adolescents who volunteer. In addition, youth who participate in community service activities tend to have a parent who also volunteers. Less is known about peer influences, but religiosity is associated with greater volunteering, and adolescents who view religion as important are more likely to volunteer. Studies indicate that volunteering, is associated with positive outcomes such as school achievement and self-esteem, and that volunteering helps in the prevention of delinquency and deviant behavior (e.g., teen pregnancy, school dropout).

Moral Emotions

According to Martin Hoffman and others, moral emotions play an important role in prosocial, moral behavior. Adolescents who experience others' emotions, concern for others, and emotions such as guilt and shame are expected to act in ways that are responsive to others' feelings, social cues, norms, and cultural values. Research on moral emotions has utilized questionnaire, observational, and psychophysiolgical methods and indicates that moral emotions of empathy/sympathy, guilt, and to a lesser degree shame, are associated with moral behavior and judgment. Moral emotions such as embarrassment and pride are less related to moral behavior.

Empathy is typically defined as an affective response that stems from the apprehension or comprehension of another's emotional state or condition, and is similar to what the other person is feeling or would be expected to feel in a given situation. It is believed that true empathy must include at least some self-other differentiation, and increased perspective-taking ability may be one reason why empathy increases from childhood to adolescence. Empathy often leads to sympathy, an emotional response stemming from feelings of sorrow or concern for another person, but sympathy can also be evoked cognitively. In addition, empathy is believed to sometimes lead to personal distress (a self-focused, aversive reaction to the emotional state or condition of another); personal distress may be elicited by empathic over-arousal that is experienced as aversive and elicits a focus on the self rather than others' needs. Thus, empathy is thought to be value-neutral, whereas sympathy is a more true moral emotion. However, empathy often leads to sympathy and may be a direct precursor of moral emotion and behavior.

Research suggests that there are age-related increases in empathy-related responding through childhood and from childhood to adolescence, but increases have not always been found in studies of adolescents. In a large meta-analytic review, Eisenberg and Fabes found that self-reported and observed empathy and sympathy were higher among females and older children, but there was no gender difference for physiological responses or nonverbal facial expressions Thus, whether or not sex differences emerge in studies likely depends somewhat on the methods used (e.g., how easy it is to discern and control the sex-role consistent response and perhaps how the moral emotion is interpreted by the individual).

Guilt is usually defined as an emotion that is typically in response to a specific behavior or action. It involves a painful or agitated feeling concerning regret over a specific wrongdoing. Guilt may enhance social relationships because it motivates people to treat one another fairly and equally and to make retribution for wrongdoing. In contrast, shame involves a negative evaluation of the self, rather than a focus on a particular wrongdoing. Shame is a more helpless, severe emotion that involves the dejection of the entire self, and may cause one to want to avoid others. Thus, shame is believed to be more deleterious to the self than guilt, and guilt is more often associated with positive developmental outcomes.

Research indicates that guilt is closely, and positively, linked to empathy and perspective taking. There is evidence that individuals high in guilt are better at perspective taking compared to individuals high in shame and personal distress. In order to experience guilt, an individual must be aware of upsetting another person either due to enacting a negative behavior or failing to follow through on a commitment. However, unlike empathy, an individual does not have to experience the feelings of another person, and the individual has to perceive him/herself as causing the distress. Nonetheless, empathy may often be the basis of guilt in that it alerts youths to the effects of their behavior on others.

Guilt and shame are closely linked, and it is possible that too much guilt may result in the feeling of shame, causing more negative attributions of the self. Moreover, when guilt is based on irrational assessments of the self and responsibilities, rather in response to hurting another person, it is likely to be more serious and maladaptive. More research is needed on when guilt becomes shame because it is likely that high levels of guilt over wrongdoings – especially if one cannot or does not make retribution – eventually will lead to more harmful feelings about the self.

Most researchers agree that differences in shame and guilt are due primarily to the degree of focus on the self. When a person experiences shame, the entire self is affected, feeling exposed and vulnerable. In contrast, guilt involves feelings of regret and remorse and does not affect one's identity. Shame and guilt both involve a sense of responsibility and the idea that one has violated a moral standard. Guilt appears to be the more 'moral' emotion because shame often involves concern about others' evaluations, rather than concern over harming another person. Guilt is more likely to result in someone trying to rectify a wrongdoing, whereas shame is more likely to cause a person to withdraw. Moreover, as stated previously, guilt is more strongly associated with empathy compared to shame, and studies indicate that shame, compared to guilt, is more closely linked to maladaptive outcomes such as aggression and depression.

Shame and guilt are affected by cognitive changes in middle childhood and adolescence. The experience of shame is affected as general representations about the self in comparison to others become more sophisticated and advanced. In early adolescence, with the advancement of more abstract thinking, children begin to make abstractions about personality characteristics and traits, and instead of thinking "I am bad at sports and math," a child may think that because he or she performs poorly in math and sports, he or she is an 'incompetent person.' In mid- to late adolescence, with increased abstract thinking, an adolescent may extend an attribution about another person with an identity related to him/herself. If he or she relates that person's behavior to the self because of a shared racial, ethnic, or cultural background, shame can result. For example, a teen may feel shame if someone of the same race and background is involved in a school shooting in his or her city. The experience of guilt also changes as children develop. In middle childhood, a child can experience guilt due to not fulfilling a promise or agreement, and in late childhood/early adolescence, guilt can be experienced when an individual breaks a general moral rule (e.g., honoring agreements). In adolescence, as thought becomes more abstract, adolescents are able to judge themselves in comparison to others and may experience guilt if they perceive themselves to have upheld a moral rule less well than someone else.

Adolescence may be a particularly important developmental period for examining guilt and its correlates. There is some evidence that gender differences in guilt emerge during adolescence, with females experiencing more than males. Moreover, as adolescents begin to develop romantic relationships and become more sexual, many teens experience guilt over their sexual activity, particularly if it violates parental or religious expectations. As abstract thinking, maturity demands, and responsibilities increase, there are more opportunities for adolescents to experience guilt, and expectations for males versus females may play some role in the amount of guilt experienced. Thus, high levels of guilt may accompany problems with adjustment experienced by many adolescents.

Moral Identity

Adolescence is often viewed as a developmental period when youths are struggling to establish their own identity, separate from their parents. Some researchers argue that one important component of identity development, or self-concept, is moral identity. Moral identity is the view of oneself in terms of moral values, behaviors, and roles. Moral identity is closely linked to cognitive development, and the study of moral identity often involves an assessment of the ways in which individuals think about morality and the self. The extent to which individuals view themselves in moral terms varies, and some research indicates that individuals who score higher on moral identity exhibit higher levels of moral behavior. However, more research is needed to determine if moral behavior results in higher moral identity or vice versa.

Research has linked moral identity to volunteering and civic engagement. Youth who volunteer tend to be concerned for future generations and have increased self-understanding. Daniel Hart and colleagues have found that youth who are designated as care exemplars by their peers (i.e., individuals committed to caring for others) are more likely to describe themselves in terms of moral goals and have self-concepts involving personal beliefs. Studies also find that adolescents who volunteer often provide moral reasons for their behavior, and volunteering has been linked to future civic engagement, voting, and prosocial, moral values. Longitudinal studies suggest that it is the actual experience of volunteering that increases moral behavior and values, not simply that volunteers tend to be higher in moral behavior and values.

Socialization Influences

As in childhood, there is reason to believe that multiple socialization agents affect youths' moral development. For example, multiple interacting systems (e.g., family, parenting, school, peers, and religious institutions) are involved in shaping the development of moral reasoning in adolescents. Much of the research has focused on the role of parenting in the socialization of adolescents' moral reasoning. However, traditional cognitive approaches hypothesize that peers have a greater role in socializing moral reasoning during adolescence because of the equal status in peer interactions. Yet, little is known about the impact of peer relationships on the development of moral reasoning in youth and even less is known about how culture impacts moral judgment. Understanding socialization factors on multiple systemic levels likely holds the potential for a greater understanding of the processes by which moral development occurs in adolescence.

Parenting Behaviors and Style and Other Familial Influences

Although the transition into adolescence is characterized by seeking independence from one's parents, the family context continues to shape the socialization of moral behavior, thinking, and feeling. Parenting behaviors that communicate warmth and support and encourage adolescents to utilize critical thinking (using the Socratic Method) are associated with higher levels of moral reasoning. Furthermore, research indicates that authoritative parenting (warm yet demanding parenting) that includes inductive (i.e., reasoning) approaches to discipline facilitate higher levels of moral decision-making, at least in Western cultures. Cognitive developmental theorists have suggested that parenting practices that create cognitive conflict about moral issues lead to higher levels of moral judgment.

Because parents are an important source of information about rules, social roles, and expectations, their responses to misbehavior are an important part of socialization and have been linked to the development of moral emotions. For example, parents can use a child's wrongdoing as a time to teach about emotions, and research suggests that parental discussion of emotions is related to empathy-based guilt reactions to misbehavior. Research suggests that parental disciplinary techniques that are degrading or are overly emotional in nature likely result in shame. In contrast, parents' focus on the act of wrongdoing and how that behavior affects others, rather than degrading the child, likely results in guilt.

The family consists of multiple relationships that create an overall emotional climate that contributes to the socialization of moral reasoning, and family cohesion and communication have been associated with higher levels of moral reasoning. It has been suggested that the quality of family relationships may be more important in moral reasoning in early adolescence, whereas the families' encouragement of perspective taking and cognitive stimulation may be more important among older adolescents. However, data are lacking to support this claim. Although aspects of the family climate hold promise for explaining the development of moral reasoning, there is a need for further research to examine specific socialization pathways. In addition, causality of influence is difficult to determine given that most research is correlational.

Peers

The transition to adolescence includes establishing autonomy from parents and spending more time with peers. Thus, peers become an important influence on the moral development of adolescents. This relationship has been the focus of traditional cognitive approaches to moral development because of the importance of balancing self and others' interests due to equivalent status friendships. Although much more is known about the influence of peers on children's moral development, peers likely play an important role in adolescent moral development as well. Peer relationships may impact moral development in youth through dialogue about moral issues with peers and the use of conflict resolution skills in handling disagreements. Therefore, the quality of the relationships with peers may also be an important factor in shaping moral reasoning and thinking. The role of conflict resolution may be different among boys compared to girls, as some researchers have found greater benefit of moderate peer conflict among males. Conflict among friends provides an avenue to utilize more abstract ways of thinking and may aid in higher levels of moral reasoning. Quality of friendship and peer acceptance have been linked to moral reasoning as well, with higher reasoning among youth who are more accepted, and who have more friends and more positive social interactions.

Religion

In general, religion has been linked to positive moral outcomes in adolescence. Studies indicate that adolescents who report higher levels of religious affiliation (extrinsic religiosity, church attendance) or belief systems (intrinsic religiosity, faith) also report more positive adjustment and behavior (socioemotional health, prosocial behavior, volunteerism) and often are viewed as more prosocial by others. The impact of religious orientation on moral development merits further examination, as it is unclear whether activities associated with religious groups or religious orientation contribute to moral reasoning. Further, the expectation of prosocial behavior or 'good will' in religious communities may provide an avenue for youth to function at lower levels of moral reasoning if such motivations are not internalized. Thus, moral development in religious contexts sometimes may be motivated by external processes that are expected rather than by encouraging an internal moral code.

The emotional climate and cognitive stimulation in religious communities may have a similar impact on moral development as has been found in parenting research. Specifically, the socialization of higher levels of moral reasoning may depend partly on encouraging adolescents to think critically and be tolerant of diverse perspectives. However, further research is needed to support such claims, and more longitudinal studies are needed to disentangle the direction of effects.

Culture

The culture in which adolescents develop also plays an important role in adolescents' moral judgment. The definition of moral reasoning may take on different meanings according to cultural norms and expectations. This may be the reason for mixed findings in cross-cultural studies of moral reasoning. Further, there may be some differences that occur within subcultural ethnic groups in moral reasoning. Some researchers argue that more collectivist societies that encourage social responsibility are higher in moral reasoning due to the focus on others rather than self. This may change across age groups depending on the expectations of the particular subculture that is associated with the transition into adolescence. However, not much is known about moral development within different ethnic groups. Further, the impact of other contextual factors such as neighborhood characteristics, socioeconomic status, and privilege likely contribute to moral reasoning, yet not much is known about these potential influences.

International research has produced mixed findings about the applicability of justice-orientated moral reasoning across cultures. More traditional cultures sometimes tend to score lower on Kohlberg's schema of moral reasoning, but this might be to its focus on abstract constructs. Although the basic stages proposed by Kohlberg have been found in 23 countries, the application to all cultures has been challenged. Many researchers and theorists argue that self-oriented societies are fundamentally different than cultures that emphasize other-oriented prosocial behavior. Therefore, studies that focus on particular aspects of moral development may produce different results across cultures in which moral development is measured. Further, it may be interesting to understand the conditions in a country that affect moral development. For example, cultural value systems may shape the interpretation of events and the application of moral reasoning, leading to more or less moral behavior.

Moral Development and Adjustment

Adolescents' levels and type of moral reasoning are important because they are related to differences in behavior and attitudes for behavior. Adolescents who reason at more mature levels tend to be more prosocial, socially competent, and tolerant of others. Moreover, justice-related moral judgment has been linked to higher-level social problem-solving skills and to more mature coping strategies. In contrast, adolescents low in moral reasoning tend to engage in more antisocial behaviors. For example, juvenile delinquents have been found to use lower stage moral reasoning compared to nondelinquent peers. Adolescents who are more aggressive typically score lower on more judgment and hold more positive attitudes toward violent groups, and are more likely to perceive intentional sports injuries as legitimate. These findings are often stronger among males compared to females.

A particular concern during adolescence is risky behavior such as drug use, sexual activity, and suicide. There is some evidence of links between cognitions about morality and adolescents' tendencies to endorse or engage in risky behavior, but only among adolescents who view these behaviors as having moral relevance rather than being a personal choice. However, it is not clear if moral reasoning affects risky behavior or if participation in risky behavior affects how adolescents categorize risky behaviors.

Prosocial moral reasoning has also been related to children's and adolescents' prosocial behaviors such as helping and sharing. In general, adolescents who use high-level prosocial (vs. lower-level) moral reasoning pertaining to others' needs, moral emotions, and/or moral principles tend to be relatively high in prosocial behavior as well as in sympathy or empathy. Especially consistent have been the negative relations between adolescents' use of hedonistic moral reasoning and their levels of prosocial behavior and sympathy. However, the level of prosocial moral reasoning tends to predict morally relevant behavior and emotion concurrently (i.e., when measured at the same age) rather than into the future.

Intervention and Prevention Programs

This section focuses on moral education and related intervention and prevention programs that are theoretically and empirically grounded. In the 1970s, Lawrence Kholberg rejected the idea of traditional character education approaches focused on teaching a list of virtues and vices. Indeed, such lists of virtues are often vague, and meanings differ across generations. Kohlberg argued that the facilitation of reasoning through moral dilemmas was the ideal moral education framework. Kohlberg and colleagues developed 'just community' schools where the goal was to enhance moral development by allowing students to participate in a democratic community where decisions were made via consensus and discussion. Often, these schools were small (a school within a school), but they often showed at least a modest effect on youths' moral reasoning. Similarly, some interventions have focused on creating a caring school environment, which has been associated with higher levels of cooperative, prosocial modes of behavior.

Many current intervention programs are aimed at decreasing aggressive behavior rather than specifically increasing prosocial, moral behavior. Nevertheless, evidence suggests that such programs can reduce aggression, improve social skills, and increase empathy and sympathy. Such programs also target cognitive skills such as understanding one's own and others' emotions, perspective taking (understanding another's point of view), reasoning about the causes of behavior (e.g., not assuming minor harm is always intentional), and chalking out strategies for dealing with social conflict. These programs often involve youths discussing moral dilemmas, similar to real-life situations that these youth may have encountered, role-playing, and problem solving.

Community volunteering and civic engagement also may be important interventions that promote prosocial, moral behavior, and empathy. As already noted, participation in volunteer programs tend to improve adolescents' academic achievement and civic engagement, and reduce school dropout and delinquency. In general, volunteering is associated with greater prosocial behavior and less deviant behavior even when controlling for background characteristics such as socioeconomic status and gender. However, the quality and length of the program (multiple months seem to be better) affect the potential benefits of volunteering.

Conclusion and Future Directions

Research suggests that multiple interacting systems (e.g., culture, family, peers) are involved in shaping the development of moral reasoning in adolescents. Further, individual differences in moral emotions and prosocial behavior affect adolescents' moral reasoning, and in turn, adolescents' moral reasoning affects prosocial and moral behavior. Intervention and prevention programs focused on reducing aggression, and promoting empathy, perspective taking, and volunteering hold promise for increasing moral behavior among adolescents.

Although empirical research on adolescent moral behavior continues to grow, there is still more to be learned about the complex nature of moral development, particularly across Western and non-Western cultures. Cross-cultural research focused on similar methods of measurement addresses the question of the universal nature of the stages of moral reasoning and the applicability of such theories across cultures. For example, Monika Keller and colleagues examined moral development in Western and non-Western cultures and found cultural differences in reasoning about moral obligations (e.g., Western societies ascribing more importance to personal autonomy vs. interpersonal obligation). Such research challenges some of the assumptions of grand theories on moral development and may produce mini theories to guide our thinking about adolescent moral development. In addition, utilizing real-life, culturally appropriate moral dilemmas (rather than hypothetical dilemmas) with adolescents is a promising approach.

Future research on adolescent moral development will likely benefit from utilizing multiple methods to examine moral reasoning and behavior across a variety of contexts, and both positive and negative influences on moral behavior should be explored. Well-designed research on moral reasoning and behavior has the potential to aid in the development and refinement of interventions aimed at enhancing prosocial, moral behavior among youth in both high-risk and normative settings. Such work may prove fruitful in promoting overall positive youth development.

See also: Civic and Political Engagement; Emotional Development; Parenting Practices and Styles; Self-Development During Adolescence.

Further Reading

Eisenberg N (1986) *Altruistic Emotion, Cognition, and Behavior*. Hillsdale, NJ: Erlbaum.

Eisenberg N, Fabes RA, and Spinrad TL (2006) Prosocial behavior. In: Eisenberg N (vol. ed.) and Damon W and Lerner RM (series eds.) *Handbook of Child Psychology, Social, Emotional, and Personality Development*, 6th edn., vol. 3, pp. 646–718. Hoboken, NJ: Wiley.

Eisenberg N, Morris AS, McDaniel B, and Spinrad TL (2009) Moral cognitions and prosocial responding in adolescence. In: Lerner RM and Steinberg L (eds.) *Handbook of Adolescent Psychology*, 3rd edn., pp. 229–265. New York: Wiley.

Gilligan C (1982) *In a Different Voice: Psychological Theory and Women's Development*. Cambridge, MA: Harvard University Press.

Hoffman ML (1980) Moral development in adolescence. In: Adelson J (ed.) *Handbook of Adolescent Psychology*, pp. 295–343. New York: Wiley.

Hoffman ML (2000) *Empathy and Moral Development: Implications for Caring and Justice*. Cambridge, UK: Cambridge University Press.

Killen M and Smetana J (eds.) (2006) *Handbook of Moral Development*. Mahwah, NJ: Erlbaum.

Kohlberg L (1969) Stage and sequence: The cognitive–developmental approach to socialization. In: Goslin DA (ed.) *Handbook of Socialization Theory and Research*, pp. 347–480. Chicago: Rand McNally.

Kohlberg L (1981) *The Philosophy of Moral Development: Moral Stages and the Idea of Justice*. San Francisco: CA: Harper and Row.

Lapsley DK and Narvaez D (eds.) (2004) *Moral Development, Self, and Identity*. Mahwah, NJ: Erlbaum.
Nucci LP and Narvaez D (eds.) (2008) *Handbook of Moral and Character Education*. New York: Routledge.
Patterson GR, DeBaryshe BD, and Ramsey E (1989) A developmental perspective on antisocial behavior. *American Psychologist* 44: 329–335.
Tangney JP and Dearing RL (2002) *Shame and Guilt*. New York, NY: Guilford.
Tangney JP, Wagner PE, Hill-Barlow D, Marschall DE, and Gramzow R (1996) Relation of shame and guilt to constructive versus destructive responses to anger across the lifespan. *Journal Personality Social Psychology* 70: 797–809.
Turiel E (1998) The development of morality. In: Damon W (series ed.) and Eisenberg N (vol. ed.) *Handbook of Child Psychology*. Vol. 3: *Social, Emotional, and Personality Development*, 5th edn., pp. 701–778. New York: Wiley.

Adolescent Sleep

J B Maas, R S Robbins, R G Fortgang, and S R Driscoll, Cornell University, Ithaca, NY, USA

Glossary

Chronotype: Natural patterns of alertness and drowsiness within a day.
Circadian: From Latin *circa diem* – 'about a day,' to follow a roughly 24-h periodicity.
Entrainment: Calibration of the internal circadian rhythms to a 24-h day in the presence of external factors (i.e., light).
Ghrelin: A hormone that stimulates hunger. Ghrelin levels increase before meals and decrease after meals. It is the counterpart of the hormone leptin, which induces satiation when present at higher levels.
Homeostasis: The maintenance of internal stability within a system.
Leptin: A hormone that tells the brain it has had enough to eat.
Phase: Position in a cycle in terms of how far it is offset from the beginning.
Ultradian rhythm: The repetition of 90–110 min cycles of different brain waves experienced each night by humans.
Zeitgeber: Any external or environmental cue that synchronizes an organism's endogenous (internal) biological clock to the earth's 24-h day.

Introduction

Adolescents are developmentally vulnerable to sleep difficulties. The causes of inadequate sleep in adolescence are manifold. Adolescents require at least as much sleep as they did as preadolescents; however, the amount of sleep adolescents get drops significantly, especially during the school week, and causes chronic sleep loss. Adolescents' daytime sleepiness increases (for some to pathological levels) even when their schedules provide for optimal amounts of sleep. Researchers have identified changes in sleep patterns, sleep–wake systems, and circadian timing systems associated with puberty that contribute to excessive daytime sleepiness (EDS).

Compounding the shifting physiological sleep rhythms during adolescence are behavioral, environmental, and psychosocial factors that influence sleep habits. These range from increased academic demands and early school start times to social pressures, the use of alcohol, distractions of the Internet, and time-consuming after-school jobs.

The Architecture of Adolescent Sleep

Whenever an adolescent falls asleep, a distinctive cycle of sleep stages follows, generally in a regular pattern. The night is basically divided into non-REM (non-rapid eye movement) and REM (rapid eye movement) sleep. REM sleep is the period in which most dreams take place. Non-REM (also referred to as 'slow-wave' sleep) is subdivided into several stages, characterized by different brainwaves and purposes.

These brainwaves are derived from electroencephalographic (EEG) signals, which are thought to represent cortical activity and which serve as a central defining measure of sleep. During adolescence, the central nervous system undergoes major changes that notably include a process called synaptic pruning. This pruning process is essentially a usage-based selection of which synapses to strengthen and which to let die, resulting in fewer synapses overall and less gray matter. Presumably reflecting this process is a decline in EEG power, or wave amplitude, over the course of adolescence. EEG dampening is seen both during wakefulness and sleep. The dampening has been linked specifically to age and Tanner stage, which is a measure of pubertal development based on physical primary and secondary characteristics, like development of genitalia. This phenomenon, essentially the volume being turned down on all electrical brain activity, is part of how we know that adolescent sleep is physiologically distinct from childhood sleep (see **Figure 1**).

Non-Rapid Eye Movement Sleep

After one's eyes close, brainwaves become slower and more regular than when fully alert. They are called alpha waves, look like the teeth of a comb, and signify a relaxed yet still wakeful state, akin to meditation. These alpha waves increase in frequency with brain maturation, from approximately 4 Hz in infancy to approximately 8–12 Hz in adolescence, where it stabilizes. Next is Stage 1 sleep, heralded by about 5 min of theta waves and a slower rate of breathing. The large muscles begin to relax. The transition to Stage 2 is sometimes marked by a fleeting sensation of falling, causing the sleeper to wake momentarily with a jerk. During this period, one disengages from the environment and becomes blissfully unaware of any outside stimuli. Researchers believe Stage 2 is the beginning of actual sleep. It is marked by spikes in brainwave activity, called sleep spindles, and K-complexes, which interrupt those previously regular waves. Stage 2 lasts 10–25 min but is revisited several times before daybreak, accounting for half the night's slumber. In adolescence, Stage 2 sleep has been known to increase.

Next comes Stage 3 sleep, which is characterized largely by slow theta brainwaves. These are interspersed throughout the next 30 min by even slower delta waves.

With the decline of theta waves, the sleeper enters Stage 4, the deepest sleep stage, which consists solely of delta waves. They will eventually comprise up to 20% of the total night's sleep. The first Stage 4 epoch of the night's sleep lasts for 30–40 min. During this stage, blood pressure drops, respiration slows, and blood flow to the muscles decreases. In Stage 4,

 doi:10.1016/B978-0-12-373915-5.00039-5

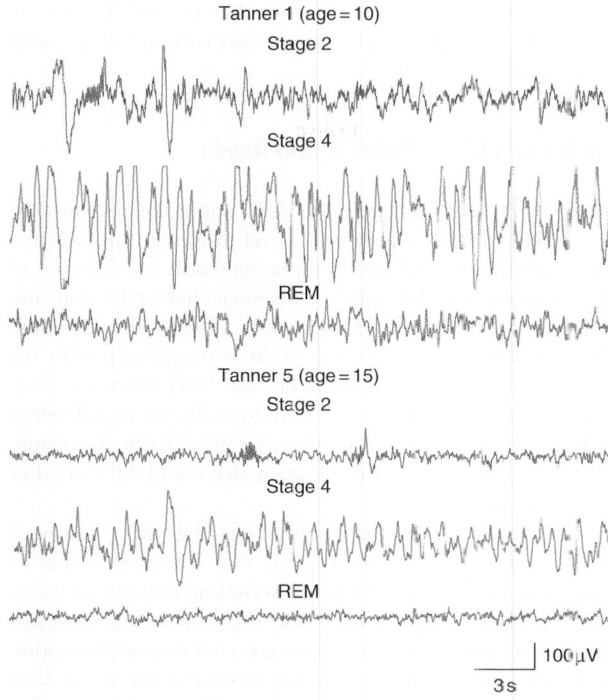

Figure 1 Comparison of Tanner stage 1 (top) and Tanner stage 5 (bottom) EEG tracings of NREM sleep stage 2, stage 4, and REM sleep. Reproduced with permission from Tarokh L and Carskadon MA (2009) Sleep in adolescents. *Encyclopedia of Neuroscience* 8: 1015–1022.

one is most completely disconnected from the external world, and thus most vulnerable. It is the closest humans get to hibernation. If aroused during this period, a person feels groggy and disoriented. During Stage 4 sleep, the secretion of growth hormone by the pituitary gland also peaks, stimulating body development and tissue repair. That is why uninterrupted deep sleep of significant duration is especially critical for adolescents, and why we sleep more when we are sick (see **Figure 2**).

Although slow wave sleep stages are of utmost importance in adolescence, these stages decline notably in quantity, by approximately 40–50%. EEG power also declines most prominently in delta waves, by about 50% between the ages of 10 and 20.

After 30–40 min of Stage 4 sleep, sleepers return to Stage 3 and then Stage 2.

Rapid Eye Movement Sleep

At this point, about 90–100 min after sleep onset in adolescents, something astonishing happens. Instead of going back into Stage 1 or 'twilight' sleep, the sympathetic nervous system becomes more active than it is in slow-wave sleep or even when awake. Blood flow to the brain, respiration, pulse rate, blood pressure, and body temperature all increase. Eyes dart back and forth under their lids and the sleeper enters the highly active stage of REM sleep. The REM period typically comes at a latency of about 150–180 min in adults, and in adolescents it is seen significantly earlier, about 100 min after sleep onset.

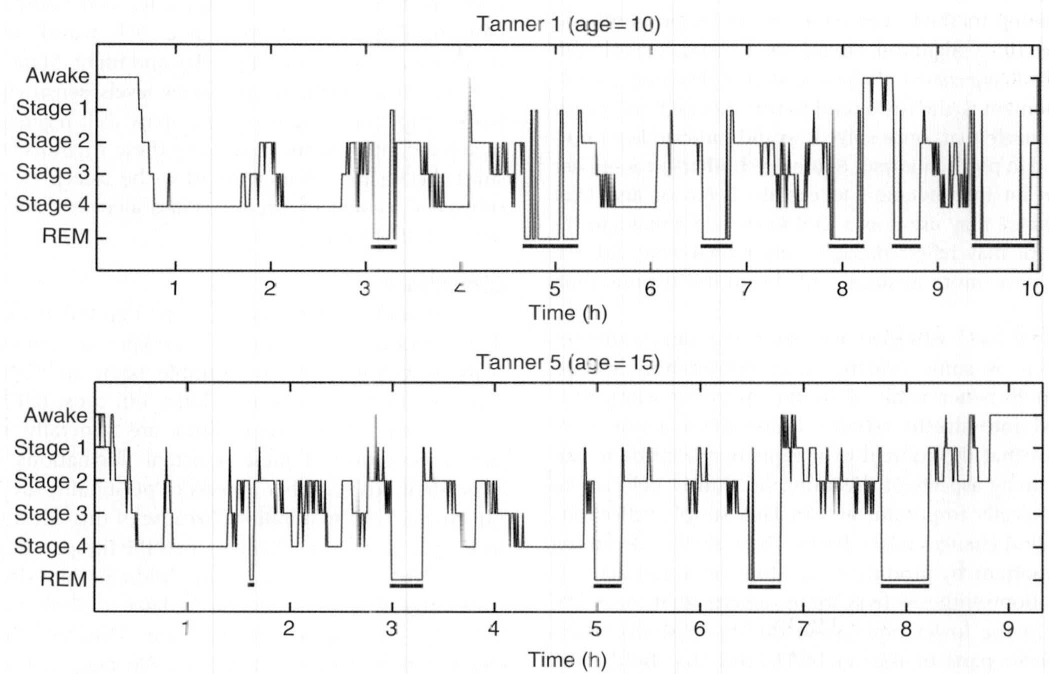

Figure 2 Sleep hypnograms of two boys, one at pubertal Tanner stage 1 (top) and the other at Tanner stage 5 (bottom). A hypnogram is a condensed representation of a session of EEG recordings. Note the differences at these ages and the changes after maturation to adolescence. There is significantly greater stage 4 sleep in prepubertal adolescents compared to postpubertal adolescents. Postpubertal adolescents have increased stage 2 sleep. Note that REM sleep increase in duration as the night progresses. There is a delayed onset of the first REM episode in the Tanner 1 preadolescent, and that first REM episode might even be 'skipped.' Reproduced with permission from Tarokh L and Carskadon MA (2009) Sleep in adolescents. *Encyclopedia of Neuroscience* 8: 1015–1022.

In REM, sleep messages from the brain's motor cortex are blocked at the brainstem. As a result, muscles relax, and one cannot move. That is why REM sleepers are described as having 'an active brain in a paralyzed body.' It is the first REM period that brings the first dream of the night. Although dreaming can occur in all stages, about 85% take place during REM sleep. REM dreams are usually the most vivid and emotional. But the functions of REM sleep exceed dreaming. The previous day's events are solidified into permanent memory traces, and sequences of learned skills (like playing a piano sonata or acquiring a new golf swing) become muscle memories, as evidenced by the timing and speed of responses seemingly done without need for conscious thought.

At the conclusion of the first REM period, the adolescent typically goes back to Stage 2 sleep, then Stage 3 and once more to Stage 4. Then back to Stage 3, Stage 2 and another REM period. The 90 min cycle, called an ultradian rhythm because it turns on a time-scale of less than 24 h, repeats itself throughout the rest of the night, with each successive REM period being twice as long as the last.

Dreams

Dreams typically last from 9 min to as long as 30 min or more and predominately occur during REM sleep. They may include visual imagery, sensations of taste, smell, hearing, or pain. Everyone has dreams, but most are not remembered in the morning.

Dreams range from the realistic and easily understood to the illogical and incomprehensible. Their interpretation and meaning have been debated throughout the centuries, and scientists are still working to shed light on their origin, purpose, and meaning. In 1932, Sigmund Freud, an Austrian neurologist, authored *The Interpretation of Dreams*, stating that understanding dream content is 'the royal road to the unconscious' – each dream is a puzzle that, once solved, would indicate key information to aid in psychoanalysis. Some psychotherapists still use Freudian dream interpretation to explain behavior and treat neuroses. Others may use it as a tool to initiate a dialogue, as dream content may reflect mood or emotional state. Adolescents often have more anxious and disturbing dreams than adults.

Researchers have struggled to divine the significance of dreams. There is some evidence that information learned before sleep is better retained in the morning when it is incorporated into dream activity. Some investigators have hypothesized that the content of dreams may well be meaningful, but many aspects of dreaming previously believed to be psychologically important are, in fact, simple reflections of physiological changes in the brain. They feel that dreaming is an unimportant by-product of random neuronal activity. Their activation-synthesis hypothesis asserts that firing of nerve cells in the lower brain stem during REM sleep randomly activates parts of the cerebral cortex that hold ideas and memories. Our brain tries to make sense of the neural activity by synthesizing the impulses into what we experience as dreams. The synthesis may involve unresolved daytime issues, but could just as well be a compilation of memories triggered at random. The fact that newborns and many lower species also spend considerable time in REM sleep lends credence to the theory that not all dreams are the result of unsettled personal events or the need to gratify basic desires.

Adolescent Sleep Patterns and Needs

Adolescents, in general, go to bed later and wake up later than adults. This has been observed across various cultures, across time, and in both genders. The phenomenon is a function of many factors, including adolescents' social lives, rebellion, and homework. Adolescence is also a time of dramatic and rapid physiological change, and the world is out of step with the adolescent's ideal circadian schedule. According to sleep researchers, the teenage brain is biologically set to fall asleep at 3 a.m. and begin to awake sometime after 11 a.m. As a result, 80% of teenagers do not get enough sleep, and 43% say they feel sleepy all day.

Sleep is all about cycles. Every day the brain follows a rhythm, and sleep is a movement that comes at a specific time – a certain phase of hormone secretions and other factors. When adolescents go to sleep and wake up at inappropriate phases, they suffer a negative impact, even if they get the appropriate amount of total sleep. Going to sleep at the wrong time affects nocturnal sleep; subsequently, waking up at the wrong time affects daytime alertness.

Circadian Rhythms

Sleep is maintained by several detailed body systems, which are responsible for a larger cycling system known as circadian rhythms from the Latin 'about a day.' Our bodies and behaviors have evolved to cycle in a 24 h world, with regular changes over the course of the day and night. Many physiological measures – including hormone levels, sensitivity to drugs, body temperature, brain wave activity, cell regeneration, and metabolic rate – work in time to these rhythms. These measures dictate the optimal times to be asleep or awake, the subjective feelings of sleepiness and alertness, and the occurrence of REM sleep.

Chronotypes

Humans and other animals feel tired and alert in correspondence with their individual chronotypes, or natural circadian patterns within a day. For example, some are night-owls and some are morning people or larks, but most fall somewhere in between. Sleep personalities are generally stable, but the orchestration of these punctual fluctuations is also age dependent, just as other aspects of personality are very stable but change with maturation. Because of this, ideal times to go to sleep and wake up change across the lifespan in predictable ways. Chronotypes are early in children (they sleep and rise early) and then get progressively later until about age 20, at which point they reverse direction. This shift in circadian rhythm and sleeping patterns has been suggested as a defining measure of the end of adolescence.

Phase shift in adolescents

If a system is rhythmic, that means that its component levels rise and fall in a regular way, like a wave, with peaks and troughs. The phase of a rhythm refers to a position in a cycle in terms of how far it is offset from the beginning. For example, the level of melatonin rises and falls during the day, and its peak is a phase that occurs at roughly the same distance from the start of the day every night, barring interference of bright light. One way to determine a circadian phase position is by measuring these melatonin levels, using plasma or saliva. The onset of melatonin secretion in dim light conditions is a good marker to tell scientists when someone's internal clock signals that it is time to go to sleep.

Evidence has mounted for a delay – or shift – in the circadian phase during adolescence. This in part explains the general pattern of going to bed and waking up later. In other words, if the oscillation begins at one time of day in early childhood, it begins later and later during adolescence, and at age 20 finally changes direction and begins at progressively earlier times. For adolescents, ideal bedtimes and wake-times are later than they are for young children and adults. Furthermore, core body temperature's trough is associated with REM sleep's peak, and in adolescents, core body temperature does not reach its trough until about 1.5 h before the usual time to wake up. Their bodies may push them to nap during early-morning classes in order to get all of the REM sleep they need.

Entrainment

Circadian rhythms are guided by what is often referred to as the brain's biological clock, actually the suprachiasmatic nuclei (SCN), which then send timing information to other bodily systems. This small region of the hypothalamus is located directly above the optic chiasm, where the visual pathways cross. In the controlled absence of external cues, the SCN follow their own 'free-running' cycle, which is generally spread across about 25 h.

Outside of the lab, though, the endogenous clock uses external information to set itself to a 24-h day, a process called entrainment. Most importantly, it uses information about light that reaches the SCN from the retinohypothalamic pathway, entering via specialized retinal receptors.

In adolescents, however, this light exposure has less of an impact than in adults, and setting the clock is more of a challenge. This is why it is often difficult for a teenager to adjust to an early school start time after a summer of sleeping in. Because light is the main zeitgeber, or time-giver, responsible for entrainment of the system to a particular sleep–wake timetable, its decreased impact makes for a much less pliable sleep schedule.

The SCN is also subject to input from the thalamus and Raphe neurons, suggesting that it is influenced by additional factors including, for example, feeding and exercise. Individual SCNs entrain in different ways (individual chronotypes) but still follow age-linked patterns.

Homeostasis

Together with the circadian system, another component affecting sleep is termed homeostasis. Although the two systems are thought to be independent, they interact to regulate sleep timing and duration. The word homeostasis refers to a tendency to maintain internal stability. When applied to sleep, it means the body's regulation of time awake and time asleep to achieve the appropriate ratio.

The process behind the building urge to sleep is called the homeostatic drive. As the duration of wakefulness increases, so does sleep pressure, until it can be dissipated during sleep. In adolescence there is a developmental change in coping with homeostatic drive for sleep. Adolescents are able to resist sleep pressure, enabling them to stay up later without becoming as drowsy as they would have during childhood. The increased tolerance to a later bedtime, even when sleepy, may contribute to the time shifts in sleeping and waking observed in this age group.

Hormones

From the SCN, circadian information travels all over the brain and affects various populations of neurons, neuropeptides, and neurohormones, such as melatonin and growth hormone, which experiences a spurt at puberty. Hormone levels fluctuate in time with circadian rhythms, and such synchronization may be especially important during adolescence, since it is the time for maturation of many endocrine systems. Throughout adolescence, the secretion of growth hormone is maximal and release of cortisol is minimal at 1 a.m., about an hour later than in adults.

Melatonin secretion

Melatonin is the hormone that is most involved in regulating the sleep–wake schedule. It is a key factor causing drowsiness and lowering core body temperature, which is in turn linked to slow wave sleep and REM. The pineal gland secretes melatonin at night – when in dim enough light conditions – at times directly controlled by the SCN, so melatonin level variation is a good indicator of endogenous clock activity.

Melatonin secretion is delayed in adolescence by about 40 min even in the transition from ninth grade to tenth. This delay makes it difficult for adolescents to fall asleep at an early hour, a task that was easier during childhood. A teenager who goes to bed early to get up for early class start times will not experience the secretion of melatonin until the later, physiologically determined hour. Slow wave sleep is associated with melatonin secretion; therefore, this teenager's slow wave sleep, a stage crucial to development, will be truncated.

Irregular Sleep Patterns

Adolescent sleep schedules on weekends are typically much different than on weeknights. On weekends, adolescents delay bedtime and wake time, and often increase total sleep time. One study analyzing sleep data from 3000 adolescents indicated that young people on weekends delay bedtime by an average of 50 min beyond their school-night bedtime. Among 18-year-olds, the average discrepancy was more than 2 h. Irregular sleep patterns during a given week result in a sleep phase shift (a tendency to prefer later bedtimes), difficulties falling asleep and poor quality of sleep.

Poor Judges of Sleepiness

Researchers have analyzed college student sleep patterns using objective at-home, sleep-monitoring devices to gather sleep data. The findings indicate that average sleep time among these adolescents was 6.47 h per night, 2 h and 28 min less than recommended. These adolescents overestimated the amount of sleep they were getting by an average of 47 min.

Consequences of Insufficient Sleep Among Adolescents

Sleep and Cognition

Sleep deprivation has deleterious implications for cognitive functioning, emotion, and adolescent academic performance. Sleep-deprived adolescents have impaired short-term memory, slower cognition, reduced ability to assimilate and analyze new information or solve abstract problems. Students who are drowsy will have trouble sustaining attention in both class and at home. Endurance and motivation plummet. Communicating and handling stress become more difficult.

Schoolwork, job performance, and social life can all suffer with sleep deprivation. Although it is difficult to isolate causation in controlled studies of sleep, it is possible that lack of sleep has wide implications. William Dement, MD of Stanford University said, "What we consider the negative aspects of adolescence – rebellion, violence, drug abuse, dropping out – are caused by or exaggerated by sleep deprivation."

One night of shortened sleep will not cause too much damage. However, sleep debt is cumulative, and habitually getting 1 or 2 h too little sleep each night can lead to chronic daytime sleepiness. Studies show that 1 week with 6 h or less sleep per night can bring cognition to the same low level as someone who is legally drunk.

Emotional Implications

Going to bed earlier protects adolescents against depression and suicidal thoughts. A study of 12–18-year-olds found those with bedtimes after midnight were 24% more likely to have depression than those who went to bed before 10 p.m. Additionally, those who slept fewer than 5 h a night had a 71% higher risk of depression and a 48% higher risk of suicidal thoughts than those who slept 8 h. Lack of sleep can lead to moodiness which affects judgment, concentration, and impulse control. The reverse causality is also true. Increased rumination, also associated with depression, may lead to later sleep onset. Adequate sleep could be a preventative measure and a treatment for depression.

Academic Implications

Quantity and quality of sleep are significant indicators of academic performance among adolescents, although other factors may be at play, such as after-school jobs. Sleep researchers found that high school students who report getting mostly B grades or better sleep 17–33 min more sleep on school nights and go to bed 10–50 min earlier than C and D/F students. They report studies showing that

1. adolescents who sleep 9 h have significantly better grades than those who sleep 6 h, have fewer learning difficulties, and are tardy less often;
2. efficient sleep (fewer awakenings at night and greater sleep quality) leads to higher grades, especially in math;
3. students struggling or failing in school (getting grades ranging from C to F) go to bed an average of 40 min later on school nights than students getting A and B marks and these students have more variation in weeknight versus weekend sleep schedules.

Adolescents who report higher-quality sleep are more receptive to teacher influence, have more positive self-images, and exhibit more motivation for academic achievement. A study of university students found a significant correlation between total amount of sleep and academic performance, and an even more significant correlation between grades and amount of deep sleep.

Although most of the published studies on sleep and school performance have methodological limitations which make it difficult to isolate causation, the evidence does suggest that self-reported shortened total sleep time, erratic sleep–wake schedules, late bed and rise times, and poor sleep quality are negatively associated with school performance for adolescents from middle school through college. Future research on the relationship between sleep patterns and academic performance must take into account a variety of other possible moderator variables such as socioeconomic status, parent involvement, school size, after-school jobs, levels of stress and motivation, and sex and age. For example, poor students may be less engaged with school and more engaged in other activities that go later into the night. Also, education and intervention strategies need to be developed to encourage students to value sleep and change their sleep behaviors.

Safety Implications

Accidents and injuries are often the result of severe sleep deprivation or complications from sleep disorders. Adolescents who have school, extracurricular activities, and a job are more often than not so exhausted that they are highly prone to injuries and accidents.

Sleep deprivation can result in microsleeps, short bouts of subconscious sleep lasting for up to 90 s. These periods of unresponsiveness to surroundings cannot be avoided by any measure of effort or intention and can be lethal when driving. According to the National Highway Traffic Safety Administration, driving when sleep deprived is akin to driving drunk and is one of the main causes of car crashes each year. Sometimes these accidents are caused by microsleeps at the wheel and other times simply because sleepiness leads to impairments in reaction time, attention, and vigilance. Young drivers of age 25 or under cause more than one-half of fall-asleep crashes, resulting in many deaths and injuries each year.

There is a very prominent circadian variation in highway accident rates. The peak in highway accidents occurs at 3 a.m., when people are the most tired. For adolescents, a peak risk time is early morning on the way to school. Susceptibility to the cognitive impairments associated with alcohol and drug use is greatly magnified among sleep-deprived adolescents. For the average teenager, having six drinks on 8 h of sleep is cognitively indistinguishable from having one drink on 6 h of sleep.

Sleep disorders, the propensity for which increases with sleep deprivation, are another common cause of accidents and injuries. Patients with obstructive sleep apnea often exhibit significantly impaired daytime alertness and frequent micro-sleeps. Many parasomnias, such as REM Sleep Behavior Disorder (RSBD), sleep-walking, or night terrors, can be direct causes of sleep-related accidents or injuries. For example, patients who sleep-walk or have RSBD may jump from their beds or walk out of their houses while sleeping, exposing them to danger.

Sleep and Health

Sleep is critical for health and proper immune system functioning. A loss of sleep may result in increased susceptibility to infection. Sleep is also critical for recovery from infectious disease. Sleeping less than 6 h a night increases susceptibility to viral infection by 50% compared to those getting adequate rest. Those who sleep less than 7 h a night are three times more likely to get a cold than longer sleepers.

Obesity

There is a significant link between sleep deprivation and the risk of obesity. Those who are deprived of sleep have lowered levels of leptin, a hormone that tells the brain when it has had enough to eat. Adolescents who do not get enough sleep overstimulate their ghrelin levels, which increases their desire for food. Adolescents who get fewer than 8 h of sleep are at a three times greater risk of obesity than those who get over 10 h. Lack of sleep decreases metabolic functioning, allowing the body to store more fat. Lack of sleep also causes fluctuations in serotonin levels, which increase feelings of hunger. This can also create a risk for early onset type 2 diabetes in adolescents. Sleep deprivation also elevates levels of visfatin, a hormone secreted by belly fat that is associated with insulin resistance.

Emotion

Sleep-deprivation can make it more difficult for adolescents to regulate their emotions and behavior and to stay out of trouble in school. Adolescents who sleep less than 8 h a night report more depressed moods than their well-rested peers. Sleep-deprived teenagers are often irritable, anxious, angry, and frustrated. Adolescents are at a high risk for emotional and behavioral disorders. The prefrontal cortex, which is associated with self-control, does not fully mature until about age 25. Inadequate sleep can exacerbate existing difficulty regulating emotions and forming relationships.

With impaired ability to manage and cope with stress, rates of substance abuse (including caffeine, alcohol, and tobacco) increase among teenagers who are not receiving adequate sleep.

Athletic and Motor Ability

Sleepiness impairs reaction time, awareness, and motor skills. Adolescents who make sleep a priority experience substantial improvements in their athleticism. In particular, those who forego early-morning workouts and practice only in the afternoon perform better due to the extra sleep.

Adolescent Sleep Disorders

Many of the sleep disorders seen in adolescents are partially the result of poor sleep habits, stress, substance abuse, circadian-rhythm shifts, respiratory malfunctions, social pressures, early school start times, after school jobs, or distractions such as Facebook.

Insomnia

Adolescent insomniacs have difficulty falling asleep and maintaining sleep. There are three main types of the disorder. Transient insomnia can last for several days and is usually caused by stress, illness, a noisy environment, or time zone changes. Short-term insomnia may last up to 3 weeks and usually results from the death of a loved one, the breakup of a serious relationship, severe stress, or major illness. Chronic insomnia lasts longer than 3 weeks and its cause may often be difficult to diagnose due to complications such as substance abuse, circadian rhythm-based sleep disorders, or sleep apnea.

Circadian Rhythm-Based Sleep Disorders

Circadian rhythm-based sleep disorders affect the sleep–wake cycle and are especially common in adolescence. These disorders are often the result of physiological and hormonal changes that appear at the onset of puberty. The disorders frequently involve daytime sleepiness, memory lapses, attention deficits, depressed mood, slowed reaction time, and poor academic performance. They can all be treated initially by solidifying good sleep hygiene. The use of bright daylight spectrum light therapy has shown to be effective in regulating sleep.

Delayed Sleep Phase Syndrome

Delayed sleep phase syndrome (DSPS) involves a pattern of markedly late sleep onset and awakening times and tremendous difficulty falling asleep at night and awakening in the early morning. Total sleep length and quality are normal, but timing is shifted more severely than the typical shift observed in adolescents (see section on Circadian Rhythms). The disorder, which is likely inherited, usually begins at puberty or early adulthood and appears in 5–10% of adolescents. It is occasionally coupled with complaints of depression. Affected persons tend to fall asleep in school and have impaired academic performance, which can be misinterpreted as laziness. About 50% of DSPS patients do not respond to conventional sleep hygiene therapy and should consult a specialist.

Non-24-Hour Sleep–Wake Cycles

An extension of the entire circadian rhythm to 25 h or longer, difficult to entrain, is prevalent in mentally retarded adolescents. Treatment to entrain the body to a 24-h cycle includes bright daylight spectrum light therapy or judicious doses of melatonin.

Excessive Daytime Sleepiness

This common adolescent complaint usually results from underlying factors like insufficient nocturnal sleep, narcolepsy, depression, or sleep apnea. EDS is often confused with laziness. With distractions like Facebook and text messaging, EDS is becoming ever more prevalent as adolescents are willing to sacrifice nocturnal sleep for these activities.

Narcolepsy

Narcolepsy is the tendency to fall asleep at inappropriate times, such as in class, while eating, or while driving. A common symptom is cataplexy, or complete loss of muscle control. Sleep attacks typically last 10–30 min and can be accompanied by sleep paralysis and/or hypnagogic hallucinations. If one parent has narcolepsy, there is a 20% chance that an offspring will inherit the disorder. Common treatments for narcoleptic patients include proper sleep hygiene, naps, sleep education, or the use of medications to reduce cataplexy and daytime sleepiness.

Parasomnias

Parasomnias are sleep disorders that involve abnormal and unnatural movements, behaviors, emotions, perceptions, or dreams. They occur at sleep onset, while sleeping, between sleep stages, or during arousal from sleep. Frequently, they represent partial arousals in the transition period between sleep stages.

Nightmares

Nightmares represent the most prevalent parasomnia disorder among adolescents. These dreams provoking fear or anxiety usually occur during REM sleep. Nightmares typically start during early childhood and diminish with age but not necessarily by adolescence. Disturbing dreams can be spurred by increased stressors, such as moving away from home. Reducing stress and keeping the bedroom cool often reduce the incidence of nightmares.

Sleep Paralysis

This inability to move or speak after waking, often accompanied by auditory or visual hallucinations, usually begins during adolescence. Some patients attribute the symptoms of pressure on the chest and restricted movement to paranormal experiences. It affects fewer than 5% of college-aged adolescents and is exacerbated by sleep deprivation and alcohol.

Sleepwalking and Sleep Terrors

These episodes, which disappear as adolescents physiologically mature, are characterized by partial arousal from nocturnal sleep. Sleepwalking is nocturnal walking while in a twilight state of arousal. Sleep terrors cause sudden uprightness in bed, inconsolable tears or screams, a quickened heart rate, and rapid breathing, as well as total amnesia following the occurrence. Affected adolescents are advised to minimize sleep deprivation, which worsens symptoms. Those affected should be evaluated for underlying psychopathology. Sedatives are often used as a stop-gap measure.

Sleep Apnea

Sleep apnea is a common and very severe cause of insomnia resulting from upper airway obstruction. Symptoms include sleep disruption, frequent awakenings, loud snoring, EDS, morning headaches, depression, and decline in school performance. During an episode, a patient snores with increasing intensity. This is followed by a silent pause, and then a loud gasp for air, sometimes accompanied by violent body movements. In adolescents, sleep apnea is usually due to enlargement of tonsils or other tissue in the oral pharynx. It is also prevalent in obese patients. Sleep apnea can be effectively treated by using a Continuous Pressure Airway Pump (CPAP) machine, which uses air pressure to keep the airway open. Some use simpler treatments, like pinning a tennis ball to the back of the patient's shirt, as sleeping on one's side helps keep airways unblocked.

Factors Promoting Healthy Adolescent Sleep

Experts' recommendations for improving sleep quality and quantity hinge on an increasing understanding of circadian and homeostatic sleep regulation processes in the body.

Individual Sleep Need

The need for sleep is genetically determined and rarely adaptable to change. When adolescents fall short of their individual sleep needs, their concentration, productivity, and work quality all decrease. After 17 to 19 h without sleep, brain activity resembles that of someone with a Blood Alcohol Content (BAC) of 0.05 (0.08 being the legal limit for intoxication in most states).

In order to determine personal sleep need, experts recommend that adolescents choose a bedtime when they are able to fall asleep and one that allows for 9.25 h of uninterrupted rest. If an alarm clock is required to wake up, if it is difficult to get out of bed or if daytime alertness is impaired, then move the bedtime earlier by 15 min for the next week. Continue adding 15 min until able to rise without an alarm clock and maintain alertness all day.

Although one night of shortened sleep will not cause significant damage, the effects of sleep loss are cumulative. One night of shortened sleep will not cause significant damage, per se; however, if sleep is reduced by 1 h for seven consecutive nights, the effect is the same as one night of complete sleep restriction.

Regular Schedule

Maintaining a regular sleep–wake schedule is vital for stabilizing and synchronizing the biological clock. With irregular sleep and wake patterns, mood deteriorates. Adolescent sleep schedules are particularly difficult to adjust and are highly susceptible to even small disruptions. It takes 4 weeks to fully synchronize the sleep and wake phases of adolescent circadian rhythms. Keeping routines regular has been associated with more restorative sleep and increased levels of alertness when compared to a 'yo-yo' schedule that allows for adequate sleep, yet at varying hours, indicating that regularity actually reduces total sleep need. Jodi Mendell and her colleagues at Saint Joseph's University also found that consistent routines resulted in fewer problematic sleep behaviors, improvements in the time to sleep onset, and reduced nighttime awakenings.

A bedtime routine such as easy stretching or a warm bath will help induce sleepiness at appropriate times.

Continuity

One long block of uninterrupted sleep is necessary for peak daytime performance. Fragmented sleep has been shown to be less physically and mentally restorative and to cause daytime drowsiness. It can dramatically compromise learning, memory, productivity, and creativity. Limit time in bed to personal sleep need in order to associate the bedroom environment with restfulness, instead of tossing and turning.

Sleep Debt

Adolescents need 1 h of sleep to repay every 2 h of wakefulness. After 16 h of being awake, a minimum of 8 h of sleep are required to fully recharge. When this is violated, as is true of many adolescents every night, sleep debt accumulates very quickly and the urge for sleep increases, causing daytime microsleeps. Adolescents will often replace lost sleep in one long block, such as sleeping for 15 h one night on a weekend. Such a significant disruption to the adolescent circadian rhythm will make regular sleep during the school week exceedingly difficult. Instead, experts recommend proper sleep hygiene such as meeting one's individual sleep need every night, keeping a regular bedtime, and getting continuous sleep as the best methods for avoiding sleep deprivation. Naps can also be helpful but carry a risk of further disturbing the sleep cycle if they extend too long. If sleep deprived, naps should not exceed 20 min or they run the risk of disturbing nocturnal sleep.

Stimulant Use

Caffeine stimulates metabolism, which keeps the body awake and alert. It is the most widely used drug in the world and is a major cause of insomnia, increasing difficulty of sleep onset and increasing frequency and duration of nighttime awakenings. Caffeine (chocolate, coffee, energy drink, soda, tea, or even certain medications such as Midol and Excedrin) after 2 p.m. might disrupt sleep. Caffeine has a half-life of 6 h, which means that 6 h after consumption, half of the consumed caffeine remains in the body. Its effect is cumulative, so consuming more than 300 mg – or three cups of coffee, cola or energy drink – will probably have an effect on sleep. For some individuals, even just one cup of coffee in the morning or a cola at lunch can be disruptive.

Adolescents commonly use stimulants such as Ritalin, Concerta, and Adderall, either prescribed or obtained as 'street drugs' to aid in alertness. Attention problems, however, are often a result of sleep deprivation, and stimulant use generally worsens these problems.

Alcohol and Tobacco

Alcohol is a depressant, meaning that it slows central nervous system activity, but it is not a sedative. Alcohol within 3 h of bedtime can affect REM sleep. Mixing alcohol with sleeping pills or tranquilizers can be lethal.

Nicotine is an even stronger stimulant than caffeine. Aside from its carcinogenic properties, nicotine increases blood pressure and heart rate, and it stimulates brain activity. Several studies clearly demonstrate that sleep improves immediately after cessation of smoking.

Bedroom Environment

Some experts say that bedroom environment has a significant effect on the length and quality of sleep.

Temperature

The ideal sleeping temperature is 65–70°. An overly heated bedroom has been shown to prevent sleep or induce nightmares: neural activity in the brain will increase in intensity and duration as body temperature rises. Conversely, a cold room keeps the body from fully relaxing because the body needs to protect its core temperature.

Light

Light is the most powerful cue for initiating and maintaining wakefulness. Because light entrains the circadian schedule, light in the bedroom at night will prevent the sleep phase, in some cases by preventing the secretion of melatonin. Experts recommend gradually lowering the brightness in the bedroom until it is as dark as possible. Even the LED digits on an alarm clock have enough luminosity to get through the thin eyelids and disrupt sleep.

Noise

Even noise as low as 60 decibels, the level of a normal conversation, can stimulate the nervous system. Most adolescents can adapt to certain recurrent noise, like a ticking clock or highway traffic. Irregular, intermittent sounds, like clinking radiators and honking taxis, can be disturbing, and experts recommend masking these sounds with a low and consistent noise from another source.

Mattress and pillow

Experts recommend that adolescents sleep on a surface that allows for the head, neck, and spinal cord to be aligned as if the sleeper was standing. The body must be well-supported at all contact points, especially the lumbar region. The mattress foundation is considered more important than whether the mattress is classified as firm or soft. A pillow should be firm enough to support the head and neck and maintain the spine's normal curve. Most people sleep in a fetal position, and it is recommended they use a 'side-sleeper' pillow, with two seams.

Stress Management

Stress is the primary cause of adolescent insomnia. Stressed teenagers have difficulty falling asleep, sleeping deeply, and maintaining sleep throughout the night. When pressured, the body produces excessive amounts of cortisol, adrenaline, and epinephrine – three of the major stress hormones. The body responds to stressful situations by activating the autonomic nervous system's sympathetic responses, which increase heart rate, slow metabolism, and depress the immune system in order to focus the body's limited energy on averting the stressor. Sustained stress can lower overall immunity and increase the risk of health problems, including high blood pressure, cardiovascular disease, and even cancer. Managing stress can promote better sleep and overall health.

Meditation and Exercise

Meditative states can produce brainwaves similar to those in Stage 2 sleep, so much so that those who meditate frequently require less nocturnal sleep than those who do not meditate. Just a short period of daily meditation has been shown to significantly lower blood pressure. Even mini-meditations throughout the day will help improve sleep.

Those who exercise regularly have a more defined circadian rhythm; they are more awake at appropriate times and drowsier at bedtime. Any type of physical activity alleviates stress, which is also helpful for sleep health. Exercise either at mid-day or in the late afternoon is most helpful for enhancing sleep. Circadian rhythms create peaks and troughs in alertness. Increased aerobic activity between 5 p.m. and 7 p.m. is ideal because the body is neither trying to accumulate heat or disperse it. This window is past the usual mid-day dip in alertness, typically between 2 p.m. and 4 p.m., when core body temperature naturally drops and reaction time slows. Morning workouts are too far from bedtime to improve sleep and leave adolescents prone to injury. Although many coaches consider two daily workouts to be essential for athletic success, some research shows that circadian rhythms promote exercise later in the day.

Presleep Routine

Experts recommend a bedtime routine to help transition from wake to sleep. The routine can include reading a book, conversing with a partner, or a warm shower or bath, which will raise body temperature. Then, when entering the bedroom (which should be kept at 65 °F), body temperature will plummet, helping to initiate deep sleep.

Proper Nutrition

Healthy eating habits throughout the day in addition to appropriate snacks before bedtime will promote good sleep, cognitive development, and linear growth among adolescents. If hungry in the evening, foods high in carbohydrates but low in protein are suggested. These types of foods contain glucose, which speeds the amino acid tryptophan to the brain, where it is converted to serotonin, a sleep-inducing neurotransmitter. This process takes 45–60 min after consumption.

Creating Sleep-Friendly Schools

Changing School Start Times

In most cases, adolescents do not get optimal sleep. Educational structure, in the United States in particular, exacerbates the physiological challenges adolescents already face when it comes to getting adequate sleep. Although bedtimes delay as children mature into adolescence, institutions often demand earlier class start times. This results in inadequate and poorly timed sleep, and adolescents manifest consequences including reduced daytime performance, poor moods, difficulty maintaining or forming new relationships, violent behaviors, and suppressed immune system functioning.

Studies of schools that have changed their start times are shedding light on the positive effects of such changes. Interestingly, in these schools that impose later class start times, bedtimes do not change, and therefore a later rising time allowed for more total sleep time. Deerfield Academy, a preparatory school in Massachusetts, instituted a later class-start time that gave students an extra hour of sleep, and a lecture on the deleterious effects of sleep deprivation on performance. Student grade point average increased, as did student alertness during first period classes – a marker of more well-rested students. Improvement was also seen in general health (20% less visits to the infirmary), athletic victories, and a 17% increase in the number of hot breakfasts consumed.

When class times necessitate a rising time that truncates sleep, alertness is significantly impaired due to students being in a circadian phase that does not support wakefulness. When compared to schools with later start times, students with an earlier start cite shorter weekday total sleep, increased sleep problems, daytime sleepiness, attention difficulties, and sleeping in on the weekends.

Sleep Education

Many schools have already made the transition to later, sleep-friendly start times. In order for these changes to be successful, all stakeholders including students, teachers, administrators, parents, and after school activity leaders must all be educated on the importance of sleep.

Sleep is not often discussed along with other health topics in school settings. Education about sleep is important at this transition phase and where instituted has been shown to correlate with better sleep practices, more total sleep, and better academic performance.

There will undoubtedly be challenges to new schedules such as coordinating elementary school start times, bus schedules, community activities, and student employment, to name a few. However, if the goal of education is to maximize adolescent potential, then creating a school environment that is conducive to the biology of adolescent students is crucial.

Many believe that functioning with a lack of sleep is an inescapable part of adolescence. However, if sleep can be incorporated into the fabric of educational structure, teens will be far more likely to operate at their peak.

Conclusion

Sleep undergoes changes of many kinds during adolescence as circadian rhythms shift and the brain matures. Adolescent brains send signals to go to sleep and wake up increasingly later. Homework and other societal factors interfere with the possibility of early bedtimes. Yet, schools are starting earlier and earlier. These factors lead adolescence to be an excessively sleepy stage of life.

Sleep researchers have suggested that schools and colleges must adapt to the physiological and psychological needs of adolescent students by creating sleep-friendly educational institutions. Teachers and other academic personnel, as well as parents, must be educated about adolescent sleep, signs of sleep loss, sleep disorders, and other alertness issues. Sleep-related education must be introduced into curricula so students can learn about the deleterious consequences of sleep deprivation on general health, motivation, and performance. Public policies must be introduced to establish later school start times for adolescents, initiatives to educate young drivers on the effect of drowsiness on driving ability, and limitations on the number of hours and the time of day that adolescents are permitted to work.

As noted by the National Sleep Foundation, sleep research has demonstrated clear relationships between sleepiness, health, safety, productivity, and performance. The field of sleep research is relatively young, and there is much to be learned about the role of sleep and the affects of sleep loss in adolescents. According to the National Institute of Health, additional studies on the neurobiology, genetics, epidemiology, and neurobehavioral and functional consequences of sleepiness are needed, particularly on the adolescent population. Interdisciplinary research is needed to further examine the role of sleep in adolescent development, health, and behavior.

See also: Cognitive Development; Memory.

Further Reading

Carskadon MA (2002) *Adolescent Sleep Patterns: Biological, Social, and Psychological Influences*. Cambridge: Cambridge University Press.

Carskadon MA, Acebo C, and Jenni O (2005) Regulation of adolescent sleep: Implications for behavior. *Annals of the New York Academy of Sciences* 1021: 276–291.

Carskadon MA, Wolfson AR, Acebo C, Tzischinsky O, and Seifer R (1998) Adolescent sleep patterns, circadian timing, and sleepiness at a transition to early school days. *Sleep* 21(6): 871–881.

Dement WC (1999) *The Promise of Sleep: A Pioneer in Sleep Medicine Explores the Vital Connection Between Health, Happiness, and a Good Night's Sleep.* New York: Delacorte.

Maas JB (1998) *Power Sleep: The Revolutionary Program that Prepares your Mind for Peak Performance*. New York: Villard.

Maas JB and Robbins RS (2010) *Sleep for Success! Everything You Must Know About Sleep but Are too Tired to Ask*. Bloomington, IN: AuthorHouse.

National Sleep Foundation (2000) *Adolescent Sleep Needs and Patterns*. Washington D.C.: National Sleep Foundation Research Report and Resource Guide.

National Sleep Foundation (2006) *Sleep in America Poll, a Look at the School Start Times Debate, Changing School Start Times*. Washington, D.C.: National Sleep Foundation.

Owens JA and Mindell J (2005) *Take Charge of Your Child's Sleep: The All-in-One Resource for Solving Sleep Problems in Kids and Teens*. New York: Da Capo.

Tarokh L and Carskadon MA (2008) Sleep in adolescents. *Encyclopedia of Neuroscience* 8: 1015–1022.

US Dept of HHHS, National Institute of Health, National Heart, Lung, and Blood Institute (2005) Your guide to healthy sleep. *NIH Publication No. 06-5271*.

Wolfson AR and Carskadon MA (1998) Sleep schedules and daytime functioning in adolescents. *Child Development* 69(4): 875–887.

Relevant Websites

www.mayoclinic.com/health/sleep/HQ01387 – Mayo Clinic: 10 tips for better sleep.

www.aacap.org – American Academy of Child & Adolescent Psychiatry.

www.Sleepnet.com – Everything you wanted to know about sleep but were too tired to ask.

www.sleepfoundation.org – The National Sleep Foundation.

www.health.harvard.edu – Harvard Health Publications.

www.powersleep.org – Sleep for success.

Autonomy, Development of

M J Zimmer-Gembeck and W H Ducat, Griffith University and Griffith Health Institute, Gold Coast, QLD, Australia
W A Collins, University of Minnesota, Minneapolis, MN, USA

Glossary

Autonomous orientation: Intrinsic motivation and personal commitments that have a foundation in a sense of volition and understanding of personal goals.
Autonomy: The term used to refer to a range of psychosocial issues related to independence, choice, volition and regulation in the domains of behavior, emotion and cognition (see **Table 2**).
Autonomy support: An awareness and sensitivity to children's and adolescents' perspectives and choices, assistance with exploration of personal values and interests, and minimizing the use of external controls and power assertion.
Heteronomy: Being controlled, coerced, compelled, or manipulated into actions that do not freely emerge from the core self.
Internalization: The adoption of values from one's social context (e.g., culture, parents, peers) as one's own values.
Self-differentiation: The balance between effective interpersonal and intrapersonal functioning or between communion with others and personal agency.

Introduction

When asked, parents often say that their greatest wishes for their children are that they grow into happy, healthy adolescents and adults who can find optimal niches within their communities. Ideal societies provide the opportunities for such progress among all children. Parents expect that their children's progress will reflect personal choices and interests, make contributions to society, and include connections to family and others, and they hope the society will support such outcomes. Not all aspects of these parental aspirations for their children are about autonomy development, but almost all include a solid foundation in adolescents' capacity for autonomous thought, self-managed behavior, and independence of mind that is balanced against the needs and desires of others at many levels of society – from family to neighborhood to community to culture. This makes the study of autonomy development during adolescence a field that includes many lines of research and much progress, but it is also one that is rife with diverse definitions, theories, frameworks, and controversies.

The development of autonomy is not only difficult to study and cohesively summarize, it also is an extremely challenging task for adolescents, often referred to as a critical developmental task. Although autonomy is a developmental and individual process influenced by changes in competencies, skills, and social conditions at any age, adolescence is a time when the task of autonomy development has primacy and urgency. Societies and families around the world recognize this by affording adolescents more rights and responsibilities. These increased rights and responsibilities not only reflect adolescents' desires for both more behavioral and emotional autonomy but they are also recognitions of (or are deemed necessary to prompt) better self-regulation of behavior and emotion, and greater independent decision-making. Greater rights and responsibilities also are triggered by recognition of greater physical and social maturity. Because of all of these individual and societal desires and necessities, autonomy and its development are a reflection of adolescents' opportunities and guidance as well as an outcome of adolescents' own choices, values, and goals. Negotiation of this developmental milestone circumscribes the quality of an adolescent's selected pathways, how good he or she will feel, and the optimization of decision opportunities. Failures in these tasks are at the very least correlates but may also be causes of many recognized problem behaviors and other difficulties.

Although the successes and failures of social systems to promote autonomy, the advantages of autonomous functioning, and the nature of autonomy development have been studied for decades, research in the past couple of decades has continued to concentrate on definitions of autonomy, different forms of autonomy (autonomous orientation, behavioral autonomy), and support for autonomy from different sources and its correlates. In addition, normative timelines of autonomous development are being detailed, and there is an escalating interest in autonomous behavior and support in multiple cultures or contexts. Such topics are diverse. However, they converge on a smaller number of overarching themes, which we address in this article. We begin by organizing themes and topics according to the most prominent theoretical views of autonomy during adolescence. We discuss how autonomy has been conceptualized and operationalized within each theory, and identify and briefly summarize some findings from areas of research related to each theoretical approach. We next contrast theories by focusing on intrapersonal versus interpersonal aspects of autonomy and assumptions of universality versus specificity of autonomous behavior, cognition, and emotion. Third, we review research on the interpersonal foundations of autonomy, including relationships with parents and peers, and the influence of involvement in organizations and leisure activities. Finally, we conclude by noting some newly emerging areas of research and identify some future research directions.

Despite continued progress in the study of autonomy, the field seems at a crossroads in definitional issues and relevance that needs to be addressed before reviewing the literature.

 Encyclopedia of Adolescence, Volume 1 doi:10.1016/B978-0-12-373915-5.00004-8

When autonomy is used as an umbrella term for many fields of related research, the practical importance of autonomy is clear. However, because of autonomy's broad domain, it is difficult to get a complete picture of it and how it is clearly distinct from other topics such as competence, efficacy, control, and support from the social context. This becomes especially important when simultaneously considering the other limitations of the empirical studies of autonomy. These limitations include the use of a variety of definitions, little replication of findings across studies, an overreliance on cross-sectional designs, the minimal evidence to support the direction of influence, few studies of pathways and processes, and an almost exclusive reliance on self-report. Other limitations include generalizability of findings – it is difficult to represent the range of diversity within one country much less to study multiple countries. Also, historical timing might matter for some aspects of autonomy. For example, a higher poverty rate or a turbulent job market may have implications for autonomy development. Although these limitations should be kept in mind throughout the remaining sections of this article, these are limitations that afflict empirical research on all difficult and complex psychological phenomena – especially when such phenomena change with age and experience, while also being multiply determined and embedded within social and cultural fields.

Theoretical Views of Autonomy and Autonomy Development

The term *autonomy* is often used to refer to psychosocial issues related to independence, choice, volition, and regulation in the domains of behavior, emotion, and cognition. Just some of the definitions found in recent studies are shown in **Table 1**. Definitions of autonomy have ranged from actions that are initiated and regulated by the core self to disengagement from parental ties and control. Even just these two definitions reflect the fact that autonomy has been defined as a core self behavior, one that involves the capacity to make personal choices, pursue goals, and regulate behavior, cognition, and emotion. Nevertheless, many also recognize that, when focusing on adolescents, such behaviors can signify increasing freedom from the constraints of childhood dependence on others. The various definitions also imply how autonomous

Table 1 A selection of definitions of autonomy and conceptually related constructs

Authors	*Construct*	*Definition*
Allen et al. (2006)	Autonomy in social relationships	Includes multiple traits such as being assertive and independent thinking, and directing own behavior.
Collins et al. (1997)	Behavioral autonomy	Active, overt manifestations of independent functioning, includes regulation of one's own behavior and decision-making.
Collins et al. (1997)	Emotional autonomy	Individuation from parents and relinquishing of dependence on them.
Collins et al. (1997)	Cognitive autonomy	A sense of self-reliance, a belief that one has control over one's own life, and subjective feelings of being able to make decisions without excessive social validation.
Daddis and Smetana (2005)	Behavioral autonomy	Expectations of timing for personal behavioral choices.
Deci and Ryan (2000)	Autonomy	The organismic desire to self-organize experience and behavior and to engage in activities concordant with one's integrated sense of self; acting from one's integrated sense of self, and endorsing one's actions.
Herman et al. (1997)	Psychological autonomy	An independent sense of identity, even while preserving connection to parents.
Noom et al. (2001)	Attitudinal autonomy	The ability to specify several options, to make a decision, and to define a goal.
Noom et al. (2001)	Emotional autonomy	A feeling of confidence in one's own choices and goals.
Noom et al. (2001)	Functional autonomy	The ability to develop a strategy to achieve one's goal.
Pomerantz et al. (2009)	Independent self-construal	A view of the self as autonomous, independent, and unique.
Pomerantz et al. (2009)	Interdependent self-construal	The self is meaningfully cast in relation to others.
Ryan et al. (1995)	Autonomy	Operating agentically and authentically from one's core sense of self; to be self-initiating and self-regulating; not independence and detachment; a need of all humans throughout the lifespan.
Skinner and Edge (2000)	Autonomy	Need to express one's authentic self and to experience that self as the source of action.
Soenens et al. (2007)	Self-determination	General tendency to act in a volitional manner.
Steinberg and Silverberg (1986)	Emotional autonomy	Individuation from parents, nondependence on parents, seeing parents as people, and deidealization of parents.
Vansteenkiste et al. (2009)	Autonomous motivation	Intrinsic motivation and well-internalized extrinsic motivation.

functioning evolves with age, depends on relationships and social context, and may impact upon the nature of relationships with others. In general, current perspectives incorporate these features by proposing that socially responsible and optimal autonomous functioning follows from the continuing maintenance of connections to others, while individuals become self-regulating, self-motivating, and independent. In this section, we briefly describe three theories on autonomy that have been influential when studying adolescents or emerging adults, and provide an overview of some empirical research founded in each theoretical perspective. The first perspective is the most classic theory of autonomy development, which has origins in the psychoanalytic perspective. The remaining two are more contemporary perspectives, with one perspective emphasizing motivation and a second emphasizing cognitive processes.

Classic, Psychoanalytic Theory of Adolescent Autonomy Development

When describing theories related to adolescent autonomy, the significant and early influence of psychoanalytic and neoanalytic theories must be recognized. In these views, drives, primarily sexual drives, promote autonomy via disengagement from the family, particularly a loosening of ties with parents. The development of autonomy is not behavioral or emotional detachment from parents, but instead it is an individuation process. Individuation is believed to stimulate and depend on behavioral or cognitive rebelliousness and defiance toward parents or other caregivers. In line with this view, conflict with parents is expected to be normal and necessary, and is the spark that ignites extrafamilial adult love objects and other intimacies.

Much of the early research on adolescent autonomy had its beginnings in this classic view. Most prominent has been the research of Laurence Steinberg and his colleagues. Their work showed that multiple aspects of *emotional* autonomy, which included nondependency on parents, individuation, and de-idealization of parents, increased with age and that adolescents reported better psychosocial functioning and academic success when they experienced a combination of emotional autonomy from parents and support within the parent–adolescent relationship.

Emotional autonomy is often differentiated from behavioral and cognitive forms. Behavioral autonomy includes self-governance, self-regulation of behavior, and acting on personal decisions. Cognitive autonomy includes a belief that one has control over one's own life and subjective feelings of decisional capacity without requiring excessive social validation. As emotional autonomy increases, there also are age-related increases in behavioral and cognitive autonomy. However, premature behavioral autonomy, defined as a relaxed curfew and other freedoms from parental monitoring, has been linked with problems in both late adolescence and early adulthood; these problems include deviant behavior, less capacity for planning, and lower subjective well-being. Similar research has also shown deficits associated with premature emotional autonomy.

This early research on emotional autonomy was not without controversy primarily because of a lack of consideration of parents and their roles in adolescent autonomy and functioning. When emotional autonomy is not examined along with positive parenting qualities (such as warmth and autonomy support), emotional autonomy does identify some adolescents who are more self-reliant but also who are more detached from parents and susceptible to peer influence. Hence, some early operationalizations of emotional autonomy comingled premature and problematic detachment from parents with more normative and healthy aspect of autonomy development.

Self and Motivation

Consistent with the psychoanalytic view of adolescent autonomy, views emphasizing the self-system and motivation attribute autonomy and related aspects of self-development to internal and internalization processes. However, diverging from psychoanalytic views, different processes of interaction between the individual and the environment are accentuated. Most prominent here is Self-Determination Theory (SDT).

In SDT, autonomy is referred to as "the extent that one is operating agentically, from one's core sense of self ... To be autonomous thus means to be *self*-initiating and *self*-regulating." Within this perspective, autonomous action or an autonomous orientation is marked by the perception of the self as the origin of action (the agent). Autonomy is evident in intrinsic motivation to engage in certain behaviors and joy in choosing to engage in certain behaviors rather than others. An innate need for autonomy energizes and motivates all individuals to seek their own course of behavior, while a need for relatedness to others simultaneously promotes behaviors that maintain connections with others.

SDT has sparked new research on adolescent autonomy. Much of this research has concentrated on the intrapersonal processes involved in volition and choice. To identify these processes, an autonomous rather than a controlled orientation is considered optimal for day-to-day engagement and disengagement from tasks, and for predicting success and well-being. An autonomous orientation has been defined as intrinsic motivation and personal commitments that depend on feelings of volition in actions relevant to one's personal standards and goals. In contrast, a controlled orientation has been defined as pressure from external contingencies such as rewards and motivation related to internal compulsions and obligations. For example, in one study of adolescent behavioral autonomy (measured as home leaving) and subjective well-being, results revealed that, although premature or late behavioral autonomy might be expected to be associated with problems, this association depended on the adolescents' motivation underlying their living situation. Living situation accompanied lower well-being and satisfaction when it was not based on one's own volition.

Overall, motivational and self theories, such as SDT and others, spotlight the desire for individual agency as a universal but they also recognize that relationships with others are critical to the enactment and recognition of agency. Although these perspectives do not view detachment and conflict with parents as necessary or even central for autonomy development, they do highlight the importance of social interactions. The opposite of autonomy is the experience of being controlled, coerced, compelled, or manipulated into actions that do not freely emerge from the core self ('heteronomy'). Successful

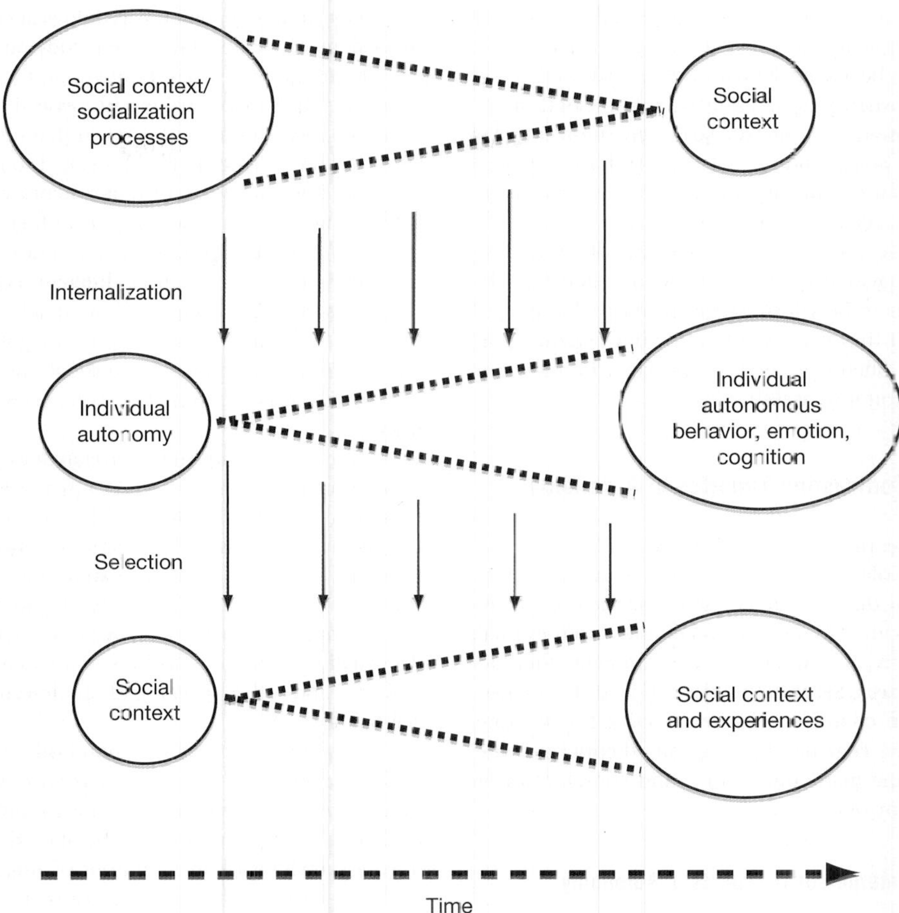

Figure 1 An illustration of the influences on social environments on autonomy development via the *internalization* of social beliefs, opportunities, values, and norms and how autonomy entails a progressive and agentic selection of contexts.

autonomous functioning includes having an adequate awareness of the self, understanding and internalizing social information and values, and having the means to regulate and modify the self. A simplified version of such an interactional process is illustrated in **Figure 1**. This shows not only how the development of autonomy has at its source the *internalization* of social beliefs, opportunities, values and norms but also how autonomy results in agentic selection of contexts. *Internalization* refers to the adoption of values from one's social context (i.e., culture, parents, and increasingly peers) as one's own values. As shown in **Figure 1**, internalization and selection processes should wane and wax, respectively, over time with a larger influence of socialization (shown as a larger circle) at younger ages and selection opportunities becoming more available with increasing age. At the same time, autonomy in its multiple forms should become more salient with increasing age.

Figure 1 illustrates how autonomy and autonomous actions can be conceptualized as distinct from but inextricably linked to the influence of and interactions with others. Autonomy development involves socialization by others, usually beginning with parents and eventually including peers and intimate partners. Such socialization promotes the internalization of others' values that in turn enhance an autonomous orientation and a feeling of agency. Yet, it is individuals' abilities to make selections, as well as their perceptions of choice and willingness that make them active in their own development and social worlds. Hence, the important message is that when autonomy is defined apart from the social context, autonomous actions can occur while dependent on or attached to another. Independence and autonomy are not equivalent.

Cognitive Elements of Autonomy

Changes in adolescents' capacities for abstract thought and their escalating abilities to consider multiple perspectives and issues in order to make more complex decisions are critical for adolescent autonomy development. Although this is recognized in all developmental theories of autonomy, the cognitive theory of autonomy, proposed by Marc Noom and colleagues, is one that makes the cognitive components most explicit. In this theory, autonomy includes understanding personal desires, values and capacity, and regulating pursuit of personal interests and goals. Hence, autonomy has attitudinal, functional, and emotional aspects. The attitudinal component encompasses understanding choices, setting goals, and making decisions. The functional component includes regulation of goal striving via strategy identification and enactment. The emotional component includes feelings of confidence when making choices and pursuing goals. These aspects of cognitive autonomy have been found to be associated with firmer goals and active coping with stress, whereas adolescents who report both more attitudinal and emotional autonomy also perceive more internal control over their choices and goals (i.e., they have a greater internal locus of control). In sum, these cognitive dimensions of autonomy clearly identify goal selection, seeking, planning, and related regulatory strategies as components of autonomy. This, along with behavioral autonomy in the form of being self-supporting and able to be self-sufficient, is often what people have in mind when they discuss autonomy but psychological views of autonomy often place equal importance on the emotional aspects of autonomy, as well.

Comparing and Contrasting Theories of Autonomy

All of the above theories identify autonomy as a positive and necessary part of adolescent growth and well-being. However, these theories can be differentiated in two ways. First, although each recognizes both the intrapersonal and interpersonal aspects of autonomy and autonomy development, they do differ in their emphasis. Second, theories can be differentiated based on the claim of universality versus criticism of more limited applicability. Together, however, the theories provide a rich account of the many dimensions and complexities of adolescent autonomy development.

Intrapersonal and Interpersonal Aspects of Autonomy

The theories and definitions of autonomy vary both in their emphasis on the specific dimension of autonomy, such as behavioral, emotional, or cognitive autonomy, and in their focus on the predominant origin of autonomy development as within the self (an intrapersonal process) or as a developmental process that is socially supported or constrained (an interpersonal process). Perspectives on autonomy that specify the normative growth of emotional autonomy from parents emphasize the importance of interpersonal process in the development of autonomy, or in other words, the relational changes (i.e., interpersonal process) between parents and their children as adolescents move from dependent to more egalitarian relationships with their parents. In contrast, cognitive approaches emphasize adolescents' ability to make their own decisions and development of autonomy around perceptions of control (i.e., intrapersonal process). Regardless of the presumed origin of autonomy – either the individual organism or the social environment and its constraints and affordances – all theories and most definitions of autonomy recognize the complex interdependency between individual and context as well as the bidirectional influence of the increasingly autonomous individual and the social environment.

One way to illustrate differences in emphasis is to examine the measures most often used by researchers connected to each theory. Measures used in different bodies of research on autonomy include (a) a focus on emotional autonomy from parents within the psychoanalytic perspective, (b) measures of an intrapersonal autonomous orientation and the need for autonomy within a motivational SDT perspective, (c) measures of autonomy support, parental psychological control, and related dimensions of relationships when studying the roles of social partners in autonomy development, and (d) measures of the cognitive and decision-making processes involved in autonomous behavior. Research has shown that different measures of autonomy are often only weakly related to each other or even unrelated. There are weak or nonexistent associations between different measures of autonomy including agency, emotional autonomy, cognitive autonomy, and autonomous expression with others (voice), as well as different associations between these measure of autonomy and parent–adolescent relationship qualities. These findings give further weight to the suggestion that autonomy has both intrapersonal and interpersonal elements that may be somewhat or even largely distinct from each other.

On the other hand, the interrelatedness between effective intrapersonal and interpersonal functioning is increasingly recognized as a marker for healthy development. From the SDT literature, consistent correlations between the quality of the social context in terms of parent and teacher autonomy support and adolescent autonomy and well-being have been found. Similarly associations have often been found between high-quality social interactions with classmates, romantic partners, and other peers and adolescent autonomy and well-being.

Of note, recent extensions upon both psychodynamic and cognitive approaches necessarily recognize that both intrapersonal and interpersonal processes are important. An alternative to each of these perspectives, motivational theories of autonomy, begin with specific definitions of autonomy striving and orientation toward autonomous causality orientations, but also often includes conceptions of the interpersonal processes that support or undermine autonomy. For example, in SDT, autonomy has been described as a universal intraindividual need that is fulfilled based on specific individual motivations or efforts toward autonomy fulfillment and supported by interpersonal relationships and social environments. Such fulfillment of the need for autonomy is encouraged by specific qualities within social contexts.

In summary, healthy autonomy might encompass psychosocial functioning in many domains, including competence in school, work, and relationships; emotion regulation and impulse control; leadership; and positive self-esteem and identity. The multiple theories and approaches suggest that this is the case. Nevertheless, we still have the nagging question of whether autonomy should be defined and measured independent of other aspects of psychosocial maturity, or whether the concept of autonomy supplements our understanding of psychosocial maturity in its many forms. Putting aside these conceptual issues for a moment, theories consistently describe the development of autonomy as dependent upon both the active human organism and the environment. Therefore, relationships with significant others are expected to aid or thwart autonomy development, but additional research is needed to determine the many interrelated processes involved.

Universality and Specificity

Adolescents and parents live in diverse places of socialization and developmental environments. Because not all of these environments can be assumed to hold the same values for individualism (autonomy and agency) and collectivism (interdependence) or provide the same structural and financial opportunities, the study of autonomy has been criticized for its possible cultural specificity. Autonomy and personal freedom are strong cultural values in most Western industrialized societies. Other cultures, and even cultural groups living within a single country, have their own unique normative values and practices that form a society and shape an individual, their family, and the community at large. Some struggle with unsafe neighborhoods or other factors that can restrict opportunities for autonomous behavior and volition. For example, Mexican, Chinese, Filipino, and European adolescents residing in the United States report different acceptability of disagreements with mothers and fathers, endorsement of parent authority, and expectations for behavioral autonomy, conflict, and cohesion. Those with Mexican and Filipino heritage expressed more respect for their parents' authority, whereas those with Chinese heritage expected to be granted behavioral autonomy later than other adolescents. Such a difference between cultures (within or between countries) is often simply described as a difference in independent (individualistic) versus interdependent (collectivistic) cultural expectations and norms, and such a cultural difference has been verified in research. Because of the often identified link between autonomy and independence researchers have rightly suggested that autonomy processes may differ between cultures, that the meaning of autonomy and striving for autonomy may not be present in the same way across cultures – or may even indicate maladjustment in interdependent cultures – and that other phenomenon such as relational harmony and interdependence may be dominant values in collectivist cultures.

Cultural distinctiveness in the expression of autonomy has been found for adolescents' expectations for autonomy, the timing of the development of autonomous decision-making, viewing parents as part of a self-schema, and for the balance of autonomy and relatedness. Cultural differences also have been found in parents' support for autonomy and in striving and values for autonomy. Overall, the broad picture is that cultures described as more individualistic and independent have adolescents who expect more autonomy and independence earlier and have parents who grant this earlier. In contrast, interdependent or collectivist cultures – most often studied are African and Asian cultures – place somewhat more value on relational harmony, collective well-being, conformity, and shared functioning when compared to valuing independent functioning. In some of these cultures, there is evidence of later onset of some behavioral indicators of autonomy, and traditional conceptualizations of autonomy supportive parenting are not clearly associated with positive adolescent outcomes. The cause of these differences is often assumed to be located within the values of the society at large, although this is rarely directly confirmed.

In separate theory and research, autonomy has been described as a universal need that may be met and expressed differently between cultures. In particular, those taking an SDT perspective have proposed that it is the definition of autonomy that helps explain the emphasis on cultural distinctiveness versus universal importance. They argue that traditional definitions of autonomy as self-reliance will differ across cultures, whereas the SDT perspective on autonomy, as behavior that is self-endorsed or volitional functioning, will be universally important. When researchers have investigated the universal nature of autonomy from the SDT perspective – as opposed to measuring behavioral forms of autonomy – there is evidence for the universal presence and positive value of volitional functioning in American, European African, and Asian adolescents. This includes having positive effects on achievement, self-management of chronic health conditions, positive perception of parents and adjustment, well-being, and life satisfaction.

There are other arguments for the universality of the need for autonomy, but these views note that it is important to balance this against the need for relatedness and belongingness. The recognition that a balance of autonomy and relatedness need fulfillment may be most beneficial for all humans, for example, has made significant advances on classic perspectives on autonomy. Well-being is enhanced for individuals with higher levels of both agency and communion, defined as independent and self-assertive behaviors plus a valuing of interpersonal relationships, cooperation, and caring.

There is now substantial support for autonomy and relatedness as complementary, universal developmental tasks. Similarly other contemporary clinical research approaches investigating *self-differentiation* – defined as the balance between effective interpersonal and intrapersonal functioning – shows consistent associations between this form of autonomy and relatedness balance and late adolescent and emerging adult well-being, academic engagement, and less risky or problem behavior. While not the focus of this review, there is a substantial body of research on John Bowlby's concept of *attachment security* applied to adolescence – which specifies the necessity for a successful balance between relatedness and exploration as a precursor to well-being – and shows the fundamental importance of attachment security for well-being across the lifespan. In accordance with this, early childhood attachment security is a prospective predictor of autonomy in adolescence.

The Important Role of Parents in Adolescent Autonomy Development

Regardless of which specific view of autonomy is in the spotlight, a key research goal has been isolating the social foundations of adolescent adaptive autonomy. Such questions satisfy intellectual curiosity but their answers also have direct relevance for real-life decisions including the implementation of best parenting and teaching practices and the design of adolescent mental health services and youth development programs.

Parenting Dimensions and Adolescent Autonomy

The important roles of social relationships and the selection of environments in the development of autonomy, which we depict in **Figure 1**, are not new ideas. Many developmental scientists have proposed that autonomy does not necessitate severing of ties with parental figures and depends on the internalization of social standards and values. Moreover, the nature and quality of social contexts are critical to the internalization of the desires of others. Adolescents must balance the need for continued conformity to the expectations of others, while understanding their own values and pursuing their personal goals. Internalization of others' standards is one bridge that enables continued connections with others and allows social adaptation, while maintaining a sense of volition without feelings of coercion. Adolescent autonomy development is partly a process of transforming socially sanctioned values into personal values in order to develop a sense of volition about selected actions, while also knowing when to resist outside influence.

In fact, most recent empirical research on adolescent autonomy has built upon this proposition by teasing apart how socially responsible autonomous functioning and self-regulation depend upon continuing, but transformed, attachments and connections to others. In some of the most recent views, autonomous functioning has been described as more likely when exchanges between adolescents and adults honor and respect the adolescents' capabilities and permit and support autonomous behaviors and decision-making while also maintaining positive emotional connections. Parents who provide high levels of support for their adolescents' autonomy are those who rarely rely on punitive, coercive parenting tactics to gain compliance or exert control and who engage in low levels of psychologically controlling behavior.

Many developmental theorists and researchers have considered whether particular behaviors of parents, peers, and teachers, and what particular styles of interacting with young people, facilitate the development of autonomous functioning. Although terminology and conceptualizations vary when describing these influential features (see **Table 2** for a partial list of terms and definitions), there are two divergent approaches to research in this area. The first is to study multiple dimensions of parenting, such as warmth, monitoring, or discipline along with intrusive or overinvolved parenting, autonomy support, coercion, psychological autonomy granting, or behavioral control. In these studies, the combination of parental warmth with autonomy support or psychological autonomy granting is expected to promote adolescent autonomy, whereas intrusive parenting, coercion, and high levels of behavioral control are expected to undermine adolescent autonomy. These studies often focus on global parenting styles in which warmth or involvement, monitoring, and discipline behaviors are combined (e.g., authoritative, authoritarian, or permissive parenting styles). The second approach is to conduct more fine-grained analyses of the multiple forms of parenting that are expected to assist adolescent autonomous functioning. This has been done to specifically identify which aspects of parents' 'autonomy' supportive actions are associated with independence and/or detachment from the family and which are associated with autonomy balanced with relatedness to others. For example, researchers have differentiated promotion of independence from promotion of volitional functioning, autonomy granting from psychological control, autonomy support from psychological control, and the multiple dimensions of emotional autonomy.

When researchers have used the first approach, most find that parents' support for behavioral and emotional autonomy are associated with adolescent competence, better mental health, well-being, and self-regulation. However, in some cases, parenting warmth and involvement overshadow any impact of parental autonomy support on adolescents' well-being. In other cases, it is combinations of parenting dimensions that are most revealing. For example, when independent

Table 2 Parenting dimensions and behaviors related to adolescents' autonomy

Authors	*Construct*	*Definition*
Ryan et al. (1995)	Autonomy support	Encouraging self-initiation, providing choice, allowing independent problem-solving, minimizing control, and power assertion.
Barber (1996)	Psychological control	Control attempts that intrude into the psychological and emotional development of the child; measured as invalidating feelings, constraining verbal expression, personal attack, and love withdrawal.
Barber and Olsen (1997)	Psychological autonomy granting	The extent to which socialization processes facilitate and do not intrude on the development of an independent sense of identity, efficacy, and worth.
Collins et al. (1997)	Parent–child conflict	Conflict stimulates realignment toward more age-appropriate expectations especially in the area of behavioral autonomy.
Eccles et al. (1997)	Autonomy support	The provision of opportunities for autonomous behavior and decision-making.
Herman et al. (1997)	Psychological autonomy granting	The extent to which parents employ noncoercive, democratic discipline and encourage the individuality of the adolescent.
Skinner and Edge (2000)	Autonomy support	Supporting freedom of expression and action, and encouraging attendance to, acceptance of, and valuing of inner states, preferences, and desires. The opposite is coercion or controlling social conditions.
Silk et al. (2003)	Autonomy granting	Allowing adolescents to make choices about activities and behavior, and encouraging the development of independence.
Reitz et al. (2006)	Decisional autonomy granting	Allowing adolescents to make their own decisions.
Soenens et al. (2007)	Promotion of independence	Allowing adolescents to make choices about activities and behavior, and encouraging the development of independence (see also autonomy granting, Silk et al. (2003)).
Soenens et al. (2007)	Promotion of volitional functioning	Encouraging behavior on the basis of self-endorsed interests, including taking adolescents' perspectives as much as possible, allowing meaningful choices, and providing reasonable rationale when choices are limited.

and joint effects of parents' acceptance-involvement, strictness-supervision (behavioral control), and psychological autonomy granting on adolescents' adjustment have been examined, both individual and joint effects of aspects of parenting were related to most of the adolescent outcomes measured. These outcomes included behavior problems (antisocial behavior, deviance, drug use, peer conformity), psychosocial development (work orientation, self-reliance, self-esteem), internal distress (psychological symptoms, somatic symptoms), and academic competence (academic self-competence and grade point average). Most significantly, the findings show that parental autonomy granting yields the highest levels of adolescent psychosocial development when parental involvement and behavioral control are also high. This has raised awareness of the possibility of nonlinear associations between parenting behaviors and adolescents' psychosocial development – although the gains in psychosocial development as parental acceptance-involvement and psychological autonomy granting increase from low to high, there are nonlinear patterns, too, with greater gains as parental acceptance-involvement increased from low to moderate and as psychological autonomy granting increased from moderate to high. Behavioral control had a weaker relation with psychosocial development, but a moderate level of behavioral control was best for adolescent psychosocial functioning.

When the second approach has been used, emotional bonds that include a number of specific types of interactions are best for promoting individuation and autonomous functioning. In one view, autonomy granting is orthogonal to parental psychological control. Autonomy granting is more closely aligned with promotion of adolescents' independence and includes parents' use of noncoercive discipline and the encouragement of expression of views and true selves within the family. Another somewhat competing view identifies autonomy support from parents as an awareness and sensitivity to their children's and adolescents' perspectives and choices, assistance with exploration of personal values and interests, and minimizing the use of external controls and power assertion. These two forms of autonomy support, which have been referred to as autonomy support for *independence* and autonomy support for *volitional functioning*, may not be orthogonal. Nevertheless, autonomy support for independence is weakly associated with controlling and coercive parenting, whereas it is autonomy support for volitional functioning that is negatively associated with controlling and coercive parenting. Such a pattern of associations illustrates how parents' autonomy support for independence may or may not be accompanied by coercive parental behaviors but that parents' support for volitional functioning is clearly in opposition to parental coercion and psychological control. Moreover, compared to parents' support for independence, it is support for volitional functioning and lack of psychological control that are more strongly associated with adolescents' self-determination and positive functioning, especially lower depressive symptoms and better self-esteem. Recently, ideas about autonomy support for volitional functioning have been extended to the romantic relationship domain and this research shows that autonomy support from romantic partners in late adolescence and early adulthood also is associated with better individual well-being.

Parent–Adolescent Relationships and Culture

As with cultural values for adolescent autonomy, there is cultural variation in parental autonomy granting practices and the timing of adolescents' autonomy expectations. For example, in Latino, Chinese American, and Filipino American cultures, parental authority and decision making are valued for longer throughout adolescence and adulthood. The granting of behavioral autonomy generally occurs later in interdependent cultures such as China than in individualist cultures. Although some qualities of parent–child interactions and certain parenting practices, such as warmth, involvement and support, are important in every culture, parents from the United States are more likely to engage in authoritative parenting, which emphasizes autonomy development in the context of warm, supportive relationships, whereas African American, Latino, and Asian parents are more likely to engage in authoritarian parenting, focusing on obedience and control.

Overall, research investigating parenting behaviors across cultures supports the existence of different definitions or constructions of adolescent autonomy and suggests that the impact of parent autonomy on adolescents may also diverge depending on culture. For example, in the United States – an independent culture – autonomy supportive parents may be defined as those who ask their child's opinion about important issues and allow their child to babysit or conduct other behaviorally independent tasks. In China – an interdependent culture – relational harmony and faithfulness to one's family may be emphasized and autonomy development may be slower and defined differently with Chinese adolescents more interdependent. Adolescents in some Asian cultures consider it more typical to have parents who allow them little participation in decision making. This may support their adoption of cultural and family values.

The Conjoint Role of Individual Maturation and Social Relationships

As their children get older, parents naturally adjust their ways of interacting with them, especially when it involves autonomy and balancing connection and support with opportunity for autonomous action. The nature and function of family relationships are transformed along with an adolescent's gains in independent functioning and attempts for more autonomy. In the United States, transformations have been found to partially be prompted by adolescents' desires and requests for more decision-making authority and behavioral freedoms, with longitudinal research showing that US parents tend to provide fewer opportunities for adolescent decision-making control than desired by their adolescents especially when referring to personal issues that are perceived to entail little harm. This often follows a three-phase developmental sequence, beginning with parental regulation of children, to gradually increasing coregulation between children and parents, to eventual self-regulation. Middle childhood and early adolescence are depicted as the period during which coregulatory processes are especially important to the eventual achievement of responsible autonomy.

There can also be a more elaborate process in which autonomy results from successive transformations of dyadic interactions in response to violated expectancies. Rapid physical, cognitive, and behavioral changes of adolescence and slower, but notable changes of mid-life for parents result in frequent violations of expectancies about the behavior of each member of the pair. Parent–adolescent dyads alter expectancies based on violations of expectancies. These altered expectations eventually reach a level appropriate to the interactions of parent and more adult-like offspring. Therefore, violations of expectancies and the family discussions, challenges, or conflicts that accompany these violations can be adaptive and can stimulate important changes in family relationships and individual development. This means that negative disruptions within families are usually time limited and result in realignment of expectancies, adaptation to the developmental changes of family members, and decreased conflict as young people transition into late adolescence and early adulthood. Emotional strains are more prominent during early adolescence than in later adolescence, adolescents' emotional experiences when interacting with family become increasingly positive in the later high school years, and expectancies of parents and adolescents gradually converge by late adolescence. Recent research has questioned whether parent–adolescent conflict is really the impetus for increasing autonomy-relatedness balance in the parent–adolescent relationship, however. In one recent study, increases in conflict co-occurred with increasing egalitarian parent–adolescent relationships, but conflict between parents and adolescents was not a precursor or even necessary for these changes to occur.

Research studies on the enactment of parental autonomy support versus psychological or behavioral control often imply the importance of conflict or at least disagreement and/or discussion of rights and responsibilities between parents and their children. It may be these multiple types of interactions between adults and adolescents that provide specific opportunities for the provision of parental autonomy support, the promotion of adolescent autonomy, and the internalization of parental values and expectations. Considering the views of all involved in this interaction is important. It is a discrepancy between adolescents' desired autonomy and parents' report of their own willingness to grant autonomy that is associated with more negative adolescent functioning and well-being. A higher level of discrepancy compared to the norm is a correlate of adolescents' poorer well-being, adjustment, and self-management. When discrepancy exists in the context of heightened stress, for example, chronic health condition, academic pressure, or pressure for an adolescent's rights, it is a particularly salient predictor of maladjustment. However, such maladjustment may be time limited. No studies have examined whether such maladjustment continues beyond adolescence.

The Early Parent–Child Relationship as a Foundation for Adolescent Autonomy

It is important to underscore that parents' roles in the promotion of adaptive adolescent autonomous functioning may begin well before the adolescent years. Even parents' support of autonomy and warmth in their preschool age children is associated with the development of greater regulation of attention, cognition, affect, and action. Similarly, attachment theorists often describe the importance of children's attachment to parents, as well as attachment in adolescence, as a core foundation that facilitates or impedes the development of adolescents' autonomy, adaptation, and regulation. In one view, a secure attachment during childhood promotes children's *meta-monitoring*, defined as the ability to monitor one's own models of self and others, reflect on these models, and revise them, if necessary. It is this capacity for meta-monitoring that is believed to be one significant force in the development of adolescent autonomy and self-regulation.

Other Relational Foundations of Adolescent Autonomy

The Roles of Peers

In addition to parents, leisure activity with peers can be the context for the enactment of autonomous behaviors, and peers can influence adolescent functioning by behaving in ways that are either autonomy granting or coercive. However, only a few researchers have focused on adolescents' behavioral, emotional or cognitive autonomy, initiative or autonomous orientation when studying peer relationships. Instead, most developmentalists have focused on peers' influences on restricting behavioral autonomy or increasing problem behaviors in the form of *peer pressure* to conform. In this way, the expectation is that resistance to peer pressure is ideal and should be a positive marker of adolescent autonomy development and maturity. Such maturity is suggested by studies that show that parents and peers have declining influence on adolescents' opinions and decisions as they get older, that resistance to peer pressure increases throughout adolescence and adolescents who report less peer influence show less problem behavior, and that adolescents who have more influence in interactions with a friend are lower in substance use, externalizing behavior, and other problems. Even in early adolescence, those adolescents whose parents increasingly involve them in decision-making are less likely to be exceedingly oriented to peer opinions and peer acceptance than those adolescents whose parents allow less involvement in decision making. However, some adolescents remain susceptible to negative peer influence even into late adolescence, and friends can influence adolescents' expectations of behavioral and emotional autonomy by serving as resources of information about appropriate beliefs about parental controls in both early and middle adolescence. In this way, friends play multiple roles in patterns of autonomy development by providing a context for conformity, but also by serving as direct socializing agents, models of autonomous behavior, and information resources about family norms and rules. It does seem, however, that there may be individual differences in the influence of friends. Aspects of peer relationships are more influential among adolescents with poorer family relationships and adolescents vary in their susceptibility to peer influence.

Leisure and Organizational Influences

In recent years, there has been growing recognition that community and youth organizations can be sources of positive youth development, including assisting with adolescents' development of socially responsible autonomous cognition and behavior, engagement, and initiative. In such work, *initiative*, defined as internally motivation attention and effort toward a goal, has been found to be strongly associated with autonomous behavior as described in SDT.

Youth organizations seem most helpful for adolescents' development of initiative when they contain certain important design elements – they are best when they provide opportunities for choice and contain low levels of coercive interactions, allow time to share personal views and discuss perspectives, provide feedback about choices and performance, and give opportunities for meaningful investment of personal resources. In this way, youth organizations can be important because they provide many opportunities for personal and interpersonal development. In fact, the benefits are usually greater than those provided by classwork and paid work. Yet, not all activities are equal. Involvement in sports and the arts promote initiative and sport participation assists with greater regulation of emotion when compared to a range of other activities (e.g., academic clubs or service to the community). Community, service, and faith activities stand out for their associations with greater interpersonal development (e.g., establishment of adult networks, teamwork, social skills) when compared to sports, the arts, and academic clubs. Moreover, and somewhat unexpectedly, time with friends also has similar benefits to participation in organized activities. Hence, time with friends and participation in organized youth programs both seem to promote positive youth developmental outcomes.

It remains uncommon for organizations to explicitly state autonomous action or initiative as specific developmental goals of program involvement. What is becoming clear is that youth programs are most beneficial when adolescents have a self-generated and intrinsically motivated commitment to the purpose, can select the work they will do within limits, have adults who assist them to make their choices, and have access to an environment where they are safe to discuss their views, listened to, and respected. There are three features of youth organizations that can facilitate agency and initiative in youth:

1. youth-based so that the motivation, direction, and goals come from the youth;
2. adults providing structure in the form of specifying rules and constraints, while emphasizing the importance of the youth based aspects of the organization; and
3. structuring organizations around a period of activity followed by the completion of a project or goal.

Moreover, similar to what is known about parent–adolescent relationships and autonomy, autonomy support from adult leaders also seems important. For example, a coach who provides rationale for rules and other aspects of a program, gives feedback about adolescents' competence, does not control or excessively criticize, as well as engaging in a range of other similar behaviors can be the spark responsible for adolescents who set and strive for goals, reflect on their own purpose and self-identity, feel able to explore their own identities, and report better well-being. It seems to be adolescents' perception that their needs for autonomy, competence, and relatedness are met that partly account for such a link between coaches' autonomy-supportive behaviors and adolescents' initiative. In general, then, the picture that is emerging is that organizations can provide positive opportunities for adolescents that sometimes may not be available to them within their families or their peer groups.

Conclusions

Research on adolescent autonomy reveals a complex and multidimensional developmental process that is normative and predictable at the same time as it is multifaceted and contextually influenced. The many theories and conceptualizations of autonomy all identify autonomous behavior, cognition, and emotion as outgrowths of the active human organism interacting within all levels of the environment from the microsystem (e.g., within families and with friends) to the macrosystem (e.g., social policies), with much of our more recent knowledge concentrated on the development of an autonomous self balanced with relatedness and a changing conception of relationships with others. Regardless of the inherent difficulties that are part of research on a complex process like autonomy development, research on autonomy has not faltered. Instead, the focus of these efforts has shifted. In particular, efforts have increasingly moved away from studying families in Western cultures to the consideration of what is universal and when diversity may be found. However, what has not changed is the variety of perspectives and approaches that can be found when reviewing the literature on adolescent autonomy.

Recent efforts have addressed some of the critical questions, including the universality versus context-specificity of all aspects of autonomy development, how relationships in many domains (e.g., family, peers, and youth organizations) can support or undermine the many different aspects of autonomy, and how autonomy and relatedness to others are balanced as children grow into adolescents and then adults. There are still other themes that require this same level of attention, however. One important issue is the examination of bidirectional effects between adolescent autonomous behavior and the behaviors of significant others. Few studies have had the opportunity to address this issue, but when they have done so, it is clear that adolescents' development of autonomous behaviors, cognitions, and emotions are influenced by their parents and other people at the same time that they have influence on their parents' and others' autonomy granting and related behaviors. In conclusion, all adolescents deserve and usually desire the opportunity for autonomy, volition and choice, in its many forms, and they also depend on and deserve support from others to uncover their talents, abilities, and strengths. Research on adolescent autonomy illustrates that these processes are simultaneously a product of the individual and their social world, making autonomy development difficult, complex, and important for adolescents in all parts of the world.

See also: Adolescent Decision-Making; Cultural Influences on Adolescent Development; Metacognition and Self-regulated Learning; Parent–Child Relationship; Socialization.

Further Reading

Beveridge RM and Berg CA (2007) Parent–adolescent collaboration: An interpersonal model for understanding optimal interactions. *Clinical Child and Family Psychology Review* 10: 25–52.

Beyers W, Goossens L, Vansant L, and Moors E (2003) A structural model of autonomy in middle and late adolescence: Connectedness, separation, detachment, and agency. *Journal of Youth and Adolescence* 32: 351–365.

Goossens L (2006) The many faces of adolescent autonomy: Parent–adolescent conflict, behavioral decision making, and emotional distancing. In: Jackson S and Goossens L (eds.) *Handbook of Adolescent Development*, pp. 135–153. New York: Psychology Press.

Hill JP and Holmbeck GN (1986) Attachment and autonomy during adolescence. *Annals of Child Development* 3: 145–189.

Kagitcibasi C (2005) Autonomy and relatedness in cultural context: Implications for self and family. *Journal of Cross-Cultural Psychology* 36: 403–422.

Larson RW, Pearce N, Sullivan PJ, and Jarrett RL (2007) Participation in youth programs as a catalyst for negotiation of family autonomy with connection. *Journal of Youth and Adolescence* 36: 31–45.

Noom M (1999) *Adolescent Autonomy: Characteristics and Correlates*. Delft, Netherlands: Eburon.

Qin L, Pomerantz EM, and Wang Q (2009) Are gains in decision-making autonomy during early adolescence beneficial for emotional functioning? The case of the United States and China. *Child Development* 80: 1705–1721.

Steinberg L and Monahan KC (2007) Age differences in resistance to peer influence. *Developmental Psychology* 43: 1531–1543.

Zimmer-Gembeck MJ and Collins WA (2003) Autonomy development during adolescence. In: Adams GR and Berzonsky MD (eds.) *Blackwell Handbook of Developmental Psychology*, pp. 175–204. Malden, MA: Blackwell.

Body Image during Adolescence: A Developmental Perspective

D C Jones, University of Washington, Seattle, WA, USA
L Smolak, Kenyon College, Gambier, OH, USA

Glossary

Appearance teasing: Critical communication between a teaser and a target that focuses on appearance. This kind of teasing is often hurtful, irrespective of the intention of the teaser.

Body image satisfaction: The degree to which adolescents evaluate positively their physical features, shape, and weight.

Body mass index (BMI): A measure of body fat based on dividing weight by the height squared.

Body shame: Within Objectification Theory, the self-surveillance associated with self-objectification may result in body shame when the woman is inevitably unable to achieve the societal ideal. This body shame involves a sense of failure and a negative sense of self-because of this inability to meet the standard.

Internalization of appearance ideals: Psychological commitment made by individuals to socially defined ideals of appearance such as thinness and muscularity.

Objectification: Within Objectification Theory, this term is used to capture the dominant societal definition of women's bodies as sexualized objects for the pleasure of men. Women's bodies are, therefore, subjected to the sexualizing gaze of others and women are expected to be pleasing to those who look at them.

Self-objectification: Within Objectification Theory, the internalization of the gaze of others. This internalization causes women to be invested in their appearance and to engage in self-surveillance or self-monitoring in order to insure that they are meeting the societal standards.

Social comparison: An evaluative process that involves seeking information and making judgments about the self relative to others on aspects such as weight and shape.

Introduction

Self-evaluations of body image are evident across the life span and are core aspects of the representation of self for children, adolescents, and adults. Yet, adolescence is the developmental period most frequently associated with body image concerns. Body image emerges as a major defining issue of adolescence because of the myriad physical, cognitive, and social changes that unfold during this developmental period. Some of the earliest and most striking changes associated with adolescence are evident in external appearance. The changes in height, weight, and secondary sexual characteristics that are a part of puberty transform the image and reality of the embodied self. With the cognitive advancements comes a new complexity to the self-concept and a growing appreciation that the self becomes the object of evaluation by others. The increased salience of peer relationships and the heightened concern with acceptance and attractiveness mean that peer experiences become an increasingly important contributor to self-evaluation and body image.

Integrating body image into one's identity and self-evaluation is a normative developmental task during adolescence, but it is a challenging one as well. Body image plays a prominent role as a risk factor for several types of adjustment problems and disorders with adolescent onset. Body dissatisfaction has been a prospective predictor of depression, drive for thinness, eating disorders, body dysmorphia, low self-esteem, and health-compromising behaviors such as dieting and steroid use. Thus, interest in body image during adolescence has been motivated by concern with its role in adjustment problems and clinical disorders.

Body image then is a central feature of adolescence and a prime issue relevant to the challenges and adaptations of adolescents. In this article, we synthesize the research literature to describe the development of body image across adolescence and to identify factors that shape developmental pathways.

 doi:10.1016/B978-0-12-373915-5.00005-X

We limit our article to research that includes specific assessment and evaluation of body image satisfaction, that is, the degree to which adolescents accept their weight and shape. Weight and shape continue to be the body image features that are of greatest concern even with the increase in obesity worldwide. We use the terms, body esteem and body satisfaction, interchangeably in the article. The primary focus is on research about adolescents in middle and high school, but we include evidence from other age groups when applicable.

The primary purpose of this article is to provide a developmentally-oriented description and evaluation of the adolescent body image literature. We begin our review of body image research with an overview of measurement issues. We then describe the framework and factors that guide the conceptual foundations of the review. This is followed by discussions of the developmental trajectory of body image, factors that influence this development, and interventions to help treat and prevent body image disturbances.

Measurement Issues

Since the definition of body image is multidimensional, measures of body image differ in the dimensions they assess. Some assessments focus on general body image or overall body esteem, whereas others measure satisfaction with specific body parts, weight and/or shape, or muscularity.

The research that we review in this article is based primarily on the two widely used formats for assessing body image. One type presents perceptually-based figure-rating scales. Typically 7–9 figures, ranging from very thin to very fat, are provided. There are separate drawings for boys and for girls. The respondent selects an 'ideal' and an 'actual' body image with the difference between the two representing body dissatisfaction. Several of these scales are available for preadolescents and adolescents. Some have been validated on very small samples; most were originally developed for adults and then adapted for use with children and adolescents. These measures often offer limited choices that may not accurately represent the respondent's body shape. There are also frequent procedural problems in that presenting the figures in ascending order may bias responses. The available muscularity-based figures have not been widely used with adolescents.

Attitudinal scales are the other type of measurement most frequently used with adolescents. The Body Esteem Scale for Adolescents and Adults was validated with over 1200 adolescents and young adults (aged 12–25). The 20-item survey yields either a total score or three subscale scores (weight, appearance, and attribution). The Body Dissatisfaction and Drive for Thinness subscales from the Eating Disorder Inventory are also frequently used. These are brief scales (9 and 7 items respectively) that were originally developed for use with adult women, but have been used extensively with adolescents.

The issue of whether the scale was originally developed for adolescents or adults is an important one. Researchers have provided at least some psychometric information on the scales that are used with adolescents but were developed for adults. However, standard indicators of reliability and validity do not tell us whether the measures have the same meaning with adolescents as with adults. There is a need for researchers to more fully investigate the meaning of body image and body change strategies with adolescents, developing or revising measures to better reflect adolescent concerns.

Conceptual Model

Efforts to describe and explain the development of body image require an understanding of multiple factors that work together in complex ways. Two conceptual frameworks inform our review of the literature on adolescents' body image: the biopsychosocial and ecological models.

The biopsychosocial model is a general framework for identifying factors across biological, psychological, and social domains that contribute to well-being. The explicit integration of three domains into the model reflects a holistic approach and acknowledges the interplay between different characteristics of the individual in the social environment.

It is the complexity of the environment that is most clearly elaborated in the ecological model. The ecological model proposes that development always takes place in a context with both individual characteristics and multiple levels of the environment influencing the trajectory of development. The levels of the environment range from the sites of daily interaction (microsystems) and their interrelations (mesosystem) to the overarching institutions and beliefs that represent the society and culture (exosystem and macrosystem).

We integrate these two frameworks into a model that guides our review of the development of body image during adolescence (see **Figure 1**). We examine genetics, puberty, and body mass index (BMI) as the biological characteristics that contribute to body image development. Individual psychological characteristics are related to beliefs, attitudes, and processes that are represented by the internalization of appearance ideals, appearance social comparisons, self-esteem, and negative affect. We differentiate the multiple levels of the social domain to include the interactions and relationships with family, friends, peers, and romantic partners as the core elements of the social relational context. As suggested by the ecological model, the qualities of the repetitive interactions in each of these primary relational contexts are considered the proximal processes shaping developmental outcomes. The relational experiences with parents and peers are also embedded in larger sociocultural contexts that represent the beliefs, values, and norms of a culture. The social–cultural context is explored through a review of cultural norms, race-ethnicity, gender socialization patterns, media influence, and school structure and organization.

We propose that the developing sense of body image during adolescence emerges from the reciprocal interaction and transformations of the individual in the relational and cultural contexts. We examine the ways in which these multiple factors affect the developing sense of body image during adolescence and the particular challenges facing adolescents as they chart their identity as embodied selves. Because cultural norms and gender roles are prominent organizing forces in the development of body image, we begin by highlighting the research on these two major domains before reviewing the literature on other factors related to body image development.

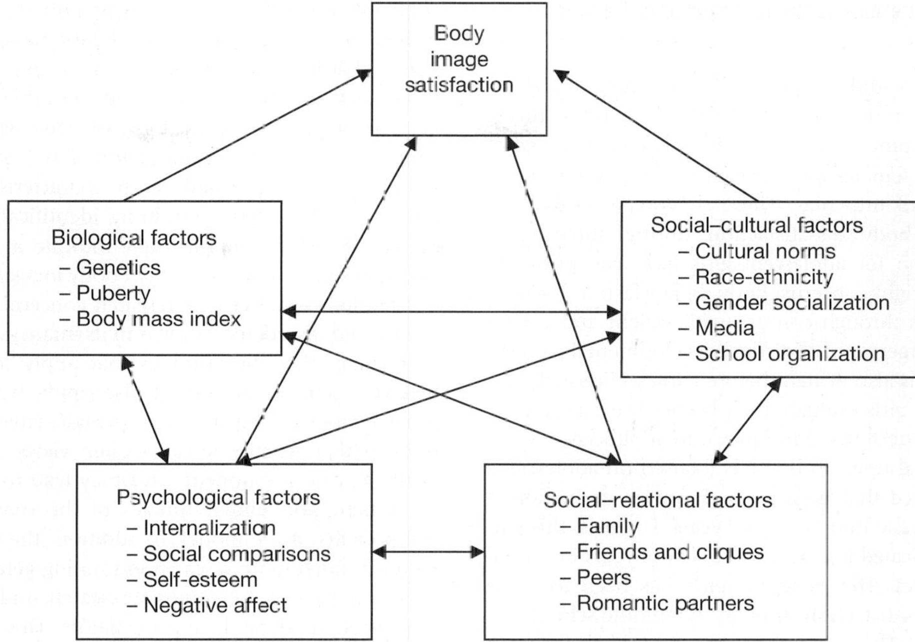

Figure 1 Factors related to the development of body image during adolescence.

The Development of Body Image Dissatisfaction

The Cultural and Ethnic Context of Body Image Development

Research on body image in diverse cultural and ethnic groups is important to those who argue that sociocultural influences shape body image. Every culture or society has an ideal body type for women and for men. The specifics of that body type reflect broader cultural values and expectations regarding the meaning of bodies, gender roles, religious values, and economic and political status. If distinct cultural norms contribute to body image, then we would expect differences between cultures and ethnic groups in preferred body types. At the same time, there are shared characteristics among cultures that create similarities in body image expectations. Furthermore, globalization and immigration have generated increasing accessibility to Western images of idealized bodies that have the potential to shape personal experience within the context of diverse cultural values.

There is accumulating evidence that many cultures around the world value thinness and muscularity. Much of the extant research on adolescent body image is derived from adolescents in countries that share historical and political cultural similarities (e.g., United States, Australia, Canada, and Britain). In these countries, adolescents tend to show patterns of body image development that are similar with special emphasis on thinness for girls and muscularity for boys. Asian countries such as Korea have traditionally valued thinness, a cultural norm that has generated body image problems even to a greater degree than in the United States. Emerging evidence from several Central and South American countries, including Argentina, Brazil, Panama, Cuba, and Guatemala, indicates that there is a strong pressure on adolescent girls to be thinner, presumably related to traditional gender roles. Although recent research in Middle-Eastern societies reveals wide variation in the prevalence of body image dissatisfaction among adolescents, dissatisfaction with weight is increasingly documented.

There is also evidence of cultural and ethnic differences that are suggestive of subcultural body image norms. For example, overweight boys in Fiji and Tonga are much less likely than Australian boys to experience body dissatisfaction. Indeed, Fijian and Tongan boys are also more likely to engage in behaviors to gain weight. The common research finding that African Americans prefer a wider range of body types may constitute a cultural norm that creates a behavioral and attitudinal difference and higher levels of body satisfaction than any other American ethnic group (such as Latino, Asian, and White adolescent and adult women). This difference is relatively small, but does not seem to be decreasing or disappearing in recent years, particularly in terms of global body esteem. Interestingly, some studies indicate that African American and Pacific Islander adolescent boys may enjoy a similar advantage in terms of body satisfaction relative to other boys, but other research has found no differences in mean levels or pattern of relationships across adolescent male ethnic groups.

The current evidence suggests that the causes of cultural similarities and differences are multifactorial and do not simply reflect Westernization. Indeed, within a region (e.g., Central America), some cultures may value curvy female bodies while others emphasize thin bodies. In cultures with frequent food shortages, heavy or even obese body types may be preferred because they signify sufficient prosperity to eat well. The factors determining the substantial cultural differences and similarities in rates, forms, and developmental trajectories of body image still remain to be elaborated.

Developmental Patterns and the Emergence of Gender Differences

Individuals bring to adolescence a clear knowledge of appearance preferences in the culture. Most of the body image research on developmental trajectories has been conducted in societies in which females are expected to be thin and males are to be lean and muscular. These stereotype ideals have implications for body dissatisfaction during adolescence. Body dissatisfaction for adolescent girls has been primarily associated with weight concerns. Body dissatisfaction for boys has dual pathways through concern with weight and greater muscularity. The emergence of distinct developmental patterns for girls and boys is also evident before adolescence such that elementary school girls evaluate their bodies more negatively than boys do, a pattern that continues into adolescence.

The longitudinal research that has focused on adolescents has clearly indicated that negative body image evaluation is heightened during the middle school years. For girls, this pattern has been replicated for the middle school years in several longitudinal studies. The trend for girls has been to show decreases in body satisfaction through the middle school and high school years. The percentage who report moderate to extreme dissatisfaction increases slightly from middle school to high school. The precise nature of the developmental trajectory during the high school years has been more variable. In some cases, there has been stability or increases in body dissatisfaction from high school into the college years. In other research, there has been a slight increase in satisfaction either across high school or around 18 years.

The developmental trajectory for boys has been confirmed in studies that have typically included boys from middle school into high school. The middle school years are the point of greatest dissatisfaction for the boys after which body satisfaction tends to increase or remain stable over the adolescent years. For example, rates of dissatisfaction have been more than twice as high for middle school compared to high school boys. Presumably, the physical changes associated with puberty bring boys closer to the male ideal image of a muscular and lean body, whereas puberty for girls takes them away from the thin ideal. For boys, the pubertal changes provide a more positive basis on which to evaluate their body image.

It is important to recognize that there appear to be gender differences in all cultural and ethnic groups. Specifically, girls tend to demonstrate more body dissatisfaction than do boys. However, this finding is tempered by the relative paucity of studies that have used body image measures specifically designed for boys, such as the Drive for Muscularity Scale.

Factors Related to Development of Body Image

Biological Factors

Genetics

There is a steady growth in interest in developmental psychology in genetic influences on behavior. The limited genetics research with female adolescents has focused on disordered eating rather than body image. However, in this research, disordered eating is defined to include body dissatisfaction. Longitudinal data have demonstrated that genetic factors have a negligible to small influence on prepubertal girls' disordered eating, but account for over half of the variance in 14-year-olds, a level that holds steady at 18 years. Cross-sectional research indicates that pubertal status moderates this age relationship. Early pubertal development is associated with more weight concerns and body dissatisfaction if puberty is assessed in terms of multiple secondary sex characteristics (rather than just menarche) hence permitting identification of the onset of puberty. These findings may indicate a role for pubertal hormones in the development of body image/eating problems.

Developmental genetic research concerning body dissatisfaction and disordered eating is in its infancy. It is important to note, then, that the critiques that apply to developmental behavior genetics in general also apply here. For example, genetic models tend to assign genetic–environment interactions, which genetics research often views as unidirectional, to the genetic component. This may lead to overestimates of the genetic and underestimates of the shared environment components of the model. In addition, the body image field requires much more research examining genetic influences at various ages, more longitudinal research, and greater attention to possible moderators and mediators. This is a rich area for future research.

Puberty

There are several reasons why researchers and theorists have considered puberty as an influence on body image. The majority of this research has focused on adolescent girls. First, there are dramatic body changes associated with puberty, including a substantial weight gain. Second, body dissatisfaction and eating disorders become more common starting in early adolescence, coincident with puberty. Third, puberty is associated with more adult-like behaviors such as dating and pressures related to an intensification of gender role expectations. Traditional gender roles associate femininity with investment in appearance and thinness and masculinity with strengthen and muscularity, characteristics that may increase the risk of body dissatisfaction. Finally, again particularly among girls, early puberty has been associated with a wide range of psychological and behavioral problems. Researchers have investigated whether body image and eating concerns are among these.

Early cross-sectional research indicated that body dissatisfaction was correlated with puberty. Specifically, girls' body satisfaction dropped as they entered puberty such that early maturers experienced the decline before on-time or late maturers. The timing of puberty also has mattered for boys. In Western cultures, late-maturing boys have been more likely to experience greater body dissatisfaction. However, factors such as weight gain or BMI have been more strongly related to body dissatisfaction than has pubertal timing for both girls and boys.

BMI

Not surprisingly, BMI, or weight to height ratio, is correlated with many forms of body image. One of the most robust findings in the research is the nearly consistent positive relationship between BMI and body dissatisfaction. For both adolescent girls and boys, higher BMI is associated with greater body dissatisfaction.

There are variations to this theme, however. Boys who are underweight also express body dissatisfaction. Thus, the relationship between BMI and body dissatisfaction for boys may be best expressed as U-shaped: under- and overweight boys are expected to be most dissatisfied with their bodies, albeit for different reasons. However, this quadratic relationship has not always been statistically significant or tested directly. Another variation is the distribution of dissatisfaction across the BMI levels. Even in the lowest percentiles of BMI, there are girls who want to be thinner. This is not true for boys who generally only want to lose weight when they are substantially overweight. This pattern suggests a greater tolerance for males to be overweight. Furthermore, the drive for muscularity has been related to lower levels of BMI among boys, indicating that underweight boys want to build muscles rather than gain weight, though the findings on this are inconsistent.

It is important to note that it is the culturally defined meaning of BMI rather than BMI itself that influences body satisfaction. In cultures where being heavy is interpreted as a sign of prosperity, heavier people are not body-dissatisfied. In Western cultures, heavier girls and boys are more likely to be body-dissatisfied because they do not meet the cultural standards for thinness or lean muscularity.

Psychological Factors

Psychological factors such as attitudes, values, affect, and self-evaluation are central to understanding the processes of body image development. Most of the research linking psychological constructs to body image has focused on risk factors that increase the likelihood of experiencing body dissatisfaction. A risk factor is a variable that has been shown prospectively to predict an adjustment outcome such as body dissatisfaction. Experimental designs or longitudinal research with statistical analyses that control for the initial levels of the adjustment outcome are needed to identify risk factors. Internalized appearance ideals and appearance social comparisons are among the prominent psychological risk factors contributing to body dissatisfaction. We will also consider the evidence related to self-esteem and negative affect.

Risk factors

Internalization of appearance ideals

Internalization of appearance ideals refers to the psychological commitment made by individuals to socially defined ideals of appearance. These ideals are different across time/history and culture. For the last 50 years, the ultra-slender female and the muscular, lean male have been the ubiquitous ideal images in Western societies that have been broadcast around the world. These internalized appearance ideals undermine body satisfaction because the ideal forms are difficult, if not impossible, to attain for most individuals and are associated with unhealthy behaviors such as dieting and steroid use in an attempt to create the perfect body shape and size.

There has been substantial support for the linkage between internalized appearance ideals and body dissatisfaction. A greater commitment to appearance ideals has been associated with heightened body dissatisfaction in cross-sectional studies of adolescent girls and boys and emerging adults. When the prospective contribution of internalized appearance ideals has been examined in longitudinal studies, the effects on body dissatisfaction have been smaller than in cross-sectional studies and the results not as consistent, especially for girls. Among adolescent boys, limited data indicate that the adoption of the muscularity ideal has been a prospective contributor to body dissatisfaction.

Social comparison

Social comparison represents an evaluative process that involves both seeking information and making judgments about the self relative to others. An important part of the social comparison process is the selection of targets for comparison. Peers and models/celebrities are typically the most frequent targets of social comparison for both boys and girls. Although information gathered through social comparison can theoretically serve as a motivating agent and enhance self-regard through a positive evaluation of the self, an interesting aspect of research on appearance social comparison has been its frequent linkage with negative self-evaluation. Adolescent boys and girls who report more frequent appearance comparisons also experience greater body dissatisfaction. Appearance comparisons to ideal images of models or 'perfect' peers at school can detract from positive body image regardless of gender, even if adolescents are of normal weight or muscularity.

There are important gender differences in appearance social comparison. First, girls compared to boys report higher levels of appearance comparisons. In addition, appearance comparisons levels typically are more strongly related to body dissatisfaction for girls. Finally, the self-evaluative process of appearance comparison for girls is a significant longitudinal factor contributing to change in body dissatisfaction, but not for boys. This evidence means that social comparison processes fulfill the requirements as a risk factor for girls, but not for boys.

Research on college students provides suggestions for understanding these gender differences. Women are more likely to select 'upward' comparisons (targets who are superior to the self) and men more 'downward' comparisons. The upward comparisons are related to negative self-statements for women and the downward comparisons are correlated with positive self-statements for men. These findings have clear implications for gender differences in the maintenance of body dissatisfaction. Further research is needed to confirm these outcomes for adolescents and determine the rates of 'naturally' occurring target selection for appearance comparisons.

Self-esteem

Global self-esteem has been defined as the overall evaluation of the self as a person of worth or value. One of the well-established findings in the empirical literature has been that adolescent girls and boys who are satisfied with their bodies also have positive self-esteem. Although the relationships have been more consistent and stronger for girls, the general trend in cross-sectional research from several countries has been for body esteem to be strongly associated with global self-esteem.

Self-esteem may help to promote positive body image, but it is also feasible that positive body image enhances global self-esteem. The few longitudinal studies that have attempted to unravel the direction of effect provide a complicated answer that is dependent on developmental timing and gender. It would appear that there is some evidence to consider self-esteem a protective factor during early adolescence for girls, but not for high school girls and boys. When older adolescents feel good about their bodies, they then have more positive self-esteem. During later adolescence, body dissatisfaction functions as a risk factor for self-esteem rather than the reverse.

It is premature to conclude that self-esteem is primarily an outgrowth of body image and that it does not contribute to body image development. The limited time frames and number of assessments may not reveal the reciprocal dynamic between self-esteem and body image satisfaction. The relational dynamics between self-esteem and body image satisfaction deserve further attention from researchers.

Negative affect

The relationship between negative affect and body dissatisfaction also reflects the reciprocal causality conundrum. The preponderance of evidence indicates that it is body dissatisfaction which is a risk factor for depression, especially for adolescent girls and not the reverse. For example, in a 2-year longitudinal study, body dissatisfaction among girls but not boys was a significant prospective predictor of the onset of depression even when stressful life events, negative affectivity, parental support, and externalizing behaviors were considered in the model. The unique contribution of body dissatisfaction to future onset of depression is especially important given the greater rates of depression for adolescent girls.

Protective factors

There has been more attention to risk factors in the research on body image than in identifying and understanding the dynamics of protective psychological factors. The focus on risk factors has been understandable given the prospective connection of body dissatisfaction to clinical outcomes. However, there has been minimal conceptualization of protective psychological factors other than the inverse of current risk factors. Nonetheless, limited research suggests some possible protective factors. A cultural acceptance of a wider range of body shapes and of a definition of beauty that emphasizes attitude rather than physical appearance, as in African American communities, may protect against body image problems. Participation in after-school activities, especially nonelite, team sports, may bolster positive feelings about physical competence and enhance body satisfaction. Work with adults indicates that adopting a feminist perspective may offer some protection for girls. Much more research is needed to identify potential protective factors.

Social Relational Factors

Family relations and body image

Families provide the primary relationships in development and play a formative role in shaping attitudes and values in their children. Parents express their expectations and beliefs about appearance in the lifestyle patterns they create for eating, dieting, exercise, and evaluation. They serve as models, critics, and advocates in the development of body image from early childhood through adolescence.

Parents serve as models in multiple ways. Their expressed evaluations about their own and each others' bodies serve as models for children and adolescents to critique themselves and others. Exercising and dieting activities of the parents serve as behavioral examples for engaging in physical activity or restricting food intake. In married couples, it has been found that there is more emphasis placed on wives to lose weight than on husbands. The impact of these types of modeling is evident across development. The body dissatisfaction of young girls and boys (ages 5–8) is related to their perceptions of mothers' body dissatisfaction. Other research indicates that parental modeling may continue to be important through adolescence, though findings are inconsistent.

Parents' positive messages about appearance and general parental support can serve as protective factors in the development of body image. Most research though has examined parents' explicit negative messages about appearance which have a deleterious effect on body image. When mothers and fathers stress the importance of being thin and exert pressure on their children to lose weight, adolescent girls and boys are more likely to initiate dieting and hold negative views about their appearance and bodies. Appearance criticism and teasing by mothers and fathers have consistently been related to greater body dissatisfaction for adolescents, particularly in cross-sectional studies. Overall, families that emphasize appearance and put pressure on attaining appearance ideals are more likely to have adolescents with greater body dissatisfaction.

Peer appearance culture

Experiences with peers represent an important social context for the development of body image among adolescent girls and boys. Adolescents bring to peer interactions the values and expectations they have learned in the family and the larger culture. They further create an appearance culture with their peers that is governed by norms and expectations which are modeled and reinforced by peers. These accumulated experiences within the peer appearance culture thus reflect and shape individual behaviors and attitudes about body image of self and others.

Friends and cliques

Friendship similarity and influence Mutual friendships and extended friendship groups known as cliques typically share similar interests and values in a variety of areas, including appearance. Friendship cliques tend to have similar body image and BMI levels, have similar attitudes toward the importance of appearance, and similar experiences in appearance change strategies such as dieting, disordered eating, and muscle building.

Friends and cliques vary in their endorsements of the peer appearance culture. When friends share a heightened concern with appearance and endorse weight/shape ideals, then patterns of heightened body dissatisfaction are evident. In cross-sectional studies, appearance-oriented cliques report talking more about dieting, acknowledging the importance of friends in the decision to diet, comparing their bodies more often with others, and teasing one another about weight and shape. In longitudinal research, perceived friend dieting is a prospective risk factor for body dissatisfaction, especially in early adolescent girls.

There is also evidence of social influence within friendships regarding body image and related issues. One source of influence occurs through conversations about appearance and body changes strategies such as dieting and muscle building. The attention and reinforcement given to appearance issues in conversations with friends highlight appearance as an important attribute, support the construction of appearance norms and ideals, and encourage evaluating the self relative to the others on physical attributes. Research verifies that girls and boys who reported more frequent conversations with their friends about appearance also reported greater body dissatisfaction. For girls, appearance conversations with friends are a prospective contributor to body dissatisfaction.

Appearance conversations can also train adolescents to be highly evaluative of appearance. Among girls, 'fat talk' ("I'm so fat") has been highlighted as a discourse style in which individuals repeatedly criticize and lament the size of their own bodies in the presence of peers. It has been suggested that 'fat talk' solicits peer assurances ("No, you're not") and promotes group solidarity. However, the repeated experiences of verbalizing these negative self-evaluations have the potential to normalize self-disparaging discourse and internalize a critical judgmental stance toward one's own body, increasing the likelihood of body dissatisfaction.

Friendship quality Positive friendship characteristics such as communication, trust, and acceptance are not correlated with body dissatisfaction among high school girls and do not appear to serve as a protective factor. Rather negative friendship qualities (alienation and conflict) are the features that are most frequently related to body dissatisfaction. In addition, the termination of friendships can be especially problematic in early adolescence. In a longitudinal study of early adolescent boys and girls, loss of friendships over a school year predicted decreases in body esteem but not in other dimensions of self-esteem. This finding indicates the vital contribution of friendships to the developing body image.

Peers

Adolescents must function at school with classmates who are not necessarily friends or network members. In the school context, research has focused on status differences among peers and the degree of acceptance within these arbitrary groups of age mates.

Popularity Adolescent experiences in schools are embedded in the social hierarchy of the peer ecology. One indicator of social status has been peer-perceived popularity, also known as social reputation. At the top of the social hierarchy are typically the popular students who have greater access to the attention and resources of the school community, many times through their association with athletics and cheerleading. Even though the evidence to connect social status to body dissatisfaction has been inconsistent, there are several ways in which popularity has been linked to body image satisfaction.

Popular students are identified by adolescents as the most prominent source of peer appearance pressure presumably because 'ideal' body shapes are evident in popular groups. Higher levels of popularity are associated with boys' reports of thinner, muscular figures, whereas heavier figures are related to lower levels of popularity. Among girls, smaller body shapes are a factor connected to popularity. In a recent study of older high school students, dieting behavior was most prevalent among popular boys and girls. Thus, the appearance ideals and appearance change strategies that are modeled by the higher status students presumably set the standards for individual evaluation.

Peer acceptance Not everyone is or wants to be popular. Most adolescents do want to be accepted and liked by peers. Although peer-based acceptance measures have been inconsistently related to body image satisfaction, individual's ratings of perceived acceptance by peers have been repeatedly related to body image.

Adolescents who think that social acceptance is achieved by conformity to body ideals are vulnerable to body dissatisfaction. These adolescents often engage in 'if only' cognitions. For girls, these beliefs have been evaluated for being thinner (If only I were thinner then boys would be more attracted to me); for boys, the focus has been on being more muscular (If only I were more muscular, then girls would pay more attention to me). The results of the research are highly consistent. When peer acceptance is perceived to be related to body concerns, girls and boys are at greater risk for negative body image.

There is a reality in the peer world that acceptance is related to body shape and size. Adolescents identify weight and shape as among the most important attributes for attractiveness for females and males. Peer acceptance has typically been associated with attractiveness and athleticism across the school years, suggesting that students who conform to appearance standards are more likely to be accepted by peers. There is strong social reinforcement then to achieve an ideal body shape among adolescents and sanctions for deviation. The effects of deviating from normative expectations or appearance ideals are evident in that overweight adolescent girls and boys are less accepted by peers and are more socially isolated than normal-weight peers.

Peer evaluations: Appearance teasing Peers directly communicate their critiques of appearance via teasing. In fact, appearance teasing is the most frequent type reported by adolescents. Furthermore, teasing about being overweight is considered by adolescent girls and boys to be the most hurtful and least humorous form even when compared to being underweight or nonmuscular. Friends and male peers are identified as the most frequent perpetrators. Because teasing generally is deemed socially acceptable especially among friends, the effects of appearance teasing can be underestimated. Appearance teasing is not innocuous banter, but is a potent way to reinforce appearance standards and critique deviations from the norm. It frequently meets several of the criteria for bullying because it occurs repeatedly, between peers of unequal social status, especially for overweight adolescents. It is not surprising then that in cross-sectional studies, appearance teasing is consistently related to lower body satisfaction for both girls and boys regardless of ethnicity or body size.

The prospective contribution of appearance teasing to body image satisfaction has not been as evident. Further research is needed to determine if the impact of appearance teasing is indirect in its effects on body image through other potential contributors such as self-esteem or negative affect.

Romantic partners

The sexual maturity that emerges during adolescence brings with it an interest in romantic partners. The body concerns of adolescents are driven in part by concerns with attractiveness to potential romantic partners. The limited research in this area of peer relations has been on primarily European American girls in heterosexual relationships.

Developmental age and normative expectations for dating figure prominently in the relationship between romantic relations and body image. Body image dissatisfaction and dieting are greater for early adolescent girls who are sexually involved with boys, especially for European-American adolescents. Dating does not appear to have this direct relationship to body dissatisfaction and dieting in high school girls when romantic relationships are more normative. It is early dating with sexual involvement then that is associated with increases in body dissatisfaction.

For high school girls, the linkage between body dissatisfaction and romantic relations is based more on the importance of being popular with boys and the perceived importance of thinness to boys. If being popular with the opposite sex and having a romantic partner are deemed as important, then adolescents are more likely to have a negative body image.

It is true that body shape and weight are important features for attracting romantic partners for males and females. Research indicates that adolescent boys have internalized the sociocultural beliefs regarding attractiveness and thinness and tend to look for romantic partners based on physical appearance more so than do girls. For adolescent boys, thinness is important in making a girl appear attractive and in deciding whether to go out with her or not. Obese girls, but not boys, are more likely to report no dating experience than their peers. These phenomena create indirect pressure on girls to be thin and increase the likelihood of body dissatisfaction.

It is remarkable how little information is available for boys, adolescents of color, and gay, lesbian, bisexual, and transgender (GLBT) students. Given the importance of romantic relationships in adolescence and adulthood, this is a serious oversight that limits our understanding of the role of romantic relationships in the development of body image.

Sociocultural Factors

Gender socialization

The gender differences in the nature, meaning, and development of body image raise the possibility that gender roles are instrumental in the development of body image. Very limited cross-sectional research suggests that among adolescent boys, masculinity may be related to the drive for muscularity. Boys who adopt masculine gender roles may find it particularly important to engage in muscle-building activities. Traditional measures of gender role adoption (e.g, the Bem Sex Roles Inventory) show only small relationships to body dissatisfaction among girls and women. However, there are data indicating that gendered 'lived experiences' of adolescent girls are indeed related to body image. Two lived experiences reflecting gendered roles and stereotypes have received particular attention: objectification and sexual harassment.

Objectification theory contends that cultural definitions of bodies differ by gender. The male body is culturally defined as active and agentic, while the female body is supposed to be passive and decorative. Adolescents have absorbed this message with data indicating that girls are more invested in the aesthetic of body image ("how I look") and boys in the functional components ("what can my body do"). Moreover, women's bodies are objectified and sexualized in the media and society. Peers and parents may also contribute to girls' awareness of their bodies' culturally defined roles as sexualized objects. There are rewards for girls and women who follow these dictates ranging from more dating to greater success at work.

According to objectification theory, these cultural pressures are internalized and lead girls to view themselves as objects to be evaluated on the basis of appearance. This objectified body consciousness is associated with self-surveillance, that is, the monitoring and preoccupation with evaluating observable body attributes. Heightened self-surveillance is associated in turn with body shame. These constructs are assessed using a new measure, The Adolescent Version of the Objectified Body Consciousness Self-Surveillance Scale (OBCA), which has three subscales: Surveillance, Body Shame, and Control.

Research indicates that, as the theory predicts, girls show higher levels of self-surveillance than boys do. This difference is evident by the fifth grade and intensifies during middle school. Furthermore, the correlation between self-surveillance and body shame is stronger in girls than in boys. However, when boys and men do experience objectification, self-surveillance, and body shame, the relationships among them are similar to those seen in girls and women. This similarity underscores the sociocultural roots of objectification and self-objectification and their impact on psychological processes.

Sexual harassment represents another lived experience that detracts from positive body esteem. Sexual harassment refers to unwanted, sexualized behaviors and comments by others that make one uncomfortable or fearful. Up to 90% of high school girls and boys report sexual harassment experience. Sexual harassment by peers of either gender predicts self-surveillance in both boys and girls. Furthermore, girls who perceive themselves as less typically feminine and less content with the feminine gender role are more likely to perceive themselves as victims of sexism, primarily from male peers. One possibility is that male peers who notice adolescent girls and boys who stray from the culturally defined path attempt to bring them back in line via sexual harassment and sexist comments about academics, sports, and gender orientation. Given the gendered nature of peer teasing and bullying, including that involving appearance, this issue deserves additional research.

Such experiences do affect behavior and attitudes. Compared to boys, girls report feeling more self-conscious and less confident following sexual harassment. Research further suggests that sexual harassment is more clearly associated with negative body image in girls than in boys, beginning in elementary school. Sexual harassment has been associated with increased body dissatisfaction in high school girls. These data are overwhelmingly cross-sectional and occasionally retrospective. Prospective data are needed to test these relationships.

Media

Adolescents use and are exposed to mass media with great regularity. Reports indicate that over 70% of girls from 9 to 14 years old and nearly as many boys read magazines at least once per month. Over three-quarters of girls report reading fashion and health/fitness magazines. Though boys rarely read such magazines, over a quarter of them read sports magazines which may feature the muscular ideal. In addition to reading magazines, the girls reported watching television 9.5 h per week while the boys watched over 12 h. Add in time surfing the Internet and playing video games, which also project gender stereotyped body shapes, and it is evident that the media have the opportunity to be a substantial influence. There is considerable evidence that the media portrayals of body shapes that adolescents view are narrow, stereotyped, and sexualized.

The exposure to media has an effect on body image as documented in several meta-analyses establishing a small to moderate effect size of media on body dissatisfaction and internalization of appearance ideals. Both longitudinal and experimental data indicate that media exposure is typically related to body image, especially among adolescent girls. In a 2-year longitudinal study, the more frequently Hispanic adolescent girls watched 'mainstream' television, the greater the drop in body image. In a naturalistic experiment, the introduction of Western television in a rural Fijian community was associated with increases in body image disparagement and weight and shape preoccupation among adolescent girls. Meta-analyses of experimental data indicate that girls under 18 years old are at least as affected by exposure to the thin ideal in media as are adult women.

At the same time, adolescents from ethnic minority groups may view these models as unrelated to them. For example, in a small study of Asian American middle and high school girls, there was no significant correlation between either the number of appearance magazines they routinely read or their investment in these magazines and body dissatisfaction scores.

Research concerning the relationship between media and body image among boys is more limited. A meta-analysis on the relationship reports significant but small effect sizes for both correlational and experimental research. These effect sizes for boys are somewhat smaller than those observed among girls and women. In the correlational studies, age is a significant moderator such that the effect was larger among older (early adulthood) than younger samples. Future research might examine why boys are less susceptible than men are; perhaps the boys recognize that extreme muscularity is partly unrealistic for pre- and peripubertal bodies. However, it is the case that investment in media is still associated with adolescent boys' body image and that efforts to understand the circumstances under which this influence is important should be continued.

Schools

Unlike appearance in the media which is typically viewed in two dimensions, appearance as part of the daily life at school is a three-dimensional, lived experience. Gender and age composition of the school, activity opportunities, and norms for inclusion are school-level factors associated with body image. Research on school-level characteristics related to body image is limited and focused on girls. The extant data suggest that girls in single-gender schools report higher levels of body dissatisfaction, perhaps reflecting an emphasis on achievement in such schools. Similarly, younger girls who come in contact with older adolescents at school are more likely to want to change their bodies. Schools that have more inclusive activities and are less cliquish are more likely to promote feelings of acceptance and weight satisfaction.

Schools are the context in which adolescents spend a good amount of time learning about and experiencing the meaning of appearance. Furthermore, schools have the potential to moderate the negative impact of societal messages about appearance and to promote more constructive peer experiences that can have a positive impact body image. In order to realize the potential of schools as contexts for positive body image development, more research is clearly needed that examines the impact of diverse structural, organizational, school climate, and demographic characteristics on body dissatisfaction.

Interventions

It should be clear by now that body image is an important issue. Poor body image contributes to a variety of diagnosable psychiatric disorders, including eating disorders, body dysmorphic disorder, and depression. Body dissatisfaction is also a factor in body change strategies including dieting which in turn contributes to obesity. Thus, body image is involved in adolescent health in a variety of ways. It is, therefore, important to prevent body image problems before they develop into disorders or health-threatening problems.

There are two general types of prevention that are especially relevant to a discussion of body image programs for adolescents. The first is universal prevention. In universal prevention, the program is aimed at large groups of healthy adolescents. There is no attempt to identify teens who might be at special risk for body image problems. These programs are often school-based. Some of them have been aimed at developing a *healthy* body image and healthy eating habits rather than simply at preventing disorders. They frequently focus on media literacy or ways in which to resist appearance pressure. Other prevention programs have adopted an ecological perspective and attempted to change the context such as appearance norms and expectations in schools where body image and eating problems thrive.

Many of the programs that have been tested are actually aimed at the prevention of eating disorders and include body image only as a component. Since participants in these programs often start out within in the normal range of body esteem or satisfaction, it is often difficult to demonstrate positive effects. Nonetheless, several of these programs have either successfully reduced body dissatisfaction or have prevented the typical middle school decline in body esteem. However, because of the emphasis on eating disorders and because researchers have underestimated the levels and consequences of body image problems among boys, most of the programs have been aimed only at girls.

The second type of prevention program is targeted at students who are identified as at risk for body image or related problems. Some researchers have argued that targeted programs, are the most effective and efficient type. Indeed, research often shows larger effect sizes for targeted than universal programs, though those for universal interventions are not negligible. Most notable among these are the dissonance-based and healthy weight intervention programs developed by Stice and his colleagues in 2006. These programs have been aimed primarily at high school and college age women. They need to be implemented and evaluated with middle school students.

The identification of risk factors for the development of body image and related problems is ongoing. That does not mean that prevention efforts should be delayed until there is a complete understanding of the developmental processes. Indeed, prevention programs can provide experimental data that help to identify risk and protective factors. Prevention programs have been shown to have some positive effects. It is, then, time to invest more resources into developing programs that might prevent either the development of body image problems or at least the negative outcomes of these body image problems for all adolescents. It is particularly time to design targeted programs for boys, ethnic minority teens, and young adolescents.

Summary

In this article, we have emphasized three major themes. First, body image concerns are a normative and prominent feature of adolescent development for both girls and boys as they integrate physical, psychological, and social changes into their self-conceptions and evaluations.

Second, body image concerns are highly gendered. Although developmental processes are similar for adolescent girls and boys, the ideal forms, the values, and the expectations in the relational and cultural contexts are tied to gender. Regardless of ethnic variations in the acceptance of diverse body types, adolescent girls are more likely to experience body dissatisfaction and sexualized objectification than boys.

Third, body image concerns reflect the interactions of the individual biological and psychological characteristics in relational and cultural contexts. Adolescents live in a world that sends powerful messages about the body. These messages are deeply rooted in cultural beliefs and media representations about what constitutes an ideal body, how important it is to achieve that body, and what means are acceptable to obtain the ideal body. The body ideal is conveyed to adolescents and reinforced by the parents, friends, peers, and (potential) romantic partners. When the external pressures and ideal expectations for appearance are internalized and when psychological energy is expended in appearance comparisons and surveillance, then adolescents are more likely to experience body image dissatisfaction

Although research on body image was initially focused on its relationship to the media and eating disorders among girls, there is now a broader understanding of the importance of body image as a developmental issue for adolescent girls and boys across race, ethnicity, and cultures and of the multiple factors that affect it. There is still much to be learned about the processes that shape body image and the intervention strategies that will promote more positive body image for all adolescents. Greater attention to the peer-relational contexts in school settings may be a productive way to attend to the norms and expectations at both relational and structural levels that make positive body image a challenge for too many adolescents. In addition, person-oriented approaches that more clearly distinguish between different developmental trajectories, their precursors and consequences could help to identify protective factors and improve the delivery of intervention programs.

See also: Gender Issues; Gender Roles; Media, Influence of; Overweight/Obesity; Peer Relations; Physical Attractiveness; Popularity and Social Status.

Further Reading

Cash TF and Smolak L (2011) *Body Image: A Handbook of Science, Practice, and Prevention*, 2nd edn. New York: Guilford.

Grabe S and Hyde JS (2006) Ethnicity and body dissatisfaction among women in the United States: A meta-analysis. *Psychological Bulletin* 132: 622–640.

Grabe S, Ward LM, and Hyde JS (2008) The role of the media in body image concerns among women: A meta-analysis of experimental and correlational studies. *Psychological Bulletin* 134: 460–476.

Jones DC (2004) Body image among adolescent girls and boys: A longitudinal study. *Developmental Psychology* 40: 823–835.

Paxton SJ (1999) Peer relations, body image, and disordered eating in adolescent girls: Implications for prevention. In: Piran N, Levine MP, and Steiner-Adair C (eds.) *Preventing Eating Disorders: A Handbook of Interventions and Special Challenges*. Philadelphia: Brunner/Mazel.

Ricciardelli LA, McCabe MP, Williams RJ, and Thompson JK (2007) The role of ethnicity and culture in body image and disordered eating among males. *Clinical Psychology Review* 27: 582–606.

Smolak L and Thompson JK (eds.) (2009) *Body Image, Eating Disorders, and Obesity in Youth: Assessment, Prevention, and Treatment*, 2nd edn. Washington, DC: American Psychological Association.

Stice E, Shaw H, Burton E, and Wade E (2006) Dissonance and healthy weight eating disorder prevention programs: A randomized efficacy trial. *Journal of Consulting and Clinical Psychology* 74: 263–275.

Brain Development

L P Spear, Binghamton University, Binghamton, NY, USA

Glossary

Amygdala: A complex subcortical region that is involved in the processing of social, emotional, and rewarding stimuli.

Brain networks: Interconnected and functionally interrelated brain regions that are sometimes widely dispersed throughout the brain.

Dopamine: A neurotransmitter substance that forms an important part of the brain reward system and that undergoes marked developmental change during adolescence.

Functional magnetic resonance imaging (fMRI): Use of scanning techniques for noninvasive assessment of regional patterns of brain activity during performance of a particular task relative to a baseline condition.

Myelination: A fatty material wrapped around axons of neurons that serves to speed information flow along the axons and to decrease the amount of energy required for this transmission.

Neurotransmitter: Chemical substances that are specialized for passing along information at synapses.

Prefrontal cortex (PFC): A slowly maturing area of the frontal cortex that projects widely throughout the brain and is thought to be critical for relatively advanced cognitive functions for which performance continues to improve during adolescence.

Synaptic pruning: A reduction in the number of synaptic connections between neurons that normally occurs during development and is thought to help refine neuronal connectivity.

Ventral striatum: A subcortical brain region that is thought to play a critical role in processing, learning about, and responding to rewards.

Introduction

Brain development is a lifelong process. Its development is most marked during the prenatal period when the embryonic precursors of the nervous system rapidly multiply, migrate, and begin to differentiate, forming a brain that at birth is similar in appearance and approaches 80% of the size of the adult brain. From that point onward, brain development had long been thought to consist largely of the gradual differentiation and refinement of connections with the continued cognitive development of the growing individual. Yet, studies conducted during the last several decades of the twentieth century, largely in laboratory animals, revealed that the trajectory of brain development changes notably during adolescence as the brain undergoes a variety of notable regressive and progressive transformations – developmental alterations that, from the limited human autopsy data available, also appeared to occur in human adolescents. Indeed, advances in imaging techniques, such as magnetic resonance imaging (MRI), that allow noninvasive imaging of youth without the use of radioactivity, have revealed compelling evidence that adolescence in humans, as in simple animal models of adolescence, is characterized by sometimes marked developmental transformations in the brain that ultimately serve to convert the relatively plastic, inefficient, and cognitively immature brain into a more efficient but seemingly less malleable adult version.

Brain Development and the Biological Roots of Adolescence

Numerous biological transformations are associated with adolescence. Major events include the physiological, hormonal, and brain changes associated with puberty – that is, the process of sexual maturation that occurs over a relatively restricted time frame, often early in adolescence. Adolescence is also characterized by other hormonal changes as well as a considerable growth spurt, along with both pubertally dependent and independent transformations in the brain. Many of these biological changes – and certain behavioral features as well – are not restricted to human adolescents, but are evident among organisms undergoing this transition from dependence on parental support to the relative independency of maturity in other species as well. In terms of the brain, not only did the basics of brain structure and function arise millions of years ago, but also the relative timing of development of these brain components across species. These across-species similarities in behavior and biology during adolescence suggest that adolescence as a developmental period has been conserved evolutionarily. The similarities provide reasonable face and construct validity for the judicious use of simple animal models of adolescence for study of adolescent brain features not amenable to analysis in human adolescents.

For instance, even with the improvements in MRI approaches that allow systematic structural and functional investigations of the developing human brain, the smallest unit of analysis in imaging studies (the voxel) typically contains millions of brain cells (neurons) and billions of connections (synapses) between them. Such complexity provides serious challenges for utilizing imaging studies to assess development of specific neural and synaptic systems at the molecular, cellular, and neurophysiological level. In contrast, these levels of analysis are more amenable to developmental study when using the invasive techniques available in laboratory animals, recognizing of course that other species lack the rich complexity of the human brain and hence only certain aspects of adolescent brain function can be modeled. Collectively, the rapid escalation of imaging studies of youth (and the limited human autopsy data available) along with the results of basic science studies conducted using simple animal models of adolescence are rapidly increasing our understanding of the adolescent brain.

Recognition of the functional importance of changes in the adolescent brain does not imply biodeterminism. Adolescence as a developmental phase is shaped by multiple forces – some of which are biological, whereas others are cultural, economic, and psychosocial. Distinctions between these types of influences are sometimes blurred, given the evidence that sociological, economic, and psychological factors bidirectionally influence and are influenced by the biology of adolescence. For example, not only do the physical changes of puberty influence how adolescents are perceived and treated by others, but conversely the timing of those physiological, hormonal, and brain changes are vulnerable to cultural/environmental and socioeconomic factors, ranging widely from whether the society is monogamous or polygamous or uses stressful initiation rituals, to nutritional status, level of exercise, and rearing conditions (e.g., whether the father or an unrelated male is present in the home). The nature of some of these neural transformations may even be dependent on the environment and experiences of the adolescent – signs of adolescent brain plasticity to be discussed later. Thus, although transformations in the adolescent brain play a critical role in influencing how adolescents think, feel, and behave, these neural alterations, in turn, are inexorably linked to, and influenced by the cultural, social, and economic environment.

Characteristic Developmental Transformations of the Adolescent Brain

The brain undergoes considerable developmental remodeling during adolescence. Changes seen are both progressive and regressive, and have a magnitude and timing that is regionally specific. A few of the major types of transformations occurring in the brain during adolescence will be described first before focusing more specifically on maturational changes within several critical target regions of the adolescent brain.

Refinement of Connectivity: Synaptic Pruning

During development, many more connections (synapses) are formed among neurons than ultimately will be maintained. The general developmental principle appears to be that specificity in neuronal connections is obtained via producing large numbers of synaptic connections, followed by eliminating ('pruning') those synapses that do not develop effective connections, while retaining those that do. This process of synaptic overproduction followed by pruning is very prevalent in the nervous system of neonates and infants and has long been thought to represent a form of developmental plasticity by which brain connections are matched to the need and to the characteristics of the environment. Production of new synapses and synaptic pruning generally continues at a much slower pace thereafter, throughout the remainder of life. This pruning is highly selective and is more pronounced in the outer layers of the brain (neocortex) than in regions underneath (subcortical regions). Within the neocortex, pruning occurs early in life in sensory and motor regions of the cortex (that receive sensory input and process motor information), but is generally delayed until adolescence within cortical regions that process information from (and send outputs to) a diversity of cortical and subcortical regions – the so-called association cortex. Such pruning can be marked during adolescence, with a loss of almost half of the synaptic connections at this time in some regions of the association cortex in the primate brain. This culling is generally more pronounced for synapses where chemicals passing along excitatory information are released (especially the major excitatory neurotransmitter in the brain, glutamate) than at synapses releasing inhibitory neurotransmitters (such as the major inhibitory neurotransmitter in the brain, GABA). While the ultimate significance of this regressive loss of synapses during adolescence remains somewhat speculative, such pruning is thought to contribute to the fine-tuning of brain connections necessary for the emergence of adult-typical networks of brain activity, along with perhaps providing an additional opportunity for the brain to be sculpted by the environment.

Speeding up of Information Flow: Myelination

Information is transmitted over relatively long distances in the nervous system via the passage of electrical impulses from the cell body of neurons along extensions of neurons called axons, with these impulses eventually providing the cue for neurotransmitter release when the terminals of these axons make synaptic connections with other neurons. The speed of the flow of electrical information along the length of an axon can be markedly enhanced by insulating ('myelinating') the axon. Via this process, nonneural brain support cells (glia) wrap many layers of a fatty membrane cover around axons, insulating them so that electrical impulses are conducted down their length much faster than when the axons are unmyelinated. This is important because when neurons integrate the information they receive, the input received first generally has a greater impact than the input that is more delayed in its arrival. Although myelination begins very early in life and continues into adulthood, there is an escalation of this process during adolescence, with relatively long axons interconnecting distant brain regions particularly targeted. As a result, there is an increase during adolescence in the speed with which input is received from distant regions relative to more local, unmyelinated connections. Such selective myelination could provide one way by which the relative influence of input from more distant regions may increase within networks of functionally interconnected brain regions during adolescence.

Increase in Energy Efficiency

The young brain of preschoolers and children requires more energy to function than at any other time in the life span. Hence, more blood flow and nutrients need to be directed to the brain of the child, with for instance glucose utilization rates more than twice that seen in infancy or in adulthood. These high utilization rates decline during late childhood/early adolescence to eventually reach the lower rates typical of the mature brain. This marked decline in brain energy needs appears driven in part by processes of synaptic pruning and myelination. Maintaining synapses is energetically costly, primarily because of the energy needed to restore baseline brain chemistry following message-conveying synaptic activity. Thus, the overall decline in the number of synaptic connections during adolescence would be expected to reduce brain energy needs. Substantial amounts of energy are also needed to restore baseline levels of ionic balance across membranes following electrical transmission down axons, with unmyelinated axons being particularly costly in this regard. Hence, the increasing proportion of myelinated axons would also lower brain energy needs. There may be other contributors to the increase in brain efficiency during adolescence as well. For instance, as discussed later, adolescence is associated with changes in the number of brain regions recruited during the performance of particular tasks to the extent that fewer neurons are recruited for a given task across age; brain energy needs associated with that task would likewise be expected to decline.

Network Development

The process of brain development is beginning to be viewed less as a developmental parade of specific brain regions coming on-line at different ages, and more as a dynamic process of emerging regional activities that interact and influence other brain regions, resulting in networks of brain regions whose activities become more strongly interrelated over time. Although little is yet known of the precise processes underlying network formation, the coordination of activities among functionally related but spatially distant regions is likely aided by maturation and myelination of the long axonal tracts that interconnect such distant regions as well as perhaps by pruning of network-inappropriate connections. Viewing brain development as an emergence of networks of brain regions that influence, compete, and interact with one another provides a more nuanced view of the developmental process than simply trying to relate a given adolescent-typical behavior pattern to the immaturity of a particular brain region.

Regional Differences in Brain Development

The relative timing of developmental transformations in the brain is regionally specific. Developmental changes tend to occur much early (i.e., during childhood) in cortical and deeper (subcortical) brain regions located toward the back of the brain that subserve basic functions (such as the processing of sensory stimuli and motor responses) than in cortical (frontal and prefrontal) and subcortical regions in the front of the brain (forebrain) whose development continues through adolescence. Regional differences in brain development can be examined in a number of ways. One approach is to use structural MRI to compare either size (volumes) of different brain regions during development, or the ratio of 'gray matter' (areas that appear gray in unstained tissue and are enriched in cell bodies and their connections) to 'white matter' (areas enriched in axonal tracts, many of which are myelinated and appear white in unstained tissue because of the high fat content of myelin). The volume of gray matter in the cortex generally increases to reach a plateau and declines moderately thereafter, with the increases in white matter volumes associated with continued myelination of axonal tracts. These gray matter declines often occur prior to adolescence in sensory and motor regions, but emerge during adolescence in the prefrontal cortex (PFC) and other cortical regions thought to be critical for cognitive functions that continue to strengthen during adolescence. Changes in gray matter volumes during adolescence are also seen in some subcortical regions as well, although typically, these changes are more modest than those seen cortically, and are characterized both by declines in gray matter in some regions and increases in others.

Diffusion tensor imaging (DTI) is another MRI technique that uses speed and directionality of water diffusion (which is greater along axon tracts – especially myelinated tracts – than across them) to examine properties of white matter presumed to be related to white matter efficiency and myelin integrity. DTI has shown that the increases in white matter seen during adolescence with structural MRI are often associated with developmental increases in myelin integrity in those regions as well.

Using both structural imaging and DTI data, a number of studies have revealed significant associations between changes in regional brain volumes or myelin integrity and adolescent cognitive and behavioral function. Another strategy to examine the functional significance of adolescent brain changes has been the use of functional MRI (fMRI). This imaging technique uses blood-oxygen-level-dependent (BOLD) signals to assess changes in regional blood flow during performance of a target task relative to a control task or baseline conditions, and is based on the principle that regions of elevated brain activity require greater blood flow to provide the energy needs to power that activity. With rapid improvements in imaging technology and strategies to design cognitive tasks suitable for use within the tight physical constraints of scanners, developmental fMRI studies began to escalate rapidly around the start of this century. They have revealed notable differences in regional activation patterns among children, adolescents, and adults during performance of a variety of cognitive tasks, as reviewed in the sections to follow.

Amygdala and Other Regions Involved in Emotional Processing

Emotionally arousing stimuli increase activity in brain regions such as the amygdala that are critical for responding to, learning about, and remembering affective, socioemotional, and stressful stimuli. Numerous fMRI studies have found that the amygdala of adolescents often responds differently to emotional stimuli, such as fearful faces, from the amygdala of adults. The nature of those age differences differs across studies, however, with reports of greater amygdala activation in response to such socioemotional stimuli in adolescents than adults in some but not all studies. This variability is likely due in part to the complexity of the different subregions that collectively comprise the amygdala complex, and the varying functions they subsume. Signs of greater amygdala activation to emotional stimuli during adolescence under some test circumstances may be linked to increased emotional reactivity, with several studies showing that increased amygdala activation to emotional stimuli is correlated with poorer affect-relevant performance during development. Although such correlations do not necessarily reflect causal associations, these findings are reminiscent of other evidence that, although adolescents under low stress/emotional circumstances may exhibit adult-typical levels of rational decision-making (so-called 'cold cognitions'), their decision-making tends to degrade under emotional, exciting, or stressful circumstances ('hot cognitions') more so than that of adults.

Adolescents may also vary from adults in their physiological reactions to emotional stimuli and in the cues about their emotional state that they derive from these physiological reactions. Stimuli with emotional or stressful content are often associated with bodily (somatic) reactions that include release of stress hormones, as well as alterations in heart rate, blood pressure, and respiratory rate associated with activation of the autonomic nervous system (ANS); these somatic signs may not only be a consequence of emotional reactions, but also to some extent may be used as cues to determine one's emotional state. Although work in this area to date is limited, some evidence has emerged that puberty/early adolescence may be associated with an increase in ANS and stress hormone reactions to emotional and stressful stimuli. Yet, at the same time, these exaggerated somatic signs may not be as strongly linked to perceived emotional expression in adolescents as in adults.

Thus, the data currently available suggest that under some circumstances, adolescents tend to be hyperreactive in their response to emotional stimuli at the level of the amygdala and perhaps in their bodily reactions to emotional stimuli relative to adults. Such immaturities in emotional processing may be one factor contributing to the greater propensity of adolescents to engage in 'hot cognitions' under emotionally stimulating and arousing conditions, increasing their propensity to engage in risky behaviors.

Reward Neurocircuitry

Rewarding stimuli of all types – ranging from positive social interactions, tasty food, and novel and exciting stimuli to drugs of abuse – all tap into phylogenetically ancient reward circuitry in the brain playing necessary roles for survival in seeking out, obtaining, and 'consuming' natural rewards. Marked transformations have been seen in this reward circuitry during adolescence in both basic science studies and human imaging work.

One important component of the reward system that undergoes considerable transformation during adolescence is the dopamine (DA) neurotransmitter system. Cell bodies of neurons that utilize DA as a neurotransmitter are found deep are the back of the brain and send axonal projections to forebrain areas that contain receptors to sense DA, including the critical, reward-related region of the nucleus accumbens (also called the ventral striatum), along with other interconnected regions such as the dorsal striatum, hippocampus, amygdala, and prefrontal cortex. The relative balance of DA receptors across these brain regions changes considerably during adolescence, with losses of up to 20–50% of the DA receptors during adolescence in some of these regions (ventral and dorsal striatum) but not others. General levels of overall DA activity also change markedly during adolescence, with 2–7-fold alterations in DA activity (DA'tone') seen during adolescence in some of these regions as well. There is still considerable controversy as to the precise role of these various components of the DA system in reward-relevant responding in the adult, let alone the significance of these adolescent-associated DA changes for the adolescent. Yet, given the marked transformations seen in this reward circuitry during the adolescent period, it would be remarkable if adolescents did not differ from those at other ages in the way they respond to rewards.

Consistent with this expectation, fMRI evidence is mounting that the adolescent brain processes rewarding (and aversive) stimuli differently than does the mature brain. The strongest evidence to date is for adolescents to show greater activation of the ventral striatum than adults when they prepare to make a response (in a laboratory experimental task) that will lead to a reward, or in response to receipt of the reward, especially when the reward is of relatively large magnitude. Such elevated activations are not always evident during adolescence, however, and may be influenced by a number of factors. The nature of the control task used to assess task-specific activation is critical. Characteristics of the target task are also undoubtedly influential, including whether reward receipt is automatic, probabilistic (as in a gambling task), or predicated on a correct response. Properties of the reward are also likely significant, including the magnitude of the reward and whether it varies across trials, as well as whether punishment is received on nonreward trials. For instance, in contrast to the enhanced neural activation of ventral striatum that is sometimes seen when adolescents process rewards of relatively large magnitude, adolescents sometimes show attenuated activation relative to more mature individuals in the ventral striatum when receiving small rewards, and in the amygdala when receiving a punishment. These findings are reminiscent of behavioral data showing young adolescents to be more sensitive to rewards and less sensitive to punishment than their older counterparts, a point to be revisited later.

The exaggerated patterns of ventral striatal activation adolescents sometimes show during *receipt* of rewards – for example, more BOLD activation to large magnitude rewards than older individuals but perhaps weaker responses to small rewards – vary from the attenuated ventral striatal response that adolescents have sometimes been shown to exhibit when *anticipating* or assessing possible reward-relevant cues. Taken together, the fMRI data available to date in this very active area of research suggest that, relative to the mature brain, adolescent reward neurocircuitry may be both underactive and overactive – depending on the task used, the nature of the reward and the context in which it is received, and what portion of the processing of rewards is being assessed. These fMRI data, like the studies of the DA system discussed earlier, emphasize the complexities of the changes in the reward system seen during adolescence, and the challenges that emerge when trying to derive simple conclusions relating age differences in brain reward processing to reward-related behaviors of the adolescent. What is clear is that the adolescent brain processes rewarding stimuli quite differently than does the mature brain. What remains to be clarified are the specific contingencies underlying these age-specific alterations and what these findings signify for understanding specific adolescent behaviors.

Prefrontal Cortex and Behavioral Control

The ability to exert inhibitory control over one's behavior, although present in young children to some extent, continues to mature through adolescence, and is thought to be one of a number of executive functions associated in part with activity in PFC and other regions of the frontal cortex. Careful neuroanatomical investigations have shown that these regions undergo considerable refinement and development during adolescence. DA input to PFC rises to a peak throughout adolescence, along with notable culling of both excitatory glutamate and inhibitory GABA synapses there, resulting in marked maturational changes in levels of neural activity and tuning sensitivity of the PFC to different types of input during adolescence. Myelination of axons projecting from PFC to other regions likely contributes to the increasing influence and network involvement of the PFC on other regions. These marked developmental alterations are thought to contribute to the improvements seen during adolescence in behavioral performance on tasks involving executive function.

The amount of focal activation deep within the PFC (i.e., in ventral PFC) has been found to increase with age when adolescents perform tasks involving response inhibition or risky decision-making, with greater activation in these ventral regions on trials when responding was successfully withheld. In contrast to the lower levels of focal activation in ventral PFC that young adolescents often exhibit during risk taking and response inhibition tasks, greater activation is seen rather diffusely across other regions of PFC and frontal cortex. Thus, maturation of behavioral control has sometimes been viewed as a shift from a pattern of broader and more diffuse activation in frontal regions to greater regionally-specific activation, with such regional shifts being particularly pronounced in PFC. Such a developmental shift from diffuse to focal activation could be related, at least in part, to age differences in task difficulty, with for instance broader activation patterns, perhaps reflecting greater effort necessary to perform the task at younger ages. However, in some circumstances, diffusely activated regions showing age-related activity declines were found to be unrelated to task performance, suggesting that the diffuse activation seen early in adolescence may reflect inefficiencies in neural recruitment rather than greater task difficulty and effort. Yet another possibility is that age differences in brain activation patterns may reflect differences in the cognitive strategies used to perform the tasks, and hence in the brain regions engaged when using these cognitive strategies.

Developmental Discontinuities in Brain Development: 'Bottom-Up' versus 'Top-Down' Systems and Puberty

In one sense, brain development can be characterized as developmental interweaving of maturing brain regions with separable developmental time-lines. In some instances, brain regions may exhibit activation patterns even early in adolescence that are somewhat reminiscent of those of adults, exemplified in the discussion thus far by the amygdala as a component of the socioemotional/affective system and by the ventral striatal component of the reward system. Yet, it should not simply be concluded that these systems are 'early maturing,' in that the activation patterns seen in these regions to highly engaging stimuli during adolescence are often different and sometimes exaggerated relative to that seen at maturity. While some researchers have emphasized the importance of one or other of these early appearing systems for behavior of the adolescent, these systems exhibit a number of anatomical and functional interrelationships, with for instance receipt or omission of rewards often having an emotional impact, and emotional context likewise having the potential to influence the salience of rewarding stimuli. Both systems are also stress-reactive, with stressors often elevating activity in amygdala and nucleus accumbens, while suppressing levels of functional activity in the PFC.

In counterpoint to these early appearing, stress-sensitive, and sometimes developmentally hyperreactive neural systems, research in brain development has also highlighted regions whose activity and influence continue to emerge during adolescence. Included are frontal cortical control regions such as the ventral PFC where, as discussed previously, focal activation during response inhibition tasks continues to build during adolescence. The PFC is well-positioned to influence a wide variety of regions, with widespread anatomic connections to other cortical areas and numerous subcortical regions as well, including DA cell body areas as well as key regions within the reward (e.g., nucleus accumbens) and socio/emotional (e.g., amygdala) systems. Synaptic pruning and refinements in synaptic functioning are pronounced in frontal regions, as are myelination of axonal tracts interconnecting this area with other regions. The resulting rewiring and refinement of PFC neural circuitry is thought to facilitate maturation of its role in executive functioning in part via an increasing influence of PFC on other regions.

One way of expressing such regional differences in brain development has been to view adolescent brain function as a developmental dissociation between the emergence early in adolescence of one or more 'bottom-up' systems that exhibit sometimes exaggerated reactivity to emotional and/or rewarding stimuli, and the progressively greater involvement of more 'top-down' cognitive control from the PFC and other regions of the frontal cortex. According to this perspective, exaggerated patterns of reactivity in early emerging 'bottom-up' regions could reflect not only developmental transitions in DA activity and other neural transformations within these reward- and affective-related regions as discussed earlier, but also relatively unconstrained activity within these 'bottom-up' systems in the absence of sufficient 'top-down' control. With the gradual maturation of networks involving 'top-down' control, activity in 'bottom-up' systems may be gradually more modulated during development, resulting in inverted U-shaped patterns over time in response to rewarding and emotional cues characterized by intensified responding to rewards and emotional stimuli that peaks during mid-adolescence at levels greater than that seen at younger or older ages.

Given the timing of expression of 'bottom-up' versus 'top-down' systems, researchers began to reason that expression of early emerging, 'bottom-up' affect and/or reward systems might be in part triggered by rises in sex hormones at the time of puberty, whereas the later maturation of 'top-down' control regions may be unrelated to pubertal processes. Indeed, there is anatomical evidence that 'bottom-up' affect and reward systems are influenced by sex hormones such as estrogen and testosterone, with receptors for these hormones found in portions of the amygdala and nucleus accumbens, as well as on DA neurons themselves. In support of a possible role of pubertal hormones in the emergence of 'bottom-up' systems, an increasing number of studies have found significant correlations between pubertal status and various adolescent-typical behaviors, including sensation seeking, alcohol/drug use, and other risky behaviors. Data linking pubertal hormones with developmental changes in affect and reward systems are beginning to emerge, and are active areas of current study.

Functional Implications of Adolescent Brain Development

The developmental transformations occurring in the brain during adolescence ultimately transform the immature brain into a more efficient mature brain that supports adult-typical neural and behavioral function. These developmental transformations may have other consequences as well, which are also outlined subsequently.

Development of Cognitive Skills

Adolescence is characterized by continued improvements in the speed of information processing and performance on tasks viewed to tap various 'executive functions' such as working memory, decision-making, attentional control, and response inhibition. As exemplified earlier in the discussion of studies of fMRI during cognitive control tasks, developmental studies have often found different brain regions to be activated during the performance of a given cognitive task in children, adolescents and adults, with the development of more efficient cognitive functions sometimes viewed as a shift from inefficient task-associated activation of diffuse neural systems to more regionally-specific activation patterns, along with the emergence of 'top-down' control mechanisms. The specific brain regions that show developmental increases (or decreases) in task-related activation during adolescence vary somewhat across studies, perhaps in part to the cognitive demands of each task. As outlined earlier, activity in the ventral portions of the PFC tends to become more focal with development during the performance of response inhibition tasks, whereas increases in focal activation of other portions of the PFC (e.g., dorsolateral PFC) and related cortical regions (such as the anterior cingulate cortex), have been reported during a variety of other executive function tasks. Maturational increases in task-related activation in PFC and other frontal regions have also been associated with elevations in coordinated network activity, as differing networks that function collaboratively with these frontal areas gain in strength, weaken, and incorporate different component brain regions during adolescence. There is, however, no overriding consensus as to the precise brain regions and associated networks linked to improvement in specific cognitive capabilities during adolescence, with specific regional activation patterns likely not only influenced by the type of task, but also its difficulty, the test context, and the control task used to establish baseline levels of brain activation from which task-specific activation is derived. Affective and attentional states of the individual are likely influential as well.

Puberty and the Attainment of Sexual Maturation

Puberty is critically associated with adolescent brain development in two ways. On the one hand, portions of the developing brain are responsible for triggering the pubertal process of sexual maturation via initiating a cascade of hormone release that ultimately results in increases in gonadal hormones (e.g., testosterone released from the testes in males; estrogen and progesterone released by the ovaries and uterus in females). The rising levels of these gonadal hormones in turn contribute to the physiological changes of puberty, including the development of secondary sexual characteristics (e.g., breast development in females, deepening of the voice in males, genital hair development). These hormones also stimulate estrogen and testosterone receptors in a variety of brain regions, influencing brain function and behavior, and perhaps stimulating maturational changes in those brain regions. Thus, there appears to be reciprocal, bidirectional interrelationships between pubertal hormone release and adolescent brain development.

Gonadal hormone release is the endpoint of a hormonal cascade that (1) begins with the release of the hormone, gonadotropin-releasing hormone (GnRH), deep within the brain in a region called the hypothalamus, with (2) GnRH in turn stimulating the pituitary gland to release gonadotropin hormones into the blood, and (3) these gonadotropins circulating through the bloodstream to reach the gonads (testes and ovaries) where they in turn stimulate the release of gonadal hormones such as testosterone and estrogen. Collectively, this three-tiered hormonal cascade is termed the hypothalamic–pituitary–gonadal (HPG) axis. The rise in activity of the HPG axis at puberty is actually the second developmental period during which notable increases in activity of this axis are seen. The first is seen prior to and for some time after birth, when high levels of gonadal hormones serve to channel differentiation of the brain (and sex organs) into a male-typical pattern, whereas low levels of these hormones result in female-typical differentiation patterns, thereby creating the subtle sex differences seen in the brain in terms of the size of certain brain regions, number of synapses, number of receptors for hormones and neurotransmitters, and so on. After this critical period of brain sexual differentiation, the HPG axis becomes relatively quiescent until its activity is reinstated at the onset of puberty – a rise in HPG activity that often occurs earlier in females than in males.

Exciting progress has been made in determining how the brain triggers the reactivation of the HPG axis at the onset of puberty. An important component of the trigger appears to be a group of small neurotransmitter-like substances called 'kisspeptins' and their receptors in the hypothalamus. Neurons that release kisspeptin have receptors for the fat hormone, leptin. Leptin rises in females as they approach puberty, stimulating the kisspeptin system and presumably signaling that the body contains sufficient fat stores to support a pregnancy and lactation. This is likely the mechanism by which body weight and amount of body fat is associated with puberty (especially in females) across a variety of species, with pubertal timing delayed in girls who are anorexic or engaged in sports encouraging low levels of body fat (e.g., ballet, gymnastics). Pubertal timing has been shown to be of significance for a number of behavioral outcomes, with for instance early puberty associated with an increase in a variety of adverse outcomes in both boys and girls, including early alcohol/drug use and more risky drinking, early and risky sexual activities, and elevations in delinquency.

Traditionally, sex differences in the brain were thought to be induced solely by 'organizational' effects of the presence or absence of gonadal hormones early in life, whereas the rise to adult levels of gonadal hormones at puberty was thought to merely serve an 'activational' role, stimulating latent sex differences in the brain that were established early in life. There is emerging evidence from basic science studies, though, that the developing brain in some instances may remain sensitive to organizational influences of these gonadal hormones through adolescence. Extension of organizational influences into adolescence raises the possibility that pubertal increases in gonadal hormones may not only activate those sex differences in the brain established early in life, but may also exert additional organizational influences, adding to the sex differences already present in the brain to produce the final sex-specific brain differentiation needed to support sexually dimorphic behaviors. Indeed, in human MRI studies correlating brain structure with pubertal development, the stage of puberty has been found to account for a modest amount of the variance in size of brain regions such as the amygdala and certain cortical areas. Likewise, the stage of pubertal development has also been correlated with a variety of behaviors as well, including not only expected rises in sexual activity and interests, but also shifts toward later sleep onset, and increases in risk taking and sensation seeking. It should be kept in mind, though, that causality cannot be determined from such correlational analyses, and that findings of reliable relationships between pubertal status and neurobehavioral function are not always evident, even during the early adolescent period where marked differences in pubertal status may be seen among individuals of the same chronological age.

Relationship to Adolescent-Typical Behavior Patterns

Changes occurring in adolescent brain not only serve as the substrate for the emergence of adult-typical functions, but also must support age-typical behaviors of the adolescent as well. As reviewed earlier, during adolescence, there are marked changes in brain reward systems, in regions processing socioemotional stimuli, in neurocircuitry critical for 'top-down' control of these regions from PFC and other forebrain regions, and in the balance of DA modulatory input to all of these areas. Given the ongoing, evolutionarily conserved neural changes in these regions, adolescents would be expected to differ from children and adults in the ways they respond to rewarding stimuli, including natural rewards such as food, social stimuli, and even novelty. For instance, in terms of food intake, adolescents across a variety of species, including humans, have the highest caloric intake relative to their body weights than at any time in the life span (ignoring here pressures for dieting among female adolescents in some cultures). This increased food intake is in part associated with the substantial caloric demands of the growth spurt of adolescence, and may be facilitated by adolescent-associated changes in brain reward systems.

Social interactions and affiliations with peers also take on increasing importance during adolescence in many species. The neural changes supporting increases in peer-directed social interactions are thought to have been conserved across species because of the adaptive functions served by this peer-directed focus – functions such as easing the transition to independence away from the family, guiding choice behavior, supporting the development of sexual activity and interests, along with providing the opportunity to practice and model other adult-typical behavior patterns.

Human adolescents and their counterparts in other species also exhibit increases in a group of related behaviors varyingly termed risk taking, novelty seeking, and sensation seeking. These behaviors are particularly prominent in adolescent males and have been speculated to serve a number of important adaptive functions that outweigh the transient age-related increase in death rates associated with these risky behaviors across a variety of species. Potential benefits of adolescent risk taking include fostering peer acceptance, enhancing the probability of reproductive success, and aiding in the process of emigration of young adolescents away from the home territory around the time of reproductive maturity, thereby avoiding the adverse consequences of inbreeding (i.e., mating with those with which they are genetically related). Indeed, generally among mammalian species (including our human ancestors), males, or less frequently, females, or both sexes, leave the natal area and enter novel, challenging, and potentially risky new areas around the time that they begin to become sexually mature. Brain changes supporting increased risk-taking and novelty-seeking behaviors during adolescence seemingly have been maintained across species, because the overall adaptive benefits of risk taking outweigh the considerable costs of this behavior for individual adolescents.

Adolescent Reward Systems: Potential Implications for Adolescent Alcohol/Drug Use and Abuse

In addition to mediating age-typical behaviors of adolescents and setting the stage for the emergence of mature neurobehavioral functions, transformations occurring in the adolescent brain may have a number of ancillary consequences, including the propensity of adolescents to use and sometimes abuse alcohol and other drugs. Alcohol and other drugs of potential abuse activate the same reward systems activated by natural rewards, such as food, fluids, social and sexual stimuli, novelty, and so on, with repeated high levels of exposure to drugs thought to 'hijack' these reward systems, resulting in the compulsive drug use associated with dependence. Given the marked developmental transformations occurring in these reward systems as discussed earlier, it might be expected that adolescents would not only vary from other aged individuals in their sensitivity to food, social reward, and novel stimuli, but also to the rewarding properties of alcohol and other drugs.

As discussed earlier in the section on 'Reward neurocircuitry,' fMRI studies have shown adolescents to sometimes show exaggerated/intensified neural (ventral striatum) response to receipt of rewarding stimuli, but an attenuated neural (amygdala) response to punishment. These findings are reminiscent of other data from studies in humans and laboratory animals showing adolescents to be more responsive to positive rewards and sometimes less sensitive to punishment than adults. In these basic science studies, adolescents were found to be more sensitive than adults not only to the positively rewarding effects of social peers and novelty, but to the rewarding effects of drugs such as cocaine, nicotine, and alcohol as well. Conversely, adolescent animals were found to be less sensitive than adults to a variety of aversive stimuli, including the aversive effects of these same drugs.

Adolescents vary from adults not only in their sensitivity to the rewarding and aversive effects of alcohol, but in their sensitivity to other alcohol effects as well. Although ethical concerns prohibit administration of alcohol to youth in controlled human studies, studies using a simple animal model of adolescence have found adolescents to be more sensitive not only to positive rewarding effects of alcohol/drugs, but also to the facilitation of social behavior seen at low doses of alcohol as well as to acute alcohol-related disruptions in brain plasticity and memory. In contrast, similar studies in laboratory animals have found adolescents to be less sensitive than adults not only to the aversive effects of alcohol and other drugs, but also to many of the intoxicating effects of higher doses of alcohol that are normally thought to serve as cues to moderate intake, including alcohol-related sedation, social impairment, and motor incapacities, along with even some 'hangover' effects.

Developmental transformations in the brain leading to an adolescent-associated insensitivity to feedback cues that would normally moderate intake could contribute to the relatively high alcohol consumption levels characteristic of this developmental stage, with per episode alcohol intakes averaging 2–3-fold higher in adolescence than in adulthood across a variety of species. Such developmental insensitivities to alcohol may be further exacerbated by additional insensitivities to alcohol associated with genetic and environmental factors. Collectively, these insensitivities may promote sufficiently high levels of alcohol exposure among vulnerable adolescents to result in a pattern of escalating alcohol use and a trajectory toward problematic use and dependence. Indeed, insensitivity to alcohol intoxication is a known risk factor for development of alcohol use disorders, presumably via increasing the propensity to drink large amounts of alcohol, thereby elevating the alcohol burden to which the brain is exposed repeatedly and increasing the likelihood of long-lasting neurotoxicity.

Relationship to Developmental Alterations in Prevalence of Psychological Disorders

During adolescence, the incidence of a number of psychological disorders increases, including anxiety disorders, depression, externalizing disorders such as conduct disorder (CD), eating disorders, and substance abuse disorders. Psychological symptoms leading to diagnoses of schizophrenia also often increase during late adolescence to early adulthood. Contributors to the rise in these disorders are undoubtedly multifactorial, and are, to some extent, disorder-specific, although comorbidity is common. Among the many potential contributing factors to the rise in psychopathology during adolescence are stressors and other environmental changes, developmental increases in gonadal hormones, and age-related differences in gene expression – all of which ultimately interact with ongoing development of the adolescent brain.

Developmental increases in the number of stressors to which youth are exposed may combine with increases in hormonal and neural reactivity to stressors early in adolescence (see earlier discussion), perhaps triggering the onset of psychological disorders among individuals who enter adolescence at greater vulnerability for these disorders. Both higher-than-normal and atypically low stress hormone levels have been associated with particular psychological disorders, with levels often unusually low in youth with externalizing disorders, but elevated among those individuals diagnosed with schizophrenia, anxiety, and (under some circumstances) depression. Rises in gonadal hormones associated with puberty may contribute to the increasing incidence in psychological disorders during adolescence, particularly for psychological disorders, such as depression, where notable sex differences in incidence emerge postpubertally. Sex-specific rises in gonadal hormones may trigger developmental changes in the brain that influence sensitivity to stressors, unmask previously latent neural vulnerabilities, or alter gene expression in critical brain regions. Indeed, gene expression changes developmentally, with evidence for stronger genetic influences on certain psychological disorders among postpubertal than prepubertal individuals. Genetic-based vulnerabilities are only evident when that gene is normally expressed during development, raising the possibility that adverse consequences of some genes conferring enhanced susceptibility to one or more psychological disorders may only begin to be detectable with developmental increases in expression of those genes during adolescence.

Ultimately, all of these influences interact with the remodeling of the brain during adolescence to alter the propensity for the emergence of psychological disorders during adolescence. The synaptic pruning and shifts in functional balance across brain regions occurring during adolescence may uncover latent neural vulnerabilities previously induced by expression of variant genes or early life exposure to adverse environmental conditions/stressors. Regionally specific alterations in gray matter volume, altered myelin integrity, and changes in synaptic signaling have been reported in the brains of youth who develop various psychological disorders, along with changes in regional fMRI activation patterns to emotional/cognitive stimuli. It is too early to see the emergence of consistent patterns in this work. Some of the neural changes reported may represent alterations in the pacing of developmental changes whose expression may wax and wane over time, perhaps as influenced by the impact of various aversive or positive experiences on the dynamically transforming adolescent brain.

The Adolescent Brain and Brain Plasticity

Development of the brain is sensitive to experience, with the result that the developing brain is customized, to some extent, to the environmental circumstances faced by the organism early in life. This 'developmental programming' of the brain has been well documented during the fetal and early postnatal periods, with the magnitude of the plasticity seen during these critical periods notably greater than the general experience/learning-related plasticity that continues throughout life. There is emerging evidence that such developmental programming may continue, to some extent, into adolescence, with this age period serving as a critical period for experience-related plasticity – especially in areas of the brain and pathway connections that undergo notable maturational change in adolescence.

For instance, the process of myelination appears to be in part experience-dependent. Basic science studies have shown that electrical activity associated with propagating nerve impulses down the axons induces release of chemical substances from the axons that can serve to stimulate nearby glial support cells to myelinate them. Indirect evidence for experience-dependent myelination is seen in DTI work showing that individuals skilled in particular tasks (e.g., professional musicians) show greater myelin integrity in performance-relevant axonal tracts, with the amount of practice in youth but not later in adulthood most predictive of the extent of these changes. Although it is important to remember that causal associations cannot be inferred from correlational studies of this nature, somewhat reminiscent findings have been seen in basic science experiments, with laboratory animals housed in enriched environments through adolescence having a larger corpus callosum, the huge bundle of largely myelinated fibers connecting the two sides of cortex, than animals housed in nonenriched environments.

Plasticity also occurs at the synaptic level. Environmentally-induced plasticity occurring during the early postnatal period in sensory regions of the cortex such as visual cortex has been shown to involve both synaptic pruning and the formation of new synapses, processes that are also seen during adolescence in frontal regions involved in executive control functions and that diminish in prevalence thereafter. In several respects, the adolescent brain appears more malleable than the adult brain. In cultures of brain tissue, axonal (presynaptic) endings from adolescent animals have been shown to extend and retract in a matter of minutes, processes that occur much more frequently and at a substantially faster pace than with axonal endings from adult animals. Moreover, although the vast majority of neurons are formed early in life, some new neurons continue to be produced from small clusters of stem cells in the brain and are thought to facilitate plasticity in certain regions (e.g., cortex; hippocampus) throughout life; this rate of new neuron formation is 4–5 times higher during adolescence than in adulthood.

From these types of studies, the evidence is beginning to mount that developmental neuroplasticity is retained into adolescence, perhaps especially in brain regions and axonal tracts normally undergoing maturational change during adolescence. Such residual plasticity could permit adolescent experiences to customize the maturing brain in ways that are not evident when similar experiences occur in adulthood. Such customization could confer not only long-lasting benefits from particular adolescent experiences, but also vulnerabilities from other experiences. Of particular concern are potential lasting consequences of the use of alcohol, nicotine, and other drugs of abuse during adolescence. It is well established that the earlier individuals begin using alcohol or other drugs, the greater the probability of developing lasting abuse/dependence disorders. The evidence is also building that a history of heavy use of alcohol, marijuana, and nicotine during adolescence is associated with signs of altered neural functioning and neuropsychological deficits, some of which outlast the period of use. Whether these effects are causal – that is, a result of excessive drug use during adolescence – or whether they may have been present prior to such use, perhaps serving as risk factors for elevated use, are areas of active inquiry in prospective human studies and in studies using animal models to examine the consequences of controlled drug exposures during development.

There is much interest in the notion of adolescence as a time of greater neuronal plasticity, particularly in brain regions and axonal tracts normally undergoing maturational change during adolescence. Much further work is needed, however, to determine the extent to which adolescence actually serves as a sensitive period for experience-dependent brain sculpting, the nature and timing of effective experiences, and the vulnerabilities and opportunities they may afford.

See also: Addictions in Adolescence; Adolescent Decision-Making; Alcohol Use; Cognitive Development; Developmental Psychopathology; Emotional Development; Executive Function; Hormones and Behavior; Motivation; Peer Influence; Puberty and Adolescence: An Evolutionary Perspective; Risk-Taking Behavior; Stress; Transitions into Adolescence.

Further Reading

Casey BJ, Getz S, and Galvan A (2008) The adolescent brain. *Developmental Review* 28: 62–77.

Dahl RE and Spear LP (eds.) (2004) *Adolescent Brain Development: Vulnerabilities and Opportunities*. New York: New York Academy of Sciences.

Doremus-Fitzwater TL, Varlinskaya, EI, and Spear LP (2010) Motivational systems in adolescence: Possible implications for age differences in substance abuse and other risk-taking behaviors. *Brain and Cognition* 72: 114–123.

Geier C and Luna B (2009) The maturation of incentive processing and cognitive control. *Pharmacology, Biochemistry and Behavior* 93: 212–221.

Giedd JN (2008) The teen brain: Insights from neuroimaging. *Journal of Adolescent Health* 42: 335–343.

Spear LP (2010) *The Behavioral Neuroscience of Adolescence*. New York: W.W. Norton.

Steinberg L (2010) A behavioral scientist looks at the science of adolescent brain development. *Brain and Cognition* 72: 160–164.

Steinberg L (2010) A dual systems model of adolescent risk-taking. *Developmental Psychobiology* 52: 216–224.

Career Development

M P Neuenschwander, University of Applied Sciences Northwestern Switzerland, Solothurn, Switzerland
B Kracke, University of Erfurt, Erfurt, Germany

Glossary

Career counseling/career guidance: Professional strategies of assessing and promoting individual career-related competencies in all phases of the lifelong career development process.
Expectancy-value theory: A theoretical approach stating that one's choices and behaviors are a function of one's expectancies and the value of the goal toward which one is working.
Occupation: Employed or self-employed paid work.
Profession: Vocational activities based on formal qualifications conducted in a regulated institutional setting.
Stage–environment fit: The match between the current level of individual's abilities, characteristics, and interests and the requirements and opportunities provided by the immediate environment.
Transitions: The diachronic and synchronic moves between social contexts.
Vocational choice: The process of making a decision on a professional career.

Introduction

Career development is a lifelong endeavor that starts in childhood and usually ends in old age after retirement from paid work. Although career development is a life-time biographical project with relevant demands in every life stage, adolescence is a period with particular challenges for the individual. Career goals have to be developed and first choices concerning educational trajectories have to be made, channeling future career options and pathways with many personal, social, and economic consequences. Even though many adolescents choose to deviate from their primary vocational decision in adult years, the first career choice strongly influences later career development in many countries. These choices have to be well prepared by exploring one's own abilities, interests, and values and available career opportunities. How adolescents cope with this task varies considerably among individuals. Personal characteristics as well as the social, institutional, and economic contexts are important for the way in which adolescents prepare for their future occupational career. Thus, these contexts define educational and professional opportunities and pathways that individuals can choose among. These contexts regulate the individual's development. In this article, after an overview on theoretical approaches towards career development, we conceptualize career development as transitions in the life course and as a stressful challenge particularly for adolescents. We discuss career development as the interplay of individual, social, and institutional contexts and finally introduce concepts of vocational guidance and policy implications.

Theoretical Perspectives on Career Development and Choice

Theories on career development have been developed since the 1950s and have stimulated many research studies and policy interventions. They conceptualize the influence of individuals or of social contexts on career development, or they focus on the relationship or fit between individuals and contexts. Some theories describe the micro processes in short time periods, whereas other theories focus on developmental processes during the life course. They give varying explanations of how individuals and their professional environment establish a good fit. Some form of dynamic balance between individuals' interests, competences, and attitudes and the professional demands is required for successful professional activities. Because individuals always develop and because professional

 doi:10.1016/B978-0-12-373915-5.00007-3

contexts change, this fit remains dynamic and needs to be reestablished in a lifelong process. Generally speaking, career choices are prepared in families, peer-groups, and schools in childhood, although the vocational choices highly depend on experiences during adolescence. To shed light on these processes, we present four highly influential approaches in career development with a special emphasis on developmental perspectives.

Trait-and-Factor Matching Approaches

In trait-and-factor matching approaches reaching back to Frank Parsons's seminal work in 1909, personal characteristics are considered to be attributed to professions. The basic idea is a close match between individual personality traits and occupational characteristics. A good fit is a precondition for a successful professional career and work satisfaction. Adolescents recognize patterns of personal competences, interests, and traits and learn professional characteristics.

Following this idea, John Holland described in the late 1950s six ideal personality types that corresponded to six ideal types of occupational activities. He proposed Realistic, Investigative, Artistic, Social, Enterprising, and Conventional personality types (RIASEC). Each personality style is characterized by specific competences, professional preferences and values, life goals, and self-concepts. The corresponding types of occupational activities, although not exhaustive, are assumed to include all the major kinds of work environments. Holland called them motoric, intellectual, supportive, conforming, persuasive, and esthetic environments.

This approach received much attention in vocational counseling and stimulated further research addressing mainly the number of dimensions. Using questionnaires, adolescents are classified into one of these personality types or they get scores on the six personality dimensions resulting in an interest profile. Based on this personality diagnosis, they are allocated to corresponding professional work types and occupations that help them planning their work career.

However, a simple and static allocation of personality types to occupational areas does not provide process-related information. First, it is still not clear how the personality types develop. Second, the person–environment fit approach does not explain how adolescents make choices and how they can be supported in their vocational choice process and career development. Nevertheless, the idea of person–environment fit is an important aspect in career development and has influenced theory and research in career development.

Decision Making Approaches

The decision making approaches do not address long-term developmental processes but rather focus on how vocational choices are made. Typically, vocational choices are a sequence of partial choices. Adolescents approach their final choice step by step, excluding alternatives or weighing options. It is of core interest how students evaluate professions and occupations and how they perceive their own competences, interests, and attitudes. The complexity and multidimensionality of vocational choices with their enduring consequences lead adolescents to choose professions and work places with incomplete information. Students typically do not have all available information about professions and occupations or even about themselves. They cannot evaluate every option. Therefore, vocational choices are only partially logical, partially spontaneous and intuitive. Cost–benefit analyses in vocational choice processes are more plausible in the context of approaches of ecological rationality. That is, vocational choices are rational because they are adapted to their life situation.

An important decision making approach with high impact is the social cognitive theory of career choice that was elaborated by Lent, Hackett, Brown, and Eccles. It stresses attitudes such as student expectations and values. The basic idea is that students' expectancies and values are main points of reference for vocational choices. Expectancies describe anticipated occupational challenges in relation to individual competences. Expectancies for success predict how well adolescents do on upcoming tasks and define the level of aspiration of the chosen profession or occupation. Values like attainment, intrinsic quality, utility, and costs express subjective students' preferences and predict the quality and content of the chosen profession or occupation. Choices are seen to be influenced by both negative and positive task characteristics. All choices are assumed to have costs associated with them precisely because one choice often eliminates other options. The relative value and probability of success of various options are key determinants of choice.

Research shows that students' expectancies and values can quite precisely predict educational pathways and vocational choices in western countries and age groups – even in long-term perspectives. For example, expectancies and values of seventh graders predict college enrollment at age 20 in the US educational system and in Western European countries. These attitudes also are reminiscent of motivational processes as proposed by Atkinson's expectancy-value-theory of achievement motivation in the 1960s: Students with inappropriate expectancies and values are less engaged in their education and have a higher risk of youth unemployment.

Modern expectancy-value theory stresses the interplay of student attitudes with contextual factors. Student expectancies are internalized from the expectancies of their parents and friends and adapted to achievement-related feedback from teachers and other persons of reference. Values are internalized from persons of reference who express their values verbally or behaviorally and they are modified by their general values and priorities to make up a coherent value structure.

Developmental Approaches

Developmental approaches stress the long preparation period of vocational choices and how these are modified in the life course. They stress the process of how individual professional dreams in childhood translate to initial vocational choices and become realized in occupations. Adults will perhaps commence further vocational training and switch to new occupational fields. They can become unemployed or take a break as parents. After retirement, they can find new challenges and become engaged in age appropriate activities. The long-term perspective of developmental approaches enables the identification of general and age-specific processes and structures in career development and to identify the thread in professional biographies.

Lifelong career development

In the 1950s, Donald E. Super presented a comprehensive theory of lifelong career development. His theory is still important because the life-course approach captures basic developmental processes and because it shows how vocational choices are situated in long-term developmental pathways. The theory includes an 'arch of career determinants' to explain vocational choices and a 'life-career rainbow' with four main developmental stages. Super's arch of career determinants describes how biological, psychological, social, and societal factors affect the self-concept and vocational choices. It explains the micro processes within the broader developmental theory and contextualizes individual processes.

The four developmental stages are exploration (about age 10–20), establishment (age 20–35), maintenance (age 35–55), and decline (after age 55). Today, this sequence looks normative and heuristic because many professional biographies have become nonlinear and are interrupted with breaks and detours. Career development results from a professional self-concept that is differentiating and integrating during the life-course. Super assumed a match between a person's self-concept and occupations. But this match is only weak, so that the person fits in varying occupational areas.

Research has confirmed the correspondence between self-concept and professional and occupational activities. For example, the academic self-concept helps to predict the person-environment fit for apprentices in Switzerland. A high professional self-concept is an effective personal resource in conflict situations, high work load and stress in work situations. However, losing an occupation lowers the self-concept. The link between self-concept und professional and occupational activities should, thus, be conceptualized as a mutual interplay.

Career goals, life goals

Career development is determined by social and biological factors, but it is also highly self-regulated. Approaches focusing on this aspect have become particularly successful in explaining career development because adolescents have many options from which to choose in this domain. Drawing on general and domain-specific values and social feedback from persons of reference, students set up career goals. Life goals are rather general in scope and have a long-term perspective, whereas career goals relate to the near or far occupational and professional future. Adolescents report personal goals in various life domains. Their most important goals in middle adolescence are related to education and occupation. Adolescents expect to achieve their educational goals first, followed by occupational and family goals and, finally, securing material assets.

Driven by their goals, adolescents influence the educational and occupational contexts where they work or learn or they choose the educational or work contexts that determine their actions and development. Thus, goals also have an indirect effect on adolescents' development. Moreover, goals have a strong motivational impact and regulate actions and development. Individuals monitor and control their actions and developmental process. Students with high self-efficacy and agency beliefs use more efficient strategies and thus achieve their goals more directly and faster. Self-efficacy beliefs are students' expectations concerning their ability to act as they want to act. In contrast, agency beliefs are expectations that an action has the desired outcome.

For vocational choices, curiosity and exploration are effective aspects of self-regulation. Adolescents who intensely explore their proper vocational interests, competences, and traits and who systematically collect information about professions and occupations choose their profession more self-confidently. They increase self-efficacy beliefs, career decidedness, and commitment to the chosen profession, and are more motivated working in their job. After intense exploration, students' career goals become more important and more concrete. But career exploration does not predict the level or the type of the chosen profession or occupation.

Contextual Approaches

Career development in the life-course is strongly determined by structural features of the social context. Social contexts define how well the person–environment match is established. The individual plays an important role in shaping the career development although choices and initiatives are always constrained by social forces and biological limitations. Glen H. Elder, Jr. and Michael J. Shanahan as well as Walter Heinz described the life course as an age-graded sequence of socially defined roles and events that are enacted and even recast over time. People generally work out their life course in relation to established, institutionalized transitions and pathways and their regulatory constraints, such as the curricula or tracks of a school and the professional careers of a firm or culture. Professional careers result from individual motives and goals restricted by the constraints of educational and occupational contexts. These constraints are weaker in transition situations when individuals can choose between available contexts and find new pathways within these contexts.

The school-to-work transition is a typical example of the interplay between the individual and his or her context. Adolescents as subjects become members of a society pondering and establishing their relation to societal institutions and contexts. They try to fulfill their personal interests and goals activating their resources and using the available institutional chances. The strong contextual effect on individuals' career development is, thus, moderated by individual motives, goals and competences and biographically based perceptions of social expectations.

Transition as a Challenge

Transitions from one context to another are core elements of career development. Even though these transitions are often planned and receive high social approval, they usually challenge individuals' coping abilities as they require adaptation to expectations of new contexts and bear the risk of failure to reach desired goals. To successfully cope with this task increases public approval, social status, and well-being. Then, the new context provides new stimulation. Selected situations bearing potential problems, such as career indecision, transition stress, selection processes, school-drop out, and unemployment as well as related psychological risks in transition situations will be discussed.

Career Indecision

Career choice in adolescence depends on the timing of identity development. Vocational choices are a challenge for students lagging behind in their identity development because their self-concept is not elaborated and they have diffuse personal values and professional goals. This challenge is accentuated in educational systems where adolescents have to choose professions early (e.g., in countries with a well established dual apprenticeship system). Research shows strong correlations between professional identity problems and career indecision in late adolescence. Female students with low professional self-efficacy beliefs and with low exploration are especially at risk with regard to career indecision. Students with insufficient social resources or with high stress (critical life-events, high school pressure, little parental support, overprotective parents) are at risk for developing professional identity problems and career indecision. Career-undecided adolescents are academically and professionally less engaged, have unclear and unrealistic professional goals, and need to change them to more realistic ones (cooling down effect). They tend to start their professional training at a later point. They perceive a lower fit between their interests or competences and their profession, have a lower self-esteem and are less happy in their profession. They are less confident to have chosen the appropriate profession and think about moving to a new professional area.

Transition Stress

School transitions, school-to-work transitions, and job mobility at the beginning of young adult careers are associated with challenges and often experienced as stressful events. Before transitions, individuals have to set up vocational goals, make plans, and find ways to realize them. They lose friends and have to establish new social relations with peers and teachers or supervisors and find social relationships in new social contexts after the transition. Parents, siblings, and close friends remain important persons of reference. Young people need social skills to become integrated in a new social context and to receive acceptance and social prestige. Moreover, they have to negotiate their work conditions with their supervisor, especially when they change their job. Research shows that this process becomes stressful when the new school, college or workplace is large and anonymous and does not support positive social relationships.

This social process overlaps with higher or modified achievement-related expectations after transition. After transition to high-school or college, students have to fulfill higher achievement standards and to learn more independently. They receive less advice and feedback about their learning process and examination preparation. Adolescents have to learn in a self-regulated manner and find control strategies to ask for help and feedback.

Then, during the transition period students have to accommodate their daily routine. They may have a longer commute between home and school, a new timetable for their classes, or less leisure time. Upon entry into occupation, in particular, the daily routine typically changes dramatically when the school schedule and work hours differ greatly. Adolescents have to elaborate a new social role and new habits after transition. They can prepare for this transition by learning from older students' experience and by thus anticipating the challenges. Once having entered the world of work, young employees have to face new challenges. They have to be mobile and flexible in terms of willingness to accept timely limited and part-time jobs to ensure their economic independence. However, frequent job changes go along with more work pressure and less commitment with the enterprise.

Selection Processes

School transitions, school-to-work transitions, and job mobility at the beginning of early adults' careers are associated with the choice of and the passage into educational and professional channels. Both individuals and institutions are interested in establishing a match between individuals' interests and competences and institutional demands. In the matching process, the number of positions offered in an academic or professional field in contrast to the supply of workers plays a crucial role. If there are fewer offers than the supply in the market, institutions select persons that more precisely match their profile. Individuals have a larger risk of not obtaining the desired position and become frustrated or even depressed.

Selection strategies of institutions vary between school systems and countries. In some European countries such as Switzerland and Germany, only students who have passed an academic examination are allowed to enter high school (Gymnasium). In many countries, selection takes place during the transition to universities, typically based on aptitude and intelligence tests or prior academic grades. In contrast, the selection process leading to apprenticeships or the job market is based on academic achievement or prior professional experience as well as on social competence and motivation. Through effective coaching, students can be prepared for these evaluations during selection periods and can be supported coping with frustration in case of not being successful.

Unsuccessful selection and disengagement in education or training often lead to downward pathways like school dropout or youth unemployment. Those pathways may end in permanent low-status occupations. Some individuals, however, undertake new educational efforts to improve chances for more prestigious occupational positions.

Individual Differences in Career Development

Career development trajectories vary among individuals and groups of individuals. The impact of structural features such as gender and socioeconomic background as well as of individual characteristics such as interests, values and individual competences will be discussed.

Gender

Population statistics show that some professions are female or male gender-typed and some professions are not. This reality of the world of work is reflected in adolescents' vocational goals. In general, adolescent boys and girls do not show the same professional preferences. They differ in their vocational interests, goals, and conceptions of their own futures. These gender differences in vocational interests, however, start at a very young age. Already in elementary school when vocational interests are not very differentiated, girls prefer jobs they perceive as being appropriate for women whereas boys prefer male-dominated professions. In mid-adolescence, when the structure of vocational interests is rather similar to that of adults, in most cultures girls score higher in the artistic and social domains while boys score higher in the realistic and investigative domains, as assessed by the RIASEC dimensions of Holland. These gender differences are also present when adolescents report on possible academic selves. Gender differences in the entrepreneurial and conventional domains are not that dramatic.

Gender differences in vocational interests and goals can be mainly explained as being a product of gender role socialization. Gottfredson's Circumscription and Compromise Theory describes how an individual's perception about gender role socialization influences career choice. The individual's learning experiences in his or her sociocultural context shapes the perception of what types of gender appropriate roles and behaviors are commonly associated with the tasks and duties of a particular occupation. Consequently, the individual develops gender stereotypes concerning occupations. At the same time, children and adolescents develop ideas about behaviors by which they want to individually express their way of being a male or a female. The combination of the perceived gender appropriateness of occupations and the own gender concept creates a limited space of careers which appear to be suitable for the individual. Gender differences are not only reported in vocational interests but also in the perceived efficacy to achieve in certain occupational fields. Girls, for instance, seem to lose confidence in their abilities associated with investigative interests. This has dramatic consequences for course choice in school and studies at university and in the end for occupations. But if girls endorse science-related career goals in adolescence they are more likely to enter careers in these fields as adults.

Gender differences are also found in how adolescents anticipate their future career paths. Girls are more confident concerning their educational goals than boys are, whereas boys report a greater number of occupational goals and are more specific in their plans to attain them. More boys than girls expect to work full time during their occupational lives. Girls tend to expect to have a partner and children at an earlier age than boys, which, in turn, affects their anticipation of career paths.

Because adolescents limit their vocational interests based on gender-stereotypes of occupations and not mainly on their abilities to fulfill the job demands, early interventions should be developed that sensitize adolescents to gender biases, broaden their options, and facilitate their pursuit of these options. Although gender stereotypes about occupations already develop in childhood, adolescence is a timely period to intervene because adolescents are open for experiences and explore several options for their future lives. Thus, they may also consider alternative occupations when they are introduced to them.

Socioeconomic Background, Migration Background, Ethnicity

Socioeconomic status (SES) strongly influences educational career trajectories. How adolescents perceive their future occupational options and how they pursue their occupational goals are partly influenced by their SES. High SES is generally related to higher educational goals and higher educational trajectories leading to more prestigious occupations. At the same time, SES affects already the chances of a successful entrance into the world of work and, by the same token, is a (negative) predictor of youth unemployment. The character of occupational aspirations such as job status and income, however, is influenced by more proximal family factors than by SES. Material conditions, parental support, involvement and aspirations as well as adolescents' academic achievement and self-concept are more influential than SES per se. However, offspring of more advantaged families have generally higher career aspirations than those from less affluent families.

The role ethnicity and migration background play for educational pathways and job entry is complex. Specific stereotypes are associated with specific ethnicities, suggesting that some ethnic groups emphasize educational success more than others, which then would be reflected partly in adolescents' educational and occupational aspirations. Moreover, there are empirical findings that migrants differ in their educational and occupational aspirations from the majority population. But despite these differences, there is a considerable cross-cultural overlap in adolescents' valuing of educational and occupational goals. The main difference between ethnicities is what traditionally is regarded as a valuable occupation in their group. Migration status is often confounded with SES and, thus, has not much information value itself for the explanation of variations in educational pathways and job entry.

Interests and Values

A young person's choice of profession is based on their personal and professional interests and values. Much research addressing the role that the fit between vocational interests and values and the success plays in one's career is based either on Holland's RIASEC dimensions or on expectancy-value theory. Adolescents who choose an apprenticeship or start college or university studies that fit their interests are more satisfied with their choice, achieve better, and tend to drop out to a lesser degree.

It is still unclear how specific interests develop. Competencies seem to have an important impact. The structure of interests and perceived competencies develop across adolescence. Both become more differentiated partly because of cognitive development, enabling more complex thinking processes that are further refined by different social experiences such as competition and grades. If an individual perceives him or herself competent in one domain he or she is more likely to invest more time in the future in this domain because the feeling of being competent is satisfying. This has been shown particularly for the choice of math and science classes in school. However, the link between competencies and interests is reciprocal. If individuals like something, they will put more effort into it and become more competent. How this link develops in future career paths is still not thoroughly examined.

Intellectual and Social Competences

Occupational interests and goals, educational and occupational aspirations, and achievements are strongly influenced by intellectual competences. Students with higher general cognitive abilities tend to have better grades, more sophisticated interests and higher scores in achievement tests, which enable them to apply for more demanding studies and/or professions. Individuals with lower ability enter less demanding educational tracks, are interested in and look for less complex jobs. Grades in school and general cognitive abilities are the best predictors of achievement in university education or in apprenticeship. Once launched into a career, higher intellectual capacities contribute to the pursuit of more successful careers as reflected in more autonomy and increasing complexity. Job demands and intellectual competencies mutually influence each other positively. While cognitive abilities are important for the level of the occupation, social competences such as the ability to cooperate, to resolve conflicts, and empathy influence adolescents' social adaptation to new situational demands after having left the school context. They help adolescents to get along with the collaborators in an enterprise and establish a good person–environment fit.

The Social Context of Career Development

The long-term and multifaceted process of the development of an adolescents' educational and vocational biography takes place in interaction with proximal social contexts. Parents, peers, and teachers provide learning opportunities, give feedback about abilities, and lend emotional as well as instrumental support for these various aspects of adolescents' vocational development.

Parents

Parents influence their adolescents' career development in different ways. First of all, parents influence their adolescents' educational trajectories by transmitting to them certain cognitive abilities and temperament characteristics via their genetic heritage. On the basis of their genetic makeup, they provide specific environments which are more or less stimulating for intellectual growth and self-determination. Second, parents' educational and occupational biographies are models for their adolescents. The work experiences, both, positive and negative ones that parents convey at home and their knowledge about occupations influence their children's images about the world of work and shape their expectations concerning their future vocational lives. Parental work values and virtues such as reliability or effort are blueprints for the development of their offsprings' attitudes towards work.

Apart from those features of parents' educational and work experiences, parental attitudes toward their children's aspirations and parental activities to support the pursuit of educational goals are of great importance for adolescents' vocational development. High parental educational aspirations for their children generally translate into high adolescent aspirations and educational achievements which in turn influence vocational aspirations. Parental and adolescent educational aspirations correspond positively, particularly when parental aspirations are accompanied by support, acceptance and closeness, encouragement and interest and involvement in adolescents' learning activities.

Because career development is a long-term multifaceted process, some features of parental support have to change over time to be adaptive to specific situational demands. Empirical findings show that in primary and middle school those students do best whose parents provide a stimulating learning environment and encourage academic achievement. In high school, those adolescents progress best in their vocational development whose parents support exploration activities which are necessary to acquire self-knowledge and knowledge about the opportunities given in the world of work. In addition to formulating high expectations concerning academic achievement, these parents provide access to appropriate career-related information and opportunities for the adolescents to explore the world of work. A continuous feature of parental behaviors stimulating the development of a career identity is their willingness to arrange situations in which children and adolescents can experience their own abilities and to give appropriate feedback to their children about their observations.

Mothers and fathers partly have different functions in supporting their children's educational and vocational development. Mothers' expectations and role modeling seem to be particularly important for the formulation of higher educational goals. If they stimulate independence their children are more likely to strive for independence and leadership. Mothers generally provide more support in the process of vocational development than fathers do. For girls, working mothers serve as important models for their own career aspirations and goals. The special role of mothers as advisors in career related issues is mostly due to the greater amount of time that mothers spend with their children, especially in dyadic interactions, as compared to fathers. Nevertheless, fathers are important role models for sons and the extent of their involvement in their daughters' education positively relates to daughters' career achievement.

Peers

From early on, peers play an important role in the development of an individual's self-concept. While the positive role of peer support for academic achievement and peers potential negative effects on adolescents' problem behaviors are thoroughly studied, the role of peers in the course of adolescents' career development has only rarely been considered. The few studies addressing this issue show that peers give feedback about certain features of jobs, such as prestige and gender-stereotypes, and that they can be important in the process of career exploration. If an adolescent expresses certain occupational goals that in terms of prestige do not fit to the expectations of their peer group, they get negative feedback and may, thus, be pushed away from that goal. This would be particularly dramatic if the intended vocation would perfectly fit to the individual's abilities and other vocations that would be accepted by the peer group might be too demanding or not demanding enough for the individual. The same holds with respect to gender stereotypes about vocations. If the goals of an individual violate the gender stereotypic expectations of their peers he or she might give up plans in order to fit to their peers' expectations. The impact of peers' judgments about the appropriateness of goals should be especially strong in early adolescence when young people tend to conform to their peers in order to keep up a high self-esteem.

Peers can have a positive impact on adolescents' career development when they serve as models showing how to cope with career relevant tasks. They can help to improve adolescents' vocational exploration and decision process by giving hints about important information sources, about appropriate behaviors in internships or during the applications process for jobs or apprenticeships. Peers also serve as a sounding board in the process of exploration and decision making itself. They provide security when they accompany the adolescent in unknown situations such as job centers or interviews with counselors, and they can exchange information about jobs or studies.

Teachers and School

Although adolescents perceive school, in general, and teachers, in particular, as being less important for their career development than their parents, both may have a positive impact. First of all, schools and teachers provide learning opportunities and give feedback about adolescents' abilities. This allows students to differentiate their academic and vocational interests. In a tracked school system such as the German one, school is a very important channel for future job opportunities because school tracks lead to different levels of entrances to the labor market with different employment opportunities. In Germany, school track is not only related to adolescents' career aspirations but also to the role teachers ascribe to themselves concerning their students' careers after their leaving school. In the lower track mainly leading to blue collar and craft jobs and in the middle track mainly leading to white collar or administration occupations, teachers generally feel more responsible for their adolescents' after-school career than in the higher track which prepares students for the transition to university. Beyond tracking, another aspect of school organization can influence adolescents' development of vocational identities, namely, gender segregation. Girls, for instance, who visit girls-only schools more often report career aspirations in sciences and expect to have more influential and prestigious jobs in general than those in mixed schools.

Beyond these peculiarities of school structure, the organization of individual schools within a track can influence students' career development. Schools vary a lot with respect to the opportunities they provide for their students to explore the world of work by integrating internships into the curriculum or special courses on career preparation. The more students experience their schools as institutions interested in their future vocational development and providing them with information, learning experiences, and support, the more they report own exploration activities and less uncertainty about their occupational options. The same holds for teachers. If students perceive their teachers as being interested in their future and providing emotional and instrumental support concerning vocational issues, they engage more in the process of exploration of occupational interests and planning and show higher occupational self-efficacy.

The Institutional Context of Career Development

Normative career trajectories are defined by the institutional contexts in a country. Although educational institutions in many countries have become open, pluralistic, and flexible, and pathways may include detours and breaks, educational institutions typically define a number of pathways by national laws and standards that specify how the school-to-work transition is organized. Rarely do students choose unexpected upward or downward pathways. In the following, we present normative pathways from school to work in an international perspective.

International Perspectives

From an international perspective, there are two main pathways for school-to-work transitions: In some western European countries such as Germany, Switzerland, and Austria, after compulsory schooling many students enter the dual vocational and educational training system (dual VET) and learn a profession. During VET, they typically search for a job corresponding to this vocation. In contrast, high-school and college curricula in the United States, Canada, and Great Britain typically focus on general education. Students learn competences to cope with the occupational demands while on the job, generally not beforehand. Students are thus qualified for a broad range of occupations and are flexible in order to switch between varying occupations, but they have little professional and practical experience and they have to learn intensively on their first job. Professional careers are less determined by students' educational qualifications than in countries with a VET system. The educational and employment systems are less linked. In Japan, we find an alternative transition pathway to college that corresponds well to the Japanese culture: The transition to high school and to university is a selection process that depends on academic entrance tests and on the prestige of the preparatory school. Students from highly prestigious high schools who have demonstrated sufficient academic achievement are allowed to move on to highly prestigious universities or companies. Supported by a broad network, employers inform teachers about the free positions in these companies and teachers encourage a few students from their class apply in the firm. Thus, the job market is highly regulated by the involved teachers.

Learning in the VET System

In several European countries, the dual vocational and educational training system (vocational school and enterprise) has become the main transition system. For example, in Switzerland, about two thirds of all apprentices enter the VET system and move on to the job market or to tertiary education (e.g., universities of applied sciences). The VET curricula and the certification system are vocation-bound; permeability between occupations is low and pathways from vocational education to employment are highly standardized. Apprentices (ages about 16 to 20) acquire theoretical knowledge in a vocational school and practical competences on the job while preparing for their full entry into work life. Apprentices are still in the role of students and have limited responsibilities. They are not yet 'full' workers, but no longer 'pure' students. During three to four days a week, apprentices participate in real production processes in their training company and earn a modest wage; for one or two days they are students in vocational schools.

Many apprentices like this combination of theoretical learning in schools and the acquisition of practical knowledge for their profession in their firm, because they acquire knowledge with high relevance to their ensuing professional life. Furthermore, adolescents' levels of maturity are reflected in their pre-professional status in society. Employers like workers who have finished an apprenticeship with a diploma because of their theoretical and practical knowledge, so they are willing to hire them. The professionally trained workers, on the other hand, are less flexible and need further training during the life course to enter new professional fields. Because companies require a high degree of flexibility, professions may lose their significance and the VET system must be transformed. From an international perspective, the two transition systems (VET vs. college bound) are thus likely to eventually converge.

Learning on the First Job

In educational systems in which colleges or universities prepare students for employment, the link between college and occupation is weak, so that the transition becomes particularly stressful. Students typically have a broad academic education that allows them to work in different professional fields. But they need specific skills for their occupation and workplace; they are not employable for stable jobs. In a floundering period, those students switch from one occupation to another in short intervals and gain the required knowledge on the job. To perform a task in their occupation, they typically receive instructions from the employer or more experienced employees. During the work process, they learn techniques, routines, and tools by imitating and by being coached by more experienced employers or workers. First-time workers learn in a self-regulated manner. In some enterprises, young employees receive formal training on the job to fulfill a function. During their professional career, they continually acquire the required competences with every new position.

Vocational Guidance: Counseling and Policy Implications

The challenges during the process of career development justify establishing professional and institutionalized help. In Germany and Switzerland, for example, 20% of adolescents who start an apprenticeship after school quit it within one year. The same percentage is reported on students quitting their university studies. Research examining the reasons for this reveal that the dropout mainly is because adolescents did not have enough information about the contents and the requirements of the apprenticeship or studies, respectively. This draws attention to the contents of vocational guidance. It should provide adolescents with sufficient information about themselves and the world of work to make good vocational decisions. Because, as shown above, vocational development is a long-term and complex process which can only be successfully managed with sufficient knowledge, vocational guidance should address other competencies as well.

The guidance process should be organized under a developmental perspective considering the cognitive abilities of the developing child and adolescent and situational conditions of making experiences potentially relevant to vocational development depending on the age of the child and related legal conditions. Considering Gottfredson's theory of circumscription and compromise (which claims that gender stereotyped vocational interests form early, in elementary school) and research findings showing that perceptions of competencies related to vocational interests also develop quite early, it seems appropriate that vocational guidance should start well before adolescence. The first steps of vocational guidance should address information about educational tracks, jobs and career on a very general level, addressing gender issues as well as the fact that careers also demand certain abilities that can be acquired in the process of learning in school.

The second step of career guidance should enable children and adolescents to gather information about themselves and the world of work. That means, on the one hand, providing them with information, and, on the other hand, making them competent to seek information by themselves with appropriate methods such as interest and competence inventories or in relevant contexts such as the Internet, internships, and visits of work settings. This information competence can be conceptualized with reference to self-regulation processes including setting goals, planning, pursuing goals, and reflecting experiences with respect to the individual goals.

The third step of vocational guidance would concentrate on decision making and teach the adolescents how to narrow the range of alternatives, to evaluate alternatives with respect to the individuals' values and interests, and finally come to a decision which can be defended when challenged. In the fourth step adolescents need to be informed about best ways to apply for jobs, apprenticeships or studies.

In this guidance process, a network of competent partners should be involved. Parents and teachers as primary facilitators of career-relevant learning opportunities should be part of this network as well as specially trained experts in issues concerning the institutional context of career development. This network would operate best if all partners had well defined functions which complement each other. Moreover, it should also be able to compensate for one partner's possible lack of abilities to guide the adolescents. This could particularly be necessary for youths whose parents are not able to take care of their adolescents' vocational development because they are lacking work experience or abilities to act planfully in favor of their children. To support the efficient work of such a network, checklists featuring optimal occupational preparation could be utilized to early identify possible problematic candidates and offer them optimal help right from the beginning of the career development process. The work of this social network should also be assisted by internet based information sources which allow the adolescents to search for information by themselves.

Conclusions

Career development has become a complex and flexible lifelong process with detours and interruptions. This process is partially regulated by the individual and partially by social and institutional contexts. Regulation efforts of the individual and the regulating structures of the context have to be of certain quality to allow a successful career development. The international comparison of the pathways from school to work on the institutional level shows that adolescents are prepared for work life by societies in different ways. These alternatives are characterized by specific challenges and stress factors and they have their peculiar advantages and disadvantages for adolescents and enterprises.

At the individual level, specific core competences can be identified that are useful for the individual to successfully cope with the transition from school to work and the establishment in a job. In general, the ability to set and pursue goals as well as problem-solving and decision making competences and self-efficacy are functional individual characteristics which enhance the chances of a successful management of the career development process. Social competences such as conflict resolution skills and team cooperation help adolescents and young adults to establish a fit in their apprenticeship or first job after transition to work life. These competencies, however, have to be acquired by the individual. Some adolescents get enough positive stimulation in their families others need compensatory or complementary help – from school or other sources. To offer this assistance, schools need concepts and strategies for teaching the transition competences and preparing students for work life. Mandatory internships to promote exploration or procedures to make teachers conscious of their role as advisors could be effective features of such school concepts. Besides schools, parents and employers would benefit from more systematic programs teaching them to assist adolescents to make appropriate vocational choices.

To gain more insight into the specific interplay between individual and institutional factors shaping career development a promising strategy could be international comparisons based on longitudinal data. More theory and data are needed to understand the complex process of individual development in social and societal contexts.

Finally, theory and research results may guide the development of programs for adolescents at risk. Special effort is needed to prevent school drop-outs, disengagement, and deviance in adolescence and to integrate these adolescents in the work system and to prevent unemployment. These strategies are not only justified by lower economic costs as a result of lower unemployment in a country but, in particular, by helping adolescents to find their place in society as citizens.

See also: Employment; School-to-Work Transitions; Vocational Training.

Further Reading

Brown D (ed.) (2002) *Career Choice and Development*, 4th edn. San Francisco: Jossey-Bass.

Bryant BK, Zvonkovic AM, and Reynolds P (2006) Parenting in relation to child and adolescent vocational development. *Journal of Vocational Behavior* 69: 149–175.

Elder GH and Shanahan M (2005) The life course and human development. In: Lerner RM and Steinberg L (eds.) *Handbook of Child Psychology*, vol. 1, pp. 665–715. New York: Wiley.

Herr EL, Cramer SH, and Niles SG (2004) *Career Guidance and Counseling through the Lifespan*, 6th edn. Boston: Pearson.

Skorikov VB and Patton W (eds.) (2007) *Career Development in Childhood and Adolescence*. Rotterdam: Sense Publishers.

Relevant Websites

http://careerplanning.about.com/
www.careercounseling.com

Cognitive Development

D P Keating, University of Michigan, Ann Arbor, MI, USA

Glossary

Analytic reasoning: A general term indicating the application of systematic rules to problem spaces, including formal reasoning, inductive and deductive reasoning, and logical systems in general.

Dual process models: A theoretical approach to cognitive processing that draws a distinction between more analytical, rational, purposeful reasoning, as opposed to processing that is more heuristic, experiential, and intuitive. Included are theoretical distinctions between processes that are more conscious and aware, believed to be guided by the prefrontal cortex (system), and that are more responsive to emotional arousal and social context.

Heuristic processes: Thinking processes that are experience based, often thought of as intuitive or instinctual; theoretically contrasted with analytic reasoning.

Metacognition: Thinking about one's own thought processes, both for self-reflection and for the conscious guidance of cognitive activity.

Myelination: The physiological process of depositing myelin on nerve pathways, which serves as an insulator and increases the speed of transmission of information; this increases substantially in early adolescence.

Prefrontal cortex (PFC): The brain region principally responsible for coordination of other brain systems as the primary locus of executive functions and judgment; the PFC shows differentially greater growth and interconnections compared to other brain regions during adolescence.

Psychometrics: The field of psychology concerned with mental measurement in the assessment of abilities and achievement.

Synaptic pruning: The process through which the most used neural circuits are reinforced and grow, and the least used circuits die off; in adolescence, this process follows a period of synaptogenesis, a proliferation of new brain cells, and contributes to experience-dependent shaping of neural circuitry.

Introduction

Systematic research on cognitive development during the adolescent years began in earnest in the 1960s, sparked by the seminal 1958 work of Jean Piaget and Barbel Inhelder on *The Growth of Logical Thinking from Childhood to Adolescence.* Embedded in Piaget's encompassing structuralist framework, this groundbreaking work focused on the development of propositional logic, which was regarded as the adult, mature form of logical reasoning. In Piagetian theory, the development of formal operations was identified as the fourth and final stage of logical development, following the earlier developmental periods of sensorimotor, preoperational, and concrete operational thinking.

Given the breadth and depth of the Piagetian theory of formal operations, it is unsurprising that an extensive array of research was conducted in the ensuing years, generating a great deal of descriptive information on how the thinking of adolescents differed from both children and adults. Much of the focus of this research was on testing explicit or implicit empirical claims embedded in the broad theory of formal operations. Several distinct but overlapping phases emerged as this work progressed, representing a series of theoretical contrasts.

The first phase can be characterized as a focus on testing the claims of the theory of formal operations, asking questions such as: How different are adolescents and children, or adolescents and adults, on performance of logical tasks? At what ages do shifts in logic task performance emerge, and in what sequence do the observed changes emerge? What additional factors have an impact on logic task performance, including content knowledge or the context of assessment?

This intensive exploration of the theory of formal operations led to four broad outcomes that are noted here and described in more detail later in this article. First, over time, a general consensus emerged that the theory of formal operations, construed as a set of testable empirical claims about the course of logical development, or cognitive development more broadly, during adolescence, was not supported in a number of key ways. Second, in pursuing this research agenda, important findings about key characteristics of adolescent thinking were sufficiently replicated to afford substantial confidence in them. Third, competing theoretical formulations arose, challenging the centrality of shifts in logical structure as the driving force of cognitive development, both in general and during adolescence in particular. In response, arguments were advanced in defense of the general theory of formal operations, including the assertions (a) that the theory was broader than the narrow set of specific empirical claims that had been tested and found wanting and (b) the view that although the claims may be wrong on some specifics, the overall systems theory remains valuable. Finally, the topic of scientific reasoning, closest to the empirical tasks developed by Inhelder and Piaget, continued to develop in ever more complex ways, even as it became less attached to the specifics of formal operations theory.

Research arising from approaches that competed with formal operations theory can be viewed as comprising the second major phase of systematic research on adolescent cognitive development. Three major areas of research in this second phase of theoretical competition can be identified and are also described in more detail later in this article: cognitive science models, in particular, human information processing models; expertise and knowledge-focused models; and

Encyclopedia of Adolescence, Volume 1 doi:10.1016/B978-0-12-373915-5.00008-5

approaches emphasizing the limits of rationality, arising from a range of dual process models, including the interactive role of socioemotional context with cognitive processing ('hot vs. cold' cognition), the distinction between heuristic and analytic cognitive processing, and increasingly brain-based analyses, especially focused on the relations between the neural substrates for prefrontal cortex activity and activity in the limbic system, both functionally and in the pace of development. Although arising from different research traditions, these varied dual process models have much in common, and this overlap is described in the section on integrative approaches later in the article.

A parallel line of research, standing outside much of the theoretical back-and-forth about formal operations and competing theoretical models of cognitive development, has focused on the development of cognitive abilities and achievement during adolescence. Cross-over between cognitive and psychometric (mental measurement) approaches to adolescent functioning has been relatively rare, but the central practical importance of psychometric assessment for influencing future developmental pathways, especially with respect to higher education, is hard to overstate. A separate treatment of adolescence research on this topic appears later in this article.

The third, contemporary phase of research on adolescent cognitive development is characterized by two broad research themes, also noted here and elaborated later in this article. The first impetus can be viewed as a drive toward integration of different models of adolescent cognitive development, based on research findings that have not supported theories focusing on particular cognitive functions as the central, encompassing explanation. Increasingly, one key test of the value of integrative approaches is the degree to which they are compatible with a growing understanding of the specifics of brain development during adolescence. It is important, though, to distinguish this from reductionist models that view cognitive development as fully explainable by neural developments. The second impetus in contemporary research is a deepening concern about the implications for policy and practice arising from our understanding of adolescent cognitive development. Three especially noteworthy topic areas in which cognitive development has had notable influence include public health, where injury or death arise in the second decade of life most frequently due to excessive risk taking or behavioral misadventure; driving safety, in which the role of expertise and its interaction with the socioemotional context are deeply implicated; and juvenile justice, where mitigation based in part on cognitive immaturity has become a central concern in recent court findings, in the United States, Canada, and elsewhere. Although space constraints do not allow an extended review of these or other examples, it is clear that an understanding of adolescent cognitive development is increasingly important for a wide range of issues in policy and practice.

Development of Reasoning

As noted in the overview section above, the initial thrust for the systematic study of cognitive functioning in adolescence arose from Piaget's structuralist theory, specifically the theory of formal operations. The theory is multifaceted and comprehensive, but the key elements can be summarized as follows. The central methodology is one of genetic epistemology, which focuses on the ontogenesis ('genetic' is derived from this meaning, not the currently more common use of molecular genetics) of how children and adolescents come to know the world. The central change that occurs in cognition over the course of development is the shift in the structure of logic used to navigate the world. The central dynamic mechanism that drives these changes is the tension between assimilation, that is, viewing the world from within the cognitive structures available at that point in development, and accommodation, that is, altering one's structural model of the world, typically in light of contradictory feedback from the world, once it is apprehended as contradictory. According to the theory, the shift from concrete operational thinking in childhood to formal operational thinking in adolescence and adulthood is a change in fundamental logical structure.

In concrete operational thinking, individuals are able to perform mental manipulations on objects in the world, such as comparing the number of elements in two differently shaped arrays, or comparing the volume of liquids in two differently shaped containers. What concrete operational thinkers are not able to do, and what the theory of formal operations argues is the central adolescent cognitive accomplishment, is to perform mental operations on those operations, or to perform what have been described as second-order operations. The most prominent organizational scheme for organizing these 'operations on operations' is that of propositional logic, which requires the application of logical operations to propositions rather than to objects. These can be fairly simple 'if–then' logical connections, on the one hand, or highly complex logical analyses that require, for example, the systematic review of all possible combinations of a set of propositions (i.e., combinatorial logic), on the other. Inhelder and Piaget tested individuals of different ages with respect to their ability to solve formal operations tasks such as displacement of volume (Archimedes' law), the interaction of weight and distance from a fulcrum on a balance task, or the construction of all possible combinations of a given set of elements. In general, adolescents were found to perform better on these and similar tasks compared with children. As noted in the overview section, the general theory of formal operations and the tasks devised to assess logical reasoning generated a wave of research comparing children, adolescents, and adults on increasingly diverse versions of these and similar logical tasks during the initial phase of research on adolescent cognitive development.

Research on Formal Operations

Initial research on the formal operations tasks tended to support the theoretical claims that children were largely incapable of solving the tasks originally devised by Inhelder and Piaget, as well as a range of variations of those tasks devised by a number of researchers. Adolescents were generally found to be more successful on them, although with wide variations in task performance across both individuals and tasks. The substantial variability across tasks posed a significant challenge to the theoretical claims, in that one might expect that once a shift to formal operational thinking occurred, it should apply equally to all tasks that made similar logical demands. The substantial variability across individuals posed a different challenge, in that it gave rise to the possibility that factors other than changes in logical structure were implicated in task performance.

In Piaget's theory, these sources of variability were attributed to a range of factors, grouped under the overarching construct of 'decalage': horizontal decalage is invoked to account for the fact that all tasks that appear to be logically equivalent are not attained simultaneously and vertical decalage is invoked to account for the observation that some individuals move rapidly through logical tasks of a specific type or in a specific content domain (such as chess), but without more generalized advances in logic task performance. The theoretical reasons for each type of decalage were not fully spelled out, and thus remained largely descriptive of observed deviations from the theoretical expectations, rather than as explanations that alleviated concerns about core theoretical claims.

Research directed toward tests of the core empirical claims of the theory of formal operations eventually coalesced into tests of three broad issues: scaling, that is, does performance on tasks occur in the predicted sequence; age of acquisition, that is, do adolescents perform logically as would be expected given the acquisition of formal operations, especially in comparison to children; and logical demands, that is, do the empirical tests of logical performance closely match the empirical claims.

Research on the scaling of the difficulty of logical tasks yielded results that did not firmly establish the accuracy of theoretical predictions. In general, confirmatory results using a variety of approaches to the scaling of task difficulty tended to be strongest when the range of difficulty was quite wide, spanning early concrete operations to late formal operations. This posed three main difficulties. First, when the lens of comparison is narrowed to formal operations only, scaling results did not make the empirical distinctions predicted by the theory. Second, when the scaling research used a wide range, it was much more difficult to isolate the cause of those differences as arising from logical changes, because they can be readily attributed to other sources, such as enhanced processing speed or additional content knowledge. Third, most of the scaling research was cross-sectional, comparing different individuals of different ages, rather than longitudinal, following the same individuals across time to ascertain their sequence of acquisition of logical task performance.

Similar issues arise in studies of the age of acquisition of formal operations, along with some new challenges. Early major challenges arose as researchers began to modify the logical tasks, to more carefully isolate changes in logic while eliminating or controlling for context and/or content knowledge differences. It was discovered that relatively simple task modifications raised or lowered the age at which successful performance on logical tasks was observed. In particular, children were often found to perform well on formal reasoning tasks when the content knowledge required for the task was readily available to them. One response to these findings was the counterclaim that these tasks no longer constituted true tests of formal logical reasoning, which should be confined to circumstances where such knowledge was unavailable, as in abstract logical reasoning, or counterfactual reasoning, where the logical premises were in fact not true, in order to assess whether individuals could still perform the logical operations being tested. Unsurprisingly, children fared quite poorly under these circumstances, but so did most adolescents and, in fact, most adults. Clearly establishing the age of acquisition of logical competence, independent of context and content, proved to be extremely difficult.

Closely related to the research on age of acquisition was a sustained debate on what qualified as adequate tests of the underlying logical competence. Some researchers argued that if the theory is about how changes in underlying logical structure lead to differences in how individuals employ their cognitive capacities in everyday life, then aspects of context and content are crucial for evaluating the generalizability of performance on logical tasks. Others argued that such modifications did not allow for pure tests of logical competence, and the appropriate tests required tasks that eliminated context and content as much as possible. Generally, these purified tasks found low levels of formal operational thinking in either adolescents or adults, in contrast with tasks with modifications that allowed individuals to make use of other cognitive capabilities, such as knowledge of how the world works. The overarching difficulty in resolving this conundrum is that the theory is one of logical competence, that is, the underlying logical structure that is hypothesized to be driving the changes in adolescent cognition, but what is assessed empirically is performance on tasks that are intended to test the underlying logical structure. Although the competence versus performance distinction is an issue in many areas of developmental research, it proved particularly problematic for the theory of formal operations because the theory focused explicitly on changes in specifically identified competencies.

Taken together, the difficulties in establishing reliable scaling evidence at a suitably fine-grained level, in confirming the age of acquisition of formal reasoning, and in the lack of consensus on what constituted a reasonable test of logical acquisition while balancing the demands of generalizability and logical purity, led to the broader conclusion that the direct empirical claims of formal operations theory were not confirmed, or perhaps not open to confirmation.

There have been two significant dissents from this consensus view. The first dissent concerns the empirical scope of formal operations theory. Testing the explicit or implicit set of empirical claims of the theory of formal operations was occasionally characterized as the North American questions – who has formal operations, when do they get it, do some get it faster than others – rather than focusing on the broad outlines of the theory that emphasizes the importance of general shifts in logical structure. From this perspective, the theory is not intended to comprise a set of formally testable claims; if true, then its value as a scientific theory of adolescent cognition is moot. The second dissent argues that even if the specific empirical claims do not hold up or are found to be untestable, the theory does advance a broader systems view, in addition to its claims about shifts in logical structure, that remain important. It is the case that Piagetian theory encompasses the paradox that open systems processes are claimed to lead to preordained logical structures. Emphasizing the systems perspective without retaining the specific structural claims accords better with prevailing views, described in the section below on integrative models, in that it accommodates the roles of other cognitive inputs and changes, including processing changes, context effects, and content knowledge, and it views the development of adolescent thinking as an emergent property of the interaction among these multiple factors.

Core Descriptive Features of Adolescent Cognition

Even though research aimed at testing the claims of the theory of formal operations eventually found the theory not to be validated in its details, it did generate a large body of work that provides a reliable descriptive portrait of major shifts in adolescent thinking. Many of these are closely aligned with the core ideas of formal operations theory, and in that sense the Piagetian model, if not the formal theory, remains highly influential. In this section, five broad features of adolescent thinking that have been identified across a number of research programs are briefly described. None of these shifts that are characteristic of adolescent thinking should be seen as a completely novel development originating in adolescence; rather, each of them has roots in earlier developments. Their increasing prevalence and sophistication, however, are sufficient to identify them as central changes in adolescent cognitive development.

Thinking hypothetically

Beginning in early adolescence, there is an increasing facility in being able to think about, and reason about, possibilities that are not grounded in concrete reality. This includes advances in thinking hypothetically, including the consideration of multiple premises and arriving at conclusions that take account of imagined, rather than directly represented contingencies. Full logical competence in propositional logic, in the Piagetian sense, is not included in the repertoire of most adolescents (or adults), but there is a marked shift in the ease with which adolescents can engage in thinking about a range of possibilities in a systematic and logical fashion. An important subset of possibilities that adolescents become capable of thinking about systematically includes thinking about different futures, for themselves and others. This new capability is likely linked to advances in identity formation, and in new-found concerns and commitments to larger social issues, which also is more clearly manifest during adolescence.

Thinking about and using abstract concepts

A closely related development in adolescence is the ability to think with and about abstract concepts. This includes both formal abstractions, such as increasingly sophisticated mathematical and scientific constructs, and informal abstractions, including constructs like society or justice, literary symbolism, as well as more everyday abstractions that underlie analogy, satire, and irony. As a consequence of these enhanced cognitive capabilities, there is an observed upsurge during adolescence in seeing the implications and making the connections among concepts from different domains of experience. In particular, the implications of new abstract concepts for thinking about the self and for thinking about society become more prevalent and frequent during the adolescent transition.

Thinking self-reflectively

One of the topic areas toward which adolescents' new cognitive frames are applied entails an increase in self-reflection, including a growing awareness of one's own thinking processes. This increase in self-reflection, which should be seen as an often latent capability rather than as a persistent habit of mind among adolescents across all contexts, takes on a variety of forms. The first, and most direct, can be categorized as thinking about thinking, which is typically studied under the rubric of metacognition. At one level, this is manifested in a growing ease with terminology that describes and distinguishes more clearly among mental states, such as knowing, imagining, inferring, guessing, and so on. This more sophisticated capability for making such distinctions has been compared with the earlier childhood acquisition of a theory of mind, which enables a clear recognition that one's own mental processes and focus are not identical to others. In the adolescent cognitive apparatus, what is added is an ability to view the internal operations of one's own mind from a reflective perspective. In other words, theory of mind enables social perspective taking, whereas the enhanced metacognitive capabilities of adolescence enable self-perspective taking. At another level, such metacognitive skills can be attended to explicitly, contributing to a greater awareness of one's own cognitive biases and dispositions, an important advance for scientific reasoning as described in that section below. These developments have important ramifications for areas closely related to cognitive development, in particular, identity development and the related focus on the underlying meaning of things, where beliefs come from, and how we know what we think we know. In this sense, the natural history of epistemology that was a focus of Piagetian metatheory is clearly evident.

Thinking in multiple dimensions

One of the most replicated findings in the study of adolescent cognitive development is that there is an increase in the number of elements or dimensions that can be dealt with simultaneously. At the most basic level, this is demonstrated as an increase in the capacity of working memory, assessed psychometrically through tasks such as digit span, or experimentally through paradigms such as dual processing tasks (e.g., remembering a list of letters after completing an intervening, competing task, such as solving arithmetic problems).

It is also evident on more complex tasks, ranging from combinatorial problems that require attention to all possible combinations of elements, to planning tasks such as the Tower of London that require joint attention to specific moves, beginning states, and target end states. The ability to attend to multiple dimensions is also an underpinning for advanced scientific reasoning, particularly on the ability to coordinate theory and evidence. These developments, especially working memory and planning capabilities, overlap substantially with the set of cognitive activities grouped together as executive function, which is described further in several sections to follow and is also the topic of a separate article.

Thinking about knowledge as relative

As a consequence of the developments described above, another important, characteristic shift in adolescent thinking is the growing awareness of knowledge as relative. The acquisition of thinking that is increasingly hypothetical, abstract, self-reflective, and attentive to multiple dimensions makes it difficult to retain the concrete, black/white certainties of childhood thought. In particular, subjecting long-held beliefs to scrutiny using these new cognitive capabilities is often experienced by adolescents variously as exhilarating, liberating, confusing, and terrifying.

A range of responses have been observed as adolescents confront these challenging new perspectives. Some settle into a balanced stance of relativism, recognizing that, even though absolute certainties can always be challenged, this does not eliminate the possibility of real knowledge and consistent values, but rather that assertions of fact or belief require conscious attention to evidence and the sources of evidence. Some adolescents experience what is perhaps best viewed as an overgeneralization of relativism, akin to the overgeneralization of grammar among early language learners who start saying 'ranned' after having consistently used the irregular 'run' at an earlier point. This overgeneralization of relativistic thinking is expressed as an epistemic commitment to skepticism, that there exists no possibility of reliable facts, values, or beliefs. More rarely, this progresses to full-on nihilism, but, more typically, these adolescents draw back from the unpleasantness of that epistemic stance. A final possibility, in response to the unsettling nature of relativism, is a longing for an earlier sense of certainty that manifests as various forms of fundamentalist thinking, often but not always religious in orientation. It does seem clear that nearly all adolescents grapple with these challenges arising from newly acquired cognitive powers, although their resolution is highly variable.

Scientific Reasoning in Adolescence

As noted in the overview section above, the currently active research area closest to the focus of Piaget and Inhelder's original proposals regarding the development of reasoning in adolescence focuses on scientific reasoning. Consistent with the Piagetian approach, early work in this area focused heavily on growing adolescent capabilities to engage in scientific analyses using more advanced reasoning. Over time, the discrepant findings described in the section above on testing formal operations theory led to a reconsideration of the centrality of shifts in logical reasoning as the driving force in the maturation of scientific reasoning capabilities. Subsequent and more recent research in this area has identified a number of important factors that require attention with respect to the development of scientific reasoning capabilities.

Understanding scientific reasoning and how it develops requires explicit attention not only to analytic capabilities, but also to strategic and metacognitive aspects, to the role of experience as it provides a context for the application of analytic efforts, and to the difficulty of maintaining sound reasoning on more complex, multivariable problems. One of the greatest strategic challenges is that the deployment of scientific reasoning is cognitively effortful and requires one to adopt a more conscious stance with respect to hypothesis generation and testing, and the evaluation of the quality and relevance of evidence. Even for working scientists, there are substantial challenges that arise from the cognitive distortions and biases that have been studied under the heading of dual process models, explained in the section below on that topic. In particular, the common pattern of attaching more significance to confirmatory than to contradictory evidence is hard for experts to avoid, and this cognitive bias is clearly observed among adolescents as they engage with scientific reasoning.

From this and other evidence, it is clear that experience and a concomitantly growing knowledge base present a double-edged sword. The ability to reason effectively about domains with which one has greater familiarity is more advanced, and has been observed among early adolescents, or even among children. On the other hand, high levels of content knowledge sometimes create a mindset that makes it difficult to challenge one's own automatic assumptions or strongly held beliefs. Maintaining a self-aware scientific stance does increase over the course of adolescence, although evincing a slow and protracted course of development, but is always under pressure to yield to more instinctual or second-nature accounts, most likely attributable to fundamental features of human cognitive architecture.

A related challenge to sound scientific reasoning has been observed as reasoning tasks grow more complex, moving beyond single variable cause-and-effect problems into scenarios where there are multiple potential causes, and most particularly if those variables interact with each other. Performance in these circumstances degrades rather precipitously. Developing a well-reasoned approach when multiple, interacting variables are involved is often beyond the grasp of older adolescents, as well as many adults.

A somewhat similar challenge has received substantial research attention, the coordination of theory and evidence. This is somewhat similar to the ability to think in multiple dimensions, as in the multivariable problems just described, but it makes additional cognitive demands in that such coordination requires an evaluative step with regard to the probative value of the evidence relative to the specific problem at hand. Especially in the face of evidence whose salience seems obvious, it is difficult to hold the theory at a sufficient distance to ask whether the evidence at hand actually speaks to particular claims of the theory. Research on this coordination shows gradual improvement over the course of adolescence, although it remains a difficult task even for late adolescents and young adults.

Two types of educational approaches with adolescents have shown promise in addressing some of these key limitations in effective scientific reasoning. The first of these builds explicit skills in reflective awareness and metacognitive perspective taking into the study of science and the scientific method. The second aims at similar outcomes, but does so by developing the notion of scientific argument, along with skills in argumentation. In this view, the tendencies to ignore the coordination of theory and evidence, and to succumb to a wide range of apparently built-in cognitive biases – such as preferring confirmatory to contradictory evidence – are directly challenged when one is required to participate in formal argumentation.

In summary, the acquisition of analytic capabilities during adolescence, which does occur, is only half the battle in developing sound scientific reasoning. Equally or more difficult is the acquisition of understanding when and how to deploy those analytic skills, extending those skills to expanded demands arising from multivariate problem spaces, and learning how to avoid a range of cognitive traps that, with relative ease, lead one to abandon analysis in favor of experientially based knowledge or in response to normative cognitive biases and distortions.

Competing Accounts: Process, Content, and Context

As described in the section above on testing formal operations theory, key challenges arose from competing models that focused on the nature and development of the cognitive processing system, on the content knowledge available (or not) to adolescents solving reasoning tasks, and on the context in which the cognitive activity occurred. As noted in the overview, these competing models became a focus of extensive research not only as challenges to formal operations theory, but as fully developed theoretical accounts in their own right. In this section, research on these approaches is described.

Information Processing

Research on the fundamental features of the human information processing system began in earnest at about the same time as the major growth in research on formal operations, but these emerging paradigms were not systematically employed to examine the development of the cognitive processing system for about a decade or so later. By the early 1970s, however, there was a burgeoning literature based on the application of these cognitive science approaches to the study of children's and adolescents' cognitive functioning.

There were several different approaches to understanding the development of the cognitive processing system, focusing on different hypothesized features of the system, especially speed of processing, core processing capacity, and the central conceptual structures within which processing was organized. In each case, there were a range of experimental paradigms the goal of which was to isolate one or another of these hypothesized features of the processing system.

Evidence rapidly accumulated showing that the speed of processing, even for extremely simple reaction time tasks that looked at information processing while controlling for motor reaction time, increased over the course of childhood and adolescence, with an apparent positive growth inflection point in early adolescence. The evidence also indicated a plateau in basic speed of processing by late adolescence or early adulthood.

A similar pattern emerged in research on processing capacity, most often measured as working memory span, with growth through childhood and into adolescence, with a similar plateau by later adolescence or soon afterward. There is less clear evidence for a growth inflection in early adolescence, although this may be due to the fact that span is less finely grained in its measurement than reaction time (i.e., items recalled vs. milliseconds of reaction time).

Disagreements arose with respect to which aspect of the system was the principal driver of cognitive change: do changes in speed make it possible to handle more items in working memory, or does expanded capacity enhance processing speed? A third perspective, often referred to as neo-Piagetian approaches, argued that both speed and capacity were substrates for changes in central conceptual structures, where the most significant changes were occurring. In this view, reorganization of the conceptual apparatus, such as in the models of numeracy in mathematics, enabled more information to be handled, and with greater efficiency and speed. Assessments of central conceptual structures also showed a growth pattern similar to what had been observed for speed and capacity of processing. This, however, expanded the competition for what should be viewed as the central driver of developmental changes in processing: speed, capacity, or conceptual structures.

More recently, longitudinal research has yielded evidence that these aspects of the system are highly interdependent, and it may prove impossible to identify a specific leading cause. A separate line of research examining relationships between changes in speed, capacity, or conceptual structures as explanations of performance differences in complex cognitive tasks found in general that the more refined and precise the parameters of each aspect became, the less variance in task performance was explained. In other words, there appear to be fundamental shifts in each of these processing features, but their coordination across the course of development is what gives rise to observed changes in cognitive activity at the more complex level of problem solving and reasoning.

This perspective accords well with an organizing model that has become the focus of contemporary research attention, namely, the coordinating role of an executive functioning (EF) system, which is described in more detail in an article focusing on that topic. Core elements of EF systems typically include working memory, inhibitory control, and planning or organization, each of which overlaps with elements identified in information processing research. Added to this, however, is a more prominent role for connectivity among the executive functions, along with a role for increased capability of metacognitive governance of the cognitive system more generally. Similarities to the findings arising from the study of scientific reasoning, described in that section above, enhance confidence that this approach is a substantial advance in our understanding of adolescent cognitive development.

Confidence in this general approach is also enhanced by evidence arising from cognitive developmental neuroscience. Details of these developments are described in a separate article on brain development in adolescence. Many of the key findings there match up readily with the research findings described above. Most prominently, increased myelination of neural pathways substantially enhances the speed of processing. Increases in internal connectivity among differing brain systems also resonates with the view that interdependency among core processing features is more likely than not. In addition, the specific developments within the prefrontal cortex (PFC) that are seen as enabling greater and more coordinated governance of the cognitive system line up well with the cognitive evidence on the increased capabilities of metacognitive guidance of cognitive activity. It is also notable that the interconnectivity observed in early adolescence appears to give a privileged role to the PFC, as it appears to take a more central role in linking together a range of neural subsystems.

Knowledge and Expertise

In parallel with the research programs on testing formal operations theory and on studying the development of the information processing system, a separate and competing line of research focused on the acquisition of knowledge and the development of expertise. There emerged a stronger and a weaker version of this approach vis-à-vis theoretical claims for the primacy of either logical structures or processing systems. The strong version was that changes in reasoning or processing are effectively secondary to the acquisition of knowledge and expertise. In this view, as one acquires knowledge and expertise in any given domain, enhanced automaticity increases the efficiency of the processing system and enables, as noted in the section on the development of reasoning, more advanced reasoning skills. Thus, changes in reasoning and processing are subsidiary skills that are enabled by growth in knowledge and expertise. The weaker version of this approach did not relegate changes in processing or reasoning to a secondary level, but did argue that cognitive models that did not take the growth of knowledge and expertise as fundamental to how cognition functions and develops were missing a key element.

The initial evidence for a central role of expertise arose from the study of children and young adolescents who had acquired high levels of performance in specific areas, such as chess or knowledge of dinosaurs. This line of research found evidence for much better and more efficient problem solving, reasoning, and memory among early adolescents who had substantial expertise in the area being assessed, often surpassing novice or minimally experienced adults. The evidence also suggested more advanced levels of domain-specific planning and metacognitive strategies among these younger subjects. This could arise from either or both of two factors: with greater knowledge and expertise, there is a greater likelihood that the individual will have seen the same or similar patterns previously, allowing one to draw on that past experience to guide current action; and such individuals may also have automated a large number of component skills, allowing spare cognitive capacity to be used to assess the situation more globally or to engage in more sophisticated planning activity. In summary, the evidence supported the claim that advancing knowledge and expertise exercised a significant influence on the functioning of the cognitive system, beyond merely having more knowledge. On the other hand, the evidence for developmental differences in processing in more tightly controlled experimental paradigms that controlled or eliminated preexisting knowledge differences indicates that other factors besides the acquisition of expertise were implicated in adolescent cognitive development.

Another feature of the research on expertise is worth noting, in that it also has implications for understanding how neural developments impact on cognitive functioning during adolescence. The '10 000 hours rule,' associated originally with the research program on expertise of K. Anders Ericsson and subsequently attaining the status of common knowledge, states that approximately that amount of time is required to achieve proficient to expert performance in virtually any domain. Although the precision of the estimate has been disputed, the general point has become widely accepted.

Developmental neuroscience has independently provided evidence of an early adolescent proliferation of synapses, or synaptogenesis, followed by a period of synaptic pruning or shaping during adolescence, in which those neural subsystems most heavily activated and engaged are selectively retained compared with subsystems not activated. Although additional research is proceeding on the possible links between the acquisition of expertise and synaptic pruning, there is a strong implication that the advances in a wide range of more adult-like skills in adolescence may arise in part from the impact of experience on synaptic pruning, akin to that observed in infancy and early childhood.

The Limits of Rationality: Dual Process Models

In only the second Nobel Prize awarded to behavioral scientists, both for the Economics Prize – the first being awarded to Herbert Simon in 1978 for his work on organizations – Daniel Kahneman was cited in 2002 for his collaborative work with Amos Tversky (who died in 1996 and was thus ineligible to share the prize) on "how human judgment may take heuristic shortcuts that systematically depart from basic principles of probability." For economic theory, this was an important breakthrough in that it called into question a core assumption about the rational maximization of self-interest in decision making that is central to classical economic theory. For cognitive scientists, it launched a vigorous line of research on biases and distortions that appear to be endemic to human cognitive architecture.

Research following the Kahneman and Tversky approach generated a lengthy list of ways in which rational analysis can go awry, including the confusion of correlation with causation (including co-occurrence, or '*cum hoc ergo propter hoc*' in classical logic, or sequencing, '*post hoc ergo propter hoc*'), errors of reverse implication ('if A then B' being incorrectly conflated with 'if B then A'), as well as more everyday heuristic biases like the 'sunk cost fallacy' – having already invested a lot, one may feel compelled to continue pursuing a goal, even if a new analysis ignoring already sunk costs would lead to a different conclusion. Many of these deviations from complete rationality arise from a fundamental feature of human cognitive actors, namely, the search for meaningful patterns. Co-occurrence, for example, may not be a reliable guide to causal connection, but it may be a leading indicator that a meaningful link may exist. From this perspective, the terminology of cognitive bias or distortion may reflect a stance of epistemic privilege allocated to total rationality, despite the theory's origins in challenging the rational actor assumption.

This line of research has often been categorized as focusing on the limits of rationality, and it eventually gave rise to a range of dual process models of cognitive activity. In this model, there are two sets of cognitive processes, one that is associated with analytic reasoning, and the other of which relies on more heuristic processes – the latter of which is also characterized as experiential processing or instinctual processing. The contrast is captured by Jonathan Evans, an early theorist of the heuristic-analytic distinction who noted that analytic reasoning is slow, is sequential, requires substantial central cognitive resources, and is responsive to instructions, whereas in each case the opposite is true of heuristic processing.

Dual process models have subsequently been applied to a wide range of adolescent cognitive functioning, from scientific reasoning to health decision making to behavioral choice. One common element is the recognition that the context of cognitive activity makes a substantial difference. Because analytic reasoning is effortful and heuristic processing appears to be the default, the former is less readily activated and requires specific circumstances to evoke it. Several different areas of research on adolescent cognition have drawn explicitly or implicitly on dual process models.

Most explicitly, contemporary research on adolescent decision making has drawn on the heuristic-analytic distinction. Not surprisingly, for adolescents as for adults, heuristic or experientially based decision making is often the default mode. Because analytic reasoning is both effortful and time consuming, and many decisions in everyday contexts do not require new analytic approaches on each repeated occasion, invoking *de novo* analytic processing could be debilitating. The difficulty, however, lies in distinguishing between situations in which heuristic processes suffice from those in which a more conscious analytic effort would be beneficial. As noted in the section on scientific reasoning above, explicit instruction on metacognitive strategies or with formal argumentation may assist in making this distinction, at least in that context. Also, as noted above in the section on expertise, the ability to automate component skills may be a key support for enabling the deployment of metacognitive strategies, and thus balancing the advantages of fast bur error-prone heuristic against slower but more reliable analytic processes presents a significant challenge. There is evidence that this may be particularly challenging for adolescents, because the analytic skills are relatively recently acquired and thus even more effortful than they are for adults, and because the executive functions of inhibitory control and planning are not fully developed, making it difficult for them to identify situations in which decisions might be better if subjected to more careful cognitive processing.

The difficulties that adolescents face in identifying situations in which more careful analytic processing might be more beneficial and of deploying such processing in those contexts are exacerbated in socioemotionally challenging contexts, associated with emotional arousal or peer pressures, or both. This distinction is often described as 'hot versus cold' cognition. Laboratory-based experimental tasks, on which much of the research on adolescent cognition is based, is believed to assess cold cognitive processes, which favor focused attention to the task and invoke more analytic or higher order processing. In contrast, cognitive activity in the heat of the moment, when emotional arousal is high or social influences are more intense, is termed hot cognition. In addition, there is independent evidence suggesting that emotion systems, affiliated with the limbic system of the brain, mature much more rapidly toward adult levels, compared with the slower growth of the PFC-supported executive functions, including self-regulation. There is increasing evidence for the maturational mismatch of prefrontal and limbic systems, which places particularly acute pressures on the adolescent's cognitive system. Enhanced reliance on heuristic processing and reduced invocation of analytic processing has been hypothesized to play a major role in the elevated levels of risky decisions observed among adolescents, a line of research that is receiving substantial attention from contemporary investigators.

Development of Cognitive Abilities in Adolescence

While the majority of researchers' focus on adolescent cognitive activity has involved efforts to understand the underlying cognitive architecture and how it changes over the course of development, a parallel line of work has focused on major products of cognitive activity, namely, the ability to perform more complex tasks. Grounded in the research traditions of educational psychology and psychometrics rather than cognitive science, this research has yielded increased understanding of how cognitive abilities develop during the adolescent period

Rate of Growth

Although precise quantitative estimates of the growth of abilities in different cognitive domains is difficult, particularly because measurement models often aim to smooth the growth curve, it does seem clear that there is an acceleration in the acquisition of abilities to do cognitive tasks around early adolescence. The complexity of the kinds of knowledge that are included in school curricula increases notably at this point in education, and the pace of acquisition appears to accelerate.

The explanations for these observed changes are varied, but to date the links from abilities to underlying cognitive processes and systems are not well established. Three leading candidates include changes in core processing, an increased knowledge base making new learning easier, and an increasing neural substrate for interconnectivity. Taking each in turn, there are general enhancements to the processing system, not only in working memory and core cognitive capacity, but also in the sophistication of core functions such as memory. These may enable more efficient acquisition of new material. A second reason may be the establishment of a critical mass of knowledge in key domains, enabling new knowledge to be added to existing conceptual frameworks rather than constructing those frameworks. Third, the evidence for increased neural interconnectivity may afford a substrate for easier knowledge transfer and for building more robust and multifaceted systems for both knowledge and problem solving.

A recurring debate on whether to emphasize maturational versus learning approaches to supporting the growth of cognitive abilities has led some to advocate for a 'wait them out' approach to education in early adolescence, with claims based on selected evidence from developmental neuroscience. In other words, not much is likely to happen until neural maturation is more complete by mid-adolescence, and intensive instruction is thus pedagogically misguided. What this view does not take adequately into account, however, is that nearly all neural developments are experience-dependent, requiring focused cognitive stimulation to advance the growth of complex cognitive abilities.

Differentiation and Specialization

A second well-replicated finding on the development of cognitive abilities in adolescence is the increase in differentiation and specialization. Not only do individual differences in general increase as some students proceed to high levels of ability while others proceed more slowly, but also the patterns of ability development across different content domains become increasingly differentiated, especially between verbal versus symbolic (mathematics, science) abilities. Much of this can be readily attributed to patterns of expertise acquisition, as described in the section above on that topic. Some of these patterns are associated with gender differences that emerge more clearly in early adolescence, most frequently reported for spatial reasoning, with boys showing more rapid growth and slightly better performance. The reliability of these findings has been controversial, and their interpretation even more so.

In any case, none of the evidence suggests that the highest levels of achievement in domains related to those skills are unattainable by adolescent girls. In the more general case, an educational challenge has been how to most effectively deal with the wide range of individual differences observed among adolescents, whatever their sources. Proponents of ability tracking, whether global (e.g. college preparatory vs. general education) or within specific academic domains have argued that this approach is the most effective in providing adequate stimulation for the most advanced students and more intensive remedial support for the least advanced. Opponents point to the social costs of tracking owing to the inevitable labeling that occurs, the restricted range of interaction among students in different tracks, and that in practice if not in theory early tracking becomes a self-fulfilling prophecy. Moreover, they argue that appropriately differentitated educational experiences can be built into educational models that do not employ tracking. Although mixed, currently available evidence suggests that tracking is detrimental for less advanced students while not especially enhancing the academic achievement of more advanced students, but the variability across schools and school systems is such that robust conclusions may be difficult to attain.

Integrative Approaches to Adolescent Cognitive Development

Although the search for the central drivers of adolescent cognitive development has not yielded a consensus candidate system, the now extensive body of research on adolescent cognitive development has revealed important points of convergence, even if only provisionally. First and foremost, the evidence for the interdependence of the development of major cognitive systems is quite strong – the mirror image of not finding a single driving cognitive factor that generates all other observed changes. Reasoning, for example, cannot be understood independent of what is being reasoned about, and the context in which the reasoning is occurring.

A second point of convergence is the emerging prominence of dual processing models. The recognition that heuristic processes are deployed as or more often than analytic processes requires that more sophisticated models of each type of cognitive activity need to be elaborated. The fact that contextual variables, especially high socioemotional investment, affect which processing system gets deployed reinforces the notion that a fuller account of adolescent cognitive development will require a better understanding of when and how different cognitive systems are used.

A third and perhaps most important point of convergence is that the integrative models, including dual process models, that have emerged through the study of adolescent cognitive development resonate strongly with findings arising out of the developmental neuroscience of adolescence. The parallels between increased speed of processing and myelination, between synaptic pruning and the development of differentiated expertise, and between the relatively more gradual development of the PFC system, including its networked organization with other neural systems, and the gradual growth in executive functions and internal self-regulation during adolescence, are unlikely to prove coincidental. A productive research approach will not be to conflate neural and cognitive systems, but rather to understand how each develops and connects with the other.

This will be especially true for those aspects of cognitive functioning that are the most specifically human. How meaning, consciousness, and identity develop as emergent properties of a complex interplay of cognitive and neural systems has not been an intensive or explicit focus of adolescent research, but the strong probability that they are in fact emergent properties of both underlying systems affords the opportunity for future focused research on these critical but hard to define aspects of the adolescent cognitive system.

See also: Adolescent Decision-Making; Brain Development; Creativity in Adolescence; Executive Function; Memory; Metacognition and Self-regulated Learning.

Further Reading

Evans J (1984) Heuristic and analytical processes in reasoning. *British Journal of Psychology* 75(4): 451–468.

Gibbons F, Houlihan A, and Gerrard M (2009) Reason and reaction: The utility of a dual-focus, dual-processing perspective on promotion and prevention of adolescent health risk behaviour. *British Journal of Health Psychology* 14(2): 231–248.

Inhelder B and Piaget J (1958) *The Growth of Logical Thinking: From Childhood to Adolescence.* New York: Basic Books.

Keating D (2004) Cognitive and brain development. In: Lerner R and Steinberg L (eds.) *Handbook of Adolescent Psychology*, 2nd edn., pp. 45–84. Hoboken, NJ: Wiley.

Klaczynski P (2005) Metacognition and cognitive variability: A dual-process model of decision making and its development. *The Development of Judgment and Decision Making in Children and Adolescents*, pp. 39–76. Mahwah, NJ: Lawrence Erlbaum.

Kuhn D (2009) Adolescent thinking. In: Lerner R and Steinberg L (eds.) *Handbook of Adolescent Psychology, Vol. 1: Individual Bases of Adolescent Development*, 3rd edn, pp. 152–186. Hoboken, NJ: Wiley.

Reyna V and Farley F (2006) Risk and rationality in adolescent decision making: Implications for theory, practice, and public policy. *Psychological Science in the Public Interest* 7(1): 1–44.

Stanovich K (2006) Rationality and the adolescent mind. *Psychological Science in the Public Interest* 7(1): i–ii.

United States Supreme Court (2005) *Roper v Simmons*. Washington, D.C.

Creativity in Adolescence

C M Callahan and T C Missett, University of Virginia, Charlottesville, VA, USA

Glossary

Algorithmic problems: Problems for which there is the possibility for a known or step-by-step solution.

Big C creativity: The unambiguous creative contributions of eminently recognized persons such as Michelangelo, Einstein, and Shakespeare.

Child prodigies: Children and adolescents who are recognized for performance at an adult professional level in a valued and demanding area such as music, chess, writing, or drawing.

Creativity: The interaction among the creator's aptitude, the creative process used, and the environment in which creativity occurs, all of which combine resulting in a perceptible product that is both novel and useful within a social context.

Divergent thinking: Part of the creative process characterized by cognitive mechanisms which enable a person to generate a wide array of useful and novel solutions to open-ended or novel problems. Divergent thinking represents a composite of four subskills including

- Originality (the ability to generate novel or unique ideas and solutions to a given problem)
- Fluency (the ability to generate many ideas and solutions)
- Flexibility (the ability to generate conceptually different ideas and solutions)
- Elaboration (the ability to provide numerous details in connection with an idea)

Extrinsic motivation: Motivation derived from the desire to achieve goals external to the task or activity itself that have been imposed by others, such as attaining a reward, a grade, an award, meeting a deadline.

Flow: The experience during the creative process of completely losing track of time, not being aware of fatigue, complete involvement in the creative activity, and intense focus on creating.

Intrinsic motivation: The ability to derive rewards and personal satisfaction from an activity itself. It is generally thought to be conducive to creativity.

Little C creativity: Everyday creative contributions demonstrated by those with the potential for high creative abilities.

> Creativity is being playful with ideas or being willing to be playful. It's kicking around possibilities, approaching at least some of the world with an attitude of "what would happen if . . .?" It's sometimes going against conventional and traditional ways of doing things, and being unafraid to challenge the status quo. Originality of thought, openness to experience, receptivity to that which is new and different or maybe even irrational, willingness to take risks in thought and action, sensitivity to the aesthetic characteristics of ideas and things – all these define creativity.
>
> (Joseph Renzulli and Sally Reis, 2009)

Introduction

When presented with an adolescent who demonstrates exceptional artistic or musical talent, or who solves complex problems by using original and highly analytic processes, or who frequently questions the status quo or conventional wisdom, parents and educators inevitably ask many questions about this individual. Is he creative? How can I help her develop her creative talents and abilities? Can I teach him, along with all his classmates, to be unafraid to take risks, and to solve problems more skillfully and effectively? Will she mature into a creative adult? Do all children have the potential for creativity? What environments promote, or hinder, his creative development?

In order to address these questions, one must first define the term 'creativity.' Creativity has been defined in numerous ways over the years by prominent theorists in the field, and a debate as to which definition best captures or operationalizes the illusive nature of this construct continues to this day. The broad and flexible process-oriented definition offered earlier by Renzulli and Reis focuses on the multiple ways in which creativity can manifest itself in an adolescent. Along a different dimension, Teresa Amabile focuses on the creative product, and she defines creativity as that which knowledgeable observers in a field agree is novel and appropriate to the task at hand. Robert Sternberg similarly defines creativity as the ability to produce work that is both novel and appropriate for a given problem. Jonathan Plucker recognizes a combination of components likely to influence creativity, focusing on the interaction among the creator's aptitude, the creative process used, and the environment in which creativity occurs, all of which combine to yield a perceptible product that is both novel and useful within a social context.

To understand creativity in adolescence, all of the components, or strands, most experts agree are likely involved in creativity must be explored. Hence, this discussion of creativity will refer specifically to the person, or adolescent, who utilizes a process that brings into being a product that is novel, useful, and appropriate to the problem or task at hand. Further, the role of environment in which creative activity occurs will be considered. With this multifaceted definition as a framework, questions posed at the outset will be explored with a focus on the developmental, social, and environmental factors that powerfully impact creativity in adolescents. In addition, the roles intrinsic and extrinsic motivation play in fostering,

 doi:10.1016/B978-0-12-373915-5.00009-7

or hindering, the creative adolescent in the process of generating a creative product will be evaluated along with other controversial issues concerning creativity in adolescence and the contributions from neuroscience regarding the brain structures supporting the creative process.

Historical Conceptions of Creativity

Long before scholars considered creativity to be a worthwhile topic to study, humans themselves endeavored to understand the inspirations for their capacity for art, music, poetry, dance, and scientific innovation. To the ancient Greeks, such creativity occurred only as the result of divine inspiration. The ancient Greeks believed in the bicameral brain. One chamber of the brain served as the vessel into which the Muse, or God, infused divine inspiration. This has been called the 'visitation of the Muse.' The other chamber allowed humans to discover and then reproduce in tangible form, or to create, only that which the Muse had inspired. The ancient Romans and other early cultures where eastern religions such as Buddhism, Hindu, and Taoism were practiced similarly viewed creativity as the human discovery and reproduction of a divinely ideal form. Inherent in these ancient views was the belief that humans could not create anything new. Rather, humans could only generate, through mimicry of ideal forms, tangible representations of what the gods had inspired. Thus, originality, which exists in most contemporary conceptions of creativity, was not historically a marker of creativity.

During the Renaissance, this view of humans as conduits for God's creative visions began to evolve. Talents and abilities for exceptional artistic and scientific expression came to be recognized as unique to individuals and, thus, independent of divine origin. Later, as the Enlightenment period emerged, an interest in imagination and scientific inquiry separate from religion arose. This period, coupled with an emphasis on individual freedom, encouraged philosophers to explore creativity more empirically. By the end of the Enlightenment, philosophers considered extraordinary creative talent to be divorced from the supernatural or heavenly world and to reside within the individual.

Throughout the nineteenth and into the twentieth century, theorists and philosophers increasingly considered creativity within a scientific context. As Darwin's theory of natural selection gained prominence, the ability to problem-solve and generate art, music, and other symbolic forms came to be seen as adaptive and potentially available, although in different measure, to all humans. The twentieth century saw an explosion of theories concerning the nature of creativity that were, and in many ways continue to be, rooted in the discipline of psychology. In turn, research into the exceptional human capacity to produce original ideas, insights, inventions, or artistic objects emerged as a distinct field of study for researchers. Researchers began to focus in earnest on the thought processes and personality characteristics that were associated with creativity.

Well into the twentieth century, researchers endeavored to understand creativity by studying eminent, or widely recognized, creative persons such as Einstein, Michelangelo, Picasso, Darwin, Freud, and others who revolutionized standards and ideas of the field in which they functioned through their work. These studies endeavored to identify the personality characteristics and personal traits that could accurately describe what A. Maslow described as 'Big C' creative individuals. Big C research continues to be important in that it provides useful information about creative expression at the uppermost level in a given domain.

However, the focus on the unambiguously recognized 'Big C' creative persons and their personal attributes drew criticism for ignoring both the cognitive processes used during creative production and the way environments enhanced or reduced creative output. This focus also drew criticism for failing to recognize 'Little c' creativity, or the kind of creativity displayed by individuals, including adolescents, in everyday life. In the case of adolescents, an exceptional science fair project, an award-winning essay in a school writing competition, or a moving interpretation of a Mozart piece, were ignored in traditional creativity research. By including such Little c creativity, critics argued, we would appropriately recognize that people can generate a product that, while not revolutionary, could surely be described as original and useful. Such criticisms highlighted the difficulties researchers and theorists had in defining the term 'creativity' in a way that could be agreed on by all.

In the last decade or so, parents, educators, and researchers have increasingly recognized creativity and innovation to be essential competencies for students who live in and are preparing to enter the world of rapid and accelerating change. Few people doubt that environmental degradation, continued poverty in all parts of the world, economic insecurities, and an increasingly technology-driven world are issues the next generation of students must creatively address. With this recognition, researchers and educators have paid increasing attention to creativity in adolescents and children, and they have begun to systematically consider whether and under what conditions creativity could be enhanced in children and adolescents. Thus, the study of creativity in children and adolescents has emerged recently as a vital area of research and educational practice.

Undoubtedly, researchers and educators have directed most of this recent interest toward Little c creativity, on those who have demonstrated the *potential* for creative accomplishment, the unique cognitive processes they use, and the characteristics of environments that most support creative thinking and productivity. Embracing Little c creativity is essential in the case of adolescents because, except in the case of child prodigies (discussed later), the relative lack of knowledge and understanding of the complexities of a domain, experience, and/or skills development in a domain due to young age preclude the demonstration of Big C creativity during adolescence.

Early research on the relation between Big C and Little c creativity generated conclusions which hold today. Generally speaking, both are typically limited to a single domain. Moreover, individuals who became Big C creative adults exhibited Little c creativity as adolescents in their personal and/or academic lives. However, the vast majority of Little c creative adolescents rarely develop Big C creative abilities despite an early showing of potential. Notably, while Little c creativity is associated with a particular area of interest, interest areas in adolescents typically evolve in the march toward adulthood.

Consequently, researchers caution educators against narrowing their focus on any one creative context or academic domain to the exclusion of other areas as this might actually limit creative opportunities for adolescents with emerging or changing areas of interest.

More recent theorists in the area of adolescent developmental psychology offer an additional theory for the development and study of Little c creativity, but not Big C creativity, in adolescents. They hypothesize that the effect of cognitive development on creative functioning operates differently in youth than it does in adults. Specifically, the developing cognitive structures underlying the ability to think formally and solve algorithmic problems arise in adolescence well before the ability to think through more open-ended and ill-defined problems fully develops. In other words, convergent thinking precedes divergent thinking developmentally. Thus, adults are not only able to fully utilize the analytic power of formal or convergent thinking but in essence can also transcend the limitations of formal thinking by incorporating the ability to think more abstractly and divergently, or creatively.

Creativity in Adolescence: The Four Ps of Creativity

In the case of adolescents, creativity is often considered from four interconnected perspectives or strands called the 'four Ps' of creativity. The first of these strands pertains essentially to the creative person or the personality characteristics typically found in adolescents with the potential for either Big C or Little c creative talents and accomplishment. The second strand focuses on the cognitive or mental processes that are operative in generating ideas and solving problems. A third strand considers the influence of the ecological press, or environment, on the adolescent and upon his or her creative mental processes. Finally, the fourth strand converges on the study of ideas expressed in the form of either language or craft and refers to what we call the creative product.

The Creative Adolescent: The Person Dimension

Just as it cannot fairly or accurately be said that all adolescents are equally intelligent, there are compelling reasons to conclude that they are not equally creative. Moreover, not all highly creative adolescents manifest their creative talents in the same way. A fifth grade student who possesses the advanced problem-solving and mathematical skills necessary to take calculus, an eighth grade student who produces unusually rich, award-winning poetry, and a tenth grade student able to beautifully interpret Mozart or write her own original music will all likely exhibit different creative and personal traits. Consequently, no consistent personality profile exists which enables a parent or teacher to identify every exceptionally creative child or adolescent.

While creative adolescents are undoubtedly a diverse group, research does seem to suggest that youth deemed to be highly creative often share some common characteristics across intellectual, emotional, and social domains as reported by adolescents themselves, parents, and teachers and as measured by personality inventories and tests of divergent thinking. Although they appear in varying degrees and at different times, the behaviors or attributes considered indicative of creativity in adolescents include

- Less social conformity, more social independence, reluctance to accept conventional wisdom, and a questioning stance toward rules and authority – more so than one would see in other adolescents who also exhibit these traits as they establish independence through normal developmental progress.
- Attraction to novel and complex ideas, tolerance for multiple perspectives and ambiguity.
- Willingness to surmount obstacles and persevere longer than others in problem-solving or creative production situations.
- Global modes of information processing – thinking abstractly, generalizing, extrapolating, and seeing the big picture.
- Keen and/or mature sense of humor.
- Unusual imagination and daydreaming.
- Obsessions about matters and topics of interest.
- Unusually high sensitivity and compassion.
- Intellectual playfulness, curiosity, finding pleasure in playing with ideas.
- Ability to look at a problem or issue from many different perspectives.
- Ability to come up with many solutions to a problem and examining a problem from a variety of angles.
- Risk-taking: consistent willingness to try something new, notwithstanding the physical, cognitive, and emotional risks that may be incurred.
- Hyperactivity or extreme energy.

Many creative adolescents with these characteristics seem somewhat 'quirky' or out of the ordinary in comparison to their less creative peers. Interestingly, creative adolescents realize they are a little 'out of step.' Nevertheless, they do not typically seem to mind being different, and they do not have negative self-concepts. In fact, research suggests that creative adolescents tend to have significantly more positive self-concepts than does the general population and seem to possess an unending supply of confidence that can be produced at will. Another prosocial attribute shared by many creative adolescents is a strong inner locus of control which enables them to attribute their creative successes to their own efforts and initiative. Generally speaking, creative children appear to be an emotionally healthy group. Notably, the personality traits of creative adolescents tend to carry over into creative adults. In longitudinal studies tracking adolescents identified as highly creative into their young adulthood, they continued to be viewed as highly, if not eminently, creative, and the personality traits that distinguished them in their youth continued to distinguish them from their less creative adult peers many years later.

While they are extremely rare, there are some adolescents who are recognized for performance at an adult professional level in a valued and demanding area such as music, chess, writing, or drawing. These individuals, called child prodigies, have in many cases grown up to be eminently creative adults. Picasso, for example, produced remarkably skillful and beautiful drawings as a child. Mozart, too, was a highly accomplished composer by the time he reached his teen years. Case studies of prodigies suggest that they, too, exhibit specific personality traits. In addition to those traits noted previously, child prodigies already display intense engagement in, curiosity about, and commitment to developing the skills within the domain for which they ultimately gain recognition. Thus, as evidenced by the hours of practice and study, the adolescents who become concert pianists, chess masters, or achieve recognition for unusual ability to solve mathematical problems have already shown signs of deep commitment to their craft at a young age. They have also developed highly advanced skills.

It is important for parents and educators to recognize that not all prodigies go on to become highly creatively productive adults. It is also important to note that many children who were not prodigies grow up to make significant creative contributions as adults. The founder of Microsoft, Bill Gates, was not known to be a child prodigy, but there is no doubt that he revolutionized the field of computer technology. Some prodigies come from highly supportive and stimulating home environments; some do not. However, in those domains that require significant practice and skills development such as music, a strong early start with the opportunity to learn and practice, commitment to expertise at a young age, and demonstrably rare progression toward expertise are usually detected in adolescence in the case of creative prodigies.

A number of instruments have been developed to measure the traits associated with the creative person. These instruments are based on extrapolations of studies of the behaviors and personalities of creatively productive individuals. The most widely used teacher rating instrument is the Creativity Scale of the Scales for Rating the Behavioral Characteristics of Superior Students (Renzulli, Smith, White, Callahan, and Harman). Other self-report instruments commonly used to assess perception of one's own creative self include the Thematic Apperception Test, the Khatena-Torrance Creative Perception Test, and the Alpha Biographical Inventory. Such self-perception tests are based on the premise that for students to express themselves creatively, they must view themselves as creative. Although the results of self-perception tests do not always correlate with actual creative production, and thus the reliability and validity of these tests are subject to debate, they are often used by schools to assess creative potential in students.

The Creative Process in Adolescence

Like the broader construct of creativity, the more specific notion of the creative process has been described in numerous ways. The individual often recognized as the father of study of creativity, J.P. Guilford, first proposed that creativity and the problem-solving process involve a critical mental process called divergent thinking characterized by cognitive mechanisms which enable a person to generate a wide array of useful and novel solutions to open-ended or novel problems.

Divergent thinking represents a composite of four subskills. The first is originality reflected in the ability to generate novel or unique ideas and solutions to a given problem. The next is fluency, which is the ability to generate many ideas and solutions. The third, flexibility, is the ability to generate conceptually different ideas and solutions. The fourth is elaboration, or the capacity to provide numerous details in connection with an idea. Divergent thinking is a topic of much interest because it appears to be an area of creativity that is amenable not only to measurement, but also to development. In other words, divergent thinking skills have been shown to be measurably improved by instructional strategies and training programs. Tests developed to measure creative thinking skills in the area of divergent thinking include written and visual measures of how many ideas or solutions an individual can think of (fluency), how original and detailed these ideas are (originality and elaboration), and how many different perspectives the individual uses when coming up with an idea or solution (flexibility). Because schools often use these tests to identify students for gifted programs, many consider them to be high-stakes instruments. Some of the more popular and reliable of these measures are The Torrance Test of Creative Thinking, the Guilford Creative Perception Inventory, and the Wallach and Kogan scales.

Using such measures of divergent thinking, some researchers have concluded that the creative abilities of adolescents often develop in a discontinuous manner showing creative peaks and creative slumps through adolescence. E. Paul Torrance's (1967) early longitudinal studies of the development of creativity in youth found a creativity 'slump' around age 5 when children start school, a peak again around the fourth grade, another slump around age 12 or 13, and a marked peak in creative performance around 16. More recent longitudinal studies of creative development of youths showed similar trends. Some researchers hypothesize that these peaks and slumps correspond to adolescents' developmental changes that generate similarly changing conformist and nonconformist tendencies. Other longitudinal studies suggest that preschool children who have high pretend behaviors tend to be more creative teens when measured using divergent thinking tests.

Not only can some aspects of creativity be measured, there is some research indicating that the creative thinking process can be enhanced for adolescents through well-designed, highly structured training programs and techniques. This is especially true in the area of creative problem solving and divergent thinking outcomes. Some of the more popular creativity enhancement programs developed to enhance certain skills within the domain of creativity are based on the expansion of the concept of divergent thinking skills into the Creative Problem Solving Model first conceived by Alex Osborne and Sidney Parnes, then elaborated on and revised by Donald Treffinger. The Creative Problem Solving Model is iterative in its use of divergent thinking and convergent thinking and the evaluative processes and dependent on not just the generation of many solutions – but also on the recognition of criteria by which successful solutions will be considered and evaluation of solutions in the light of those criteria. Programs based on the model include Destination ImagiNation, Odyssey of the Mind, and Future Problem Solvers. Generally speaking, these programs endeavor to foster creative and critical thinking skills, develop teamwork and collaboration, encourage real-life problem solving, and nurture research and inquiry skills, all in an effort to generate a creative product for a competition.

These programs have been shown in some studies to improve student performance on tests of divergent thinking such as those identified previously. Similarly, creativity enhancement programs have also been shown in some cases to improve both the quality and quantity of ideas and real-world products for many students. Moreover, students participating in these programs report perceptions that participation helped them develop creativity and problem-solving skills. Because of the success these programs have had in enhancing creative thinking and production, along with the enjoyment students experience, many schools incorporate them into the curriculum or support them as extracurricular opportunities.

Another model that has been translated into an instructional model for classrooms is Synectics. First developed by Edmund Gordon as a tool for developing creativity in business settings, this instructional model is based on the use of analogy and metaphor to consider seemingly different concepts as related, thus encouraging unusual and potentially useful connections. An example is the development of Velcro from considering the burdock plant. Most often used in group settings, evidence suggests that the strategy can help students develop unique responses in problem-solving settings, to retain newly learned information, to generate creative ideas in the writing process, and to explore solutions to social and disciplinary problems.

Parents and educators must exercise caution, however, before unequivocally concluding that creativity-enhancing programs do, in fact, increase creativity in adolescents. It is not clear that the creativity and problem-solving skills attained in these settings are either transferable to other contexts or enduring. Additionally, the research might alternatively suggest that participants in creativity-enhancing programs tend to be more creative to begin with. Many of the studies lack control groups that could be compared to those who have participated in such programs. Finally, there is no research base to support the conclusion that creative performance on tests of divergent thinking or a program designed to enhance problem-solving skills predict greater creative products in adults.

Some researchers have proposed that the emphasis on divergent thinking comes at the expense of convergent thinking. They caution that the ability to generate many ideas is not the same as the ability to produce a superb idea or a singularly effective solution to a problem. This means that if an adolescent is able to generate numerous ideas from multiple perspectives, but is unable to turn one into a practical solution to a given problem, her creative abilities do not ultimately serve her well. In other words, a unique, but bizarre or impractical, solution is not creative because it is not appropriate. Consequently, it appears that producing a novel and appropriate solution to a problem most likely involves both divergent and convergent thinking, and each of these mental processes are important. In fact, training programs with evidence of the greatest improvement in creative thinking abilities have attended to developing both divergent and convergent thinking skills.

The Creative Product

> The starting point, indeed the bedrock of all studies of creativity, is an analysis of creative products, a determination of what it is that makes them different from more mundane products.
>
> D.W. MacKinnon

Most conceptions and definitions of creativity include allusion to and judgment in relation to an observable product or idea. That is, peers, parents, teachers, and others who evaluate creativity typically judge an adolescent's creative skills and talents based on the end result of productivity in a task – be it art, music, science, writing, ideas, performance, or solution to a problem. Consequently, adolescents who think creatively but do not express unusual thoughts, or beautifully play an instrument but let no one hear the melody, or write moving prose but do not share their words, will not be recognized for their creative gifts.

Most theorists agree that products generated in response to open-ended, or heuristic, problems and tasks are more likely to reflect creativity. For example, Mihaly Csikszentmihalyi proposes that discovered problems, rather than presented and algorithmic problems, or those for which there is the possibility for a known or step-by-step solution, are more likely to result in creative products. This seems to occur because the creator is unconstrained and not limited to a formulaic response, and is therefore more likely to inject novelty into a product or solution. Similarly, products resulting from tasks relevant to an adolescent's life, style, and preferences tend to exhibit greater creativity.

Although the creative product is arguably the bedrock of all creativity studies, and as shown earlier it has received some attention by researchers, it has garnered relatively less attention than studies of the creative person and process. More recently, theorists have acknowledged this shortcoming and have attempted to develop techniques, tools, and criteria for assessing creative products. Many of these efforts have been directed toward making it more possible to systematize or quantify beliefs about which products are creative and to derive more methodical means for assessing creative products. Terese Amabile's Consensual Assessment Technique, for example, proposes "a product or response is creative to the extent that appropriate observers independently agree it is creative." Appropriate observers are those familiar with the domain in which the product was created or the response articulated and possess meaningful experience and training in the domain. In the case of adolescents, appropriate observers are often parents, teachers, coaches, and in some cases, peers. Joseph Renzulli and Sally Reis developed the *Student Product Assessment Form*, a product evaluation scale used for the purpose of assessing creative outcomes and products in areas such as novelty, usefulness, appropriateness of the resources used, and overall effort. Although these assessment tools have demonstrated reliability and validity when comparing teacher evaluations to evaluations of experts in various domains in which students completed products, theorists caution that alone they are insufficient to ascertain whether or not an adolescent has the potential for high degrees of creativity.

The impact of intrinsic and extrinsic motivation on the creative process and product

> It is nothing short of a miracle that the modern methods of instruction have not yet entirely strangled the holy curiosity of inquiry; for this delicate little plant, aside from stimulation, stands mainly in need of freedom; without this it goes to wreck and ruin without fail. It is a very grave mistake to think that the enjoyment of seeing and searching can be promoted by means of coercion and a sense of duty.
>
> Albert Einstein

Teresa Amabile proposed three components of the creative process essential for the production of creative products: intrinsic task motivation, domain-relevant skills (expertise and talent in the task domain such as music, art, or writing), and creativity-relevant cognitive skills conducive to the production of novelty. Her research has supported the principle that intrinsic motivation is generally conducive to creativity, but extrinsic motivation appears to be detrimental in many cases. Of course, this general principle has exceptions. Because the impacts of intrinsic and extrinsic motivation have implications for adolescents in nearly every context including home and school, they warrant attention.

Intrinsic motivation is the ability to derive rewards and personal satisfaction from an activity itself. On the topic of intrinsic motivation, J.D. Salinger said, "I love to write. It's just that I want to write for myself." In adolescents, intrinsic motivation is manifest as a deep curiosity about the activity or problem to be solved, a perception that the task at hand is stimulating, and the feeling of strong self-direction rather than external control. When the adolescent has a strong personal interest in the creative activity, there is the sense of engaging in play rather than work. For many students, engagement in the creative activity produces feelings of joy, even mania. Adolescents report feeling completely focused and able to persist in a task when engaged in intrinsically motivated creative endeavors. Consequently, they feel more able to overcome obstacles associated with the difficulty of the task or problem.

Mihaly Csikszentmihalyi refers to this experience of completely losing track of time, not being aware of fatigue, complete involvement in the creative activity, and intense focus on creating as *flow.* Flow produces such a rewarding and pleasurable mental state that people seek to return to it. In adolescents, the concepts of flow and intrinsic motivation have significant bearing on their academic experiences. Research suggests that adolescents are most intrinsically motivated and in a flow-like state during sports and extracurricular activities of their own choosing. It is lowest when they receive direct instruction, doing homework, or in the case of the teenage adolescent, at jobs. Moreover, adolescents do not reach flow-like states when they are alone nearly to the degree that adults do. Flow also seems to increase when adolescents are with a peer group or with an adult such as a coach, parent, or teacher, who pushes them to rise to a challenge.

Intrinsic motivation and flow are the aspects of creativity least responsive to training efforts. It is difficult to teach an adolescent to be deeply and personally interested in a topic or domain. Hence, some educational environments are particularly detrimental to flow. Specifically, flow has been shown to be comparatively low for adolescents in most classrooms, but even more so in classrooms characterized by lectures and note-taking. As more fully described later, teachers can provide an educational environment and employ teaching strategies more likely to draw upon their students' intrinsic motivations.

Extrinsic motivation is derived from the desire to achieve goals external to the task or activity itself. In other words, extrinsically motivated behavior is narrowly directed toward achieving a goal that has been established and is controlled by others, whether that goal is attaining a reward, a grade, an award, meeting a deadline, or achieving the approval of an observer such as a parent, teacher, or coach. Thus, for example, when adolescents are asked to compete for prizes based on creative production, the end result of such extrinsic motivators has generally been generation of less creative products.

While it is generally agreed that extrinsic motivation has an undermining effect on creativity, many theorists believe that in certain circumstances it can play a role in positively influencing creativity. For example, Sternberg proposes that extrinsic motivation can increase concentration on and completion of certain tasks. On more algorithmic tasks, the offer of extrinsic rewards coupled with explicit instructions on how to make a more creative product by elaboration and increasing fluency have increased creativity. In such cases, extrinsic control may be viewed as providing helpful instructions. Others recognize that often intrinsic and extrinsic motivation coexist. Michelangelo possessed deep love of his art but also produced great works of art under intense pressure and with rewards from religious and political leaders. Such synergistic extrinsic motivators act in concert with intrinsic motivators to provide helpful information or increase a person's sense of competence. In turn, this synergy enables a person to engage in the often tedious development of the skills necessary to gain the necessary technical expertise in a domain to which the adolescent was initially attracted with intrinsic interest and motivation.

The Creative Environment or Press

Environment is recognized as playing a vital role in adolescent creativity. Because most environments can be altered or manipulated, it is an area researchers consider in their creativity-enhancement efforts.

Family and peers

The family environment is one context that appears to impact creativity in adolescents. Children from stimulating, flexible, and supportive homes exhibit habits of mind necessary to creative production. Research supports the notion that parents who feel personally secure and unconstrained by societal expectations such as sex role stereotyping have more creative children. Moreover, when parents are intensely involved in supporting their child's creative ambitions, when they encourage these ambitions with positive reinforcement, and when parents tolerate significant independence, their children are more creatively productive.

In a similar vein, peer pressure can operate positively on creative behaviors in cases where the peer group encourages divergent thinking and production. This is seen in the types of creativity-enhancing programs described earlier. Moreover, adolescents experience flow more frequently when they work on topics and activities of interest with peers. Conversely, peer groups that demand conformity or discourage independent and creative thought can also hinder and reduce creativity.

Creativity in the educational environment

> There is little a teacher can aspire to do that will be more important to the quality of the intellectual lives of his or her students throughout their adulthood than to foster in them a deep sense of wonder about the world and existence.
>
> (Robert J. Sternberg, 1999)

Given our understanding of the impact of intrinsic and extrinsic motivation on creativity in adolescents, it should come as no surprise that the educational context plays a large role in an adolescent's creative production. As many highly creative adolescents can attest, it is not easy being creative in school. Many of the personality characteristics – nonconformity, the tendency to challenge authority, and the motor restlessness that accompanies creative impulses – often find resistance in the classroom from both teachers and peers. This is particularly true in the classrooms of educators who seek to establish conformity and provide few opportunities for independent, interest-oriented work.

Most educators sincerely desire to improve the academic experiences of their students. However, they may need help in recognizing and understanding the nature of the creative adolescent and suggestions for providing an educational environment that provides increased opportunities for creative expression. Nourishing educational environments can take many forms. Specifically, research strongly suggests that academic environments attentive to students' academic interests and that allow students some control over their own learning tend to be more conducive to creativity. Thus, teacher planning should incorporate self-directed, rather than teacher-directed, learning activities, and teachers should remain amenable to a less structured atmosphere where students explore their own interests and choose topics of study. Open-ended tasks tend to generate more creative products. Group work should be utilized to increase the likelihood of flow. Curriculum and instructional practices should incorporate problem solving across all disciplines from kindergarten through high school. Based on research of teacher characteristics shown to be conducive to student gains in divergent thinking, several recommendations are warranted. Teachers should encourage and train students to be more observant, ask more questions about their surroundings, challenge the assumptions of a discipline, as well as encourage multiple solutions to a problem, multiple interpretations of text, and varied approaches to expressing learning. Further, teachers can encourage creative expression by those students who appear 'quirky' even when they challenge the conventional wisdom and the status quo, and even when their unique personalities pose some frustrations for the classroom environment. This recommendation is particularly warranted, given that the research showing these personality characteristics associated with the creative adolescent often generates disfavor on the part of teachers.

The Relationship between Creativity and Intelligence

> The relationship between creativity and intelligence is worth considering. The question is theoretically important, and its answer probably affects the lives of countless children and adults.
>
> (Robert J. Sternberg, 1999)

The relationship between creativity and giftedness (i.e., those with high IQs) in children and adolescents has received considerable attention. This interest derives largely from this question: Are creativity and intelligence basically identical, distinct, or related constructs?

Before addressing the relationship between creativity and intelligence, a distinction must be drawn between traditional and more contemporary conceptions of giftedness. Although educational research abounds with definitions of giftedness, as with creativity, generating a definition that is accepted by all has proved difficult. Traditionally, giftedness was equated with high intelligence. Consequently, high IQ test scores have dominated operational definitions of giftedness. Specifically, students scoring in the top 3–5% on IQ tests have traditionally been called gifted.

More recently, eminent thinkers in the fields of creativity and giftedness have broadened traditional definition of giftedness to reflect dissatisfaction with this narrow, IQ-based definition and have incorporated creativity into their definitions of giftedness. One school of thought views creativity as one of the many forms of intelligence. For example, in his theory of multiple intelligences, Howard Gardner expressed the belief that people could be intelligent in many different ways and identified creative functioning as a distinct form of intelligence. Thus, just as some students can be academically intelligent or gifted, still others can be creatively gifted.

Others view creativity as one of the several interrelated components of giftedness. Joseph Renzulli, for example, includes the interaction among above-average academic ability or achievement, task commitment or motivation, and creativity in his three-ring conception of giftedness. Renzulli distinguishes the school-house gifted student, or the student who gets As and scores high on IQ tests, from the creatively productive one, but concludes both are gifted.

Robert Sternberg proposes intelligence as one of the six elements of creativity, the others being knowledge, thinking styles, personality, motivation, and the environment. These six elements interact to generate creative behaviors. Giftedness, on the other hand, constitutes an exceptionally high level of performance as indicated by success achieved through a balance of analytical, creative, and practical skills that enable a person to excel in some valued area of life's endeavors.

While there is some disagreement, theories and research efforts directed toward answering the more specific question – are creativity and intelligence (as opposed to the more broad term 'giftedness') related – generally suggest that creativity and intelligence as measured by IQ tests are in fact related and overlapping, but distinct in several important ways. Specifically, intelligence appears to be a necessary, but not sufficient, component of creative ability. The notion that a minimum amount of intelligence is required before one can exhibit creative problem-solving behaviors or creative output is referred to as the threshold effect. Research strongly suggests low levels of intelligence generally correspond to uniformly low levels of creativity. Moreover, all levels of creativity are found in individuals with higher levels of intelligence. It appears that while highly creative individuals are generally above average in intelligence, in individuals with IQ scores above 120, IQ does not appear to exert any considerable influence on creativity. Students who score extremely high on intellectual aptitude tests are not necessarily highly creative as indicated by tests of creativity. Some researchers even propose that the skills needed for highly analytical problem solving, namely convergent thinking skills, may hinder the divergent thinking skills associated with high creativity.

While students with high IQs tend to be more academically successful in school, to obtain higher degrees, and are more likely to ultimately pursue professional occupations than their less intellectually gifted peers, they do not necessarily go on to make significant creative contributions to their fields as adults. On the other hand, many adolescents who demonstrate high levels of creativity, but are not necessarily the best students, in many cases demonstrate creative accomplishment as adults. It is said, for example, that Picasso exhibited strong drawing abilities as a child but he did not perform exceptionally well academically.

In any discussion of highly creative and highly intelligent adolescents, the question of whether these abilities are innate or developmental inevitably arises. Currently, a debate exists as to whether some individuals are born with more intelligence and creativity than others, whether a supportive environment and the ongoing role of practice, commitment, and study lead to differences in intelligence and creativity, or whether some combination of nature and nurture are at play. At this point, most scholars endorse the view that nature contributes significantly to exceptional intellectual and creative abilities, while nurture supports the development of these abilities. Nevertheless, a robust body of literature continues to support the proposition that intelligence and creativity have significant biological and neurological correlates. Neuroscience, or the research that illuminates our understanding of how the brain develops and works, may ultimately provide some answers to the question of whether creativity is innate or developed.

Finally, the role of chance in creative or intellectual accomplishment often arises in the nature versus nurture discussion. Some theorists speculate that the role of luck and fate contribute, at least in part, to the development of creativity in some adolescents and not in others who might be equally capable of creative development. The accidents of birth and environment that foster creativity are viewed by some as critical variables. For example, first born and only children are disproportionately represented in many realms of Big C creative achievement, while later-born children may have an advantage in originality. Others recognize that for some, simply being in the right place at the right time opens the door to creative opportunities available only to a small number of people. In-depth biographical case studies have been used to demonstrate how creative individuals have been greatly affected by chance associated with such variables as having a talent in a domain that is ripe for change. This might explain why some adolescents without stimulating and supportive homes, such as George Bernard Shaw and H.G. Wells, nevertheless show themselves to be capable of great creative achievement. Still others have had the good fortune to have mentors who have recognized unusual talents and pushed adolescents to pursue them. Nevertheless, it seems clear that without high potential for creative accomplishment and the motivation to achieve, no amount of good luck will lead to the realization of great creative potential.

Undoubtedly, the debate as to whether creativity is innate or can be nurtured is not likely to be settled any time soon. However, many researchers, parents, and educators firmly believe that certain aspects of creativity can be enhanced. Similarly, most agree that environments in which adolescents have some independence in their learning and creative endeavors support the development of creative potential. Thus, at a minimum, parents and educators can potentially encourage and foster their adolescent children's or students' creative capabilities by explicitly teaching skills associated with creativity and by providing a stimulating and encouraging environment.

Conclusion

> In answering the question, How are poems made? my instinctive answer is a flat, "I don't know." It makes not the slightest difference that the question as asked me refers solely to my own poems, for I know as little about how they are made as I do of anyone else's. What I do know about them is only a millionth part of what there must be to know.
>
> Lowell, as cited in Teresa Amabile

Creativity has proved itself to be an illusive construct. While we can define creativity operationally and describe interconnected features – the person, the process, the product, and the environment – that are generally thought to contribute to fully understanding the construct, much is yet to be done to fully understand how creative adolescents maximize their potential and become creative adults. Many developments in the study of creativity have led to suggestions as to how creativity in adolescents can be assessed, and thus enhanced, in the home and educational contexts. But, much work remains to be done to bring us to complete understanding of the dimensions of the environment that can be manipulated to maximize creative potential. Defining and assessing creativity remain the subjects of much dispute among researchers and theorists because creativity appears to be something more complicated than its component parts. As a result, clearly defining creativity in a manner acceptable to all continues to elude us; it is as if we know creativity when we see it but we cannot completely describe it. Thus, while researching the component parts of creativity has offered theorists valuable information about creative adolescents, the environments that best motivate their creative production, the cognitive processes that facilitate their creative endeavors, and the quality of their creative products, establishing a fully encompassing definition agreeable to all continues to elude us. Nevertheless, as the field continues its efforts to understand creativity, and is increasingly informed by the research available to date, a precise answer to the question, "What is creativity?" continues to be a worthwhile pursuit.

See also: Cognitive Development; Motivation; Personality Traits in Adolescence; Schools and Schooling.

Further Reading

Amabile TM (1996) *Creativity in Context*. Boulder, CO: Westview.

Clapham MM (2004) The convergent validity of the Torrance Tests of Creative Thinking and creativity interest inventories. *Educational and Psychological Measurement* 64: 828–841.

Dolliinger SJ, Urban KK, and James TA (2004) Creativity and openness: Further validation of two creative product measures. *Creativity Research Journal* 16: 35–46.

El-Murad J and West DC (2004) The definition and measurement of creativity: What do we know? *Journal of Advertising Research* 44: 188–201.

Feldman DH, Csikszentmihalyi M, and Garnder H (1994) *Changing the World: A Framework for the Study of Creativity*. Westport, CT: Praeger.

Fishkin AS, Cramond B, and Olszewski-Kubilius P (eds.) (1999) *Investigating Creativity in Youth*. Creeskill, NJ: Hampton.

Gardner H (1993) *Creating Minds: An Anatomy of Creativity Seen Through the Lives of Freud, Einstein, Picasso, Stravinsky, Eliot, Graham, and Ghandi*. New York: Basic Books.

Hunsaker SL (2005) Outcomes of creativity training programs. *Gifted Child Quarterly* 49: 292–299.

Renzulli J and Reis S, with Thompson A (2009) *Light Up Your Child's Mind*. New York: Little, Brown.

Ryhammar L and Brolin C (1999) Creativity research: Historical considerations and main lines of development. *Scandinavian Journal of Educational Research* 43: 259–273.

Sternberg RJ (ed.) (1999) *Handbook of Creativity*. Cambridge: Cambridge University Press.

Yang C, Wan C, and Chiou W (2010) Dialectical thinking and creativity among young adults: A postformal operations perspective. *Psychological Reports* 106: 1–14.

Relevant Websites

www.creativelearning.com – Creative Learning Center.
www.idodi.org – Destination ImagiNation.
www.fpsp.org – Future Problem Solvers Program.
www.nmum.org – National Model United Nations.
www.odysseyofthemind.com – Odyssey of the Mind.

Disabilities, Physical

J Magill-Evans and J Darrah, University of Alberta, Edmonton, AB, Canada

Glossary

Activity: Execution of a task or action by an individual. It includes tasks such as mobility, dressing, and communication that impact a person's functional independence (as defined by the World Health Organization's *International Classification of Functioning, Disability and Health*).

Developmental physical disabilities: Impairments of movement present from birth or acquired prior to age 5 years and present throughout the person's life.

Functional abilities: Activities associated with independence. They include mobility, self-care activities, such as dressing, eating, and bathing, and social roles such as relationships, working, and recreation.

Participation: Involvement in life situations. It includes involvement in life roles such as being a student, employment, relationships, living arrangements, etc. (as defined by the World Health Organization's *International Classification of Functioning, Disability and Health*).

Secondary conditions: Conditions that may arise in the course of living with the original disability, for example, weakening of the bones due to medications to treat breathing difficulties for persons with muscular dystrophy, muscle contractures for persons with cerebral palsy.

Stigma: Negative perceptions of a person as a result of labeling, stereotyping, separation, status loss, and discrimination within the context of unequal power.

Universal design: Products and environments usable by the broadest range of people possible without specialized design or adaptation.

Introduction

The birth of a new baby is an exciting and challenging time as the parents and baby get to know and understand each other. When infants have developmental physical disabilities, parents' joy and excitement can be mixed with concern about their infant's development. Infants may need difficult tests and procedures. For example, infants with spina bifida often require immediate surgery to repair lesions in their spine and to prevent pressure building in their brains. Parents of babies who receive an early diagnosis of cerebral palsy may worry about their infant's ability to move and explore their environment. For other children and families, concerns and tests may not occur until later in childhood when the child starts having trouble moving (e.g., muscular dystrophy) or after the child has trauma to their spine (e.g., spinal cord injuries).

The physical disabilities associated with these four diagnoses cannot be cured. Historically, the emphasis of intervention and research was focused on childhood, but now all of these physical disabilities are viewed as life span conditions, presenting with different problems at different life stages. For example, in adolescence, physical challenges such as reduced mobility may increase, and secondary conditions such as fatigue and pain may raise new concerns. In addition to physical problems, social environmental factors external to the person, such as other people's attitudes, can result in nonphysical concerns such as stigma. Some of the additional challenges that adolescents with physical disabilities may encounter are described in this article. The information in this article does not apply to physical injuries acquired after childhood nor conditions that affect primarily vision, hearing, or internal systems (e.g., cystic fibrosis, Crohn's disease). Adolescents with these challenges may have different life experiences and expectations compared with adolescents who have grown up with the four developmental physical disabilities described.

Cerebral Palsy

Cerebral palsy is a group of conditions that occur in about two to three infants per 1000 births. The primary disorder affects the development of movement and posture due to an insult to

 doi:10.1016/B978-0-12-373915-5.00011-5

the developing fetal or infant brain. Most cases of cerebral palsy are prenatal in origin. The physical disorders of cerebral palsy can be accompanied by disturbances of sensation, perception, cognition, communication, and behavior, and by medical problems such as epilepsy and swallowing difficulties.

Damage to an immature brain and nervous system may limit a person's functional abilities and restrict their independence. Although the initial insult to the developing brain is not progressive, secondary conditions can cause persons with cerebral palsy to experience a continued loss of functional abilities in adolescence and adulthood. For example, adolescents with cerebral palsy who have walked as their main mobility option as children may choose to use a wheelchair as an adolescent or young adult because of secondary musculoskeletal conditions such as arthritic changes that cause pain.

It is important to remember that the label cerebral palsy does not describe a person's functional abilities – two people with cerebral palsy can have very different levels of independence. The same is true for the other labels described in this article. Traditionally, cerebral palsy was classified according to the type of muscle tone (e.g., spastic, hypotonic) and the part of the body affected (e.g., diplegia – affecting the legs primarily, quadriplegia – affecting arms and legs, and hemiplegia – affecting the arm and leg on one side). The more contemporary classification of cerebral palsy describes a person's functional abilities (e.g., able to walk in the community without mobility aids) rather than the traditional anatomical descriptions of their deficits (e.g., hemiplegia). Two commonly used classification systems are the Gross Motor Functional Classification System to describe movement and sitting abilities and the Manual Ability Classification System to describe hand function.

Most persons with cerebral palsy live into adulthood. Adolescence and adulthood bring new challenges, as secondary musculoskeletal conditions such as arthritis, muscle shortening, and pain may change and further limit their functional abilities.

Spina Bifida

Three to four babies per 10 000 births in the United States have a diagnosis of spina bifida. The incidence of this neural tube defect has decreased dramatically in the last 20 years since the discovery of the role of folic acid. If pregnant women take folic acid prior to and during pregnancy, 75% of the cases of spina bifida can be prevented.

There are different types of spina bifida, and the degree of physical involvement depends on both the type of lesion and the level of the lesion on the spinal cord. The most common lesion is myelomeningocele. With this lesion, the nerves in the spinal cord and spinal fluid bulge out of the spine, forming a pouch on the back. Children with spina bifida can also have hydrocephalus, a build-up of fluid in the brain. Surgery is usually performed very soon after birth to close the gap in the spine, protect the nerves, and to place a shunt to drain excess fluid from the brain.

The nerves damaged in spina bifida most often are those that control the legs. The muscles are often floppy. Persons with spina bifida may use braces, crutches, walkers, or a wheelchair to assist with their mobility. Because sensation is also damaged, care must be taken to protect the skin from sores due to pressure. Bowel and bladder control can also be compromised. Catheters to drain the bladder, medications to control emptying and filling of the bladder, and routines to control bowel movements are used. If nerves controlling the muscles of the trunk are damaged, curvature of the spine (scoliosis) can develop as the person grows.

The life expectancy of persons with spina bifida has increased in the last two decades because of improved management of medical problems associated with shunt revisions and infections from continuous catherizations. Seventy-five percent of persons with spina bifida live at least until early adulthood, but medical complications continue into adulthood.

Childhood Muscular Dystrophy

Muscular dystrophy is a group of hereditary neuromuscular diseases that cause progressive muscle weakness. Duchenne muscular dystrophy is the most common form, which is diagnosed on average around 3 to 4 years of age when parents may notice that their son is more clumsy and is having difficulty going up stairs or getting up from the floor. Duchenne muscular dystrophy is a genetically inherited, X-linked recessive disorder affecting 1 in 3500 boys. Children with this disease initially have normal developmental milestones, but as the disease progresses and muscles become weaker, they require braces and walkers to continue walking. Most children need to use a wheelchair by 10 years of age, eventually using a wheelchair full-time. At adolescence, the scoliosis progresses more rapidly and weight gain may become an issue. In the adolescent years, breathing is affected by sleep-related breathing problems, resulting in difficulties concentrating at school and morning drowsiness. As the diaphragm muscles become weaker, adolescents and their parents must make decisions about ventilation. Ventilation is provided only at night initially through a portable noninvasive ventilator with a gradual need to also use it during the day. Because the heart is also a muscle, it is affected in most persons over the age of 18. With interventions such as noninvasive ventilation and medications, the average life expectancy for persons with Duchenne muscular dystrophy is in the mid- to late-20s and may extend to the early 40s.

Spinal Cord Injuries

Spinal cord injuries requiring hospital treatment in children under the age of five are rare (annually, around two per 1 million children) and are usually the result of falls or traffic accidents. The prevalence of spinal cord injuries during adolescence is also low. The amount of paralysis and loss of sensation and function depends on where the spinal cord is damaged, similar to spina bifida. A fracture high in the spinal cord (cervical spine), more likely in young children, results in both arms and legs being affected, while fractures lower in the back result in the legs and trunk being affected. Many persons with spinal cord injuries use wheelchairs for mobility. The onset of puberty is not affected by having a spinal cord injury. This diagnosis is different from cerebral palsy and spina bifida because the child has experienced typical development. It differs from muscular dystrophy because it is not a deteriorating disorder. Compared to the three other diagnoses presented, persons with spinal cord lesions have less additional problems but they can be at risk for infections, skin breakdown, and secondary musculoskeletal conditions such as muscle contractures, spasticity, and scoliosis. The extent of the medical complications is usually associated with the level of spinal cord injury and with the age of injury.

Common Secondary Physical Challenges of Adolescents with Developmental Physical Disabilities

All adolescents, with or without a developmental physical disability, face issues related to physical functioning as they experience puberty, an adolescent growth spurt, and a changing physical appearance. Common issues include weight (over- or underweight) and fitness levels. Adolescents with developmental physical disabilities face these same issues plus additional physical challenges.

Weight has important implications for health. Adolescents with cerebral palsy can be overweight, particularly if they have very limited mobility. On the other hand, adolescents with cerebral palsy who are severely involved can have feeding, swallowing, and breathing challenges, placing them at risk to be underweight. Increased weight is common in adolescents with spina bifida likely related to movement limitations, premature puberty limiting physical growth, and a lower basal metabolic rate. Adolescents with muscular dystrophy may also have increased weight due to steroid use and loss of physical activities as their muscle weakness progresses. As the disease progresses further and affects the muscles for eating, swallowing, and breathing, loss of appetite and weight loss can occur for these adolescents. Adolescents with spinal cord injury can also have an overweight issue because of wheelchair use and limited activity. Adequate and well-monitored nutrition is an important part of management and intervention for persons with these diagnoses. In addition, both recreational and monitored physical activity opportunities should be available to encourage increased levels of activity.

Young persons with developmental physical disabilities are less physically fit physiologically than their nondisabled peers and at risk for developing lifestyle-related diseases. Meaningful inclusion in physical education classes can be challenging and other opportunities for conditioning and fitness may be limited. Fitness activities are important to decrease the risk of secondary conditions such as osteoporosis, limited joint range, and obesity. Physical fitness programs are receiving increased attention as an intervention strategy for adolescents with physical disabilities. Although physical conditioning can improve physiological responses such as muscle strength and heart rate, the long-term effects of improved physical fitness on functional independence and independent mobility have not been well understood.

Fatigue is a poorly researched area with young persons with disabilities and needs more attention. Adolescents with developmental physical disabilities are often faced with a trade-off between independence in the areas of activities and participation, and having enough energy to do the things that matter most to them. For example, they may choose to spend more time completing their homework and accept help with tasks such as dressing or lunch preparation that consume energy and time.

Musculoskeletal changes can also limit functioning of adolescents. For example, adolescents with Duchenne muscular dystrophy develop an increasing scoliosis which may affect their breathing and postural comfort. Adolescents with more severe cases of cerebral palsy, spina bifida, or spinal cord injuries can also develop scoliosis. Osteoporosis weakens bones and increases the risk of fractures, and is a risk if the person is sedentary and inactive.

With all four diagnoses, a person's physical functioning changes as they age. Walking is a good example. Adolescents with cerebral palsy and spina bifida who walked as children may choose to use a wheelchair or other mobility device as they get older in order to preserve energy for other things, or because of increased musculoskeletal problems such as joint pain, arthritis, or deterioration of balance. All children with Duchenne muscular dystrophy lose the ability to walk as their condition deteriorates. Changes in mobility supports are not always negative, but rather are choices to fit different circumstances. Some researchers suggest that encouraging walking over other forms of mobility may actually contribute to challenges such as joint pain and arthritis later in life. Adolescents are encouraged to consider using different mobility options in different environments rather than the same mobility choice in all environments. Adolescents without disabilities can choose to walk, run, take the bus, ride their bike, rollerblade, skateboard, or drive a car to get around. Their choice is often influenced by environmental factors such as time, distance, and cost. In the same manner, an adolescent with a physical disability may choose to use canes in the classroom, a wheelchair to move between classes, and a power scooter to keep up with his friends at the mall. It is important that adolescents with physical disabilities do not feel that they have 'failed' if they choose a mobility option other than walking. One way to encourage this perspective is to provide mobility choices early in childhood and to continue to respect them in adolescence and adulthood.

Changes in physical functioning affect more than mobility options for adolescents. Adolescents may require more assistance with personal care activities and may compromise their health to avoid being different and disclosing their need for assistance. In particular, adolescents with muscular dystrophy require more and more assistance with personal care activities due to progressive muscle loss. These adolescents can direct their personal care and use environmental control technology to help them to maintain the much-desired independence.

Many adolescents with developmental physical disabilities also have challenges with learning which are likely associated with their physical disabilities (e.g., pressure on the brain from fluid buildup; lack of oxygen to the brain). This is less likely in adolescents with spinal cord injuries that did not involve traumatic brain injuries. Individualized assessments of the cognitive and perceptual skills of adolescents with developmental physical disabilities are needed to identify and capitalize on their strengths and to provide appropriate accommodations at every stage of their education.

Diagnoses and Physical Impairments: Only Part of the Picture

Knowledge of the etiology and physical impairments associated with the four diagnoses described is important in order to understand implications for functioning and to be aware of the normal life span course. This knowledge is only part of our understanding of persons with physical disabilities. General knowledge of a diagnosis does not provide specific information about the functional abilities of an individual with any of the diagnoses described. Although the future functional abilities of a person with spina bifida, Duchenne muscular dystrophy, or spinal cord injury can be predicted more accurately than the abilities of a person with cerebral palsy, a description of the anatomical and medical challenges does not fully capture the functional independence of individuals in their home, school, and leisure pursuits. The International Classification of Functioning, Disability and Health (ICF) is a classification system used across many sectors (health, education, social service, public policy) to describe not the disease of the person but rather their functional health status. The abilities of all people, disabled or not, can be classified using the ICF. In addition to assessing the anatomical and physiological strengths and weaknesses of a person, it also describes their *activities* or day-to-day functional abilities such as mobility, dressing, communicating, and their *participation* or success in life roles such as relationships, employment, and living arrangements. The framework of the ICF also acknowledges the influence of *contextual factors* on a person's health status and independence. *Environmental* contextual factors can be physical (e.g., accessibility issues), social (e.g., government policies for persons with disabilities), or attitudinal (e.g., acceptance by coworkers). All of these factors, in specific situations, can either facilitate a person's activities or participation or act as a barrier to the person's functioning. *Personal* contextual factors are the least well developed part of the framework, representing features of the individual that are not part of the health diagnosis. They include factors such as age, gender, race, fitness, and coping styles.

The ICF framework cautions against assuming a direct relationship between the severity of physical impairment and the resulting functional abilities of a person. For example, a person with cerebral palsy who cannot walk may be functionally independent in an environment that supports a powered wheelchair. The idea that a person's functional abilities are influenced by both the person's disease and the environmental context reflects the new interactional perspective of disability described in contemporary literature such as the United Nation's Convention for Persons with Disabilities. It suggests that a person's functional independence is a reflection of the fit between the person's abilities and the environmental supports or barriers. The following sections provide examples of the contextual factors that can influence the experiences of adolescents.

Environmental Contextual Factors

Social Attitudes and Policies

Policies and legislation define the length of mandatory education and determine how adolescents are viewed within the legal system. They indicate the age when an adolescent can drive, drink, participate in consensual sex, or give informed consent. Social attitudes based on race, socioeconomic status, and cognitive abilities can be barriers. Adolescents in general are stigmatized, being treated in a particular way simply because of their age, by adults who hold more power in society. Adolescents with developmental physical disabilities experience the same barriers and stigma but to a greater degree and in more areas. To allow these adolescents to participate as fully as possible in education, legislation and policies were required to address attitudinal barriers and to ensure their inclusion.

Inclusive education can trace its roots to civil rights movements that aimed to address discrimination and segregation and implementation of rights. The United Nations addressed the right of all people to education in the Universal Declaration of Human Rights. Inclusive education was legislated in the United States (Public Law 94–142) in the 1970s and in the United Kingdom in the early 1980s, while other countries used policies to address segregated education of persons with disabilities. Disability rights activists have ensured that rights are maintained and implemented in practice. Legislation continues to be updated (e.g., the Individuals with Disabilities Education Act in the United States) to support education for all persons in their least restrictive environment. The United Nations Convention on the Rights of Persons with Disabilities looks at inclusion in all areas of life.

Currently, many adolescents with developmental physical disabilities (including almost all of those with spinal cord injuries) are educated in the same classrooms as their peers without disabilities, particularly if they do not have severe cognitive deficits. With supports such as an aide, extra time for exams, or special technology in the classroom to compensate for their movement disability, they learn alongside their peers. An inclusive environment is one in which all students, irrespective of abilities, are valued, accepted, and safe. All students belong and can participate and interact with others. However, being physically located in the same classroom or the same building does not ensure that adolescents are truly included.

Barriers to inclusion for adolescents with developmental physical disabilities include larger class sizes with a peer group who varies from class to class, leaving them with inconsistent peer supports. Teachers focus on content areas and every class may have a different teacher, making consistent supports and accommodations difficult to achieve. More importantly, adolescents can face stigma that alters interactions with others in their environment because of others' attitudes toward disabilities.

According to Link and Phelan, stigma arises from five processes – labeling, stereotyping, separation, social status, and discrimination. The adolescents may be labeled based on how they move (e.g., clumsy) or their diagnosis (e.g., cripple), indicating a difference from the norm. The label may be associated with a stereotype. The adolescent is seen as disabled first and not as an individual. The stereotype may be that adolescents with disabilities require and are grateful for help, that they are less able, or less active. The adolescents may also experience separation when they are given separate transportation to school, excluded from extra curricular class activities that require mobility, sent to the library during physical education classes, or assigned to special education classes. The adolescents may also be assigned a lower social status based on comparison to the norms associated with higher status (e.g., athletic skill, good looks, popularity). In an effort to avoid loss of status, adolescents with disabilities may avoid disclosing details of their condition in order to pass as more able or avoid other adolescents with disabilities in an effort to move up the social hierarchy. Discrimination or being denied access to opportunities may occur when adolescents are not given opportunities to participate in particular activities (e.g., overseas field trip options) or prepare for particular careers (e.g., law enforcement) because of perceptions that they would not be interested or able. It can also occur when curriculum or leisure opportunities are designed for only those who are able bodied.

Adolescents with disabilities are vulnerable to stigma in situations where they lack power. They describe situations where they were perceived as having a stigma and lacking power, resulting in physical or emotional bullying. Depending upon the environment, adolescents with disabilities may have options that make them less vulnerable to stigma. They can develop advocacy skills, identify resources to help them address stigma in their environment, and become leaders. They may create alternative social networks with other persons who share the same or similar challenges where they are safe and valued. They may also choose to label persons without disabilities (e.g., 'neurotypicals') and make deliberate choices to choose environments and situations where they do not experience ongoing stigma. For example, adolescents may become active in sports that are only for persons with disabilities and attend social gatherings that are primarily for persons with disabilities.

Relationships with Others

Family

Stereotypes also exist about how families, which include an adolescent with a physical disability, function. Traditionally the literature suggested that families with adolescents with disabilities were more stressed and at risk for dysfunction compared to families of adolescents without disabilities. Contemporary research suggests that an array of functioning styles exist among all families. Families of adolescents with disabilities are more similar than different when compared to families who have adolescents of the same ages without disabilities. Families that include a member with multiple disabilities or more severe limitations, single-parent families, and families with lower socioeconomic background or from ethnic minorities may have more challenges. However, every family needs to be considered individually in terms of their relative strengths, challenges, and need for supports without using stereotypical assumptions.

Another common perception of parents of adolescents with disabilities is that they are overprotective. This is true of some parents, while others support their adolescents in whatever endeavors they choose, encouraging them to overcome barriers. Parents' ability to foster the autonomy of their adolescents, and in particular fathers' ability, is associated with the young person's greater perceptions of maturity in early adulthood. It is important that parents encourage their adolescents to take charge of managing their health and personal care and making decisions. This can be harder for parents when the adolescent is losing function and becoming more physically dependent. However, they can help their adolescents learn to direct their care.

Families may have very close relationships with their adolescent with a disability, especially if the adolescent has a limited social network. As noted later in the section on self-perceptions, this closeness may support positive feelings of self-worth if family interactions are healthy. When parents are expected to assist with bathing, toileting, and other personal care activities, adolescents can find this embarrassing. For those who acquire a spinal cord injury during adolescence, adolescents need and seek the support of their parents during the adjustment period, although there can be struggles over who should control the rehabilitation process. Many times during the adjustment process, adolescents express their anger and frustration in interactions with parents rather than to other caregivers.

Friends and social networks

Friendships are an important contextual factor for all adolescents. When asked what constitutes success in their lives, young adults with developmental physical disabilities have identified friendships as a key component. There are barriers to spending time with friends, some of which are common to all adolescents (e.g., transportation) and some of which are unique (e.g., stigma, limited verbal communication, and concerns about contracting respiratory infections or other communicable diseases). School absence due to extended sickness or surgeries and frequent medical appointments can disrupt social relationships.

Adolescents with developmental physical disabilities have a variety of friends. On average, adolescents with spina bifida tend to have larger social networks than adolescents with cerebral palsy. The size of the network is not as important as the quality of the relationships. Adolescents who acquire a spinal cord injury report the key role of friends in motivating and supporting them during their adjustment period. Social networks may or may not include others with disabilities either from choice or due to limited opportunities to experience different networks of friends. With the increased acceptance of inclusion, it can be difficult to make connections with other adolescents with the same diagnoses who share similar challenges, even though these friendships could empower adolescents in dealing with the stigma they may face. Connections are made through diagnosis-specific camps or support groups, or through electronically mediated support groups. For instance, the Spina Bifida Association has a youth and adult on line group, and Ability Online is designed solely for persons with disabilities.

Adolescents with milder forms of physical impairments may choose not to disclose their disability or all aspects of their disability (e.g., not disclosing bowel and bladder issues) to their friends or acquaintances. They selectively choose to whom they should disclose details, doing so when it is necessary or important to the relationship. They may also choose to disclose their disability when it helps them avoid nonpreferred activities (e.g., avoiding gym class when there is a substitute teacher).

Dating and intimate relationships are problematic for adolescents with physical disabilities. They start dating and have sexual relationships later and at a lower frequency than do their peers. This may be associated with lower social self-efficacy, mobility problems, speech problems, or difficulty in finding a sexual partner due to society's attitudes. Parental protectiveness may be a factor, as many parents do not discuss sexuality with their adolescents and generally do not integrate sexuality into their adolescent's life.

In terms of school, adolescents with cerebral palsy or spina bifida rate their behavioral conduct more positively than peers, indicating that they may be less likely to have challenging relationships with school staff. Adolescents with muscular dystrophy have also rated their relationships with teachers as more positive than their peers. Given that adolescents with physical disabilities may receive more support in a school setting from persons such as educational aides, these positive relationships may color their perceptions. In terms of functioning at school, those without physical impairments report significantly better functioning than those with spinal cord injuries, who report better functioning than adolescents with spina bifida. Thus, there are indications of challenges within the school environment.

Physical Environment

The physical environment includes both man-made environments and natural environments. Within man-made environments, adaptations such as sidewalks with curb cutouts, ramps, elevators, and wheelchair accessible washrooms make it easier for persons who use walkers or wheelchairs to move independently in their schools, jobs, and communities.

Increasing use of universal design principles in newer buildings are making buildings and activities more accessible to all persons regardless of age or physical abilities. Public buildings must have alternatives to stairs. Light switches, elevator buttons, and door handles are placed to allow easy access from a wheelchair or from standing, and many doors have power assist. Transit systems have added kneeling buses and designated space on regular buses for wheelchairs, allowing adolescents to travel to and from school with classmates irrespective of their physical skills. In the United States, legislation such as the Americans with Disabilities Act has been instrumental in improving transportation and building accessibility for persons with disabilities.

For adolescents, continued barriers may include school lockers that are too high or too small to accommodate assistive technology devices needed in classes. Small community schools with two storeys may not be able to accommodate full-access classrooms on the second floor for disabled students, contributing to their 'difference.' Crowded school hallways may be difficult to maneuver. Leisure centers may have limited accessible changing areas, and exercise equipment may not be designed to accommodate wheelchair users.

Natural environmental barriers can make mobility difficult when there are snow banks blocking access to the street or to bus stops. Steep hills and rough or muddy areas can also be barriers. These types of barriers are challenging to overcome but can be addressed through policies (e.g., regular snow removal, sidewalk maintenance), technology (e.g., power wheelchairs; alternative tires on wheelchairs), and a good support system (e.g., friends to push).

Personal Contextual Factors, Mental Health, and Quality of Life

Adolescence is marked by a number of transitions which can be stressful. Adolescents often move into new educational settings which are more impersonal with larger class and school sizes and expectations to be self-directed and to achieve. At the same time they are developing sexually and establishing their own identity and social network independent of their families. They are dealing with issues of meaning and purpose in their lives and setting directions for their future adult life. Adolescents with developmental physical disabilities must navigate these same transitions while dealing with stigma.

Self-Perceptions, Self-Efficacy, and Self-Identity

Because of stigma, adolescents with major disabilities are stereotyped as having negative self-perceptions. The average overall self-worth of adolescents with cerebral palsy, spina bifida, or spinal cord injuries is similar to normative values or comparison groups. Clearly, these adolescents experience positive and supportive interactions that outweigh negative stereotypes and/or they place little importance on the areas in which they experience limitations. It could also be argued that they are unrealistic in their self-appraisals. However, they demonstrate an awareness of their abilities as seen on domain-specific self-perception scores such as athletic competence where they rate themselves markedly lower and behavioral conduct where they rate themselves positively. Adolescents can and do perceive themselves positively in the presence of a major disability. Information on self-perceptions is limited for adolescents with muscular dystrophy.

It is important to consider gender when looking at self-perceptions. Adolescent males with physical disabilities often have scores on measures of self-perceptions and patterns of scores that are similar to males without disabilities. Females with disabilities follow a similar pattern of high and low domain scores as female peers without disabilities but score markedly lower on social acceptance. The differential importance of domains needs to be considered. Overall, it is important to consider each person with a developmental physical disability individually and determine how they perceive themselves.

Self-perceptions are related to the concept of self-efficacy or the belief in one's capabilities to perform tasks or actions that influence events in one's life. Like self-perceptions, self-efficacy is domain-specific. Efficacy expectations can determine the types of settings an adolescent chooses to engage in (e.g., higher education) and his or her persistence with difficult tasks prior to completion.

Bandura's conceptualization of self-efficacy identifies four sources of efficacy information; past performance, vicarious experiences, verbal persuasion, and emotional arousal. The most influential source is past performance experiences. For example, if adolescents have overcome physical barriers in the past, they are more likely to be confident that they can move around their new high school environment. Vicarious experiences through knowing of other persons with disabilities who succeeded in specific areas of interest can increase confidence. Positive portrayals of persons with disabilities in sport (paralympic athletes), science (Stephen Hawking), and advocacy (Rick Hansen, Christopher Reeve) can provide these experiences. Hearing of others with muscular dystrophy who survived into adulthood can increase self-efficacy related to health behaviors. Verbal persuasion or suggestion that the adolescent can indeed cope with a previously difficult situation is another source of efficacy information. For persons with disabilities, having high levels of social support is associated with higher self-efficacy. The last source of information is emotional arousal where negative emotions from stressful situations such as being stigmatized can lower self-efficacy. Adolescents may choose to avoid integrated social settings or work settings that are not ready to accommodate their disability. There is limited information about the actual self-efficacy of adolescents with developmental physical disabilities, so much remains to be learned about domain-specific self-efficacy.

Most adolescents with developmental physical disabilities do not focus on their disability when considering their identity. They are more likely to focus on their personal characteristics rather than on physical limitations. This may be in part due to having no life experiences without physical limitations, so physical limitations are a taken for granted part of who they are.

Risk Behaviors

Risk behaviors for adolescents with developmental physical disabilities are not well researched. As a group, adolescents with a broad range of chronic conditions (e.g., diabetes, asthma, seizures, arthritis, mental disorders, physical disabilities) have reported more health risk behaviors (e.g., smoking, drug use) than their peers. However, it is not clear if this is true for adolescents with the diagnoses discussed in this article. Like all adolescents, a proportion of them will engage in risky or antisocial behaviors. Behavior problems may be increased by steroid use as an intervention. Some adolescents with Duchenne muscular dystrophy have reportedly engaged in risk behaviors (drinking, drug abuse, shoplifting) because they had no future, but there is no sense of how frequently this happens. Up to 15% of young adults with a spinal cord injury before age 18 report substance use as a coping strategy.

Mental Health

Having a developmental physical disability does not determine the mental health of an adolescent. However, it can be one of a number of risk factors. Mental health is underevaluated as the physical challenges garner more attention from health professionals and are generally the reason for referrals and evaluations. Physical challenges can make communication difficult for adolescents with some forms of cerebral palsy and it can be hard to determine their emotional well-being. For persons with spina bifida and hydrocephalus, changes in mood and activity level may be considered symptoms of a blocked shunt, and this explanation needs to be ruled out before considering that the adolescent may be experiencing depression. For adolescents with muscular dystrophy who are losing more and more muscle control, it may be assumed that they are experiencing depression if they begin sleeping more while the adolescent may be coping well psychologically, but decreased oxygen supply is making them much more tired.

Recent research suggests that young people with developmental physical disabilities have a higher rate of depression than expected in the general population, but this needs further evaluation. It is important for family members, teachers, and health care professionals to have conversations about adolescents' mental health. If depression is recognized, it can be challenging to find interventionists who are comfortable with adolescents with physical disabilities and can understand the social environment and stigma with which they may be coping daily.

As many as a quarter of persons with physical disabilities may have delays in emotional functioning and coping. Adolescents may less frequently use coping styles that focus on problem solving. However, other adolescents with physical disabilities may actually perceive themselves as more mature than their peers because of having successfully dealt with major decisions or difficult surgeries and procedures that their peers have not experienced.

Quality of Life

Quality of life is a multidimensional construct that considers physical, mental, and social components. Overall, adolescents and adults with a variety of muscular dystrophies are relatively satisfied with their quality of life or life satisfaction with lower scores in physical and social dimensions. In one of the few studies of only adolescents with muscular dystrophy and using a quality of life measure with few items addressing physical function, adolescents' quality of life did not differ from peers, except for leisure activities. Quality of life remains relatively stable even when the disease progresses, requiring ventilation support. On average, adolescents with cerebral palsy, spina bifida, or spinal cord injuries report lower quality of life in some areas than their peers, though as many as one third report a good quality of life. Lower scores may be due to the way in which quality of life is measured with the inclusion of disease effects on physical function rather than looking primarily at life satisfaction or well-being. Care must be taken to understand what constitutes good quality of life for persons who experience lifelong physical disabilities.

Beyond Adolescence: An Uncharted Future

All adolescents must make important decisions during adolescence that will have an impact on their future. They must choose a course of studies that will prepare them for post secondary education or employment. They must take responsibility for their health and personal well-being. For adolescents with developmental physical disabilities, the future can be uncertain in terms of how long they will live and what supports they will need, as well as what supports will be available to them as they move into adulthood. Research suggests that supports decrease rather than increase as adolescents move into adulthood.

Health Transitions

Adolescents with developmental physical disabilities have usually been seen by a pediatric rehabilitation team to support their health and development, beginning at the time of their diagnosis. Except for adolescents with muscular dystrophy, during adolescence, the frequency of contact with this team decreases. In the latter stages of adolescence, adolescents and their families transition to services appropriate for adults. This can be stressful as many general practice physicians do not have an in-depth understanding of the management of developmental physical disabilities and do not have the support of rehabilitation specialists. With this transition, adolescents take on an active role in their health care, explaining the nature of their health issues and how they have been managed in the past. They may have to play an educational role with their physician and participate in important decisions. It is sometimes challenging to find health care providers such as family physicians and dentists who are willing to accept young adults with disabilities as patients.

Employment

Adolescents typically earn income through some form of job whether it is inside or outside the home. This work provides experiences in time and money management, relating to employers and fellow employees, and acquiring some basic work skills. These experiences lay the basis for future employment. Adolescents with developmental physical disabilities are much less likely to have these part-time experiences, and this may be one of the many factors that place them at greater risk for unemployment in adulthood. Typically, young adults with disabilities have less success at finding full-time employment in adulthood compared with young adults without disabilities. Besides their physical limitations, factors such as education, transportation challenges, fatigue, and stigma may be factors contributing to their challenges in finding full-time employment.

Support Programs

Programs designed to support adolescents with disabilities can be invaluable in providing many important services but may actually restrict their independence and participation as young adults. Providing modified programs and alternative educational experiences for adolescents with developmental physical disabilities may close future avenues for learning and employment without the adolescent or their parents appreciating the consequences of their educational placements. Having adolescents progress from grade to grade with their peers provides social opportunities for inclusion but may result in a poor academic foundation for future studies. The adolescent may need a longer time than peers without disabilities to fully grasp course content, yet could achieve the same level of academic learning given this accommodation.

Similarly, transportation programs for persons with disabilities designed to support community participation and independence can actually be a barrier to social participation. Due to inflexible schedules related to high demands for the service and limited resources, transportation must be planned and scheduled well in advance. Social activities of adolescents are often flexible and spontaneous, resulting in a mismatch of the service and the need.

In some settings, once adolescents turn 18 and leave home, they become eligible for income assistance that includes a living allowance and supplementary health benefits. The program is designed to help them be independent. This assured income in many cases discourages persons with physical limitations from realizing their full employment potential because of rigid rules regarding how much can be earned while still being eligible for health benefits. Many entry-level jobs for which they qualify do not provide health benefits and do not provide enough income to cover their health care costs. The income assistance program then becomes a disincentive to seeking full-time employment.

Surviving Longer

In general, persons with developmental physical disabilities live into adulthood due to advances in medical care. This shift has been most dramatic for persons with Duchenne muscular dystrophy although less dramatic than for persons with cystic fibrosis, one of the most common lethal genetic disorders beginning in childhood. From relatively early in their lives, adolescents with Duchenne muscular dystrophy know that they face a shortened life. Until recently, relatively few adolescents could expect to live into early adulthood. While adolescents still face the specter of impending death, they can now consider life as an adult though the length remains uncertain. Gibson frames this as facing both a shortened and shifting life expectancy. Further education beyond high school, leaving home, and personally meaningful forms of productivity and leisure during these additional years is possible. However, Gibson found that men with Duchenne muscular dystrophy lived meaningfully in the day-to-day environment, but many viewed future-oriented activities (e.g., education) as a waste of time. Adolescents may become more future-oriented as they are raised with expectations of a shifting life expectancy and if there are sufficient resources available to support meaningful social participation and productivity. Like cerebral palsy and spina bifida, even muscular dystrophy is no longer a disease of childhood but more a life span condition. This opens up new opportunities and new challenges for persons with developmental physical disabilities.

Conclusions

Adolescence with a developmental physical disability includes many of the same challenges and opportunities encountered by adolescents without disabilities. In the light of longer survival, there is increasing interest in how they navigate adolescence and lay the basis for a successful healthy adulthood. While much has been learned about adolescents' experiences, there are still many unknowns. More research is needed to challenge stereotypes and to ensure that the perspectives of the adolescents themselves are heard, perhaps through qualitative research. It is important to consider all aspects of the adolescent and not focus primarily on the physical aspects of the individual which have received the most attention to date. Environmental contextual factors also require attention to ensure future supportive relationships, employment, and post secondary educational opportunities. There are common issues for adolescents across all four of the diagnoses described in this article, supporting the need to focus more on function and participation.

See also: Physical Attractiveness; Self-Development During Adolescence.

Further Reading

Anderson CJ, Vogel L, Chlan K, and Betz R (2008) Coping with spinal cord injury: Strategies used by adults who sustained their injuries as children or adolescents. *Journal of Spinal Cord Medicine* 31(3): 290–296.

Darrah J, Magill-Evans J, and Galambos N (2010) Community services for young adults with motor disabilities – a paradox. *Disability and Rehabilitation* 32(3): 223–229.

Gibson BE, Zitzelsberger H, and McKeever P (2009) 'Futureless persons': Shifting life expectancies and the vicissitudes of progressive illness. *Sociology of Health and Illness* 31(4): 554–568.

Link B and Phalen J (2001) Conceptualizing stigma. *Annual Review of Sociology* 27: 363–385.

Livingston M, Rosenbaum P, Russell D, and Palisano R (2007) Quality of life among adolescents with cerebral palsy: What does the literature tell us? *Developmental Medicine and Child Neurology* 49: 225–231.

Magill-Evans J, Darrah J, Pain K, Adkins R, and Kratochvil M (2001) Families with adolescents and young adults with cerebral palsy – the same as other families? *Developmental Medicine and Child Neurology* 43: 466–472.

O'Sullivan D and Strauser D (2009) Operationalizing self-efficacy, related social cognitive values, and moderating effects: Implications for rehabilitation research and practice. *Rehabilitation Counseling Bulletin* 52: 251–258.

Ozek M, Cinalli G, and Maixner W (eds.) (2008) *Spina Bifida: Management and Outcome*. Milan: Springer.

Vuillerot C, Hodgkinson I, Bissery A, et al. (2010) Self-perception of quality of life by adolescents with neuromuscular diseases. *Journal of Adolescent Health* 46: 70–76.

Wiegerink D, Roebroeck M, Donkervoort M, Cohen-Kettenis P, and Stam H, and the Transition Research Group (2008) Social, intimate, and sexual relationships of adolescents with cerebral palsy compared with able-bodied age-mates. *Journal of Rehabilitation Medicine* 40: 112–118.

Relevant Websites

http://www.ablelink.org – Ability Online.

http://www.canchild.ca/en/measures/gmfcs.asp – Gross Motor Function Classification System.

http://idea.ed.gov/ – Individuals with Disabilities Education Act.

http://www.who.int/classifications/icf/en – International Classification of Functioning, Disability and Health.

http://www.macs.nu – Manual Ability Classification System.

http://www.muscle.ca/national/home.html – Muscular Dystrophy Canada.

www.ninds.nih.gov/disorders/cerebral_palsy – National Institute of Neurological Disorders and Stroke.

www.spinabifidaassociation.org – Spina Bifida Association of America (youth and adult alliance listserv).

http://www.un.org/disabilities/convention/conventionfull.shtml – United Nations Convention on the Rights of Persons with Disabilities.

Emotional Development

J Kim, D Riser, and K Deater-Deckard, Virginia Polytechnic Institute and State University, Blacksburg, VA, USA

Glossary

Downregulation: Cognitive appraisal involving changing the meaning of the event so as to decrease its emotional impact.

Emotion regulation: The ability to modulate one's emotional arousal such that an optimal level of engagement with the environment is fostered.

Heritability: A statistical estimate of the contribution heredity makes to a particular trait or ability.

Nonshared environment: A set of conditions or activities that lead to differences between one child in a family and another child in the same family.

Shared environment: A set of conditions or experiences that lead to similarity between children being raised in the same family.

Introduction

Emotions and their development play a crucial role in the daily lives and experiences of adolescents. Emotion is commonly defined as a psychological state of specific duration that involves behavior expression, conscious experience, and physiological arousal. Adolescents experience more extreme, intense, and fleeting emotions and are less happy in general compared to adults, due to changes arising from hormones and brain development. Emotions arise from a process of appraisal of situations which in turn influence motivation and behavior. Biological and social/cultural influences on emotions and their regulation, including genetic and cognitive factors, figure prominently in adolescent development. Healthy emotional development is strong tied to adolescents' well-being, as well as to their risk for developing behavioral and emotional disorders such as conduct disorder or depression. There are small age and sex differences in emotional development and functioning over adolescence, with older adolescents and girls showing better regulation of emotions compared to younger adolescents and boys – but there also is wide variation between adolescents in their levels of emotion expression and regulation within both sexes and at all ages.

Definition of Emotions

In 1884, William James began the exploration of emotions in human development and experience by asking "What is an emotion?" Today, this question still captures our interest, and research is forever attempting to better answer this question. Emotions and emotion development are integral parts of healthy development and overall well-being across the life span. The development and use of emotions plays a particularly important role in adolescence as youths use emotion and emotion regulation to navigate their constantly broadening experiences of the world. Emotion is commonly defined as a psychological state of specific duration that involves behavior expression, conscious experience, and physiological arousal. Frequently, emotions occur when an individual is in an interaction that is important to him or her, particularly to his or her well-being.

The expression of one's own emotions and the understanding of emotions in others are essential in several key areas, such as gaining emotional competence skills, building friendships and social skills, and developing appropriate emotion as one matures. Emotions are important to a variety of functions in children and adolescents. For instance, success in communication of emotions and understanding the emotions of others are linked to healthy social functioning. The development of emotions in adolescents is influenced by many factors, including genetic inheritance, environmental conditions, parenting relationships, and peer interactions.

Some of the important mechanisms of emotion expression and understanding include emotional competence, emotion regulation, and emotion reactivity. Emotional competence involves being aware of one's own emotion state and the emotional state of others, using appropriate emotion vocabulary, having sensitivity to others' experiences, and being aware of the role of emotions and their expression in relationships. Emotion regulation consists of effectively managing emotions and arousal to adapt, cope, and reach goals. Finally, emotional reactivity is the way an individual responds to events and can include both facial expressions and physiological reactions, such as increased heart rate when excited, or flushed cheeks when embarrassed.

Adolescence and the Development of Emotions

The understanding, expression, and regulation of emotions change across the life span and these changes are particularly evident in childhood and adolescence. In adolescence, there are many physical changes taking place that have implications for changes in emotion development. Emotions continue to change in their occurrence and causes in childhood and adolescence. In particular, adolescents tend to experience more extreme and more fleeting emotions than adults and are less happy overall. Indeed, emotions in adolescence are characterized by turmoil and can change instantly with little provocation.

Emotions during adolescence, likely in part due to the influx of hormones, are characterized by overall increased intensity – in both positive and negative emotional states. Early in adolescence there is an increase in multiple hormones as children enter puberty. These hormones include thyroxine, adrenal androgen, testosterone, and estrogen. Not surprisingly, many developmental problems of adolescence tend to involve emotional extremes and poor emotional control. Adolescents are at an increased risk of depression, suicide, and delinquency. The brain may not adequately inhibit negative emotions or the body's hormonal response to stress may be inappropriate. Poor self-regulation of negative emotions, including sadness and anger, can also put youths at an increased risk for suicide or delinquency.

The frontal regions of the cerebral cortex increase their connections and integrated activity with the temporal lobes during middle childhood indicating greater neural efficiency. The brain undergoes a growth spurt in the frontal lobes of the cerebral cortex in late adolescence, around 17 years of age, and this growth continues into early adulthood. This area of the brain is in control of logic, planning, and emotion regulation. Therefore, adolescence is characterized by slowly developing better control of emotions and their expression. Adolescents, with the frontal lobes not having achieved full development, are much more likely to engage in sensation seeking and risky behaviors.

Nominal Categories and Structures of Emotions

Emotions have typically been categorized as either primary or secondary. Primary emotions involve both positive and negative emotions which are for the most part innate, including smiling, laughter, anger, sadness, and fear. Secondary emotions involve a higher-order set of feelings and are typically referred to as self-conscious emotions such as embarrassment, pride, guilt, and shame.

Primary emotions are the more basic human emotions, are universal across all human cultures, and are seen very early in a child's development. Basic emotions promote survival and aid in communication and social interaction. The primary emotions are broadly divided into positive and negative emotions. Positive emotions include enthusiasm, joy, and happiness. These emotions involve expressions such as smiling or laughter. Smiling begins between 3 and 8 weeks of age as a response to external stimuli. Laughing is well developed by 4 months of age and is useful to maintaining positive emotions and well-being. These positive emotions promote healthy social interactions and the overall survival of a child. Negative emotions include anger, disgust, fear, and sadness. Anger and sadness are present very early in childhood and help express needs to caregivers through nonverbal cues. Fear generally manifests around 3 months of age and begins with wariness until eventually being evident through responses such as stranger anxiety which emerges around 7–9 months of age. Both positive and negative emotions involve social referencing or reading the emotional cues of others early on and continue to be highly influenced by relationships throughout development.

The frequency with which specific emotions are experienced seems to change in childhood and adolescence. There is some evidence that negative emotion increases after middle childhood, and early to middle adolescence is marked by an increase in the frequency or intensity of negative emotions and a decrease in positive emotion. Older adolescents seem to experience less emotional lability (i.e., change from day to day) than do young adolescents.

Secondary emotions, or self-conscious emotions, include emotions that involve injury to or enhancement of the way we view ourselves, known as our sense of self. These higher-order emotions include guilt, shame, pride, embarrassment, and envy. Self-conscious emotions can involve having a negative view of one's self and one's behavior as in the case of shame or embarrassment. However, self-conscious emotions may also involve an individual feeling happiness in themselves and their personal achievements, as is the case with pride.

Secondary emotions are more complex and require the ability to differentiate and integrate several aspects and roles of a situation, particularly the role of personal responsibility. These emotions generally tend to emerge in early childhood and become more developed throughout childhood and adolescence. Though these emotions relate to how individuals view themselves, they are still frequently influenced by how others view the individual and by social interactions.

Behavioral Consequences of Emotion

Emotions are an important part of human experience. Nico Frijda explained that emotions have behavioral consequences through emotion regulation (control of emotional reactivity; regulation of emotional arousal and expression), action initiation/guidance, and attention shift. Frijda defines emotion as a state of action readiness, which is a motivational state. Emotion, by its very nature, is change in action readiness to maintain or change one's relationship to an object or event. Motivation, or motivational change, is one of the key aspects of emotions. Obviously, emotions have much to do with action. Frijda outlines emotion processes as follows: An event occurs and we interpret that event. The interpretation of that event is our appraisal. The appraisal leads to action readiness, affect, and arousal, and these three responses are what motivate behavior. For example, the appraisal may gear us (action readiness) to flee (behavior) a dangerous situation (situation appraised as 'dangerous').

Motivation for action – changes in motivation and motivational processes – is an important part of emotions. Emotions involve two traditional hallmarks of motivation: the phenomena of intent and of energizing of behavior. Intent refers to the phenomena of functional equivalence of behaviors – that is, their sharing of a common end state. Energizing refers to the feature that behavior does occur, even when it demands effort and other costs, that it seeks to continue in spite of interruptions and obstacles, and that resources are marshaled to accomplish all this. Motivation shapes the fine grain of emotions: How they feel, what states of readiness they harbor, what behavior follows (if any), and what autonomic changes occur. Emotions themselves consist of two separate processes: the changes in motivation and the appraisal processes that trigger them. The appraisal processes provide objects and events with emotional value or meaning. Different emotions arise in response to different meanings. Situation meaning is inferred in part from how people consciously experience emotional situations and in part from the observed effects of earlier experiences, current context, and current subject conditions (such as fatigue and alertness) on emotions. The processes causing motivational change are sensitive to the outcomes of the appraisal processes; different appraisals tend to play on different modes of action readiness.

Acceptability is one of the factors that influence changes in motivation. Unacceptable actions are suppressed or toned down, or an alternative is sought. Acceptability represents some balance between the harms brought by doing and the harms brought by not doing, and depends on the urgency or importance of the aims at hand. In balancing costs and benefits, anticipated emotions (i.e., 'virtual emotions') play key role. For example, one abstains from hurting someone else not only because of actual empathic distress or guilt feeling, but also because empathic distress and guilt feeling are expected to be forthcoming if one did hurt. Many social emotions, such as shame, guilt, and jealousy, seem to function in a way that action results from anticipating future emotions. That is, we behave properly and prudently in order not to feel shame or guilt later.

In addition, whether action follows emotions or not is also determined by the availability of meaningful action. Not seeing the possibility for meaningful action can deeply affect emotional motivation. For example, if one finds no meaningful outlet for anger, it may lead to harming oneself. By contrast, if actions are readily available, motivation may be enhanced from irritation to outright rage. As goal formation takes time, effort, invention, and overcoming practical obstacles, the urgency and importance of the emotion must be worth the effort. An event is felt as important when it affects concerns to a serious degree. An event that is perceived as having great importance affects beliefs that influence daily decisions, expectations of what will happen next in the course of life, and interactions with other people. Emotions arise in response to events that are important to the individual's concerns. One example of the conditions under which such an event occurs is when the sense of self is affected – by humiliation, trauma, or shattering of beliefs. The sense of self represents the conception of what counts in how one views oneself, and what counts in guiding decisions. It influences how events are evaluated and how one could or should respond to them.

Finally, the influences of three factors – acceptability, availability, and importance – on the emotion–action link depend in part on social norms, as well as the model provided by others who do what they do. In particular, whether or not an issue is appraised as important strongly depends on the beliefs that shape appraisal, and the nature and strength of many beliefs depend on information that is socially distributed and approved. The role of social influences is particularly potent in determining emotional action because so much of that action takes place in a social context, under the direct eye of others, and under the direct sway of the norms of the moment. For example, emotions such as respect, consideration, distrust, and contempt modify the norms of what is or is not acceptable.

Genetic and Environmental Influences on Emotion Development

Genetic Contributions

Researchers often study family members whose degrees of biological relatedness are known to investigate the contributions of heredity and environment to individual differences. Heritability, by definition, is a statistical estimate of the contribution heredity makes to a particular trait or ability. Shared environment refers to a set of conditions or activities that lead to differences between one child in a family and another child in the same family. In contrast, nonshared environment refers to a set of conditions or experiences that lead to similarity between children raised in the same family.

There is a substantial literature supporting the heritability of emotionality. Genetic studies consistently find evidence for a moderate to substantially high genetic contribution to internalizing symptoms in adolescence, including persistent feelings of sadness, despair, loneliness, and hopelessness as well as fearfulness and anxiety. Longitudinal research examining gene–environment influences on intraindividual change in internalizing symptomatology in a sample involving twin-, step-, and adoptive-adolescent siblings indicates that increases and decreases in internalizing symptomatology were accounted for by nonshared environmental factors that were specific to each child within the same family. However, there was no evidence for a genetic or shared environmental contribution to intraindividual change in internalizing symptomatology over a 4-year period during adolescence. In contrast, stability in internalizing symptomatology (test–retest correlation about 0.6) was accounted for by both genetic and nonshared environmental factors, suggesting that the gene–environment processes underling continuity in internalizing symptomatology are clearly in place by adolescence.

Similar findings were reported in another longitudinal study using a community sample of adoptive- and nonadoptive siblings. Intraindividual changes in early adolescents' internalizing symptomatology were attributable to nonshared environmental sources of variance. Therefore, the findings indicate that nonshared environment is crucial to changes in internalizing symptomatology in adolescence. That is, environmental influences that affect adolescents' feelings of loneliness, sadness, and isolation are most likely to be individual-specific within families. Such findings, however, do not rule out the possibility that shared experiences in the family (such as parental divorce) have an influence on an individual adolescent's internalizing symptomatology. Instead, they suggest that the influence of shared experiences may not lead to similar internalizing symptoms for siblings in the same family because the siblings may react differently to the same shared event.

With respect to negative emotions such as anger and aggression, researchers have found moderate to substantial genetic and nonshared environmental variance. The candidates for nonshared environment processes include harsh reactive parenting, peer rejection, and delinquent peer affiliation. Longitudinal studies have shown that the development of externalizing symptomatology is linked to problems in parent–child interaction, particularly, the presence of harsh and coercive parenting. For example, research indicates strong phenotypic associations between children's aggressive behaviors and their parenting environments. However, much remains to be learned about whether such nonshared environmental processes can be identified and replicated across studies.

Influences of Parenting Behaviors and Family Environments

Family influences on the development of emotion can be seen in parenting practices, emotional family climate, and different emotional learning experiences. Particularly, supportive parenting and parental involvement play an important role in the development of emotional competence in adolescents. For example, parents' warmth and positive expressivity were related to adolescents' effortful control – a temperamental characteristic contributing to emotion regulation – which in turn predicted low levels of aggression and delinquency. On the other hand, harsh parenting and lack of parent involvement are associated with impulsivity, aggression, noncompliance, moodiness, and low self-esteem among adolescents. In addition, attachment seems to be specifically influential for the effectiveness of emotion regulation, because attachment patterns established in early life represent specific ways of interactive regulation behavior with the caregiver. In adolescence, secure attachment is associated with effective emotion regulation and social competence shown in interactions with parents and peers.

Studies of maltreating families reveal that child maltreatment presents a significant threat to the optimal development of emotional understanding and regulation, partly due to the absence of such sensitive interactions between the caregiver(s) and the child. In maltreating families, parents are less likely to be available to provide support and scaffolding when their children are upset, from which children can learn constructive strategies to regulate their emotional states. An unpredictable and disorganized environment, as found in maltreating homes, might make children particularly vulnerable to experiencing negative emotions. Specifically, maltreated children and adolescents tend to be more angry, frustrated, reactive, and irritable than their nonmaltreated peers. In particular, physically abused children and adolescents may experience overwhelming emotional arousal that leads to difficulties managing and processing negative emotionality. Indeed, existing literature indicates that maltreated children and adolescents evidence numerous deficits in the recognition, expression, and understanding of emotions.

Research has demonstrated that when parents have high conflicts between themselves, that can have deleterious effects on adolescents–those adolescents tend to display more aggressive and acting-out behaviors than other adolescents with parents whose marital relationships are more positive and supportive. Adolescents may be affected directly by marital conflict by witnessing fights and arguments between parents. In particular, the history of conflict between the parents influences adolescents' emotional security, as evidenced by emotional reactivity. Homes with a continuous high level of conflict are likely to sensitize adolescents to be concerned about their own security because such conflicts last a long time, increase the probability of future conflicts, and have a detrimental effect on parent–child relationships. Being concerned about one's own security is adaptive for adolescents as it allows them to cope with threats that are brought upon by interparental conflict.

Interestingly, studies by Mavis Hetherington and colleagues have shown that boys are more susceptible to the negative effects of martial conflict than girls. It appears that boys are more likely to be directly exposed to parental bickering and physical abuse than girls. That is, parents quarrel more often with each other, and their quarrels are longer, in the presence of their sons. The effects of marital conflict on adolescent emotional development can be indirect. Marital difficulties seem to diminish the ability of parents to provide authoritative parenting, which is eventually related to problems in emotional health among adolescents.

Finally, family economic environments seem to influence family processes, which in turn, are related to adolescent emotional development. In particular, prior research has demonstrated the negative impact of persistent poverty on adolescent emotional adjustment. For example, Rand Conger and colleagues studied rural families struggling with the economic crisis that affected midwestern parts of the United States during the 1980s. Their findings indicate that the harmful effects of family economic hardship on adolescent emotional adjustment were mainly mediated by poor parenting behaviors and parental negativity toward adolescents. As the parents face economic problems, they felt helpless and became depressed and irritable, and they had more conflicts in their marriages. This was true across families living in diverse geographic areas and diverse ethnic groups. Studies of poor African American families in Southern parts of the United States demonstrated that parents experiencing marital conflicts showed more negative and less nurturing behaviors in their interactions with their adolescent children. Such negative parenting behaviors were, in turn, related to adolescents' emotional problems such as low social competence, and high emotional maladjustment including depression and anxiety.

Influences of Peer Relations

Emotion development and emotion regulation are largely social processes that occur within the context of social interactions. Social relationships require the appropriate expression and interpretation of emotion. Peers and close friends actively influence one another throughout childhood and adolescence. In early adolescence, adolescents learn and practice many social skills in the context of small groups of friends. These relationships also enhance individual adolescents' coping and emotional adjustment.

Emotional expression and regulation affect adolescents' interactions with their peers through the ways in which peers understand, interpret, express, and react to one another. In particular, adolescents must regulate their own emotions correctly in order to accurately interpret social and emotional cues in the environment. Adolescents who exhibit good emotion regulation and emotional competence are likely to have better social skills and show socially appropriate behavior. In contrast, adolescents high in negative emotions or lacking emotion regulation are at a greater risk of not only behavior problems but also of poorer social skills which can in turn lead to poor social relationships.

Research suggests that emotional development interacts with social functioning to predict adolescents' overall functioning. It has been found that adolescents high in social functioning tend to exhibit low negative emotions and better emotion regulation skills. In contrast, adolescents with high rates of negative emotions are more likely to have low social functioning. Nancy Eisenberg and colleagues have demonstrated that children and adolescents who show high levels of negative emotions and poor emotion regulation are likely to face more difficulty in handling social situations and their emotion arousal in these situations. Furthermore, these children and adolescents show overall low social competence, low levels of prosocial behavior, and high levels of problem behavior.

The relationship between social and emotional development is of a reciprocal nature. Not only that appropriate emotion regulation and high emotional competence predict better social functioning, but also that social experiences influence emotion regulation and emotional competence. Peers act as socializers of emotion by reacting to the emotions of one another, expressing emotions to one another, and discussing emotions. It is in peer relationships that adolescents are able to develop their ability to regulate emotions in social settings, and exhibit emotional competence by correctly expressing their emotions to others and accurately interpreting the emotions expressed by others. Emotion regulation and emotional competence may also affect the continuity of social functioning through negative emotion expression or poor emotion regulation, which leads to negative social interactions and peer rejection over time. Such negative social experiences can in turn increase problem behaviors and have negative effects on adolescents' overall emotional development.

Being rejected by peers has harmful consequences for adolescents' emotional development. Peer victimization occurs when an adolescent is bullied by other peers – including physical victimization as well as relational victimization (in which peers try to damage or control their relationships with others). Victimized adolescents are more likely to be anxious, depressed, and lonely and tend to have more negative perceptions of their competence. Prior research also suggests that some children, whether they are actively rejected by peers or not, seem to actively avoid interaction with peers. Their peers reject many, but not all, of these withdrawn children. Studies demonstrate that such patterns of withdrawal from social interaction in childhood appear to be stable over time and context, and predict subsequent emotional maladjustment including depression, anxiety, loneliness, and poor self-esteem.

Emotion and Psychopathology

Adolescence is a crucial time for emotion development, with overall emotion development and regulation making huge strides between middle childhood and adolescence. Understanding the role of emotion development in internalizing and externalizing symptomatology becomes all the more crucial, as the period of adolescence puts youths at a greater risk for developing certain types of psychopathology and symptomatology. Emotion development and functioning has been implicated in both internalizing and externalizing symptomatology, as well as in many clinical disorders. Emotions play a powerful role in both psychological health and physiological health. For example, emotions can exert negative or positive effects on overall health in adolescents through physiological changes, such as increased heart rate or cortisol levels. Emotions can also affect psychological well-being through the effects of extreme sadness or joy on an individual's mood. Positive emotions can buffer the effects of stress on adolescents, whereas negative emotions (in particular prolonged negative emotions) can exacerbate the effects of stress and negative life experiences.

Emotion regulation and subsequent socioemotional development play important roles within overall adolescent risk and resilience. For instance, adolescents who report more intense and labile emotions and less effective regulation of these emotions also reported more depressive symptoms. Furthermore, good emotion regulation capabilities can act as a protective factor against trauma and other risk factors, whereas poor emotion regulation may act as a risk factor leading to more negative emotions, poor coping, and poorer social interactions. In particular, emotion regulation and emotional competence may act as adaptive factors in the face of adversity and may promote more positive coping strategies and thus healthy adjustment throughout development. For example, prior research has shown that children's optimal emotion regulation is negatively affected by maltreatment and interadult violence, and children's poor emotion regulation is related to higher levels of anxious/depressed symptoms and social problems. More importantly, there is evidence that emotion regulation mediates the link between earlier child maltreatment and emotional adjustment outcomes such as anxious/depressed symptoms. Overall, past research points out that emotion regulation can both directly and indirectly affect emotional adjustment among children and adolescents, through its influences on the ways in which youth process and control their reactions to their environments.

Sex Differences in Emotional Development

Sex differences are evident in emotion development in multiple aspects of overall emotionality. It is a common belief – across cultures, ages, and genders – that females are more emotionally expressive than males, especially with respect to sadness and fear. Some studies seem to support such sex differences particularly for behavior expression across different emotion components (both positive and negative emotions, possibly with the exceptions of anger) and intensity of emotional expression. As far as anger is concerned, males tend to use more direct 'acting out' or retaliatory strategies, whereas females tend to use strategies such as avoidance, interpersonal reconciliation, turning against the self, and nonaggressive strategies. In contrast, for sadness, females behaviorally manifest sadness more than do males in that they will cry more, whereas males will withdraw more from sad or depressing situations and engage in distracting activities such as physical exercise. In addition, females are more accurate at recognizing emotional expressions than are males, and females tend not only to verbally self-report more embarrassment and shame, but also to actively attempt more interpersonal reconciliation when such emotions occur.

Sex plays a key role in the types of emotions displayed and experienced by adolescents. Male adolescents are less likely than female adolescents to disclose their fearful emotions during times of distress. Risk factors in family environments seem to have differential effects on adolescent emotional adjustment between boys and girls. For example, male adolescents respond to parental divorce with increases in conduct problems, whereas female adolescents tend to show increases in depression. Harsh parenting may inhibit aggression in girls while promoting it among boys. Some sex differences also are obtained in the quality and effects of sibling relationships. Female siblings are no less negative and conflictual but are more supportive and positive in their sibling relationships than are male siblings. Moreover, in times of stress, compassionate caring relationships can protect adolescents from emotional maladjustment. Male adolescents receive less emotional support from either male or female siblings during difficult transitions such as a parental divorce or remarriage.

Sex differences also have been observed in levels of emotion regulation, indicating that girls develop emotion regulation skills earlier and show better emotion regulation skills than do boys. Girls show higher empathy, more prosocial behaviors, and more effective regulation of negative affect than do boys. Although relatively few researchers have examined the role of sex in relation to the linkages between emotion regulation and children's social and behavioral adjustment, available findings imply that emotion regulation may interact with sex when predicting adjustment outcomes. For example, Nancy Eisenberg and her colleagues found that among children in early and middle childhood, correlations between emotion dysregulation and conduct problems were stronger for boys than for girls (correlations about 0.4 for boys versus correlations about 0.1 for girls). In contrast, poor regulatory skills were significant predictors of peer victimization among girls but not among boys.

Some studies have found effects of emotion regulation and emotion development to be effective in preventing unhealthy adjustment or risk behaviors in males but not females. In intervention studies targeting inner-city African-American youths, social–emotional programs that emphasized communication, social networking, stress management, empathy, and role models were effective in preventing adolescent boys from engaging in multiple risk behaviors, including violence. However, this effect was not found for adolescent girls. Thus, previous studies indicate that different aspects of emotion and social development may influence boys and girls differently as protective factors against risky behaviors. Overall, boys show lower levels of emotion regulation than girls do. However, emotion regulation appears to play a more important role as a protective factor for adjustment problems among boys.

Sex differences in emotion regulation may be in part due to the fact that caregivers may respond in different ways to boys and girls. For example, caregivers may pay more attention to an inhibited boy than an inhibited girl, reinforce autonomy and self regulatory behavior in boys more than girls, and encourage emotional control more in boys in part by interactions with parents and in part due to cultural norms of males being less emotional. These differences may stem from girls being taught more relationship-oriented strategies for regulating emotion, whereas boys are taught more active and instrumental strategies such as distracting activities. In addition, although girls are typically found to be better regulated than boys particularly during childhood, it is unclear as to whether these are innate differences in reactivity levels or due to sex-specific socialization of emotional behaviors.

Research involving self-reports of emotional experiences suggests that females are more emotionally expressive and show more detailed representations of their own emotions. Similarly, research using physiological measures of emotional arousal and attention suggests that females are more reactive to emotional stimuli than males. Some recent studies suggest that sex differences in emotional responding among late adolescents and young adults may be in part due to sex differences in emotion regulation. Specifically, in these studies, fMRI signals from prefrontal cortex regions of the brain were used to identify sex differences in control-related regions that are more active during cognitive regulation when compared to responses to negative emotion pictures. The findings indicated that males showed greater downregulation (i.e., cognitive appraisal involving changing the meaning of the event so as to decrease its emotional impact) and less activity in prefrontal regions than women responding to negative images. Therefore, although males and females do not report differences in the frequency with which they utilize cognitive emotion regulation in everyday life, when they are instructed to regulate, males seem to be able to regulate their negative emotion with greater efficiency or less effort than do females. Specifically, these studies suggest that sex difference in emotional responding might be attributed to both enhanced emotional reactivity and/or reduced capabilities to cognitively regulate in terms of reappraisal.

Overall, though the findings on sex differences in emotional development are somewhat mixed and underdeveloped, it is evident that social development and emotional development both influence each other and influence the healthy development and adjustment of both males and females. It also should be noted that even when research identifies sex differences in a particular domain of emotions, there is generally a great deal of overlap between males and females. That is, individual differences within each biological sex group seem to be far greater than differences between male and female groups.

Conclusions

To summarize, emotions and their development play a crucial role in the daily lives and experiences of adolescents. There are wide-ranging differences between adolescents in their predominant emotions – expressions of underlying states and traits – that are elicited by specific situations, but that also remain fairly stable across time and contexts. There are biological and social/cultural influences on emotions and their regulation, including genetic and cognitive factors, and qualities of personal relationships with others (including parents, siblings, and peers). The variety of influences on emotional development and functioning are strongly tied to adolescents' well-being, as well as risks for developing behavioral and emotional problems and disorders that range from antisocial conduct problems to mood disorders such as depression. There are age and sex differences in emotional development and functioning over adolescence, although it is important to emphasize that there also is a great deal of continuity over time, and similarity between females and males. What remains unknown is how specific mechanisms linking biological and environmental influences operate, coupled with learning and shifts in the context of adolescents as they grow older, to explain why adolescents who appear to be at little risk for emotional difficulties end up maladjusted and why those who seem to be at great risk turn out so highly resilient. Tackling these questions lays the foundation for a future developmental science in adolescent emotional development that will be exciting and challenging.

See also: Emotion Dysregulation; Social Competence.

Further Reading

Coan J and Allen J (2007) *Handbook of Emotion Elicitation and Assessment.* USA: Oxford University Press.

Crockett LJ and Crouter AC (eds.) (1995) *Pathways Through Adolescence: Individual Development in Relation to Social Contexts.* Hillsdale, NJ: Erlbaum.

Hetherington EM and Arasteh JD (eds.) (1988) *Impact of Divorce, Single Parenting, and Stepparenting on Children.* Hillsdale, NJ: Erlbaum.

Kavanaugh RD, Zimmerberg B, and Fein S (eds.) (1996) *Emotion: Interdisciplinary Perspectives.* Mahwah, NJ: Erlbaum.

Manstead ASR, Frijda N, and Fischer A (eds.) (2004) *Feelings and Emotions: The Amsterdam Symposium.* Cambridge, UK: Cambridge University Press.

Petrill SA, Plomin R, DeFries JC, and Hewitt JK (eds.) (2003) *Nature, Nurture, and the Transition to Early Adolescence.* New York: Oxford University Press.

Executive Function

E Mezzacappa, Children's Hospital Boston, Boston, MA, USA

Glossary

Gray matter: In gross anatomical terms, the *gray matter* of the central nervous system is formed by *neurons*, which in turn consist of *cell bodies*, and prolungations known as *dendrites* and *axons*.

Meta-cognitive skills: These skills encompass a range of processes that involve awareness/knowledge of self and others, learning, and (self) regulation. The skills subsumed under *executive function* are a subset of meta-cognitive skills devoted primarily to (self) regulation of goal-directed behavior.

Myelin: An electrically insulating material produced by *glial cells* that form a layer around the *axon* of a neuron. The main purpose of myelin is to increase the speed at which neural impulses propagate along axons. In gross anatomical terms, myelin is what forms the *white matter* of the central nervous system.

Synapses: Synapses are the communicative junctions between neurons. Nerve impulses travel down the *axon* of one neuron across the synapse, generally via chemical mediators known as *neurotransmitters*. On the receiving end of the synapse, *dendrites* pick up the incoming chemical signal and pass it along to the cell body of the receiving neuron.

Introduction

Adolescence, a social construct, is a transitional period in human development between childhood and adulthood during which social roles across multiple domains progress from dependent to independent. Cultural and secular influences help to define when these transitional social processes begin and when social maturity is reached, as in the case of norms for when dating and marriage are considered appropriate. Within cultures and historical epochs, the transitional period to achieve social maturity may also differ across the various social domains, as in the age when individuals are allowed to vote or to own property.

Puberty, a biological construct, represents a period in human development characterized by marked physical growth and changes that culminate in reproductive – sexual maturity. It too is subject to cultural, environmental, and secular influences. For example, for reasons as yet poorly understood, the average age of pubertal onset has been declining in recent decades, particularly for children who reside in the urban centers of industrialized societies. Although associations are commonly drawn between the onset of puberty and adolescence, in modern industrialized societies, development of the latter is prolonged well beyond the point when sexual–reproductive maturity is attained. Adolescence is therefore an extended period in human development when the growth of individuals is influenced by important biological and social-contextual factors. In the case of typical development, these factors and their influences lead first to sexual-reproductive maturity, and ultimately to social independence.

In this article, we examine executive function in adolescence. We will describe what matures functionally before and during adolescence, as well as what matures biologically to support the observed changes in functional capacities that occur over the course of development into adolescence. We examine the social implications of these developmental changes in executive function and how they may support progress toward social independence; and to the extent possible, we place these changes in the context of environmental and gender influences. Finally, we examine particular risks and vulnerabilities during adolescence related to the rapidity of dyssynchronous maturational changes in the brain, and how these interact with the complex cognitive and social demands that routinely occur during this period of human development in a way that can sometimes lead to poor or frankly problematic outcomes.

Background, Concepts, and Definitions

Executive function is a pragmatic construct that encompasses the processes and skills required of an individual to anticipate, plan, initiate, monitor, modify, and terminate goal-directed, that is, voluntary–purposeful, behavior. These processes and skills can in turn be broken down into subsystems, both structurally and functionally. These subsystems, while distinct in some ways, must be well integrated structurally and functionally in order for individuals to effectively guide their behaviors over time and across contexts. In this section, we identify various executive and related subsystems by their structural and functional characteristics; keeping in mind at all times that the explicit separation of these processes, skills, and neural networks is solely for clarity of presentation, since they are always intimately interrelated, structurally and functionally, in the service of self-regulation and social adaptation.

Processes and skills involved with limbic influences and with social cognition are also included in this discussion. While generally not considered a part of executive function per se, some of the structural and functional components of social cognition overlap considerably with those of executive function; while those involving limbic influences are crucial to understanding the role played by emotion and motivation in regulating goal-directed behavior. Furthermore, the processes and skills required for effective self-regulation and

 doi:10.1016/B978-0-12-373915-5.00016-4

social adaptation in general, and during adolescence in particular, make separating executive function, limbic influences, and social cognition problematic at best, and reductionistic otherwise.

Executive function more narrowly construed consists of 'top-down' regulatory processes; named this way because of their assignment to the higher-level meta-cognitive skills, and because of the anatomical location in the brain of structures such as the frontal lobes that are believed to support their manifestations.

The Fronto-Parietal Network

Within the realm of top-down control, two subunits are identified. The fronto-parietal network supports the first subunit. This network, summarized in **Table 1**, involves 'cold' executive skills and processes such as working memory, inhibitory control, the capacity to focus attention and screen out the effects of interfering information, and the ability to formulate and to adjust action plans.

Working memory subsumes the active, flexible representation of information required to carry out goal-directed action plans in contextually appropriate ways. Inhibitory control and resistance to interference are required to prevent distraction from goal-directed behavior and for preventing prepotent (impulsive) responses from being carried out, thus allowing time for the formulation and execution of alternative responses. Stated differently, the fronto-parietal network regulates the moment-to-moment decisions involved in the planning and execution of goal-directed behavior.

The Cingulo-Opercular Network

The second subunit contributing to 'top-down' control, supported by the cingulo-opercular network, can be thought of as an appraisal or evaluative network that integrates both 'cold' cognitive and 'hot' emotional processes relevant to the regulation of goal-directed behavior. This network, summarized in **Table 2**, is structurally and functionally interposed between the fronto-parietal network and the limbic network. The cingulate gyrus, a midline structure, and the operculum, a region around the lateral sulcus that encompasses parts of the inferior frontal, orbitofrontal, inferior parietal, and superior temporal lobes, provide the structures that comprise this network. This network facilitates bidirectional communication between the 'cold' top-down processes indentified earlier, and the 'bottom-up' or 'hot' emotional processes arising in the limbic network to be discussed in the next section. In this manner, emotions, expectancies, memory, motivation, and goal salience emanating from the limbic network can be managed, and these in turn can influence the allocation of cognitive resources to guide behavior that is both contextually appropriate and personally meaningful.

For example, the cingulo-opercular network is critical in decision-making about pros and cons, and whether to engage in behaviors or not in the first place. It also plays a key role in the detection of conflicts and discrepancies between individual goals and what is contextually acceptable, the detection of errors that occur during the course of behavior, and the management of emotions such as frustration or joy that may result from behavior or the reactions elicited by it. Through its

Table 1 Cognitive processes and regulation of goal-directed behavior

'Top-down' ('cold') regulatory processes		
Cognitive regulatory tasks	*Intermediate processes*	*Fronto-parietal network*
Moment-by-moment regulation of goal-directed behavior	Maintain active representations of context-relevant rules and goal-relevant instructions	Dorsal frontal cortex
Determine:		Dorsolateral prefrontal cortex
– What to focus on	Select relevant information	Inferior parietal lobe
– What to ignore	Suppress irrelevant information	Intraparietal sulcus
– What to do (next)	Inhibit inappropriate or ineffective actions	Lateral parietal cortex
– What not to do	Activate or substitute appropriate, effective actions	Medial cingulate cortex
– How to do what should be done		Striatum (basal ganglia)
		Thalamus

Table 2 Integrative processes and regulation of goal-directed behavior

'Integrative' regulatory processes		
Overall regulatory tasks	*Intermediate processes*	*Cingulo-opercular network*
Identify goals	Maintain response state	Anterior cingulate cortex
Appraise appropriateness and salience of goals in context	*Monitor and manage:*	Anterior insular cortex
(Should I? – Shouldn't I?)	– Conflicts	Cerebellum
Formulate and carry out action plans	– Discrepancies	Medial prefrontal cortex
Assess outcomes	– Errors	Orbitofrontal cortex
(Oops! – Darn! – Great!)	– Expectancies	Striatum (basal ganglia)
Reevaluate goals and action plans as needed	– Frustration – Joy	Thalamus
	– Salience	Ventrolateral prefrontal cortex

relations with both fronto-parietal and limbic influences, the cingulo-opercular network supports maintenance of a response state, so long as this is needed to accomplish the goals of self-directed behavior. Stated differently, this network supports the processes needed to evaluate and to sustain focused, effortful goal-directed behavior.

The Limbic Network

The limbic network, summarized in **Table 3**, supports the influences on regulation of goal-directed behaviors provided by emotions, expectancies, memory, motivation, and goal salience. Temperamental or intrinsic reactive tendencies are captured here as well. Structures of the limbic network are sensitive and responsive to cues for perceived danger, fear, and the possible experience of pain and punishment – broadly construed; as well as for the prospective attainment of pleasure and reward. Through this system and its interface with the cingulo-opercular network, the ability to inform and to make choices based on personally meaningful preferences is supported.

The Default Network

The 'default' network of the brain is a relatively recent discovery. Its name was originally coined based on the assumption that the brain was operating in a 'default mode', since the activity of this network was first observed during neuro-imaging studies while subjects were in a 'restful' state prior to engaging in experimental tasks. Following its discovery, further investigation of this network has revealed that it supports several critical functions. Perhaps the most basic and pervasive of these functions is that of coordinating the activity of all other neural networks, including those described here, when these are called into action. For the purposes of this discussion, we focus on two other functions of this so-called default network; namely, sentinel and contemplative functions, each closely related to our discussion of executive function and social adaptation in adolescence. These functions and the principal structural components of the default network are summarized in **Table 4**.

The sentinel function of the default network reflects the capacity of individuals to maintain a proactive state of general openness and readiness to receive and process information regardless of its source, or its nature. This state is not directed to any one particular source of information or task. In fact, the activity of the sentinel function diminishes once a specific focus of attention is identified or a specific goal-directed activity is undertaken.

The contemplative function of the default network reflects the capacity of individuals to engage in mental simulations, including those that involve generating alternative perspectives that place the subject somewhere other than within themselves in the here and now. For example, these simulations allow persons to imagine themselves in the past or in the future. They can place themselves in the mental shoes of another person, they can act according to the rules of law and morality even when they are not being observed, and they can simulate different outcomes of goal-directed behavior before any are carried out. It is apparent from this description that both the sentinel and the contemplative aspects of the default network

Table 3 Emotional processes and regulation of goal-directed behavior

'Bottom-up' ('hot') regulatory processes		
Emotional regulatory tasks	*Intermediate processes*	*Limbic network*
Determine what matters (more/most) Manage response biases and reactive tendencies related to temperament and prior experiences	Access memory for prior experiences Approach tendencies – Responses to prospects of reward and experiences of pleasure Avoidance tendencies – Responses to danger, fear, and to prospects of punishment and experiences of pain	Amygdala (avoidance – fear) Hippocampus (memory) Nucleus accumbens (reward) Ventral tegmental area (reward)

Table 4 The intersection of executive function and social cognition

Regulating goal-directed behavior in context: executive function and social cognition		
Social regulatory tasks	*Intermediate processes*	*'Default' network*
Maintain a general state of awareness and openness toward external and internal sources of information Anticipate and evaluate actions, reactions, events, and consequences before they happen	Engage in flexible, self- and socially relevant mental explorations and simulations Generate alternative perspectives that place the subject somewhere other than within themselves in the here and now	Dorsomedial prefrontal cortex Hippocampus Inferior parietal lobe Lateral temporal cortex Posterior cingulate cortex Ventromedial prefrontal cortex

are critical to social cognition and to those aspects of executive function that are important to successful social adaptation.

For clarification and completeness, it bears mentioning here that in the case of social cognition, the default network differs in some important ways from the mirror neuron network; yet another recently discovered brain system that is crucial to social cognition and social adaptation, but that we will not discuss in detail. The most prominent difference concerns the observation that while mirror neurons and their network are intimately related to motor and to sensory neural systems, the default network has no such direct connections with either the motor or sensory systems of the brain. Functionally then, while the mirror neuron system appears to support processes of imitation and possibly empathy, through perception and action, the default network on the other hand presumably allows individuals to contemplate the meaning and ramifications of behaviors, be they their own (actual or simulated) or those of others.

Development of Executive Skills

Overview and General Principles of Development

The development of executive skills, like other complex meta-cognitive skills such as language, is prolonged, and evolves over decades. Since the developmental trajectory of executive skills is so prolonged, the contributions to their proficiency made by experience and learning are considerable. In fact, executive skills, like all other meta-cognitive skills, are learned gradually, and rehearsed and refined repeatedly within social contexts over the course of human development.

It is a generally accepted principle that in the case of meta-cognitive skills, our genetic endowment specifies basic blueprints for the neural architecture needed to support these skills, while experience shapes their emergence, development, and ultimate proficiency. A prime example is language. Humans are endowed with the genetic code that specifies the basic neural architecture to support the use of symbols for communication. However, if the developing child is not exposed to language and other forms of symbolic communication, they will not develop or demonstrate these capacities on their own. So too is the case for executive processes and skills. Without the influence of appropriate experiences and learning, these skills will not develop to their fullest potential, thereby limiting how they ultimately can contribute to the regulation of goal-directed behavior and to social adaptation.

Development of individual meta-cognitive skills can be broadly characterized by the form of the developmental trajectory, that is, when in life a skill first emerges, and how quickly it then develops in proficiency and complexity in relation to the age of the child or adolescent over time; as well as by the end point achieved in maturity, that is, the ultimate level of proficiency attained. Variations along these dimensions may be observed in relation to differences in the prevalent experiences that children and adolescents are exposed to. Furthermore, another fundamental aspect in the development of complex meta-cognitive skills concerns the observation that as individual skills develop, they must also become integrated with other meta-cognitive skills, in order to be useful to their fullest extent in the service of guiding and regulating complex goal-directed behavior and social adaptation.

As a general rule, the development of complex meta-cognitive skills can be described functionally and biologically as proceeding through stages. These stages are not so distinctly marked in actuality, but nonetheless they capture the key aspects of fundamental developmental processes involving meta-cognitive skills. These general developmental stages are summarized in **Table 5**, from the emergence of singular basic skills to the full integration of mature meta-cognitive skills. In **Table 6**, we focus more directly on the functional and biological changes that occur to support the development and integration of meta-cognitive skills during adolescence.

The human brain in late infancy–early toddlerhood already presents in readily identifiable fashion all the gray matter regions and corresponding interconnecting nerve fiber tracts of the adult brain. The biological and functional maturation of gray matter regions involved in the regulation of goal-directed behavior, and their interconnections, undergo considerable changes that culminate in adulthood with full structural and functional integration of these processes.

The first stage involves the emergence of particular meta-cognitive skills or their precursors in their earliest and most basic forms. At this stage, these newly emerging skills are not elicited consistently and reliably in the service of regulating goal-directed behaviors. Biologically, the emergence of these meta-cognitive skills is associated in human brain

Table 5 General development of higher brain functions

Functional stages	*Biological stages*
Emergence	*Emergence*
Earliest evidence for specific meta-cognitive skills or their precursors	Regional peaks in gray matter production are observed
Establishment	*Establishment*
Consistent, reliable performance of basic forms of specific skills is noted	Stabilization of synapses and enhancement of local–regional connectivity occurs
Elaboration/Evolution	*Elaboration/evolution and integration*
Increasing complexity and sophistication of specific meta-cognitive skills is observed	Reductions in synaptic density and related gray matter thinning provide more rapid, efficient processing Myelination supports enhanced local and long-range connectivity within and between brain regions and across neural networks
Integration	
Occurs among various specific skills with other interdependent and related skills	

Table 6 Development of higher brain functions in adolescence

Functional stages	*Biological stages*
Elaboration/evolution Increasing complexity and sophistication of specific meta-cognitive skills *Integration* Occurs among the various specific skills with other interdependent and related skills such as those supporting language and social cognition *Result* Enhanced capacity for successful, independent self-regulation and social adaptation	*Elaboration/Evolution and Integration* Sexually dimorphic changes in brain development begin with puberty: 1. *Gray matter*: New proliferation and increased synaptic density, most prominent in fronto-parietal regions; followed by pruning and reduced synaptic density – Females typically attain peak synaptic density and subsequent gray matter thinning earlier than males 2. *White matter*: Increased myelination within (interneuronal) and between (axonal) gray matter regions enhance connectivity in and among brain regions and networks – Rates of myelination are higher in males, who also display greater axonal girth on average than females *Result* Rapid, efficient processing and communication, within and among brain regions and neural networks

development with corresponding peaks in the production of gray matter and increased synaptic density in cortical regions known to support those particular skills. As children practice these emergent skills in the service of regulating goal-directed behaviors, in conjunction with support from adults in their environment, these skills will gradually become more proficient and better established, and the child will eventually be able to elicit them more independently to guide their goal-directed behaviors. Biologically, the consolidation of individual meta-cognitive skills coincides with the stabilization of synapses and enhanced connectedness within the gray matter regions that support the proficiency of those particular skills.

From this point forward, once basic meta-cognitive skills have become well established, they must gradually attain the proficiency needed to guide and regulate the increasingly complex goal-directed behaviors required to support adaptation toward social independence that occurs during adolescence. This growth in functional capacities also necessitates that each developing meta-cognitive skill becomes increasingly well integrated with other high-level, complex skills, such as those involved with language and social cognition.

The biological processes of synaptic stabilization and enhancement in connectivity within gray matter regions continue, as the functional complexity of singular meta-cognitive skills improves, along with pruning of synapses and thinning of gray matter to remove superfluous local and regional connections; while long-range connectivity and integration with brain regions that support other complex meta-cognitive skills is enhanced both anatomically and functionally through the myelination of axons, a process that greatly enhances the speed and efficiency of neural transmission of information.

More specifically, with the onset of puberty and the associated gender differences in gonadal hormone production, both gray and white matter in the adolescent brain develops in sexually dimorphic ways. In both genders, a second peak in the production of gray matter is observed that is especially apparent in the frontal, parietal, and temporal cortices. This peak corresponds to an increase in synaptic density and typically results in more overall gray matter production in males than in females.

Following this new proliferation, there is a period of intensive, experience-driven pruning of synapses and an overall thinning of cortical gray matter. Synapses and circuits that are more routinely utilized are stabilized, while those that are not are pruned. The end result of these reductions in synaptic density is the formation of brain regions that are capable of more rapid and efficient processing of information.

Additional contributions to the apparent thinning of gray matter are presumably due to the interposition of white matter resulting from interneuronal myelination within the gray matter regions themselves. On average, females demonstrate these peaks and reductions in synaptic density and the corresponding eventual thinning of gray matter about 2 years earlier than males.

The production of myelin along nerve cell axons is thought to be largely responsible for enhancements in the functional connectivity and the efficiency of communication between gray matter regions and networks observed as the brain matures during adolescence. The process of myelination, like gray matter production, is noted to be more intense in males, and typically results in axons of greater girth in males. These gender differences in the rates of maturation of gray and white matter that are typical of the sexually dimorphic brain are hypothesized to underlie observations that females on the whole display observably better cognitive control and less overt aggression during adolescence than do males.

Factors Influencing the Development of Executive Skills

Although executive skills have been portrayed thus far as developing slowly from childhood through young adulthood, the earliest experiences and factors that may affect how these skills develop occur prenatally. Adequate maternal nutrition and avoidance of toxins during pregnancy are crucial for healthy fetal development in general. The absence or relative deficiency of certain nutrients in the mother's diet has been associated with a range of poor developmental outcomes. Deficiencies in dietary folic acid, for example, have been associated with malformations involving the central nervous system such as spina bifida, referred to as neural tube defects.

Toxic exposures during pregnancy can also result in a wide variety of problems postnatally, some of which are readily apparent in infancy, while others manifest more clearly later in childhood. Fetal alcohol syndrome, for example, involves poor growth of the brain and alterations in the morphology and size of the head and the face, as well as serious cognitive deficits, and occurs from excessive prenatal exposure to alcohol. Absent such gross malformations, prenatal exposure to lesser amounts of alcohol, to cigarette smoke, as well as to lead emanating from maternal bone stores, to name a few common environmental neurotoxins, can each result in problems that manifest later on in young children as milder cognitive deficits, and as emotional and behavioral problems, some of which may be partly rooted in the problematic development of executive skills resulting from prenatal exposure to these and to other neurotoxins.

The relevance of broad-ranging contextual influences captured by socioeconomic status is repeatedly noted in studies reporting that children from more disadvantaged backgrounds demonstrate less proficient executive function. In these cases, the influence of poverty may act both pre- and postnatally to adversely affect a range of factors, from the adequacy and quality of nutrition to the (greater) likelihood of exposure to neurotoxins such as environmental lead and cigarette smoke, the latter also occurring postnatally as second-hand smoke, to the quality of the parenting and the education that children are routinely exposed to.

Nowhere is the importance of parenting itself to healthy child development more apparent than in accounts of children raised in orphanages under conditions of extreme psychosocial deprivation. Many of these children show impairments in cognitive and social-emotional development reminiscent of those seen in autism and in mental retardation. Collectively, studies of children who subsequently receive interventions such as placement in high-quality foster care, also speak to the plasticity of young children as they respond to variations in their care-giving environments. In less dramatic fashion, large-scale studies conducted in the United States by the Early Childcare Research Network of the National Institute of Child Health and Human Development found that maternal responsiveness and learning stimulation prior to and during the preschool years predicted the competence of children's sustained attention and inhibitory control, as well as their readiness for primary school, defined by their academic and social competence assessed in the first grade.

It is unusual for adults to intentionally impart specific executive skills directly to children when they interact with them. Instead, two concepts originally introduced by the Soviet psychologist, Lev Vygotsky, namely, 'scaffolding' and the 'zone of proximal development,' capture how many such skills are transferred by adults to children in day-to-day activities. Scaffolding is the process by which tutors, that is, parents, caregivers, and teachers, assist the goal-directed activity of children so that they can successfully execute and complete tasks that are otherwise beyond their capabilities. Scaffolding is optimal when it occurs within the child's zone of proximal development. The zone of proximal development involves challenges that are just outside the realm of the child's capabilities. Scaffolding then regulates children's motivation and engagement in goal-directed tasks, and it regulates the strategies and cognitive resources that are brought to bear in the execution of these challenging tasks.

Scaffolding is often described as being either directive or elaborative. Directive scaffolding essentially simplifies a complex task and thus brings it within the realm of capability for the child, such that simple(r) solutions will be successful. For example, in the case of a complex multistep task, the tutor might intervene by saying to the child, 'First do this, then do this,' etc. Elaborative scaffolding on the other hand enhances the (external) cognitive resources available to the child through the tutor, who introduces their own problem-solving strategies to the child, often in the form of questions. So in the case of the same multistep task, rather than prescribe what should be done and how, instead the tutor might ask, 'What do you think we need to do first here?' This leads to the possibility for discussion about multiple alternative solutions that can be 'simulated' in the context of the discussion before any one solution is actually implemented.

Directive scaffolding works well for promoting early cognitive control of goal-directed behavior in toddlers. Elaborative scaffolding becomes more and more important in promoting healthy development of cognitive control as children approach the preschool years and beyond; and is the form of scaffolding more closely related to later competence across a range of executive skills. In fact, this form of learning remains relevant throughout childhood, adolescence, and young adulthood. What differs developmentally is the complexity of the challenges and tasks to be mastered.

Investigators have begun to explore the role of variations in genetic endowment to observed variations in executive skills. Genes that regulate the activity of the neurotransmitter dopamine, a key chemical mediator of the cingulo-opercular network, have been the most closely studied so far where executive skills such as the ability to inhibit prepotent responses and substitute more effortful ones instead, are concerned. Of perhaps even greater interest in this regard are very recent findings that parenting influences on the development of executive skills may interact with these variations in genetic endowment and affect how the genes are expressed behaviorally. In particular, children who may be genetically predisposed to less effective executive control also appear to be more susceptible, for better and for worse, to variations in the quality of the parenting they receive than those who are not predisposed.

Development of Particular Executive Skills

Inhibitory control, resistance to interference, and working memory comprise critical elements in the cognitive control needed to flexibly guide and regulate goal-directed behavior and promote effective social adaptation. Many consider these to be the most fundamental, ubiquitous executive processes and skills. In this section, we examine the progressive development of these elements by highlighting the developmental proficiency of cognitive control at four time points: late infancy, late toddlerhood–early preschool age, primary school age, and finally, adolescence. We also examine in some detail the increasingly important contributions to the regulation of goal-directed behavior in adolescence made by emotions and the integration of meta-cognitive processes and skills such as social cognition, and how these processes must interact with executive skills in the service of effective social adaptation.

Late infancy

During the latter half of the first year of life, infants learn to reach for attractive objects such as toys. This action pattern is initially dominated by what is termed 'line of sight,' meaning that infants will reach for objects according to their visual input. If an obstacle such as a clear plastic pane is placed along the line of sight between the infant and the object, the infant will perseverate in reaching for the object by trying to go through the clear pane. At around 10 months of age, after one or two such failed attempts, the typically developing infant will reach around the pane and successfully retrieve the object; a simple modification to the basic action pattern of reaching along the line of sight, considered a precursor to cognitive control of goal-directed behavior.

Late toddlerhood and the preschool years

Playing interactive games is increasingly important developmentally as infants become toddlers and the latter become preschoolers. Games come with rules that become more complex as children get older, thereby providing many occasions for them to learn and practice emerging executive skills in the context of enjoyable activities. By observing children playing games, we can see what many consider to be the first manifestations of true cognitive control. One such game used in developmental studies, the 'Opposites Game,' illustrates this well. In the 'Opposites Game,' children are shown easily recognizable pictures in pairs of 'opposites': a boy and a girl, a winter scene and a summer scene, the sun and the moon, etc. First, children must identify what they see according to what is actually represented in the picture. Then in a second round, they must say the opposite of what they see. Children in the age range of 24–30 months are dominated in their responses by the identity of the picture. They are able to describe the picture, but they cannot inhibit this tendency and say its opposite. Between 30 and 36 months of age, many typically developing children show the emerging capacity to inhibit the dominant tendency to identify the picture and say its opposite instead. Successful responding in this game is no longer the modification of a simple action pattern. Here, a prepotent response to the identity of the picture is inhibited even in the face of continued interference by the picture's presence, and an alternative, more effortful response, the naming of the opposite picture, is substituted instead. The rule set for this game is also more complex, in that it contains two (competing) parts, and the child must remember which of the two parts to follow and act on, making it more taxing to working memory as well. By 4 years of age, most typically developing children can play this game and others like it, error-free.

Primary school age

In primary school, great importance is placed on the ability of young students to follow directions and rules independently, so that teachers may focus on imparting curricular materials and not on the external regulation of their students' behaviors. A commonplace, everyday example of successful cognitive control in the primary school classroom setting is seen whenever a student raises his or her hand and waits to be recognized, instead of calling out to gain the teacher's attention. Here again, one sees elements similar to those the child must elicit to play the 'Opposites Game'; namely, inhibiting the prepotent tendency to call out for attention, and raising one's hand instead. However, in the case of the classroom, as compared to the 'Opposites Game,' the process is further complicated by several factors. First, the child must elicit this control independently. Then, there is the introduction of delayed responding, in that the child cannot speak out until recognized; and finally, there is perceived competition with other children who also vie for the teacher's attention to be recognized. Therefore, the child must independently initiate and then sustain inhibition over time. He or she must also maintain the action plan for the alternative, more effortful response of hand raising while at the same time managing the emotions associated with the hope of being recognized first, a factor that might otherwise compel the child to speak out prematurely. However, the child must also keep in awareness the possibility that if he or she chooses at some point to speak out before being recognized, then there is the risk of sanction and loss of the teacher's positive regard, at least temporarily.

Adolescence

In adolescence, the primacy of peer relations, as one manifestation of the progression toward social independence, provides many opportunities to examine the crucial role played by cognitive control and closely related social cognitive processes operating together in the service of social adaptation. Take for instance the situation of an argument between close friends. Each peer wishes to be 'right,' and at the same time, each does not want to offend the other or jeopardize their relationship. In order to do this successfully, each peer must monitor their thoughts and related emotions carefully, and prevent these emotions from leading to impulsive utterances or actions that will be heard or experienced as insulting or offensive. At the same time, in an effort to resolve the argument in mutually and personally favorable ways, they must formulate alternative approaches that take into account their own goals, the perceived perspectives of their friend, and the imagined consequences of their choices. Here, one clearly sees the importance of an intact system supporting cognitive control capable of managing potentially intense emotional arousal that is also well integrated with the systems supporting social cognition, highlighting the fact that development and successful social adaptation require a multitude of metacognitive skills working together more or less seamlessly.

Cognitive control alone cannot effectively deal with the situation we have just portrayed. All the elements of the frontoparietal, cingulo-opercular, limbic, and default networks described previously and summarized in **Tables 1** through **4** are brought into play by this common scenario. Successful inhibitory control and the capacity to resist the influence and ongoing interference of (intense) emotions must preclude impulsive responses that could quickly result in deterioration of the argument and any related poor outcomes, and therefore afford time for reflection and the formulation of alternative, more adaptive responses. Each peer must maintain active representations in working memory of their desired goal(s), the rules governing – in this case – interactions among friends, personal and other perspectives concerning the disagreement, and the range of possibilities that could result in either favorable or unfavorable resolution of the conflict.

In sum, from infancy to adolescence, there is a steady progression of cognitive control from its infant precursors to its central role in regulating complex, affectively laden social interactions among adolescents. These developing processes mature to support regulation in the face of the ever-increasing complexity of challenges encountered as children's social world expands. Effective social adaptation in adolescence requires that cognitive control be well integrated with other high-level meta-cognitive processes such as social cognition. Yet, despite their best intentions, and despite their display of a range of well-developed individual meta-cognitive skills, adolescents often make choices that lead to suboptimal outcomes. What accounts for these poor choices?

Risks and Vulnerabilities

Complementary theories have been advanced to explain the apparent shortcomings in executive function that can occur in adolescence. Each of these theories is based on circumstantial evidence gleaned from brain imaging studies of children, adolescents, and adults, that focus either on general aspects of maturation in and across different parts of the brain or on brain images collected while participants across the age range from childhood to adulthood perform cognitively or emotionally challenging tasks.

The first of these theories involves the observation that while 'top-down' control is indeed improving steadily from childhood through adulthood, concurrent with development of the neural networks that support these skills, 'bottom-up' influences on the regulation of goal-directed behavior experience a surge of activity with the onset of puberty. Compared to children and adults, adolescents show heightened activation of the amygdala to emotional stimuli and heightened reactivity to potentially rewarding situations that is mediated through the nucleus accumbens and ventral tegmental areas of the brain. This means that adolescents are more inclined to respond to the emotional content and salience of situations, be it positive or negative, than either children or adults; resulting at times in an imbalance between 'top-down' and 'bottom-up' influences on behavioral regulation, such that the latter can prevail in decision-making. This creates fertile circumstances for impulsive responses that are guided more by emotions than by thoughtfulness. Furthermore, this heightened limbic network reactivity to emotional salience occurs in the context of a partial, transient decline in top-down control processes related to the increases in synaptic density and gray matter that occur with the onset of puberty. This imbalance gradually resolves as the maturational processes of synaptic pruning and myelination restore functionality, and promote connectivity and integration of functioning, until adult levels are ultimately attained.

The second, complementary, explanatory theory for the poor decision-making sometimes noted in the behavior of adolescents, particularly under circumstances of high emotional arousal, is predicated on observations that integration of complex meta-cognitive skills and the networks that support them is still incomplete at this stage of development. In the face of emotionally challenging tasks, for example, healthy adults recruit an extensive array of well-connected regions from both the fronto-parietal and cingulo-opercular networks in order to manage input arriving from limbic regions. The involvement of the cingulo-opercular network in particular renders these processes efficient and rapid, given its structural and functional interposition and integrative role between the front-parietal and limbic networks. By contrast, adolescents do not show such well-distributed integration across the fronto-parietal and cingulo-opercular networks in emotionally arousing situations. They do not consistently recruit cingulo-opercular regions. Instead, they rely more heavily on fronto-parietal regions to directly manage limbic input, an inherently slower and less efficient means of managing emotional arousal. The resulting delays in the interposition of top-down control means that emotionally guided behavior is more likely to break through under circumstances of high affective arousal.

If we return now to the scenario of the two friends arguing, applying these explanatory theories, we can better imagine how the argument, instead of being constructively resolved, could turn sour in various ways. The prospect of 'winning' the argument could result in poorly managed arousal emanating from reward circuits that promote exuberant, impulsive behaviors and utterances; while exaggerated emotions related to feelings and perceptions of being insulted or threatened, and subsequent overarousal of the amygdala, could lead to unchecked reactivity in the form of aggression or hostility, either verbal or physical. In each instance, delay in the interposition of top-down control means that any heightened emotional arousal could more easily result in a variety of impulsive, regrettable behaviors on the part of either participant.

Now with some underlying bases for beginning to understand the variations in self-regulatory capacities often observed during adolescence, it is not so difficult to go from the scenario of our two peers in an argument, to more serious risky behaviors that adolescents frequently engage in; including experimentation with alcohol and illicit drugs, as well as unprotected sexual activity, with its own attendant risks of sexually transmitted diseases and unwanted pregnancy. In both cases, based on the concerted workings of the two theories presented earlier, when these behaviors do occur, it is presumed that emotionally guided choices, which condition the perception of risk as well, prevail because of the salience of the behaviors and perceived outcomes leading to intense activation of the limbic network. This coupled with delay in the interposition of cognitive control emanating from the fronto-parietal and cingulo-opercular networks that could inhibit such behaviors a priori and then promote the formulation and implementation of more adaptive responses, enhances the likelihood that such risk-taking behaviors would occur.

Concluding Remarks

Adolescence is an extended period in human development marked by important biological and social-contextual contributions to changes that result in sexual–reproductive maturity, and ultimately social independence. Development of cognitive control and its integration with other meta-cognitive processes involves inherently dys-synchronous biological maturational processes in the brain. Furthermore, because these meta-cognitive skills have protracted developmental trajectories and because adolescence itself may represent a sensitive period for development of certain kinds of skills, in particular those related to social cognition, variations in the prevalent experiences that adolescents are exposed to will contribute substantially to observed variations in cognitive control and related meta-cognitive skills critical to effective, independent social adaptation.

We are just beginning to explore and to understand the interplay of the biological, genetic, and experiential influences that affect brain development before, during, and after adolescence. How experience interacts with genetic endowment and with the inherently dys-synchronous biological changes occurring in the brain during adolescence, will ultimately affect everything from the most basic manifestations of cognitive control to the sophisticated levels of self-regulation that are required in complex social interactions.

Since adolescence is an inherently high-risk period in human development, and it is clear that experience plays an important role in shaping brain–behavior relations, it is also important that we consider interventions, before and during adolescence itself, to reduce the risk for adverse outcomes that may result from poorly developing cognitive control. Interventions aimed at parenting practices, such as those described earlier regarding the role of scaffolding with younger children, support the relevance of utilizing experience to deliberately shape various aspects of cognitive control.

New and exciting areas of intervention and prevention to complement those that have focused on parenting include classroom-based curricula rooted in Vygotskyan principles, cognitive training of specific meta-cognitive skills, and the use of meditation and mindfulness. Classroom-based interventions that incorporate deliberate promotion of a range of executive skills have been utilized with considerable success in preschool. Children receiving these interventions demonstrate better self-regulation in the classroom and better academic and social competence when compared to children exposed to traditional preschool curricula, suggesting that by improving executive skills, there is a transfer of effects to meaningful skills of everyday life. Meditation and mindfulness training have been used successfully in young adults to improve attention and executive skills, and should be methods that are readily adaptable for use in adolescents.

Among cognitive training interventions, those directed at working memory are perhaps the most studied and have been applied successfully with a wide age range of participants from childhood through late adulthood. Working memory training conducted in typically developing children, in healthy adults, as well as in children and adults who suffer from a range of neuropsychiatric conditions such as attention-deficit hyperactivity disorder ADHD and dementia, results in improvements of the meta-cognitive skill itself and in the transfer of treatment effects to ecologically important skills such as fluid intelligence, complex reasoning skills, mathematic skills, and better regulation of attention. Despite the promise of these approaches, there is much yet to be learned about when and how to conduct these interventions, singularly and in combination, and for whom these interventions will produce the greatest impact, as we seek to improve the developmental success of children and adolescents.

See also: Adolescent Decision-Making; Brain Development; Cognitive Development; Emotional Development; Metacognition and Self-regulated Learning; Social Cognition.

Further Reading

Blakemore SJ (2008) The social brain in adolescence. *Nature Reviews – Neuroscience* 9: 267–277.

Blakemore SJ and Choudhury S (2006) Development of the adolescent brain: Implications for executive function and social cognition. *Journal of Child Psychology and Psychiatry* 47: 296–312.

Buckner RL, Andrews-Hanna JR, and Schacter DL (2008) The brain's default network: Anatomy, function, and relevance to disease. *Annals of the New York Academy of Sciences* 1124: 1–38.

Casey BJ, Jones RM, and Hare TO (2008) The adolescent brain. *Annals of the New York Academy of Sciences* 1124: 111–126.

Fair DA, Cohen AL, Dosenbach NUF, et al. (2008) The maturing architecture of the brain's default network. *Proceedings of the National Academy of Sciences* 105(10): 4028–4032.

Fair DA, Dosenbach NUF, Church JA, et al. (2007) Development of distinct control networks through segregation and integration. *Proceedings of the National Academy of Sciences* 104(33): 13507–13512.

Lewis C and Carpendale JIM (eds.) (2009) Social interaction and the development of executive function. *New Directions in Child and Adolescent Development*. 123: entire issue.

Luna B (2009) Developmental changes in cognitive control through adolescence. *Advances in Child Development and Behavior* 37: 233–278.

Paus T (2005) Mapping brain maturation and cognitive development during adolescence. *Trends in Cognitive Sciences* 9: 60–68.

Posner MI and Rothbart MK (2009) Toward a physical basis of attention and self-regulation. *Physics of Life Reviews* 6: 103–120.

Gender Issues

E A Daniels, University of Oregon, Bend, OR, USA
C Leaper, University of California, Santa Cruz, CA, USA

Glossary

Ambivalent sexism model: Gender-related prejudice includes a combination of hostile sexism (negative attitudes toward women who violate traditional gender roles) and benevolent sexism (valuing feminine-stereotyped attributes in women and a paternalistic belief that men need to protect women).
Expectancy-value model of achievement: Achievement motivation in a particular domain is highest when individuals expect success and value the domain.
Gender schema theory: People pay attention to information relevant to their own gender and to recall information consistent with their existing beliefs.
Social cognitive theory: Learning occurs through observing role models and inferring incentives for particular behaviors; when behaviors are practiced and mastered, self-efficacy ensues.
Social identity theory: People value characteristics associated with their ingroup and encourage assimilation to ingroup norms in others.
Social role theory: The gendered division of roles in the larger society shapes people's expectations about their own gender roles.

Introduction

During adolescence, girls and boys undergo important changes related to their gender that can shape their self-concepts, beliefs, goals, and social relationships. For example, with the onset of puberty, girls and boys undergo physical transformations that can affect their self-image and how others treat them. This is a period when girls and boys become increasingly interested in their sexual attractiveness to one another (or possibly to the same sex). Adolescence is also a period when more flexible and egalitarian conceptions of gender might emerge or when adherence to conventional gender roles may strengthen. Adolescent girls' and boys' gender-related beliefs can guide their motivation to pursue particular activities, such as sports, or certain academic subjects. In dating relationships, adolescents may rely on traditional gender scripts as they navigate first romantic relationships. With dramatic increases in gender equality during the last half century, however, adolescents in the United States and other Western societies are increasingly able to transcend many gender-role restrictions.

The following gender-related issues during adolescence are reviewed in the present article: self-concept and attitudes, academic achievement, athletic participation, body image, sexuality and sexual orientation, friendship intimacy, and aggression and violence. Before addressing each of these topics, factors that influence the salience of gender during adolescence are reviewed.

Factors Influencing the Salience of Gender During Adolescence

A combination of cultural, interpersonal, cognitive-motivational, and biological factors influence many of the gender-related issues that youth face during adolescence. Like many other topics in psychology, much of the research on gender-related issues that youth face during adolescence is based on ethnic majority youth in Western cultures including the United States, Canada, Northern Europe, Australia, and New Zealand. As a result, much of the research reported on in this article is based on these youth. Less research has been done with ethnic minority groups in Western cultures and with cultural groups in other parts of the world. It is important to note that cultural context is a crucial factor in understanding adolescents' experiences in general as well as in understanding gender-related issues.

 doi:10.1016/B978-0-12-373915-5.00017-6

Cultural Factors

The relative division of labor and roles among women and men in a given society is an important cultural factor in adolescents' gender-related experiences. As articulated in social role theory, the gendered division of roles in a society shapes the kinds of expectations about gender roles that individuals formulate for themselves and about others. For example, men are still more likely than women to hold positions of power (e.g., US Presidents, corporate CEOs), whereas women are still more likely than men to be responsible for childcare and housework. These societal patterns can shape how adolescents think about the kinds of roles that they will adopt. Consistent with the social role theory, cross-cultural research suggests that gender socialization practices are less rigid in more gender-egalitarian societies.

The extent that a society organizes roles and behaviors according to gender affects the salience that gender will have as a social category organizing individuals' thinking. Being a member of one's gender group – that is, being a girl or a boy – is perhaps the most fundamental group identity that individuals experience during childhood and adolescence. The beliefs and knowledge that individuals form about gender are known as gender schemas. According to gender schema theory, individuals tend to pay more attention to information relevant to their own gender, and they store information in memory in ways to make it consistent with their existing gender schemas.

Interpersonal and Cognitive-Motivational Factors

People learn about the cultural norms regarding gender roles from various social agents, including family members, teachers, peers, and the media. Although contemporary adolescents living with their mother and father will typically observe both parents working outside of the home in Western contexts, fathers may be more likely than mothers to hold high-prestige occupations. It is even more likely that a gendered division of labor occurs inside the home of dual-career parents with most mothers still being primarily responsible for childcare and housework. Thus, as adolescents approach adulthood themselves, their ideas about family roles may be partly influenced by what they have observed in their home.

The importance of gender as a social category is also emphasized in social identity theory, which further addresses the impact of one's gender-group identity on motivation. According to social identity theory, people tend to value characteristics associated with their ingroup and they tend to encourage ingroup members to assimilate to the group's norms. Throughout childhood, girls and boys primarily affiliate with same-gender peers. Although cross-gender contacts increase during adolescence, friendships usually are mostly with same-gender peers. In these peer groups, gender-stereotyped social norms are often enforced among peers.

Social cognitive theory is another approach that is helpful for understanding gender development. According to this theory, many aspects of gender development occur through observing role models and perceiving incentives for particular kinds of behavior. In turn, by practicing a behavior, individuals develop a sense of self-efficacy (a feeling of personal competence and agency) that increases motivation to continue the behavior. For example, if children observe in their environments that mostly women take care of babies, they are likely to infer that caretaking is associated with the female role. This may lead girls to play with dolls in childhood and to seek out babysitting jobs in adolescence. As a consequence, girls may be more likely than boys to develop competence and feelings of self-efficacy regarding caregiving.

Biological Factors

Biological factors related to pubertal maturation contribute to the salience of certain gender-related issues during adolescence. These include changes in cognitive development during adolescence. For example, youth may develop more abstract thinking abilities, especially if they attend secondary schooling, that allow them to better understand certain aspects of gender roles (discussed later). Furthermore, with the onset of puberty, youth experience major changes to their anatomy, physiology, and physical appearance. Puberty leads to the development of secondary sex characteristics in girls (e.g., breasts, increased body fat) and boys (e.g., facial hair, greater muscle mass and height). However, there is a high degree of within-gender variability and between-gender overlap in many of these physical changes (e.g., the height difference between the tallest and shortest males is larger than the difference between the average female and male).

On average, girls enter puberty 2 years before boys do. The timing of maturation can be especially important for girls and boys. Early-maturing girls are at risk for poor body image (described later in the article) as well as substance use, delinquency, and early sexual activity due to contact with older peer networks. Early-maturing boys tend to have increased body image, but are also at risk for substance use, delinquency, and early sexual activity because of older peers. Late maturation for boys (but not girls) tends to be especially negative. These boys are at risk for teasing and bullying. They tend to have higher rates of alcohol use and delinquency as well as lower grades in school than boys who develop 'on time'. Finally, puberty is associated with increased sexual interest and sexual behavior. As addressed later in the article, physical changes and sexual interest affect how adolescents view themselves and one another.

Gender-Related Beliefs

Self-Concepts and Attitudes

Gender-related self-concepts refer to people's self-perceived personality traits, abilities, and interests, whereas gender-related attitudes refer to their views about the kinds of behaviors that other females and males should adopt. Gender-related self-concepts and attitudes are not always consistent with one another. For example, an adolescent may endorse gender-egalitarian attitudes but personally have gender-stereotypical interests. As reviewed in the course of this article, many adolescents hold gender-stereotyped beliefs regarding certain academic subjects, sports, body image, sexuality, and interpersonal relationships.

The emergence of abstract thinking can set the stage for some adolescents to reflect upon the social origins of gender roles. This awareness may lead some adolescents to reject these social conventions and to explore and to adopt more flexible views of gender roles. Accordingly, adolescence is a period when gender-role transcendence is possible. However, many youth internalize traditional gender norms as personal values. For them, adolescence can be a period of continued (or possibly increased) gender-role rigidity.

Research suggests that gender-role flexibility is more likely if youth perceive support for gender-egalitarian roles from family members, peers, teachers, and the media. For example, parents' encouragement may facilitate greater willingness to disclose personal feelings (a feminine-stereotyped behavior) in boys or more interest in athletic participation (a masculine-stereotyped behavior) in girls.

On average, gender-role flexibility in beliefs and behavior is more likely among girls than boys. Correspondingly, gender-role conformity pressures in the family and peer group are usually stronger for boys than girls. Social scientists attribute these patterns to men's greater status and dominance in society. The attributes associated with the dominant group can enhance one's status, whereas the characteristics related to the subordinate group can diminish one's status. Hence, when girls adopt masculine-stereotyped qualities, it may enhance their status; but when boys adopt feminine-stereotyped qualities, it may diminish their status.

During the course of identity exploration, adolescents commonly judge themselves according to how well they meet cultural gender expectations. Social change in cultural attitudes about appropriate behavior for females over the last several decades has made it far more acceptable today in many Western contexts for girls to be ambitious, independent, athletic, and have other masculine-stereotyped (i.e., self-assertive) characteristics. In contrast, boys continue to be sanctioned for being gentle, nurturing, or displaying other feminine-stereotyped (i.e., affiliative) qualities. In Western societies, both self-image and peer acceptance tend to be highest for highly self-assertive boys and girls who display a mixture of self-assertive and affiliative behaviors.

Sexism

Gender stereotypes often lead to sexist views and behaviors. Gender-based prejudice and discrimination are the cognitive and behavioral components of sexism, respectively. According to the ambivalent sexism model, gender-based prejudice includes both hostile and benevolent forms. Hostile sexism refers to negative views toward individuals who violate traditional gender roles. For example, some people disparage girls who enter traditionally masculine domains such as science or sports. Benevolent sexism includes valuing feminine-stereotyped attributes in females (e.g., nurturance) and a belief that traditional gender roles are necessary to complement one another. Benevolent sexism also includes the view known as paternalism that females need to be protected by males. Benevolent sexism contributes to gender inequality by limiting women's roles. Thus, in the ambivalent sexism model, girls and women are punished for violating traditional gender norms (hostile sexism) and are reinforced for adopting traditional roles (benevolent sexism). Only a few studies have examined sexist attitudes in adolescent samples; among these, the suggestion is that both hostile and benevolent sexism may increase in prevalence from early to late adolescence.

As reviewed later in this article, reported experiences with sexist discrimination, such as gender bias and sexual harassment, tend to increase during adolescence. The trend may be due both to increased rates of sexist events with age and to increases in the cognitive ability to recognize a sexist event when it occurs. Also, studies suggest that learning about feminism and the women's movement may help increase girls' ability to detect sexist events.

Academic Achievement

Overall Achievement

In North America, Australia, and many parts of Europe, girls on average get better grades in school than boys do, although this difference is small. Girls are also less likely than boys to repeat a grade, and girls are more likely to achieve higher rankings, earn more academic awards, and take college preparatory classes. Finally, related to their stronger academic performance, girls are somewhat more likely than boys to finish high school. Socioeconomic status is an important factor in these patterns. Boys and girls from middle and upper socioeconomic backgrounds perform similarly in academics and are equally likely to finish high school and enroll in college. Girls from working-class and low-income backgrounds may perform more poorly in school than their middle-class peers, but they are likely to complete high school and enroll in college. In contrast, working class and poor boys, who are more apt to be ethnic minorities, are more likely to perform poorly in school, drop out of high school, and disengage from academics. Therefore, socioeconomic status *and* gender are important factors in understanding academic achievement.

Traditional gender roles may be related to average gender differences in overall academic performance and success. In the socialization of girls, there is often greater emphasis on compliance to adult authority. In contrast, many boys experience pressure among their male peers to maintain an image of masculinity based on appearing tough that can include opposition to teacher authority. Researchers have found that agreeableness and social dominance goals are positively and negatively related, respectively, to academic achievement during adolescence.

Achievement in Specific Academic Subjects

Gender-stereotyped beliefs can affect girls' and boys' attitudes toward achievement in particular academic subjects. In turn, gender-related variations in academic achievement are related to the kinds of occupations that women and men later choose. Gender-related differences in achievement, therefore, can perpetuate the gendered division of labor in adulthood. One of the many strides toward gender equality in the United States and other Western nations has been the narrowing of the gender gap in many academic domains such as mathematics and the biological sciences. Only a few decades ago in the United States, boys were outperforming girls in these subjects.

However, recent reports indicate negligible average differences between girls and boys in high school math and biology grades and test scores. A small average gender gap remains, however, in test scores in the physical sciences (favoring boys) and in reading and writing (favoring girls).

In addition to historical changes within the United States in girls' and boys' math and science achievement, there are also cultural variations. A recent cross-cultural analysis of math and science standardized test scores indicated considerable variability in the pattern of gender difference across nations. In some countries, there was no average difference; in other nations, there was an average difference that favored boys; and in some countries, there was an average difference that favored girls. Thus, there is an emerging consensus among developmental researchers that a large portion of the variation in academic achievement is attributable to social and cognitive-motivational factors.

Parents, teachers, and peers may hold gender-stereotyped beliefs about adolescents' interests and abilities. Consequently, they may differentially encourage girls' and boys' achievement in different academic subjects. For example, longitudinal research in the United States has found that many parents tended to hold higher expectations for boys than girls in math, and that parents' expectations predicted later math motivation even after controlling for initial math performance: Girls of parents with low expectations became less interested in math and took fewer advanced math courses in high school. Other studies have highlighted the potential impact of peers. Conformity pressures can undermine boys' and girls' achievement in certain areas. For example, many boys may avoid feminine-stereotyped subjects such as reading to maintain an image of masculinity. Conversely, peer support may help to sustain interest in cross-gender-typed subjects. For example, girls who perceived peer support for science were more likely to maintain their own interest in science over time.

Despite significant advances over the years, women remain underrepresented in many fields related to science, technology, engineering, and math (STEM) in the United States and other Western nations. When considering gender disparities in STEM-related careers, it is therefore important to consider factors related to school achievement as well as occupational aspirations. Among girls who do well in math and science during high school, many are not motivated to pursue occupations related to these subjects. The expectancy-value model of achievement helps explain these patterns. According to the model, individuals are motivated to pursue domains in which they feel competent (expect success) and find interesting (value). When certain subjects are stereotyped for the other gender, it may undermine the personal value that an individual may attach to that domain. In this regard, many adolescents associate math, science, and computers with males and associate reading and writing with females. Therefore, girls may devalue math, science, and computers and boys may devalue reading and writing. The potential impact of gender stereotypes on adolescents' academic self-concepts is implicated in other studies finding corresponding average gender differences in self-perceived competence and interest in these subjects. To the extent that youth feel less confident or less interested in certain subjects, they are less likely to pursue those fields. However, studies also point to possible ways to foster adolescents' interest in particular academic subjects. For example, one study in Germany found that high school girls' interest in physics increased when practical applications were highlighted in the curriculum.

Athletic Participation

Girls' and Boys' Participation in Organized Sports

Sports are an important activity context in many adolescents' lives. According to a nationally representative study in the United States of 12–18-year-olds' time use, these youth spent more time per week ($\sim$4 h) in sport activities than in all other organized activities combined. Girls' involvement in organized sport in the United States is higher today than ever before. This is largely due to historic increases in girls' athletic participation since the passage of Title IX of the Education Amendments of 1972, which required equal opportunity for girls and boys in all school programs receiving federal financial support. During the last 40 years, girls' involvement in high school sports in the United States has increased from approximately 3% to approximately 40%. Boys' participation in high school sports has remained approximately 50% during this period.

There are both similarities and differences in the kinds of sports that are popular for girls and boys in the United States. Basketball, track and field, baseball/softball, and soccer are among the top five most popular high school sports for both girls and boys. However, football is the most popular among boys and is rarely played among girls. In contrast, cheerleading squads are popular among girls and are pursued relatively infrequently among boys (98% female). Boys' and girls' differential involvement in these two sports reflects traditional gender roles, with males being more physically aggressive (in football) and females being more supportive (in cheerleading).

Despite increased sport opportunities for girls and women, sports remain a highly gendered activity context. As previously noted, proportionally more boys (50%) than girls (40%) in the United States participate in high school sports. Also, whereas participation in organized sports declines during the course of adolescence for boys and girls, the trend is stronger for girls. According to the World Health Organization, these trends are seen across the world. Finally, within the United States, gender disparities in physical activity and sport participation are even more pronounced for girls of color and low-income girls.

Girls are more likely than boys to report barriers to participating in sports and physical activities. Some cited barriers include time pressures (e.g., too much homework, responsibilities at home), structural limitations (e.g., problems obtaining transportation, facilities, and equipment), interpersonal impediments (e.g., parental belief that sport is not as important for girls as for boys), and psychological factors (e.g., low confidence in their physical abilities or knowledge about how to play). A United Nations report on women, gender equality, and sport found that physical barriers to females' participation in sport, including a lack of access to facilities and resources, are a worldwide problem. In addition in many parts of the world, sports are considered to be more important for males and in some regions, female sport participation directly violates social norms for appropriate female behavior. Lack of access to sport facilities and prohibitive social attitudes jointly limit girls' opportunities to participate in sport activities.

Benefits and Costs of Sport Participation for Girls and Boys

There are several positive outcomes associated with sport participation. For example, sport involvement has been linked to positive academic performance, school engagement, and future educational aspirations. Research has also found a positive longitudinal relationship between high school sport involvement and psychological adjustment. This pattern may be likely because sport participation is highly valued in US high schools, and athletes often hold high status positions in their peer groups.

Some benefits associated with athletic participation are especially likely among adolescent girls. Research shows that girls' involvement in sports and physical activities is related to increased self-esteem, self-efficacy, and feeling self-reliant. In addition, several studies show that adolescent girls and college women who play sports are more likely than nonathletes to report more satisfaction with their bodies. In addition, female high school athletes are less likely than nonathletes to report eating disorders. Adolescent girls who are involved in sports also show a number of positive behaviors related to sexuality. Female athletes engage in fewer risky sexual behaviors and do more to protect their sexual health than do their nonathletic peers.

Despite the various psychological, social, and physical benefits associated with involvement in sports, positive outcomes are not an automatic byproduct of participation. There are negative attitudes and behaviors that may increase with athletic involvement. For example, some research in the United States suggests that high school athletes are more likely than nonathletes to drink alcohol. However, this pattern may vary across ethnic groups or communities; for example, it appears more likely for European American than African American athletes. For girls, there is evidence that participation in lean sports (in which being slender is believed to be an advantage, such as distance running) is related to self-objectification, which involves focusing on how one's body appears rather than what it can do. Further, some female athletes are at risk for developing disordered eating problems. This includes dancers, girls and women who play aesthetic (in which bodies are judged as part of the competition, such as figure skating) and lean sports, and elite athletes (who play in professional leagues or compete at national or international events).

For boys, sport fields have historically been a place to learn about and prove one's masculinity, and boys achieve status among their peers based on their athletic ability. For many male athletes, there is a locker room culture that promotes misogyny and homophobia. Those who are less athletically skilled tend to be lower on the dominance hierarchy in US high schools, and can be targets for bullying and homophobic taunts. High status male athletes at the top of the social hierarchy in some communities are more likely to hold rape-tolerant attitudes and to commit sexual violence against females.

In an effort to cultivate positive sport environments, researchers and youth sport advocates have created models for optimal sport contexts as well as specific sport programs with a positive youth development focus. These programs focus on teaching sports skills along with life skills in a safe, fun, supportive, and challenging environment that involves caring relationships, well-trained adult leaders, facilitated and experiential learning, and moderate-to-vigorous physical activity.

Body Image

The US National Eating Disorders Association (NEDA) identifies four components that define body image:

1. how you see yourself when you look in the mirror or picture yourself in your mind:
2. what you believe about your own appearance;
3. how you feel about your body, including your height, shape, and weight; and
4. how you sense and control your body as you move, which includes how you feel in your body, not just your thoughts about your body.

NEDA characterizes a positive body image as having an accurate perception of and appreciating one's shape as well as feeling proud of and comfortable in one's body. Individuals with a positive body image also understand that physical appearance does not dictate one's value as a person, and these individuals refuse to spend excessive time worrying about food and weight. In contrast, a negative body image is characterized as having a distorted perception of one's shape, feeling ashamed, self-conscious, and anxious about one's body, viewing one's body as a personal failure, and feeling uncomfortable in one's body. People with negative body image are at an increased risk for developing an eating disorder, suffering from depression, low self-esteem, and obsessions with weight loss.

Pubertal Timing and Body Image

Girls who mature earlier tend to be shorter and heavier in appearance relative to their female peers, which is inconsistent with Western cultures' value on thinness in females. This can cause negative body image, eating disorders, and depressed mood. Late-maturing girls might experience teasing and negative body image in early adolescence because of their lack of physical development. By late adolescence, however, they tend to have more positive body image than other girls because they generally have a lean body build that is favored in many Western groups. Early-maturing boys grow and put on muscle earlier than their male peers, giving them an advantage in sport activities, which also gives them more status among their peers. These boys tend to be more popular than other boys and more attractive to girls because of their advanced development of facial hair, deeper voice, and other secondary sex characteristics.

Body Image Concerns Among Girls

Concern with body shape and size starts very early among girls and primarily centers on attaining a thin ideal body shape emphasized in many Western societies. One study found that at age 10, approximately 81% of American girls were afraid of being fat. To attain the thin body ideal, approximately 40–60% of US high school girls are on diets.

However, there are differences among ethnic groups within the United States. On average, African Americans are more accepting as a group of a range of female body shapes and sizes, whereas European Americans tend to highly value female thinness. Recent research, however, has found body dissatisfaction, weight dissatisfaction, perceived overweight, low body pride, and disordered eating in all ethnic groups in the United States.

Body image is a central concern among many adolescent girls in the United States, and a basis for self-evaluation as well as evaluation by others. During puberty, rapid physical maturation occurs, including hormonal and physical changes. For girls, body fat increases which is incompatible with cultural standards of beauty (i.e., a thin ideal body shape). Dissatisfaction with physical appearance is particularly concerning because physical appearance satisfaction is the most significant predictor of global self-esteem among adolescents. Therefore, dissatisfaction with appearance has implications for adolescents' overall psychological adjustment, and this is especially true for girls.

Body Image Concerns Among Boys

The cultural ideal for body shape among males in many Western cultures is the athletic, V-shaped body including well-developed pectoral muscles, arms, and shoulders, and a narrow waist. Body image concerns among boys and men often involve gaining more muscle mass in pursuit of the athletic ideal body shape. Weight is also a concern for many males, especially boys who enter puberty late and perceive themselves as being underweight. One American study of teen boys found that about 40% were dissatisfied with their weight and about a third of boys were dissatisfied with their body shape. Further, almost one-third of the normal-weight boys in the study were dissatisfied with their weight, and more than two-thirds of those thought they were underweight. These boys wanted a bigger chest and arms and a smaller stomach. Some boys take anabolic steroids in pursuit of the muscular ideal body shape. In the United States, it is estimated that this occurs among 3–11% of teenage boys. The potential risks of steroid use include serious medical conditions (e.g., cardiac and neuroendocrine problems) and psychological effects (e.g., mood disorders, aggression).

Just as among girls and women, body fat is not a desired body characteristic among boys and men. Yet, the desire to be thin is more pronounced among females as a group than males with notable exceptions. Several sports involve weight restrictions including gymnastics, running, body-building, rowing, swimming, dancing, and being a jockey. Males and females involved in these sports are at heightened risk for eating disorders, although their weight loss behaviors may be tied to a desire for athletic success rather than the mental health problems associated with eating disorders.

Body Image and Popular Media

For both females and males, media constitute an important source of information about physical attractiveness. Societal factors strongly influence the development and maintenance of body image through the construction of an appearance-oriented culture that values and displays cultural ideals of beauty and body shape. Media images play a key role in shaping and reinforcing societal standards of beauty. They influence individuals' beliefs about ideal body shapes and their assessment of whether their own bodies match the ideal.

Magazines targeted at girls and women heavily emphasize which female bodies are valued and considered sexually attractive. There is a strong message in these magazines that women's bodies should be very slender, and if girls and women do not match this ideal then they should work to achieve it through dieting and fitness routines. Indeed, these magazines contain high volumes of advertisements and articles promoting weight loss. Even girls who are infrequent readers of magazines report that the media affect their concept of the ideal body shape. Media images of men are more lean and muscular today than ever before, and the frequency of seeing men without their shirts on in media seems to be on the rise. Boys and men tend to report more body dissatisfaction after viewing muscular media images of men if they compare themselves to these images.

Eating Disorders

Eating disorders are associated with a negative body image. In the United States, as many as ten million females and one million males struggle with an eating disorder such as anorexia or bulimia; 90% of these individuals are adolescent girls and young women between the ages of 12 and 25. Anorexia is characterized by self-starvation and excessive weight loss. Bulimia involves a cycle of binge eating and compensatory behaviors to undo the effects of eating (e.g., self-induced vomiting). Millions more struggle with binge eating disorder (or compulsive overeating), which involves uncontrolled, impulsive, or continuous eating beyond the point of feeling comfortably full without purging behaviors. People with an eating disorder typically become obsessed with food, body image, and weight. Eating disorders can become chronic and sometimes even life threatening, but they are treatable problems, especially when intervention occurs early on.

Adolescence may be an especially vulnerable period for the development of anorexia among girls. Indeed, the majority of individuals who suffer from anorexia are female. Narrow standards for female beauty that stress a thin-ideal body shape contribute to this problem. While the number of individuals who meet the full clinical standard for anorexia is somewhat modest ($\sim$1 in 200 American adolescents), researchers estimate that 40% of newly identified cases of anorexia in the United States are among girls 15–19 years old. Of particular concern is the high mortality rate associated with anorexia, which is higher than any other mental illness. About 10% of teens with anorexia are boys. Boys, however, are less likely to be diagnosed and treated for an eating disorder perhaps because of the stereotype that eating disorders are a female problem. Far more common than full-blown eating disorders are disordered eating practices in which both girls and boys engage. More than one-half of teenage girls and nearly one-third of teenage boys use unhealthy weight control behaviors such as skipping meals, fasting, smoking cigarettes, vomiting, and taking laxatives.

According to the US National Eating Disorders Association, a number of factors can contribute to eating disorders.

Psychological factors include low self-esteem, feelings of inadequacy or lack of control in life, depression, anxiety, anger, or loneliness. Interpersonal factors consist of troubled family and personal relationships, difficulty expressing emotions and feelings, a history of experiencing weight-based teasing, or a history of physical or sexual abuse. Social factors include cultural pressures that value thinness and having a 'perfect body,' narrow definitions of beauty that include only women and men of specific body weights and shapes, and cultural norms that value people on the basis of physical appearance and not other qualities. Other factors that can contribute to eating disorders include possible biochemical or biological causes and genetics (i.e., there is some evidence that eating disorders run in families).

Sexuality and Sexual Orientation

Sexual Scripts

Dating and sexual relationships typically begin and increase during adolescence. Girls and boys in the United States have traditionally learned different sexual scripts, which are cognitive frameworks for understanding how sexual experiences should occur. Benevolent sexist attitudes (i.e., the view that women need men's protection) often emerge as adolescents turn to traditional dating scripts. Because many girls internalize traditional gender attitudes, they often endorse benevolent sexism. In general, both girls and boys expect the boy to be the initiator of the sexual behavior, whereas the girl is supposed to set limits on how far the sexual encounter should go. Girls are often taught to recognize and restrict boys' sexual desire, but not taught to recognize or appreciate their own sexual feelings. Whereas boys gain status among their peers for being sexually active and 'scoring,' girls run the risk of being ostracized for the same behavior and labeled a 'slut,' reflecting a double standard in attitudes toward sexual behavior. This double standard is common worldwide.

Sexual Behavior Among Heterosexual Youth

Whereas all adolescents experience similar biological changes in reaching sexual maturity, beliefs about adolescent sexuality vary across cultures and communities within particular societies. Restrictive cultures, including a number of Arab countries, strongly prohibit sexual activity before marriage. To discourage such a possibility, boys and girls are often segregated in schools and other social domains. Strong social norms, and sometimes the threat of physical punishment and public shaming, severely limit girls' and boys' contact with each other. Girls, in particular, may be harshly sanctioned for premarital sexual activity in restrictive cultures. Their virginity is considered a matter of family honor and they risk physical violence and even death for violating this social norm. Boys' virginity is also valued in restrictive cultures, but they are far less likely to be punished for premarital sexual activity. In direct contrast, permissive cultures encourage and expect adolescent sexual activity. The people of the Trobriand Islands in the South Pacific were classified as permissive by anthropologists studying them in the 1950s. More recently, researchers have found that many formerly permissive cultures have become less permissive with globalization and religious missionary work. Semirestrictive cultures, like the majority culture in the United States, have prohibitions on premarital adolescent sexual activity, but they do not tend to enforce them.

During adolescence, many youth in permissive and semirestrictive cultures engage in sexual activities for the first time. These may include kissing, touching genitals, sexual intercourse, oral sex, and anal sex. The average age of first intercourse for American youth is 16.9 years for boys and 17.4 years for girls. According to a nationally representative survey of ninth through twelfth grade students in public and private schools in the United States, the percentage of high school students who reported ever engaging in sexual intercourse has steadily declined over the last two decades from 54% in 1991 to 46% in 2009. Rates of reported sexual intercourse were similar for girls and boys. Although 46% of youth reported ever having had sexual intercourse within the past year in 2009, only 34.2% reported having had sex in the prior 3 months. Thus, incidences of sexual intercourse appear to be sporadic. Also, the incidence of sexual intercourse varies across different ethnic groups and communities. For example, on average, African American youth begin having sex at 15.8 years, followed by European Americans at 16.6 years, Hispanics at 17.0 years, and Asian Americans at 18.1 years.

Sexual Minorities

As tolerance for sexual minorities has increased in many Western cultures, adolescence has become a safer period of 'coming out' for many lesbian, gay, bisexual, or transgender (LGBT) youth. Coming out involves recognizing one's same-sex attractions and disclosing one's sexual identity to family members, friends, and others. This process can be difficult and painful for youth if they confront homophobia (fear or antipathy toward sexual minorities) and heterosexism (prejudice and discrimination against sexual minorities). As a result, many sexual-minority youth can feel extremely isolated from their family members and heterosexual peers. Also, they may defer exploring and expressing their sexual identity until early adulthood.

Sexual identity trajectories appear to differ for sexual-minority girls and boys. In addition, there is a great deal of diversity in the pathways to sexual-minority identification among sexual-minority youth of different socioeconomic backgrounds, ethnicities, and historical cohorts. Research with US youth has found that sexual-minority boys resemble heterosexual boys in the timing of their first sexual behaviors, which tends to be soon after the onset of puberty. In contrast, sexual-minority girls engage in same-sex sexual behaviors later than boys do. One study found that sexual-minority girls' first sexual behaviors were more likely to occur in a romantic relationship as compared to sexual-minority boys. In the same study, sexual-minority males were more likely to purse same-sex sexual contact before labeling themselves as nonheterosexual. The opposite pattern was found among sexual-minority females who were more likely to label themselves nonheterosexual before pursing same-sex sexual contact.

The mental health of LGTB youth has been a concern among psychologists because of heightened rates of depression and suicidal ideation in these youth. A recent study found that experience with heterosexism was associated with increased rates of symptoms of depression among LGTB boys and girls as well as increased risk of self-harm and suicidal ideation among LGTB males. Thus, peer rejection based on rigid adherence to traditional gender-role beliefs – rather than sexual orientation per se – appears to account for higher rates of emotional distress among sexual-minority youth. Accordingly, some school-based interventions have been successful when they targeted homophobic social norms.

Friendship Intimacy

Affiliation and assertion are two interpersonal goals that underlie social behavior. Affiliation refers to the need to connect with others, whereas assertion refers to the need to exert control and influence over others. Although individuals may favor one goal over the other, affiliation and assertion are not mutually exclusive. Collaboration refers to the joint pursuit of affiliative and assertive goals as seen, for example, when individuals cooperatively build on one another's discussion topic or activity. Average gender differences in affiliative and assertive goals are seen during childhood and adolescence. Girls are more likely than boys to value affiliative goals or a combination of affiliation and assertion. In contrast, boys are more likely than girls to pursue power-assertive goals (i.e., emphasizing assertion while downplaying affiliation).

Affiliative and assertive goals are important factors when considering the development of intimacy during adolescence. The emphasis on power-assertion associated with traditional masculinity norms can impair the development of intimacy in many boys' relationships. By focusing on being dominant and appearing tough, many boys become unwilling to express vulnerable feelings or express affection with same-gender friends. Traditional masculinity norms are also associated with homophobic attitudes that can further impair boys' intimacy because boys learn to suppress their emotions to avoid being labeled gay. In contrast, girls are more likely than boys to offer personal disclosures to friends and parents. Also, females are more likely than males to be recipients of self-disclosure from both girls and boys. That is, adolescents are more likely to disclose to female friends or mothers than to male friends or fathers, respectively.

Research in the United States, Canada, Europe, and similar societies suggests that there may be more variability in the expression of intimacy among boys than girls in same-gender friendships. In most girls' friendships, self-disclosure appears to be the primary pathway toward emotional closeness. Shared disclosure is also a pathway toward emotional closeness in the friendships of many boys. But for other boys, shared activities (e.g., playing sports) appear to be an alternative pathway to friendship closeness.

Self-disclosure is generally associated with positive socioemotional adjustment and relationships satisfaction in friendships and romantic relationships. However, recent research has highlighted how excessive disclosure in friendships can lead to negative outcomes. Corumination occurs when two friends repeatedly dwell on personal problems together. This process may lead to anxiety and depression in adolescents (perhaps especially among girls more than boys).

Aggression and Violence

Direct and Indirect Aggression

Gender-related variations in various forms of aggressive behavior occur during adolescence. Researchers distinguish between direct and indirect forms of aggression. Direct aggression refers to overt and face-to-face aggression including physical aggression (e.g., hitting, shoving) and verbal aggression (e.g., insults). On average, both physical aggression and verbal aggression are more common among boys than girls during adolescence. Furthermore, cross-cultural research indicates a general pattern for greater physical aggression among males than females, but the magnitude of the difference varies across cultures.

Indirect aggression (also known as relational or social aggression) refers to behaviors such as spreading negative gossip and social exclusion. Contrary to earlier proposals that indirect aggression is more common among girls than boys during adolescence, the research evidence indicates no meaningful gender difference. However, there is an average difference inasmuch that girls' use of aggression is primarily limited to indirect forms, whereas boys' use of aggression is more likely to involve both direct and indirect forms.

Sexual Harassment

During adolescence, many direct and indirect aggressive behaviors may be forms of sexual harassment. Physical sexual harassment includes unwanted touching or sexual coercion. Verbal sexual harassment occurs through the expression of demeaning, homophobic, or unwanted comments with sexual themes. These comments might be made directly to the person or indirectly through negative gossip.

Survey studies in the United States and Canada indicate that most adolescents experience or instigate sexual harassment. According to recent surveys, overall rates of reported sexual harassment are similar for girls and boys; however, girls are more likely than boys to report feeling distressed by these experiences. There are average gender differences in reported incidences of particular forms of sexual harassment. For example, homophobic comments are directed more to boys than girls, whereas unwanted touching is more common for girls than boys. Both girls and boys are more likely to identify cross-gender than same-gender peers as perpetrators of sexual harassment; however, boys are more likely than girls to experience same-gender sexual harassment. Furthermore, sexual-minority youth are especially at risk for sexual harassment.

Romantic relationships are another relationship context in which aggressive behavior can occur. Studies in the United States and other Western cultures find that boys as well as girls may instigate aggression in dating relationships, although it is more common among boys than girls. According to some estimates from studies in the United States, approximately 25% of adolescent dating relationships experience some form of psychological or physical abuse. However, there are variations across communities within the United States in rates of dating violence. Furthermore, cross-cultural research indicates that rates of sexual harassment and sexual violence are inversely related to the degree of gender equality in the society.

Repeated sexual harassment and dating violence can be very stressful for youth and it is associated with adjustment problems. Possible consequences in girls and boys include increases in emotional distress, suicidal thoughts, substance abuse, externalizing behaviors, and disengagement from school and other activities. In addition, among girls, sexual harassment may lead to negative body image and self-harm. Furthermore, abusive dating experiences may lead some girls to expect demeaning behaviors as normal in heterosexual relationships; and these girls may be at risk for dysfunctional and abusive relationships later in adulthood.

Summary

Gender is an important social category that affects adolescents' lives in multiple ways. Gender identities and gender schemas shape the kinds of ideas and behaviors that adolescents may consider appropriate for themselves and others. Stereotyped beliefs may lead to sexism, including prejudiced attitudes and discriminatory behaviors. Gender-related variations during adolescence occur in academic achievement, athletic participation, sexuality, body image, dating relationships, friendship intimacy, and aggression. Many aspects of gender development are shaped by the kinds of roles allocated to women and men in society.

With increased gender equality, opportunities have broadened for girls in many Western societies. For example, girls' participation in athletics and achievement in math and science have dramatically increased. However, there are some areas, such as body image, where things have become worse in recent decades. These contradictions reflect the complicated set of factors that shape gender development. For example, whereas parents and schools may be doing a good job getting girls to participate in sports, the media is simultaneously bombarding them with unrealistic and hypersexualized ideals of beauty.

Finally, it is worth noting that there has been relatively slower gender-role change among adolescent boys than girls in recent decades. This is partly due to higher status associated with masculine-stereotyped attributes and activities than with feminine-stereotyped attributes and activities. For example, girls' participation in sports can increase their self-esteem and confidence in competitive settings; also sports are a highly valued activity in our culture. Similarly, doing well in math and science allows girls a wider range of occupational options, including many high-paying and prestigious positions in technology fields. Conversely, boys' demonstration of feminine-stereotyped attributes, such as emotional disclosure, or their pursuit of feminine-stereotyped roles, such as helping with childcare, are often viewed as diminishing their status in the eyes of their peers and family. Whereas gender-role change may be slower among boys than girls, it is occurring. Men are increasingly sharing childcare responsibilities at home. As this occurs, boys are being increasingly exposed to models that may affect how they conceptualize their own gender role.

See also: Academic Achievement; Achievement Motivation; Body Image during Adolescence: A Developmental Perspective; Bully/Victim Problems during Adolescence; Eating Disorders; Gender Roles; Media, Influence of; Peer Influence; Peer Relations; Puberty and Adolescence: An Evolutionary Perspective; Romantic Relationships; Sexual Orientation; Sexuality; Sport Participation.

Further Reading

Blakemore JEO, Berenbaum SA, and Liben LS (2009) *Gender Development*. New York: Taylor & Francis.

Kimmel MS (2007) *The Gendered Society*, 3rd edn. New York: Oxford University Press.

Leaper C (2012) Gender development during childhood. In: Zelazo P (ed.) *The Oxford Handbook of Developmental Psychology*. New York: Oxford University Press.

Rose AJ and Rudolph KD (2006) A review of sex differences in peer relationship processes: Potential tradeoffs for the emotional and behavioral development of girls and boys. *Psychological Bulletin* 132: 98–131.

Tolman DL, Striepe ML, and Harmon T (2003) Gender matters: Constructing a model of adolescent sexual health. *The Journal of Sex Research* 40: 4–12.

Wood W and Eagly AH (2002) A cross-cultural analysis of the behavior of women and men: Implications for the origins of sex differences. *Psychological Bulletin* 128: 699–727.

Genetics

A C Edwards and D M Dick, Virginia Commonwealth University, Richmond, VA, USA

Glossary

Allele: Natural variation in the genetic sequence. Allelic variation can take the form of a change in a single nucleotide or longer stretches of DNA.

Deoxyribonucleic acid (DNA): Genetic material. DNA molecules consist of two polynucleotide chains bound together as a double helix. The DNA sequence includes both noncoding and gene-encoding regions. DNA is tightly bound into chromosomes, which are located in the nucleus of eukaryotic cells.

Dominant: An allele that determines the observed phenotype in a heterozygous condition. Only one copy is necessary to result in the phenotype, for example, AA and Aa have equivalent phenotypes under true dominance.

Epigenetics: Genetic variation that is not due to DNA sequence variation, but rather to phenomena such as methylation, which affects gene expression.

Heritability: The proportion of total phenotypic variance that can be accounted for by genetic factors.

Heterozygous: Containing one copy of two different alleles (e.g., Aa).

Homozygous: Containing two copies of the same allele (e.g., AA or aa).

Phenotype: The observed outcome under study. Can be the manifestation of both genetic and/or environmental factors.

Recessive: An allele whose phenotype is only observed when no dominant allele is present (aa).

(Homologous) recombination: A process that occurs during meiosis in which the DNA strand is broken and rejoined to another, homologous, DNA molecule. Recombination frequency varies across the genome: it can happen often in recombination hotspots, or very seldom, resulting in blocks of linkage disequilibrium.

Ribonucleic acid (RNA): RNA is a single-stranded polynucleotide molecule similar to that of DNA. Different types of RNA have diverse roles; for the purposes of this article, we will be concerned primarily with messenger RNA, which serves as an intermediate between DNA and protein. DNA is transcribed into RNA, which is then translated into a protein.

Introduction

The so-called 'central dogma' of genetics states that deoxyribonucleic acid (DNA) is transcribed into ribonucleic acid (RNA), which is then translated into protein. This process is unidirectional, proceeding from DNA to protein. We now know that this is a simplified schematic for a complicated phenomenon. At each level of the process, there are different types of molecular or cellular variation that can have consequences for phenotypes relevant to adolescence. In addition, environmental processes can have far-reaching impacts on the way in which genes influence phenotypes. The relationship between genes and the environment is far more bidirectional than once thought, and the concept of 'nature *versus* nurture' has been replaced with the more realistic notion of 'nature *and* nurture'. Some genes' effects are dependent on environmental circumstances; indeed, the environment can have an astounding degree of control on where and when some genes are expressed, or whether some genes are expressed at all. This new area of study is called 'epigenetics'.

Nearly every cell in the body contains two copies of 'instructions' in the form of DNA – one inherited from an individual's biological mother and another from the biological father. These instructions are distributed across 46 chromosomes, which are tightly packed DNA molecules. The DNA sequence itself is made up of four nucleotides, which are often denoted simply by the letters A, T, C, and G – the first letters of their full names, adenine, thymine, cytosine, and guanine, respectively. Of the 46 chromosomes, there are 22 pairs of autosomal chromosomes, and one pair of sex chromosomes. Boys inherit a Y chromosome from the father, and an X chromosome from the mother; girls have two copies of the X chromosome.

Everyone has a slightly different copy of these instructions, due to variations in the DNA sequence. That said, the vast majority of the DNA sequence is shared across people. It is thought that about 99% of the DNA sequence is shared, although this estimate has been revised downward several times as we learn more about DNA structure. Nonetheless, most of the DNA sequence is shared. However, the total DNA sequence consists of about 3 billion base pairs, so the 1% that is unshared constitutes about 3 million possible locations where there is variation. These sequence variants, which are called alleles, can fall within or between genes, and the observed effect can depend on their location. Some DNA sequence variation produces an easily observed outcome, such as a single gene that controls the ability to roll your tongue or that results in a disorder, such as cystic fibrosis (see below); in other cases, a subtler outcome is observed, such as when a variant subtly affects the rate of transcription of a certain RNA molecule, which may have small effects on a downstream behavior. The vast majority of allelic variation actually lies outside genes and has no known effect on behavior.

Mendelian Inheritance

Gregor Mendel was the first to describe the process of genetic inheritance, well before DNA was discovered or genes were readily identified. Mendel figured this out by conducting

 doi:10.1016/B978-0-12-373915-5.00018-8

breeding experiments with pea plants, wherein he investigated phenotypes such as pea color (yellow versus green) and texture (wrinkled versus round). These phenotypes are (luckily for Mendel) determined by single genes, and by crossing two phenotypically distinct 'true breeding' plants, which we would now recognize as homozygous, Mendel was able to discern a pattern by which the traits were inherited. He observed that when two 'true breeding' plants were crossed (such as one parent with wrinkled peas crossed to one with round peas), all the observed offspring (called the F1 generation) had the round phenotype. However, when these offspring were crossed with one another, their offspring (called the F2 generation) had a 3:1 ratio of round to wrinkled peas. He deduced that this pattern would result if there were two 'elements' (which we now call alleles) involved in the transmission of the phenotype. These, and more complicated experiments, including an extended series of crosses wherein he examined multiple phenotypes, led to Mendel's understanding that alleles could be dominant, like the round pea allele, or recessive, like the wrinkled pea allele.

Essentially, Mendelian inheritance refers to the fact that parental alleles assort independently of one another and then segregate during gamete formation. Each gamete has only one of the two possible parental alleles at every position, or locus. When maternal and paternal gametes combine, the resulting fertilized egg has two copies of the DNA 'instructions' described earlier, one from each parent. A Mendelian trait is one that is controlled by only one locus in the genome; an individual's phenotype for such a trait can be predicted if parental genotype is known. An example of a Mendelian trait in humans is the recessive disorder cystic fibrosis. If both parents carry one copy of the disease-conferring allele (they will be unaffected since the disorder is recessive, necessitating two copies of the deleterious allele), there is a 25% chance that their offspring will be affected with cystic fibrosis. This likelihood can be demonstrated using a Punnett Square (**Figure 1**). The Punnett Square is named for its inventor, Reginald Punnett, and is used to determine possible offspring genotypes given parental genotypes. If the mode of inheritance (i.e., dominance, additivity, etc.) is known, the corresponding phenotypes can be predicted as well.

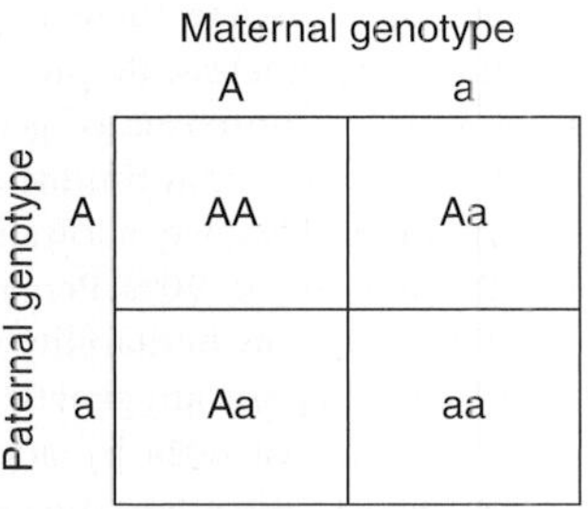

Figure 1 In a Punnett Square, the alleles for one parent are shown along the top of the square and the alleles that the other parent carries are shown along the left side of the square. Because offspring receive one allele from each parent, this allows one to easily work out what the four possible genotypic outcomes are for potential offspring based on the parents' genotypes. In this example, both the mother and father carry one copy of the recessive disease-conferring allele, 'a'. In 25% of cases, their offspring would not carry any copies of the disease-conferring allele, and would have a genotype of 'AA'. In 50% of cases, the offspring would carry one copy of the disease-conferring allele (the 'Aa' genotype). In 25% of cases, the offspring would inherit two copies of the disease-conferring allele, have the 'aa' genotype, and would be affected with cystic fibrosis.

The probability increases to 50% if one parent carries two copies of the disease-conferring allele and has affected him or herself. Probability of disease calculations depends on whether the disease-conferring allele is dominant or recessive, and on whether the gene is located on a sex chromosome.

Quantitative Traits

The alleles influencing quantitative genetic traits are inherited the same way as Mendelian traits: offspring randomly receive one or the other allele from each parent, for every gene. However, the resulting phenotype is not as straightforward as being either affected or unaffected with cystic fibrosis. The phenotype for a single quantitative trait – say, height – can be influenced by many different genes, with each gene contributing to only a fraction of the total variance in height. The hallmarks of quantitative traits are that they are continuously distributed in a population (for example, as a bell curve), are influenced by many genes, and those genes are individually of relatively small effect: that is, no single gene can be held accountable for much of the phenotypic variance in a given trait. Furthermore, these quantitative traits are also influenced by environmental factors, and in many cases, by complex interactions between the environment and genotype. The nature of quantitative traits means that different combinations of alleles can result in the same phenotype in two different individuals. For this reason, mapping genes associated with a quantitative trait is far more complicated than mapping genes associated with a Mendelian trait, as we discuss later in the article.

Genetic Approaches to Behavior

Basic Genetic Epidemiology

Many phenotypes are influenced by both genes and the environment. The most basic goal of genetic epidemiology is to estimate the extent to which genetic and environmental influences impact a trait of interest. The heritability of a trait is the proportion of the total variance in that trait that is due to genetic influences. The premise underlying genetic epidemiological studies is that different types of family members resemble one another to varying degrees and also share different proportions of their genes. This makes it possible to estimate the degree to which genetic factors are responsible for familial resemblance.

The simplest example comes from twin studies. Monozygotic (MZ), or 'identical', twins share all of their genetic variation in common, while dizygotic (DZ), or 'fraternal', twins share on average half of their genetic variation common by descent. This means that the additive genetic variance for DZs is approximately half that of MZs. However, for dominant genetic effects, different alleles do not contribute equally to the phenotypic outcome. Thus, dominance variance results in DZ twins being less phenotypically similar than does additive genetic variance. If the DZ correlation is less than half the MZ correlation, it implies that dominant genetic influences are involved.

Twins raised together also share environmental influences. Those experiences that serve to make them more similar are called common, or shared, environment. Experiences that make individuals different from one another are called unique, or nonshared, environment. Some of these experiences may be objectively nonshared, such as when one twin has exposure to a peer group that the other twin does not. However, experiences that are objectively shared but that have the effect of making twins more different from one another are also considered 'unique' environmental influences, such as if one child reacts to a parental divorce by acting out, while the co-twin reacts by being more well behaved. All of these factors – additive and dominant genetics, common environment, and unique environment – have an effect on the variance of a phenotype, as depicted in **Figure 2**. However, it is only possible to simultaneously estimate three components of variance when only twin data are available. Typically, an a priori decision is made to test for dominant or common environmental influences depending on whether the DZ correlation is greater than (indicating common environment) or less than (indicating dominance) half the MZ correlation. For the purposes of this article, we will restrict our discussion to additive genetic, common environment, and unique environmental variance. This is in large part because far more phenotypes in adolescence show evidence of common environment, with few showing evidence for dominance.

By comparing the correlation between MZ twins to that between DZ twins, we can estimate the heritability of a trait using simple arithmetic:

$$r_{MZ} = a^2 + c^2$$

$$r_{DZ} = \frac{1}{2}a^2 + c^2$$

where r_{MZ} is the correlation between MZ twins, r_{DZ} the correlation between DZ twins, a^2 the genetic variance ('a' stands for additive genetics), and c^2 is the common environmental variance. Since DZ twins share only half of their genetic variation identical by descent, and MZ twins share all their genetic variation, the genetic variance contributing to DZ correlation is half that contributing to MZ correlation. As one example, say we are interested in the heritability of height. We measure the height of a group of MZ twins and find that the correlation between twins' heights is 0.95. Next, we measure a group of DZ twins, and their correlation is 0.50. Plugging these numbers into the aforementioned equations produces the following:

$$r_{MZ} = 0.95 = a^2 + c^2$$

$$-r_{DZ} = 0.50 = \frac{1}{2}a^2 + c^2$$

$$0.45 = \frac{1}{2}a^2$$

By working through the math, we find that $a^2 = 0.90$; that is, the heritability of height is about 90%. Common environmental factors – say, nutrition in this example – account for the remaining 5% of the twin correlation. If the correlation between MZ and DZ twins is the same, then the heritability of that trait would be 0. If the DZ correlation is exactly half the MZ correlation, there is no evidence for common environmental effects, as $\frac{1}{2}$ the MZ correlation is exactly what we would expect based on genetic similarity alone. Finally, if MZs are not exactly identical on the outcome of interest (assuming no measurement error), then unique environmental influences must be important.

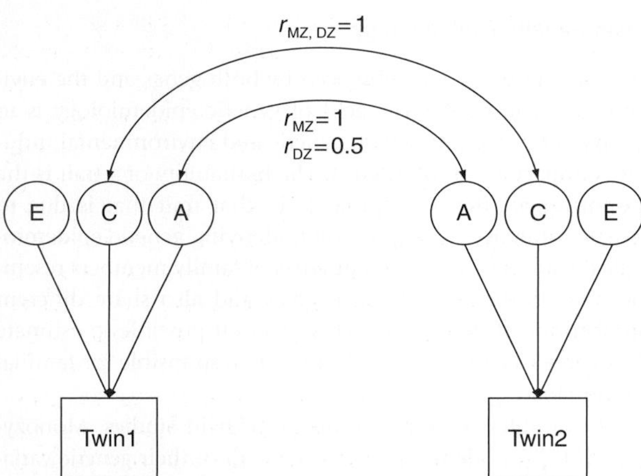

Figure 2 Latent additive genetic factors (A), common environmental factors (C), and unique environmental factors (E) contribute to the observed variance of a given phenotype. Since MZ twins share all their genes, their genetic correlation is equal to unity; since DZ twins share on average half of their genetic variation, their genetic correlation is 0.5. Twins reared together have a shared environmental correlation of 1.0, regardless of zygosity. By definition, there is no unique environmental correlation between twins. Hence, A and C contribute to the phenotypic correlation between twins, but E does not.

Most studies of heritability of commonly studied traits in adolescence show evidence of genetic influence, though exact heritability estimates often vary across studies. Broad ranges for heritability estimates in adolescence likely reflect many factors, including the span of age range of participants in any given study, and the measure/informant used to assess the outcome. This is more relevant in research on childhood and adolescence, where multiple informants are more often used to assess behavior (e.g., self, parents, teachers) than in research on adult outcomes, where there is greater reliance on self-report measures. Nonetheless, despite methodological differences, there is a broad consensus of genetic influences across most traits of interest. Pubertal timing, a trait of strong relevance to the study of adolescence, shows strong evidence of genetic effects, in the range of 60–90%. Personality domains, as measured by the Big Five, show heritability estimates in the range of 30–60%. IQ shows significant genetic influence, with heritability estimates upward of 80% by adolescence. Twin studies of early onset anxiety disorders suggest that they are moderately heritable, with estimates in the range of 15–50%, and heritability estimates for depressive symptoms in adolescence are approximately 40–60%. There is also some evidence of sex differences for heritability of depression, which is interesting, since the prevalence of depressive symptoms between the sexes becomes evident in adolescence. Perhaps surprisingly, alcohol dependence in early adolescence shows little evidence of genetic effects, being predominantly influenced by environmental factors. However, measures of alcohol consumption show significant genetic influence across adolescence, and alcohol problems by later in adolescence and young adulthood show heritability estimates in the range of 50%. Childhood conduct disorder and antisocial behavior also show a heritability of about 50%. ADHD is considered one of the most heritable psychiatric disorders, with an average heritability of about 75%.

Advanced Genetic Epidemiology

Establishing the extent to which genetic and environmental influences impact a trait of interest is the most basic question addressed by genetic epidemiologic methods. It is important to remember that this basic question was critical in changing the predominant paradigm in the previous century, during which most psychiatric and behavioral outcomes were thought to be the result of environmental factors. Understanding the critical role that genetics plays in most outcomes of interest was an incredibly important step forward in understanding basic etiology. However, heritability estimates provide population-based estimates and are not specific to any given individual. For example, if a trait is 50% heritable, that does not mean that 50% of the reason any given individual expresses that outcome is due to their genetic make-up and 50% is due to their environment. Rather, it means that 50% of the variation across the population in that outcome is due to differences in genetic influences. **Figure 3** illustrates the concept of population-based estimates, using the analogy of factors that contribute to the area of a rectangle.

The area for any given rectangle is influenced by its length and width. In the first population of rectangles, all of the rectangles have different areas, but the biggest factor contributing to differences in area across the rectangles is length. In the second population of rectangles, the rectangles also differ in area, but in this case, it is differences in width that are largely responsible for the differences in area. A parallel can be drawn to understanding heritability estimates. Most psychological outcomes are influenced by both genetic and environmental influences. Heritability estimates indicate the relative influence of genetic and environmental effects in differences observed between individuals across a population. But they do not pit genetic and environmental influences against each other, as some critics of behavior genetics have erroneously concluded. It makes no more sense to talk about whether something is genetic versus environmental than it does to ask if the area of a rectangle is due to width or length.

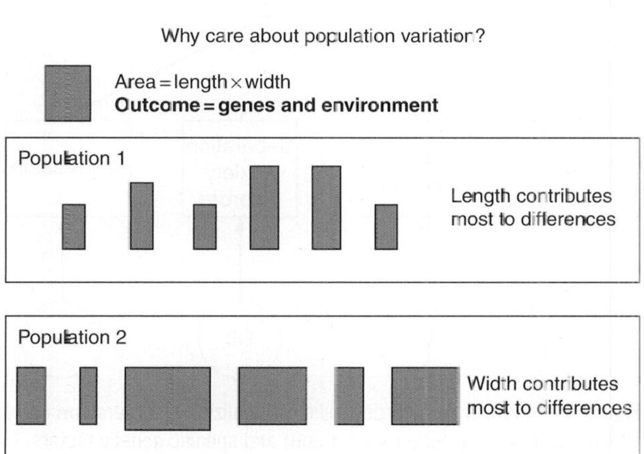

Figure 3 Understanding variation at the population level, rather than individual specific estimates. The area of a rectangle is a function of its length and width. In the first population of rectangles, the primary factor contributing to the differences in area between the rectangles is their length. In the second population of rectangles, the primary factor contributing to variation in area across the rectangles is differences in their width. For any one rectangle, the area is always a function of its width and length, but across the population, we can estimate the extent to which variation is due to differences in width and/or differences in length.

Although it is relevant to know to what extent variation between individuals is due to genetic and environmental influences, it does mean that heritability (and environmental) estimates are necessarily specific to that population under study. Those point estimates depend on the characteristics of the population under study – including factors such as age and environmental circumstances. However, heritability is not a static concept, as evidenced even by the range of estimates yielded for any given trait, as indicated earlier. Heritability might be quite low in a situation where environmental factors are strongly influential, and the heritability of a trait may differ across developmental stages.

Most twin studies now focus on more interesting and complex questions about *how* genetic and environmental influences act and interact to contribute to behavioral outcome. These include questions about how genetic influences may vary as a function of specific, measured environments (gene–environment interaction), as well as the extent to which our genetic predispositions shape the way we experience the world (gene–environment correlation). They address the dynamic nature of genetic and environmental influences across time and development, and the extent to which genetic and environmental influences impact covariation across traits. Many of these questions are particularly relevant to the study of adolescence, as illustrated in the following paragraphs.

Gene–environment correlation and interaction

Parsing genetic and environmental influences into separate sources represents a necessary oversimplification, as genetic and environmental influences are ultimately intertwined. Most measures of the environment show some degree of genetic influence, illustrating the active role that individuals play in selecting and creating their social worlds. To the extent that these choices are influenced by an individual's genetically influenced temperaments and behavioral characteristics, an individual's environment is not purely exogenous, but rather, in some sense, is yet another extension and reflection of the individual's genotype. This concept is called gene–environment correlation.

One particularly relevant example is adolescent peer group substance use and deviance. Multiple genetically informative samples have demonstrated that a genetic predisposition toward substance use is associated with the selection of other friends who use substances. Genetic effects on peer group deviance show a strong and steady increase from childhood to adulthood, suggesting that as individuals get older and have increasing opportunity to select and create their own social environment, genetic factors assume increasing importance.

The concept of gene–environment correlation is different from gene–environment interaction, which refers to the phenomenon where the importance of an individual's genotype varies as a function of their environment (alternatively characterized as the environment being differentially influential dependent on an individual's genotype; these two conceptualizations of gene–environment interaction are statistically indistinguishable). Heritability estimates essentially average across environments; accordingly, if there is reason to believe that the importance of genetic effects might vary as a function of the environment, this information can be incorporated into the twin model to test for significant differences in heritability as a function of the environment. Adolescent substance use provides one area where gene–environment interaction effects have been found to be particularly important. Environments that exert more social control and present less opportunity to engage in substance use consistently show reduced evidence for the importance of genetic effects. In this sense, the environment is essentially constraining the expression of a predisposition toward substance use/problems. For example, genetic influences on adolescent substance use are more important among adolescents who report lower parental monitoring. Genetic influences are exacerbated among adolescents who report affiliation with more deviant and/or substance using peers. In this case, the environment appears to offer greater opportunity to express genetically influenced predispositions. These analyses demonstrate the critical role that the environment can play in shaping the manifestation of individuals' temperaments and predispositions, especially in adolescence when individuals have more opportunities to directly influence their environments.

Changing genetic influence across development

In general, heritability appears to increase from adolescence to young adulthood across many behavioral domains, including externalizing behaviors, anxiety symptoms, depressive symptoms, IQ, social attitudes, and alcohol consumption. The only domain that yields no evidence of heritability changes across time is attention-deficit/hyperactivity disorder. The robust finding of increases in the importance of genetic influences across development likely reflects, in part, active gene–environment correlation, as individuals increasingly select and create their own experiences based on their genetic propensities, as discussed earlier.

In addition to changes in the relative magnitude of importance of genetic and environmental influences, another dynamic change is that different genes may be acting at different time points. By assessing twins' phenotypic covariance across different time points, researchers have found that, even in cases where the overall heritability of a trait remains stable across time, the genetic factors influencing that trait are often changing. For example, we have found that genetic influences on depressive symptoms at age 14 decrease in importance by age 18 (genetic attenuation), and genetic influences not apparent at age 14 become important by age 18 (genetic innovation). It appears that genetic innovation becomes particularly pronounced at puberty. Accumulating evidence suggests that genetic influences on many psychiatric and substance use disorders are likely to be developmentally dynamic, with genes becoming more and/or less important across different developmental stages.

Comorbidity of phenotypes

Overlap across different psychiatric outcomes and behavioral disorders is usually the rule rather than the exception: for example, ADHD and CD are often comorbid, as are anxiety and depressive disorders. Such cases of comorbidity are increasingly becoming the focus of twin studies, which seek to clarify the etiology of these epidemiological findings. By conducting multivariate analyses that tease apart the phenotypic covariance of these traits, researchers can test the extent to which the phenotypic association between traits is due to shared genetic and/or environmental factors. In many cases, observed comorbidity appears to be due in large part to shared genetic effects.

One example of a genetic factor common to multiple phenotypes is illustrated in **Figure 4**, which depicts a genetic liability influencing multiple manifestations of internalizing behavior.

A similar pattern has been observed across externalizing disorders, including alcohol dependence, antisocial behavior, childhood conduct disorder, and illicit substance use. One study of adolescent twins found that the genetic correlations between conduct disorder, alcohol dependence, and illicit drug dependence were around 0.60–0.80. Another found that ADHD, CD, and oppositional defiant disorder are strongly genetically correlated ($r_G = 0.46–0.74$). Perhaps surprisingly, there is also evidence that major depression and CD are genetically correlated during adolescence, as are anxiety/depression and alcohol use. More generally, the childhood/adolescent externalizing domains of attention problems, delinquency, and aggression have been demonstrated to have genetic correlations upward of 0.70, while internalizing domains (e.g., withdrawal, somatic complaints, anxiety) are variably genetically correlated (about 0.25–0.70).

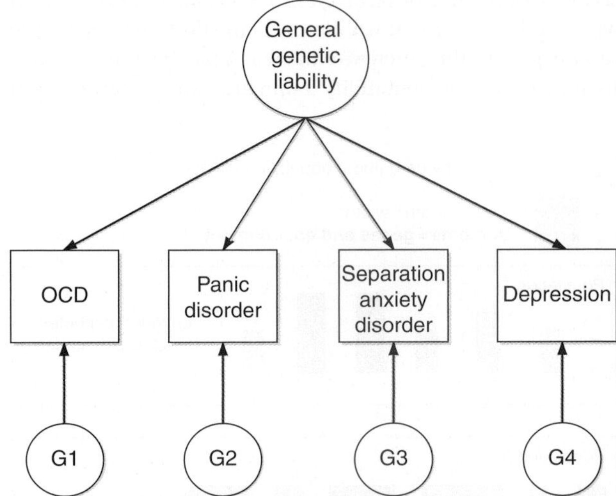

Figure 4 Internalizing disorders, like externalizing disorders, are likely influenced by both general (or common) and specific genetic factors. Here, measured internalizing phenotypes are depicted in boxes. All of the disorders are influenced by a general genetic factor, represented by the circle at the top of the figure. This genetic factor might load differentially onto each internalizing disorder. In addition to the general factor, each disorder is also influenced by genetic factors *specific* to that disorder, which are depicted by the circles labeled G1–G4. For example, both obsessive-compulsive disorder (OCD) and panic disorder are influenced by the general genetic liability factor; genetic influences represented by G1 influence liability to OCD but not panic disorder, and G2 influences liability to panic disorder but not OCD.

These multivariate studies indicate that shared genetic influences contribute susceptibility toward the development of multiple disorders, and different environmental influences might result in diagnostically distinct outcomes. Thus, the clinical distinctions made across internalizing or externalizing disorders, for example, might be useful for treatment, but do not necessarily accurately reflect the common biological etiology of these traits. These findings have further clinical implications: individuals who present with one disorder are likely at increased genetic risk for the development of genetically related disorders. Intervention, prevention, and treatment strategies could conceivably be tailored to address correlated risk.

Gene-Finding Methods

While twin studies can be used to estimate the effects of latent (i.e., unobserved) genetic variation, other approaches are needed to identify chromosomal regions or specific genes influencing a particular phenotype.

Two primary strategies have been used for gene identification: linkage and association studies. Linkage studies traditionally offered the advantage that they enabled researchers to scan the entire genome for possible regions containing genes influencing a trait of interest, without any a priori knowledge of where these genes may reside. This was accomplished by testing genetic markers approximately evenly spaced throughout the genome. Early studies using linkage methods in psychiatric disorders were largely unsuccessful and led to much early disappointment and frustration. This was based, in part, on the use of linkage methods that required specification of a disease model (e.g., mode of inheritance, penetrance, disease allele frequency in the population). Although these methods had been used successfully to map genes for hundreds of Mendelian disorders, studying complex phenotypes introduced a number of new complications, including the involvement of many genes of small effect, genetic heterogeneity, environmental influences, and phenotypic imprecision. Subsequently, linkage methods were created that were better suited for the many complexities inherent in complex phenotypes. The basic idea behind these methods is to search for genetic regions that are more likely to be shared among affected individuals, suggesting that there is a gene in the region that contributes to that outcome.

Although linkage analyses are theoretically useful for identifying chromosomal regions likely to harbor genes influencing the phenotype of interest, linkage peaks are broad, sometimes containing hundreds of genes, and linkage is imprecise in its ability to localize the underlying susceptibility variant. In addition, we expect that many genes involved in complex behavioral phenotypes may have effect sizes too small to be detected in linkage analyses. Accordingly, the second method of analysis, association analysis, has become increasingly popular.

Association analyses provide a useful tool for several purposes, including testing the role of potential candidate genes, fine-mapping in regions of linkage, and more recently, genome-wide analyses. Allelic association refers to a significantly increased or decreased frequency of a particular marker allele with a disease trait. The most commonly used association design is the case-control study. Case-control studies compare the frequency of alleles between a group of unrelated, affected individuals and a group of matched controls. The controls should be matched to the cases with respect to numerous factors, such as age, gender, and ethnicity, so that they differ only in disease status. In this way, differences in allele frequencies between the two groups are interpreted as evidence that the gene is involved in disease status.

The advantage of this approach lies in its relative simplicity. The necessary statistics are straightforward and the method is generally powerful for detecting genes of smaller effect than those that can be identified with linkage analysis. Case-control studies are also fairly easy to implement in terms of sample collection. The primary disadvantage of this approach is its sensitivity to the existence of population stratification. Population stratification refers to the mismatching of cases and controls for population substructure, for example, ethnicity. If cases and controls are mismatched on ethnicity (or another relevant variable) and ethnic groups differ in disease risk, then spurious genetic associations can result.

Association studies traditionally focused on a particular candidate gene of interest, selected based on hypothesized involvement in relevant biological pathways. However, as genotyping costs have decreased and technology has advanced, genome-wide association studies (GWAS) have become increasingly common. These studies proceed in the same manner as a traditional candidate gene association study, in that researchers evaluate whether phenotypes differ significantly as a function of genotype at a given marker. However, rather than only assessing a marker (or markers) within a single gene that is considered a strong candidate based on prior knowledge, GWAS assess multiple markers across the entire genome, often surveying over one million markers. Because marker coverage is so extensive, GWAS are atheoretical in that they do not rely upon prior hypotheses about the biology underlying the phenotype of interest, and are therefore able to identify novel genes associated with the phenotype.

Although GWAS are certainly a powerful tool for gene identification, they have their own limitations. Because so many markers are assayed, statistical corrections for multiple testing must be imposed, and the most appropriate correction method is not always clear. Very large sample sizes are needed to provide adequate statistical power for the analyses. As with traditional candidate gene association studies, phenotypic definition is very important. Furthermore, researchers must consider the possibility that different alleles are segregating in different populations, which can lead to failure to replicate across studies. GWAS are currently producing a wealth of data that must be thoroughly mined to determine which results are meaningful. And despite their power, GWAS have not rendered traditional association studies obsolete: results from GWAS can be used to lay the foundation for nuanced questions about pathways of risk, and smaller-scale association studies can be more affordable – and informative – to address these more focused questions.

Gene finding for adolescent outcomes

Gene finding efforts, in the form of both targeted association studies and GWAS, are underway for most major psychiatric disorders and many behavioral outcomes of relevance to adolescence. ADHD is one outcome that has been extensively studied using the candidate gene strategy. Many of these studies have focused on genes related to dopamine, since the neural circuitry involving this neurotransmitter has been implicated in the etiology of ADHD; in addition, medications targeting dopaminergic neurotransmission are often effective in alleviating symptoms. Variation in the gene encoding one of the dopamine receptors, DRD4, has been relatively consistently associated with risk of ADHD. Although a number of studies have failed to replicate this finding, on balance, the association is statistically significant. Likewise, meta-analyses of studies on another dopamine transporter, DRD5, suggest that this gene also contributes to ADHD liability. In addition to these receptor genes, the dopamine transporter is a biologically plausible candidate gene, in part because medication acting on the transporter is helpful in treating ADHD. Indeed, many studies suggest that variation in the gene encoding this protein is associated with the disorder. ADHD is one of the success stories in gene-finding efforts for psychiatric disorders and the use of the candidate gene strategy.

Additionally, GWAS studies are underway for CD, alcohol dependence, and depression and anxiety, though most of these rely on adult populations and/or retrospective report of behavior in childhood/adolescence. Most analyses have yielded some genes that are thought to be promising, in terms of their potential involvement in susceptibility for the given outcomes, but they await replication in independent studies. **Table 1** briefly describes genes that have been reliably associated with various psychopathologies.

Gene finding: The next step

As stated previously, most major gene identification efforts for psychiatric disorders currently focus on adult psychiatric outcomes. One of the next research priorities will be to study how risk associated with particular genes changes across development, and how environmental factors influence genetic risk. These endeavors can be informed by genetic epidemiology. For example, the twin literature indicates that childhood conduct

Table 1 Genes associated with phenotypes relevant to adolescence

Phenotype	*Gene*	*Gene-finding method*	*Gene function (if known)*
Intelligence	***CHRM2****	Association analysis	Influences acetylcholine activity in the central and peripheral nervous system
	SNAP-25	Association analysis	Involved in the release of neurotransmitter into the synapse; may play a role in learning and memory
Personality	***SNAP-25***	Association analysis	Involved in the release of neurotransmitter into the synapse; may play a role in learning and memory
ADHD	***CDH13***	Linkage study	Cadherin; regulated neural cell growth
	CNR1	GWAS	Cannabinoid receptor
	DAT	Association analysis	Dopamine transporter
	DRD4	Association analysis	Dopamine receptor
	DRD5	Association analysis	Dopamine receptor
	HTR1B	Association analysis	Serotonin receptor
	SNAP-25	Association analysis	Involved in the release of neurotransmitter into the synapse; may play a role in learning and memory
CD	*CYP19*	Association analysis	Converts testosterone to estrogen
	DAT	Association analysis	Dopamine transporter
	ESR1	Association analysis	Estrogen receptor
	GABRA2	Association analysis	Gamma-aminobutyric acid receptor
	MAOA	Association analysis	Degrades monoamines
	SERT	Association analysis	Serotonin transporter
AUD/SUD	ADH (multiple genes in the family)	Association analysis	Degradation of ethanol
	ALDH (multiple genes in the family)	Association analysis	Degradation of ethanol
	CDH13	GWAS	Cadherin; regulated neural cell growth
	CNR1	GWAS (cannabis dependence)	Cannabinoid receptor
	GABA receptors	association analysis, GWAS	Influence the body's response to ethanol
	GABRA2	GWAS (cannabis dependence)	Gamma-aminobutyric acid receptor
Anxiety disorders	***COMT***	Association analysis	Degrades catecholamines
	HTR2A	Association analysis	Serotonin receptor
Depression	*BDNF*	Association analysis	Brain-derived neurotrophic factor; involved in neuronal survival
	COMT	Association analysis	Degrades catecholamines
	MAOA	Association analysis	Degrades monoamines
	PCLO	GWAS	Presynaptic protein; involved in monoamine neurotransmission
	SERT	Association analysis	Serotonin transporter

Bolded genes have been associated with multiple phenotypes.
**CHRM2* has been associated with a general liability to externalizing in a linkage study.

disorder and adult alcohol dependence are strongly genetically correlated. Thus, genes associated with risk to alcohol dependence have been investigated regarding their association with conduct problems earlier in development. Results indicate that some genetic variants associated with adult alcohol dependence – for example, *GABRA2* and *CHRM2* – are indeed associated with childhood conduct disorder before alcohol problems ever begin to manifest. In addition, in some cases, the effects of these genetic risk variants vary as a function of environmental conditions, such as exposure to deviant peers, or low levels of parental monitoring.

Accordingly, as genes are identified in large-scale gene finding projects, there remains a wealth of questions that must be addressed about how these genes impact behavioral outcome across development and in conjunction with the environment. One area that has received a lot of attention is the study of gene–environment interaction (**Figure** 5).

In 2002, a research group led by Avshalom Caspi published a landmark study of measured genotype-by-environment interaction. This longitudinal study examined the interaction between childhood maltreatment (occurring between ages 3–11) and genotype in the promoter region of the *MAOA* gene, which encodes an enzyme that metabolizes monoamines such as dopamine and serotonin. The outcomes of interest were various measures of antisocial behavior, such as conduct disorder and violent disposition. Caspi and colleagues found that individuals with the *MAOA* risk variant (which confers lower enzymatic activity) were more likely to exhibit antisocial behavior; however, this difference was only observed when incidence of childhood maltreatment was taken into consideration: among individuals who did not experience maltreatment, there were no differences in antisocial behavior as a function of genotype.

The most widely studied example of a measured gene-by-environment interaction comes from the literature on unipolar depression. In 2003, the same research group that examined *MAOA* and childhood maltreatment found that individuals with a particular genetic variant in the promoter region of the serotonin transporter gene were more likely to be depressed as adults than were individuals who did not carry this variant. Critically, this increased genetic risk was only observed under conditions of increased environmental risk, which was defined as having experienced a certain number of stressful life events. In the intervening years, researchers have reported both significant main effects and gene-by-environment interaction effects at this locus. However, many studies have failed to replicate these findings. Recent meta-analyses, which incorporate findings across different studies in an effort to maximize statistical power, indicate that, on balance, the evidence does not support the existence of a gene-by-environment interaction at this locus. A probable explanation for these discrepant findings is that many gene-by-environment studies are statistically underpowered; in addition, the use of distinct measures of environmental risk across studies makes direct comparison difficult. These are issues that the field is currently working to address. There is broad consensus that specific gene-by-environment interactions exist, but given small effect sizes of the relevant genes, in conjunction with the complicated genetic and environmental etiology of these phenotypes, the methods by which these studies are conducted can be improved. Nonetheless, characterizing the risk pathways associated with identified genes will be critical in eventually translating this information into improved prevention and intervention programs.

Conclusions

We now know that most behavioral phenotypes can be considered 'complex traits'. That is, they are influenced by a wide variety of genes, most of which have small individual effect sizes; genetic effects can be interdependent; and these genetic

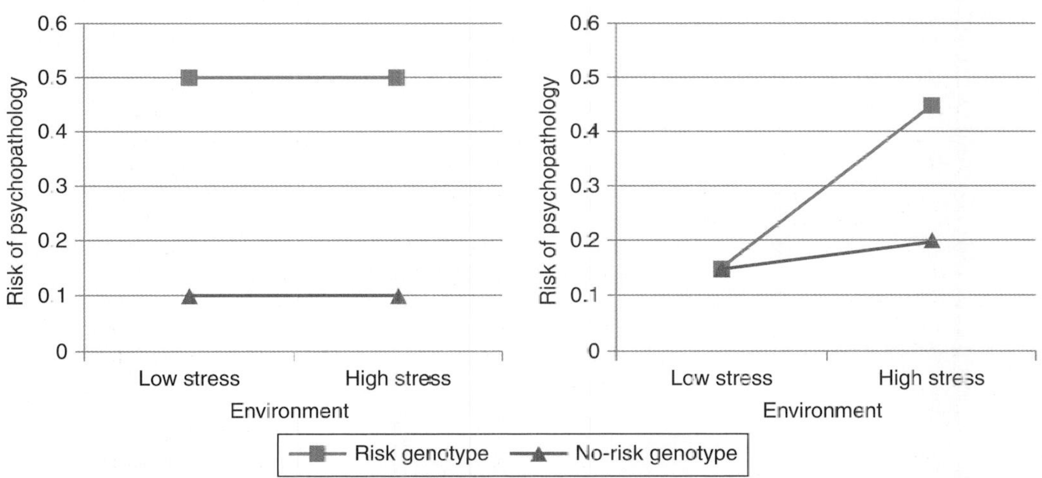

Figure 5 Allelic effects are often sensitive to the environment, and might only be observable under certain environmental conditions, in which case a genotype-by-environment interaction is present. In the figure on the left, main effects of genotype are observed: individuals with the risky genotype are more likely to exhibit psychopathology than are individuals without the risky genotype, regardless of whether they are exposed to environmental stress. The figure on the right depicts a gene-by-environment interaction: no difference in risk of psychopathology is observed, regardless of genotype, if individuals are in a low-stress environment. However, given a high-stress environment, individuals with the risky genotype are far more likely to exhibit psychopathology than are individuals who do not have the risky genotype.

influences are environmentally sensitive. Twin and family studies enable us to quantify latent genetic variation influencing these complex traits, which include phenotypes such as intelligence, adolescent substance use, and adolescent depression. Other statistical genetic methods are used to identify specific genetic variants that are associated with variation in these traits, that is, with high cognitive ability, or with increased risk of developing alcohol problems. A wealth of research has been conducted toward these ends, and many of the genes that influence phenotypes discussed in this article have roles in neurotransmission or neural development. In addition, the use of GWAS now enables us to identify novel genes that might be involved a given trait, advancing our understanding of the underlying biology. However, finding genes is not an endpoint, but rather, opens a host of new questions that can be addressed about how the risk associated with that gene changes across development and in conjunction with the environment. Because most of the gene identification efforts underway are focused on adult outcomes, it will be particularly important to take these genes to well-characterized longitudinal samples in order to understand their risk at earlier developmental phases. The overarching goal of these lines of research is to further our understanding of the etiology of traits related to the human condition. Great progress has been made on this front, and advances in technology and biology hold the promise of an even more precise understanding of complex phenotypes.

See also: Adolescent Sibling Relations; Depression and Depressive Disorders; Intellectual Disabilities (Mental Retardation).

Further Reading

Caspi A, McClay J, Moffitt TE, et al. (2002) Role of genotype in the cycle of violence in maltreated children. *Science* 297: 851–854.

Caspi A, Sugden K, Moffitt TE, et al. (2003) Influence of life stress on depression: moderation by a polymorphism in the 5-HTT gene. *Science* 301: 386–389.

Dilalla LF and Gottesman II (eds.) (2004) *Behavior Genetics Principles: Perspectives in Development, Personality, and Psychopathology*. Washington D.C.: American Psychological Association.

Falconer DS and Mackay TFC (1996) *Introduction to Quantitative Genetics*. Essex: Longman.

Kendler KS and Prescott CA (2006) *Genes, Environment, and Psychopathology: Understanding the Causes of Psychiatric and Substance Use Disorders*. New York: The Guilford Press.

Kim YK (ed.) (2009) *Handbook of Behavior Genetics*. New York: Springer.

Neale BM, Ferreira MAR, Medland SE, and Posthuma D (eds.) (2008) *Statistical Genetics*. New York: Taylor and Francis.

Plomin R, DeFries JC, McClearn GE, and McGuffin P (2008) *Behavioral Genetics*. New York: Worth Publishers.

Zhang TY and Meaney MJ (2010) Epigenetics and the environmental regulation of the genome and its function. *Annual Review of Psychology* 61: C1–3.

Relevant Website

http://www.nebi.nlm.nih.gov/omim – Online Mendelian Inheritance in Man (OMIM).

The History of the Study of Adolescence

R M Lerner, M J Boyd, M K Kiely, C M Napolitano, and K L Schmid, Tufts University, Medford, MA, USA
L Steinberg, Temple University, Philadelphia, PA, USA

Glossary

Biological reductionism: A form of explanation that contends that all phenomena of behavior and development can be interpreted through reference to underlying biological characteristics (e.g., genes) or processes (e.g., evolution).
Grand theory: Theories of "everything"; that is, grand theories seek to explain all features of a field of scientific inquiry. For example, Behavioristic theories seek to explain all facets of human behavior and development, including cognitive development, personality development, ego development. the development of parenting, etc.
Metatheory: A theory about theories; a philosophical position that frames lower-order theoretical or empirical statements. Metatheories are pre-empirical, whereas theories pertain to empirically verifiable statements.
Mid-level theory: Theories of a selected set of features of a field of scientific inquiry. For example, Piaget's theory pertains to cognitive development but not to personality development, ego development, or the development of parenting.
Nativism: Theories of human behavior and development that contend that biological characteristics (e.g., genes) or processes (e.g., evolution) are the fundamental bases of development.
Plasticity: The potential across ontogeny for systematic change in the structure or function of attributes of the individual.
Positive Youth Development (PYD) Perspective: The belief that the potential for plasticity among all youth constitutes a fundamental resource for healthy development.
Recapitulation theory: A change in the timing of developmental events such that there is a universal acceleration of development that pushes ancestral (adult) forms into the juvenile stages of descendants.
Relational fields of inquiry: Areas of scholarship wherein, implicitly or explicitly, the key unit of analysis in understanding the development of the person is his or her relation with both molecular (e.g., biological) and molar (social group, cultural, and historical) levels of organization; in such a relational frame, no one level of organization is seen as the "prime mover" of development.
Relational models of development: Conceptions that recognize the fundamental, integrative character of influences across the levels of organization comprising the ecology of human development.

Introduction

In the opening sentence to the Preface to the first edition of his classic, *A History of Experimental Psychology*, Edwin G. Boring reminded readers that "psychology has a long past, but only a short history" (1929: ix), a remark he attributed to the pioneer of memory research, Hermann Ebbinghaus. A similar statement may be made about the study of adolescents and their development. The first use of the term adolescence appeared in the fifteenth century. The term was a derivative of the Latin word *adolescere*, which means to grow up or to grow into maturity. However, as recounted by Rolf Muuss, more than 1500 years before this first explicit use of the term adolescence, both Plato and Aristotle proposed sequential demarcations of the life span, and Aristotle in particular proposed stages of life that are not dissimilar from sequences that might be included in contemporary models of youth development. He described three successive, 7-year periods (infancy, boyhood, and young manhood) prior to the full, adult maturity.

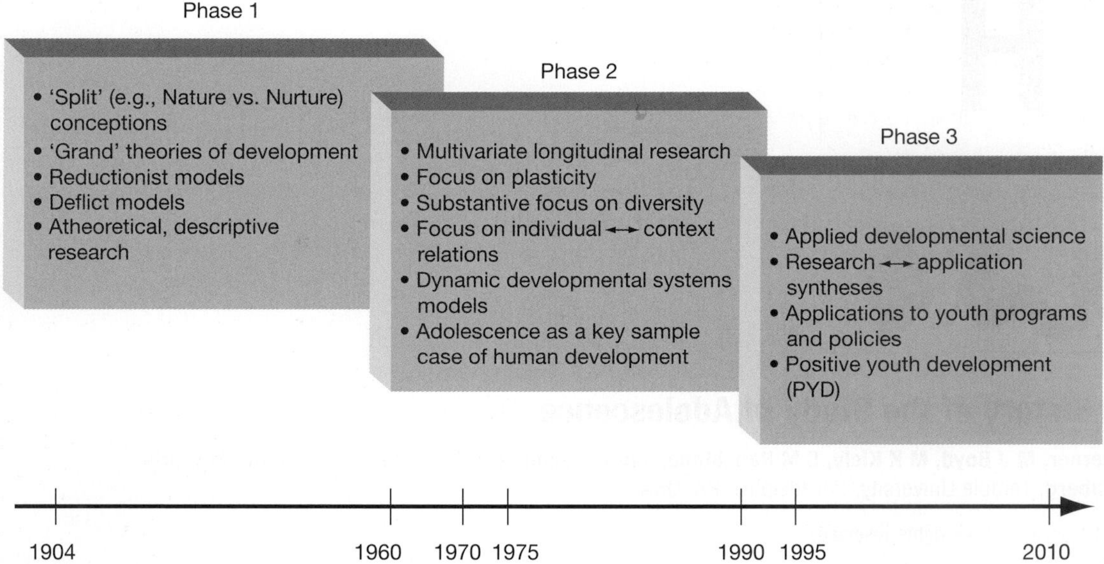

Figure 1 Three phases in the history of the scientific study of adolescent development (Lerner and Steinberg, 2009, p. 4).

About 2000 years elapsed between these initial philosophical discussions of adolescence and the emergence within the twentieth century of the scientific study of this period of life with the publication in 1904 of G. Stanley Hall's two-volume work: *Adolescence: Its Psychology and its Relations to Physiology, Anthropology, Sociology, Sex, Crime, Religion, and Education*. Across the subsequent century, 100 plus years, the history of the scientific study of adolescence has had three overlapping phases. These phases in the history of the field are illustrated in **Figure 1**.

To elucidate the historical phases depicted in **Figure 1**, we describe the contributions of individuals, organizations, and historical changes in shaping the substance and direction of the scientific study of adolescence. We note how researchers and practitioners from multiple disciplines and different countries contributed to understanding adolescent development.

The First Phase of the Scientific Study of Adolescence

G. Stanley Hall (1844–1924) contributed one of the earliest papers on child psychology and also wrote the first text on adolescence (a two-volume work entitled *Adolescence*, 1904). His often overlooked text on old age (*Senescence*, 1922) attests to the ground-breaking life-span perspective he brought to the study of human development. One of the most prominent and influential psychologists at the turn of the century, Hall had his most specific influence on developmental psychology. Hall saw development from a nativist point of view. A pure nativist stance contends that human behavior and development derive from nature or inborn (intrinsic) characteristics (e.g., heredity and genes). Hall's theory was one of recapitulation. He believed that the changes characterizing the human life cycle are a repetition of the sequence of changes a person's ancestors followed during their evolution.

As we note again subsequently, although Hall's specific views about the role of nature in shaping adolescent development have not maintained an influence on the thinking of contemporary developmental scientists, other facets of his scholarship were important within its era and, as well, have significant implications for the contemporary study of adolescence. For instance, Hall's *Adolescence* launched the scientific study of adolescence and introduced the field to evolutionary (Darwinian) thinking. In addition, Hall discussed the role of social change in adolescent development, and Pinquart and Silbereisen note that this scholarship remains useful in elucidating the nature of adolescent development in periods of social change. Recent theory and research about the impact of social change on youth development by Silbereisen and Chen is a case in point regarding the applicability of Hall's ideas for studying features of development among contemporary adolescents, for instance, regarding the fit between developmental needs and the resources available for healthy development that may be present in changing social ecologies.

Furthermore, Hall believed that adolescence represented a specific period in ontogeny after childhood. As such, Hall was the first person, within a scientific theory of development, to conceive of adolescence as a distinct portion of the life span (according to Rolf Muuss, the term had, however, initially appeared in the first half of the fifteenth century). Moreover, Hall's demarcation of adolescence as a distinct period of ontogeny was discussed in a manner consistent with a life-span view of human development. That is, Hall saw the capacities and changes of childhood continuing into adolescence, but at a more rapid and heightened pace.

Studying Adolescence after Hall

As we have noted, although other scholars of Hall's period, such as Thorndike in 1904, did not accept his nativist view of development, on either empirical or methodological grounds, other theorists of adolescent development used a conceptual lens comparable to Hall's, at least insofar as his biological reductionism and his deficit view of adolescence were concerned. Anna Freud, for instance, saw adolescence as a biologically-based, universal developmental disturbance. Erik Erikson viewed the period as one wherein an inherited maturational ground plan resulted in the inescapable psychosocial crisis of identity versus role confusion. When theorists rejected the nature-based ideas of psychoanalysts or neopsychoanalysts, they proposed equally one-sided, nurture-oriented ideas (and hence also used split conceptions) to explain the same problems of developmental disturbance and crisis. For example, Boyd McCandless presented a social learning, drive reduction theory to account for the developmental phenomena of adolescence (e.g., regarding sex differences in identity development) that Erik Erikson interpreted as associated with maturation.

Although the developmental theory of cognition proposed by Piaget involved a more integrative view of nature and nurture than these other models, he also saw nature and nurture as separable (and hence split) sources of development, ones that just happened to interact (but, because they were separate and split, did not alter the status or quality of each other over the course of their interaction). The predominant focus of Piaget's ideas was on the emergence of formal logical structures and not on the adolescent period per se. The absence of concern in Piaget's theory with the broader array of biological, emotional, personality, social, and societal concerns that had engaged other theorists' discussion of adolescence did not stop a relatively minor and historically transitory interest in Piaget's ideas as a frame for empirical understanding of the adolescent period. However, as Steinberg and Morris have explained, only a short while after this period of heightened interest in using the onset of formal operations as an explanation for everything adolescent, the influence of Jean Piaget's theory on mainstream empirical work in the study of adolescence would become as modest as that associated with the other grand theories of the period, such as those authored by Erikson.

The waning of these grand theories across the first phase of the study of adolescence, a phase that lasted about 70 years, was due at least in part because the sorts of Cartesian 'splits' emphasized in the ideas of these theorists created false dichotomies – not only nature versus nurture, but, as well, continuity versus discontinuity, stability versus instability, constancy versus change, or basic versus applied – that limited the intellectual development of the field. Willis Overton has noted that, as seen through the contemporary, postmodern lens of relational models of development, conceptions that recognize the fundamental, integrative character of influences across the levels of organization comprising the ecology of human development – such as those theories proposed by Urie Bronfenbrenner or by Glen H. Elder, Jr. – have come to the fore. From the perspective of such relational models, split ideas are regarded as counterfactual (or, at best, egregiously flawed) scholarship. Such split models use unidimensional conceptions of human development to focus on, at best, ecologically invalid assessments of components of youth behavior or, at worst, counterfactual characterizations of the bases of individual structure and function.

Accordingly, these theories were limited by the fact that they either focused exclusively on nature (e.g., genetic or maturational), as in the work of Sigmund or Anna Freud or Hall, focused exclusively on nurture, as in the work of McCandless, or weakly combined multiple sources of influence in ways that retained an emphasis on one or the other sources of development (usually on nature) as the prime basis of development, as in the ideas of Erikson. As such, these theories were becoming increasingly out of step with empirical evidence, indicating that variation associated with complex relations between organismic (biological) and contextual (proximate to distal) ecological variation, including culture and history, was involved in the course of adolescent development. While this evidence began to accumulate during the first phase in the scientific study of adolescence, it would not be until the end of the second phase and the emergence of the third phase of development of the field that these data, and other findings related to them, would be integrated into dynamic, integrative models of development. Indeed, during the first phase of the field, the major empirical studies of adolescence were not primarily theory-driven, hypothesis-testing investigations. Instead, they were atheoretical, descriptive studies. As such, even theory and research were split into separate enterprises. Moreover, there was also a split between scholars whose work was focused on basic developmental processes and practitioners whose focus was on community-based efforts to facilitate the healthy development of adolescents.

In other words, the divergence between the 'grand' theories of the adolescent period and the range of research about adolescence that would come to characterize the field at the end of the twentieth century actually existed for much of the first phase of the field's development. The classic studies of adolescence conducted between 1950 and 1980 were not investigations derived from the theories of Hall, Anna Freud, McCandless, Piaget, or even Erikson (work associated with the ideas of James Marcia notwithstanding). Instead, this research was directed to describing (note, *not* explaining) patterns of covariation among pubertal timing, personal adjustment, and relationships with peers and parents, both within and across cultural settings, as with the work of Paul Mussen and his colleagues at the Institute for Human Development at the University of California-Berkeley; the diversity in trajectories of psychological development across adolescence (e.g., as in the research of Albert Bandura, Jack Block, Elizabeth Douvan and Joseph Adelson, and Daniel Offer); and the influence of history or temporality (i.e., as operationalized by time of testing- or cohort-related variation) on personality development, achievement, and family relations, as in the research of Glen Elder or in the work of John R. Nesselroade and Paul B. Baltes. Writing in 1988, Anne C. Petersen described the quality of the classic empirical work on adolescence by noting that such scholarship encompassed two domains, research with adolescent participants on behavioral and psychological processes, or descriptive studies of specific groups of adolescents.

Despite its separation from the grand theories of adolescence that dominated the field during its first phase of scientific development, this body of early research, and the subsequent scholarship it elicited, made several important contributions to shaping the specific character of the scientific study of adolescence between the early-1980s and late-1990s. This character involved the longitudinal study of individual-context relations among diverse groups of youth, the deployment of innovative quantitative and qualitative, ethnographic methods, and the use of such scholarship for purposes of both elucidating basic developmental processes and applying developmental science to promote positive youth development across the adolescent period and within the diverse settings of their lives.

These contributions to the study of adolescence acted synergistically with broader scholarly activity within developmental science pertinent to the theoretical, methodological, and applied features of the study of human development across the life span. A classic paper by Beatrix Hamburg in 1974 did much to provide the foundation for this integration, making a compelling case for viewing the early adolescent period as a distinct period of the life course and providing an exemplary ontogenetic window for understanding the key individual-context relational processes involved in coping and adaptation.

The emergence of the relationship between the specific study of adolescence and more general scholarship about the overall course of human development provided the bridge to the second phase in the study of adolescent development. Indeed, in a review of the adolescent development literature written during this second phase, Petersen, predicted that, "Current research on adolescence will not only aid scientific understanding of this particular phase of life, it also may illuminate development more generally." (1988: 601) Future events were consistent with Petersen's prognostication.

The Second Phase of the Scientific Study of Adolescence

From the late 1970s through this writing, the adolescent period has come to be regarded as an ideal 'natural ontogenetic laboratory' for studying key theoretical and methodological issues in developmental science. There are several reasons for the special salience of the study of adolescent development to understanding the broader course of life-span development.

The Emergence of Adolescence as the New Focal Period within the Life Span

The prenatal and infant periods exceed adolescence as ontogenetic periods of rapid physical and physiological growth. Nevertheless, a first reason for adolescence emerging in the 1970s as an ontogenetic period engaging the focused interest of developmental scientists was that the years from approximately 10 to 20 – 'the adolescent decade' – not only include the considerable physical and physiological changes associated with puberty but, as well, mark a time when the interdependency of biology and context in human development is readily apparent. Second, and in a related vein, as compared to infancy, the cognitive abilities, social relationships, and motivations of adolescents can, through reciprocal relations with their ecology, serve as active influences on their own development.

Third, the study in adolescence of these relations between active individuals and their varied and changing contexts serves as an ideal means to gain insight into bidirectional, mutually influential person–context relations. Indeed, Willis Overton, as well as other developmental scientists working during the 1970s and early- to mid-1980s (for instance, Paul B. Baltes, K. Warner Schaie, Urie Bronfenbrenner, Richard M. Lerner, John R. Nesselroade, Klaus Riegel, and Arnold R. Sameroff), began to forward developmental models that rejected reductionist biological or environmental accounts of development and, instead, focused on the variables from interdependent, or fused, levels of organization as constituting the developmental system and its multilayered context. Scholars such as Andrew Collins, Laurence Steinberg, Marc Bornstein, E. Mavis Hetherington, Eleanor Maccoby, Gilbert Gottlieb, Esther Thelen, Linda Smith, and Arnold Sameroff made major contributions to the development of such conceptual and theoretical frameworks.

These developmental systems models have provided a metatheory for research on adolescent development, and have been associated with more mid-level (as opposed to grand) theories, models that have been generated to account for transformations in individual-context relations within selected domains of development. Instances of such mid-level developmental systems theories are the stage-environment fit model of Jacquelynne Eccles, used to understand achievement in classroom settings; the goodness of fit model, of Alexander Thomas, Stella Chess, and Jacqueline V. Lerner, used to understand the importance of temperamental individuality in peer and family relations; and models forwarded by scholars such as William Damon and Peter Benson that were used to link the developmental assets of youth and communities in order to understand positive youth development.

A fourth and related reason for the focus by developmental scientists on the study of the adolescent period arose because of the growing emphasis on developmental systems theoretical models. By the end of this second phase in the study of adolescence (during the second half of the 1990s), these dynamic, developmental systems models were regarded as defining the cutting edge of theory in developmental science. The multiple individual and contextual transitions into, throughout, and out of the adolescent period involve the major institutions of society (i.e., family, peers, schools, the workplace, and the neighborhood or community). As such, the study of the individual's relations to these contexts engaged scholars interested in the dynamics of both ecological and individual levels of organization. Focus on adolescents' varied relations across the ecology of human development afforded a rich opportunity for understanding the nature of multilevel systemic change.

Finally, there was also a practical reason for the growing importance of adolescence in the broader field of developmental science. As noted by Steinberg and Morris, the longitudinal samples of many developmental scientists who had been studying infancy or childhood had aged into adolescence. In addition, scholars became engaged in the study of adolescents because of interest in age groups other than adolescents! For example, interest in infants often entailed the study of teenage mothers and interest in middle and old age frequently entailed the study of the 'middle generation squeeze,' wherein the adult children of aged parents cared for their own parents while simultaneously raising their own adolescent children.

The Emerging Structure of the Field of Adolescent Development

The scholarly activity that emerged at about the close of the 1970s was both a product and a producer of a burgeoning network of scholars from multiple disciplines in the United States and internationally. In 1981, the late Herschel Thornburg launched a series of biennial meetings (called the 'Conference on Adolescent Research') at the University of Arizona. During these meetings (which occurred also in 1983 and 1985), the idea for a new scholarly society, the Society for Research on Adolescence (SRA), was born The first meeting of SRA was held in Madison, Wisconsin in 1986.

In turn, although focused on development across the life span, the International Society for the Study of Behavioral Development (ISSBD), founded in 1969, has included in its biennial meetings and journal (the *International Journal of Behavioral Development*, or *IJBD*) a great deal of research around the globe that pertains to adolescence (Hartup, 1996). Moreover, many of the presidents of ISSBD have been prominent scholars of adolescent development (for instance, Anne C. Petersen and Rainer K. Silbereisen). In addition, the European Association for Research on Adolescence (EARA) was formally launched in 1991. It has held biennial meetings since its inception, and has served as a means to make visible the basic and applied research about adolescence that is ongoing across Europe.

Moreover, government organizations around the world and the international philanthropic community paid increasing attention to the importance of theoretically predicated, adolescent research to improving health and to enhancing public policy. For instance, the National Institute of Child Health and Human Development, which is part of the US National Institutes of Health, issued in the latter portion of the first decade of the twenty-first century a request for proposals to study and enhance positive youth development. In turn, in 2009, a major international foundation, the Jacobs Foundation in Zurich, Switzerland, launched a new award – the Klaus J. Jacobs Research Prize – to recognize career achievements in the study of productive youth development.

Impetus to this growth in scholarly interest in the study of adolescence was also stimulated by the publication in 1980 of the first handbook for the field. Edited by Joseph Adelson, the *Handbook of Adolescent Psychology* was published in 1980 as part of the Wiley Series on Personality Processes. The volume reflected the emerging multidisciplinary interest in the field (with chapters discussing levels of organization ranging from biology through history, including an interesting historical chapter on youth movements), the growing interest in systems models of adolescent development (e.g., in the chapters by Glen Elder and by Anne Petersen and Brandon Taylor), the importance of longitudinal methodology (in a chapter by Norman Livson and Harvey Peskin), and the increasing interest in diversity (i.e., there was a five-chapter section on 'Variations in Adolescence'). Importantly, as reflected in several chapters on the problems of adolescence, there was still ample representation in the volume of the deficit view of adolescence. Nevertheless, the 1980 *Handbook* included information pertinent to normative development and to developmental plasticity, that is, to the potential for systematic change across development, change that, within developmental systems models, was regarded to derive from individual-context relations. Finally, presaging an emphasis on positive youth development that would crystallize during the third phase in the history of the field, there were several chapters that discussed the positive individual and social features of youth development.

The publication of a handbook, the organization of a successful scholarly society, and the initiation of that society's scholarly journal – all underscored the growing interest in and the scientific maturity of research on adolescent development. This intellectual milieu and the scholarly opportunities it provided attracted a broad range of scholars to the field, some for reasons that had little to do with adolescence per se, but others because they came to see themselves as experts on the second decade of life. By the mid-1980s, a growing cadre of scientists would identify themselves as adolescent developmentalists.

The Study of Adolescence as a Sample Case for Understanding Plasticity and Diversity in Development

Scholars interested initially or primarily in the instantiation of developmental processes within other periods of the life span (infancy, e.g., Jeanne Brooks-Gunn; or adult development and aging, e.g., Paul Baltes or John Nesselroade) or in disciplines other than developmental psychology (life course sociology, e.g., Orville G. Brim, Jr., Linda Burton, or Glen Elder) became adolescent developmentalists as well. As suggested by Steinberg and Morris, the one scientific concern that arguably was most significant in transforming the field of adolescent development beyond a focus on this single developmental period into an exemplar for understanding the breadth of the human life span was the emerging focus within developmental science on the ecology of human development, a perspective championed by Urie Bronfenbrenner and his colleagues and students. The integrated, designed, and natural ecology was of interest because its study was regarded as holding the key to understanding the system of relations between individuals and contexts that is at the core of the study of human development and providing evidence that theories about the character of interactions within the developmental system were more useful in accounting for the variance in human ontogeny than theories whose grounding is exclusively nature (e.g., behavioral genetic or sociobiological) or exclusively nurture (e.g., social learning or functional analysis).

A second set of broader issues that engaged developmental science in the study of adolescence pertained to understanding the bases, parameters, and limits of the plasticity of human development (which, as we have noted, reflects the potential across ontogeny for systematic change in the structure or function of attributes of the individual). The presence of plasticity across the life span legitimates an optimistic view about the potential for interventions into the course of life to enhance human development. In the second phase of the history of the field, the focus on plasticity encouraged growth in scientific activity in the application of developmental science to improve life outcomes, and gave impetus to the idea that positive development could be promoted among all people and, in regard to the adolescent period, among diverse youth.

This idea of 'Positive Youth Development' (PYD) flourished in the third phase of the history of this field. That is, because plasticity means that the particular instances of human development found within a given sample or period of time are not necessarily representative of the diversity of development that might potentially be observed under different conditions, the PYD perspective is based on the belief that the potential for plasticity among all youth constitutes a fundamental resource for healthy development; if supportive families, schools, communities, programs, and policies could be created for youth, their potential for plasticity could be actualized as change in positive directions.

Finally, while the coalescing of developmental scientists interested in positive youth development would not occur until the third phase of the history of the field, within the second phase, developmentalists pursuing an interest in the developmental system and the plasticity in ontogenetic change that it promoted recognized the need to develop and deploy methods that could simultaneously study changes in (at least a subset of) the multiple levels of organization involved in the development of diverse individuals and contexts. Accordingly, multivariate longitudinal designs were promoted as key to the study of the relatively plastic developmental system, as were the development of empirical tools, such as change-sensitive measures, sophisticated data analysis techniques, and strategies such as triangulation of observations within and across both quantitative and qualitative domains of inquiry.

Defining Features of the Study of Adolescence During Its Second Phase

Four defining features of the second phase of the science of adolescent development are worth noting. First, during its second phase, the empirical study of adolescence emerged as a 'relational' field of inquiry. That is, it became an area of scholarship wherein, implicitly or, at times, explicitly, the key unit of analysis in understanding the development of the person was his or her relation with both more molecular (e.g., biological) and more molar (social group, cultural, and historical) levels of organization. In such a relational frame, no one level of organization was seen as the 'prime mover' of development.

A second distinctive feature involves the confluence of the multiple levels of organization involved in the developmental system which provide the structural and functional bases of plasticity and of the inevitable and substantively significant emergence of systematic individual differences; that is, such individuality serves as a key basis of the person's ability to act as an agent in his or her own development. Accordingly, the field of adolescence has become an exemplar within the broader study of human development for the study of individual differences and for the person-centered approach to research on human development, a perspective championed by David Magnusson and his colleagues (e.g., Håkan Stattin and Margaret Kerr).

Third, although there remains a focus within the contemporary adolescent literature on problems of this developmental period, the focus on plasticity, diversity, and individual agency – and the strength or capacity of an adolescent to influence his or her development for better or for worse – means that problematic outcomes of adolescent development are now regarded as just one of a larger array of outcomes. Indeed, it is this plasticity that provides the theoretical basis of the view that all young people possess strengths, or, more simply, the potential for positive development.

In sum, the second phase in the scientific study of adolescence arose in the early to mid-1970s, as developmental scientists began to make use of the burgeoning empirical research on adolescents; that is, because this work involved the study of both individual and contextual variation, developmental scientists began to see that the adolescent years provided a 'natural developmental laboratory' for elucidating issues of interest across the entire life span. Indeed, at the beginning of the 1970s, the study of adolescence may not have been seen as an important period for developmental inquiry, the reliance on adolescence research to inform fundamental questions in developmental science about how links between diverse individuals and changing contexts textured the course of change across individuals, families, and generations, prompted research on adolescent development to emerge as a dominant force in developmental science. By the end of the 1970s, the study of adolescence had finally come of age.

Across the past four decades, there has been a sea change in scholarly regard for the study of adolescent development. Among those scholars whose own careers have begun more recently, the magnitude of this transformation is probably hard to grasp. To those who have been witness to these events, however, the change has been nothing short of astounding. Adolescent development was once regarded as a minor topic within developmental science, one that was of a level of importance to merit only the publication of an occasional research article within prime developmental journals or minimal representation on the program of major scientific meetings. Now, the study of adolescent development is a distinct and major field within developmental science, one that plays a central role in informing, and, through vibrant collaborations with scholars having other scientific specialties, being informed by other areas of focus.

In essence, then, the study of adolescence in its second phase was characterized by an interest in developmental plasticity among diverse youth. Because of this focus, interest also arose in the application of science to real-world problems, a focus that would burgeon in the next phase of the history of the field. Finally, however, the second phase also was marked by the development and use of more nuanced and powerful developmental methods, ones aimed at providing sensitivity to the collection and analysis of longitudinal data pertinent to the multiple levels. Together, these intellectual facets of the second phase in the study of adolescent development created the scientific bases for the emergence of a subsequent phase, one that – at this writing – characterizes the contemporary status of the field.

The Third Phase of the Scientific Study of Adolescence

At the time of the publication in 2004 of the second edition of the *Handbook of Adolescent Psychology*, this third phase in the history of adolescence seemed to have just crystallized. As a consequence of the unprecedented growth in theoretically informed research about the adolescent period, an analysis of the third edition of this work, albeit published only 5 years later, reflected the fact that the field as unequivocally embedded within this third period of its growth, as one that, as noted, involves burgeoning interest within the United States and internationally in applied developmental science. Such work involves evidence-based applications of research about adolescent development. Such scholarship is pursued in numerous university- or community-based centers within the United States and, more recently (within this third phase), throughout the world.

For instance, the Center for Applied Developmental Science, directed by Rainer Silbereisen, at the Friedrich Schiller University in Jena, Germany, is an exemplary case in point.

In addition, as represented by the chapter in the third edition of the *Handbook* by neuroscientist Tomas Paus, another important development during the past decade has been the rapid expansion of research on the developmental neuroscience of adolescence. Despite the claims of some nonneuroscientists that the notion of 'the adolescent brain' is some sort of myth, the fact that there are significant changes in the brain during adolescence is no longer debatable – if indeed it ever was. In fact, it appears that the brain changes characteristic of adolescence are among the most dramatic and important to occur during the human life span. Whether neurobiological differences between adolescents and adults should inform how society treats young people is open for debate, but whether such differences are real is not (Steinberg, 2009).

In this regard, it is important to note that 'different' does not necessarily mean 'deficient'; that while there are some universals in adolescent brain development, there are also important individual differences; and that the process of brain maturation in adolescence (or during any period, for that matter) unfolds within an environmental context that influences the course of neural development and moderates its expression in emotion, behavior, and cognition. In much the same way that research on adolescent behavioral development was initially dominated by studies of problematic development, we currently have a better understanding of the ways in which adolescent brain development may contribute to psychopathology and problem behavior than we do of the ways in which it may contribute to normative development and positive functioning. Moreover, researchers have paid more attention to the study of universals and processes of biological maturation than to individual differences and environmental influences. As the field matures, and as collaborations between neuroscientists and nonneuroscientists become more common, attention to these issues will most likely increase.

As epitomized by the growth in scholarship about the developmental neuroscience of adolescence, the third phase in the historical development of the scientific study of adolescence is marked by its own distinctive features. Nevertheless, it is also the case that, as we have explained, the roots of this third phase were established within the second phase, and by some of the scientific innovators whose work in this phase we have noted. For instance, more than a third of a century ago, in 1974, Bronfenbrenner explained the importance of a science of development that involved the full and bidirectional collaboration between the producers and consumers of scientific knowledge. In turn, David Hamburg and Ruby Takanishi proposed in 1996 that the quality of life of adolescents, and their future contributions to civil society, could be enhanced through collaboration among scholars, policy makers, and key social institutions, for instance, community-based youth serving organizations (e.g., scouting, 4-H, Boys and Girls Clubs) schools, and the media. In our view, the Hamburg and Takanishi vision has been actualized.

The idea that the adolescent period provides the ideal time within life to study the bases of positive human development frames what has become a defining feature of the field in its current, third phase. As shown in **Figure 1**, the study of adolescent development is today characterized by a synthetic interest in basic and applied concerns about youth development. In sum, in what has emerged as the third phase in the history of the scientific study of adolescence, the field of adolescent development serves as an exemplar of developmental science that is of service to policy makers and practitioners seeking to advance civil society and promote positive development. Indeed, we are in a phase of science defined by theoretically framed, research-based applications to programs and policies that advance understanding of the basic, individual-context relations process of adolescent development and, as well, that enable policy makers and practitioners to collaborate with scientists to enhance the course of development. Evidence-based practice, policy, and advocacy aimed at understanding the bases of, and as well promoting positive, healthy development among all youth may be the hallmark of this third period.

The Future History of the Developmental Science of Adolescence

The study of adolescence today represents the exemplar within developmental science wherein excellent conceptual and empirical work is undertaken with a collaborative orientation to making a contribution both to scholarship and to society. These collaborations, involving the understanding and support of young people, are vital endeavors – for both science and society. The future of civil society in the world rests on the young. Adolescents represent at any point in history the generational cohort that must next be prepared to assume the quality of leadership of self, family, community, and society that will maintain and improve human life. Scientists have a vital role to play in enhancing, through the generation of basic and applied knowledge, the probability that adolescents will become fully engaged citizens who are capable of, and committed to, making these contributions.

High-quality scientific work on adolescence is in fact being generated at levels of study ranging from the biological through the historical and sociocultural. Above all, the study of adolescent development at its best both informs and is informed by the concerns of communities, of practitioners, and of policy makers. The developmental science of adolescence is now (at this writing), and we believe will continue to be, a field wherein the best theoretically predicated, research-based information possible is used to promote and advocate for the healthy and positive development of young people everywhere.

Acknowledgments

The preparation of this article was supported in part by grants from the National 4-H Council and the Thrive Foundation for Youth. Material for this article is based on prior historical accounts by Lerner (2002), Lerner and Steinberg (2004, 2009), and Steinberg and Lerner (2004). These references may be consulted for complete documentation of and references to the historical literature reviewed in the article.

See also: Adolescence, Theories of; Cognitive Development; Globalization and Adolescence; Initiation Ceremonies and Rites of Passage.

Further Reading

Adelson J (ed.) (1980) *Handbook of Adolescent Psychology*. New York: Wiley.

Boring EG (1929) *A History of Experimental Psychology*. New York: Appleton Century Crofts.

Bronfenbrenner U (1979) *The Ecology of Human Development: Experiments by Nature and Design*. Cambridge, MA: Harvard University Press.

Hall GS (1904) *Adolescence: Its Psychology and its Relations to Physiology, Anthropology, Sociology, Sex, Crime, Religion, and education*, vols. 1 and 2. New York: Appleton.

Hamburg B (1974) Early adolescence: A specific and stressful stage of the life cycle. In: Coelho G, Hamburg DA, and Adams JE (eds.) *Coping and Adaptation*, pp. 101–125. New York: Basic Books.

Hamburg DA and Takanishi R (1996) Great transitions: Preparing American youth for the 21st century – the role of research. *Journal of Research on Adolescence* 6(4): 379–396.

Hartup WW (1996) The International Society for the Study of Behavioural Development after 25 years: Retrospect and Prospect. *International Journal of Behavioral Development* 19: 243–254.

Lerner RM (2002) *Concepts and Theories of Human Development*, 3rd edn. Mahwah, NJ: Erlbaum.

Lerner RM and Steinberg L (eds.) (2009) In: *Handbook of Adolescent Psychology*, 3rd edn., vols. 1 and 2. Hoboken, NJ: Wiley.

Petersen AC (1988) Adolescent development. In: Rosenzweig MR (ed.) *Annual Review of Psychology*, vol. 39, pp. 583–607. Palo Alto, CA: Annual Reviews, Inc.

Pinquart M and Silbereisen RK (2005) Understanding social change in conducting research on adolescence. *Journal of Research on Adolescence* 15(4): 395–405.

Silbereisen RK and Chen X (2010) *Social Change and Human Development: Concept and Results*. Thousand Oaks, CA: Sage.

Steinberg L (2009) Should the science of adolescent brain development inform public policy? *American Psychologist* 64: 739–750.

Steinberg L and Lerner RM (2004) The scientific study of adolescent development: A brief history. *Journal of Early Adolescence* 23(1): 45–54.

Steinberg L and Morris AF (2001) Adolescent development. *Journal of Cognitive Education and Psychology* 2(1): 55–87.

Hormones and Behavior

C M Worthman, Emory University, Atlanta, GA, USA

Glossary

Hormones: Chemicals produced in the body at one location (usually a gland such as the adrenal, ovary, or testis) which produce an effect on the activity of another location, called the target tissue. Target tissues have receptors where the hormone binds to generate a sequence of cellular responses. Most but not all hormones are transported through the body via the bloodstream.

Limbic system: A set of loosely defined structures located around the border of the cortex in the ancient core of the brain, including the hippocampus, amygdala, fornix, cingulate gyrus, and hypothalamus, among others. Structures in this group have connections to regions throughout the brain and are associated with emotion and affective processing, long-term memory formation, behavior, and endocrine and autonomic regulation.

Prefrontal cortex: The frontal lobes is a core area for high-level processing that integrates internal states (sensory information, affective processing), with thoughts and intentions to make decisions and guide actions. During adolescence, this region undergoes distinct maturational changes involving growth, pruning, and hence reorganization.

Steroid hormones: A class of small compounds whose distinctive structure permits them to move directly through membranes and whose powerful actions are due to their capacity to alter gene transcription in the nucleus of cells in target tissues. They include gonadal (testosterone, estradiol) and adrenal (cortisol, adrenal androgens) secretions involved, among other things, in reproduction and stress responses.

Stress reactivity: The cognitive-emotional and associated neuroendocrine sensitivity to stressors. High reactivity is linked to greater endocrine and autonomic stress responsiveness that increase the strength and duration of hormonal (cortisol) and physical (heart rate) reactions to stress. As such, reactivity reflects the psychological and physiological impact of stressors on an individual.

Abbreviations

ACTH	Adrenocorticotropic hormone
CRF/CRH	Corticotrophin releasing factor/hormone
DALY	Disability-adjusted life years
DHEA	Dehydroepiandrosterone
DHEAS	Dehydroepiandrosterone sulfate
DNA	Deoxyribose nucleic acid
FSH	Follicle stimulating hormone
GH	Growth hormone
GHRH	Growth hormone releasing hormone
GnRH	Gonadotropin releasing hormone
HPA	Hypothalamo–pituitary–adrenal axis
HPG	Hypothalamo–pituitary–gonadal axis
HPT	Thyrotropic or hypothalamo–pituitary–thyroid axis
IGF-1	Insulin-like growth factor
LH	Luteinizing hormone
NPY	Neuropeptide-Y
POMC	Pro-opiomelanocortin
SRIF	Somatotropin release-inhibiting factor, or somatomedin
STA	Somatotropic axis
T4	Thyroxine
TRH	Thyroid releasing hormone
TSH	Thyroid stimulating hormone

Introduction

Behavioral maturation is a major part of adolescence that, together with the many concomitant physical changes of puberty, transforms children into young adults. Because the outcomes represent the future of the society, virtually every group on record attempts to manage the process to achieve desired goals. Ethnographic and historical accounts document a wide variety of strategies to guide and influence adolescent development, from structured formal interventions (rituals, schools) to age/stage-specific activities and expectations (labor and task assignment, recreational options, skills attainment), to adjustment of daily settings (living arrangements, apprenticeship, altered supervision/monitoring, exposure to peers). These situations and demands may or may not mesh with individual inclinations and abilities, and the resulting tensions and strains on adults and the adolescents themselves not infrequently lead to adult perceptions of adolescents as unruly and difficult. Thus, the discovery of hormones and their role in puberty during the early–mid twentieth century fostered a popular attribution of the emotional–behavioral turmoil around adolescence to 'raging hormones.'

The insight that adolescence is a stressful period of heightened vulnerability has emerged more recently. Even as the adolescent confronts new demands, capacities, and expectations, the maturation processes of physical (growth, reproductive) and cognitive-emotional systems themselves are not fully synchronized and proceed on different schedules. Gaps among

 doi:10.1016/B978-0-12-373915-5.00020-6

physical, emotional, cognitive, and behavioral attainments complicate the process of adolescent adjustment. The most obvious and dramatic changes in body morphology (size and shape), physiology, and behavior relate to reproductive maturation, leading to a focus on the role of gonadal hormones in these transformations. Hence, much of the early work on hormones and behavior in adolescence focused on the hormones involved in reproductive maturation, particularly the so-called 'sex hormones,' testosterone and estradiol. But recognition that the hormones of stress may be intimately involved with adolescent behaviors has been informed by growing evidence of the role of activity and stress reactivity of the stress response system in adolescent social cognition and behavior.

This survey commences by reviewing why the psychobehavioral health of adolescents is of particular importance today. The following sections explain the regulation and developmental course of hormones of significance in puberty and adolescence. To streamline the enormous complexity of the neuroendocrine system, discussion will focus on three key elements of adolescent maturation: reproduction (the gonads), stress (adrenals), and affective-cognitive processing (brain). The term 'neuroendocrine' here recognizes the fact that the nervous and endocrine systems essentially form a functional unit. The dynamics of hormones and behavior in adolescence must be understood to operate within a network of interacting developmental, physiological, perceptual, and social forces. A heuristic model of these developmental biosocial dynamics is provided to walk the reader through the complexities. Then, translation of the insights gained from hormone-behavior dynamics for addressing the practical problem of adolescent mental health is applied to the urgent matter of depression. A consideration of the implications for global youth concludes the discussion.

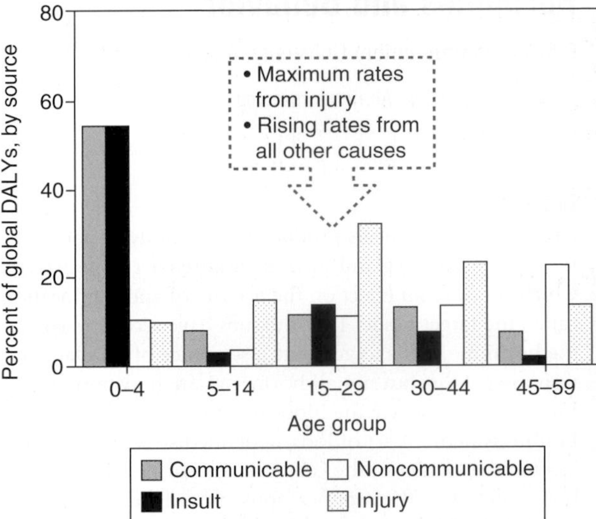

Figure 1 Distribution of the burden of disease by source across age groups under age 60 years. Burden is calculated in terms of disability-adjusted life-years (DALYs). Based on data in Mathers and colleagues (2006, Table 3C9, pp. 228–233). Sources of burden: communicable disease (gray), insult (black), noncommunicable disease (white), and injury (dotted).

A Brief Global Epidemiology of Adolescence

Youth are the cornerstones of any society's future, and this is especially true today. Recent trends have created a demographic bind. On the one hand, human population expansion has created the largest global cohort of youth ever seen, comprising over one billion aged 15–24 plus 1.2 billion aged 5–14 in a total human population of over 6.5 billion in 2005. On the other hand, increased longevity and declining fertility have contributed to population aging and diminished the global proportion of young people. Matters concerning youth therefore assume dual importance, for the sheer numbers and human potential youth represent, and for their future significance in aging populations.

Whatever the demographics, understanding youth behavior is critical because the major threats to their health during this period have their origins in behavior rather than infectious or chronic disease. Mortality is at its lowest in the teen and young adult years, but the rapid physical and psychobehavioral changes of puberty and adolescence alter the risks of health-related behavior problems, including sexual and physical risk-taking, substance use, suicide, and mood disorders. The age distribution of the burden of morbidity and mortality (expressed in terms of disability-adjust life years, **Figure 1**) reveals that rates of injury and insult are at their highest during the period of late adolescence and early adulthood, exceeded only by the high burden of insult associated with birth and malnutrition in infancy. Note also that the burden of communicable disease increases by 50% and that from noncommunicable diseases triples between ages 5–14 and 15–29. Behavior plays key roles in these expansions to burden. For instance, rates of suicide increase dramatically, particularly in young men. The rising importance of romantic and peer relationships contributes to sexual risk-taking with consequences for reproductive health such as sexually transmitted diseases or premature childbearing. Sensation seeking and initiation of substance use contribute to increasing rates of accidents. A pressing question has been *why* youth are prone to behaviors that risk their present and future welfare, and where the key points of leverage may lie to optimize successful, healthy pathways through adolescence.

Another special historical circumstance is relevant. As a group, global youth today are physically maturing earlier than perhaps any time in human history, owing to widespread improvements in health and nutrition. It also appears that early-maturing populations such as those in Europe, the United States or Japan progress through puberty more rapidly than their later-maturing ancestors and contemporaries. Consequently, the association of earlier exposure to the physiological and bodily changes of puberty to the ongoing neurocognitive and behavioral maturation of adolescents remains an important but unresolved question. Do the accelerated timing and pace of puberty fuel a growing mismatch between physical and psychosocial development? How and how much are physiological and neurocognitive maturation synchronized at puberty, and what is the role of social expectations, constraints, and opportunities in producing asynchronies between physical and psychosocial maturation? Puberty brings a final phase of growth and the beginning of the adult productive and reproductive career with concomitant demands on forming and conducting social relationships, performing social roles, and making effective and responsible decisions. Thus, the connection of physical and psychosocial maturation is a critically important one.

Hormones in Developmental Processes

The key purpose of hormones is to make things happen. Hormones by definition are secreted in one place to have an effect on another. Thus, hormones mediate short-term projects such as digesting a meal, as well as long-term ones such as growing up or having a baby. Understanding about the role of hormones in behavioral maturation at adolescence is evolving along with insights about sites and mechanisms of endocrine action, the impact and mediation of experiential effects, and processes of brain maturation. To understand the effects of endocrine changes during this period requires a view of puberty as part of an ongoing process of development that begins *in utero*. During gestation and the first few postnatal months, hormones influence the structure of neural pathways in the brain that will form the basis of behavior regulation. Such irreversible effects on structure and shaping of adult behavior comprise the organizational effects of hormone action, which may not be expressed until later exposure to the hormones produced in puberty. Reversible endocrine stimulation of behavior expression comprises the activational effects of increased hormonal outputs. Much of the work on organizational effects has focused on the possible action of gonadal steroid hormones in mediating sex differences in behavior via their early organizational effects on the brain, followed by activational effects in puberty and adulthood. Now, however, imaging studies of brain development strongly suggest that the brain undergoes an adolescent period of growth and reorganization that is subject to organizational effects by hormones as well.

Overview of Endocrine Regulation and Production

To understand hormone–behavior interactions, first it is useful to review endocrine regulation and production within the neuroendocrine continuum. The four classic endocrine systems outlined in **Figure 2** establish dynamic feedback between the brain and the body's endocrine activity via a three-step process involving the hypothalamus, pituitary, and target organ. The brain produces releasing hormones (CRH, GnRH, GHRH/SRIF, TRH) from the hypothalamus that trigger secretion of hormones from the pituitary (ACTH, LH and FSH, GH, and TSH) that in turn stimulate production of cortisol, gonadal steroids testosterone and estradiol, IGF-1, and T4. Circulating levels of these hormones provide feedback to the brain about target organ activity, and releasing hormone production is adjusted accordingly. These four pathways are known respectively as the hypothalamo–pituitary–adrenal (HPA), hypothalamo–pituitary–gonadal (HPG), somatotropic (STA), and thyrotropic or hypothalamo–pituitary–thyroid (HPT) axes. More recently, the importance of distributed endocrine activity that has central nervous system effects has been recognized, such as the production of leptin by white fat or of cytokines by lymphocytes. The HPG axis shows the most dramatic changes during puberty, but the STA is also involved in the growth spurt and likewise, the HPA exhibits alterations in its activity.

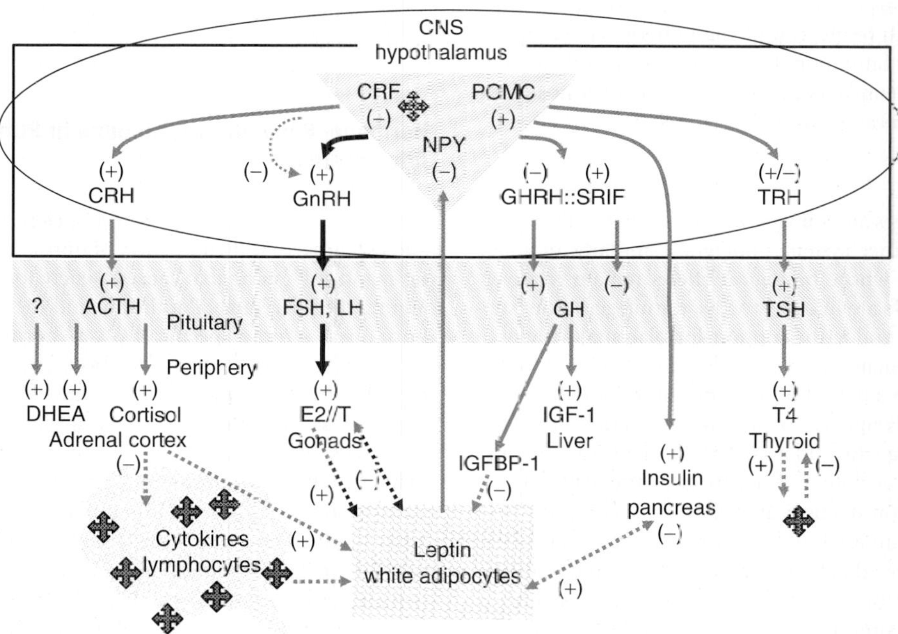

Figure 2 Overview of classic endocrine systems. These four endocrine systems represent functional axes that each operate via a three-step process involving the hypothalamus, pituitary, and target organ. More recently, the importance of distributed endocrine activity that has central nervous system effects has been recognized, such as the production of leptin by white fat or of cytokines by lymphocytes.

Developmental Trajectories

The reproductive axis

During gestation, gonadal activity plays a key role in sex differentiation. Specifically, morphological and functional sex differentiation is triggered by an early cascade of genetic factors and the reproductive axis becomes functional, reaching adult levels of gonadotropins by mid-gestation and declining thereafter until after birth, when they rise again during the first year of life. Similarly, the gonads actively produce testosterone or estradiol during gestation and show another surge during the first months after birth. The axis becomes quiescent in the second year, and remains so until nighttime pulses in gonadotropins signal the onset of puberty. Gonadotropin production mediates brain regulation of the reproductive axis but it is the gonadal steroids they stimulate that exert organizational and activational effects on the brain and the body.

How does the body know when to begin puberty? Answering that question could net a Nobel Prize. This biological puzzle is important because puberty is triggered by distinct but elusive neuroendocrine mechanisms that act as the pace makers of human development. The mechanisms are necessary because the systems regulating reproductive maturation have been profoundly suppressed to create the distinctively human phenomenon of prolonged childhood. Something must reverse the decade-long quiescence to close the childhood phase and permit the final stages of maturation to proceed. A suite of permissive factors (nutritional status, stress, physical health) modulates pubertal timing, but nevertheless the pace maker appears to be located in the central nervous system. Girls enter puberty slightly earlier than boys and experience rises in estradiol reflecting ovarian activation that gradually reaches levels sufficient to establish ovarian cyclicity. Menarche is an early marker of such cyclicity, but it takes years for the axis to achieve routine ovulation and robust, stable ovarian cycles. Males, by contrast, experience systematic increases in testosterone and attain adult levels in mid-late puberty. However, the external signs of maturation (voice change, beard growth) appear only at sustained, well-elevated levels of testosterone and thus they manifest relatively late in puberty.

The adrenals

The dramatic changes attending reproductive maturation claim attention, yet another system undergoes similarly dramatic endocrine changes whose biological effects remain relatively cryptic. The adrenals are intensely active during gestation, supplying most of the endocrine support for placental activity to regulate fetal and maternal metabolism and exchange. After birth, they undergo a period of reorganization. Both gestation and the early years appear to be sensitive periods for HPA organization during which maternal stress, maltreatment, and trauma alter basal activity and reactivity of the axis. Diurnal patterns of cortisol production, as well as sensitivity of the HPA axis to challenge, are established during the first year of life. During adolescence, the HPA undergoes age- and puberty-related increases in basal levels of cortisol as well as changes in stress reactivity. Although reactivity tends to increase during adolescence and move toward an adult pattern of HPA response to stressors, both sexes exhibit hyporesponsiveness around age 11, followed by marked sex differences around age 13 when boys remain nonreactive and girls become hyperreactive. Current evidence suggests these changes are more closely related to age than to pubertal status.

The HPA axis is essentially an on-demand system that mobilizes the body's response to challenges. HPA responsivity to challenge, in terms of how much cortisol is released and for how long, is a key feature that is determined by both psychological and biological factors. Appraisal of the stressor provides the trigger for HPA response: the more intense the internal perception of challenge, the greater the HPA response. But the HPA axis itself may be more or less responsive to stimuli or regulatory feedback that alters the strength and duration of cortisol release. Given these sources of individual variability, HPA reactivity to challenge has been used as an important index of functional regulation of the axis and the burden of stressors under everyday conditions for each individual.

Weak androgens are another set of adrenal hormones (see **Figure 2**), the most prominent of which is DHEA and its sulfated form, DHEAS. These have a distinctive developmental trajectory. DHEA/S rise postnatally and then decline to low levels during the second year. They then increase slightly yet distinctly at adrenarche, between ages 6 and 8. The onset of puberty is paralleled by a more rapid ascent that continues until around age 25, so that DHEAS becomes by far the most prevalent form of circulating steroid hormone. The regulation of adrenal androgens is not entirely clear, nor is their function (at puberty, they stimulate growth of axillary and pubic hair), yet their profile of developmental change is remarkably pronounced across the life course. The developmental course of DHEA/S production is independent of the reproductive axis: when adrenarche was discovered nearly 40 years ago, some thought it may be a preliminary phase of puberty, but clinical evidence has established that the two are dissociated. DHEA/S is implicated in widespread neuromodulatory and neuroprotective actions, and a small literature finds tenuous links to risk for mood and behavior problems in adolescents that will not be reviewed here.

Hormone–Behavior Interactions in Puberty and Adolescence

Historically, western science and society have characterized adolescence as a difficult period of unrest, unruliness, exploration, and risk-taking that causes anxiety for parents and alarm among the guardians of authority and the status quo. 'Raging hormones' – more specifically, 'sex' hormones produced by activating gonads – often have been pegged as the cause of teen tension and trouble and thus, these difficulties are regarded as endemic to puberty itself. Gonadal hormones often have been found guilty by association because dramatic behavior changes appear to coincide with surges in their production, going from virtually zero in late childhood to adult levels in mid-late adolescence. But this logic has unraveled in the face of mounting evidence. The major changes in behavior and behavior problems occur after puberty starts. Moreover, direct correlations between hormone levels and behavior are rarely found. Nevertheless, pubertal hormones are known to have organizational and activational effects on the neuroregulation of emotion, but the pathways by which these effects are manifested involve social–experiential factors as well.

Other complexities cloud the ability to link behavioral changes of adolescence to the neuroendocrine changes of puberty. During this time, the activity and architecture of several neuroendocrine systems undergo maturation, production of multiple hormones is altered, the patterns of endocrine activity (not just the average) determine its physiological significance, and individuals vary enormously in timing, course, and extent of change. Both early organizational effects and genetic background contribute to this variation. Recall, too, that the processes of maturation occur on somewhat different schedules and are either partially synchronized or largely independent of one another. Furthermore, pubertal changes both affect and are affected by the contexts in which they occur.

An Integrative Biosocial Approach

Thus, developmental science has come to regard hormone–behavior interactions in adolescence as participating in a network of contributory factors, rather than as a simple cause–effect relationship. A heuristic model of these complexities is provided in **Figure 3**, using the example of gonadal steroids. If we are to understand the connections between endocrine change and psychobehavioral outcomes, at least several candidate pathways must be considered. First is endocrine mediation, whereby maturational processes activate the GnRH pulse generator that in turn drives gonadotropin release to increase output of testosterone and/or estradiol. These hormones then moderate neurological mechanisms involved in behavior and behavior regulation, including an influence on the structures involved in social cognition and emotion regulation. This chain of events comprises what have been regarded as the activational effects of gonadal steroids. Second, another possibility is central mediation, namely, the same maturational processes that trigger the onset of puberty also involve alterations in the central mechanisms organizing behavior independent of gonadal maturation. Logically, it could also be that gonadotropins themselves exert effects on these mechanisms, although there is no evidence supporting that link. Recent brain imaging does, however, support the importance of a central pathway via adolescent maturation of the brain itself. Third is maturational cuing: body changes signaling pubertal status alter self perceptions, expectations, and evaluations. In addition, changing appearance affects perceptions and responses in social contexts and existing relationships that set up both positive (opportunity) and negative (challenge) stressors. Novel stressors, in turn, directly affect social cognition and emotional-evaluative processes. These cognitive-evaluative processes mediate the impact of each avenue of maturational cuing on the central regulation of behavior. Social mediation comprises the fourth pathway, whereby social contexts and relationships produce opportunities, demands, and stressors that directly influence the central regulation of behavior. This pathway recognizes the important role of norms, relationships, and contexts in adolescent behavior and behavior changes, independent from hormones per se. All of these pathways operate in concert, so the question has become how they work together and what determines the relative contributions of one pathway or another. A critical dimension not represented in this model is time: puberty and adolescence are framed within ongoing developmental processes that extend from conception through aging. Thus, what happens during this time is shaped by prior experience and development while it also shapes future social and physical trajectories through adulthood.

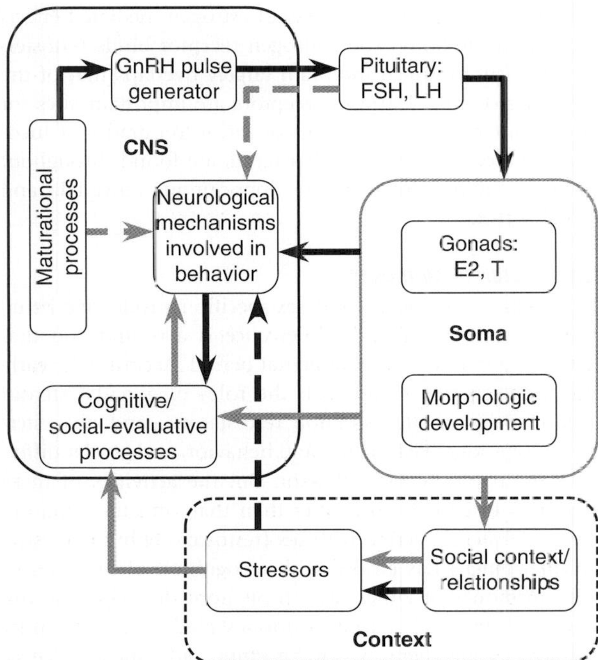

Figure 3 Multiple pathways linking puberty and behavior change in adolescence. Four types of pathways are shown, including endocrine mediation (solid black line), central mediation (dashed gray line), maturational cuing (solid gray line), and social mediation (dashed black line).

Central Mediation

Brain maturational changes in the second decade play a major role in the behavioral changes observed in adolescence. Innovative technologies for imaging brain structure and activity have opened new windows onto brain architecture and activity that are revolutionizing understandings of its development as well as of brain function and its roles in cognition and behavior. At birth, the human brain is relatively large and grows much more rapidly than does the rest of the body, attaining 50% of adult size by age 1 and 95% by age 10. However, growth in size is only a small part of brain development, which mainly involves the structuring and restructuring of anatomical arrangements within the brain. Connectivity is a major determinant of how the brain operates, so processes that shape how cells and regions of the brain talk with each other comprise the most powerful determinants of mature function. Prominent aspects of these processes are pruning and myelination. Pruning is the removal of nerve connections (synapses) or neurons to sculpt fine and large patterns of connectivity among neurons. Myelination most simply may be thought of as the process of insulating the wiring of the brain to enhance both speed and specificity of connections among brain regions. Together, pruning and myelination represent potent means of shaping patterns of activity and transmission, and hence function.

During development, neuronal and synaptic overproduction and pruning drive structure, while myelination matures transmission speed. The number of unmyelinated neurons, or gray matter, expands rapidly in fetal and infant development and then undergoes pruning in a dynamic 'use it or lose it' process whereby synapses (nerve connections) and neurons that are exercised or activated are retained. Those that do not 'work' expire. Recent imaging studies have revealed another wave of gray matter overproduction in early puberty, at age 11 in girls and 12 in boys, followed by some thinning. A thickening of cortical gray matter indicates the production of new nerve cells, while cortical thinning reflects the maturational processes of pruning and myelination that sculpt regional and overall brain functioning. Such thickening and then thinning of the cerebral cortex happens at different times in adolescent development for different functional areas, but occurs primarily in the frontal lobe, a region responsible for 'executive functions' such as reasoning, planning, and impulse control. Myelination of neuronal fibers and tracts is progressive and proceeds from the front to the back of the brain, as reflected in the expansion of white matter that commences in early childhood and attenuates after age 12. However, the frontal lobes also show another phase of myelination during the teen years, which is thought to support maturation of cognition and executive functions, although development of sensory, auditory, language, and spatial functions is largely complete. Overall, then, anatomical changes in the brain, represented in part by gray matter decreases and white matter increases, provide clear evidence that adolescence is an important period of brain development.

In sum, adolescence is a phase of extensive brain development that involves several systems and changes in synaptic density and myelination. These processes are particularly evident in the frontal lobes; indeed, the prefrontal cortex is the latest area of the brain to develop mature synaptic density and myelination. Additionally, limbic structures involved in affect and memory develop during adolescence, manifested most notably in increasing volume of the amygdala and hippocampus. These maturational patterns have important implications for understanding adolescent affective-behavioral attainments and vulnerabilities. Executive function, or the ability to implement rational analysis and planned intentions and to manage countervailing feelings and impulses in the control of behavior, is particularly challenging for adolescents. This is not just a matter of maturation in specific brain regions, but also of consolidation of tracts linking different regions of the brain to facilitate and coordinate complex, timely processing and behavior regulation. The collaborative function of different brain regions that is seen in adults is not yet formed in adolescents, whose brains literally must work harder to accomplish such tasks. In part, this is due to the apparent asynchrony in the emergence at puberty of affective-appetitive drives and the development of cognitive-regulatory systems. For example, the amygdala plays a central role in affective processing and managing the dynamics between emotion and cognition, and is critical to memory consolidation. Interactions between the prefrontal cortex and the amygdala produce the assignment of emotional valences to facial expressions, and adolescents show a series of shifts in such processing. Maturation of amygdale–prefrontal connections may underlie the dramatic social and emotional changes in early adolescence.

Endocrine Mediation

For hormones to affect behavior, they must influence brain activity, directly or indirectly. Steroid hormones such as estradiol, testosterone, or cortisol are particularly potent because they can pass directly through membranes to exert their effects within the cell, at the level of gene expression. Target tissues contain cellular receptors that act as transcription factors: these receptors bind the steroid, transport it to the nucleus, and directly regulate DNA transcription. The distribution and density of receptors determine the sites, specificity, and intensity of endocrine action. Thus, for example, in emotion regulating regions of the brain such as the hippocampus, cortisol binds to two classes of receptors (mineralocorticoid and glucocorticoid) that mediate its concentration-dependent actions. In another example, testosterone exerts its actions indirectly in some tissues through its aromatization to estradiol and binding to estrogen receptors within the target tissue.

The brain is richly furnished with steroid receptors. There are two major recognized estrogen receptors, the alpha-receptors concentrated in the hippocampus and connecting regions, beta-receptors scattered throughout the brain including cerebral cortex, plus a membrane receptor, G protein-coupled estrogen receptor (GPR30), concentrated in the hypothalamus and pituitary. Several other proteins also are known to bind estrogen to create a diverse array of estrogen-mediated effects throughout the body. The androgen receptor binds testosterone; its distribution in the brain largely overlaps that of the estrogen receptors. Estrogen receptors are important sites for testosterone action in cells that convert it to estradiol. Glucocorticoid receptors, on the other hand, are found throughout the brain, and particularly in the hippocampus, amygdala, and frontal cortex.

Gonadal steroid hormones

The emergence of sexual and sex-specific reproductive behaviors during puberty and adolescence is a central and dramatic feature of this developmental period. Accordingly, early endocrine research focused on the roles of gonadal steroid hormones (especially estradiol, testosterone, and progesterone) in reproductive function and behavior, and gender differences in cognition and behavior. But the activities of these hormones extend much further than that, and the equation of gonadal steroid action with sex (testosterone in men, estradiol in women) has eroded with recognition of the roles of both hormones in either sex. Throughout development and adulthood, gonadal steroid hormones play active regulatory roles in shaping neuronal architecture and function. These hormones influence a wide range of neurodevelopmental processes, from dendritic growth, cell death, and synaptic formation and elimination, to expression of neuropeptides and receptors. The activity of several neurotransmitter systems (including dopaminergic, serotonergic, cholinergic, and noradrenergic neurons) is modulated by gonadal steroid hormones. These systems play key roles in the regulation of higher-order functions that inform behavior, such as cognition and emotion regulation. Several of them, as well as others regulated by gonadal steroids (oxytocin, vasopressin, endogenous opioids), are directly involved in social responsiveness. The actions of gonadal steroid hormones are particularly evident in the limbic system (amygdala, hippocampus, striatum), cerebellum, and cortex and influence many behaviors, such as verbal, motor, and spatial abilities, aggression, emotion regulation, and some dimensions of learning and memory. For example, sex differences in fear conditioning are associated with attenuation in women by estrogen suppression of long-term potentiation in the hippocampus. Similarly, the amygdala has a high concentration of androgen receptors and shows sex differences in its activation patterns: activation to angry faces correlates with circulating testosterone in men but not in women.

Pubertal increases in gonadal steroid hormones change the processing of social experience. Strong specific effects of gonadal steroids on target brain regions include sexual behavior, social bonding, and social memory. Given the pattern of receptors and target tissues, it is unsurprising that emotional and behavioral responsiveness to social stimuli constitutes an important arena of gonadal steroid hormone influence at adolescence. For instance, in both females and males, sexual responsiveness to a social stimulus is enhanced with increased circulating androgen levels. Adolescents characteristically manifest heightened self-awareness and sensitivity to peer acceptance and rejection. Gonadal steroid hormones, particularly androgens, also have been linked to social dominance and status-seeking behaviors. Some animal models indicate that these endocrine effects are greatest during early encounters with a novel stimulus, suggesting a basis for the formation of patterns of social behavior during adolescence.

Recent imaging studies are beginning to reveal links of brain development with endocrine and other pubertal changes. Amygdala volume *increases* in boys but *decreases* in girls with pubertal progression as indexed by testosterone levels. However, cortical thinning is greater with increasing testosterone in girls but not boys. Interactions between the amygdala, critical for processing emotional information, and frontal cortical regions important for risk evaluation and impulse control may follow different courses in females and males during puberty-related brain development. If a thinner cortex is related to better executive control over the emotional processing centers of the amygdala, then this helps explain differences in emotional processing between boys and girls, depending on pubertal status and brain maturation. Adolescents also exhibit alterations in reward-related behavior that are thought to contribute to increasing emotional and behavioral problems such as mood disorders and drug abuse. Brain imaging studies have reported conflicting results about adolescent maturational change in reactions to experience by reward-related structures such as the striatum and medial prefrontal cortex (mPFC). One argument points to evidence of increased activation to suggest that rewards are more salient to adolescents, which enhances reward-related brain activation and thence greater reward-seeking behavior. Another argument points to evidence of reduced reward-related brain reactivity and suggests a blunted response to reward among adolescents that, in turn, motivates them to seek more rewarding experiences in order to maintain reward circuit activity at an optimal level. A recent imaging study by Forbes and colleagues examined the association of reward-related brain function to every day real-world experience, and found that reward-related brain function changes with puberty and is associated with positive affect and depressive symptoms. Specifically, testosterone correlated negatively with reward-related brain reactivity to receipt of reward; hence, increased reward-seeking in adolescence may act to compensate for these changes.

Glucocorticoids

Appropriate levels of glucocorticoids (cortisol is the dominant form in humans), neither high nor low, are necessary for normal brain development. But glucocorticoid levels are highly responsive to stressors, particularly psychosocial stress. Thus, the timing of exposure to stressors directly influences their impact on the developmental course of HPA function and on glucocorticoid-sensitive structures (hippocampus, frontal cortex, amygdala) involved in affective, cognitive, and behavioral regulation. During gestation, glucocorticoids are involved in shaping brain architecture (e.g., neuronal remodeling, myelination, glial maturation). In accord with the animal literature, prenatal stress (maternal stress, depression, adversity, or treatment with glucorticoids) results in fetal programming of the HPA and persistently increased basal HPA activity. Such prenatal adversity has been linked to perturbations in neurological, cognitive, and behavioral development that include social insensitivity, sleep disturbance, and attention deficit hyperactivity disorder, along with increased risk for psychiatric problems such as substance abuse and mood and anxiety disorders.

Converging lines of evidence in animals and humans point to the importance of early caregiving quality for establishing HPA regulation that is robust to everyday challenges. Responsive and sensitive parenting provides social regulation of infant HPA development, while early harsh conditions conduce to dysregulated HPA activity. Such effects appear to be enduring and affect later functioning. For example, increased HPA activity in adolescents whose mothers suffered from postpartum depression is responsible for the association between early adversity and late depressive symptoms. Recent evidence suggests a particular sensitivity of the adolescent brain to elevated glucocorticoids and thus to stress. This sensitivity is greatest in the frontal cortex, where development is proceeding apace. Gene expression studies have found that levels of glucocorticoid receptor mRNA in the prefrontal cortex are high in adolescents compared to earlier and older age groups. Additionally, the effects of early adversity on HPA function may also emerge in adolescence as youth face developmental stressors inherent to that maturational period. Thus, girls born with low birthweight who then experience childhood adversity show both greater cortisol reactivity and risk for depression at adolescence.

HPA activation is most reliably linked to two conditions, social challenge/threat and perceived lack of control. The increased salience of social stimuli and heightened emotional reactivity, along with all the physical changes, are each promoted by surging gonadal steroids and contribute to increased adolescent self-consciousness and hypersensitivity to peer relations. Such sensitivities activate the HPA and likely contribute to the greater HPA stress reactivity that adolescents experience. Individual differences in cognitive-affective responses to stressors can further exacerbate the burden of stress, and here the effects of prior experience and predispositions come into play. Heightened HPA activity in adolescence also has a bearing on HPG actions, because glucocorticoids have suppressive effects on HPG function at the level of the brain and gonads. Stress responsiveness is gender (social) and sex (biological) differentiated and merits much more study. At birth, HPA regulation differs in males and females, the ACTH : cortisol ratio being greater in infant boys, and sex differences in responses to stress persist. HPA response to stressors like public speaking or mental arithmetic is greater in males than females, and is also moderated by partner support in males but not females. HPA reactivity is more sensitive to social rejection in women and to achievement challenges in men, especially in youth. The role of sex and gender differences in exposure and responses to different stressors during adolescence remains underexplored. Acute or chronic psychosocial stress can disrupt the reproductive axis and delay puberty and maturation. Interactions of gonadal steroid hormones and glucocorticoids may contribute to the complexities of psychobehavioral changes and vulnerabilities during adolescence.

Maturational Cuing

The pathbreaking ability to image brain structure and function along with techniques for minimally invasive hormone sampling have drawn scientific attention away from earlier foci on psychological and social processes mediating pathways between puberty and behavior. Self as well as peer perceptions of maturational status also play a role in forging these pathways. The bodily changes of puberty that visibly manifest the maturational status of the adolescent also mobilize self- and other-expectations for new behaviors, competencies, relationships, and statuses to be performed and mastered. Earlier studies relied on morphologic changes to track pubertal status and focused on the effects of pubertal timing on social relationships and behavior problems as a way to test whether pubertal changes led to selection or recruitment into different social roles and peer groups. The expectation was that asynchrony with their peers exacerbates the inherent stresses of pubertal transition for early and later maturers. Indeed, it appears that early or late pubertal transition pushes some vulnerable individuals toward behavior problems.

Subsequent studies confirmed that view and have gone on to show that maturational timing is a modulator of typical stress during this period of transitions. Both hyper- and hypoactivity and reactivity of the HPA axis are associated with problem behaviors in adolescence that range from disruptive behavior and aggression to alcohol abuse. These problems may have neuroendocrine bases. Recent findings by Susman and colleagues demonstrate interactions between pubertal timing and reactivity in relation to problem behavior in boys, but not girls: later-maturing boys with high cortisol reactivity have increased antisocial and rule-breaking behavior. Another arm of the stress response system showed a different pattern of response. This arm is known as the sympathetic–adrenal–medullary (SAM) system and involves direct neural release of catecholamines into the bloodstream by another region of the adrenal, the medulla. A marker of SAM activity, salivary amylase, showed a different pattern: low SAM reactivity in early-maturing boys was related to rule-breaking and conduct disorder symptoms. The distinct central pathways regulating the HPA and SAM systems permit nuanced responses to stressors in which the two arms operate partly independently and partly synergistically. Clearly, maturation of these two systems during adolescence, their respective roles in meeting the stressors endemic to that period, and their interactions with reproductive maturation are important areas for future investigation.

Understanding the effects of maturation cuing that are mediated by hormones therefore is not simply a matter of their effects on physical-maturational status but also of how maturation of other neuroendocrine systems interacts with the new challenges and opportunities encountered in adolescence.

Social Mediation

Many aspects of behavior change in adolescence are shaped by forces independent of hormones. Adolescence radically transforms the social landscape and field of action. Established relationships must be recast and many new ones formed. The importance and content of familial, peer, and other extrafamilial relationships shift. New, more diverse, and more complex and demanding settings are to be explored and claimed. Social networks are to be negotiated, expanded, and remodeled. Figuring out how to behave, identifying social niches and life aspirations, and successfully navigating among all these dimensions of everyday life are major tasks of adolescence. Putting together real-world complexities with the neuroendocrine and morphological dynamics reviewed earlier makes it clear why adolescence appears to be a stressful period. Gendered dimensions of all these tasks also create differences in demands, expectations, options, and opportunities that shape developmental trajectories and color the adolescent experience with gendered rewards and stressors. Indeed, gender differences in susceptibility to stress may be related in part to differences in the types of social stress that are encountered. A survey of the myriad developmental tasks of adolescence should not obscure the important point that adolescents show extraordinary resilience in meeting all these challenges. Those few who fare poorly merit close attention, but the great majority who do well suggest that adolescents could provide an excellent model for understanding resilience, including its endocrine correlates.

Then, too, adolescent behavior problems may be in the eye of the beholder. Adults, whether parents, teachers, or law makers, have expectations and views on social norms that may not be shared, and indeed may be challenged, by the adolescent who is just growing into them. Indeed, many parents find parenting an adolescent stressful, particularly if the adolescent is of the same sex or in the midst of self-formation (individuation), or the parent is divorced or less invested in work or marriage. Often, parent–adolescent conflict and adolescent adjustment problems occur against a background of previous adversity or family difficulty.

Unsurprisingly, there are neuroendocrine dimensions to these linkages. The role of neuroendocrine functioning is to support the successful pursuit of individual goals such as survival, mating, or belonging, while meeting ongoing demands and vicissitudes of daily life. The evidence reviewed previously outlines some of the many pathways by which neuroendocrine systems build upon experience for adaptive development to meet these roles. Social relationships and conditions are the most decisive determinants of adaptive demands and challenges, as well as the opportunities and resources to meet them. The importance of early caregiving and adversity on psychological and neuroendocrine responsivity to stressors has already been reviewed. Social relationships and quality of life circumstances continue to be important for shaping the course of adolescent development. But the hormone–social behavior interactions may run both ways: previously formed patterns of social cognition and related neuroendocrine profiles may drive the course of social relationships in adolescence, while social experiences in adolescence may shape neuroendocrine development in this sensitive period. For example, established individual patterns of HPA activity appear to influence the quality of relationships girls form during adolescence. Diminished HPA activity reflected in low basal cortisol is associated with poor-quality social relationships with parents, siblings, or peers for adolescent girls, but not for boys. Contrastingly, the established association between testosterone and behavior in boys depends on the social context of their closest peers. High levels of testosterone in boys whose peers ranked as positive social influences are associated with leadership qualities reflected in socially assertive and dominant behaviors. But high testosterone levels in boys whose peers ranked as behaviorally deviant (rule breaking, substance use) are associated with nonaggressive symptoms of conduct disorder.

Translation to Adolescent Mental Health: The Case of Depression

Worldwide, depression ranks among the top ten sources of lifetime morbidity, a burden that underscores the importance of tracing the genesis of depression to guide efforts at prevention. Rates of depression begin to escalate during adolescence. One of the most outstanding phenomena in developmental epidemiology of western populations is the transition from gender equivalence in rates of depression during childhood to a female preponderance that emerges around age 13. The coincidence with mid-puberty has suggested a role for HPG maturation. And indeed, pubertal increases in both estradiol and testosterone have been associated with risk for depression in girls, with each having independent and additive effects in which testosterone exerts the greater impact.

Depression is also a stress-related disorder: onset is commonly associated with exposure to adversity and depression is associated with altered HPA activity. Thus, the accumulating evidence for increasing levels of cortisol and gender-specific changes in HPA reactivity during puberty has suggested that these changes may play a role in gender-differentiated vulnerabilities to psychopathology, including depression. Accordingly, girls, but not boys, who exhibit greater HPA responses to stress, also report more depressive symptoms.

But the story is more complex and has developmental roots extending back to gestation. Stress during gestation and early childhood influence vulnerability to challenge by shaping the development of reactivity to experience and HPA regulation, as reviewed previously. But these cognitive and neuroendocrine effects are grounded in epigenetic and gene–environment interactions that establish functional characteristics of the neuroregulatory systems that govern experiential processing, appraisal, and thus reactivity. From genetic epidemiology, depression has appeared to be a genetic disorder, showing 37% familial heritability. But the other 63% is related to individual-specific environmental effects. A new generation of research on interactions between environment and genetic polymorphisms for molecules involved in neuroendocrine regulation and on the impact of early environment on gene expression has begun to illuminate the biological bases of those environmental effects.

This work has dealt a final blow to old nature–nurture, gene–environment distinctions and deterministic accounts in favor of nuanced contextualized views of biobehavioral development. A well-studied example of gene–environment interaction involves polymorphisms in the regulation of a key modulator of neurotransmission (the serotonin transporter gene) that influence reactivity to stress and thence alter the risk for depression. These findings are exciting because they point to sites for translation into social conditions over which humans may have some control. Epigenetics, on the other hand, involve variation not in genes, but in the expression of genes. A cascade of environmentally sensitive mechanisms imprint each person's genetic code with molecules that determine whether and how that genetic information will be read. A powerful example concerns the impact of parental care on the child's HPA function through epigenetic programming of glucocorticoid receptor expression. For instance, the epigenetic signature has been found whereby childhood abuse alters HPA stress responses and risk for suicide by altering the regulation of glucocorticoid receptor expression in the hippocampus.

Conclusions

The study of hormones and behavior in adolescence has yielded useful lessons. They include, first, that hormones do not 'cause' behaviors. Rather, hormone-behavior dynamics are only to be understood in the contexts of prior developmental events and an interactive biosocial network of which such dynamics form a part. Second, early experiences are formative, particularly for stress reactivity systems. Many associations of hormones and behavior at adolescence are activational, based on organizational effects of these same hormones on target tissues such as the developing brain earlier in life. We now know, however, that a wave of brain development occurs during adolescence and opens a window of sensitivity to organizational effects of hormones at that time. Conversely, adolescent behavior, including psychosocial reactivity to environmental stressors, can also drive hormonal profiles. Third, although reproductive maturation is a signal feature of puberty and adolescence, neuroendocrine systems that handle stressors and stress are also crucial to psychobehavior maturation in this period. Issues of stress, adaptation, and resilience are central to adolescence. Fourth is the insight that biological systems are designed to capture information from the environment of which social contexts are defining features. Hormones play a central mediating role by reflecting regulatory mechanisms influenced by prior experience and by orchestrating the allocation of the body's material and cognitive resources to meet demands in view of ongoing priorites. Specific mechanisms involving gene–environment interactions and epigenetics are known to mediate the interface of person and context, often via modulation of neuroendocrine activity. Fifth, greater insight into hormone–behavior interactions provides insight into the sources, as well as prevention and treatment, of adolescent mental health problems such as depression. In sum, hormone-behavior dynamics reflect the inherent interdependence of body, mind, and context in human development.

Global Perspectives

This discussion of hormones and behavior offers insights but has limitations worth considering in view of conditions among contemporary global youth. Virtually all research represented in this article draws upon studies conducted in western settings that represent but a small fraction of humanity. Some evidence-based theories of development and hormone–behavior interactions at adolescence may hold across the range of human cultural, ecological, and economic-political diversity, but that is an empirical question for future science to address. Many more lessons likely will be learned in the process. Meanwhile, consider the challenges for global youth in view of our knowledge about lifetime interactions of social context, experience, and neuroendocrine development in the formation of hormone–behavior interactions in adolescence. Globalization and urbanization have refashioned the conditions of childcare by transforming family formation, parental wage labor involvement, and daily life patterns. Concomitantly, worldwide efforts for universal schooling have transformed childhood and adolescence: in 2002, youth worldwide spent on average 10.5 years in school. These global shifts also have opened up media, mobility, and economic landscapes for adolescents and youth. Nevertheless, nearly half of adolescents have grown up and live in poverty, and 15% of youth ages 15–24 are undernourished and 15% are unemployed.

Evidence in the aforementioned reviews shows that factors ranging from gestational stress and low birthweight, to early caregiving, adversity, and uncertainty in childhood and adolescence, and family, peer, and other extrafamilial adolescent relationships all shape neuroendocrine and behavior development before and during adolescence. Global trends touch on each one of these factors. Developmental science is just beginning to explore the biosocial pathways of resilience and risk by which adolescents negotiate a rapidly shifting world of uncertainty, opportunity, and adversity.

See also: Brain Development; Genetics; Transitions into Adolescence.

Further Reading

Angold A, Costello E, Erkanli A, and Worthman C (1999) Pubertal changes in hormone levels and depression in girls. *Psychological Medicine* 29: 1043–1053.

Booth A, Granger DA, Mazur A, and Kivlinghan KT (2006) Testosterone and social behavior. *Social Forces* 85: 167–182.

Booth A, Granger DA, and Shirtcliff EA (2008) Gender- and age-related differences in the association between social relationship quality and trait levels of salivary cortisol. *Journal of Research on Adolescence* 18: 239–260.

Bramen JE, Hranilovich JA, Dahl RE, et al. (2011) Puberty influences medial temporal lobe and cortical gray matter maturation differently in boys than girls matched for sexual maturity. *Cerebral Cortex* 21: 636–646.

Cameron JL (2004) Interrelationships between hormones, behavior, and affect during adolescence: Understanding hormonal, physical, and brain changes occurring in association with pubertal activation of the reproductive axis. *Annals of the New York Academy of Sciences* 1021: 110–123.

Caspi A, Hariri AR, Holmes A, et al. (2010) Genetic sensitivity to the environment: The case of the serotonin transporter gene and its implications for studying complex diseases and traits. *American Journal of Psychiatry* 167: 509–527.

Dahl RE, Gunnar MR, Dahl RE, and Gunnar MR (2009) Heightened stress responsiveness and emotional reactivity during pubertal maturation: Implications for psychopathology. *Development and Psychopathology* 21: 1–6.

Forbes EE, Ryan ND, Phillips ML, et al. (2010) Healthy adolescents' neural response to reward: Associations with puberty, positive affect, and depressive symptoms. *Journal of the American Academy of Child and Adolescent Psychiatry* 49: 162–172.

Gunnar MR, Wewerka S, Frenn K, et al. (2009) Developmental changes in hypothalamus–pituitary–adrenal activity over the transition to adolescence: Normative changes and associations with puberty. *Development and Psychopathology* 21: 69–85.

Lupien SJ, McEwen BS, Gunnar MR, et al. (2009) Effects of stress throughout the lifespan on the brain, behaviour and cognition. *Nature Reviews Neuroscience* 10: 434–445.

Mathers CD, Lopez AD, and Murray CJL (2001) The burden of disease and mortality by condition: Data, methods, and results for 2001. In: Lopez AD, Mathers CD, and Ezzati M, et al. (eds.) *Global Burden of Disease and Risk Factors*. New York: World Bank/Oxford University Press.

McGowan PO, Sasaki A, D'Alessio AC, et al. (2009) Epigenetic regulation of the glucocorticoid receptor in human brain associates with childhood abuse. *Nature Neuroscience* 12: 342–348.

Nelson EE, Leibenluft E, McClure E, and Pine DS (2005) The social re-orientation of adolescence: A neuroscience perspective on the process and its relation to psychopathology. *Psychological Medicine: A Journal of Research in Psychiatry and the Allied Sciences* 35: 163–174.

Patton GC, Coffey C, Sawyer SM, et al. (2009) Global patterns of mortality in young people: A systematic analysis of population health data. *Lancet* 374(9693): 881–892.

Rowe R, Maughan B, Worthman CM, et al. (2004) Testosterone, conduct disorder and social dominance in boys: Pubertal development and biosocial interaction. *Biological Psychiatry* 55: 546–552.

Sisk CL, Foster DL, Sisk CL, and Foster DL (2004) The neural basis of puberty and adolescence. *Nature Neuroscience* 7: 1040–1047.

Steinberg L (2008) A social neuroscience perspective on adolescent risk-taking. *Developmental Review* 28: 78–106.

Susman EJ, Dockray S, Granger DA, et al. (2010) Cortisol and alpha amylase reactivity and timing of puberty: Vulnerabilities for antisocial behaviour in young adolescents. *Psychoneuroendocrinology* 35: 557–569.

Impulsivity and Adolescence

J Weiser and B Reynolds, The Ohio State University, Columbus, OH, USA

Glossary

Behavioral disinhibition: The inability to inhibit a prepotent behavioral response to stimuli.

Contingency management programs: Treatment programs that use positive reinforcement with tangible rewards such as money, privileges, and vouchers to encourage behavior change.

Delay discounting: The preference for a smaller, immediate reward over one that is larger and delayed. The devaluing of a reward by the product of its delay.

Dopamine (DA): A neurotransmitter that acts in conjunction with the limbic system to promote reward/sensation seeking and other impulsive behaviors.

Methylphenidate: An AD/HD medication which improves PFC functioning and, as a result, reduces behavioral disinhibition and delay discounting.

Myelination: The coating of neurons in myelin in order to reduce interference and enhance efficiency of neural function.

Neuroplasticity: The developmental process by which the brain adapts to its environment.

Nucleus accumbens (NAc): The reward center in the limbic system of the brain which contributes to multiple components of impulsive behavior, such as delay discounting, decreased ability to evaluate consequences, sensation seeking, impatience, and immediacy.

Prefrontal cortex (PFC): A region of the brain responsible for executive function, devoted mainly to planning and impulse control, analyzing reward and value information, and regulating attention

Serotonin (5-HT): A neurotransmitter that acts in cooperation with the PFC as an inhibitor of impulsive behavior.

Synaptic pruning: The selective elimination of brain cells (i.e., neurons) and the connections a person uses the least, based on his or her experiences.

Introduction

When thinking of the concept of impulsivity, many different behaviors can come to mind. One example would be an unplanned decision which serves to gratify present desires and does not adequately take the future into account. Another behavior that comes to mind is doing something dangerous simply to experience the sensation of doing something new. Yet, other behaviors may involve the inability to inhibit a response to stimuli or to maintain attention. As such, impulsivity is a broad and multifaceted behavioral concept that is pertinent to nearly everyone's life.

From a developmental perspective, there is evidence that certain types of impulsive behavior (e.g., sensation seeking) may increase during adolescence, a life stage falling roughly between the ages of 10 and 20. As a period of many biological and social changes, adolescence is a unique age range involving both opportunities and vulnerabilities. In extreme instances, the influence of impulsivity can have consequences that extend far beyond the immediacy of an individual decision. For example, a desire to experience new sensations may result in poor decisions behind the wheel of a car, leading to a tragic end, or to experimentation with drugs or alcohol and eventual addiction. Given the potential long-term consequences of impulsive behavior during adolescence, considerable research has been devoted to the measurement of impulsivity and to better understanding the link between these behaviors and various problematic conditions or outcomes.

In the following sections, we define impulsive behavior and discuss the multidimensional nature of this construct, along with some of the measures that have been developed to assess these different dimensions. Also, we will explore certain physiological aspects of impulsivity in the context of the developing adolescent brain and how certain developments during this life period may influence impulsive behavior. Finally, we will discuss ways to reduce impulsive behavior in clinical populations.

Impulsivity Defined

Unfortunately, there is no single, universally accepted definition of impulsivity. Conceptualizations of impulsive behavior tend to range from very narrow definitions that include only behavioral disinhibition to more inclusive definitions that accept a broad range of behaviors associated with maladaptive outcomes. For the purposes of this article, we will adopt a more inclusive definition provided by the International Society for Research on Impulsivity (ISRI), which defines impulsive behavior as follows:

> human behavior without adequate thought, the tendency to act with less forethought than do most individuals of equal ability and knowledge, or a predisposition toward rapid, unplanned reactions to internal or external stimuli without regard to the negative consequences of these reactions.

There are several features of this ISRI definition that are worth highlighting. First, by impulsive behavior, we are referring to maladaptive human behaviors that are not the result of misunderstanding the possible consequences of these actions when compared to most individuals. Therefore, a behavior may not be considered impulsive (even if highly maladaptive) if the person did not have sufficient information to understand the negative outcomes associated with that behavior. For example, the act of smoking cigarettes during adolescence might be considered impulsive, even if it takes a degree of planning and thought to obtain the cigarettes and if the adolescent is from a region with a high level of public awareness about the health risks associated with smoking. However, that same behavior (i.e., smoking) may not be considered impulsive if it occurs in a different region where there is little or no awareness of the negative consequences associated with smoking. Therefore, impulsivity describes behavior that is outside the norm and that occurs despite awareness of the potential for negative consequences.

Another important feature of the ISRI definition of impulsivity is the breadth of behaviors that can be considered impulsive. For instance, behaviors like risk taking, sensation seeking, decision-making that reflects immediate gratification, an inability to sustain attention toward goal behaviors, and an inability to inhibit inappropriate behaviors (i.e., disinhibition) – all can be considered different types of impulsive behavior that would be relevant to different types of situations. This approach clearly embraces a multidimensional description of impulsivity. However, to varying degrees, each of these impulsive behaviors reflects a breakdown in what is known as Executive Functions, or the cognitive processes that serve to regulate a person's thoughts, decisions, and activities. As such, there is an underlying commonality across these behaviors involving cognitive function.

A final consideration when defining impulsive behaviors is that the term 'impulsivity' describes behaviors that are maladaptive and serve to significantly increase the likelihood of negative outcomes. For example, everyone exhibits some propensity for risk taking or making decisions in the interest of immediate gratification; however, only maladaptive instances of risk taking or immediate gratification would be considered impulsive. In fact, in some cases, these behaviors may be most adaptive or functional. Therefore, impulsivity must be defined within the context that the behavior occurs. In future discussion, impulsive behavior will refer to behaviors that are not appropriate for a given context and that are linked with negative outcomes.

Impulsivity Measured

There are two primary methods for researchers to measure impulsivity: self-report measures and laboratory-behavioral tasks. Both methods conceptualize impulsivity as a multidimensional construct, meaning that there is more than one type of behavior that can be considered impulsive.

Self-report measures are valuable because they allow the participant to evaluate his or her own behaviors and cognitions. One benefit of the self-report method is that these measures can easily be given to large groups of individuals at a relatively inexpensive cost. However, an issue with this method is the potential that participants will misrepresent themselves, as this measure does not evaluate the actual behavior of interest but rather a participant's report of his or her behavior. This concern might be especially warranted for children and adolescents who may be less capable of accurately describing their own behaviors. One widely used self-report measure is the Barrett Impulsivity Scale (BIS-11), which is a 30-item questionnaire that measures three subtraits of impulsivity: cognitive impulsiveness, motor impulsiveness, and nonplanning impulsiveness. Another important self-report measure is the UPPS Impulsive Behavior Scale. The UPPS characterizes four dimensions of impulsivity. The measure is named after the four dimensions it assesses, which are urgency, (lack of) premeditation, (lack of) perseverance, and sensation seeking. Both the BIS and the UPPS have been demonstrated to measure adolescent and adult impulsivity.

As mentioned before, an alternative approach to measuring impulsivity is to use laboratory-behavioral tasks. These assessments uniformly differ from the self-report measures in that the participant completes a behavioral task that assesses the actual behavior of interest. This ability to measure the actual behaviors in question is a strength of these assessments over the participant's report of his or her behaviors. Some issues with this method are that it is more labor-intensive to administer and complete, and that the assessments should be completed in the same manner each time, that is, the researcher needs to control for variables that could affect behavior during the task (e.g., noise, time of day). Laboratory-behavioral tasks have been organized into three separate dimensions of impulsivity: impulsive decision-making, impulsive disinhibition, and impulsive inattention. Each of these dimensions reflects a distinct type of behavior that might be relevant to different types of situations. Unlike the self-report measures, there is little consensus on specific, widely accepted laboratory-behavioral instruments.

Research indicates that for both adults and adolescents, the dimensional structure of impulsivity using self-report and laboratory-behavioral measures is consistent. That is, the dimensions of impulsivity identified through factor analyses with adult samples are replicated with adolescents, suggesting that the types of impulsive behavior people exhibit are similar across these two age groups. However, as will be discussed further, the degree of certain types of impulsive behavior, such as sensation seeking, that are exhibited may be different across adults and adolescent age groups.

The Biology of Impulsivity

The brain is an extremely complex organ – it controls all of the body's activities. Certain areas of the brain correspond to different roles, cognitions, and actions, and the brain stimulates and communicates with these areas using neurotransmitters. The areas of the brain and the neurotransmitters we will be focusing on in this article are those demonstrated to have an influence on a person's impulse control and risk-taking behavior.

The neurobiological side of impulsivity reflects an interaction between the prefrontal cortex (PFC) regions of the brain and parts of the limbic system, including the ventral tegmental area (VTA), nucleus accumbens (NAc), and amygdala (**Figure 1**). Behavioral self-control versus impulsivity is determined by a competition between the goal-directed, impulse control function of the PFC and the automatic, reward processing regions of the limbic system. Specific neurotransmitters also play a role in impulsive behavior. The neurotransmitters most widely connected to impulsivity are dopamine (DA) and serotonin (5-HT), and we will discuss

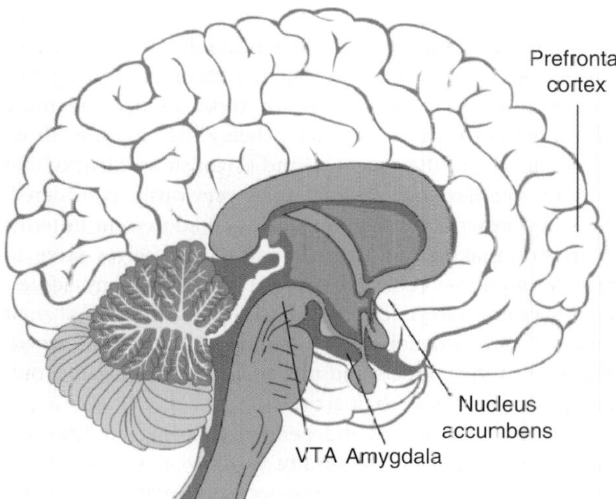

Figure 1 Location of the brain regions related to impulsivity. One neural pathway, which contributes to reward and sensation seeking as well as impulse control and inhibition, includes the ventral tegmental area (VTA), the nucleus accumbens (which is a part of the ventral striatum), and the prefrontal cortex. The amygdala is involved in an individual's response to novel stimuli. Image courtesy of the National Institute on Alcohol Abuse and Alcoholism.

the role each of these transmitters plays in impulsive behavior, sensitization, and the influencing of neuroplastic processes. Adolescence is a time of great development for not only the brain in general but also the PFC and its systems in particular.

The systems of the PFC play an important role in executive function, as they are devoted mainly to planning and impulse control. The PFC is divided into five parallel subcircuits. Three of the most relevant subcircuits are the dorsal lateral prefrontal cortex (dlPFC), orbital frontal cortex (OFC), and anterior cingulated cortex (ACC). All the three of these regions contribute to impulse regulation, and they also enable a person to draw information from past experiences to make a present decision. The dlPFC forms the foundation of executive function, as it controls attention as well as organizes behavior to solve complex problems. The OFC, along with the dlPFC, integrates and regulates sensory, affective, and associative information. The ACC is critical for motivation. More generally, the PFC has been demonstrated to receive sensory input, analyze reward, and value information to plan events and behaviors, and to incorporate patience and understanding of long-term, abstract rewards in the decision-making process. Damage to the PFC is associated with behavior that is more heavily affected by immediate rewards and a failure to plan, and abnormal PFC functioning due to other causes has been implicated in mood disorders, schizophrenia, substance abuse and addiction, as well as other disorders.

In contrast to the executive role of the PFC, the NAc and amygdala contributes to multiple components of impulsive behavior, such as delay discounting, decreased ability to evaluate consequences, sensation seeking, impatience, and immediacy. The NAc is the reward center that is heavily innervated in DA, a potent promotivational neurotransmitter. These DA innervations are from cells that extend from the VTA to the NAc. In a somewhat different role, the amygdala aids the PFC in the decision-making process by contributing motor, autonomic, affective, and hormonal information. In the presence of weak inhibitory responses from the PFC, the amygdala is able to condition the brain to respond automatically to stimuli, and it is thought to contribute to the craving triggered by stimuli associated with drugs for an addicted individual.

Much like the brain regions described earlier, there are two reciprocal systems of neurotransmitters that affect the way people respond to stimuli and the power given to either the PFC or limbic motivation systems. DA is a neurotransmitter that plays a large role in impulsive behavior. The release of DA into the NAc is prompted by various stimuli such as drugs, natural rewards, rewarding situations, and stressful or negative stimuli. Release of DA into the NAc carries with it a feeling of novelty and pleasure, and the DA systems as a whole promote reward/sensation seeking and other impulsive behaviors. Again, the NAc and other parts of the limbic system are innervated by DA from the VTA, and thus work in conjunction to promote rewarding sensations and potentially impulsive behavior. Conversely, 5-HT acts in cooperation with the PFC as an inhibitor of impulsive behavior. While the role of 5-HT in impulsive behavior is complex, activity has generally been found to be decreased in people who engage in addictive, suicidal, or otherwise impulsive behaviors.

Beyond the more general underpinnings of impulsive behavior described earlier, the adolescent is also going through puberty. Large-scale body changes are taking place during this time, and sex hormone levels increase dramatically. For example, levels of testosterone (a sex hormone) increase in both males and females during adolescence, with the increase in males being substantially greater than that of females. Increased testosterone is associated with an increase in adolescent impulsivity and risk taking. Increased reward seeking also correlates strongly with pubertal development.

The Adolescent Brain, Development, and Impulsivity

The adolescent brain undergoes a great deal of development. As discussed previously, adolescence is a life stage when a person exhibits more impulsivity or sensation seeking than in childhood or adulthood, and this change in behavior is largely due to the continued development of the PFC through adolescence. As such, the relative strength of the limbic reward DA system is greater than that of the inhibitory 5-HT PFC systems.

The prefrontal cortex, a person's primary center of executive function and impulse control, is the last region of the brain to mature, going through most of its major changes in late adolescence. Being that it is late to develop, the PFC is competing against the already-mature areas of the limbic reward system discussed previously. The weakness of the PFC and its inhibitory ability during adolescence is not only due to its lack of development but also due to the nature of the developments taking place. For example, the brain selectively eliminates the cells (i.e., neurons) and the connections a person uses the least, based on his or her experiences, in a process known as synaptic pruning. This pruning makes the adolescent less efficient at implementing impulse control and utilizing executive functions in decision-making than that of an adult. It has also been demonstrated that the PFC undergoes myelination even into adolescence. Myelination is the coating of neurons in myelin in order to reduce interference and enhance efficiency of neural function. These continued developments in the adolescent brain allow the adolescent to learn and adapt to his or her environment quickly, and eventually these changes will result in more efficient functioning of the PFC and greater impulse control. During the period of adolescence, however, the actual acts of myelination and synaptic pruning cost the developing brain resources that could be applied to utilizing the PFC.

However, the developments of the adolescent brain are not without some evolutionary benefits. For the adolescent, this is a time of concentrated adaptation and learning about the environment, when the lessening of inhibition brought about in part by changes in the brain can aid the adolescent in learning about environments that are different than that in which he or she grew up. The propensity for sensation seeking during adolescence may foster new and varied life experience. The rapid, unplanned nature of impulsive thinking and sensation seeking may help the adolescent find novel solutions to problems. The inclination toward sensation seeking and urgent, unplanned responses could also play a role in taking the adolescent away from his or her original environment, thus diversifying the gene pool. These examples, though they include behaviors that could be considered impulsive in some contexts, are not maladaptive from an evolutionary perspective and therefore would not be considered 'impulsive.'

While there have been evolutionary benefits from the neural developments that take place during adolescence, there are also great risks in current society. For example, if an adolescent experiments with drugs or alcohol during this delicate stage of development, PFC development could be altered in such a way as to make the adolescent more susceptible to addiction later in life. That is, the adolescent, with already reduced executive function, is at increased risk of initiating use of drugs or alcohol and thereby changing his or her brain to favor automatic, immediate rewards.

In addition to the physical changes taking place in the brain, the neurotransmitters, DA and 5-HT, play an influential role in adolescent impulsive behavior. The DA and 5-HT systems mature at different times with the 5-HT system, like the PFC, maturing later. The inhibitory influence of 5-HT and the PFC is proportionately less potent than the much stronger, promotivational DA systems. The DA system is at its most active during the time of adolescence. There is also an increased risk for addiction during adolescence, as the DA system is liable to pharmacological sensitization, meaning that the adolescent and subsequent adult would be more sensitive to changes in the DA system than one who had not experimented with addictive drugs.

In summary, key regions of the brain related to self-control are not yet fully developed during adolescence, which contributes to impulsive behavior throughout this period of life. There may be certain advantages to these adolescent developments, but there are also associated risks like experimentation with drug use. These high-risk behaviors may lead to long-term consequences and vulnerabilities that extend well beyond adolescence.

Environmental Aspects of Impulsivity

In conjunction with biological changes, the adolescent also experiences numerous environmental changes. During this age, there are many occasions for teens to become more socially independent, encounter beliefs different from those of childhood and their parents, and establish an identity that is more complex and abstract than previously considered. These new experiences require a lot of an adolescent in terms of decision-making, and may in-and-of-themselves serve to increase impulsive behavior. More specifically, many adolescents may not adequately consider the ramifications of their actions in new situations because of a lack of relevant experience, even if they understand that there may be negative outcomes associated with their actions.

In terms of increased independence during adolescence, one factor stands out: the ability to drive a motor vehicle. Obtaining a driver's license allows teens to leave their parents' house more easily, spend more time with friends, and make independent decisions that affect their well-being. This change also adds more responsibility to the teen's life. Not only is the teen in control of a moving vehicle, but he or she has to make decisions about how, where, and with whom to spend his or her time. This greater degree of responsibility also extends into other areas of the adolescent's life. For example, he or she enters high school and has to consider what comes next – college, career, the military, or any one of a large number of choices.

Greater independence also allows the teen to encounter beliefs and experiences separate from his or her parents. The time adolescents spend with their families drop sharply during this age, and the relationships with their parents become more ambivalent. Parents are a source of security for adolescents, but they are also sources of conflict, as the adolescent is trying to reconcile his or her emerging autonomy with his or her parents' values The increasing social distance and ambivalence toward parents increases the risk that the adolescent will lose some of the support and guidance provided by parents in childhood.

The adolescent also has an awareness and drive to understand and define himself or herself. During this developmental period, the adolescent's identity becomes more complex and abstract. Adolescents are better able to integrate contradictions into their identity and understand many more aspects to concepts or situations. They also value more abstract, trait-focused descriptors when describing themselves and use less of the concrete descriptions characteristic of childhood (i.e., adolescents will describe themselves as 'honest' or 'smart,' while younger children use statements like "I have a brother named John and I live in Columbus, Ohio"). This new consideration of identity leads adolescents to be more self-conscious not only of what they think of themselves, but also others' opinions of who they are becoming.

Adolescent Impulsivity: Opportunities and Vulnerabilities

As described earlier, there is an increase in certain types of impulsive behavior that are concurrent with the neurological, hormonal, and environmental changes that occur during adolescence. In particular, there is an increase in sensation-seeking and risk taking. The adolescent is driven to pursue novel, stimulating, and sometimes dangerous activities. There is a strong link between sensation seeking and pubertal development. An increase in delay-discounting, the preference for smaller, immediate rewards over larger, delayed ones, also takes place during this time. Many younger adolescents favor the more immediate rewards; however, as they age into later adolescence, teens increasingly tend to choose the larger, delayed rewards. This change correlates with development of the PFC discussed in the previous sections.

There are positive and negative aspects associated with increased impulsivity in adolescents. For example, as mentioned earlier, natural rewards release DA into the NAc of the brain. If an adolescent perceives winning a competition (academic, athletic, or otherwise) as a reward, the reward centers may provide an extra incentive. In that way, the reward drive of the NAc can push the adolescent to achieve greater and greater natural rewards. Similarly, sensation seeking can give the adolescent the drive and opportunity to have many new experiences and take positive risks Risk taking allows the adolescent to develop skills that he or she might not have otherwise attempted had there been greater concern about the risk of failure, and it can help adolescents understand and cope with such failure when their efforts prove unsuccessful. It allows the adolescent to have experiences outside that of his or her normal life and family, and helps him or her explore and build a more varied identity. The successful resolution of risks can help bolster the adolescent's self-esteem and contribute to a positive self-image. Failures, however, can lead to a negative self-image, as well as many other problems.

On the flip side, the drive toward impulsive choice, risk taking, and sensation seeking also poses many dangers for adolescents. For example, motor vehicle accidents are the leading cause of death for North American teenagers. While sensation seeking and risk taking in the situations mentioned previously can be positive and constructive, those same behaviors behind the wheel of a car can prove deadly. The top four causes of death for US residents of all ages are heart disease, cancer, stroke, and chronic lower respiratory diseases. Cigarette smoking can significantly increase the risk of all of these conditions, and up to 90% of adults who smoke cigarettes initiate the habit during adolescence. From earlier discussion, an adolescent might experiment with smoking for a number of reasons: It is a new experience; valuing the short-term, pleasurable feeling of tobacco use; being socially accepted by his or her peers; and other reasons. The adolescent's tendency toward impulsive choice can value these short-term, immediate rewards over larger, delayed rewards such as better health in adolescence and adulthood, freedom from addiction, and money savings. Similarly, teen suicide is the third leading cause of death for US adolescents, and impulsivity, described earlier by the ISRI as a "predisposition toward rapid, unplanned reactions to internal or external stimuli without regard to the negative consequences of these reactions," would seem to be relevant to this problem. Research has demonstrated that impulsive choice, interacting with depression, and other mood disorders, place some adolescents at high risk for suicide. Impulsive choice and sensation seeking also play a role in other adolescent health concerns such as drug and alcohol use and unprotected sex.

Reducing the Effects of Impulsivity with Treatment

As described previously, the behaviors associated with impulsivity can provide developmental, social, and evolutionary advantages to the adolescent. Behaviors like sensation seeking, delay discounting, and reward seeking serve developmental purposes and are part of normal developmental change. However, when the impulsive behaviors are coupled with situations in which an adolescent has access to health-compromising opportunities (such as drugs, alcohol, or cigarettes), or the tendency toward impulsive behaviors is strong enough to be maladaptive otherwise, then certain actions can be taken to temper the unwanted effects of impulsivity.

Computer programs developed to help victims of traumatic brain injury recover better brain functioning have recently been shown to reduce certain types of impulsivity. These programs, called cognitive rehabilitation programs, help to strengthen the user's PFC through the repetition of tasks that involve memorization, recall, and categorization. As related to impulsive behavior, it is believed that the enhancement of executive functioning through strengthening of the PFC increases the participant's inhibitory ability. This is especially helpful in adolescents, where not only are the motivational, proreward drives stronger than the inhibitory drives, but there is a high degree of brain plasticity. As discussed previously, environmental influences play a large role in synaptic pruning throughout adolescence, with those areas the adolescent utilizes most receiving the most attention. It is likely that adolescents undergoing cognitive rehabilitation programs will experience a strengthening of the PFC as well as more long-lasting benefits due to stimulation of this area during this important developmental period.

Medication has also been shown to reduce certain forms of impulsivity. Though it may initially seem counterintuitive, stimulants are often used as a treatment for attention deficit/hyperactivity disorder (AD/HD) – which is characterized by high levels of impulsivity as a core feature of the diagnosis. Stimulants, such as Ritalin and methylphenidate, improve PFC functioning and, as a result, reduce behavioral disinhibition and also choice preference for smaller, immediate rewards at the expense of larger, delayed rewards. Such an approach to reducing extreme impulsive behavior may be well suited for situations in which a quick solution is required.

Knowledge of impulsivity and the still developing adolescent brain can also be useful in drug and alcohol treatment programs designed for use with adolescents. One such example of a treatment that may be especially effective for adolescents is contingency management (CM). CM programs use positive reinforcement to encourage behavior change. For example, patients are rewarded for appropriate changes in behavior using tangible reinforcers such as money, privileges, and vouchers to be exchanged for purchase items. In the case of substance use, these natural rewards offered by the CM program are meant to be stronger and more salient in terms of controlling behavior than those rewards gained from the use of drugs or alcohol. The longer the participant remains abstinent, the more rewards he or she receives, as prolonged abstinence is desired. Rather than attempting to reduce impulsivity, CM takes over the reward drive and attempts to use it for positive change.

Conclusions

In this article, we discussed the complex concept of adolescent impulsivity. There is no widely accepted definition for the term, and we chose a more inclusive approach, bringing behaviors like sensation seeking, impulsive decision-making, disinhibition, and inattention under the term of impulsivity. We also discussed the ways in which people measure these behaviors – chiefly through self-report and laboratory-behavioral measures. Certain brain systems are involved with different aspects of impulsivity, with the prefrontal cortex having the responsibility for inhibition and impulse control, and certain areas of the limbic system, like the Nac, contributing to sensation and reward-seeking drives. We also discussed the roles certain neurotransmitters play in impulsivity, with dopamine contributing to impulsive behavior and serotonin having an inhibitory role. Biologically, the adolescent brain is susceptible to impulsive behaviors due to the development taking place in the PFC, making it relatively weaker when compared to the developed, DA innervated Nac. Along with biological changes, there are many social changes taking place in the life of the adolescent. Greater independence and self-awareness along with greater levels of impulsive choice and sensation-seeking make this a period wrought with both opportunities for growth and vulnerabilities for development. Finally, we discussed some ways to temper impulsive behavior as well as use reward sensitivity for positive behavior change. Impulsivity is a concept made up of many different behaviors. As we have discussed, behaviors that might be considered impulsive in certain contexts can be highly adaptive in other settings. Therefore, the study and understanding of impulsive behavior during adolescence should be informative for parents, administrators, or anyone else working with adolescents.

See also: Risk-Taking Behavior.

Further Reading

Chambers RA and Potenza MN (2003) Neurodevelopment, impulsivity, and adolescent gambling. *Journal of Gambling Studies* 19(1): 53–84.

Crews FT and Boettiger CA (2009) Impulsivity, frontal lobes and risk for addiction. *Pharmacology, Biochemistry and Behavior* 93(3): 237–247.

d'Acremont M and Van der Linden M (2005) Adolescent impulsivity: Findings from a community sample. *Journal of Youth and Adolescence* 34(5): 427–435.

Evenden J (1999) Impulsivity: A discussion of clinical and experimental findings. *Journal of Psychopharmacology* 13(2): 180–192.

Evenden JL (1999) Varieties of impulsivity. *Psychopharmacology* 146(4): 348–361.

McClure SM, Laibson DI, Loewenstein G, and Cohen JD (2004) Separate neural systems value immediate and delayed monetary rewards. *Science* 306(5695): 503–507.

Reynolds B, Penfold RB, and Patak M (2008) Dimensions of impulsive behavior in adolescents: Laboratory behavioral assessments. *Experimental and Clinical Psychopharmacology* 16(2): 124–131.

Steinberg L, Albert D, Cauffman E, Banich M, Graham S, and Woolard J (2008) Age differences in sensation seeking and impulsivity as indexed by behavior and self-report: Evidence for a dual systems model. *Developmental Psychology* 44(6): 1764–1778.

Steinberg L, Graham S, O'Brien L, Woolard J, Cauffman E, and Banich M (2009) Age differences in future orientation and delay discounting. *Child Development* 80(1): 28–44.

Whiteside SP and Lynam DR (2001) The five factor model and impulsivity: Using a structural model of personality to understand impulsivity. *Personality and Individual Differences* 30(4): 669–689.

Intellectual Disabilities (Mental Retardation)

M H Fisher, University of Massachusetts Boston, Boston, MA, USA
M M Griffin and R M Hodapp, Vanderbilt University, Nashville, TN, USA

Glossary

Dual diagnosis: Comorbidity of intellectual disability and mental health disorder in an individual.
Etiology: The cause of intellectual disabilities, including organic and undifferentiated.
Inclusive education: Placement in the general education classroom with individualized supports and accommodations.
Intellectual disability: Significantly subaverage intellectual functioning which leads to impairments in adaptive behavior, all of which are first manifested during childhood.
Psychopathology: Behaviors symptomatic of mental illness or psychological impairment.

Introduction

Just as all children experience adolescence as the transitional phase to adulthood, so too do children with intellectual disabilities (ID). They experience those same physical, mental, and social changes that characterize adolescence for all other children. Yet for individuals with ID, this transition also presents some unique challenges and issues. Thus, legal responsibilities generally conferred during adolescence (e.g., driver's license) may not be attained by individuals with ID, whereas other legal concerns apply only for (some) adolescents with ID and their families (e.g., establishing conservatorship).

To address issues encountered by adolescents with ID, we first discuss the definition, different levels of functioning, and the various causes of ID. In the second section, we address social concerns that arise during adolescence, including issues related to friendships, social vulnerability and exploitation, and sexuality. We then summarize the legal issues that especially pertain to adolescents and young adults with ID, as well as their school and postschool experiences. We next examine families of these individuals, before describing mental health concerns related to adolescents with ID. Throughout the article, we describe intervention options and emphasize that adolescents and young adults with ID have experiences that are both similar to and divergent from those attained by their same-aged peers.

The experiences of adolescents with ID do differ in some ways from one culture or country to another. However, because the majority of the work in this subfield has been done by Western researchers, this article focuses primarily on the experiences of adolescents in Western countries (e.g., United States, Great Britain).

Diagnosing and Classifying Adolescents with Intellectual Disabilities

This section addresses the definition of ID, as well as two ways to differentiate individuals within the overall population. Each issue will become important as we proceed to examine different issues of adolescents with ID.

Definition

Both the 'old' (DSM-IV-TR) and the 'new' (DSM-V) versions of the *Diagnostic and Statistical Manual of Mental Disorders* describe ID as subaverage intellectual functioning that is associated with or results in impairments in adaptive behavior, with onset during childhood or adolescence. The first criterion is an IQ score of 70 or below on an individually administered test. Second, individuals must exhibit concurrent impairments in performing age-appropriate adaptive behaviors (e.g., daily living skills, socialization). Third, these characteristics must be present before the individual is 18 years of age.

Although this three-pronged definition is generally accepted, professionals continue to debate the most appropriate way to operationalize and emphasize each criterion. For example, the American Association on Intellectual and Developmental Disabilities (AAIDD) deemphasizes the significance of IQ scores. Arguments also relate to the cut-off score of IQ 70, suggesting that there are few differences in functioning between individuals slightly below versus slightly above this arbitrary number. Further, AAIDD highlights the role of adaptive behavior in the definition of ID, even as debate continues as to the specific behaviors that constitute such behavior, the correct number of adaptive domains, and how one best measures these domains. Concerns also exist regarding the relation between adaptive and intellectual functioning and the potentially limited opportunities that certain individuals have to develop adaptive skills.

Levels of Functioning

Historically, professionals have classified individuals according to their level of impairment. These categories correspond to a range of IQ scores, including mild (IQ = 55–70), moderate (40–54), severe (20–25 to 40), and profound (below 20–25) impairment.

Alternatively, AAIDD has reframed this classification, focusing not on IQ scores per se, but on the intensity of support needed by each individual. Individuals with ID are classified based on whether they need intermittent, limited, extensive, or pervasive support. These classification systems describe the variety that exists in the functioning levels among different individuals.

 doi:10.1016/B978-0-12-373915-5.00025-5

Etiology

Similarly varied are the etiologies, or causes, of ID. Traditionally, professionals have categorized the causes of ID into two groups, undifferentiated and organic. Undifferentiated ID – also called 'cultural–familial' or 'sociocultural–familial' ID – refers to those individuals for whom the cause of the disability is unknown. Hypothesized causes include polygenetic inheritance, environmental deprivation, undetected organic cause(s), or some combination of these factors. In contrast, organic ID refers to individuals for whom a clear, organic cause of the disability has been identified. These include hundreds of causes that can occur pre-, peri-, or postnatally. Prenatal causes include over 1000 genetic disorders, as well as fetal alcohol syndrome (FAS) and all accidents in utero. Perinatal causes include prematurity, anoxia, and other birth-related complications. Postnatal causes include both sickness (e.g., meningitis) and accidents (e.g., head trauma).

Over the past few decades, much progress has been made in identifying behavioral characteristics of most persons with specific organic conditions, most notably, different genetic ID conditions. We now appreciate, for example, that persons with Williams syndrome show sociability – even hypersociability – and language strengths, even as other areas (e.g., visual-spatial skills) are markedly delayed. Similarly, individuals with Prader–Willi syndrome usually show marked hyperphagia (i.e., excessive overeating) and a variety of behavior problems (tantrums, obsessions–compulsions). Such behavioral characteristics – which can relate to cognitive, linguistic, personality, adaptive, or maladaptive functioning – greatly influence these individuals' experiences as they progress through adolescence.

Social Concerns Related to Adolescents with ID

Although adolescence can cause social difficulties for all individuals, adolescents with ID may face additional challenges concerning friendships, social exploitation and abuse, and handling their developing sexuality.

Friendships

As they age, individuals with ID find it increasingly difficult to make and maintain friendships. Despite this difficulty, adolescents with ID report having reciprocal friendships with classmates, but these friendships differ qualitatively from those of individuals without disabilities. Compared to friendships of other adolescents, friendships for those with ID tend to be less stable, more prone to conflict, and often involve fewer intimate disclosures. When one individual has a disability and the other does not, an asymmetrical, hierarchical pattern of role distribution often develops. That is, the individual without disabilities becomes the leader, the individual with ID the follower. These friendships also tend to display less mutual engagement and responsiveness.

Part of the problem may be that adolescents with ID differ in their views of what constitutes friendship. To them, a friend is a person who provides help with school-related activities such as tutoring or school guidance. To adolescents without ID, in contrast, friends are those with whom they can share secrets and thoughts, and create a certain intimacy. Students with ID thus seem less likely to consider the emotional aspects of friendships and are more likely to emphasize help and mutual entertainment. Adolescents with ID are more likely to interact with friends at school, those without disabilities more often at home.

Adolescents with ID may also have trouble maintaining friendships due to difficulties in social competence. For example, adolescents with ID may not be as adept as their peers at reading nonverbal social cues (e.g., cues for ending a conversation). Furthermore, their interests may differ: while other adolescents are thinking of gaining independence from their parents and going to college, adolescents with ID often have few plans for moving away from home. Finally, their interests may not be age-appropriate, as they may still be more interested in watching 'children's' TV shows and going on outings with adults, rather than engaging in more age-appropriate hobbies with same-aged peers.

Compared to their same-aged peers without ID, then, adolescents with ID generally have fewer friends, and their friendships are often less intimate, less empathetic, and more often with same-sex relatives. With fewer peer contacts outside of school hours, most socialization of adolescents with ID occurs only while at school. Finally, compared to peers without disabilities, these adolescents more often experience social rejection. However, there are programs that address this issue directly and effectively; Best Buddies is one such example. Best Buddies is a nonprofit organization whose mission is, in part, to foster one-to-one friendships between people with intellectual and developmental disabilities and their typical peers.

Social Vulnerability and Bullying

As implied previously, adolescents with ID are more often socially vulnerable, a situation which sometimes results in social victimization and bullying. Research has shown that students with ID are at a higher risk for bullying than students without ID. High rates of bullying among individuals with ID have also been reported internationally, with studies being conducted in the United Kingdom, Australia, and Israel. Such victimization comes about for several reasons. First, adolescents with ID are often perceived to be easy targets. In several studies, these students report that they can better make friends if they engage in 'conformist' behavior, in giving things to others, and in performing services for potential 'friends.' With smaller networks of friends, individuals with ID have fewer peers to protect them from the poor intentions of others.

Other personal characteristics also predispose adolescents with ID (compared to other adolescents) to be bullied. Heightened risks relate to low self-esteem, a tendency to look toward others for guidance, and lessened abilities to realize that potentially dangerous situations are developing. Poor social skills are also likely to cause children with ID to be ostracized by other peers. Furthermore, individuals with more severe disabilities are likely to have motor skills deficits, or physical or health impairments which may make them targets for bullies who see them as weaker victims. Students with ID who are picked on are also often reported to have co-occurring behavior problems.

Intervention options

To intervene effectively, the excessive rates of bullying experienced by adolescents with disabilities must first be recognized.

But studies find that parents and teachers significantly underestimate the amount of bullying experienced by students with ID while at school. Although many schools have now adopted 'zero tolerance' programs against bullying, specific procedures may be needed to stop the bullying of individuals with disabilities. By including adolescents with ID in regular education classrooms, these students may gain protection from bullies, especially if students with ID can form closer relationships to peers without disabilities. Individuals without disabilities will also come to know their peers with ID.

Adolescents with disabilities can also benefit from training in social skills and assertiveness. Such programs should fulfill two roles. First, they should encourage adolescents with ID to disclose any experience of abuse or victimization, including formal and informal ways to deal with the teen's complaints. Second, such programs should include preventative measures, designed to empower adolescents with ID to resist abuse and peer victimization. Programs such as the 'decision-making curriculum' can teach adolescents to be assertive and resist coercion. By helping participants to become aware that they are being abused and can stop the abuse, these programs also empower students with ID.

Abuse

At all ages, individuals with ID are at increased risks of experiencing abuse. In addition (and compared to persons without disabilities), those with ID are at increased risk of experiencing multiple forms of abuse (not just one type), more instances of abuse (not just one occurrence), and abuse by multiple perpetrators (not just one person). While among other children the risks of abuse decrease with increasing chronological age, rates of abuse for children with ID either remain the same or increase as they get older. Further, while younger children usually experience abuse within the home, abuse among adolescents with ID more often occurs in the individual's social environment by such perpetrators as neighbors, school personnel, or the adolescent's or family's friends. Typically, the adolescent with ID knows the perpetrator. Adolescents with ID have been found to be most at risk of experiencing physical, sexual, and emotional abuse.

Risks of experiencing abuse also relate to the adolescent's level of functioning. Although seemingly counterintuitive, higher rates of abuse occur among adolescents with lesser degrees of disability. Thus, compared to those with severe to profound ID, adolescents with mild ID are at greater risk of abuse.

Given the retrospective nature of most studies, it remains difficult to determine if the child's disability was a cause or consequence of the abuse. Compared to those without disabilities, for example, individuals with ID are 3.8 times more likely to experience physical abuse. But did the maltreatment cause the individual's ID or was maltreatment partially a result of the individual's already existing ID? Similarly, individuals with behavior disorders are 7.3 times more likely to experience physical abuse; again, we do not know whether the behavior disorder is a result of years of maltreatment, or if maltreatment is a response to the child's behavior problems.

Finally, etiology may matter, as adolescents with certain disabilities seem more at risk than others. Due to their tantrums, obsessions–compulsions, and other severe behavior problems, for example, adolescents with Prader–Willi syndrome may be at greater risk of experiencing physical abuse at the hands of caregivers. Alternatively, young adults with Williams syndrome are often indiscriminately friendly, even toward total strangers. Such social disinhibition might greatly increase the risk of sexual abuse, especially among females.

Physical abuse

Compared to those without disabilities, adolescents with ID are also more likely to experience physical abuse. Most often, such abuse involves threats of abuse, theft, and being forced to do something against their will; less frequently as actual attacks against the person. Adolescents with ID (vs. those without) are also more likely to experience repeated abuse, and males with ID are more likely to be physically abused than females.

Sexual abuse

While both male and female adolescents with ID are (compared to adolescents without disabilities) at increased risk of experiencing sexual abuse, girls with ID are more often reported as victims. Further, adolescent girls with ID more often experience severe forms of sexual abuse (e.g., penetration), whereas adolescent boys with ID experience less severe forms of sexual abuse.

Adolescent girls with ID are also at greater risk of experiencing sexual abuse than are girls without disabilities. Compared to girls without ID, adolescent girls with ID are found to report higher incidences of sexual harassment, unwanted sexual touching, and being forced to touch someone sexually. The perpetrator of the abuse also differs. Whereas friends more often abuse girls without disabilities, girls with ID more likely report abuse by their friends and service providers, family acquaintances, and other adults who are known to them.

Going beyond the risk factors faced by all adolescent girls, adolescent females with ID are also at risk because they lack sexual knowledge and sex education. In addition, many adolescent girls with ID have experienced a lifelong physical and emotional dependence on adult caretakers, thus leading to compliance and an inability to discern whether certain behaviors are abusive or not. Individuals with impaired verbal abilities are often sought as targets, as the perpetrator assumes that the individual will be unable to report abusive incidents. Finally, the risks of sexual abuse among these adolescents more generally are related to cultural, community, and familial responses to ID. As individuals with disabilities are often considered to be asexual or incapable of sexual expression, many adolescents are punished for healthy sexual expression (e.g., parents seek to prohibit masturbation) and are often denied appropriate sexual education. Such attitudes lead adolescents with ID to have inadequate knowledge about sexuality, sexual abuse, and self-protection skills. Studies show, for instance, that while some individuals with mild ID can recognize inappropriate touching, they are often unable to report what they would do if they were faced with an abusive situation. These individuals thus lack the necessary self-protection skills to avoid sexual abuse.

Sexuality

Similar to peers without disabilities, adolescents with disabilities have sex drives and sexual interests, and are just as likely to experiment with sexuality. Consequently, adolescents with ID need to learn about appropriate sexual behavior, including the appropriateness of behaviors in certain situations, and what is and is not acceptable touching. Unfortunately, adolescents with ID are rarely included in sexual education programs.

Aside from experiencing new sexual feelings, adolescents with ID have the added challenge of feeling comfortable with bodies that may not be amenable to the idealized body image. This unsatisfactory body image could lead to lowered self-esteem and doubts involving attractiveness to partners, self-sufficiency, and the ability to reproduce and be a good parent.

While many are concerned about an individual with ID's ability to parent, this is a rite of passage that many experience. Today, concerns related to the heritability of ID and competence in parenting are addressed when considering the reproductive choices of adolescents and adults with ID. Researchers estimate that about a quarter of children whose parents have ID will themselves inherit ID. Additionally, for those women with ID who have children, some are competent mothers, and some are not–mirroring mothers without disabilities in the general population. Of particular challenge to parents with ID are such skills as adequately monitoring their children, and adapting to the host of new or unanticipated situations that parenting inevitably presents. Fortunately, parents with ID can become effective parents, through the help of a supportive friend without ID and through a variety of behaviorally oriented programs that teach parenting skills. Further research is needed, however, to increase maintenance and generalization from these training programs.

Intervention options

Adolescents with ID should be provided with appropriate sex education. Compared to sex education for teens without disabilities, however, programs should be tailored to meet the comprehension needs of adolescents with ID. Programs should start with basic information (e.g., naming body parts) and teach about developmental changes experienced during adolescence. These courses should also extend to comprehensive sexual health education, including information about contraception, sexually transmitted diseases, and pregnancy.

Finally, adolescents with ID need to be educated about birth control options. For those with ID, barrier contraception may not be the best choice, as motivation to use this method may be limited. Similarly, oral contraceptives may also not be optimal, as adolescents with ID may experience side effects different from those without ID. Consequently, the most popular contraceptive method for women with ID is depot-medroxy-progesterone acetate. Finally, while sterilization of youth with ID remains a controversial, complex topic, many parents and caregivers still make this choice today.

Transition Issues Concerning Adolescents with ID

Although for many adolescents the transition from childhood to adulthood is stressful, for those with ID, the transition to adult life presents unique challenges. This section addresses various aspects of transition, including relevant legal issues, schooling, and behavioral interventions. We also discuss critical adult outcomes for adolescents in transition: employment, postsecondary education, and residential options.

Legislation and Other Legal Issues Relevant to Adolescents with ID

Several legal issues directly affect the ways in which adolescents with ID participate in school, work, and community environments. This section addresses legislation that applies to individuals with ID, issues relevant to adolescents, and concerns specific to adolescents with ID and their families.

Individuals with Disabilities Education Act

Of all the legislations affecting the rights of young adults with ID, the Individuals with Disabilities Education Improvement Act (IDEIA, 2004) is arguably the most critical. IDEIA includes regulations regarding the education of students with disabilities from birth through age 21, as well as certain provisions that specifically apply to adolescents. Under this legislation, students with disabilities are entitled to a free appropriate public education provided in settings with typical peers (to the maximum extent appropriate). Under IDEIA, each student with a disability is required to have an Individualized Education Program (IEP), a plan that describes the instruction and related services necessary to meet the student's needs. The team that develops this plan should be composed of involved educators, service providers, and parents. Also, students are encouraged to participate as appropriate. An IEP should include the student's present level of performance, measurable goals, and the specific plan to meet those goals.

IDEIA also includes certain provisions that apply to adolescents who are preparing to transition from school to adult life. These transition services are a coordinated set of activities for a young adult with a disability. Such services focus on improving the student's academic and functional skills and facilitate the transition to postschool activities (e.g., postsecondary education). Just as other school-provided instruction and services should be individualized for each student, transition services should be tailored to each student's particular strengths, needs, and preferences.

To that end, IDEIA mandates that each student's IEP must include a plan to provide the appropriate transition services before the student becomes 16 years old. This plan must include measurable goals related to various areas of adult life (e.g., employment). It must also include the services needed to support the student in meeting these goals (e.g., vocational training). Additionally, transition plans are most effective if they include the agencies that will support students after transitioning out of school (e.g., the state Vocational Rehabilitation agency). Finally, transition plans must document that students have been informed of their right to make decisions regarding their IEPs a year before reaching the age of majority (18 years), when they are legally considered adults.

Americans with Disabilities Act

Like IDEIA, the Americans with Disabilities Act (ADA) also pertains to individuals with ID, and is particularly relevant in adolescence because it addresses discrimination within the workplace. The ADA prohibits discrimination against people with disabilities and requires that employers make reasonable accommodations for qualified job applicants or employees. However, employers are not required to make accommodations that would pose an unreasonable expense or hardship. In this way, ADA differs from IDEIA, which requires schools to provide accommodations that are identified as necessary in the student's IEP, regardless of cost.

Legal issues related to independence and adulthood

Many issues relate to the rights and responsibilities typically conferred at milestones in adolescence. For example, adolescents are eligible to obtain a driver's license at age 16; however, young adults with ID rarely obtain licenses. Similarly, new rights and responsibilities typically arise at the age of majority; however, for adolescents with ID, some of these rights and responsibilities may be assumed by a conservator.

Learning to drive and travel independently

For adolescents in the United States, learning to drive is a rite of passage. For most young adults with ID, however, the inability to pass the written test precludes them from obtaining a license. Although some training programs now successfully prepare adolescents with ID for the written test, most do not access this training and do not obtain a driver's license. Although some find alternatives (e.g., biking, public transportation), the independent travel of adolescents with ID (vs. peers without ID) is generally much more restricted.

School Experiences of Adolescents with ID

Unlike the high school experiences of typical students, students with ID are influenced greatly by provisions in IDEIA. Their instruction and classroom placement is guided by their IEPs, and students with ID may continue their secondary schooling through age 21. Also unlike other adolescents, most students with ID do not receive a general education diploma; the National Center on Educational Statistics (NCES) reports that, among all disability categories, students with ID received the lowest percentage of regular high school diploma, with a 37% total. Depending on the state, students with ID may receive Special Education diplomas or certificates of attendance. Young adults with ID who attend high school past age 18 may continue to learn in a traditional classroom environment; however, many also participate in community-based training. Community-based classrooms are located throughout the local community and are age-appropriate settings where students can learn practical employment skills.

In addition to instruction in academic and employment skills, adolescents with ID also often receive training in other areas. For example, students with maladaptive behaviors will need training to minimize and replace them with more appropriate behaviors. Students may also need to learn skills for independent living, typical social interactions, and self-determined behavior.

Teaching adaptive behaviors

Many adolescents with ID need to be taught adaptive behaviors, those skills necessary to function safely and independently (e.g., money handling). Several assessments have been developed to determine an individual's level of adaptive behavior. For example, the Vineland Adaptive Behavior Scale assesses adaptive skills across the domains of communication, daily living skills, and socialization. Although adolescents with ID all have their individual strengths and limitations, most will need instruction in one or more adaptive behaviors. Behavior Skills Training (BST) is one effective way of teaching such behaviors. BST involves direct instruction on the target skill, modeling the skill, role-playing the skill with the student, and providing feedback on the student's performance.

Teachers and caretakers can help students maintain these behaviors over time in a variety of ways. They can develop prompts for the student (e.g., a picture schedule), and teach the student to use these tools to guide their behavior. They can also teach students to request help from natural supports in the environment (e.g., a classmate). For example, if students cannot determine which behaviors are needed to successfully buy lunch in the cafeteria, they could ask a nearby classmate for help. Students can also learn self-management skills to help maintain adaptive behaviors. For instance, students who have trouble remembering what they need to bring to school could use a checklist to remember the necessary materials. Although each student will have individual support needs, these strategies can help students maintain adaptive behaviors they have learned.

Teaching social skills

Just as many adolescents with ID must be taught certain adaptive behaviors, many also need to be taught appropriate social skills. Such skills may be influenced by limited cognitive abilities, limited receptive or expressive communication, maladaptive behaviors, or a combination of these factors. Regardless of the reason, many adolescents with ID do not behave similarly to their typical peers without appropriate modeling of social skills.

Unfortunately, those students with the least developed social skills are often placed in the most segregated classroom settings. While these settings may address the students' academic needs, they generally do not feature typical peers who can model appropriate social behaviors (e.g., initiating a conversation; maintaining eye contact during conversations). Especially for students with less-developed social skills, explicit training may be necessary. These students may also benefit from increased opportunities to interact with typical peers in extracurricular settings or through peer mentoring programs. Social skills training and increased opportunities to interact with typical peers promote the ability of adolescents with ID to make and sustain social connections.

Promoting self-determination

Self-determination involves the capacity of individuals to determine their own actions and make self-directed decisions about their lives. Because many adolescents with ID have not developed this capacity, instruction in self-determination can help these young adults behave in a more self-directed manner. Self-determination interventions generally focus on goal setting, decision-making, problem solving, self-awareness, and self-advocacy.

Transition Outcomes

Although the postschool outcomes have recently expanded for students with ID, many continue to have limited experiences in the community and remain socially isolated. Even compared to students with other disabilities, those with ID are least likely to participate in employment training, to become employed, or to continue their education after high school. Only 52% of young adults with ID in the United States are so engaged.

Employment experiences

Employment has long been considered a primary outcome for young adults with ID. However, according to American Community Survey data (collected by the US Census in 2007), only 36% of people with disabilities ages 16–64 were employed. This contrasts sharply with the 75% rate for this age group among people without disabilities. Furthermore, median salaries among working people with disabilities were just 65% of the salaries earned by people without disabilities. Similarly low levels of employment have been reported in England, with only 17% of people considered working-age were employed. Although historically, adults with ID worked mostly in segregated environments (e.g., sheltered workshops), recent decades have seen a new emphasis on inclusion within the community.

Through school or personal connections, adolescents with ID may access a host of inclusive work-based opportunities. School instruction helps students explore which careers interest them, and students learn job skills in a community-based classroom. Many adolescents with ID gain valuable experience through job-shadowing, or observing someone who is currently employed in a career of interest. Volunteering or interning is also an excellent way for prospective workers to gain experience in an authentic workplace environment. Within the contemporary model of work-based learning, each option can prepare adolescents for paid employment. For those who need support at the workplace, service agencies can also provide assistance from job coaches. For those not requiring this level of support, success can be promoted through accommodations and natural supports within the workplace (i.e., people already present who informally help).

Postsecondary education options

Historically limited to segregated educational settings, students with ID are increasingly attending inclusive postsecondary education (PSE) programs at colleges throughout the country. Whereas previously students with ID would not have had access to inclusive education after exiting high school, over 150 PSE programs now offer this option across the United States. Rather than requiring a regular high school diploma to matriculate, these programs offer alternatives to the conventional college admission process. PSE programs exist in a variety of settings (e.g., community and 4-year colleges) and have different emphases. Some focus on academics, others employment skills, and still others opportunities that include both. Such inclusive PSE programs offer young adults with ID a 'college experience' akin to that of their typical peers.

Supported and independent living

Although living independently constitutes a third hallmark of adult life, many young adults with ID need some support to live away from their parents. While many may not attain full independent living, most can enjoy supported living with the appropriate supports. Services provided by state Vocational Rehabilitation and Developmental Disabilities agencies can support young adults with ID to live on their own or in shared residences.

Issues Related to Families of Adolescents with ID

Families of adolescents with ID are in some ways the same as families of typical adolescents, even as they also encounter challenges that require different knowledge, skills, and supports. Like the parents of most typically developing children, parents of children with ID provide critical, primary support from birth through childhood. By the time individuals with disabilities reach adolescence, family members are 'old pros' at raising a child with special needs. Typically, the support provided by parents begins to taper during adolescence, as young adults become more independent. Adolescents with ID, however, may continue to require higher levels of parental and familial support. As the needs change for these individuals, parents begin to face new and different challenges.

Disability researchers have now begun the important work of studying the experiences of families of individuals with ID. Although a specific subfield has yet to develop, certain findings show how families cope with the adult service system, help their offspring attain age-appropriate milestones, and deal with conservatorship, protection, and other issues.

Adult Service Systems

Once adolescents exit high school, they are no longer entitled to many services they once received under IDEIA. When navigating the adult service system, parents often face long waiting lists and few services that are appropriate for their adolescent's needs. Parents also become responsible for coordinating all of the services their child might receive. As they learn that they will be losing most of the supports they had for years received within the school system, parents realize that they will be assuming primary responsibility for caring for their adult son or daughter.

Parents are often unfamiliar with the adult service world, and often uninformed about post-high-school options. They worry about finding appropriate residential and vocational placements for their offspring, and face financial concerns as they are placed on waiting lists for services. More generally, parents with adolescents with ID experience increased stress as their child reaches the adult years. More interventions are needed that might ease parental stress as their offspring transition from high school into the adult years.

Attaining Age-Appropriate Milestones

Because IDEIA guarantees students with disabilities educational services through age 21, many students with ID remain in public schools through their adolescence. In contrast, typical high school students graduate and either begin working or enroll in college. These are options as well for adolescents with ID, although young adults with ID (vs. those without disabilities) attain their milestones at different ages and often need increased levels of support to reach these goals.

Parents play key roles in facilitating the transition from high school to adult life. Considered as a group, adults with ID are less likely to find regular full-time employment, thus increasing their time at home with unstructured activities and increasing their financial dependence on their parents. For those who do obtain jobs, parents still need to secure and coordinate the additional supports that are needed for job success (e.g., job coaches).

Related issues pertain to where and how adults with ID will live. Although persons with ID are living increasingly longer lives, most adults (about 60%) continue to reside in their parents' home, with few individuals (<10%) living independently without supports. Just as with employment, parents bear the brunt of planning for, coordinating, and achieving supported or independent living arrangements for their offspring.

Conservatorship and Protection

Although typically conferred to young adults at the age of majority, increasing legal rights do not always occur for young adults with ID. For those unable to care for themselves, a conservator may be assigned to manage the individual's care and protection. Appointed by a judge, the conservator provides for the conservatee's basic needs (e.g., food, clothing, shelter), as well as other health care, transportation, recreation, or financial needs. Often for young adults with ID, a parent or other relative will assume the conservator role. This arrangement can, however, prove difficult. Adolescents with ID see their peers achieving autonomy in decision-making, and feel they too should be allowed to make independent decisions. Assuming such rights, however, is hindered by their financial and physical dependence on their caregivers, and the parents' need to protect their child.

Parents and adolescents with ID thus often experience tensions, as their adolescent desires greater independence and autonomy, while parents attempt to protect the adolescent from the perceived dangers of adult life. Worrying about the dangers their child could face, parents are often reluctant to relinquish control. Indeed, parental concerns for their adolescent's safety is a main barrier to allowing young adults with ID to attend postsecondary education, obtain a job, or live independently.

Other Members of the Family

As parents of adolescents with ID assume myriad roles and responsibilities on behalf of their adolescent with ID, other responsibilities may fall to siblings, grandparents, or other extended family members.

Though only a few studies examine adolescent siblings of people with ID, most are doing well, yet they experience some increased depression and anxiety compared to siblings of individuals without disabilities. As siblings transition to the adult years, most report close and positive relationships with their brother/sister with ID. Further, these individuals often consider their sibling with disabilities when making major life choices and transitions. In one study, siblings of individuals with ID took the sibling into account when making decisions related to going to college (64%), dating (41%), and moving away from home (58%). Female siblings, who (compared to male siblings) are most likely to be their brother/sister with ID's future caregiver, are also more likely to marry and have children later in life – and to divorce less often – compared to other, same-aged females in the general population.

Mental Health Concerns Related to Adolescents with ID

The transition to adolescence is a difficult time for many individuals, with and without disabilities. Brain changes that occur during the adolescent years make some individuals more susceptible to a variety of psychiatric conditions. As such, symptoms of several psychiatric disorders are often first manifested during adolescence. Adolescents often become moody and irritable, displaying more mood swings, school problems, and even suicidal thoughts. While the extent to which such brain changes occur in adolescents with ID is unknown, they do experience increases in psychiatric conditions during adolescence.

Dual Diagnosis

Those individuals with ID also diagnosed with a psychiatric disorder are considered to have a 'dual diagnosis.' Compared to individuals without disabilities, individuals with ID display psychiatric disorders or emotional and behavioral problems at higher rates. Unfortunately, prevalence estimates vary greatly in the ID field, as psychiatric conditions among those with ID are often difficult to diagnose or remain undiagnosed. As such, estimates of individuals with ID who have a dual diagnosis range from 10% to 50%. Overall, as many as one-third or more of all people with ID have "significant behavioral, mental, or personality disorders requiring mental health services" (DM-ID, 2007).

The misidentification of mental health conditions in individuals with ID leads to inadequate mental health treatment. Individuals with dual diagnosis often fall through the cracks in service delivery systems, as neither the mental-health nor the developmental-disability service systems assume responsibility for providing treatment, services, and support. Misidentification of mental health disorders can also occur. Three reasons include diagnostic overshadowing, atypical manifestation of the mental illness, and the unavailability of proper assessments to measure symptoms among individuals with ID.

Diagnostic overshadowing

Diagnostic overshadowing occurs when an individual's mental health concerns are attributed to the individual's primary diagnosis of ID rather than to a concurrent psychiatric disorder. For example, if an individual with ID displays symptoms of depression, anxiety, or a behavioral disorder, a professional might simply attribute these behaviors to intellectual disabilities per se, rather than assessing the individual for a psychiatric diagnosis. When the individual's mental health problems are attributed to the person's ID, clinicians then fail to properly identify and treat the mental health conditions.

Diagnostic overshadowing can also occur when a mental health condition is misdiagnosed. Indeed, studies show that clinicians' perceptions of clients with ID affect three areas of diagnostics: (a) *severity* (how severe the symptoms are); (b) *category/diagnosis* (the individual's specific disorder(s)); and (c) *treatment* (how the disorder should be treated). The more severe the symptoms, the more likely a clinician is to provide a mental health diagnosis to an individual with an ID. Unfortunately, the underdiagnosis of mental health conditions often leads to the mistreatment (or nontreatment) of these conditions. This prolongs the suffering of those individuals with ID who have concurrent mental health conditions.

Atypical manifestation of mental illness

Individuals with ID may also sometimes display atypical symptoms – behaviors that do not generally denote a particular psychiatric disorder among adolescents who do not have ID. Some have suggested, for example, that depression among young adults with ID can sometimes be associated with self-injury, aggression, or screaming; these behaviors might be the 'behavioral equivalents' of depression in individuals with ID. Unfortunately, these behaviors are often considered problems that are addressed through behavioral interventions, rather than through psychiatric treatments. Consequently, the individual will not receive the proper treatment. Furthermore, while some maintain that certain psychiatric disorders are more difficult to diagnose in adolescence because of common features of this stage of life (e.g., moodiness, impulsivity), there is no research pertaining to this difficulty among adolescents with ID.

To better address the issue of potential atypical symptoms, the field is now examining age, gender, living status, and etiological causes and correlates of maladaptive behavior in individuals with ID. Some research has found that behavior problems are more closely related to psychiatric disorders when individuals have more severe forms of ID. Further, individuals with certain etiologies display behaviors that are related to certain psychiatric conditions (e.g., autism spectrum disorder in fragile X syndrome, anxiety disorders in Williams syndrome).

Individuals with certain genetic syndromes often show developmental changes in their maladaptive behavior and psychopathology as they get older. Young children with Prader–Willi syndrome are typically described as pleasant, friendly, and affectionate, whereas older individuals often develop temper tantrums, impulsivity, stubbornness, underactivity, fatigue, food-stealing, compulsions, and difficulties with peers. These behaviors could be misattributed to the onset of hyperphagia, rather than to the development of a psychiatric condition. Once they reach adulthood, individuals with PWS also display heightened risks for affective disorder, psychosis, and thought disturbance.

Assessment

A third diagnostic issue concerns the psychiatric classification system itself. Do traditional diagnoses – as described in the DSM and International Classification of Diseases (ICD) diagnostic manuals – apply to adolescents and young adults with ID? Such issues are difficult to resolve, especially as some individuals with ID struggle with expressing abstract thoughts and feelings, as well as reporting specific information about the onset, duration, frequency, and severity of their symptoms. In addition, many diagnoses are based on information gathered during a psychiatric interview with the patient, and professionals have raised concerns about the validity of interview responses given by individuals with ID.

In recent years, professionals have addressed this issue in multiple ways. Some have created alternatives to typical psychiatric interviews, developing assessments specially designed for individuals with ID (e.g., Psychiatric Assessment Schedule for Adults with Developmental Disability). Others have modified the criteria for diagnoses in the DSM-IV-TR and ICD codes, tailoring them for use with individuals with ID. For example, The *Diagnostic Manual-Intellectual Disability: A Textbook of Diagnoses of Mental Disorders in Persons with Intellectual Disability* (DM-ID, 2007) was developed by the National Association for the Dually Diagnosed (NADD) and the American Psychiatric Association (APA) to serve as an adaptation of the DSM-IV-TR to aid in the diagnosis of mental disorders in individuals with ID. This manual provides a description of each disorder and a summary of the DSM-IV-TR diagnostic criteria. It then provides adaptations of the diagnostic criteria to be applied for persons with ID. The DM-ID also provides alternative assessment methods for providing a diagnosis.

Beyond assessment adaptations related to a formal diagnosis, other tools have been developed to assess the behavior of individuals with ID (e.g., Aberrant Behavior Checklist, Reiss Screen, and Developmental Behavior Checklist). Additionally, professionals may conduct a Functional Behavioral Assessment (FBA) to obtain information about specific problem behaviors exhibited by an individual. The FBA can identify patterns in an individual's problem behavior and interventions that might be effective in decreasing this behavior.

Types of Psychopathology

Individuals with ID are at risk for all forms of major mental illness, including mood disorders, anxiety disorders, schizophrenia, attention deficit/hyperactivity disorder (ADHD), and autism spectrum disorders (ASD). The prevalence of these diagnoses varies widely across studies. For example, prevalence rates of depression among all individuals with ID (regardless of age) range from 1% to 30%; anxiety disorder from 1% to 25%; psychotic disorders from 5% to 25%; ADHD from 7% to 21%; and ASD from 2% to 41%.

Although only a few longitudinal studies have been conducted, age may relate to some changes in prevalence rates of mental illness among individuals with ID. First, mental illness has been shown to decrease over the life span among boys with ID (compared to girls) and among individuals with mild ID (compared to those with severe or profound ID). Second, compared to younger individuals with Down syndrome, adolescents (ages of 10–19) may have higher rates of internalizing behaviors (especially withdrawn behaviors). Further, females between the ages of 14 and 19 displayed more internalizing behaviors than males, and children between the ages of 10 and 13 displayed more externalizing behaviors. Finally, compared to when they are younger, individuals with ID are more likely to be diagnosed with depression and emotional disorders during adolescence. More research is needed to understand the nature, prevalence, and correlates of psychopathology throughout the life span of individuals with ID.

Intervention Options

Clearly, mental health issues are important to consider in understanding the behavior and lives of adolescents with ID. Dual diagnosis of adolescents with mental illness and ID presents unique intervention challenges to professionals who work with this population.

Various options are available to treat individuals who are dually diagnosed with ID and mental illness. The first relates to pharmacological treatments. Such treatments are recommended based either on specific symptoms or on the individual's diagnosis. As with all recommendations for medication, professionals should exercise caution in recommending this treatment course for adolescents with ID. Professionals should conduct appropriate medical assessments and consider psychosocial conditions, environmental factors, current medications, history of previous interventions, and family history. Furthermore, formative assessments should take into account critical factors such as dosage levels, the fidelity with which the recommended regimen is being followed, and any side effects of the medication.

Several additional issues should also be noted. First, many mental health professionals have not received adequate training in working with individuals with ID. Additionally, most only work with individuals with ID occasionally. This lack of training and experience could lead to inappropriate prescriptions because professionals may not be aware of which medications or dosages are most appropriate.

For the general population, medication is most effective when paired with other (environmental) interventions; this may also prove the case for individuals with ID. Such interventions include behavioral and cognitive therapies. Recommendation of these interventions should be made following a thorough evaluation of the individual and problem behaviors. To determine the most appropriate interventions, professionals should collect multidisciplinary evaluations across the individual's home, school, and community settings.

Conclusion

Throughout this article, we have argued that adolescents with ID are 'the same and different' from other, typically developing adolescents and young adults. Like all young adults, these individuals are attempting to assume adult roles, to pursue additional educational and job opportunities, and to live on their own and establish their own, independent lives. In contrast to other young adults, however, those with ID more often have difficulties in establishing friendships, being bullied, abused, or taken advantage of, and appropriately expressing their sexuality. Although postschool opportunities and potential job opportunities have expanded exponentially in recent decades, most adults with ID continue to live in their family home and many require extra supports to live more independently or to pursue higher-level work. Families too struggle to foster in their offspring more independent, productive, and meaningful lives, experiencing even more intensely the 'push-and-pull' of giving their offspring independence while protecting them from the many dangers such independence entails. Such issues are further exacerbated by each adolescent's level of functioning, etiology-related behaviors, and mental health concerns. Ultimately, researchers, educators, and clinicians need to better understand adolescents with ID and their families, as we together help these individuals experience challenges that are both unique and universal on their transition from childhood into the adult years.

See also: Adolescent Decision-Making; Autism and Aspergers; Bully/Victim Problems during Adolescence; Developmental Psychopathology; Disabilities, Physical; Peer Influence; Peer Relations; Quantitative Research Methods; School-to-Work Transitions; Transitions to Adulthood.

Further Reading

American Association on Mental Retardation (2002) *Mental Retardation: Definition, Classification, and Systems of Supports*, 10th edn. Washington, DC: Author

Dykens EM (2000) Annotation: Psychopathology in children with intellectual disability. *Child Psychopathology and Psychiatry* 41: 407–418.

Emerson E and Hatton C (2008) *People with Learning Disabilities in England*, CeDR Research Report 2008. Lancaster, UK: Centre for Disability Research.

Fletcher R, Loschen E, Stavrakaki C, and First M (eds.) (2007) *Diagnostic Manual-Intellectual Disability (DM-ID): A Textbook of Diagnosis of Mental Disorders in Persons with Intellectual Disability*. New York: The National Association for the Dually Diagnosed.

Hodapp RM and Dykens EM (2005) Problems of girls and young women with mental retardation (intellectual disabilities). In: Bell DJ, Foster SL, and Mash EJ (eds.) *Handbook of Behavioral and Emotional Problems in Girls*, pp. 239–262. New York, NY: Kluwer Academic/Plenum.

Individuals with Disabilities Education Act of 2004, 20 U.S.C. 1400 *et seq.*

Jopp DA and Keys CB (2001) Diagnostic overshadowing reviewed and reconsidered. *American Journal on Mental Retardation* 106: 416–433.

Khemka I and Hickson L (2006) The role of motivation in the decision making of adolescents with mental retardation. In: Switzky HN (ed.) *International Review of Research in Mental Retardation* 31: 73–115

Murphy NA and Elias ER (2006) Sexuality of children and adolescents with developmental disabilities. *Pediatrics* 18: 398–403.

Rehabilitation Research and Training Center on Disability Statistics and Demographics (StatsRRTC) (2009) *Annual Disability Statistics Compendium: 2009. Rehabilitation Research and Training Center on Disability Demographics and Statistics.* Hunter College, http://www.disabilitycompendium.org.

Rojahn J and Meier LJ (2009) Epidemiology of mental illness and maladaptive behavior in intellectual disabilities. *International Review of Research in Mental Retardation* 38: 239–287.

Taylor JL (2009) The transition out of high school and into adulthood for individuals with autism and their families. *International Review of Research in Mental Retardation* 38: 1–32.

Wagner M, Newman L, Cameto R, and Levine P (2005) *Changes Over Time in the Early Post-secondary Outcomes of Youth with Disabilities. A Report of Findings from the National Longitudinal Transition Study (NLTS) and the National Longitudinal Transition Study-2 (NLTS2).* Menlo Park, CA: SRI International.

Wehmeyer ML, Agran M, Hughes C, Martin JE, Mithaug DE, and Palmer SB (2007) *Promoting Self-determination in Students with Developmental Disabilities.* New York: Guilford.

Relevant Websites

www.aaidd.org – American Association for Intellectual and Developmental Disabilities.

http://idea.ed.gov/ – Individuals with Disabilities Education Act.

http://www.thenadd.org/ – NADD: An association for persons with developmental disorders and mental health needs.

http://nces.ed.gov/ – National Center for Education Statistics, Institute of Education Sciences, U.S. Department of Education.

http://www.thearc.org/ – The Arc of the United States.

Literacy and Reading Behavior

R K Parrila and H Stack-Cutler, University of Alberta, Edmonton, AB, Canada

Glossary

Aliterate: A person who knows how to read but is not inclined to do so.

Emoticon: A symbol or combination of symbols used in a text document to express an emotion or reveal the writer's state of mind.

Functional literacy: Skills needed to allow an individual to find relevant information, to interpret, to analyze, and to synthesize information from different sources, to write clear and coherent prose, and to use their reading skills to acquire knowledge, new competencies, and personal satisfaction from literacy activities.

Health literacy: An individual's ability to read, understand, and use health-care information to make decisions and follow instructions for treatment (reading and consumption skills).

Illiterate: An individual who cannot with understanding read and write a short simple statement on his or her everyday life.

Literacy: The ability to understand and produce written texts to some minimally acceptable standard.

New literacies: The forms of literacy made possible by digital technology developments.

Reading literacy: The ability to understand, use, and reflect on written texts to achieve one's goals, to develop one's knowledge and potential, and to participate effectively in society.

Introduction

In the developing world, the economics of literacy, both national and personal, have drastically changed after the Second World War. The opportunities for economic well-being that were widely available in North America, Japan, and in most European countries for a labor force with very basic literacy skills have all but disappeared. All over the developed and developing world, the fastest growing professions are those with greater than average demands for reading and writing skills, and the fastest declining professions are those with lower than average demands. In the next 10 years, more than two-thirds of all new jobs are expected to require some postsecondary education, with the jobs requiring the most education (and offering the highest pay) growing the fastest in numbers. As a result, the jobs that today's adolescents are going to compete for require better reading and writing skills than ever before in history.

Before leaving school, the adolescents of today must acquire sophisticated literacy and numeracy skills to be successful in the employment market and in their private lives as partners and citizens. In colleges, universities, and work places, they are expected to find and understand complex information from different sources; judge credibility of the source; evaluate relative merit and evidence for different arguments; and to write, write, and write, be it term papers, proposals, memos, contracts, letters to customers, and so on. In their private lives, they make contributions to the social media in writing, their future homes will likely be full of electronics that require programming (and come with dense manuals using both print and graphic information), and more and more of the information they need or desire has to be located on the World Wide Web, which is replete with irrelevant information. Adolescents without the sophisticated literacy skills these activities require will have limited participation options.

It is clear that the literacy skills most in demand are not the basic reading and writing skills that are usually meant in conversations about illiteracy (see below). In most countries, the vast majority of adolescents can read words and simple sentences accurately (see **Figure 1**). Most can also write simple sentences without much trouble. What they need are skills that allow them to find the relevant information;

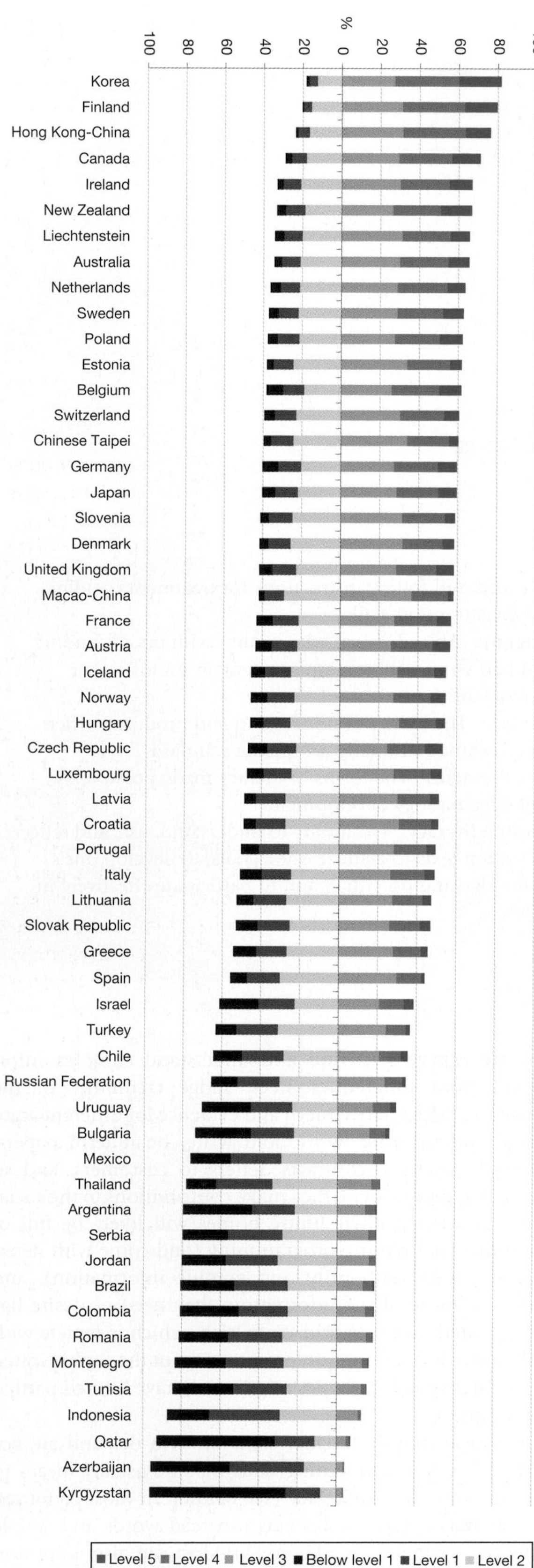

Figure 1 Percentage of children performing at five levels of literacy skills in different countries in PISA (2006) assessment.

interpret, analyze, and synthesize information from different sources; write clear and coherent prose; and use their reading skills to acquire knowledge and new competencies, and perhaps also personal satisfaction from literacy activities. We call these skills *functional literacy* and argue that in most parts of the world, the critical twenty-first century literacy issue is not whether adolescents are literate or illiterate, but whether they have the functional literacy skills expected of them as citizens.

The remainder of this article is divided into four main somewhat independent sections. The first section examines briefly how the concept of literacy has evolved over time. The second section focuses on reading and literacy learning and development in adolescence that make the behaviors possible. The third section takes a global perspective and examines what we know about adolescents' reading and literacy behaviors around the world. We then conclude with a discussion of literacy and reading crisis in developed and developing worlds.

Reading and Literacy

Literacy is a concept claimed and defined differently by a variety of academic fields. Perhaps the most common understanding of literacy is that it is a set of measurable skills – particularly reading and writing skills. In English, it is based on the term literate, as is exemplified by the definition in the *Oxford English Dictionary*: The quality or state of being literate; knowledge of letters; condition in respect to education, especially the ability to read and write.

Traditionally, the English word, literate, meant to be familiar with literature, erudite, well educated. It is, however, the second meaning of literate, one who knows the letters, and the use of literacy as an antonym of illiteracy that has been more the focus over the last 50 years. In this sense, literacy is the ability to understand and produce written texts to some minimally acceptable standard. However, the standards and methods that each country uses to establish that one has the ability to read and write vary widely. In some instances, a yes/no answer to the question 'can you read and write' or 'can you read this sentence' is used as the criteria for establishing literacy rates. In others, attending a school for some number of years suffices to qualify an individual as literate. Still in others, the ability to read a newspaper is the standard of basic literacy skills.

Whatever the definition, historically, substantial benefits have been attached to basic levels of literacy. For example, in some Northern European countries, obtaining a marriage license from the church required that the applicant was able to read the catechism, a simple book about the principles of religion written in question–answer format. Apparently, in twelfth and thirteenth century England, the ability to read a passage from the Bible could entitle a common law defendant to be tried before an ecclesiastical court – a significant benefit given that the sentences in these courts were more lenient than those in secular ones, where hanging was a likely sentence. In both of these examples, the skill level required went beyond knowing the letters, but not always much beyond. This, as well as the juxtaposition with illiteracy, is also reflected in the perhaps first global definition of literacy accepted in the UNESCO's General Conference in 1958:

> (a) A person is literate who can with understanding both read and write a short simple statement on his (her) everyday life. (b) A person is illiterate who cannot with understanding both read and write a short simple statement on his (her) everyday life.

The focus has since shifted to the more complex task of applying the basic skills in relevant ways, or what we called above functional literacy. In 1975, UNESCO suggested that people have functional literacy skills if they can engage in the activities in which literacy is required for effective functioning of their group and community, and can use reading, writing, and calculation for their own and the community's development. A more elaborate definition followed in 2003:

> Literacy is the ability to identify, understand, interpret, create, communicate, and compute using printed and written materials associated with varying contexts. Literacy involves a continuum of learning in enabling individuals to achieve his or her goals, develop his or her knowledge and potentials, and participate fully in the community and wider society. *(Definition of literacy agreed during a June 2003 meeting organized by the UNESCO Institute for Education)*

This latter definition is very similar to the one used in Program for International Student Assessment (PISA) studies we discuss later.

Expansion in Two Dimensions: Depth and Breadth

With expansion from basic to functional literacy skills, there is also a growing agreement that literate competence includes competence with the more specialized intellectual and academic language that provides access to a large variety of texts and communication. Universal education historically focused on basic literacy skills, whereas the more advanced skills were reserved to a selected few, for example, to students in elite lyceums and universities. Opponents of making the advanced skills accessible to all were worried that the schools might succeed in educating people to the point where there would be a surplus of highly literate individuals who then would undermine the existing social hierarchy. Whatever the political justification, in most parts of the world, economic and technological development have resulted in increased demand for all individuals to have advanced literacy skills, making the old concerns absurd at best.

With technological development comes also expansion in the breadth of literacy skills in demand. Adolescents use both traditional text and digital media to communicate and gather information. Texts vary by subject (e.g., language arts, biology, history) and genre (e.g., textbooks, technical manuals, fiction), by complexity of the language used, and by the mode of presentation (e.g., paper, computer screen, or cell phone, with pictures and graphics or without, with interactive features or not, etc.). Literacy definitions that focus only on traditional texts do not capture the full picture of how adolescents produce and use texts today, particularly in the developed world.

One approach to accommodating the changes is to expand the skill sets covered. In the United States, for example, the National Council of Teachers of English and the International Reading Association added 'visually representing' to the list of required competencies. In Scotland, in turn, literacy was defined as the ability to read and write and use numeracy, to handle information, to express ideas and opinions, to make decisions and solve problems, as family members, workers, citizens, and lifelong learners. In this last sense, the term literacy now covers most of the outcomes we would attribute to good education. Similar expanded definitions that talk about dealing with information and communication in general rather than in 'letters' are currently being promoted in many other jurisdictions.

The second approach is to talk about multiple literacies. For example, adolescents use various digital devices in school, at work, and for their own pleasure and learning. This has led to an argument that the definition of literacy should include the ability to use such tools as word processing programs and text messaging. Others, however, have called for new terms to cover these new skill sets, such as computer literacy, multimedia literacy, information literacy, and digital literacy. Sometimes, the term *new literacies* is used to refer to the forms of literacy made possible by digital technology developments. Commonly recognized examples of new literacy skills include those needed for such practices as instant messaging, blogging, participating in online social networking, creating and sharing videos, podcasting, manipulating and sharing images, emailing, digital storytelling, participating in online discussions, conducting and collating online searches, reading and commenting on fan fiction, and processing and evaluating online information, most activities that many adolescents frequently engage in and often are better at than their parents or teachers.

Similarly, skills needed to contribute to and critically consume information in different content areas have led to the widespread use of terms such as scientific literacy, health literacy, technological and technical literacy, and cultural literacy. How much each of these involves reading and writing varies. For example, health literacy is usually used to refer to an individual's ability to read, understand, and use health care information to make decisions and follow instructions for treatment (reading and consumption skills); scientific literacy tends to include understanding as well as being able to contribute in writing; and technological and cultural literacy definitions may have little to do with either reading or writing per se. All of these literacies, however, are functional literacies in that the focus is on using and producing information in daily lives and pursuits, rather than basic literacies as defined previously.

Literacy and Reading Skills in Adolescence

Adolescents develop physically, cognitively, and socially quite rapidly during the teenage years. They take on new roles as employees and romantic partners, experiment and prepare for future adult roles while simultaneously navigating the complex social world, emotional fluctuations, and physical changes of adolescence. All these changes impact the social context of literacy, how adolescents manage the literacy tasks, and what literacy tasks they engage in.

The literacy tasks and requirements also change themselves, both in school and out of school. At school, the texts that adolescents are asked to read become longer and more complex both structurally and ideationally, and thus require increasingly sophisticated reading strategies and more motivation to understand; sentences increase in length and complexity and require that students recognize and understand what cohesive devices (words such as *which, who, that, if, or,* and *because*) indicate about the relationships between ideas in them; many topic area texts are full of long, morphologically complex words that require different strategies to decipher and understand than simpler words in elementary school; and texts in specific topics may require not only topic area knowledge but also specific reading strategies and skills; for example, the critical analysis skills learned in language arts class may not serve students well with the chemistry book or even with the history book.

Out of school, the complex social networks require engagement in new literacy activities such as creating blogs, connecting through social networking sites, and interacting with friends through chat rooms, email, and instant messaging. New interests and roles may require searching for information both online and from books. Entrance to the work force brings new and largely unexpected literacy challenges. In the following sections, we examine first the psychological changes that make it possible for adolescents to tackle the new demands, and then the social context within which the new skills are applied.

Adolescents as Readers; Psychological Context

Adolescence comes with multiple physiological changes that propel several interrelated processes. Physical changes in adolescence result in heightened self-awareness as social and sexual beings. As adolescents experiment with and construct their multiple new identities, they frequently rely on and are influenced by print-based information. They can learn about bodily changes and sexual feelings and behaviors by reading fictional and nonfictional accounts of the processes they are going through. They can also learn about the sexual mores and behavioral expectations of their and other societies. They can get vicarious information from different texts that may or may not be sanctioned by parents and teachers. Some of these experiences can play an important role in adolescents' construction of positive social, gender, and racial identities. Others may have negative repercussions: exposure to beauty and fashion magazines, for example, has been associated with increased drive for thinness and dieting, and decreased psychosocial well-being in young females.

Neurological changes in the brain, in the frontal lobes in particular, continue during adolescence and likely contribute to the further development of many cognitive functions that are important for reading, including self-regulation, selective attention, decision-making, and working memory. Similarly, important aspects of social cognition, such as self-awareness and perspective taking, are likely associated with the same developmental changes in how the brain functions. It is easy to understand how regulatory and memory processes can impact both reading comprehension and reading involvement (together with motivation). Comprehension of more complex texts that adolescents are expected to read requires simultaneous use of cognitive strategies to ensure understanding and self-monitoring to detect when breaks in understanding occur either because of text internal conflicts or perhaps because of conflicts between the reader's expectations and the text content. Research evidence indicates that particularly text internal conflicts are difficult for early adolescents to detect, and that error detection improves during adolescence.

One reason for this improvement could be better working memory that allows for superior online processing of information while reading. Many aspects of memory are critical for reading comprehension as reading requires simultaneous storing and processing of incoming information within the text and integration of that information with prior knowledge held in long-term memory. In general, research indicates that adolescents with good and poor comprehension skills perform similarly on short-term memory tests, but not in working memory tasks that require storing and processing of verbal information; this in spite of the fact that they do not seem to exhibit memory problems with nonlinguistic tasks. There is also evidence that working memory problems are not due to differences in overall memory capacity but, instead, may reflect difficulties in selecting the relevant information and suppressing the irrelevant information, connecting memory problems with selective attention, inhibition, and decision-making problems. These results point to executive functioning as the likely source of developmental differences during adolescence.

Other aspects of cognitive development, such as increased reasoning ability, self-awareness, and perspective taking likely also lead to qualitatively different reading experiences during adolescence. Increased reasoning ability may be particularly important for making the right inferences required for building a coherent representation of a complex text. We also know that the ability to understand less direct expressions, such as idioms and metaphors, develops during adolescence, together with the ability to recognize different text structures and locate important information from the text. While some of these developments are no doubt related to cognitive development, others are also promoted by increased experience with different kinds of texts and contents.

Finally, the concept of motivation has been central in the adolescent literacy research. Motivation is usually defined as separate from interest (with motivation being a general disposition and interest being more topic-specific) as a cluster of reading related personal goals, values, and outcomes that disposes engagement in reading instead of some other activities. Motivation can naturally be both situation- and material-specific – an adolescent may be highly motivated to read at home the sports pages of the newspaper but will not touch the social studies text, or vice versa, whereas another will only read at school and only the prescribed material. Motivation and engagement in reading may also influence reading skill development in that motivated students benefit more from reading instruction they receive. Students who are motivated and engage more in reading benefit from increased print exposure by developing automaticity with words, learning new words, and learning new text structures. The argument about automaticity and word learning is easy to understand when we consider that according to some estimates, a motivated active reader can read around 5 million words every year in their leisure time, whereas an unmotivated inactive reader may be limited to some hundreds of words. Practice matters also in literacy development.

Motivation may be closely related to self-efficacy, one's experienced competence as a reader, and the development of intrinsic motivation is related to actual competence. When students are able to successfully complete the assigned reading tasks and are aware of their skills and limitations, we can expect that both their self-efficacy and intrinsic motivation will increase. Strategy instruction may be a central instructional factor in this equation; students with high self-efficacy tend to look at difficult reading tasks as challenges and use the strategies they know actively to master them.

Interestingly, several studies have indicated that motivation to read declines in adolescence. If real, this decline may have to do with three conditions. First, a move from self-contained and supportive elementary education classrooms to more teacher-centered and less personal junior high classrooms may reduce social support that increases intrinsic motivation for reading and learning. Students who have a caring teacher and sense of belonging in their classroom are more likely to adopt prosocial goals, which are then highly correlated with intrinsic reading motivation and self-efficacy. These findings may also explain why peer tutoring has been found to improve reading scores in early adolescence. Second, the changing reading tasks and lack of instruction may turn out to be too much of a challenge for adolescents who do not have strong basic reading skills. Repeated failures may lead to disengagement with the reading tasks and engagement in other competing activities. Finally, it may be that reading motivation per se does not change, but the goals do. Some small-scale studies of adolescents' literacy practices suggest that they are indeed extensively involved in different social media literacy exchanges such as instant messaging, carrying on multiple conversations simultaneously (while also completing homework assignments and listening to music). In this case, the socially motivating literacy activities are not those traditionally valued by teachers and parents (and examined by researchers), but the 'new literacy' activities that likely are less valued in schools.

Adolescents as Readers: Social Context

Leisure reading and writing as social activity

Part of the adolescent identity construction process is the conception of themselves as readers. Boys and girls can have increasingly separate leisure reading interests, as well as different conceptions of the purpose of reading. Both genders become more responsive to recommendations from peers and spend increasing amounts of leisure reading time with digital media compared to print media. Leisure reading in particular may also be seen as a 'feminine' or 'schoolish' activity, with more boys than girls reporting no reading for pleasure and finding reading in public undesirable.

Out of school, however, much of their literacy time is spent online creating blogs, connecting through social networking sites, and interacting with friends through chat rooms, email, and instant messaging. The recent development of and access to electronic devices promote socially-oriented multimodal literacy activities and shape the way youth use language. Using chat mediums, such as instant messaging, motivates adolescents to engage in decoding, encoding, interpretation, and analysis, among other literacy processes. Within this medium, adolescents manipulate their tone, voice, word choice, and subject matter to fit their audience and communication needs, often switching from one chat partner to another in order to sustain interesting conversations and discontinue those that are not of interest to them. Written exchanges are often done in a speech-like quality, rather than in a more formal writing style. Other strategies used to express thoughts and keep other users engaged include emoticons, font size, and color, and dividing sentences up between messaging exchanges. During these exchanges, a skilled user must keep conversations interesting, respond quickly, spell words correctly to ensure correct meaning of thoughts, and balance multiple conversations simultaneously, working spatially across windows. Critically analyzing users' word choice allows those responding to do so at an appropriate level. The way readers use texts impacts the meaning they associate with them. For instance, adolescents use instant messaging to enhance their social relationships by staying on top of discussions and news that reflects their offline lives. Users find exchanges meaningful when they use them to gather information and social leads.

Writing and reading fanfiction is another online activity that promotes digital literacy practices. The authors of these texts research other materials to ensure that they are credible and authentic before including information into their own work. Often an online editing collaboration is available, which includes others reading fanfiction texts and providing feedback, consulting sites for help with ideas or formats and style guides.

Web 2.0 – a more enriched version of the Internet that supports linking and remixing multimedia content – is another outlet that socially engages youth with literacy by providing them with opportunities to socialize and collaborate with others to express their personal opinions and create knowledge. Partly as a result of Web 2.0 and increased availability of various technological tools, multimodal ways of learning and understanding – where text is related to audio, visual, and spatial presentations, as can be seen in media and electronic hypermedia – are becoming more commonplace among adolescents. These multiple ways of expressing themselves and interacting with others engage adolescents in unconventional literacy experiences that encourage the development of socially responsible and independent, yet collaborative, thinkers.

Work reading

When adolescents enter part-time or full-time employment, they encounter reading requirements that can be both at a higher level than and different from the requirements they are familiar with in schools. Some studies indicate that at US workplaces, almost all the reading requirements for entry-level jobs are higher than the reading ability level of most high school students and can exceed the reading requirements of most college coursework because of the technical nature of the reading.

Given the complex reading and writing requirements of many entry-level jobs, adolescents need the ability to learn new literacy skills to cope with job demands when they enter the workplace. While reading requirements may be higher for entry-level jobs than for higher levels, typically, the opposite is true for writing skills: the higher the level of job responsibility, the higher the requirement for strong writing skills. However, even those in clerical and sales positions have to write frequently. More than half of those in clerical and service jobs and more than three quarters of those in managerial and professional levels report that they frequently write memos and reports. As income and prestige rises, so does writing requirements. At the same time, blue-collar workers' reading and writing skills have become increasingly important as technologies have driven more record keeping and decision-making to them.

Attention to the reading and writing process is, if anything, more important in workplace settings than in school settings. At the workplace, constraints of time, space, and budgets – all become factors in reading and writing. For example, a wide range of social factors influence the ways in which writing must be accomplished in workplace settings. Research shows that workers have to learn a variety of different writing styles to accommodate for multiple texts (e.g., letters, memos, reports, proposals), develop flexible processes for getting writing tasks accomplished when working alone or in groups (and sometimes in very large groups) and under different situational constraints, and be highly attuned to the social dimensions of written communication. Concise, logical prose is valued at workplaces.

Anything that can be done to educate students to have robust reading and writing skills may help to prepare them for future success with literacy demands at the workplace. While prose literacy (fiction, nonfiction, drama, and poetry) continues to be an important part of adolescents' education, other forms of literacy also need to be taught in order for adolescents to be competitive at the workplace. The increased use of technology is leading to higher and different reading requirements for success in life than existed in the past, especially in the areas of document literacy, quantitative literacy, and technological literacy. This trend will continue for the foreseeable future. Advanced levels of literacy skills required to perform well at the workplace reflect the literacy skills needed to cope with everyday adult life as well. Because of the constant flow of ever-changing information, as adolescents of the twenty-first century enter into adulthood they will be exposed to increasing reading and writing demands, and will need to adapt to new technologies and ways of learning; more so than any other generation of the past.

Adolescent Literacy Facts Around the Globe

The three most widely used sources of comparative literacy data – UNESCO statistics, the CIA World Factbook, and the PISA studies – give a slightly varying picture of the literacy rates of the world's adolescents. It is not a straightforward task to obtain an accurate understanding of global literacy and reading behaviors. Various studies and sources of data define literacy differently, and countries have dissimilar social and cultural contexts, data collection methods and quality, and different expectations for the adolescents. Even when data collection methods are standardized across countries, as with PISA data below, comparing countries' literacy rates must be done with caution as the testing format, the tasks required, and the material read, among others, can all affect the performance of adolescents differently across the countries.

The UNESCO Institute for Statistics collected literacy data for adolescents 15–24 years of age around 1990 and again in 2000. UNESCO concluded that the most populous countries – Bangladesh, Brazil, China, Egypt, India, Indonesia, Mexico, Nigeria, and Pakistan – often have the most problems with illiteracy, at least in terms of sheer numbers of illiterate adolescents. Between the two data collection points, there was an overall global literacy increase of 4% for adolescents, meaning that there were 30 million less illiterate adolescents in 2000 than in 1990.

The CIA World Factbook mirrors the trends of the assessment results from UNESCO, with developing countries having lower literacy rates than developed countries. Specifically, in five countries, less than one-third of the population aged 15 and above can read and write: Burkina Faso (21.8%), Chad (25.7%), Afghanistan (28.1%), Niger (28.7%), and Guinea (29.5%). An additional 15 countries have literacy rates of less than 50%. Most of these 20 countries that still struggle with basic literacy are located in sub-Saharan Africa.

On the other end of the performance spectrum, the CIA World Factbook reports that 100% of the population aged 15 and above can read and write in Finland, Georgia, Greenland, Liechtenstein, Luxembourg, and Norway, with many other countries not far behind with literacy rates of 99% or higher. It is important to remember that the standard for literacy used to obtain these numbers has little to do with functional literacy skills as discussed previously. Perfect 100% literacy rate is only possible if the criterion is school attendance, or many special needs populations are excluded.

The data from PISA is likely the most relevant in terms of assessing functional literacy skills, or reading literacy as PISA calls it. In PISA, *reading literacy* is defined as understanding, using, and reflecting on written texts in order to achieve one's goals, to develop one's knowledge and potential, and to participate in society. Proficiency levels range from Level 5, in which students can perform complex literacy tasks (e.g., critically evaluating text and developing hypotheses, drawing on specialized knowledge) to Level 1, where students can perform only the least complex reading tasks provided by PISA (e.g., locating a single piece of information, making a simple connection with their everyday knowledge). While assessing more relevant skills than UNESCO or CIA, the PISA assessment is more limited in its coverage, with most participating countries being among the better performers in UNESCO and CIA assessments. Thus, what PISA likely tells us best is how the more advanced reading skills and functional illiteracy are distributed among the more developed countries; not insignificant given the role these skills play in knowledge-based economies.

Figure 1 shows the country-level reading data from PISA 2006. PISA 2006 compared the performance of 15-year-old students across 56 countries, most of whom belong to the Organization of Economic Co-operation and Development (OECD) that sponsors the PISA studies.

As indicated in **Figure 1**, there clearly are large differences between the countries in literacy performance of adolescents. Of the 56 countries that participated in the 2006 PISA assessments, Korea, Finland, Hong Kong-China, Canada, and Ireland had the highest percentage of students performing at Level 3 or above. These are students whose reading skills likely are sufficient to pursue higher education. At the other end of the scale, Tunisia, Indonesia, Qatar, Azerbaijan, and Kyrgyzstan had the lowest percentage of students performing at these levels. These latter countries often also have more than 50% of students performing at or below Level 1, that likely indicates lack of functional literacy skills (but not illiteracy per se). The three populous countries – Brazil, Indonesia, and Mexico – that UNESCO reported as having a high number of illiterate citizens and participated in PISA were all in the bottom third in **Figure 1**, with close to half of the adolescents lacking functional literacy skills. We should also note that scores for the 2006 PISA were not available for the United States; however, in the 2003 assessment, US adolescents performed nineteenth highest of 40 participating countries.

Adolescent Literacy Crisis

Many adolescents struggle with reading tasks because they lack in word recognition automaticity, making the process of accurate word reading too slow to support comprehension. Others have never been given an opportunity to learn to read in the first place. Still others, however, fail because they have not developed, or were never taught, the strategies and processes required to comprehend increasingly more complex and abstract texts that adolescents are required to read. Assuming access to proper education, the first group consists usually of individuals with specific learning disabilities; their issues are beyond the scope of this article. The second group consists of adolescents who are illiterate in the sense discussed earlier, and the third of those whose struggles are best described as functional illiteracy.

If we define illiterate to be those who lack basic reading and writing skills, the problem is naturally closely associated with access to basic education. In 2010, UNESCO estimated that 759 million youth and adults – 16% of the world's population aged 15 and older – lack basic literacy skills. In most parts of the world, the number of adolescents lacking basic literacy skills has been going down over the last 20 years; the exception is sub-Saharan Africa, where poverty, social unrest, and armed conflicts have resulted in an increase rather than a decrease in the number of illiterate adolescents.

Functionally illiterate adolescents have basic reading and writing skills, but they cannot locate the relevant information, to interpret, analyze, and synthesize information from different sources, or to write a coherent argument to promote their point of view. They may also lack the reading skills needed to benefit from educational opportunities and to use reading to acquire new competencies; many are also very unlikely to read for personal satisfaction and may qualify as 'aliterates,' or individuals who know how to read but are not interested to do so. In many cases, these adolescents, with the help of direct instruction provided in elementary school, learned the basic reading skills early in their school careers. However, they may struggle with the changing reading tasks in secondary schools, particularly if relevant literacy skill instruction is not provided.

While illiteracy is still an issue in several developing countries, the adolescent literacy crisis in most countries is that of a fight to keep the functional literacy skills of adolescents abreast with the increasing needs of the society and the labor markets. A failure to do so becomes a personal crisis when an adolescent is not able to pursue his or her goals and aspirations due to insufficient reading and writing skills. It is a societal crisis when economic development is hindered by the lack of skilled employees.

Poor Adolescent Literacy as a Societal Crisis

Figure 1 can indicate society-level literacy crisis in two different manners depending on where the goal is set. If we take performance on Level 1 and below as an indicator of functional illiteracy that will restrict the economic growth and severely limit participation in information society, it is clear that countries with 50% functional illiteracy rates have a long road ahead to developing modern economies. Many of these countries are the same that until recently have or still do struggle with basic illiteracy rates. They also have a very small proportion of adolescents at the two highest levels (Levels 4 and 5) that according to PISA studies mark the likely future innovators and knowledge workers. It is naturally possible to have a system that produces both a reasonably high number of adolescents with excellent literacy skills while also leaving a high number of adolescents without functional literacy skills. Many reasons can contribute to this kind of polarization, including financial or other selection methods to quality-tiered school systems, cultural and language differences, and family poverty (particularly through early involvement in paid labor). Interestingly, some of the richest countries in **Figure 1** – Germany, Japan, United Kingdom, France, and Austria – seem to exhibit this pattern (for reasons that are beyond this article). However, it is mostly the developed countries with strong public education systems that have both the largest proportion of high performers and the least low performing students, suggesting that offering a high-quality education to all children is the most likely route to also producing a 'literacy elite' to drive future economic development.

While **Figure 1** does not include data from the United States, the discussion of adolescent literacy crisis has probably been the liveliest there and can be used to exemplify many of the complexities behind adolescent literacy levels. National assessments that have been going on for decades in the United States indicate that while that nation's students seem to be doing better in the early grades (e.g., grade 4 assessments), the same is not true for the later grades; for example, some estimates indicate that a third of grade 8 and 12 students read below the proficient level (defined roughly as being able to obtain knowledge from challenging subject matter texts), whereas another third may not reach the basic level (defined roughly as being able to understand the text literally and to make simple inferences). In addition, achievement varies among ethnic groups and socioeconomic classes, with large differences between European American and Latino, African American, and American Indian students, and between schools in high-poverty areas and schools in more affluent areas. A comparatively large proportion of the 3000 secondary students who drop out of school every school day are visible minority students with poor reading skills.

Some observers have also noted that the US crisis is not limited to the low end of the performance scale. Data from international comparisons of 16–18-year-olds indicate that the top 10% of US students cannot compete with the top 10% of 16–18-year-olds in other industrial countries. Approximately 25% of high school graduates are not able to handle college reading tasks (although many college text books are written with language supposedly accessible for high school students) and require remedial reading courses. In community colleges, from 40 to 60% of freshmen experience reading and writing problems, and 25% of them leave school without graduating mainly because they cannot read well enough to do the course work.

Keeping in mind what we learned above about the literacy requirements at the work places, it comes as no surprise that US companies estimate spending over 3 billion dollars a year to bolster literacy skills of entry-level workers. Simply put, the skills needed to succeed in colleges and work places have changed over the years, but the skills taught in high schools have not kept up with the demands.

Illiteracy as a Personal Crisis

Whether the crisis is about functional literacy skills in developed nations or about basic literacy skills in developing nations also has an impact on what role issues such as socioeconomic status, minority status, and gender plays in the crisis.

About two-thirds of all adolescents who lack the basic reading and writing skills are estimated to be women, perhaps reflecting the fact that girls still have limited access to basic education in many parts of the developing world. Illiteracy puts a toll on women's ability to actively participate in activities that contribute to life improvements. Specifically, health reports in developing countries indicate that literacy levels are important predictors of employment, community participation, and health status, especially for women's and children's health. Female literacy rates also are important for women's overall well-being and longevity. All countries listed in the top 10 for women's well-being have a 90% literacy rate or higher. Women's illiteracy has an impact on the decisions they make for themselves and their families with regard to important health and social issues such as HIV/AIDS prevention, children's education, and reproduction. Illiterate women, for example, average 6–8 children per family, compared to two by literate women. Numerous studies have shown that lower female literacy rates are linked to a higher risk for infant mortality, poorer family nutrition and living conditions, little autonomy in the household, and lower earning potential. When girls do not receive as much as basic education, they will be later ill-equipped to meet the demands of a daily life even in the most underdeveloped societies.

In developed countries, personal consequences of functional illiteracy are significant. Initial poor learning is difficult to compensate later and adolescents who do not acquire the necessary reading skills at school face limited options not only in terms of employment but also in terms of personal enjoyment and social interactions. Their participation in any postsecondary education is problematic as almost no form of training is any longer free of substantial reading requirements (e.g., take a look at the safety manuals vocational colleges require their students to master). Job-related continued education and training may also be out of reach for these adolescents. Several studies have established that low levels of literacy skills in adolescence are associated with poor educational, employment, and health outcomes, as well as with higher levels of incarcerations. Interestingly, two large-scale longitudinal data sets from Britain indicate that adolescents with poor numeracy skills do not fare any better: they leave full-time education at the earliest opportunity, are more than twice as likely to be unemployed than those with sufficient numeracy skills, and are more at risk for poor mental and physical health outcomes. In brief, these data indicate that having poor numeracy (mathematics) skills has negative consequences, equal to those of poor literacy skills, in all areas of life.

There are some specific risk factors that are associated with an individual's likelihood of experiencing poor functional literacy outcomes and the associated negative outcomes. First, boys tend to do worse than girls in reading tasks but even more so in writing. While some observers have suggested that gender differences may be more of a measurement issue (assessment tools favor girls) than a real literacy skill issue, it seems unlikely that all the studies showing the differences would be biased to favor girls. Other explanations that have been suggested include conceptions of masculinity that are incompatible with reading and writing (e.g., reading is viewed as a feminine activity), lack of relevance of reading and writing tasks used in schools (reading and writing are viewed as 'schoolish' as opposed to useful in real life), and neurobiological differences (e.g., girls in general have stronger neural connections in their temporal lobes than boys) between boys and girls that affect all language tasks. The first two reasons would affect the engagement in reading, whereas the last may affect outcomes of the engagement; however, it is important to note that research is still inconclusive on why the gender gap exists.

To complicate the issue, several authors have argued that the literacy crisis is limited to only some of the boys – more specifically, to those from lower socioeconomic status (SES) and minority backgrounds. Several studies, including the aforementioned PISA studies, have shown that both SES and minority status are associated with reading outcomes. The explanations for differences include cultural, resource access, and language differences. Whatever the reasons, the differences are real; for example, in one recent analysis in the United States, only 13% of African-American and Hispanic junior high students were deemed to be proficient readers compared to 41% of European-American students. Perhaps the real functional literacy crisis is exposed by combining the risk factors: disturbingly low achievement has been reported for boys from poor minority families. Their options for economic advancement are the most severely limited.

Conclusion: 'Reading Wars' for the Twenty-first Century

Sometime ago, one of us attended a presentation by an educational technology expert that predicted waning importance of text reading skills and increasing importance of all kinds of new literacy skills emphasizing multimodal presentation. The basic message was that the literacy education we give to children in our school has to move aggressively toward these new skills. On substantial hindsight, the presenter was only half correct: the importance of new literacy skills has indeed increased in developed countries. At the same time, however, the more traditional text reading and writing skills have not become less important, and all educational systems face a significant challenge in teaching adolescents these skills to the level needed for functioning in society. In the developing countries, the basic literacy skills have improved, but the problem of illiteracy remains a significant issue, affecting millions of adolescent girls.

The outcomes related to adolescents' reading performance are many (e.g., economic development, educational pursuits). The countries on top of the PISA scale often are also those with knowledge-base economies and highly skilled labor force, however, those conditions naturally do not guarantee economic success. Economic conditions are related to literacy levels also through the investments that a country can make on basic education as richer countries tend to spend much more per student than poorer countries. Given this, it is probably not surprising that the poorer the country the more likely it is to do less well in these comparisons. At the same time, it is important to consider that investment in basic education may be the way out of poverty, as exemplified by the performance of South Korea since the Korean War.

On a personal level, new literacies have not opened up many new doors to success that do not also require sophisticated text reading and writing skills. The task is not to master one set of skills instead of the other, but to master a diverse set of skills to levels never required before. The reward is increased social, educational, and professional opportunities for those who succeed. The reading wars worth fighting are those against illiteracy in developing countries and those for increased functional literacy levels in developing countries.

See also: Schools and Schooling.

Further Reading

Alexander PA and Fox E (2010). Adolescent reading. In: Kamil ML, Pearson PD, Moje EB, and Afflerbach P (eds.) *Handbook of Reading Research*, vol. IV. Mahwah, NJ: Erlbaum.

Alvermann DE and Moore DW (1991) Secondary school reading. In: Barr R, Kamil ML, Mosenthal PB, and Pearson PD (eds.) *Handbook of Reading Research*, vol. II, pp. 951–983. White Plains, NY: Longman.

Carnegie Council on Advancing Adolescent Literacy (2010) Time to act: An agenda for advancing adolescent literacy for college and career success. New York: Carnegie Corporation. Available from http://carnegie.org/publications/

Guthrie JT and Wigfield A (2000) Engagement and motivation in reading. In: Kamil ML, Mosenthal PB, Pearson PD, and Barr R (eds.) *Handbook of Reading Research*, vol. III, pp. 403–422. Mahwah, NJ: Earlbaum.

Kamil M (2003) Adolescents and Literacy: Reading for the 21st Century. Washington, DC: Alliance for Excellent Education. Available from http://www.all4ed.org

Snow CE and Biancarosa G (2003) Adolescent literacy and the achievement gap: What do we know and where do we go from here? (Adolescent Literacy Funders Meeting Report). New York, NY: Carnegie Corporation. Available from http://carnegie.org/publications/

UNESCO (2008) International literacy statistics: A review of concepts, methodology and current data. Montreal: UNESCO Institute for Statistics. (Available from http://www.uis.unesco.org).

Relevant Websites

https://www.cia.gov/library/publications/the-world-factbook/ – CIA World Factbook.
http://www.reading.org – International Reading Association.
http://www.ncte.org/ – National Council of Teachers of English.
http://www.pisa.oecd.org – PISA.
http://www.unesco.org – UNESCO.

Memory

W Schneider, University of Würzburg, Würzburg, Germany

Glossary

Autobiographical memory: Content of long-term memory that relates to personal experiences of a given person.
Basic memory capacity: Refers to the amount of information people can actively process at one time.
Domain-specific knowledge: Prior knowledge about a domain or content which is relevant for a given memory problem/task.
Memory strategies: Special techniques used by learners to facilitate the storage and retrieval of to-be-learned materials.
Metamemory: Knowledge about memory processes and contents.

Introduction

Memory development in children and adolescents has been one of the most-studied topics in all of cognitive development. Experimental studies on the development of memory are nearly as old as scientific psychology. Around the turn of the nineteenth century, numerous studies were carried out in Europe to investigate developmental and individual differences in children's memory. Whereas most early studies were 'basic' in nature, trying to assess age differences in various aspects of memory, others were driven by educational interests. For instance, the early finding that no reliable sex differences could be found in various memory components facilitated the introduction of coeducation in several European countries.

Major insights concerning the 'general' course of memory development were derived from a classic large-scale study conducted by Brunswik and colleagues in the early 1930s. This study is aimed at providing a general description of short-term and long-term memory in school-age children and adolescents. A large variety of memory tasks were presented to a sample of about 700 participants, ranging from 6 to 18 years of age.

As can be seen from **Figure 1**, a curve of the general development of immediate memory ('memory strength') based on an aggregation of all memory scores indicated linear and steep rises in memory performance for participants from 6 to 11 years of age, followed by a plateau in performance during pre- and early adolescence. The developmental curve regarding general improvements in memory performance has been replicated in several other studies of the early research period and also basically validated in modern longitudinal work.

Models of Memory

One major difference between early and contemporary memory studies is that the latter are based on a theoretical framework distinguishing between various memory components or systems. Before reviewing core findings regarding memory development, we briefly discuss relevant terms and concepts related to the theoretical framework.

Classic memory models emphasize the fact that memory processes are time-dependent. Thus, a distinction is made between a 'sensory register' (SR), a short-term store (STS), and a long-term store (LTS). New information first enters the SR, where it forms memories of very short duration (less than a second). It then moves on to the STS, a system of limited capacity. Activities of the STS are called 'control processes' (e.g., rehearsal). They keep alive selected information which is then transferred to the LTS. Various content-specific taxonomies have been offered to describe the organization of the LTS. Generally, a distinction is made between declarative and nondeclarative memory. Whereas the former has been defined as the conscious remembering of facts and events, the latter refers to unconscious memory for skills (i.e., procedural memory). Declarative long-term memory is composed of two

 doi:10.1016/B978-0-12-373915-5.00024-3

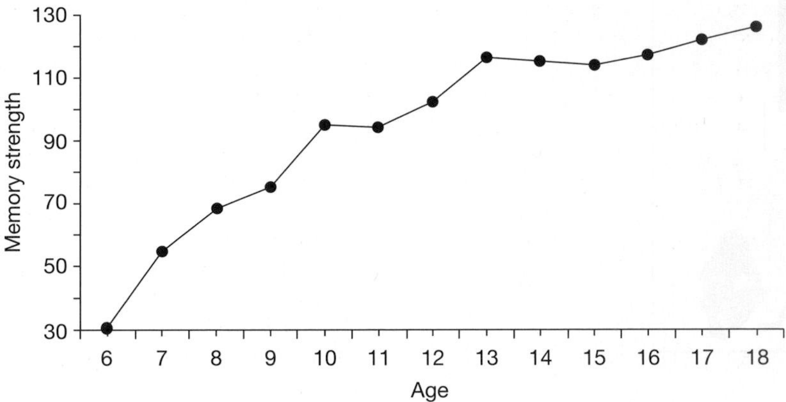

Figure 1 Memory development in children and adolescents (slightly modified after Schneider and Pressley (1997)).

different but interacting components, episodic and semantic memory. Whereas episodic memory refers to an individual's autobiographical record of past experiences, semantic memory focuses on our 'world knowledge,' that is, knowledge of language, rules, and concepts. Both systems are similar in that they can be accessed consciously.

An alternative distinction concerning the nature of LTS emphasizes the impact of awareness, separating explicit from implicit memory. Explicit memory involves conscious recollection of previous experiences and can be tested directly using free recall, cued recall, and recognition. Implicit memory is an unconscious form of retention, or 'memory without awareness,' that is assessed with tasks testing memory indirectly. The distinction between these two LTS components is supported by numerous experiments with brain-damaged patients, showing severe impairment in explicit memory but preserved functioning in implicit memory. Although the distinction has been questioned in several scientific debates, it seems to have withstood the test of time. One should note, however, that the two systems are not completely distinct. Under ordinary circumstances, explicit and implicit memory operate in parallel, and also coexist in situations where behavior no longer requires conscious awareness.

Accordingly, implicit memory may also contribute to performance in tasks aiming to assess deliberate memory. For instance, research on expertise in the domain of motor performance has shown that procedural motor memory creates the automaticity of lower-level functions to free up space for higher-level functions, indicating that unconscious functioning seems necessary for some skilled motor performance.

Most of the research presented in this article is related to explicit, declarative memory. However, a short summary of implicit memory development in children and adolescents is given before moving on to findings describing the development of explicit, declarative memory in children and adolescents.

Development of Implicit Memory

As noted previously, implicit memory is 'memory without awareness.' Developmentally, it has been claimed that implicit memory is present from the start of life, and does not change much over the years. This conclusion was drawn from studies focusing on perceptual priming. Most of these developmental studies involved the use of fragmented pictures, perhaps pictures of a dog, which should be identified by the participants. This is very difficult to do initially, but as more of the picture is completed, it becomes increasingly easier to identify the pictures. After a series of such picture-identification tasks has been given, children are provided with degraded pictures of both previously seen vs. unseen objects. The typical finding is that repetition priming is observed. That is, participants identify fragmented pictures of previously seen pictures much faster than fragmented pictures of previously unseen objects. Interestingly, most developmental studies failed to find age differences in implicit picture-fragment completion tasks. Thus, perceptual priming effects seem comparable for older and younger participants. However, recent research on age differences in perceptual priming indicates that processes such as encoding and storage show at least slight age-related improvements from young to middle childhood, continuing until early adulthood. Overall, however, developmental differences in perceptual priming observed within the age range of 5–15 years are rather small.

In order to draw firm conclusions about the developmental invariance of priming, other types of implicit memory testing such as conceptual priming are needed. For instance, a conceptual measure of implicit memory provides participants with a list of category names and requires them to produce the first exemplars of the categories that come to mind. The typical finding from studies with adults is that prior presentation of a category exemplar increases the likelihood of that word being named as a category instance. Given that these tests emphasize the semantic relationships between studied and tested items and thus require conceptually driven processing, one should expect age differences in conceptual priming. That is, older children and adolescents should show more priming because the semantic categories are more meaningful to them than to younger children. However, the research situation is not clear.

Whereas some of the few studies that examined developmental trends in conceptual priming claimed that priming is age-invariant, other researchers have argued that the unexpected finding of age-invariant conceptual priming could be either due to the rather narrow age ranges or to the predominance of familiar semantic categories in those studies. In fact, subsequent studies using a larger range of age groups and also different semantic categories showed that reliable age differences in conceptual priming were found for atypical but not for typical category exemplars. Accordingly, although there is substantial evidence for the age invariance of priming effects, performance on conceptual priming tasks changes with age. However, these changes seem related to changes in conceptual knowledge rather than caused by changes in the priming mechanism per se. More studies using novel materials are needed to examine this issue further.

Development of Verbal Explicit Memory

Most studies in the field of memory development have addressed developmental differences in episodic memory that, unlike implicit memory, involves conscious awareness. This memory system usually refers to memory for episodes and events in one's life. Research from the last four decades indicates that children and adults organize memory for recurring events in the form of 'scripts' or general event representations.

Event Memory

To study young children's memory for recurring events, a suitable method is to ask them questions about familiar routines such as attending birthday parties and going grocery shopping. In developmental studies on event memory, children are typically asked to tell the experimenters what happens during such events, and are then prompted when necessary. The empirical evidence shows that children as young as 3 years already demonstrate general and temporally organized knowledge for recurring events. This research thus indicates that children's episodic memory is organized around general event representations from a very early age on.

Other studies with young children have demonstrated that novel and unusual events can also be remembered over longer periods of time, indicating that episodic memory is not constrained to routines and recurring events. Although the ability to remember specific events for a longer period of time is already evident in preschoolers, it undergoes further changes with development, affecting both the number of events remembered and the robustness of memories for specific events. In sum, the numerous studies on the development of event memory show that the ability to learn, store, and recall episodic information develops rather early in childhood, and progresses at a similar pace for the majority of children until late adolescence. Although one can still speculate about the type of growth function involved, the available evidence suggests linear improvement with age, with no inflections during adolescence.

Autobiographical Memory

There is a widespread view in adult literature that event knowledge is hierarchically organized in a general autobiographical memory system. Although little is known about genesis and early development of autobiographical memory, there is reason to assume that the factor most important to the emergence of autobiographical memory is the development of the 'cognitive self' late in the second year of life. Alternative hypotheses about the delayed onset of autobiographical memory focus on the role of emerging language and social interaction, in particular, the sharing of experiences with others linguistically. According to this argument, the lack of early memories is not the result of basic structural changes in the memory system with development, but due to the absence of abstract knowledge structures for describing the temporal and causal sequences of events.

Overall, findings from several developmental studies indicate that the primary function of autobiographical memory is to develop a life history in time, and to do that by telling others about events of the past. Representing events of one's life is clearly a social process that begins early in development. The capacity to organize information more coherently in memory is critical to most memory advances in childhood and adolescence, and seems closely related to the emergence of the cognitive self. Subsequent advances in language and social cognition seem very important for developmental changes in autobiographical memory. An interesting aspect of autobiographical memories is that they simultaneously reflect elements of the original experience as well as interpretations of those events that occurred during dialogues with significant others. Given that autobiographical memory is reconstructive memory, with social interactions and long-term knowledge affecting original encodings, there is always the risk of memory errors. The accuracy of autobiographical memory is crucial in the context of forensic investigations, and numerous studies have been carried out to investigate developmental trends in eyewitness memory.

Eyewitness Memory

Eyewitness memory represents one specific form of event memory that emphasizes the accuracy rather than the amount of information recalled about an experienced event. In most developmental studies, children and adolescents witnessed events either staged at their schools, or videotaped events, or were asked to recollect some potentially traumatic experiences, such as visits to the doctor or the dentist. During the interview period following the event, participants were typically first questioned using general prompts, usually followed by more specific questions. With children being increasingly called upon to provide testimony in legal cases, issues about how much and how accurately they remember, and the degree to which they are influenced by suggestion, has become a high-priority research interest. In general, the developmental patterns for episodic memory and eyewitness memory are highly similar in that older children and adolescents can generally provide more detailed and narratively coherent memories than do younger children. Regarding age differences in eyewitness memory, most investigations revealed that levels of recall to general questions are generally low, and that free recall increases considerably with age. However, despite low levels of free recall, what preschoolers and kindergarteners do recall is usually accurate. Thus, despite age differences, most young children possess the cognitive capacity necessary for accurate testimony. Age differences may diminish or even disappear under certain conditions, for instance, if an event is particularly salient or personally meaningful to young children. In most studies, levels of correct recall increased when more specific cues were provided, unfortunately in most cases also accompanied by an increase in the number of inaccurate responses, thus reducing overall accuracy, particularly in younger children. However, even young school children can enhance the accuracy of their testimony by screening out wrong answers when given explicit incentives for accuracy. This finding indicates that young children can regulate their memory reporting to produce a more accurate record of past events when they are allowed and encouraged to screen out wrong answers (e.g., by saying 'I don't know') and when they are explicitly motivated to do so. Although eyewitness memory improves with age, differences seem most pronounced for the period between 4 and 7 years of age. Most studies that additionally included samples of adolescents and young adults illustrated that older elementary school children's free recall of witnessed events is comparable to that of adolescents and adults.

An important topic in children's eyewitness memory concerns age differences in susceptibility to suggestion. In most suggestibility paradigms, participants witness an event and are later asked sets of misleading questions, suggesting an inaccurate 'fact.' Most studies that have looked for developmental differences in suggestibility have found them, with preschool children being particularly prone to suggestion, much more than school children, adolescents, and adults (see **Figure 2**).

How long do memories of witnessed events last? Are there developmental differences in long-term recall and forgetting rates? This seems like an important question, given that in forensic interviews, children, adolescents, and adults are asked to recall experiences or events they witnessed weeks, months, or even years earlier. Several studies investigated participants' memories of specific events for periods ranging from several weeks to 2 years. Although the results of these studies are not totally consistent, they indicate that age differences in the accuracy of recall increase with increasing delays, at least when delays are longer than 1 month. This finding is in accord with contemporary experimental research on long-term retention and forgetting, and may be explained by Fuzzy Trace theory. This theory proposes that memory representations exist on a continuum from literal, verbatim representations to fuzzy, gistlike traces, and that multiple-memory traces exist for any event one experiences. Given that verbatim traces, favored by young children, deteriorate more rapidly than the gist, or fuzzy traces preferred by older children and adolescents, greater losses of information over delays should be expected for younger as compared to older participants.

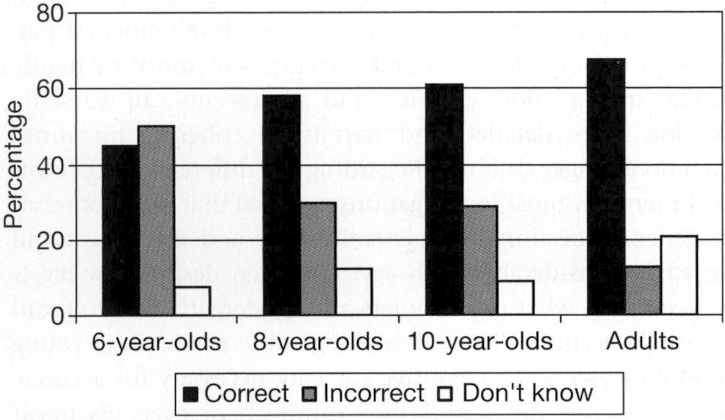

Figure 2 Percentage of correct and incorrect responses to recognition questions (based on data from Cassel, Roebers, and Bjorklund (1996)).

Developmental studies on recall of stressful and traumatic events have shown that developmental differences are typically evident, with older children and young adolescents tending to be more accurate and complete than younger children in their reports for nonstressful and stressful events. However, even young children's memories of stressful experiences such as a visit to the doctor for a physical examination seem quite accurate, with higher levels of distress frequently associated with better memory. Direct comparisons of reports of traumatic and nontraumatic events given by children and adolescents revealed that narratives about traumatic events were about twice as long as those referring to nontraumatic events experienced at about the same time, regardless of age. Although the range in ages of the participants in these studies was large, age differences in recall were not pronounced. The results of this research suggest that the memory reports about traumatic and nontraumatic experiences differ qualitatively, with narratives about traumatic events being more complete and better integrated.

Important Determinants of Verbal Memory Development

One important difference between early research on memory development and more recent approaches concerns a shift from an emphasis on describing developmental differences in memory to an emphasis on identifiying the underlying mechanisms of change. The vast majority of studies on memory development since the mid-1960s have been carried out with older children and adolescents, mainly dealing with explicit memory, that is, conscious remembering of facts and events. It was repeatedly found that particular clear improvements in declarative memory can be observed for the age range between 6 and 12 years, which roughly corresponds to the elementary school period in most countries. Although increases in memory performance were also found during adolescence, they seemed to be less pronounced.

In order to explain these rapid increases in memory performance over time, different sources or determinants of memory development have been identified. According to most contemporary memory researchers, changes in basic capacities, memory strategies, metacognitive knowledge, and domain knowledge – all contribute to developmental changes in memory performance. There is also broad agreement that some of these sources of development contribute more than others, and that some play an important role in certain periods of childhood but not in others. In the following sections, evidence concerning the relevance of these sources for memory development is summarized.

The role of basic capacities and working reminiscence

Development of short-term memory

One of the oldest and most controversial issues concerning children's information processing is whether the amount of information they can actively process at one time changes considerably with age. Age differences in the capacity of the STS were typically found in developmental studies that used memory span tasks. Such tasks require that participants must

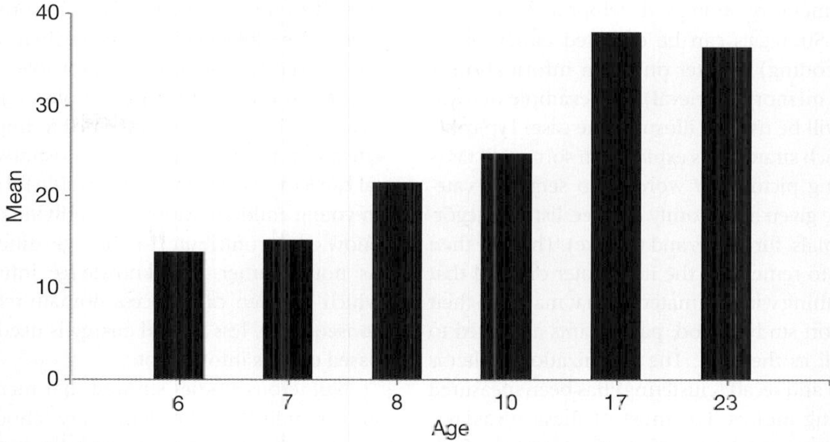

Figure 3 Development of sentence span, as a function of age (data from Munich Longitudinal Study, Schneider, Knopf, and Sodian, 2008).

repeat, in exact order, a series of rapidly presented items such as digits or words. Age differences in memory span are very stable.

Empirical findings indicate that the digit span of 2-year-olds is about two items; of 5-year-olds about four items; of 7-year-olds about five items; and of 9-year-olds about six items. The average memory (digit) span of adults is about seven items. Recent findings from the Munich Longitudinal Study using the same sentence span measure for the same participants from age 4 to age 23 showed continuous span increases until the age of 17 (see **Figure 3**). Obviously, memory span for sentences improves considerably between late childhood and late adolescence, with no further increases thereafter.

The robustness of these span differences makes very attractive the interpretation that the actual capacity of the STS is increasing with age. As appealing as this is, however, it is too simple. Research over the past three decades has made it clear that memory span is not a domain-general phenomenon that is essentially identical regardless of what type of information is being remembered. Rather, how much a person knows about the stimuli he or she is remembering definitively affects memory span, with knowledge presumably having its effect by influencing the speed of processing. This suggests that the memory span is domain-specific, varying with the person's knowledge about the to-be-remembered material.

However, there is also indication that age differences in the memory span (and increases in processing speed) are due to a presumably domain-general mechanism. One reason for the regular age-related improvements observed on most memory-span tasks is that older children and adolescents typically have a larger vocabulary and know more about most domains under investigation. When age differences in task-relevant knowledge are experimentally controlled for, age differences in the memory span no longer occur. It has been well established by now that the speed of information processing increases with age across a wide range of tasks.

Development of working memory

A popular model of working memory that accounts for age differences in the memory span primarily in terms of the speed of processing has been developed by Allan Baddeley and colleagues. This conceptualization of working memory has at least three subcomponents: these are the central executive, the visuo-spatial sketchpad, and the articulatory or phonological loop. Whereas the central executive represents an attentional control system, coordinating the various working memory activities, the visuo-spatial sketchpad is thought to process and retain visual and spatial information, and also to hold any verbal information stored as an image. The articulatory loop is a temporary phonological store which maintains and processes verbal and acoustic information (speech sounds), lasting about 1–2 s. As decay in this store is rapid, verbal information needs to be rehearsed by subvocal articulation. There is evidence that the basic modular structure of this working memory model is present from 6 years of age and possibly earlier. Working memory span indicates the capacity to maintain relevant information in the face of interference, and may be conceived as the combination of STS and controlled attention. In general, children's performance on working-memory tasks shows the same age-related increase in their performance as their performance on memory-span tasks, although the absolute level is comparably lower. Given that most studies on working memory development were restricted to children and did not simultaneously include samples of adolescents and young adults, it remains unclear whether peak performance has been already reached in adolescence.

Overall, there is converging evidence that developmental changes in memory capacity and working memory are due to significant increases in information processing speed which are most obvious in early ages, with the rate of changes slowing thereafter. Age differences in the speed of processing are influenced by maturational and experiential factors. Maturational factors place biological limits on how quickly children and adolescents can process information and retain items in their STS. However, the speed of processing is also influenced by experiential factors (e.g., knowledge base), making it clear that development of basic memory abilities is a result of the dynamic interaction between biological and experiential factors that vary over time.

Effects of memory strategies

Memory strategies have been defined as mental or behavioral activities that achieve cognitive purposes and are effort-consuming, potentially conscious, and controllable. A lot has been learned about memory strategy development in about 50 years of research. Strategies can be executed either at the time of learning (encoding) or later on when information is accessed in long-term memory (retrieval). The example of organizational strategies will be used to illustrate the case. Typically, the development of such strategies is explored in sort-recall tasks that involve organizing pictures or words into semantic categories. Participants are given a randomly ordered list of categorizable items (e.g., animals, furniture, and the like). They are then told that their task is to remember the items later on, and that they are free to do anything with the materials that may help their recall. Following a short study period, participants are asked to recall as many stimuli as they can. The organization of items during study (sorting) and recall (clustering) has been measured using various clustering indices. For most of these measures, values close to 1 represent almost perfect organization of stimuli, whereas values close to 0 indicate random responding.

Early research on the development of memory strategies as well as subsequent studies confirmed a specific trend in strategy development. Typically, deliberate strategies were not observed in children younger than 5 or 6 years of age. The lack of strategic behaviors in very young children was labeled mediation deficiency, indicating that children of a particular (preschool) age do not benefit from memory strategies, even after having been instructed how to use them. Although slightly older children such as kindergarteners and young school children also did not utilize strategies spontaneously, their problem was different. These children were shown to suffer from a production deficiency. That is, they failed to use (or to produce) strategies when given 'neutral' instructions but could be easily trained to do so, usually with corresponding improvements in memory performance. Much research in strategy development has concerned the factors responsible for production deficiencies, the subsequent failure to transfer an acquired strategy to a new situation, and ways in which to improve children's strategy effectiveness. This research demonstrated that insufficient mental capacity was partially responsible for production deficiencies in young children. Moreover, individual differences in domain knowledge contribute to the age differences in strategy use. As noted earlier, rich knowledge influences the speed with which children can process domain-related information. As a consequence, less mental energy is needed to execute a strategy based on this information.

Numerous studies showed that memory strategies develop most rapidly over the elementary school years. Older children are more likely to actively rehearse items, and to group items on the basis of meaning and to study same-category items together, with higher levels of sorting and clustering yielding higher levels of recall. However, the ages of strategy acquisition are relative, and variable within and between strategies. In general, rehearsal strategies seem to develop somewhat earlier than semantic categorization strategies, although both techniques are usually demonstrated by advanced elementary school children. For instance, a semantic categorization task was also included in the Munich Longitudinal Study (LOGIC) already mentioned previously and presented to the same participants at ages 4, 6, 8, 10, 12, 17, and 23. As a major result, it was not only shown that sorting and clustering were already at their peak by the age of 12, but that recall performance did not improve much in later years (see **Figure 4**).

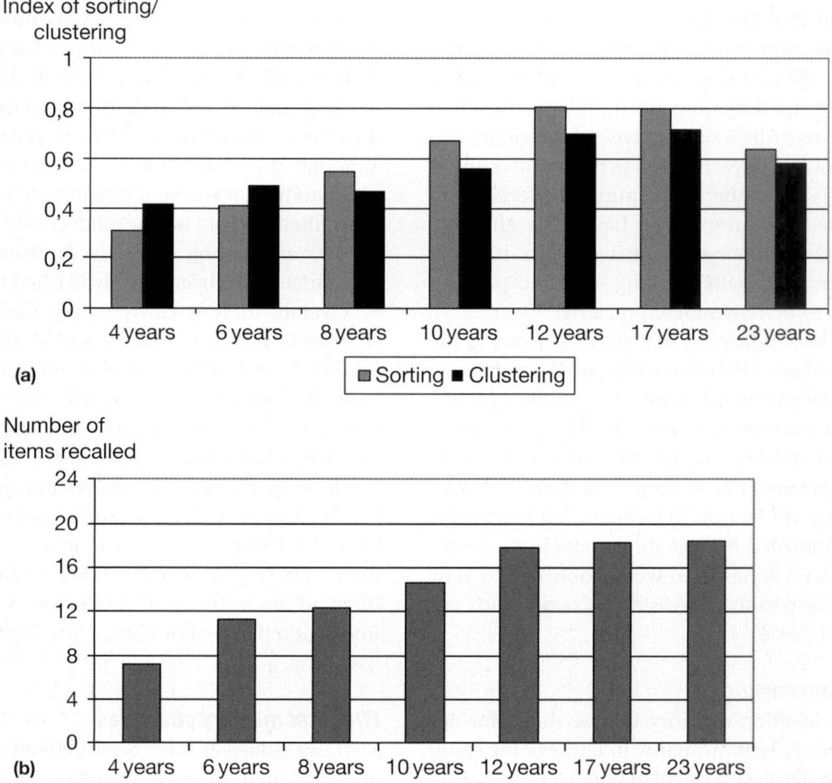

Figure 4 (a) Sorting during encoding and clustering during recall. (b) Free recall (sort-recall task). Data from Munich Longitudinal Study.

A rather new line of research based on longitudinal data has broadened our knowledge concerning the nature of developmental changes in memory strategies. In particular, this research showed that findings based on cross-sectional studies and analyses of group data do not give us the whole picture about individual strategy changes over time. For instance, there is evidence from the LOGIC Study that the impression of gradual developmental increases in strategy use and recall derived from cross-sectional studies cannot be confirmed by longitudinal data. Although that impression was confirmed on the group level (which suggested gradual increases of strategy use and recall over time), individual stabilities for the strategy and recall variables over time were surprisingly low. A closer inspection of individual change data revealed that gradual, steady increases could be rarely observed. Less than 10% of the children showed a gradual improvement in the use of organizational strategies (sorting and clustering), as suggested by the group data. In comparison, more than 80% of the children 'jumped' from chance level to near perfection between subsequent measurement points. These findings thus confirm that children go from chance levels of sorting to perfection, but they do so at different points in time. Once a jump occurs, it tends to be stable, particularly when it occurs in late childhood and early adolescence.

Although these findings suggest that strategy development mostly occurs during childhood, this does not mean that all kinds of memory strategies are already fully developed by early adolescence. For instance, the situation seems different for elaboration strategies typically used to facilitate the learning of factual information. Two general categories emerge from an inspection of various elaborative techniques. Transformational strategies involve the introduction of relationships into to-be-learned material that are not always naturally connected to the materials. In contrast, nontransformational elaborations are additions to to-be-learned content that are naturally and meaningfully connected with the content. The best known transformational elaborations are imagery or verbal mnemonics that can be used in paired-associate learning, for instance, in the case of vocabulary learning. Typical examples illustrating the utility of nontransformational strategies include the construction of images representing the content of a text, and self-interrogation strategies after having read specific prose materials.

Both transformational and nontransformational elaborative strategies have been studied developmentally. There are clear developmental increases in noninstructed use of these procedures. In particular, especially impressive increases were reported for the period between late childhood to late adolescence. Obviously, most older adolescents use elaboration strategies spontaneously, whereas older children and young adolescents more strongly depend on instructions to construct elaborations. Although older grade-school children can be taught many elaboration strategies, they do not transfer these strategies as readily as adolescents. Another rather new line of research explored whether children and adolescents use more than one strategy for remembering at a time, and whether the use of multiple strategies can benefit their recall. Several studies revealed that even young children (kindergarteners) may take advantage of more than one strategy when dealing with a memory task. Other studies demonstrated that children are more likely to use multiple strategies with age, and that the number of strategies children used on a memory task was related to the amount recalled. Multiple strategy use is the common finding when samples of adolescents are given memory tasks.

Taken together, research conducted during the last four decades has convincingly shown that age-related effects in the frequency of use and quality of strategies play a large role in memory development between the early school years and adolescence. However, there is now an increasing realization that the use of encoding and retrieval strategies largely depends on children's strategic as well as nonstrategic knowledge. There is also broad consensus that the narrow focus on developmental changes in strategy use should be replaced by an approach that takes into account the effects of various forms of knowledge on strategy execution.

The impact of metacognitive knowledge

About 40 years ago, the term metamemory was introduced to refer to knowledge about memory processes and contents. From a developmental perspective, this concept seemed well-suited to explain young children's production deficiencies on a broad variety of tasks. Whereas young children do not learn much about the advantages of memory strategies, school children are regularly confronted with various memory tasks that eventually help them discover the advantages of strategies and improve their metamemory.

Two broad categories of metacognitive knowledge have been distinguished in the literature. Declarative metacognitive knowledge refers to what people factually know about their memory. This type of knowledge is explicit and verbalizable and includes knowledge about the importance of person variables (e.g., age or IQ), task characteristics such as task difficulty, and strategy knowledge. In comparison, procedural metacognitive knowledge is mostly implicit (subconscious) and refers to one's self-monitoring and self-regulation activities while solving memory problems.

Empirical research exploring the development of declarative metamemory revealed that children's knowledge of facts about memory increases considerably over the primary-grade years, but is still incomplete by the end of childhood. Recent studies also showed that increases in knowledge about strategies are paralleled by the acquisition of strategies and that metamemory–memory behavior relationships tend to be moderately strong. Thus, what people know about their memory frequently influences how they try to remember. However, although late-grade-school children know much about common strategies, there is increasing evidence that many adolescents and adults (including college students) have little or no knowledge of some more complex, important, and powerful memory strategies such as those related to the processing of text information.

The situation regarding developmental trends in procedural metacognitive knowledge is not entirely clear. Several studies explored how children use their knowledge to monitor their own memory status and regulate their memory activities. There is evidence that older children and young adolescents are better able to predict future performance on memory tasks than are younger children, and that there are similar age trends when the task is to judge performance accuracy after the test has been taken. Also, older children seem better able to judge whether the name of an object that they currently cannot recall would be recognized later if the experimenter provided it (feeling-of-knowing judgments).

However, although monitoring skills seem to improve continuously across childhood and adolescence, it is important to note that developmental trends in self-monitoring are less pronounced than those observed for declarative metamemory. Contrary to earlier assumptions, recent research shows that even young children are well able to monitor their progress in memory tasks. It appears that the considerable developmental improvements in procedural metamemory observable in elementary school children and young adolescents are mainly due to an increasingly better interplay between monitoring and self-regulatory activities. That is, even though young children may be similarly capable of identifying memory problems compared to older ones, in most cases, only the older children will effectively regulate their behavior in order to overcome these problems. For instance, developmental studies on the allocation of study time examined whether school children and adults were more likely to spend more time on less well-learned material. All of these studies reported an age-related improvement in the efficient allocation of study time. That is, older children and adolescents (from age 10 on) spent more time studying hard items than they spent studying easy items, despite the fact that even many young children were able to distinguish between hard and easy pairs.

Metamemory–memory relations

One of the main motivations to study metamemory has been the assumption that there are important relationships between knowing about memory and memory behaviors. However, early investigations did not find substantial links between the two components. More recent research has shown that the relation one finds between memory and metamemory is considerably stronger than previously assumed, and that moderate to high correlations between metamemory and memory behavior can be found. The strength of relation varied as a function of type of task (e.g., organizational strategies or memory monitoring), task difficulty, when metamemory was assessed (before or after the memory task), age, and the interaction of these various factors.

Taken together, research on the role of metacognitive knowledge in memory development has created a large body of evidence supporting the utility of the concept. Mainly due to methodological improvements, more recent work on the metamemory–memory link has provided evidence for rather strong relations among metamemory, memory behavior, and memory performance.

Effects of domain knowledge

Surprisingly, one of the most obvious sources of individual differences in memory performance, prior knowledge of task-related content, was discovered relatively recently. Since the late seventies, however, a large number of developmental studies have demonstrated that the amount of knowledge in a particular domain such as chess, physics, or sports determines how much new information from the same domain can be stored and retrieved.

Prior knowledge of related content affects memory in several ways. It not only influences how much and what people recall, but also affects their execution of basic processes and strategies, their metacognitive knowledge, and their acquisition of new strategies. Rich domain knowledge can also have nonstrategic effects, that is, diminish the need for strategy activation. Interestingly, domain knowledge can serve as an explanation for other memory changes. Increasing domain knowledge improves efficiency of basic processes, acquisition and execution of strategies, and metacognitive knowledge.

Evidence for the powerful effects of domain knowledge on memory performance comes from studies using the expert–novice paradigm. These studies compared experts and novices in a given domain (e.g., baseball, chess, or soccer) on a memory task related to that domain. From a developmental perspective, the major advantage of the expert–novice paradigm is that knowledge and chronological age are not necessarily confounded, a problem inherent in most studies addressing knowledge-base effects. Several studies demonstrated that rich domain knowledge enabled a child expert to perform much like an adolescent or adult expert and better than an adult novice – thus showing a disappearance and sometimes reversal of usual developmental trends. It was repeatedly shown that experts and novices not only differ with regard to quantity of knowledge but also regarding the quality of knowledge, that is, in the way their knowledge is represented in the mind. Moreover, several studies also confirmed the assumption that rich domain knowledge can compensate for low overall aptitude on domain-related memory tasks, as no differences were found between high- and low-aptitude experts on various recall and comprehension measures. Perhaps the most robust finding in the literature on knowledge effects is that experts in an area learn faster and more when studying 'new' information in their domain of expertise than do novices.

How is such a rich knowledge base acquired? The few available longitudinal studies indicate that expertise is based on a long-lasting process of motivated learning. Building up a rich knowledge base requires not only cognitive abilities but also high levels of interest and motivation. In several domains, it is the amount of practice and not so much the level of general aptitude that determines exceptional performance. However, even though most available developmental studies on expertise highlight the importance of deliberate practice in developing domain-specific expertise, they do not support the assumption that individual differences in basic abilities (such as memory capacity) can be completely neglected when it comes to predicting the development of exceptional performance.

Overall, research on the effects of domain knowledge conducted during the last 30 years has convincingly shown that any explanation of memory development must reserve a large place for increasing knowledge of specific content. Domain knowledge is a powerful determinant of memory and learning. It increases steadily and greatly from infancy to adulthood and contributes to the development of other sources of memory competencies such as basic capacities, strategies, and metacognitive knowledge. Research on the development of domain knowledge has illustrated the fact that the sources of memory development interact in numerous ways, which sometimes makes it very difficult to disentangle the effects of specific sources from that of other influences. The importance of these interactions was highlighted in the Model of Good Information Processing developed by Michael Pressley and colleagues, which emphasizes the interplay of intact neurology (basic capacities), strategic, knowledge-base, and motivational components in determining cognitive performance.

Development of Visuo-Spatial Memory

As noted earlier, the vast majority of studies on memory development focused on verbal memory. Given that there is considerably less research on the development of other memory components such as people's visuo-spatial memory skills, findings from this domain are mostly ignored in contemporary reviews of the state of the art.

What do we know about developmental trends in visuo-spatial memory? First of all, it is important to note that there seem to be several visuo-spatial memory systems, and not just one. Although the working memory model developed by Allan Baddeley and colleagues (see above) suggests that the retention of visual and spatial material is organized by the same underlying system, namely, the 'visuo-spatial sketchpad,' the empirical evidence based on studies with children and adults does not support this assumption. Meanwhile, most researchers agree that the visuo-spatial component of working memory consists of a visual cache which passively stores visual information, and an 'inner scribe' which actively rehearses spatial and sequential movement as well as visual information. Thus, findings indicate that developmental pathways for processing visual and spatial information differ considerably.

Overall, studies testing visual short-term memory and working memory in children and adolescents found reliable age differences, with older participants outperforming younger ones. However, one interesting outcome of some studies dealing with recognition memory for unfamiliar faces was that the developmental curve for face recognition displays a temporary dip in performance during early adolescence. While performance on such recognition tasks improves steadily from 5 to 10 years, it seems to exhibit a temporary dip in accuracy around 11–12 years, recovering to adult level by 16 years. Although the reasons for this phenomenon (which also generalizes to nonfacial pictures) are not entirely clear, it could be that in the course of development, the child changes from a more basic (and already mastered) cognitive strategy to a new and potentially more efficient strategy, which still needs to be mastered. Another possible explanation refers to the fact that early adolescence is a time of dramatic physiological changes, and that these pubertal changes are directly responsible for the disruption in visual recognition memory at this age. Overall, the age effects found in these developmental studies were rather small and far less pronounced than those observed for verbal memory. Given that the empirical evidence for this interesting observation (temporary dip in accuracy) is still scarce, replication studies testing the full age range are needed.

Other studies used picture-reconstruction tasks to disentangle memory for visual and spatial components. Children of different ages and adolescents were first shown large picture frames that contained several small pictures of familiar objects and were then asked to remember the items and their locations. There were clear-cut age effects in the ability to associate a picture with its location in that older participants outperformed younger ones. However, memory for locations, that is, memory for the original positions of the small pictures (regardless of their identity) was generally well developed and did not vary as a function of age. All in all, it appears that there is little development in the nature of the spatial knowledge system itself. Developmental changes in permanent visuo-spatial memory mainly reflect an increasing coordination of the knowledge system with action and with spatial markers in the world.

Memory and Brain Development

Many memory researchers meanwhile have recognized that the development of memory cannot be isolated from development of the brain. We still do not know much about the neuropsychology of memory development, both at the level of description and explanation. Neuropsychological research can influence memory development research in a number of ways. We know from brain research that the functions of the frontal lobe include planning, organizing, strategic operations, and sustaining attention. It is sometimes referred to as the 'executive' of the brain. Frontal gray matter increases throughout childhood, peaks in early adolescence, and then declines throughout adolescence. In comparison, the temporal lobes subserve functions of language, emotion, and memory. The temporal gray matter does not peak until late adolescence. A memory-relevant structure in the medial temporal lobe is the hippocampus that is involved in short-term memory storage and retrieval. Human capacity for these functions undergoes considerable changes from ages 4 to 18 years. However, the relationships between changes in these abilities and changes in brain morphology are not well understood.

Neuropsychological research focusing on the hippocampus has shown that new memories are kept in the hippocampus before being transferred to the cerebral cortex for permanent storage. This may explain the finding that patients with a brain damage to their hippocampal region can memorize faces and places, which are stored in the cortex, but find it very difficult to form new short-term memories. Other studies exploring the role of the hippocampus investigated memory development following bilateral hippocampal damage early in life. Individuals with such damage did not show the severe deficits in semantic memory that might be expected if the hippocampus was crucial for both episodic and semantic memory. On the other hand, their performance on episodic memory tasks such as delayed recall of information was markedly impaired. One explanation for the relative preservation of semantic memory following early hippocampal injury is that transient projections exist during normal development between the rhinal cortex and the hippocampus that are retained because the hippocampus lesions occurred before the time when these projections are usually retracted. This explanation thus reflects the plasticity of developing memory systems. One conclusion from their research is that the hippocampus and related medial temporal lobe structures are not only important for adult memory but also contribute significantly to memory development in infancy, childhood, and adolescence. They propose that normal memory development involves a sequence in which semantic-like memory emerges first, whereas episodic memory develops only later with progressive development of the hippocampus. Accordingly, development of memory abilities appears to unfold in a sequence, beginning with novelty preferences and/or familiarity-based recognition, followed by recall, then by flexible memory, and ultimately by source memory.

Research on the neural substrates for (visuo-spatial) working memory indicates that these appear to be very similar in children, adolescents, and adults, with frontal and parietal areas of particular importance. For instance, one study investigated memory in children and adolescents aged from 9 to 18 years, and reported that changes in working memory capacity were correlated with increased activity in the superior frontal sulcus and intraparietal cortex. Age was correlated with increased brain activation during the working memory task but not with the amount of cortex activated. Although this finding suggests that there may not be much change in the neural substrates recruited by visuo-spatial memory with age, the situation seems different for verbal working memory. There is evidence from neuropsychological research that frontal lobe development extends beyond the adolescent years. In a study that assessed children's and adolescents' performance on various working memory tasks, developmental changes were observed on those tasks associated with the frontal lobe, whereas no improvement was found on tasks largely supported by more posterior neural substrates. One conclusion from this research is that working memory tasks should be grouped largely on task demands, irrespective of working memory domain.

Recent neuropsychological studies addressing implicit memory development point to an independent memory system. It seems that the brain systems mediating perceptual and conceptual priming are fully developed early in life, which clearly contrasts with the continuous development of the explicit memory system. There is substantial evidence in cognitive neuroscience that perceptual and conceptual priming do not depend upon the medial-temporal and diencephalic brain structures that mediate intentional declarative memory. Although early Russian research already pointed to young children's surprisingly well-developed 'involuntary' memory, contemporary findings on implicit memory provide a convincing explanation for dissociations between involuntary and voluntary memory that are found throughout the life span.

Conclusions

Although memory development is a rather mature field, there is still much to learn, and the centrality of memory to all other aspects of cognition makes it likely that the ontogeny of memory, in one form or another, will continue to be a primary focus of cognitive development. As has been shown previously, generalizations in the field of memory development are difficult given the great variability of memory phenomena, attributes, modalities, and contents. Given the evidence of numerous studies, however, it appears that memory strategies, domain-specific knowledge, and metacognitive knowledge represent major sources of interindividual differences in verbal memory performance, regardless of chronological age. Remarkable intraindividual changes in verbal memory development are apparent during the elementary school years, reaching a peak in late adolescence. In comparison, similar changes in nonverbal memory have not been observed.

Recent longitudinal research on memory development further indicated that the assumption of general verbal memory concepts may oversimplify the case. For instance, several studies that concerned the issue whether the concept of verbal memory represents a domain-general skill or consists of domain-specific verbal abilities did not support the view of a unitary concept. Instead, they indicate that relations among various facets of verbal memory such as strategic memory, memory capacity, and text recall are only moderate in early childhood and continue to be so until early adulthood. These findings are consistent with the position that deliberate verbal memory may be better thought of as a set of specific abilities ('modules') rather than as a domain-general concept.

Overall, although the field of memory development constitutes one of the oldest and most active research areas in the field of cognitive development, there are still many open issues that need to be clarified in future research. We still need more precise cross-sectional experimental studies to better understand the role of mediators of memory development, and also more longitudinal studies which should be combined, when possible, with parallel experimental studies that bring hypothesized mediators of developmental change under experimental control. Accordingly, it should be possible to study both memory development and the development of memory by this integration of methods.

See also: Brain Development; Cognitive Development; Metacognition and Self-regulated Learning.

Further Reading

Cassell WS, Roebers CM, and Bjorklund DF (1996) Developmental patterns of eyewitness responses to increasingly suggestive questions. *Journal of Experimental Child Psychology* 61: 116–133.

Courage ML and Cowan N (eds.) (2009) *The Development of Memory in Infancy and Childhood*. Hove, UK: Psychology Press.

Schneider W and Bullock M (eds.) (2008) *Human Development from Early Childhood to Early Adulthood. Findings from a 20 Year Longitudinal Study*. New York: Psychology Press.

Schneider W, Knopf M, and Sodian B (2008) Verbal memory development from early childhood to early adulthood. In: Schneider W and Bullock M (eds.) *Human Development from Early Childhood to Early Adulthood. Findings from a 20 Year Longitudinal Study*, pp. 63–90. New York: Psychology Press.

Schneider W and Pressley M (1997) *Memory Development Between Two and Twenty*, 2nd edn. Mahwah, NJ: Erlbaum.

Metacognition and Self-regulated Learning

M Hasselhorn and A S Labuhn, German Institute for International Educational Research, Frankfurt am Main, Germany

Glossary

Metacognition: Knowledge about and control of one's own cognitive activities.
Self-efficacy beliefs: People's beliefs about their capabilities to perform in a certain manner to attain personal goals.
Self-evaluation: Evaluating personal progress against a goal or standard.
Self-monitoring: Mental tracking of one's performance during learning or engaging in task.
Self-regulated learning: Learning process that is guided by metacognition, strategic action, and motivation to learn.

Introduction

During adolescence, the developmental task of planning for one's own life and making related decisions becomes more and more prominent. Adolescents differ strongly with regard to the individual quality and effectiveness of their plans and the regulation and control of their behavior. Research on metacognition and self-regulation provides a conceptual framework for describing and explaining these differences.

Metacognition and self-regulation are generally treated as two separate concepts in the psychological literature. This is less grounded in the fact that they relate to different phenomena and mechanisms of human behavior, but rather in the different lines of research they come from. As the older of the concepts, metacognition has emerged from developmental psychological research into memory, where it was introduced in the early 1970s as a significant mechanism for explaining the increase of cognitive human abilities with age. In contrast, the concept of self-regulated learning derives from educational–psychological research into learning. Both concepts share the common feature of referring to late-developing, higher-order competencies that are especially useful to explain individual differences among adolescents.

Metacognition

Theoretical Framework

Metacognition is used as a collective term describing a number of phenomena, activities, and experiences related to the *knowledge* and *control* of one's own cognitive functions (e.g., perception, learning, memory, understanding, and thinking). Metacognition can be distinguished from other types of cognition by the fact that in metacognition, cognitive states or functions are the objects of reflection themselves. 'Awareness' constitutes a crucial element of defining metacognition.

Early definitions of the term already contain the two-component-perspective of metacognition that is still valid today, according to which *knowledge* about one's own cognitive functions, products, and goals on the one hand can be distinguished from *control of one's own* cognitive activities on the other hand. As reasonable as this distinction between metacognitive knowledge and metacognitive control might be with respect to defining the term, it is insufficient as regards a description of the research area of metacognition. A distinction of at least five subcategories of metacognition has proved to be appropriate here. The first two subcategories indicate that the traditional knowledge component of metacognition shows two facets that are qualitatively distinct, that is, *systemic* knowledge and *epistemic* knowledge. The systemic knowledge domain comprehends knowledge about rules of functioning, influential factors, and strengths and weaknesses of one's own cognitive functions. If persons know under what conditions they can learn certain subjects particularly well, this indicates a high quality of their systemic knowledge. Knowledge about one's own knowledge and its gaps is principally independent from this, as well as the knowledge about knowledge acquisition and its possible use and the knowledge regarding one's own current cognitive state and willingness (disposition) to learn. These kinds of knowledge relate to the epistemic knowledge domain of metacognition.

Executive metacognitions form a third subcategory: they are identical with the control component in the traditional two-component perspective. This subcategory subsumes planning abilities, monitoring, and governing and thus the regulation of one's own cognitive activities (e.g., learning processes).

Further subcategories of metacognition have been introduced that seem adequate for consideration. On the one hand, this relates to the *sensational category* and to the *metacognitive experience* on the other. Sensation describes an awareness of one's own current possibilities of cognitive action, which is indispensible to executive monitoring processes. This sense can probably be a consequence of sufficient experience-based knowledge as well as an expression of an 'intuitive' sense. While this intuitive sensation need not be in any way conscious, metacognitive experiences by contrast refer to conscious cognitive sensations (e.g., 'being confused' about information that appears to be contradictory) or affective states regarding one's own cognitive activity (e.g., 'being downcast' about something you do not understand).

Relevance of Metacognition for Cognitive Behavior

A complicated networking of the different subcategories of metacognition results from an individual's learning processes. Owing to this intrinsic networking structure, it is in many cases

 doi:10.1016/B978-0-12-373915-5.00026-7

hardly possible to empirically separate the different aspects of metacognition. Nevertheless, metacognitive measures (e.g., knowledge about strategies and their usefulness and limitations, accuracy of the prediction of one's own memory performance, allocation of learning time, feeling of knowing judgments) prove to be predictors of observable cognitive achievement. Early meta-analyses on the coherence between metacognition and cognitive achievement have investigated all of the existing publications reporting data on the correlation between metacognition measures and achievement indicators and established a mean correlation of $r = 0.41$.

More recent works reveal the existence of different mechanisms regarding the effects of metacognition on learning outcomes. For instance, reading a text can evoke a metacognitive experience because the individual perceives inconsistencies between different paragraphs. Or when trying to summarize the contents of a text, you become aware that you have not understood its contents (metacognitive monitoring) and begin to plan and conduct activities directed toward surmounting this lack of comprehension. Regardless of all the different triggers and metacognitive components involved in such learning processes, at least one of two characteristics is nearly always involved: the individual learning process is *reflected* upon and *strategic activities* are performed.

From the perspective of research on metacognition, it is important that reflection can refer to the past as well as to the present: the former refers to thinking about actions, while the latter relates to thinking while acting. Both types of reflection are coequally the origin and a consequence of metacognition. Thus, thinking about actions is a consequence of executive metacognition as well as being the origin of metacognitive experience and systemic knowledge. In a similar way, the metacognitive activity of thinking while performing a learning action discloses a metacognitive sensation while at the same time it generates epistemic knowledge. The reflection thus links different metacognitive competencies on the one hand, while linking metacognition with learning outcome, and learning achievement, on the other hand. At the same time, it renders the learning process conscious and provides for the actual use of accessible learning strategies.

Developmental Changes and Individual Differences

Considerable interindividual differences as well as intraindividual variations can be observed regarding the quality and intensity of using metacognitive competencies. Interindividual differences in metacognitive competencies can largely be explained by three classes of influential factors: (1) by biological mechanisms of maturity, (2) by social influence, and (3) by the degree and intensity of a person's own activities.

Presumably, maturity-based mechanisms, for instance, lead to the emergence of a realistic self-perception at the age of 8 years, and around the tenth or eleventh year, they result in a reflective self-abstraction that was already observed by Piaget about 70 years ago. Development in the area of metacognition, however, cannot simply be allocated in an age-related grid. The different facets of metacognition and the diverse contents within the different subcategories are also subject to highly disparate developmental processes. Generally speaking, though, the growing age and the enhanced acquisition of knowledge of children and youths correspond to an increased functioning ability of metacognition, and the final stage of development is by no means reached with the onset of adolescence. For example, there is evidence that many adolescents (including college students) demonstrate little knowledge of powerful and important learning strategies when the task is to read, comprehend, and remember complex text materials. However, despite this kind of observation of suboptimal metacognitive competencies among young adults, there is an overall increase of such metacognitive knowledge during the adolescent years.

During the 1990s, it became more and more obvious that the aim of explaining individual differences in real-life behavior and its self-regulated control cannot be fulfilled to satisfaction by referring to the knowledge and executive skills that are addressed by the concept of metacognition. Although it was demonstrated that these cognitive entities and skills are necessary to predict the quality and effectiveness of adolescents' daily behavior and its regulation, further competencies in the area of motivation and volition were revealed to contribute to both the efficiency of the usage of available metacognitive competencies and the acquisition of more elaborated metacognitive knowledge and executive skills. As a consequence, the broader concept of self-regulation became more prominent, because it refers not only to metacognition but also to a number of motivational and volitional mechanisms.

Self-Regulation and Self-Regulated Learning

An active, self-responsible, and reflective attitude is essential to meet the demands of a rapidly developing society. In recent years, Barry Zimmerman elaborated on self-regulation in one of the most important fields of adolescents' activities, that is, learning with regard to school requirements or skill acquisition. He defined self-regulated learning as referring to self-generated thoughts, feelings, and actions that are planned and cyclically adapted to the attainment of personal goals. Self-regulation thus implies that thoughts, feelings, and actions are adapted to the goals people set for themselves.

Theoretical Framework

In most recent theoretical contributions, self-regulated learning is considered in terms of a dynamic interaction of cognitive, metacognitive, and motivational aspects of learning. Representing a social-cognitive perspective, Barry Zimmerman defined self-regulated learning by a cycle of three sequential phases: forethought, performance, and self-reflection. The *forethought* phase refers to processes that precede learning activities. The key self-regulatory categories associated with this phase are task analysis and sources of motivation, such as self-efficacy beliefs. Closely related to the task analysis, goal setting, and strategic planning are important self-regulatory subprocesses that ideally take place before a learner engages in a task. The *performance* phase involves processes that relate to and occur during action and fall into two major categories: self-control and self-observation. Self-control refers to various strategies the learner uses to complete the task, and self-observation includes metacognitive monitoring or self-recording one's performance. *Self-reflection* occurs after engaging in a task or after a learning session and is directly related to the person's performance. The major categories of this phase are self-judgments and self-reactions that are based on those judgments. A key type of self-judgment is self-evaluation, which refers to comparing the learning outcome with a goal or standard. As a reaction to this comparison, certain affects such as satisfaction or dissatisfaction arise. The self-reflection processes, in turn, influence the subsequent self-regulatory cycle, for example, the motivational and emotional preconditions, the use of more appropriate strategies, or the modification of personal goals.

Empirical Evidence for the Relevance of Self-Regulatory Processes

An increasing body of research has proved the strong link between the capacity to self-regulate one's learning and several key variables of personal development and skill acquisition, such as self-efficacy, intrinsic task interest, goal orientation, and self-satisfaction. Moreover, there is evidence for the relation between self-regulated learning (SRL) processes and academic achievement as well as for a relation between SRL and the domain of sports and motor skill acquisition. In the broad field of SRL research now hundreds of studies demonstrate the relevance of key self-regulatory processes for personal and academic development.

To assess the role of self-regulatory processes during learning and performance, social-cognitive researchers have suggested a microanalytic measurement approach. This approach is used to study human belief, reasoning, and behavior during actual performance and thereby provides insights into the processes that underlie overt behavior. In 2002, Anastasia Kitsantas and Barry Zimmerman used the microanalytic approach to demonstrate that there is an association between several self-regulatory processes and performance outcomes. They compared practice and performance of expert, nonexpert, and novice volleyball players. Regarding the self-regulatory process of planning, it was found that the experts' plans about daily training routines had a more sophisticated structure than either that of nonexperts or novices. Additionally, experts included a number of key components of volleyball skills in their practice (e.g., warm-up, pepper drills, and specific skill training), whereas most nonexperts had only a single component in their plans, and the novices' plans did not include even one key component.

The relevance of self-evaluation for skill development was also of interest in this study. To investigate self-evaluative judgments, all participants were asked whether they self-evaluated their performance after practice sessions, and if so, what this evaluation was comprised of. Based on the reasonability of their answers, two coders classified each student as either a self-evaluator or a non-self-regulator. The number of self-evaluators was higher for the experts than for nonexperts or novices, which emphasizes that sophisticated self-evaluation can be associated with high levels of skill development.

Moreover, participants' adaptations after missing three serves in the practice session were assessed by questions such as "When you make an error serving overhand, do you change anything during your next overhand serving attempt?" The researchers found that more experts thought about their errors and were more likely to change their strategy or procedure than either nonexperts or novices. Furthermore, experts were more likely to seek out social assistance by coaches or teammates than the nonexperts or novices. This form of social assistance has been referred to as 'adaptive help-seeking' in self-regulation literature and can be considered an appropriate way of adaptation within a cyclical SRL model.

From a social-cognitive perspective, self-efficacy beliefs play a key role in a cyclical SRL model inasmuch as these self-motivational beliefs have an influence on processes of all phases of self-regulation: forethought, performance, and self-reflection. Adolescents who believe they can successfully perform on given tasks use more cognitive and metacognitive strategies, work harder, persist longer, and persevere in the face of challenge. We can therefore assume that students' self-efficacy beliefs influence their academic motivation and performance through their use of key self-regulatory processes such as planning, goal setting, using adequate strategies, self-monitoring, and self-evaluation.

Barry Zimmerman and his colleague investigated the role of adolescent girls' homework practices in their self-efficacy beliefs regarding their use of specific learning processes (e.g., organizing, memorizing, monitoring), perceptions of responsibility for academic outcomes, and academic achievement. Homework practices were predictive of students' self-efficacy beliefs regarding their capacity to learn and their perceptions of personal responsibility for learning. Both self-efficacy for learning and perceived responsibility beliefs played an important mediating role between students' homework practices and their academic achievements.

Experimental studies also provide evidence for the impact of self-regulatory processes on learning and development. In terms of personal goals – be they academic goals, health-related goals, or goals in everyday life – Peter Gollwitzer argues that goal attainment is facilitated when people plan their goal-striving in advance. He suggests that effectively regulating one's goal striving – by making so-called 'if–then plans' (i.e., forming implementation intentions) – is a powerful means of enhancing self-regulation. In contrast to simple goal intentions (e.g., "I intend to achieve outcome x"), implementation intentions specify when, where, and how responses lead to goal attainment. Through their if–then structure of "When situation x arises, I will perform response y!", implementation intentions directly link anticipated situations with goal-directed responses. A meta-analysis reported a medium-to-large effect-size of $d = 0.65$. This result highlights the additional facilitation of goal achievement through implementation intentions as opposed to simple goal intentions.

A wide range of domains exist wherein implementation intentions guide people toward their goals. If–then plans can support successful goal-striving also in challenging achievement situations, as a study from Gollwitzer's lab demonstrated. In a setting with female high-school students who had to complete a math test, half of the students were asked to form a mere achievement goal intention: "I will correctly solve as many tasks as possible!" The other half of the students supplemented this goal intention with an implementation intention designed to strengthen the females' academic self-efficacy: "And if I start a new task, then I will tell myself: I can solve this task!". Those participants who formed implementation intentions were found to show a better performance in the math test than girls who formed mere achievement goals.

Taken together, a number of studies using different research methodologies were able to highlight the key role of self-regulatory processes in a number of different domains, including academic performance and sports.

Developmental Changes and Individual Differences

When we look at developmental changes in self-regulated learning, it is important to note two aspects. First, the proposed definition of SRL focuses on students' metacognition, motivation, and behavior in *academic* learning. That is, although children acquire the capacity to self-regulate as well as relevant precursors of academic skills before they enter school, the theory and research on self-regulated learning predominantly deals with the use of self-regulatory skills in an academic context. Second, it is not only by definition reasonable to investigate self-regulatory processes during academic learning episodes. Most developmental theorists assume that young children do not self-regulate their learning in a formal manner. This does not mean that they are incapable of age-typical forms of self-regulation, but those components relevant in academic self-regulated learning obviously evolve at later stages of development and are not fully available before adolescence. For example, young children rarely reflect on their performance, but are rather overly optimistic about their capabilities. Preschool children's belief that they can achieve anything if only they try hard enough is an important motivator of early learning experiences in skill acquisition. It has been reported from various western societies that at the age of about 8 years, children become progressively more realistic about their capabilities. Interestingly, developmental gains in accuracy have often gone along with a decreasing pleasure in learning, suggesting that being overly optimistic serves to protect achievement motivation in early stages of development.

With self-monitoring, self-reflection, and attribution being critical components of self-regulated learning, most researchers study SRL processes in school aged children and older students. In 1990, Barry Zimmerman and his colleague examined fifth, eighth, and eleventh grade students' use of 14 self-regulatory strategies, assessed by a structured interview. Verbal and mathematical self-efficacy was found to increase with age and grade. Moreover, the use of a number of learning strategies was related to students' grade levels, but the pattern of results appeared to be complex, reflecting developmental trends in academic self-regulation. For example, a significant decline occurred in students' text revision, whereas there was an increase in the revision of notes across the grades. These data indicate that students shift their preferred reviewing activities from text to self-recorded notes. Similarly, there was a decline in students' reliance on adults' (generally their parents') assistance, which went along with an increase in students seeking assistance from their teachers. With higher levels of perceived competency, students seem to adapt their help-seeking behavior and decide to consult more expert professionals. Taken together, findings from this study indicate that students' efforts to strategically regulate their learning are associated with higher perceptions of mathematical and verbal self-efficacy and increase when they advance in school. Regarding metacognitive skills, an increase between the ages of 14 and 20 has been observed in several empirical studies. However, there is also evidence for some decline in self-regulatory processes in adolescence.

In 2009, Eunsook Hong and colleagues investigated Chinese adolescents' reported homework value and motivation as well as their use of self-regulatory and metacognitive strategies during homework completion. The researchers found that older Chinese students perceived homework as less useful, enjoyed doing their homework less, expended less effort, persisted less, and reported less planning and self-checking than younger students did. While knowledge of metacognitive strategies is assumed to improve with age at the elementary level, students in this study reportedly used such strategies less in high school compared to middle school. As Chinese students receive a variety of drill-and-practice types of homework assignments, this may have contributed to the decline in valuing homework and the use of strategies when they progressed to an age where autonomy and independence become most important. Still, other studies from Western countries also found a decline in effort and persistence in homework completion. Similarly, Italian researchers recently found a progressive decline in self-efficacy from junior to senior high school.

As these studies show, in many individuals, self-regulated learning decreases in the phase of adolescence and young adulthood: that is, students have shown higher levels before this drop and are thus actually capable of self-regulation. Therefore, we can assume that the decline found in several studies is predominantly caused by motivational reasons that are associated with the characteristics of the developmental phase of adolescence, when students are increasingly faced with issues that distract them from learning and deliberate practice. As a result, many youths are reluctant to expend effort to reflect on their learning activities, to apply self-regulatory strategies, and, if necessary, to adapt their procedure to optimize learning outcomes. Thus, although the capability to regulate one's learning is assumed to increase over adolescence, this is not always reflected by improved self-regulatory or metacognitive performance.

Beside these age-related differences, a number of recent studies have addressed the question whether there are gender differences in self-regulated learning in adolescence: Do girls and boys differ in their use of self-regulatory processes? When reviewing the literature, it becomes apparent that this question is too general for a precise answer. Therefore, our question should be: In what SRL processes precisely have gender differences been found?

By now, a substantial body of research exists on gender differences in cognitive and metacognitive as well as motivational aspects of SRL. Whereas much of the data on cognitive and metacognitive SRL processes reveal higher levels of self-regulatory skills in girls, research on competency-related beliefs presents a more mixed pattern of results. Male students tend to be more 'self-congratulatory' particularly in academic domains that stereotypically favor boys.

Findings from an early SRL-study by Zimmerman and his colleagues illustrate this summary: Regarding the use of self-regulated learning strategies, girls reported significantly more record keeping and monitoring, environmental structuring, goal setting and planning than the boys. At the same time, boys perceived greater verbal self-efficacy than girls. Although girls showed well-developed self-regulatory behavior, they felt less confident about their capabilities than boys did, which is a provocative, but well-documented pattern of results.

In a recent developmental study with 1432 Swiss high school students between the tenth and twelfth grades, the Swiss researcher Bruno Leutwyler investigated students' use of metacognitive learning strategies. He found that the self-reported use of monitoring and evaluation strategies was more frequent in girls, but tended to converge between genders during high school. Regarding metacognitive planning strategies, the more frequent use reported by girls remained stable over time.

Beginning in the late 1990s, Frank Pajares and his colleagues have focused on gender differences in writing self-beliefs. Their results confirmed the advantage of girls concerning the use of self-regulatory processes. Girls expressed more confidence for self-regulation in elementary school and in middle school. More precisely, girls felt more efficacious about their capability to self-regulate their study behavior (e.g., using strategies such as finishing homework assignments in time or self-motivation when there are other interesting things to do). These findings are consistent with research in the associated domain of self-discipline conducted by Angela Lee Duckworth and Martin Seligman. Results from a study with adolescent students indicate that girls were more self-disciplined than boys according to delay of gratification measures and self-reports, as well as teacher and parent ratings.

Although converging evidence documents a more frequent use of self-regulatory behavior such as planning, monitoring, structuring, and applying strategies in girls, female learners do not necessarily feel more confident about their capabilities. On the contrary, it has been found that they are less likely to attribute their success to their abilities. Instead, in mathematics, for example, girls tend to attribute their success to effort, which can turn out to be a less adaptive motivational pattern, especially when task difficulty increases. Moreover, in subject areas such as mathematics or science, higher levels of self-efficacy or related competency beliefs have been found in boys.

Returning to our initial question: In what SRL processes have gender differences been found? Even though the empirical data are often more complex when taking a closer look, we can summarize that the most obvious gender differences occur according to the two main domains of self-regulated learning: cognitive and metacognitive processes of SRL on the one hand, and motivational processes of SRL on the other hand. Regarding subprocesses of the former domain, girls most often show higher levels of self-regulatory skills, whereas regarding subprocesses of the latter domain, results are mixed with a tendency toward more adaptive patterns in boys.

Self-Regulated Learning Interventions as a Means of Promoting Skill Development

Timothy Cleary and Barry Zimmerman have introduced a promising approach to promoting self-regulated learning in individual students, 'Self-Regulation Empowerment Program (SREP).' This program combines the diagnostics and promotion of self-regulatory skills. The SREP is an application of social-cognitive theory and research and is based on the assumption that students' motivational beliefs and behaviors depend on the nature of the educational setting or a given task, that is, motivation and performance are assumingly context-specific. Within the SREP program, self-recording serves as a powerful means of increasing students' awareness of their learning progress. Self-recording refers to the act of actually recording (e.g., on paper or white board) observations made through self-monitoring. For example, students can be taught to record the number of points they have lost in tests or quizzes on a self-recording form. The instructor can use this information to identify specific reasons for difficulties and to enable the student to develop solutions for improving performance. Another self-recording technique suggested by the authors of SREP is graphing. Graphing refers to plotting learning outcomes (e.g., school grades) and (optionally) recording the strategies used to achieve these outcomes. This method emphasizes the link between the strategies the learner applies and his or her performance outcomes. Anecdotal findings from a case study illustrate the usefulness of the program.

In 2003, Lynn and Douglas Fuchs and their colleagues conducted a study with third graders in the domain of mathematics. The researchers assessed the contribution of self-regulated learning strategies, when integrated in problem-solving transfer instruction. The self-regulatory strategies incorporated goal setting and self-evaluation and were combined with instructional sessions including the acquisition of problem-solution rules as well as transfer. While the problem-solving transfer treatment alone failed to produce effects on the far-transfer measure of problem-solving performance, the combination of problem-solving transfer and self-regulated learning led to an improved performance on this measure. Obviously, including SRL strategies is a useful method of strengthening the problem-solving transfer treatment because these strategies help improve metacognitive processes and increase perseverance in the face of challenge.

Another group of SRL researchers from the University of Darmstadt (Germany) demonstrated that the combination of mathematical problem-solving and self-regulation is also effective for adolescents. Their training consisted of six 90-min sessions conducted on a weekly basis. The results of an evaluation confirm that it is possible to improve mathematical problem-solving and self-regulation competencies by administering this short training to adolescents. Positive effects were observed for self-regulation and for mathematical problem-solving performance, highlighting the need to train self-regulatory process context-specifically, that is, closely intertwined with domain-specific skills.

Based on Steve Graham and Karen Harris's self-regulated strategy development model (SRSD) and their extensive work on teaching cognitive and self-regulatory writing strategies to children, German researchers from the University of Giessen investigated the potential benefits of integrating additional self-regulation procedures into a well-developed writing strategy program designed to improve fourth graders' composition skills. Six classes were randomly assigned to three conditions: strategy plus self-regulation, strategy-only, and control. Strategy instruction involved the following components based on the self-regulated strategy development model: activation of background knowledge, direct instruction and group discussion of strategies, cognitive modeling of each step involved in the strategy, reciting mnemonics to retrieve each step from memory, guided, collaborative, and independent practice in drafting and rewriting stories, progress feedback, and verbal scaffolding of instructional support during the training period. Students in the strategy plus self-regulation group received this training in combination with self-regulatory procedures such as self-monitoring of strategic planning, self-assessment, self-monitoring of revision activities, criterion setting, and setting procedural goals. The strategy plus self-regulation group showed a better writing composition performance than the two comparison groups both at a posttest and at a follow-up after 5 weeks. They also outperformed the other groups at a transfer task. In conclusion, writing interventions appear most likely to enhance children's skill development if they include key processes of self-regulation.

The purpose of a study in the domain of science education from our own laboratory was to investigate the connection between self-regulation and the acquisition of content knowledge within regular lessons. A quasi-experimental design was used to evaluate the effectiveness of a teaching unit that was designed taking into account Zimmerman´s theory of self-regulated learning. The participants were 199 seventh graders in a German comprehensive school. The study centered on a lesson unit on the topic of nutrition that was developed in collaboration with a group of science teachers. Students in the control group received regular instruction on the subject matter (i.e., nutrition), whereas teachers in the experimental group combined key self-regulatory processes with their classroom instruction. They focussed on goal setting, self-efficacy beliefs, motivation, and learning strategies. These components were combined with teaching subject matter and therefore trained context-specifically. For both groups, the teaching unit consisted of eight lessons. Teachers of both groups were trained separately before the intervention and they were provided with manuals and a detailed schedule for each lesson. To assess transfer of self-regulatory processes, a subsequent unit was taught to both groups identically without explicitly training self-regulation.

The results confirmed that self-regulated learning can be enhanced in classrooms through this brief intervention. Although teaching of self-regulatory processes during the lessons seemed to reduce the available time for the actual presentation of content knowledge, trained students scored as high as students in the control group on the knowledge test. In addition, learning in the second teaching unit was improved by the preceding intervention. The results of a follow-up testing after 6 months revealed that although self-regulation had slightly decreased, the experimental group still scored higher than the control group. Moreover, trained students outperformed the students in the control group on the knowledge test.

To conclude, this study highlights the fact that multiple components of self-regulated learning can be enhanced within daily activities in science education. Students can benefit both in terms of their self-regulatory skills and the acquisition of content knowledge.

Taken together, the results of the several intervention studies as presented earlier are in line with recent theories of self-regulated learning, which assume that across different domains, learning results are greatly enhanced when content knowledge is taught in combination with key strategies of self-regulated learning.

Component Competencies of Self-Regulated Learning in Adolescents

Nearly all contemporary models of complex skill acquisition and academic learning either explicitly or implicitly acknowledge the critical role of self-regulatory competencies as described previously. Moreover, the same competencies are relevant for many daily activities like diary writing or planning a weekend trip. Although the social-cognitive perspective of most of the theoretical approaches to self-regulation are more concerned with socially embedded processes than with stable individual dispositions, it is also possible to describe individual differences in the effectiveness of self-regulated behavior from a more dispositional perspective. Accordingly, it seems helpful to look at the component competencies of self-regulated learning in some detail in order to understand individual differences in the success probability of most goal-directed activities that can be observed among adolescents.

Despite the already mentioned age-related differences in the efficiency of self-regulated learning during adolescence, more pronounced individual differences have been found *between* adolescents of the same age group. Those differences can be observed in adolescents' behaviors in a variety of situations and domains. These variations are attributed at least partly to differing individual dispositions. A number of terms are often used to refer to these dispositions, the most frequent being 'aptitudes,' 'abilities,' 'capabilities,' 'capacities,' 'skills,' 'proficiencies,' and last but not least, 'competencies.' These terms are used synonymously to label the individual preconditions necessary, or even sufficient, to achieve specific goals. This broad definition of the concept of competencies has two important aspects. First, it emphasizes the individual preconditions on which competencies are based. Second, it emphasizes the goal-specificity of competencies, which means that in order to describe a competency in greater detail, one must answer the question of what objectives the competency is oriented toward achieving. Like many other scientifically productive constructs, the concept of competencies is fuzzy. This fuzziness becomes apparent if one considers the stability of an individual competency. While the preconditions for the development of individual competencies are by no means elusive phenomena that change from one situation to the next, it would be wrong to conclude that they are inherited or largely unalterable.

From the perspective of self-regulated behavior, the most important components of the related individual dispositions are metacognitive, motivational, and volitional competencies. To begin with the metacognitive competencies, people differ with regard to their metacognitive knowledge as well as the availability of executive skills as described in more detail earlier. Those who have better knowledge and more sophisticated executive skills are more competent with regard to the reflection of the antecedents and consequences of their own behavior. There are many reports of positive associations between metacognitive competencies and cognitive performance in a variety of domains. In addition, self-reported levels of self-control competencies are even related to measures of social adjustment. Longitudinal studies have shown that low ratings of self-control at early adolescence are associated with later tendencies to delinquency. Some authors thus have argued that a poor level of self-regulation in adolescence lies at the root of much antisocial behavior and aggression.

However, self-reports and rating of self-control competencies are not only estimations of available metacognitive skills. In addition, motivational and volitional dispositions are critical preconditions for successful goal-directed activities. Especially, the quality of the individual achievement motive system forms one of the most important motivational preconditions for successful learning not only in the academic domains but also in most areas of skill acquisition (e.g., sports, music). The achievement motive system can be described from three perspectives: first, by looking at the extent to which the motive is characterized either by a success orientation or by a fear of failure; second and closely related to the first, by looking at the preferred attributions of successful versus nonsuccessful outcomes of one's own behavior; and third, by looking at the individual's self-concept of competencies. Relatively stable individual differences in achievement motives become identifiable in early adolescence which are attained via a series of stages. At each stage, the course can shift toward a success orientation or toward a fear of failure. Even more than with the metacognitive preconditions described earlier, what occurs at these potential turning points is determined by the individual's experiences in his or her social context. When adolescents receive feedback that is not based on social comparisons with peers or criteria set up to measure their performance against achievement standards (reference norms), but rather on the level of performance achieved by themselves up to that point, this has a number of positive effects on the further development of their learning motives. This leads to more realistic achievement goals, more beneficial causal attributions and self-assessments, higher self-concepts of ability, and stronger control beliefs as well as enhanced willingness to exert effort. The use of individual reference norms to evaluate the outcomes of their own behavior has a positive effect on the development of the achievement motive system.

Even with adequate motivation, one still sometimes fails to realize behavior objectives. One of the main reasons discussed in the research for the incomplete realization of intentions are impeding emotions and suboptimal volitional processes. To illustrate this, we again refer to the area of academic learning outline in more detail earlier: The question of what volitional preconditions develop until adolescents can perhaps best be approached in relation to the strategies of volitional behavioral control. In this regard, high levels of volitional competency rely on the capability of ignoring information irrelevant to the particular learning objective at hand (*attention control*) and on the focussed processing of the information relevant to their goals (*encoding control*). Other aspects that are characteristic to volitional competencies are whether subjects can motivate themselves to carry out their intended activities (*motivational control*), whether they can influence their emotional state in such a way as to increase their efficiency (*emotional control*), whether they are capable of stopping thoughts of failure and abandoning goals that have proved impossible to reach (*activation control*), and whether they are capable of translating their current objectives – despite competing behavioral impulses – into action (*initiation control*).

Although we know more about the benefits of metacognition and self-regulated behavior in the domains of academic learning than in most other areas of daily life of young people, it seems obvious it is helpful for being successful in life if the related competencies are well developed.

Summary

Both metacognition and self-regulated learning are concepts with high relevance for personal development, skill acquisition and, not least, they play a key role in lifelong learning. Since metacognitive and other self-regulatory processes have been shown to be strongly related to academic achievement, they are often studied during academic learning episodes. The milestones in the development of self-reflective behavior and learning activities take place before children enter adolescence. One of the most important steps can be seen in the evolvement of a reflective self-abstraction in 10- or 11-year-old children. This prerequisite for self-reflective action was already observed by Piaget about 70 years ago. After individuals have acquired the basic components and precursors of metacognition and, in a broader sense, of self-regulated learning, the further development and differentiation of those skills and capabilities becomes a highly individually varying process which strongly underlies contextual influences. Accordingly, traditional developmental models that clearly describe an age-related line of metacognitive and self-regulatory development are not as useful for the period of adolescence as compared to childhood. Therefore, many researchers have been particularly interested in the interindividual differences *within* an age group because of their predictive power for academic success.

Given the strong influence of context factors as, to name but a few, the parental home, peers, and the learning environment, measurable changes in brain development, are not easily described directly on the level of behavior. For example, although we would predict age-related gains in metacognition and self-regulation, longitudinal studies have revealed inconsistent findings, with some showing even a decline in those capabilities over adolescence: Although an increase in metacognitive skills and strategy use between the ages of 14 and 20 has been observed in several empirical studies, others report a progressive decline in other self-regulatory variables during this period. We can assume that, once acquired, students do not lose their capability to self-regulate when they pass through adolescence. Instead, the decline may be predominantly caused by motivational reasons that are associated with the characteristics of the period of adolescence, when students are increasingly faced with issues other than academic learning that attract their attention. The substantial *interindividual* variability in motivational characteristics makes it difficult to describe systematic *intraindividual* developmental changes in metacognitive and self-regulatory variables over adolescence.

Taken together, the growing age and the enhanced acquisition of implicit and explicit knowledge in young individuals correspond to an increased functionality of metacognition and self-regulated learning. However, the use of the advantages of these capabilities strongly depends on motivational and volitional as well as on contextual factors.

See also: Achievement Motivation; Executive Function.

Further Reading

Bandura A (1997) *Self-efficacy: The Exercise of Control*. New York: Freeman.

Duckworth AL and Seligman MEP (2006) Self-discipline gives girls the edge: Gender in self-discipline, grades, and achievement test scores. *Journal of Educational Psychology* 98: 198–208.

Gollwitzer PM (1999) Implementation intentions: Strong effects of simple plans. *American Psychologist* 54: 493–503.

Gollwitzer PM, Gawrilow C, and Oettingen G (2010) The power of planning: Effective self-regulation in goal striving. In: Hassin R, Ochsner K, and Trope Y (eds.) *Self-Control in Society, Mind, and Brain*. Oxford University Press.

Graham S and Harris KR (2003) Students with learning disabilities and the process of writing: A meta-analysis of SRSD studies. In: Swanson HL, Harris KR, and Graham S (eds.) *Handbook of Learning Disabilities*, pp. 323–344. New York: Guilford.

Kitsantas A and Zimmerman BJ (2002) Comparing self-regulatory processes among novice, non-expert, and expert volleyball players: A micronanlytic study. *Journal of Applied Sport Psychology* 13: 365–379.

Kitsantas A and Zimmerman BJ (2006) Enhancing self-regulation of practice: The influence of graphing and self-evaluative standards. *Metacognition and Learning* 1: 202–212.

Schunk DH and Zimmerman BJ (eds.) (2008) *Motivation and Self-Regulated Learning: Theory, Research, and Applications*. New York: Erlbaum.

Waters HS and Schneider W (eds.) (2010) *Metacognition, Strategy Use, and Instruction*. New York: Guilford.

Weinert FE (2001) Concept of competence: A conceptual clarification. In: Rychen DL and Salgamik LH (eds.) *Defining and Selecting Key Competencies*, pp. 45–65. Göttingen: Hogrefe.

Zimmerman BJ (2000) Attaining self-regulation: A social cognitive perspective. In: Boekaerts M, Pintrich PR, and Zeidner M (eds.) *Handbook of Self-Regulation*, pp. 13–39. San Diego, CA: Academic Press.

Zimmerman BJ and Martinez-Pons M (1990) Student differences in self-regulated learning: Relating grade, sex, and giftedness to self-efficacy and strategy use. *Journal of Educational Psychology* 82: 51–59.

Relevant Websites

http://metacognition.org/ – Metacognition.org website.

http://www.des.emory.edu/mfp/self-efficacy.html – Information on Self-Efficacy.

http://en.wikibooks.org/wiki/The_Practice_of_Learning_Theories/Self-Regulated_Learning – The Practice of Learning Theories/Self-Regulated Learning.

http://findarticles.com/p/articles/mi_m0NQM/is_2_41/ai_90190493/?tag=content;col1 – Becoming a self-regulated learner: an overview.

http://www.idea-frankfurt.eu/homepage – IDeA (Center for Research on Individual Development and Adaptive Education of Children at Risk) founded by the German Institute for International Educational Research (DIPF) and Goethe Universität Frankfurt.

Motivation

M E Ford, George Mason University, Fairfax, VA, USA
P R Smith, Madison Learning, Seattle, WA, USA

Glossary

Capability beliefs: This component of motivation provides advice about what goals to pursue at what level of effort and persistence through judgments about whether one has the knowledge, skills, and biological capabilities needed to attain a goal.

Context beliefs: This component of motivation provides advice about what goals to pursue at what level of effort and persistence through judgments about whether the environment will support efforts to pursue a goal.

Emotions: This component of motivation energizes and regulates action and, for each evolved emotion pattern, includes three subcomponents integrated into a functional unit: a *biological* component that supports energy production and action requirements; an *expressive* element consisting of characteristic facial and vocal expressions, gestures, and body language; and an *affective* element that is the conscious 'feeling' part of the emotion.

Motivation: The organized patterning of four closely interrelated sets of psychological processes: personal goals, capability beliefs and context beliefs (collectively known as personal agency beliefs), and emotions. Motivation plays a leadership role in human behavior and development.

Personal agency beliefs: Unified patterns of capability and context beliefs.

Personal goals: This component of motivation comprises thoughts about desired and undesired future states and outcomes.

Possible selves: Imagined future identities – a manifestation of the personal goal component of motivation. Possible selves include both desired and feared identities.

Social purpose: A motivational pattern directed by one or more integrative social relationship goals (belongingness, social responsibility, equity, and resource provision). Social purpose functions as a 'meta-amplifier' for the entire motivational system.

Thriving: A term used to describe a motivational pattern in which each of the four components of motivation have been 'amplified.' The components of the thriving pattern are an active approach goal orientation, personal optimism, mindful tenacity, and emotional wisdom.

Thriving with social purpose: A motivational pattern that integrates thriving and social purpose into a unified whole. Thriving and social purpose are mutually reinforcing qualities of motivational systems that expand and strengthen the capacity for effective leadership of self and others.

Introduction

As illustrated by the contents of this encyclopedia, motivational issues are at the heart of nearly every major topic in the study of adolescent development. Theory and research on identity development, career decision making, and civic engagement are organized around adolescents' self-directed exploration of goals, values, and social roles. Efforts to understand the nature of family, peer, and educational influences on adolescent behavior are largely concerned with the motivational impact of these socialization agents. Studies of deviance, drug use, and risky behavior in youth typically focus on motivational concepts and propositions. Even studies of biological development in adolescence tend to focus on motivation-rich topics like body image, sexuality, and neural-hormonal influences on decision making and behavior.

What Is Motivation?

Motivation plays a leadership role in human functioning and development. That is why it is a central theme in so many research and intervention efforts. Nevertheless, it has been a struggle to reach consensus on precisely what motivation is all about. That is because motivation is not just 'one thing.' Rather, humans have complexly organized motivational systems with several integrated components (analogous to our circulatory or digestive systems). After reviewing all contemporary theories of motivation in psychology, education, and business, Martin Ford developed the following definition of motivation as part of his integrative Motivational Systems Theory:

> Motivation is the organized patterning of four closely interrelated sets of psychological processes: *personal goals*, which are thoughts about desired and undesired potential future states; *capability beliefs* and *context beliefs* (collectively known as *personal agency beliefs*), which include thoughts about the anticipated consequences of pursuing those goals; and *emotions*, which include affective states related to the possible consequences of pursuing those goals.

The collaborative nature of the work these processes carry out can be represented using a simple formula and a triangle graphic that emphasizes the leadership role played by personal goals (**Figure 1**).

Together, these closely allied processes help adolescents imagine future possibilities and then decide which alternatives to pursue at what level of effort and persistence. For example, exploration of educational and career options will involve thoughts about the 'fit' of those alternatives with one's personal interests and identity, as well as 'reality checking' with respect to emotions and personal agency beliefs ("Can I succeed in this field? Will people support me if I choose this pathway?" "Does this feel 'right' for me?"). Similarly, assessing the attractiveness

 doi:10.1016/B978-0-12-373915-5.00028-0

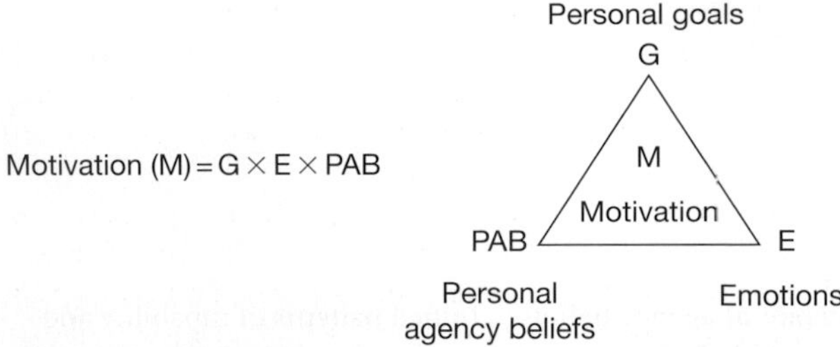

Figure 1 The formula for human motivation from Motivational Systems Theory emphasizes the dynamic interactions among personal goals, emotions, and personal agency beliefs. The graphic representation of this formula emphasizes the leadership role played by personal goals in 'motivational headquarters,' with emotions and personal agency beliefs serving primarily in an advisory capacity. Reproduced with permission from Ford and Smith (2007).

of a potential romantic partner will involve not only thoughts about the compatibility of that individual with relevant personal goals (such as intimacy and security), but also sorting out evaluative thoughts and feelings such as excitement ("Am I attracted to this opportunity only because it's new?") and self-doubt ("Will I be rejected if I pursue this opportunity?").

When an adolescent experiences a strong sense of purpose, empowering emotions, and feelings of confidence and support from others, motivation will be at its peak. Imagine, for example, a young person engrossed in an intensive episode of online social networking, or enrolling in a new school and being welcomed into a club (or a gang) that provides opportunities to pursue special interests or satisfy compelling emotional needs. Conversely, if 'mixed messages' emerge from one or more of the elements in 'motivational headquarters' (see **Figure 1**), that can inhibit or terminate goal pursuit. That is why it is important to keep in mind that, although research on adolescent motivation has often focused on just one component of motivation, all of these processes are always working closely together as a *motivational system*. Moreover, motivational systems also must work in partnership with three other sets of functional processes that comprise the overall person–environment system:

1. knowledge and skill-related capabilities;
2. biological processes; and
3. environmental elements.

The fact that motivation involves a system of dynamically interacting components explains why research on motivation often yields complex, nonlinear findings, and why traditional methods that rely on 'averaging' techniques can be quite deceptive. Adolescent motivation is best understood by looking at the configuration of multiple, contextually relevant processes within particular individuals, followed by an identification of subsets of adolescents who manifest shared motivational dynamics and developmental trajectories. Consider, for example, trying to make a prediction about whether your adolescent son or daughter will engage in risky sexual behavior. It is hard to imagine being able to make a reliable prediction without having information about the content, strength, and stability of each motivational component and how they will 'play out' in situations with different sets of contingencies and skill requirements.

Why Do We Have These Motivational Systems?

Our minds and bodies evolved to enable us to control aspects of our world, ourselves, and others that are important to us, thereby insuring our individual and collective vitality. As Eric Klinger and W. Miles Cox explain in their *Handbook of Motivational Counseling*:

> If animals evolved with a motile strategy to go after the substances and conditions they need, the most basic requirement for their survival is successful goal-striving. In that case, all animal evolution, right up to humans, must have centered on natural selection of whatever facilitated attaining goals. This must mean that everything about humans evolved in the service of successful goal-striving – including the human anatomy, physiology, cognition, and emotion.

This evolutionary perspective helps explain why personal goals function as 'the leader' within the adolescent's developing mind and body. Fundamentally, humans are self-directed, continuously learning creatures that require mechanisms for making sound decisions not only about current opportunities and circumstances but also about the future. *That is how we are designed*. That design principle, along with enabling biological and cognitive developments during the second decade of life, is what makes it possible for adolescents to develop enriched self-concepts and to engage in an intensive period of 'identity development' (see the articles on Self-Concept and Identity Development in this encyclopedia) – that is, to imagine 'possible selves,' explore alternative futures, and make commitments intended to make those goal thoughts a reality.

Consistent with this premise, adolescents are generally most aware of the impact of their motivational systems when they are actively engaged in the self-directed pursuit of their core personal goals. Dreaming about the future, feeling strong emotions, making meaningful choices, striving to make things better, connecting with other people – these are the things that are at the heart of the adolescent experience. Conversely, when adolescents do not have a sense of self-direction, autonomy, and connection, they tend to feel 'lifeless' – bored, alienated, depressed, or even suicidal.

The earliest-evolving motivational systems involved pursuit of what might be thought of as *preinstalled goals* regulated by homeostatic control systems (e.g., regulation of body temperature around a set point of 98.6 °F; regulation of water and salt levels at life-sustaining levels). Although not the focus of this article, these systems are very much a part of adolescent motivation and are heavily implicated in certain types of concerns prototypically associated with adolescence (e.g., obesity, eating disorders, alcohol and drug abuse; see Volume 3 of this encyclopedia).

The focus of this article is on what we have been calling *personal goals* – future states and outcomes that we are not only capable of mentally imaging, but that we are able to 'see' ourselves pursuing as actors in a 'life movie' for which we are the writer and director. This imaging process involves both empowerment and constraints. An adolescent may have high aspirations that go far beyond the possibilities suggested by current circumstances. At the same time, those aspirations may need to be pursued within the framework of significant biological, cognitive, or resource limitations. Parents, teachers, and mentors may be key factors in opening up new options and pathways, but other 'cast members' in the adolescents' emerging life story may be unresponsive or create obstacles to goal attainment. That is why *personal agency* has been such an important theme in research on adolescent development. When young people experience a loss of personal agency – as suggested by terms such as hopelessness and futility – the results can be motivationally debilitating. Conversely, when adolescents engage the world with a sense of self-efficacy and trust in the world around them, those beliefs – in conjunction with the emotions linked to those beliefs – help maximize their motivational potential.

The Role of Consciousness in Adolescent Motivation

It is important to understand that the vast majority of activity in 'motivational headquarters' (as represented by the triangle in **Figure 1**) occurs beneath awareness as part of our ongoing implementation of familiar routines associated with everyday activity. Being able to 'automatize' habitual patterns of behavior has great adaptive value. However, as circumstances change and new opportunities arise, this *self-organizing* tendency can also make it difficult to alter habits and routines that are no longer adaptive (or only adaptive in limited circumstances). Significant behavior change typically requires a powerful investment of conscious energy focused on key motivational components. For example, an adolescent experiencing a lack of energy and meaning in their daily activities may need to seek a better understanding of whether they are making choices and investing their time in ways that are aligned with their core personal goals (as illustrated by the assessment tools at www.implicitself.com). A young person suffering from a 'crisis of confidence' as they enter a new level of schooling or a new social context may need help bringing their thoughts and feelings about personal strengths and weaknesses into awareness where they can be discussed, assessed, and empirically tested.

Another key aspect of consciousness as it relates to motivation is the time frame in which one can imagine pursing personal goals. The time dimension is also related to the magnitude of change that can be envisioned. Preadolescents can easily imagine incremental changes over a relatively short time span (e.g., starting a new school year, hanging out with a new friend, trying a new activity). However, one of the emergent capabilities in adolescence is the ability to also think about the outcomes of goal pursuit over a much longer time period, and in doing so to imagine transformational changes in capabilities, contexts, activities, and identities. Indeed, one of the most commonly used criteria for assessing maturity during this age period is the degree to which an adolescent engages in preparation to pursue longer-term life goals, such as those related to career, family, and health outcomes. This 'broadening of the motivational horizon' is a defining feature of adolescent development.

The ability to think about hypothetical futures in ways that are less constrained by current realities can have a downside, however, for adolescents who are still developing the neural mechanisms responsible for regulating those thoughts and associated. For example, young people who can envision the potentially exhilarating outcomes associated with a risky behavior but have not yet developed the ability to regulate those impulses in the face of possible legal or health consequences may be at greater risk of life-changing errors in judgment than more mature adolescents who can think about the future in broader, deeper ways. Adolescents who have developed the ability to engage in elaborate fantasies about their social lives and how others will react to them may become irrationally despondent about minor (or even imaginary) flaws or transgressions. As Mark Leary warns in *The Curse of the Self*, the ability to think self-consciously not only facilitates motivation and identity development, but it also makes it possible for adolescents to become self-absorbed, to ruminate about imagined failures and shortcomings, to worry excessively about the past and the future, and to become obsessively concerned about their self-image and social reputation.

Personal Goals

Erik Erikson proposed that identity formation is the central developmental task for adolescents. Translating this proposal into motivational terms, we would assert that the central developmental task for adolescents is developing self-awareness of their core personal goals and how they relate to consequential choices in various life domains (e.g., work, religion, politics, leisure, friendships, gender roles, intimate relationships). Without this fundamental self-knowledge, responses to work and relationship problems will tend to be expedient rather than thoughtful and satisfying. Achievements will tend to be ephemeral rather than cumulative and meaningful. Choices and commitments will tend to be disconnected and shortsighted rather than strategic and facilitative of good developmental outcomes.

In the early days of psychology, it was taken for granted that identifying and classifying a person's underlying motives was a central question for anyone seeking to understand or improve human behavior. As a result, several pioneering scholars developed wide-ranging motivational taxonomies, highlighted by Abraham Maslow's hierarchical scheme that included Physiological and Safety needs at the bottom of the hierarchy and Belongingness-Love, Esteem, and 'Self-Actualization' needs at the upper levels of the hierarchy (Maslow also proposed the less familiar categories of Aesthetic and Cognitive needs).

Although these early motivational taxonomies proved to be of limited utility, the need for such tools remained. Whether one focuses on 'needs' (personal goals with primarily internal origins) or 'values' (personal goals with primarily social origins), having meaningful concepts and a rich vocabulary for thinking about and discussing personal goals can greatly facilitate successful goal pursuit, especially for adolescents, as that is the age period during which both the capability for thinking about the longer-term implications of core personal goals and the need to do so emerge. In that spirit, Martin Ford and C.W. Nichols developed a *Taxonomy of Human Goals* grounded in contemporary motivational science that provides a comprehensive accounting of the high-level goal content that people may experience in their thinking about desired (and undesired) future outcomes (see **Table 1**).

Based on data from the *Assessment of Personal* Goals, the measure designed to estimate the strength of each of the 24 goal categories in the Taxonomy of Human Goals, it is evident that certain goal categories are particularly compelling to adolescents and young adults, both generally and in comparison

Table 1 The Ford and Nichols taxonomy of human goals

Integrative social relationship goals	
Belongingness	Building or maintaining attachments, friendships, intimacy, or a sense of community; avoiding feelings of social isolation or separateness
Social responsibility	Keeping interpersonal commitments, meeting social role obligations, and conforming to social and moral rules; avoiding social transgressions and unethical or illegal conduct
Equity	Promoting fairness, justice, or equality; avoiding unfair actions
Resource provision	Giving approval, support, assistance, advice, or validation to others; avoiding selfish or uncaring behavior
Self-assertive social relationship goals	
Individuality	Feeling unique, special, or different; avoiding similarity or conformity
Self-determination	Experiencing a sense of freedom to act or make choices; avoiding the feeling of being pressured, constrained, or coerced
Superiority	Comparing favorably to others in terms of winning, status, or success; avoiding unfavorable comparisons with others
Resource acquisition	Obtaining approval, support, assistance, advice, or validation from others; avoiding social disapproval or rejection
Affective goals	
Entertainment	Experiencing excitement or heightened arousal; avoiding boredom or stressful inactivity
Tranquility	Feeling relaxed and at ease; avoiding stressful overarousal
Happiness	Experiencing feelings of joy, satisfaction, or well-being; avoiding feelings of emotional distress or dissatisfaction
Bodily sensations	Experiencing pleasure associated with physical sensations, physical movement, or bodily contact; avoiding unpleasant or uncomfortable bodily sensations
Physical well-being	Feeling healthy, energetic, or physically robust; avoiding feelings of lethargy, weakness, or ill health
Cognitive goals	
Exploration	Satisfying one's curiosity about personally meaningful events; avoiding a sense of being uninformed or not knowing what's going on
Understanding	Gaining knowledge or making sense out of something; avoiding misconceptions, erroneous beliefs, or feelings of confusion
Intellectual creativity	Engaging in activities involving original thinking or novel or interesting ideas; avoiding mindless or familiar ways of thinking
Positive self-evaluations	Maintaining a sense of self-confidence, pride, or self-worth; avoiding feelings of failure, guilt, or incompetence
Task goals	
Mastery	Meeting a challenging standard of achievement or improvement; avoiding incompetence, mediocrity, or decrements in performance
Task creativity	Engaging in activities involving artistic expression or creativity; avoiding tasks that do not provide opportunities for creative action
Management	Maintaining order, organization, or productivity in daily life tasks; avoiding sloppiness, inefficiency, or disorganization
Material gain	Increasing the amount of money or tangible goods one has; avoiding the loss of money or material possessions
Safety	Being unharmed, physically secure, and free from risk; avoiding threatening, depriving, or harmful circumstances
Subjective organization goals	
Unity	Experiencing a profound or spiritual sense of connectedness, harmony, or oneness with people, nature, or a greater power; avoiding feelings of psychological disunity or disorganization
Transcendence	Experiencing optimal or extraordinary states of functioning; avoiding feeling trapped within the boundaries of ordinary experience

Reproduced with permission from Ford and Smith (2007).

with older adults. Social relationship goals within both the integrative and self-assertive clusters are of special concern to adolescents, especially those involving the creation of meaningful friendships and group membership identities (Belongingness) and socially relevant personal identities (Individuality). Consistent with these motives, concerns about social evaluation (Resource acquisition) and self-evaluation (Positive self-evaluation) are prominent in many adolescents' goal profiles. Self-determination is also a compelling goal category for many adolescents, consistent with the autonomy-related tasks associated with this developmental period.

Perhaps not surprisingly, the largest age differences for any single goal category are consistently found for Entertainment goals. That helps explain why boredom is so aversive to many adolescents and why thrill-seeking is much more commonly observed in this age range than in later age periods. Relative to adults, young people are also somewhat more heavily invested in Physical Well-Being goals (consistent with cultural images of youthful vitality) and Material Gain goals (consistent with adolescents' anticipation of taking on adult roles).

It is important to emphasize, however, that there are vast individual differences among adolescents in their personal goal profiles. Each young person is truly unique in terms of the constellation of issues, activities, and experiences they find most fascinating and fulfilling, and in the methods they use to explore and discover what aspects of life fit best with their core personal goals. That is one of the things that makes this developmental period so interesting. It is often not until adolescence, when opportunities for autonomy increase and the development of capabilities for long-term planning and reflection accelerate, that the core personal goals that organize identity and personality development become clearly evident. Aligning those underlying motivational forces with the choices and pathways that adolescents pursue is the key to laying the foundation for an engaging and meaningful future.

Personal Agency Beliefs

Personal goals are thoughts that represent *desired* (and undesired) future outcomes that people wish to experience (or avoid). However, deciding whether to actually pursue an imagined goal also depends a great deal on the *expected* outcomes of goal-seeking activity. Among the variety of terms used to label expectancies about the consequences of personal goal seeking (e.g., self-efficacy, outcome expectancies, perceived competence, perceived control) is the integrative concept of *personal agency beliefs*, or PABs. PABs assess whether personal goals are realistic and attainable, and for those goals that are being actively pursued, the likelihood that further progress can be made.

There are two distinct types of personal agency beliefs. *Capability beliefs* reflect judgments about whether one has the knowledge, skills and biological capabilities needed to attain a goal. In contrast, *context beliefs* focus on whether the environment will support efforts to pursue a goal. PABs thus make it possible to bring all of the major components of human functioning into the decision-making process in 'motivational headquarters,' as shown in **Figure 2**.

Over the past several decades, motivation scholars have focused much of their attention on the PAB component of motivational systems, as illustrated by well-researched topics such as self-efficacy, self-determination, self-worth, and learned helplessness (or learned optimism). PABs are also featured in theories of personal causation, effectance motivation, reactance, causal attributions, and optimal experience.

The basic premise underlying all of these theories – for which there is now extensive empirical evidence – is that, to develop and maintain strong motivational patterns, it is necessary to have a fundamental belief that *the future can be better than the present*. This requires a belief that there are pathways that can lead to a better future as well as a belief that one has the capabilities and support needed to successfully follow those pathways. For example, school motivation is strengthened when adolescents have faith in their capabilities and in the people responsible for helping them negotiate the transition to adulthood. Career exploration is more vigorous when options are seen as relatively unconstrained by limitations of ability and opportunity. Conversely, many types of developmental dysfunction in adolescence have been attributed to negative or weak personal agency beliefs (and the emotions associated with those PAB patterns), including academic failure and school dropout, delinquency, substance abuse, eating disorders, and suicidal ideation (see Volume 3 of this encyclopedia).

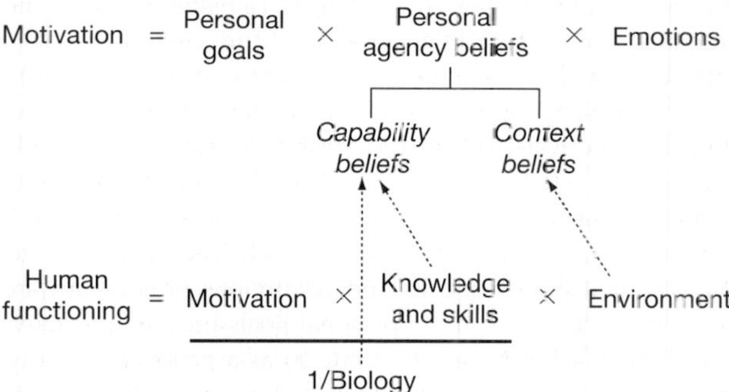

Figure 2 Illustration of how judgments of biological functioning, knowledge and skills, and the environment are represented in 'motivational headquarters.'

Personal Agency Belief Patterns

Capability and context beliefs are quite distinctive in terms of their focus (within the self vs. outside the self); nevertheless, they operate as a unitary system, like an advisory board. While it is possible to look at each advisor separately, the motivational outcome remains rather unpredictable until you get a joint perspective. This important principle is illustrated by the personal agency belief patterns shown in **Figure 3**.

Adolescent scholars and helping professionals have tended to focus primarily on the developmental impact of negative PABs, as illustrated by the vast range of studies focused on the potentially debilitating impact of unfavorable self-concepts, low self-esteem, and perceptions of alienation. Although there is much individual complexity and variability, there is substantial evidence supporting the view that when adolescents' habitual thought patterns are infused with negative capability and/or context beliefs, that increases the risk of conduct problems and emotional disorders. These problems can also be amplified by the increased self-consciousness adolescents experience as a natural result of their expanded cognitive capabilities, and by the tendency for feelings of self-worth to be closely intertwined with body image during adolescence – an age period when qualities associated with physical appearance are inherently unstable and worrisome (see the article on Body Image in this encyclopedia).

It is important to note, however, that exaggerated PAB appraisals can also lead to significant problems. When adolescents are overconfident, they do not feel a need to reflect on possible negative outcomes or to prepare for potential risks and challenges – for example, by engaging in responsible driving, contraception, and studying habits.

Context beliefs		Capability beliefs: Strong	Capability beliefs: Moderate or variable	Capability beliefs: Negative
	Positive	R Robust pattern	E Encouraged pattern	F Fragile pattern
	Moderate or variable	T Tenacious pattern	C Cautious pattern	I Insecure pattern
	Negative	A1/A2 Antagonistic or accepting pattern	D Discouraged pattern	H Hopeless pattern

Figure 3 The Motivational Systems Theory taxonomy of personal agency belief patterns. Reproduced with permission from Ford and Smith (2007).

Emotions

Emotions are a significant part of all motivational patterns. Emotions, in turn, are composed of three subcomponents integrated into a functional unit. At the heart of each emotion pattern is a *biological* component that supports the energy production and action requirements (e.g., increased or decreased heart rate, accelerated breathing) associated with the pursuit of an activated goal in a particular set of circumstances. Fundamentally, emotions evolved to facilitate immediate action (e.g., fear responses are generally well underway before we are even conscious of them). Newer emotions (e.g., guilt and shame) emerged over evolutionary time as changing conditions of living produced new action requirements for survival, reproduction, and well-being.

In addition, emotions include an *expressive* element, as evidenced by the fact that there are characteristic facial and vocal expressions, gestures, and body language associated with different kinds of emotion patterns. These expressive features help communicate what is being felt to others, which is an important way that people influence how others respond to them. Each emotion pattern also includes an *affective* element. That is the conscious 'feeling' part of the emotion that evolved to help sustain the motivational impact of emotions. Feelings are conscious experiences that arise from the brain's mapping of the bodily changes caused by the triggering of an emotion. Consistent with the biochemistry of these bodily changes, each feeling has a valence – some variation on pleasure or pain. That is why we tend to think of emotions as being 'positive' or 'negative' even though the feelings associated with each emotion pattern are qualitatively unique.

As Antonio Damasio (*Looking for Spinoza: Joy, sorrow, and the feeling brain*) has explained, at the core of each feeling is an idea of the body being in a certain way – a reference to the biological and expressive components of the emotion pattern. However, feelings tend to get linked to thoughts and perceptions in learned associative networks rather than existing in some 'pure' state. This helps explain how emotions can play such a pervasive motivational role in our daily lives, and why emotions are such an important aspect of adolescent development (see the article in this encyclopedia on Emotional Development). Feelings arise from emotions, but they are not just conscious manifestations of an emotional state. Feelings are closely linked to a variety of relevant perceptions and thoughts, with the range and depth of possible cognitive associations expanding significantly during the adolescent age period. That developmental shift can produce unfamiliar emotional experiences that are far more powerful than anything the adolescent has experienced in the past. The results can be emotionally enriching but also psychologically dangerous. Without the perspective of experience (e.g., the realization that feelings are context-specific and that even very powerful emotions will tend to fade over time), it is easy for adolescents to assume that profound feelings of despair, shame, or self-loathing will never go away.

Moreover, feelings can make certain kinds of perceptions and thoughts more accessible even if they are not directly related to that particular feeling. For example, when an adolescent feels good about some accomplishment or good fortune, they will tend to focus on pleasant experiences, have an optimistic mindset, and think more broadly and creatively. In contrast, when negative feelings cannot be resolved, the adolescent's thought patterns will tend to narrow and become infused with negative memories and expectations. That is why chronic negative emotions are a much greater concern with respect to adolescent motivation than emotional volatility, despite the image of adolescence as a period of 'storm and stress.'

Thriving with Social Purpose

Because adolescence involves many new and increasingly consequential challenges, much of the research on adolescent motivation has focused on what parents would generally regard as 'developmental disasters' – school dropout, teen pregnancy, attempted suicide, drug abuse, criminal activity, and the like. However, for the majority of adolescents – and even for most of those who suffer some sort of major developmental 'setback' – the more salient long-term question is how to make the most of the motivational 'gifts' we have inherited from our ancestors. We are all goal-directed by nature. Our minds and bodies naturally generate motivating thoughts and emotions on a continuous basis. So, how can we help adolescents not only to survive the transition to adulthood, but also to thrive both as an individual and as a contributing member of society? In other words, what are the qualities that differentiate 'ordinary' motivational patterns from those characteristic of a more optimally functioning motivational system?

Consistent with the idea that optimal functioning is associated with a configuration of multiple elements within an integrated system, Martin Ford and Peyton Smith have coined the phrase *Thriving with Social Purpose* (TSP) to summarize what happens when the four components of human motivation – personal goals, capability beliefs, context beliefs, and emotions – are 'amplified' in dynamic, mutually reinforcing patterns that reliably facilitate developmental growth. TSP modes of functioning facilitate goal pursuit in the present while also providing a motivational foundation for longer-term success and well-being. The centerpiece of the TSP motivational pattern is an active approach goal orientation informed by a fundamental concern for others (*social purpose*). This orientation is supported and strengthened by a firm belief in one's ability to make progress toward meaningful goals (*personal optimism*), a persistent tendency to imagine alternative pathways when progress is challenged (*mindful tenacity*), and intentional efforts to align emotions and circumstances in ways that will best facilitate goal progress (*emotional wisdom*).

In the next section, the parameters associated with amplified motivational processing (the concepts in brackets in **Figure 4**) are described for each element in the overall motivational system. Taken together, these processes compose a *thriving* pattern of functioning that facilitates productive engagement with relevant contexts and continuous progress toward personal goals. When those personal goals include integrative social relationship goals (see **Table 1**) as a persistent priority, the resulting *social purpose* facilitates an even broader and more meaningful pattern of optimal functioning by enhancing not only the well-being of the individual but also the welfare of the social systems of which that individual is a part.

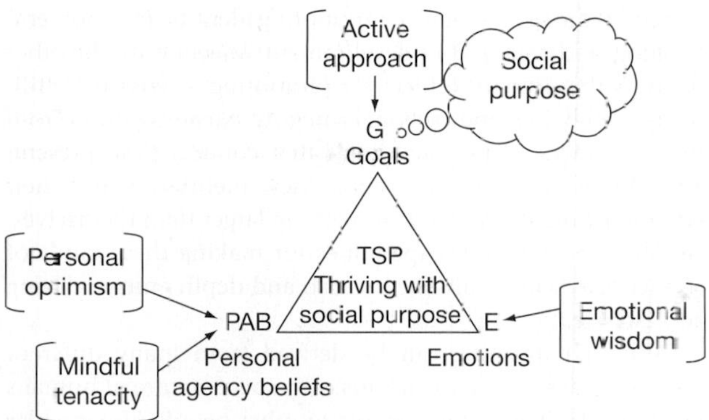

Figure 4 A diagram representing the amplified motivational components constituting the Thriving with Social Purpose pattern of human motivation. Reproduced with permission from Ford and Smith (2007).

Thriving Motivational Patterns

Active Approach Goal Orientation

The key to establishing a thriving motivational pattern is the cultivation of strong leadership qualities in the personal goal component of system functioning. Such qualities include a clear understanding of one's core personal goals and the ability to stay focused on those goals. Consistent with theories of identity development, which emphasize the critical importance of exploring developmental options in consequential life domains, goal amplification also includes a willingness to explore alternatives, take psychological risks, and maintain a persistent bias toward initiating action (as opposed to becoming mired in evaluative thoughts and feelings or having external circumstances dictate options and opportunities). Collectively, this *active approach* goal orientation promotes engagement with a wide variety of social, cultural, educational, and vocational opportunities while also facilitating continuous self-improvement.

Ample research supports the hypothesized importance of an active approach orientation for optimal functioning. Notably, this work has been conducted within the context of a variety of different motivation theories. Of particular note within the adolescent motivation literature is research indicating that an active approach goal orientation is closely linked to school achievement. But regardless of the developmental domain, there is a common motivational theme: when adolescents think about the uncertainties and challenges of the future as something positive to be embraced rather than something negative to be feared, they are more likely to explore, learn, minimize stress, and enhance their developmental potential.

Personal Optimism

PABs can facilitate and further strengthen the orientation to seek out and explore opportunities and challenges. But they can also 'put on the brakes' if fundamental doubts arise about personal capabilities. The key here is to develop goal-striving habits of sufficient diligence and persistence to make the contingency between effort and success reliably apparent. That is how young people develop trust in their ability to make progress toward meaningful goals through their own efforts.

The use of the modifier 'personal' in the phrase *personal optimism* is important because there is little evidence to support the notion that optimism in general is associated with effective functioning, either in terms of performance accomplishments or general well-being. A positive world view will have little motivational impact if that view does not include personal agency as its centerpiece. In contrast, a vast body of evidence linking capability beliefs to optimal functioning has emerged in recent years, with much of that research having been conducted with adolescents and young adults.

It is also important to understand that personal optimism is very different from 'wishful thinking.' Personal optimism combines positive expectations with realistic representations of current circumstances. It is this coupling of motivating 'feed-forward' information and accurate feedback messages that makes it possible for adolescents to stay focused on the planning and problem solving needed to facilitate effective goal pursuit, and to insure that the challenges they seek out are 'optimal' (i.e., developmentally and personally appropriate).

Mindful Tenacity

The confident, self-directed motivational messages flowing from an active approach goal orientation and a genuine sense of personal optimism are necessary but not sufficient to maintain an overall thriving pattern. To facilitate optimal functioning, there must also be a motivational bridge connecting the internal psychology of the person to the external environment. Context beliefs provide that bridge. As with capability beliefs, context beliefs have the greatest positive impact when they are grounded in reality but persistently hopeful about the future. When both of these information channels are flowing, an adolescent can feel discouraged and disconsolate in the present and yet still maintain motivation by focusing on future pathways and possibilities that are more hopeful than the (objectively) unresponsive conditions that are currently thwarting goal progress.

Although family, school, peer group, and cultural contexts can vary dramatically from one occasion to the next (as illustrated by the contents of Volume 2 in this encyclopedia), in a broad sense most young people are developing in circumstances that are moderately or inconsistently responsive rather than consistently responsive or consistently unresponsive. Under these circumstances, the optimal PAB pattern is one characterized by *mindful tenacity*. This pattern combines generally positive capability beliefs with hopeful but realistic context beliefs, thus providing adolescents with the motivational strength to persist in the face of challenges and obstacles. Because persistence under these conditions means continuing to imagine alternative pathways for progressing toward a goal, amplified context beliefs are closely linked to creative thought. The imagination process, which is fueled primarily by intrinsic motivational qualities, provides a potential source of inspiration, whereas continued persistence, which is maximized by a synergistic combination of intrinsic and extrinsic goals, provides the necessary perspiration.

Emotional Wisdom

Emotions serve a dual function in supporting a thriving steady state pattern. One primary function is to *energize* the motivational system, thus facilitating action. However, emotions must also *regulate* the kind and amount of energy that is communicated to the rest of the mind and body. In this respect, emotions are like the channel and volume settings on a television set. Amplified emotional functioning means being able to intentionally control both the 'emotional channel' that the person is tuned to and the volume (up or down) to maximize the ability of emotions to facilitate progress toward personal goals. Too much emotion, too little emotion, or simply the wrong kind of emotion for the circumstances, and things could go badly. In contrast, when people are skilled at maintaining such control – which also implies awareness and understanding of the optimal channel and volume for different circumstances – they can be thought of as manifesting *emotional wisdom.*

Because of their relative lack of experience with a variety of new roles, responsibilities, and cultural expectations, adolescents as a group are notoriously lacking in emotional wisdom. However, some adolescents are more skilled than others with respect to the building blocks of emotional wisdom, that is, reflective understanding, emotional empathy, and emotional regulation. These are the adolescents who are recognized by adults as 'maturing quickly' and having the best chance to move successfully into peer leadership, peer mentoring, and peer counseling roles. Conversely, adolescents with limited emotional awareness and emotional regulation skills are more likely to have adjustment problems, use hard drugs, and have multiple sexual partners.

Emotions operate continuously as long as a person is conscious. To facilitate optimal functioning, the 'preset' emotional channels that are generally on throughout the day should be positive emotions such as interest, affection, and gratitude (i.e., assuming they are situationally appropriate). This can be accomplished by aligning daily activities with core personal goals, thus insuring that goal pursuits are generally emotionally engaging and meaningful. The consequences of such alignment for adolescent development can be dramatic. Positive emotions facilitate an active approach goal orientation and broaden the range of information, ideas, and actions that people are open to considering, thus facilitating the creative thinking and behavioral flexibility associated with mindful tenacity. In addition, positive emotions facilitate enduring growth in personal and social resources, including motivational and contextual resources such as personal optimism and social support.

Another facet of amplified emotional functioning is empathy, which can be thought of a uniquely social version of the 'tuning' process involved in emotional wisdom. Empathy is particularly important for promoting those aspects of effective functioning that involve the person's identity as a part of a larger social system (e.g., as a friend, family member, team player, or concerned citizen). Empathy, and more generally interpersonal competence, is thus closely connected to the final component of the TSP framework, which focuses on integrative social goal content.

Social Purpose

From a motivational perspective, optimal functioning has two essential qualities that operate in mutually reinforcing fashion. *Engagement,* which is the primary focus of the thriving pattern, is the key dynamic in promoting identity development, learning, and competence development. *Meaning,* on the other hand, is the primary vehicle for promoting a sense of fulfillment, well-being, and personal integrity. Meaning flows from the attainment of personal goals that connect past, present, and future and that help people view themselves and their accomplishments as part of something larger than themselves. Notably, the cognitive capabilities for making these kinds of connections with adult-like breadth and depth emerge during adolescence.

Although meaning can be derived from many different kinds of goal content, the intrinsically social nature of humans makes goals that connect people to other people of particular interest in understanding motivation and optimal functioning. As shown in **Table 1**, there are four types of integrative social relationship goals that connect people to each other and the larger social units of which they are a part: belongingness, social responsibility, equity, and resource provision. Whenever these types of goals are activated and pursued, *social purpose* is manifested, the effective pursuit of which is widely regarded as being essential for individual and societal development. As noted earlier, this is one of the strongest motivational themes found in the expressed interests and concerns of adolescents.

Social purpose also appears to be linked with other goals representing intrinsically meaningful aspects of human experience. For example, in a study conducted by a research team at Stanford University contrasting the motivational profiles of highly caring and relatively uncaring youth, the adolescent exemplars of social purpose were three to five times more likely than their counterparts to endorse goals related to intellectual and task creativity, unity, understanding, and individuality, suggesting that caring for others may be part of a larger pattern of seeking to engage life in ways that are rich in meaning. In contrast, adolescents with little investment in integrative social goals manifested motivational patterns that are rarely associated with optimal functioning, including a self-absorbed, hedonistic pattern; a hypermasculine pattern focused on power and control; and a pragmatic-defensive pattern oriented toward stability maintenance.

Developmental Implications of TSP Motivational Functioning

As shown in **Figure 4**, social purpose transcends the impact of other motivational amplifiers by functioning as a 'meta-amplifier' for the entire system. Analogous to changing a black-and-white photograph into a color photograph, social purpose enables young people to experience life differently, with transformative implications for behavior and development.

TSP Contributes to Health, Well-Being, and Longevity

Research on altruism and social bonding in adolescence (and across the life span) makes it clear that TSP is 'good for you.' Compared to young people who do not often display TSP qualities, adolescents who are motivationally thriving and who are genuinely concerned about the welfare of others have better mental and physical health outcomes in adulthood, more satisfying lives, and greater emotional stability. Conversely, non-TSP modes of functioning (e.g., avoidance, defensiveness, self-absorption) are associated with excessive stress and less optimal health outcomes.

Social purpose also appears to reinforce an intrinsic motivational orientation, a pattern that is itself often linked to indices of adjustment and well-being. In addition, a strong sense of social purpose provides balance with respect to self-assertive social relationship goals, which are generally quite salient during the adolescent years. The positive consequences associated with a generous investment in helping goals are largely attributable to their ability to amplify positive emotions such as affection and compassion that reinforce concern for others and limit the impact of negative emotional states.

TSP Enables Imagination and Creativity to Flourish

An adolescent's life is filled with ups and downs and bumps and bruises. Sometimes it is quite adaptive to be cautious and detached. Nevertheless, when an adolescent's general motivational orientation is to actively pursue the goals that capture their imagination with confidence, tenacity, and productive energy, their capacity for creativity and positive change will be maximized. Moreover, when young people are naturally inclined to focus not just on themselves but also on the broader impact of their actions for others, their thinking becomes more flexible and inspired. That is a key reason why adolescents who engage in prosocial activities tend to do better in their academic and social lives at school.

Life Meaning Flows Naturally from TSP Experiences

Thriving with social purpose is a way of approaching life's opportunities and challenges that appears to contribute directly to a sense that 'life is worth living.' This psychological experience of life meaning is difficult to engineer, and yet it is a natural consequence of both the thriving and social components of TSP functioning, as life meaning flows from self-directed goal-seeking that produces personally fulfilling and socially worthwhile consequences. That is an important benefit for adolescents, who for the first time are cognitively equipped to reflect on broader questions related to life meaning.

Adolescents Respond Best to Parents, Teachers, and Mentors with TSP Qualities

The topic of adolescent motivation encompasses not only the psychology and behavior of the adolescent but also the qualities of those responsible for cultivating motivation and optimal functioning in adolescents. As it turns out, the TSP framework is a useful tool in this regard as well, as adolescents are generally more motivationally receptive and personally engaged when learning from parents, teachers, and mentors who convey TSP-related qualities such as hope, optimism, trust, empathy, and authentic concern. Such interactions are emotionally satisfying and developmentally impactful. In contrast, just as non-TSP adolescents can be significant sources of stress for the adults they interact with, adolescents find it hard to respect adults who convey non-TSP qualities like egocentrism, defensiveness, and negativity.

This makes sense given the rapidly growing evidence from evolutionary scholars that humans are naturally designed to engage in active pursuit of personal goals that facilitate not only their own growth and development but also the interests and well-being of others. We have an innate urge to cooperate with and follow the lead of those who are helpful – and who have a reputation for being helpful. Adolescents resonate to caring adults who express firm, guiding values; a combination of self-confidence and acceptance of others; and emotional warmth. In short, TSP motivational patterns are 'contagious.' Adults who are themselves thriving with social purpose provide the optimal context for promoting motivational strengths and positive developmental trajectories in adolescence.

See also: Achievement Motivation; Autonomy, Development of; Body Image during Adolescence: A Developmental Perspective; Creativity in Adolescence; Emotional Development; Impulsivity and Adolescence; Self-Development During Adolescence.

Further Reading

Benson PL and Scales PC (2009) The definition and preliminary measurement of thriving in adolescence. *The Journal of Positive Psychology* 4: 85–104.
Deci EL and Ryan RM (2002) *Handbook of Self-determination Research*. Rochester, NY: University of Rochester Press.
Elliot AJ and Dweck CS (eds.) (2005) *Handbook of Competence and Motivation*. New York: Guilford.
Ford M (1992) *Motivating Humans*. Newbury Park, CA: Sage.
Ford ME and Smith PR (2007) Thriving with social purpose: An integrative approach to the development of optimal human functioning. *Educational Psychologist* 42: 153–171.
Fredrickson BL (2009) *Positivity*. New York: Crown.
Leary MR (2004) *The Curse of the Self*. New York: Oxford University Press.
Markus H and Nurius P (1986) Possible selves. *American Psychologist* 41: 954–969.
Pajares F and Urdan T (2006) *Self-efficacy Beliefs of Adolescents*. Greenwich, CT: Information Age Publishing.
Post SG (ed.) (2007) *Altruism and Health: Perspectives from Empirical Research*. New York: Oxford University Press.
Snyder CR and Lopez SJ (eds.) (2002) *Handbook of Positive Psychology*. New York: Oxford University Press.
Steinberg L (2001) We know some things: Parent–adolescent relationships in retrospect and prospect. *Journal of Research in Adolescence* 11: 1–19.
Steinberg L (2007) Risk taking in adolescence: New perspectives from brain and behavioral science. *Current Directions in Psychological Science* 16: 55–59.
Tomasello M (2009) *Why We Cooperate*. Cambridge, MA: MIT.
Yeager DS and Bundick MJ (2009) The role of purposeful work goals in promoting meaning in life and in schoolwork during adolescence. *Journal of Adolescent Research* 24: 423–452.

Relevant Websites

http://www.implicitself.com – Provides assessment tools derived from Motivational Systems Theory: the *Assessment of Personal Goals*, the *APG Personal Application Guide*, and the *Assessment of Personal Agency Belief Patterns*.
http://www.psych.rochester.edu/SDT/ – Provides resources related to Self-Determination Theory, including a broad range of theoretical and applied publications and questionnaires.
http://www.des.emory.edu/mfp/AdoEd5.html – Provides information and several downloadable chapters from the book *Self-efficacy Beliefs of Adolescents*.
http://www.positivityratio.com/ – Provides resources related to Barbara Fredrickson's 'Broaden-and-Build' theory of positive emotions, including information related to her provocative 'positivity ratio' hypothesis.
http://people.virginia.edu/~jdh6n/ – Provides resources related to Jonathan Haidt's groundbreaking work on various aspects of human flourishing.
http://ccare.stanford.edu/ – Provides information and resources related to a major interdisciplinary scientific effort to understand and promote qualities of compassion and social purpose in humans.

Music Listening in Adolescence

T Ter Bogt and S Soitos, Utrecht University, Utrecht, The Netherlands
M Delsing, Nijmegen, The Netherlands

Glossary

Argot: The special vocabulary of a social group.
Cultivation theory: A media theory postulating that the more exposure an individual has to a given medium (e.g., type of music or television show), then more likely the person is to accept messages conveyed by that medium.
Media practice model: This model postulates that individuals actively select and interact with media that match their personality, tastes, or interests (rather than having these shaped by the media).
Meter: A musical term referring to the regular rhythm or pattern of beats per measure in a musical composition.
Priming theory: A media theory postulating that activation of a particular thought or feeling may trigger related thoughts or feelings.
Timbre: A musical term referring to the quality or 'color' of a musical note.

Introduction

Music is integral to the development of the human species. People in all known cultures throughout history have always sung and made music. The oldest musical instruments, bone and ivory flutes that were excavated in Geissenklöstele in the Southwest of Germany, are about 35 000 years in age, providing evidence for musical mastery among the earliest humans in Europe. It appears to be a universal human practice to embellish various social gatherings with different types of appropriate music attuned to the occasion. Talented musicians across cultures are often highly regarded or even idolized. It should be noted, however, that the capacity to listen to and enjoy music and to respond to music by singing and dancing is present in nearly all humans. Only a tiny minority of humans, an estimated 4%, suffers from a condition known as tone-deafness or amusia: the inability to discern music in sound.

Our Musical Brain

Humans are characterized by their exceptionally large brains with areas specifically equipped to recognize and process auditory information. The human brain is a formidably complex organ and neurocognitive sciences have only begun to map the brains topography and the functions of different areas.

Representation of Language and Music in the Brain

Our capacity to listen to and produce highly complex rhythmic, harmonic, and melodic sound – music – and understand and use a highly sophisticated system of symbols – language – are unique features of humankind. To evolutionary scientists, the advantages of language are obvious: it is a perfect medium to communicate and hence, synchronize and gear behaviors of different people to each other, a skill that is highly valuable for a species that depends on cooperation for its survival. The functions of music are less obvious. Steven Pinker has even referred to music as 'auditory cheesecake,' a pleasant dessert derived from the evolution of language development. The perception of intonation in speech and melodic contour in music may recruit the same neural structures, and while the building blocks of language and music are different, words and pitches/chords, respectively, our brains analysis of the 'correct' sequential structure of these building blocks – syntax – draws on the same neural resources. However, recent neurocognitive research – for example, studies of individuals with brain lesions as an effect of accidents – has also introduced evidence that language and music are distinct phenomena that do not share the same processing components. Problems with language and music do not always co-occur, implying that at least some brain components are specialized in the processing of music or language.

Music Modules in the Brain

Though types of music vary endlessly, some music universals exist and our brain seems to be attuned to these universals. Across cultures tonal scales are used, that is, pitches with stable intervals form a scale of usually five to seven tones, repeated through octaves. A limited number of tones can blend into a harmony, and pitches outside this tonal system are perceived as 'false.' Universally, music is further characterized by the specific grouping and repetition of tones, its tempo, and the occurrence of rhythmic patterning through the repetitive emphasis in the order of tones. With regard to the perception of music, it has been proposed that the processing of music recruits at least two different and specialized brain modules: those for the tonal (pitch, melody) and temporal (meter, rhythm) dimensions of music.

Older studies have identified the primary auditory cortex, located on the right temporal lobe as important for the processing of auditory material. In a groundbreaking 1962 study, Brenda Milner found that patients who had their right temporal lobe removed in order to treat severe cases of epilepsy showed dysfunctions in tonal memory, and the perception of timbre, loudness, and time relations in music. More recently, it has been found that the right anterolateral part

Encyclopedia of Adolescence, Volume 1 doi:10.1016/B978-0-12-373915-5.00029-2

of Heschl's gyrus is crucial for that very basic component of music perception, encoding of pitch. However, other areas besides the right temporal lobe play an important role in music perception. For example, reception of pitch intervals implicates both the right and left temporal lobe, and the same holds for recognition of the melodic patterning of a piece of music. Rhythm perception predominantly recruits neural structures in the left hemisphere of the brain, but discerning meter is again located in the right hemisphere. In sum, our musical capacities draw on the activation of a whole network of regions across both the right and left side of the brain. Some of these neural networks may exclusively be used to perceive music. Others may also be functional for the processing of other types of auditory information or speech as well.

The Evolutionary Function of Music

As humans we are highly dependent on others in our group, as the group is more productive in the securing of basic needs such as food, shelter, and fending off danger. The earliest vocalizations of *Homo sapiens* may have developed in two divergent routes, with language as an efficient way to communicate relevant information, and music as a tool to communicate emotion and secure bonding; hence both types of vocalizations have survival benefits. Further, music may not only be a bonding device, but individual mastery of music and dance may also have reproductive benefits.

Reproductive Benefits

Charles Darwin observed that some male animals vocalize during the breeding season, and that the sound they make is used to attract females. Vocalization is, hence, a sexual dimorphic trait, more often present in males than in females. This idea of music's benefits in sexual selection processes has been revived by Geoffrey Miller in 2000 who argued that among humans musical skills such as singing and dancing are seen as good indicators of health and fitness, and that virtuosity in these modes is 'sexy.' Musicians have to expose themselves to their audience and this implies extraversion, control over nervousness, and confidence. Virtuosic performers of music and dance show great motor control and creativity in music hints at a flexible and intelligent mind. These are all attractive traits for the mating game. Last but not least, music is an emotion-eliciting medium, and therefore the format of a love song, so dominant in popular music, is a fine instrument in courtship.

While in the animal kingdom male vocalization predominates, among humans not only male talent is highly regarded but also female musical genius is considered to be very attractive, for similar reasons. However, even though we like our female performers, Miller indicated that among humans the male display of musical virtuoso is far more evident. From an exploratory analysis of more than 7100 works in classical music, jazz, and popular music, he concluded that males produce ten times more music than females, and that this courtship display peaks around the age of 30, when male mating efforts and activity are at their highest. It must be noted though that the music industry was and is a bastion of male dominance. Cultural pressures can have prevented the full female display of musical talent, and music may not be as sexually dimorphic among humans as some evolutionary biologists and psychologist have thought.

Survival Benefits

Not only sexual selecting but also natural selection can contribute to the survival of music behaviors. Developing music skills in a playful manner may also have benefits for individual. Learning to play music alone or with others involves skills such as focusing attention for prolonged periods of time, pattern detection, fine-tuning and integration of simultaneous auditory, visual and kinesthetic input and output, coordinating one's behavior with others, and hence anticipating and responding to music in movement. In that sense individually or collectively making music may be play, but it facilitates skills and behaviors that are adaptive, both individually and group-wise.

Making or listening to music can be extremely pleasurable and people can even experience the 'chills,' an emotion that is grounded in objective physiological markers, such as blood flow changes in several brain areas. Moreover, music making and listening can induce the release of the hormone oxytocin, a neurotransmitter facilitating birth and breastfeeding in females, but, more generally, fostering feelings of well-being, trust, and bonding with others, in both females and males. In addition, humans have an exceptional talent in discerning rhythm. When we hear a piece of music that is familiar in our social setting, nearly everybody can join in and clap their hand in unison. Music is a tool that facilitates coordinated movement. In sum, music's effects transcend individual pleasurable emotional states and foster group cohesion and coordinated action.

Another line of thought also places music in the parent–infant link. Newborns are totally dependent on their caregivers and a strong emotional bond between them is necessary. So-called infant directed speech (IDS), the emotionally expressive type of sing-song speech caregivers use when addressing small infants, is a universal phenomenon. It is not only an emotionally pleasant way to address children, but also infants are confronted with a wide range of vocal and facial expression conveying emotional states that induce their own emotional and social development. Again, IDS, as a musical language, promotes skills and behaviors that are adaptive individually and socially.

In evolutionary sciences, it is a basic assumption that for behaviors to be evolutionary adaptive they must bring greater benefits than costs. Music seems to be evolutionary relevant as it singles outs individuals as sexually attractive and helps bonding, cooperation, and coordination in humans that as a species depends on those social behaviors.

Music Listening Among Adolescents

Exposure and Importance

The biological and evolutionary aspect of music has universal features that cross national and cultural boundaries. Our knowledge of, more specifically, adolescent music involvement is limited to populations from Western countries, due to the fact that most research on the importance and functions of music listening has been conducted in the United States and in some European countries.

In prosperous, industrialized countries technical innovations have facilitated music listening. In the early part of the twentieth century, most music listening occurred by way of the radio. After the Second World War, the listening habits of large populations in the United States and Western Europe began to change. There were sharp increases in the sales of vinyl 45 rpm and 33 rpm records, followed by the advent of audio cassettes and compact discs that made choosing and listening to the music of choice far easier. In the 1980s, music listening partly shifted to music watching, as companies such as MTV Networks expanded a huge international network of music television. Listening patterns have been further revolutionized with the introduction of personal audio players, first in the form of the Sony Walkman (1979) and in the 1990s through the advent of personal audio players using digital formats for the storage of music. The personal computer has also become an important music machine and since the late-1990s young people legally or illegally down- and upload enormous amounts of digitalized music material. In recent years, the mobile phone has become an entertainment center with different communicative and media uses. The result of the market penetration of these technical innovations is that adolescents can listen to their favorite music virtually anywhere, anytime.

Music listening time is difficult to estimate as listening often is a background activity. Hence, studies focusing on music listening as the prime activity and studies assessing music listening as fore- and background activity vary widely in their estimation of average listening time. Adolescent listening time diverges by gender, age, region, and ethnicity, but across countries it has been found that a conservative estimate of average listening time among adolescents is between 2 and 3 h daily. In some communities and among older adolescents, these figures may be as high as 4–5 h daily, and girls have a slight edge over boys in terms of listening duration. Studies in life-course perspectives have found that music importance and involvement is already present in childhood, increases during the early adolescent years, and peaks in late adolescence and emerging adulthood. For most people, music remains important throughout life but not on the levels common between ages 16 and 22. Most adolescents rate music as an important or very important medium, but for 5–20% of adolescents, music is not significant. However, even this group of musically low-involved youth may occasionally use music to enhance their mood and fend off boredom (see below), but they have little knowledge of music genres, music history, and artists, and stick to the most popular chart music.

When comparing the importance of different media in adolescence (TV, print, gaming, Internet surfing, music), it has been shown that in terms of exposure and perceived importance, music is the most important medium for adolescents. For children under the age of 12, television is the dominant medium. For adolescents, music (on radio, CDs, DVDs, computer, personal audio) is at least as important as television in terms of exposure, but more important in terms of functionality. For example, for mood management, music, and less so TV programs, is a key media element. Computers and mobile phones have become more important carriers of entertainment and these devices blur the boundaries between picture and sound. While using a computer, one can watch, listen, and in the meantime communicate with peers. When computers are at stake, it is difficult to assess which 'medium' is dominant, as computers comprise a series of older and new medias. It must be noted that music listening, music video watching, and up- and downloading of music belong to the most important computer uses. It is further interesting to note that, though virtual or real communities may arise as a result of shared interests, for the choice of friends and identification with adolescent crowds, music, and less so TV programs or games, remains a key media element in Internet and real-life environments.

Functions of Music Listening

In their seminal 1998 book *It's Not Only Rock'n Roll*, Peter Christenson and Don Roberts made a strong case for the importance of music in adolescence when they referred to music as 'equipment for living.' Obviously, for adolescents, music has the same functions as for people in general, that is, advanced skills in playing music, singing, and dancing imply reproductive benefits. Teenagers with these skills are generally more popular, socially embedded, and attractive for potential romantic partners. In addition, rock concerts, music festivals, or dance parties are proof that music is also a great bonding device. However, in adolescence, music has several overlapping functions that are specific for this period of life or probably more important during this phase of life than in others.

Atmosphere creation

Music lubricates adolescent social life. Hardly any social gathering of adolescents is without music. Music creates atmosphere, fills in gaps between conversations, and is in itself a popular topic of conversation. Adolescent leisure is about fun with same sex and other sex friends, but this is also a life phase where pairing, romance, and sexuality become highly significant. A large share of the leisure time of adolescents and young adults revolves around going out, partying, and dancing. Pop music with prominent rhythmic qualities promotes dancing and provides a pleasing background for flirting and courtship.

Mood management

Music is not only important socially; most music listening in fact takes place individually. The most important individual function of music listening is mood management. Music is a powerful medium capable of eliciting a wide range of emotions. Hence adolescents can use music to get into a mood that fits the moment. Music is most often used to get into a more relaxed mood and to release tension. It helps to relieve boredom and makes tasks that are generally viewed as annoying – homework, cleaning up one's room – less unpleasant. Even depressed or angry music can be used to get into a better mood. Music is also an effective way to get energized, for example, when preparing to go out, or during exercise. Music tastes (see below) vary widely and the types of music used to enhance mood may be very different. What is noise to some may be relaxing to others.

Connectedness

Even listening to music alone seems to have social effects. Adolescents report they listen to music to make them feel part of an imaginary community of other fans of the same type of music. That young people can feel connected to others even in their physical absence by listening to music is further proof of its great bonding capacity.

Coping

Because of music's capacity to enhance moods, relieve boredom and loneliness, it is often used as a strategy to cope with problems. At least three processes may be at work when using music for coping with trouble. First, the qualities of the music itself are important to change mood, for example, airy, energetic music may help to lift feelings of gloominess and depression. Second, adolescents may feel the lyrics of the music they listen to reflect their situation, and in that sense music is used to contemplate on and work through problems. Third, young people may perceive the artist singing these lyrics as a person who cares for them and expressively voices problems they face themselves. By listening to music, young people can feel lovingly addressed and comforted by their favorite artist and the sentiments that seem to express feelings of hurt, loneliness, confusion, angriness, desperation, and uncertainty they are feeling themselves.

In his studies on heavy metal fans in the 1980s and 1990s, Jeffrey Arnett has studied the fact that adolescents may not only choose uplifting music when troubled, but may also wallow in music that is musically and lyrically dark, gloomy, depressing, or angry, aggressive, and rebellious. However, it has been suggested that the net result for most young listeners is positive as comparisons to the persons and situations described in these songs may dwarf the magnitudes of one's own problems. This identification with the artists and fellow fans enhance the sense that one is not alone with one's problems. Music eliciting negative emotions may be used in a purgative way and help to give meaning to and help work through negative emotions and experiences. Most young people using dark music to cope with problems find that this strategy works. For the small minority for whom sad and angry music deepens their own feelings of angst, alienation, and aggression, these negative music effects may be an indicator of serious personal problems.

Knowledge

Though, obviously, school is the prime institution to gain academic knowledge, music is an important source of information for adolescents. Artists display what is cool and what is not, what to believe and what to not, how to act and avoid awkward behavior. As many young people strongly identify with their artist of choice, these artists are important and highly credible informants. In their performances and in video clips, artists and bands promote a diverse range of codes for dress, haircuts, makeup, and accessories. Further, guides are given for bodily postures, movement schemas, and argot, and, last but not least, artists may influence attitudes and worldviews.

In the 1970s British authors noticed that fans are affected by musicians and bands and adopt sets of style codes as central elements in their subculture. The structure of these 'homologous' styles of dress, demeanors, and attitudes is highly different and linked to differences in music taste that is also a key element of a set. For example, hippies, heavy metal fans, punks, and hip-hop fans may all have a specific way of dressing, moving, speaking, and believing that is to some extent coherent, and with some variation shared within the group. Artists and bands have been shown to be effective in promoting appearance codes and clothing styles, leading companies to promote consumer goods as diverse as perfume, soft drinks, and alcohol through artists.

Identity

In adolescence, identity formation is an important developmental task. Adolescents have to establish more autonomy from parents, define close friendships anew with other peers, develop romantic relations, and acquire more definite values and beliefs. It has been noted already that music is a source of information as well as entertainment and provides cultural background that influences identity formation. Listeners may be influenced by lyrics, attitudes, and ideas expressed by artists. There is also more subtle identification with the image projection of an artist or band. Music is used to develop, negotiate, and maintain a sense of self through identification with artists or bands and their work. Additionally, there is a symbiotic learning relationship with other fans that appreciate the same type of music. During adolescence, young people may experiment with different styles and dress codes and consequently their demeanors and attitudes may be subject to change. Notably, research has established that from age 12 onward music taste is remarkably stable, thus forming basic codes influencing adolescent identity. Radical changes in identification thus set are rare. These stable adolescent demographics provide social scientists with ideal conditions for study of musical influences.

Friendship formation and social identity

In one of the first social scientific books on pop music, *The Sociology of Rock* (1978), Simon Frith noted that music may help to define identity by showcasing an individual's persona in terms of a 'badge' function. Among adolescents, this 'badge' idealization through music is crucial to establishing and maintaining social relations. Peers receiving these 'badge' messages immediately form an adequate picture of the other's personality on the basis of musical information presented. Hence, music functions as an important factor in the choice of friends and shared music preferences influence the formation of adolescent crowds. Music functions as a marker, not only of individual identity, but also of social identity. It highly influences the choices of group identity among adolescents. Studies suggest that adolescents not only express what kind of music they like but also convey which types of music they dislike, individually and as a group. Obviously, adolescents tend to favor the music that is popular in their own group and mark other groups' choices as 'bad' music. In this way, they differentiate themselves from other groups. Music helps to sustain a positive evolution within peer circles leading to increased self-esteem. This is not to say that music choices only divide and differentiate. Awareness of shared music taste or noticing unfamiliar but interesting music choices in other groups may also bridge differences between groups.

Importance of the functions of music

An estimated 20% of all adolescents can be qualified as high-involved – meaning that for them music is crucial to their identity. About 75% of adolescents define themselves as medium-involved in music and 5% list music as not particularly important in their lives. When rating the importance of the different functions of music listening, it is clear that music is first and most important a medium for regulating emotions. Nearly all adolescents, even the musically low-involved, use music to enhance their mood, get rid of a bad temper, and fend off boredom. Both the high-involved and the medium-involved groups tend to also use music to cope with stress and feelings of depression and loneliness. They are mildly positive on using music for identity purposes with the high-involved group more so than the medium-involved group. The use of music as a marker of social boundaries is deemed the least important factor among all three groups. For the younger groups, knowledge of and identification with their favorite artists is particularly important. These fans are more prone to pick up clues on 'cool' behavioral and attitudinal styles than musically less-involved adolescents. What is 'cool' for fans may be detested by adolescents not into that particular type of music or artist. Hence, even though they may not be aware of it, music differentiates youth through behavioral and attitudinal styles.

Music Taste and Its Origins

Long before adolescents' use of music to define social boundaries was studied, sociologists examined the role of cultural behavior in relation to social structure. In the early twentieth century, classical sociologists such as Georg Simmel and Max Weber argued that the selective appreciation of material and symbolic goods is a marker for group boundaries, and that taste differentiation mirrors social differences. In the same vein, Herbert Gans in *Popular Culture and High Culture* (1974) and Pierre Bourdieu in his seminal study *La Distinction* (1979) found that audiences for cultural commodities can be divided into different taste cultures with different socioeconomic foundations. A significant body of research has explored the antecedents of music taste finding that preference choices are not only related to socioeconomic status (SES) but also to characteristics such as gender, age, ethnicity, and personality factors.

The Structure of Music Taste

Evolving nature of musical styles

Though earlier forms of popular music found mass audiences (e.g., jazz), current 'pop music' emerged as rock 'n roll in the mid-1950s. Rock is a hybrid of older forms of American Black and White working-class music types, that is, country, gospel, and blues. In the 1960s, American, British, and local melodic and catchy forms of popular music were no longer called rock 'n roll but referred to as 'pop music,' a term that became universal. Pop is difficult to define outside of its catchiness, easy-to-listen quality, and mass appeal. Indeed, even now any song from a whole range of different genres within current popular music can be characterized as 'pop.' In the 1960s, pop music developed into a wide array of genres, sometimes close to the Black or White roots of modern popular music, sometimes entirely new. The loudest form of guitar, drum, and bass driven pop sporting manic singers grew into rock music, a predominantly White genre. The even more strongly rhythmic, melodic, voice driven form of pop, highly dependent on keyboards and horns, developed into soul, funk, and later, hip-hop and R&B music. These are predominantly Black genres. In the 1970s, disco emerged as hyperrhythmic dance music that was revolutionized by the advent of synthesizers and other digital devices, turning it into electronic dance music. In addition to popular music, art music, that is, classical music, has appealed to a mostly highly educated audience.

Empirical Studies in Adolescent Music Taste

Social scientists have shown that the structure of adolescent music taste taps into and sometimes parallels these divisions and grand lines in the development of pop music. In the 1990s and early 2000s, studies of the structure of musical preferences were conducted in the United States and Europe. These studies have generally confirmed a four- or five-factor 'deep' structure of styles. This chart would include, first, a 'popular, chart-based, girlish' style, sometimes including country and religious music; second, a 'boyish, rock' style that is intense and rebellious, defined by rock, alternative, and heavy metal music; third, 'Afro-American' and 'Afro-Caribbean' music encompassing rap/hip-hop, soul/funk, and electronic/dance music; fourth an 'elitist' preference for complex music, such as classical music, jazz, and folk music; and sometimes, a fifth style consisting of ultrarhythmic 'dance music.' While artists may come and go, and specific genres wax and wane, there seems to be great commonality in the structuring of popular music preferences in Europe and North America.

Despite the consistency of musical styles in these studies, there can be changes across time in the prominence of certain styles or types of music encompassed within a style. An investigation of music preferences of large representative samples of Dutch adolescents (12–18 years) across 2 decades indicated that in 1989 a simple three-factor structure was visible (see **Table 1**). The Pop factor included not only mainstream pop music but also a cluster of other highly rhythmic and danceable music very popular during the 1970s and 1980s – soul, reggae, and disco – or had just emerged as new pop music – hip-hop and house. A second overall style comprised Rock music, such as rock and heavy metal, and alternative rock in the form of punk and new wave. A third factor included music with a long-standing high reputation – classical music – and, interestingly, also older African American music such as blues,

Table 1 Structure of music taste in Dutch adolescents 12–18 in 1989

I *Pop*	*II* *Rock*	*III* *High brow*
Pop	Rock	Classical
Disco	Hard rock	Jazz
House	Punk	Soul
Hip-hop	New wave	Blues
Soul		
Reggae		

Source: Jongeren 1989, Qrius Research, Amsterdam.

jazz, and soul. Sociologists stress that cultural commodities do not have a definite fixed status in the cultural field, and music can be upwardly mobile. Richard Peterson noted that in the 1960s and following decades, the cultural elite adopted pop cultural artifacts, and in the process turned from being 'snobs' into 'omnivores.' The clustering of classical music with music of (Black) working-class origin – jazz, blues, and soul – is indicative of this development.

Twenty years later, in 2009 (**Table 2**), pop, rock, and high-brow overall styles materialized again in the taste structure of Dutch adolescents. Pop consisted of mainstream top 40 pop and the Dutch varieties thereof. Rock steadily comprised rock, metal, and different types of alternative rock, and the high-brow style again held the cluster of classical music, jazz, and soul, in addition to singer-songwriter music. In the 1990s and early 2000s, Afro-American music, such as hip-hop and R&B, was hugely popular and now composed a separate factor of Black music, subsuming also reggae and Latin pop. Different types of electronic dance music – house, trance, and techno – clustered in the Dance factor. The demographic composition of Dutch youth is changing and second generation immigrant adolescents tend to favor music that is connected to their parents' country of origin. The Ethnic pop factor comprised pop music from Turkey and Morocco, thus indicating by extrapolation that in other countries the Ethnic factor may include music from those adolescent's parent's country of origin.

Not surprisingly, adolescents who favored pop also liked Black and dance music that was well represented in the pop charts. Also preferences for dance and Black music are highly correlated. Rock fans overall dislike pop music but, interestingly, are relatively fond of high-brow music. The people labeled omnivores by Richard Peterson not only like classical music and older and newer forms of Black music but they sometimes show even broader taste in music that includes pop, rock, and dance. An estimated 10–20% of adolescent fall within this category.

The popularity of music styles 1989–2009

Figure 1 depicts the popularity of different styles among Dutch adolescents in the period from 1989 to 2009. Pop music is indeed popular, reigning across 2 decades as the most preferred musical category. In the early years of the new century, enthusiasm for different types of Afro-American music peaked. Both hip-hop and R&B were massively popular among Dutch teens (and across the globe). Though never as popular as Afro-American music types, dance music climbed in popularity during the period from 1995 to 2005. Different types of rock

Table 2 Structure of music taste in Dutch adolescents 12–18 in 2009

I *Pop*	*II* *Rock*	*III* *Black*	*IV* *High brow*	*V* *Dance*	*VI* *Ethnic*
Pop	Rock	Hip-hop	Classical	House	Turkish pop
Dutch pop	Heavy metal	R&B	Jazz	Trance	Moroccan pop
	Alternative rock	Reggae	Soul	Techno	
		Latin pop	Singer-songwriter		

Source: Jongeren 2009, Qrius Research, Amsterdam.

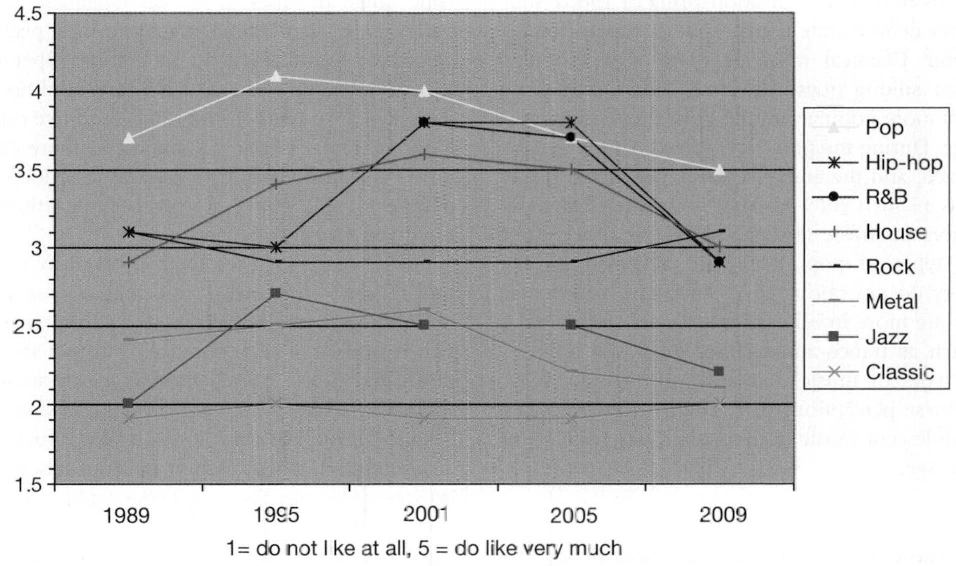

Figure 1 Popularity music genres 1989–2009. (Source: Jongeren 1989, Jongeren 1995, HBSC 2001, HBSC 2005, Jongeren 2009, Qrius Research, Amsterdam and Trimbos Institute/Utrecht University, Utrecht.)

music have huge fan bases, but on average, 'rock' maintains a median position. A more radical rock genre such as heavy metal has highly dedicated fans, but generally this genre is rated poorly. Jazz and, even more so, classical music are music types for specialized audiences. In particular, classical music was and is highly unpopular among adolescents. This hierarchy of the popularity of pop music has been found to be consistent in European countries other than the Netherlands although some cross-national differences may exist and deserve further analysis.

Origins of Music Taste

Music taste has been related to a number of personal and cultural factors, including gender, age, personality, education, and social class/SES. Current research delving into the relationship between individuals and their cultural background as pertaining to music preference can be enlightening. However, caution must be used when interpreting the associations found. For example, the question of how gender relates to music taste is fraught with difficult suppositions. Are women and men drawn to different music preferences because their brains are more attuned to specific types of music or are women and men socialized to find certain types of music more to their liking? When educational level is found to be significant for preferences, it may be because more highly educated adolescents prefer more complex music, or that in different schools or neighborhoods different music is popular. These types of associations are open to further interpretation and the factors discussed below should not be understood as causal forces.

Gender

Rather stereotypically, girls are more drawn to melodic, romantic music and boys to noisy, rebellious music. From the 1970s onward, it has been found that girls tend to like the most popular forms of pop or chart music more than boys, who gravitate to music within the rock field. When considering the rather broad style of Afro-American music, girls prefer the melodic strains of R&B, the latest offspring of 1960s' soul music, while boys demonstrate a greater attraction to louder forms of hip-hop. Classical music is often more popular among girls than among boys. Music to dance to such as disco was always more popular among girls. But even stereotypes can change. During the past 2 decades the audience for rock has feminized, and the audience for dance has masculinized. **Figure 2** is a Dutch 2009 example for gendered similarity and differences in music taste. Indeed, girls more often prefer different types of pop, R&B, and singer-songwriter material, but they do not rate rock or alternative rock lower than boys. Boys are more into heavy metal, and surprisingly, dance music such as trance and techno. Boys and girls do have views on types of music that are prototypically male or female, and these perceptions drive their preferences. But the history of adolescent music testifies that these prototypes are subject to change.

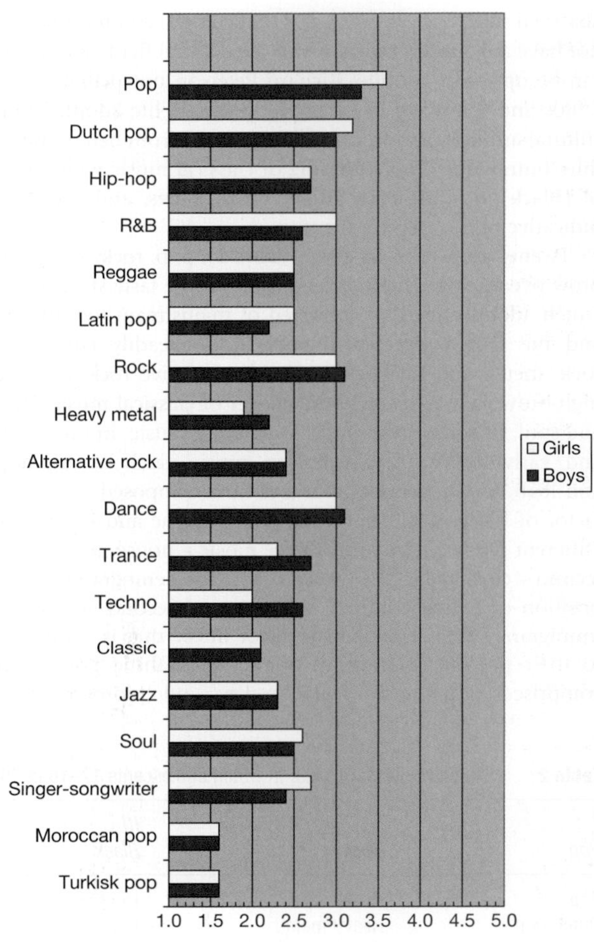

Figure 2 Male and female taste among Dutch 12–18 year olds in 2009. (Source: Jongeren 2009, Qrius research, Amsterdam.)

Age

Twelve year olds know and can discern a wide range of popular music genres, and the knowledge of music types and artists increases further as adolescence develops. Scholars find that children are fairly 'open-eared,' that is, tolerant to a relatively wide range of types of music. Open-earedness declines in adolescence when adolescent conformity peaks and peers are all-important influences on preferences. Open-earedness again increases in late adolescence and early adulthood, when young people, helped by their increased cognitive capacities (among other factors), develop an interest in more complex types of music and form a definite musical taste identity. As listeners mature to older ages, the reverse indications of less open-earedness may occur.

With regard to three types of stability concerning music preferences – for artists and bands, for genres, and for music styles – studies indicate that adolescents relatively easily switch in their artist preferences, but that the appreciation of music genres and overall styles is highly stable. Early adolescents may trade in Slipknot or Marylin Mason for U2 or the Kings of Leon, but they keep on liking rock. Others may be fond of Snoop Doggy Dog or the Sugababes as teens and end up loving Marvin Gaye or Eryka Badu when older but still consistently choose music in the Afro-American tradition. Alternatively, artists may mature, and keep their audience with them throughout their life. From Chuck Berry, the Beatles, and Stones to Madonna, Prince, and George Michael, all great artists still appeal to the audiences they obtained at a much younger age.

Liking one of the grand music styles discussed above is a very stable and almost a fundamental personality characteristic. Once a type of music is defined as prototypical of taste, preferences of new music depend on the similarity to that prototype. This is not to say that music taste does not develop at all. Listeners may develop a far richer and more detailed knowledge of music and its makers, but odds are that they develop this interest in the same stream of music they already liked when they were adolescents. Late adolescence and early adulthood are a critical period for the development of taste. Music that is preferred during that phase of life is remembered best and liked most when listeners reflect on their preferences later on in life.

Personality

Traditionally, researchers have been particularly interested in what personality factors draw adolescents to 'defiant' musical genres like heavy metal, hard rock, grunge, and punk because preferences for these types of music have been shown to be associated with problem behaviors and/or major psychological issues. Preferences for these genres are linked with higher levels of sensation seeking. Sensation seeking, which is assumed to have a biological base, refers to the tendency to search out and savor novel and intense sensory stimulation. More recently, researchers have employed a broader perspective by including a wider range of music genres and personality characteristics in their investigation. One study correlated US college students' scores on the 'Big 5' personality domains (see article on Personality in this encyclopedia) with their preferences for four broad music categories (Reflective and Complex, Intense and Rebellious, Upbeat and Conventional, and Energetic and Rhythmic). Preferences for the Reflective and Complex and the Intense and Rebellious categories were positively related to Openness to Experience, suggesting that individuals who enjoy listening to classical music and jazz or to rock and heavy metal tend to be inventive, curious about different things, enjoy taking risks, have active imaginations, and value aesthetic experiences. Preference for the Upbeat and Conventional category was positively associated with Extraversion, Agreeableness, and Conscientiousness and negatively with Openness to Experience, suggesting that individuals who enjoy listening to mainstream pop and dance music are cheerful, socially outgoing, reliable, enjoy helping others, and tend to be relatively conventional. Preference for the Energetic and Rhythmic category was positively related to Extraversion and Agreeableness, suggesting that individuals who enjoy rap/hip-hop and soul tend to be talkative, full of energy, and tend to be pleasant and accommodating in social situations. A more recent study of Dutch adolescents replicated these basic findings, thus confirming the cross-national robustness of the reported associations between music taste and personality.

The *uses and gratification* theory assumes that people are attracted to the types of music that have the capacity to satisfy their needs. For example, extraverts who have a desire to socialize with peers and to have fun are drawn to popular genres like hip-hop, R&B, and Top 40 which are frequently played at parties and social gatherings of youngsters. Similarly, the desire for variety, intellectual stimulation, and unconventionality of individuals scoring high on openness may attract them to relatively complex genres like jazz and classical music or other nonmainstream genres like gothic and punk. Some of the associations between personality characteristics and music preferences may also be explained from a psychological *model of optimal stimulation*. Extraverts, who are believed to have a relatively high level of physiological arousal, may be particularly attracted to genres like hip-hop and trance because these musical styles move them toward their optimal arousal level. In contrast, emotionally unstable adolescents may tend to avoid overstimulation and may thus be attracted to more traditional styles of music (e.g., classical).

Parents and peers

The generation that was in their teens during the rock 'n roll and beat music eras of the late 1950s and early 1960s became adults with generally deep involvement with pop music. For this generation, differences in music taste with their parents, who sometimes outright hated the new rock and pop music, were overall extremely large. But their own children grew up in a household in which pop music was a natural auditory background. Parents are indeed able to transfer their taste to their children. It may not be the fondness of particular artists or bands that they convey, but they can pass on broad preferences in types of music to their children. It has been noted before that music preferences mark and legitimize social boundaries. Parents liking high-brow music such as classical music and jazz are particularly interested in socializing their children into these high-status types of music, but transmission is not confined to high-brow music. Parents can also socialize their children into rock, Black music, or dance music. Girls are probably somewhat more sensitive to the tastes of their mothers and fathers than boys, who seem to base their taste more in their peer group.

For adolescent music choice and taste, peers show more influence than parents. In particular, in early adolescence young people tend to conform to the taste of their peers, later on there is more freedom and willingness to develop individual taste. However, adolescents are not helpless victims and forced to adapt to the taste of their friends. Music is one of the criteria for friendship formation and teen crowd aspiration; adolescents may actively seek peers that have a similar taste that they wish to be associated with. Throughout adolescence, selection and peer influence are entwined processes.

Social class, socioeconomic status, and education

Music preferences are also related to social class and education. Studies of British youth in the 1970s found that male working-class youth tended to like rock 'n roll and its 'heavier' derivatives, while middle-class youth were more oriented to progressive rock or 'hippie music.' In other studies, heavy metal for boys and soul and disco for girls have been characterized as genres with a disproportionately working-class fan base. Knowledge of music can be used by adolescents to gain social prestige when their school results are below average. However, the place of music in the cultural field can change. Heavy metal, once music for alienated lower class American and European youth gained popularity among the college crowd, and today, at least in Europe, metal and other loud forms of rock are also popular among youth with higher SES and education.

Research across different countries has corroborated time and again that high-brow music (e.g., classical, jazz) draws audiences with disproportionately high social status and educational levels. The newer forms of dance music, house, trance, and techno are more popular among adolescents with lower educational attainment and SES. Researchers have generally found adolescents with higher social status/education tend to have a more wide-ranging musical taste, that is, that they both recognize and indicate an affinity for a wider variety of music genres, both high-brow and popular, than those of lower status and educational attainment.

Music Taste and Problem Behavior

Influence or Selection?

Artist's behavior, music videos, and song lyrics may have a direct influence on young people. *Priming theory* assumes that stimuli can activate cognitive schemas, and that repeated activation leads to strengthening of these schemas. Thus, attitudes and behaviors can be shaped by media exposure. *Cultivation theory* argues that adolescents exposed to high levels of media content may adopt the worldview presented in the media as their subjective reality. If frequent and positive references to risk behavior occur, the effect may be to normalize these behaviors by creating the impression they comprise a common aspect of adolescent life. *Social cognitive theory* postulates that people tend to learn from and imitate other people. Social learning is far more probable, when

1. the attitudes and behaviors displayed by the models are relevant for the observers;
2. these role models are attractive and have a high status; and
3. the role models seem to benefit from displaying these attitudes and behaviors.

Hence, adolescents may find their beloved pop artists attractive role models and imitate them. Further, pop music taste is not developed in isolation; in shaping their preferences adolescents are influenced by their peers, not only with regard to music itself but also with regard to sets of attitudes and behaviors that are linked to music preferences and form a broader lifestyle. Processes of learning, imitation, and 'contagion' are even more complex as they may not only concern adaptation of behaviors that are in fact present in peer crowds, but individuals may also comply to rules that they *believe* are dominant in their social scene. That is, a false sense of consensus may shape adolescents' attitudes and behaviors.

Listeners are not passive victims, intimidated by media messages or peers. The *media practice model* posits that music choices reflect the needs and preferences of listeners. Adolescents may select the type of music that fits them and actively choose friends with similar preferences. When adjusting to their social environment, they actively choose to adopt attitudes and behaviors from peers that they like and hold in high regard. Music's beneficial effects and functions have been noted, but music preferences can also indicate problem behaviors. Our discussion of influence versus selection implies, once more, that caution is needed when interpreting associations. Music may or may not be a causal factor in the relationship with problem behavior.

In the 1990s, two genres stood out as 'problematic.' The brashest, loudest form of rock – heavy metal – and Afro-American music – ganstarap – had the reputation of spoiling youth, that is, propagating substance use, violence, suicide, uncommitted sex, gender stereotyping, and misogynist behaviors. Research has corroborated that fans of these types of music, at least in the United States, were prone to more internalizing problem behaviors, such as depression and suicide ideation (heavy metal) and/or externalizing behaviors such as aggression and norm-breaking behaviors (heavy metal, hip-hop). Part of this last association can be explained by the fact that fans of these types of music are characterized by their higher tendency for sensation seeking or disinhibition, in itself strong predictors of risky behaviors. It may also be that fans enveloped in these youth cultural scenes, individually or as a group, adopt risk behaviors that are frequently portrayed by artists themselves or in their lyrics and music videos.

It must be noted though that even for music labeled as 'problematic' results are not entirely consistent: in some studies, no relations have been found between 'problem music' and externalizing behaviors; in others, liking hip-hop and R&B was associated with decreased problems. Cross-national differences in these associations may also exist. Across Europe, relations between liking heavy metal or hip-hop and various problem behaviors have been mixed. In Europe, young people eager for thrills and excitement seem to gravitate more toward dance music and the dance music scene.

Links Between Music and Problem Behavior

Substance use

Content analyses of music lyrics have confirmed that alcohol and drug use are often themes laced into pop music. Over the past 2 decades, a substantial increase in substance use references has been noted, and both alcohol and illicit drugs are generally portrayed in a favorable way. In particular, country music and even more so hip-hop is fraught with substance use references.

Experimental research and observational studies have shown that music tempo, music lyrics with substance use references, and exposure to smoking, drinking, and drug using media models may unconsciously enhance substance use. Correlational studies have reported that adolescents who listen to loud, energetic, and rebellious music show a propensity for risky substance use. US studies from the 1980s and 1990s indicated that heavy metal fans were more likely to be substance users. More recent US studies indicate that preferences for heavy metal, hip-hop, techno, and reggae are positively associated with smoking, drinking, and cannabis use. For Europe, the stronger currents of rock and Afro-American music may or may not indicate higher substance use. Across Europe the strongest links between music preferences and tobacco, alcohol, and illicit drug use have been found for the more energetic and louder form of dance music such as techno and hardhouse. Overall, preferences for mainstream pop and classical music are associated with less substance use. Though boys and girls tend to like different types of music, it seems that the links between music preferences and substance use are highly similar.

In the dance scene and in other youth cultural scenes as well, music and substance use are both parts of a broader lifestyle. It is therefore difficult to claim that the link between music and substance use is directly caused by media use. However, within these youth cultural scenes that are often characterized by a special fondness for certain types of music, substance use contagion effects may be present.

School success and dropout

In Swedish and US studies in the 1990s, liking heavy metal has been linked to decreased motivation for school, lower grades, and potentially school dropout. In addition, African American boys enveloped in hip-hop may get the impression that there are alternate ways to social success than school. Preferring hip-hop may decrease school motivation. Conversely, in European studies, it has been found that adolescents liking chart pop or classical music overall have a more favorable attitude toward school. It has been suggested that adolescents with problems with school are drawn to rebellious music, more so than the other way around; in other words, associations between music and antischool attitudes may be explained by selection effects.

Externalizing problems: aggression and norm-breaking

After a few well-publicized tragic massacres at high schools and universities with heavy metal or gothic fans involved, this particular loud rock music has been singled out as a problem genre. In the 1990s, aggressive content in heavy metal and hip-hop videos, and aggressive music lyrics have been linked in experimental studies with increases in aggressive feelings and thoughts. Theoretically, feelings and thoughts may translate into aggressive behavior, but this claim has not yet been substantiated scientifically.

In correlational research in both the United States and Europe, associations have been found between liking louder forms of rock and Afro-American music and rebelliousness and norm-breaking behaviors. Obviously, in correlational studies the direction of effects can never be established, that is, these results should not be interpreted as if music causes problems. However, in longitudinal research it has been established that a fondness for these types of music in early adolescence may also mark later adolescent problem behavior. Metal or hip-hop may be part of a wider, lower SES type of adolescent lifestyle with risky aspects. Young people with a broad taste in music, omnivores, are also more prone to externalizing behaviors. It has been speculated that omnivores form a distinct group of higher SES bohemian youth, and in their unconventionality more often cross legal lines.

It has been noted already that part of the association between loud music and problem behavior can be explained by the personality characteristics of its listeners, that is, rebelliousness, sensation seeking, or disinhibition. But in most research that controls personality characteristics for the effects of music preference remains. Again a subcultural explanation is likely: on the basis of their music preference, adolescents become part of different cliques and crowds and within these youth groups they adopt prevailing attitudes and attractions to risky or even problematic behaviors. Scenes with a risky reputation may foster their members' risk behaviors.

Internalizing behaviors: depression and suicide

After a few equally well-publicized tragic adolescent suicides and suicide attempts, heavy metal music was once again accused of stimulating internalizing distress. In the 1990s in US correlational studies, heavy metal has indeed been linked to depression and suicide ideation, but also fans of country and classical music were more prone to these cognitions and feelings. Recently these links have been confirmed in European studies for more extreme types of rock music and classical music. Interestingly, once again omnivores are more vulnerable with regard to internalizing distress.

Depressed adolescents may like to play depressing music, but for most of them, the net effect is a better mood. Even depressing music can be comforting. Therefore, depressing music cannot simply be conceptualized as a factor stimulating depression and suicide. Most young people are helped by listening to music that reflects their own feeling even if it is sad. For a tiny group, sad music may magnify feelings of depression and angst. For this last group, wallowing in musical sadness may be an indicator of deep personal problems. Further scientific study is needed to investigate whether for this type of listener enveloping oneself in sad music indeed deepens depression and promotes suicide.

Sexual stereotyping

Content analysis of popular music and music videos show a high amount of sexually suggestive, if not openly provocative, lyrics and images. References to sex have become far more explicit over the past decades. In particular, hip-hop music clips have become notorious for their frequent display of macho types of males in opulent surroundings and sexy women in submissive roles. Cross-sectional and longitudinal investigations have found that frequent exposure to sexual media content may accelerate adolescents' initiation and continuation of sexual activity. Media messages may contribute to gender stereotypes, that is, views of men as sex driven and tough, and of women as sex objects. Television has received much attention in research but studies on the effects and correlates of music video watching and music listening are much scarcer. It has been found though that stereotypical pop music and music videos can amplify stereotypical gender schemas, foster beliefs that gender relationships are adversarial, and that appearance is all-important. Fans of hip-hop and dance music are more often characterized by stereotypical attitudes. With regard to stereotyping, media effects may be real and adolescents liking to be exposed to specific music may be influenced by its typecasting of male and female roles.

Music and problem behavior: conclusion

Experimental research has uncovered real effects of music, and correlational studies hint at associations between music preferences and adolescent problem behaviors. It must be noted, though, that in general, effects that have been described in experimental research are short term and that currently it is unknown whether music can have more lasting effects on cognitions, emotions, attitudes and behaviors that have been labeled as problematic. Further, effects, if at all present, are generally small. The same holds for the correlations between music preferences and problem behaviors emerging from survey research. In popular media, in particular 'defiant' types of music such as heavy metal, gothic, and gangstarap are routinely described as causing troubles in young people. Scientific evidence backing these claims is at this date inconclusive. The great majority of fans even of problem music do not display more problem behavior as a result of listening to music, but it may be that a small group is affected negatively by 'problematic' music. Future research should investigate which young people are vulnerable to negative music influences. Music may well be of influence indirectly, as adolescents get tied to their circle of friends partly on the basis of their music taste. Music choice may bring them in contact with risky social scenes that influence their own risky behaviors.

Adolescents in the middle of the process of gaining more autonomy vis-à-vis their parents may use this thrilling and rebellious symbolic resource to distance themselves from their parents and to create their own youth culture. What is fun for them may be obnoxious for their parents, and should be so. Further, much adolescent risk or problem behavior is adolescence limited. When entering romantic relations, higher education, or work, adolescents as young adults 'mature out' of these problem behaviors. It has been hypothesized that music preference may mark or, at worst, slightly increase adolescent-limited problem behavior, but that it is not a driving factor in more extreme and enduring patterns of problem behavior that have their roots in more fundamental genetic, educational, and personality characteristics. Problematic individuals may seek 'problematic' music, but even most fans of 'problematic' music are healthy, nonproblematic young people spicing up their life with music that is exciting, *because* it is bad, wild, sexy, illegal, and unconventional.

Conclusion

Music is an important medium in adolescence, as it reflects the adolescent life situation as no other medium does. Most adolescents are exposed to their favorite music on a daily basis. It helps to improve their mood, to cope with problems, and to construct and maintain personal and social identity. Connections have been found between music preferences and adolescent risk behaviors, but even so, for most adolescents, problematic or nonproblematic, music is 'equipment for life.'

Acknowledgments

The authors wish to thank Henkjan Honing who commented on a draft of this text.

See also: Brain Development; Media, Influence of; Personality Traits in Adolescence.

Further Reading

Christenson PG and Roberts DF (1998) *It's not only Rock and Roll: Popular Music in the Lives of Adolescents*. Cresskill, NJ: Hampton.

Delsing MJMH, Ter Bogt TFM, Engels RCME, and Meeus WHJ (2008) Adolescents' music preferences and personality characteristics. *European Journal of Personality* 22(2): 109–130.

Honing H (2011) *Musical Cognition*. New Brunswick, NJ: Transaction Publishers.

Justlin PN and Sloboda J (2009) *Handbook of Music and Emotion*. Oxford: Oxford University Press.

Miranda D and Claes M (2004) Rap music genres and deviant behaviors in French-Canadian adolescents. *Journal of Youth and Adolescence* 33: 113–122.

Mulder J, Ter Bogt TFM, Raaijmakers QAW, and Sikkema P (2010) From Death Metal to R&B? Consistency of music preferences among Dutch adolescents and young adults. *Psychology of Music* 38: 67–83.

North AC and Hargreaves DJ (2008) *The Social and Applied Psychology of Music*. Oxford: Oxford University Press.

Peretz I (2006) The nature of music from a biological perspective. *Cognition* 100: 1–32.

Rentfrow PJ and Gosling SD (2003) The do re mis of everyday life: The structure and personality correlates of music preferences. *Journal of Personality and Social Psychology* 84: 1236–1256.

Ter Bogt TFM, Simons-Morton BG, Godeau E, et al. (2010) Dance is the new Metal: Adolescent music preferences and substance use across Europe. *Substance Use and Misuse*.

Thompson WF (2008) Music, Thought, and Feeling: Understanding the Psychology of Music. Oxford: Oxford University Press.

Wallin N F, Merker B, and Brown S (2001) *The Origins of Music*. Cambridge: MIT.

Nutrition in Adolescence

M Braun and B B Brown, University of Wisconsin-Madison, Madison, WI, USA

Glossary

BMI: Body Mass Index, a measure of weight that is adjusted for height and age. BMI scores are used to identify underweight, normal weight, and overweight or obese individuals.

Diet: Description of an individual's food intake in terms of the quantity and quality of nutrients ingested, as well as the distribution among common nutritional categories (e.g., fats, fiber, carbohydrates).

Food pyramid: An arrangement of common foods into groupings that have different nutrient emphases, represented in a diagram according to the number of recommended daily servings (from fewer servings at the top of the pyramid to more servings for foods at the base).

Macronutrients: The chemical compounds consumed as food in relatively large quantities to meet the body's energy needs.

Micronutrients: Nutrients required in small amounts to maintain healthy body development and functioning.

Introduction

Few things are more fundamental to human life than eating. Like breathing, regular intake of food is necessary for individual survival. To remain viable, the human organism must do more than simply ingest food. It must maintain a nutritious diet that meets the needs of body systems and fosters healthy physical and psychological development. This is especially true in adolescence because of the dramatic changes occurring to body systems during this stage of life. The regular (daily) need for food and the complexities of food preparation (in contrast to the simple act of breathing) have elevated eating from a simple survival tactic to a complex social activity. Eating is part of individuals' lifestyles and patterns of social interaction, allowing nutritional needs to sometimes take a back seat to other facets of eating behavior.

In this article, although we are attentive to the social agenda of eating, our focus remains squarely on nutrition. We begin by summarizing research concerning the nutritional needs of adolescents and the basic elements of good nutrition. We then describe common eating patterns among young people, with attention to both historical changes and social or cultural differences in these patterns. We consider how eating is not merely a matter of feeding body systems but a social activity, shaped by the norms and traditions of one's family and society. Finally, in the light of evidence that adolescents typically follow suboptimal patterns of eating and nutrition, we consider research on efforts to improve young people's eating habits and nutritional intake. Our focus is on normative patterns of eating and their implications for adolescent nutrition. Many adolescents manifest disordered eating processes, which have more severe implications for nutrition. These are addressed in a different article in Volume 3 of the encyclopedia.

Nutrition and Development

Good nutritional habits are fundamental to good health. This basic principle is routinely affirmed in studies that examine the linkage between diet and physical or psychological outcomes. For example, a diet rich in fruits and vegetables, nonfat dairy products, and whole grains has been shown to lower blood pressure among adults with hypertension. Conversely, among overweight adolescents in Saudi Arabia, a majority of food calories (in one study) was derived from carbohydrates; nearly another third came from fats and only 13% from healthier foods, classified as proteins. In a sample

 doi:10.1016/B978-0-12-373915-5.00030-9

of US youth, higher intake of sugar-sweetened beverages (which have little nutritious value) was associated with more problematic insulin regulation, higher systolic blood pressure, greater waist circumference and BMI scores, and lower concentrations of HDL ('good') cholesterol.

Nutrition is associated with individuals' mental health and physical health. In an Australian study, mothers rated how frequently their adolescents consumed a wide variety of foods, and then completed a standard instrument measuring internalizing and externalizing behaviors. Through factor analyses, the authors reduced the list of food items into two major factors, labeled a healthy diet (high consumption of fruits, vegetables, legumes, and whole grains) and a Western diet (high levels of fast food, red meat, potatoes, refined grains, fattened dairy products, and soft drinks). Controlling for several background variables, levels of healthy eating were not significantly related to problem behaviors, whereas the level of Western eating was significantly associated with both internalizing and externalizing behaviors.

In addition to these contemporaneous associations, studies point to long-term effects of nutrition on physical health. Diets in childhood and adolescence that are low in cholesterol and fats, especially saturated fats, have been shown to lower the risk of heart-related ailments in adulthood. Higher sugar-sweetened beverage consumption in adolescence is associated with higher serum uric acid levels and systolic blood pressure, which are implicated in many health problems in adulthood. Studies affirm that poor nutrition during adolescence can precipitate such adult chronic illnesses as hypertension, diabetes, and cardiovascular disease. By the same token, good eating in adolescence can have health dividends for years or even decades later.

Special Significance of Nutrition in Adolescence

These are basic principles that apply throughout the life span, but there are also factors that heighten the salience of nutrition in adolescence in particular. Puberty initiates a remarkable period of growth and bodily changes, featuring a rapid acceleration in height, the maturation of the reproductive systems, and considerable sexual dimorphism, highlighted by increased muscle mass in boys and body fat in girls. The extensive bone growth of this period heightens the demand for calcium intake. Likewise, the initiation of menstrual cycles and accompanying changes in reproductive systems increases the requirements for certain micronutrients. Adolescents' diets must adjust to meet these nutritional demands.

Scholars specifically note the need for a well-rounded diet that includes low-fat dairy products, fruits, and vegetables, along with routine, weight-bearing physical activity, to promote good bone growth. In a study of Spanish early adolescents, investigators found that shifting from their normal to a Mediterranean diet – featuring comparatively high amounts of legumes, cereals, fruits and vegetables, and fish, a lower content of meat and meat products, and a higher monounsaturated versus saturated fat ratio – for a month improved the young people's dietary calcium utilization. By enhancing peak bone mass, the investigators argued, this diet might not only enhance immediate bone growth but also fend off long-term conditions such as osteoporosis.

Adolescents' diets must serve the needs of cognitive and physical growth. During this period, there are considerable changes in brain structure and function that can be enhanced, in part, by nutritional eating. Using data from the National Health And Nutrition Examination Survey (NHANES) in the United States, investigators have demonstrated that an increase in polyunsaturated fats or carbohydrates and a decrease in cholesterol is associated with high levels of performance on standard cognitive tests.

Adolescents tend to consume more calories to accommodate this period of heightened growth. Parents are often amazed at how quickly food disappears from their kitchen and how frequently their children seem to be eating, but these are common signs of the physiological changes their children are negotiating. Not only does caloric intake increase in adolescence, but it becomes more gender-differentiated. Males need more calories than females to sustain their growth through most of this life stage, but caloric intake varies widely among individuals and depends significantly on the level of physical activity. Young people must be careful, however, not to consume more calories than they need because if they eat food with more calories than required for their growth status and level of activity, they will gain weight.

Gender-Differentiated Nutritional Needs

The increased sexual dimorphism that occurs during adolescence signals the need for more differentiated diets as well. Already noted is males' general need for a higher number of calories. Because pubertal development tends to occur over a longer time period for males, they also require more nutrients related to bone growth (e.g., calcium) and such micronutrients as zinc, vitamins A and E, and some B vitamins. Females, on the other hand, tend to require more iron and folic acid. In cultures that emphasize certain body shapes or sizes, nutritional needs may conflict with social norms for physical appearance or beauty. This can jeopardize young people's healthy physical and cognitive development. Women, who are more frequently confronted with societal standards of beauty, are more susceptible to these problems than males are.

Elements of Good Nutrition

Good nutrition involves a balance among several elements: total caloric intake, distribution of items among the major groupings of foods and beverages, ingestion of adequate levels of specific nutrients (especially micronutrients), and healthy eating patterns – including spacing meals across the day and eating at optimal times of day.

Total Caloric Intake

As already noted, total caloric intake can be expected to rise during adolescence and may be particularly high during the early phases of puberty when young people negotiate a growth spurt. The specific calorie count will vary by gender, the stage of pubertal development, and (especially) the amount of regular exercise or activity. Sedentary youth need about 1500 calories per day to sustain their growth and satisfy other body requirements during early adolescence, and about 1800 calories in middle adolescence. Very active youth need a calorie intake of 2200 in early adolescence and 2400 in middle adolescence.

Distribution Among Food Groups

Adolescents need to create a daily menu from a diverse array of foods, so as to maximize their chances of obtaining the appropriate mix of macronutrients. Various organizations and agencies have attempted to categorize foods into distinct food groups. Although there is no complete consensus on the specification of these groups, similar categories do appear across schemes. These include fruits and vegetables (sometimes combined and sometimes left separate), healthy oils and fats (differentiating unsaturated from saturated fats), dairy products (typically emphasizing milk but often including yogurt and cheese), red meats (sometimes combined with beans or other major sources of protein), and grains (sometimes differentiating between whole grains – considered more healthy – and refined grains – considered less healthy). Additional elements that are considered in some but not all schemes are fish–poultry–eggs, beverages (other than milk), and exercise. The Harvard School of Public Health's Healthy Eating Pyramid combines a set of less nutritious foods (red meats, butter, refined grains, potatoes, salt, sugary drinks, and sweets) into a single category with the caution: use sparingly. These food groups are useful to individuals in planning a balanced menu, especially if they are accompanied by age- and gender-specific guidelines for the number of daily portions or servings that should be derived from each group. They are also instrumental in studies of nutrition and diet patterns, as participants are often asked to catalog their daily or weekly food intake in terms of servings per category.

From childhood through late adolescence, the number of servings per food group tends to rise (although more for some food groups than others), before receding again modestly in adulthood. In several groups, the number or range of recommended servings is higher for males than females (lean meats, fruits, vegetables, and grains). Likewise, the number of servings varies directly with an adolescent's average level of physical activity. There is general consensus, however, that an adolescent's menu should be drawn primarily from the food groups encompassing fruits, vegetables, whole grains and, to a lesser extent, unsaturated fats and milk or dairy products.

Adequate Levels of Specific Nutrients

A problem with organizing dietary recommendations by food group is that healthy diets depend less on the specific foods eaten than on the nutrients contained in these foods. A different categorical scheme is used to capture fundamental nutritional elements, which include carbohydrates, protein, fat, minerals, vitamins, fiber, and cholesterol. Carbohydrates are found in foods from several of the primary food groups (fruits, vegetables, whole grains). Nutritionists typically encourage adolescents to draw more than half their daily calories from this element, and on average, just over half of adolescents' calories do come from carbohydrates. Proteins are particularly important when adolescents are in the throes of their growth spurt, around 11–14 for females and 15–18 for males. Youth in the United States tend to consume about twice as much protein as they need.

Adolescents in the United States also consume more than recommended levels of fat, especially saturated fats – a trend that seems to be spreading beyond North America. There are notable ethnic differences in the United States in fat consumption, with daily rates appearing much higher among African American than European American youth. The minerals category includes calcium (already noted for its role in bone development), iron (especially important for girls past menarche), and zinc (which plays a significant role in sexual development). Because iron and zinc are most readily available in meats or poultry, vegetarian adolescents are at special risk for suboptimal levels of these minerals.

Micronutrients, mainly vitamins, are found in a variety of different foods. Some, such as vitamin C, are easy to acquire through fruits and some vegetables. Others, such as vitamin E, are more challenging because they are most prevalent in nonnutritious foods unprocessed plant oils that are generally consumed in moderate quantities. Folate, which helps adolescents negotiate the physiological changes of puberty, is most readily accessible in ready-to-eat cereals, orange juice, bread, and milk. Adolescents who skip breakfast can easily fall short of recommended levels of this nutrient. Fiber, which assists in digestion and wards off major diseases such as certain cancers, also is often lower than desired levels in adolescents because it is common in breakfast items such as cereal and fruit.

Achieving the Proper Balance

The challenge for many adolescents is eating an appropriate balance of foods that allows them to achieve the appropriate levels of all key nutrients without ingesting unhealthy levels of calories. Overeating to acquire all vital nutrients can be as problematic as maintaining an appropriate calorie level without reaching recommended levels of certain nutrients. Studies of adolescent males in the United States, for example, suggest that they generally achieve adequate levels of macronutrients but often fail to acquire appropriate levels of micronutrients. In one investigation, over half of the male participants had suboptimal amounts of vitamins A and B6, and three-quarters consumed inadequate amounts of magnesium, phosphorus, and zinc. Participants classified as overweight had significantly lower protein and carbohydrate intake than normal weight participants.

In a survey of Irish youth, high consumption of foods with added sugars, such as soft drinks, was associated with low levels of several micronutrients. This illustrates a common observation that if adolescents fill up on foods with little nutrient value, they may fail to acquire adequate levels and the appropriate balance of nutrients needed to nurture their physical and cognitive growth and to sustain other daily functions. Contributing to this situation is adolescents' often inadequate understanding of the elements of good nutrition. In Bangladesh, for example, researchers found a generally low level of dietary knowledge among adolescents. Over half were unable to name foods that provided major sources of energy and protein, and over one-third were unaware that they needed to consume extra nutrients during their adolescent growth spurt. Research on youth in Hong Kong suggests that better knowledge about food does not necessarily seem to correlate with more nutritious eating habits. This begs the question of whether or not adolescents' common eating patterns conform to the nutritional needs of this phase of life.

Eating Patterns in Adolescence

Nutritional Deficiencies

Surveys of large, nationally representative samples of youth in North America suggest that their food consumption often does not conform to the recommended amounts and distribution among food groups and nutritional elements. Among youth in the United States, for example, studies indicate that mid-adolescent males generally have adequate daily servings of grains, vegetables, dairy, and meat, but they are low on fruit. Early adolescent males and girls in both age groups tended to fall short of recommended amounts in all categories of the food pyramid. In fact, only 5% of mid-adolescent boys, 2% of early adolescent boys, and none of the girls in the survey met the stipulated minimum number of servings of all five major food group categories in the food pyramid. Within specific categories, not more than 38% of boys and 25% of girls met minimum recommended servings. Moreover, the content of servings in specific categories was not always healthy. Potato (typically, fried) was by far the leading vegetable; few of the grains servings came from whole-grain products (which provide more nutritional value than refined grains).

It is somewhat surprising that family income had only a modest impact on these general patterns of food consumption. Ethnic differences were more noticeable. European-American youth had a higher intake of whole grains and total grains, as well as higher consumption of soft drinks than other groups. Latino youth were comparatively low in eating dark green leafy vegetables but, along with African American adolescents, high in consumption of whole milk. Setting aside fat content, African Americans drank relatively little milk.

A comparable survey of Canadian youth showed similar trends. Most fell below recommended levels of food groups included in the Canadian Food Guide to Healthy Eating. Although, on average, they consumed reasonable levels of macronutrients, they fell short on micronutrients and fiber. Comparing the 40% of survey participants who were classified as having poor diets to the smaller group judged to have superior diets, the investigators found relatively low rates of ingesting protein, fiber, and low-calorie beverages, and high intakes of carbohydrates, fat, and foods with high concentrations of added sugar. Those with poor diets also were less physically active, less likely to eat breakfast, and more likely to eat meals away from home than their peers with better diets.

Studies of youth in other parts of the world reveal similar nutritional deficiencies in adolescents' diets. Less than half of the participants in a study of adolescents in the United Kingdom had five or more portions of fruits and vegetables per day. About a third of this sample reported inadequate exercise and a tendency to skip breakfast, along with too few servings of fruits and vegetables. In fact, only 10% of boys and 2% of girls were judged adequate on all three indicators of healthy eating and lifestyle. Among Irish youth, an increase in eating foods high in sugar was accompanied by a decrease in amounts of dairy products, fruits, vegetables, and other high-fiber foods in their diet. Intake of micronutrients fell as ingestion of sugary foods rose among German and Norwegian adolescents. Consumption of fruits and vegetables was below recommended levels for most participants in a survey of Hong Kong adolescents. In Canada, glycemic levels have been found to be inversely associated with adolescents' consumption of dairy products, fruits and vegetables, and meat alternatives, but directly related to the amount of grains and pure-sugar foods (e.g., candy) that adolescents eat.

Common Changes in Eating Patterns

A common theme across many of these studies is the tendency for adolescents to skip breakfast. The NHANES study revealed that 30% of US youth regularly skipped breakfast and 36% focused primarily on ready-to-eat cereal for this meal. This pattern may be partly explained by the conflict between adolescents' circadian rhythms, which incline them to go to bed late and not awaken fully until mid-morning, and the demand to be at school relatively early in the morning. Adolescents tend to sleep past the breakfast hour when they have the opportunity or sleep as long as possible before rushing to get ready for school (leaving little if any time for eating). Not only does skipping breakfast deprive young people of nutrients and energy calories that could help them concentrate and learn better in school, but it also affects digestion patterns that contribute to the likelihood of this group being overweight or obese – especially in comparison to those who concentrate on ready-to-eat cereals for breakfast. Ironically, cereal eaters display higher levels of micronutrients and lower rates of obesity than youth who normally eat a more elaborate breakfast.

The tendency to skip breakfast is only one of the numerous changes in eating patterns common to adolescence, especially in the United States. Most of these changes undermine adequate nutrition during this important stage of life. Other patterns commonly noted by researchers and practitioners include

- eating more meals away from home;
- increased portion sizes at meals (which can lead to consuming more calories than needed);
- general decline in consumption of fruits and vegetables;
- shift away from high-fiber fruits and vegetables to fried and nutrient-poor foods such as fried potatoes;
- decreased consumption of dairy products;
- increased ingestion of foods with added sugar, especially soft drinks or other sweetened beverages; and
- higher percentage of calories obtained from snack foods.

These patterns tend to result in an overconsumption of fats, especially saturated fats that elevate cholesterol levels, and underconsumption of micronutrients. Some of these patterns deserve additional commentary.

The increase in meals eaten away from home is not necessarily a problem, except that restaurants preferred by many teenagers and families of teenagers serve a relatively unhealthy menu. This is especially true of fast-food establishments. In fact, studies have demonstrated an inverse relationship between adolescents' ingestion of fast food and the amount of whole grains, fruits, and vegetables in their diet.

Young people are more likely to order soft drinks than milk with their meals away from home – again, especially at fast-food establishments. North American restaurants routinely offer free refills on soft drinks or coffee, but not on milk, which provides a monetary incentive to move away from dairy products that are a vital source of calcium. Despite the need for calcium-rich diets in middle adolescence, at this age, boys' average consumption of soft drinks matches their consumption of milk and exceeds their consumption of fruit juices or fruit drinks. One survey of Canadian youth indicated that nearly one-fifth of daily calories come from beverages. Research in the United States indicates that milk consumption is comparatively low among ethnic minorities, especially African Americans. Low income may be a factor in this pattern, but African Americans also have higher levels of lactose intolerance than other ethnic groups, exacerbating the need for these young people to locate other sources of calcium for their regular diet.

Diminished dairy consumption continues from middle adolescence into late adolescence and young adulthood. Findings from Project EAT, a large-scale study of youth in the Midwest of the United States, indicate that during the transition to young adulthood, mean daily calcium intakes of females and males decreased by an average of 153 mg and 194 mg, respectively. Numerous factors appeared to temper this disturbing drop in calcium levels, including the simple availability of milk at mealtimes, a taste preference for milk, stronger personal commitment to health and nutrition (including healthy weight control behaviors), and peer support for healthful eating in middle adolescence. The more time late adolescents spent watching television, the lower their likelihood was of drinking milk.

The shift from milk to soft drinks is also exacerbated by adolescents' increasing reliance on snacks as a major food source. In fact, soft drinks constitute the most commonly chosen snack by adolescent females. Almost all adolescents in a US survey acknowledged having at least one snack a day; a majority had more than one. Snacks accounted for between one-fourth and one-third of daily energy calories. The prevalence of snacks, as well as the proportion of daily calories derived from snacks, has risen dramatically over the past 30 years. Not surprisingly, common snack foods are not particularly nutritious, featuring high levels of sugar, sodium, and fat, and low amounts of micronutrients.

Snacking alone cannot account for micronutrient deficiencies in adolescents, but these deficiencies are a significant concern. Data from the NHANES study indicate that about 60% of male European American youth met or exceeded minimum daily requirements for vitamin D, but males from other ethnic groups, as well as all females (across ethnic groups) failed to display required levels. Ethnic differences are apparent regarding other vitamins. For example, African American adolescent girls display lower levels of vitamins A and D, calcium, and magnesium than do European American girls. Generally speaking, intake of these micronutrients decreases across adolescence, thus expanding with age the portion of women displaying nutritional deficiencies and exacerbating long-term health risks.

Information on changes across adolescence in eating behaviors primarily relies on cross-sectional data, but there are a few relevant longitudinal studies. Project EAT, for example, tracked participants from age 15 to 20, attempting to discern factors that could account for the general decrease across middle and late adolescence in fruit and vegetable consumption. The investigators found that, controlling for basic demographic variables as well as factors affecting fruit and vegetable consumption at base line, the amount eaten in these food groups in late adolescence was positively associated with (mid-adolescent) concern for health and taste preference for fruits and vegetables, and negatively related to the amount of television viewing and the availability of snack foods at home. Additional predictors of fruit consumption for males were parent and peer support for healthy eating, the frequency of eating meals at home, and the simple availability of fruit at home. Although the investigators did not determine how these various factors work together to influence changes in fruit and vegetable consumption, the general message was that such changes are related not simply to personal attitudes but to a variety of lifestyle issues and social network characteristics.

These findings do not diminish the importance of socioeconomic factors, which were controlled in the Project EAT analyses. Data from the same sample, for example, found that about 10% of adolescents acknowledge food insecurity – an uncertainty that any food will be available for them to eat on a routine basis. These young people are less likely to eat breakfast or have other meals with the family, more likely to eat fast food and have foods with high fat content and, not surprisingly, more likely to be overweight. Ethnic minority youth were over-represented among those expressing food insecurity. It is noteworthy that food-insecure and food-secure youth did not differ in the importance they accorded to healthy eating, but the former group did regard healthy eating as less convenient. This is hardly surprising when the sheer presence of food is uncertain.

Trends Over Time

Changes in eating and nutritional patterns from childhood to adolescence, or across adolescence, need to be placed in the context of historical changes. Here, information is limited, but some patterns are apparent. We know, for example, that US adolescents' consumption of fast food has risen considerably since the beginning of the twenty-first century. Increasing work demands for parents, more extensive after-school involvements of youth, and a simple rise in the number of fast-food restaurants in most neighborhoods, help to account for this historical trend.

More long-term analyses reveal that over the past 30 years, the total daily calorie intake has increased between 150 and 300 calories. Most of this increase is accounted for by liquid sugars (soft drinks and other sweetened beverages). Between 1970 and 1995, per-person consumption of soft drinks rose 70%. Of course, higher intake of foods with these added sugars, combined with lower intake of foods with more essential nutrients, results in weight gain, which helps to explain the sharp rise in adolescent obesity over the same time period.

Vegetarian Adolescents

Most studies of adolescents' eating habits fail to recognize important differences among subgroups who consciously follow a different diet. The most obvious of these subgroups is the small cadre of youth who subscribe to vegetarian eating principles. Although incidence rates are uncertain, about 2% of North American youth and 5% of young people in Europe claim to be vegetarian. One problem in establishing incidence rates is that vegetarianism encompasses a variety of diets, all distinctive because of the absence of red meat but still quite different. Vegan diets, by contrast, eschew any animal-based foods. These differences inspire caution when comparing vegetarian and nonvegetarian adolescents because differences are not necessarily applicable across all vegetarian subgroups. Nevertheless, some general patterns are noteworthy.

Vegetarian diets tend to conform more closely than nonvegetarian diets to recommended daily servings of most food groups. Vegetarians are especially low in consumption of junk foods (low-nutrient, high-fat items). They have lower consumption of saturated fats and high-cholesterol foods, giving them a long-term advantage concerning heart disease. Vegetarian girls also tend to reach menarche later than other girls, which carries some long-term health benefits in decreased risk for several cancers.

There are some drawbacks to vegetarian diets for adolescents. First, they tend to be low in calories, compelling ingestion of more high-calorie foods to accommodate energy demands; many adolescents will choose cheese or fried foods over more healthful legumes, nuts, or whole grains. Second, substandard levels of protein and calcium are common among strict vegetarians. Third, intake of several micronutrients, particularly zinc and vitamin B-12, may be inadequate.

Cultural Considerations

The general eating patterns and maturational or historical changes in adolescents' eating behavior that are highlighted in most studies tend to mask considerable ethnic or cultural differences that exist both within and across nations of the world. The dearth of studies from many nations or regions exacerbates our limited understanding of these differences. Adolescents' food preferences are heavily influenced by culture and tradition, as well as the simple availability of certain foods in different climates or ecologies. Because of this, a food pyramid appropriate for one nation or culture may not be at all sensible for another group of adolescents. Health Canada recognizes this by providing different recommendations for First Nations, Inuit, and Métis than for the nation's other residents. Other providers of general nutritional guidelines are likely to follow suit as more culture-specific information becomes available.

In multicultural societies, adolescents often complicate the issue by challenging traditional food practices within their families. In the United States, researchers report that African American and Latino parents often prepare traditional ethnic dishes for home meals, but when the family eats out, adolescents tend to select menu items more consistent with fast food fare and parents tend not to interfere with their choices. This inclination to indulge fast-food appetites diminishes the importance of more ethnic-specific dishes that not only may be more nutritious but also more attuned to the specific nutritional needs of a particular ethnic or cultural group. How, then, do family and cultural traditions, affect adolescent nutrition? To address this, we turn our attention to the sociocultural aspects of eating.

Eating as a Social and Cultural Event

Eating is not just a nutritional necessity but also a social event, shaped by the norms, values, and preferences of significant social units in adolescents' lives. Although a substantial portion of young people's food intake occurs outside the home, the family unit remains the primary venue for meals in that more meals are eaten with the family than any other social unit or context. Accordingly, researchers have concentrated on family dynamics and family traditions in examining social influences on adolescent nutrition.

Family Norms and Values Concerning Food

Parents play an especially significant role in adolescent nutrition because they tend to choose the timing, place, and content of meals and snacks. Of course, parental authority over these matters tends to diminish across adolescence. Studies suggest that between a quarter and a third of adolescents rarely eat dinner with their family, if at all, and the proportion increases across adolescence. Still, parents have an opportunity to form their child's food preferences and eating habits for a decade prior to adolescence, and once formed, these predilections are likely to carry over to a considerable extent as young people grow older. There is even some evidence that disordered eating behaviors can be transmitted from mother to child.

In a literature review of over 60 studies of family influences on children's nutrition patterns, several important patterns emerged. First, that parental intake of fruits and vegetables was positively associated with adolescents' consumption of these food groups. Second, there was a positive association between parental occupational status and adolescents' fruit consumption. Parental education levels also were positively correlated with the amount of fruits and vegetables that an adolescent ate. This reflects the fact that low-income families often have to settle for cheaper foods, which constrains the capacity to provide children with healthy quantities of fruits and vegetables. In more general terms, parents serve as role models of the types of foods that are preferred, and when and where they are eaten.

Adolescents' eating behavior may also reflect the nature of the parent–child relationship. When parents subscribe to an authoritative parenting style, their offspring tend to eat more fruit. Adolescents whose parents practice more of an authoritarian parenting style show more of a preference for less healthy foods. Perhaps they find high-sugar/low-nutrition foods more comforting amid the harsher family environment, but it also may be the case that these foods serve as a safe way to rebel against oppressive family rules. Parents can exacerbate poor nutritional habits if they employ food as a reward for good behavior or withhold food as a punishment for bad behavior.

Sharing Meals Together

Despite multiple ways in which parents and families can influence adolescent eating behaviors, the vast majority of relevant research has concentrated on family meals. Sharing a meal together has long been considered one of the fundamental features of family life. It represents a gathering of individuals around a nurturing activity, encouraging communication and support among family members. It is a context for socialization (learning appropriate manners and family values), connection (sharing stories of daily activities), and planning (discussing future activities for the self or the whole family). It is also a context in which offspring learn about food selection and preparation, thus cultivating their gastronomic tastes and preferences. Time spent together eating can enhance family cohesion and stability. Considering these factors, it should be no surprise that youth who regularly eat meals with their family and have a regular meal schedule within their family are less prone to deviant activity and more successful in school than youth from families who do not have regular and consistent meal schedules. This effect remains significant even controlling for general family functioning and the quality of parent–child relationships.

The positive effects of family meals extend to nutritional issues as well. Across a number of studies, there is remarkable convergence in the effects of eating meals – especially dinner – with the family on a regular basis. The more this occurs, the more likely adolescents are to eat breakfast and lunch, which is important because eating these meals is associated with better nutritional intake. Better nutrition itself is a second direct correlate of eating with the family. Researchers report higher intake of healthy food featuring both macronutrients and micronutrients, which is partly a function of higher quality meals when eating with the family but probably involves food choices when not with the family as well. Third, fast food is less common among adolescents who eat more often with their family. Finally, young people who are overweight or obese report eating fewer dinners with the family.

A common practice in some families is to watch TV while eating together. About a third of US adolescents report this as an occasional or common occurrence. Some question whether or not this compromises the efficacy of family meals. Adolescents in families in which television is part of family meals tend to report less nutritious food patterns than their peers whose families keep the TV off during mealtimes. However, their eating habits are still healthier than adolescents who rarely or never eat with the family. In the Minnesota Project EAT sample, watching television did not compromise the protective effects of eating meals with the family against adolescent drug and alcohol use.

The benefits of regularly sharing dinner or other meals with family members are tempered by the realization that this practice is no longer the norm for US adolescents, nor has it been for decades. Some evidence suggests that it is becoming rarer in other nations as well. Is it possible to reverse this trend, or are there better ways to ameliorate the nutritional habits of adolescents?

Improving Adolescent Nutrition

Careful scientific study over the past 20 years has clarified and cataloged the importance of nutrition in adolescent development and the specific nutritional needs during this stage of life. More recent research has documented evolving trends in adolescents' eating behavior, pointing to a number of disturbing nutritional deficiencies among adolescents in several nations. This work needs to be expanded to a broader scope of adolescents, but it is sufficient to underscore the need for families, health practitioners, educators, and community agencies to take steps to improve the diet and eating habits of young people. The most disturbing evidence of nutrition-related problems among this age group is the rapid rise in obesity rates. At this point, about one in six adolescents in the United States is obese; another one in six is overweight. Comparable figures are lower in other industrialized nations, but still disturbingly high in most cases.

There have been many efforts to address the nutritional needs of adolescents, but in most cases, intervention programs have not been subjected to rigorous scientific assessment. Many programs feature small and esoteric samples from which generalizations would be difficult. From the information available, programs typically have had only modest success. So, there is a limited corpus of work on which to base recommendations for improving adolescent nutrition.

In focus groups, adolescents have provided four major reasons for not eating a more nutritious diet. First, they lack the time needed to procure healthy foods and prepare nutritious meals. Second, eating healthy is inconvenient. The attraction of nonnutritious alternatives – from fast-food restaurants, convenience stores, or vending machines – is that they are quick and close, not to mention cheaper in many instances than healthier food sources. Third, adolescents acknowledge that they lack self-discipline. The ease and attraction of unhealthy alternatives is too much to resist on a regular basis, especially if friends and/or family members are inclined toward less nutritious fare. Finally, there is little sense of urgency. Focus group participants express the belief that they do not need to worry so much about nutrition while they are young and in good health. They can focus on this issue later in life. To be effective, any intervention effort has to address these factors that undermine adolescents' attentiveness to the issue.

Although recommendations must remain tentative, there seem to be three major factors underlying most professionals' efforts to enhance adolescents' healthy eating behavior: providing good food, teaching good eating habits, and promoting lifestyles that foster proper nutrition. We illustrate the major issues in each area.

Provide Good Food

The most obvious and fundamental factor in improving adolescents' eating is to ensure that good food is easily available. Several investigators have found that adolescents are more likely to make nutritious food choices when their homes are stocked with healthy foods. For parents, this is a relatively simple matter of keeping a good supply of fresh fruits and vegetables, buying more whole-grain items, and stocking the refrigerator with low-fat dairy products. Other research indicates that good nutrition is negatively associated with the availability of unhealthy foods, suggesting that in addition to keeping high-nutrient foods on hand, parents should limit the supply of low-nutrient choices such as soft drinks and other high-sugar beverages, salty snacks, candy, and so on.

Additionally, meals eaten out should only occasionally involve fast-food establishments or other restaurants offering a menu dominated by low-nutrition foods.

These same principles could be adopted in other contexts in which adolescents spend much of their time – most notably, schools and after-school programs. Many schools in the United States have stopped preparing hot lunches and signed contracts with vendors to supply meals and stock-vending machines with food and beverage items. In most cases, high-calorie, relatively nonnutritious options dominate the menus and vending machine choices in these schools. Although an attractive source of revenue for the schools, these practices should be curtailed in the interest of students' health. In fact, many schools are rolling back these programs in response to parent or community pressures.

In addition, schools can be instrumental in encouraging adolescents to change their diets toward healthier foods and eating habits through special meal programs. For example, one school offered a group of 15-year-olds a nutritious breakfast at school for a brief period of time. They measured participants' eating habits before, during, and after the intervention, finding that shortly after the program ended, students tended to return to their preprogram breakfast habits. Nevertheless, compared to a nonintervention control group, the participants were more likely to eat lunch, maintained a healthier diet, and, unlike the control group, did not gain weight over the study period. Even short-term provision of good foods can have longer-term effects on adolescent nutrition.

Teach Good Eating Habits

Eating well is not an inherent behavior, especially when there are tasty or socially attractive, nonnutritious alternatives. Especially in adolescence, as young people gain more autonomy over their eating behaviors, it is important to offer instruction about good nutrition. This education can begin at home. One study examined the extent to which young people in the United States modeled their parents' eating behavior by comparing parents' and children's food intake over a 24-h period. Parents' diet choices were more strongly correlated with children's than adolescents' food choices, although the correlation was stronger in some food categories (especially, fruits and vegetables, saturated fats, cholesterol, calcium, and soft drinks) than others. The findings were consistent across socioeconomic levels, although Hispanic adolescents were slightly more consistent with parents' behavior than were youth in other ethnic groups.

Another study indicated that mothers' concern with good eating did not affect adolescents' food choices, but adolescents' perception of maternal concern was a factor. With adolescents, parents may need to be more open about their interest in a child's healthy eating if they want it to have an impact on adolescents' behavior.

Schools are an obvious source of instruction in nutritious eating. Information can be incorporated into the curriculum in health classes, science courses, home economics or home management classes, and other places. In addition to this direct approach to instruction, schools may be successful with more indirect educational programs. One example involves three high schools in the United States that initiated a labeling program for items sold for school meals and snacks. All items received a green, yellow, or red label indicating whether they were considered high, moderate, or low in nutritional value. Compared to a prelabeling base line period, the investigators found that purchase of red items declined sharply (from 83% to 47% of total purchases), whereas selection of yellow items increased markedly (from 18% to 48%). Multiple and innovative approaches to nutrition education may be most effective with this age group.

Older adolescents may respond to a more direct educational approach. An intervention program aimed at increasing college students' knowledge of nutrition and healthy diet choices (as well as prevention of chronic diseases) proved successful in increasing participants' intake of fruits and vegetables and diminishing the amount of fried potatoes that they ate. Females were more responsive to the intervention than males were.

Physicians also can be important sources of nutrition education. In one study, patients making routine visits to their primary care physician were asked to take a short lesson about healthy eating, and then complete a brief questionnaire about health issues or concerns (all on a Personal Data Assistant) while waiting to see the doctor. The physician then used this information to initiate conversations about various health topics during the examination. Follow-up analyses indicated that patients in the PDA condition increased their calcium intake and exercise regimen significantly more than a nonintervention control group.

Even eating establishments may have a role in nutrition education. For example, several restaurants and fast-food establishments publish some basic nutritional information about items on their menu. A recent study of such programs in one set of restaurants indicated that providing customers with this information did not change the eating habits of adolescents. Reasons for this program's lack of success are unclear, and the efficacy of the program deserves a broader assessment, but it is possible that this is not the most effective venue for encouraging better nutrition habits among adolescents.

For the most part, the studies we highlight indicate the potential positive effects of the various types of educational programs in different domains of adolescents' lives. Not all programs are successful, however, nor are successful ones frequently able to inspire dramatic changes in adolescents' eating behavior. Indeed, scholars argue that educational programs are not likely to have much impact unless they are accompanied by broader environmental changes that encourage adolescents to pursue good nutrition as part of a healthy lifestyle.

Promote Lifestyles that Foster Good Nutrition

Good nutrition is valuable in its own right, but it is better viewed as part of a broader array of behaviors that encompass a healthy adolescent lifestyle. Several studies indicate that healthy eating and regular physical exercise are significantly correlated. Indeed, the number of calories adolescents need is contingent on their level of physical activity. Likewise, as other articles in this encyclopedia indicate, health is enhanced by positive relationships with peers and family members. A healthy diet is likely to inspire adolescents to be more physically active and to engage more vigorously in social activities with family and peers. Close family relationships will encourage adolescents to stay home more often for meals, which should lead to or reaffirm existing healthy eating patterns. Evidence to date of linkages among these components of healthy adolescent development is still modest and tentative, but it is sufficient to urge interventionists to structure nutrition education and intervention programs as part of a larger effort to inspire healthy adolescent development.

Conclusion

Because of the dramatic physical, cognitive, and social changes that individuals undergo at adolescence, nutrition is an especially salient issue in this stage of life. The complex nutritional needs of this age group and their metamorphosis across adolescence may not be well understood by young people or those who guide them through this life stage. Conditions of contemporary life often mitigate against optimal eating behaviors. The challenge for parents, educators, medical professionals, and adolescents themselves is to create an environment that helps young people appreciate the need for proper nutrition, and then gives them the opportunity to maintain healthy eating behaviors.

See also: Eating Disorders; Overweight/Obesity.

Further Reading

Gidding SS, Dennison BA, Birch LL, American Heart Association, et al. (2006) Dietary recommendations for children and adolescents: A guide for practitioners. *Pediatrics* 117: 544–559
Satter E (2005) *Your Child's Weight: Helping without Harming.* Madison, WI: Kelcy
Woodruff SJ and Hanning RM (2008) A review of family meal influence on adolescents' dietary intake. *Canadian Journal of Dietetic Practice and Research* 69: 14–22.

Relevant Websites

http://www.hc-sc.gc.ca/fn-an/food-guide-aliment/index-eng.php – Canada's Food Guide.
http://www.epi.umn.edu/let/pubs/adol_book.shtm – Electronic copy of Stang J and Story M (eds.) (2005) *Guidelines for Adolescent Nutrition Services.*
http://www.thenutritionsource.org – The Nutrition Source, Harvard School of Public Health.

Personality Traits in Adolescence

M A G van Aken, Utrecht University, Utrecht, The Netherlands
R Hutteman and J J A Denissen, Humboldt University, Berlin, Germany

Glossary

Ego control: The threshold or operating characteristics of an individual with regard to the expression or containment of impulses, feelings, and desires.
Ego resiliency: The dynamic capacity of an individual to modify his/her modal level of ego-control, in either direction, as a function of the demand characteristics of the environmental context (resourceful adaptation vs. little adaptive flexibiliy).
Five factor theory: Number of propositions about the nature, origins, and developmental course of the five personality factors from the Five Factor Model (or Big Five): Extraversion, Agreeableness, Conscientiousness, Emotional Stability (sometimes reversed labeled Neuroticism), and Openness to Experience.
Mean-level stability: Consistency across time in the average level of a trait within a sample, irrespective of rank-order differences.
Personality traits: Individual differences in the tendency to behave, think, and feel in certain ways that are consistent across time and situations.
Rank-order stability: Consistency across time in the rank-order differences between individuals within a sample, irrespective of mean-level trends occurring in the general population.

Introduction

Adolescence has traditionally been viewed as a period of storm and stress in intra- and interpersonal functioning. During this period of the life span, some youths show increases in conflict with parent, drops in self-esteem, engagement in risk-taking behavior, and mood disruptions. Although the view on adolescence as a conflict-ridden period now is somewhat outdated, numerous questions still remain about changes that occur. Is it the personality of youths that changes? And if so, how fundamental are these changes for later development? In this article, we focus on personality development during adolescence. We first start with a definition of personality from a trait perspective. After that, we look at stability and change in personality traits during adolescence. Finally, we look at the implications of personality traits for psychosocial functioning and adaptation during adolescence.

Most developmental psychologists are familiar with the construct of temperament, which can be defined as "individual differences in behavior that appear early in life." Some researchers supplement this definition with the notion that temperamental factors (also in adulthood) are somehow more biological or genetic in origin. Researchers usually use the term temperament when they talk about personality differences in young children (<3 years) and have developed age-specific measurement scales to assess them. However, several researchers have focused on temperament in adolescence, and found four broad factors for adolescence (surgency, negative affectivity, effortful control, and affiliation). Behavior genetic studies have obtained similar heritability estimates for temperament and personality traits which are inconsistent with the notion that temperament is somehow more 'genetic' in origin. Several authors have also stressed the similarity between the structures of temperament and personality traits in childhood and adolescence. For example, a factor akin to the factor extraversion, one of the factors in the Five Factor Model (FFM) in adults, is also found in children, at which age it is sometimes called surgency. Given the large overlap between personality and temperament, especially when focusing on traits, we see no reason to differentiate between the two constructs. Therefore, for this article, we consider temperament and personality as two labels for similar individual differences, and we use the label of personality traits to denote these differences during adolescence.

Definitions of Personality

McAdams (see Further reading) distinguishes between three different perspectives in thinking about the development of personality. In a way, these standpoints can be seen as three layers of psychological individuality, with each layer being superimposed onto the other with an increasing level of complexity and sophistication.

The first layer is that of the person as actor and refers to personality traits, which are defined as individual differences in the tendency to behave, think, and feel in certain ways that are consistent across time (i.e., are stable) and situations (i.e., are domain-general). The second perspective is that of the person as agent, and refers to a layer of characteristic adaptations that include goals, plans, and values. This can more be seen as the motivational perspective on personality, in which human agency is placed at the center of personality inquiry. Issues within this domain concern people's choices, motivations, or goals. In adolescence, such motives and goals may focus particularly on education and choices of a future profession, as well as issues of social belongingness and identity. Personality traits influence how adolescents differ in the way that they deal with the specific developmental tasks they encounter. For example, some adolescents may be wary of new situations and new stimuli, and may therefore be careful in trying out illicit substances. Others may have a high need to be affiliated to others and may therefore be inclined to follow the choices their peers make. Still others may have a strong tendency to live up to environmental expectations regarding task fulfillments and may therefore suffer from not being able to cope with the higher standards of secondary education.

The third layer is that of the person as author and refers to the integrative life narratives in which individuals give their life a unique and culturally anchored meaning. Such a life narrative provides a person's life with a sense of unity, purpose, and meaning, and as such integrates the dispositional traits and the characteristic adaptations, or the outlines and the detail of individual variability. Narratives may include representations of traits or motivations, but they typically contain more complex and temporally sequenced themes. Given that the development of identity constitutes one of the main developmental tasks during adolescence, the third layer of personality is certainly highly relevant for this phase in life. However, because other articles in this encyclopedia deal with this issue more specifically, we do not present it in detail here.

In a way, traits form a broad stylistic background against which other features of individuality are expressed. As stated previously, dispositional traits appear even in early human life, and they are also observed among nonhuman animals, such as pigs and dogs and even among octopuses and guppies. During the past two decades, the FFM of personality has been accepted as a working taxonomy of the major trait domains. The FFM consists of five broad dimensions which form the basic tendencies in the Five Factor Theory of Robert McCrae and Paul Costa (which will be described in more detail later): extraversion (the tendency to react with positive affect and vigorous behavior to rewards and social situations), emotional stability (sometimes labeled neuroticism, the susceptibility to react to threats and dangers with negative emotions and general distress), conscientiousness (individual differences in self-control), agreeableness (the tendency to maintain harmonious relationships with others), and openness to experience (the motivation to explore and reflect about the outside world). Although the FFM was discovered in research on adult personality, the five factors can also be used to describe the personality of adolescents, and developmental precursors of extraversion, emotional stability, and conscientiousness can be identified in even younger children. We therefore use the FFM to review existing research on personality development during adolescence.

A somewhat different approach toward studying personality is to focus on personality types rather than on personality traits. Three personality types, which are based on the theory on ego-resiliency and ego-control by Jack and Jeanne Block, are consistently found in research: undercontrollers, overcontrollers, and resilients. Undercontrollers are characterized by a low level of ego-resiliency (comparable to self- or emotion-regulation) combined with a low level of ego-control (comparable to impulse control); overcontrollers by a low level of ego-resiliency and a high level of ego-control; and resilients by a high level of ego-resiliency and a flexible level of ego-control (that can be adjusted to the specific requirements of certain circumstances). Several studies have shown that these types are also present in adolescence and have implications for their functioning. However, since the three personality types are also distinguishable in terms of the traits from the FFM (resilients high on all dimensions, undercontrollers low on agreeableness and conscientiousness, overcontrollers high on agreeableness and conscientiousness and low on emotional stability) and the theoretical implications of the results within these studies are largely comparable to those described for the FFM-traits in this article, we focus only on the latter.

Many early theories on personality development assumed that personality development proceeds in qualitative and ordered stages. For example, Freud believed that children's personality moved from the oral phase to the anal phase, and that the personality of some individuals would get stuck or 'fixated' in a certain stage. Almost all contemporary personality researchers, by contrast, assume a model in which a more continuous course of development is formulated. If anything, the period of adolescence is important in the sense that from the preteen period onward, a clear and consistent structure of personality traits (i.e., the five factors) seems to appear. In addition, individual differences in goals and attitudes become more apparent and more stable. This signals clear signs of consistent and stable individual differences in characteristic adaptations (or in psychosocial functioning).

As for the assessment of personality traits, it has now generally been accepted that psychological self-reports for children and adolescents can be obtained from as early as age 10 onward. Research indicates that as of that age, factors such as acquiescent responding or difficulties in verbal comprehension are no longer strong enough to call into question the possibility of a coherent and differentiated assessment of personality using children's self-reports. Children as young as 5–7 years of age have even been found to be able to provide reliable and valid self-reports on the five personality factors when researchers use a procedure in which puppets were used to interview the children about their self-perceptions about key aspects of their lives.

In addition to self-reports, researchers can use information from either lay judges who are acquainted with the adolescent (e.g., parents or teachers) or who are professional experts in dealing with the trait in question (e.g., doctors). Information can also be obtained from peers, using either descriptions of single targets or sociometric ratings of entire groups. Finally, personality can be measured by collecting objective behavioral data related to the trait in question (e.g., number of fights as an index of aggressiveness). All these different sources, which may be biased and/or based on limited information, can be supplemented by self-descriptions provided by children and adolescents as an additional and unique source of insight into individual differences in personality.

In this article, we focus on the development and the relevance of the first layer of personality during adolescence, that is, on personality traits. However, since the notion of characteristic adaptations and narrative identity (Layers 2 and 3) also relates to the functioning or adaptation of adolescents, we elaborate somewhat on the relation between these layers later, when we come to the section on the implications of personality traits on psychosocial functioning and adaptation.

Stability and Change of Personality During Adolescence

Scholars have studied stability and change of personality during adolescence in two ways. First, studies on mean-level change of personality trait expression look at how groups of individuals change in their average trait levels. For example, all children between ages 10 and 16 may show a normative mean-level increase in height. Second, studies on rank-order consistency and change compare the continuity of individuals' relative trait score (i.e., compared to the average level of their peers). In the following sections, we first review mean-level change and stability in adolescence, followed by an overview of rank-order change and stability in adolescence.

Mean-Level Stability During Adolescence

When a strict definition of traits focusing on individual differences between people is applied, mean-level change in personality trait expression does not technically constitute personality change. For example, if all individuals in a cohort demonstrate identical increases in physical height, individual differences between them are retained (e.g., if Peter is the fourth tallest person in his class at both age 10 and 16). It is, however, interesting to study such changes because mean levels of personality trait expression of a given population constitute the background against which individual differences manifest themselves. For example, for estimating whether a person has become relatively more antisocial between the ages 12 and 16, it is useful to have information about the typical trajectory of aggressiveness during that period. After all, during adolescence, an increase in antisocial behavior is normative according to Terrie Moffit's theory on adolescence-limited antisocial behavior. Therefore, an increase in relatively minor delinquent activities in adolescence may not indicate that a teenager is developing an antisocial personality, as this constitutes (normative) mean-level change during this life phase.

Brent Roberts and his colleagues conducted the first meta-analysis on mean-level changes in personality trait expression in 2006. Only longitudinal samples ($n = 92$) were included in their analysis, representing a broad range of birth cohorts. They classified traits according to their position in the FFM, with an additional distinction between two facets of extraversion: social dominance and social vitality. In addition, they compared results between adolescents (10–18) and different older age groups. The most notable finding from this meta-analysis was that mean-level changes in trait expression were not most prominent in adolescence. In fact, from the eight age-groups that were defined in this meta-analysis, the three periods after adolescence (18–22; 22–30, 30–40) often showed more change in mean-level personality. For Extraversion, significant amounts of mean-level change were found in all four age periods, but was highest between ages 18 and 22. For Agreeableness, none of the age periods showed much change. For Conscientiousness, significant amounts of change were found between ages 22–30 and 30–40. For Emotional Stability again there was change in these periods, but here also for the ages 10–18 and 18–22. For Openness, a significant amount of change was found only for the age period between 18 and 22. In sum, maturation of personality certainly does not seem to be done by the age of 18, and in fact seems to be even stronger in emerging and early adulthood. Because this is also the time period with the highest density of social role changes, theories have been developed that personality maturation is associated with the fulfillment of adult social roles. If one accepts this premise, adolescence loses its theoretical significance as the main period for personality development, because many of these adult social roles are not taken on until after adolescence by (western) individuals (i.e., only after emerging adulthood or thereafter).

However, the finding that adolescence is not the period in which the largest changes in personality development take place does not mean that there are no mean-level changes at all during this period. In fact, during adolescence and most other periods of the life span, personality 'matures' in that mean levels of traits move in a direction that is generally seen as desirable in interaction partners. In other words, in adolescence, people on average become easier to interact with; agreeableness, social dominance (one of the extraversion facets), openness, and emotional stability (slightly) increase during adolescence.

Some studies on big five personality development between ages 11 and 17 have found gender differences in this development in the form of larger mean-level changes in girls than boys. These gender differences might be explained by the faster cerebral cortical development of adolescent girls as opposed to adolescent boys, which is thought to result in an advance of girls' intellectual and social-cognitive functioning. However, timing differences between boys and girls cannot explain differences in development of individual traits, as some researchers have not only found the pattern to differ in timing, but for some traits also in direction. If these gender differences are replicated, they would have to be explained in terms of different expectations that the environment (both proximal institutions such as the family or the peer group, but also broader in terms of socioeconomic status group or ethnic culture) has for personality development in boys versus girls, and differences in person–environment interactions that result from these expectations. For example, the environment could expect girls to become more agreeable and conscientious during adolescent development (living up to the stereotype of a sociable and responsible girl), whereas for boys, environmental pressure would lead to less extraversion and openness, and as such more focusing on serious business involving school and career orientation.

As stated previously, social role theory can be used to explain gender differences in personality development. Two other schools of thought have sought to explain the specific direction of mean-level changes in personality across time. First of all, Costa and McCrae's Five Factor Theory of personality suggests mean-level changes to be intrinsically human in nature, stemming from endogenous, genetic factors residing within every individual. Such a genetically fixed program of personality change could be seen as evolutionary adaptations to facilitate important life history transitions (e.g., development of reproductive capacities). In nature, these transitions follow a predictable pace, so it may be plausible that accompanying personality changes can be characterized by a similar level of predictability. Testing this perspective, one study compared mean-level age changes between samples from Turkey, Germany, Great Britain, the Czech Republic, and Spain. Although these countries differ in terms of cultural practices, socioeconomic circumstances, and historical heritage, mean-level differences between age groups were found to be remarkably similar.

An alternative perspective that tries to explain the quasi-universal nature of mean-level personality maturation, based on Social Investment Theory, states that investing in social institutions is the driving mechanism underlying personality maturation. According to this perspective, as people take on responsibility in social roles in the form of establishing stable romantic relationships, starting a career, and becoming involved in community life, they are expected to become more socially dominant, agreeable, conscientious, and emotionally stable. For example, having a job requires people to be on time for meetings and regulate aggressive impulses against customers and coworkers. These types of social roles are mainly (expected to be) adopted during young adulthood. This would explain the finding that personality maturation (in the form of mean-level change) is more prominent in young adulthood than in adolescence. However, some mean-level changes are found in adolescence. These changes might be explained by those social roles that are already beginning to be adopted during adolescence, such as starting to work part-time.

Rank-Order Stability During Adolescence

The second main approach to study personality development is by focusing on the rank-order of an individual within a certain population regarding a specific trait. This approach focuses on differences between individuals at a specific time point, irrespective of mean-level trends occurring in the general population. In the following paragraphs, we start by reviewing general patterns of personality continuity. After that, we discuss sources of rank-order personality change, as well as possible explanations for this phenomenon.

An earlier meta-analysis, published in 2000, indicated that the rank-order stability of personality traits increases with age. In adolescence, rank-order stability is already somewhat more stable as compared to early childhood. Specifically, the average stability coefficient was 0.35 for the period between ages 0 and 3, compared to 0.47 between ages 12 and 18 and 0.51 between ages 18 and 22. This should not be taken as proof, however, that change is no longer possible, as such a conclusion would only be warranted by retest stabilities around 0.80 (i.e., the reliability of many personality questionnaires). Indeed, rank-order consistency only peaks in late adulthood, where it is 1.5 times larger than in adolescence. This relatively low level of rank-order consistency compared to other periods of the life span suggests that adolescence is not a crucial period in which personality dispositions are becoming more crystallized, but rather a period of exploration.

Issues of personality stability and change might be related to processes in the third layer of personality (i.e., identity): It is typically assumed that a lot of identity exploration takes place during adolescence. Identity change might lead to a subjective perception of general instability in intrapersonal domains. In other words, exploring one's ideological and vocational choices in life might give rise to the impression that one has 'changed as a person,' even though one's underlying style of behavior (as captured by trait levels) remains the same. That is, instability in identity might overshadow the consistency in personality traits.

Another way in which the first and third layer of personality overlap is that as adolescents start to develop a stable sense of identity, their personality may increase in stability. Identity has been found to become increasingly stable as people grow older, and this might act as an active force promoting personality stability. For example, once an adolescent has decided that learning for school is something for 'nerds' (a group to which he does not want to belong), he may start to avoid behaving in a conscientious way.

In the following sections, we discuss possible sources of rank-order personality change in adolescence. By definition, such influences can only be nonnormative in nature, as normative influences are universal within a certain population and can thus only affect mean-level changes in trait expression. We review four sources of differential change.

Genetic factors

Given the prominent role of genes in personality stability, it may be surprising that they can also promote personality change. This may seem counterintuitive, as the genetic code (as captured in the DNA) does not change across life. Consistent with this, studies have indeed found that genes mostly contribute to personality stability. However, genetic factors have been found to account up to 30% of individual differences in personality change. This can occur because gene expression is a dynamic phenomenon, with genes being turned on and off during various stages of development, with resulting changes in associated personality traits. For example, Huntington's disease is a neurological disorder caused by a rare allele of the so-called Huntington gene that is passed from parents to offspring at birth. Physical symptoms in the person suffering from this disease commonly become noticeable only in a person's 40s, causing profound personality changes. Comparable to this, there might be the possibility that new genes become active and affect personality during puberty.

Social relationships

According to the so-called social looking glass self-perspective of Charles Horton Cooley, people become how others perceive them to be. Indeed, social relationships constitute a key influence in shaping human development, particularly in adolescence, in which peer pressure is an especially salient issue. Another type of relationship that first becomes prominent in adolescence can be found in the domain of mating. Because mating and reproducing are highly salient evolutionary tasks confronting humans, it is not surprising that romantic relationships have been shown to exert an important influence on personality trait development. There is some evidence that as individuals start a first romantic relationship, they decrease in neuroticism and increase in conscientiousness.

Importantly, these changes seem to persist even in people who later discontinued their romantic relationships, suggesting that the formation of a first romantic relationship represents a formative experience toward personality maturation. It is unclear what mechanism is responsible for the conservation of this formative experience, but it could be that some kind of cognitive reprogramming plays a role (e.g., the knowledge that one is able to attract and retain a mate can give security in future romantic interactions). This is relevant for adolescence because many individuals experience their first romantic relationship during this period of life, although for some other people, such changes do not take place until emerging adulthood or even later.

In spite of the theoretical importance of early family experiences, behavior genetic studies have generally found the effect of shared parenting influences (i.e., those influences that have a similar effect for children within one family) on personality to be quite limited. This is not to say that parents do not matter; rather, the effect of their parenting behaviors may differ between children because (a) siblings may react differently to the same behaviors of their parents, and (b) parents may adjust their parenting behaviors to match the personality of the child.

Social relationships have been found to have an influence on rank-order changes in personality in adolescence through the quality of these relationships. Recent findings on the Munich LOGIC-study (a longitudinal study in which children were followed from age 3 onward to the age of 23), revealed that conflict with father at the age of 17 years was related to decreases in emotional stability, conscientiousness, and self-esteem 6 years later. In addition, conflict with mother at the age of 17 years was related to decreases in emotional stability and self-esteem. Quality of the relationship with best friend appears to play a role as well, in that conflict with best friend was related to decreases in extraversion and self-esteem, whereas perceived support from best friend was positively associated with changes in extraversion.

However, the reverse has also been found in several studies where personality traits in adolescence were found to predict the quality of social relationships. For example, big five personality traits at age 12 have been found to predict support from parents and peers at age 17. Extraversion, agreeableness, and conscientiousness are predictive of certain aspects of social relationships such as the number of peer relationships and conflict with peers. This might suggest a reciprocal association between social relationships and change in personality traits during adolescence.

Work experiences

Being a successful worker in most professions requires that people act in a socially responsible matter. According to the social investment perspective mentioned earlier, it can be expected that success in the work domain is related to increases in personality maturity. This is especially true for conscientiousness, which has been found to be a trait that has been repeatedly shown to predict work-related success. However, work-related changes in personality would seem less consistent with the biological perspective of Five Factor Theory, because modern-day work experiences seem to share little resemblance with evolutionary pressures that could have resulted in uniform mean-level changes in humans.

A growing body of evidence is consistent with the notion that work experiences can shape personality development. For example, one study showed that women who increased their participation in the labor force became more agentic and more norm-adhering as they grew older. In another study, they showed that positive work experiences were associated with increases in emotional stability, extraversion, and conscientiousness in a sample of young adults. In that study, it was also shown that increases in work satisfaction are associated with changes toward personality maturation, whereas engaging in counterproductive work behaviors is associated with decreases in emotional stability and conscientiousness.

In addition to the effects of full-time work, part-time work has also been found to exert influence on personality development in adolescence and young adulthood. Part-time work has long been thought to have a negative influence on adolescents' development, as it would prevent adolescents from participating in developmentally beneficial activities and would confront them with stressors. However, part-time work in adolescence has recently been found to be associated with resilience and psychological well-being in early adulthood, perhaps by preparing adolescents for stressful occupations in adulthood. Moreover, some studies have found that part-time work experiences in emerging adulthood are associated with decreases in aggressiveness. Whether part-time work experiences have a negative or a positive effect on adolescents' (personality) development probably depends on various other factors such as the nature and the amount of the work, the reasons to start with the work, and the age and the demographic background of the adolescents.

Life events

It has long been thought that negative (or traumatic) life events represent an important influence on personality development. Through some process, the resulting negative effect has been hypothesized to be related to subsequent personality changes. This has often been referred to as the 'scarring' hypothesis, where the experience of serious psychopathology would lead to lasting changes in personality. Some recent studies indeed suggest that serious life events during adolescence may lead to a deviation of the normal personality development during that period. Normative decreases in fear and frustration were less strong for adolescents who experienced one or more serious life events. It is still unknown, however, what kinds of life events may lead to subsequent personality changes and what processes account for their potential consolidation (e.g., brain processes, establishment of cognitive schemata).

Personality and Adaptation in Adolescence

To understand the association between personality and adaptation in adolescence, one can invoke the distinction made in the beginning of this article between personality traits (in McAdams's terms, the person as actor) and characteristic adaptations (the person as agent). The layer of characteristic adaptations is superimposed on the layer of personality traits, with an increasing level of complexity. This increasing complexity when going from personality traits to characteristic adaptations is a result of the fact that personality traits interact with the social environment; personality is also becoming 'translated' in the functioning of children and adolescents through interactions with the environment.

Three mechanisms through which this 'translation' occurs are described in the literature in terms of three systematic transactions between persons and their environment. First, *proactive* transactions reflect the processes by which people select social environments that are consistent with their personality. Second, *reactive* transactions reflect the tendency for people to react to and interpret similar environments in a consistent way, fitting with their personality. Third, *evocative* transactions reflect the tendency for certain personality dimensions of a person to evoke reactions from others. These mechanisms can be observed in several life domains for adolescents.

Personal Relationships

The quantity and quality of relationships is associated with almost all of the five personality dimensions from the FFM and also differs between the three personality types. These associations have been documented clearly in adulthood, but empirical research is also beginning to show them in childhood and adolescence.

The three transactions mentioned previously can be described in terms of three processes by which personality can have an effect on relationship outcomes. First, proactive transactions can be seen when personality has a direct, proactive effect on relationships, for example, by determining the initiative of an adolescent to become exposed to certain peers, or to invest in them. Second, evocative transactions are seen when the personality of an adolescent evokes specific behavior from relationship partners that affect the quality of that relationship (or even its continuity). For example, adolescent undercontrollers may be rejected by their classmates as a result of their impulsive and perhaps hostile behaviors. Third, reactive transactions are seen when certain personality traits shape a person's reaction to the behavior of relationship partners. For example, an adolescent low on agreeableness may have difficulties handling interpersonal closeness and therefore may react awkwardly to expressions of affection by their romantic partners.

Fairly uncharted territory is the extent to and mechanisms with which adolescents' personality traits may determine the quality of their relationship with their parents, including parenting. The few studies that are reported show that both adolescents' and parents' personality exert a significant impact on the quality of their mutual relationship. In addition, newer studies suggest parents' and adolescents' traits to be equally important for the warmth in their relationship, but adolescents' personality is a stronger predictor of the amount of control.

School and Work

Effects of personality have also been reported in the domain of school achievements and work success. These findings mostly concern the academic or occupational success of adults, but several studies also report associations earlier in life. The dimension for conscientiousness has repeatedly been found to determine attentional capacities and striving for high standards, which in turn may influence school achievement. Neuroticism has also been mentioned often, but seems to be more related to job success than to school achievements earlier in life.

Again, the three processes mentioned earlier might underlie these associations. People might proactively choose educational and work settings or experiences that fit their personality, or, conversely, they might leave settings that do not fit. However, people might evoke different reactions from the environment that affect their selection into certain educational or work settings on the basis of their personality. A third process is that people may perceive and interpret work-related situations differently based on their personality profile. For example, highly optimistic individuals may perceive difficult tasks as challenging, whereas others react with learned helplessness. Such differences in appraisal have been found to determine the subsequent outcome of the stress process.

It should be noted that these mechanisms have been found more often in relation to occupational success than to educational success. Studies on the personality determinants of educational success in children and adolescents are not that frequent.

Problem Behavior

More studies have been reported on the association between personality and problem behavior than on the two domains mentioned earlier. From a Big Five perspective, a higher score on extraversion has been found to be related to more externalizing behaviors, as have lower scores on agreeableness and conscientiousness. A higher score on neuroticism has been found to be related to internalizing behaviors, as have lower scores on extraversion and agreeableness. Studies have also focused on the three personality types and found that overcontrollers show internalizing problems, whereas undercontrollers show externalizing problems.

Several studies report interactions between personality and support in the prediction of problem behavior. For example, studies on the interaction between personality and parenting report that a higher level of warmth between parents and children mitigates the development of internalizing problems in overcontrollers, whereas a higher level of coercion aggravates the development of externalizing problems in resilients and undercontrollers. Similarly, personality has been found to moderate the effects between parenting and problem behavior. For example, parental rejection has been found to be more related to depression in overcontrolled girls than in resilient girls.

Personality and Personality Disorders

An interesting and recent addition to the literature on personality in children and adolescents concerns the connection between 'normal personality' and personality disorders, as classified in psychiatric diagnosis systems such as the Diagnostic and Statistical Manual of Mental Disorders (DSM) and the International Classification of Diseases (ICD). The reasons for this addition are twofold. First, as we know more and more about the development of personality, there is also more attention to the development of personality disorders. This concerns issues of stability and change, but also questions about the precursors of personality disorders. Second, it is likely that the new version of the DSM-classification (DSM-V) may result in a procedure to diagnose personality disorders in terms of scores on continuous dimensions (instead or in addition to a categorical classification), which would blur the line between normal and pathological personality.

What is the relation between normal and psychopathological personality development? Some models start with the assumption that personality is an exogenous factor, leading to subsequent development of pathological outcomes. For example, according to a *vulnerability* model, certain personality dimensions (e.g., emotional instability) could be considered as risk factors that make the individual vulnerable to the development of certain forms of psychopathology, especially in combination with triggering factors in the environment. In a *protective* model, certain personality dimensions (e.g., resiliency) might buffer against the effects of environmental stressors. A third possible association is specified by the *maintenance* model, in which it is assumed that personality dimensions are not so much associated with the initial development of psychopathology, but rather influence the course and prognosis of a disorder.

Finally, somewhat different from these models (in which personality and personality disorders are still separate entities), is the spectrum hypotheses. Here, personality pathology is seen as representing a quantitatively more extreme score of the entire spectrum of possible personality scores within a population, without assuming any kind of qualitative differences between 'normal' and 'abnormal' personality. Consistent with this, several studies have shown that a common structure underlies normal and pathological dimensions and that the latter are therefore just more extreme manifestations of the former.

Conclusion

Adolescents differ from one another in meaningful ways in the way they think, behave, and feel in reaction to various situations. These differences in personality traits are fairly stable over adolescence both in their mean level and in their interindividual rank order. However, stability is not perfect: growth toward a more adaptive personality can be seen, and individual adolescents may change in comparison with their age mates. These individual differences can have profound effects on the way adolescents function in the domains of relationships, school and work, and their psychosocial functioning, even into the area of psychopathology.

Perhaps, the weakest part of our knowledge regarding personality traits in adolescence concerns the psychological mechanisms behind stability and change in personality. Stability and change seem to be influenced by genetic factors and also by environmental factors such as relationships and work, and to some extent also by idiographic life events.

These three sorts of influences are nicely summarized in the work of Chris Fraley and Brent Roberts, who describe a model for three mechanisms underlying personality change. The first mechanism mentioned in this model, developmental constancies, is based on the idea that people have constant factors which influence their personality throughout their lives. Such factors may be of genetic origin (note that of course genetic influences are not always immediately notable during the first years of life, but might as well become prominent in a later phase, e.g., during adolescence), but they may also result from formative early experiences that leave a lasting mark on personality (e.g., in the form of stable working models underlying attachment in adolescence). The second mechanism addresses the effects of social relationships and work experiences and refers to person–environment transactions. This mechanism is based on the assumption that personality traits and environmental factors influence each other in a reciprocal fashion. Although several studies show such transactional mechanisms during adolescence (e.g., where adolescents' family relationships affect and are affected by problem behavior), studies are needed on environmental effects on personality traits. The third mechanism described in this model is that of the stochastic or contextual processes. This mechanism takes account of the large influence of accidental factors on personality development, such as life events during adolescence or major incidental changes to the environment. An empirical test of this model showed that all the three mechanisms play a role in explaining the development of neuroticism (one of the Big Five factors). Transactional mechanisms played the smallest role, followed by the mechanism of the developmental constants, the largest influence being exerted by stochastic processes, or coincidence. As said, studies on the factors that affect personality change during adolescence are needed to shed a clearer light on this issue.

In this article, we have demonstrated the importance of considering individual differences in personality in the development of adolescents, and have made clear that, although we already know much about the developmental course and implications of these individual differences, we still have to learn about the psychological mechanisms behind these.

See also: Developmental Psychopathology.

Further Reading

Block J and Block JH (2006) Venturing a 30-year longitudinal study. *American Psychologist* 61: 315–327.

Denissen JJA, Asendorpf JB, and van Aken MAG (2008) Childhood personality predicts long-term trajectories of shyness and aggressiveness in the context of demographic transitions in emerging adulthood. *Journal of Personality* 76: 67–99.

Fraley RC and Roberts BW (2005) Patterns of continuity: A dynamic model for conceptualizing the stability of individual differences in psychological constructs across the life course. *Psychological Review* 112: 60–74.

McAdams DP and Olson BD (2010) Personality development: Continuity and change over the life course. *Annual Review of Psychology* 61: 517–542.

McCrae RR and Costa PT (2003) *Personality in Adulthood: A Five-Factor Theory Perspective*, 2nd edn. New York: Guilford.

Roberts BW and DelVecchio WF (2000) The rank-order consistency of personality traits from childhood to old age: A quantitative review of longitudinal studies. *Psychological Bulletin* 126: 3–25.

Roberts BW, Walton KE, and Viechtbauer W (2006) Patterns of mean-level change in personality traits across the life course: A meta-analysis of longitudinal studies. *Psychological Bulletin* 132: 1–25.

Roberts BW and Wood D (2006) Personality development in the context of the Neo-Socioanalytic Model of personality. In: Mroczek D and Little T (eds.) *Handbook of Personality Development*, pp. 11–39. Mahwah, NJ: Erlbaum.

Shiner R and Caspi A (2003) Personality differences in childhood and adolescence: Measurement, development, and consequences. *Journal of Child Psychology and Psychiatry and Allied Disciplines* 44: 2–32.

Physical Attractiveness

T E Davison and M P McCabe, Deakin University, Melbourne, VIC, Australia

Glossary

Body image: Perceptions an individual holds of his or her appearance, typically measured by the level of satisfaction with body shape or size.
Cultural ideal: The hypothesis that there is a standard of physical attractiveness commonly held by members of a particular cultural group or society, for example, the presence of a thin cultural ideal for Western females.
Objective attractiveness: Ratings of attractiveness made by judges, typically consisting of average scores of multiple judges using a rating scale.
Self-concept: The way in which an individual perceives himself or herself. A global construct, typically viewed as multidimensional.
Self-esteem: A component of emotional well-being, consisting of views of self-worth, self-acceptance, and self-confidence.
Subjective attractiveness: Self-ratings of attractiveness, consisting of individuals' judgments about their own level of attractiveness.
Universal ideal: The hypothesis that the different culturally groups agree on what is considered physically attractive, with judgments based on similar characteristics, for example, facial attractiveness defined by average and symmetrical features.

Introduction

For individuals in Western society, physical appearance is important. Television, magazines, music videos, and other media give a strong message about the desirability of physical attractiveness, with the predominance of advertisements featuring beautiful, slender, blemish-free young people, looking confident, popular, and having fun. A lucrative industry has developed to help individuals to improve their attractiveness, offering fashion, hairstyling, cosmetics, skin treatments, low fat food, exercise programs, cosmetic dentistry, and even surgical options.

What are the consequences of these societal influences to look beautiful on young people? Does being attractive offer any advantages or disadvantages in life? Are there cultural differences in how beauty is defined and the importance of being attractive? In this article, we explore the role of physical attractiveness in the lives of adolescent boys and girls, looking at what influences perceptions of attractiveness and the impact of physical attractiveness on how young people view themselves and how they are viewed by others, particularly their peers.

Defining Terms

Physical attractiveness has been explored by researchers in different fields, who have found that appearance-related constructs are important in understanding such varied phenomena as interpersonal dynamics, psychological development, and pathological eating behaviors. This varied literature demonstrates that there are a number of distinctions that can be drawn in what is meant by the term physical appearance, which lead to different lines of investigation.

Body Image Versus General Physical Attractiveness

The term *body image* is normally concerned with subjective views of one's appearance, which typically focus on perceptions of or attitudes to one's weight and body shape. Young people, particularly girls, tend to report being highly dissatisfied with their bodies, preferring a slimmer physique, while boys often desire a more muscular body. The normative nature of this dissatisfaction for Western adolescents is well documented in the literature. Research on body image has been particularly important in understanding the development of eating disorders.

Less commonly considered is the concept of *general physical attractiveness*, which examines aspects other than simply physique. While our views of our body size and shape play an important role in determining how attractive we consider ourselves, physical attractiveness is a broader construct that includes other important dimensions. Thus, adolescents may be dissatisfied with their bodies, but still consider themselves to be attractive, perhaps due to factors such as facial features, hairstyle, complexion, grooming, or clothing style. Facial characteristics make a particularly strong contribution to general physical attractiveness, and are typically more important to overall ratings of attractiveness than physique. This article focuses on general physical attractiveness, while the rapidly growing field of body image is reviewed in another article.

Objective Versus Subjective Physical Attractiveness

This distinction refers to the source of judgment of a person's attractiveness. Researchers typically measure *objective physical attractiveness* by asking multiple judges to provide independent ratings of a target individual's physical attractiveness, say on a scale of 1 to 10 from 'very unattractive' to 'very attractive,' and calculating an average rating. Generally, interrater reliability of these judgments is quite high, indicating that we share a common consensus on attractiveness. Adolescent boys and girls tend to use similar criteria as adults in making their judgments of physical attractiveness. As we discuss later, it is likely that there are differences between cultural groups, with particular physical characteristics being more valued in some cultures than others. Objective physical attractiveness has been an

 doi:10.1016/B978-0-12-373915-5.00032-2

important aspect of research by evolutionary theorists, with it being seen as a strong contributor to sexual behavior, while social psychologists have long been interested in whether we respond differently to attractive versus unattractive individuals.

In contrast, *subjective physical attractiveness* is measured by asking subjects to rate their own level of attractiveness, with questions such as 'how good-looking are you?' One would expect that the way we view our appearance would be similar to how others might rate our attractiveness. However, a classic study by Alan Feingold in 1988 suggested that the association between objective and subjective attractiveness is in fact rather small.

This article is concerned with both objective and subjective aspects of general physical attractiveness. We will consider factors that influence perceptions of attractiveness and review the evidence to determine the impact of attractiveness on adolescents' daily lives. First, we need to consider how judgments of physical attractiveness are made, what attributes or features are used to determine whether an individual is attractive or unattractive. An important consideration is the extent to which standards for attractiveness vary across countries and between ethnic groups, or whether there is a universal ideal that applies to all males and females.

Standards for Attractiveness

Evidence for a Cultural Ideal for Attractiveness

Many people have argued that physical attractiveness is a culturally defined phenomenon. Charles Darwin suggested from his review of different cultures that there is no universal standard of female beauty, with the criteria used to determine attractiveness varying between different cultural groups. Clearly, standards of attractiveness have also changed over time, as illustrated by changes in the body shapes depicted in Western art. However, the high interrater agreement on physical attractiveness within a particular cultural group indicates that beauty is not in the eye of the beholder, but rather there are cultural standards of attractiveness that we learn and use. These standards are clearly reflected in media images.

For Western women and adolescent girls today, a key attribute defining attractiveness is slimness. Thinner females are consistently rated as more attractive than heavier females. This cultural ideal is at odds with the developing bodies of adolescent girls, who evidence an increase in body mass and accumulation of fat around the hips and thighs as a normal consequence of puberty. The 'ideal' body has become increasingly difficult for females to obtain over the past 40 years. This may place girls today at a particular risk of a disturbed body image and may be associated with an increased likelihood of eating disorders.

While physique is also important in defining male attractiveness, body *size* is less important than body *shape*. Attractive males are those with a broad chest and shoulders and narrow waist, a shape consistent with physical strength and muscle development. There is also some suggestion that height is associated with attractiveness among boys, with taller boys rated as more attractive. In contrast to girls, pubertal development generally serves to bring boys' bodies closer to, rather than further away from, the tall, muscular ideal.

Although the existence of these standards for male and female bodies is thought to be a Western phenomenon, there is growing evidence of weight concerns among girls in other cultural groups, for example, in Eastern Europe, the Middle East, and Asia. Body image concerns reported by boys in non-Western cultures have been similar to those found among Western cultures. However, studies have also found some variation in standards for attractiveness in different ethnic groups. For example, African, African American, Pacific Island, and Caribbean adolescents have reported a larger ideal female body size than is typically reported by members of other ethnic groups, and have reported less negative attitudes toward obese males. Research in the United States has indicated that Black Americans rate themselves as more attractive overall than do White Americans. One study also suggested that African American girls held more flexible views of attractiveness, allowing for more variability in what is considered attractive than other American girls. However, African and Asian subcultures may place more importance on other aspects of physical appearance, such as skin color and hair texture.

Most research examining ideal images of physical attractiveness focuses on the existence of a thin ideal for females and a lean, muscular ideal for males, with other aspects of attractiveness receiving less attention. However, when asked to define attractiveness, adolescents refer not only to weight for girls and body build for boys, but also appear to consider height and facial attributes, with particular importance given to facial attractiveness. Facial features are often more important than physique when making evaluations of an adolescent's overall physical attractiveness. The importance of facial attractiveness has been demonstrated in studies that found that facial attractiveness was a better predictor of psychosocial functioning than multiple measures of bodily attractiveness combined. Compared to cross-cultural research on physique, there is less evidence that the importance of facial characteristics and other aspects of appearance is culturally determined. Indeed, there appears to be remarkable similarity in judgments of attractiveness based on people's faces.

Evidence for a Universal Ideal for Attractiveness

Research has compared ratings of attractiveness between ethnic groups (e.g., different groups living in the United States), and between countries, and found that people generally agree on who is attractive. When evaluating the attractiveness of an adolescent, groups of adults or other young people tend to give consistent ratings. This has led some authors to suggest that there could be a universal standard by which attractiveness is judged. Men across cultures tend to prefer women with a low waist-to-hip ratio. In addition, people across cultures rate faces with proportions that are close to average proportions as more attractive than more distinctive faces that deviate from the norm. Symmetrical faces and bodies – where the left and right sides are highly similar – also seem to be seen as more attractive.

Women who are rated attractive are more likely to have faces that are more 'feminine' than average, which include features such as small chins, large eyes, high cheekbones, small noses, and full lips. Women who look relatively young are also consistently rated as more attractive than older looking women. These features are considered attractive for females across many different cultural groups, including those with little exposure to Western standards of beauty. However, there is less consistency in what makes a man's face attractive, and there is no clear preference for masculine faces, with some studies suggesting that many women prefer men with more feminine faces. Most studies have focused on attractiveness in adult faces. However, research conducted by Tamsin Saxton and her colleagues in 2009 found that young adolescents living in the United Kingdom preferred average, symmetrical and feminine faces for both boys and girls their own age.

Other evidence supporting the view that attractiveness is not culturally determined comes from studies with young children. Even babies of 2 and 3 months old seem to make similar judgments of attractiveness as adults, with research showing babies spent more time looking at those pictures of women who had been rated as attractive by adult raters, and spent less time looking at unattractive women.

Gender Differences

Adolescent boys tend to rate themselves as more physically attractive than girls, who are more critical of their own general appearance. However, this gender difference is less marked than differences between boys and girls in body image measures, such as dissatisfaction with their body size and shape, which is much more widespread among girls. Interestingly, there is a smaller gender difference in self-ratings of attractiveness among adults, suggesting that adolescent girls are particularly vulnerable, not only to negative attitudes toward their bodies, but also regarding their general appearance. The gender difference found in self-ratings of physical attractiveness appears to be found across countries.

Cross-cultural research suggests that men throughout the world are more concerned about women's physical attractiveness than women are with men's appearance. Male attractiveness usually depends on his level of skills and prowess as well as his physical appearance. The lower subjective attractiveness that is reported by females compared to males in research is unlikely to be due to differences in actual physical attractiveness, because limited evidence suggests that judges tend to rate early adolescent girls and boys as similarly attractive, and late adolescent girls and young women as better looking than males of the same age.

In 1998, Alan Feingold and Ronald Mazzella conducted a meta-analysis study that integrated 222 studies from the previous 50 years. These authors found that a male advantage in self-rated physical attractiveness only became apparent in research in the 1980s and 1990s. In the 1970s, there was only a marginal gender difference, and in research prior to 1970, females rated themselves as more attractive than males, suggesting changing sociocultural factors that influence perceptions of attractiveness. It has been argued that females make more negative evaluations of their attractiveness than do males because society focuses on physical features as a key criterion for success for females; in contrast, males are more likely to achieve acceptance and regard through intelligence, academic and job success, sporting ability, wealth, and status. Certainly, evidence suggests that girls receive more praise from others for their appearance than boys.

Despite the aforementioned findings, there are reasons to believe that gender differences in self-rated attractiveness may be on the decline. In recent years, messages related to the importance of male physical attractiveness appear to be increasing, as the male body has become increasingly objectified. There is evidence that boys are becoming progressively more fashion conscious and more attentive to their hairstyle, clothing, and overall appearance. Magazines for adolescent boys now promote the importance of physical appearance, with narrowly defined standards for how males should look. In addition, skin care products and dietary products are now heavily marketed to males. Many adolescent boys spend considerable time 'working out' in gyms and health clubs to achieve a more muscular physique, with some turning to anabolic steroids or even cosmetic surgery to enhance their appearance. Given the increased emphasis on an ideal male body shape in recent years, it is likely that many males may, like females over the past 30 years, feel they fail to meet the ideal muscular and masculine body portrayed in the media, which may, in turn, impact the way they perceive their general attractiveness.

Sociocultural Influences on Boys and Girls

The importance ascribed to physical attractiveness is learned early in life, with children highly aware of the cultural criteria for attractiveness. Even very young children know of the importance of societal requirements for attractiveness and what those standards are. Sociocultural influences are important in determining adolescents' standards of beauty, particularly regarding physique, and in suggesting how important appearance should be in their lives. Such influences include the messages and images portrayed by the media, as well as input from peers, family members, schools, and others in adolescents' social surroundings. Attractive young people are vastly overrepresented in the entertainment world of television, movies, and magazines. The role of the media is argued to be a particularly important factor in determining body image concerns, with research focusing on the thin ideal for females, and perceived pressure from the media to achieve thinness. It has been commonly noted that the physically attractive stereotype for females that is transmitted in the media includes a thin body shape that is unrealistic for most to attain. Young people may not be aware when viewing images in the media that many are unrealistic, for example, that the images of models in magazines have been digitally altered or 'air-brushed.' Research in body image has suggested that adolescents, particularly those who are less attractive, compare their own appearance to those of models in advertisements and magazines, with negative consequences about their views of their own bodies.

As noted by author and researcher Susan Harter, "Pick up any teen magazine . . . and you will be assaulted by an outrageous number of ads for makeup, perfume, skin cream, hair products, diets, provocative clothing." However, little is known about the impact of media messages on our perceptions of general physical attractiveness. Society may offer more subjective standards for attractiveness than the relatively unvarying standard for body size, with adolescents able to change their overall appearance with clothing and hairstyles, in order to create a particular image. However, as mentioned earlier, overall attractiveness appears to be heavily influenced by facial characteristics, with similar key features considered attractive across cultural groups. Further research is required into understanding sociocultural influences on perceived attractiveness because, as outlined subsequently, the way adolescents view their level of attractiveness plays a crucial role in how they view themselves more generally.

Attractiveness and Self-Concept During Adolescence

Developmental theorists, such as Erik Erikson, place a strong emphasis on adolescents' physical attributes as a vital source of their identity and self-concept. Physical characteristics appear to be central to an adolescent's sense of self, and are more important than other aspects such as social or academic qualities. This is in contrast to the increase in importance in later years that is placed on internal characteristics such as intelligence and success. The role of physical appearance in adolescence takes on additional importance when placed within the context of the substantial physical changes that occur during puberty.

Developmental psychology has suggested that the early years of adolescence are characterized by heightened self-consciousness and concern about evaluations from peers. Self-esteem at this stage of life is likely to reflect perceptions of how adolescents feel they are evaluated by significant others, with appearance being a common focus of perceived evaluations. Given these characteristics of adolescence, negative evaluations made by boys and girls of their own physical attractiveness are likely to have a significant impact on their sense of self-worth. Indeed, research has suggested that physical appearance is an important predictor of the overall sense of worth as a person, or self-esteem, throughout adolescence.

Subjective Attractiveness and Self-Esteem

There is a large body of evidence that supports the relationship between low self-esteem and a negative body image among girls, whose developing bodies are often viewed as failing to meet the ideal slim female body shape. Body image is commonly viewed as an important aspect of global female self-esteem. However, the picture for males is less clear, with no consistent link between how males view their bodies and their sense of self-worth.

Less research has looked at the impact of self-ratings of general attractiveness on how adolescents feel about themselves. Self-rated attractiveness has been found to be related to self-esteem among college students, with those individuals who perceive themselves as attractive reporting higher self-esteem. Our preliminary work has suggested that perceptions of general attractiveness, which includes facial attractiveness and overall appearance, may be more important to self-esteem among boys than their specific view of their physique. This has been confirmed in the limited research on this topic. Seeing themselves as unattractive appears to be more important in understanding low self-esteem among boys than girls, whose low self-worth is more strongly related to negative feelings about the size and shape of their bodies.

There has been limited research on the relationship between self-esteem and attractiveness in other cultural groups, although research by T. Joel Wade in the United States has suggested that self-rated physical attractiveness was more strongly linked to the self-esteem of White adolescents than to Black adolescents' self-esteem. The author noted that overall, Black American adolescents rated their level of attractiveness more highly. He argued that Black adolescents may have more flexible standards of attractiveness, and so a less attractive appearance will have fewer negative consequences for their sense of self worth.

Objective Attractiveness and Self-Esteem

So far, we have considered the impact of adolescents' own views of their physical attractiveness on their sense of self. It is also important to consider whether boys and girls who are rated by others as less attractive report lower self-esteem, but only limited research has looked at this issue. Evidence to date suggests that there is no relationship between objective physical attractiveness and self-esteem among adolescent boys or girls. Research with adults has suggested that while self-ratings of attractiveness are highly important in understanding levels of self-esteem, there is no relationship between self-esteem and levels of attractiveness as rated by others.

However, there may be some negative consequences for attractive girls. A study by Caroline Davis and her colleagues in Canada found that young women who were rated as attractive by others were more preoccupied with their weight than their less attractive peers. The authors speculated that attractive girls are more likely to identify with and aspire to the cultural thin ideal, with a sense of being attractive forming an important part of their self-identity. This study has been replicated with adolescent girls, but the effect was found only among Caucasian girls, and not for African American or Hispanic girls. It has been argued that attractive Caucasian girls are praised for their looks and subsequently their appearance and being considered attractive by others becomes an important defining characteristic. Consequently, these girls may feel more pressure to attain and maintain an ideal body, as defined by the media and the broader society.

Attractiveness and Relationships with Others During Adolescence

As we have seen, low self-esteem among adolescents is strongly related to negative views of their own general physical attractiveness (among boys) or body size and shape (among girls). However, being judged by others as attractive or unattractive does not appear to have a substantial impact on adolescents' feelings of general self-worth. A rather different picture is found when we consider the impact of attractiveness in the social domain, where highly attractive boys and girls operate at a significant advantage. Firstly, we review the literature on how adolescents' ratings of their own attractiveness impact on their peer relationships.

Subjective Attractiveness and Interpersonal Functioning

Self-rated attractiveness appears to be important in understanding the social functioning of adolescents. Peer relationships play a more important role during early adolescence than in childhood, with friendships becoming more intimate and complex, and sexual interests emerging. This parallels the increase in concerns about how boys and girls appear to others, and a focus on 'fitting in' with their peer group, with social conformity peaking in early adolescence. Conforming to the norms of appearance, including aspects such as body size, clothing, and hairstyle, is a central concern at this stage of development. Developmental theorists have suggested that adolescents assume that others, their 'imaginary audience,' are highly engaged in evaluating their appearance, and so are sensitive to possible indications of rejection from others. This may have particularly negative ramifications for girls, given the high proportion who are dissatisfied with the changes taking place in their bodies following puberty. Adolescents who perceive themselves as unattractive may be at a disadvantage regarding the development of their interpersonal skills and in forming positive relationships with other boys and girls.

Research with college students has suggested that those young people who considered themselves unattractive were more likely to report concerns about interacting with members of the opposite sex than those with more positive views of their attractiveness. However, self-rated general attractiveness appears to be less important in understanding social interactions than ratings of satisfaction with their body size and shape. Although there has been only limited research examining the impact of perceived attractiveness on social functioning among early adolescents, it does appear to play a more important role than is the case for older adolescents or young adults. Reviews have found that popularity with the opposite sex is related to perceived attractiveness, with those adolescents who hold positive views of their own attractiveness being rated as more popular.

Our own research found that boys and girls who saw themselves as attractive reported more positive relationships with the opposite sex. This relationship continued to be strong even when controlling for self-esteem, suggesting that it was not simply due to higher levels of self-worth among adolescents with positive self-rated attractiveness. General physical attractiveness was more important than concerns about their body size in understanding adolescent relationships. We also found that subjective attractiveness was important in understanding the relationships girls formed with other girls. Those girls who viewed themselves as unattractive reported poorer same-sex relationships. But appearance did not appear to be important in the relationships boys formed with other boys. During adolescence, girls' ratings of their general attractiveness appear to be more closely linked with concerns about how others evaluate them. It has been speculated that the process of comparing their appearance to that of other people around them contributes to girls' negative ratings of their own attractiveness and impacts their relations with other girls in their social group. More research is required to better understand the strong influence of subjective attractiveness on relationships during adolescence.

Objective Attractiveness and Interpersonal Functioning

While there has been only limited research on the impact of self-rated attractiveness in the social domain, many social psychologists have demonstrated that an individual's actual physical appearance impacts significantly on the way that others perceive and interact with him or her. This is an important issue, as an adolescent's physical appearance is a highly salient personal characteristic in social interactions.

In 1972, Karen Dion and her colleagues in the United States demonstrated that attractive college students were rated as more socially desirable than unattractive students, and were expected to have happier and more successful lives. Since that seminal study, a large number of research projects have demonstrated the presence of a physical attractiveness stereotype, with findings that attractive individuals are viewed as more intelligent, better adjusted, and with better social skills. This literature supports the notion that people do indeed judge books by their covers. Further, attractive individuals tend to receive more favorable treatment from others than those who are unattractive.

Attractiveness appears to be associated with the development of more intimate social relationships for young men and women, with attractive female college students being more likely to be in a current steady relationship than their less attractive peers. Young men and women have indicated a preference for interacting with attractive individuals, with male students observed to be more socially responsive when conversing with attractive rather than unattractive females. Unattractive young adults tend to receive more negative evaluations from their peers and have reduced opportunities for social contact, and they report higher levels of loneliness and social anxiety. Physical attractiveness appears to have important social implications, not only in Western society, but also in traditional cultures. For example, attractive Ache women have greater reproductive success than their less attractive peers.

Physical attractiveness exerts an influence very early in life. Even infants and toddlers provoke different reactions from others based on their level of attractiveness. Studies have found that mothers and fathers of attractive infants show more affection toward them and engage in more interaction compared to parents of less attractive infants. Physical attractiveness has been found to impact strongly on peer relationships in childhood, with a number of studies of children from middle childhood through early adolescence suggesting that attractive girls and boys are viewed more positively by their peers, and engage in more positive social interactions than less attractive children. Children in research projects have indicated that they would prefer an attractive child as their friend, even when he or she had no social or athletic skills. Appearance plays a role, not only in new friendships, but also continues to be important after significant periods of interaction, when children know one another well. Studies in elementary schools have found that attractive children are more likely than less attractive children to be socially accepted and popular.

During adolescence, physical attractiveness appears to become an even stronger predictor of social interaction and popularity. Some studies have found that outward appearance is the primary basis of friendships and evaluations of others made during adolescence. Attractive adolescents are rated as more popular and are better liked by their peers than those who are less attractive. A recent study found that physical attractiveness in early adolescents was more important in understanding popularity than factors such as academic performance, rebellious behaviours, or athleticism. Similarly, adolescents have reported they feel more pressure to conform to appearance norms (such as clothing and hairstyle) than to obtain good grades, and spend a large amount of time in grooming activities. The strong relationship between objective attractiveness and positive peer relationships has been found among both boys and girls, and throughout the period of adolescence, although the effect appears to be strongest during early adolescence. Physically attractive boys and girls who are just beginning adolescence integrate more with members of the opposite sex than is observed among their less attractive peers. Attractiveness also impacts on dating and the development of romantic relationships during later adolescence, with boys particularly likely to be influenced by physical appearance when selecting potential dates. Most research in this area has taken place in the United States or Western Europe, although attractive adolescents have also been found to have improved social functioning in Mexico.

In 2000, Judith Langlois and her colleagues published an important review of research about the impact of attractiveness. This review found strong evidence that attractive children were judged more positively by others across a range of measures. For example, attractive children were perceived as having greater social appeal, viewed as more interpersonally competent and better adjusted psychologically, and were also judged to be more academically competent. This suggests that attractiveness is not only important for judgments relevant to adolescents' social functioning, but may also influence judgments made of their academic performance.

Teachers' initial judgments of academic competence among their new students have been found to be related to the adolescents' objective physical attractiveness. Attractive students were judged to have higher academic functioning than unattractive students. While it is perhaps not surprising that appearance impacts on judgments in the absence of significant additional information about the new students, these early impressions appeared to have a lasting impact. Teachers' initial reactions to the appearance of the students were related to the actual educational outcomes achieved by the adolescents at the end of the academic year. This is consistent with other research indicating that attractive children tend to perform more highly on tests of ability and achievement. Similarly, positive outcomes, such as greater success in the workplace, are found among attractive young adults, indicating the widespread impact of objective physical attractiveness in the lives of males and females.

Conclusions

This article has described the critical role of physical attractiveness for adolescent girls and boys. Appearance has long been considered a key component of global self-concept for girls. However, there appears to be increasing pressure on boys and young men to look attractive. There is growing evidence that feeling unattractive is associated with poor self-esteem among boys as well as girls, although boys are less likely to report negative views of their appearance. Over the past 40 years, social psychologists have demonstrated that people judge attractive and unattractive individuals quite differently, with appearance clearly serving as a powerful stimulus for social evaluation. As a result, attractive adolescents receive more positive treatment from both their peers and teachers. These effects are just as strong for boys as for girls. Attractiveness, whether self-rated or rated by others, is associated with a broad range of achievements throughout the life span. It is likely to be associated with social, academic, vocational, and interpersonal success. We know that achievements at an early age impact on later achievements. Thus, it would appear that attractive children have a substantial advantage over less attractive children. This finding appears to apply in a range of cultural settings, but is most apparent with Caucasian boys and girls in Western societies. Clearly, beauty may have consequences that are more than just skin deep.

See also: Academic Achievement; Body Image during Adolescence: A Developmental Perspective; Gender Issues; Gender Roles; Peer Relations; Self-Esteem; Social Competence.

Further Reading

Colabianchi N, Levers-Landis CE, and Borawski EA (2006) Weight preoccupation as a function of observed physical attractiveness: Ethnic differences among normal-weight adolescent females. *Journal of Pediatric Psychology* 31: 803–812.

Davison TE and McCabe MP (2006) Adolescent body image and psychosocial functioning. *Journal of Social Psychology* 146: 15–30.

Feingold A and Mazzella R (1998) Gender differences in body image are increasing. *Psychological Science* 9: 190–195.

Langlois JH, Kalakanis L, Rubenstein AJ, et al. (2000) Maxims or myths of beauty? A meta-analytic and theoretical review. *Psychological Bulletin* 126: 390–423.

Lerner RM, Delaney M, Hess LE, Jovanovic J, and von Eye A (1990) Early adolescent physical attractiveness and academic competence. *Journal of Early Adolescence* 10: 4–20.

Patzer GL (2008) *Looks: Why They Matter More Than You Ever Imagined*. New York: Amacom.

Saxton TK, Burriss RP, Murray AK, Rowland HM, and Roberts SC (2009) Face, body and speech cures independently predict judgments of attractiveness. *Journal of Evolutionary Psychology* 7: 23–35.

Wade TJ (1991) Race and sex differences in adolescent self-perceptions of physical attractiveness and level of self-esteem during early and late adolescence. *Personality and Individual Differences* 12: 1319–1324.

Puberty and Adolescence: An Evolutionary Perspective

B Bogin, Loughborough University, Loughborough, Leicestershire, UK

Glossary

Adolescence: A stage in human life cycle covering the years after the onset of puberty until the onset of adulthood (approximately ages 9–19 years). The adolescent phase is characterized by a growth spurt in height and weight, the development of secondary sexual characteristics, sociosexual maturation, and intensification of interest and practice in adult social, economic, and sexual activities.

Biocultural reproduction: The human type of cooperative breeding, which is the pooling of resources such as food and shelter which increase the reproductive success of adults in the social group.

Childhood: A stage in the human life cycle that occurs between the end of infancy and the start of the juvenile growth period (about the ages 3.0–6.9 years). Children are weaned from all breast-feeding (or bottle feeding) but must be provided specially prepared foods due to immaturity of their dentition and digestive systems. Children require intensive care by older individuals due to the child's motor, neurological, and cognitive immaturity.

Juvenile: A stage of growth and development of some mammals that occurs between the end of infancy (cessation of feeding by lactation) and the onset of adulthood (reproductive maturity). The human juvenile stage is an exception, in that it begins at approximately ages 7.0, after the human childhood stage, and ends at about age 10 years in girls and 12 years in boys, when human adolescence begins.

Natural selection: Defined by Darwin (1859) as the differences in fertility (production of offspring) and mortality (deaths of offspring) between individuals of a population. Physical or behavioral traits that increase fertility and/or decrease mortality will become more frequent in the population over time. Traits that reduce fertility and/or increase mortality will decline in frequency from generation to generation.

Puberty: In biology, a short-term physiological event, taking place over a few weeks, of the central nervous system, which reinitiates positive feedback within the hypothalamic–pituitary–gonadal axis and promotes sexual maturation. In people, puberty occurs at the end of the juvenile stage and the beginning of the adolescent stage of the life cycle (approximately age 9–10 years).

Rites of passage: Culturally patterned ritual or ceremonial activities to mark such events as birth, puberty, adulthood, courtship, marriage, death, accession to office, admission to membership, and expulsion. In various forms, rites of passage are found in all human societies, although particular individuals may or may not participate in them. Rites of passage seem to be unique to the human species.

Sexual selection: Defined by Charles Darwin (1871) as, "... the advantage which certain individuals have over other individuals of the same sex and species, in exclusive relation to reproduction." The 'advantage' may take the form of a physical trait, such as bright plumage in birds or horns/antlers in some mammals, or may take the form of a behavioral trait such as singing or dancing, as found in many animals including the human species.

Introduction

What happens during puberty to a boy?

He says goodbye to his childhood enters adultery.

An incorrect answer to an examination question.

In this article, we discuss puberty and adolescence from a biological and anthropological perspective. This perspective differs from that taken by many social and psychological treatments. Each view of puberty and adolescence has merits. The emphasis here is on those aspects of puberty and adolescence which are best explained in terms of human evolution and the patterns of culture found in human societies throughout time and around the world.

The nature of human puberty and adolescence are best understood as part of the entire pattern of human biological growth. **Table 1** lists the stages of human development from conception to death, their approximate ages, and several defining features of each stage. Human development before birth follows many of the patterns seen in other animal species, but after birth there are some special features. Humans share with other social mammals, such as most monkeys and apes, three postnatal life stages: infancy, juvenile, and adult. Human life history is unusual due to the addition of childhood, adolescence, and grandmotherhood (postmenopausal stage) as biologically and behaviorally definable stages of the life cycle. The pattern of human growth in height from birth to adulthood is shown in **Figure 1** (body weight follows very similar curves). The distance curve (part a) indicates the amount of height achieved at a given age. The velocity curve (part b) indicates the rate of growth at a given age. The velocity curve best illustrates the human postnatal growth stages of infancy (I), childhood (C), juvenile (J), and adolescence (A).

Definitions of these life stages may be given in terms of how people of different ages are fed, especially in the traditional human societies of hunter-gatherers, horticulturalists, and

Table 1 Stages in the human life cycle (modified From Bogin B, *Patterns of Human Growth*, 2nd edn. Cambridge University Press, 1999)

Stage	*Duration*	*Events*
First trimester of pregnancy	Fertilization to week 12	Embryogenesis
Second trimester of pregnancy	Months 4 to 6	Rapid growth in length
Third trimester of pregnancy	Month 7 to birth	Rapid growth in weight and organ maturation
Neonatal period	Birth to 28 days	Extrauterine adaptation, most rapid rate of postnatal growth and maturation
Infancy	Month 2 to end of lactation (usually by 36 months)	Rapid growth velocity with steep deceleration in velocity with time, feeding by lactation, deciduous tooth eruption, many developmental milestones in physiology, behavior, and cognition
Childhood	3–6.9 years	Moderate growth rate, dependency for feeding, mid-growth spurt, eruption of first permanent molar and incisor, cessation of brain growth by end of stage
Juvenile	7–10 (girls) or 12 (boys) years	Slower growth rate, capable of self-feeding, cognitive transition leading to learning of economic and social skills
Puberty	Brain: 9–10 years Body: girls, 10 years; boys, 12 years	In the brain, puberty is an event of short duration (days or a few weeks) that reactivates the hypothalamic GnRH pulse generator leading to a massive increase in sex hormone secretion; on the body, puberty is noted by a darkening and increased density pubic hair
Adolescence	The 5–8 years following onset of puberty	Adolescent growth spurt in height and weight, permanent tooth eruption virtually complete, development of secondary sexual characteristics; sociosexual maturation, intensification of interest and practice in adult social, economic, and sexual activities
Adulthood		
Prime and transition	18–20 years for women to 45 years (end of child-bearing) and from age 21–25 years for men to about age 50 years	Commences with completion of skeletal growth; homeostasis in physiology, behavior, and cognition; menopause for women by age 50
'Grandmotherhood'	10–20 years following menopause	Culturally defined stage of women's life often characterized by investments of time and energy in the caring for grandchildren
Old age and senescence	From end of child-bearing years to death	Decline in the function and repair ability of many body tissues or systems
Death		

pastoralists. Human biology and behavior evolved in these types of societies, which represent 99% of human history. Even though large-scale agricultural and industrial societies dominate today, these ways of life appeared only in the past few thousand or few hundred years. Typical social behaviors in much of the industrialized world of today such as bottle-feeding infants and separate infant–mother sleeping arrangements did not exist during the evolutionary development of our species.

Human growth and development between birth and adulthood may be divided into four stages: (1) infancy, (2) childhood, (3) juvenile, and (4) adolescent. Infancy lasts from birth to age 30–36 months and is characterized by breast-feeding, with complementary foods added by age 6–9 months. The transition to childhood by about age 3 years is characterized by the termination of maternal lactation and the completion of deciduous tooth eruption. The limitations of a deciduous dentition and small digestive system require that children eat easy to chew and nutrient dense foods. Older members of the social group acquire, prepare, and provision these foods to children. This style of cooperative care frees the child's mother from lactation and much care and feeding of the child. The mother may then accumulate new reserve capacity, such as fat stores and bone mass lost during pregnancy and lactation, and in time, devote her reserves to a new pregnancy and lactation of a new infant. The childhood stage ends at about age 6.9 years.

The juvenile stage spans age 7 years to onset of the adolescent growth spurt (approximately age 10 for girls and age 12 for boys in healthy, well-nourished populations). Juvenile mammals are sexually immature, but physically and mentally capable of providing for much of their own care. Human juveniles have the physical capabilities to eat the adult-type diet, as the first permanent molars and the central incisors have erupted by age 7 years. In many human societies, juveniles perform important work including food production and the care of children, but still require food provisioning by older people to achieve energy balance. Puberty takes place near the end of the juvenile stage and we have more to say about this event below.

Adolescence includes the years of postpubertal growth (approximately ages 10–18 years for girls and ages 12–21 years for boys, including the adolescent growth spurt). Adolescence ends with the eruption of the third molar (if present) and/or the termination of growth of the skeleton. Adulthood and reproductive maturity follow.

Human growth velocity in body length stands in contrast to all other mammals, even our closest genetic cousins the African apes. The childhood stage of relatively moderate and stable

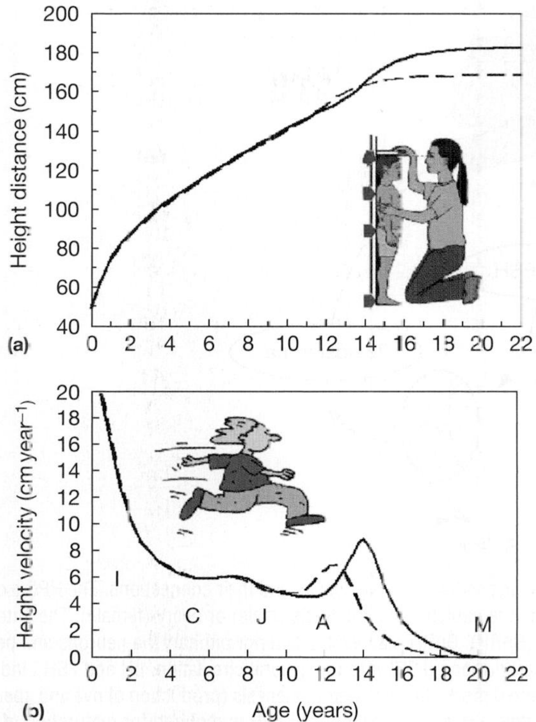

Figure 1 Average distance (a) and velocity (b) curves of growth in height for healthy girls (dashed lines) and boys (solid lines). Distance is the amount of height achieved at a given age. In part (a), the image shows a child's height being measured. Velocity is the rate of growth at a given time, in this case shown as centimeters per year. In part (b), the running figure represents 'velocity.' The velocity curves show the postnatal stages of the pattern of human growth. Note the spurts in growth rate at mid-childhood and adolescence for both girls and boys. The postnatal stages: I, infancy; C, childhood; J, juvenile; A, adolescence; M, mature adult (original figure of the author).

growth velocity and the adolescent growth spurt in virtually all skeletal dimensions are not found in other mammals. The termination of breast-feeding takes place earlier in humans than in the chimpanzee, bonobo, or orangutan. Human female reproductive maturity takes place during the later part of the adolescent stage, and this differs from the apes as well. Healthy, well-nourished girls achieve physiologically defined fecundity (i.e., 80% of menstrual cycles release an ova) at a median age of 18 years. The worldwide median age of human first birth is 19 years. This is up to 6 years later than in the other apes. Human boys may produce fertile spermatozoa by 13.5 years, but are not likely to become fathers until after age 20 years. Even though sexually mature and capable of producing sufficient quantities of food to exceed their own energy requirements, teenage boys and girls remain immature in terms of sociocultural knowledge and experience. To gain sufficient experience for successful adulthood, adolescent boys and girls in all societies engage in many types of economic, social, sexual, and ideological apprenticeships, or rites of passage as they are called by anthropologists. These informal and formal settings for learning lead to greater adult reproductive and sociocultural success. We discuss these apprenticeships/rites of passage in more detail below.

It is hypothesized that the childhood and adolescence stages of human life history evolved due to the selective advantages for increased reproductive fitness. In essence, this reproductive fitness hypothesis predicts that childhood and adolescence: (1) enhance the fertility of mothers, (2) improve the survival of mothers, and (3) lower the mortality of offspring prior to adulthood. This hypothesis emphasizes that early weaning and the transfer of responsibility to other social group members for the feeding and care of children frees the mother to reproduce more quickly than any ape, without increasing the risks for morbidity and mortality of the children. There are also benefits for increased brain growth and learning, but these are secondary outcomes of the selection for increased fertility of the mothers.

Puberty Defined

Physiologically, puberty is a short-term event (taking place over a few weeks) of the central nervous system, which reinitiates positive feedback within the hypothalamic–pituitary–gonadal (HPG) axis and promotes sexual maturation. Puberty is also defined socially, to mean the period of time when sexual development and its related behaviors and emotions are taking place. In this article, we use the physiological definition for puberty and use the term 'adolescence' to refer to the period of time for sociosexual maturation between puberty and adulthood.

Biology of Puberty

Much of human biology is associated with our brain. Adult humans have brains which are 3–4 times larger than the brains of adult chimpanzees. The human advantage is evident at birth and differences increases over time as human brain grows rapidly during infancy and childhood, but chimpanzee brains grow much less after birth. The large and fast growing human brain requires a relatively large amount of metabolic input, for example, energy and oxygen. The human newborn uses 87% of its resting metabolic rate (RMR) for brain growth and function. By the age of 5 years, the percent RMR usage is still high at 44%, whereas in the adult human, the figure is between 20 and 25% of RMR. At comparable stages of development, the RMR values for the chimpanzee are about 45, 20, and 9%, respectively. A trade-off seems to take place between the supply of energy required to support the growth of human brain versus energy to support the growth of rest of the body. The trade-off is seen in **Figure 1b** as the rapid deceleration of growth velocity during infancy. Relatively slow growth continues through childhood and juvenile stages. Rapid growth returns following puberty, after the brain has almost completed its own growth in size.

The hypothalamus is a brain center of neurological and endocrine control (**Figure 2**). During fetal life and early infancy, the hypothalamus produces relatively high levels of gonadotrophin-releasing hormone (GnRH). This hormone causes the release of luteinizing hormone (LH) and follicle-stimulating hormone (FSH) from the pituitary gland, and these hormones stimulate the ovaries or testes to secrete their estrogen or androgen hormones. The latter promote body growth.

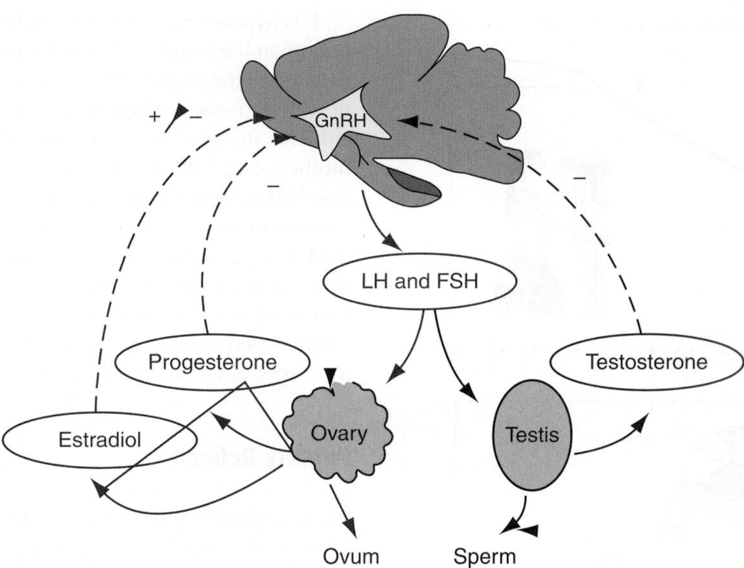

Figure 2 The hypothalmic–pituitary–gonadal (HPG) axis. This simplified cartoon indicates the principle tissues and their connections. The HPG axis is composed of the hypothalamus and its neural connections with the rest of the brain, the pituitary, and the testis (male) or ovary (female). The anterior hypothalamus is responsible for the synthesis of gonadotropin-releasing hormone (GnRH). GnRH reaches the anterior pituitary via neurons and portal veins and stimulates the release of luteinizing hormone (LH) and follicle-stimulating hormone (FSH) into the general circulation. LH and FSH bind to receptors in the ovary and testis and regulate gonadal function by stimulating sex steroid production and gametogenesis (production of ova and sperm). In the male, LH causes testosterone to be produced from the Leydig cells of the testes. LH in combination with FSH is required for maturation of spermatozoa. FSH stimulates testicular growth and increases production of androgen-binding protein by Sertoli cells. Androgen-binding protein concentrates testosterone near the sperm, enabling normal spermatogenesis. In the female, LH stimulates ovarian production of estrogen and progesterone. An LH surge midway in the cycle causes ovulation, and sustained LH secretion stimulates the corpus luteum to produce progesterone. FSH exerts primary control over development of the ovarian follicle, and FSH and LH are responsible for follicular secretion of estrogen. The solid lines indicate the stimulatory cascade from hypothalamus, to pituitary, to gonads. The broken lines and '–' symbols indicate the inhibitory feedback loops. The '+/–' symbols of the estradiol feedback loop indicate the variation of inhibitory/stimulatory feedback during the menstrual cycle (with permission of Prof. C. Rivier, unpublished).

The effect that GnRH production has on the pituitary is associated with the frequency, or 'pulse,' of its release from cells in the hypothalamus. In 1975, Melvin Grumbach and colleagues reported that the gonadotrophin-releasing hormone pulse generator has an on–off–on pattern of activity during postnatal development in humans. Rodents do not show this pattern, instead having a progressive and uninterrupted increase in GnRH production from birth to sexual maturation. Since 1975, much research has been focused on the mechanisms that control this on–off–on pattern (**Figure 3**). The current understanding of the control of puberty (also called 'gonadarche' in the literature) is that one or perhaps a few centers of the brain change their pattern of neurological and endocrinological activity, and their influence on the hypothalamus. The human hypothalamus becomes, basically, inactive in terms of sexual development by about age 2–3 years. The 'inhibitor' has not been identified but likely is located in the brain and certainly not in the gonads. Human children born without gonads, as well as rhesus monkeys and other primates whose gonads have been surgically removed at birth, still undergo both GnRH inhibition in infancy and hypothalamus reactivation at puberty.

In most species of primates, puberty is followed within a few months or a year by reproduction. In humans, there is a greater delay between puberty and first reproduction, usually on the order of 5–10 years. This interval is the human adolescent growth stage. In humans, the hormones responsible for sexual maturation also cause the adolescent growth spurt in stature and other skeletal dimensions. The ubiquitous nature of the adolescent growth spurt is unique to the human species. Not even our closest genetic relative, the chimpanzee, has anything like it.

Another neuroendocrine event precedes puberty. This event is called adrenarche and is the postnatal onset of secretion of the androgen hormones dehydroepiandrosterone (DHEA) and DHEA-sulfate (DHEA-S) from the adrenal gland. The mechanism controlling adrenarche is not understood because no known hormone appears to cause it. In humans and chimpanzees, adrenarche occurs between the ages of 6–10 years (median age is 7 years). In some other primates, such as the rhesus monkey, the upregulation of DHEA and DHEA-S begins just before or after birth. DHEA acts as an antiglucocorticoid with a wide variety of effects, including promoting immune function, altering glucose metabolism, and being neuroprotective, all suggesting a selective benefit, but the evolutionary origins of adrenarche are not known. It is suggested that adrenarche and DHEA-S may play a role in ape and human evolution in terms of extended brain development and prolonged life span compared with other primates. In humans, adrenarche has been related to the adiposity rebound (regaining of body fat) at the transition between the childhood and juvenile stages of the life cycle.

Current evidence indicates that there is no connection between the occurrence or timing of adrenarche and puberty. Perhaps the evolution of adrenarche may be explained as a mechanism for mental maturation. By this we mean that the physical changes induced by adrenarche are accompanied by a change in cognitive function, called the '5- to 7-year-old shift' by some psychologists, or the shift from the preoperational to concrete operational stage, using the terminology of Piaget. This shift leads to new learning and work capabilities in the juvenile. Adrenarche may function to mark the transition from the childhood to the juvenile growth stage.

Human Adolescence

Biological adolescence begins with puberty and lasts for 5–10 years. The physiological transition in the brain and hormonal system from juvenile to adolescent stages cannot be seen without sophisticated technology. The effects of puberty, however, can be noted easily as visible and audible signs of sexual maturation. In both sexes, there is a sudden increase in the density of pubic hair and often other body hair. In boys, there may be an increased density and darkening of facial hair. The deepening of the voice (voice 'cracking') is another sign of male puberty. In girls, a visible sign is the development of the breast bud, the first stage of breast development, which often precedes the appearance of dense pubic hair. The pubescent boy or girl, his or her parents, and relatives, friends, and sometimes everyone else in the social group can observe one or more of these signs of early adolescence.

Other notable features of adolescence include a growth spurt in height and weight, the completion of permanent tooth eruption, development of secondary sexual characteristics (fat and muscle typical of each sex, **Figure 4**), and the intensification of interest in and practice of adult social, economic, and sexual activities leading to sociosexual maturation.

Adolescence ends with (1) the cessation of skeletal growth in length, usually due to the closing of the epiphyses of the long bones; (2) the completion of dental development (eruption of the third molar, if it is present, which takes place between 18–21 years of age); and (3) sociosexual maturation, meaning both the biological and social ability for successful parenthood. On a worldwide basis, including living and historical societies, the age of onset of adulthood averages 19 years for women, which is best measured as the median age at first

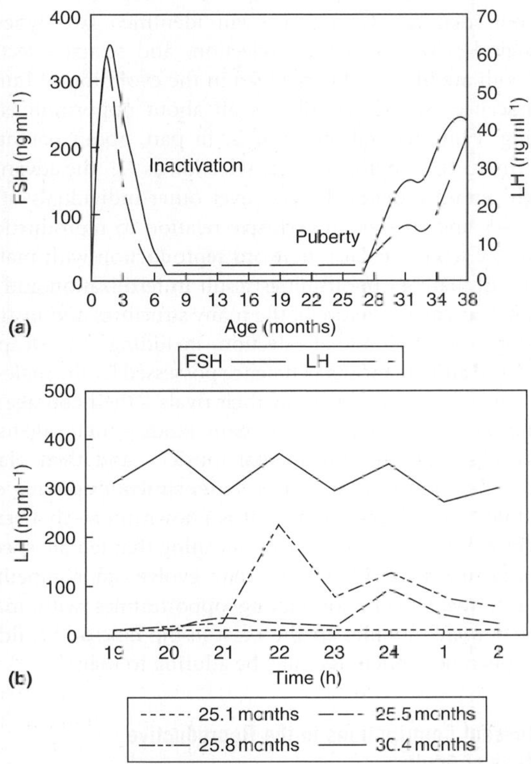

Figure 3 (a) Pattern of secretion of FSH and LH in a male rhesus monkey (genus *Macaca*). The testes of the monkey were removed surgically at birth. The curves for FSH and LH indicate the production and release of GnRH from the hypothalamus. After age 3 months (i.e., during infancy), the hypothalamus is inactivated. Puberty takes place at ~27 months, and the hypothalamus is reactivated.
(b) Development of hypothalamic release of GnRH during puberty in a male rhesus monkey with testes surgically removed. At 25.1 months of age, the hypothalamus remains inactivated. At 25.5 and 25.8 months, modest hypothalamic activity is observed, indicating the onset of puberty. By 30.4 months, the adult pattern of LH release is nearly achieved. This pattern shows increases in both the number of pulses of release and the amplitude of release. In human beings, a very similar pattern of infant inactivation and late juvenile reactivation of the hypothalamus takes place. Adapted, with some simplification, from Plant TM (1994) Puberty in primates. In: Knobil E and Neill JD (eds.) *The Physiology of Reproduction*, 2nd edn., pp. 453–485. New York: Raven.

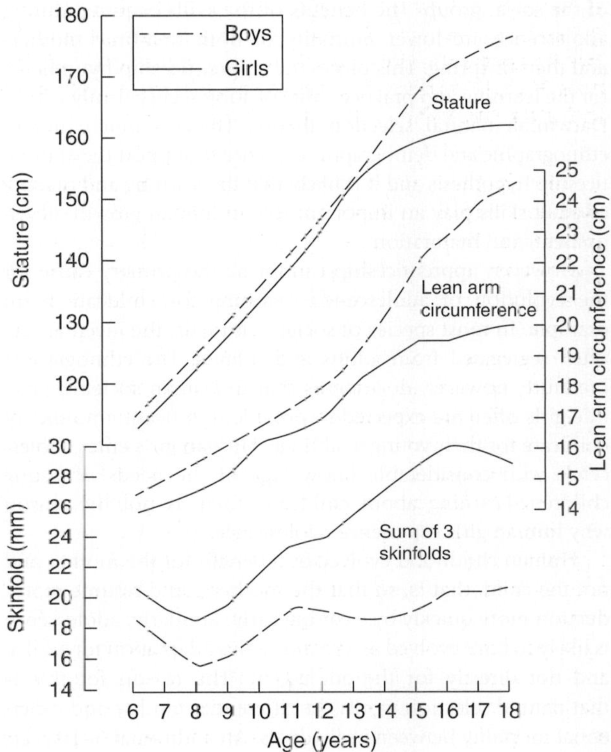

Figure 4 Mean stature, mean lean arm circumference, and median of the sum of three skinfolds for Montreal boys and girls. Notice that sexual dimorphism increases markedly after puberty, from 12–13 years onward. Reproduced from Baughn B, Brault-Dubuc M, Demirjian A, and Gagnon G (1980) Sexual dimorphism in body composition changes during the pubertal period: As shown by French-Canadian children. *American Journal of Physical Anthropology* 52: 85–94.

successful reproduction. The age at adulthood for men is more difficult to measure. Skeletal growth completion for men occurs between 21 and 25 years of age. Adolescent boys can father offspring, and as young as age 13 years in some notorious cases. But, few men become fathers before age 20–25, and many wait longer. We discuss the factors influencing age at fatherhood below.

Biocultural Perspective on Human Adolescence

Clearly, the human pattern of growth and maturation following puberty is quantitatively different in terms of amount, rate, and duration from the pattern for other mammals. Human adolescence, however, is more than skeletal growth and reproductive system maturation. It is also a stage of the life cycle defined by several changes in behavior and cognition that are found only in our species.

Evolution of Human Adolescence

Some theorists hypothesize that the adolescent stage of human growth evolved to provide the time to learn and practice complex economic, social, and sexual skills required for effective food production, reproduction, and parenting. In this perspective, adolescence is a time for an apprenticeship, working and learning alongside older and more experienced members of the social group. The benefits of the skills acquired during adolescence are lower mortality of both first-time mothers and their offspring. This places the 'apprenticeship hypothesis' for the learning and practice value of adolescence firmly within Darwinian natural selection theory. There is much human ethnographic and demographic evidence to support the apprenticeship hypothesis and it is likely that the learning and practice of adult skills play an important role in human growth, development, and maturation.

However, apprenticeship cannot be the primary cause for the evolution of adolescence. Learning for childcare is an example. In most species of social mammals, the juveniles are often segregated from adults and infants. The ethnographic literature, however, documents that in human societies juvenile girls often are expected to provide significant amounts of childcare for their younger siblings. Human girls enter adolescence with considerable knowledge of the needs of young children. Learning about childcare, then, is not the reason why human girls experience adolescence.

Human childhood evolved as a benefit for the mother and not the child, that is, so that the mother could resume reproduction more quickly by weaning early. Similarly, adolescence is likely to have evolved as a reproductive adaptation for adults, and not directly for the adolescent. The reason for this is that natural selection works on differential fertility and differential mortality between individuals. An additional 5–10 years of infertility, or reduced fertility, associated with adolescence could not evolve for all humans, since those individuals who 'cheated' by terminating growth at an earlier age would begin reproducing sooner and would be at a reproductive advantage. All other primates do, in fact, begin reproducing at earlier ages than humans, and none of the nonhuman primates has a human-like adolescent growth spurt, nor many of the other biological and behavioral features of human adolescence. Clearly, a juvenile primate does not need to pass through a lengthy period of adolescence, with apprenticeship type learning, just to be reproductively successful. What factors, then, could give rise to adolescence and further delays in reproduction?

The answer may lie in a type of multilevel model of selection for mating and parenting. Multilevel models in evolutionary biology include selection at the level of the individual and at the level of the social group. Such models allow for time lags between the stage of life when selection takes place and the accrual of reproductive benefits later in life. The complex pattern of human individual growth and development, combined with equally complex human social and cultural behavior, seems to be better explained by multilevel evolutionary models rather than simpler models, for example, those focusing only on fertility or mortality of the adolescent.

Human mating and parenting are of course related, but they are not identical. Charles Darwin identified two types of biological selection, natural selection, and sexual selection, and both are likely to be involved in the evolution of human adolescence. Sexual selection is all about opportunities for mating, while natural selection is, in part, about parenting. Darwin, in 1871, defined sexual selection as "... the advantage which certain individuals have over other individuals of the same sex and species, in exclusive relation to reproduction." Today we would replace the word reproduction with mating, as not all mating opportunities result in fertilization and offspring. Darwin also wrote of the many structures and instincts developed through sexual selection, including, "... weapons of offence and the means of defence possessed by the males for fighting with and driving away their rivals – their courage and pugnacity – their ornaments of many kinds – their organs for producing vocal or instrumental music – and their glands for emitting odors; most of these latter structures serving only to allure or excite the female." It is known today that sexual selection also works for females, meaning that female-specific physical and behavioral traits may evolve via competition between the females for mating opportunities with males. Some human examples are the waist-to-hip ratio and childlike voice pitch of women that may be alluring to men.

Adolescent Contributions to the Reproductive Success of Adults

Earlier we described the cooperative care of human children by older group members. In biology, such care of offspring by nonparents is called cooperative breeding. It is found in some species of birds and mammals (e.g., wolves and hyenas) and it works to increase net reproductive output. In those species the cooperative breeders are close genetic relatives of the mother. A genetic connection may exist in human cooperative breeding, but often it does not as people have social and cultural rules about marriage and kinship, and these, rather than genes, define the rights and obligations that people have to each other. Due to these social rules, it may be better to call the human type of cooperative breeding biocultural reproduction, because it enhances the social, economic, political, religious, and ideological 'fitness' of the group as much or more than it contributes to genetic fitness.

Human juveniles may hunt, gather, or produce some of their own food intake, but overall they require provisioning to achieve energy balance. In contrast, human adolescents are capable of producing sufficient quantities of food to exceed their own energy requirements. Some of the food that adolescents produce may be used to fuel their own growth and development, creating larger, stronger, and healthier bodies. The surplus production is shared with other members of the social group, including younger siblings, parents, and other immediate family members (defining families in the broad anthropological sense). Adolescent contributions enhance the fertility of adults and the survival of infants, children, and juveniles. The biological trade-off is the delay of years between puberty and first birth for the adolescents. For their valuable services in food production, the adolescents receive care and protection to safeguard their health and survival. This is important because adolescents are immature in terms of sociocultural knowledge and experience.

Girls and Boys: Separate Paths Through Adolescence

The multilevel nature of the evolution of human adolescence may be seen by considering the trade-offs related to biocultural reproduction and the different sequence of biological and behavioral events experienced by adolescent girls and boys. The differences allow each sex to improve opportunities for mating and parenting. Mating will eventually lead to the birth of offspring, but producing offspring is only a small part of reproductive fitness. Rearing the young to their own reproductive maturity is a surer indicator of success. The developmental paths of girls and boys during adolescence may be key in helping each sex to both produce and rear its own young successfully.

The order in which several pubertal events occur in girls and boys is illustrated in **Figure 5** in terms of time before and after peak height velocity (PHV) of the adolescent growth spurt. In this figure we use the Tanner Maturation Staging System for the development of secondary sexual characteristics. This system is based on five stages. Prepubertal maturation is denoted as Stage 1, for example, B1 – the absence of breast development in girls, or G1 – the absence of testes or penis enlargement in boys. The adult appearance is stage 5.

In both girls and boys, puberty begins with changes in the activity of the hypothalamus and other parts of the central nervous system (the HPG axis). These changes are labeled as 'CNS puberty' in the figure. Note that the CNS events begin at the same relative age in both girls and boys, that is, 3 years

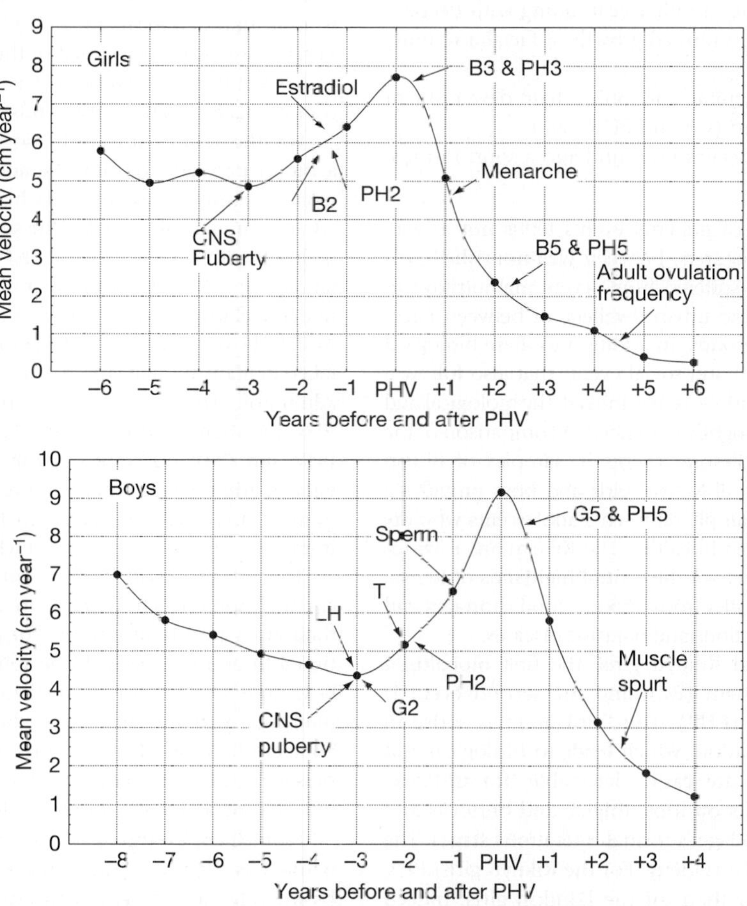

Figure 5 The ordering of several sexual maturation events for girls (top panel) and boys (bottom panel) during the adolescent growth spurt. The velocity curves are calculated using data derived from a sample of healthy, well-nourished girls and boys living in Guatemala. Girls achieve adult levels of fertility near the end of the adolescent growth spurt. Boys are fertile early-on during the growth spurt. See text for an explanation of each labeled event (original figure by the author).

before PHV. This is also the time when growth rates change from decelerating to accelerating. In girls, the first outward sign of puberty is the development of the breast bud (B2) and wisps of pubic hair (PH2). This is followed, in order, by

1. a rise in serum levels of estradiol which leads to the laying down of fat on the hips, buttocks, and thighs;
2. increased velocity of the adolescent growth spurt;
3. further growth of the breast and body hair (B3 and PH3);
4. menarche (first menstruation);
5. completion of breast and body hair development (B5 and PH5); and
6. attainment of adult levels of ovulation frequency.

The path of pubertal development in boys starts with a rise in serum levels of luteinizing hormone (LH) and the enlargement of the testes and then penis (G2). This genital maturation begins, on average, only a few months after that of girls. However, the timing and order of other secondary sexual characteristics is unlike that of girls. About a year after CNS puberty, there is

1. a rise in serum testosterone levels (T) which is followed by the appearance of pubic hair (PH2);
2. about a year later motile spermatozoa may be detected in urine;
3. PHV follows after about another year, along with deepening of the voice, and continued growth of facial and body hair;
4. the adult stages of genital and pubic hair development follow the growth spurt (G5 and PH5); and
5. near the end of adolescence boys undergo a spurt in muscular development.

The sex-specific order of pubertal events tends not to vary between early and late maturers, between well-nourished girls and boys and those who suffered from severe malnutrition in early life, between rural and urban dwellers, or between European and African ethnic groups. In addition to these biological events there are behavioral and social events that also follow a predictable course during adolescence. Indeed, the biological and cultural events are usually tightly correlated. A comparison of the biocultural timing of adolescent events in samples of British (London) and Kikuyu (rural Kenya) girls and boys provides a case study. The London sample represents adolescents who are relatively well nourished and healthy. The Kikuyu are a Bantu-speaking, agricultural society of the central highlands of Kenya. Kikuyu adolescents may suffer from periodic food shortages and a higher incidence of infectious and parasitic diseases.

For both London and Kikuyu girls, the first biocultural event is breast development (B2), and the second event is pubic hair development (PH2). The third event is a rise in serum estradiol concentration, which leads to biological and behavioral changes that are easily detectable, for instance, in the form of fat deposits on hips, thighs, and buttocks and new levels of cognition (Piaget's formal operations stage). The fourth event is peak height velocity. For the Kikuyu girls, PHV occurs about 2 years later than for the London girls. Indeed Kikuyu girls achieve each adolescent event later than English girls, varying from a few months delay in the case of reaching the B2 stage to a 2.6-year delay in menarche (13.2 years for London and 16.8 years for Kikuyu).

For many Kikuyu girls, the fifth biocultural event is clitoridectomy, which removes the tip of the clitoris. About 40% of girls underwent this operation, at the time that Carol Worthman undertook this research in 1979 and 1980. Clitoridectomy takes place just after PHV, at about breast stage 3, and just before menarche. The operation is a rite of passage. In various forms, adolescent rites of passage are found in all societies, although particular individuals may or may not participate in them. Rites of passage are symbolic activities, generally understood to have social functions, but which also have biological sequelae. Kikuyu clitoridectomy is timed so that it precedes the onset of sexual activity and marriage which follow menarche. London girls may experience some adolescent rites of passage after PHV, such as Anglican Confirmation, the school prom, a first job, and other events that may be less well defined and less traumatic than clitoridectomy.

The sixth event is menarche, which is taken as a sign of impending sexual maturation in all cultures. In many cultures, menarche often precipitates intensified instruction about sexual behaviors and the practice of these behaviors.

For both London and Kikuyu boys, the first two biocultural events are enlargement of the testes (G2), and a rise in serum concentration of luteinizing hormone. The third event is a rise in the serum concentration of testosterone, which precipitates a cascade of physical and behavioral changes. The fourth event is pubic hair development (PH2). As was the case for the girls, English boys experience each of these events, on average, at an earlier age than Kikuyu boys. The overall delay for all adolescent events for Kikuyu boys tends to be about 1 year.

For the Kikuyu, the fifth biocultural event is separation, a rite of passage requiring the adolescent boys to leave their nuclear family household and begin living in an age-graded adolescent male household. The separation to the 'boys' house' is closely correlated with age at first nocturnal emission or ejaculation. Separation takes place at about the same age that girls undergo clitoridectomy. The sixth event is peak height velocity. At PHV boys achieve about 92% of total adult height, which is taken in many human cultures as an indicator of entry into early adulthood. The spurt in muscle mass (PMV) of boys follows PHV by about 2 years (**Figure 5**). This means that between PHV and PMV boys are not capable of performing physical tasks of adult men. In most cultures, boys at this stage of development are often considered to be biologically and socially immature, and still in need of much training and education.

The seventh biocultural event for Kikuyu adolescents is circumcision, which is done to all young men and marks their entry into final training for adulthood. Circumcision is timed to occur along with the spurt in muscle mass. London boys do not undergo a circumcision rite of passage, but within that same year they usually graduate from secondary school. That event, which London girls also experience, is a rite of passage in most industrialized societies and often marks entry into the social and economic world of adults.

From these examples we may see that the adolescence, as defined as the time span of the adolescent growth spurt, is a biologically and socially significant event for both sexes. The order of adolescent events, however, is different for each sex. The reasons for the variation between boys and girls seem to be related with the way each sex prepares for mating (sexual selection) and parenting (natural selection).

Why Do Girls Have Adolescence?

In human societies, adolescent girls gain knowledge of sexuality and reproduction because they look mature sexually, and are treated as such, several years before they actually become fertile. The adolescent growth spurt serves as a signal of maturation. Early in the spurt girls develop pubic hair and fat deposits on breasts, buttocks, and thighs. They appear to be maturing sexually. About a year after peak height velocity, girls experience menarche, an unambiguous external signal of internal reproductive system development. However, most girls experience 1–3 years of anovulatory menstrual cycles after menarche. Nevertheless, the dramatic changes of adolescence stimulate both the girls and the adults around them to participate in adult social, sexual, and economic behavior. For the postmenarchial adolescent girl, this participation may be 'low risk' in terms of pregnancy.

Some girls, of course, may become pregnant and there are other social and psychological risks of adolescent sexual behavior. Teenage mothers and their infants are at risk because of the reproductive and emotional immaturity of the mother. This often leads to a low-birth-weight infant, premature birth, and high blood pressure in the mother. The likelihood of these risks declines and the chance of successful pregnancy and birth increases markedly after age 15 years and reaches its nadir after age 18 years. Due to these biological and social risks, most human societies carefully regulate, according to age and sex, the onset and type of sexual behavior that is permitted by adolescents.

Another evolutionary reason for the delay between menarche and adulthood in girls is that human female fertility tracks the growth of the pelvis. Marquisa LaVelle Moerman reported in 1982 that the crucial variable for successful first birth is size of the pelvic inlet, the bony opening of the birth canal. Moerman measured pelvic X-rays from a sample of healthy, well-nourished American girls who achieved menarche between 12 and 13 years. These girls did not attain adult pelvic inlet size until 17–18 years of age. Quite unexpectedly, the adolescent growth spurt, which occurs before menarche, does not influence the size of the pelvis in the same way as the rest of the skeleton. Rather, the female pelvis has its own slow pattern of growth, which continues for several years after adult stature is achieved.

Why the pelvis follows this unusual pattern of growth is not clearly understood. Perhaps another human attribute, bipedal walking, is a factor. The evolution of bipedalism is known to have changed the shape of the human pelvis from the basic ape-like shape. Apes have a cylindrical-shaped pelvis, but humans have a bowl-shaped pelvis. The human shape is more efficient for bipedal locomotion but less efficient for reproduction because it restricts the size of the birth canal. It may take human women longer than an ape to grow a large enough pelvis to achieve full reproductive maturity. That time of waiting provides adolescent girls with many opportunities to practice and learn important adult behaviors that lead to increased reproductive fitness in later life. Cross-cultural studies of reproductive behavior show that human societies acknowledge (consciously or not) this special pattern of pelvic growth. The age at marriage, and first childbirth, clusters around 19 years for women from such diverse cultures as the Kikuyu of Kenya, Mayans of Guatemala, Copper Eskimos of Canada, and the United States from the colonial period to the 1950s.

Why Do Boys Have Adolescence?

The adolescent development of boys is quite different from that of girls. Boys become fertile well before they assume the size and the physical characteristics of men. Analysis of urine samples from boys 11–16 years old show that they begin producing sperm at a median age of 13.4 years. Yet cross-cultural evidence indicates that few boys successfully father children until they are into their third decade of life. In the United States, for example, only 3.09% of live-born infants in 1990 were fathered by men under 20 years of age. In Portugal, for years 1990, 1994, and 1999, the percentage of fathers under 20 years of age was always below 3%. In 2001, Portugal stopped presenting results concerning the percentage of fathers below 20 because there were too few of them. Among the traditional Kikuyu of East Africa, men do not marry and become fathers until about age 25 years, although they become sexually active after their circumcision rite at around age 18.

The explanation for the lag between sperm production and fatherhood is not likely to be a simple one of sperm performance, such as not having the endurance to swim to an egg cell in the woman's fallopian tubes. More likely is the fact that the average boy of 13.4 years is only beginning his adolescent growth spurt (**Figure 1**). Growth researchers have documented that in terms of physical appearance, physiological status, psychosocial development, and economic productivity, the 13-year-old boy is still more a juvenile than an adult. Anthropologists working in many diverse cultural settings report that few women (and more important from a cross-cultural perspective, few prospective in-laws) view the teenage boy as a biologically, economically, and socially viable husband and father.

The delay between sperm production and reproductive maturity is not wasted time in either a biological or social sense. The obvious and the subtle psychophysiological effects of testosterone and other androgen hormones that are released after gonadal maturation may 'prime' boys to be receptive to their future roles as men. Alternatively, it is possible that physical changes provoked by the endocrines provide a social stimulus toward adult behaviors. Whatever the case, early in adolescence, sociosexual feelings including guilt, anxiety, pleasure, and pride intensify. At the same time, adolescent boys become more interested in adult activities, adjust their attitude to parental figures, and think and act more independently. In short, they begin to behave like men.

However – and this is where the survival advantage may lie – they still look like boys. One might say that a healthy, well-nourished 13.5-year-old human male, at a median height of 160 cm (62 in.) 'pretends' to be more childlike than he really is. Because their adolescent growth spurt occurs late in sexual development, young males can practice behaving like adults before they are actually the size of an adult and perceived as mature by other adults. The sociosexual antics of young adolescent boys are often considered to be more humorous than serious. Yet, they provide the experience to fine-tune their sexual and social roles before their lives or those of their offspring depend on them. For example, competition between men for women favors the older, more experienced man. Because such competition may be fatal, the childlike appearance of the immature but hormonally and socially primed adolescent male may be life-saving as well as educational.

Genetic and Environmental Influences on Puberty

In 2009 Ken K. Ong and colleagues reported that a region on human chromosome 6 called *LIN28B* is the first specific region of the human genome associated with the timing of puberty. Each copy of the major allele for *LIN28B* is associated with 0.12 years earlier menarche. This same genome region is linked with earlier breast development in girls, earlier voice breaking and pubic hair development in boys, a faster tempo of height growth in girls and boys, and shorter adult height in women and men. Earlier puberty often results in shorter adult stature due to the completion of skeletal maturation at a younger age.

Prior to the discovery of *LIN28B*, there were many less direct indications of genetic influences on the timing of puberty. Studies of parents and offspring and twin studies contrasting monozygotic (identical) versus dizygotic (fraternal) twins showed that the greater the genetic similarity between people the more similar they were in terms of pubertal events. Medical disorders with a genetic basis influence the age at puberty and even its absence. These findings pertain to individuals and family members, or to pathological medical conditions. While these are important contributions to the biology of puberty, they tell us little about the wide variation within and between human populations in the timing of puberty and the duration of adolescence.

The study of secular trends in human growth and development tell us more about population variation in puberty. In human biology, the phrase 'secular trends' refers to changes in the mean size, shape, or rate of maturation of the members of a population from one generation to the next. Such trends can be positive (e.g., increasing size or decreasing the age at puberty) or negative (decreasing size or increasing the age at puberty). The word 'secular' has two meanings: (1) worldly, especially pertaining to the material, nonspiritual world, and (2) just once in an age, indicating a relatively long span of time. Secular trends in human biology are aptly named because the factors influencing these trends are related to the material conditions of life and these conditions do act on human growth over long spans of time.

Secular trends in growth and maturation are some of the best examples of the effect of the environment on growth. Increases in stature and reductions in the age of menarche have taken place during the past century and a half in virtually all affluent countries and more recently in many developing countries. In North America and Western Europe, the adult height increases average about 0.6 cm per decade and the decline in the age at menarche averages about 1 or 2 months per decade. An example of the secular trend in Sweden is shown in **Figure 6**.

Sometimes the changes are greater. For example, in Poland age at menarche declined from 1955 to 1978 by about 4.15 months per decade for girls living in villages and towns. For city girls, the decline was 3 months per decade. Despite the greater rate of decline for village and town girls, the city girls have always had the earliest mean age at menarche. In 1955 the mean ages were 14.3 years in villages, 13.9 in towns, and 13.4 in cities. In 1978 these mean ages were 13.5, 13.1, and 12.9 years, respectively. Polish researchers attribute the differences between locales to the lower quality of nutrition and health care, and greater physical labor, in towns and villages compared with cities. The overall decline in age at menarche in all locales attests to improvements in the quality of life in all three areas with time.

Even negative secular trends are best explained by environmental factors. Between 1978 and 1988, Poland suffered considerable political and economic turmoil. The age at menarche in all regions increased by an average of 1.7 months during the decade. Such reversals in secular trends are common during times of deterioration in the biological and socioeconomic environment. By 2008 the political and economic climate had improved and the mean age of menarche for urban girls declined again to 12.4 years.

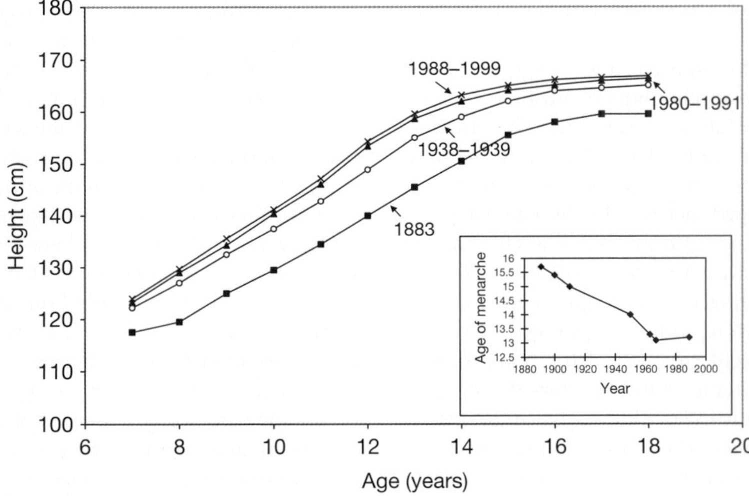

Figure 6 Secular trends in height and age of menarche (inset) in Swedish girls since the 1880s. Height has increased and age of first menstruation has decreased. Courtesy of Prof. Sara Stinson, Queens College, New York.

Several studies find that earlier puberty is related to smaller size at birth and rapid growth between birth and 2 years of age. Other research shows that persistent overweight due to excess body fat throughout the childhood and juvenile stages is associated with earlier puberty. These studies suggest that nutritional balance from the prenatal to the juvenile stages is an important regulator of the tempo of growth and pubertal development. Psychosocial stress caused by restrictive or abusive parenting, poverty, and racism also is linked with earlier puberty in otherwise well-nourished groups of girls. A specific example is the earlier average age of breast development and menarche in African American girls compared with European American girls. On average, African American girls have more body fat, are of lower socioeconomic status, and have greater exposure to racism. These observations are somewhat counterintuitive to the findings of the secular trend studies, which show that better environments lead to earlier menarche. Researchers in this area are actively trying to understand these relationships. There are several other environmental factors that influence the timing of puberty, including artificial lighting and adoption of infants and children from developing nations by parents from wealthy nations. An important area of research is the link between precocious or delayed puberty and exposure to endocrine disruptors, such as estrogen-like compounds in industrial pollutants (PCBs and PBBs), cosmetics, food, and drugs.

Risks of Puberty and Adolescence

The evolution of any new structure, function, or stage of development may bring about many biosocial benefits; however, it also incurs risks. Human puberty and adolescence comes with its own set of specific risks. Among the most common and serious of these are psychiatric and behavioral disorders. The onset of such problems tends to peak during adolescence. Most mammalian species terminate all brain growth well before sexual maturation, but human adolescents show enlargement and pruning of some brain regions leading to structural changes in the cerebral cortex. Some scholars hypothesize that the increase in brain-related disorders may derive from these cortical changes, which affect the adolescent brain's sensitivity to reward.

The reward system of the brain may lead adolescents toward risk-taking behavior. One perspective on this is expressed by Laurence Steinberg who in 2004 wrote of

> ... a disjunction between novelty and sensation seeking (both of which increase dramatically at puberty) and the development of self-regulatory competence (which does not fully mature until early adulthood). This disjunction is biologically driven, normative, and unlikely to be remedied through educational interventions ....

A less biologically deterministic perspective on risk-taking is expressed by Dan Romer who in 2010 wrote that

> Individual differences in impulsivity underlie a good deal of the risk taking that is observed during adolescence ... However, early interventions appear able to reduce the severity and impact of these traits by increasing control over behavior and persistence toward valued goals ....

Whether inherently biological or shaped by social intervention adolescence is a time of life with a high level of risk for certain diseases, of the mind and the body, and greater mortality. The later is often due to exposure to ritualized violence, such as serving as combatants in warfare, or being exposed to inherently dangerous but socially normative behaviors, such as automobile driving, alcohol consumption cigarette smoking, and sex, without appropriate instruction and regulation by the society.

Conclusions

In this article, we have taken a biocultural approach to the study of human puberty and adolescence. We reviewed the pattern of human postnatal growth and development – the stages of infancy, childhood, juvenile, adolescence – and set these basic principles in their evolutionary context. Puberty as a physiological and sociocultural event was defined. Adolescence was defined as the time span from puberty to adulthood. Several hypotheses were discussed concerning how the new life stages of the human life cycle represent feeding and reproductive specializations, which secondarily allow for the human style of learning and cultural behavior.

The biocultural perspective of human development focuses on the constant interaction taking place during all phases of human development, both between genes and hormones within the body and with the sociocultural environment that surrounds the body. Research from anthropology, developmental psychology, endocrinology, primate behavior, and human biology shows how the biocultural perspective enhances our understanding of human development.

See also: Initiation Ceremonies and Rites of Passage.

Further Reading

Bogin B (1999) *Patterns of Human Growth*, 2nd edn. Cambridge: Cambridge University Press.

Bogin B (2009) Childhood, adolescence, and longevity: a multilevel model of the evolution of reserve capacity in human life history. *American Journal of Human Biology* 21: 567–577.

Darwin C (1871) *The Descent of Man and Selection in Relation to Sex*. London: John Murray.

Ellison PT (1982) Skeletal growth, fatness, and menarcheal age: A comparison of two hypotheses. *Human Biology* 54: 269–281.

Hawkes K and Paine RR (2006) *The Evolution of Human Life History*. Santa Fe, New Mexico: School of American Research Press.

Helander EA (2008) *Children and Violence: The World of the Defenceless*. Basingstoke, UK: Palgrave Macmillian.

Ken K Ong, et al. (2009) Genetic variation in *LIN28B* is associated with the timing of puberty. *Nature Genetics* 41: 729–733.

Locke JL and Bogin B (2006) Language and life history: A new perspective on the development and evolution of human language. *Behavioral Brain Science* 29: 259–325.

Moerman ML (1982) Growth of the birth canal in adolescent girls. *American Journal of Obstetrics and Gynecology* 143: 528–532.

Paus T, Keshavan M, and Giedd JN (2008) Why do many psychiatric disorders emerge during adolescence? *National Reviews Neuroscience* 9: 947–957.

Plant TM (2008) Hypothalamic control of the pituitary–gonadal axis in higher primates: key advances over the last two decades. *Journal of Neuroendocrinology* 20: 719–726.

Romer D (2010) Adolescent risk taking, impulsivity, and brain development: Implications for prevention. *Developments in Psychobiology*, Feb 19 [Epub ahead of print].

Steinberg L (2004) Risk taking in adolescence: What changes, and why? *Annals of New York Academy of Science* 1021: 51–58.

Weisner TS (1987) Socialization for parenthood in sibling caretaking societies. In: Lancaster JB, Altmann J, Rossi AS, and Sherrod LR (eds.) *Parenting Across the Life Span: Biosocial Dimensions*, pp. 237–270. New York: Aldine de Gruyter.

Worthman CM (1993) Biocultural interactions in human development. In: Perieira ME and Fairbanks LA (eds.) *Juvenile Primates: Life History, Development, and Behavior*, pp. 339–357. New York: Oxford University Press.

Relevant Websites

http://kidshealth.org/kid/grow/body_stuff/puberty.html – KidsHealth, all about puberty.

http://www.nhs.uk/Conditions/Puberty/Pages/Introduction.aspx – NHS: Introduction to puberty.

http://www.livestrong.com/article/12450-puberty/ – Lance Armstrong Foundation: Overview of puberty.

http://www.patient.co.uk/doctor/Precocious-Puberty.htm – PatientPlus UK: Precocious puberty.

Quantitative Research Methods

W Wu and T D Little, University of Kansas Lawrence, KS, USA

Glossary

Generalizability: The degree to which the findings can be generalized from the study sample to the entire population.

Latent variables: The variables that are not directly observed or measured but are rather inferred from manifest variables.

Manifest variables: The variables that can be observed or directly measured.

Power: The probability of rejecting a null hypothesis when it is false, often denoted by $1 - \beta$.

Quantitative research: The systematic investigation of quantitative properties and phenomena and their relationships. The objective of quantitative research is to develop and employ mathematical models, theories, and/or hypotheses pertaining to phenomena.

Quasi-experimental design: The type of an experiment in which one has little or no control over the assignment of the treatments or other factors being studied. The key feature in the design is lack of random assignment.

Reliability: The consistency of your measurement, or the degree to which an instrument measures the same way each time it is used under the same condition with the same subjects.

Stratification: The process of grouping members of the population into relatively homogeneous subgroups before sampling.

Structural equation modeling: Statistical technique for testing and estimating predicted relationships among manifest and latent variables using a combination of statistical data and theoretical assumptions.

Type I error: The probability of rejecting a null hypothesis when it is true, often denoted by α.

Validity: Best available approximation to the truth or falsity of a given inference, proposition, or conclusion.

Introduction

Scientific knowledge is only as sound as the research methods used to obtain it. Research methods encompass three broad categories: design issues, measurement issues, and analysis issues. In our overview of research methods, we selectively outline key features and elements within each of these three areas. Because of our need for brevity, we have assembled a selective list of further readings for more in-depth coverage of these topics. Our goal is to provide a panoramic view of the broad research methods terrain.

Research methods can be classified along a number of different dimensions: qualitative–quantitative, exploratory–confirmatory, descriptive–inferential, manifest–latent, nonmetrical–metrical, and so on. Although the qualitative–quantitative distinction is perhaps the most commonly invoked taxonomy, space precludes us from a detailed survey of the techniques that would traditionally fall under the qualitative header. The principles of research methods that we discuss, however, are relevant to all modes of inquiry regardless of which taxonomy one uses.

Design Issues

Defining a universe of generalization (i.e., a population) and sampling from it is generally a first step in any research study. Even with single-subject designs, a population of behaviors, times, or locations is defined and then a plan to sample from the population is developed. Most studies of adolescence focus on individual adolescents (ages 10–20 or so) and then sample from this defined population. All persons who are eligible to be selected in a sample define the universe of generalization for a study's results. When the sample is drawn randomly and is targeted to be representative, the study's results will be maximally generalizable to the population.

 doi:10.1016/B978-0-12-373915-5.00034-6

Studies of US adolescents that are not nationally representative are less generalizable than regionally representative samples, for example. Nonrepresentative samples are often referred to as convenience samples. Although convenience samples are the norm in the published literature, they should not be considered as preferred or optimal. Even randomly selected convenience samples are limited in their sphere of generalizability. The population in this case is the local catchment area of youth who could have been a part of the sample. To the degree that one knows and can measure the characteristics that define the local population and the larger population, one can use weights to make the local sample reflect the characteristics of a nationally representative sample. Key characteristics of samples that are often used in weighting include gender, race/ethnicity, age, and socioeconomic status (SES). Other relevant characteristics that can be used include intellective skill, parental status, and geographic status (rural, urban). A sample that is not representative is said to be selective. A selective sample is a biased sample. When the sample is biased, the accuracy of the conclusions (i.e., validity) and the generalizability of the findings are diminished.

A related selection threat to the validity of generalizations is a phenomenon known as selective attrition. In any longitudinal study, participants will drop out or otherwise refuse to participate. If the persons who no longer participate in the study are disproportionately different from the original sample (e.g., persons of lower SES often drop out more than persons of higher SES), the sample will be selective and the validity of the conclusions will be compromised.

Quasi-Experimental Designs and Randomized Experimental Designs

Causal inference is a central topic of many studies (e.g., does X cause, predict, or lead to change in Y). Three criteria must be satisfied to make a causal inference of $X \rightarrow Y$. First, X and Y must covary with each other. This covariation can be linear or nonlinear (though we mostly assume a linear relationship). This criterion is tested using a variety of statistical methods (e.g., analysis of variance, regression). Second, X must precede Y in time. This criterion can be satisfied by experimentally manipulating X before Y. Third, no other variables can completely explain the relationship between X and Y. In other words, with the effect of all other variables controlled, the $X \rightarrow Y$ relationship still exists. This criterion is most difficult to assess because it is typically impossible to exhaust all other variables.

If we randomly assign participants to experimental conditions (e.g., treatment and control), this third criterion will be satisfied on average (but should be verified analytically). With random assignment, the influence of other variables is assumed to be equally spread across the study conditions. If this assumption is valid, then only the experimentally controlled variables can explain the group difference after treatment (i.e., the treatment effect). There are many variants of randomized experimental designs. The randomized pretest–posttest design is the most widely used. In this design, the individuals, who are randomly assigned to experimental and control conditions, are evaluated twice: before and after treatment. This design can inform both the change on an outcome (change between the pre- and posttest in control group) and the treatment effect (difference in change between the pre- and posttest across groups).

In many situations, however, random assignment is not available or feasible. For example, one cannot randomly assign participants to felon versus nonfelon. In such cases, quasi-experimental designs are used. Quasi-experimental designs incorporate design features to eliminate the influence of any potential threats to validity such as maturity, history, regression to mean, and selection bias. There are dozens of quasi-experimental designs. To highlight the principles of such designs, we describe the basics of three commonly used quasi-experimental designs: regression discontinuity design (RDD), nonequivalent control-group design (NCGD), and interrupted time series (ITS) design. As with all quasi-experimental designs, there are many variants of them, and combining design features is often used to further strengthen causal inference.

Regression discontinuity design

The basic idea of the RDD is that participants are assigned to treatment condition based only on a cutoff score on an assignment variable (best continuous) that is measured prior to treatment. For example, English as a second language students are to be assigned to a remedial writing program based on their arrival time in a native English school. The students who arrive early (e.g., before noon) are assigned to the program while the students who arrive late are not. Once the assignment variable is controlled, only the treatment effect is responsible for the difference between the groups. A treatment effect is usually manifested as a vertical discrepancy between the regression lines for the treatment and control groups *at the cutoff point*. The likelihood of such a discrepancy occurring *at the cutoff point* by chance is infinitesimal, which allows valid and generalizable conclusions about an intervention. The RDD assumes that (1) the assignment rule is perfectly followed and (2) the relationship between the treatment and the outcome is correctly specified (e.g., specified as linear when it is linear). If either assumption is violated, RDD cannot address the bias completely.

Nonequivalent control-group design

NCGD is similar to randomized pretest–posttest design, except that participants are not randomly assigned to experimental groups. NCGD is therefore susceptible to selection bias. If the probability of being assigned to treatment group for each participant can be calculated, it can be used to adjust for selection bias. Measured covariates related to selection bias can be used to predict the probability using methods such as logistic regression. This predicted probability is called a propensity score. The propensity score is then used in a variety of ways to reduce or eliminate potential selection bias (e.g., matching, stratification, covariance adjustment, and weighting). The covariance adjustment and weighting approaches assume linear relationship between the propensity score and the outcome. Stratification and matching do not have this limitation. Matching is more accurate than stratification in balancing groups; however, stratification is easier to implement and almost as efficient as matching. Another threat to NCGD is selection by maturation interaction. Adding an additional pretest can help control for this threat.

Interrupted time series

ITS is a sound design when there are only a small number of units or when an intervention naturally occurs. With ITS, the same variables are repeatedly measured over a large set of occasions and the treatment occurs at a designated occasion. If there is a treatment effect, one can detect an interruption at the treatment point. The series of observations before and after treatment can differ in many different ways. Commonly expected changes include change in intercept, slope, or both. In some cases, the variance of observations or the cyclical pattern might differ before and after the treatment. The treatment effect can be immediate or delayed in time (i.e., the interruption occurs after the treatment point).

Power to Detect an Effect

Besides dealing with potential threats to the validity of a study, a planned study must have sufficient power (typically 80%) to detect an effect. Three factors interact with one another to influence power: (1) sample size – as sample size increases, power increases, (2) effect size – as effect size increases, power increases, and (3) type I error rate (α) – the risk that an effect is in fact a chance occurrence. The type I error rate is usually fixed at a normal level (0.05 or 0.01). Effect size is a measure of the strength of an effect, or how far an effect size is from the null hypothesis (usually zero). Effect sizes are estimated based on past research, pilot work, or Cohen's norms of 1988. A power analysis determines the needed sample size to achieve a level of power to detect an effect of a certain size given a fixed alpha level.

Power analysis can be conducted before (a priori) or after (post-hoc) data collection. An appropriately conducted a priori power analysis prevents one from either missing a true effect due to insufficient sample size or oversampling the population so that even trivial effects are significant. Post-hoc power analyses should be interpreted cautiously because they do not necessarily provide an accurate estimate of true power.

Summary of Design Issues

All research designs attempt to minimize potential threats to the validity of any scientific conclusions. Unfortunately, all research designs contain one or more threats to validity. As early methodologists such as Campbell argued, some threats to validity are plausible, while others are so unlikely that attempts to control for them are not warranted. Threats to validity can be dealt with in two ways. One way is to measure the plausible threats and statistically control for their potential influence on the focal outcome analysis of interest (e.g., propensity scores). The second way is to incorporate explicit design features that attempt to control the plausible threats to validity (e.g., randomized control group design). Both the design and the statistical approaches can be merged to provide even further controls for validity threats. Finally, all research designs are only as valid and generalizable as the population that a given sample represents. Too often, conclusions about a study are stated as if they apply to a much larger universe of generalization than is warranted by the weaknesses in the sampling of units. Here, sampling units include the sampled individuals as well as the sampled contexts, occasions, and measured variables, for example.

Measurement Issues

Measurement tools are indirect reflections or indicators of underlying latent variables (i.e., constructs). Hence, all measured/manifest variables are proxies of a given latent variable. For example, responses to a questionnaire item such as how often do you say mean things to others is a proxy for the theoretical construct of aggression. Constructs are not directly measurable – they are theoretical abstractions that we presume exist and have utility to help us understand the phenomena we choose to study. Measured variables (e.g., observations, instrument recordings, or responses to stimuli) are the manifest indicators of latent constructs.

Researchers provide theoretical definitions of constructs and generate lawful statements about (a) the expected relationships among constructs or (b) the expected influence of one construct on another construct. In this regard, the constructs are used as the building blocks of a given theory. Each construct, however, must have at least one measured indicator that can be tangibly recorded. Measured variables and latent variables come in many different classifications and go by many different names, depending on the discipline or scientific tradition. **Table 1** provides an incomplete list of the names of variables that are used. We classify these variables into three general categories: covariates, predictors, and outcomes. Each variable type can be measured with different scales of measurement.

Each class of variable presented in **Table 1** can be measured on different metrics or scales. Commonly, these scales are broken down into nominal, ordinal, interval, and ratio. For the most part, however, the scales can be classified into two classes. The first we label categorical, where the levels of a variable reflect distinct classes or groups (i.e., differences in kinds). The second we label metrical, where the levels of a variable reflect magnitudes or degrees (i.e., differences in amounts).

Each measured indictor is created by following very specific operational characteristics that are specified by the researcher. These operational blueprints are based on the theoretical definitions. To establish that an operational definition of a construct adequately corresponds with the theoretical definition of a construct, a researcher must estimate and evaluate (a) the reliability of the indicators' scores, (b) the validity of the indicator as a reflection of a construct, and (c) the validity of the construct as a meaningful abstraction for understanding the focus of a study.

Some researchers reify the measured variable and treat it as if it were the construct. Such reification of the measured variable assumes that its scores are error-free (reliable) and accurate (valid). These two assumptions must be carefully examined in order to produce meaningful and generalizable research findings. In nearly all disciplines, some constructs are not easily measured and in some disciplines, nearly all constructs are not easily measured. When a construct is not easily measured, the degree of reliability and validity of measurement must be clearly established.

Table 1 A simple taxonomy of the types of variables and their role in an analysis

Covariates	*Predictors*	*Outcomes*
Control variables	Independent variables	Dependent variables
Nuisance variables	Instrumental variables	Endogenous variables
Conditioning variables	Exogenous variables	Outcome variables
Confounding variables	Predictor variables	Response variables
Suppressor variables	Process variables	Criterion variables
Moderator variables	'Causal' variables	Mediator variables
	Regressor variables	
	Mediator variables	
	Moderator variables	
	Treatment variables	
These variables are used as statistical controls to account for their influence on other variables so that the influence among the other focal variables can be seen clearly. These variables are often seen as potential confounding influences that may create or mask a hypothesized relationship.	These variables are treated as the focal variables that are the primary determining influence on an outcome variable. They reflect the hypothesized process or mechanism that gives rise to the outcome variables.	These variables are also focal variables but reflect the outcome of interest. They are the end result of the predicted relationships that one tests after controlling for potential confounds.

Note: These categorizations are simplified and the precise technical meaning varies across disciplines and individual researchers.

Both classical and modern measurement theories share the common idea that scores on a given indicator or item can be divided into a proportion that is systematic and meaningful (a true score) and a proportion that is unrelated to the construct (a combination of noise and indicator-specific variance). In fact, a key feature of measurement and analysis is partitioning the difference sources of variance to quantify their respective amounts.

Reliability refers to the consistency of the scores that are collected – the reproducible aspects of the scores. Internal consistency measures, such as Cronbach's alpha, index the consistency by comparing scores on multiple items or indicators of a construct. Cronbach's alpha assumes that the items or indicators are all about equally good at measuring the underlying construct (i.e., essential tau-equivalence). McDonald's omega is a similar measure of internal consistency but it allows that some items or indicators may carry more information about the construct than others (i.e., congeneric indicators).

Test–retest reliability is another technique that unfortunately is still commonly used. Test–retest reliability requires that a measure be administered to a selected sample and then a repeat administration is given at some specified interval (e.g., 1 week or 1 month later). Many measures in the social and behavioral sciences have been developed using test–retest reliability assessment. The unfortunate consequence of this practice is that most measures in the social and behavioral sciences are not sensitive to change. A key issue for measurement development in the developmental sciences is developing measures that are sensitive to change.

Blind devotion to reliability in the development of a measurement tool generally will undermine the validity of the measure. For developmental research in particular, the more critical concern of measurement should be on the change and age sensitivity of the measure. With modern latent variable analysis methods, the question of reliability should be an ancillary concern to the question of validity.

In the same way that experimental validity refers to the accuracy of a study (the design issues discussed previously), measurement validity refers to the accuracy of the measurement tool – the degree to which the scores accurately reflect the construct that one intends to measure. Whereas reliability focuses on the intrinsic value of the scores, validity focuses on the extrinsic meaning of the scores. Are the scores meaningful and accurate reflections of one's standing on the underlying latent construct? Validity in this context is generally classified into three categories: content validity, criterion validity, and construct validity.

Content validity refers to the quality of the indicators as reflecting a construct. For many, content validity and reliability are often conflated. These concepts are correlated, but content validity delves into the behavior of each indicator as a reflection of an underlying construct. Generally speaking, good content validity is characterized by indicators that possess large amounts of true score variance and small amounts of specific variance. In factor analysis and structure equation modeling, such indicators have pronounced loadings on their respective factors/constructs and do not have correlated specific variances or secondary loadings on other factors or constructs.

Criterion validity refers to the qualities of the construct in relation to other constructs and in relation to any manipulations. Traditionally, criterion validity is described as a high correlation between a focal construct and a well-established criterion construct. More generally, however, criterion validity involves the degree to which the set of expected/predicted relationships for a specific construct are met. High levels of criterion validity are reflected in the overall patterns of relationships that conform to expectations.

Lastly, construct validity refers to the overall utility of a construct to *d.e.p.i.c.t.* a phenomenon. That is, construct validity is the degree that a construct, across numerous studies, can *d*escribe, *e*xplain, *p*redict, *i*mprove, and *c*ontrol the behavior or phenomenon under scrutiny and the degree to which these aspects of a construct are adequately tested across various studies and contexts.

Summary of Measurement Issues

To paraphrase E. L. Thorndike, if something exists at all, it exists in some amount. Measurement is the rule-bound assignment of numbers to manifest indicators of that which exists. Measurement should never be haphazard in the sense of throwing together a set of items on cocktail napkins at a professional meeting. Instead, measurement should be thoughtfully and planfully pursued. Focus groups, pilot work, and professional critique should all be included in the development of a measurement tool. Even existing tools can often benefit from adaptation to a specific research context. In this regard, if something is worth measuring, it is worth the time and effort to measure it well.

Analysis Issue

A wide variety of data analysis techniques have been developed to address different research questions and different types of dependent variables (DVs) and independent variables (IVs). Given the space limits, we focus on the techniques that are most commonly used in research on adolescence. We reviewed the articles published in the *Journal of Research on Adolescence* in 2008. The vast majority of the studies were quantitative. The analysis methods range from classical statistical methods such as correlations, *t* test, analysis of variance (ANOVA), chi-square test, multiple regression, and logistic regression to more advanced methods such as path analysis, SEM, multilevel modeling (MLM), which is the general term for hierarchical linear modeling (HLM), growth curve modeling (GCM), and latent class analysis (LCA).

The aforementioned methods fall in the following frameworks of quantitative methods: general linear model, generalized linear model, path analysis, latent variable analysis (SEM), analysis for dependent observations, longitudinal data analysis, and approaches for classifying individuals. In the following sections, we discuss the major analysis techniques in each of the frameworks.

General Linear Model

General linear models have traditionally been the most widely used analysis tools in the social sciences. General linear models include a wide range of analysis techniques such as *t*-test, ANOVA, and multiple regression (MR). Among which, multiple regression is the most general and flexible approach.

The *t*-test and ANOVA are used to test null hypothesis regarding group means (e.g., are females greater than males in their social skills?). *t*-test can handle one categorical IV with two groups. ANOVA can handle more than one IV with more than two groups. In addition, one can examine interaction effects among IVs using ANOVA. The basic idea of ANOVA is to partition the total variance of the outcome variable into different components: variance due to each effect and variance due to chance. If the variance due to an effect is substantially greater than the variance due to chance, one can conclude that the effect is significant. A variety of ANOVA designs exist depending on whether individuals are measured under more than one condition.

MR is mainly used to assess the degree of relationship between a continuous DV and a set of IVs. IVs can be continuous, categorical, or both. The *t*-test and ANOVA are just special cases of multiple regression with categorical IVs. The general regression model expresses the DV as a linear combination or weighted sum of the IVs:

$$Y = \beta_0 + \beta_1 X_1 + \beta_2 X_2 + \cdots + \beta_p X_p + e \qquad [1]$$

where Y is the DV; $X_1, X_2, \ldots, X_p$ are IVs: $\beta_1, \beta_2, \ldots, \beta_p$ are regression weights; β_0 is the regression constant, or intercept; and e is the residual. This general form specifies that the relationships are linear, but, by including a variable that is a nonlinear function of an IV (e.g., a powered function of the IV such as X^2 or X^3), the nonlinear relationship between an IV and DV can be modeled.

Three strategies are available for building a regression model: standard, hierarchical, and stepwise. Standard regression enters all IVs into the equation at once. Hierarchical regression enters the IVs one at a time or as a set at a time based on some theoretical considerations. Stepwise regression is a purely data-driven approach which enters or deletes IVs one at a time based on whether or not an IV has significant prediction of the outcome above and beyond other variables already included in the model. A stepwise approach is no longer recommended because it does not take theory into consideration, is sample-specific, and does not necessarily lead to a model that best predicts an outcome variable.

All these methods follow the standard assumptions of the general linear model, and particularly that the DV is continuous and normally distributed. Generalized linear models are even more general in that the DV can be categorical or have different distributions.

Generalized Linear Model

In the general linear models, a continuous DV can be expressed as a weighted sum of the IVs. Other types of DV, such as dichotomous, count, and ordinal variables, cannot be linked directly to a linear function of IVs. However, this problem can be solved by transforming the DV using some nonlinear function. The transformation is called a link function which can take different forms depending on the type of outcome variable. In the following, we illustrate models for two common outcomes: binary and count. Logistic regression is often used to analyze binary outcomes. Poisson regression is often used to analyze count outcomes.

Logistic regression

Logistic regression (LR) examines the relationship between a categorical DV (e.g., mature/immature/pseudomature, use drug/not use drug) and a set of IVs (e.g., age, smoker, weight). LR predicts the *probability* of being a case ($\hat{p}(Y=1)$) instead of predicting whether someone is a case or not. For example, peer rejection and antisocial behavior predicted the probability of dropping out of school for eighth graders. Here, a case is a student who dropped out of school.

Probability of being a case is a logistic instead of linear function of the predictors. To linearize the relationship, the logistic transformation uses the logarithmic of the ratio of (a) the probability of being a case ($\hat{p}(Y=1)$) and (b) the probability of being a noncase ($1 - \hat{p}(Y=1)$), as shown in eqn [2]. This ratio is called the odds ratio and the logarithm of the odds ratio is called a logit.

$$\text{logit} = \log\left(\frac{\hat{p}(Y=1)}{1-\hat{p}(Y=1)}\right) = \beta_0 + \beta_1 X_1 + \beta_2 X_2 + \cdots + \beta_p X_p \qquad [2]$$

where β_0 represents the predicted value when all of the Xs are equal to 0, $\beta_1 - \beta_p$ are regression coefficients. For continuous predictors, β_p indicates that for one unit change in *p*th IV, the logit changes by β_p units holding the other IVs constant. Because the logit is difficult to understand, researchers often prefer to interpret the effect of the IVs in terms of the odds ratio. For one unit increase in X_p, the odds ratio will increase by a factor of e^{β_p}.

The predicted probability can be then used to classify units given assigned threshold, say 50%. For example, if a student has a predicted probability of dropout >50%, s/he is assigned to the high-risk group. Otherwise, s/he is assigned to the low risk group. The accuracy of the classification can be gauged by three indices: *correct classification* = proportion of cases and noncases who are correctly classified, *sensitivity* = proportion of cases who are classified as cases, and *specificity* = proportion of noncases who are classified as noncases. Depending on the nature of a study, any index can be used. Often, characteristic curve (ROC) is used to find an optimal balance between sensitivity and specificity.

Poisson regression

Poisson regression is used to analyze count data (e.g., the number of drinks per week; the number of arrests per year). Poisson regression is used to answer the questions such as what factors can predict the frequency of an event. Count data follow a Poisson distribution which is positively skewed and usually contains a large proportion of zeros. Logarithmic transformation can linearize the distribution, thus the link function is log. The log outcome rate is then expressed as a linear function of a set of predictors (see eqn [3]).

$$\log(\hat{Y}) = \beta_0 + \beta_1 X_1 + \beta_2 X_2 + \cdots + \beta_p X_p \qquad [3]$$

where β_p reflects the amount of change in the logarithm of the predicted number of events for a unit change in X_p.

Although generalized linear models are very flexible, they are limited to only one regression equation for a single outcome variable, which is also true for general linear models. This limitation is conquered in path analysis.

Path Analysis

Superior to general and generalized linear models, path analysis allows simultaneous analysis of multiple linear equations. Path analysis is efficient and flexible. It can be used to answer a variety of research questions that cannot be addressed by general and generalized linear models (i.e., these models are special cases of path analysis). For example, moderation and mediation models that involve multiple outcomes are easily specified and estimated in path analysis (illustrated in details below).

The best way to depict a path analysis is through path diagrams. **Figure 1** provides illustrations of a number of path diagrams of models already discussed or that will be discussed. Suppose that investigators find an adolescent's academic achievement is correlated with the number of days of school attended, but academic achievement is also correlated with positive comments that teachers make to the adolescent about her/his performance in class. If all the three variables are intercorrelated, it illustrates **Figure 1(a)**. If investigators suspect that both days attended and teacher comments contribute to academic achievement, the appropriate model is presented in **Figure 1(b)**. Other investigators could question the order of effects between these two predictors. Do days attended affect teacher comments (controlling for teacher comments at baseline) or do teacher comments encourage better attendance (cross-lagged model, **Figure 1(c)**)?

Mediation and moderation

Mediation is defined as a case where the effect of an IV (*X*) on a DV (*Y*) is transmitted by a third variable (*M*). We say that *M* mediates the effect of *X* on *Y*. *M* is thus called a mediator. Using the previous example as an illustration, perhaps teacher comments do not affect academic achievement directly, but it changes attendance, which in turn changes academic achievement (meditational model, **Figure 1(d)** or **1(e)**). Note that more than one mediator is possible.

It is challenging to establish true mediation. Modern discussions on mediation have simplified how it is tested and described. Mediation exists if the indirect effect of *X* on *Y* via *M* is significant, regardless of whether a direct effect of *X* on *Y* exists or not (see **Figure 1**). Mediation should be tested in path analysis as a simultaneously estimated set of equations, and the product of the pathways (*a* and *b* in **Figure 1(d)**) involved should be tested for significance using bootstrapped estimation. The bootstrap approach is superior to all other methods because the distribution of *ab* is often highly skewed. Baron and Kenny's four-step approach of using simple regression to establish mediation is no longer acceptable in practice.

Moderation is defined as a case where the strength of the effect of an IV (*X*) on the DV (*Y*) changes as a function of a third variable (*Z*). *Z* is called a moderator that changes the effect of *X* on *Y*. Again, as in the previous example, perhaps attendance affects academic achievement, but only for those who encounter relatively high numbers of positive teacher comments (**Figure 1(g)** or **1(h)**). Moderation can be tested by adding the product between *X* and *Z* in the model and evaluating its significance **Figure 1(h)**. Simple slopes analysis that gives the slope of *Y* on *X* at each value of *Z* can be done to probe a significant interaction.

Moderator-oriented research focuses on when certain effects will hold or change in strength. Mediator-oriented research focuses on the mechanism(s) for how and why effects occur. A moderator is often introduced when *X* and *Y* have a weak or inconsistent relationship. A mediator is often introduced when *X* and *Y* have a strong relationship. Researchers sometimes confuse these ideas with each other and with

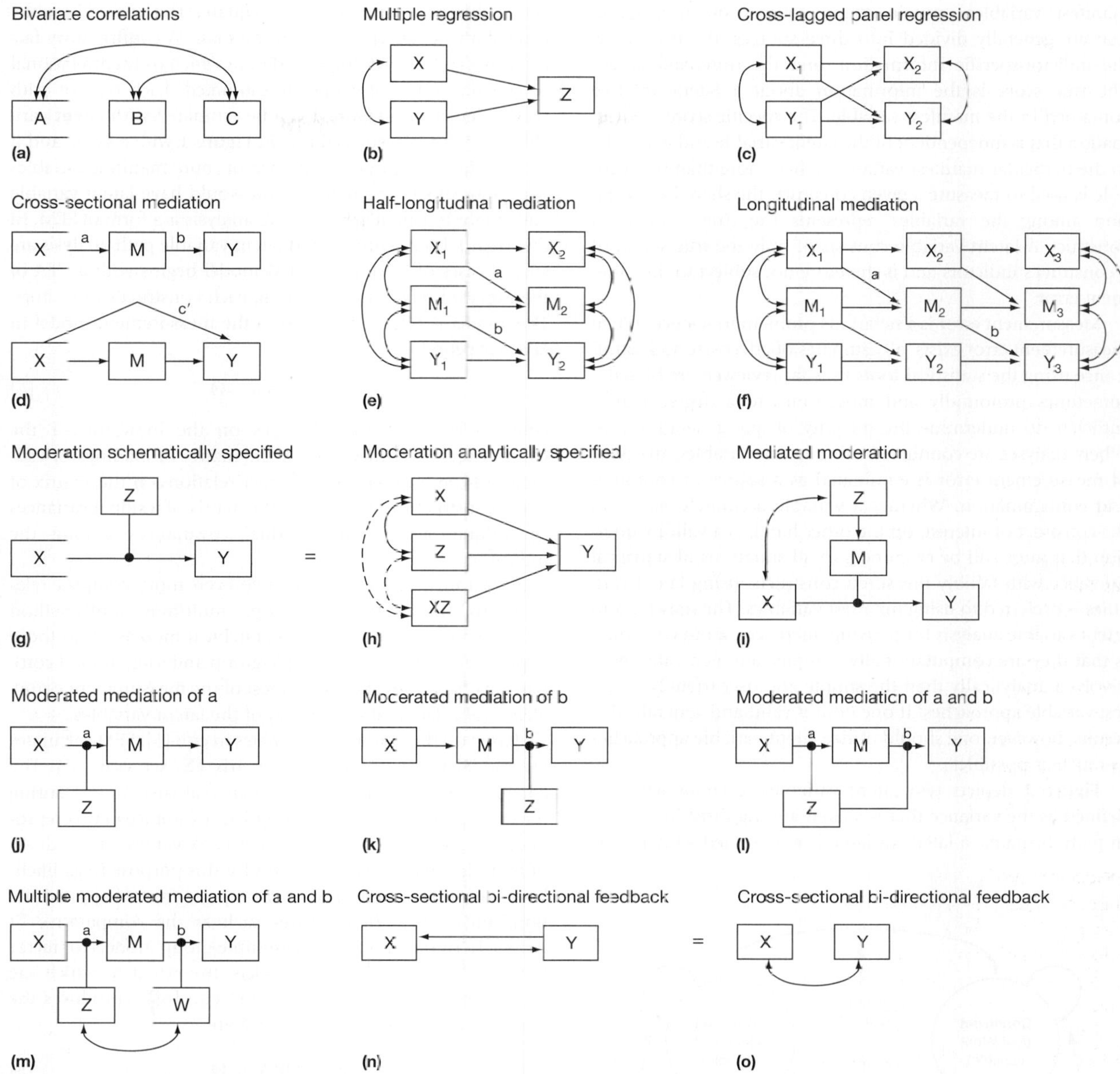

Figure 1 A simple taxonomy of statistical analysis models and names for them.

additive effects of multiple predictors. Here, the additive effect is the simple linear combination of unique effects that contribute to an outcome. One's standing on the outcome is directly related to one's standing on the multiple predictors.

Moderated mediation and mediated moderation are also possible. A mediated moderator occurs when a moderation effect is transmitted by a third variable (e.g., the moderation effect of Z on $X \rightarrow Y$ is mediated by M, see **Figure 1(i)**). For example, teacher comment might not change the effect of attendance on academic achievement directly but through student's self-concept.

A moderated mediation occurs when a mediation effect is not constant across different contexts. If any effect involving M in the $X \rightarrow M \rightarrow Y$ model (a, b, or both paths) varies across different levels of another variable, then the mediation is moderated (see **Figures 1(j)–1(m)**). For example, perhaps attendance mediates the effect of teacher comments on academic performance. However, this mediation effect varies as a function of student's self-concept.

Latent Variable Analysis

All of the methods introduced earlier assume that the variables are measured without measurement error (i.e., with 100% reliability). Because nearly every measured variable in the social and behavioral sciences, no matter its role (see **Table 1**), is affected by measurement error, this assumption is untenable. Each measured variable represents an abstraction that cannot be directly assessed. This abstraction is referred to as the latent variable. Manifest variables are proxies of the latent variable.

Manifest variables contain many sources of information that are generally divided into three sources: the true score, the indictor-specific information, and the unreliable noise. The true score is the information about a latent variable contained in the manifest variable. The specific score is information that is independent of the latent variable and is specific to the particular manifest variable. When more than one variable is used to measure a given construct, the shared information among the variables represents the true score of a construct. A latent variable consists of only the true scores of a construct's indictors and is therefore not subject to measurement error.

Measurement error is a nefarious problem in science. When measurement error exists, all estimates of effect size and significance using the statistical tools thus far reviewed are biased – sometimes profoundly and most times to a degree that is sufficient to undermine the integrity of any generalizations. When analyses are conducted using latent variables, the issue of measurement error is eliminated as a source of confound and contamination. Whether a variable accurately measures the construct of interest, on the other hand, is a validity question that must still be examined. In all situations of statistical inference with fallibly measured constructs, using latent variables is preferred to using manifest variables. The drawback to latent variable analysis for drawing inferences about constructs is that they are computationally complex and generally more involved analytically than the simple and user-friendly manifest variable approaches. If one desires valid and generalizable results, however, one should utilize latent variable approaches as much as possible.

Figure 2 depicts two latent variables, each of which is defined as the variance that is shared among three indicators. In path diagrams, a latent variable is represented with a circle and a manifest variable with a square. The curved double-headed arrow reflects a variance estimate. A confirmatory factor analysis (CFA) is a form of SEM in which only correlational or covariance relationships are estimated. Each type of path model depicted in **Figure 1** can be estimated with latent variables. If you replaced each box in **Figure 1** with a circle and if each circle was represented by two or more manifest variables like those shown in **Figure 2**, you would have latent variable path analysis. Latent variable path analysis is a form of SEM. In this regard, both manifest and latent variable path analysis are special cases of SEM. Every SEM model begins with a CFA of the expected relationships among each construct's indicators. This model is often referred to as the measurement model in SEM (see eqn [4]).

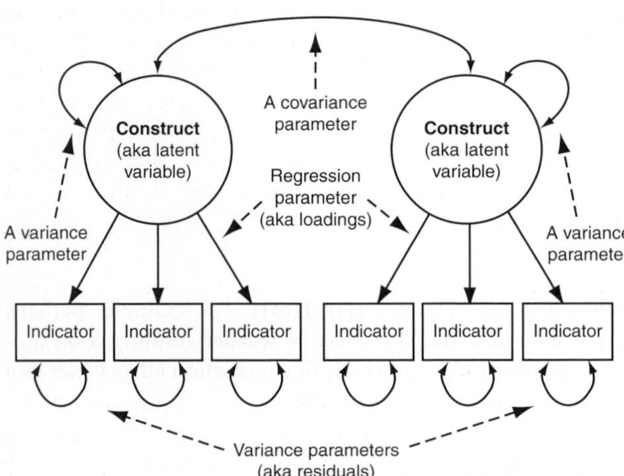

Figure 2 Drawing conventions for constructs.
- Circles (or ovals) respresent the unobserved/latent constructs.
- Boxes (or rectangles) represent the measured/manifest indicators (e.g., items, parcels, scales).
- Curved double-headed lines are variables if they start and stop on the same circle or same square.
- Curved double-headed lines are covariances if they start and stop on different circles or squares.
- Straight single-headed lines are directed, regression-like relations.

$$y = \mathbf{T} + \mathbf{\Lambda}\boldsymbol{\eta} + \mathbf{\Theta} \qquad [4]$$

where y is the vector of scores on the indicators, $\mathbf{T}$ the column vector of intercepts, $\mathbf{\Lambda}$ the matrix of loadings or estimates of the indicator-to-construct relations, $\boldsymbol{\eta}$ the matrix of latent construct scores, and $\mathbf{\Theta}$ is the matrix of residual variances or unique factors, and residual covariances among the indicators.

SEM can flexibly accommodate even more complex relationships among indicators (e.g., multitrait, multimethod models) and constructs (e.g., hierarchical models) than those depicted in **Figure 1**. In multiple-group and longitudinal comparisons, SEM provides a direct test of the measurement equivalence (*aka*, factorial invariance) of the latent variables.

Based on the parameter estimates in eqn [5], SEM calculates the model implied covariance matrix ($\hat{\mathbf{\Sigma}}$, see eqn [5]). The adequacy of the model can be often evaluated by measuring the extent to which the model implied covariance matrix reproduces the observed covariance matrix. A variety of goodness of fit indices have been developed for this purpose (e.g., likelihood ratio test statistic, root mean square error of approximation, and relative fit measures such as the comparative fit index). In some cases, such as multiple-group models for factor invariance and longitudinal models, the extent to which the model implied mean vector ($\hat{\mu}_y$, see eqn [6]) reproduces the observed mean vector is also important.

$$\hat{\mathbf{\Sigma}} = \mathbf{\Lambda}\mathbf{\Psi}\mathbf{\Lambda}' + \mathbf{\Theta} \qquad [5]$$

$$\hat{\mu}_y = \mathbf{T} + \mathbf{\Lambda}\mathbf{A} \qquad [6]$$

where $\mathbf{A}$ is the column vector of latent construct means, $\mathbf{\Psi}$ the matrix of variances and covariances among the constructs, and $\mathbf{\Lambda}'$ is the transpose of $\mathbf{\Lambda}$.

Multilevel, Nested Data

The analytic approaches described previously assume independent observations (i.e., a given observation has no effect on another observation or shares a common influence). This assumption often does not hold. For example, the data for the students within the same classroom are correlated with each other (i.e., not independent) because they share the same context (e.g., same teachers, physical space, and shared interactions). This type of data is variously called clustered, nested, hierarchically structured, or multilevel data (e.g., individuals are clustered or nested in classrooms). The degree of correlation among the individual data due to the fact that they are from the same cluster (e.g., classroom) is called the intra-class or within-class correlation. Not accounting for the within-class correlation typically produces standard errors of parameter that are underestimated, which inflates type I error rate (i.e., one is more likely to detect an effect when it is actually not there).

Multilevel models (MLM) account for the within-class correlation by allowing the relationship among variables to differ across the different levels or clusters. These models are also called random coefficients modeling and HLM; MLM can be done on manifest variables or latent variables (which is sometimes called MSEM). MLMs examine the relationships among variables at each level, the variability of the relationships across levels, and possible interactions across levels. MLMs address: (1) what are the average within-level parameter estimates (fixed effects)? (2) Do these estimates vary across levels (random effects)? (3) What covariates can explain the difference in the relationships between levels?

As an illustration, eqns [7] and [8] present a two-level regression model for hierarchical data with adolescents nested within the neighborhood.

Level 1 (adolescent):

$$y_{ij} = \beta_{0j} + \beta_{1j}x_{ij} + e_{ij} \qquad [7]$$

Level 2 (neighborhood):

$$\begin{aligned} \beta_{0j} &= \gamma_{00} + u_{0j} \\ \beta_{1j} &= \gamma_{10} + u_{1j} \end{aligned} \qquad [8]$$

where i indicates adolescent and j indicates neighborhood. y_{ij} is the outcome variable, for example, adolescents' educational values. x_{ij} is a covariate at the adolescent level, for example, adolescents' gender. β_{0j} and β_{1j} represent the intercept and slope for the effect of adolescents' gender on educational values in neighborhood j. γ_{00} and γ_{10} represent the average intercept and slope across neighborhoods (fixed effects). u_{0j} and u_{1j} represent deviation in the intercept and slope for neighborhood i from the average intercept and slope. The variances of u_{0j} and u_{1j} capture the variability of the intercept and slope across neighborhoods (random effects). Covariates at the neighborhood level (e.g., neighborhood income) can be added to the level-2 equation to explain interneighborhood differences in the intercept and slope.

Longitudinal Data Analysis

The advances in MLM and SEM provide convenient and flexible ways to analyze longitudinal data. Longitudinal data involve repeated observations or measures over time (e.g., repeated measures on academic achievement over grades). Longitudinal data allow researchers to measure change which is a fundamental concern of practically all scientific disciplines. Longitudinal data can be analyzed in three ways: (a) as traditional repeated measures of individual differences, or panel models; (b) as growth curve models of the individual differences in the intraindividual (within person) trends of change, for example, the individual change in academic achievement; or (c) as within person models of each person, or p-technique analyses. Space limit does not allow a comprehensive discussion of those methods. In the following sections, we highlight some of the basic models and basic concepts related to longitudinal modeling, focusing on the second approach.

The second approach can be implemented using a two-level MLM because the repeated measures (level 1) are nested within individuals (level 2). Intraindividual change is modeled at first level. The interindividual differences are captured at the second level. Interestingly, such models can also be specified in the SEM framework as a latent growth curve model with equivalent results under most of the conditions. A variety of change trajectories can be modeled, ranging from linear, curvilinear (e.g., quadratic) to nonlinear (e.g., s-shaped curve). More waves of repeated measures are usually required to estimate more complex change trajectories. If distinct periods of growth exist over the course of a study (e.g., before and after an intervention), the growth trajectories should be divided into pieces representing each period. Different growth curves are then fit to the pieces simultaneously. This type of model is very useful and often referred to as spline or piecewise growth curve model.

Covariates or predictors of intraindividual and interindividual changes can also be included. Covariates that explain intraindividual change must vary across time and individuals (i.e., time-varying covariates). For example, stress level can be a time-varying covariate to the change in depression over time. Covariates that explain individual difference in intraindividual change are constant across time but different across individuals (i.e., time-constant covariate). For example, adolescents' perception of their connection with their parents and teachers predicts their growth in math achievement from grades 8 to 12.

In the SEM framework, one can parallel the change process of two or more outcome variables and examine how the change processes covary with one another (e.g., change series in adolescent and peer alcohol use were found positively related to each other). Longitudinal panel models of parallel constructs are useful in examining longitudinal mediation effects to answer questions such as whether change in M mediates the effect of change in X on the change in Y or whether the mediation effect of M varies across time (e.g., a prevention program increased the rate of change for perceived importance of a team leader, which in turn increased the change rate of nutrition behaviors of high school football players across years).

Latent Class Analysis

When there is unknown heterogeneity among participants (i.e., when distinct subgroups exist but one does not know how many or who belongs to which subgroup), various methods can be used. Cluster analysis, mixture distribution modeling, and LCA can each be used to identify underlying subgroups or subpopulations. Latent class and mixture modeling treat group membership as a latent variable and thus are model-based approaches to subgroup identification. Instead of assigning participants to a specific group (as is done in traditional cluster analysis which is a data-based approach), these model-based approaches estimate the probability of membership in each group, which adds to 1.0 for each individual. Given that the number of subpopulations is usually unknown, solutions with different number of subgroups are audited.

The solution that offers an optimal balance between model fit and parsimony as well as substantively interpretable subgroups is selected. Note that the idea of mixture modeling can be applied to longitudinal data analysis to identify subpopulations of change trend. This technique is named growth mixture modeling (GMM). For example, using GMM, three classes of change trajectory of alcohol drinking behavior were identified among young adults: low use of alcohol, early onset, and increasing use of alcohol. The differentiation of the three classes has important implications for effective prevention of drinking problems. Four developmental typologies of identity formation were also identified: pathmakers, guardians, searchers, and consolidators.

Missing Data Analysis

Missing data are a ubiquitous aspect of research methods. Missing data can arise for many reasons, such as nonresponse, coding errors, and dropout from a study. The validity of missing data analysis techniques depends on many factors such as the proportion of missing data, the pattern of missing data, and the missing data mechanism. Three types of missing data mechanism are possible: missing completely at random (MCAR), missing at random (MAR), and missing not at random (MNAR). MCAR refers to missingness that is unrelated to any variables either measured or unmeasured. If missingness is determined by an observed variable that is related to the variables in the statistical model, then the data are MAR. If missingness is related to the underlying values that are missing (i.e., are due to a variable that is not measured), the mechanism is called MNAR.

Traditional methods attempt to fix the problem by getting rid of the missing data (e.g., listwise deletion and pairwise deletion) or use a naïve approach to filling in the data (e.g., mean substitution). The traditional approaches give unbiased parameter estimates only when missing data are MCAR, which is rarely a tenable assumption. None of the traditional approaches can recover the uncertainty due to missing data. As a result, the standard error estimates are biased and statistical inference is misleading.

Modern approaches to missing data analysis use information about the MAR source of missingness to recover the missing information and estimate the uncertainty due to the missing data. To do this, modern approaches use either full information maximum likelihood (FIML) or multiple imputation (MI). FIML addresses the missing data issue by utilizing all of the available observations to construct the likelihood function and obtain the parameter estimates as well as their standard errors. FIML deals with missing data and estimates a statistical model in one step. On the other hand, MI attempts to fill in the data with the uncertainty of missingness accounted for in the imputation process. Specifically, MI involves estimating multiple copies of the imputed data. The statistical model is run on each imputed dataset. The final parameter estimates are then computed by combining (i.e., taking the average) across the analyses. The standard errors of a parameter estimate are computed by combining the within-imputation variance of the parameter and the variance of the parameter across imputations. In this way, the uncertainty due to missing data is well recovered.

Both MI and FIML methods can provide unbiased parameter and standard error estimates assuming MAR, normal distributions, and large sample sizes. However, even if those assumptions are not satisfied, MI and FIML are superior to traditional missing data techniques. In addition, including the variables (auxiliary variables) that are related to variables in the model can improve the accuracy of imputation as well as statistical power. Although the best way to deal with missing data is to prevent them in the first place, in order to achieve maximally generalizable results, current best practice dictates that one must analyze data based on either MI-created datasets or FIML estimation of model parameters.

Modern missing data procedures also have tremendous implications for future directions in research design and analysis because of the power and potential of intentionally missing data designs, including three-forms protocols, controlled administration in longitudinal studies, and accelerated longitudinal models.

Summary of Analysis Issues

Both general and generalized linear models assess the relationship between a DV and a set of IVs by expressing the DV or a transformed DV as a linear combination of the IVs. Both models can be used to explore the influencing factors for an outcome as well as make prediction on the outcome variable, given known information on the IVs. In addition, important theoretical questions such as those related to mediation and moderation can be answered using the approaches in the two frameworks. General and generalized linear models are fundamental statistic tools. However, they have at least three limitations: (1) they cannot handle multiple outcome variables simultaneously; (2) since they operate at the manifest variable level, the effect of measurement error is confounded in the parameter estimates; and (3) if the observations are not independent of each other, they will give biased standard error estimates and consequently misleading statistical inference. Solving for these limitations has led to the development of path analysis, SEM, and MLM. Path analysis allows multiple DVs and multiple equations to be handled simultaneously in one model. SEM partitions measurement error from observed score and examines the relationships among latent variables. In addition, using latent categorical variables, one can capture the underlying heterogeneity in participants in terms of their profiles or change trajectories. MLM takes into account the dependency of individuals and thus produces unbiased standard error estimates. The emergence of MLM and SEM has been particularly advantageous for longitudinal data analysis. One can now evaluate intraindividual change trend and interindividual difference in the change trend in one step. Finally, advanced missing data approaches such as MI and FIML can be used to improve the accuracy of parameter estimates from all types of data analysis.

Concluding Thoughts

Clearly, a topic as broad as research methods is difficult to cover in detail. We have selectively covered key topics and ideas that are at the heart of all research methods. For the most part, research methods involve codified logic and common sense. The scientific method toward epistemology demands logically and internally consistent theory coupled with empirical verification of testable hypotheses. In this regard, theory is the methodologist's best friend. Theory dictates the research question and the measurement tools (and operational characteristics of the constructs under view). With the question and measurement tools in hand, an appropriate design to test the research question can then be created. One can borrow from the many designs that have already been carefully vetted and considered in terms of threats to validity and the strength of generalizability, or one can adapt and modify, based on the needs of the question. From this latter perspective, we advocate that the research methods be adapted to the question rather than the question be adapted to the methods. When questions are adapted to the methods, the answer is no longer the answer that was originally sought and often does not shed light on the original motivating question. Similarly, the analytic tools that are available should be adapted to the design rather than the design dictated by the analysis tool. Here, the unconsidered reliance on ANOVA-based designs for scientific inquiry, for instance, often can undermine the growth of scientific knowledge. Optimally, a productive program of research incorporates experimental and nonexperimental designs as well as mixed methods of inquiry. From this perspective, a productive program of research would incorporate nearly all the design, measurement, and analysis tools that we have reviewed under this rubric of research methods.

See also: Adolescence, Theories of.

Further Reading

Bickel R (2007) *Multilevel Analysis for Applied Research: It's Just Regression!.* New York, NY: The Guilford.

Brown TA (2006) *Confirmatory Factor Analysis for Applied Research.* New York: Guilford.

Charmaz K (2006) *Constructing Grounded Theory: A Practical Guide Through Qualitative Analysis.* Thousand Oaks, CA: Sage.

Cohen J, Cohen P, West SG, and Aiken L (2003) *Applied Multiple Regression/Correlation Analysis for the Behavioral Sciences,* 3rd edn. Mahwah, NJ: Erlbaum.

Collins LM and Lanza ST (2010) *Latent Class and Latent Transition Analysis with Applications in the Social, Behavioral, and Health Sciences.* New York: Wiley.

Denzin NK and Lincoln Y (eds.) (2005) *Handbook of Qualitative Research.* Thousand Oaks, CA: Sage.

Enders CK (2010) *Applied Missing Data Analysis.* New York, NY: Guilford.

Hoffman JP (2003) *Generalized Linear Models: An Applied Approach.* Boston, MA: Pearson/Allyn and Bacon.

Jaccard J and Jacoby J (2010) *Theory Construction and Model-building Skills: A Practical Guide for Social Scientists.* New York, NY: Guilford.

Klein RB (2010) *Principles and Practices of Structural Equation Modeling,* 3rd edn New York, NY: Guilford.

Little TD, Bovaird JA, and Slegers DW (2006) Methods for the analysis of change. In Mroczek DK and Little TD (eds.) *Handbook of Personality Development,* pp. 181–211. Mahwah, NJ: Erlbaum.

MacKinnon DP, Fairchild AJ, and Fritz MS (2007) Mediation analysis. *Annual Review of Psychology* 58: 593–614.

McDonald RP (1999) *Test Theory: A Unified Treatment.* Mahwah, NJ: Erlbaum.

Raudenbush SW and Bryk AS (2002) *Hieracrical Linear Models: Applications and Data Analysis Methods.* Thousand Oaks, CA: Sage.

Shadish WR, Cook TD, and Campbell DT (2002) *Experimental and Quasi-experimental Designs for Generalized Causal Inference.* Boston, MA: Houghton Mifflin.

Shavelson RJ and Webb NM (1991) *Generalizability Theory: A Primer.* Newbury Park, CA: Sage.

Singer JD and Willett JB (2003) *Applied Longitudinal Data Analysis: Modeling Change and Event Occurrence.* New York: Oxford.

Relevant Website

www.QuantKU.edu – Links to calculators.

Resilience

M D Resnick and L A Taliaferro, University of Minnesota, Minneapolis, MN, USA

Glossary

Cognitive style: The manner in which individuals think or engage in cognitive activity, including their ways of attending to stimuli, processing, and storing information.

Divergent thinking: A mode of processing information that involves generating all logical possibilities and considering unusual or creative solutions to problems.

Emotional intelligence: The degree of ability an individual has to identify and control one's own and other people's emotions.

Perinatal: The period after birth, especially infancy.

Protective factors: In resilience theory, factors that protect an individual from the negative effects of personal or environmental characteristics.

Vulnerability factors: In resilience theory, factors that increase a person's susceptibility to the adverse consequences of environmental stressors.

Introduction

Resilience is a concept that originated in physics. Once transplanted into the field of developmental science and social behavioral research a generation ago, it inspired the investigation of key protective factors, opportunities, and experiences that enable young people to resist stress and even thrive in the face of adversity. Increasingly, it is the basis for programs, policies, and public health practice that seeks to employ the dual strategy of reducing risk while enhancing protective factors that place (or keep) young people in a healthy developmental pathway.

Resilience Defined

The word resilience comes from the Latin *resilientia* meaning the 'action of rebounding.' The *Oxford English Dictionary* defines resilience as 'The action or an act of rebounding or springing back.' The field of physics first adopted the term resilience to describe the capacity of materials to retrieve their initial shape following exposure to external pressure (i.e., flexibility and elasticity). More broadly, resilience represents the capacity of dynamic systems to withstand or recover from significant disturbances. Therefore, scientists can examine resilience at many levels, over varying time frames, and from different disciplinary perspectives. Some scientists might use terms like equilibrium or homeostasis when they are considering this process of 'righting oneself,' either as a system or as an individual. In developmental science, resilience refers to positive adaptation in the context of significant threats to development (i.e., adversity). Most developmental research focuses on resilience within individuals, although researchers also apply the concept to systems within which individual and collective development occurs such as families, classrooms, schools, or communities. In short, the term is widely applicable, well beyond its traditional, specific use in describing the ability of materials to resist stress or insult, or the capacity of objects to resume their form or function following challenging or demanding circumstances.

History of Resilience in Developmental Science

The science of resilience in human development emerged in the 1960s and 1970s. Pioneering scientists shaped an arena of study through their desire to understand, prevent, and treat mental health problems among young people. Researchers addressing developmental psychopathology studied children at risk for maladaptation due to such factors as perinatal hazards, parental psychopathology, psychosocial disadvantage, and loss. These innovative thinkers observed that many

 doi:10.1016/B978-0-12-373915-5.00035-8

children appeared to develop well despite their status as members of a known risk group with elevated probability of some undesired outcome, or their known exposure to psychosocial adversities associated with problems such as family violence or poverty. Rather than focusing their attention on the characteristics that increased the likelihood of adverse outcomes, imagination and curiosity moved these scholars to ask different kinds of questions, propelling them away from an exclusive focus on risk – such as how is success possible contrary to expectation, or, what accounts for desirable versus undesirable outcomes among individuals or groups seemingly exposed to similar challenges? This line of inquiry inspired efforts to understand processes that avert or ameliorate psychopathology and foster desirable outcomes among children facing threats to positive development. These early investigators studied children they termed resilient to understand the intriguing and often mysterious variations in human behavioral responses to adversity or challenge.

Recognizing and systematically studying resilient children reversed many negative assumptions and deficit-focused models about the development of children growing up under threats of disadvantage and adversity. In particular, the acknowledgment and intrigue with resilience, positive outcomes, and/or resistance in the face of challenge nurtured a set of research questions that defied a pattern of inquiry in the social behavioral sciences that for years had favored the examination of negative outcomes, risk factors, and failure. These scholars shifted their focus from presumptions of near-inevitability about young people becoming casualties of negative factors, to frameworks of understanding that incorporated the possibility of youth demonstrating healthy development contrary to prediction and expectation.

Early conceptualizations of resilience implied that children who functioned well despite exposure to stressful life experiences were remarkable or special. Scholarly work and mass media portrayed these children as so constitutionally tough that they would not succumb under the pressures of stress and adversity. Some of this early literature depicted these youth as *invulnerable or invincible*. While this portrayal refuted the assumption that disadvantage was destiny, this notion of invulnerability was misguided for three reasons:

1. resistance to stress is relative, not absolute;
2. the foundation of resistance includes both environmental and constitutional factors;
3. degree of resistance varies over time and according to circumstance.

Rather than a rarely seen quality or set of processes, resilience actually represents a common phenomenon that usually results from the operation of basic human adaptational systems. If these systems remain functional and protected, then youth experience robust development even when faced with severe adversity. However, if these systems become impaired, then youth show greater risk for developmental problems.

Researchers use the term resilience to describe three types of phenomena:

1. good developmental outcomes despite high-risk status (beating the odds, better than predicted development);
2. sustained competence under stress (stress-resistance, coping); and
3. recovery from catastrophic adversity (bouncing back, self-righting) or severe deprivation (normalization).

Recently, researchers have explored the possibility of positive transformation after adversity, such that adaptive functioning actually improves following a traumatic experience. At the core of any research on resilience resides the question: Is this system performing the way it should perform? Investigators incorporated a protracted perspective to this fundamental question when they brought resilience into a developmental framework and asked: Is this system developing well?

The assessment of resilience requires two types of judgment. The first involves an inference that addresses the threat side. To consider an individual resilient, the person must have experienced significant threat(s) to his or her development. Demonstrable risk requires exposure to current or past hazards with the potential to derail normative development. These risk factors can be biological or psychosocial hazards that increase the likelihood of poor or negative outcomes. As examples, risk factors associated with developmental problems include poverty, family instability, schizophrenia in a biological mother, and witnessing or experiencing violence. Risk factors often co-occur – a well-studied phenomenon whereby one risk factor is frequently accompanied by others. Researchers have developed ways of assessing this kind of 'cumulative risk,' or the clustering of risk factors, finding both additive and sometimes exponential risk for poor outcomes on multiple indicators of development. Clearly, the piling on of risk factors increases the vulnerability of individuals or systems to poor outcomes, but thresholds vary as to 'how much is too much' in terms of experiencing damage or harm.

The second judgment involves criteria researchers use to assess or evaluate the quality of adaptation or a developmental outcome as 'good' or 'OK.' Controversy remains about who should define resilience and what standards researchers should apply. Many investigators define resilience based on an observable history of meeting a society or culture's major expectations for behavior among children (or teens or adults) of a certain age. In other words, are individuals or groups generally 'on time' when it comes to achieving certain milestones or developing various competencies? The criteria used by other investigators focus on the absence of psychopathology or a low level of symptoms and impairment. The first definition allows for an examination of indicators of thriving, well-being, functional effectiveness, and achievement. The second is focused on the relative absence of risk (but speaks nothing to the issue of competence and capacity). In fact, some investigators include both criteria. A related issue involves whether to define resilience based on external adaptation criteria (e.g., academic achievement or the absence of delinquency), internal criteria (e.g., psychological well-being or low levels of distress), or both criteria.

These issues of definition and assessment of resilience have varied over time. Generally, the history of behavioral research on resilience can be described in terms of four waves of investigations. The first wave began over 30 years ago and now wanes in prevalence. That initial wave was descriptive and sought to identify correlates and predictors of good adaptation among young people considered at risk for different reasons. The second wave is increasingly reflected in the literature and focuses on identifying processes and mechanisms that explain adaptation in the context of risk or adversity. Put another way, the first wave of investigations helped to answer the question of 'what' made a positive difference, while the second wave addressed the 'how' and 'why' of resilience. The third wave, still in its early phase, involves interventions designed to create or enhance resilience by strengthening protective processes. In some respects, this is akin to the earliest application of the concept of resilience – involving the tempering of steel to make it more resistant to stress. Here, the evaluation of these interventions seeks to better understand the events, opportunities, and experiences that young people need to do well and to answer the interventionist question: "What works best with whom?" The fourth wave, in an even more nascent phase of development, includes the integration of multiple levels of analysis including, but not limited to, gene–environment interactions, social interactions, and person–media interactions. Beyond purely descriptive work, the research increasingly relies on longitudinal analyses to understand resilience processes and mechanisms, building upon single point-in-time studies that effectively identified the elements that needed to be examined over time, but not necessarily clarifying the mechanisms by which resilience is strengthened or undermined.

Longitudinal Research on Resilience

The origin of resilience research in developmental science derived from studies investigating the impact of parental schizophrenia on the development of children. Researchers found that among children at high risk for psychopathology, a subset showed healthy adaptive patterns. Rather than dismissing these youth as atypical or outliers and continuing a focus on risk and risk factors, investigators labeled them 'resilient' or 'stress-resilient' and sought to identify factors that differentiated vulnerable children who became ill from resilient children who did not become ill or even thrived.

Emmy Werner's Kauai longitudinal study represents a landmark investigation in resilience research. Her study began in 1954 and followed a cohort born in 1955 on the island of Kauai from birth to adulthood. Investigators monitored the impact of various biological and psychosocial risk factors, stressful life events, and protective factors on development. The principal goals involved assessing long-term consequences of perinatal complications and adverse rearing conditions on development and adaptation. Researchers categorized young people as high risk if they were born into poverty and experienced moderate to severe perinatal stress, or lived in a family environment characterized by discord, divorce, parental alcoholism, or mental illness. Some 10% of these high-risk children became competent, confident, and caring young adults and comprised the resilient group. Three clusters of protective factors differentiated resilient youth from other high-risk youth who demonstrated serious and persistent problems in childhood and adolescence, including

1. at least average intelligence and dispositional attributes that elicited positive responses from others (such as calm and humor);
2. emotional ties with parent substitutes that encouraged trust, autonomy, and initiative; and
3. an external support system that rewarded competence and provided a sense of coherence, consistency, and meaning.

During their 30s, the resilient group showed educational and vocational accomplishments equal to or exceeding the low-risk group from affluent, secure, and stable environments. Shared qualities characterizing resilient children in adulthood included personal competence and determination, support from a spouse or mate, and reliance on faith and prayer.

The Rochester Longitudinal Study, conducted by Arnold Sameroff, began in 1970 to examine the effects of parental mental illness, social status, and other family cognitive and social variables on the development of children from birth through age four. Researchers categorized children into four groups based on their mother's diagnosis: (1) schizophrenia, (2) neurotic-depression, (3) personality-disorder, or (4) no mental illness. Social status and severity or chronicity of a mother's mental illness produced the greatest impact on child development. Children of more severely or chronically ill mothers and lower socioeconomic status (SES) African American children showed worse cognitive and social-emotional competence than comparison groups. Further, children challenged by multiple, simultaneous family risk factors demonstrated much worse outcomes than those facing fewer risks. In fact, among studies of children reared by a parent with mental illness, the most consistent correlates of positive child outcomes include warm relationships with adults within and/or outside the family, and a child's intellectual skills and capacity to elicit positive responses from adults, due to temperament and/or behavior.

The Project Competence studies conducted by Norman Garmezy, Ann Masten, and colleagues focused on adaptation among normative and high-risk samples of children. These studies searched for risk and protective factors associated with competence in middle childhood and adolescence. Researchers identified several correlates of school competence within three domains:

1. individual attributes (female gender and higher IQ);
2. demographic factors (higher socioeconomic status, higher level of maternal education, and intact family); and
3. positive family qualities (global parenting quality, family sociability, family stability/organization, and family cohesion). Competent youth also demonstrated better interpersonal awareness and social comprehension, a more reflective cognitive style, more divergent thinking, and greater ability to appreciate and generate humor.

Sir Michael Rutter and his associates compared parenting problems and psychosocial difficulties among women reared in foster institutions since early childhood, and women from the general population. Institution-reared women with a nurturing spouse in a supportive marriage showed levels of good parenting commensurate with the comparison group. However, institution-reared women without good marital support demonstrated higher rates of poor psychosocial functioning and poor parenting. Marital support represented a less critical factor associated with good parenting for women in the comparison group. These researchers subsequently sought to identify mechanisms that enabled some of the institution-reared women to create and sustain a successful marriage. Positive school experiences represented the most influential protective factor. Social relationships, athletic prowess, musical success, and scholastic achievement increased the likelihood that institution-reared women would exercise planning and intentionality in choosing a spouse and a career. In other words, the experience of success at school enhanced these women's feelings of self-esteem and self-efficacy, and increased their sense of control over their life circumstances.

Glenn Elder and colleagues used archival data from the Berkeley Guidance Study and Oakland Growth Study to investigate the long-term impact of the 1930s' Great Depression on youth. The Berkeley cohort was comprised of children during the Great Depression, while the Oakland cohort consisted of adolescents. Researchers compared these young people who experienced the profound economic hardship of the Great Depression with their peers unaffected by economic misfortune. Among the Oakland cohort, males and females from economically deprived homes were more likely to seek advice and companionship from persons outside their immediate family than the comparison group. For economically deprived youth, personal attributes such as intelligence (for males) and physical attractiveness (for females) served as buffers against risk, and achievement motivation more highly correlated with ability than among noneconomically deprived youth. Similarly, for the Berkeley cohort, an easy temperament, physical attractiveness (for females), and positive mother–child relationships buffered the impact of risk factors on a variety of outcomes.

As a final example, the Rochester Child Resilience Project assessed the correlates and antecedents of resilience among low-income, urban children who experienced significant life stress. Emory Cowen, Peter Wyman, and colleagues identified variables that consistently differentiated resilient children from youth who exhibited poor outcomes. Resilient children demonstrated an easy or relaxed temperament, high IQ, empathy, and proficiency in social problem-solving and perceived themselves as generally competent. Families of resilient youth showed sound parent–child relationships, and parents maintained a sense of efficacy as well as good mental health.

These longitudinal studies demonstrate that most young people possess self-righting tendencies that enable them to become functionally effective individuals despite having backgrounds characterized by severe disadvantage. What this generation of research has achieved, collectively, is to identify protective processes predictive of positive outcomes across multiple social groups and across a variety of social settings and situations.

Protective Processes

In both cross-sectional and longitudinal studies (as noted previously), resilience researchers assess positive features of development in young people and their environments. In contrast to risk-centered social behavioral research, the very concept of resilience and associated research into protective factors place an emphasis on strengths, capacities, hope, and potential. Protective processes refer to represent mechanisms that moderate, ameliorate, or alter a person's reaction to a stressful situation or chronic adversity so he or she demonstrates more successful adaptation than would occur in the absence of protective factors. Researchers identify four types of protective processes, including mechanisms that

1. reduce the impact of risk or a person's exposure to risk,
2. reduce negative chain-reactions preceding bad events or experiences,
3. increase self-esteem and self-efficacy through achievement, and
4. promote positive relationships and new opportunities providing needed resources or new directions in life.

The accumulated body of research over a generation consistently suggests a 'short list' of commonly observed correlates and predictors of resilience including

- One or more effective parents
- Connections to other caring, competent adults
- Cognitive, attention, and problem-solving skills
- Effective emotion and behavior regulation
- Positive self-perceptions; self-efficacy; self-worth
- Beliefs that life has meaning; hopefulness
- Religious faith and affiliations
- Aptitudes and characteristics valued by society (e.g., talent, attractiveness)
- Prosocial friends
- Socioeconomic advantages
- Effective school, a sense of connectedness to school
- Effective community (e.g., safe, with emergency services, recreation centers, options for young people).

This list suggests protective processes that explain human adaptation and resilience. Some of these factors clearly reside within the adolescent (e.g., cognitive abilities and executive functioning), some reside within the family or close relationships (e.g., effective parenting, connectedness to prosocial others), and some are embedded in community or cultural contexts (e.g., good schools). These pervasive predictors of resilience imply fundamental protective systems for human adaptation and development that can enhance capacity for resilience when confronted with various adversities. Thus, resilience rarely requires extraordinary resources, but instead emerges from interactions among basic adaptive systems that foster and protect human development. Beneath this observation is the challenging fact, arising from research and evaluation studies, that not all individuals, groups, or systems respond in the same way to risk and protective factors, and varying levels of intensity are needed in order for protective factors to have positive effects, based on the intensity of risk exposure, and normal variation that is inherent in all human beings and social groups.

Discontinuities in Research

Many forces in the lives of young people show similar patterns – maltreatment hurts all children and good parenting benefits all youth. However, several social mechanisms remain highly significant in some contexts, but prove unimportant under different circumstances. For example, some experiences perceived by preschool children as highly stressful, such as admission into a hospital, remain associated with much less stress for older children. Researchers have identified optimism as a correlate of life satisfaction and low depression among whites, but not among Asians. In some instances, the same process may actually reflect antithetical patterns in different samples. In general, among mainstream youth in low-risk settings, parental strictness represents a detrimental influence that inappropriately inhibits and produces guilt in adolescents. However, maternal behaviors that undermine a young person's autonomy often benefit inner-city youth living in high-risk environments who may experience overprotective behaviors as expressions of care and concern that increase a sense of safety.

Though many investigators identify high intelligence and an easy temperament as protective factors associated with resilience in youth, some research distinguishes these characteristics as vulnerability factors. Benefits of intelligence may vary depending on environmental conditions. Some researchers have found that among low-income adolescents, intelligence did not create protective effects. Instead, more intelligent young people exhibited more sensitivity than others to negative environmental forces. Facing low levels of stress, intelligent adolescents performed much better in school than did less intelligent youth. However, under conditions of high stress, more intelligent youth showed competence levels similar to those of their less intelligent counterparts.

Research on temperament discovered similar discrepancies. In many situations, 'difficult' children elicit more criticism and hostility from parents than 'easy-tempered' children who elicit more positive parent–child interactions. One attribute that can elicit more negative responses from parents is high levels of activity, related to both sleep patterns and play. Highly active infants can exhaust parents. But in another context, high activity levels can elicit positive responses from adults. For example, highly active infants in a poor-quality institution fared better than less active infants because their activity elicited stimulating interactions with staff. Likewise, studies show that children with temperaments that produce little behavioral reaction to stress (therefore considered a more 'easy' child) may respond to stressful situations with negative affect or depressive symptoms.

Distress Among Resilient Youth

Competence and intellectual functioning among resilient youth may function as vulnerability factors, protective factors, or both. Considerable research indicates that young people functioning well in stressful circumstances often show higher levels of emotional distress, compared to their peers experiencing low stress. For example, investigators found that very competent children and adolescents in high-risk environments performed worse on measures of mental health and school achievement than less competent youth in low-risk environments. Resilient youth may manifest effects of stress associated with experiencing adversity and challenge in more developmentally 'advanced' internalizing symptoms. Thus, even if a young person's behavior appears resilient, he or she may struggle with inner distress such as depression or anxiety. Typically, these 'quietly disturbed' young people capture the attention of adults less frequently than youth engaged in externalizing, acting-out behaviors.

These findings indicate that unlike the early concept of the invincible or invulnerable child, severe life stresses and adversity will likely show some kind of impact. Experiencing high stress, some young people may react with emotional distress as well as behavioral difficulties. Others may feel depressed and/or anxious, but still function well and meet societal expectations, since some youth can successfully cope with challenging environments despite experiencing distressing emotions. In fact, the highest form of resilience may constitute the capacity to maintain competence despite significant inner distress.

Variation is inevitable. Resilience never represents an 'across-the-board' phenomenon. Resilient young people and youth in general do not exhibit uniformly positive or negative adaptation on all measures, for all outcomes. Accordingly, scientists have started to distinguish specific domains in which youth demonstrate resilience by using such terms as academic resilience, social resilience, or emotional resilience. Because resilient youth may experience distress, and untreated depression or anxiety can derail the life trajectory of these young people, intervention efforts should consider the unique profile of each adolescent. Interventions must meet the needs of youth who demonstrate behavioral competence, yet remain psychologically vulnerable. Admittedly, this task of tailoring interventions to the specific qualities and characteristics of individual young people is enormously complex, requiring time, capital, and human investments that can easily exceed the capacities of programs or services to be responsive in this way.

Promoting Resilience in Youth

Protective processes identified in the study of resilience can inform development of targeted interventions. An approach to prevention and promotion of healthy youth development focused on resilience emphasizes building skills and capacities that facilitate young people's capacity to successfully negotiate high-risk environments. Specifically, individuals may promote resilience in youth through three major avenues: (1) reducing risk exposure, (2) increasing resources and assets, and (3) mobilizing and facilitating powerful protective systems. Frequently, efforts can prevent or reduce young people's exposure to risk or adversity. Such activities may involve providing good prenatal care, reducing neighborhood violence, or preventing bullying at school. Even in the presence of risks, efforts can increase protective factors and resources, or enhance their effectiveness, to offset risk. For example, schools may provide students meals, health care services, computers, books, tutors, and competent teachers with the talents and capacities to connect well with their students. Researchers can also direct intervention efforts at powerful adaptive systems by promoting their development or restoring their function. Examples include developing programs to improve parent–child or teacher–student relationships, helping and supporting parents going through a divorce to facilitate positive outcomes for their children, and promoting self-regulation among youth to enhance school success. Increasingly, the strategy of resilience-focused programs is grounded in a 'dual strategy' approach of reducing risk while enhancing protective factors. The following are examples of this kind of approach.

Seattle Social Development Project

Researchers at the University of Washington initiated the Seattle Social Development Project (SSDP) in 1981 to reduce childhood risk factors associated with school failure, drug abuse, and delinquency. SSDP included a three-part intervention for teachers, students, and parents in grades 1–6 in public schools located in high-crime areas. Researchers designed interventions to reduce risks and increase protection at the individual, peer, family, and school levels. Teachers in intervention classrooms received training on proactive classroom management, interactive teaching, and cooperative learning. Proactive classroom management emphasized clear standards and expectations for behavior and participation. Interactive teaching methods enhanced teachers' abilities to design lesson plans that motivate students and to monitor learning. Cooperative learning addressed commitment to school, positive peer influences, and recognition of student progress. Children in the intervention group received training in Grade 1 to enhance cognitive, social, emotional, and behavioral skills. In grade 6, they developed and practiced skills recognizing and resisting social influences to engage in problem behaviors, and to generate and suggest possible alternatives to such behavior, while maintaining friendships. Finally, parent training enhanced skills in managing difficult child behavior, supporting academic achievement, and reducing risks for child substance use.

At age 18, 6 years after the intervention, compared to control students, fewer youth in the intervention group reported violent delinquent acts, heavy drinking, sexual intercourse, having multiple sex partners, and a pregnancy or causing a pregnancy. Intervention participants also reported greater commitment and attachment to school, better academic achievement, and less school misbehavior than those of control students. The intervention group showed significantly greater bonding to school than that of the control group at ages 13 and 18. Thus, researchers hypothesized that enhanced school bonding during the secondary school years mediated relationships between the intervention and health behavior outcomes observed during adolescence. Further, at age 21, 9 years after the intervention ended, the intervention continued to produce broad effects on positive functioning in school and at work, emotional and mental health, as well as reductions in criminal behavior. These findings suggest that early and continued, multifaceted interventions can guide children on a positive developmental path that youth maintain throughout adolescence into early adulthood.

Fast Track Project

Fast Track is a comprehensive 10-year intervention project targeting children at risk for conduct disorders to prevent serious antisocial behavior and related problems. Researchers identified three successive cohorts (1991, 1992, and 1993) of high-risk children in kindergarten at four sites across the United States. The program extended from first through tenth grade, and provided interventions at the family, child, classroom, peer group, and school levels. During elementary school (grades 1–5), the intervention included a universal teacher-led classroom curriculum designed to increase social and emotional competence by developing emotional awareness and understanding, peer-related social skills, social problem-solving, and self-control. Further, high-risk youth and their families received five additional programs: (1) parent training to promote positive family–school relationships and to teach parents skills to manage difficult child behavior; (2) home visits to foster parents' problem-solving skills, self-efficacy, and life-management skills; (3) child social skills training; (4) child tutoring in reading; and (5) child friendship enhancement in the classroom.

The adolescent phase of the intervention program (grades 6–10) addressed four core domains associated with successful adolescent adjustment: (1) peer affiliation and influence, (2) academic achievement and orientation, (3) social cognition and identity development, and (4) parent and family relations. The program included standard and individualized activities for high-risk youth and their families. Individualized services sought to strengthen protective factors and reduce risk factors in areas of particular need for each youth, and included academic tutoring, mentoring, support for positive peer-group involvement, home visiting and family problem-solving, and liaisons with school and community agencies.

Children and parents receiving intervention services showed multiple improved competencies. Compared to the control group, children in the intervention group demonstrated improved social, cognitive, and academic skills, and their parents showed reduced use of harsh discipline. Intervention effects were reflected in behavioral improvements during the elementary school years and beyond. During elementary school, compared to youth in the control group, children in the intervention group displayed significantly less aggressive behavior at home, in the classroom, and on the playground; a greater percentage became free of conduct problems or showed a developmental trajectory of decreasing conduct problems; and fewer youth were placed in special education. Group differences continued through adolescence. By eighth grade, fewer intervention group boys had arrest records. Psychiatric interviews with intervention participants after ninth grade indicated that the intervention reduced serious conduct disorder by over one-third. Success of Fast Track resulted in the program's implementation in several school systems across the United States, as well as schools in Great Britain, Australia, and Canada.

Chicago Child–Parent Center Program

The Child–Parent Center Program (CPC) was established in 1967 through funding from Title I of the Elementary and Secondary Education Act (1965). This school-based preschool and early school-age intervention provides comprehensive educational and family support services to economically disadvantaged children living in high-poverty neighborhoods. The program emphasizes parent involvement and the development of literacy skills. CPC's guiding assumption exhorts that a stable and enriched learning environment during early childhood (ages 3–9) is integral to school success.

Evaluation studies found that relative to children in a matched comparison group, participants in the CPC program showed higher rates of high school completion, more years of completed education, lower rates of school dropout, and lower rates of juvenile arrest for violent and nonviolent charges. Time spent in the program showed direct effects on academic achievement. Relative to children with less extensive participation in CPC, children who participated from preschool through the second or third grade experienced lower rates of grade retention in grades K-12 and were less often classified as needing school remedial services. The CPC program had the strongest effect on boys. The group of predominantly African American males involved in CPC experienced a 47% higher rate of high school completion than males in the comparison group. Key factors contributing to the success of the CPC program included early intervention, parent and community involvement, program continuity/long-term support, and individualized attention/small classes.

Advocacy for Life and Learning in Youth (RALLY)

Harvard University's RALLY Program represents a school- and after-school-based, inclusive model of intervention and prevention designed to build middle school students' competence and resilience through relationships with positive adults. The program emphasizes helping young people build academic, social, and psychological strengths. The RALLY approach defines five goals and principles: (1) facilitate young people's development, resiliency, and academic success; (2) establish a variety of relationships and opportunities shown to support resilience, developmental growth, and academic success; (3) connect the diverse worlds of school, after-school, family life, and community; (4) integrate mental health, youth development, and education to reduce fragmentation among service systems and stigma of participation in intervention and prevention activities by involving *all* students; and (5) provide a system of early detection to support students' needs as early and intensively as necessary. RALLY employs 'prevention practitioners' to address the educational, mental health, and physical health needs of students and families. These developmental specialists focus on three primary areas: building relationships with and supporting students, linking a child's different worlds, and providing academic support in classrooms.

RALLY defines a three-tiered model of intervention and prevention for all students by differentiating between high-intensity (Tier 1), targeted (Tier 2), and inclusive (Tier 3) students. Tier 1 students are considered high-risk for behaviors such as aggression, academic failure, drop-out, depression, early sexual activity, or substance use. RALLY practitioners provide these youth with weekly individualized tutoring or mentoring and academic support, and interact regularly with their parents or guardians. Rather than removing Tier 1 students from their normal environment to procure services and assistance, practitioners bring a network of services to schools so these youth may remain in their regular environments and achieve success. Students are selected for Tier 2 if they show early signs of high-risk behavior. Prevention practitioners provide Tier 2 students with targeted interventions such as academic or support groups, crisis intervention, after-school programs, and referrals for mental and physical health services. Tier 3 comprises entire classrooms or all students not assigned to Tiers 1 or 2. Practitioners' time with Tier 3 students involves briefly checking-in to provide youth an opportunity to discuss their achievements or concerns and a space to develop trusting relationships with practitioners.

Evaluation of the RALLY Program did not involve a comparably rigorous design as used in evaluation of the preceding programs. Nonetheless, RALLY produced selected positive effects on academic outcomes such as doing schoolwork and thinking about life and the future. Also, students showed increases in empathy, trust, peer support, and emotion regulation skills. Thus, the program positively impacted participants' resiliency and social-emotional competencies as perceived by students, practitioners, and teachers; practitioners and teachers also reported decreases in behavioral problems.

Future Research

The future of resilience research will include combining psychosocial and biological approaches to examine biopsychosocial pathways of resilience. To date, most research has focused on social and psychological variables. However, building on more recent advances in neuroscience as well as in assessment technology, researchers now have an increased capacity to consider biological factors as mediators of risk, and as processes underlying vulnerability and protective factors. Identifying genes that contribute to protection or vulnerability and that moderate associations between adversity and competence will open further avenues of research for interdisciplinary teams that have the capacity to undertake and evaluate complex, multidimensional, and long-term interventions. Studying psychobiological reactions to stress will also inform resilience research. Questions to consider in future investigations may include the following: Do stressful or challenging tasks activate different areas of the brain among competent and noncompetent youth; and do resilient and nonresilient youth who experience the same type and level of adversity show different patterns of brain structure and functioning?

In addition, exploring gene–environment interactions to enhance the identification and description of risk, vulnerability, and protection processes comprises another broad area of inquiry. Studying gene–environment interactions involves identifying genes as well as specific environmental factors that contribute to resilience. Future work in this area may involve (1) examining the relative contributions of genetic versus environmental influences regarding the operation of different protective and vulnerability factors; (2) understanding mechanisms involved in each of these operations; and (3) identifying genetic markers that confer protection or vulnerability and describing processes underlying their effects. Future research may examine in greater depth the interplay of nature and nurture in development by elucidating how chronic and severe adversity shape brain development, personality, and cognitive development, as well as how biological factors affect psychological processes. Researchers studying resilience will remain interested in atypical outcomes, in understanding success or difficulty contrary to expectation. Therefore, investigators will want to explain the mechanisms that contribute to positive development despite genetic liabilities and risk, as well as the mechanisms involved in adverse developmental outcomes despite favorable genes and conditions.

Another area of future research involves disentangling the specific pathways or the mechanisms that contribute to competence and confidence in young people, such as intelligence and positive parenting. The field would benefit from interdisciplinary research that identifies how specific protective factors impact different aspects of successful outcome, as well as adaptation in different environments or among particular subgroups. Such research would enhance the understanding of 'context-specific' protective and vulnerability processes in child development and help to answer the ongoing and very complex questions around which opportunities, resources, and experiences work best, with whom, when, at what intensity, and for what period of time. Other domains requiring further investigation include identifying additional personal characteristics that facilitate resilience such as practical and emotional intelligence; exploring processes and capacities underlying skill development (e.g., capacities that aid in learning); and examining the social-cognitive constructs associated with resilience such as empathy, altruism, personal authenticity, hope, optimism, and 'flow.' Intervention research may focus on exploring the effectiveness of attachment-based interventions in schools; illuminating factors that enable teachers to cultivate the best in their high-risk students; using positive peer relationships to foster resilience; and developing strong networks among parents, school personnel, and neighborhood groups.

The perspective of social epidemiology and the role of social capital also warrant further consideration in resilience research focused on young people. Social epidemiology examines the social determinants of health, specifically the processes through which societal conditions affect health and well-being. Social capital refers to connections within and between social networks with the understanding that the quality of social networks, support, and the structure of opportunity within neighborhoods and communities contribute to resilience and vulnerability. The application of these perspectives to resilience also invites intelligent debate on the underlying political questions raised by resilience research: how much attention should be devoted to helping young people adapt to stressful social contexts? What is the proper role of seeking social change and contextual transformations that will make environments more conducive to life, health, and growth? How can successful approaches to enhancing resilience, healthy development, and well-being be sustained in the face of competing agendas and constrained resources?

These questions, the burgeoning interest in resilience, and the use of the dual strategy of risk reduction and enhancement of protective factors through clinical-, school-, and community-based programs and policies, suggest that the concept of resilience will generate considerable attention and interest for a long time. An idea once grounded in the physical sciences has become central to the work of scholars and practitioners across a variety of disciplines. Pioneers, who decades ago challenged risk-focused paradigms of inquiry, have created the framework for exciting and innovative work that is still unfolding, with great promise for promoting and protecting the healthy development and life chances of young people.

See also: Coping; Modes of Intervention; Personality Traits in Adolescence; Social Competence; Social Support.

Further Reading

Luthar SS (2006) Resilience in development: A synthesis of research across five decades. In: Cicchetti D and Cohens D (eds.) *Developmental Psychopathology: Risk, Disorder, and Adaptation*, 3rd edn. Hoboken, NJ: Wiley.

Masten AS (2007) Resilience in developing systems: Progress and promise as the fourth wave rises. *Development and Psychopathology* 19: 921–930.

Masten AS (2009) Ordinary magic: Lessons from research on resilience in human development. *Education Canada* 49: 28–32.

Olsson CA, Bond L, Burns JM, Bella-Brodrick DA, and Sawyer SM (2003) Adolescent resilience: A concept analysis. *Journal of Adolescence* 29: 1–11.

Resnick MD (2000) Protective factors, resiliency and healthy youth development. *Adolescent Medicine: State of the Art Reviews* 11(1): 157–164.

Rew L and Horner SD (2003) Youth resilience framework for reducing health-risk behaviors in adolescents. *Journal of Pediatric Nursing* 18: 379–388.

Rink E and Tricker R (2005) Promoting health behaviors among adolescents: A review of the resiliency literature. *American Journal of Health Studies* 20: 39–46.

Rutter M (1990) Psychosocial resilience and protective mechanisms. In: Rolf J, Masten A, Cicchetti D, Nuechterlein K, and Weintraub S (eds.) *Risk and Protective Factors in the Development of Psychopathology*. New York, NY: Cambridge University Press.

Rutter M (2006) Implications of resilience concepts for scientific understanding. *Annals of the New York Academy of Science* 1094: 1–12.

Sameroff AJ and Rosenblum KL (2006) Psychosocial constraints on the development of resilience. *Annals of the New York Academy of Science* 1094: 116–124.

Werner EE (2000) Protective factors and individual resilience. In: Shonkoff J and Meisels S (eds.) *Handbook of Early Childhood Intervention*, 2nd edn. Melbourne, Australia: Cambridge University Press.

Werner EE and Smith RS (1992) *Overcoming the Odds: High Risk Children from Birth to Adulthood*. Ithaca, NY: Cornell University Press.

Self-Development During Adolescence

S Harter, University of Denver, Denver, CO, USA

Glossary

Intrapsychic conflict: The perception that contradictions within one's personality, for example, cheerful versus depressed, cause concern and distress.

I-self: Those cognitive processes that define how the individual thinks about the self, processes that change with the substages of adolescent development.

Me-self: The object of one's thinking about the self, self-descriptions and self-evaluations such as domain-specific self-concepts and global self-esteem.

Self-concept: An evaluation of one's performance in specific domains such as scholastic competence, social acceptance, and physical appearance.

Self-esteem: An evaluation of one's overall worth as a person.

Introduction

'Adolescence'. It is instructive to first inquire into the origin of this designation that defines the ranks of millions of teenagers. The term 'adolescence' is derived from two Latin parts of speech, 'ad,' which means 'to' or 'toward,' and 'olescere,' which means 'to grow.' Thus, adolescence is the period during which teenagers are *growing toward* adulthood. In thinking about this developmental trajectory, what are the psychological stepping stones along that path of *self* development?

In addressing these questions, it is useful to conceptualize adolescence *not* as a single stage, the typical textbook presentation. Rather it is more fruitful, and faithful to the adolescent's experience, to delineate three substages, early adolescence, mid-adolescence, and late adolescence. In this article, I describe how the self evolves over these three substages of adolescence, highlighting three different themes:

a. I first describe the *normative developmental features* of self-description and self-evaluation. These features include the salient content of the self, the organization of self-constructs, the valence and accuracy of self-representations, the nature of social comparisons in forming self-judgments, and sensitivity to others as sources of information that may be relevant to self-representations. Given that the self is not only a *cognitive* construction but a *social* construction crafted in the crucible of interactions with significant others, normative developmental manifestations of the self will necessarily be affected by the socialization of parents and peers, to name the two key influences.
b. Second, I describe the *normative-developmental liabilities* at each substage. The very fabric of development involves advances to new stages that may bring with them normative liabilities that should *not* be interpreted as pathological, liabilities that will dissipate as even more advanced developmental skills are acquired. Movement to a new stage of cognitive development produces numerous liabilities given that the individual is not yet facile at exercising or controlling new cognitive acquisitions. Consider the analogy to learning athletic skills. The novice typically overhits or underhits a ball, in many sports. Just as it takes practice to hone physical skills so it takes mental exercise to perfect cognitive abilities.
c. Third, I indicate how at each developmental substage more serious forms of *psychopathology* may emerge given that self-development can be seriously derailed particularly due to socialization influences. These are to be distinguished from normative-developmental liabilities in their severity and the extent to which they compromise the functioning of the adolescent at each period; they are also more resistant to change. These characteristics will take us into the realm of clinical interpretation and intervention.

The I-Self and the Me-Self

In addressing these themes, this article, in places, draws upon a distinction between the I-self and the Me-self. The majority of scholars who have devoted thoughtful attention to the self have come to a similar conclusion: Two distinct but

 doi:10.1016/B978-0-12-373915-5.00036-X

intertwined aspects of the self can be meaningfully identified, self as subject (the I-self) and self as object (the Me-self). William James, a prominent historical scholar of the self first introduced this distinction. He defined the I-self as the active knower, whereas the Me-self was the object of one's knowledge. Think of the mirror as providing one metaphor. The I-self is you, the observer, the perceiver, the thinker, who gazes into the physical or psychological mirror. The Me-self is the image of you in the mirror. The Me-self is more than your observed physical characteristics, but includes your psychological attributes, most notably, those that define the self. The distinction between the I-self and the Me-self has proved amazingly viable and appears as a recurrent theme in most treatments of the self.

Until the past decade, major empirical attention had been devoted to the Me-self as reflected in self-descriptions and self-evaluations. More recently, the I-self has become more prominent in accounts of self-development. Both the structure and content of the Me-self at any given developmental level necessarily depend upon the particular I-self capabilities, namely, those cognitive processes that define the knower. Thus, the cognitive-developmental changes in I-self processes will directly influence the nature of the self-theory that the adolescent constructs.

Developmental Differences in Self-Representations During Adolescence

The period of adolescence represents a dramatic developmental transition, given pubertal and related physical changes, cognitive-developmental advances, and changing social expectations. Cognitively, adolescents develop the ability to think abstractly and to think about the contents of their thoughts, for example, "what am I really like?" Piaget, the foremost cognitive-developmental psychologist of the twentieth century, described how the capacity to form abstractions emerged in early adolescence. These newfound acquisitions, according to Piaget, should equip the adolescent with the skills to create a formal theory. This observation is critical to self-development, given that many personality theorists have claimed that the self is a theory, a personal epistemology, a cognitive construction. From this perspective, a theory of the self should meet those criteria by which any good theory is evaluated, namely, the degree to which it is parsimonious, empirically valid, internally consistent, coherently organized, testable, and useful. For Piaget, entry into adolescence should make the construction of such a theory possible, be it a theory about elements in the world or a theory about the self.

However, as will become apparent, the self-representations during early and middle adolescence fall far short of these criteria. They are not coherently organized, nor are the postulates of the self-portrait internally consistent. Moreover, many self-attributes fail to be subjected to tests of empirical validity; as a result, they can be extremely unrealistic. Nor are self-representations particularly parsimonious. Thus, Piaget's framework fails to provide an adequate explanation for the dramatic developmental changes in the self-representations that can be observed across the substages of adolescence. Rather, a neo-Piagetian approach is needed, meaning that one must understand how cognitive-developmental changes in I-self processes result in very different Me-self organization and content at each three age levels: early adolescence, mid-adolescence, and late adolescence. For each substage, I first describe the normative-developmental changes in self-representations and self-evaluations, after which the normative liabilities of each period will be explored, followed by pathological implications.

Early Adolescence

Verbal Cameo of Normative Self-Representations and Self-Evaluations

> I'm an extrovert with my friends: I'm talkative, pretty rowdy, and funny. I'm fairly good-looking if I do say so. All in all, around people I know pretty well I'm awesome, at least I think my friends think I am. I'm usually cheerful when I'm with my friends, happy and excited to be doing things with them. I like myself a lot when I'm around my friends. With my parents, I'm more likely to be depressed. I feel sad as well as mad and also hopeless about ever pleasing them. They think I spend too much time at the mall with my friends, and that I don't do enough to help out at home. They tell me I'm lazy and not very responsible, and it's hard not to believe them. I get real sarcastic when they get on my case. It makes me dislike myself as a person. At school, I'm pretty intelligent. I know that because I'm smart when it comes to how I do in classes, I'm curious about learning new things, and I'm also creative when it comes to solving problems. My teacher says so. I get better grades than most, but I don't brag about it because that's not cool. I can be a real introvert around people I don't know well. I'm shy, uncomfortable, and nervous. Sometimes I'm simply an airhead. I act really dumb and say things that are just plain stupid. Then I worry about what they must think of me, probably that I'm a total dork. I just hate myself when that happens.

With regard to the *content* of the self-portraits of young adolescents, interpersonal attributes and social skills that influence interactions with others or one's social appeal are typically quite salient. Thus, our prototypical young adolescent admits to being talkative, rowdy, funny, good-looking, and downright awesome. Presumably, these characteristics enhance one's acceptance by peers. In addition to social attributes, self-representations also focus on competencies such as one's scholastic abilities (e.g., 'I'm intelligent'), as well as emotions (e.g., 'I'm cheerful' and 'I'm depressed').

From a developmental perspective, there is considerable evidence that the self becomes increasingly differentiated. During adolescence, there is a proliferation of selves that vary as a function of social context. These include the self with father, mother, close friends, romantic partners, and peers, as well as the self in the role of student, on the job, and as an athlete. As the cameo reveals, the adolescent may be cheerful and rowdyish with friends, depressed and sarcastic with parents, intelligent, curious, and creative as a student, and shy and uncomfortable around people whom one does not know. A critical developmental task, therefore, is the construction of multiple selves that will undoubtedly vary across different roles and relationships.

Both cognitive and social processes contribute to this proliferation of selves. Cognitive-developmental advances described earlier promote greater differentiation. Moreover, these advances conspire with socialization pressures to develop different selves in different relational contexts. For example, bids for autonomy from parents make it important to define oneself differently with peers and parents. As one moves through adolescence, one is more likely to be treated differently by those in different relational contexts.

Many of the self-descriptions in early adolescence represent abstractions about the self, based upon the new-found cognitive ability to integrate trait labels into higher-order self-concepts. For example, as the prototypical adolescent reveals, one can construct an abstraction of the self as 'intelligent,' combining such traits as smart, curious, and creative. Alternatively, one may create an abstraction that the self is an 'airhead' given situations where one feels dumb and 'just plain stupid.' Similarly, an adolescent could construct an abstraction that he/she is an 'extrovert' (integrating the traits of rowdy, talkative, and funny) as well as an 'introvert' in certain situations (when one is shy, uncomfortable, and nervous). With regard to emotion concepts, one can be depressed in some contexts (combining sad, mad, and hopeless) as well as cheerful in others (combining happy and excited). Thus, abstractions represent more cognitively complex concepts about the self in which various trait labels can now be appropriately integrated into even higher-order generalizations.

Although the ability to construct such abstractions reflects a cognitive advance, these representations are highly *compartmentalized*; that is, they are quite distinct from one another. Therefore, the young adolescent can only think about each of them as isolated self-attributes, one at a time. The young adolescent lacks the ability to *integrate* the many single abstractions that are constructed to define the self in different relational contexts. As a result, adolescents will engage in black and white thinking, isolating attributes in their conscious self-portrait. Fragmentation of self-representations at this period is the rule rather than the exception.

Another manifestation of these compartmentalized abstract attributes can be observed in the tendency for the young adolescent to be unconcerned about the fact that across different roles, certain self-descriptors are potentially inconsistent, as the prototypical self-description implies (in contrast to middle adolescence where there is considerable concern.) However, during early adolescence, the inability to integrate seemingly contradictory characteristics of the self (intelligent vs. airhead, extrovert vs. introvert, depressed vs. cheerful) has the psychological advantage of sparing the adolescent conflict over opposing attributes in his/her self-theory.

Interview research by Harter has pointed out to young adolescents the potential contradictions in their self-attributes that they did not detect in constructing their self-portrait. As one young adolescent put it, when confronted with his self-descriptors indicating that he was both caring and rude, "Well, you are caring with your friends and rude to people who don't treat you nicely. There's no problem. I just think about one thing about myself at a time and don't think about the other until the next day." When another young adolescent was asked why opposite attributes did not bother her, she succinctly exclaimed, "That's a stupid question. I don't fight with myself!" As will become apparent, this pattern changes dramatically during middle adolescence.

The differentiation of role-related selves can also be observed in the tendency to report differing levels of self-esteem across relational contexts. In the prototypical cameo, the young adolescent reports that with friends, "I like myself a lot"; however with parents, I "dislike myself as a person." Around "people I don't know well, I just hate myself." Although the concept of self-esteem is typically reserved for perceptions of global self-esteem, Harter's research has introduced the construct of relational self-esteem, which differs across relationships.

Within the social realm, young adolescents often compare themselves to others. However, during early adolescence, there is a shift from more conspicuous to more subtle forms of social comparison as they become more aware of the negative social consequences of overt comparisons; for example, they may be accused of boasting about their superior performance. As the prototypical young adolescent describes in the cameo, "I get better grades than most, but I don't brag about it because that's not cool."

Normative Liabilities of Self-Development During Early Adolescence

As with the entry into any new developmental level, there are liabilities associated with emerging self-processes. For example, although abstractions are developmentally advanced cognitive structures, they are removed from concrete, observable behaviors and therefore more susceptible to *distortion*. The adolescent's self-concept, therefore, becomes more difficult to verify and is often less realistic. When the self becomes a collection of abstractions, uncertainties are introduced, since there are few objective and unambiguous facts about one's various self-attributes. Although the young adolescent may have multiple hypotheses about the self, he/she does not yet possess the ability to correctly deduce which are true, leading to distortions in self-perceptions. This also contributes to vacillating and unrealistic self-perceptions in which at one point in time, one may feel totally intellectually awesome, whereas at another point, one may feel like a total dork. Thus, vacillations cause the young adolescent to question which is the 'real me,' raising questions about the nature of his/her true self.

Finally, there are normative liabilities that are associated with educational transitions. Most adolescents shift from an elementary school to either a middle school or junior high school that typically draws upon several elementary feeder schools. Thus, they must now move into a group of peers, many of whom they have previously not known. Certain educational practices represent a mismatch given the adolescent's needs. At a time when young adolescents are painfully self-conscious, the school system heightens social comparison, for example, publicizing each student's performance, which can diminish one's sense of self. Moreover, in middle and junior high schools, poorer performance is attributed to lack of scholastic *ability* (as opposed to effort in the elementary school setting), leading many young adolescents to feel that they do not have the aptitude or intelligence to succeed.

Pathological Self-Processes and Outcomes During Early Adolescence

Beginning in early adolescence, there is a heightened concern with how *others* view the self. This represents a normative process articulated by another historical scholar of the self,

Charles Horton Cooley, who described the 'looking glass self,' in which others are the social mirrors into which we gaze for information about how others view the self. If significant others provide support for those attributes that the young adolescent feels truly define the self, then one will experience the self as authentic. However, the construction of a self that is too highly dependent upon capitulating to the demands of others can lead to the creation of a false self that does not mirror one's authentic experience. It is noteworthy that not until early adolescence does the concept of acting as a false self becomes salient in the consciousness of young teenagers.

False self behavior is particularly likely to emerge if parents make their approval contingent upon the young adolescent living up to unattainable standards of behavior. This phenomenon, labeled 'conditional support,' is somewhat of a misnomer because adolescents do not perceive conditionality, in the face of unrealistic demands, to be 'supportive.' Rather, it reflects the psychological hoops through which young adolescents must jump in order to conform to the parental agenda. They learn to suppress their true-self attributes, in a desperate attempt to garner the needed approval from parental caretakers. Those experiencing high levels of parental conditionality express hopelessness and low levels of self-esteem and depression. Furthermore, chronic and severe abuse, with its origins in childhood, puts one at even more extreme risk for suppressing one's true self, leading to various displays of false-self behavior.

There are other dynamics that represent barriers to authenticity among victims of abuse. They may develop a malignant sense of inner badness that is often camouflaged by the abused child's persistent attempts to be good. If one's true self, corroded with inner badness, were to be revealed, it would be met with scorn and contempt. Therefore, it must be concealed at all costs. Although these dynamics are observed in childhood, beginning in adolescence there is much more conscious awareness that one is being false or phony, which exacerbates feelings of low self-esteem, hopelessness, depression, and in some, suicidality.

A larger model of the determinants, correlates, and consequences of self-esteem

An overall model of these processes (see **Figure 1**) becomes increasingly relevant at early adolescence and beyond (see Harter studies). Findings reveal that lack of both parental support and peer support can lead to pathological levels of low self-worth, depressed affect, and hopelessness, that in turn may provoke suicidal ideation if not suicidal behaviors.

The peer culture looms large in adolescence. Peer support and approval, or its absence, is a powerful predictor of the depression/adjustment composite that includes self-esteem, affect/mood, along a continuum of depressed to cheerful, hope (hopeless to hopeful), that predicts suicidal thinking. Lack of peer approval is more directly linked to perceived inadequacies in the domains of physical appearance, likability by peers, and athletic competence. That said, parental support does *not* decline in importance during adolescence. Previous textbook portrayals of adolescence imply that parental influences decline as one moves into adolescence. However, nothing is further from the truth when one examines the impact of parental support on self-esteem, hopelessness, and depression.

Peer rejection, humiliation, and implications for the high-profile school shootings

The role of peer *rejection*, not merely the lack of peer approval, is telling. In Harter's studies, initial interest in peer rejection began with an analysis of the emerging profiles of the, now, 12 high-profile cases of school shootings by white, middle-class, male older children and adolescents, from small cities or suburbs. They have gone on shooting sprees killing peers, and in a few cases, school officials who were random victims, rather than specifically targeted individuals. What became evident, in the analysis of media reports, is that all of these male youth killers had a history of peer rejection and *humiliation*. Surprisingly, there is virtually no literature on humiliation. Yet, humiliation is a daily event in most schools and neighborhoods. For the school shooters, extreme feelings of chronic humiliation by peers, due to excessive teasing, taunting, and physical insults eventually led them to psychologically 'snap,' provoking random deaths and, in the case of the Columbine teens, to suicide.

An examination of the media accounts of the school shooters made it obvious that many of the determinants in the model could be found in the lives of these adolescents. They displayed inadequacies in the domains of peer acceptance, athletic ability, and scholastic competence. They experienced low peer and parental approach, exhibited low self-esteem, and

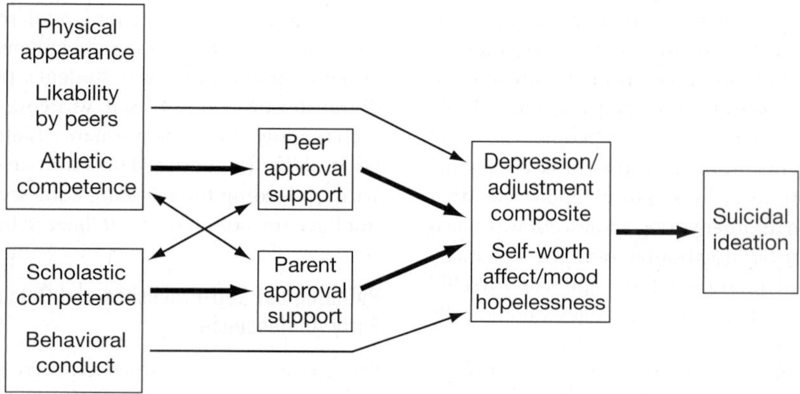

Figure 1 General model of the predictors of depression/adjustment.

were hopeless about their future, and often depressed. Some experienced suicidal tendencies. Thus, humiliation can put one at pathological risk for endangering not only others' lives but also one's own.

A critical feature of the humiliation experience is the necessary role of an *audience* where observers laugh at the victim, often joining in the harassment and mockery. The bullying literature links such harassment directly to revenge and violence. However, a more thoughtful analysis addresses the critical role of humiliation as a key *emotional* link or mediator between harassment and retaliation.

Pathological eating disordered behavior

One self-concept domain robustly affects global self-esteem across ages within Western cultures, namely, perceived physical appearance or attractiveness. A review of the inextricable link between perceived appearance and self-esteem makes it very apparent that this link is profoundly impacted by cultural standards of appearance for each gender. That our culture touts physical attractiveness as the measure of one's worth as a person has been amply demonstrated in contemporary society, as well as historically. These relationships are not merely statistical but are very much embedded in the consciousness of individuals who are aware of this link. Evidence reveals that those who fervently endorse current cultural values (e.g., being attractive will lead to higher self-esteem, meeting standards of appearance will make people more popular and successful) report more negative views of their appearance, lower self-esteem, and more eating disordered behaviors.

The seeds of these cultural values are sown in early adolescence (if not earlier) as teenagers become well aware of the prevailing norms of attractiveness. For adult females in the 2000s, the standards are punishing. One must be tall, very thin, weigh very little (around 110–115), have ample breasts, and of course a pretty face and an acceptable hair style, an unattainable combination for more than 90% of the female population. What is new within the last two decades is the fact that the bar has been raised for males in our society. No longer is a man's appeal to be judged by his status, wealth, position, and power but by physical standards of attractiveness, as well. Muscular build, abs, biceps, physique, hair, on the head as well as on the face, have all come to define the new ideals for men.

These standards are not lost on young adolescents who experience the futility of their inability to emulate the models, singers, and movie stars in the limelight. Standards of attractiveness become particularly salient during early adolescence as pubertal and social changes that signal impending adulthood. Those not meeting the gold standard are at serious risk for low self-esteem, pathological forms of depression, suicidal thinking, and potentially life-threatening eating disorders.

Middle Adolescence

Verbal Cameo of Normative Self-Representations and Self-Evaluations

What am I like as a person? You're probably not going to understand. I'm complicated! With my really close friends, I am very tolerant. I mean, I'm understanding and caring. With a group of friends, I'm rowdier. I'm also usually friendly and cheerful but I can get pretty obnoxious and intolerant if I don't like how they're acting. I'd like to be friendly and tolerant all of the time, that's the kind of person I want to be, and I'm disappointed in myself when I'm not. At school, I'm serious, even studious every now and then, but on the other hand, I'm a goof-off too, because if you're too studious, you won't be popular. So I go back and forth, which means I don't do all that well in terms of my grades. But that causes problems at home, where I'm pretty anxious when I'm around my parents. They expect me to get all As, and get pretty annoyed with me when report cards come out. I care what they think about me, and so then I get down on myself, but it's not fair! I mean I worry about how I probably should get better grades, but I'd be mortified in the eyes of my friends if I did too well. So, I'm usually pretty stressed-out at home, and can even get very sarcastic, especially when my parents get on my case. But I really don't understand how I can switch so fast from being cheerful with my friends, then coming home and feeling anxious, and then getting frustrated and sarcastic with my parents. Which one is the real me? I have the same question when I'm around boys. Sometimes, I feel phony. Say I think some guy might be interested in asking me out. I try to act different, like Beyonce. I'll be a real extrovert, fun-loving and even flirtatious, and think I am really good-looking. Its important to be good-looking like the models and movie stars. That's what makes you popular. I know in my heart of hearts that I can never look like her, so why do I even try. Its makes me hate myself and feel depressed. Plus, when I try to look and act like her, then everybody, I mean *everybody* else is looking at me like they think I am totally weird! They don't act like they think I'm attractive so I end up thinking I look terrible. I just hate myself when that happens! Because it gets worse! Then I get self-conscious and embarrassed and become radically introverted, and I don't know who I really am! Am I just acting like an extrovert, am I just trying to impress them, when really I'm an introvert! But I don't really care what they think, anyway. I mean I don't want to care, that is. I just want to know what my close friends think. I can be my true self with my close friends. I can't be my real self with my parents. They don't understand me. What do they know about what it's like to be a teenager? They treat me like I'm still a kid. At least at school, people treat you more like you're an adult. That gets confusing, though. I mean, which am I? When you're 15, are you still a kid or an adult? I have a part-time job and the people there treat me like an adult. I want them to approve of me, so I'm very responsible at work, which makes me feel good about myself there. But then I go out with my friends and I get pretty crazy and irresponsible. So, which am I, responsible or irresponsible? How can the same person be both? If my parents knew how immature I act sometimes, they would ground me forever, particularly my father. I'm real distant with him. I'm pretty close to my mother though. But it's hard being distant with one parent and close to the other, especially if we are all together, like talking at dinner. Even though I am close to my mother, I'm still pretty secretive about some things, particularly the things about myself that confuse me. So I think a lot about who is the real me, and sometimes I try to figure it out when I write in my diary, but I can't resolve it. There are days when I wish I could just become immune to myself!

Self-descriptions increase in length, as adolescents become increasingly introspective and morbidly preoccupied with what others think of them. The unreflective self-acceptance of earlier periods of development vanishes, what were formerly unquestioned self-truths now become problematic self-hypotheses. The tortuous search for the self involves a concern with 'who am I,' a task made more difficult given the multiple Me's that crowd the self-landscape. There is a further proliferation of selves as adolescents are able to make finer differentiations; the cameo adolescent describes a self with really close friends (e.g., tolerant) versus with a group of friends (e.g., intolerant) and a self with mother (e.g., close) versus father (e.g., distant). New roles, for example, self at a job, also requires the construction of corresponding new context-specific attributes (e.g., responsible).

Furthermore, additional cognitive I-self processes emerge that give the self-portrait a very different look. Abstractions that define the self are no longer isolated from one another. During mid-adolescence, one acquires the cognitive ability to actively *compare* abstractions, particularly those that involve opposing self-attributes. These opposites can take the form of seemingly contradictory abstractions about the self (e.g., tolerant vs. intolerant, extrovert vs. introvert, responsible vs. irresponsible, good-looking vs. unattractive, as in the cameo).

However, the major limitation at this substage is that the individual cannot yet truly integrate such self-representations in a manner that would resolve these observable (e.g., they cannot yet reconcile their recognition that they are both depressed and cheerful). Therefore, awareness of these opposites causes considerable intrapsychic conflict, confusion, and distress. To illustrate, our prototypical adolescent agonizes over these contradictions: "Am I just acting like an extrovert, am I just trying to impress them, when really I'm an introvert?" "So which am I, responsible or irresponsible? How can the same person be both?"

In addition to such confusion, these seeming contradictions lead to very unstable self-representations that are also cause for concern (e.g., "I don't really understand how I can switch so fast from being cheerful with my friends, then coming home and feeling anxious, and then getting frustrated and sarcastic with my parents. Which one is the real me?"). The creation of multiple selves, coupled with the emerging ability to detect potential contradictions between self-attributes displayed in different roles, naturally ushers in concern over which is the true self.

Normative Liabilities During Middle Adolescence

Mid-adolescence brings a preoccupation with what others think of the self, a task made more challenging given the proliferation of multiple selves. To complicate matters, adolescents falsely assume that others are as preoccupied with their behavior and appearance as they themselves are. As our prototypical respondent exclaims, "Everybody, I mean everybody else is looking at me like they think I am totally weird!" Those overly preoccupied with how multiple others evaluate them are more likely to construct an unrealistic portrait of their true self, a vacillating view of themselves given different messages from significant others that leads them to experience conflict, confusion, and distress. The contradictory feedback that adolescents may receive from different sources will produce volatility in self-esteem.

The penchant for introspection may also contribute to lowered self-esteem in that it facilitates the comparison of one's ideal and real self-concepts. William James described how self-esteem is a product of the comparison between one's perceived adequacies and one's aspirations. If one's ideal self exceeded the perception of one's real self-attributes, then low self-esteem would ensue. A heightened awareness of the discrepancy between how one perceives the self to be in reality (e.g., "I can get pretty obnoxious and intolerant") and how one would ideally like to be (e.g., "I'd like to be friendly and tolerant all of the time. That's the kind of person I want to be, and I'm disappointed in myself when I'm not") can erode self-esteem. The realm of physical appearance is particularly critical. Thus, this adolescent wants to look like Beyonce, knows she does not, and this sets up another painful discrepancy between how she would ideally like to look and how she feels she does look. In reality, she does not value her appearance, which falls far short of the cultural standards for beauty.

Adolescents' lack of realism can also be observed in their penchant to assert that their thoughts and feelings are uniquely experienced, a form of adolescent egocentrism. No one else can possibly understand or experience the ecstasy of their rapture, or the intensity of their despair. Parents are typically singled out in this regard. As the prototypical adolescent exclaims, "My parents don't understand me. What do they know about what it's like to be a teenager?"

The liabilities of this period, therefore, are legion, given the conflict and confusion over contradictory attributes, concern over which characteristics define the true self, distortions in self-perceptions, as well as discrepancies between the real and ideal self-concepts, which can all contribute to lowered self-esteem. An appreciation for these normative processes can help to interpret the unpredictable behaviors, shifting self-evaluations, and mood swings that are observed during this age period. Such displays are less likely to be viewed as intentional or pathological and are more likely to meet with empathy and understanding if normative cognitive-development changes can be invoked as partly responsible. For many parents, as well as other adults working closely with teenagers, their seemingly inexplicable reactions often lead to perplexity, exasperation, and anger, provoking power struggles and altercations that strain the adolescent–adult relationship. The realization that this normative stage will not persist forever may provide temporary comfort to adults who feel beleaguered and ineffectual in dealing with adolescents. Indeed, it gives a more charitable rendering of their behavior.

Pathological Self-Processes and Outcomes in Mid-Adolescence

Female adolescents are more likely to suffer from processes that move into the realm of pathology. An intense preoccupation with attempts to meet the impossible standards of beauty, coupled with very negative perceptions of one's body image, can lead to extremely low self-esteem, depression, and in the extreme, pathological eating disordered behaviors. Dramatic gender differences in both depression and eating disordered behavior of clinical proportions emerge in middle adolescence. Among male adolescents, there is the potential for the escalation of violence, as in the high-profile cases of school shootings by white, middle-class, adolescents is apparent. Intense rejection by peers, at a time when both self-consciousness and the need for approval are so salient, sets the stage for violent ideation that can turn to action. The fragile and vacillating self-structures of this particular period can, in the face of humiliation, lead some adolescent boys to act on their thoughts more impulsively, leading to violence toward others.

While the fragmented self is a normative liability of this period of middle adolescence, those with a history of severe and chronic physical and sexual abuse may lead to pathological outcomes. The continuing effects of abuse on the self-system are legion. From a developmental perspective, a history of abuse can serve to further fragment the fragile multiple selves, provoking a pathological construction of *multiple personalities*. As a result, there is no core self at the helm, there is little communication between multiple personalities, precluding the ability to develop an integrated self. As a result, there is the risk for 'Dissociative Identity Disorders' that represent severe pathological conditions that may require years of treatment.

Late Adolescence

Verbal Cameo of Normative Self-Representations and Self-Evaluations

I'm a pretty conscientious person, particularly when it comes to things like doing my homework. It's important to me because I plan to go to college next year. Eventually I want to go to law school, so developing good study habits and getting top grades are both essential. (My parents would rather I go into teaching, but law is what I want to pursue, I think, I'm not really positive.) Every now and then I get a little lackadaisical and don't complete an assignment as thoroughly or thoughtfully as I could, particularly if our high school has a big football or basketball game that I want to go to with my friends. But that's normal, I mean, you can't just be a total 'grind'. You'd be pretty boring if you were. You have to be flexible. I've also become more religious as I have gotten older, not that I am a saint or anything. Religion gives me a sense of purpose, in the larger scheme of things, and it provides me with personal guidelines for the kind of adult I'd like to be. For example, I'd like to be an ethical person who treats other people fairly. That's the kind of lawyer I'd like to be, too. I don't always live up to that standard; that is, sometimes I do something that doesn't feel that ethical. When that happens, I get a little depressed because I don't like myself as a person. But I tell myself that it's natural to make mistakes, so I don't really question the fact that deep down inside, the real me is a moral person. Basically, I like who I am, so I don't stay depressed for long. Usually, I am pretty upbeat and optimistic. I guess you could say that I'm a moody person. I'm not as popular as a lot of other kids You have to look a certain way, have the right body type, wear the right clothes, to be accepted. At our school, it's the jocks who are looked up to. I've never been very athletic, but you can't be good at everything, let's face it. Being athletic isn't that high on my own list of what is important, even though it is for a lot of kids in our school. I try to think that, anyway. But I don't really care what they think anymore, at least I try to convince myself that I don't. I try to believe that what I think is what counts. After all, I have to live with myself as a person and to respect that person, which I do now, more than a few years ago. I'm pretty much being the kind of person I want to be. I'm doing well at things that are important to me like getting good grades. That's what is probably most important to me right now. Having a lot of friends isn't that important to me. I wouldn't say I was unpopular, though. While I am basically an introvert, especially on a date when I get pretty self-conscious, in the right social situation, like watching a ball game with my friends, I can be pretty extroverted. You have to be adaptive around other people. It would be weird to be the same kind of person on a date and with my friends at a football game! For example, when our team has a winning season and goes to the playoffs, everyone in the whole school is proud, what the team does reflects on all of us. On a date, the feelings are much more intimate, just between you and the other person. As much as I enjoy my high school friends and activities, I'm looking forward to leaving home and going to college, where I can be more independent, although I'm a little ambivalent. I love my parents, and really want to stay connected to them, plus, what they think about me is still important to how I feel about myself as a person. So leaving home will be bittersweet. But sometimes it's hard to be mature around them, particularly around my mom. I feel a lot more grown-up around my dad; he treats me more like an adult. I like that part of me because it feels more like my true self. My mom wants me to grow up, but another part of her wants me to remain 'her little baby'. I'll probably always be somewhat dependent on my parents. How can you escape it? But I'm also looking forward to being on my own.

With regard to the content of the self-representations that emerge in late adolescence, many of the attributes reflect personal beliefs, values, and moral standards inculcated by significant others, that have become internalized, or alternatively, constructed from older adolescents' own experiences. These characteristics are exemplified in the prototypical cameo, where the adolescent expresses the desire to go to college, which requires good grades and discipline in the form of study habits. Although classmates tout athletics as the route to popularity, there is less concern at this age with what others think ("I used to care but now what I think is important"). In addition, there is a focus on one's future self, for example, not only becoming a lawyer, but also an ethical lawyer, as a personal goal. Noteworthy in this narrative is the absence of an explicit reference to the likely *origins* of these goals, for example, parental encouragement or expectations that one pursue a career. That the impact of significant others is not acknowledged suggests that older adolescents have come to 'own' values as personal choices, rather than attribute them to the social sources from which they may have been derived.

Another new feature of the self-portrait of the older adolescent is reflected in that now opposing attributes are no longer described as contradictory characteristics that cause distress. Thus, being conscientious as a student does not appear to conflict with one's lackadaisical attitude toward schoolwork: "That's normal, I mean, you can't just be a total 'grind.' You'd be pretty boring if you were. You have to be flexible." Nor does introversion conflict with extroverted behaviors. "You have to be adaptive around other people. It would be weird to be the same kind of person on a date and with my friends at a football game!"

Cognitive acquisitions allow the older adolescent to overcome some of the liabilities of the previous period, where contradictory attributes caused internal conflict. Cognitive advances promote the construction of integrated, higher-order abstractions. For example, the fact that one is both introverted and extroverted can be integrated through the construction of a higher-order abstraction that defines the self as 'adaptive.' The observation that one is both depressed and cheerful or optimistic can be integrated under the personal rubric of 'moody.' Similarly, the attribution that one is 'flexible' can allow one to coordinate conscientiousness with the tendency to be lackadaisical. The higher-order concept of 'ambivalence' integrates the desire to be independent yet still remain connected to parents. Moreover, 'bittersweet' reflects a higher-order abstraction combining both excitement over going to college and sadness over leaving parents. Such higher-order abstractions provide new self-labels that bring meaning and therefore legitimacy to what formerly appeared to be troublesome contradictions within the self.

Finally, evidence from longitudinal studies reveals that self-esteem improves in later adolescence. Several interpretations of these gains have been suggested. Reductions in the discrepancy between one's ideal self and one's real self should improve self-esteem. As the prototypical adolescent indicates, he/she has more self-respect now, compared to a few years ago and observes that "I'm pretty much being the kind of person I want to be. I'm doing well at things that are important to me like getting good grades and being ethical." Gains in personal autonomy and freedom of choice may also play a role, in that the older adolescent may have more opportunity to select performance domains in which he/she is successful. Such freedom provides more opportunity to select those support groups that will provide the positive regard necessary to promote or enhance self-esteem. Increased role-taking ability may also cause older teenagers to behave in more socially acceptable ways that enhance favorable attitudes of others toward the self that are internalized as positive self-esteem.

Parents are still part of this equation. Whereas it has been common in treatments of adolescent development to suggest that as the influence of peers increases, the impact of parental opinion declines, findings do not support the latter contention. As our cameo subject reports, "What my parents think about me is still important to how I feel about myself as a person." The correlation between classmate approval and global self-esteem does increase during adolescence; however, the correlation between parental approval and global self-esteem, which is high in childhood, does not decline during adolescence.

Normative Liabilities During Late Adolescence

Many of the limitations of mid-adolescence would appear to be overcome as a result of changes during late adolescence. Attributes reflecting personal beliefs, values, and standards become more internalized. The focus on future selves also gives the older adolescent a sense of direction. The ability to construct higher-order abstractions provides for a meaningful integration of single abstractions that previously represented potential contradictions in the self-portrait. The older adolescent can also resolve potentially contradictory attributes by asserting that he/she is flexible or adaptive. Moreover, older adolescents are more likely to normalize potential contradictions. However, conflict will be more likely to persist if the new skills that allow for an integration of seeming contradictions within the self-portrait are not fostered by significant others in the socializing environment.

Pathological Self-Processes and Outcomes in Late Adolescence

Many of the pathological processes described earlier can be observed, albeit in a somewhat different form, due to developmental advances. Preoccupation with impossible cultural standards of attractiveness looms even larger as the older adolescent anticipates emerging adulthood, where one must confront new standards in order to be socially acceptable and successful in the new adult world order. For females, failure to meet these standards can lead to potential eating disorders. In addition, older adolescents are *less* likely to report the vacillations that were observed during middle adolescence, a mixed blessing, because perceived negativity becomes more stable and entrenched in their core belief system.

Male adolescents are clearly at continued risk for violence, particularly the type of violence that emanates from peer rejection and chronic humiliation. However, unlike the impulsive acts of the school shooters in middle adolescence, the violent acts of those who were older teens, for example, Eric Harris and Dylan Kleibold from Columbine, Colorado, were far more *planful*. For over a year, they had developed their strategies for revenge.

In addition, an examination of the media accounts of the 12 high-profile school shooting cases suggests that the dynamics may be different from what we normally consider to be delinquent, conduct-disordered behavior that comes to the attention of teachers, school officials, school psychologists, law officers, peers, and parents. In most of these cases, there had been few obvious warning signs. The male shooters had *not* been in serious trouble with the law, they were *not* identified as trouble-makers in the school, they did *not* have clinical diagnoses that would have placed them in inpatient treatment, nor had they been placed in special classes for disruptive students who had a penchant for acting out.

Thus, there is a need to discriminate the form of violence exhibited by the school shooters from acts that have been committed by known delinquents and conduct-disordered youth who have come to the attention of school and mental health professionals. These latter youth commit different types of crimes, for example, drive-by shootings to target one individual in contrast to the random injury and killing of as many classmates as possible, in the case of the high-profile school shooters. The dynamics would appear to be very different, and deserve our attention.

The construction of multiple selves, while a normative process, can also have pathological implications. It was pointed out in the section on middle adolescence that the effects of abuse can lead to clinical symptoms that prevent one's multiple selves from being integrated. In the severest cases, this can lead to Dissociative Identity Disorder (what used to be terms Multiple Personality Disorder). Abuse impacts the negativity of those attributes judged to be at the core of the self, in contrast to less important or more peripheral attributes. Normatively, when asked to rate their self-attributes, older adolescents will define their most important, central core attributes as *positive*. They assign any negative characteristics to the periphery of the self, namely, as less important self-attributes. This is, therefore, a normative, self-protective strategy. In contrast, abused female patients, hospitalized for treatment, identified *negative* attributes as their core self, relegating what few positive characteristics they could identify as peripheral or less important self-descriptors. Herein, we can detect another deleterious effect of abuse on self-processes requiring clinical intervention to restore a more positive balance of self-perceptions.

Concluding Observations

Having completed the discussion of the three stages of adolescence, it should not be concluded that self-development has reached its maturity. Classic stage theories have implied such endpoints. Freud's final goal was to reach the genital stage, and for Piaget, attaining formal operational skills marked his last period of development, both achieved at the end of adolescence. However, an entire new stage of *emerging adulthood* has recently been posited in Western cultures, particularly for college-bound youth. Most in this age group (18–25) readily acknowledge that they have not met the primary criteria for adulthood proper: (a) becoming financially independent of parents, (b) taking responsibility for their actions, and (c) making their own independent decisions. Nor have they met such challenges as forging an occupational identity, creating meaningful moral or spiritual values, navigating romantic waters toward the goal of a committed relationship, curbing risk-taking behaviors rampant at this period, and coping with their vulnerability to depression. Thus, there are many challenges ahead for the self.

Cross-Cultural Issues

Three themes are noteworthy. First, emerging adulthood is not a universally experienced stage of development; it exists only in those cultures that postpone adult roles and responsibilites. In more traditional, non-Western cultures, youth are more quickly thrust into adult roles at puberty (e.g., work responsibilities, owning property, marriage, raising children), and such relatively abrupt transitions are signaled by rituals and rites of passage.

Second, Western ideals of beauty for women, our punishing standards of attractiveness, are not universally acknowledged across cultures. The goals of being tall, extremely thin, and large-breasted, where bodies are typically on display, are rejected by some but accepted by others. For example, the traditional *Japanese* conceptualization of the desirable female shape rests in an appreciation for the kimono which communicates that a woman's body should be concealed rather than displayed. Modesty and simplicity define physical beauty. In *South Africa*, notions of beauty interact with health concerns where HIV and AIDS are pandemic. Thinness is a sign of ill-health and thus, a larger figure is considered attractive. In *Jamaica*, to be full-figured is to be fully of vitality, and the combination of flesh and curves in motion is essential to a culturally critical form of recreation, dancing. Heavier women are not only considered attractive, but a sign that their husbands are good providers by maintaining their wives' ideal body weight.

In stark contrast, modern-day *Chinese* woman totally embrace the American standards of attractiveness and the body ideal. In fact, they are desperately attempting to emulate the look, which is a symbol of status, wealth, and success. To achieve these goals, they are flocking to plastic surgeons in droves, demanding tummy tucks, breast augmentation, rounded eyes, or a higher nose bridge. Moreover, they subject themselves to painful procedures in which leg bones are literally shattered and a metal rod is inserted in order to gain a few inches of height. Another cultural transformation can be observed in the exposure of *Fiji's* fishing villages to American-controlled TV (around 1990) where families watched American sitcoms, music videos, and advertising. More travel to Fiji by Western women made beauty ideals more palpable to those in service industries who had opportunities to observe them. Within a decade, Fiji women began to defect from their traditional larger body size which would be judged overweight in the United States, and are now trying to emulate Western standards of attractiveness.

A third cross-cultural distinction can be observed in how the *self is construed* in *individualistic* (typically Western where the United States is the prototype) cultures versus more *collectivistic* (typically Eastern where Asians are the prototype) cultures. The individualistic culture promotes the *independent* self that is *distinct* and unique, it should stand out in a crowd. Self-esteem is highly important and is based on individual accomplishments and personal success. High self-esteem is supported by many *self-enhancement strategies* and *self-serving biases* that often constitute distortions. That is, self-appraisals are not necessarily realistic. In contrast, collectivistic cultures promote an *interdependent* self defined by connectedness to others and the commitment to the pursuit of in-group goals, to insure social harmony. Self-esteem is not a major concern or goal. Rather, *self-effacing* tendencies are the norm, where modesty and self-criticism prevail. Thus, the American focus on the ego, also reflected in narcissistic tendencies, is not mirrored in many Eastern cultures. These cultural differences are shaped during childhood and adolescence, given parenting practices and other socialization experiences with peers, and represent a fascinating new area for study.

See also: Self-Esteem; Social Support.

Further Reading

Fischer KW (1980) A theory of cognitive development: The control and construction of hierarchies of skills. *Psychological Review* 87: 477–531.

Harter S (1999) *The Construction of the Self. A Developmental Perspective*. New York: Guilford.

Harter S (2006) The self. In: Damon W and Lerner R (series eds.), and Eisenberg N (vol. ed.) *Handbook of Child Psychology: Vol 3. Social Emotional, and Personality Development*. 6th edn., pp. 505–570. New York: Wiley.

Harter S (2011) *The Construction of the Self: A Developmental Perspective*, 2nd ed. New York: Guilford.

Harter S, Low S, and Whitesell NR (2003) What have we learned from Columbine: The impact of the self-system on suicidal and violent ideation among adolescents. *Journal of Youth Violence* 2: 3–26.

Self-Esteem

S Thomaes, A Poorthuis, and S Nelemans, Utrecht University, Utrecht, The Netherlands

Glossary

Dark side of self-esteem: The positive link between favorable forms of self-esteem and aggression and violence.

Epiphenomenon: By-product (the epiphenomenon view of self-esteem holds that self-esteem is the outcome of one's life circumstances, but has no importance by itself).

Implicit self-esteem: Nonconscious attitude toward oneself as a person.

Narcissism: Excessive self-love and self-perceived superiority.

Self-efficacy: The belief that one is able to successfully complete the tasks one faces.

Self-esteem: Global self-evaluation of worth or value.

Sociometer theory: The theory that posits that self-esteem measures the quality of our social relationships.

State self-esteem: Global self-evaluation of worth or value in the moment.

Trait self-esteem: Global self-evaluation of worth or value over time.

Introduction

People differ in how much worth or value they place on themselves. Whereas some people place much worth on themselves and are generally satisfied with the person they are, other people place much less worth on themselves and are not so satisfied with the person they are. These differences between people reflect differences in self-esteem. How is self-esteem different from the many related thoughts and feelings that people have about themselves? How does self-esteem emerge, and what leads some adolescents to have higher or lower self-esteem than others? Does self-esteem have a pervasive impact on adolescent well-being and adjustment, as is often believed? And why should we care about self-esteem anyway?

For decades, self-esteem has been among the most widely studied traits in adolescent psychology. Accordingly, psychologists have obtained a wealth of important knowledge about adolescent self-esteem. At the same time, recent advances in theory and measurement motivate more and more researchers to test longstanding ideas and conventional wisdom about adolescent self-esteem on its merits. Some ideas have turned out to be correct. Other ideas – even the most obvious and prosaic ones – will need to be refined in the light of the current empirical evidence. In this article, we discuss the meaning, development, causes, and consequences of adolescent self-esteem, and we highlight some of the controversies that surround the topic.

What Is Self-Esteem?

In common-day language (e.g., in newspapers, magazines, television shows, Internet discussion boards, self-help books, and school meetings where parents discuss the well-being of their children), self-esteem is often used as an umbrella term that diffusely refers to such traits as feeling confident, secure, strong, competent, or proud. In psychology, self-esteem is more narrowly defined as one's overall evaluation of worth or value as a person. This definition involves two important elements. First, self-esteem involves an evaluation. The evaluation can be positive, negative, or somewhere in between. The evaluation includes a cognitive component (i.e., how one thinks about oneself) and an affective component (i.e., how one feels about oneself). Second, self-esteem refers to one's global worth as a person. Self-esteem should not be equated with more specific self-evaluations in certain domains of functioning such as sports (e.g., "I am good at sports"), school ("I am not that good at school"), or physical appearance (e.g., "I like the color of my eyes, but I do not like the way my body looks"). Rather, self-esteem is the summary self-evaluation of all competencies, traits, and values that define oneself as a person.

Making things a bit more complicated, there exist several terms in psychology which are related to self-esteem but have a different meaning. The term self-efficacy is different from self-esteem, in that it more specifically refers to the belief that one is able to successfully complete the tasks one faces (rather than the belief that one is a worthy person). For example, it is possible that an adolescent believes that he or she is able to perform successfully at school, with friends, or in other important life-domains (which reflects high self-efficacy), but is still rather unsatisfied with oneself as a person (which reflects low self-esteem). Other terms such as self-image, self-concept, or simply self-view are sometimes used as synonyms for self-esteem, but more typically they refer to beliefs that people have about themselves that do not involve an evaluation of worth. For example, a belief such as "I am an outgoing person" is part of one's self-image, self-concept, or self-view. However, it does not involve an evaluation of worth, and so it does not speak to one's self-esteem.

As most people will recognize from their own experience, the positivity of one's self-esteem is not to be taken for granted, or something that constantly remains the same. People may feel very good about themselves at one moment (perhaps because they accomplished something well, or they feel that someone likes, values, or admires them) and then feel 'normal' or even much worse about themselves at the next moment (because the initial thrill of the positive event has disappeared or because a more negative event has occurred). Yet at the same time, each person has a certain baseline, or average level of self-esteem that is relatively stable over time. To distinguish between these two manifestations of self-esteem,

 doi:10.1016/B978-0-12-373915-5.00037-1

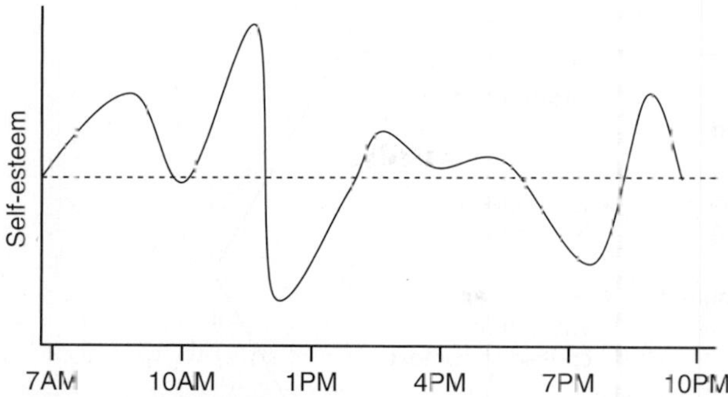

Figure 1 State self-esteem (solid line) varies from moment to moment; trait self-esteem (dotted line) is relatively stable. The figure depicts hypothetical data.

psychologists use the terms trait self-esteem (i.e., one's enduring self-evaluation of worth or value over time) and state self-esteem (i.e., one's self-evaluation of worth or value in the moment). Thus, state self-esteem is variable and fluctuates around a relatively stable level of trait self-esteem, as depicted in **Figure 1**.

Self-Esteem Motive

Having high self-esteem feels good and having low self-esteem feels not so good. It is perhaps for this reason that people (especially people in Western, individualistic societies) generally are strongly motivated to pursue high self-esteem. This motivation is not something that people are consciously aware of. Rather, the tendency to pursue high self-esteem is like an unconscious motivation that guides many of our feelings, thoughts, and actions (much like people can long for pizza, buy one, and eat one, while being unaware of their underlying motivation to obtain nutritious and fat food that may help them to survive in times of scarcity). The motivation to pursue self-esteem is very common among adolescents. For example, adolescents often use impression-management strategies (e.g., they exaggerate their accomplishments or skills) to boost their public image. When they hold a positive public image, it is much easier for them to hold favorable self-views. Thus, adolescents often influence others to think well of oneself as a means of creating favorable self-views. In addition, often without knowing it, many adolescents hold a self-serving bias – a tendency to claim credits for success (so that one's self-esteem is boosted) while blaming external factors for failure (so that one's self-esteem is protected from harm). For example, when adolescents perform well at school, they may think this is because they are smart. When they perform badly at school, they may think this is because they did not do their best, because they were tired, or because their teacher is unable to make proper exams!

Measuring Self-Esteem

How do we know the level of an adolescent's self-esteem? Because self-esteem involves a person's own internal thoughts and feelings about oneself (and does not involve behaviors that can be seen), the standard way to measure self-esteem is by means of self-report. Two different self-report questionnaires are commonly used to measure trait self-esteem in adolescents: the Self-Esteem Scale (developed by Morris Rosenberg) and the Self-Perception Profile for Adolescents (developed by Susan Harter). The preferred measure depends on the purposes of the researcher. The Self-Esteem Scale is preferred when the researcher is exclusively interested in adolescents' self-esteem (not in domain-specific forms of self-evaluation). Its items are positive or negative statements about oneself (e.g., "On the whole I am satisfied with myself," "At times I think that I am no good at all"), and adolescents report their agreement with these statements on a four-point scale.

The Self-Perception Profile for Adolescents is preferred when the researcher is not only interested in self-esteem per se, but as well in other, domain-specific forms of self-evaluation (including scholastic competence, social acceptance, athletic competence, and physical appearance). The items of this questionnaire comprise two contrasting statements (e.g., "Some teenagers really like the kind of person they are BUT OTHER teenagers often don't like the kind of person they are"; "Some teenagers are not happy with the way they look BUT OTHER teenagers are happy with the way they look"). Adolescents first choose whether the first or second statement is most true for them, and then they indicate whether that statement is 'sort of true' or 'really true' for them.

Both the Self-Esteem Scale and the Self-Perception Profile for Adolescents are good-quality questionnaires with several positive features (e.g., both questionnaires are reliable, and measure well what they intend to measure). However, they are limited in one respect. They can only be used to determine the degree to which an adolescent's self-esteem is high versus low. In the past decade, psychologists have come to believe that there is more to self-esteem than whether it is high or low. For example, people differ in the degree to which their (state) self-esteem is stable from one moment to the other, in the degree to which their self-esteem is a realistic, warranted reflection of their competencies and relationships, and in how much importance they place on having high self-esteem. As will be discussed in a later section, these three aspects of self-esteem (stability, reality, and perceived importance) are very important, but they cannot be measured using standard self-esteem measures.

Development of Self-Esteem

One may perhaps assume that self-esteem is such a fundamental aspect of our social and psychological functioning that even very young children should already have a sense of self-esteem. This is not the case. The skills needed to be able to form self-esteem are quite complex (as will be discussed in this section), and they are gradually acquired throughout the earlier stages of children's development. Most of our current knowledge of the development of self-esteem was obtained in research by Susan Harter and her coworkers (see suggested reading for a reference to her main work on this topic). This section describes the development of self-esteem from the preschool years up into adolescence (**Figure 2**).

Toddlerhood and Early Childhood

Up into the early school years, children lack the skills to form a global representation of their worth as a person, which is the defining characteristic of self-esteem. They cannot yet reflect on whether they are 'satisfied with who they are as a person' because they cannot yet think in such abstract terms. This

Toddlerhood and early childhood	Middle and late childhood	Adolescence
• Behaviorally manifest self-esteem • Specific self-evaluations • Inflated self-evaluations	• Actual self-esteem (from age 7 or 8) • More realistic self-evaluations	• Self-esteem decreases • Self-esteem varies from context to context • Self-esteem is unstable

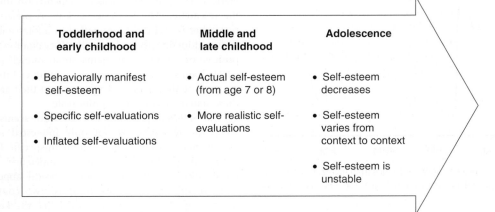

Figure 2 Main developments in self-evaluation from toddlerhood into adolescence.

said, young children do show various behaviors that can be seen as early expressions of an emerging sense of worth and value (and they are typically judged as such by parents and teachers). Such behaviors are labelled 'behaviorally manifest self-esteem.' For example, young children may show pride ("mom, look, I drew a crocodile and it looks very real!"), initiative, and confidence (representing high behaviorally manifest self-esteem); or instead they may show doubt, passiveness, and a lack of confidence (representing low behaviorally manifest self-esteem).

Furthermore, although young children cannot yet evaluate their global worth as a person, they do make more specific evaluations of themselves from about 2 or 3 years old. For example, a 2-year-old child may say "I am strong!" or "I am good at jumping!" Later in the preschool and early school years, children's self-evaluations become more inclusive. For example, previous self-evaluations of being strong and good at jumping may now be combined into "I am good at sports." Another characteristic of young children's self-evaluations is that they are unrealistically positive. Ask kindergarteners who is the best in class at drawing, and most if not all of them will say that they are themselves. To be sure, this is not because all kindergarteners have big egos. Rather, they have not yet acquired the cognitive skills to distinguish their ideal competencies (defining the person who they want to be) from their actual competencies (defining the person who they actually are).

Middle and Late Childhood

From about age 7 or 8, a number of important developments take place. First, from this age, children typically become able to form actual self-esteem. Thus, besides making self-evaluations of specific behaviors or attributes, they now can also form a global sense of worth and value as a person. Individual differences in self-esteem now rapidly emerge, with a majority of children thinking very positively about themselves and a minority thinking somewhat negatively about themselves. Second, from age 7 or 8, children become increasingly motivated to hold favorable self-views and to avoid unfavorable self-views. For example, they become more concerned about creating positive images in the eyes of others, and they become more sensitive to receiving criticism, being ridiculed, or experiencing shame (a developmental trend that becomes even more pronounced in adolescence). Third, children's self-evaluations become more realistic from this age. Most children can now distinguish who they want to be from who they actually are. An 8-year-old talented drawer may still tell you he is the best drawer in class (righteously so), but less gifted individuals will accurately say they have no exceptional skills at drawing. This said, although most children develop more realistic self-evaluations, some others maintain an unrealistically positive, inflated sense of self for extended periods of time (some of them may even maintain inflated self-evaluations for the rest of their lives).

Adolescence

Adolescence is a period full of physical, cognitive, and social changes, and these changes are reflected in children's self-evaluations as well. From the earliest stages of adolescence, children's social skills and attributes come to have a strong impact on their self-evaluations. For example, when young adolescents (11–13-year-olds) are asked to describe themselves, they may say they are easy-going, talkative, and fun-loving, or shy and uncomfortable with others – labels that describe how they relate to others. Young adolescents' self-esteem is also very much dependent on how they believe they are viewed by others, even more so than is normal in other stages of development. Although peers have a strong impact on young adolescents' self-esteem, parents remain important as well. Young adolescents' self-esteem often varies among social contexts. They may have high self-esteem when with friends (who share the same interests and values), lower self-esteem when with parents or teachers (who may not approve of all things they say or do), and still lower self-esteem when with unknown peers (who, at times, can be very critical). At a somewhat later age, in middle adolescence, adolescents often experience conflict between the contrasting views they may have of themselves and which they find difficult to reconcile. For example, a 15-year-old girl may worry over whether she is a responsible person (as she is in her job) or an irresponsible person (as she is when coming home too late after visiting a friend). Finally, adolescents' self-esteem, and more precisely, their state self-esteem, is less stable than it is at other ages. It is not uncommon for adolescents to experience intense state self-esteem 'highs' and 'lows,' sometimes within a single day. Such strong fluctuations in state self-esteem are especially likely to occur following social events, such as when one is valued and admired or, instead, criticized and ridiculed by peers.

Perhaps the most notable self-esteem change that occurs in adolescence is that, on average, self-esteem becomes lower. Many individuals (and especially girls) come to experience at least some level of self-doubt and insecurity when they go through adolescence, which typically influences their self-esteem to decline. Does this mean that low self-esteem is the norm rather than the exception in adolescents? Fortunately not. Rather, most adolescents come to hold more moderate levels of self-esteem than the typically high levels of self-esteem they held in childhood. Only a few individuals actually come to hold very low self-esteem in adolescence. These individuals often are more diffusely troubled and suffer from depressive symptoms as well. Several factors may explain the downward shift in adolescent self-esteem. First, in most countries, the onset of adolescence is also the time when children transition from primary school into secondary school. This means they lose many of their former peer relationships, need to form new peer relationships, and need to adjust to their new school routines that emphasize more social comparison and competition – stressful changes that can challenge self-esteem. Second, the standards and expectations that adolescents face become increasingly difficult to meet. For example, it becomes increasingly important to obtain good grades in school, but not everyone is able to obtain good grades. Failure to meet standards will often lead to less approval (e.g., from teachers or parents) which, in turn, will lead to lower self-esteem.

Importantly, adolescent girls' self-esteem typically shows a much stronger decline than does adolescent boys' self-esteem. This gender gap in self-esteem that originates in adolescence tends to persist throughout the life span. What causes adolescent girls to lose self-esteem? First, in adolescence, girls come to attach greater importance to their physical attractiveness, while at the same time, many girls evaluate their attractiveness more negatively than they did in childhood (perhaps because they now compare themselves to idealized standards for women's attractiveness). This implies that girls, who attach more importance to how they look, are at greater risk to lose self-esteem. Second, adolescent girls tend to be more judgmental and critical of one another than are adolescent boys (e.g., girls tend to be more judgmental of one another's physical appearance), and so they may harm one another's self-esteem more than boys do.

Antecedents of Self-Esteem

What factors lead some adolescents to have higher self-esteem than others? Are there perhaps certain early-life experiences that have an enduring impact on self-esteem? What current experiences or circumstances influence adolescents to have higher or lower self-esteem? Does self-esteem have genetic origins? And why do people hold self-esteem anyway? These are some of the most fundamental questions one can possibly ask about self-esteem. Over the past one or two decades, psychologists have found a number of answers. Some of these answers were perhaps more or less predictable, others were outright surprising.

Parenting and Genetic Influences

Conventional wisdom holds that parents have a strong impact on their children's level of self-esteem. Consistent with that notion, early research has found that parents who are cold and rejecting or exceedingly critical have a somewhat higher chance of having children with low self-esteem. The reverse is also true: parents who are warm and loving or parents who regularly praise their children have a somewhat higher chance of having children with high self-esteem. Furthermore, parents who show conditional regard for their children (i.e., parents who provide love and affection when their children display certain desired behaviors, but withhold their love and affection when their children do not display those behaviors), tend to have children whose state self-esteem strongly fluctuates from one moment to the other (i.e., children with unstable state self-esteem).

One limitation of this early research, however, is that it failed to consider the possibility that children's self-esteem is also influenced by parental genes rather than by parental behaviors alone. Recent research that did consider this possibility found that genes have in fact a stronger impact on children's self-esteem than do parental behaviors. In fact, whereas genetic influences account for about 30–50% of individual differences in self-esteem, shared environmental influences (e.g., parental behaviors) only account for about 10%. Consider the example of two families that each has an adopted (and thus genetically unrelated) child. In the one family, parents tend to be cold and rejecting, while in the other family, parents tend to be warm and loving. Will the lucky child in the latter family develop higher self-esteem than the unlucky child in the first family? Possibly, but not necessarily. A more important factor is the child's genetic makeup – for example, how much positive attitudes to self such genetic makeup contributes.

Peer Influences and Sociometer Theory

Can we conclude that self-esteem is almost exclusively determined by genes? No, we cannot. For example, self-esteem is also strongly influenced by how much adolescents are liked and valued by their peers (or more precisely, by how much they believe they are liked and valued by their peers). Adolescents who think they are well liked and valued by most of their classmates, who are satisfied with the friendships they hold and with the social groups they belong to, are likely to form high levels of self-esteem. Adolescents who believe they are rejected or disliked by their classmates, or who are dissatisfied with their friendships or the social groups they belong to, are likely to develop more moderate levels of self-esteem. Why so? What is the reason that self-esteem is strongly dependent on the perceived quality of one's social relationships?

Human beings are social animals. Our ancestors were more likely to survive and reproduce when they lived in social groups (e.g., because social groups provided the opportunity to share food or other resources, provided protection against danger, and provided access to opposite sex partners), and so we are all born with a 'need to belong' – a fundamental need to have positive social relationships. An influential psychological theory, called sociometer theory, holds that the main reason people have self-esteem is that it measures the quality of our social relationships. Self-esteem functions to inform us about how much we are liked and valued by others. It is important to have such a measure because it may alarm us when our need to be liked and valued is not adequately fulfilled and we should do something about it (just like feelings of hunger alarm us when our need for nutrition is not adequately fulfilled and we should do something about it). The sociometer function of self-esteem works in the short run (e.g., when adolescents are approved by peers in the moment their state self-esteem increases) and in the long run (e.g., when adolescents become better liked by peers, they gradually develop higher levels of trait self-esteem). Because adolescents are even more concerned about obtaining interpersonal approval than are people of other ages, it is easy to see why adolescents' self-esteem is so strongly dependent on the quality of their social relationships.

Competence-Based Influences

What about the impact of having (or lacking) certain competencies, skills, or strengths on adolescents' self-esteem? Does it benefit self-esteem if one is a good athlete or a good student, and does it harm self-esteem if one is a poor musician or not the best-looking kid in class? There is no simple answer to this question. Adolescents' competencies, or their perceptions thereof, only impact self-esteem to the extent that they are also considered important by the individual. Thus, for those who believe it is important to be a good athlete, it will definitely benefit their self-esteem if they are one. However, for those who believe it is not particularly important to be a good athlete, it will hardly benefit their self-esteem, even if they are able to run 100 m in 10 s. It follows from this line of reasoning that it can seriously harm adolescents' self-esteem if they fail or lack competencies in a domain that they consider important. The self-esteem of a talented music student who desperately wants to get into conservatory, but fails the entry audition, may be seriously harmed, even if his of her musical skills are actually quite good.

In summary, adolescents' level of self-esteem is influenced by a number of factors. Genes and the (perceived) quality of one's social relationships are especially important. Competencies, skills, and experiences with parents and peers fine-tune adolescents' level of self-esteem to somewhat higher or lower levels.

Consequences of Self-Esteem

Few traits in psychology have received such a 'good press' as self-esteem. For a long time, researchers, clinical psychologists, policymakers, teachers, and parents assumed that high self-esteem had many benefits. They thought that high self-esteem would help youths to behave responsibly and make wise decisions, to love others as they love themselves, to have good relationships with family and friends, to fulfill their academic potential, and more generally, to have success in life. Sometimes, the belief that self-esteem is an unmitigated good went too far. For example, in the 1980s, the California State government funded a task force to increase the self-esteem of Californians, claiming that self-esteem is "the likeliest candidate for a social vaccine, something that inoculates [youth] against the lures of crime, violence, substance abuse, teen pregnancy . . . and educational failure."

In more recent years, the actual importance and benefits of self-esteem have become controversial. Some psychologists even argued that self-esteem is an epiphenomenon – something that goes up when life goes well and goes down when life goes badly, but that has no importance by itself. Roy Baumeister and his colleagues wrote an extensive literature review on the consequences of self-esteem in several important life domains. This review (see Further Reading) has become the most authoritative source of current knowledge on the importance of self-esteem. In the following sections, we discuss the main conclusions of the review insofar as they pertain to adolescents. Where more recent research evidence is available, it will be discussed as well.

School Performance

One major domain of adolescents' functioning is their school performance. It is often believed that high self-esteem causes adolescents to perform well at school or at least to make the best of their academic potential. There are several good reasons to believe why this should be the case. For example, high self-esteem may well lead adolescents to take up and learn from challenging learning experiences rather than to avoid them, to persist after initial failure on a task, or to be highly motivated to perform well in school to maintain or further enhance their positive feelings of worth. Consistent with such a view, early research found that adolescents' self-esteem and their academic performance are positively correlated. Adolescents who have high self-esteem tend to have higher grade point averages and to perform better at standard academic achievement tests than their peers with lower self-esteem. Does this mean that self-esteem is a cause of good school performance? No. This conclusion can be drawn from two types of research. Research that measures adolescents' self-esteem and school performance over longer time periods shows that high self-esteem has only a very minor or no impact on subsequent academic performance. The reverse effect is much stronger. Thus, high self-esteem tends to be an outcome rather than a determinant of good school performance. Furthermore, research that evaluates the effectiveness of self-esteem boosting intervention programs on academic performance typically finds that increases in self-esteem (if obtained at all) fail to lead to subsequent increases in school performance. Thus, although the assumption that high self-esteem is a psychological resource that should help adolescents to perform well at school may be intuitively compelling, the actual research evidence is disappointing. Adolescents may well come to perform better at school when they hold positive academically-related beliefs about themselves (e.g., when they believe they are good at math, they may actually come to perform better at math), but not when they hold high self-esteem.

Social Relationships

There are several reasons to assume that high self-esteem should cause adolescents to have good-quality social relationships. It is well thinkable that adolescents with high self-esteem find it relatively easy to make contact with others, and that peers like to interact with adolescents who are self-confident and secure about themselves. Seemingly consistent with that notion, self-esteem is positively related to how popular adolescents think they are. Thus, high self-esteem adolescents think very positively about their own social standing in the peer group. However, research that uses objective measures of popularity (e.g., research that asks peers rather than adolescents themselves to report how popular they are) consistently shows that high self-esteem adolescents are not more popular than are adolescents with lower self-esteem. It appears that high self-esteem adolescents create their own social illusion. Other studies have focused on the link between self-esteem and adolescents' friendships. Although high self-esteem adolescents often have more intimate and secure friendships than do low self-esteem adolescents, research that examined whether high self-esteem is a cause or determinant of good-quality friendships found no support for such a view. Perhaps the correlation between self-esteem and the quality of friendships is spurious, which means that there is some other, unknown factor that leads adolescents to hold both high self-esteem and good-quality friendships.

Aggressive and Antisocial Behavior

It has been long thought that low self-esteem predisposes youth to behave aggressively. Low self-esteem individuals experience frustration, and they vent that frustration by lashing out aggressively against others, so it was reasoned. However, a low self-esteem explanation of aggression does not coincide with anecdotal impressions of youth who engage in extreme forms of aggression and violence. For example, case studies of perpetrators of school shootings show that these individuals rarely feel worthless, inadequate, or inferior. Instead, they more often hold overly positive, inflated self-views, and are absorbed with themselves. Research that focuses on more common forms of aggression (e.g., physical aggression, excluding or humiliating others, bullying) is generally consistent with the latter view. There is little evidence that low self-esteem leads adolescents to be aggressive. There is much more evidence that aggressive youth hold inflated, narcissistic forms of self-esteem. Narcissists (individuals who feel superior to others, who feel entitled to privileges, and who demand attention and admiration) become especially aggressive when they receive a blow to their egos, such as when they feel criticized or rejected. The link between inflated self-esteem and aggression has been called the 'dark side of self-esteem.' A different story may apply for socially undesirable behaviors that do not involve aggression, such as cheating, lying, stealing, or school disciplinary problems. Although the magnitude of observed relationships is not strong, there is fairly consistent evidence that low self-esteem causes or predisposes adolescents to engage in such antisocial but nonaggressive behaviors.

Unhealthy Habits

What about adolescents' unhealthy habits and lifestyles? Many adults are concerned that their teens abuse alcohol or other drugs. If low self-esteem feels bad, then low self-esteem adolescents may perhaps be inclined to look for options that provide relief from their misery, such as abusing alcohol or other drugs. On the other hand, high self-esteem adolescents often underestimate danger and are prone to take risks. The bulk of research shows that high and low self-esteem adolescents are equally likely to drink alcohol or smoke marijuana (most research on adolescent drug abuse focuses on smoking marijuana). Besides alcohol and drugs, smoking cigarettes might provide a means for low self-esteem adolescents to gain much-wanted status or approval in certain peer groups. However, the research evidence is inconclusive. Although some studies found a minor link between low self-esteem and smoking tobacco, several other studies found no such link at all. If low self-esteem predisposes adolescents to start smoking, its effects are very small.

Sex

Many adults are also concerned that their teens have sex at a young age (e.g., before the age of 15). High self-esteem makes people less susceptible to peer pressures, such as peer pressures to have sex, and so one might assume that high self-esteem should help adolescents to refrain from having sex at a young age. Research suggests otherwise. For boys, self-esteem does not influence the age of first sexual intercourse. For girls, self-esteem does have an influence, but in the opposite direction of the high self-esteem hypothesis. High self-esteem girls are more (not less) likely to have their first sexual intercourse at a young age than do low self-esteem girls. In a similar vein, high self-esteem does not reduce the chance of engaging in risky sexual behaviors (e.g., having sex without a condom), does not reduce the chance of sexually transmitted diseases, and does not reduce the chance of teen pregnancy.

Happiness

So far, the evidence about the benefits of high self-esteem is very weak. This said, it probably goes too far to state that self-esteem is a mere epiphenomenon. High self-esteem does have a few important benefits. As mentioned before, high self-esteem feels good. High self-esteem adolescents experience more positive feelings (e.g., feelings of hope, pride, connectedness) and less negative feelings (e.g., feelings of sadness, anxiety, frustration) than do low self-esteem adolescents. Furthermore, they report being happier and more satisfied with the way they are leading their lives. High self-esteem is not only associated with how happy adolescents are in the moment; it is also a good predictor of how happy they will be as adults. The flipside of happiness is depression. Adolescents who experience depression feel sad or 'empty' for longer periods of time, and they often lose their interest in everyday activities. Research shows that high self-esteem can protect adolescents from developing depression later in adolescence or in adulthood. High self-esteem seems to provide a resource of positive feelings that individuals can draw on (perhaps especially so in times of sorrow and misfortune) to remain happy and satisfied with their lives. Low self-esteem is not a recipe for depression, but the chances for low self-esteem adolescents to develop depression are definitely higher than for high self-esteem adolescents.

Eating Problems

High self-esteem can also keep adolescents from developing eating problems. Eating problems can involve excessive weight-loss behaviors (as in anorexia nervosa) or binge–purge behaviors (as in bulimia nervosa), and are relatively common in adolescence (especially in adolescent girls). Research shows that girls who have low self-esteem are more likely to develop eating problems in adolescence than are girls with higher self-esteem. Other traits such as perfectionism and considering oneself overweight even further increase the likelihood that low self-esteem girls develop eating problems. Girls with eating problems also appraise their attractiveness more harshly than do others. This should not be taken to suggest that eating disordered adolescents underestimate their attractiveness; rather, whereas healthy girls overestimate how attractive others find them, girls with eating problems estimate very accurately how attractive others find them.

Conclusion

The benefits of high self-esteem (and the corresponding costs of low self-esteem) are less strong and pervasive than once assumed. It may have been theoretically plausible or intuitively compelling to believe that self-esteem functions as a social vaccine that inoculates youth against many problems, but research suggests otherwise. Self-esteem is more often an outcome than a cause of good adjustment. If self-esteem does have a causal impact on adolescent functioning, its effects are generally weak or modest. This said, there are exceptions to this general pattern, the most important exception being happiness. High self-esteem feels good and helps adolescents to be happy and satisfied with their lives. Thus, self-esteem is neither a social vaccine nor an epiphenomenon. It is a trait with a few benefits, but these benefits should not be overestimated.

Controversies and New Developments

For several decades, self-esteem has been among the most popular research topics in adolescent psychology. In the past two decades alone, several thousand publications on adolescent self-esteem have appeared (**Figure 3**). One would perhaps assume this means that all debates and different viewpoints would have settled down by now. Perhaps disappointingly, this is not the case. Many controversies and unresolved issues continue to exist, and there are some exciting new developments that will continue to fascinate psychologists in future decades.

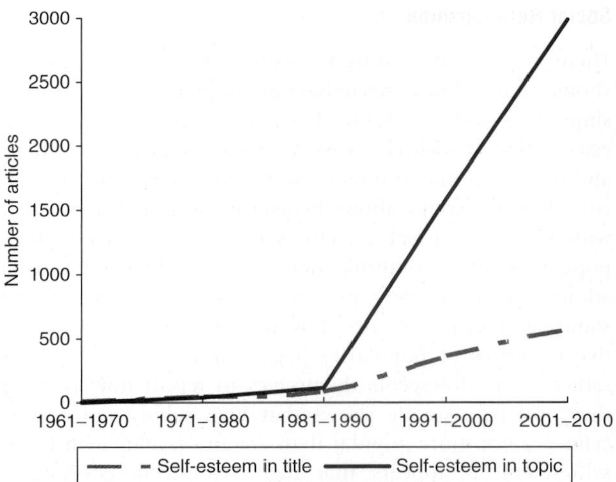

Figure 3 Number of publications per decade on adolescent self-esteem. The two lines depict the number of publications with self-esteem in the topic (i.e., title, abstract, or keywords) and in the title alone. Based on citation databases included in Web of Knowledge.

There Is More to Self-Esteem Than Whether It Is High or Low

There are several important aspects of self-esteem that have been neglected in the past. Consider the differences in the self-esteem of these two girls. Elizabeth is a 14-year-old girl. She is generally satisfied with the person she is. This is not something she constantly seeks to communicate to others; rather, she simply makes the impression to genuinely value herself. Her self-esteem is also well grounded in reality. Elizabeth is good at school, is a promising pianist, and is well liked by most of her classmates. However, she is not as good at sports. Although this is surely disappointing to her, it hardly affects her overall feelings of worth. Heather is also a 14-year-old girl. She thinks of herself as a special person, and feels better and more deserving than others. However, her self-esteem appears somewhat artificial and unreal. Her competencies are no better than those of others, but she enhances her self-views by trying to impress others or garnering admiration. At the same time, Heather is very sensitive to being negatively evaluated by others. She responds with excessive emotion to criticism or other events that challenge her superior sense of self.

What can be said about these girls' self-esteem? On the one hand, they both hold high self-esteem. When they would complete standard self-esteem measures (e.g., Rosenberg's Self-Esteem Scale or Harter's Self-Perception Profile for Adolescents), both of them would probably obtain high scores. On the other hand, Elizabeth's and Heather's self-esteem seems quite different. Elizabeth holds stable self-esteem, her self-esteem is accurate and justified given her competencies and the quality of her relationships, and she seems not particularly concerned about her self-esteem. In contrast, Heather holds unstable and inflated self-esteem, and she does seem very concerned about maintaining high self-esteem. In the past, psychologists hardly ever distinguished between stable and unstable self-esteem, realistic and unrealistic self-esteem, and the different concerns adolescents may have about their self-esteem. This is unfortunate in that it has rendered us a rather one-sided view of what self-esteem actually entails. Over the past decade, more and more researchers have come to study multiple aspects of adolescents' self-esteem – including the extent to which self-esteem is stable, realistic, and object of concern. This 'new look' promises to yield a much improved understanding of adolescent self-esteem, and the way it is involved in psychological functioning and well-being.

Implicit Self-Esteem

Thus far, we talked about self-esteem as a self-evaluation of worth that people are consciously aware of. This is the typical view of self-esteem. However, some researchers argue that self-esteem also has so-called implicit aspects that people are not consciously aware of (and thus, these implicit aspects cannot be measured using standard self-report questionnaires). Implicit self-esteem can be defined as the nonconscious attitude people have toward themselves as a person, an attitude that unknowingly influences people's feelings, judgments, and behaviors. Consider the following example. On a sunny day, a girl walks across a street. Her shadow keeps following her wherever she walks. She does not pay conscious attention to her shadow at all, but she is continuously catching quick glimpses of it. The girl experiences positive emotions. Why would this be the case? The most straightforward explanation is that people simply tend to feel good on sunny days. Scholars who study implicit self-esteem, however, would argue that the girl's positive emotions were also influenced by her positive implicit self-esteem: unknowingly, the girl was primed with an image of herself (i.e., her shadow), and because she has positive implicit self-esteem, this image automatically triggered positive associations which made her feel good. In similar ways, implicit self-esteem may influence the way people react to experiences that activate feelings or thoughts about themselves, such as receiving praise or criticism. Such experiences often trigger knee-jerk reactions (e.g., when receiving criticism people often immediately experience negative feelings), and these knee-jerk reactions may be guided by implicit self-esteem. Other researchers, however, have been very cautious with assuming that implicit self-esteem exists. They believe that psychologists should not study traits or processes that people are not consciously aware of. They also question the quality of the instruments that are used to measure implicit self-esteem (e.g., computer-based categorization tasks that assess how easily participants associate positive vs. negative words with themselves). The near future will tell whether or not implicit self-esteem turns into an important topic of study in adolescent psychology.

Generational Differences in Self-Esteem

Another controversy concerns the question of whether youths have come to hold higher self-esteem over the past decades. From the 1960s up to now, Western societies have increasingly come to emphasize individualism and a focus on the self rather than on the groups that one belongs to. Sociologists argue that it has become more important for people in Western countries to grow up as independent and self-reliant individuals, to make the best of their competencies, and to stand out from the crowd. It is not farfetched to assume that this shift in societal norms and expectations may have influenced how people think about themselves. Indeed, some researchers who compared today's generation of young people with previous generations labeled today's young people 'Generation Me.' Today's youths are more assertive (i.e., they are more ready to come up for themselves), and make more positive predictions about their future accomplishments (e.g., they believe they will be better spouses, parents, and workers) than previous generations. In addition, researchers have argued that today's youths are more satisfied with themselves and like themselves better than did youths in the past. For example, today's youths are somewhat more likely to agree with the item (taken from the Rosenberg Self-Esteem Scale) "I take a positive attitude toward myself" and to disagree with the item "Sometimes I think that I am no good at all." However, other researchers have argued that these observations are much ado about nothing. They emphasize that generational self-esteem differences are very small. They are also hesitant to believe that generational self-esteem differences, if they exist at all, are caused by societal trends and differences in the norms and expectations that are set for children (note the similarity with the debate on climate change, where proponents argue that current temperature levels are very high compared to the past, and opponents argue that this phenomenon reflects naturally occurring change, and is not externally influenced).

Self-Esteem Intervention

A final controversy is whether self-esteem is a trait that can and, perhaps more important, should be nurtured by psychologists. This may seem a rather surprising controversy, given that self-esteem boosting is a very common goal for both preventive interventions (i.e., interventions that aim to reduce the chance that maladjustment will occur in the future) and therapeutic interventions (interventions that aim to reduce the severity of maladjustment once it has occurred already). One might perhaps assume that psychological interventions are only employed on a large scale if they have known positive effects (just as treatments for physical problems are only employed on a large scale if they have known positive effects). However, research that measures the effectiveness of self-esteem boosting attempts has found very inconsistent results. A meta-analysis (a research technique to analyze the combined results of several studies on a certain phenomenon) that was conducted to make sense of these inconsistent results concluded that interventions to boost self-esteem can sometimes be effective (i.e., can sometimes bring about actual change in self-esteem), but their effectiveness is generally small and conditional upon a great number of other factors (such as the type of participants targeted by the intervention and the type of intervention used). Preventive interventions (e.g., school-based programs that aim to enhance the self-esteem of each individual in an entire classroom) usually have no effect on self-esteem.

Even aside from this issue of limited effectiveness, one may ask whether psychologists should try to boost young people's self-esteem anyway. If self-esteem was a cause of many positive outcomes, then it probably would be worth the effort and expenses to invest on a large scale in self-esteem interventions. However, now that we know (as discussed in the previous section) that the actual benefits of self-esteem are rather limited, does it still make sense to try to boost youths' self-esteem? The answer depends on what one tries to reach by boosting self-esteem. Self-esteem helps adolescents to be happy and can prevent some adolescents from developing depression. Thus, if an individual suffers from both low self-esteem and depressive mood problems, it may be a good idea to try to boost that individual's self-esteem. Similarly, low self-esteem often contributes to adolescents' eating problems, and thus, an intervention to boost self-esteem may be well recommended for individuals who suffer from both low self-esteem and eating problems. However, because self-esteem is not a major cause of most other domains of functioning and well-being, there is little reason to continue to focus interventions in these domains on boosting self-esteem. In fact, such interventions may even have unwanted side effects if they cultivate inflated, unstable, or self-deceptive forms of self-esteem. Consider the case of interventions for aggressive and violent behavior. Many current aggression intervention programs rely on boosting self-esteem. However, aggressive youths are much more likely to hold grandiose and inflated self-esteem than to hold low self-esteem. If aggression intervention programs inadvertently cultivate such inflated self-views, they may perhaps increase rather than decrease youths' aggressive behavior problems.

Conclusions

Adolescence is a time of change in many domains of functioning, and the domain of self-esteem is no exception. From the onset of adolescence, children's self-esteem becomes increasingly dependent on interpersonal influences (e.g., the opinions of peers) and becomes relatively unstable from one moment to another. Perhaps even more important, adolescents come to hold lower self-esteem than they held in childhood and than they will hold in adulthood. Multiple factors may explain this temporary drop in self-esteem, including stressful changes at school and teens' critical evaluation of the way they look (which is especially true for girls).

Although traditional wisdom held that self-esteem has a very strong, causal impact on adolescents' positive development, research shows that the actual impact of self-esteem is rather disappointing. High self-esteem has a number of benefits (most importantly, high self-esteem helps adolescents to be happy), but does not cause adolescents to perform better at school, to have better social relationships, or to refrain from unhealthy or risky habits and lifestyles (e.g., using alcohol or other drugs). Future work will increasingly distinguish between multiple aspects of self-esteem. Now that psychologists have come to acknowledge that self-esteem has multiple aspects (and does not only vary from high to low), we are likely to obtain a much better understanding of adolescents' self-esteem and how it is involved in their psychological functioning and well-being.

See also: Academic Achievement; Depression and Depressive Disorders; Parenting Practices and Styles; Popularity and Social Status; Risky Sexual Behavior; Self-Development During Adolescence; Sexuality.

Further Reading

Baumeister RF, Campbell JD, Krueger JI, and Vohs KD (2003) Does high self-esteem cause better performance, interpersonal success, happiness, or healthier lifestyles? *Psychological Science in the Public Interest* 4: 1–44.

Damon W (1995) *Greater Expectations: Overcoming the Culture of Indulgence in America's Homes and Schools*. New York: Free Press.

DuBois D and Tevendale H (1999) Self-esteem in childhood and adolescence: Vaccine or epiphenomenon? *Applied and Preventive Psychology* 8: 103–117.

Harter S (1999) *The Construction of the Self: A Developmental Perspective*. New York: Guilford.

Kernis MH (ed.) (2006) *Self-Esteem: Issues and Answers*. London: Psychology Press.

Leary MR and Baumeister RF (2000) The nature and function of self-esteem: Sociometer theory. *Advances in Experimental Social Psychology* 32: 1–62.

Relevant Websites

Prominent classic self-esteem researchers

William James – http://www.des.emory.edu/mfp/james.html

George Herbert Mead – http://www.brocku.ca/MeadProject/

Prominent current self-esteem researchers

Susan Harter – http://www.du.edu/psychology/people/harter.htm

Jennifer Crocker – http://rcgd.isr.umich.edu/crockerlab/people/jcrocker.htm

Mark Leary – http://www.duke.edu/~leary/

Sexual Orientation

S T Russell, E M Thompson, and R D Harris, University of Arizona, Tucson, AZ, USA

Glossary

Coming out: Disclosing the nature of one's LGBTQ identity to others. Because most people are presumed to be heterosexual, coming out is not a discrete life event but a lifelong process. Coming out may also be experienced by heterosexual family members of LGBTQ persons; when a child or sibling comes out, often family members experience coming out as the parent or sibling of a LGBTQ person.

Compulsory heterosexuality: The explicit or implicit societal pressure to be heterosexual, resulting in the ignorance of or devaluing of sexual minorities' behavior, orientations, identities, or relationships, and the labeling of these as deviant.

Heteronormativity: A societal system based on the presumptions that there are natural roles for males and females, and that heterosexuality is the natural sexual orientation.

Homophobia: This term literally means 'fear of homosexuals,' but in recent decades, it has come to be used to indicate prejudice against sexual minority people.

LGBTQ: Abbreviations for lesbian, gay, bisexual, transgender, questioning. Questioning usually refers to young people who have not developed a stable sense of their sexual identity.

Queer: An historically pejorative term that has been reclaimed by LGBTQ groups as an affirmative identity when used among themselves.

Queer theory: A body of scholarship that emerged from feminist and gay and lesbian studies which challenges the idea that gender and sexuality are essential qualities of persons; queer theory is concerned with social constructions of sexuality based on normative categories of gender and sexuality.

Sexual behavior: Actual sexual behavior between people. Sexual practices may or may not be consistent with a person's sexual identity or orientation.

Sexual identity: Personally and outwardly identifying oneself as heterosexual, gay, lesbian, bisexual, transgender, queer, and so forth. A consistent, enduring sense of the meanings that the sexual orientation and sexual behavior have for a person.

Sexual minority: An umbrella term used to include persons representing many sexual identities; it has been used to include persons who have not self-identified based on a sexual identity but are in the minority based on their behavior, desires, or experiences.

Sexual orientation: A person's sexual or emotional attractions to other persons who are of the same sex (a same-sex sexual orientation), the other sex (a heterosexual orientation), or both same and other sex (a bisexual orientation). Realization of these attractions or desires may be outwardly expressed and incorporated into one's sexual identity, or there may be private acknowledgment but no public expression.

Introduction

Sexual orientation is defined as one's attractions, desires, and arousals toward others based on their sex and gender: individuals may be attracted the same, other, or both sexes. Thus, sexual orientation by definition is understood as internal to oneself, but it is important to note these desires and attractions are shaped and guided by social, cultural, and interpersonal interactions. What we know about sexual orientation in adolescence has come from research during the last quarter century, with growing attention in the last decade. Recent research with younger populations has highlighted the need to distinguish sexual orientation from how one sexually identifies or expresses oneself – that is, the sexual identity that one claims (e.g., as heterosexual, gay, lesbian, or bisexual) – or one's sexual behavior. Specifically, sexual orientation does not always match sexual behavior or chosen sexual identity labels. Human developmental research on adolescent sexual orientation has considered how sexual orientation develops, alongside the development of one's identity and behavior. By contrast, a growing body of research at the level of social groups considers the meaning and implications of differences based on sexual orientation for mental and emotional health as well as behavioral risk. Thus, there has been growing attention to sexual orientation differences or disparities in health and behavior. The most recent developments in the field have focused on the role of contexts for understanding well-being associated with sexual orientation – that is – how families, schools, and communities shape sexuality development and health and behavior based on adolescents' sexual orientations.

Adolescence is the period during which sexual orientation emerges, a process that coincides with a time of great change for youth; it is a time of dramatic physical/biological, cognitive, and social development. The biological and cognitive changes interact with changing social expectations for appropriate roles and behaviors, with increasing expectations of responsibility and independence in the transition from childhood to adulthood. In addition to fundamental developmental tasks of identity, autonomy, achievement, and intimacy or changing relationships, adolescents also must navigate sexuality development, including the onset of sexual thoughts, urges, and attractions. These changes take place in the context of intensified expectations and pressures regarding gender (what it means to be a man or woman), as well as growing awareness of sexuality norms and expectations. Thus, sexual orientation development takes places during the period of intense biological and physical change, as well as social changes and developing awareness of social norms related to gender and sexuality. All of these changes are situated within cultural contexts that shape norms and values regarding gender and sexuality. Each of these factors plays a role in an adolescent's experience of sexual orientation and its development.

In this article, we discuss the theories of origin, definitions, and meanings of sexual orientation and its expression in the forms of personal identity and behavior. We consider difficulties scientists have encountered in the study of sexual orientation, including identifying populations and measuring sexual orientation. Then, we review developmental models of sexual orientation and identity. We end this article by considering sexual orientation development for contemporary young people.

Terminology and Historical Perspectives

In the late nineteenth and early twentieth centuries, Western psychologists were especially interested in what made some people homosexual: this thinking was based on the presumption that heterosexuality is typical or 'normal.' Psychoanalysts conducted case studies and concluded that homosexuality was a genetic aberration and a mental disease. Even though scientists had shown that same-sex sexual behavior was common across cultures and historical times, and has been evident even in the lives of those who identify themselves as heterosexual, it was not until 1973 that homosexuality was no longer officially diagnosed as a mental disorder.

Because the origins of understandings of homosexuality were rooted in medical notions of abnormality and disease, the term 'homosexual' is typically understood in the light of this medical history and is considered by many to be pejorative when applied to contemporary people. Thus, the word 'homosexuality' is an appropriate noun referring to a general state of being, while 'homosexual' is best used in reference to behavior rather than to individuals. In the 1960s and 1970s, the gay rights movement emerged, and along with it came a shift in personal identities related to homosexuality; since that time people with same-sex orientations typically prefer the contemporary sexual identity labels such as 'gay,' 'lesbian,' or 'bisexual.' Contemporary developments in sexual orientation have expanded to include other alternative and more inclusive orientations (e.g., 'queer,' 'mostly straight'), and scientists in recent years have encouraged a broader focus on same-sex sexuality by introducing the term 'sexual minority,' which is used as an inclusive or umbrella term for same-sex sexualities that acknowledges the stigma associated with same-sex sexuality. The historical changes in identity labels paralleled the emergence of queer theory in the academy, which has not only reclaimed once pejorative terms like queer, but also proposes a flexible and fluid understanding of both gender and sexuality.

From the historical beginnings of this area of study, there has been significant attention to the origins of sexual orientation. Broadly speaking, there are two groups of thought on the origins of sexual orientation: essentialism and social construction. An essentialist view of the origins of sexual orientation emphasizes biology or innate physiological drives, focusing on genetic makeup, brain development, and hormones as the basis for our sexual attractions, desires, and arousals. The idea that people are 'born that way' comes from this perspective: it is believed that sexual orientation is a fundamental or essential character of our physical makeup. The essentialist perspective downplays the influence of social forces and interpersonal relationships in shaping and defining sexual orientation. In contrast, a social constructivist view of sexual orientation emphasizes societal influences, focusing on the roles of family, culture, and norms as the foundation for sexual orientation and its development. The idea here is that our sexual orientation is influenced by or develops out of interpersonal and social interactions, and is shaped by social and cultural values, beliefs, and opportunities. Social constructionist understandings of sexual orientation view sexuality as constructed and created by various influences in society; in its purest form, the social constructivist views rejects the notion that there are physiological underpinnings of sexual orientation.

There continue to be debates about and between these theoretical perspectives on sexual orientation. In fact, some contemporary scholars argue that essentialism and social constructionism cannot be reconciled. However, there are alternate conceptualizations that bring these theoretical perspectives together. Specifically, interactionist theories of sexual orientation incorporate essentialist and social constructionist views. According to these theories, there is some degree of biological inclination in one's sexual desires or arousal, but society and social groups also influence the manifestation or enactment of sexual orientation through sexual identity and behavior. Interactionist theories are compelling because they have support in recent research on the personal meanings and understandings of sexual orientation. For example, individuals often describe deeply physical and emotional urges, even early in childhood before such urges are understood as related to sexual orientation. Such accounts often include personal examples of the ways that social influences shape sexual identities or behaviors. Thus, an interactionist perspective appears consistent with the way many contemporary people describe their sexual orientations, identities, and experiences; that is, sexual orientation is often described as an interaction between the desires that a person feels are 'natural' for him or her on the one hand, and the social experiences that create opportunities for sexual identity development or sexual behavior on the other.

With these theoretical perspectives as a background, the next section considers the definitions of sexual orientation and related constructs in more depth, followed by a description of contemporary challenges and strategies for measuring sexual orientation in research.

Defining and Measuring Sexual Orientation

Describing a cohesive yet succinct definition of sexual orientation is complicated. The term is often inaccurately equated with sexual identity: it is sometimes erroneously used to mean the difference between homosexuality and heterosexuality. However, the scientific exploration of sexual orientation is extensive and includes the dynamic interaction of the self, society, and contextual influences. Using the definition that sexual orientation encompasses an individual's sexual attractions, fantasies, and arousals, it follows that each person develops a subjective internal model of the behaviors, attributes, and stimulations that are sexually and emotionally compelling, and this conceptualization orients one toward the sexual experiences that are felt to be most rewarding. Yet, sexual orientation is not always consistent with sexual behavior. For example, a person may claim a heterosexual or 'straight' sexual identity, but be primarily attracted to the same sex while engaging in sexual behavior with both sexes. The recent attention to 'down low' (men whose identity is heterosexual but who engage in same-sex sexual behavior) is a contemporary example of the complex interplay between sexual orientation, identity, and behavior. Further, social norms dictate the expression and exploration of sexual orientation, making the construct difficult to accurately capture and interpret. Thus, although same-sex sexuality is generally stigmatized, recent examples of 'girls kissing girls' challenge or disrupt that stigma at the same time, for many women, the phenomenon does not appear to be an indicator of an enduring same-sex sexual orientation, or of a lesbian or bisexual identity.

At the core of the construct of sexual orientation are the interrelated meanings of sex and gender. First, the term sex refers to the biological or physiological characteristics that define males and females, including the sexual organs that one has – having a penis and testes traditionally associated with being a male and having a vagina and ovaries associated with being a female. Research in recent years has acknowledged that this binary understanding of sex is not applicable to everyone: there is growing awareness that some people have a combination of male and female biological characteristics ('intersex' is the word that is used to describe combinations of male and female biological or physical features). Gender, on the other hand, can be understood as the roles, behaviors, and attributes that are considered appropriate by a social group, society, or culture based on sex. With this understanding of gender as a social construction, it is important to distinguish gender as an intrapsychic identification and outer expression rather than as an objective marker of specific physical characteristics. In other words, gender is more closely related to how one identifies with and expresses one's sex (which may not necessarily directly match one's biological sex).

We note here that an additional and important construct is gender identity, or an individual's self-concept as male or female. In broad terms, transgender is an identity label used by people who identify with a gender that is inconsistent with their biological sex. We do not include a detailed discussion of transgender identity in this contribution: the discussion here of sexual orientation applies to all persons, regardless of sexual or gender identities. However, it is often the case that transgender people and issues are often understood to be aligned with the public, political, or justice issues relevant for other sexual minorities. For example, the label 'LGBT' is an inclusive term for lesbian, gay, bisexual, and transgender.

Finally, sexual behavior refers to acts of sex. In contrast, sexual orientation refers to how one thinks, feels, and desires about sexual behavior; and sexual identity is one's overall sense of and identification with a sexual self or sexual label. Each individual has a sex, gender, sexual behavior, sexual orientation and sexual identity, yet these terms, categories, and experiences are not always aligned. The figure provides a simple graphic representation of these dimensions of sexuality through three overlapping circles. In the center of the figure, there is an inverted triangle that represents the overlap of each of the three circles, representing sexual behavior, sexual identity, and sexual orientation. Often it is assumed that most people's experiences are represented in this overlapping space of clear coherence between identity, behavior, and orientation; however, both empirical research and theoretical perspectives (most notably queer theory) have challenged the idea that the space in the middle is most common or typical. Rather, research and theory have shown that the interplay between these three dimensions is complex, and that this interplay is dynamic and may change over time.

The point here is that understandings of sexual orientation are based in a complex interplay between personal feelings and desires, and the ways that those feelings and desires are interpreted and understood within a person's social context or culture. Thus, a crucial point when defining sexual orientation is a consideration of the gender and sexuality norms in the dominant culture or society. In most Western cultures, sexual orientation is typically understood in exclusively binary terms: a person is either male or female, and has desire for either males or females, and therefore can only be either heterosexual or gay/lesbian. This way of thinking makes the possibility of sexual fluidity, changes in personal sexual orientation across time, and bisexuality atypical or invisible, rather than simple dimensions of variation in the human experience of sexual orientation. Yet, there are other cultures in which understandings and expressions of gender or sexual orientation are not based on rigid binaries (e.g., some Southeast Asian cultures incorporate fluidity into notions of gender, and some Native American cultures accommodate 'two-spirit' identities for persons who fulfill mixed or multiple gender roles).

Recent research on sexual orientation has moved away from the binaries of male versus female and heterosexual versus gay or lesbian and has argued instead for conceptualization along a continuum (or along multiple intersecting continua: e.g., attraction, behavior, or fantasy, in the past, present, or future). Such work has focused on sexual behavior among Americans and has highlighted variability between individuals' reported sexual behavior, sexual identity, and sexual orientation: many more individuals report some same-sex attraction and behavior than individuals who identify themselves as 'gay' or 'lesbian.' These findings have been used to argue that the conceptualization of sexual orientation as a binary is no longer appropriate: that is, few individuals are either exclusively gay/lesbian or heterosexual, and the majority of individuals fall somewhere in between the two ends of a broader continuum.

In recent years, bisexuality, or having interest in both sexes, has received increased attention in both social science research and popular culture. Research on bisexuality has highlighted the complicated relationship between sexual attraction and behavior, especially in cultures that emphasize monogamy. Serial monogamy is a common form of partnering: that is, persons may have several monogamous partnerships across the life span, separated in time and sequence. Understandings of bisexuality point out that although an individual may be presumed to be heterosexual (or gay/lesbian) based on their relationships, monosexual orientation should not be presumed.

Just as defining sexual orientation is a challenging task, measuring sexual orientation is equally complex, especially during adolescence. Even if there were no social or cultural influences, accurately self-reporting one's sexual orientation in adolescence (or adulthood) would not be a simple task. This challenge is only confounded by the intensification of gendered expectations and pressures during adolescence, along with social pressures regarding heterosexuality. It is the period during which youth learn what it means to be men and women; for example, adolescent boys learn what it means to be a man: stereotypically, to be self-reliant, void of emotion, and tough. A part of being a man is also being attracted to women and not being attracted to men. Young women also experience similar pressures related to heterosexuality, pressures that signal the norms of womanhood. Thus, the emphasis and regulation during adolescence of gender and sexuality norms regarding heterosexuality likely deters youth from self-disclosing and reporting same-sex orientation (i.e., same-sex desire or attraction).

Historically, the measurement of sexual orientation has been based on binary understandings. Measures that rely on individual self-reports of sexual identity (e.g., "Which best describes you: gay/lesbian, straight, or heterosexual?") do not capture the essence of sexual orientation, which includes desires, feelings, fantasies, and attractions and can be directed at persons of either or both sexes. More nuanced measurement of sexuality and sexual orientation that are sensitive to the unique experiences of adolescents are needed. During the last decade, scientists have recommended that studies include measures of three dimensions: sexual identity, orientation (measured as attractions or desires), and behavior. Standard measures have been offered, with supporting empirical evidence from large-scale survey studies. For example, a national US study from the mid-1990s showed that roughly 5% of adolescent girls and 7% of adolescent boys reported romantic attractions to the same sex, yet far fewer reported ever having been in a romantic relationship with the same sex (just over 2% of girls and 1% of boys). A nationwide study in Canada shows that while only 2–3% of youth report gay, lesbian, or bisexual identities, many young people are not sure (6%) or are 'mostly heterosexual' (3% of males and 9% of females); as a result, 89% of males and 82% of females report that they are '100% heterosexual.'

Finally, there remain debates about the degree to which standard measures fully capture the complexities of each of these dimensions. One form of measurement that has shown significant promise in accessing youths' experiences of sex and sexuality is the narrative, a method that allows young people to tell their sexual story through writing or voicing their experiences. Research utilizing this methodology has been able to tap into experiences of sexuality and the development of one's sexual orientation that have otherwise been difficult to extrapolate from closed-ended questionnaire measures.

Sexual Orientation Development

There are multiple perspectives from which to conceptualize the development of sexuality and sexual orientation in adolescence. In this section, we review contemporary understandings of the development of sexual orientation and its associated dimensions of identity and behavior. Because models of sexual identity development have been influential for understanding adolescent sexual orientation, we include specific attention to those models, their limitations, and what they offer to current thinking regarding adolescence.

Broadly speaking, from a developmental perspective, the biological and physiological changes of adrenarche and puberty set the stage for physical change and cognitive capacities that precede sexual awareness and physical experience. Sexual orientation development is typically conceptualized from this perspective: the development of internal desires and motives regarding sexuality are viewed as strongly linked to the physiological and cognitive changes that lead into adolescence. On the other hand, the development of one's sexual identity (e.g., understanding and labeling oneself as gay, bisexual, straight, etc.) involves social and cultural processes in which the young person makes meaning of sexual impulses and feelings, and interprets these experiences in the context of relevant cultural meanings and scripts for sexuality and identity. We consider developmental understandings from both perspectives subsequently.

As much as we know social experiences matter to the development of one's sexual orientation, it has been established that there is a bodily or physical experience of one's sexual orientation, and these physical experiences are developmental as well. Although there is some cultural variation, it has been found that in middle childhood, typically between the ages of 6 and 10, a major physiological transition occurs and creates a consciousness around one's sexuality. Adrenarche is the early sexual maturation stage that is present in humans and only a small number of other primate mammals; it signals the beginnings of the hormonal transitions that lead to the physical and cognitive changes of puberty. Based on cross-cultural studies, scholars have suggested that the cognitive awareness and understanding of sexual attraction emerges with the changes of adrenarche. That is, there is evidence that sexual attraction and desire are possible by the beginning of the second decade of life, even before the observable physical changes associated with puberty. These changes are the beginnings of the development of sexual orientation.

It is based on emerging sexual orientation that sexual identity and behavior develop and are enacted. Sexual identity is clearly social or interpersonal in nature, because it is defined as the identity a person claims based on their sexual orientation. The sexual identity one claims is dependent in large part on the socially available sexual identity categories and constructs. For example, there is clear evidence that youth may come out as gay or lesbian (or disclose their same-sex sexual identities) at younger ages than in the past. The explanation is not presumed to be due to a dramatic historical change in the course of sexuality development for the human species; rather, scientists generally agree that youth come out at younger ages because of the dramatic changes in visibility of same-sex identities (gay, lesbian, bisexual, queer, and questioning) and the associated possibilities for understanding oneself in terms of those identities. Thus, young people come out at younger ages because it is now possible to be a 'gay adolescent,' whereas such an identity was not historically or culturally possible a century ago.

Compared to the development of sexual orientation, the developmental origins of sexual behavior have been understudied. This lack of attention can be traced to understandings of sexuality and sexual expression as relevant or appropriate only in adulthood, and to the social regulation of sexuality in childhood. There is little empirical research on sexuality and sexual behavior or expression in childhood, and therefore there are few models for understanding how sexual behavior or expression is enacted or develops across childhood and into adolescence. Further, sexual behavior historically has been conceptualized also as a binary: inexperience or innocence versus onset or initiation. In this way, attention to sexual behavior has been focused on self-directed sexual initiation, which is understood in typical circumstances to take place in adolescence or adulthood. In the absence of an understanding of sexuality as a range of expressions and experiences that might include some that are relevant during childhood, most understandings of sexual behavior begin at the point of 'sexual debut,' which has historically been presumed to mean first heterosexual intercourse experience.

Developmental Models of Sexual Identity

Compared to studies of the development of sexual orientation, there has been comparatively more research on the development of sexual identity; most work in this area has focused on adults, and most has focused on the development of gay or lesbian identities. Stage models of identity development – that is, identifying the steps in the development of sexual identity – dominated psychological research from the 1970s to the 1990s. These models primarily functioned from the perspective that heterosexual identity was the presumed reference group or standard, and that when individuals question their heterosexuality or when they deviate from this standard, they go through a number of stages or developmental milestones. First, individuals feel different and confused by their desires or orientation. Such individuals then deny, avoid, change, or accept these divergent feelings. Next, individuals begin to take up or claim their same-sex orientation; however, at this stage, they do not necessarily experience pride or complete integration (e.g., an individual may maintain a negative view of homosexuality). Finally, individuals synthesize or integrate their same-sex identity into their larger self-concept. At this stage, their increased contact with other lesbian or gay people may serve to further connect them to the lesbian and gay community, and solidify their lesbian/gay identities.

Stage developmental models served an important guiding framework for theorizing and understanding LGB identity formation. However, in practice, these models have been largely discarded for several reasons. First, the traditional stage models are based on assumptions that development is linear: these models do not account for variability in the sequence and progression of stages. Second, the models do not account for important differences in sexual identity development that have been shown for men and women (and, by extension, that may be relevant based on race, ethnicity, social class, or other characteristics that may play a fundamental role in the development of sexual identity). Third, the models presume that there is a singular (and thus preferred) outcome or end state; in so doing, the models undermine the possibilities of individual differences in the outcome of the development of sexual identity, and ignore the possibility that some people may not experience a clear resolution in their sexual identity development.

A final limitation of the stage models of sexual identity development is that they were written with the implicit assumption that sexual identity development took place in adulthood, among persons who had completed the complex developmental transitions of adolescence. The contemporary reality of the developmental nature of sexual orientation in Western societies is that individual awareness and sexual identity development are happening at younger ages. Yet, the stage developmental models were based on assumptions about fully mature adult cognitive and identity processes that are not necessarily appropriate when applied to adolescents. Thus, another major limitation of the stage models is that they were not designed with unique adolescent developmental challenges in mind.

In general, these models are regarded as outdated. However, some aspects of these models may remain useful: they outline possible developmental stages which represent developmental challenges or questions that people might experience when they are taking on a marginalized or stigmatized identity. These models became troublesome when they were held up as a sequence of stages that culminated in optimal development for sexual-minority individuals. Youth may come out during adolescence or even preadolescence and do not have the same integration and stability of identity that people have if they come out during their twenties. In other words, adolescents are experiencing the multiple developmental challenges at the same time that they are developing their sexual identities. Nevertheless, elements of these models (confusion, questioning, self-labeling, assumption, and identification) could be recast as possible developmental tasks, milestones, or challenges related to sexual identity development.

Recent work has demonstrated that differential developmental trajectories more accurately reflect the process of sexual identity development. Specifically, several factors have emerged as vital for understanding sexual identity development: individual differences (e.g., gender) and context (e.g., emotionally oriented or sexually oriented), and the timing, spacing, and sequencing of sexual identity milestones. Furthermore, research also suggests that this process is not as fixed as previously conceptualized. For example, sexual questioning may and does reoccur in both heterosexual and sexual-minority individuals. Environmental, personal, and contextual changes in an individual's life may elicit feelings and questions regarding their sexual identity, and attention should be given to this reality. Such research also suggests that the integration of an LGB identity is not always an individual's personal goal. Rather, contemporary thinking about sexual identity demonstrates that the process is not static, and it may not be the same for every individual.

The classic stage models focus on sexual-minority identity formation; until recently, little attention was paid to heterosexual identity formation. This is primarily because heterosexuality is the socially normative and acceptable identity, and having a sexual orientation was thought of as relevant only for those who deviate: sexual minorities. Some contemporary scholars have focused on heterosexual identity development, arguing that like same-sex identity, heterosexual identity is influenced by culture, biology, context (i.e., microsocial and macrosocial), gender norms and socialization, religion, and heterosexual privilege (i.e., the advantages that heterosexuals have based on the system of heteronormativity). Under this model, heterosexual individuals are expected to act in ways consistent with the gender role associated with their sex, engage only in heterosexual romantic intimacy and sexual behavior, and avoid same-sex sexual exploration. Within that context, individuals engage in active exploration of sexual needs, values, and preferences (consistent with the norms of the individuals' social context), or they may follow a path characterized by absence of exploration (due to identity confusion). Based on these experiences, a deepening of and commitment to one's identified sexual needs, values, and preferences develops, leading into the congruent synthesis of a heterosexual identity into one's comprehensive identity. This model of heterosexual identity development is thus grounded in and defined by its existence in heteronormative society where heterosexuality is assumed; although heterosexuality may be explored and questioned, it is not conflicted as is the case for sexual-minority identity development. Research corroborates this model and suggests that a singular and homogeneous self-evident heterosexual identity does not simply exist a priori, but that both young men and women explore their heterosexuality through distinct and diverse processes.

Additionally, recent work suggests that for many, sexual orientation and identity are fluid and flexible, rather than static or unchanging. In other words, sexual attraction, desires, preferences, and identities can change one or more times at various stages of the life span; for some, this may be experienced as flexible noncommittal sexual orientation or identity. For example, a currently identified heterosexual woman may be in a sexual-romantic relationship with a man, while simultaneously experiencing same-sex attractions. Researchers have proposed that binaries of sexual orientation and identity labels are no longer useful: that is, it is difficult and unrealistic to determine a singular, 'true' sexual orientation or identity.

During the last decade, researchers have begun to highlight the growing number of youth who identify with alternative sexual identity labels. At the same time that there has been more research and popular culture attention to nonbinary or fluid understandings of sexuality, more youth appear to be adopting alternative labels: mostly straight, queer, unlabeled, questioning, and variations on bisexual identities. The researchers who have emphasized these alternative sexual identities have conducted work primarily based on narrative methodologies, giving space for young people to talk and/or write about their understandings of their sexual orientations. Research has begun to suggest that female sexuality may be more fluid than previously thought or more responsive to social and cultural factors. The implications of this fluidity are that females may be more likely to have a disconnect between their sexual behavior, orientation, and identity, resulting in shifts in their sexual identities over the life course (and these shifts may become especially prominent in adolescence – a time period characterized by increased awareness of and significant change in one's sexual feelings and behaviors). Still, other research demonstrates that the normative sexual identity labels – gay, lesbian, and bisexual – continue to hold meaning for nonheterosexual adolescents in labeling their sexual identities. Thus, recent studies have highlighted variability in sexual orientations and identities on the one hand, along with continuity in the relevance of historic sexual identity labels on the other.

Sexual Orientation and Contemporary Adolescence

Clearly, the last decades have been times of significant social change regarding sexuality and same-sex sexuality in contemporary societies. Yet, the typical contexts in which adolescents grow and develop – their families, schools, faith communities, and peer groups – continue to be influenced by historically traditional gender and sexuality norms. Thus, in many contemporary societies and for contemporary youth, we see evidence of dramatic social change, along with tensions in understandings and acceptance around diversity in sexual orientations.

Gender and sexual norms are internalized at young ages and are perpetuated through external rewards and punishments given by others in their social world. The internalization of these norms happens so early that most young people cannot recognize the social forces that influence them; instead, young people come to think of these gender and sexual norms as normal and natural. Thus, heterosexuality is normalized in the major institutions that shape adolescents' lives: family, school, faith, and in the media. Recent research shows, for example, that when parents or peers are rejecting of same-sex orientation during adolescence, LGB delay coming out, and as young adults have lower esteem about their sexual orientation and report more mental and behavioral health problems. In other words, nonheterosexual adolescents must navigate their developing identities within multiple contexts that may range from rejecting to supportive. Not surprisingly, from the very earliest studies, research on sexual orientation in adolescence has focused on problems and risk in the context of a heteronormative and homophobic society. Research on adult health disparities clearly shows that sexual-minority adults are at dramatically disproportionate risk for emotional, behavioral, and physical health problems across the adult life span. These disparities are presumed to have their origins in adolescence given the similar statistics about the health and well-being of queer adolescents.

There are two competing trends that shape the everyday experiences of youth in their social settings (i.e., relations with peers and in the school environment): youth with same-sex sexual orientations are coming out at younger ages, yet attitudes about same-sex sexuality become more favorable only as adolescents get older. Thus, there appears to be a developmental tension between individual awareness of sexual orientation and adoption of alternative sexual identities which may conflict with the social pressures of conformity to gender and sexuality norms that are particularly strong during early adolescence. These pressures coincide in the early teenage years in ways that may explain the tensions that are evident for contemporary queer youth. Thus, although some have argued that the social changes of recent decades have resulted in unprecedented freedoms for nonheterosexual adolescents, this view ignores the developmental reality of conformity to social and cultural norms around gender that can be at odds with the developmental course of sexuality development for individual teenagers. In the context where social change and openness are occurring and youth are accepting of their same-sex sexuality, there remains a tension to conform – a tension that may be especially salient for contemporary adolescents.

Research in schools, among peer cultures, and in family contexts has shown that gender nonconforming boys are especially at risk for social isolation, discrimination, and harassment/violence, and much of this has to do with their perceived sexual orientation as gay. Boys who do not conform to traditionally masculine gender-role norms are less likely to gain peer acceptance than their nonconforming counterparts. Gender-atypical boys also suffer from greater self-image problems and are more frequently the victims of homophobic behavior such as name-calling or bullying. More extreme cases have resulted in severe violence against gender nonconforming youth.

Sexual-minority youth are socialized to live and conform to heterosexual lives, and this has implications for their mental health and well-being. The family is one such context that has historically privileged and normalized heterosexuality. In families, even though most families eventually adjust, coming out as an adolescent has historically been met with some form of family disturbance. Particularly during the coming out period, parent–adolescent relationships can be strained, and this family stress has negative consequences for sexual-minority youth. For example, research has shown strong associations between a family's rejection of a child based on sexual orientation and health risks among sexual-minority adolescents and young adults. Family rejection or strain is closely tied to parents' expectations and images of their child's family life course; when a child comes out, many parents feel that their imagined future family life is undermined or that their family history is being rejected.

Other developmentally normative adolescent sexuality experiences remain elusive for many sexual-minority youth. Dating and romance are typically thought to be developmentally normal, meaningful, and important for adolescents' interpersonal development, but may be limited or abbreviated for sexual minorities. The initiation of intimacy and romance is understood to be a core developmental task during the adolescent years; it provides young people with experiences to learn about trust, communication, commitment, mutuality, and emotional expression, capacities that will serve them the rest of their lives. However, sexual-minority youth have historically been unable to form and maintain romantic relationships openly and easily.

Yet, many same-sex oriented youth engage in dating and romance. Due to the primacy of heterosexual dating scripts for teens, they may feel pressure to participate in heterosexual dating despite or in spite of their same-sex desires. For example, one study based on a national survey of youth found that although same-sex attracted adolescents were much more likely to report same-sex relationships, they were equally as likely as heterosexual adolescents to be involved in heterosexual relationships. However, sexual-minority youth in heterosexual relationships experienced high rates of anxiety and depression (similar to those sexual-minority youth who did not date at all). Feeling the need to conform to heterosexuality during adolescence might set a course for adult intimate relationships that could explain, for example, elevated rates of high-risk sexual behavior on the one hand, or possibilities for alternative relationship forms on the other. These findings highlight the fact that romantic relationships and intimacy play important roles in adolescence, and have some of the same developmental benefits for sexual minority youth that they do for young heterosexuals. Little prospective research exists that follows sexual minority youth into adulthood, yet we suspect adolescent dating and romantic experiences for sexual minority youth have lasting influence on their adult relationships.

Conclusions: Possibilities

Research has consistently shown there are disparities based on sexual orientation, identity, and behavior, but what are the possibilities present in this tension? The earliest research on sexual orientation in adolescence focused on risk based on same-sex sexuality; the focus on risk was consistent with the social invisibility and marginalization of sexual-minority people in those times. Although discrimination and inequality persist, social change since that time has been dramatic. There have been large shifts in societal attitudes regarding same-sex sexuality: for example, US polls show that over the last decade (2001–10), attitudes about the acceptability of same-sex relationships have increased from 41% to 52% in the general population. At the same time, there has been an increasing visibility of LGB people in the media, along with growing public attention to issues relevant to sexual minorities, including military service and marriage for same-sex couples. Even a decade ago, the possibility for same-sex marriage may have seemed unlikely, but in that period of time, several countries and US states now issue marriage licenses to same-sex couples, and many other nations and localities provide state-level spousal rights to unmarried couples. Recent studies show that these geographic differences in family policies for sexual minorities matter for the well-being of adult gay and lesbian couples; it is likely that these social changes make a difference for young people and their self-acceptance and willingness to come out to others.

These social changes have created growing awareness of same-sex sexuality, and have provided greater possibilities for adolescents, especially sexual minorities, in understanding their developing sexuality. For the first time there are conceptual models that include attention to the exploration and development that takes place among heterosexual youth regarding their sexual orientations and identities. Sexual-minority youth for the first time have access to role models; prior generations had few role models or visions of happy and successful adulthoods from which to imagine their futures. There is even the possibility of a 'questioning' sexual identity; some young people claim a sexual identity that is defined by development and change. Thus, contemporary youth have access to possibilities for identities and self-expression that are historically unprecedented. Such changes may promise new opportunities for health and adjustment in adolescence and across the adult life span.

See also: Bully/Victim Problems during Adolescence; Discrimination, Racial and Ethnic; High School; Self-Esteem.

Further Reading

DeLamater JD and Hyde JS (1998) Essentialism vs. social constructionism in the study of human sexuality. *Journal of Sex Research* 35: 10–18.

Diamond LM (2006) What we got wrong about sexual identity development: Unexpected findings from a longitudinal study of young women. In: Omoto AM and Kurtzman HS (eds.) *Sexual Orientation and Mental Health: Examining Identity and Development in Lesbian, Gay, and Bisexual People*, pp. 73–94. Washington, DC: American Psychological Association.

Diamond LM and Savin-Williams RC (2009) Adolescent sexuality. In: Lerner R and Steinberg L (eds.) *Handbook of Adolescent Psychology, Vol 1: Individual Bases of Adolescent Development*, 3rd edn., pp. 479–523. Hoboken, NJ: Wiley.

Hammack PL and Cohler BJ (2009) *The Story of Sexual Identity: Narrative Perspectives on the Gay and Lesbian Life Course*. New York: Oxford University Press.

Hammack PL, Thompson EM, and Pilecki A (2009) Configurations of sexual identity among sexual-minority youth: Context, desire, and narrative. *Journal of Youth and Adolescence* 38: 867–883.

Morgan EM, Steiner MG, and Thompson EM (2010) Processes of sexual orientation questioning among heterosexual young men. *Men and Masculinities* 12: 425–433.

Pascoe CJ (2005) 'Dude, You're a Fag': Adolescent masculinity and the fag discourse. *Sexualities* 8: 329–346.

Russell ST, Clarke TJ, and Clary J (2009) Are teens 'post-gay'? Contemporary adolescents' sexual identity labels. *Journal of Youth and Adolescence* 38: 884–890.

Savin-Williams RC (2005) *The New Gay Teenager*. Cambridge, MA: Harvard University Press.

Striepe MI and Tolman DL (2003) Mom, dad, I'm straight: The coming out of gender ideologies in adolescent sexual-identity development. *Journal of Clinical Child and Adolescent Psychology* 32: 523–530.

Thompson EM and Morgan EM (2008) 'Mostly straight' young women: Variations in sexual behavior and identity development. *Developmental Psychology* 44: 15–21.

Tolman DL and Diamond LM (2001) Desegregating sexuality research: Cultural and biological perspectives on gender and desire. *Annual Review of Sex Research* 12: 33–74.

Relevant Websites

http://www.apa.org/pi/lgbt/index.aspx – American Psychological Association: Lesbian, Gay, Bisexual, and Transgender Concerns.

http://psychology.ucdavis.edu/rainbow/html/facts.html – Facts about sexual orientation, Dr Gregory Herek, University of California, Davis.

http://www.apa.org/pi/lgbt/resources/just-the-facts.aspx – Just the Facts about Sexual Orientation and Youth.

http://www.apa.org/topics/sexuality/orientation.aspx – Online Pamphlet on Sexual Orientation from American Psychological Association.

http://sexetc.org/ – Website about sex education written by youth.

http://kidshealth.org/teen/sexual_health/guys/sexual_orientation.html# – Youth-friendly blog about youth sexuality.

Social Cognition

W M Rote and J G Smetana, University of Rochester, Rochester, NY, USA

Glossary

Behavioral self-blame: The belief that one's own behavior is the cause of an undesirable outcome and can be modified to avoid negative outcomes in the future.
Crowds: Reputation-based groups of adolescents that share activities, interests, abilities, or personal characteristics with one another but are not necessarily friends.
Egocentrism: The tendency to view the world from one's own perspective and focus on one's own thoughts and feelings.
Informational assumptions: Beliefs about the nature of reality; what one correctly or incorrectly believes to be the facts regarding a specific phenomenon.
Meritorious earning: Gaining status or wealth due to hard work and effort.
Nurturance rights: Children's right to care and protection.
Personal domain: Activities and behaviors that are not legitimately controlled by others but are instead a personal choice.
Perspective-taking: The ability to understand and coordinate one's own perspectives with those of others.
Self-determination rights: Children's right to exercise control over different areas of their lives.
Theory of mind: An understanding that people are cognitive beings with thoughts, beliefs, emotions, and desires that can be different from one's own.

Introduction

Adolescence is a time of increasing involvement in the world outside the family. Teens become more interested in peers, they desire more personal freedom, and they become more able to think abstractly about ideological issues. Research on adolescent social cognition reflects these issues and advances in social reasoning. Social cognition runs the gamut from abstract thinking about government, rights, and fairness to issues such as friendship and personal choice. It refers both to the influences of social interaction on cognitive development as well as age-related changes in adolescents' thinking about social issues. In this article, we touch on all of these topics and discuss what developmental scientists currently know about adolescent social cognition in a variety of areas. We begin with definitions of the topic.

Definitional Issues and Scope

Definitions and Different Meanings of Social Cognition

Adolescent social cognition is defined as adolescents' understanding of their social world. While this definition appears straightforward, there are actually two distinct ways of conceptualizing and researching the topic. Researchers identified with the first perspective examine how social interaction shapes and influences cognitive development. They typically focus on children and adolescents' understanding of others' internal states, such as their beliefs, desires, emotions, and intentions (also known as *theory of mind*). They document the social factors that contribute to a more advanced theory of mind and examine how these changes affect social competence. Researchers from the second perspective focus more on children's thinking about social issues. They document age-related changes in children's and adolescents' conceptions of social institutions, individual rights, and social relationships as well as changes in their understanding of self and others as psychological systems. Although generally distinct, there also may be some overlap between these two perspectives. However, in studying adolescence, the second perspective is much more prevalent, as little research has examined how theory of mind changes in adolescence.

Age Trends Versus Individual Differences

When examining children and adolescents' understanding of their social world, researchers can either focus on more normative development or on individual differences. One popular approach to the study of normative social-cognitive development is to describe age-related, qualitative changes in the structure of this reasoning. Indeed, some of the most well-known theorists of social cognition, such as Lawrence Kohlberg and Robert Selman, have focused on describing such changes. Researchers may also examine typical development by describing more continuous changes (both increases and decreases) in social understanding with age. Both are important to understand.

As most people are aware, however, normative trends are just that; they describe average differences in abilities that do not necessarily reflect the thinking of any one individual. Therefore, in addition to focusing on age trends, research also has been concerned with predicting and describing individual differences in social cognition. These studies focus on a wide variety of topics, ranging from the online processing of social cues to the way parents and peers affect adolescents' thinking about social and personal issues. Importantly, while research on normative trends mainly describes the 'what' and 'when' of social cognition, research on individual differences often examines the factors that influence 'why' different individuals think the way they do and differ from one another in their thinking.

Global Trends Versus Contextualized Approaches

A distinction can also be made between research focusing on global trends versus contextual differences. Individuals' social

 doi:10.1016/B978-0-12-373915-5.00040-1

experiences worldwide share many similarities. Social life in all cultures is marked by the presence of social norms that structure and organize social interactions, and all individuals have experiences of fairness and unfairness, pain, and joy. Individuals also have interactions that emphasize relatedness as well as separateness with others. These shared experiences may result in similar ways of thinking that are evident in universal patterns of social reasoning. This type of research typically acknowledges differences in the timing or scope of social reasoning but emphasizes changes in universal patterns of thinking.

In contrast, research examining contextual differences in social reasoning focuses on group differences and their effects on those patterns. Studies comparing the social reasoning of adolescents from different cultures, ethnicities, and social classes often examine individual differences, as well as the way context or situational variation affects social thinking. No matter what kind of contextual variation is considered, however, the best of the contextualized approaches describe not only how people vary, but also the features of their environment that promote differences in thinking and how those contextual differences are reflected in variations in social reasoning.

The rest of the article will focus on specific topics of social cognition and what developmental scientists currently know about adolescents' thinking about those issues. Although we do not discuss specific studies, we hope that you will notice how these different approaches to social-cognitive research are reflected in the types of information presented.

Reasoning about Interpersonal Relationships

Obligatory Aspects – Morality

Moral reasoning focuses on the rights and welfare of others. We describe morality as the obligatory aspect of interpersonal relationships because actions that are viewed as causing harm or unfairness to others or that violate their rights generally have a prescriptive basis – we are morally obligated to do (or not to do) these things. Although people sometimes violate moral codes in real-life situations, doing so is not taken lightly. There are a variety of research programs that investigate moral reasoning in adolescence, but most either view morality as developing in global, universal stages or as developing in parallel with other types of social reasoning.

Global stage theories

Based on research by Lawrence Kohlberg, some researchers view moral development as progressing in a sequence of universal, hierarchical stages. According to this view, during middle childhood, moral reasoning reflects concerns with punishment avoidance, obedience, and instrumental needs. During early to mid-adolescence, moral understanding may enlarge to include concerns with interpersonal norms, such as relationships, trust, and meeting the expectations of others. Further development during adolescence leads to a broader conventional understanding of morality involving a shift from an interpersonal focus to a concern with the good of society as a whole. At this point, being morally right means upholding laws, contributing to society, and fulfilling duties and agreements. Empirical evidence shows that most adolescents never progress beyond this conventional level of reasoning. Theoretically, however, there are two further stages, which are referred to as principled or postconventional reasoning. These stages involve a view of rights and justice that is universal and independent of societal convention or law.

Kohlberg's theoretical approach dominated the research on adolescent moral development for several decades, but it is no longer the leading view. There are several reasons for this. For one, few individuals develop principled moral reasoning, leading to questions about how broadly applicable the model is. Kohlberg's reliance on hypothetical dilemmas also led researchers to question their applicability to moral reasoning in real-life situations. Similarly, Carol Gilligan claimed that Kohlberg's theory is biased against women and does not accurately assess women's orientation toward care rather than justice, which is seen as a male orientation. Although Gilligan's claims regarding sex differences in moral development have been not supported, her research has highlighted the need to employ broader definitions of morality that include care. Furthermore, individuals are not necessarily consistent in their moral reasoning about different issues and in different contexts, which violates a basic tenet of Kohlberg's theory. More generally, the notion that all individuals follow a similar sequence of thinking progressing from personal concerns through conventionality to universal rights fell out of favor as the field moved toward a more nuanced consideration of cultural and contextual variations in thinking.

Social domain theory

Another theoretical approach that has received a great deal of attention more recently is called social domain theory and is based on research by Elliot Turiel, Larry Nucci, and Judith Smetana, as well as others. The basic notion here is that individuals construct different systems of social knowledge that develop in tandem over time. Morality is one of those systems and includes issues that affect the rights and welfare of others. Conventions are another such system and consist of more arbitrary norms and expectations (like manners and etiquette) that structure social interactions. Finally, personal concerns comprise a third system of knowledge and entail concerns with autonomy and a sense of self. These three types of concerns – with morality, social conventions, and self and personal issues – develop out of different social interactions and apply to individuals in different cultures, although individuals may vary in what they treat as a social convention or personal issue. These concepts become more sophisticated with age, but even children as young as age four are able to distinguish (at least in rudimentary ways) moral issues from conventional and personal issues. By adolescence, teens view the rights and welfare of others as universal givens that are not contingent on rules or laws. In contrast, conventions are seen as relative to social contexts and dependent on the rules and dictates of authority. Furthermore, as discussed later, personal concerns are viewed as a separate type of social knowledge reflecting developments in conceptions of the self.

Much of the research described in this article stems from this second theoretical approach and examines how individuals coordinate overlapping moral, conventional, and personal concerns when making social judgments in different contexts.

Interpersonal Aspects

We now turn to adolescents' thinking about other interpersonal behaviors and issues, such as friendships, exclusion from social groups, and victimization. These issues may have moral dimensions, because they often have implications for the rights or welfare of others, but they also include other considerations, such as personal choice or group norms.

Friendship

Children's conceptions of friendship change during childhood and adolescence. Most of the social-cognitive research on friendships has focused on global changes in thinking. Children and preadolescents focus on the concrete aspects of friendship, such as shared interests and abilities, similar activities, and sharing toys. Early adolescents still emphasize these concrete aspects of friendship, but they also include more psychological aspects, such as trust, intimacy, and faithfulness. Early adolescents also begin to focus more on their friends' personalities and sharing personal experiences. The importance of psychological intimacy increases throughout adolescence, with middle and late adolescents describing friendship almost entirely in terms of authenticity, self-disclosure, loyalty, and commitment. However, older adolescents also learn to balance intimacy in friendships with a need for independence. Girls consistently focus more on intimacy and self-disclosure than boys, especially as they grow older.

Exclusion

People can be excluded from social groups for many reasons. For adolescents, the most typical reasons include the unattractiveness of the individual, punishment or retribution, threat or danger of the individual to the group, and group loyalty. Adolescents typically view exclusion from social groups as a moral issue and evaluate it as wrong when it is presented in the abstract. They are also more likely than younger children to evaluate exclusion from friendships based on race as wrong. Similar to reasoning about other types of moral issues, however, adolescents are more likely to believe that exclusion is acceptable when it is described as in conflict with other concerns, such as group functioning. Early adolescents, in particular, value peer approval and maintaining group processes at the expense of excluding others. Adolescents are also more likely to view exclusion as legitimate and as a personal choice in the context of intimate relationships, such as friendships or dating, than in group contexts, like memberships in sports or clubs. As adolescents grow older, they become better able to coordinate moral concerns with unfairness with the conventional concerns of group norms and functioning. This leads to an increasing tendency to judge exclusion as wrong regardless of the context. Adolescents' evaluations of exclusion are also influenced by stereotypes and gender norms. Adolescents attempt to use person-specific information when making social decisions. When information about a person is lacking or ambiguous, however, teens rely on stereotypes to help determine whether punishment or exclusion is justified.

Adolescents' thinking about the permissibility of exclusion on the basis of sexual orientation has also been examined. While adolescents are relatively accepting of homosexuality, they are less comfortable about it when thinking about situations involving close interaction. Thus, teens view it as less wrong to exclude homosexuals than heterosexuals from peer groups, although there is no such difference in evaluations of teasing or harassment. Additionally, acceptance of homosexuality generally is greater among girls than boys, especially with age.

Teens' personal experiences also influence how they view exclusion. Adolescents who belong to high status peer groups judge peer exclusion as less wrong than do teens belonging to low status groups or no peer group. Although most teens view race-based exclusion as wrong, racial identity does appear to play some role in evaluations of more subtle race-based exclusion. For instance, experience with peer exclusion increases the likelihood of evaluating race-based exclusion as morally wrong for minority youth but not for majority youth. Furthermore, when reasons other than race are provided for exclusion, minority youth are more likely than majority youth to view race-based exclusion from a friendship as wrong.

Victimization

In addition to being excluded, adolescents can be harassed or victimized by others in the peer group. Although victimizing others is seen as wrong, the majority of adolescents believe that victims cause their own victimization. Only about a third of early adolescents believe that victimization is due to characteristics of the aggressor or environment. Of the remaining majority, about half of early adolescents studied believe that victims are in control of the behaviors that cause them to be victimized (such as being annoying), with the rest attributing victimization to characteristics of victims that are out of their control (such as physical features).

In situations of victimization, most adolescents blame the victim rather than the aggressor. However, being victimized affects the type of blame adolescents attribute to the victim. Both victims and nonvictims make behavioral self-blame attributions, believing that the causes of harassment are transitory and controllable. Compared to nonvictims, however, adolescents who have been victims of peer harassment blame themselves more and believe that their harassment is due to their own character; they perceive the causes of personal harassment to be stable and uncontrollable. These characterological self-blame beliefs are potentially maladaptive. Ethnic minority or majority status also moderates this effect. Adolescents in the numerical ethnic minority at a school tend to be victimized more than majority adolescents within the same school, independent of the ethnic makeup of the school. Nevertheless, victims in the numerical ethnic majority at a school may blame themselves more for their harassment. Because they see themselves as deviant from the dominant ethnic group norms, they tend to experience lower self-esteem, more loneliness, and greater peer-rejection than victims in the numerical ethnic minority.

Reasoning About Government, Society, and Politics

In most democratic societies, people are given the right to vote by the end of adolescence, if not before. Because of this, as well as age-related advances in moral and conventional reasoning, there has been much interest in examining adolescents' thinking about government, laws, and individuals' rights within society.

Rights

During adolescence, teens develop an increased focus on personal freedom and rights, along with a more complex understanding of what rights are, who deserves rights, and when they should be upheld. Regardless of ethnicity or country of origin, all adolescents advocate rights and do so based on concerns with fairness, autonomy, and democratic decision-making. However, there are some age-related changes in how adolescents view rights. Early adolescents, like younger children, generally define rights as the freedom to choose activities like recreation and play. They sometimes focus on legal rights. Middle adolescents are much more concerned with the freedom to make one's own decisions and with rights to free speech and civil liberties. This shift toward valuing personal freedom is also reflected in adolescents' thinking about nurturance rights (children's rights to care and protection) versus self-determination rights (children's ability to exercise control over different areas of their own lives). Studies comparing youth in different and diverse cultures have found that both younger children and adolescents endorse nurturance rights, but endorsement of self-determination rights increases dramatically during adolescence. Indeed, although both younger children and adolescents generally view nurturance rights as more important than self-determination rights, there is an increase during adolescence in endorsing self-determination rights over nurturance rights when they are in conflict. Similarly, with age, adolescents become more likely to view laws that dictate individuals' behavior as infringing on personal freedoms.

Adolescents' thinking about who deserves rights and when they should be upheld also changes with age; it shifts from focusing on direct equality (uniform distribution for everyone) to coordinating equality with equity (distribution based on need). For instance, adolescents become less likely to ground rights in personal prerogatives and more likely to base rights on individuals' mental or physical competencies. This is largely because older adolescents are more likely to consider context and situational differences in their reasoning about rights than are younger adolescents. Furthermore, adolescents increasingly support the role of government as protecting individual rights and civil liberties and view this goal as more important than maintaining equality. Indeed, late adolescents are significantly more likely to endorse violating a law that restricts civil liberties than are early adolescents. Finally, although all adolescents sometimes subordinate rights to other moral concerns, such as welfare or equality, younger adolescents tend to see it as more acceptable to violate individual rights to maintain equality than do older adolescents.

Laws and Social Conventions

As they develop, adolescents oscillate between affirming and rejecting the importance of laws and social conventions. These shifts reflect increasingly more sophisticated ways of understanding the role of social conventions in structuring social life and can be linked with actual deviant behavior. Preadolescents generally affirm the importance of social conventions based on concerns with obeying rules and authority. Early adolescents reject this concrete view; a fuller understanding of the arbitrary nature of many social conventions leads teens to view social conventions as 'nothing but' social expectations. During middle adolescence, teens begin to understand that social conventions are important because people exist in social systems that have different roles and hierarchical structures. However, late adolescents once again reject social conventions because they view societal standards as existing purely because certain behaviors have been reified through habitual use. Finally, in young adulthood, social conventions are again affirmed as important, because they are viewed as arbitrary but necessary uniformities that help to coordinate social interaction and smooth societal functioning.

Government

Adolescents' thinking about government reflects a combination of reasoning about moral issues such as rights and conventional issues such as societal rules. Both children and adolescents consider different democratic forms of government, including consensus (all people must agree), direct (majority rule), and representative democracy (rule by elected officials), to be fairer than nondemocratic forms of government, such as oligarchy (rule by the wealthy) and meritocracy (rule by the most intelligent). These evaluations have been found in children and adolescents across cultures, not just those living in democratic societies, and are justified based on the need for government accountability and for everyone to have a voice. Children do not prefer one type of democracy above others, but adolescents view direct and representative democracy as fairer than consensus democracy. This change, although sometimes justified with democratic reasons, is mainly due to adolescents' increased understanding and concern with practicality in government.

Economic Inequality

Adolescents' thinking about economic inequality becomes more varied during adolescence. From childhood until early adolescence, there is an increase in beliefs about meritorious earning, or that economic standing is based on hard work and effort. However, endorsement of this belief decreases slightly during adolescence. Older adolescents are less likely to attribute wealth or poverty to level of work than are younger adolescents and are more likely to offer a mix of personal and situational reasons for economic inequality. Indeed, sociopolitical reasoning becomes significantly more complex and integrated over the course of adolescence. Beliefs about the causes of economic inequality also vary based on social class and access to societal opportunities. Poor, inner-city adolescents more often attribute economic standing to personal factors such as effort and motivation. In contrast, middle and upper class youth more often provide social reasons for economic standing that attribute wealth or poverty to societal forces beyond individual control. Additionally, teens who attribute economic inequality to situational causes feel more compassionate toward those less fortunate than themselves.

Gender Equality and Inequality

Adolescents' reasoning about gender equality and inequality has also been studied. Compared to girls or adults of either gender, adolescent boys in the United States more strongly endorse gender norms, even when the norms conflict with concerns for fairness. Similar trends have been observed in India. In the United States, gender norms are considered social conventions. However, researchers have examined whether gender norms in family relationships and traditional cultural practices are considered moral matters or social conventions in the context of more hierarchically organized cultures characterized by traditional gender roles. In studies conducted in India, Benin, West Africa, and among the Druze Arabs in Israel, adolescents (both boys and girls) typically grant authority to males (for instance, husbands in families or male traditional authorities) for conventional reasons and view authority as alterable. At the same time, many individuals (and more often, those who are disadvantaged by the gender arrangements) judge the practices as unfair, based on moral reasons. They advocate adherence to unfair practices primarily for pragmatic reasons such as fear of punishment. Males, particularly those in the dominant positions, tend to take the protagonist's gender into account more than females do and view traditional male authority as less alterable.

Civic Engagement

Civic engagement is addressed in more detail elsewhere in this volume; we focus here only on social-cognitive approaches. Involvement in community service improves adolescents' understanding of the social order, their reasoning about moral and political issues, and their compassion for those less fortunate. In particular, it inspires more reflection on personal responsibility and justice. Contrary to common perceptions of teenagers as apathetic and uninvolved, adolescents typically view community service as morally obligatory and as highly worthy of respect. Additionally, adolescents who participate more in volunteer activities view community service as more moral (more obligatory and worthy of respect). Adolescents also believe that they have a strong obligation to engage in political activity such as voting, although primarily for conventional rather than moral reasons, such as maintaining social order and following customs. Activities such as protesting or boycotting are seen as considerably less obligatory, less important, and less worthy of respect than more traditional forms of civic engagement. However, the more adolescents know about and participate in politics, the more they treat standard political activities and behaviors like protesting as moral matters.

Tolerance

A bedrock belief of democratic society is that people should be allowed to hold different opinions and voice dissenting beliefs. But for different opinions to be voiced, individuals must have at least a modicum of tolerance for dissent. Therefore, considerable research has examined attitudes toward tolerance and its development. Specifically, research examines how people feel about others who think or act differently from how they think or act.

Like adults, adolescents are generally tolerant of dissent in abstract situations, but become much less tolerant when the dissent is described in more specific situations. Also similar to adults, adolescents' tolerance depends on whether dissent is described as pertaining to beliefs, acts, or people. Adolescents are more tolerant of holding dissenting beliefs than of expressing those beliefs, but tolerance for both increases throughout adolescence. They are also more tolerant of expressing dissenting beliefs than engaging in acts based on those beliefs. These differences reflect adolescents' attempts to coordinate respect for cultural conventions with moral issues such as individual rights and the welfare of others.

Adolescents are also more tolerant of people than of the acts they perform. That is, adolescents distinguish, at least to some extent, between persons and their behaviors. They may evaluate a dissenting act negatively while still maintaining that the actor is a good person. Additionally, with age, adolescents become more tolerant of dissenting others. They shift from the relative intolerance of childhood to greater tolerance in early adolescence to actually suspending judgment of dissenting others until they have more information in late adolescence. In particular, older adolescents take into account people's justifications for their actions. Dissenting others are viewed more negatively if their behavior is due to a different moral belief (e.g., that the act is fair) than if it is due to a different informational assumption about the way the world works (e.g., that the act helps someone).

Information about disliked acts is also very important in determining tolerance for people and behaviors in other cultures. By late adolescence, teens may believe that a behavior is unfair or unjust. But if they recognize that the behavior is in accordance with the norms or beliefs of the culture, they will be relatively tolerant of the person and the practice. This is especially true if adolescents understand that the disliked acts are viewed as beneficial and consensual within the culture, rather than as merely normative. If late adolescents dislike a behavior and believe that there is disagreement about the act within the culture, however, they will judge the actor negatively. Thus, although tolerance increases in general across adolescence, only late adolescents take into account dissenting others' beliefs about the acts and the cultural context in which a dissenting act is performed.

Some teens are also more tolerant in general of disliked people and groups. As previously mentioned, tolerance depends a great deal on understanding the beliefs of others. Consequently, tolerant youth tend to display a broader knowledge and understanding of disliked groups than do intolerant youth. Additionally, when evaluating disliked groups, tolerant adolescents tend to focus on individual rights, whereas intolerant adolescents focus more on evaluative judgments and the negative effects of dissent. Regardless of their tolerance, however, the more negatively adolescents perceive a group, the less likely they are to believe that that group has rights.

The Self and Personal Issues

Personal reasoning changes greatly during the second decade of life. Adolescents form a more nuanced understanding of the psychological world, including more complex conceptions of self, identity, and the perspectives of others. They also develop a larger personal sphere, desiring more control over various aspects of their lives. Although reasoning about the self and personal issues may appear to be very different from reasoning about social relationships and institutions, they share many similarities. Indeed, social domain theory defines personal issues as one of the three primary domains of social reasoning. Furthermore, changes in adolescents' thinking about personal issues impact their relationships with parents, peers, and the broader social world.

Concepts of Self

Adolescents' conceptions of the self become more abstract, psychological, and integrated over time. Early adolescents increasingly distinguish between physical and psychological reality, viewing the self primarily in mental terms and as a volitional entity independent of physical activity. Consequently, trait-like self-descriptions, which are common in middle childhood, give way to psychological descriptors such as 'friendly' or 'smart' in early adolescence. This increased focus on a psychological understanding of the self also paves the way for the emergence of different role-related selves. For instance, adolescents may describe themselves as outgoing with friends but shy in class. False-self behavior, where individuals may act inauthentically in certain contexts and report different levels of self-esteem in different relationships, also emerges at this age. Early adolescents are not yet able to identify and integrate contradictory aspects of their personality descriptions, however. Thus, they may describe themselves as both outgoing and shy in different relationships or contexts, but they will not recognize the contradiction.

Middle adolescence is a time of increased introspection, and multiple role-related selves may proliferate. Middle adolescents also come to recognize the contradictory aspects of their self-descriptions, yet they are unable to coordinate them. This leads to feelings of internal conflict and confusion. It is not until late adolescence or early adulthood that adolescents are finally able to integrate different aspects into abstract, higher-order self-conceptions. At this point, opposing descriptions of the self are no longer viewed as contradictory because they can be explained by higher order constructs. For instance, late adolescents might describe themselves as flexible or bad at group discussions to explain why they are outgoing with friends but shy in class. Late adolescents also begin to integrate and internalize abstract beliefs, such as moral values, into their self-conceptions.

Personal Choice/Jurisdiction

Personal issues are behaviors that are not legitimately regulated by others and are instead viewed as matters of personal choice. Personal issues pertain to privacy, control over one's body, and choices and preferences. Among American adolescents, the latter include issues like choice of friends, personal appearance, and leisure activities. Although the specific behaviors that make up the personal domain show some cultural variation, the need for a personal domain is described as universal, because having jurisdiction over personal issues allows individuals to develop a sense of agency, efficacy, and uniqueness. Personal concepts have been studied and are evident in a variety of cultures worldwide, including many that are considered to be collectivist.

Age-related changes

Children begin to identify areas of personal control in early childhood. However, during adolescence, the boundaries of personal jurisdiction greatly expand. This is not to say that adolescents believe that they should have free reign over all behaviors; adolescents generally believe that parents legitimately can control moral, conventional, and prudential (risky) issues. However, adolescents believe that parents do not have the right to control personal issues. (Parents agree to some extent, but much less than children would like.) As they grow older, adolescents view a broader range of behaviors as part of their personal domain. This pattern has been observed among adolescents from a wide variety of ethnicities and cultures, although minority adolescents in the United States (as well as youth in other cultures such as China) typically expect to gain control at slightly later ages than their European American peers.

Additionally, there are individual differences in how much personal control adolescents expect, reflecting variations around the normative patterns. Thus, although all adolescents desire more control over personal issues with age, some teens (particularly early adolescents) will cede more control to parents, although less over personal than other issues. And across different studies, there appears to be a small subset of adolescents who reject parental authority over almost all types of behavior; this pattern is associated with greater deviance, less parental monitoring and support, fewer parental rules, and lower levels of self-efficacy.

Effects on relationships/behavior

The expansion of the personal domain in adolescence is associated with increases in parent–adolescent conflict. Like adolescents, parents believe that teens should have areas of personal control and that this control should increase with age. They lag behind their adolescents in their beliefs about how much control teens should have and the particular behaviors for which this control is seen as appropriate, however. This discrepancy is the cause of much every-day bickering. Adolescents typically assert that issues like cleaning their bedroom, how late to stay out at night, when to do homework, whether to get a tattoo or piercing, who they chat with online, and what they do with friends are all personal issues. In contrast, parents may view these same behaviors as family or cultural conventions or as prudential issues of safety or health. Thus, the moderate amounts of parent–child conflict that are typical during early and middle adolescence are mainly a result of adolescents' increasing desire for personal jurisdiction and their attempts to renegotiate the boundaries of the personal domain.

These age-related increases in adolescents' desires for more control over personal issues have been observed among teens in a broad range of Western and non-Western cultures and among American youth of different ethnicities. Chinese adolescents appear to have less frequent and intense conflicts with parents over personal issues, however, and are less likely to resolve conflicts by gaining power than are European-American adolescents. Similarly, Chilean and Filipino parents are slower to grant adolescents autonomy than are their American counterparts. Indeed, the more acculturated minority teens and parents are to American society, the earlier adolescents expect autonomy over personal issues and the more likely parents are to grant it to their children.

Parents' thinking about the boundaries of the personal domain has been linked with their parenting styles. Permissive parents are lax in defining the boundaries of legitimate parental and social control and compared to other parents, tend to treat more issues as personal. Authoritative parents maintain appropriate boundaries between moral and conventional issues and grant adolescents some control over personal issues. However, they focus on the prudential or conventional dimensions of multifaceted issues and do not view adolescent control over these issues as appropriate, especially for early adolescents. Authoritarian parents overextend the boundaries of the personal domain and also moralize conventional issues (that is, treat social conventions as moral matters in their judgments). Authoritarian parenting has been linked with more intense parent–adolescent conflict, perhaps because adolescents with authoritarian parents experience larger discrepancies between how much control they want and how much control their parents are willing to give.

Adolescents are also better off when their personal freedom is restricted to some extent and in developmentally appropriate ways. Across ethnicities, one long-term consequence of giving adolescents too much personal control too early in adolescence is greater depression in late adolescence. In contrast, adolescents who gain more personal control from middle to late adolescence tend to be better adjusted. This is a fine line to walk, however; parental overcontrol of personal issues is linked with adolescent internalized distress.

Influences on personal reasoning

Adolescents' behavior can also be linked with reasoning about personal control. This is especially true in terms of adolescents' thinking about prudential issues and their risky behavior. Most adolescents believe that parents can legitimately control prudential behaviors like drinking alcohol and using illegal drugs. In contrast, frequent drug-users are more likely to view drug and alcohol use as a personal choice. They also view these behaviors as less wrong and less harmful than do other adolescents. Not surprisingly, high drug users are therefore less likely than other adolescents to believe that parents or the law have legitimate authority over their risky behavior.

Siblings and peers also influence adolescents' reasoning about personal control. Compared with first-born adolescents, later-born teens expect more autonomy over personal issues at earlier ages, especially in single-parent or step-parent families. For parents, though, the opposite is true. They view more issues as personal for their first-born than for their later-born children. Not surprisingly, later-born adolescents therefore report more conflict with their parents than do first-born teens, although at younger ages.

Adolescents tend to be similar to their friends in their beliefs about how much control their parents or they legitimately should have. This may occur both via selection effects and because adolescents notice and compare their own freedoms to those of their close friends. Similarly, crowd membership is linked with personal reasoning. Adolescents in different crowds have different patterns of beliefs about how much control teenagers versus parents should have over prudential, moral, and personal issues. American high school students identify with peer crowds like jocks, preps, nerds, loners, goths, and normals based on the crowd's similarities to adolescents' interests and identity. Crowds then channel adolescents' behavior and thus are likely to further differentiate adolescents' authority beliefs.

Disclosure and secrecy

As adolescents' need for personal control increases, so too does their desire for privacy. At least in the United States, adolescents spend increasing amounts of time unmonitored and away from parents. (This may be less the case for youth in some other cultures, where school days are longer and peer interactions are less important.) Selective control of information becomes an important way that adolescents can increase their privacy and felt autonomy. Indeed, parents' knowledge of adolescents' behavior outside the home comes mainly from adolescents' voluntary disclosure of information rather than from parental efforts at solicitation or control. Despite their desire for more autonomy, adolescents fully disclose to parents about some of their behavior, primarily because they feel obligated to do so, and also because they hope to change their parents' opinions or feel they would get caught otherwise.

However, adolescents also frequently avoid discussing the subject or employ partial disclosure techniques like omitting important information or telling parents only if asked. This happens because adolescents fear parental disapproval and punishment (particularly for prudential issues) or view the information as harmless or private (for personal issues). But nondisclosure is also influenced by ethnicity. Mexican American teens focus more on fear of parental disapproval or punishment as a reason not to share information with parents, whereas keeping secrets because of beliefs that their parents will not listen, understand, or care occur more among Chinese American than Mexican or European American teens. Although research has not yet been conclusive, partial disclosure appears relatively harmless and may function as an alternative route to autonomy for some adolescents. In contrast, adolescents rarely lie, but when they do, it is strongly linked with poor psychosocial adjustment. Disclosure and secrecy are strongly influenced by the parent–adolescent relationship. Youth with warm, supportive, accepting parents disclose more and lie less to parents.

Perspective-Taking Ability and Social Interaction

Perspective taking is defined as the ability to understand and coordinate one's own perspectives with those of others. It is the basis for reasoning about interpersonal relationships and other's rights and is an important influence on social behavior. Perspective-taking skills increase with age and show considerable development during the adolescent years.

Perspective-taking ability

Robert Selman has conducted extensive research examining the development of perspective-taking abilities. He describes social perspective taking as developing in five sequential stages. The first three stages occur in childhood; the last two stages develop during adolescence. By late childhood, children can consider other people's views and recognize that people have different perspectives on the same situation. Early adolescents develop the ability to simultaneously consider their own and other's perspectives and understand that others can do the same. Finally, middle adolescents are able to evaluate their own and other's perspectives in the context of the social system and generally held societal beliefs. The same sequence of development has been found in both normally developing and disturbed adolescents, although the latter appear to develop more slowly.

Interpersonal negotiation

Contrary to what one might expect, higher levels of perspective-taking ability do not necessarily predict better interpersonal relationships. The concept of interpersonal negotiation, or the ability to think about and devise strategies for solving social conflicts, has been used to explain this discrepancy. Interpersonal negotiation skills improve throughout childhood and adolescence; girls are better at this than are boys. Originally, it was thought that levels of perspective taking and interpersonal negotiation develop in tandem, with interpersonal negotiation mediating the influence of perspective taking on interpersonal relationships. The discrepancies between perspective taking and interpersonal negotiation are larger than expected, however, and interpersonal negotiation is much more influenced by context and experience than is perspective taking. Adolescents demonstrate more mature interpersonal negotiation abilities when reasoning about hypothetical than actual dilemmas, when thinking about conflicts with peers than with adults, and when the dilemmas are focused on personal rather than work-related issues.

An additional problem with using interpersonal negotiation to bridge the gap between perspective-taking ability and interpersonal relationship quality is that adolescents' level of interpersonal negotiation does not always correspond strongly with their actual behavior. Bipolar adolescents report poorer social skills than other adolescents but have similar levels of interpersonal negotiation skills when reasoning about hypothetical dilemmas. Additionally, adolescents' interpersonal negotiation abilities as assessed on hypothetical dilemmas predict their interpersonal negotiation skills in real-life situations, but neither type of interpersonal negotiation is consistently related to externalizing behavior.

Personal meaning

Recently, researchers have begun to focus on the role of personal meaning to explain these inconsistencies in the associations among perspective taking, interpersonal negotiation, and social behavior. Personal meaning is the emotional component of social interactions and combines individuals' cognitive perspective-taking competencies with their personal experiences to determine behavior. Personal meaning does not vary consistently with age. Rather, it is influenced by contextual factors like parenting and peers and by biological factors like temperament and brain development.

Ethnic Perspective Taking

Ethnic perspective taking refers to a person's understanding of ethnicity and the distinguishing features that make up ethnic group membership. Like perspective taking in general, ethnic perspective taking becomes more complex and nuanced with age. Children tend to focus on concrete aspects of ethnic identity such as skin color or language spoken. During adolescence, teens develop an appreciation for the experiential differences that distinguish ethnic groups, such as cultural values and environment. They begin to recognize that ethnic understanding is contextually driven, with parenting and ethnic rearing environment greatly influencing an individual's perception of ethnic identity. Members of ethnic minorities also tend to develop a group consciousness during adolescence, shifting stereotypes of their ethnicity from negative to positive and blaming those in power for their disadvantaged position.

Adolescents also become better able to differentiate and coordinate these multiple conceptions of ethnic groups with age. Ultimately, adolescents' conception of ethnicity includes physical characteristics, ethnic experiences and values, and personal feelings toward ethnic groups. Additionally, exposure to different ethnic groups increases adolescents' ethnic perspective-taking abilities and the complexity of their intergroup understanding. Nevertheless, adolescents' understanding of their own ethnic group tends to be more nuanced than their understanding of other ethnicities.

Egocentrism

Most research on adolescent social cognition focuses on how adolescents' cognitive skills and understanding increase with age, but some research focuses on possible distortions or biases in adolescents' social reasoning. An example is the research on adolescent egocentrism, or the tendency to view the world from one's own perspective and focus on one's own thoughts and feelings. In particular, two specific types of social-cognitive biases have been investigated. The imaginary audience refers to adolescents' perceptions that others are constantly watching and evaluating their actions and are just as concerned with the adolescents' behavior and appearance as the adolescents are. The personal fable refers to adolescents' belief that their experiences are unique and that they are invulnerable.

Originally, adolescent egocentrism was described as related to cognitive development. Egocentrism was hypothesized to emerge in early adolescence along with the development of early formal operational thought and to subside by middle to late adolescence as formal operations stabilized. However, little support for this hypothesis has been obtained. Egocentrism is present in childhood and does not appear to change along with cognitive development. It is also more prevalent among females than males and is influenced by factors, such as social class and parental education, although the effects vary by gender.

This led some to view adolescent egocentrism as an adaptive aspect of the separation-individuation process. According to this view, the personal fable promotes individuation through inspiring an active focus on one's own uniqueness, whereas the imaginary audience promotes connectedness by encouraging behavior that is accepted by the peer group. However, the empirical evidence for this reinterpretation is limited, which has led some recent researchers to attribute the findings to the demand characteristics of the measures. Thus, whether egocentrism is a distinctively adolescent phenomenon and a normal consequence of development or an individual difference variable that changes in strength from person to person remains unclear.

Theory of Mind

Similar to perspective taking, theory of mind focuses on the understanding that people have mental states (such as desires or beliefs) that are not always known by others and that guide their behavior. The basic concept that thoughts and feelings are private and that different experiences lead to different beliefs is in place well before adolescence. Little is known about whether there are more sophisticated developments in theory of mind during adolescence, although there is some evidence that the speed and contextual invariability of adolescents' mentalizing abilities develop during this time, along with greater variability in intraindividual differences.

Conclusions

As indicated by the broad scope of this article, adolescent social cognition is a complex topic, and many avenues of research have been pursued. Research on some topics, notably victimization and civic engagement, almost exclusively focuses on individual differences in social reasoning. Most areas, however, focus on both normative age-related changes and contextual variations in social reasoning.

Although we divided the article into discrete topics, the areas covered here are actually quite interrelated in real-life situations. For instance, adolescents' developing notions of personal jurisdiction underlie changes in their conceptions of individual rights and freedoms. Similarly, developmental advances in perspective-taking ability are important for developing greater tolerance of others. In many real-life situations, adolescents must recognize and juggle competing concerns with issues of personal choice, group processes, and the rights or welfare of others. Therefore, to understand adolescents' social-cognitive development, we must consider their thinking about various social issues as well as how they differentiate and coordinate different concerns over time.

Explaining the development of social cognition is a difficult task. We know now that social reasoning does not develop in a straightforward, unified, and stage-like way. Adolescents' thinking about different social issues does, indeed, become more abstract and complex with age, but in a much more differentiated way than originally thought. And the pathways are considerably more convoluted than global stage models suggest. Development leads to a more complex, nuanced, and integrated understanding of social issues, but only after periods of confusion and questioning.

There have been great strides in incorporating an understanding of context into studies of adolescents' social reasoning. As reviewed in this article, much research has documented the effects of family environment, peer interaction, socioeconomic status, and ethnicity, as well as personal characteristics (such as sex and race) and individual behavior on adolescents' developing social cognition. In addition, researchers have begun to investigate how adolescents themselves take contextual differences into account when reasoning about social issues. Across all these topics and influences, however, an underlying message emerges. Social cognition is complex and therefore, development during the second decade of life primarily involves adolescents' ability to handle situational variability and complexity – to coordinate multiple competing concerns and resolve incongruities in their beliefs and actions. Over the teen years, adolescents become better able to abstract and generalize about social issues and at the same time, more willing to adjust their social judgments to different situational requirements and contexts.

See also: Adolescent Moral Development; Civic and Political Engagement.

Further Reading

Goossens L, Beyers W, Emmen M, and van Aken M (2002) The imaginary audience and personal fable: Factor analyses and concurrent validity of the 'new look' measures. *Journal of Research on Adolescence* 12: 193–215.

Harter S (1999) *The Construction of the Self*. New York: Guilford Press.

Helwig CC (2006) Rights, civil liberties, and democracy across cultures. In: Killen M and Smetana JG (eds.) *Handbook of Moral Development*, pp. 185–210. Mahwah, NJ: Erlbaum.

Killen M, Margie NG, and Sinno S (2006) Morality in the context of intergroup relationships. In: Killen M and Smetana JG (eds.) *Handbook of Moral Development*, pp. 155–183. Mahwah, NJ: Erlbaum.

Nucci L (2002) The development of moral reasoning. In: Goswami U (ed.) *Blackwell Handbook of Child Cognitive Development*, pp. 303–325. Oxford: Blackwell.

Nucci LP (2008) *Nice is Not Enough: Facilitating Moral Development*. New York: Pearson.

Selman RL, Beardslee W, Schultz LH, Krupa M, and Podorefsky D (1986) Assessing adolescent interpersonal negotiation strategies: Toward the integration of structural and functional models. *Developmental Psychology* 22: 450–459.

Smetana JG (2011) *Adolescents, Families, and Social Development: How Teens Construct Their World*. West Sussex, England: Wiley.

Smetana JG and Villalobos M (2009) Social-cognitive development during adolescence. In: Lerner RL and Steinberg L (eds.) *Handbook of Adolescent Psychology*, 3rd edn., vol. 1, pp. 187–208. New York: Wiley-Blackwell.

Wainryb C (2006) Moral development in culture: Diversity, tolerance, and justice. In: Killen M and Smetana JG (eds.) *Handbook of Moral Development*, pp. 185–210. Mahwah, NJ: Erlbaum.

Relevant Website

http://en.wikipedia.org/wiki/Social_cognition

Social Intelligence

K V Petrides, University College London (UCL), London, UK

Glossary

Construct validity: The degree to which a measurement instrument measures what it claims to measure.

Multitrait–multimethod matrix: A validation strategy evaluating the extent to which different methods for assessing the same construct converge and identical methods for assessing different constructs diverge.

Operational definition: A definition predicated on the directly measurable operations that produced the concept being defined. For example, *pulse* is defined as the number of heartbeats per minute.

Sampling domain: The main elements, facets, or components that a construct is hypothesized to comprise; in psychometrics, the 'universe of items,' which the test developer has to sample randomly in order to derive a representative assessment.

Trait social intelligence: A constellation of social self-perceptions located at the lower levels of personality hierarchies; in lay terms, an individual's perception of his or her social abilities.

Veridical scoring criteria: A logically objective basis for determining whether a response to a test item or task is correct or incorrect.

Introduction

The notion that intelligence tests do not capture the totality of variation in human cognitive abilities is almost as old as the first IQ test. One of the earliest attempts to describe an intelligence beyond the confines of the traditional cognitive type was by E.L. Thorndike who postulated the existence of a social intelligence (SI), which he defined as "the ability to understand men and women, boys and girls – to act wisely in human relations."

Thorndike hypothesized two general types of SI, viz., 'understanding of others,' which involves a cognitive appreciation of others without entailing any action, and 'behavioral effectiveness' or 'wise social action,' which involves action on the part of the perceiver. Initially, the new concept was warmly received and spawned the development of many tests, but interest subsided soon after measurement problems loomed up.

It is not generally acknowledged that Thorndike's definition of SI appeared in a popular magazine unaccompanied by any empirical research. Scientific research subsequently highlighted severe problems with the operationalization of this construct. Researchers soon began to point out that there was no concrete evidence of a unitary and distinguishable SI domain. In 1960, Lee Cronbach concluded that "After fifty years of intermittent investigation, SI remains undefined and unmeasured."

Attempts to Measure Social Intelligence

Most tests of SI were designed to assess the 'understanding of others' component of the construct. Two such attempts stand out and merit special mention. The sociologist Chapin designed a scale of 'social insight' that correlated moderately (between $r = 0.25$ and $r = 0.40$) with abstract intelligence and more strongly with rankings of occupational groups and ratings of leadership ability. Despite some promising findings, this scale received very little attention in the literature, and the evidence for its validity remained scant and conflicting.

The second attempt was made by O'Sullivan and Guilford, who developed the 'Six Factor Tests of Social Intelligence,' a measure that was based on Guilford's 'Structure-of-the-Intellect' model. While some reliability and construct validity evidence was initially reported for these tests, interest in them waned quickly due to theoretical criticisms of Guilford's model and general lack of construct validity.

Efforts to measure the 'wise social action' or 'behavioral effectiveness' component of SI met with limited success too. Tentative evidence of a coherent and distinguishable SI-related factor was quickly called into question due to persistent problems with low reliability. It also became clear that it was particularly difficult to devise SI items that could be scored according to truly veridical criteria. Last, many researchers began to focus exclusively on the specific facets of SI (e.g., behavioral effectiveness), thus drastically restricting the meaning of the construct.

Research has been conducted with a multitude of SI tests and conceptualizations. For example, highly specific behavioral measures based on interviewing performance (which cannot, on its own, constitute a sufficient indicator of the broad construct of social intelligence) have been tested with mixed results, including limited convergent validity and negative correlations with academic performance. Numerous self-report measures of SI or 'social skills' or 'social competence' have also been developed. Setting aside important validity limitations, like low-to-zero correlations with cognitive ability, these questionnaires suffer from the same weaknesses as questionnaires of emotional intelligence (EI). Most of the latter are, on the whole, invalid for the purposes for which they have been developed, because intelligence, competencies, and skills cannot be validly assessed via self-report measures of the type "I am good at controlling my emotions." An important exception is the Trait Emotional Intelligence Questionnaire, which has been expressly developed to operationalize EI as a personality trait.

More recently, a number of multitrait–multimethod (MTMM) studies have been reported in the literature

Encyclopedia of Adolescence, Volume 1 doi:10.1016/B978-0-12-373915-5.00041-3

attempting to combine different measurement approaches in the operationalization of SI. No major breakthrough has been achieved through this avenue of research, which reiterated shortcomings like lack of standardized measures based on adequate sampling of the universe of social situations, nonconvergence among the multiple indicators used to operationalize the construct, and unstable patterns of correlations with IQ that are also confounded by individual differences in verbal ability and working memory. Ultimately, the findings of methodologically sophisticated MTMM studies, utilizing multiple measures analyzed via Structural Equation Modeling techniques, have corroborated the problematic nature of the construct.

Summarizing the Problems with the Construct of Social Intelligence

At the heart of the nexus of empirical limitations identified in the scientific literature is the simple fact that, like other false intelligences (creative, emotional, intrapersonal, interpersonal, etc.), SI is an intuitive, but nevertheless, invalid concept. In **Table 1**, I have provided a concise summary of the empirical literature on SI. What is striking about this table is the extent of the disagreement in definitions, measures, and conclusions drawn about what appears to be a gamut of widely different pseudo-constructs all labeled as 'social intelligence.' The numerous specific problems with SI, examples of which I list below, are symptomatic of two fundamental underlying errors discussed at the end of this section.

1. The richness and subjective nature of the various SI facets prevent the development of assessments that can provide comprehensive coverage of the sampling domain of the construct through items that can be scored according to truly veridical criteria. For example, both the 'behavioral effectiveness' and the 'wise social action' components of SI seem to be as much a function of the actor as they are of the observer, not to mention the particular context and timing of the interaction.

   The existence of veridical scoring criteria is a *sine qua non* for the operationalization of the facets of intelligence. The absence of such criteria in the field of SI opened up the way to a bewildering array of makeshift tasks and tests, so removed from everyday experience (e.g., hypothetical interactions described in decontextualized vignettes) that they are very unlikely to be tapping into any psychologically meaningful reality. This was compounded by the introduction of psychometrically baseless scoring procedures, like 'consensus,' 'expert,' and 'target' scoring, which suffer from a number of known and unknown biases and artifacts, and whose underlying mathematical properties are unknown (in the sense that they are not predicated on formal models of psychometric theory).

   More specifically, according to *consensus* scoring, a respondent's score on an item is established with reference to a normative group, with higher scores allocated for agreeing with the majority of the group. Some obvious limitations rendering this method unsuitable for intelligence testing include the fact that the consensual response to an item may vary from place to place and time to time as well as the fact that it is impossible to construct difficult items that only a minority in a sample can answer correctly. Another alternative is *expert* scoring, whereby higher scores are allocated for agreeing with a group of experts. Limitations rendering this method problematic include the fact that experts cannot possibly have more insight into the internal world of a typically developed individual than the individual herself as well as the fact that experts are often unable to reach agreement. Last, the method of *target* scoring has been proposed, whereby higher scores are allocated for accurately describing what a target individual feels. Limitations rendering this method problematic include the fact that there may be extensive individual differences in targets' ability to express themselves or to introspect as well as the fact that many items of interest do not have an external target (e.g., experiencing social anxiety).
2. Different measures of SI tend to show unacceptably low levels of convergence.
3. A large number of not always compatible definitions have been proposed, suggesting that the strength of belief by lay people (i.e., nonpsychometricians) in the existence of new domains of intelligence cannot be construed as a priori evidence of validity. In other words, a collective 'gut feeling' that some type of intelligence exists does not mean that it can also be scientifically operationalized. It now seems clear that the nontraditional intelligences that have been emerging at regular intervals in the second half of the twentieth century have mainly comprised personality traits (e.g., neuroticism relabeled as low EI and extraversion relabeled as high SI).
4. Unsuccessful attempts to differentiate between abstract knowledge pertaining to social interactions and the ability to apply such knowledge in everyday life. That is to say, no distinction is made between the capacity to think in socially intelligent ways, the capacity to behave in socially intelligent ways, and the motivated use of these capacities to pursue socially desirable outcomes.
5. Unwillingness to acknowledge that several of the constituent elements of SI may not be stable traits, but rather context-specific skills (i.e., less 'trait-like' and more 'state-like').

So why has SI research been plagued for so many years by such an overwhelming combination of problems? I suggest the answer is twofold: First, people are often reluctant to abandon their intuitions and preconceptions, even in the presence of solid and extensive contradictory evidence. Yet, empirical facts cannot be rejected simply because they defy our gut feelings. A reluctance to forsake refuted intuitions has sustained haphazard research on this barren topic for over 80 years, the main contribution of which has been the recurrent identification of the problems outlined earlier.

The second reason why the field of SI has encountered so many difficulties is because of a longstanding tendency that sees mainly well-established personality traits (but also interests, values, and motives) arbitrarily relabeled as intelligences. Under this view, individuals who enjoy interacting with others are no longer sociable, but 'socially intelligent,' individuals

Table 1 Tabulated literature review on social intelligence

Author	*Sample size*	*Study focus*	*SI measures*	*Other measures*	*Findings*	*SI definition and conclusion*
Keating (1978)	117	To investigate the empirical coherence of SI domain by means of correlating measures of cognitive ability and social intelligence	Three measures: 1. Defining Issues Test (DIT; Kohlberg) 2. Social Insight Test (SIT; Chapin) 3. Social Maturity Index (SMI; Gough)	Three cognitive ability measures: 1. Concept mastery test (part 1 and 2) 2. Standard Progressive Matrices 3. Remote Associates Test	Cognitive ability measures predicted social competence better than social measures Intradomain correlations are no higher than interdomain correlations: Intradomain $r = 0.28$ Interdomain $r = 0.33$	No identifiable social factor was isolated in this study
Ford and Tisak (1983)	620 (2 schools; Sample 1; Sample 2)	To identify a domain of SI, based on Keating's (1978) methodological model, through analysis of four tests of cognitive competence and six tests of SI	Six measures: 1. Hogan's Empathy Scale (Social Competence Nomination Form; SCNF) 2. Self-ratings 3. Peer-ratings 4. Teacher-ratings 5. Goal attainment scaling (Kiresuk and Sherman, 1968) 6. Competence interview	Four measures of cognitive competence: 1. Overall grades (GPA) 2. Three tasks on mathematical and verbal skills from the Differential Aptitude Test (DAT; Sample 1) and the Science Research Associates Test (SRAT; Sample 2)	Social measures predicted a behavioral measure of social effectiveness better than measures of cognitive competence Intradomain correlations: Sample 1 = 0.36 Sample 2 = 0.33 Interdomain correlations: Sample 1 = 0.26 Sample 2 = 0.21 Evidence that SI is multifaceted	An empirically coherent domain can be identified, if SI is defined as behavioral effectiveness
Marlowe (1986)	188	To examine the main subdomains of SI To investigate the extent to which SI is independent of verbal and quantitative intelligence	Six measures: 1. Social Interest Index (SII; Grever et al., 1973) 2. Social Self-Efficacy Scale (SSES; Sherer et al., 1982) 3. Texas Social Behavior Inventory (TSBIA; Helmreich and Stapp, 1974) 4. Interpersonal Reactivity Index (IRI; Davies, 1983) 5. Perceived Decoding Ability Scale (PDA2; Zuckerman and Larrance, 1979) 6. Social Skills Survey – Peer (SSSP; Marlowe and Weinberg, 1983)	Cognitive ability measure: 1. Shipley-Hartford Institute of Living Scale (SH; Shipley, 1940)	Analysis revealed 5 subdomains: Prosocial attitude Social skills Empathy skills Emotionality Social anxiety SI found to be separate from general intelligence; however, 'social intelligence does not appear to constitute a single domain, but rather two distinct domains' (social self-perception and social skills)	SI is multidimensional and separate from general intelligence

Barnes and Sternberg (1989)	38	To examine how nonverbal decoding ability relates to SI using a couples task (Sternberg and Smith, 1985)	Four measures: 1. Empathy Scale (Hogan, 1969) 2. Social competence nomination form (SCNF; Ford, 1982) 3. Social competence factor (Sternberg et al., 1981) 4. Self-monitoring scale (Snyder, 1974)	One nonverbal decoding measure: Judgments and confidence ratings of 2 × 24 photos ('couples' and 'supervisors'; Sternberg and Smith, 1985) Two cognitive ability tests: 1. Henmon-Nelson Test of Mental Ability 2. Embedded Figures Test	Decoding skills found to be an important part of SI However, low reliability suggests a weak general SI factor	Definition of SI: 'the ability to decode accurately social information' Proposed components underlying SI: – meta-performance – knowledge acquisition
Brown and Anthony (1990)	83	To examine the relationship between social and academic intelligence	Four measures: 1. Self-rated personality 2. Peer-rated personality 3. Self-rated social–behavioral effectiveness 4. Peer-rated social–behavioral effectiveness	Three academic performance variables: 1. Grade Point Average (GPA) 2. Academic Assessment Program English (ACT) 3. Academic Assessment Program Mathematics (ACT)	Results support Ford and Tisak's (1983) behavioral effectiveness criterion Self-assessments of SI appear to have little linear relationship to peer assessment Intercorrelations: – SI measures: 0.34 – Academic performance variables: 0.49 – SI with academic performance: 0.15	Academic and social intelligence represent different, albeit partly overlapping, domains SI consists of at least two different components (self- versus other-perceptions)
Kosmitzki and John (1993)	Sample 1 = 55	To explore the origins of SI by investigating people's implicit conceptions of the construct Correlational analysis of 18 items ranked by participants as possible SI definitions or facets	18 items based on literature reviews (e.g., Walker and Foley, 1973 and Orlik, 1978) ranked according to their relevance as SI definitions or facets	n/a	SI items grouped into cognitive and behavioral components: Cognitive: - perspective taking - understanding people - knowing social rules - openness to others Behavioral: - good at dealing with people - social adaptability - interpersonal warmth Intracorrelation: - 0.32 for components - 0.39 for definitions Rejected components: - manipulating others - being good at influencing, motivating, and leading others	People's implicit conceptions of SI include cognitive and behavioral components

(*Continued*)

Table 1 (Continued)

Author	*Sample size*	*Study focus*	*SI measures*	*Other measures*	*Findings*	*SI definition and conclusion*
	Sample 2 = 105	Factor analysis of the 18 items	18 items in third-person format rated by observers who were well acquainted with targets	n/a	Three factors identified: – Social intelligence – Social influence – Social memory Neither social influence nor social memory was related to SI as understood by participants	
Wong, Day, Maxwell and Meara (1995)	Sample 1 = 134	To establish the convergent and discriminant validity of cognitive and behavioral dimensions of SI	1. Recognition of the Mental State of the Speaker subtest from the George Washington Social Intelligence Test (Moss et al., 1955) 2. Expression Grouping subtest from the Four Factor Tests of SI (O'Sullivan and Guilford, 1976) 3. Perceived Decoding Ability Scale-Form 1 (Zuckerman and Larrance, 1979)	1. Cognitive ability measure: Wechsler Intelligence Scale-Revised (WAIS-R; Wechsler, 1981) 2. Heterosexual Interaction Measures – videotaped interaction between student and confederate 3. The Survey of Heterosexual Interactions	Three dimensions of SI – social perception – social knowledge – social behavior Evidence that SI dimensions can be discriminated from cognitive ability, but only in a homogeneous (high IQ) sample Poor convergent validity of the cognitive factors of SI	SI is likely a multidimensional construct comprising the components of social perception, social knowledge, and social behavior Improved measures will need to be developed before definitive conclusions can be drawn
	Sample 2 = 227		Three measures of Social knowledge: 1. Etiquette measure based on expert books 2. Nonverbal (pictorial) tasks 3. Self-report questionnaire Three measures of Social perception: 1. Verbal measure – Social translations subtest from the Four Factor Tests of SI (O'Sullivan and Guilford, 1976) 2. Nonverbal measure – Expressions Grouping subtest (see Sample 1 above) 3. Self-report questionnaire	1. Cognitive ability measure based on verbal and spatial analogies (Kerwin, 1989) 2. Self-report measure of cognitive ability		

			Three measures of Social insight: 1. Verbal – Judgment in Social Situations subtest from George Washington Social Intelligence *Test* (Moss et al., 1955) 2. Nonverbal – Cartoon Predictions Subtest from Four Factor Tests of SI (O'Sullivan and Guilford, 1976) 3. Self-report questionnaire			
Jones and Day (1997)	176	To assess the discriminability of social-cognitive flexibility from academic problem solving and crystallized social knowledge	Social-cognitive flexibility measures: 1. Pictorial: video clips (Jones and Day, 1997) 2. Verbal: Social Situations Questionnaire (Jones and Day, 1997) 3. Self-report: Battery of Interpersonal Capabilities (BIC; Paulhus and Martin, 1987) 4. Teacher-reports: Battery of Interpersonal Capabilities (BIC; Paulhus and Martin, 1987) Crystallized Social Knowledge measures: 1. Pictorial: Expression Grouping Subtest from the Four Factor Tests of SI (O'Sullivan and Guilford, 1976) 2. Verbal: Social Translations Subtest from the Four Factor Tests of SI (O'Sullivan and Guilford, 1976) 3. Self-report: Perceived Decoding Abilities Scale (PDAS; Zuckerman and Larrance, 1979) 4. Teacher reports (PDAS)	Academic problem-solving measures: 1. Pictorial: Ravens (Raven, 1971) 2. Verbal: Analogies drawn from the Scholastic Aptitude Test (SAT) 3. Self-report questionnaires based on concepts of fluid cognitive ability (Sattler, 1992) 4. Teacher-reports based on concepts of fluid cognitive ability (Sattler, 1992) 5. Teacher-ratings based on the Teacher-Child Rating Scale (T–CRS: Hightower et al., 1986)	– Academic problem solving was discriminable from social-cognitive flexibility, but not from crystallized social knowledge – Significant correlations between crystallized social knowledge and academic problem solving – Teacher reports of social behavior suggested that flexible application of social knowledge is important to social competence	SI can be split into a crystallized component involving declarative and procedural social knowledge and a social-cognitive flexibility component involving flexible knowledge application SI is distinct from academic problem solving

(*Continued*)

Table 1 (Continued)

Author	*Sample size*	*Study focus*	*SI measures*	*Other measures*	*Findings*	*SI definition and conclusion*
Lee, Wong, Day, Maxwell and Thorpe (2000)	208	To replicate research on the multidimensionality of SI and its discriminant validity vis-à-vis cognitive ability To investigate if a distinction between crystallized and fluid components is applicable within SI	Four measures: 1. Judgment in Social Situations subtest from George Washington Social Intelligence Test (Moss et al., 1955) 2. Cartoon predictions subtest from the Four Factor Tests of Social Intelligence (O'Sullivan and Guilford, 1976) 3. Perceived Decoding Ability Scale – Form 1 (Zuckerman and Larrance, 1979) 4. Social Knowledge measures (Wong et al., 1995)	Two cognitive ability tests: 1. Crystallized IQ: Wechsler Intelligence Scale-Revised (WAIS-R; Wechsler, 1981) 2. Fluid IQ: verbal and spatial analogies (Kerwin, 1989)	Cognitive and social intelligence may be representing distinct domains SI comprises two different dimensions: Social Inference and Social Knowledge Social Inference is equally related to crystallized ($r = 0.27$) and fluid ($r = 0.30$) IQ Social Knowledge is closer to crystallized ($r = 0.40$) than fluid ($r = 0.24$) IQ	SI is bidimensional and distinguishable from academic intelligence. The social inference component of SI relates to both fluid and crystallized IQ and the social knowledge component relates more closely to crystallized IQ

Note: Entries in this table are necessarily succinct and present only specific findings of interest. They are not intended as a summary of the original research articles, which interested readers are urged to consult.
Source: Copyright © K V Petrides (2011).

who tend to worry about things are no longer neurotic, but 'emotionally unintelligent,' etc. It is, therefore, important to clarify the meaning of two terms that are essential to this discussion. *Intelligence* concerns the mental ability to infer and apply relationships learnt from experience. The defining characteristic of its assessment is maximum-performance measurement based on veridical scoring procedures. *Personality traits* concern cross-situational consistencies in behavior. The defining characteristic of their assessment is typical-performance measurement based on self-reports.

Mere relabeling does not alter the underlying nature of a construct. It has long been known that personality traits are not amenable to maximum-performance measurement (since they concern typical performance) and, consequently, it was unsurprising that false intelligences also proved resistant to such techniques and approaches. Most problems identified in the scientific literature, many of which I mentioned previously, are symptoms of this specific underlying cause.

Social Intelligence in Adolescence

Social relationships are crucial during the adolescent years, and a number of constructs that are relevant to SI have been the subject of concerted research attention. Much work has focused on social competence, which is of pivotal importance in adolescence, when youngsters begin to form intimate relationships with their peers. In turn, relationships with peers, and also with adults, can facilitate or inhibit emotional development and social participation. Peer difficulties are known negatively to affect subsequent personal adjustment and to lead to a range of unwelcome developmental outcomes (e.g., antisocial behavior, dropping out of school, and psychopathology). In contrast, emotion perception, which features saliently in several models of affective social competence, is consistently linked to prosocial behavior and satisfactory peer relationships.

There can be no doubt that social relations and related variables, like social competence or social skills, are implicated in important and multifarious ways in adolescent development and behavior. What obfuscates, however, is to arbitrarily lump all these ideas together and label them 'social intelligence.' For example, social competence comprises cognitive, affective, and social elements, the majority of which lie outside the domain of human cognitive ability. Those specific aspects of social competence (or social skills) that bear a relationship to cognitive ability reflect, in fact, general intelligence applied to social situations. Consequently, there is little to be gained by invoking some ill-defined and elusive umbrella construct that mixes up distinct variables under an 'intelligence' label.

Social interaction is tightly intertwined with emotional development throughout childhood and adolescence. Preadolescents begin to differentiate between genuine and managed emotional expression, which fosters increased social awareness and sensitivity to social roles. Later on, adolescents begin to gain awareness into their own emotional cycles and how these bear on their relationships with both peers and adults. Overall, the deep links between social and emotional development necessitate a succinct overview of research in the cognate field of EI, not least because it has been more extensively studied during the adolescent period.

Relationships with EI

The problems encountered in the SI literature also plagued the early literature on EI, which is understandable given the overlap between the two constructs. Thus, it has been pointed out that the subjective nature of emotional experience undermines the quest for EI tests based on truly veridical scoring criteria; that there exist antithetical definitions of the construct; that different measures of the construct do not converge; and that extant tests fail to differentiate between abstract knowledge about emotions and the ability to apply such knowledge in everyday life.

Trait EI

Acknowledging that the concept of EI comprises various permutations of personality traits (as opposed to mental abilities) has led to the formulation of the construct of trait EI, which is defined as a constellation of emotional self-perceptions located at the lower levels of personality hierarchies. In simple terms, trait EI concerns people's perceptions of their emotional abilities. Trait EI theory connects the construct to mainstream research on differential psychology, and has been used as the main reference framework in areas as diverse as nursing, psychoneuroendocrinology, relationships, behavioral genetics, and work, among many others. In the following section I focus specifically on research conducted with, adolescent samples.

Trait EI in Adolescence

Unlike SI, there is a fairly large, and growing, literature on EI in adolescence. Here, I summarize the main findings of this literature, with a view to extrapolating some conclusions to the field of SI (especially trait SI, as discussed later on).

Academic performance

The absence of strong correlations between measures of personality and cognitive ability does not preclude the possibility of them having simultaneous effects on criteria like academic performance. Therefore, even though trait EI is conceptualized as orthogonal (i.e., unrelated) to cognitive ability, it is quite possible that it can have indirect, and even small direct, effects on academic achievement. Indeed, it has been shown that IQ may moderate the relationship between trait EI and achievement, such that high trait EI scores are associated with better academic performance in low IQ adolescents only. In other words, the trait EI effect may not be present in adolescents with average or high IQ scores. This suggests that such effects as trait EI might have on academic achievement are likely to assume prominence when the demands of a situation outweigh an adolescent's intellectual resources.

Modest direct correlations ($r = 0.20$, $p < 0.05$) between trait EI and academic performance in high school and university samples have also been reported, raising the possibility that the effects of trait EI may vary across educational levels as well as across subjects, like those of other personality traits (e.g., agreeableness). Thus far, the picture emerging appears to be consistent with the trait EI hypothesis that the construct's direct impact on academic achievement is modest and likely to be more relevant to specific groups of vulnerable children (e.g., those with low cognitive ability or learning disabilities).

Trait EI, social behavior, and mental health in adolescence

Research has shown that high trait EI in adolescence is linked to more peer nominations on prosocial behaviors (e.g., 'cooperation') and fewer nominations on antisocial behaviors (e.g., 'aggression'). It has also been shown that trait EI predicts emotion perception, operationalized as recognition of facial expression, which itself correlates with prosocial behavior and peer acceptance. At high school, high trait EI pupils are less likely to have unauthorized absences (truancy) and to have been excluded or expelled from school due to breaches of discipline. A related line of research has revealed negative links between trait EI and Internet addiction, video gaming abuse, and gambling.

The fact that high trait EI adolescents enjoy fulfilling personal relationships during a period when they are so important to personal development is significant because peer acceptance, social networks, and social status offer a shield against antisocial behavior, delinquency, and psychopathology. With respect to the last of the three, trait EI is a strong negative correlate of, and a potential protective factor against, depression, psychosomatic symptoms, and even self-harming behaviors and suicidal ideation.

Much of the research revealing socially desirable outcomes for high trait EI adolescents is heavily reliant on self-report methodologies and often suffers from shortcomings relating to item overlap and common method variance. Several studies employing more elaborate designs as well as nonself-report (especially objective) criteria have revealed that high trait EI is not always adaptive and that there are circumstances and contexts where high scores are associated with maladaptive outcomes. For example, high trait EI individuals experience stronger negative emotions than their low trait EI peers when faced with a negative event or poor decision outcome, and they are also more sensitive to negative mood induction. It is also worth mentioning that there is little evidence to support the typical, yet untested, assumption in the literature that high trait EI has a causal positive influence on external criteria.

Trait Social Intelligence

Just as trait EI resolved many of the problems identified in the field of EI, the construct of trait social intelligence (trait SI) can help resolve the similar problems identified in the field of SI. Trait SI is defined as a constellation of social self-perceptions located at the lower levels of personality hierarchies. This definition allows us to connect the construct to mainstream models of differential psychology. Simply put, trait SI concerns people's self-perceptions of their social skills and abilities.

Sampling Domain of Trait SI

In psychology, constructs are defined operationally (see **glossary** for definition), rather than via dictionary definitions. When proposing a new construct, it is vital to establish a sampling domain and to develop a valid measurement vehicle for this domain. The effort to establish a sampling domain for trait SI is facilitated by the relative straightforwardness of the field that, having never attracted quite so much interest outside the confines of differential psychology, has remained relatively coherent. Furthermore, there exist in-depth reviews as well as measures seeking to operationalize SI and related constructs, all of which can inform the process of identifying the core components of the construct. A full consideration of this body of evidence suggests that it is possible to derive complementary, but for the most part, mutually exclusive sampling domains of trait SI and trait EI.

The sampling domain of trait SI is presented in **Table 2**, along with a brief description of its 14 facets (more details are given in the text below). Most of these facets are linked to established literatures, which trait SI can help unify in the same way that trait EI helped bring together diverse literatures pertaining to emotional traits. It is important to remember that trait SI facets do not reflect actual cognitive abilities, but rather self-perceptions.

Communicative anxiety: High scorers seem to enjoy communicating with strangers, so much so that many actually take pleasure in public speaking. Low scorers, on the other hand, routinely have difficulties communicating with those they do not know well. For them, voicing opinions in formal meetings

Table 2 The adult sampling domain of trait social intelligence

Facets	*High scorers view themselves as...*
Communicative anxiety (low)	... effective and relaxed communicators.
Managing others	... persuasive and influential.
Negotiating	... good at bargaining and conflict resolution.
Networking	... people–connectors and able to make new acquaintances easily.
Perspective taking	... adept at identifying with others and seeing things from their perspective.
Savoir vivre	... well-mannered and refined.
Social adaptability	... socially flexible and able to relate to people from different backgrounds.
Social attentiveness	... tuned in to other people and with superb listening skills.
Social confidence	... self-assured extraverts who excel at socializing.
Social forecasting	... able to predict other people's viewpoints, reactions, and behaviors.
Social empathy	... caring and willing to go out of their way to help others.
Social relationships	... being popular and skillful in building relationships with others.
Teamwork/cooperation	... cooperative and valuable team members.
Understanding others	... able to 'read' other people and understand their needs and aspirations.

Source: Copyright © K V Petrides (2011).

creates anxious feelings. Even when they do manage to rise above their fears, they sometimes cannot express themselves clearly.

Managing others: Though dealing with compliant people is simple for almost anyone, those who score highly on this facet find it easy to persuade even opinionated others to follow their lead. Low scorers do not enjoy managing individuals who are vocal in their opinions, and experience difficulty in dealing with people who are upset. Unlike those who know how to make others see their point of view, low scorers often admit that managing others is a weakness.

Negotiating: The negotiating facet concerns one's willingness and ability to bargain and resolve disagreements between people. Individuals who score highly on this facet are the 'wheelers and dealers' of the world. They find bargaining and negotiating enjoyable and are often capable of settling disputes. Low scorers, on the other hand, find deal-making stressful and tend to regard bargaining and dispute resolution as difficult.

Networking: People with high scores on this facet make new acquaintances and contacts quickly and easily. In contrast, those with low scores have a hard time connecting with others, and may perceive networking events as a waste of time and resources.

Perspective taking: Perspective taking concerns the inclination to 'walk in someone else's shoes.' High scorers can easily identify with others and sense their thoughts, feelings, and aspirations. Low scorers, on the other hand, have difficulty understanding other people and their viewpoints.

Savoir vivre: High scorers on the *savoir vivre* facet are well-mannered and know how to behave appropriately. Low scorers tend to be unsure what constitutes socially appropriate behavior and may find the notion of 'good manners' snobbish.

Social adaptability: High scorers on the social adaptability facet get along well with people from any background and can adapt to most social situations they find themselves in. In contrast, low scorers adjust their behavior to suit social situations only with difficulty. They find it harder to socialize with people from different backgrounds and/or tolerate those they do not like.

Social attentiveness: Social attentiveness concerns listening and paying attention to what others say. While those who score highly on this facet are regarded as 'good listeners' and have little difficulty remembering past conversations, low scorers are easily distracted and may find it tiresome to listen to others for long.

Social confidence: Socially confident individuals seek out social events and have a knack for the social chit-chat that makes interaction enjoyable. In contrast, those who avoid social events tend to score low on this facet. When these individuals find themselves in a gathering, they may be more prone to embarrassment and try to avoid attention.

Social forecasting: Some of us are good at predicting other people's reactions, while others are surprised by them. Those with high scores on the social forecasting facet can anticipate other people's feelings, viewpoints, and behaviors. In contrast, those with low scores have difficulty guessing how others will behave or what their attitudes and aspirations are likely to be.

Social empathy: People who score highly on the social empathy facet are often described as 'caring' and ready to go out of their way to help others. In contrast, those with low scores tend to put themselves first.

Social relationships: Having a wide circle of friends and being popular at the workplace are hallmarks of a high score on the social relationships facet. These individuals enjoy the give and take of human interaction and are known for their skill in navigating social situations. In contrast, those with low scores sometimes find it difficult to get along with others and tend to be overall less popular.

Teamwork: In contrast to high scorers, who find it enjoyable and preferable to work as part of a team, those with low scores on this facet would rather work alone. They prefer competition to cooperation and may find it difficult to be productive when they are forced to work in teams.

Understanding others: High scorers can read others 'like an open book.' For them, it is easy to guess what others think, feel, and want. In contrast, those with low scores have difficulty understanding other people.

In the context of this article, it is worth emphasizing the significance of demonstrating empirically the extent to which each of these facets is manifest among adolescents. Related trait EI research has shown that the sampling domain of that construct is largely invariant between adolescence and adulthood. However, it cannot be simply assumed that this will also be the case for the trait SI facets above, not least because the development of social aspects of personality tends to lag behind that of emotional aspects, which may have implications for early adolescence in particular. Any qualitative differences between the adolescent and adult sampling domains will, of course, be complemented by quantitative differences, with the expectation that adolescents will tend to exhibit lower scores than adults. In all, it remains important to embark on an integrated investigation of intra- as well as interindividual variability in the trait SI facets, although scattered evidence already exists highlighting the role that many of them play during the formative years of adolescence.

The Trait Social Intelligence Questionnaire (TSIQue) was designed to provide a comprehensive coverage of the sampling domain presented in **Table 2**. By comprehensive, I mean that there should be no questionnaire measures of social intelligence, competence, or skills that do not overlap substantially with the TSIQue.

Trait SI theory resolves many of the problems that have been plaguing the various models included in **Table 1**. A consistent sampling domain replaces the ad hoc selection of facets, questionnaire measurement replaces a bewildering range of makeshift assessments, and an explicit set of theoretical propositions replaces a host of ambiguous hypotheses that are tested with no definitive outcomes. In short, trait SI offers a general, testable, and falsifiable theory that integrates the construct of social intelligence into the mainstream taxonomies of personality with potential benefits for the field of adolescent psychology and beyond.

See also: Cognitive Development; Peer Relations; Personality Traits in Adolescence; Popularity and Social Status; Social Competence.

Further Reading

Jensen AR (1998) *The g Factor*. Westport, CT: Praeger.

Keating DK (1978) A search for social intelligence. *Journal of Educational Psychology* 70: 218–233.

Kihlstrom JF and Cantor N (2000) Social intelligence. In: Sternberg RJ (ed.) *Handbook of Intelligence*, 2nd edn, pp. 359–379. Cambridge, UK: Cambridge University Press.

Petrides KV, Pita R, and Kokkinaki F (2007) The location of trait emotional intelligence in personality factor space. *British Journal of Psychology* 98: 273–289.

Saarni C (1999) *The Development of Emotional Competence*. New York: Guilford.

Thorndike EL (1920) Intelligence and its uses. *Harper's Magazine* 140: 227–235.

Walker RE and Foley JM (1973) Social intelligence: Its history and measurement. *Psychological Reports* 33: 839–864.

Waterhouse L (2006) Inadequate evidence for multiple intelligences, Mozart effect, and emotional intelligence theories. *Educational Psychologist* 41: 247–255.

Weis S and Süß H-M (2005) Social intelligence: A review and critical discussion of measurement concepts. In: Schulze R and Roberts RD (eds.) *Emotional Intelligence: An International Handbook*. Göttingen: Hogrefe & Huber.

Relevant Websites

http://www.indiana.edu/~intell/ – "Human Intelligence" including historical influences, current controversies and teaching resources. Supported by Indiana University.

www.psychometriclab.com – London Psychometric Lab at UCL.

http://www.personality-project.org/ – The Personality Project.

Spirituality, Religion and Healthy Development in Adolescents

S Burg, R A Mayers, and L J Miller, Columbia University, New York, NY, USA

Glossary

Conjunctive faith: Fowler's fifth stage, involving a deeper understanding of self and integration of one's own beliefs and those of others.

Hypothetical thinking: A process of cognitive reasoning, often associated with the theory of Jean Piaget, in which individuals generate all logical possibilities in a situation and use this information to solve problems.

Intuitive reflective faith: Stage 4 in Fowler's theory, involving a more personal understanding of faith, less reliance on parental values or opinions, but also some insensitivity to the thoughts and existence of others.

Spiritual awakening: A state of enlightenment or consciousness in which one appreciates the connection to a supreme being or the submergence of the self into a spiritual force.

Spiritual individuation: The process of developing spiritual and self-awareness in which one finds a personal spiritual path toward the establishment of one's spiritual identity and sense of connectedness.

Vision quest: A rite of passage in some Native American cultures involving a journey into the wilderness, often accompanied by fasting or deprivation, in search of spiritual vision. This rite is mimicked in some contemporary programs for youth, often targeted at youth having challenges negotiating adolescence.

Introduction

Much like the vaunted separation between church and state, researchers have long been loathe to cross the line which divides the traditional sciences from the exploration of spiritual and religious pursuits. However, the past 15 years have marked a burgeoning of scholarship on spirituality and its protective qualities across the life span. An abundance of recent data support the assertion that religious participation and spiritual well-being often play an important role in promoting healthy life choices, mental health, and overall wellness. Adolescence is a critical developmental stage during which life-long health practices and healthy decision-making patterns are often determined. This not only offers great potential for the development of protective factors but also poses the risk that life-long detrimental behaviors may be established. Acknowledging the impact of religious and spiritual practices upon the healthy development and well-being of adolescents will allow this often overlooked factor to be considered alongside the other elements which influence adolescent health and development.

This article provides the reader with a broad overview of the current state of the art in this area of study, focusing on promising areas of inquiry such as the amelioration of adolescent depression and reduction of substance use. We will also explore theories of spiritual development and examine the potential for clinical applications to improve health outcomes in light of this developmental trajectory.

The Problem of Defining Spirituality

Most empirical research to date has examined the effects of religiosity as defined by one's adherence to and participation in the traditional exercises of an established faith, or 'organized religion.' This is largely due to a lack of consensus on a universal definition of spirituality that can be operationalized and measured. Work in this area has thus largely focused on tangible and easily measured aspects of religious practice, such as frequency of attendance at religious services, classification of sect or denomination, or self-reported importance of religion.

Efforts to focus on spirituality as distinct from religious practice have been few and far between, although more recent work has attempted to address this. There are several reasons for this omission. Spirituality outside of and distinct from the validation of a corresponding religion and religious practice, especially in the Western world, has often been viewed as a marginal pursuit outside the academic mainstream. Second, the tools that exist to specifically measure aspects of spirituality are limited in number and lack widespread adoption. Third, several studies have demonstrated a personal antipathy toward religion and spirituality among many social scientists. Finally, there has been little consensus in the literature as to a standard or commonly recognized definition of spirituality.

As stated above, there has been little agreement among researchers seeking a unified definition of spirituality. Perez and colleagues define spirituality as a multidimensional construct composed of "the frequency of an individual's spiritual or religious practices, personal conviction of God's existence based on experience, and a highly internalized relationship between God and the self." This again invokes religion, and may not be applicable to the growing number of individuals who report being 'spiritual, but not religious.' Alternate, more inclusive definitions might focus on the belief in a power operating in the universe that is greater than oneself, a sense of interconnectedness with all living creatures, an awareness of the purpose and meaning of life, and the development of personal, absolute values.

Although religiosity and spirituality are strongly correlated they do not refer to the same concept. One line of demarcation between religiosity and spirituality seen in the literature is that between public and private practice. As distinct from religiosity, spiritual belief is often seen to inhabit the realm of personal, or private observance. Such observance may include personal prayer, the independent study of texts, or more diffusely, one's commitment and connection to the divine. In addition, some research differentiates between qualities of personal experience, to include transcendence, an ongoing relationship with the Divine, and translation of spiritual values into daily relationships with fellow people. Conversely, a public observance of one's faith might include attendance at a house of worship, participation in community activities, or religious school attendance. These public forms of observance are more likely to be viewed as elements of formal religious practice. For the purposes of this article, we will focus upon the personal experience of spirituality, unless otherwise specified.

Measurement Tools

Although true empiricism in spiritual research is made difficult by the complex and multidimensional nature of the subject, there are a growing number of research tools devoted to the measurement of spiritual experience. The most widely used instrument to date is the Spiritual Well-Being Scale (from Paloutzian and Ellison in 1982). However, it repeatedly refers to God, limiting its applicability across cultures. In addition, the Fetzer Institute developed the very comprehensive Multidimensional Measure of Religiousness and Spirituality, which is increasingly widely used. One subscale of this instrument, the Daily Spiritual Experiences Scale (from Underwood and Teresi in 2002), measures personal spiritual experience and is often used in studies focusing on mental health. The widespread adoption of these instruments will provide greater standardization across studies. The current burgeoning of new measures will likely reveal the more fine-grained contribution of spiritual and religious dimensions. Finally, there is not currently a commonly accepted measurement tool that focuses on the adolescent population. As evidence grows for the unique effects of spirituality during this life stage, it would be useful to have a scale which targets this population.

Defining the Adolescent Population

Although definitions vary, adolescence commonly refers to youth between the ages of 10 and 19, with those aged 10–14 representing younger adolescents, and individuals aged 15–19 comprising older adolescents. Under this convention (US Department of Health and Human Services), those aged 20–24 are considered young adults, while those younger than 10 are grouped as children. The lack of standardization in these definitions throughout the body of spiritual research, as well as the significant changes in spiritual and religious practice and in health conditions during these developmental stages, may contribute to a disparity in results among the extant data.

Overall, adolescents place great importance in their spiritual lives. One study reported that 95% believe in God, 85–95% state that religion is important in their life, over 50% attend religious services at least monthly, and close to 50% pray alone frequently. Interestingly, the importance placed on spiritual belief tends to decline somewhat as adolescents age. One of the few studies employing a longitudinal design revisited subjects after 5 years (ages 13–17 to ages 18–23) and showed a reduction from 84% to 78% reporting a belief in God and from 49% to 44% reporting that their religion was important in shaping their daily lives.

The effects of religious and spiritual practice and belief tend to be stronger among girls, with female adolescents showing higher rates of both general religiosity and personal spiritual experiences than males with 68% of females rating religion as important compared to 57% of boys. In the United States, Black high school students reported higher levels of religious importance than White students (56% vs. 26%). However, the limited work examining race and ethnicity does not point to a greater correlation between these practices and positive health outcomes. One study of Kuwaiti Muslim adolescents aged 15–18 replicated the finding that females tend to be more religious than males, especially telling considering the great emphasis placed upon male religious observance among Muslims. Studies have shown little correlation for level of education, or health status among individuals within the same culture.

Prevalence and importance of spirituality show mixed results when examined across cultures (**Figures 1** and **2**). Generally, developing countries tend to show a greater level of reported spirituality than wealthier populations, although the high levels of spirituality in the United States stand out as an exception. Although there is a widespread belief in God, adolescents in developed countries tend to place less importance in formal religious practice than those in developing countries, with many reporting that they are 'spiritual but not religious.'

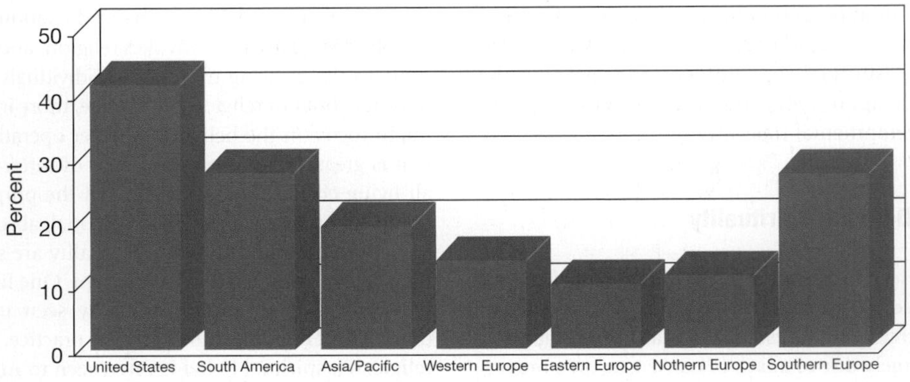

Figure 1 Religious participation among 14-year-olds in 1999.

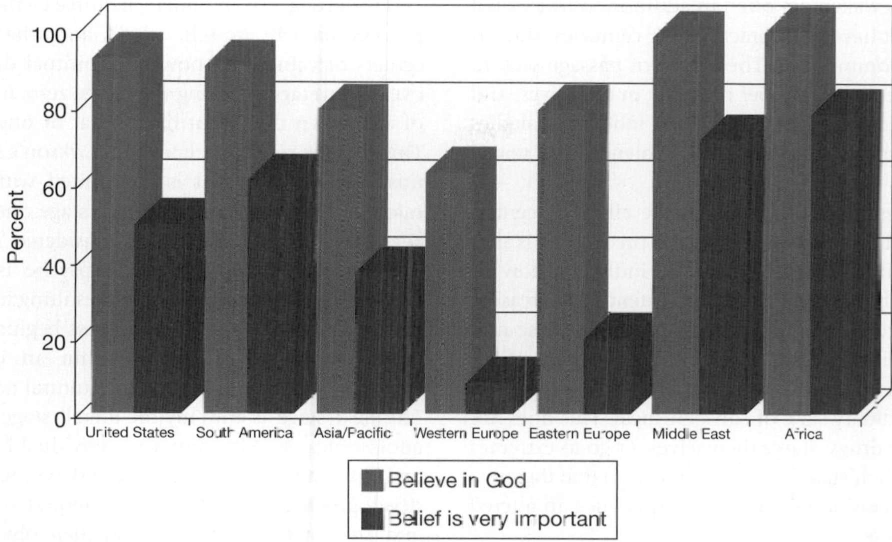

Figure 2 The importance of belief for adolescents aged 18–24, from 1999 to 2001.

Understanding Spiritual Development

As children and adolescents grow, they frequently develop a personal relationship with the divine. This relationship manifests itself in a form which is personal and sacred to each individual. This spiritual relationship holds a similar place in their emotional development relational lives as other important relationships such as those with members of their family. The more safe and secure one feels in their relationship with the Divine, the more likely they are to feel safe and confident in their own lives, supporting exploration, growth, and individuation. Conversely, a less secure spiritual relationship is likely to foster self-doubt and a sense of Divine criticism. In this way, the nature of a child's or adolescent's spiritual world can play a significant role in successful development and overall well-being.

It has long been posited that children lack inner spiritual worlds of any sophistication due to their developmental immaturity. This idea suggests that children could mimic the spiritual practices of their parents and religious communities, but that their spiritual lives equated to simplistic 'God talk.' However, this idea has been brought into question as increasing attention has been paid to this area of study. While there is not overwhelming quantitative data supporting a sophisticated personal spirituality among children, much qualitative research suggests that it exists. This disparity may be due to the inability of children to create complex cognitive structures that would allow them to express their spirituality in a way that would be understood as having a high degree of development. In one well-documented qualitative study, Tobin Hart demonstrated the existence of a highly developed personal spiritual world among children and young adolescents. As Hart explains, "While modern conceptions generally locate 'knowing' in the head, sacred traditions identify the most essential knowing with the heart."

Another study by Hart and Nelson asked 450 undergraduate students of varying majors to recall their spiritual lives as children. They found that a large number recalled feeling spiritual at a young age, suggesting a widespread occurrence. These early spiritual experiences tended to fall within four categories referred to as awe and wonder, wondering, relational spirituality, and wisdom, reflecting a deep capacity for spiritual experience despite the lack of a well-developed means of expression.

Adolescence marks a period of individuation, to include spiritual reflection and differentiation. For some adolescents, this may involve a deepening of faith, for others a process of testing, rejecting, or reclaiming. Many adolescents form a set of personal spiritual bearings through adoption of a range of religious understandings. Through a process of spiritual syncretism, they attempt to reconcile learned models with their own personal experiences.

Adolescence has been referred to as a period of spiritual awakening, during which a blossoming of spiritual attunement and importance often occurs. This is consistent with many cultural practices, such as Bar and Bat Mitzvah, and Vision Quest, which imbue the developing adolescent with greater spiritual capacity and related responsibility. While studies have generally shown that religiousness declines during adolescence, personal spiritual practice often increases, especially among girls.

Rites of Passages

Rites of passages are transitional periods in a developing adolescent's life which act as a ceremonial and spiritual bridge connecting them to the next phase of their development and historically marking the division between childhood and adulthood. For more than 10 000 years, such rites of passages have been used as pathways toward the development of spiritual consciousness. As societies have progressed, there has been less emphasis on these events as integral to the transition to adulthood.

Despite or perhaps due to this shift, there has been an effort to create new rites of passages to help introduce our youth into their own spiritual awakening, often in addition to traditional religious events that have been practiced for centuries, such as Bar Mitzvah and Communion. These rites of passage seek to guide young people toward deeper meaning in their lives, and to act as a defense against such common modern maladies as cynicism, materialism, substance use, violence, and sexual deviance.

In order for these rites of passage to be effective, certain precautions must first be taken. One such precaution is that there must be a shift in the attitude of the individual toward faith, in order that the process can work as intended, increasing the possibility of growth. A second necessity is that these rites acknowledge the spiritual needs of the individual who is about to embark upon them. A third priority is that the rites provoke or include a nonordinary state of consciousness. This does not mean one must use drugs, starve themselves, or go to extremes in order to change their state of mind, but instead that there is a recognition of humans' innate desire to experience an altered state of consciousness.

Such states of consciousness can transpire through activities such as walking in nature, spending an extended time alone, or even viewing an intense movie. Last, these rights of passage must include some aspects of the 'psychological death and rebirth process.' This process reflects the ongoing transitions one experiences throughout life and helps provide a 'map for the life process.' This can be seen reflected in the commonalities shared between many rites of passage such as the involvement of elders and one's community, a significant celebration upon completion, and the incorporation of mental and/or physical labor.

More recently, several programs supporting spiritual rites of passage have been developed outside of traditional religious entities, acknowledging the potential for positive growth for the developing adolescent and a window of opportunity for growth in adolescence. Programs such as Rites of Passage Experience (ROPE), David Oldfield's Journey program, and California's Vision Quest program are designed to mimic some of the positive outcomes experienced through participation in more traditional rites of passage that may be less prevalent in modern societies. These programs often focus on fostering self-reliance, offering participants the opportunity to discover their strengths and self-worth by successfully accepting responsibility, and overcoming obstacles to achieve a goal. These adolescents often report experiencing a sense of wonder and connection to something greater than themselves. Many graduates of these programs show greater self-esteem and confidence in their ability to make positive choices in the future.

Models of Spiritual and Religious Development

One of the leading theories of spiritual development is Fowler's theory of faith development. In this model, Fowler builds upon the work of other developmental theories including Erikson's psychosocial theory, Piaget's theory of cognitive development, and Kohlberg's cognitive theory of moral development. Fowler holds that these developmental stages occur in the same pattern and progression for all individuals and are correlated with certain ages of development.

Fowler suggests that there are three elements at work in this process, namely the self, others, and what he terms "shared centers of values and powers." Spiritual development occurs over seven stages, starting with stage zero, from birth to 2 years of age, when the infant has primal or undifferentiated faith. This stage broadly correlates with Erikson's stage of trust versus mistrust, as the infant is confronted with determining the safety of its environment. During stage one, which lasts from ages 3 to 7, the child's faith is considered 'intuitive or projective.' At this point, the child's psyche is unprotected and exposed to its own unconscious, resulting in the birth of imagination. In this stage, self-awareness begins, as the child integrates perception of reality within an internal paradigm, allowing them to understand the cultural norms of the society. The next stage is the 'mythic-literal' stage, which lasts until adolescence. At this point, the individual begins to synthesize and internalize relevant rituals and symbols. At this stage of development, these symbols are interpreted at a simplistic level and are not recognized beyond their obvious external attributes. Individuals in stage two believe that the universe operated in a wholly just manner, with all actions equally reciprocated and balanced in cause and effect. In addition, during stage two, deities are always depicted as anthropomorphic. Fowler suggests that there are those who remain in stage two for their entire lives.

The first three stages correspond closely with the child's evolving cognitive abilities and mirror the first three stages in Piaget's theory of development; sensorimotor, preoperational, and concrete operational. Stage three, which Fowler terms synthetic conventional faith, begins at adolescence and is correlated with formal operations, Piaget's final stage of development. At this developmental stage, the ego is dominant and the individual is able to use logic and hypothetical thinking to create and evaluate ideas. However, many individuals do not use these abilities to ascertain their own personal faith and instead conform to the beliefs of those around them, leaving them spiritually underdeveloped. In Fowler's words, "At Stage 3 a person has an 'ideology,' a more or less consistent clustering of values and beliefs, but he or she has not objectified it for examination and in a sense is unaware of having it." Stage three therefore can be equated with the conventional religious beliefs of most individuals. Based on his population sample, Fowler concluded that one quarter of adults do not evolve beyond stage three.

Fowler's fourth stage of faith development reflects intuitive reflective faith and generally occurs during one's mid-20s to late 30s. At this point, the individual no longer conforms to external influence and begins to take personal responsibility for their own faith and beliefs. This can cause the individual to struggle, inflicting angst and doubt. At this point, the individual might endure a 'psychic undoing,' where everything that the individual once took as absolute truth begins to be questioned, causing a crisis of faith.

Fowler's fifth stage occurs when the individual develops 'conjunctive faith,' most often occuring during a midlife crisis. During this stage, the individual is propelled by disillusionment and tragedy. Success at this stage allows the individuals to regain that which they had previously abandoned, as they begin to rededicate themselves to their faith.

After stage five, there is a conspicuous gap before one enters the sixth stage, termed 'Universal Faith.' There are very few people who reach this stage. When an individual reaches stage six, they have achieved enlightenment; the individual no longer has apprehensions between their highest possibilities and perceived loyalties, and thus becomes an activist in their own right and of their own unique model. Historical figures who are said to have reached this stage include Abraham Lincoln, Mother Teresa, Martin Luther King, Jr, and Mahatma Gandhi.

Another leading theory of spiritual development is Oser's stages of religious development. While this theory is not solely concerned with spirituality, it seeks to explain the development of spirituality in the context of belief in religion or a higher power. It is important to understand how spirituality develops in relation to religion, as the two are so closely related for many people. Oser's approach consists of five hierarchical stages, without regard to age. In the first stage, "the ultimate being does it...," individuals believe they must always obey the will of their chosen Divinity, and that their personal actions have minimal effect on the action of this higher power. For most individuals, this stage occurs during early childhood. During the second stage, "the ultimate being does it, if ..." the individual places a higher emphasis on the capacity of their actions to affect the will of a higher power. Individuals at this stage believe they have influence through praying, doing good deeds, and obeying religious doctrines. In the third stage, "the ultimate being and the human kind do ..." and the Divine is no longer seen as having a distinct sphere of action and is not in responsible for all that occurs. At this stage, the individual's will is the crucial element in social relations and individual matters.

The fourth and fifth stages, "human kind does through an ultimate being's doing," are combined because Oser believes they blend into each other. These stages most often occur during adulthood, and at this point, it is believed that the Divine is not only the basis of the universe, but of each individual's existence. Individuals in this stage believe that their lives are given more meaning through their belief and relationship with a higher power, and through their actions which honor God. The fifth stage occurs very rarely and is typified by the presence of the higher power in every action no matter how vast or minute. This stage is quite similar to Fowler's final stage of faith development, and Oser offers the same esteemed historical individuals as examples of such attainment.

Parenting, Peers, and Spirituality

A substantial literature has shown that parental love and support are associated with increased spirituality in the offspring. Studies have indicated that spirituality in children can be influenced both by the personal spirituality of the parents, and by parental love, suggesting a parental love is related in substance to spirituality. As children near adolescence, they tend to select peers who have similar levels of personal spirituality, and tendency to engage in contemplation or questioning around spiritual understanding. The relationship between parental spirituality and child spirituality becomes in part mediated by peer spirituality as the individual enters adolescence. However, parental support of spiritual individuation and questioning, as well as a willingness to share personal spiritual experience and struggle, is an important factor influencing a positive association with spirituality in adolescents.

Research shows that the process of spiritual individuation can be enhanced through adult support of adolescent individuation, whether parents, mentors, teachers, or youth leaders. Parental interest and tolerance of questioning personal spiritual beliefs, and a willingness to share in the examination of culturally dictated spiritual beliefs exert a strong influence on the spiritual experience of the adolescent.

Adolescent Morbidity and Mortality

Recent research has indicated that direct personal experience of spirituality in relationship with a higher power is among the most robust protective factors against health-damaging behaviors in adolescents. The influence of one's parents and peers can thus have a great positive impact upon the developing adolescent through sharing of adult spiritual experience, tolerance of and interest in spiritual questioning and contemplation. and embodiment of spirituality through relationships of love, commitment, and interest.

Studies have repeatedly shown that a primary threat to the health of adolescents is a high incidence of dangerous and risky behavior such as drug and alcohol use, reckless driving, and unprotected sex. These behaviors contribute to a high level of unintentional injury, resulting in extensive morbidity and mortality, and accounting for nearly 45% of adolescent and young adult deaths. In addition, among youth aged 10–24, homicide and suicide are the second and third leading causes of death, respectively, accounting for 26% of annual deaths within this age group. Each of the three leading causes of death for adolescents and young adults – unintentional injury, homicide, and suicide – are potentially preventable. If adolescents who engage in religious or spiritual practices are less susceptible to these risky behaviors, these practices may significantly reduce negative health outcomes. Accordingly, the unique epidemiological attributes of the adolescent and young adult population present an important opportunity for spiritually based interventions to be particularly effective, as behavior well established during this developmental stage tends to last.

Current data suggest that personal spirituality and religious behavior are inversely associated with depression and substance use, with the protective benefits approximately twice as great in magnitude as those found in adults. This is particularly noteworthy because adolescence marks a frequent window of onset of lifetime course of depression and substance abuse. More specifically, the most robust protective dimensions are: (1) a direct personal relationship with the Divine and personal sense of relationship to the transcendent and (2) ongoing sense of spiritual community, through religious youth groups or collective practice of religion. Rigid adherence to creed has not been shown to protect against pathology in adolescence, and in some cases poses risk for morbidity, specifically with respect to substance abuse and sexual risk-taking behavior.

Although, in general, findings on adolescents are consistent with those found in adults, with respect to some disorders the findings diverge partly or oppose completely. For example, several studies have shown that frequent religious practice and personal devotion both act to reduce the anxiety of adults. However, studies show religious or spiritual practice to be an uncommon predictor for adolescent anxiety. It is therefore evident that we must continue to expand upon research which focuses upon the adolescent population as its own unique entity. The body of research on spirituality and its protective qualities generally has been parsed by the conceptualization of the variables on religiousness.

Although research examining these protective factors across cultures is limited, one study of Kuwaiti Muslims showed a positive correlation for both sexes between religiosity and physical and mental health and happiness, and exhibited a strong negative correlation between religiosity and both anxiety and depression.

As we stated, female adolescents tend to report higher levels of spiritual importance. Females also seem to exhibit a greater correlation between these higher measures of spiritual devotion and a reduced prevalence of depression and negative or risky behavior. The causes behind the marked and pervasive differences observed in the impact of spiritual and religion devotion by gender are poorly understood, and there is little concurrence among posited theories. Perhaps adolescent girls are deeply impacted by the initiation of menarche, and the related perception of their role in the process of creation. Perhaps this increased sense of connection to one's world is sufficient to create some space for comfort and freedom. Others have suggested that the sociomoral characteristics of females may cause them to internalize the religious experience in a different way. This is clearly a potent area for future study.

Spirituality as a Protective Factor for Adolescents

The use of alcohol, tobacco, and illicit substances is of great concern for the health and well-being of the adolescent and young adult populations. A significant amount of future morbidity and mortality is linked to early adoption of the use of alcohol and other substances, as well as reckless risk-taking behavior. As these risk behaviors are within an area in which religious and spiritual belief and practice has been shown to exert an impact, it may be valuable to support certain of these practices and beliefs. Studies show such behavior to correlate significantly with a reduction in the prevalence of adolescent substance use. Specifically, some studies have shown a moderate direct negative correlation between reported importance of religion/spirituality and use of illicit substances and alcohol among teens. There are several potential explanations for these phenomenon. Certain practices may act as initiators of social bonding and interaction, both protective factors. Alternatively, a supportive social network is one of the most robust predictors of overall well-being, for all populations, positively influencing mood and self-esteem.

Since greater levels of religiosity are strongly correlated with belonging to a drug-free peer group and to lower levels of peer risk-taking, data suggest that the peer group interaction is an important mechanism of this action. This may be especially true when experienced in tandem with religious teachings supporting a substance-free life. An interesting and widespread example of this phenomenon is apparent in the State of Utah, where 69% of Utah residents are Latter Day Saints, a faith that teaches abstinence from drugs and alcohol. It is clear to see the impact of such social norms and beliefs: the adolescent population of Utah has a significantly lower rate of drug and alcohol use than the country as a whole.

Substance use and risk taking are among a broad range of unhealthful behaviors which have been shown to be ameliorated by spiritual or religious practice. Adolescents who reported a greater personal importance of religion were shown to have fewer incidents of misbehavior in school, even when potential effects of parenting are accounted for. In contrast, religious importance was not shown to be a predictive factor for higher grades, but frequency of religious attendance was. Importance of religion has also been shown to correlate positively with the likelihood of a high school student having plans to attend college. This suggests that these youth have a greater sense of self-worth, placing a greater importance on future success.

While much of the empirical work examining the effect of religion and spirituality upon potentially harmful adolescent risk-taking behaviors attempts to posit a theoretical framework for the mechanism of any mediating action, a lack of longitudinal research focusing on religion, spirituality, and risk behavior and health outcomes in the adolescent population prevents us from drawing conclusions as to the directionality of causation between practice and health.

A range of interpretative frameworks have been proposed. Oetting and colleagues, along with several other research teams, have suggested that adolescents may develop and maintain religious social networks through participation in religious activities and through living in communities in which religious values are normative. For instance, the researchers show that children shopping at a local store are less likely to buy alcohol in a religious community under the eyes of the clerk and surrounding adults.

Another factor to consider is the presence and strength of parental support. This may be strongly associated with adolescents' religious attendance, in that adolescents tend to attend religious services together with their families. This might therefore independently account for some of the affective and behavioral differences in religious versus nonreligious teens. In one study of rural youth in which parental social support was controlled for, neither religious importance nor attendance appears to be correlated with depression or self-esteem. However, these have both been strongly correlated with use of alcohol, cigarettes, and marijuana. The crucial factor here thus appears to be importance of religion, and not just attendance. Even after accounting for parental social support, higher importance of religion resulted was shown to exert a primary effect.

Another mechanism of potential action that shows promise is the presence and strength of an individual's sense of personal agency, the belief in one's ability to take effective action in a prospective situation. A personal relationship with a higher power may positively influence people's belief in the capacity to exert agency over one's life. Studies have demonstrated that certain positive agency-related beliefs reduce depressive symptoms in adolescents. One interesting conundrum is that much of the concept of personal agency is related to the belief in and ability to exercise an internal locus of control. However, many basic religious tenets require surrender of the will to a higher power. While this may seem to be in conflict, results show a strong significant direct effect of spirituality on personal agency. One way that this may be explained is that many people with a personal relationship with a higher power may perceive obstacles or crises as intentional challenges to be overcome with faith and God's support. This would render God's will and the impact of increased personal agency as allies toward the same end.

One of the most consistently reported and easily measured correlates of religious or spiritual observance among this population is a reduction in depression and a concurrent reduction in suicide rates. Adolescents' frequency of religious attendance and reported importance both show strong negative correlations with depressive diagnoses, with attendance showing a stronger effect. In one of the few longitudinal studies to look at this, it appears that religiosity may have a bidirectional effect with depression in adolescents.

Religious attendance may act to reduce depression through a system of social support, as discussed earlier. Also, greater religious attendance is often indicative of a stronger family unit. For example, greater religious attendance has been correlated with a lower rate of divorce. Positive social relationships within the family unit may act to protect the adolescent from negative life events and stressors. Religious organizations may promote certain social norms, and may also promote certain healthy lifestyles. The influence of these positive relationships may also act to reduce potential stressors

Another potential mediating factor that results in a lower rate of suicide among those who are religiously observant may be the perceived moral acceptance of such ideation and behavior. As such, the view of suicide as a sinful act may be a deterrent. In addition, the concept of fate or destiny may be a comfort, and may also lead adolescents to exert less self-blame in negative situations.

Further, some have suggested that personal spirituality provides adolescents with a sense of connectedness, which may be especially important during this period of rapid change and potential feelings of alienation. Propensity toward spiritual connection has also been shown to have genetic underpinnings. It would be interesting to examine these feelings of connectedness in such a way as to parse the implications of social networks. Much of the impact of an adolescent's social network may be due to a sense of connection.

Areas for Future Study

Positive psychology, a relatively nascent field that examines human flourishing and thriving, includes a theoretical framework that extends to embrace spirituality in children and adolescents. Kelly and Miller have shown that life satisfaction in children is highly related to daily spiritual experience of a transcendent and personal nature. Among the dimensions of personal spirituality and religions to have been examined by researchers, an ongoing daily relationship with the Divine appears the most robust in relation to life satisfaction, well exceeding the contribution of secular variables such as social class, education, and parental support. We encourage further study in this critical area as a means to better understand and better foster resilience in children and adolescents.

Acknowledging religiosity as a contributing factor in much of the current strife and cultural animosity seen in today's world, further research which expands upon the beneficial aspects of the spiritual lives of adolescents offers great promise. The unifying factors of religious and spiritual life must be incorporated with a greater emphasis on cross-cultural study. This offers the promise of a healthier, better adjusted youth, as well as a potential common ground for understanding.

See also: Developmental Psychopathology; Initiation Ceremonies and Rites of Passage; Parent–Child Relationship; Parenting Practices and Styles; Peer Influence; Religious Involvement.

Further Reading

Boyatzis C (2010) Spiritual development parenting and the family. In: Miller L (ed.) *Handbook of Psychology and Spirituality*. Oxford University Press (In Press).

Cupit CG (2004) Criteria for a comprehensive model of spiritual development in educative care. *International Journal of Childrens Spirituality* 9(3): 293–305.

Eaude T (2003) Shining lights in unexpected corners: New angles on young children's spiritual development. *International Journal of Children's Spirituality* 8(2): 151–162.

Fowler J (1981) *Stages of Faith: The Psychology of Human Development and the Quest for Meaning*. Harper Collins: New York, NY

Hyde B (2008) The identification of four characteristics of children spirituality in Australian Catholic School. *International Journal of Children's Spirituality* 13(2): 117–127.

Kelley B, Athan A, and Miller L (2007) Openness and spiritual development in adolescents. *Research in the Social Scientific Study of Religion* 18: 203–232.

Kelley B and Miller L (2007) Life satisfaction and spirituality in adolescents. *Research in the Social Scientific Study of Religion* 18: 233–261.

Mahdi L, Christopher N, and Meade M (1996) *Crossroads: The Quest for Contemporary Rights of Passage*. Chicago, IL: Open Court Publishers.

Miller L and Athan A (2007) Spiritual awareness pedagogy. *International Journal of Children's Spirituality* 12: 17–35.

Miller L and Kelley B (2005) Spirituality oriented psychotherapy with youth: A child-centered approach. In: Roehlkepartain EC, King PE, Wagner L, and Benson PL (eds.) *The Handbook of Spiritual Development in Childhood and Adolescence. Spirituality in Childhood and Adolescence*. Thousand Oaks, CA: Sage.

Stages of Adolescence

K Salmela-Aro, University of Helsinki, Helsinki, Finland

Glossary

Early adolescence: Early adolescence is a time when biological changes start the pubertal development. Pubertal development related to sexual and reproductive activity is the paramount of early adolescence. Early adolescence is about the age of 11–13 years.

Middle adolescence: Middle adolescence is the phase on the road of transformation. While most of the girls cross their puberty stage, boys are still on the road to maturing physically. Brain development is a major physiological process in middle adolescence. Friends play a pivotal role during middle adolescence. Middle adolescence is about the age of 14–17 years.

Late adolescence: Late adolescents become gradually more emotionally stable. They develop a greater concern for others and start thinking about their purpose in life. They become interested and concerned in serious love relationships and can integrate both emotional and physical intimacy in their love relationship and will now develop a clear sexual identity. They can think ideas, set goals for themselves, and can express their own ideas to others and are confident about them. Late adolescence is about the age of 17–19 years.

Emerging adulthood: Emerging adulthood is a new conception of development for the period from the late teens through the 20s with a focus on ages 18–25 proposed by Jeffrey Arnett. These are the years of identity explorations, self-focus, possibilities, feeling in-between, and instability. At the end of this phase, transition to young adulthood takes place. The most central feature of emerging adulthood is that it is a time when young people explore possibilities for their lives in a variety of areas, especially love and work. However, the new stage is controversial and conditional.

Introduction

Adolescence is the phase of transition from being a child to an adult and it is roughly considered to be the period between 11 and 19 years of age. A central task of adolescence is to develop a sense of oneself as an autonomous individual. The drive for such autonomy derives from internal, biological processes, marking the transition to more adult roles and from the shifts in social roles and expectations that accompany these underlying physiological and cognitive changes. The adolescent experiences not only physical growth and change, but also emotional, psychological, social, and mental change and growth. Adolescence can be broadly categorized into three stages: early adolescence (11–13 years); middle adolescence (13–17 years); and late adolescence (17–19 years). Moreover, a stage of emerging adulthood has been introduced covering the years from 18 to 25. However, why does adolescence, which is already a substage between childhood and adulthood, need to be divided into further substages of early, middle, and late adolescence?

It is the relation between shifts in the child and shifts in the context that mark new stages. Puberty is a biological achievement of the child, but adolescence is a socially designated phase between childhood and adulthood. Puberty is universal but adolescence is not, either in historical or cross-cultural perspective. In many cultures, adolescence is directly tied to biological changes, but in modern, post-industrial cultures, it is more closely tied to age-based transitions into middle and high schools. Depending on the culture, sexual participation can be encouraged at an early age before biological maturity or discouraged until individuals are well into adulthood. In western societies, adolescence is generally recognized. Depending on the system, desires for autonomy and intimacy can be fostered or thwarted moving the adolescent into better or worse future functioning. Negative psychological changes associated with adolescent development often result from a mismatch between the needs of developing adolescents and the opportunities afforded for them by their social environments.

The three stages of adolescence – early, middle, and late – do differ in biological, emotional, social, and cognitive ways which is the basis for recognizing the stages within adolescence and the demarcations between these substages. There has been, however, a shift in adolescence-development research from stage-oriented approaches to process-oriented approaches. In many developmental domains, the underlying process is assumed to involve fairly continuous, progressive changes, rather than transformations from one qualitative stage to another. Development in many areas is now conceptualized as involving more continual change. It has been argued that there is accumulating evidence that stages inaccurately depict the processes involved in some domains, and in others represent at best a categorical abstraction of what is actually a more continual process. In addition, the process-oriented approach also recognizes that the processes must involve interactions between individual and the social context. However, as will be evident from the changes taking place in adolescence, the three substages are a useful way of conceptualizing adolescent development.

Early adolescence is a time when biological changes start the pubertal development. The peak of pubertal change is roughly around 12. Pubertal development related to sexual and reproductive activity is the paramount change of early adolescence, while brain development is a major physiological process in middle adolescence. Biologically, early adolescence is determined by physical growth, hormonal changes, and brain development, while in middle adolescence, the communication between the brain's functional and emotional centers

 doi:10.1016/B978-0-12-373915-5.00043-7

rapidly develops. In turn, physiological changes are no longer so prominent in late adolescence.

Emerging adulthood is proposed as a new conception of development for the period from the late teens through the 20s with a focus on ages 18–25. These are the years of identity explorations, self-focus, possibilities, feeling in-between, and instability. At the end of this phase, transition to young adulthood takes place. The most central feature of emerging adulthood is that it is a time when young people explore possibilities for their lives in a variety of areas, especially love and work.

Stages of Adolescence from Different Perspectives

Stages of adolescence can be conceptualized from a biological perspective, considering features of physical, sexual, brain, and related emotional development. They can also be organized around characteristics of social or cognitive development. Researchers have also considered the distinctive features of identity and mental health development during early, middle, and late adolescence, as well as emerging adulthood. Each of these approaches will be considered in this section, along with an overview taking into account all domains.

However, one has to bear in mind that there is heterogeneity in adolescent development and different trajectories emerge. Age is the most conventional marker for developmental changes and phases of adolescence but, as many have noted, chronological age does not appropriately index many developmental phenomena. Therefore, for each developmental domain, researchers typically identify the best developmental markers, and individual change is considered within the framework of each set of markers. Consequently, the boundaries between the three stages of adolescence are shifting rather than stable.

Physical and Sexual Development

A wide variety of indices of physical development have been used to define physical maturity. They include height and weight, onset of menarche, skeletal age, pubertal stage, and total body water as a percentage of body weight. Consequently, the adolescent years are not just marked by growth in height, but also involve many other physical changes such as development of bones, muscles, and organs. The assumption underlying the incorporation of the anthropomorphic measures and secondary sexual characteristics of relative maturity is that the external changes of physical development have a significant effect on behavior because they signal to adults and peers and to adolescents themselves that the adolescents are more mature and that their behavior should change to fit their new status.

Early and middle adolescence are stages of dramatic physiological changes. The exact age a child enters puberty depends on a number of different factors, such as a person's genes, nutrition, and gender. The change from prepuberty to full reproductive capacity is heterogeneous. Pubertal development related to sexual and reproductive activity is the paramount change in early adolescence and it continues into middle adolescence. Probably the most dramatic changes are the biological changes associated with puberty. These changes include dramatic shifts in the shape of the body, increases in hormones, and changes in brain architecture. These biological shifts are directly linked to changes in sexual interest, cognitive capacities, and physical capacities. The onset of puberty is marked by the development of secondary sexual characteristics, a hormonally controlled process. Before there are any visible changes, the endocrine glands are producing hormones that bring about sexual development. This process is set in motion when the hypothalamus prompts the pituitary to begin secreting gonadotropin hormones. These hormones stimulate the testes in boys and ovaries in girls to increase production of their respective sex hormones, testosterone and estrogen. The onset of puberty is a prominent change in both males and females as it marks sexual maturation. Testosterone in males and estradiol in females play a significant role in pubertal development. Breast development is one sign that a girl is entering puberty. This will be followed by the first menstrual period (menarche). For girls, the average age for menstruation is in early adolescence, about the age of 12. However, it can take place between the age of 10 and 16. Before having the first menstrual period, a girl will normally have an increase in height, pubic, armpit, and leg hair growth, clear or whitish vaginal secretions, and increased hip size. At first, the menstrual periods typically are irregular. It is important to remember that fertility usually comes in early adolescence before emotional maturity and pregnancy can occur, thus before an adolescent is prepared for parenthood. During puberty, various endocrine glands produce hormones that cause bodily changes and the development of secondary sex characteristics. In girls, the ovaries begin to increase production of estrogen and other female hormones and end-of-growth spurt, and female body shape with fat deposition takes place in middle adolescence. In boys, the testicles increase production of testosterone. The adrenal glands produce hormones that cause increased armpit sweating, body odor, acne, and armpit and pubic hair. This process is called adrenarche. Unlike girls, boys exhibit no clear-cut signs that they have entered puberty. However, boys will normally experience faster growth, especially in height, increased shoulder width, growth of the penis, scrotum (accompanied by reddening and folding of the skin), and testes, voice changes, pubic, beard, and armpit hair growth, and nighttime ejaculations.

In late adolescence, physiological changes are not so prominent compared to early and middle adolescence as in late adolescence puberty is usually complete. In girls, it is complete usually by the age of 17, while for boys, the end of puberty often takes place in late adolescence. Any increases in height after late adolescence is uncommon. However, among boys, continuous increase of muscle bulk and body hair takes place in late adolescence. Although full physical maturity has been reached at this time, educational and emotional maturity remain ongoing.

Brain Development

There is now growing evidence that maturational brain processes are continuing well through adolescence. Even relatively simple structural measures, such as the ratio of white to gray matter in the brain, demonstrate large-scale changes during all stages of early adolescence into the late adolescence years. The impact of this continued maturation on emotional, intellectual, and behavioral development has yet to be thoroughly studied, but there is considerable evidence that the second decade of life is a period of great activity with respect to changes in brain structure and function, especially in regions and systems associated with response inhibition, the calibration of risk and reward, and emotion regulation. Contrary to earlier beliefs about brain maturation in adolescence, this activity is not limited to the early adolescence period, nor is it invariably linked to processes of pubertal maturation. Brain development is a major physiological process in all stages of adolescence, according to new imaging studies.

Recent research using magnetic resonance imaging (MRI) has found that the teenaged brain is not a finished product, but a work in progress. New findings show that the greatest changes to the parts of the brain that are responsible for functions such as self-control, judgment, emotions, and organization occur in middle adolescence. This may help to explain early adolescents' poor decision-making, recklessness, and emotional outbursts. Two particular observations about brain development in adolescence are especially pertinent to our understanding of psychological development during this period. First, much brain development during adolescence is in the particular brain regions and systems that are key to the regulation of behavior and emotion, and to the perception and evaluation of risk and reward. Second, it appears that changes in arousal and motivation brought on by pubertal maturation precede the development of regulatory competence in a manner that creates a disjunction between the adolescent's affective experience and his or her ability to regulate arousal and motivation. To the extent that the changes in arousal and motivation precede the development of regulatory competence, the developments of early adolescence may well create a situation in which one is starting an engine without yet having a skilled driver behind the wheel.

In middle adolescence, a second wave of overproduction of gray matter takes place. Following the overproduction of gray matter, the brain undergoes a process called 'pruning' in which connections among neurons in the brain that are not used wither away, while those that are used, stay. It is thought that this pruning process makes the brain more efficient by strengthening the connections that are most often used and eliminating the clutter of those that are not used at all.

Brain development is also related to adolescents' emotional development. Adolescents differ from adults in their ability to read and understand emotions in the faces of others. Recent research shows that adolescents and adults actually use different regions of the brain in responding to certain tasks. Pictures of fearful expressions shown to adolescents between the ages of 11 and 17 while they had their brains scanned using functional magnetic resonance imaging (fMRI), showed that their frontal lobes (the seat of goal-oriented rational thinking) are less active and their amygdala (a structure in the temporal lobe that is involved in discriminating fear and other emotions) is more active. Early adolescents (under age 14) often misread facial expressions, interpreting fear, for example, as sadness or anger or confusion. In middle adolescence, they answer correctly more often and exhibit a progressive shift of activity from the amygdala to the frontal lobes. The judgment, insight, and reasoning power of the frontal cortex, is not brought to bear on the task as it is in adults. The largest part, the cortex, is divided into lobes that mature from back to front. The last section to connect is the frontal lobe, responsible for cognitive processes such as reasoning, planning, and judgment. Normally, this 'mental merger' is not completed until somewhere between the ages of 25 and 30 – much later than it was earlier assumed to take place.

There are also gender differences in brain development. The part of the brain that processes information expands during childhood and then begins to thin, peaking in girls in early adolescence at roughly 12–14 years old and in boys in middle adolescence about two years later. This suggests that girls and boys may be ready to absorb challenging material at different stages, and that schools may be missing opportunities to reach them. Consequently, early and middle adolescence obviously differ by gender in brain development.

Cognitive Development

What lies at the core of adolescent cognitive development is the attainment of a more fully conscious, self-directed, and self-regulating mind and abstract thinking. Psychological development occurs in a background of rapid physical change including puberty, the pubertal growth spurt, and accompanying maturational changes in other organ systems. During early adolescence, individuals show marked improvements in reasoning (especially deductive reasoning), information processing (in both efficiency and capacity), and expertise. The transition from concrete thinking to formal logical operations begins. Early adolescence marks the beginning of more complex thinking processes (also called formal logical operations) including abstract thinking (thinking about possibilities); the ability to reason from known principles (form new ideas or questions); the ability to consider many points of view according to varying criteria (compare or debate ideas or opinions); and the ability to think about the process of thinking. Indicators that show a progression from simpler to more complex cognitive development include the following: the use of a more complex thinking is focused on personal decision making in school and home environments. The early adolescent begins to demonstrate the use of formal logical operations in schoolwork and begins to question authority and societal standards. The early adolescent begins to form and verbalize his/her own thoughts and views on a variety of topics usually more related to his/her own life, such as which sports are better to play, which groups are better to be included in, what personal appearances are desirable or attractive, and what parental rules should be changed.

During middle adolescence, developing adolescents acquire the ability to think systematically about all logical relationships within a problem. Growing verbal abilities, identification of the law with morality, and the start of fervent ideology (religious, political) take place in middle adolescence. However, each adolescent progresses at different rates in developing his/her ability to think in more complex ways and develops his/her own view of the world. Some adolescents may be able to apply logical operations to schoolwork long before they are able to apply them to personal dilemmas. With some experience in using more complex thinking processes, the middle-stage adolescent often expands to include more philosophical and futuristic concerns. The middle-stage adolescent often questions and analyzes more extensively, thinks about and begins to form his/her own code of ethics (i.e., What do I think is right?), thinks about different options and begins to develop an individual identity (i.e., Who am I?), thinks about and begins to systematically consider possible future goals and plans (i.e., What do I want?), and begins to think of the long term. In middle adolescence, the use of systematic thinking also begins to influence relationships with other people.

In turn, during late adolescence, complex thinking processes are used to focus on less self-centered concepts as well as personal decision-making. Individuals can carry out complex abstract thinking, and they have increased impulse control. Further development of personal identity takes place, including further development or rejection of religious and political ideology. The late adolescent has increased thoughts about more global concepts such as justice, history, politics, and patriotism. Late adolescents often develop idealistic views on specific topics or concerns, and they may debate and develop intolerance of opposing views. Late adolescents also begin to focus on making career decisions and establishing a role in adult society.

Social Development

Adolescence is described as a period in which independence is achieved, in particular, in individualistic cultures. The main developmental task of adolescence in this realm is to reach autonomy (changes in models of asserting autonomy, expression of autonomy). A decrease of the time spent in a relationship with parents takes place in adolescence while increasing the significance of peers and a romantic partner. These important changes in social development take place in different phases of adolescence. Through social development, adolescents co-regulate their behaviors and emotions with peers, parents, romantic partners, and teachers.

Patterns of peer relationships

During the transition into adolescence, young people spend increasing amounts of time alone and with friends, and there is a dramatic drop in the amount of time adolescents spend with their parents. Despite these changes in time allocation, adolescents' relationships with their parents influence their interactions with peers.

In early adolescence, emotional separation from parents takes place and strong peer identification begins. As early adolescents pull away from their parents in a search for identity, the peer group takes on special significance. It may become a safe haven, in which the adolescent can test new ideas and compare physical and psychological growth. In early adolescence, the peer group usually consists of nonromantic friendships, often including 'cliques', gangs, or clubs. Members of the peer group often attempt to behave alike, dress alike, have secret codes or rituals, and participate in the same activities. In general, during early adolescence, friends begin to value loyalty and intimacy more, becoming more trusting and self-disclosing.

Crowds emerge during early adolescence. They are large collections of peers defined by reputations and stereotypes. Crowds contribute to identity development by influencing the ways in which adolescents view themselves and others, and influencing adolescents' behavior by establishing norms for their members. For most adolescents, crowds become less important, less hierarchical, and more permeable between middle and late adolescence.

Cliques, in turn, are much smaller groups of peers that are based on friendship and shared activities. Members of a clique tend to be similar in terms of age, race, socioeconomic status, behaviors, and attitudes. Clique membership seems to be somewhat stable over time in terms of the defining characteristics of the group. Popular adolescents usually have close friendships and tend to be friendly, humorous, and intelligent, while rejected adolescents are often aggressive, irritable, withdrawn, anxious, and socially awkward. Peer victimization can lead to the development of poor self-conceptions as well as the internalization and externalization of problems. Although adolescents who are victimized tend to have few friends, those who have a best friend or a friend who is strong and protective seem to suffer less from the effects of victimization. Despite these harmful effects of peer rejection and victimization, there is evidence that unpopular adolescents can become more popular and accepted in later adolescence, as adolescents become less rigid in their expectations of 'normal' behavior and more tolerant of individual differences among their peers.

Young people are most influenced by peers in middle adolescence, compared to early and late adolescence. During middle adolescence, cliques change from being single-sexed to mixed-sexed. As the youth moves into mid-adolescence and beyond, the peer group expands to include romantic friendships. During middle adolescence, friendships evolve into more intimate, supportive, and communicative relationships. Close friendships typically begin within same sex pairs, but as adolescents mature, many become intimate friends with members of the opposite sex, usually around the time that they start dating. Social competencies such as initiating interactions, self-disclosure, and provision of support increase as adolescents mature into middle adolescents, and are related to the quality of friendship. There is some evidence that among girls, friendship intimacy is fostered by conversation, whereas among boys, it is gained through shared activities. Tolerance of individuality between close friends increases with age, whereas friends' emphasis on control and conformity decreases. By middle adolescence, most adolescents have had a romantic boyfriend or girlfriend.

In late adolescence, development of social autonomy takes place and intimate relationships become more important. In late adolescence, cliques are often transformed into groups of dating couples. During late adolescence, friendships evolve into more intimate, supportive, and communicative relationships.

Patterns of family ties

Studies of changes in family relations during adolescence continue to focus on parent–adolescent conflict, although a number of investigations examine changes in closeness and companionship as well. Three types of parent–adolescent conflict are often examined: conflict rate, conflict affect, and total conflict (rate and affect combined). However, the results provide little support for the commonly held view that parent–child conflict rises and then falls across adolescence, although conclusions regarding pubertal change as well as conflict affect are qualified by the limited number of studies available. Two diverging sets of linear effects emerge, one indicating a decline in conflict rate and total conflict with age, and the other indicating an increase in conflict affect with both age and pubertal maturation. In meta-analyses, conflict rate and total conflict decline from early adolescence to mid-adolescence and from mid-adolescence to late adolescence; conflict affect between adolescents and parents increases from early adolescence to mid-adolescence. A positive linear association between conflict affect and pubertal maturation has been found. However, effect-size patterns vary little in follow-up analyses of potential moderating variables, implying similarities in the direction (although not the magnitude) of conflict across parent–adolescent dyads, reporters, and measurement procedures.

During early adolescence, there is an increase in mild conflict such as bickering and squabbling between parents and adolescents. This increase in mild conflict is then often accompanied by a decline in closeness, and especially, in the amount of time adolescents and parents spend together. These transformations that take place in parent–adolescent relationships have implications for the mental health of parents as well as for the psychological development of adolescents, with a substantial number of parents reporting difficulties adjusting to the adolescent's individuation and autonomy-striving. Finally, the process of disequilibration in early adolescence is typically followed by the establishment of a parent–adolescent relationship that is less contentious, more egalitarian, and less volatile. Parents' 'authoritative' – warm and firm – parenting style is related to higher levels of competence and psychosocial maturity among early adolescents. Authoritative parenting is associated with a wide range of psychological and social advantages in adolescence. Adolescent development is affected by an interplay of genetic, familial, and nonfamilial influences, and efforts to partition the variability in adolescent adjustment into genetic and various environmental components fail to capture the complexity of socialization processes.

The sibling relationship in adolescence is an emotionally charged one, marked not only by conflict and rivalry, but also nurturance and social support. As children mature from childhood to early adolescence, sibling conflict increases, with adolescents reporting more negativity in their sibling relationships compared to their relationships with peers. High levels of conflict in early adolescence gradually diminish as adolescents move into middle and late adolescence. As siblings mature, relations become more egalitarian and supportive, and as with the parent–adolescent relationship, the sibling relationships become less influential as adolescents expand their relations outside the family.

Romantic relationships

A central challenge for an adolescent is to create an integrated self-image, which includes a representation of self as a romantic partner. In the initiation phase, triggered by pubertal maturation, peers provide norms for romantic relationships. The initiation phase symbolizes a turning point in adolescent social activities. During this phase, the early adolescent needs to become reoriented to and reacquainted with the opposite gender. The basic objectives in this first phase are to broaden one's self concept and to gain confidence in one's ability to relate to potential partners in a romantic way. Thus, the focus is on the self, not on the romantic relationship. Romantic dating occurs in the context of and with the assistance of same-sex peers. In early adolescence a stage of simple interchanges between opposite sex peers is motivated by pubertal maturation. Then middle adolescents quickly move to a stage of casual dating which fulfills their needs for affiliation as well as sexuality. During middle adolescence, romantic participation is linked to social status in the peer group. During the second phase, the status phase, adolescents are confronted with the pressure of having the 'right kinds' of romantic relationships. Dating the 'wrong' people can seriously damage the adolescent's standing in the group. Romantic relationships may thus be used to obtain or increase peer acceptance and, as such, may hinder the establishment of a mutually rewarding romantic relationship. They then proceed to stable relationships, in which attachment needs emerge alongside sexuality and affiliation. The third phase, the affection phase, is characterized by a shift of focus from the context in which the relationship exists toward the romantic relationship itself. Romance becomes a personal and relational affair; at the same time, the influence of the peer group wanes. Partners in affection-oriented relationships generate deeper feelings of commitment to their relationship, express deeper levels of caring for each other, and typically engage in more extensive sexual activity. The adolescent's peer network in this phase is reduced from a large crowd of same-sex peers to a smaller circle of mixed-sex friends. The latter may, for example, offer the adolescent advice on how to start a relationship and provide emotional support after a relationship has ended. In late adolescence, the stage of committed relationship emerges as late adolescents are increasingly able to provide care-taking roles for their partner. They form dyadic romantic relationships and they are expected to maintain the depth of relationships typical for the affection phase, yet adopt a more pragmatic perspective. Central issues of this phase concern the possibilities of remaining together with a romantic partner for a lifetime. Typically, while the romantic partners consider themselves to be inseparable as a couple, they remain distinctive personalities.

The incidence of romantic relationships varies across the three sub-periods of early, middle, and late adolescence. The percentage of adolescents who report having a romantic relationship increases during the adolescent years. Involvement in dating increases notably between the ages of 12 and 18. For example, about one-third of 13-year-olds, half of the 15-year-olds, and two-thirds of the 17-year-olds report having a 'special' romantic relationship in the previous 18 months. By middle adolescence, most individuals have been involved in at least one romantic relationship. Late adolescents commonly report more frequent interactions with romantic partners than with parents, siblings, or friends. A shift in dating takes place particularly in middle adolescence during the ages of 15 and 17 in the features and implications of romantic relationships. This apparent mid-adolescence shift is related to cognitive and emotional maturation, achievements regarding identity and autonomy, increasing diversification of social networks, and conceptual changes associated with impending adulthood. Middle adolescence is characterized by a need to establish sexual identity through becoming comfortable with one's own body and sexual feelings. Through romantic friendships, dating, and experimentation, adolescents learn to express and receive intimate or sexual advances in a comfortable manner that is consistent with internalized values.

Prior to adolescence, interactions typically occur with peers of the same gender; most friendship pairs are of the same gender. Affiliation with mixed-gender groups typically follows in early to middle adolescence and facilitates the progression from same-gendered friendships to dyadic romantic relationships. Across the teenage years, young people spend increasing amounts of time with other gender peers and romantic partners. By early adulthood, time with romantic partners increases further at the expense of involvement with friends and crowds.

The timing of involvement with a romantic partner is often attributed to the onset of puberty. Cultural norms also affect dating. For example, Asian Americans start romantic relationships later than adolescents in the past 18 months than adolescents in African American, Hispanic, Native American, and European American groups. However, less is known about the developmental course of the relationships of gay, lesbian, and bisexual adolescents. The average age of the first 'serious' same-gender relationship is 18 years.

Self-Identity

The goal of adolescence is achieving a coherent identity and avoiding identity confusion. An important developmental task of adolescence is to create an individual and sexual identity. Identity is multidimensional and may include physical and sexual identity, occupational goals, religious beliefs, and ethnic background. Adolescents explore these dimensions and usually make commitments to aspects of their identity as they move into early adulthood. Early adolescence is a period of disorganization. One needs to free oneself from the dictates of internalized parents. In early adolescence, young people seek connections, networks, supportive relationships, and groups. The capacity to invest and to connect oneself to various social relations provides the foundations and supports necessary for later identity explorations and commitments. This group identity formed in early and sometimes also in middle adolescence is important before achieving a more autonomous sense of identity in late adolescence.

Marcia's four identity statuses – diffusion, moratorium, foreclosure, and achieved status – display differential profiles with regard to progressive development. Contribution to progressive development comes mainly from the increase in achievement and the decrease in foreclosure, less from the decrease in diffusion, and not at all from the increase or decrease in moratorium. Achieved status is not, however, the end-point of development for everyone: a substantial number of late adolescents still remain in one of the other statuses.

According to Erikson, during the fifth psychosocial crisis, an adolescent learns how to satisfactorily and happily answer the question of 'Who am I?' During successful early adolescence, as a mature time perspective is developed, the young person acquires self-certainty as opposed to self-consciousness and self-doubt. Early adolescents report more daily fluctuations in self-esteem than younger or older individuals, but self-esteem becomes stable over time. They come to experiment with different – usually constructive – roles rather than adopting a 'negative identity' (such as delinquency). They actually anticipate achievement, and achieves rather than being 'paralyzed' by feelings of inferiority or by an inadequate time perspective. In turn, in late adolescence, a clear sexual identity – manhood or womanhood – is established. The adolescent seeks a role model (someone to be an inspiration) and gradually develops a set of socially congruent and desirable ideas. In Western culture, adolescence often affords a 'psychosocial moratorium'. However, there is much cultural variety. Middle adolescents do not yet have to 'play for keeps', but can experiment, trying various roles, and thus hopefully find the one most suitable for them. Middle adolescence is marked by individuals describing themselves in ways that are occasionally discrepant, but these discrepancies tend to decline in late adolescence, with adolescents forming a more constant view of themselves. Self-concepts become more differentiated and better organized in late adolescence. Global self-esteem often increases slightly over the period of late adolescence. According to Marcia, identity is mainly formed in the late adolescence, between the ages of 18 and 22. Arnett argues that real work on identity actually is conducted in emerging adulthood.

Mental Health

Although the majority manage adolescence well, some have difficulties in adapting to the transitions and changes of this age period. Negative affects are common during early and middle adolescence, and early and middle adolescents also report fewer positive affects than others. Stress evokes more negative responses among early and middle adolescents compared to children and adults An inverted U-shaped developmental curve of externalizing in adolescence appears, with prevalence rates peaking during the middle adolescent years and then declining. A different picture describes internalizing problems. Half of adults' mental health problems have begun before the age of 14 and three-quarters before adulthood. Mental health problems are twice as common in adolescence as they are in childhood. In early adolescence, mental health problems are more common among boys than girls, whereas the gender difference is reversed throughout the rest of adolescence. During early adolescence, ADHD and behavior problems are common, while in middle adolescence anxiety, mood and addiction problems are most common. Comorbidity is typical: young people often have many problems simultaneously. Anxiety is also quite typical during early adolescence, but then it usually has a concrete focus, while in middle adolescence, it is typically related to the social context. Social phobia increases in adolescence and particularly the panic disorder increases. Behavior disorders increase in early adolescence and peak in middle adolescence and then decrease. Vandalism is more common in early adolescence, while aggressive behavior characterizes middle and late adolescence; it is about five times as common among boys compared to girls. Substance abuse usually begins in middle adolescence, while eating disorders begin usually in early adolescence.

The prevalence of depression increases during early adolescence and continues to increase, albeit less dramatically, during adulthood. There is evidence that, in comparison to childhood, depression rises dramatically during the adolescent years.

Several concepts, such as depressive mood, depressive symptoms, clinical depression, and depressive disorder, have been used to study depression during adolescence. A depressed mood is fairly common during adolescence, particularly among adolescent girls, with the likelihood of depressed mood ranging by 25–40% for girls and 20–35% for boys. A depressive disorder or clinical depression, in turn, is categorically defined as a list of different depressive symptoms (e.g., loss of sleep, lack of interest in day-to day activities, changes in appetite, concentration problems, suicidal thoughts) that must be present for a specified time period (e.g., at least 2 weeks). The prevalence of major depressive disorder (MDD) ranges from 0.4% to 12% among adolescents.

Studies of middle adolescents have shown that the incidence of depression among adolescents is greater for females than males. These sex differences have been reported to emerge during early adolescence, between the ages of 13 and 15 years, and prior to this age, rates appear to be similar for young boys and girls. The prevalence of depressive symptoms among females in this age range is approximately double that among males. The prevalence of depressive symptoms among adolescents increases with age. The increase is far more severe for females than males. The increase among males, though less striking, is also notable, indicating a rapid emergence of depressive symptoms in middle adolescence.

Previous research has also shown statistically significant mean-level developmental trends in depressive symptoms across the adolescent years. Depressive symptoms seem to increase between the ages of 13 and 15, reach a peak at the age of 17–18, and then decrease in adulthood, particularly among females. In addition to an increased risk of suicide, youths who are depressed are at a higher risk for mental disorders such as anxiety, behavior disorders, and substance abuse. They are also more likely than other youths to engage in unsafe sexual practices and other risk behaviors. Further, youths who are depressed tend to experience difficulty relating to peers.

Emerging Adulthood

It is commonly said that adolescence begins in biology and ends in culture, because the transition into adolescence is marked by dramatic biological changes of puberty, while the transition to adulthood is less clearly marked. Transitions to adulthood have been defined by entrance into labor force and parenthood. As these transitions occur at later ages in contemporary society, Arnett has proposed that the period between the ages at 18 and 25 should be treated as a separate developmental period, which he labels emerging adulthood. However, there is a wide debate about whether it really is a legitimate, widely experienced, distinctive stage. Arnett's claim rests on the significant demographic diversity and instability of this period, as well as increases in identity exploration that typically occurs at this time. Until recently, however, most of the research on adolescent development has focused on early and middle adolescence, with less research focusing on transitions out of adolescence. Thus, the utility of distinguishing between late adolescence and emerging adulthood remains to be empirically determined. The research on adolescent brain development which shows that brain maturation is not complete and new research demonstrating that mature decision making does not emerge until the middle twenties, also has the potential to reshape the definitions of adolescence and the transitions to young adulthood.

The third decade of life is a period during which individuals are faced with more transitions and life decisions than at any other stage of life. These include moving from education to work, starting a career, initiating an intimate relationship, and starting a family. It has also been found that people perceive these transitions and role changes as important markers of the transition to adulthood. Many of these transitions take several years to complete and are made up of many successive stages. First, a career development trajectory typically includes a complex set of decisions concerning education and career. Another typical feature of age-graded environments is that the transitions associated with different domains of life interact with one another. For example, educational and career transitions may have consequences for the timing of interpersonal transitions, such as bringing a child into the family.

On the basis of the life span, age affects the urgency of the normative tasks faced by young people; as older individuals are closer to the deadlines set for major developmental tasks, they might be assumed to feel more pressure to take these tasks seriously into account when thinking about their future. With increasing proximity to normative deadlines, individuals feel pressured to invest more effort into attaining certain developmental goals. Emerging adulthood is a time of identity exploration, self-focus, transition, and instability. Recentering has been proposed as the process during which emerging adults make the transition from dependent adolescents to independent young adults. At the end of this phase, transition to young adulthood takes place. The most central feature of emerging adulthood is that it is a time when young people explore possibilities for their lives in a variety of areas, especially love and work. The developmental tasks of emerging adults include both salient (i.e., friendship, academic, conduct) and emerging (i.e., occupational and romantic) developmental tasks. At the end of this period, most people have made their life choices in terms of love, partnership, and family.

However, both the length of the education period and the initiation of parenthood have been extended in recent decades. Biologically, adolescence appears to be occurring at earlier stages for an increasing number of individuals, whereas the typical social transitions to adulthood, such as completing education or training, embarking on a career, and living independently from one's biological family of origin, are occurring at later ages now than in the past. As a result, the period of adolescence is much longer nowadays than it used to be. Historical changes (secular trends) in biological processes have expanded the number of years that individuals in technologically advanced societies spend in a stage that can be referred to as adolescence.

Conclusion

In this article, I have presented and discussed various stages of development in adolescence. Many changes take place in adolescence, such as rapid physical growth, brain changes, sexual maturation and development of secondary sexual characteristics, motivational, emotional, and cognitive development, maturation of judgment and self-regulation skills, and changes in educational and social contexts. Based on these differences in changes, it is evident that adolescence can be further divided into substages of early, middle, and late adolescence. These three substages differ in biological, emotional, social, and cognitive ways, which is the basis for recognizing the stages within adolescence and the demarcations between these substages. The degree of distinctiveness of substages differs across the various changes or developmental trajectories that occur in adolescence. Moreover, in many developmental domains, the underlying process is fairly continuous, rather than exhibiting transformations from one qualitative stage to another. Components within each stage are often interrelated. For example, maturing sexual capacities engender stronger social interests in romantic relationships, or maturing cognitive capacities abilities in early and middle adolescence, shape the nature of identity explorations at a later stage. For heuristic purposes, however, it is possible to provide an integrative sketch of the common features of each stage. These sketches underscore the dramatic changes that occur across the adolescent period.

Early Adolescence

The onset of puberty is a major developmental milestone of early adolescence, considered by many as the developmental change that signals one's transition into adolescence from childhood. Early adolescence is a phase in which emotions change rapidly and adolescents have difficulties with their emotional regulation. Socially, early adolescence is a phase in which social status in the peer network plays a very important role and peer networks are reciprocal. In early adolescence, the importance of peers rapidly increases and simultaneously, the importance of family decreases. Cognitively, early adolescence is a phase when memory capacity and risk taking increases.

Middle Adolescence

Middle adolescence is the phase when a child is on the road of transformation. There are many changes that occur. While most of the girls cross their puberty stage, boys are still on the road of maturing physically. Middle adolescence is the time when a teenager is developing a unique personality and opinions. Friends play a pivotal role during these years and middle adolescents take great care to maintain their identity in the peer group. This apparent mid-adolescent shift is related to cognitive and emotional maturation, achievements regarding identity and autonomy, increasing diversification of social networks, and conceptual changes associated with impending adulthood. In middle adolescence, even though emotional regulation still needs attention, adolescents are better able to identify and define their own and others' emotions. In middle adolescence, the importance of romantic peers increases and adolescent social identity also begins to develop. In addition, middle adolescence is a phase in which worldview and future-oriented planning develops. Cognitively, middle adolescence is a phase when complex memory strategies, perception, control and planning processes become more rapid and accurate, and impulse control increases.

Late Adolescence

Late adolescents finally come quite close to adulthood to have a firm identity and more stable interests. Soon-to-be-adults attain greater emotional stability finally and have a more developed sense of humor. They are able to keep a little patience when there is a delay in gratification of their desires, and are able to think ideas through. They learn to express their feelings in words, compromise, and make independent decisions. Unlike in earlier stages, late adolescents show greater concern for others. They become more self-reliant and take pride in their work. They start finalizing their thoughts about the role they want to play in their lives and become more concerned about their future.

However, as we look for changes in these different domains, it is evident that these changes take place simultaneously in many domains. For example, the apparent mid-adolescence shift is related to brain development and related cognitive and emotional maturation, achievements regarding identity and autonomy, increasing diversification of social networks, and conceptual changes associated with impending adulthood. Pubertal development related to sexual and reproductive activity characterizes early adolescence, which is also related to changes in social development. Consequently, these changes go hand in hand.

Although little has been said in this article about cultural differences, the nature of these stages – early, middle, and late adolescence as well as emerging adulthood – is likely to differ across cultures. Moreover, there is huge variety in the timing as well as gender differences. The content of stages is not universal, but depends on the social roles available to young people and the general cultural interpretation of biological, cognitive, and emotional changes likely to occur across adolescence.

Adolescence may well be a sensitive or critical developmental period for both normative and maladaptive patterns of development. Several aspects of development during this period are especially significant in this regard, among them: the role of puberty in a fundamental restructuring of many body systems and as an influence on social information-processing; the apparent concentration of changes in the adolescent brain in the prefrontal cortex together with the enhanced interregional communication between the prefrontal cortex and other brain regions; and the evidence for substantial synaptic pruning. Taken together, these developments reinforce the emerging understanding of adolescence as a critical or sensitive period for a reorganization of regulatory systems. As we look to the future of research on cognitive and affective development in adolescence, the challenge facing researchers will be integrating research on psychological, neuropsychological, and neurobiological development. What we now have are interesting pieces of a complicated puzzle, but the pieces have yet to be fit together in a way that moves the field out of the realm of speculation and toward some measure of certainty.

See also: Brain Development; Cognitive Development; Depression and Depressive Disorders; Puberty and Adolescence: An Evolutionary Perspective; Romantic Relationships; School-to-Work Transitions; Transitions into Adolescence; Transitions to Adulthood.

Further Reading

Eccles JS and Midgley C (1989) Stage-environment fit: Developmentally appropriate classrooms for early adolescents. In: Ames RE and Ames C (eds.) *Research on Motivation in Education*, vol. 3, pp. 139–186. New York: Academic Press.

Erikson E (1959) Identity and life cycle. *Psychological Issues* 1: 1–171.

Salmela-Aro K (2009a) Personal goals and well-being during critical life transitions: The 4 Cs – channeling, choice, co-agency and compensation. *Advances in Life Course Research* 14: 63–73.

Salmela-Aro K (2009b) School burnout: Antecedents and consequences. In: Schoon I and Silbereisen R (eds.) *Transition from School to Work: Globalisation, Individualisation, and Patterns of Diversity*. Cambridge: Cambridge University Press.

Sameroff A (2010) A unified theory of development: A dialectic integration of nature and nurture. *Child Development* 81: 6–22.

Steinberg L and Morris A (2001) Adolescent development. *Annual Review of Psychology* 5: 83–110.

Relevant Websites

http://www.rcpsych.ac.uk/mentalhealthinfoforall/youngpeople/adolescence.aspx
http://www.nlm.nih.gov/medlineplus/ency/article/001950.htm
http://www.childdevelopmentinfo.com/development/teens_stages.shtml
http://www.stanford.edu/group/adolescent.ctr/
https://www.earlyadolescence.org/
www.pathwaystoadulthood.org/

Transitions into Adolescence

E Trejos-Castillo, Texas Tech University, Lubbock, TX, USA
A T Vazsonyi, Auburn University, Auburn, AL, USA

Glossary

Cliques: Small social groups.

Gray matter: One of the most important components of the central nervous system which contains nerve cell bodies.

Intrapersonal: Developmental changes that occur within the individual.

Maturation: A variety of individual changes according to a biological plan, both bodily changes and psychological ones.

Myelin: The fatty material that covers and protects the nerves and allowing the conduction of impulses between the brain and body parts.

Resiliency: The ability to recover from negative events experienced in the environment by developing positive coping skills in effect overcoming these challenges.

Secular trends: Changes in the timetables of developmental events or processes across different historical periods (e.g., how the start of pubertal development has declined over the past century)

Social-relatedness: An individual's capacities and needs to relationally connect to other individuals to develop close and personal social relationships.

Transition: The multitude of changes and processes at work during the journey from childhood to adolescence or from adolescence to adulthood.

Introduction

The study of adolescence as a passageway from childhood to adulthood is relatively new from a historical standpoint. Ancient philosophers such as Plato described adolescence as a transitory and volatile state children went through before becoming adults – *'a spiritual drunkenness.'* In ancient times, children were expected to follow the standards and ideals of the society to become good men/women and responsible and productive citizens. As part of their upbringing, children helped with household chores, participated in farming activities, and were trained on the main occupation the family leaders practiced. Anthropologists have documented that across ancient and Middle-Ages societies, adolescence was not conceived as a separate stage between childhood and adulthood; indeed, it has been argued that despite being an economic asset for families, children grew unnoticed until they reached puberty, and bodily transformations along with their readiness to marry and start their own families marked their entrance into adulthood.

The smooth transitioning from childhood to adulthood up to the eighteenth century – mostly due to the stability of family livelihood – contrasted with the tumultuous development of children during the nineteenth century which was magnified by the Industrial Revolution. Many scholars have argued that the division of labor during the Industrial Revolution made a significant differentiation between home chores and work activities creating then a transitioning point in how children were raised, educated, and introduced into societal activities. With the rising cultural, social, and economic trends, the transitioning into adolescence was marked by more clearly defined gender roles and gender expectations for boys and girls, the establishment of a formal school system, and the restrictions imposed on youth labor.

Postindustrial societies focused on production and financial expansion while placing an increased weight on education of youth for specialized jobs. As a consequence, scholars have posited that the age of marriage was pushed back from 16–18 years old to 18–20 years old, which in turn, extended the adolescence period as the timing of marriage determined the entry into adulthood across most societies. The division of labor brought along scientific advances and the emergence of new professions (e.g., medical doctors, teachers, engineers) with the creation of a structured schooling system that extended the years adolescents spent learning and acquiring formal

 doi:10.1016/B978-0-12-373915-5.00013-9

training. New professions and services expanded social classes creating at the same time new sociopolitical interests that reflected back on the youth who, by mid-nineteenth century, were seen as the most important productive force of society.

With the seminal work published by G. Stanley Hall, the understanding of adolescence took a remarkable turn in the early twentieth century with the premise that the adolescent experienced not only biological changes but also a more complex transformation that was affected by the context and the social interactions. Indeed, new economic, demographic, scientific, and sociopolitical trends were key factors in the understanding of the changing youth populations and the multilevel transformations they were going through during adolescence. For instance, by the 1950s, public education had become a mandatory activity among adolescents, and with the development of psychological theories about human development, schooling became even more specialized with the establishment of school levels, age requirements, grading and degree systems extending schooling to around age 24.

Changes in the schooling system, as argued by many scholars, had started a trend in the length of adolescence extending the transitioning into adulthood to the early twenties. Multiple changes in modern society have made the study of transitions into adolescence a new phenomenon. The growth of mass media, technology, global marketing, leisure and educational opportunities as well as scientific advancements have been identified by researchers as key issues for revisiting the understanding of the transition into adolescence.

Transitioning into Adolescence: Developmental Milestones and Social Contexts

Traditionally, adolescence has been described as a passage from childhood to adulthood, marked by the gradual unfolding of biological, cognitive, psychological, and social transformations. From a more contemporary point of view, adolescence is described as a developmental phase that takes place from the ages of 10 through the early twenties divided in three periods: *early* (10–14), *middle* (15–17), and *late* adolescence (18–21). Though many perspectives can be adopted to understand this transitional period, the literature on the transition into adolescence can be generally divided into two main trends. One trend characterizes the process as the steady accumulation of physical, emotional, and behavioral transformations that collectively mark the shift from childhood to adolescence. This view describes development as a series of smooth changes that build on previous characteristics and that follows a predictable pattern. For instance, the capacity to remember symbols, solve basic problems, and learn new skills becomes enhanced gradually from childhood to adolescence with the emergence of new capacities such as abstraction, information-processing skills, and learning speed.

A second trend characterizes the transition into adolescence as the emergence of salient and distinct characteristics that are qualitatively different from childhood. For example, puberty denotes a clear transition into adolescence with the appearance of prominent physical characteristics for males and females. Along with physiological changes, two other developmental milestones mark the transition into adolescence: cognitive maturation (moving from concrete to formal operations, self-consciousness, and career planning) and socioemotional development (exploration of identity, romantic relationships, social roles, etc.). These abrupt changes require the individual to gradually reorganize behaviors and knowledge across different social contexts such as family, school, romantic relationships, and life circumstances including peer relationships, gaining independence from parents, and navigating the school system.

Understanding the onset of adolescence also includes examining individual–environment interactions and to what extent these impact youth. Individuals transitioning into adolescence are embedded in a particular sociopolitical environment, in a cultural context, and during a specific historical period which might directly or indirectly result in temporary or permanent changes in their lives. Transitions occur simultaneously at different levels, causing temporary disruptions in how adolescents experience changes in their inner (e.g., identity, self-perception) and outer worlds (e.g., relationships with parents, peers), and thus, significant variations might occur across individuals that might influence the normative or nonnormative nature of those transitions. The maturation of reproductive organs in preparation for future parenthood is a normative transition during adolescence; however, having a baby at age 15 is not a normative event associated with transitioning into adolescence. Similarly, in today's society, working during high school is seen as a normative event, since adolescents strive to gain financial independence from parents, whereas dropping out of school to marry and financially support a family is nonnormative at this life stage.

In this article, we describe the transition into adolescence from the perspective of abrupt shifts that qualitatively differentiate a new developmental stage. We focus on three main normative developmental transformations: physiological maturation, cognitive development, and socioemotional development. Along with those, we also discuss social contexts in which those developmental transitions take place, namely the family, social networks including peers and romantic relationships, and school. Finally, we provide a brief overview of the main challenges adolescents face during this transitional stage in contemporary societies.

Developmental Milestones

Physiological Development

Perhaps most noticeable during the onset of adolescence are the rapid physical transformations such as increases in height and weight and the maturation and enlargement of sexual organs that are triggered by hormonal changes. Other physiological signs of pubertal changes are the appearance of secondary sexual characteristics which are different for males and females. In males, some of the signs of sexual maturation include growth of facial and pubic hair, deepening of voice, broadening of shoulders and chest, enlargement of bone frame and muscle mass, increased physical strength, increased activity of sweat glands, and sperm production. Among girls, signs of sexual maturation include breast enlargement, widening of hips, changes in weight and accumulation of fat around buttocks, hips, and thighs, growth of pubic hair, and the menstrual period. Pubertal changes are generally experienced about 2 years earlier in girls than in boys. Boys tend to grow for a longer period than girls and as they continue to physically develop, other differences become more salient, such as greater height and longer limbs in males compared to females.

Great variation exists across adolescents in terms of the onset of puberty; generally, girls experience puberty between the ages of 8 and 13 years and boys between the ages of 10 and 15. However, some adolescents show signs of secondary sexual characteristics at an earlier age (before ages 9 for boys and 8 for girls) or a later age (after ages 13 for girls and 15 for boys). Researchers have found variations in timing of pubertal development which seems to be occurring earlier in contemporary adolescents than three to four decades ago. Early pubertal development has been associated with fat and sugar intake, obesity, and dietary habits during childhood, and also with hormones added to food and preservatives, hormonal residues and chemical pollutants in waterways, excess intake of medicines, and stress. Earlier onset of puberty has also been reported among adopted adolescents, particularly ones adopted from poor countries where they might have experienced nutritional or emotional deprivation early in life; other stressors include relocation, adapting to a new family, and acquisition of a new language.

Even though much attention is paid to sexual maturation and visible physical changes during puberty, significant changes occur in other body organs that impact the behavioral and emotional development of the adolescent. The brain, for example, goes through a series of changes, including reduction of gray matter and greater production of myelin that are associated with the development of more refined cognitive abilities during adolescence. In addition, studies have found that other areas of the brain that are responsible for controlling emotions and impulses as well as reasoning, planning, and decision-making start to mature during adolescence.

Cognitive Development

Over the course of adolescence, brain maturation allows further development of cognitive abilities including reasoning and abstract thinking, self-regulation, and the ability to foresee consequences of their behaviors. A salient aspect of transitioning into adolescence is the increasing awareness and understanding by youth of identity and self-identification. Both factors are central for an individual's social adaptation and display of behaviors and attitudes socially and culturally identified for males and females. At the same time, adolescents become more confrontational about moral and societal principles, values, and expectations which seem to be a result of adolescents' growing capacity to reflect and reason about complex matters. Self-reflective thinking allows adolescents to move from simply understanding the other person's perspective to developing a mutual and shared perspective that incorporates a third-person perspective as well as social expectations and values.

The development of higher cognitive abilities coincides not only with pubertal changes and brain maturation, but also with the entry into middle school and/or high school. Transitioning into a new school context brings with it additional challenges such as academic demands and expectations, growing social networks (peers, friends, significant others), and vocational exploration. As adolescents become more aware of their 'place in the world,' they also experience a greater need to evaluate potential occupations and vocational inclinations. Thus, during adolescence, a more comprehensive evaluation of personal values, interests, and abilities takes place related to future professional paths.

Socioemotional Development

In general, physical transformations dominate observable changes during adolescence, whereas affective changes are less visible, yet equally profound. The development of intrapersonal skills is one crucial milestone during adolescence to support both emotional and social adaptations to the environment, to individuals in the environment for the purpose of facilitating interactions and exchanges with others. Research has shown that a number of intrapersonal characteristics, including emotional wellness, self-esteem, self-expression, personal control, independence, autonomy, goal setting, emotion regulation, and decision-making, among others, support adaptations, and thus promote interpersonal relationships. Socioemotional development is particularly salient during the onset of adolescence, when youth are faced not only with physiological and cognitive changes but also with contextual changes (school, social networks). Teens begin to develop a sense of who they are and identify what they want or enjoy; in turn, this matures into a personal identity. They also become more observant of how their own actions and behaviors impact their immediate surroundings, both at home and school, as well as their relationships with family members and peers.

Parent–adolescent relationship transitions

An extensive body of scholarship has identified parents as the principal socializing agents responsible for adolescents' social interactions and behavioral outcomes. Parents attempt to transmit their wisdom about familial values, rules, and norms, while at the same time negotiate an adolescent's incorporation of extrafamilial values, beliefs, and desires, largely from peers. In turn, these equip adolescents with requisite skills to face the environment outside the home, to successfully deal and cope with challenges posed by individuals outside the home. The parent–adolescent bonds have a determinant impact on adolescent intrapersonal development and social adjustment; this extends into young adulthood as well. Studies have shown that low-quality parent–adolescent relationships are precursors of emotional problems, missing social skills, poor peer interactions as well as negative relationships with romantic partners. In contrast, positive parent–child relationships provide the foundation for healthy social and emotional development, the basis for social interactions, emotional and sexual development, and emerging partner relationships during adolescence.

During the transition into adolescence, parent–adolescent relationships experience tremendous amounts of change, driven in part by autonomy striving by teens, and at the same time, by an increased ability by the adolescent to take perspective, to empathize. Autonomy striving is designed to allow adolescents to develop the necessary skills to become independent adults. The amount of time parents and adolescents spend together in leisure activities, daily chores, and school and social activities steadily declines from early to late adolescence, paralleling the new importance of peers, and later, of partners. Time spent alone also increases, where adolescents spend more time in solitary activities like reading, watching TV, and physical activities, for instance. Studies show that closeness, communication, and desire for companionship from parents decline, while levels of conflict increase. They also show that by late adolescence, youth seek to reconnect with parents, trying to reestablish closeness, communication, and support, while at the same time decreasing conflictual exchanges.

It has also been suggested that adolescents develop a unique world view, different from the one of their parents, as a way of exploring and establishing their identity and personality. Researchers agree that for the most part, the source of conflict between parents and adolescents appears to revolve around daily household chores, leisure activities, preferences in clothing, and disapproval of peers, friends, or romantic partners. Theorists have emphasized that though parent–adolescent conflict increases during adolescence, the quality of the parent–adolescent relationship as well as core values acquired in the family remain almost intact over time.

Social networks and relationships

Growing social networks and the development of new relationships with friends, peers, and romantic partners are very important during adolescence. During adolescence, friendship relationships go through important qualitative changes as friends represent a main source of emotional support and personal disclosure of secrets, worries, and fears. Friends are chosen more carefully by adolescents who strive to find loyalty, companionship, intimacy, and safety to foster long-lasting relationships. Friends and peers, thus, play the important role of supporting social adaptation and school transitions, academic success, goal attainment, self-definition and identity, and modeling future relationships during adulthood.

Transitioning into adolescence affords new opportunities for establishing relationships with peers and other adults outside the home; these opportunities also introduce new and different demands on the adolescent who is faced with needing to incorporate them, along with all the other changes occurring in their lives. Group affiliation and participation in activities with peers gain greater significance as a way of fulfilling the adolescent's need for self-disclosure and intimacy, social comparison and identification, belongingness, and establishing social status. Peer group affiliation in cliques (small social groups) is usually based on shared values and interests and could positively and negatively affect adolescents' behaviors.

With the increases of individuation and autonomy during the transition into adolescence, youth strive for 'space' outside the home to facilitate being able to socialize with peers, and also to remove themselves from potential regulatory attempts by parents or caregivers. Positive outcomes of peer affiliations include developing social skills, adapting to the school environment, and developing leadership and collaboration skills; negative effects include substance use and experimentation, engaging in antisocial behaviors, and neglecting academic responsibilities. Neighborhoods (e.g., parks, community centers, sport activities) have been identified as preferred places for adolescents to meet and establish new relationships with other youth and to 'test' and display their developing social identities. Studies have shown that peer group affiliation and the establishment and maintenance of friendships precede dyadic romantic relationships during adolescence.

The initiation of romantic relationships during adolescence is directly influenced by peer and friend relationships; expectations and values regarding dating and expressing love toward a romantic partner are a common focus of conversations with peers and friends. Besides being preoccupied with physical changes, adolescents stress out about psychological issues such as sexual attractiveness, sexual orientation, sexual roles in society, and the idealization of romantic and sexual relationships. Some studies have shown that cultures (including more traditional ones) characterized by a sense of collectivism and strong family bonds tend to delay the development of romantic relationships until late adolescence. In contrast, Western cultures appear to encourage autonomy and participation in mixed-gender activities at a relatively early age; this would support transitioning to romantic relationships earlier during adolescence, and in fact, dating among US teens starts as early as 13–14 years of age.

Studies have documented that sexual initiation has dropped gradually during the past decades from the early twenties to around 17 years of age or even younger. Early pubertal development has been identified among the potential causes of early sexual initiation along with social factors such as mass media influences, sexual education, and the changing values regarding sexual behaviors. Significant consequences of early sexual intercourse during adolescence include pregnancy, parenthood, sexual transmitted diseases, sexual abuse, and emotional consequences.

School, career, and vocational development

In the United States, the transition into adolescence overlaps with the transition into secondary school. In general, teenagers start *middle-school* (sixth to eighth grade) around the ages of 11–14 years old and high school (ninth to twelfth grade) around the ages of 15–18 years old. Entry into secondary school represents a main event in the lives of adolescents who are at the same time struggling with pubertal changes, cognitive and emotional maturation, and the expansion of social relationships. Middle-schoolers might experience multiple concerns in their adaptation to the new school environment, such as keeping up with schedules, greater academic demands, managing extracurricular activities, crowded hallways, dealing with older peers, adapting to different testing and grade reporting systems as well as adjusting to a more impersonal school environment.

During this transitional period, adolescents become more aware of male–female physical differences, are more sensitive to their body image and how they are perceived by others, might experience stress related to personal safety, and develop a stronger need for peer group affiliation. Transitioning into high school also bring new challenges for adolescents as they might experience greater academic competition, a need to adapt to a larger and even more impersonal context than in middle school, and choosing between a multitude of curricular and extracurricular opportunities. Greater concerns are also experienced regarding self-sufficiency and associated responsibilities, peer influences, sexual attraction, future goals, and academic pressure to graduate and enter college.

Becoming an independently functioning individual is an important competence adolescents strive to master during the transition to adulthood. Studies have shown that early adolescents start thinking about and exploring careers based on their personal interests and likes or dislikes; at this early stage, career goals are rather tentative and flexible, where different options are being evaluated. By middle to late adolescence, youth are expected to define a career path in preparation for future educational and occupational attainment and are faced with a series of important choices and decisions. Societal demands regarding career goals, financial difficulties, vocational satisfaction, and employment opportunities have become more salient for contemporary adolescents who are preoccupied with joining the workforce. For instance, about one-third of American adolescents have held at least one part-time job by age 15, whereas 80% of youth report having held down a job by the time they graduate from high school.

Employment during adolescence provides youth with important experiences that support the development of time and money management skills, discipline, and work habits; these are prerequisites for gaining financial independence from parents. At the same time, employment also presents challenges for adolescents, including negative interpersonal processes in the work environment and reduced time to complete school work and study for exams. The research shows that higher involvement in school activities and extracurricular or after-school activities might be reflected on lower grades as well as increased absenteeism at school. Some have suggested that employment is related with family conflict because work demands might reduce opportunities to spend more time with family members and family activities; in addition, disagreements about spending decisions might increase conflict with parents. Whereas adolescent employment represented a way of gaining 'adult' role status and saving for college or career attainment in past times, studies suggest that employment today represents a way of exploring financial independence and fulfilling personal needs, including transportation, clothing, or expenses related to leisure pursuits.

Physical and mental health

Though physical and mental health problems can develop at any stage in one's life, adolescence is a particularly sensitive stage for the development of health problems that can be triggered by genetic liabilities and a history of family health problems or exposure to toxins in the environment. Health problems can be also related to the significant physical and emotional transitions experienced during adolescence; in addition, social relationship may also influence changes in adolescents' eating, exercising, and sleeping habits. Unfortunately, the lack of positive coping skills may put adolescents at a higher risk for making unhealthy choices with regard to their physical and mental health. For instance, national statistics show that tobacco, alcohol, and substance use have increased among adolescents; similarly, body image issues, eating disorders, and self-medication are problems commonly affecting adolescents today.

Adolescent health is an area of public concern around the globe. Scholars have raised awareness about the need to support knowledge acquisition in youth about physical and mental health as well as developing healthy habits and positive coping skills. Technological advances have increased the time adolescents spend playing video games, listening to music, and navigating the Internet, whereas the time spent in outdoor activities and sports have declined considerably, affecting nutritional and physical activity habits. New technologies and mass media are part of adolescents daily lives creating at times 'unrealistic' life expectations and modeling negative problem-solving behaviors as accepted coping skills. In addition, nutritional habits, sleep deprivation, unrealistic standards of physical beauty, and a lack of parental and social support are putting contemporary adolescents at a higher risk for developing physical and mental health problems such as disordered eating and anxiety disorders, obesity, depression, and suicide among others.

Contemporary Challenges in the Transition into Adolescence

Through history, the transition into adolescence has been shaped by historical, cultural, and sociopolitical shifts. A salient concern on the transition into adolescence nowadays relates to whether changes in the family and school systems as well as globalization and technological transformations are associated with nonnormative physical, cognitive, and socioemotional development in adolescents. On the one hand, some empirical evidence has suggested an increased trend in psychosocial disorders, substance use, and crime/delinquency among adolescents during the past decades. On the other hand, other studies have documented that trends in emotional disorders and mainly nonaggressive externalization problems reported from the mid - 1970s to late 1990s have been rather similar and steady among adolescents. Though the literature in general is not conclusive about changing trends in youth outcomes, the challenges faced by children transitioning into adolescence in today's society are key issues that warrant additional attention.

Family

In general, official data show that adolescents today are more likely to live in households headed by a single parent, a stepparent, a grandparent, or an extended family member than 20 years ago – it is estimated that about 4.5 million children live with their grandparents and about 1.5 million with other relatives in the United States. Both the meaning and attitudes about diverse family structures have changed dramatically over the course of the past two decades; evidence suggests that changes in family systems and associated family relationships directly or indirectly influence adolescents' outcomes. Nonnormative events such as parental divorce or separation, parental job instability, and relocation contribute to increased perceived stress among adolescents, and thus, a greater likelihood of adverse effects on emotional and behavioral adjustment as well as school achievement.

Studies have shown that those effects decline over time in the presence of positive parenting (good relationships and support, open communication) by the resident parent, by the nonresident parent, or both; thus, demonstrating the importance of family relationships on adolescents' well-being. A significant challenge experienced by contemporary families relates to youth exposure to media content on sexual topics which increases awareness and sensitivity about sexual issues among adolescents. Parents today strive to stay up-to-date with technological advances balancing efforts to censure media content; at the same time, they are more proactively taking actions to ensure the psychological well-being of their teenage children.

Gender Identity and Self-Concept

More than before, adolescents are immersed in a rapidly changing world with mixed messages coming from multiple socializing agents (e.g., peers, Internet, media) urging them to fulfill social expectations about being 'a man' and 'a woman' that might inaccurately resemble adult roles. Contemporary gender roles are perceived by adolescents as more flexible. Modernization has brought about greater opportunities for adolescents to communicate their developmental needs in regards to gender identification, and also to confront traditional values and cultural expectations regarding gender roles and sexual scripts. Some researchers have argued that in the quest for constructing one's self-concept, contemporary adolescents have sought the opportunity to develop a parallel, virtual world(s) that allows them more flexibility in exploring their identities through language, role playing, and identity simulation. Today's changing society has also made adolescents more aware of additional factors in the development of identity and self-concept, such as ethnic and/or racial background, geographical location (e.g., rural, urban), and generational statuses (e.g., native born, immigrant).

Technology and Media

Compared to youth from a few decades ago, adolescents today are growing up with greater access to the radio, television, Internet, interactive videogames, and technological devices (e.g., mobile phones, computers, PDAs). Indeed, access to technology and media has increased among younger adolescents, particularly in urban areas. Changes in new technologies not only shape adolescents' day-to-day lives but also create expectations that challenge long-established norms and values. For example, adolescents today are bombarded with mixed messages about the importance of physical attractiveness, physical fitness, and body image in contrast with the importance of healthy physical and emotional development. With the influence of the media, adolescents have also become an active consumer force. Through advertisement and marketing, mass media have increased the consumption of material goods and services among youth, as a mechanism of transitioning to independence (e.g., use of mobile phones).

With the proliferation of computers and widespread communication technology (cell phones), *Cyberspace* has become an important context that facilitates socializing, not only locally, but across states and even cultures/countries. The Internet offers adolescents extensive opportunities for interactions (blogs, instant messaging, e-mail, chat rooms), self-diversification, and less constrained and monitored environments by parents, but also less structured and committed relationships, including romantic relationships. On the other hand, studies have shown that adolescents are attracted to cyberspace as it is perceived as a 'safer' environment to explore issues such as sexuality, identity, or self-image. The current evidence on potential effects by the Internet on early adolescent psychological well-being remains inconclusive, although some studies on late adolescents have found relationships among Internet use and peer status, social introversion and withdrawal, depression and anxiety, and delayed maturity.

Vocational and Professional Goals

The continuing transformations across societies along with globalization trends have made the job market increasingly competitive, demanding that youth acquire higher educational levels and develop additional skills, including foreign language competence, technological knowledge, and computer literacy. Paralleling these demands, governmental policies and commercial values continue to reshape the content of curricula which drives the restructuring of the educational system. This means that youth are faced with both positive new opportunities and new challenges at the same time.

Extended curricula and after-school programs have increased the time adolescents spend at school, providing them with additional learning opportunities. With volunteering and service-learning being incorporated into school curricula, adolescents are exposed to real-life experiences that positively affect the educational process and shape future work expectations. Official data have documented important changes in the number of females attending colleges and universities across countries which in turn has impacted the job market and the positions held by women worldwide.

Conclusions

Understanding the complex transformations occurring during the transition into adolescence is a grand task. Now more than ever, we are concerned with the effects by global, systemic, or contextual changes on children transitioning into adolescents, including immigration, globalized economies, political restlessness, environmental problems, and a decrease in natural resources due to rapid development and population growth. In an era replete with rapid social changes, youth face unique challenges in their trajectory toward adulthood which provide both opportunities for risk and resiliency. Research has identified a number of factors that increase risk for adjustment behaviors, including engaging in unhealthy behaviors, lack of parental supervision, negative peer pressure, and the influence by modern technologies and mass media.

In a number of societies, the norm is that both parents must work, and thus are able to devote less time to their children; a natural consequence is that youth are less consistently supervised and that they seek social interactions and social support from peers. Glamorization of sexual and romantic relationships in mass media which portrays weak or superficial bonds as acceptable and which glorifies risk-taking behaviors as an acceptable coping mechanism (e.g., early sexual initiation, sexual intercourse, and alcohol) has led to adjustment problems and negative developmental outcomes among youth.

Despite these known risks, intrapersonal characteristics combined with strong relationships with parents emerge as key factors promoting resiliency. Studies have shown that a number of personal assets, including self-confidence, positive coping skills, self-efficacy, self-regulation, along with parental closeness and monitoring, adult mentoring and guidance, community service, and faith-based groups, provide adolescents with the tools to thrive. Recent studies have also shown that these protective processes associated with resilience do not appear to be context- or culture-specific, but rather encompass a common set of core factors that serve similar functions across different ethnic and racial groups.

In general, theoretical work and empirical research show that transitions occurring during adolescence are highly influenced by family and peer interactions, the school and community contexts as well as individual characteristics. To date, our knowledge on transitions during adolescence continues to expand as new methodologies and scientific tools become available to advance the understanding of the unique events shaping our children into adolescents and in their journey to adulthood.

See also: Adolescence, Theories of; Cognitive Development; Cultural Influences on Adolescent Development; Middle School; Parent–Child Relationship; Peer Relations; Puberty and Adolescence: An Evolutionary Perspective; Stages of Adolescence; Transitions to Adulthood.

Further Reading

Benson PL and Pittman KJ (2001) *Trends in Youth Development: Visions, Realities and Challenges*. Norwell, MA: Kluwer.

Graber JA and Brooks-Gunn J (1996) Transitions and turning points: Navigating the passage from childhood through adolescence. *Developmental Psychology* 32: 768–776. doi:10.1037/0012-1649.32.

Larson R (2000) Toward a psychology of positive youth development. *American Psychologist* 55: 170–183.

Lerner R and Steinberg L (eds.) (2009) *Handbook of Adolescent Psychology*, 3rd edn. New York: Wiley.

Lerner RM, Taylor CS, and von Eye A (eds.) (2002) *Pathways to Positive Development Among Diverse Youth. New Directions for Youth Development: Theory, Practice, and Research*. San Francisco: Jossey-Bass.

Transitions to Adulthood

A L Howard, University of North Carolina, Chapel Hill, NC, USA
N L Galambos, University of Alberta, Edmonton, AB, Canada

Glossary

Churning: A process of frequent movement in and out of employment that generates negative long-term consequences for employment, such as lower wages, fewer job skills, and reduced self-confidence.
Collectivism: A cultural belief system typical of Asian and other non-Western cultures in which citizens are encouraged to prioritize the goals, needs, and beliefs of the family and community. Obedience, conformity, and co-operation are valued.
Cycling: The pattern of repeatedly moving out of and returning to the parental home.
Emerging adulthood: A perspective on the transition to adulthood in which the late teens to mid-twenties represent a distinct stage of development between adolescence and adulthood.
Individualism: A cultural belief system typical of North American and other Western cultures in which citizens are encouraged to achieve social and financial independence and prioritize their own needs above the needs of others.
Relationship inertia: A process in which romantic couples' relationships gradually solidify – often ending in marriage – due to the accumulation of constraints that make it more difficult to break up than to stay together.
Role transitions: Markers of the transition to adulthood that have historically signaled the passage from adolescence to adulthood, including marriage, obtaining full-time employment, and becoming a parent.
Turning points: Salient developmental experiences that often lead to changes in patterns of behavior, emotion, or cognition. Turning points linked to transitions in development are especially likely to result in change.

Introduction

Picture the road to adulthood taken by typical teenagers in mid-twentieth-century North America: By age 17 or 18, most were finishing high school and expecting to face the responsibilities of adulthood. Many young men and, to a lesser extent, young women, entered the work force or went to college, moving away from their parents' home in either case. On average, men were married by age 22 and women by age 20, and had their first children a year or two later. By their mid-twenties, these former teenagers had become adults with their own families and independent households.

In contrast, as a group, contemporary young people follow a multitude of roads in making their journey to adulthood, and this diversity or heterogeneity of pathways is one way in which the transition to adulthood is set apart from other transitions across the life span. Some enter the work force as adolescents and do not complete high school, let alone pursue postsecondary education. Others encounter bouts or long periods of unemployment, particularly when growing up in poverty. Still others stay at home while attending college, working full- or part-time, or taking time off to consider options and travel around the world. Many move away from their parents' homes and select from a variety of independent and semi-independent living arrangements: college dormitories, apartments with roommates or alone, cohabitation with a romantic partner, and in some cases, back into parents' homes after a brief stint of independent living. Some marry young or have children out of wedlock at a young age. In addition, initial choices may be modified, resulting in frequent movement in and out of school, work, relationships, and living arrangements. Much diversity is explained by differences in education and socioeconomic status. Young people with postsecondary degrees and higher incomes follow paths that are similar to one another, and in stark contrast to the paths taken by young people with less education and fewer social and economic resources.

This structured diversity between and within socioeconomic classes is amplified by a lack of normative ages for settling into traditional adult roles. It is no longer the case that young people feel compelled to secure full-time employment, marry, and begin raising children by their early twenties. Of course, the constraints placed on lower-income youth mean that they tend to settle into adult roles earlier in the transition to adulthood. On average, however, first marriages are now delayed until about age 26 for women and age 28 for men in the United States, significantly lengthening the period between total dependence on one's parents and total independence and running one's own household.

In this article, we explore diversity in the transition to adulthood for contemporary young people. Much of the research discussed in this article derives from North American samples, however, limiting the generalizability of the information presented here to other countries and cultures. We focus on specific challenges that young people face with respect to family, education, work, and romantic relationships. We also discuss their mental health during this period and refer to ways in which cultural backgrounds might affect the transition to adulthood.

Making the Transition

Understanding how people navigate the challenges of transitional events in their lives is critical to the study of human development. Individual differences in the ways that transitions

 doi:10.1016/B978-0-12-373915-5.00014-0

are experienced help us to understand positive and negative outcomes that occur later on in the life course. For example, some adolescents thrive when they move out of their parents' homes, benefiting from the opportunity to make their own choices and take responsibility for their own households. Others are unprepared, and experience deep loneliness and anxiety as a result of being away from the comfort and familiarity of the family home. The transition to adulthood is probably best described as a set of transitions. Young people's transitional challenges include leaving the parental home, pursuing vocational or career-oriented education, moving into full-time employment, cohabiting with a romantic partner, getting married, and forging new relationships with parents as independent adults. All of these transitions are further marked by the demands of new social groups and behavioral expectations that are different from those found in former, more familiar, settings.

The ways in which young people navigate transitions to adulthood are determined in part by individual differences in their earlier life experiences and adaptive resources. For example, some adolescents are more emotionally and socially mature than others and better able to cope with new demands; these are personal resources that might work to ease the transition to adulthood. In contrast, individuals who had difficulties dealing with the challenges of adolescence might also have a harder time adapting when they enter the transition to adulthood. Although such individual differences might shape how the transition to adulthood is experienced, contexts such as the family, peers, school, work, and community also play a role, as events and people in these contexts might serve to promote or hinder an adaptive transition. Moreover, all of these contexts are nested within the political climate, economic conditions, and ideological norms of the cultures in which young people live, and these larger contexts also help to shape the experience of the transition to adulthood.

As an example of how the cultural context might shape the transition to adulthood, consider that Western societies tend to promote individualism, and young people in these societies focus on accomplishing personal goals that will allow them to be financially and socially independent and to make choices and decisions with their own interests in mind. In contrast, many non-Western societies promote collectivism, and young people in these societies are encouraged to put the well-being of their family and community ahead of personal goals. Conformity, obedience, and attending to family responsibilities are expectations that shape the experience of the transition to adulthood for young people in collectivist societies. To further complicate this picture, many young people face competing demands from both individualist and collectivist societies. For example, young people living in North America who originate from ethnic backgrounds that emphasize collectivism must balance the demands of their ancestral society with the expectations of the majority culture. These cultural differences contribute to the diversity in the transition to adulthood that young people experience in today's world.

Markers of the Transition to Adulthood

There are many possible markers of entrance into adulthood, some of which are objectively measured sociological criteria, and some of which are more psychological in nature (pertaining to subjective perceptions of whether or not one has reached adulthood). Traditional sociological criteria for becoming an adult are familiar to most people, and consist of a series of role transitions that mark the passage from adolescence to adulthood. They include completing education, settling into a career, getting married, and becoming a parent. Marriage in particular is a transition that has historically marked the passage to adulthood in most cultures around the world. Despite the ubiquity of such role transitions, contemporary young people in Western societies no longer agree that transitions such as marriage and parenthood are the most important determinants of whether or not one has reached adulthood, possibly due to the much later ages at which young people now make these transitions. Thus, role transitions are generally ranked as the least important criteria by young people making the transition to adulthood; that is, subjective or psychological adulthood does not require having made these transitions. Role transitions have also fallen in importance as criteria for adulthood among youth in non-Western countries (e.g., China, Israel, Argentina), but to a lesser extent than among Western youth. Therefore, other criteria must be considered when attempting to explain the psychological nature of transition to adulthood for contemporary youth.

Other markers of the transition to adulthood could include biological transitions such as reaching puberty, growing to one's full height, and engaging in sexual intercourse for the first time, and chronological or legal transitions such as obtaining a driver's license and reaching the age of majority. As with role transitions such as marriage, however, young people in cultures surveyed do not rank biological and chronological transitions as especially important aspects of the transition to adulthood. Instead, they focus on intangible psychological criteria that emphasize social, emotional, and behavioral maturity rather than completion of arbitrary rites-of-passage. One such category of transitions is norm-compliance. Transitions in this category focus on behavioral regulation, social responsibility, and staying away from harmful activities. They include avoidance of getting drunk, using illegal drugs, vulgar language, multiple sexual partners, and drunk driving. Another category of transitions reflecting behavioral maturity concerns taking on family responsibilities. Transitions in this category emphasize one's ability to function as the head of a household, performing duties such as caring for children, supporting a household financially, and physically protecting a family.

Finally, two categories that define a successful transition to adulthood can be described as sets of intangible qualities that reflect culturally imposed values. Criteria for independence, including accepting responsibility for one's actions, becoming financially independent, and establishing a relationship with parents as an equal, are consistently ranked above other aspects of the transition to adulthood by young people in Western and non-Western societies. Young people in collectivist cultures, however, tend to rank more highly criteria for interdependence, such as becoming less self-oriented, developing greater consideration for others, and making life-long commitments to others. Altogether, while there are many possible markers of entrance into adulthood, young people tend to view independent behaviors and, in some cases, interdependent behaviors, as evidence that one has become an adult.

Emerging Adulthood

An important perspective on the transition to adulthood is Jeffrey Arnett's concept of emerging adulthood, first proposed in 2000. He argues that the developmental experiences of young people in their late teens and early twenties living in industrialized societies have undergone sweeping changes since the mid-twentieth century, making the years between adolescence and adulthood fundamentally distinct. Emerging adulthood is described as a new developmental stage, for which there are five distinguishing features:

1. instability, or unpredictable movement in and out of different life situations;
2. identity explorations, or the freedom to try out different lifestyles, behaviors, and self-concepts;
3. self-focus, or more interest in self-actualization than in contributing to the well-being of others;
4. feeling 'in between' adolescence and adulthood, not yet adult but no longer a teen; and
5. infinite possibilities, or the expectation that many different futures are available.

These features derive from the few expectations placed on emerging adults to enter specific social roles; there is little pressure to marry and settle into a long-term career and parenthood until at least the late twenties. The need for higher education in our technologically advanced world has contributed to the existence of this period.

Emerging adulthood is characterized by diversity: young people consider different options for work, postsecondary education, living arrangements, romantic relationships, and worldviews. Options are often attempted, abandoned, and exchanged for others. Arnett argues that the freedom to explore options in different domains of life is a major advantage of emerging adulthood over other stages of development. Whereas adolescents' choices are largely dictated by their parents and guardians, emerging adults choose whether to drop out of school, enter the workforce, move in with their boyfriend or girlfriend, quit a job, or go back to school. Whereas adults' choices are restricted by their commitments in marriage and parenthood, emerging adults are free to pursue their own interests and try out educational and work possibilities that involve relocation, travel, and income disruption. In general, Arnett maintains that despite the stress and frustration of navigating the challenges of the transition to adulthood, emerging adulthood is a positive experience for most young people.

By drawing attention to a neglected age group, Arnett has generated considerable support for his concept of emerging adulthood from research communities in psychology, sociology, and related disciplines. At the same time, it has proved to be a controversial perspective, as several scholars have pointed out the limitations of Arnett's conceptualization of the emerging adult experience. One issue is that emerging adulthood is presented as a stage of development, in which all young people are expected to eventually become fully adult. Contemporary developmental theories reject stage-based conceptions of human development, instead emphasizing that pathways through the life course may take different forms for different people within different domains of functioning. Human development is domain-specific, highly adaptive, nonlinear, and in some cases, reversible. For example, a highly educated emerging adult with a prosperous career may move back into the parents' home after an emotionally incapacitating break-up of a long-term romantic relationship. Although this person is 'adult' in terms of education and employment, he or she is simultaneously 'adolescent,' regressing to the role of a dependent child.

Another consideration is that emerging adulthood may only be experienced by young people in developed, industrialized societies, and only by relatively affluent people within those societies. Young people in developing countries who lack resources even to supply themselves and their families with clean water, food, clothing, and shelter probably do not have the resources to engage in extensive identity explorations. Nor do they have safety nets in place to allow them the freedom to drop out of school or quit a job if the experience is found to be unfulfilling. Invariably, the stagnant economies and high rates of poverty typical in developing countries limit the opportunities available for youth. Similarly, young people in developed nations may be excluded from the experience of emerging adulthood due to lack of resources. Undereducated, unskilled, and otherwise marginalized youth have more difficulty succeeding in a society that demands ever-increasing levels of education for all kinds of employment. Indeed, many young people do not have access to postsecondary education or parents with sufficient resources to support the exploratory activities that define Arnett's emerging adulthood.

Finally, several scholars have debated whether emerging adults' freedom to explore options in work, school, and relationships allows them to flourish in adulthood or flounder in a vicious cycle in which they are "forever emerging but never adult" (Hendry and Kloep, 2007: 77). The consequences of the so-called freedom to explore in emerging adulthood include prolonged dependence on parents, underemployment among highly educated young people, and declining wages. With fewer jobs providing long-term security, frequent movement in and out of employment and educational settings may not be a choice that young people are making, but rather a prolonged moratorium from true adulthood that is imposed by society. The consequences may also extend to parents, many of whom face the financial and emotional burdens of supporting grown-up children who continue to live at home.

Despite these limitations, emerging adulthood appears to be a very real experience for many young people in countries around the world. Globalization, increased economic prosperity, and advances in higher education in developing nations are likely to lead to more young people experiencing an extended period of time for exploring opportunities between adolescence and adulthood. In Latin America, for instance, there is already evidence in favor of emerging adulthood. Still, there are differences between the rich and the poor and between rural and urban young people in their access to such opportunities. Child marriage, extreme poverty, and lack of educational and economic opportunities will work against a universal period of emerging adulthood.

Education and Work in the Transition to Adulthood

It is no longer the norm for young people to start a full-time job after high school or college, gradually acquire promotions, pay raises, and seniority, and retire after 40 years of service to a single employer. On the contrary, changes to global economic conditions, constant adaptation to new technologies, and competition with foreign businesses have drastically altered the employment landscape for young people in industrialized societies. It is now typical to move in and out of several jobs, some with long-term career opportunities and others that are unskilled and offer low pay and limited benefits. Many people also experience spells of unemployment between jobs. A further complication arises from the role of postsecondary education during the transition to adulthood. The vast majority of North American adolescents approaching the end of high school expect to obtain a four-year college education, including adolescents from low-income and otherwise disadvantaged backgrounds. As more and more desirable job opportunities require a post-secondary education, high school students are increasingly encouraged to attend college, in some cases irrespective of academic ability, preparedness, and motivation. College completion rates, however, fall far below the number of students who aspire to a postsecondary degree. Contemporary young people are faced with a daunting challenge: Higher expectations for educational attainment and high-paying careers in an unstable yet demanding job market ill-equipped to meet their expectations.

Two competing perspectives describe the nature and consequences of this challenge for young people making the transition to adulthood. The first perspective derives from literatures in sociology and labor market economics, and refers to young people's experience with the worlds of education and work during the transition to adulthood as churning. From this perspective, frequent movement in and out of jobs, in and out of unemployment, and in and out of labor force participation leads to long-term negative consequences in the form of lower wages, insufficient job training, and reduced self-confidence. The churning trap is most commonly experienced by young people with less education. For some, frequent movement may be seen as beneficial, to the extent that diverse work experiences maximize employability in a range of occupations. Movement in and out of postsecondary education may also be seen as churning, when re-enrollment in college programs is a response to limited opportunities for good jobs.

The second perspective suggests greater optimism for young people facing an increasingly unpredictable employment and educational landscape. In his depiction of emerging adulthood, Jeffrey Arnett presents instability in work and school, among other domains, as exploration. He argues that the lack of specific and restricted expectations for young people in their late teens to mid-twenties provides freedom to explore a range of interests. With respect to work and school, emerging adults have the freedom to try out different job opportunities and educational programs before committing to a single area of interest for long-term employment. Even among youth who do not actively seek to explore a variety of opportunities, Arnett argues that instability in general tends to result in a successful transition to adulthood, by challenging young people to navigate obstacles and detours on the road to adulthood.

Transition to University

Perhaps due to the large number of high school students who enroll in college and university programs, the transition to university is a special case of the transition to adulthood that warrants attention. Although transitional periods in general are challenging and can generate stress, students making the transition to university face several concurrent challenges within a short period of time as they begin their first year. New academic demands, leaving home, changes in family and peer relations, new financial stresses, and increased opportunities to experiment with risk behaviors such as binge drinking are all features of the first year of university that are common to many students. These concurrent challenges have not gone unnoticed, and there is now a growing literature documenting the significant mental health difficulties experienced by students making the transition to university. Several studies show high rates of depressive symptoms, anxiety, eating disorders, and sleep problems, including sleep disturbances and inadequate sleep. Although other lines of research suggest that mental health problems decline as young people move through the transition to adulthood, the short-term effects of disturbances to students' psychological well-being may have a range of negative consequences, such as poor academic and social adjustment, academic failure, and drop-out. Despite the perception that college and university students are a privileged group, they face significant challenges that distinguish their experiences from the experiences of young people making the transition to adulthood outside of the college context.

Relations with Parents in the Transition to Adulthood

Family relations during the transition to adulthood can be stressful for parents and their children. As young people search for ways to become autonomous individuals, parents struggle to maintain close relationships with their adult children. Ideally, parents are supportive of their children's burgeoning independence, and recognize the importance of gradually reshaping the parent–child relationship such that young people come to relate to their parents almost as equals, rather than as authority figures. Despite the freedom to make one's own choices that characterizes the transition to adulthood, parental support is key to ensuring that the transition is successful.

Leaving Home

The most significant aspect of the transition to adulthood for the parents of young people in transition is the process of leaving home. Traditionally, the process was initiated by marriage, with men and women in their late teens and early twenties moving out to establish independent households with their new spouses. As average ages at first marriage have risen in the past few decades, however, marriage is no longer seen as the only – or even the primary – reason to move away from parents. In Western societies, moving out on one's own satisfies the need to establish social and financial independence from parents. However, this independence may be more an illusion than a reality, as many young people who move out remain dependent on their parents. For example, college students living in dormitories often have their costs of living covered by parents.

In recent decades, a trend of cycling – that is, moving out and moving back in – has emerged among young people in their late teens and early twenties. Many young people who move out of the parental home to go to college move back home after entering the workforce and finding it financially burdensome to live independently. Young people who cohabit with romantic partners often move back in with their parents after the relationship has ended. Despite the value placed by western societies on independence, many contemporary parents do not appear to view their adult children moving back home as a problem. Provided that adult children are either attending college or working and saving money, parents are willing to supply room and board and relieve some of the economic barriers faced by young people living independently during the transition to adulthood.

The diversity of the transition to adulthood is certainly evident in patterns of home leaving. Although many young people do leave home shortly after high school, there are differences among those belonging to ethnic minority groups and lower-income families. Young people from Asian, Hispanic, and African American ethnic backgrounds stay at home longer, and in many cases are more likely to stay at home until marriage. Similarly, young people in European countries stay at home longer than Americans, owing to cultural differences in the perceived importance of independence and the quality of relationships with parents. Young people from low-income families often lack the resources to leave home early, and instead continue to live with their parents into their early twenties. Cycling in and out of the parental home is also less common among lower-income youth, due in part to lower rates of college attendance.

For the substantial minority of young people who do live with parents during their early twenties, a possible consequence is the sense of being stalled in their progress toward independent adulthood. Young people who move out tend to describe the relationship with their parents more favorably than young people who stay at home, but dissatisfaction among those who stay at home may be linked to parents' attempts to maintain a hierarchical household structure in which parents hold authority over children. Indeed, the higher rates of European youth living at home suggest that parents and children are able to strike a power balance that facilitates amicable living conditions. In general, parents who are able to respect their grown children's privacy and boundaries, relinquish control, and acknowledge their children's adult status may offset many of the difficulties associated with living at home during the transition to adulthood.

Intimacy and Relationships in the Transition to Adulthood

The romantic relationships of young people making the transition to adulthood are qualitatively distinct from adolescents' relationships. In adolescence, relationships are short-lived and focus on companionship, sharing recreational activities, and experimenting with sexual behaviors. By the early twenties, however, young people become more interested in longer-term relationships that involve deeper emotional intimacy, security, and commitment. Current research on intimate relationships across the life span originates from the psychoanalytic and developmental theories of mid-twentieth century scholars, Harry Stack Sullivan and Erik Erikson. Sullivan argued that intimate friendships are precursors to intimate romantic relationships, preparing adolescents to initiate relationships with opposite-sex partners when sexual interest emerges around puberty. This sequence of events, according to Sullivan, marks a successful progression toward maturity. Erikson proposed that people undergo a series of psychosocial challenges as they progress toward adulthood, including the challenge of acquiring a capacity for intimacy in relationships. He argued that successful adult friendships and romantic relationships depend on the ability to be emotionally intimate with friends and romantic partners. Features of intimate relationships include self-disclosure, partner responsiveness and reciprocity, compromise, and mutual support. During the transition to adulthood, relationships with friends, family, and romantic partners are more intimate than they were in adolescence. However, young people interact primarily with romantic partners and potential romantic partners during the transition to adulthood.

Marriage and Cohabitation

Most contemporary young people do not stay with the first significant romantic partner of their transition to adulthood, and many feel that experiencing multiple relationships prior to marriage is an important preparatory step. However, marriage is a relationship goal for most people, and probably the most significant step that young people take in their romantic relationships during the transition to adulthood. Despite the lack of importance placed on role transitions such as marriage in determining whether or not one feels like an adult, the fact is that marriage is a major event in the transition to adulthood for most people. However, as later ages of marriage suggest, the process of searching for a marriage partner is a lengthy endeavor for many young people. Since they are no longer expected to marry in their late teens or early twenties, young people put off marriage for many reasons: to finish college, establish financial independence, or because they do not feel ready or mature enough for the commitment.

Later ages of marriage in recent decades came with increasing numbers of young couples cohabiting without being married. The prevalence of cohabitation is due in part to its widespread societal acceptance, and many marriages are now preceded by cohabitation. As with every other aspect of the transition to adulthood, there is great diversity in the nature of cohabitations. Some couples cohabit because they have a mutual understanding that they will get married in the near future. Other couples cohabit because they feel that it is important to 'try out' living together before considering marriage. Still others cohabit for conflicting reasons, that is, one person may feel that marriage is an inevitable end point of the cohabitation, while the other has no such intention in mind. Many couples do not make a deliberate decision to cohabit; in these cases, couples gradually slide into a cohabiting relationship after a series of events – spending several nights a week together, gradually leaving belongings at one or the other's home, and the approaching end of one partner's lease. Scott Stanley and his colleagues refer to this effect as relationship inertia, and argue that many contemporary young people end up married to their spouses without having explicitly intended to do so because relationship constraints – financial obligations, shared property, pregnancy – make inertial movement toward marriage easier than breaking up.

Regardless of the reasons for cohabiting, cohabitations frequently end in marriage. Unfortunately, studies show that the marriages of couples who formerly cohabited are consistently poorer than the marriages of couples who did not cohabit prior to marriage, at least in North America. Problems such as poorer marital communication, lower marital satisfaction, higher levels of domestic violence, and higher rates of divorce are more prevalent in marriages that begin with cohabitation. Interestingly, these problems are much less prevalent in European marriages preceded by cohabitation, possibly because it is more common for couples to cohabit as an explicit alternative to marriage. Although rare among North American couples, this type of cohabitation involves a formal commitment between partners with the mutual understanding that a legal marriage is not a goal of the relationship. One reason that marriage may be desirable, and why marriages preceded by lengthy cohabitation may be problematic, is the ambiguity of cohabitation in contrast to marriage. Historical and cultural traditions around the world have provided a basis for the expectations and responsibilities of marriage to be extremely clear. Similarly, the meaning of marriage to members of a society is unambiguous because they agree on the parameters that define marriage, and what the marital experience involves. Cohabitation, at least in North America, is not understood in this way. There is no agreement on what cohabitation means in general or even to a specific couple with respect to expectations, responsibilities, and commitment. This ambiguity may contribute to problems observed later as couples drift gradually into marriage without ever arriving at a mutual understanding of the nature of their relationship.

Risky Behaviors and Mental Health in the Transition to Adulthood

The ambiguities and challenges of the transition to adulthood inevitably lead to the question: How are young people doing in terms of risky behaviors and psychological well-being? We know that the early twenties are a peak time for some risky sexual and substance use behaviors. Freedom from parental supervision and living and socializing in situations where other young people congregate constitute a recipe for experimenting with sex, alcohol, and drug use. Those who choose to spend their evenings out are more likely to engage in more heavy alcohol use and to report illicit drug use. Of course, such opportunities are not taken by everyone. Young people who are highly religious or who disapprove of alcohol and drug use are less likely to engage in risky activities. Religious beliefs and attitudes about substance use, then, are personal characteristics that young people bring to the transition to adulthood that help to determine how they make that transition.

Although increased freedom during the transition to adulthood helps to explain the prevalence of some risky behaviors, we know from large representative studies of cohorts of high school students in the United States followed for many years after high school (the monitoring the future studies) that entrance into marriage and parenthood is associated with decreases in such behaviors. It is almost as if these role transitions mark an end to the formerly carefree, self-focused existence of many young people making the transition to adulthood, and create new responsibilities that they become eager to adopt. In fact, even becoming engaged is associated with reductions in substance use, a trend that is reversed among the newly divorced. Thus, we can view engagement, marriage, and parenthood as role transitions that protect against some behaviors that pose a threat to health and well-being.

With respect to mental health, epidemiological studies show that people in the 18- to 24-year-old age group are more likely than other age groups to experience psychiatric conditions such as substance use (especially alcohol) disorders, personality disorders, and major depression. Substance use disorders are more common among young men, whereas major depressive disorders are more common among young women. Sleep problems are also prevalent among individuals in their twenties. The prevalence of psychiatric disorders suggests that the transition to adulthood is an important and vulnerable period for the development of mental illness.

At the same time, longitudinal studies that have tracked adolescents into the transition to adulthood have shown that, on average, symptoms of depression and anger decrease and self-esteem increases. The conclusion is that mental health typically improves from about age 18 to age 25. How do we reconcile the fact that the transition to adulthood is a peak period for the emergence of serious mental illness at the same time that the average young person shows improvement in mental health over time? We think that there is a divergence of pathways, with a small proportion of people beginning to face serious mental health challenges but the rest of the population in this age group stabilizing at a relatively healthy level as they move through the transition and experience some success. Indeed, some role transitions, specifically, marriage and becoming gainfully employed, explain improvements in mental health during this period. Divorce and unemployment are associated with decreases in mental health at the time that these role transitions are experienced.

Continuities in Adaptation from Childhood Through Young Adulthood

The transition to adulthood is not only a time during which new stresses and personal and interpersonal difficulties arise that can impact mental health, but it also presents a window of opportunity for positive change. Whether the transition leads the individual in new directions, positive or negative, partly depends on experiences in childhood and adolescence as well as on access to resources and individual competencies. Longitudinal studies tracking individuals from childhood through adolescence and the transition to adulthood are needed to learn more about how earlier events, experiences, and adaptive capacities affect how young people navigate the route to adulthood. Furthermore, studies that follow people through their twenties and into young adulthood (the thirties) are critical for telling us about the impact of the transition to adulthood on later life successes. Few studies have followed this course.

Project Competence, a study that followed school-age children for 20 years, is one exception. Based on this study, Ann Masten and her colleagues report considerable continuity in adaptive functioning from childhood, through adolescence, emerging adulthood, and into young adulthood. That is, people who were more competent in childhood (in academic, social, and behavioral domains) showed similar levels of competence in the same domains in their twenties and thirties. By the same token, people who were not doing well in childhood tended to also show less competence as emerging and young adults. Some people in the study had faced earlier adversities such as significant life stressors, which might have hindered the development of competence, but they showed resilience nevertheless (they were competent) from childhood through young adulthood. Such resilience was traced to their access to core resources such as higher IQ, socioeconomic status, and quality parenting while they were growing up. Continued access (or non-access) to resources over time helped to explain continuities in competence (and lack of competence) across the 20-year period of the study. Although there was continuity of competence over time, a small proportion of people experienced dramatic change in competence during the transition to adulthood. Several young people who were not competent in their twenties took a turn for the better, proving to be competent by young adulthood, in contrast to their peers who showed low competence throughout the transition to adulthood. Such changes in direction are called turning points, and beg the question: What accounts for the positive change by young adulthood? Project Competence showed that positive change was experienced by people who, in their twenties, had plans for the future, were self-reliant, and had supportive relationships with a variety of adults. Thus, the transition to adulthood for them was a time during which they had access to or developed resources that seemed to promote competence in their futures.

Conclusion

The diversity of pathways that makes the transition to adulthood stand out also implies that it can be told as a different story for each person who has experienced it. Differences in demographic characteristics are what stand out the most. The transition to adulthood takes place in different work and education settings: college, full-time employment, unemployment, and 'time off' out of the labor force. It takes place in different living arrangements: parents' homes, college residences, apartments with and without room-mates, and in shared accommodations with romantic partners. It also takes place in different romantic relationship contexts: dating, cohabitation, and marriage.

The heterogeneity of the transition to adulthood is an important reminder that to understand development across the life span, we must look beyond typical patterns. Instead, we must focus on differences between people navigating challenges such as those of the transition to adulthood. In this article, we showed that each of the demographic differences noted earlier has implications for the way the transition to adulthood is experienced. Certainly, there is structured diversity in paths taken through the transition to adulthood, and many differences are explained by education and socioeconomic status. However, a focus on heterogeneity will generate new questions and further articulate the experiences of young people within and across income levels: How do the experiences of college students differ from those who enter the workforce right after high school? Are young people from different cultural backgrounds influenced differently by their families and peers?

We must also focus on differences within individuals to see how these challenges change the course of their development over time. In this article, we showed that patterns of change have important implications for success in adulthood. In romantic relationships, marriages preceded by cohabitation are poorer than marriages not preceded by cohabitation. Access or lack of access to resources during the transition to adulthood, such as reliable social supports, may mean the difference between a person who recovers from adversity earlier in life and goes on to a successful adulthood and someone who does not. A focus on changes over time within individuals will also generate new questions: Do young people find it harder to cope with instability in the job market if their mental health declines over time? Do young people find it more difficult to cope with stresses at school and work if they have to change residences frequently? What kinds of transitional experiences lead to positive developments in life and career satisfaction, romantic relationships, and parenting? A continued search for sources of individual differences and variation in patterns of change throughout the life course will lead us to understand the roots for success in the transition to adulthood as well as how this transition sets the stage for outcomes in later life.

See also: Autonomy, Development of; Employment; Risk-Taking Behavior; Romantic Relationships; School-to-Work Transitions; Self-Development During Adolescence; Transitions into Adolescence.

Further Reading

Aquilino WS (2006) Family relationships and support systems in emerging adulthood. In: Arnett JJ and Tanner JL (eds.) *Emerging Adults in America: Coming of Age in the 21st Century*, pp. 193–217. Washington, DC: American Psychological Association.

Arnett JJ (2000) Emerging adulthood. *American Psychologist* 55: 469–480.

Arnett JJ (2004) *Emerging Adulthood: The Winding Road from the Late Teens Through the Twenties*. New York, NY: Oxford University Press.

Bachman JG, O'Malley PM, Schulenberg JE, Johnston LD, Bryant AL, and Merline AC (2002) *The Decline of Substance Use in Young Adulthood: Changes in Social Activities, Roles, and Beliefs*. Mahwah, NJ: Lawrence Erlbaum.

Blanco C, Okuda M, Wright C, et al. (2008) Mental health of college students and their non-college-attending peers. *Archives of General Psychiatry* 65: 1429–1437.

Galambos NL, Barker ET, and Krahn HJ (2006) Depression, self-esteem, and anger in emerging adulthood: Seven-year trajectories. *Developmental Psychology* 42: 350–365.

Galambos NL and Martínez ML (2007) Poised for emerging adulthood in Latin America: A pleasure for the privileged. *Child Development Perspectives* 1: 109–114.

Hendry LB and Kloep M (2007) Conceptualizing emerging adulthood: Inspecting the emperor's new clothes? *Child Development Perspectives* 1: 74–79.

Landow MV (ed.) (2006) *College Students: Mental Health and Coping Strategies*, New York: Nova Science Publishers.

Masten AS, Burt KB, Roisman GI, Obradović J, Long JD, and Tellegen A (2004) Resources and resilience in the transition to adulthood: Continuity and change. *Development and Psychopathology* 16: 1071–1094.

Settersen RA, Furstenberg FF, and Rumbaut RG (eds.) (2005) *On the Frontier of Adulthood: Theory, Research, and Public Policy*. Chicago, IL: University of Chicago Press.

Shanahan MJ (2000) Pathways to adulthood in changing societies: Variability and mechanisms in life course perspective. *Annual Review of Sociology* 26: 667–692.

Stanley SM, Rhoades GK, and Markman HJ (2006) Sliding versus deciding: Inertia and the premarital cohabitation effect. *Family Relations* 55: 499–509.

Worth S (2005) Beating the 'churning' trap in the youth labour market. *Work, Employment and Society* 19: 403–414.

Relevant Websites

www.pisa.gc.ca/yits.shtml – Canadian Longitudinal Youth in Transition Survey.

www.arts.ualberta.ca/transition – School-Work Transition Project.

www.transad.pop.upenn.edu – The Network on Transitions to Adulthood (MacArthur Foundation).

Country abbreviations

BEL.	Belgium
BOS. & HERZ.	Bosnia and Herzegovina
KOS.	Kosovo (disputed)
LIECH.	Liechtenstein
LUX.	Luxembourg
N. MAC.	North Macedonia
MON.	Montenegro
NETH.	Netherlands
NZ	New Zealand
SM	San Marino
SLVN	Slovenia
SWITZ.	Switzerland
UAE	United Arab Emirates
UK	United Kingdom
US	United States of America
VAT. CITY	Vatican City

ANIMAL ATLAS

ANIMAL ATLAS

Derek Harvey

Senior Editor Jenny Sich
Senior Art Editor Rachael Grady
Senior Cartographic Editor Simon Mumford
Senior Contributing Editors Ashwin Khurana, Anna Streiffert-Limerick
Editor Kelsie Besaw
US Editor Megan Douglass
Designers Vanessa Hamilton, Elaine Hewson, Greg McCarthy, Lynne Moulding
Illustrators Jon @ KJA Artists, Adam Brackenbury, Adam Benton, Arran Lewis, Kit Lane
Creative Retoucher Steve Crozier
Managing Editor Francesca Baines
Managing Art Editor Philip Letsu
Production Editor Gillian Reid
Production Controller Sian Cheung
Jacket Designer Akiko Kato
Design Development Manager Sophia MTT
Picture Research Myriam Megharbi, Sneha Murchavade, Sakshi Saluja
Publisher Andrew Macintyre
Associate Publishing Director Liz Wheeler
Art Director Karen Self
Publishing Director Jonathan Metcalf

First American Edition, 2021
Published in the United States by DK Publishing
1450 Broadway, Suite 801, New York, NY 10018

21 22 23 24 25 10 9 8 7 6 5 4 3 2 1
001–316690–Apr/2021

Published in Great Britain by Dorling Kindersley Limited

A catalog record for this book is available from the Library of Congress.
ISBN: 978-0-7440-2779-2

Printed and bound in the UAE

For the curious
www.dk.com

This book was made with Forest Stewardship Council™ certified paper—one small step in DK's commitment to a sustainable future. For more information go to www.dk.com/our-green-pledge

CONTENTS

A WORLD OF ANIMALS

INVERTEBRATES

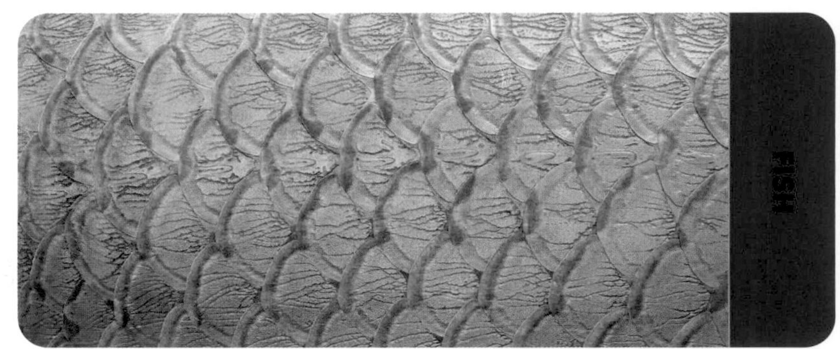

FISH

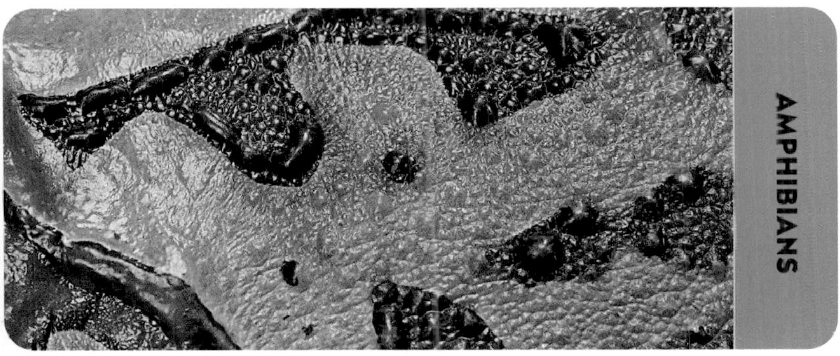
AMPHIBIANS

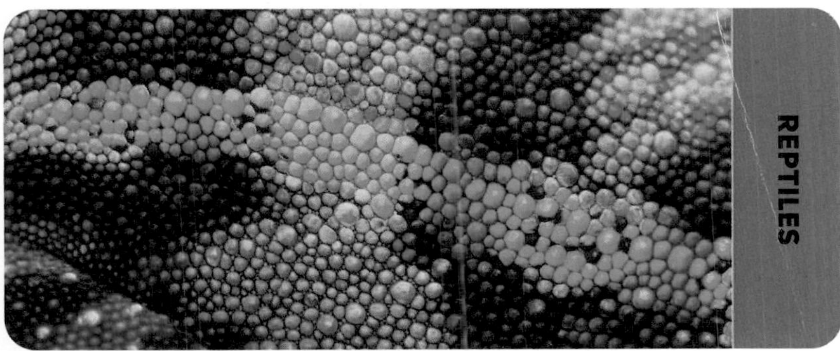
REPTILES

BIRDS

MAMMALS

Foreword

This atlas of animals is about the living world, from the freezing poles to the tropical equator, from the highest mountain to the deepest sea. But this is no ordinary atlas because it shows where the animals live, as well as what they look like, and the forests, deserts, and oceans that are their homes.

Our planet is a very special part of our solar system: it is the only one with life, and its breathtaking variety should fill us all with wonder. Animals of one kind or another survive almost everywhere on its surface, whether on land or underwater. Scientists have described more than 1.5 million species, and reckon there are many times this number still waiting to be discovered. Some, like the humpback whale or the osprey, range so far and wide that they span the entire globe. Others, like giant tortoises in the Galápagos Islands, live in less space than a single sprawling city. But all animals only succeed in places that supply what they need to survive and produce their babies, and many have very particular requirements. This means that koalas only live in Australia, where they eat eucalyptus leaves and nothing else, and parrotfish only swim in tropical coastal seas where they can munch on coral.

The animals in this book completely depend upon these wild places, but wilderness—the forests, grasslands, even unspoiled oceans—is disappearing. Since humans started building their civilizations

5,000 years ago, nearly two-thirds of the wilderness has gone. Cities have replaced trees, water and air have become polluted, and some animals have been hunted so much that very few are left. Many species have disappeared completely along with the wilderness, and others have been left threatened with extinction. This book tells the story of some of them—but also explains what is being done around the world to help. Today, more people than ever are concerned about the future of planet Earth and its extraordinary variety of animals. These animals are what make our world such an amazing place—we must look after them.

Derek Harvey

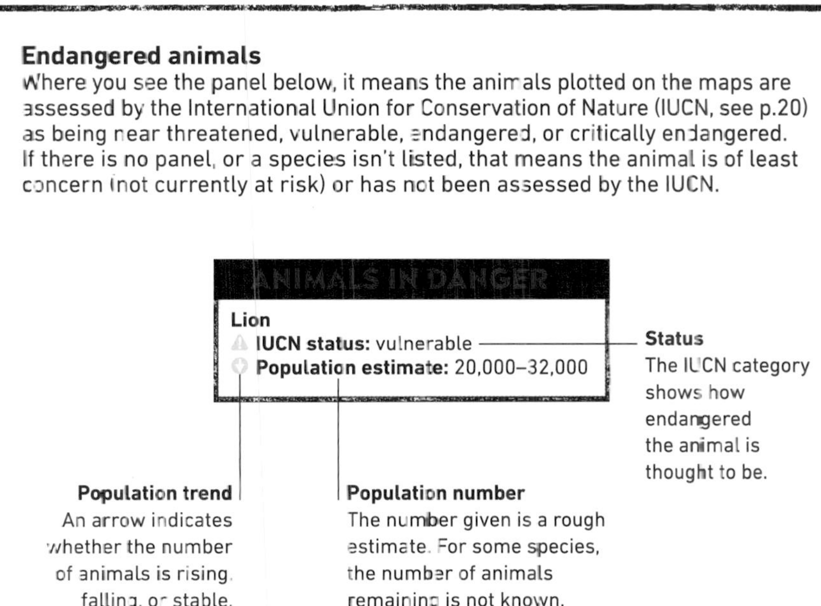

Endangered animals
Where you see the panel below, it means the animals plotted on the maps are assessed by the International Union for Conservation of Nature (IUCN, see p.20) as being near threatened, vulnerable, endangered, or critically endangered. If there is no panel, or a species isn't listed, that means the animal is of least concern (not currently at risk) or has not been assessed by the IUCN.
ANIMALS IN DANGER
Lion
IUCN status: vulnerable
Population estimate: 20,000–32,000
Status
The IUCN category shows how endangered the animal is thought to be.
Population trend
An arrow indicates whether the number of animals is rising, falling, or stable.
Population number
The number given is a rough estimate. For some species, the number of animals remaining is not known.

A WORLD OF ANIMALS

Amazing animals

Earth is teeming with life. Even places inhospitable to humans, such as the deepest oceans or hottest deserts, are alive with extraordinary animals. Wherever on the planet animals live, they have adapted to survive in their habitats.

Birds
Warm-blooded bodies and the power of flight mean that feathered birds have reached more parts of the world than any other group of land-living backboned animals, other than humans.

Reptiles
Like fish and amphibians, reptiles are cold-blooded, relying on the sun to warm their scaly bodies. They include crocodilians, turtles, lizards, and snakes.

Variety of life

Animals are classified into major groups with shared characteristics: invertebrates, fish, amphibians, reptiles, birds, and mammals. Some of these groups contain more species than others, but all are represented around the world. Some are more widespread than others, too: invertebrates exist almost everywhere, but reptiles do not inhabit the coldest places and amphibians do not reach remote islands.

Mammals
Humans are warm-blooded mammals, but we share this group with thousands of other species. All mammalian mothers produce milk to feed their babies and most mammals are covered in fur.

Fish
Half of all vertebrate species (animals with a backbone) are fish. Half live in saltwater oceans and half in freshwater lakes and rivers. They typically have a scaly body, fins for swimming, and gills for breathing underwater.

Ladybug

Sailfish

Invertebrates
These animals without a backbone make up the biggest animal group. They include worms, snails, insects, and many more. They live in every place capable of supporting animals.

Cheetah

Monarch butterfly

Oarfish

Amphibians
With their moist, scaleless skins, amphibians are mainly found in wet, freshwater habitats. They include frogs, toads, salamanders, newts, and worm-shaped caecilians.

California sea lion

Red-eyed tree frog

NEW SPECIES

Every year, scientists discover and name new species of animals found across the world, from forests to coral reefs. As exciting as these finds are, experts believe that approximately 90 percent of animal and plant species on Earth remain unknown. Listed below are some of the most recent amazing discoveries.

Wasp mantis
Found in the Peruvian Amazon in South America, this praying mantis has a body shape that makes it look like a stinging wasp. First described in 2019, it even moves and walks like a wasp, which helps to keep danger away.

Wakanda fairy wrasse
This purple-and-blue fish from an East African coral reef reminded the scientists who first described it of the outfit worn by Marvel's Black Panther. So in 2019 they named it Wakanda, after the superhero's fictional African kingdom.

Mini frogs
Scientists who discovered three tiny Madagascan frogs, each smaller than a fingernail, described them in 2019. The three species are some of the smallest frogs found in the world and were called *Mini mum*, *Mini scule* and *Mini ature*.

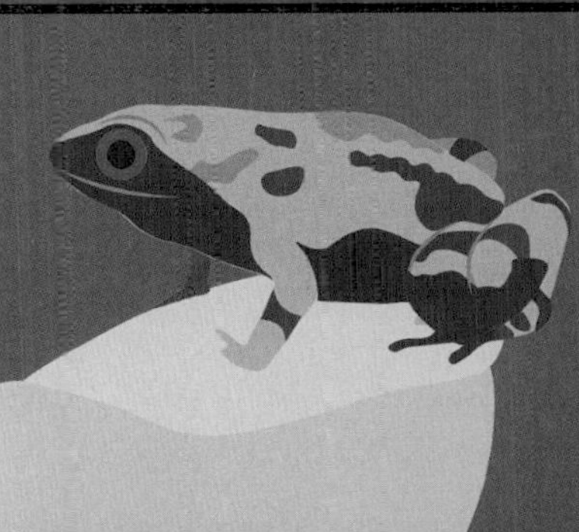

Salazar's pit viper
As fans of the Harry Potter books, the scientists who described this Indian snake in 2020 had a good option to name it. The venomous pit viper was named after the character Salazar Slytherin, who—in the story—could communicate with snakes.

Alor Myzomela
Sadly, by the time they are named some new species are already under threat of extinction. Described in 2019, this striking bird—a honeyeater—located in eucalyptus forests on the Indonesian island of Alor is threatened by deforestation

Biomes

The same type of habitat, such as a desert or tropical rainforest, can occur in different parts of the world. These habitats—called biomes—look alike, even though different animals may live there. Each color on this map represents a different land biome.

Tundra

Close to the poles, conditions are so cold that the ground is frozen for much of the year, so few trees can grow. This open landscape, home to animals such as Arctic hares, is called the tundra.

Mediterranean woodland

Woodland trees with thick, leathery leaves grow in places with warm, dry summers and mild winters, such as in the Mediterranean home of the asp viper, as well as in southern Africa and southern Australia.

Taiga

Covering the largest land area is a stretch of cold, northern forest called taiga. It is dominated by evergreen coniferous trees, and is home to many animals, such as the wolverine, which range widely south of the Arctic.

Temperate forest

Much of the forest in this temperate zone has trees that are deciduous, growing leaves in the mild summers and losing them in cold winters. North American porcupines and other animals that live here must cope with seasonal changes.

Temperate grassland

Grasslands usually grow when conditions are too dry for forest but too wet for desert. Temperate grasslands—home of the prairie chicken—are warm in summer and cold in winter, but stay green all year.

Tropical grassland

In the tropics, many grasslands are at their greenest during the rainy season. In places such as Africa, they support some of the biggest herds of hoofed mammals, including wildebeest, zebras, and giraffes.

Ocean habitats

Conditions in ocean habitats are affected mainly by depths: animals living in deeper waters must cope with higher pressures, colder temperatures, and perpetual darkness.

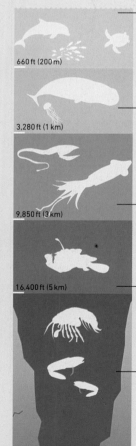

660 ft (200 m)

3,280 ft (1 km)

9,850 ft (3 km)

16,400 ft (5 km)

32,800 ft (10 km)

Sunlit zone
Here there is enough sunlight for algae—the "plants" of the ocean—to grow and support the underwater food chain. Most ocean life is found in the sunlit zone.

Twilight zone
It is too dark for algae to grow here, but just enough light reaches for animals to see. Many predatory fish live in the twilight zone.

Midnight zone
No light reaches below 3,280 ft (1 km), so many animals here produce their own light through a process called bioluminescence.

Abyssal zone
Near the cold, dark ocean floor, animals mostly rely on food sinking down from above.

Hadal zone
The ocean floor contains cracks called trenches that descend to nearly 32,800 ft (10 km). The pressures and temperatures in this zone are at their most extreme. Very specialized animals have adapted to live here.

Where animals live

The world is made up of a variety of different habitats, from magnificent tropical forests and freezing, treeless tundras on land to colorful, sunlit coral reefs of the seas and cold, dark ocean depths. Each habitat has its own unique climate and supports its own ecosystem of plant and animal life.

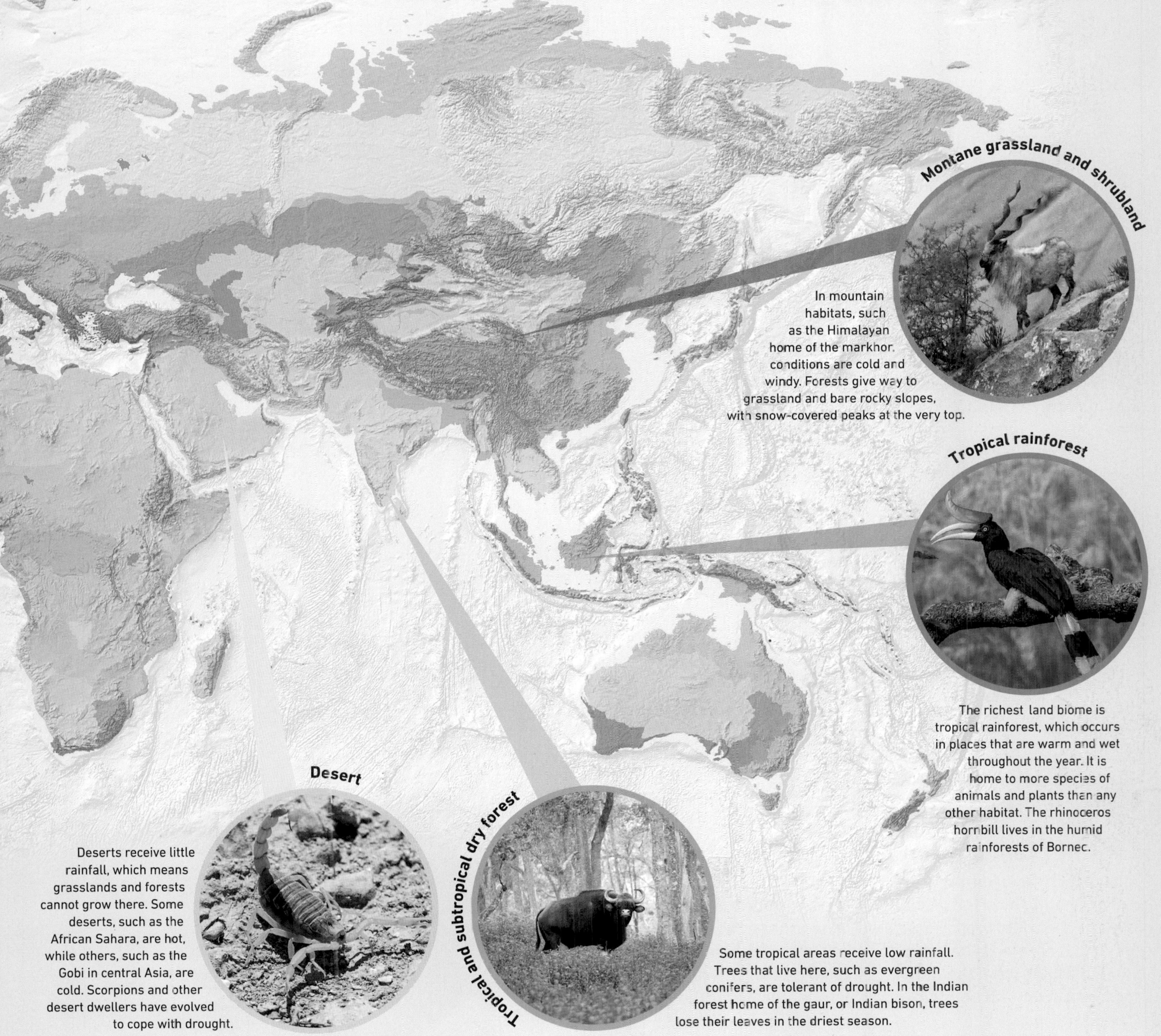

Montane grassland and shrubland

In mountain habitats, such as the Himalayan home of the markhor, conditions are cold and windy. Forests give way to grassland and bare rocky slopes, with snow-covered peaks at the very top.

Tropical rainforest

The richest land biome is tropical rainforest, which occurs in places that are warm and wet throughout the year. It is home to more species of animals and plants than any other habitat. The rhinoceros hornbill lives in the humid rainforests of Borneo.

Desert

Deserts receive little rainfall, which means grasslands and forests cannot grow there. Some deserts, such as the African Sahara, are hot, while others, such as the Gobi in central Asia, are cold. Scorpions and other desert dwellers have evolved to cope with drought.

Tropical and subtropical dry forest

Some tropical areas receive low rainfall. Trees that live here, such as evergreen conifers, are tolerant of drought. In the Indian forest home of the gaur, or Indian bison, trees lose their leaves in the driest season.

Global origins

Over million of years, Earth has changed dramatically. Continents have split apart and crashed into each other, and large regions have flooded to create smaller islands. This has had an impact on where animals live today, sometimes leaving close cousins in different parts of the world.

Changing Earth

Earth's outer layer, the crust, is split into tectonic plates, which move very slowly, carrying the land masses with them. Over billions of years, this slow movement has changed Earth's surface beyond recognition. This globe shows how Earth looked 300 million years ago, when the land was joined in two supercontinents called Gondwana and Laurasia.

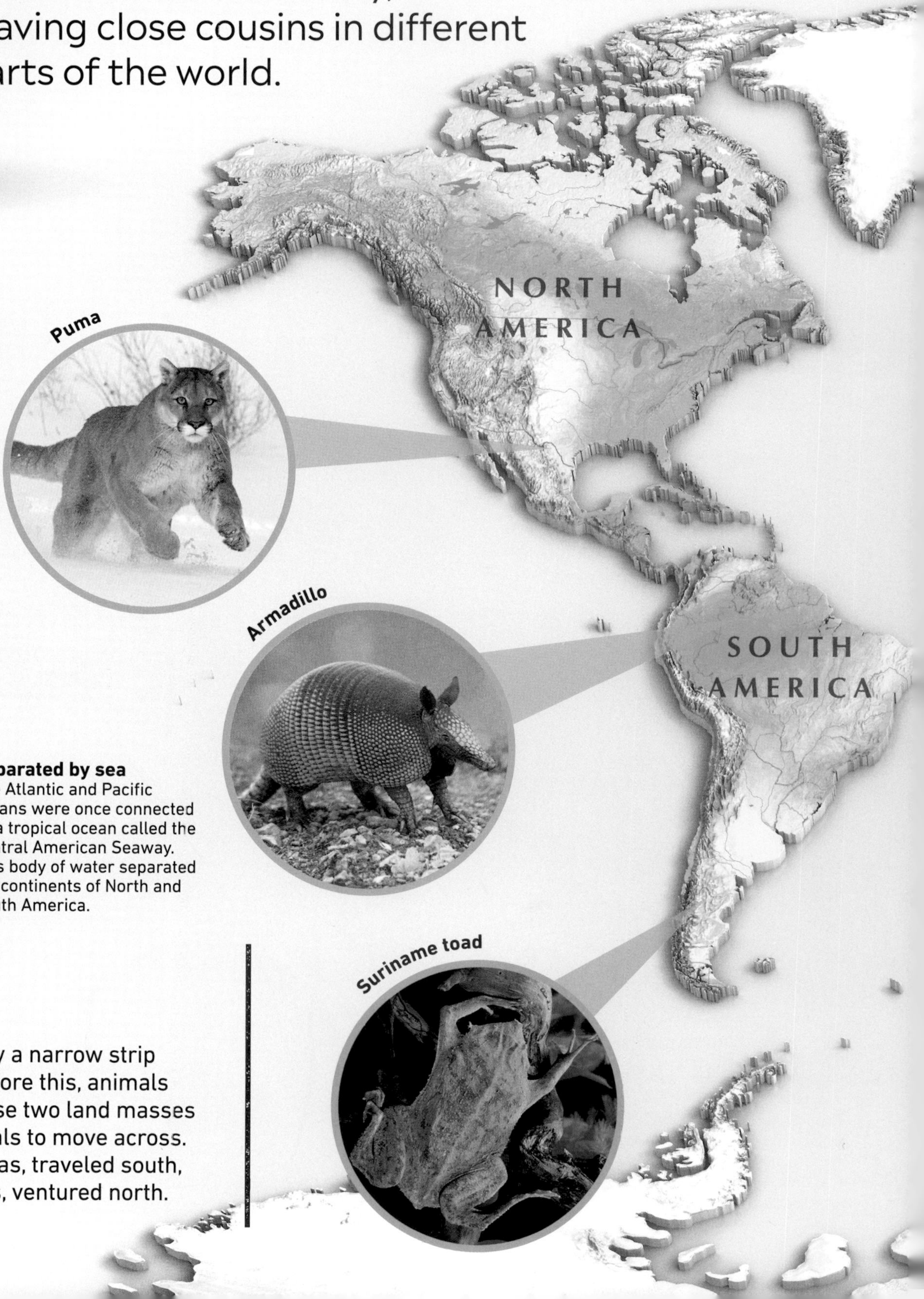

Puma

Armadillo

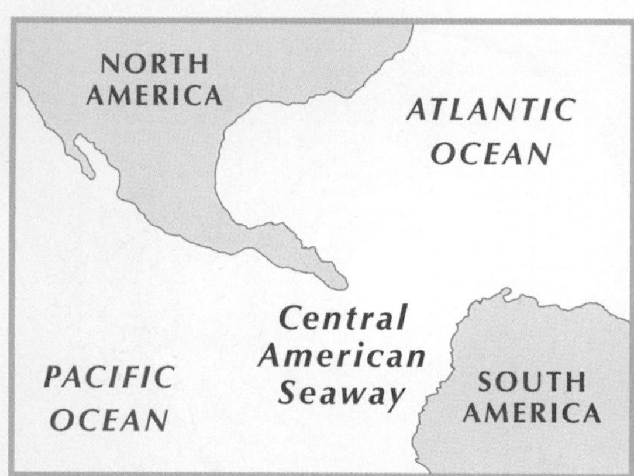

North and South America more than 2.8 million years ago

Separated by sea
The Atlantic and Pacific oceans were once connected by a tropical ocean called the Central American Seaway. This body of water separated the continents of North and South America.

Suriname toad

Continental collision

Today, North and South America are joined by a narrow strip of land that formed 2.8 million years ago. Before this, animals on each continent were separated. When these two land masses collided, it created a passage for some animals to move across. Some animals from the north, including pumas, traveled south, and some from the south, such as armadillos, ventured north.

Separated by flooding

Earth has experienced many ice ages, when large parts of the globe were covered with ice. When temperatures increased, melting ice caused sea levels to rise. Lots of islands around the world, like Sumatra and Borneo in Indonesia, formed in this way. In the process, animals there separated and evolved into different species, including the graceful pitta in Sumatra and blue-banded pitta in Borneo.

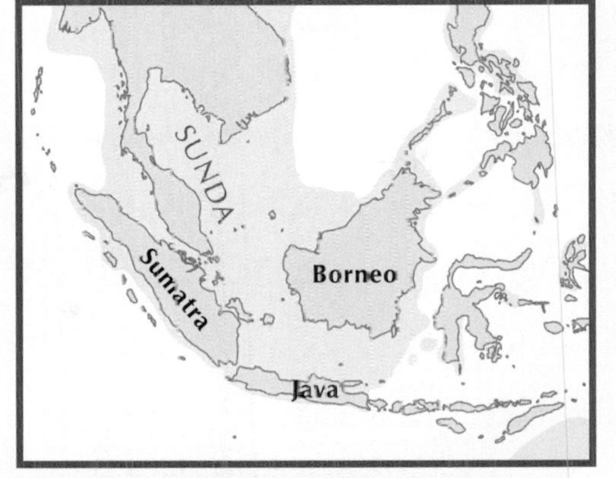

The Sunda Shelf in Southeast Asia about 20,000 years ago

Emerging islands
When sea levels were lower, Sumatra, Borneo, and neighboring islands were part of one land mass called the Sunda Shelf. With rising sea levels, much of the region became submerged (seen in a lighter color), leaving behind islands.

Graceful pitta

Blue-banded pitta

African clawed frog

Splitting up

South America and Africa were once joined, but started to drift apart 100 million years ago, separating animals. This explains why some animals are related, even with the vast Atlantic between them. One example is the Pipidae amphibians, which include South American Suriname toads and African clawed frogs.

New ocean
The matching shapes of South America and Africa is a clue that they were once joined. Volcanic activity in this area caused tectonic plates to move, pushing apart these land masses.

South America and Africa about 95 million years ago

Under threat

All around the world, animals are in decline and many species are facing extinction. As the human population grows bigger—using more space, eating more food, and polluting the environment—it becomes harder for animals to survive.

Biodiversity hot spots

Some places on Earth are especially rich in plant and animal species. These biodiversity hot spots are highly vulnerable to threats such as deforestation and climate change because many of the species that live there are found nowhere else in the world. This map shows some of the world's most important hot spots, on land and in the sea.

Amazon rainforest

The Amazon rainforest is a biodiversity hot spot containing thousands of species of insects, birds, and other animals, in a huge variety of different habitats. However, this spectacular South American region is under threat, mainly from the farming industry, which is clearing land for grazing cattle and to grow animal feed.

Rich habitat
The bright, airy canopy of the rainforest is so different from the dense vegetation growing underneath, they are like two separate habitats—with different species of animals living in each.

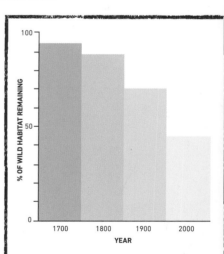

Many species
The Amazon rainforest is teeming with countless different creatures, from jaguars, anteaters, and colorful birds to tiny insects and not-so-tiny spiders. Many of the plant and animal species in this rich habitat rely on other species for things like food, shelter, and protection.

100
50
0
% OF WILD HABITAT REMAINING
1700
1800
1900
2000
YEAR

Declining wilderness

Since the Industrial Revolution, when humans started burning more fuel for energy and clearing habitats on a scale greater than ever before, wild animals have lost more than 50 percent of their living space. The wilderness has been converted to cities, farms, roads, and other developments.

Deforestation
Trees are felled to clear land for crops and livestock, or to develop buildings, dams, and open up mines. Their timber is also sold to make products, such as paper. An estimated 15 billion trees are cut down each year, resulting in the loss of forest habitats for animals and plants.

Climate change
Burning fossil fuels, such as coal, releases carbon dioxide and other greenhouse gases into the atmosphere. The increasing levels of these gases is causing the world to warm up, threatening habitats on land and in the oceans, including the vital polar ice habitat of penguins.

Building on the wilderness
When humans build towns, cities, and roads, they are carving up the wilderness to leave smaller and smaller patches of natural habitat. Some animals, such as predators that are high up in the food chain, need large areas in which to roam. They cannot survive in the isolated patches of habitat that remain.

Overfishing
Some fish are under threat because so many are taken out of the ocean that their numbers cannot recover. Other species are caught up in nets and discarded as unwanted bycatch. The sharks pictured here have been targeted for their fins, considered a delicacy in some countries.

Poaching
Many kinds of wild animals are hunted for their meat, or because their bodies supply something that is considered valuable. Elephants have long been targeted for their ivory tusks, and rhinoceroses for their horns. This is illegal but it still takes place, driving some species to the edge of extinction.

AN AREA OF **RAINFOREST** ALMOST THE **SIZE OF SWITZERLAND WAS LOST** DURING 2019 ALONE

26% **OF MAMMALS** ARE THREATENED **BY EXTINCTION**

Melting ice

Climate change is heating up the Arctic quicker than anywhere else in the world. As sea ice melts, polar bears move onto land with limited access to seals, their primary food source. Without seals, polar bears are at real risk of starvation. If nothing is done, the global population of polar bears could halve to 10,000 by 2050.

Conservation

Despite the threats that animals face, habitats are being saved and species brought back from the edge of extinction. Conservation schemes safeguard wildlife, by protecting wild areas or breeding rare species.

Conservation in action

Today, national parks in Madagascar are helping protect the critically endangered greater bamboo lemur—one of the world's rarest primates. Reduced habitat destruction, daily monitoring, and local educational programs have been instituted to help save this rare species. This is just one example of how organizations all over the world have worked to save species since the 1960s.

Distinctive tufts
The greater bamboo lemur is recognizable by the white tufts around its ears.

Rainforest reliance
This species relies on rainforest where giant bamboo grows. The bamboo, which makes up 95 percent of its diet, is being lost in forest clearance.

IUCN Red List

A global body called the International Union for the Conservation of Nature (IUCN) keeps a Red List of Threatened Species. Each of the more than 120,000 species listed is assigned a threat level in order to figure out which ones need help most urgently.

Least concern
Unlikely to face extinction in the near future

Near threatened
Close to a threat of extinction in the near future

Vulnerable
Faces a high risk of extinction in the wild

Endangered
Faces a very high risk of extinction in the wild

Critically endangered
Faces an extremely high extinction risk in the wild

Extinct in the wild
Survives only in captivity or far outside its natural range

Extinct
Very likely that the last individual has died

Species saved

Conservationists have used different methods to protect species from threats and help them recover, including setting aside protected wild areas, stopping hunting, or taking animals into captivity so they can breed safely there. Many species that were once on the brink of extinction have been saved, and today the populations of many of those species are growing.

Flying high
With a wingspan of 10 ft (3 m) the California condor soars to heights of up to 15,000 ft (4,600 m). It's the biggest flying bird in North America.

California condor
Hunting and lead poisoning helped drive North America's biggest bird of prey to extinction in the wild in 1978. But captive breeding increased numbers, and birds could be released back into protected areas.

Blue whale
Once relentlessly hunted, the blue whale became one of the world's rarest species as its numbers plunged in the early 1900s. It is still endangered but, since a hunting ban in 1966, whale populations are now increasing.

A horse apart
Its stocky body, high mane, white nose, and shorter legs set the Przewalski's horse apart from domesticated horses.

Przewalski's horse
The world's only truly wild species of horse was hunted to extinction but survived in zoos, and today it is the focus of a captive breeding program. In the 1990s, some were released back into their wild habitat in Mongolia.

Mauritius kestrel
In the 1970s, deforestation and introduced animals, such as mongooses and cats, meant that this island bird of prey was down to just four individuals—making it the world's rarest bird. They were taken into captivity for breeding, which has raised the population to hundreds.

100,000 NATIONAL PARKS AND WILDLIFE RESERVES EXIST IN THE WORLD TODAY

OF EARTH'S LAND IS PROTECTED

Sea otter
The thick, protective fur of the sea otter made this animal a target for hunters: it was hunted until there were just a thousand or so left. A hunting ban and better protection of the seas helped it recover.

Extinction in the wild

For some species in captivity, there is no true wild for them to return to. The last wild Père David's deer probably died in China more than 200 years ago, but some animals survived in a hunting park and were brought to England. The fenced herds alive today are all descended from these.

INVERTEBRATES

Invertebrate facts

Tiny animals without backbones first appeared more than 600 million years ago. These early invertebrates lived in water, and many still do. Today, the diversity of invertebrates found throughout the world is staggering, from squids and starfish to worms and spiders.

INVERTEBRATE **TYPES**

There are around 35 main groups of species in the animal kingdom. Just one of these groups, the vertebrates, contains all the fish, amphibians, reptiles, birds, and mammals. The other 34 groups are invertebrates—animals without an internal, jointed skeleton. Six of the main invertebrate groups are shown here.

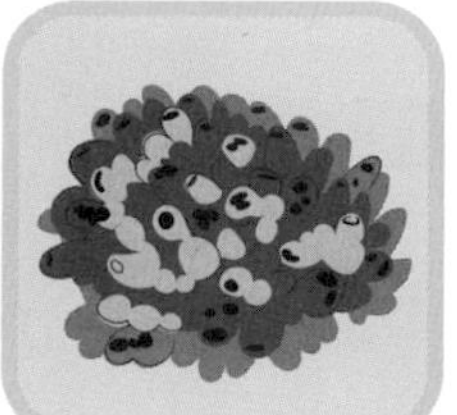

Sponges
These primitive ocean organisms cannot move, and gather food by filtering it from the water.

Cnidarians
From jellyfish and anemones to corals, these sea creatures all have stinging tentacles to catch small prey.

Echinoderms
With their "spiny skin," these marine animals include starfish, sea cucumbers, and sea urchins.

Mollusks
From slugs to squids, mollusks live in damp habitats or in the sea. Many have a hard shell.

Worms
Found in water and on land, some—such as earthworms—are made up of many identical, soft-skinned segments.

Arthropods
With their tough outer skeletons and jointed legs, arthropods include insects, spiders, and crabs.

ALMOST
97%
OF ALL ANIMALS ARE
INVERTEBRATES.

INVERTEBRATE **NUMBERS**

There are approximately 1.3 million known invertebrate species, but there could be many millions more. The vast majority of invertebrates belong to two groups: arthropods and mollusks.

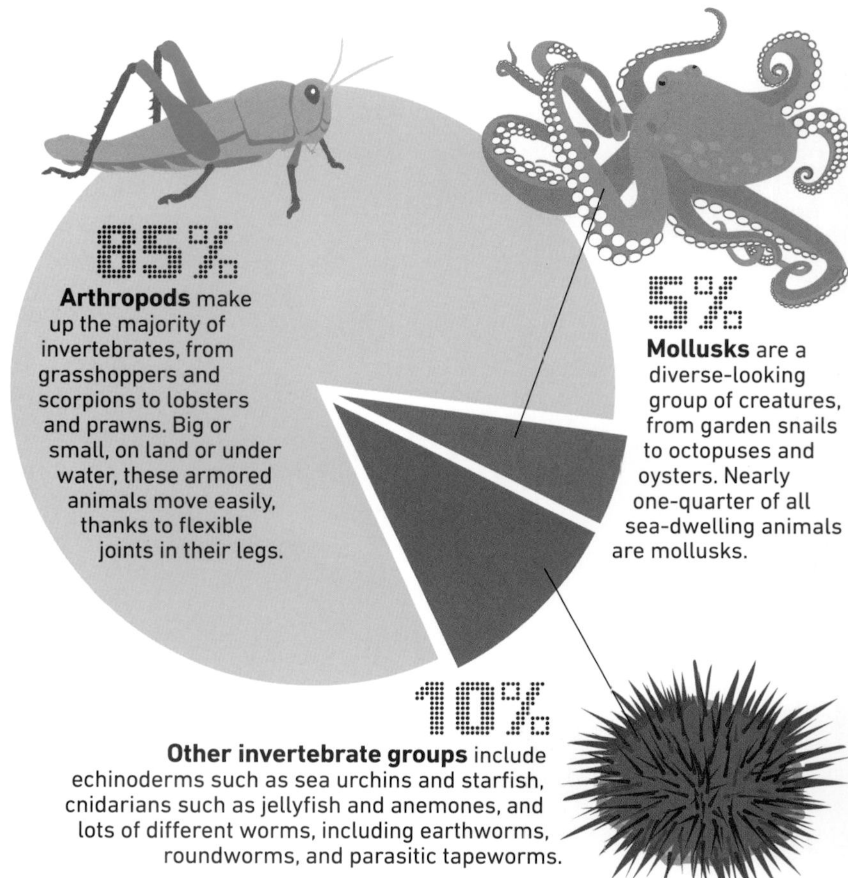

85%
Arthropods make up the majority of invertebrates, from grasshoppers and scorpions to lobsters and prawns. Big or small, on land or under water, these armored animals move easily, thanks to flexible joints in their legs.
5%
Mollusks are a diverse-looking group of creatures, from garden snails to octopuses and oysters. Nearly one-quarter of all sea-dwelling animals are mollusks.
10%
Other invertebrate groups include echinoderms such as sea urchins and starfish, cnidarians such as jellyfish and anemones, and lots of different worms, including earthworms, roundworms, and parasitic tapeworms.

EXTREME HABITATS

Some invertebrates can withstand—and even thrive—in incredibly hostile conditions, from barren, icy Antarctica to vast, unexplored regions thousands of feet below the ocean's surface.

Antarctic midges are insects that measure only $\frac{3}{8}$ in (1 cm), yet are the largest native land animal in Antarctica. They live at temperatures of 5°F (-15°C), spending nine months of the year frozen solid.

Tube worms, a type of marine segmented worm, live on the Pacific Ocean seafloor near hydrothermal vents—volcanic areas where sections of Earth's crust are moving apart. They grow up to 10 ft (3 m).

BODY SHAPES

Invertebrate body shapes fall into three main categories based on symmetry.

Bilateral symmetry
Many insects, from ladybugs to butterflies, have two halves that mirror each other.

Radial symmetry
Invertebrates such as starfish have several lines of symmetry around a central point.

No symmetry
Invertebrates like sponges have no lines of symmetry. They have irregular body shapes.

SMART OCTOPUS

The coconut octopus uses tools, such as discarded coconuts or clam shells, to hide in while watching for prey such as crabs. Living on sandy bottoms in bays or lagoons in the western Pacific Ocean, this clever creature, which extends to about 6 in (15 cm), is also able to pick up and carry these tools more than 66 ft (20 m).

BIGGEST INVERTEBRATE

COLOSSAL SQUIDS LIVE IN THE SOUTHERN OCEAN, AND CAN REACH 40 FT (12 M) LONG.

SMALLEST INVERTEBRATE

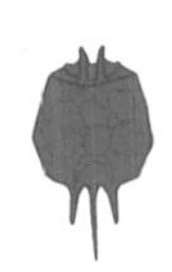

Rotifer

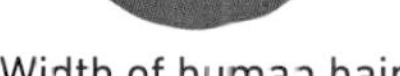

Width of human hair

ROTIFERS ARE AMONG THE WORLD'S SMALLEST ANIMALS AT 0.001 IN (0.05 MM) LONG.

FASTEST INSECT

The fastest insect relative to its body size is the tiger beetle. This ½ in- (1.4 cm-) long animal covers 120 times its body length in just a single second.

USAIN BOLT **OLYMPIC SPRINTER:** 5 BODY LENGTHS IN ONE SECOND

This long-legged creature runs so fast it temporarily goes blind from the speed.

TIGER BEETLE: 120 BODY LENGTHS IN ONE SECOND

HIGHEST JUMPER

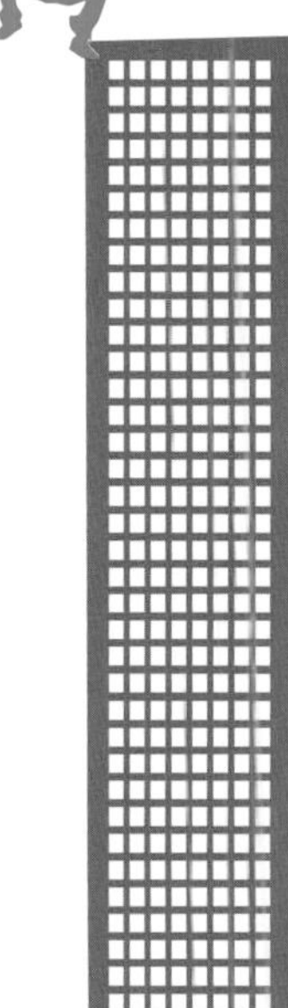

THE TINY **FROGHOPPER** CAN LEAP MORE THAN 23 IN (60 CM) IN THE AIR. THAT'S THE EQUIVALENT OF A **HUMAN JUMPING 630 FT** (190 M), OR A **40-STORY BUILDING!**

HIGH LIFE

THE **MOUNT EVEREST JUMPING SPIDER** LIVES UP TO 22,000 FT (6,700 M) ABOVE SEA LEVEL, ON THE SLOPES OF **MOUNT EVEREST**.

LONGEST MIGRATION

THE **GLOBE SKIMMER DRAGONFLY** MIGRATES 4,400 MILES (7,080 KM) THROUGH THE AIR **WITHOUT LANDING**.

BIGGEST SWARM

The desert locust gathers in swarms of up to 8 billion. Living in parts of the Middle East, Asia, and Africa, they are known to destroy crops.

Giant Pacific octopus

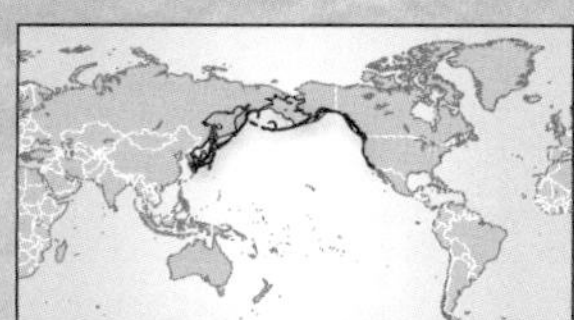

Weighing as much as two grown men, the giant Pacific octopus is the largest of all octopus species, and one of the biggest ocean predators without a backbone. It is an agile, intelligent hunter, capable of catching prey as big as sharks.

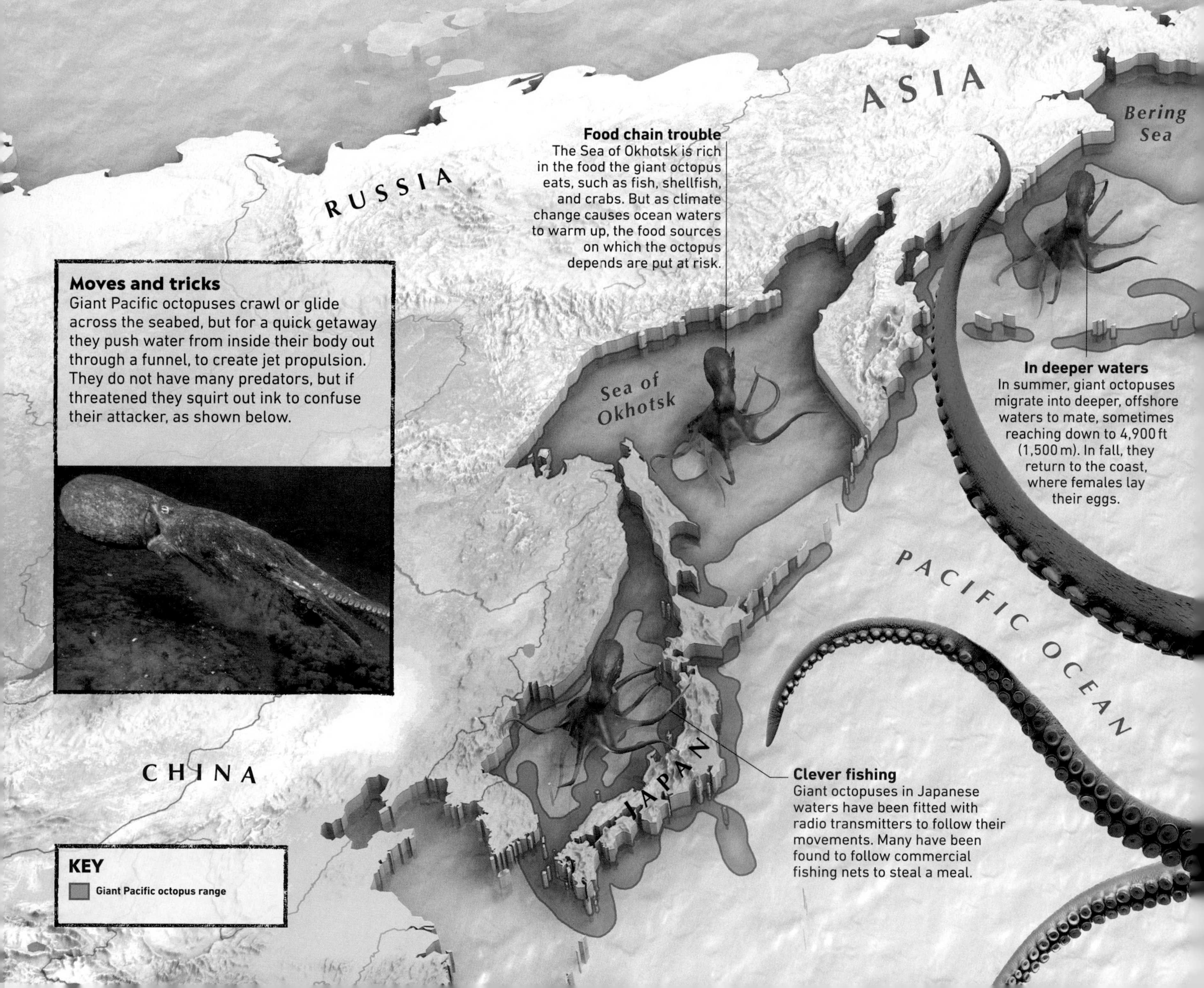

Moves and tricks
Giant Pacific octopuses crawl or glide across the seabed, but for a quick getaway they push water from inside their body out through a funnel, to create jet propulsion. They do not have many predators, but if threatened they squirt out ink to confuse their attacker, as shown below.

Food chain trouble
The Sea of Okhotsk is rich in the food the giant octopus eats, such as fish, shellfish, and crabs. But as climate change causes ocean waters to warm up, the food sources on which the octopus depends are put at risk.

In deeper waters
In summer, giant octopuses migrate into deeper, offshore waters to mate, sometimes reaching down to 4,900 ft (1,500 m). In fall, they return to the coast, where females lay their eggs.

Clever fishing
Giant octopuses in Japanese waters have been fitted with radio transmitters to follow their movements. Many have been found to follow commercial fishing nets to steal a meal.

KEY
Giant Pacific octopus range

Cold-water hunter

A big, speedy predator, the giant Pacific octopus thrives in the cold, oxygen-rich waters around the northern rim of the Pacific Ocean, mostly in seas that are rarely deeper than 1,640 ft (500 m). The octopus grabs prey with its arms, then uses its beak to inject venom into the prey. This immobilizes the prey and softens its flesh, which the octopus then can lick out with its rasping tongue.

Octopus nursery

Each female octopus lays up to 100,000 eggs in an underwater cave or crevice. She guards the eggs, which hang in clutches, until they hatch about six months later and she dies. The tiny hatchlings then spend about two months drifting among the ocean's plankton, before descending to the seabed, where they develop into adult shape and size.

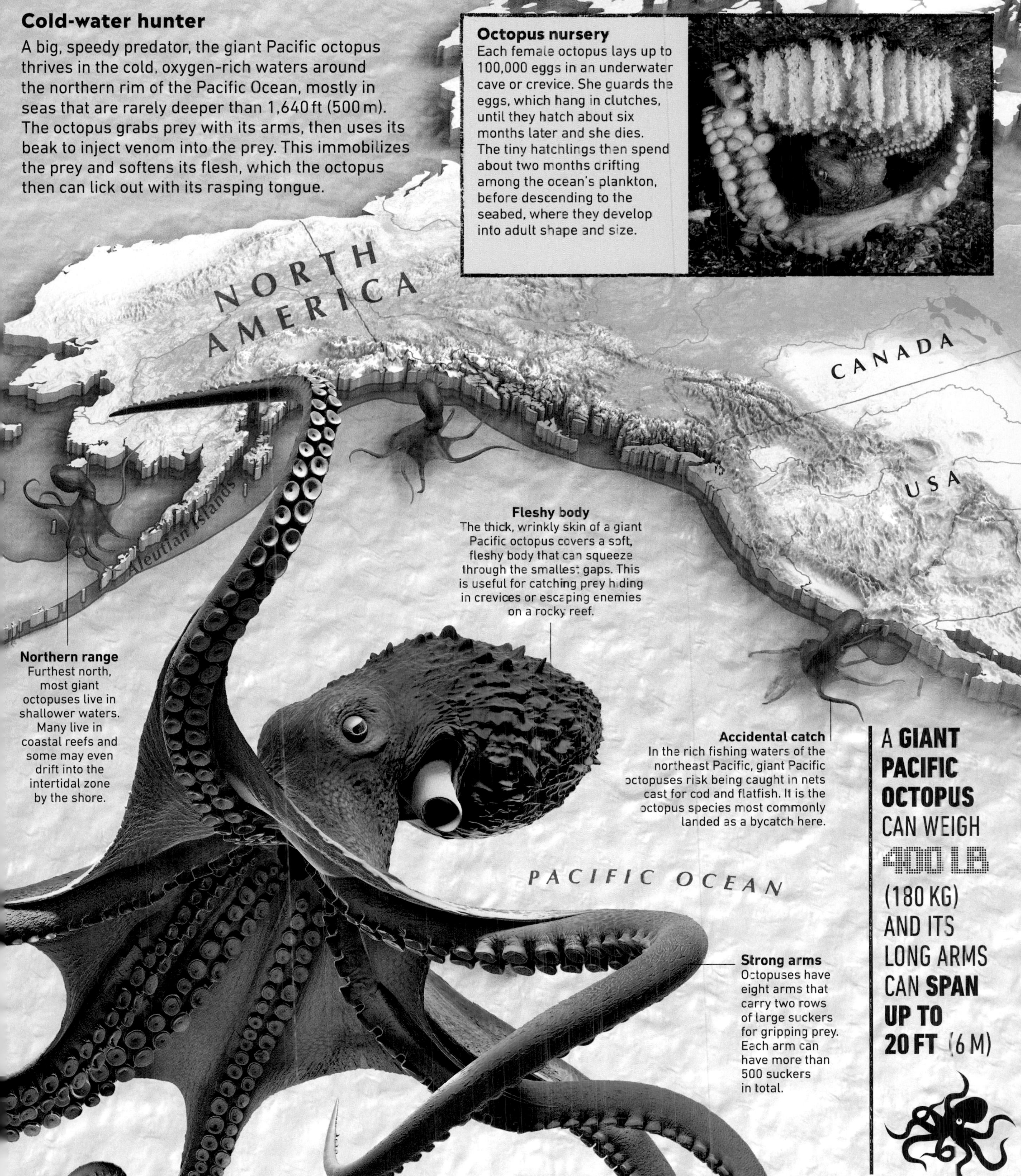

Fleshy body
The thick, wrinkly skin of a giant Pacific octopus covers a soft, fleshy body that can squeeze through the smallest gaps. This is useful for catching prey hiding in crevices or escaping enemies on a rocky reef.

Northern range
Furthest north, most giant octopuses live in shallower waters. Many live in coastal reefs and some may even drift into the intertidal zone by the shore.

Accidental catch
In the rich fishing waters of the northeast Pacific, giant Pacific octopuses risk being caught in nets cast for cod and flatfish. It is the octopus species most commonly landed as a bycatch here.

Strong arms
Octopuses have eight arms that carry two rows of large suckers for gripping prey. Each arm can have more than 500 suckers in total.

A **GIANT PACIFIC OCTOPUS** CAN WEIGH **400 LB** (180 KG) AND ITS LONG ARMS CAN **SPAN UP TO 20 FT** (6 M)

European lobster

Lobsters are crustaceans, a group of invertebrates with armor-like, jointed exoskeletons protecting their soft bodies. One of the largest lobster species, the European lobster lives in shallow coastal seas across most of Europe and northern Africa.

North Sea
The North Sea is the biggest expanse of shallow continental waters in the northeast Atlantic. It is rich in lobsters' favorite food, such as crabs, starfish, and sea urchins.

Long antennae
Lobsters use their antennae to feel their way around on the seabed in murky, dark waters.

North Sea

ATLANTIC OCEAN

Warmer waters
Like many European marine species, the European lobster reaches the southern limits of its range in the waters off the coast of Morocco in northwest Africa. It cannot tolerate the warmer tropical seas further south.

The Azores
This group of small volcanic islands marks the westernmost part of the European lobster's territory.

Uneven-sized claws
The fatter claw of a lobster is stronger for slow crushing, while the slimmer one is better for faster cutting. Both are used for breaking up food or in self-defense.

Lobster movements
Most lobsters migrate into deeper waters to spawn, but one of the most spectacular migrations happens every fall off the coast of the United States, when huge numbers of spiny lobsters move in single file over the seabed to reach their spawning grounds.

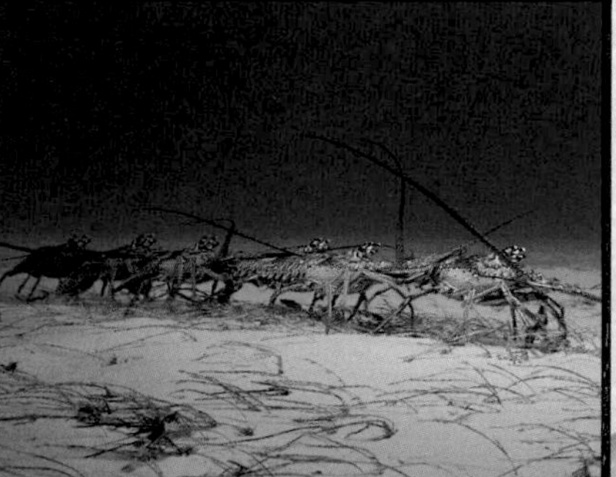

KEY
European lobster range

Norwegian Sea
Warm ocean currents flowing up from the tropical Atlantic into the Norwegian Sea help keep waters ice-free, so lobsters live as far north as the Arctic Circle.

Life on the seabed
A lobster needs water to help support its weighty body, which is far too heavy for the lobster to move around on rocky shores or beaches. Lobsters mostly crawl across the seabed, where they live in crevices or burrows. When needed, they escape by quickly swimming backwards. Even a big lobster might be swept away by strong currents in deeper water, so they don't go too far offshore.

Coastal crustacean

Like many other marine animals, the European lobster stays mainly in coastal seas. Lobsters are fished for food, but despite some local overfishing, especially in the North Sea, the overall population is stable.

Black Sea
Rivers flowing into the cool Black Sea make it less salty than the ocean. European lobsters can survive here, but in fewer numbers and only in western areas.

Salty environment
A warm climate evaporates water from the Mediterranean Sea and makes it slightly saltier than the Atlantic Ocean. Lobsters can take these conditions, and range widely across this region.

Eastern Mediterranean
The Mediterranean Sea reaches a depth of over 16,400 ft (5,000 m) in the middle. Lobsters keep to shallower coastal waters, ranging as far east as the Greek island of Crete.

FEMALE **EUROPEAN LOBSTERS** CAN LIVE UP TO **THE AGE OF**

OVERFISHING IN THE **NORTH SEA** HAS MADE **LOBSTER NUMBERS** THERE **DROP BY**

Caterpillar diet
Postman butterflies become poisonous very early in their life. Their caterpillars eat leaves of passion vines, which contain toxic cyanide. The poison stays in their bodies without harming them, even as they turn into butterflies. Adults also only feed on passion vines, but on the nectar and pollen of its flowers.

Guiana Highlands
In this area of tabletop mountains rising steeply from rainforests, the butterflies have little or no white in their color pattern—similar to those of the Andean mountains.

Central America
In the rainforests from Guatemala to Panama, postman butterflies have red bands on their forewings and white bands, sometimes tinged with yellow, on their hind wings.

Andes
High up in the mountain valleys and foothills of the northern Andes range, the butterflies' hind wings have less white; some have no white in their pattern at all.

Guiana Highlands

Amazon

Regional colors

Some species of butterfly have many different varieties according to where they live. The postman butterfly, for example, has more than 20 variations. Some of these are shown on this map, in the areas where they live.

Postman butterfly

The postman butterfly lives in varied habitats from Central to South America. Across its range, its exact pattern of red, black, and white varies from place to place. A flash of color from any postman butterfly is a sign that it is poisonous, so helps keep predatory birds away.

THERE ARE ABOUT **20,000 SPECIES OF BUTTERFLY** IN THE **WORLD**

AT NIGHT, POSTMAN BUTTERFLIES GATHER TO **SLEEP IN GROUPS** KNOWN AS **COMMUNAL ROOSTS**

Amazon Basin
Across the lowlands of the great Amazon River Basin, local postman butterflies often live along rivers and streams. Here, they have white patches on their forewings, sometimes broken into spots.
Wings at rest
Like most day-flying butterflies, postman butterflies rest with their wings raised so their tips almost touch. Flapping their wings helps spread a scent that deters predators.
Master mimics
Closely related to the postman butterfly, the red postman (above) is a separate species, but matches the local color pattern of the postman wherever it lives alongside it. As they are both poisonous, this mimicry reinforces the warning for potential predators and helps both species survive.
KEY
Postman butterfly range
Amazon Basin
Andes
SOUTH AMERICA
Wetlands
In Brazil's Pantanal wetlands, the postman lives near water. Here it has white stripes on the hindwings, looking more like those along Brazil's southwest coast and in Central America.
Sucking nectar
Butterflies have a flexible tube called a proboscis for drinking liquid nectar from flowers. Usually kept coiled up, it unrolls when the butterfly is ready to feed.
Passion flower
Wing pattern
The colors of the postman butterfly come from tiny pigmented scales that cover the surface of the two pairs of wings. Its wingspan can measure up to 3 in (7.5 cm).

Plant pollinator

Bees are essential for keeping our planet green. They transfer pollen from flower to flower, pollinating many crops that we depend on for food. This mining bee is busy harvesting pollen from an apple blossom tree in Wisconsin. But climate change is affecting bee behavior, and intensive farming and pesticides are destroying bee habitats, such as wildflower meadows, trees, and hedgerows.

Tarantulas

Many big spiders are called “tarantulas,” but all true tarantulas have fat hairy bodies and belong to a family called the theraphosids. Found in all warm parts of the world, there are nearly 1,000 species: the smallest is no bigger than your thumb, but the biggest can span a large dinner plate with its legs.

THE OLDEST **MEXICAN** RED-KNEED TARANTULA IS KNOWN TO **HAVE LIVED** FOR 28 **YEARS**

GOLIATH TARANTULA **FANGS** CAN GROW UP TO 1½ IN (3.8 CM)

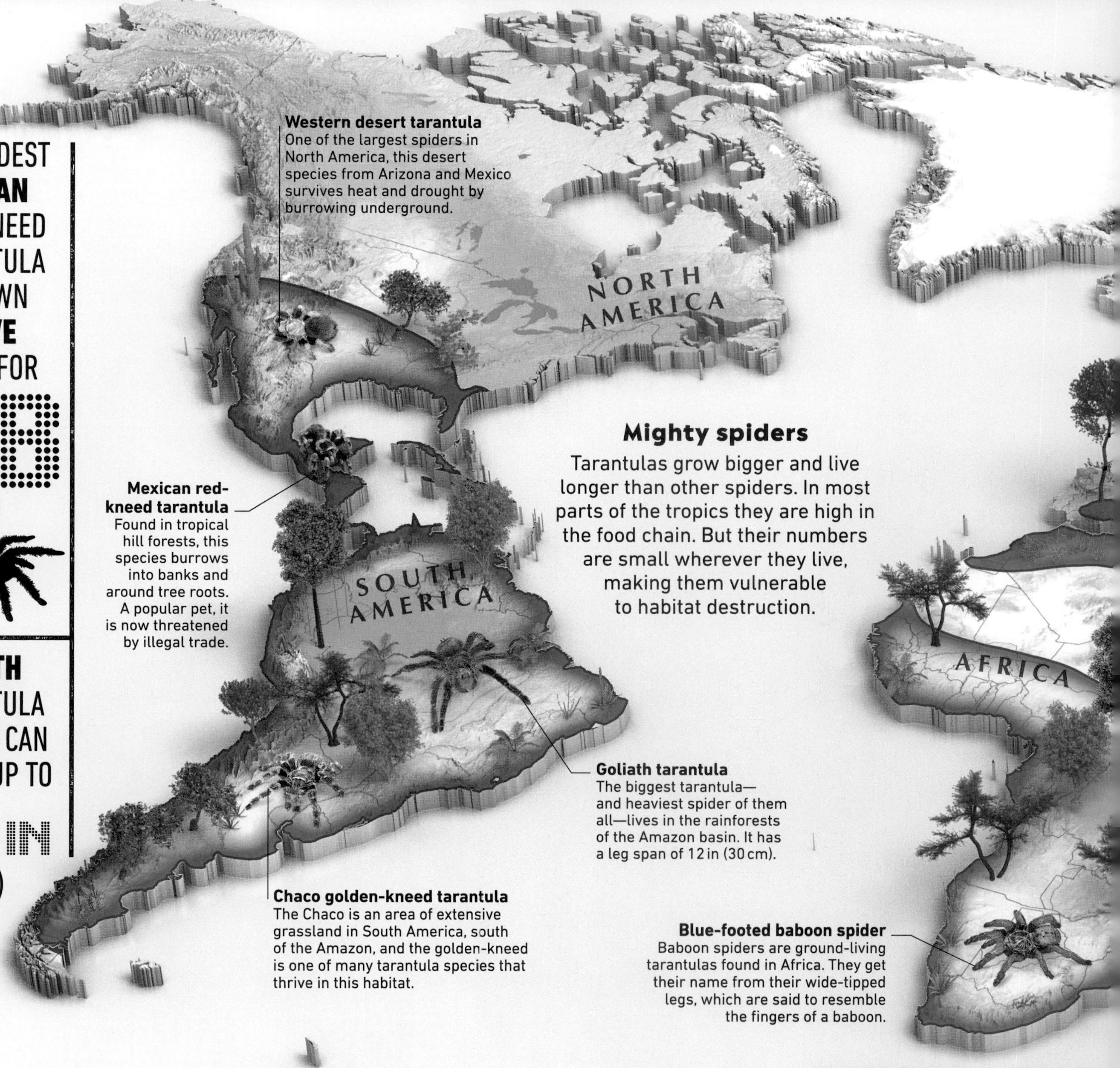

Western desert tarantula
One of the largest spiders in North America, this desert species from Arizona and Mexico survives heat and drought by burrowing underground.

NORTH AMERICA

SOUTH AMERICA

AFRICA

Mexican red-kneed tarantula
Found in tropical hill forests, this species burrows into banks and around tree roots. A popular pet, it is now threatened by illegal trade.

Mighty spiders

Tarantulas grow bigger and live longer than other spiders. In most parts of the tropics they are high in the food chain. But their numbers are small wherever they live, making them vulnerable to habitat destruction.

Goliath tarantula
The biggest tarantula—and heaviest spider of them all—lives in the rainforests of the Amazon basin. It has a leg span of 12 in (30 cm).

Chaco golden-kneed tarantula
The Chaco is an area of extensive grassland in South America, south of the Amazon, and the golden-kneed is one of many tarantula species that thrive in this habitat.

Blue-footed baboon spider
Baboon spiders are ground-living tarantulas found in Africa. They get their name from their wide-tipped legs, which are said to resemble the fingers of a baboon.

Venomous fangs
Spiders use their fangs to inject venom that disables their prey. Tarantula venom can be deadly to small creatures, but is usually no more serious to a human than a bee sting.

Hairy legs
All spiders have hairs or bristles, but tarantulas are hairier than most. Many hairs are touch-sensitive, used in detecting movement of prey. In American species, such as this one, they are barbed to irritate and can be scattered in self-defense.

Indian tree tarantula
One of many species of climbing tarantulas, this spider with striking markings lives in tree holes, where it mainly preys on large insects.

Queensland whistling spider
Like some other Australian tarantulas, the whistling spider makes a hissing sound by rubbing stiff bristles at the base of its fangs, to deter predators.

Ambush tactics

Tarantulas ambush prey, rather than trapping them in webs. The largest ones are big enough to kill small vertebrates; in this photo, two Peruvian tarantulas are feeding on a tree frog.

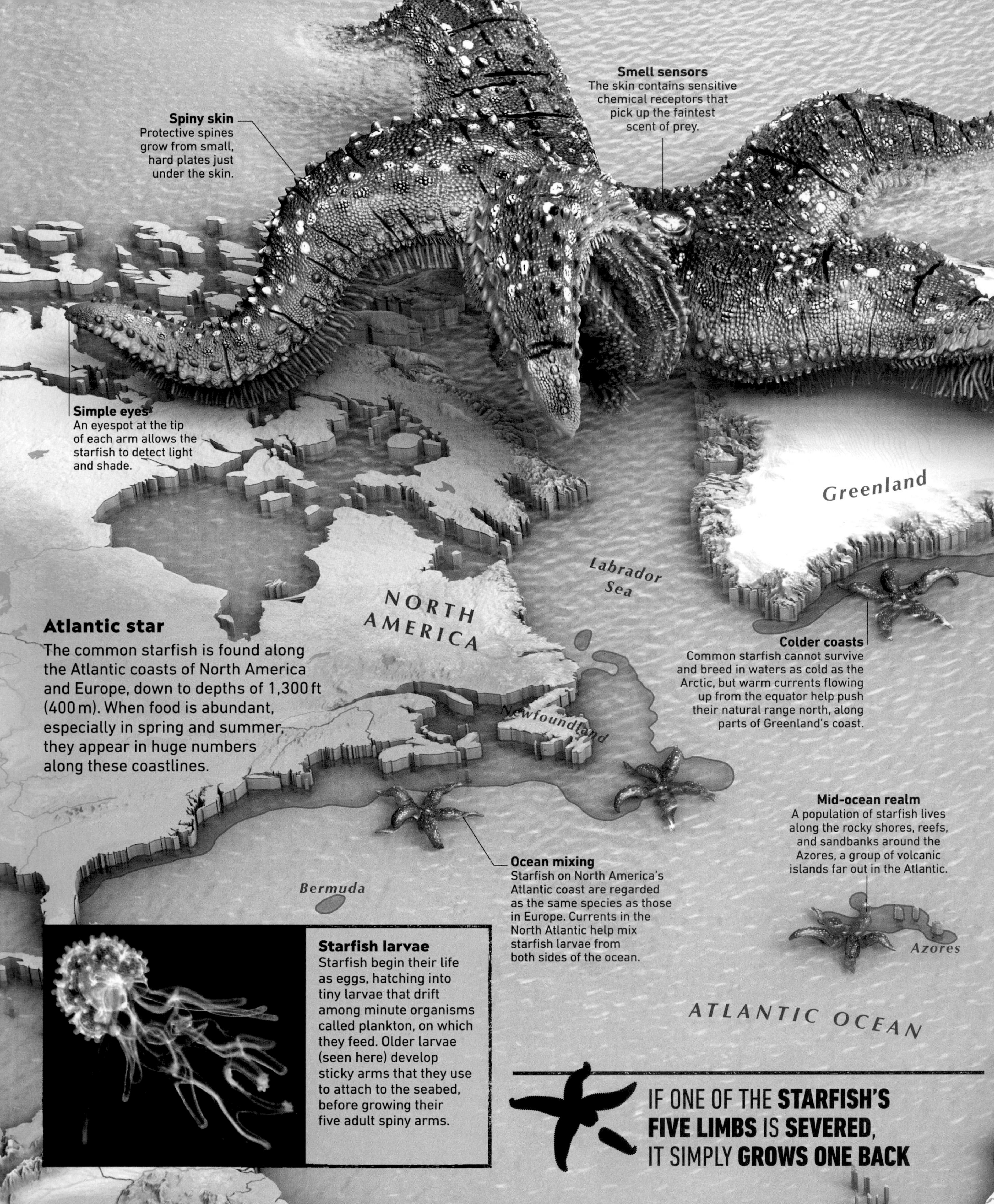

Spiny skin
Protective spines grow from small, hard plates just under the skin.
Smell sensors
The skin contains sensitive chemical receptors that pick up the faintest scent of prey.
Simple eyes
An eyespot at the tip of each arm allows the starfish to detect light and shade.
Greenland
Labrador Sea
NORTH AMERICA
Atlantic star
The common starfish is found along the Atlantic coasts of North America and Europe, down to depths of 1,300 ft (400 m). When food is abundant, especially in spring and summer, they appear in huge numbers along these coastlines.
Colder coasts
Common starfish cannot survive and breed in waters as cold as the Arctic, but warm currents flowing up from the equator help push their natural range north, along parts of Greenland's coast.
Newfoundland
Mid-ocean realm
A population of starfish lives along the rocky shores, reefs, and sandbanks around the Azores, a group of volcanic islands far out in the Atlantic.
Ocean mixing
Starfish on North America's Atlantic coast are regarded as the same species as those in Europe. Currents in the North Atlantic help mix starfish larvae from both sides of the ocean.
Bermuda
Azores
Starfish larvae
Starfish begin their life as eggs, hatching into tiny larvae that drift among minute organisms called plankton, on which they feed. Older larvae (seen here) develop sticky arms that they use to attach to the seabed, before growing their five adult spiny arms.
ATLANTIC OCEAN
IF ONE OF THE STARFISH'S FIVE LIMBS IS SEVERED, IT SIMPLY GROWS ONE BACK

Common starfish

Along with sea cucumbers and urchins, the common starfish belongs to a group of animals called echinoderms, which live only in the ocean. Like many marine animals commonly spotted on or near the seashore, the starfish actually spends most of its life in deeper waters, as it needs to be underwater to spawn.

Many tiny feet
Like other echinoderms, starfish move from place to place using tiny sucker-like tube feet. The underside of their arms is covered in hundreds of these feet, which bend from side to side to push the animal slowly along the seafloor.

Norwegian fjords
Norway's long coastline is carved by narrow, deep inlets called fjords. The muddy and sandy bottoms of these coastal habitats are full of common starfish.

Northern delights
Even along the Kola Peninsula, above the Arctic Circle, warm currents keep waters ice-free. Here, starfish feed on the plentiful scallop-beds.

Colors
The skin of the common starfish is usually orange, but some are in shades of brown or purple.

North Sea water
The North Sea is slightly less salty than the open ocean because many rivers flow into it. Common starfish still thrive here, even in river estuaries.

The Baltic Sea
The common starfish is one of the few echinoderms that can survive in the very low salt levels of the Baltic.

Mussels on the menu
The common starfish preys on lots of different invertebrates, but has a special liking for two-shelled mollusks, such as mussels. They pull the shells apart with their arms, then stick their extendable stomach through the opening to digest the meat inside.

FISH

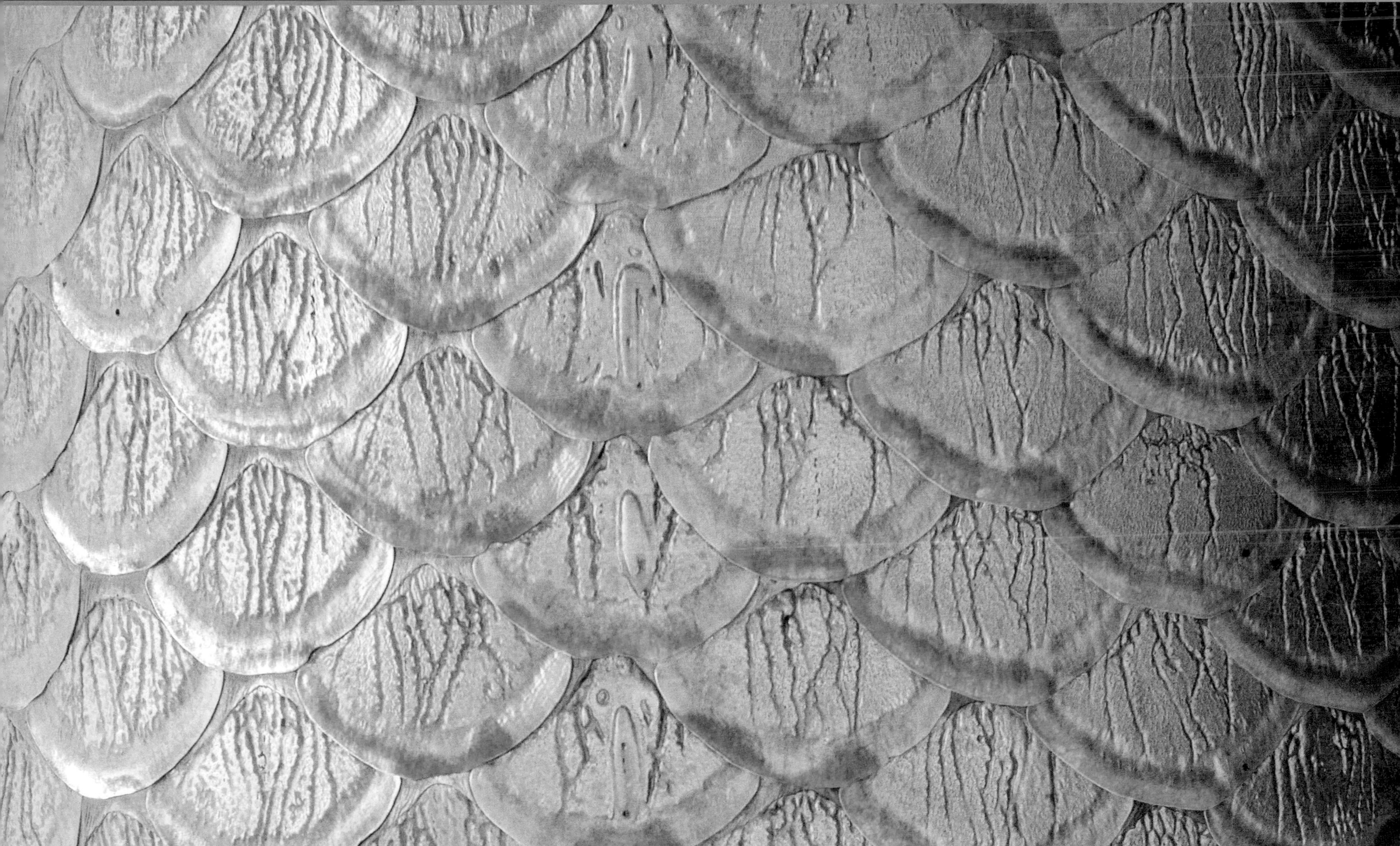

Fish facts

Fish evolved more than 500 million years ago, and were the first animals to evolve a backbone. They can be found in a variety of places, from vast oceans to small freshwater lakes. Some fish live on bright coral reefs, while others lurk thousands of feet deeper in pitch-black oceanic trenches.

WHAT IS A FISH?

Vertebrates
The typical fish skeleton consists of a spinal column, skull, ribs, and fin supports.

Cold-blooded
Fish may swim in warm or cold water, but their bodies are the same temperature as the water they live in.

Breathe with gills
Gills located on the side of a fish contain blood that absorbs oxygen from the water.

Scaly skin
Most fish are covered in protective, overlapping plates called scales. Some fish do not have scales.

Live in water
Some fish swim in salty oceans, others need fresh water to survive. Some move between the two.

FISH **TYPES**

ESTIMATED NUMBER OF FISH SPECIES:

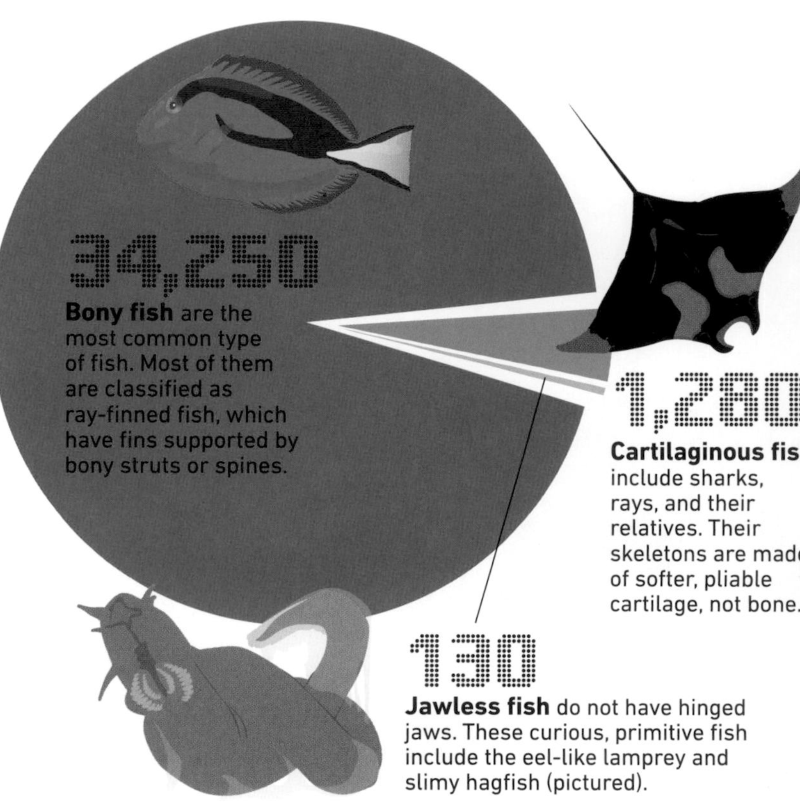

34,250
Bony fish are the most common type of fish. Most of them are classified as ray-finned fish, which have fins supported by bony struts or spines.

1,280
Cartilaginous fish include sharks, rays, and their relatives. Their skeletons are made of softer, pliable cartilage, not bone.

130
Jawless fish do not have hinged jaws. These curious, primitive fish include the eel-like lamprey and slimy hagfish (pictured).

THE **GULF CORVINA** IS THE LOUDEST FISH—WITH A CALL OF **202** DECIBELS, IT'S **LOUDER THAN A PLANE TAKING OFF!**

EXTREME HABITATS

Some fish have evolved to survive in the most inhospitable conditions, from the frozen Arctic to dried-up riverbeds.

Arctic cod can survive in sub-zero temperatures, using an antifreeze protein in their blood. This allows them to find food beneath the ice in polar regions, without any competition.

Mudskippers are found in the Indian and Pacific oceans, but they actually prefer the land—and even climb trees! They can keep breathing on land for up to two days at a time.

Lungfish live in rivers and lakes in Africa, Australia, and South America. During dry seasons, they burrow into mud, before cocooning themselves in a mucus that traps life-saving moisture.

LONGEST **MIGRATION**

DORADO CATFISH MIGRATE **7,200 MILES** (11,600 KM) INLAND, FROM THE ANDES TO THE AMAZON AND BACK.

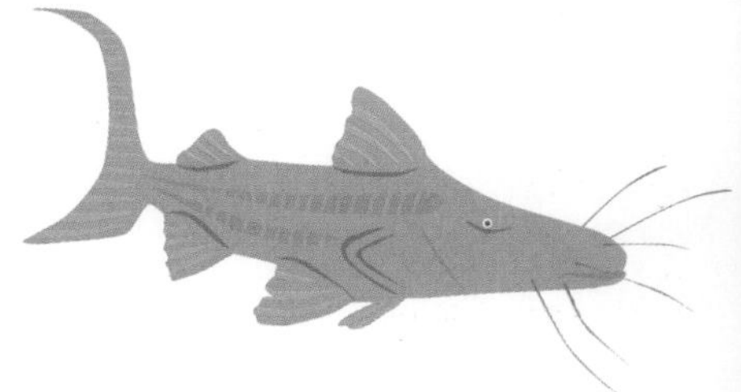

SWIMMING LIKE A FISH

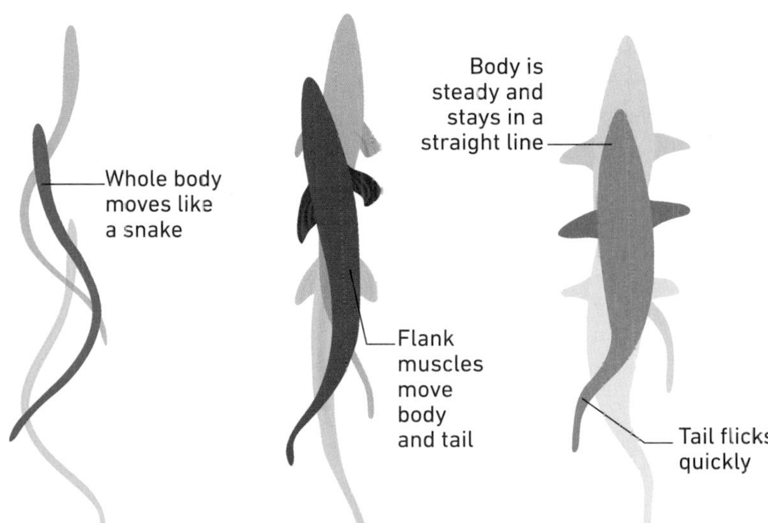

Whole body moves like a snake

Body is steady and stays in a straight line
Tail flicks quickly

Side to side
Long, thin fish, such as eels, propel themselves using a series of fast S-shaped movements through the water.

Body and tail
Many fish, including salmon, swim with the help of their body and tail, using their powerful flank muscles to move forward.

Strong tail
The fastest fish, from tuna to sharks, maintain a straight, streamlined body, while their flank muscles flick their tail from side to side.

SMALLEST FISH

PAEDOCYPRIS PROGENETICA
IS THE SMALLEST-KNOWN FISH, WITH FEMALES MEASURING JUST 5/16 IN (7.9 mm).

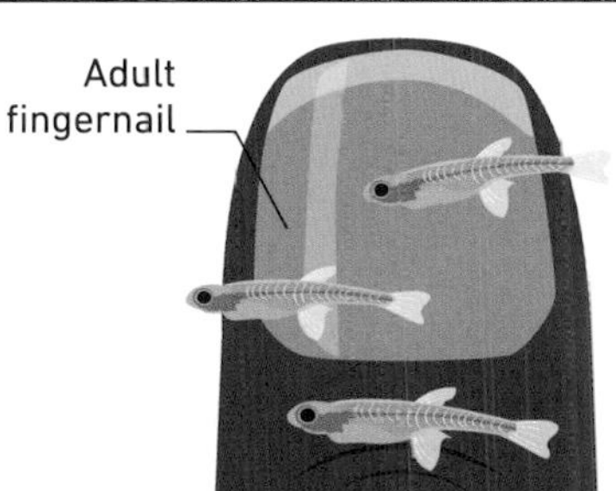

Adult fingernail

ENDEMIC SPECIES

Some fish are native to a specific habitat and do not stray from there—they are endemic to that region. This is because these fish have evolved to adapt in that area only, and they cannot survive for long anywhere else.

Coelacanths were thought to be extinct for 65 million years, but in 1938 scientists discovered them off the coast of southeastern Africa. Since then, an Indonesian coelacanth has also been found.

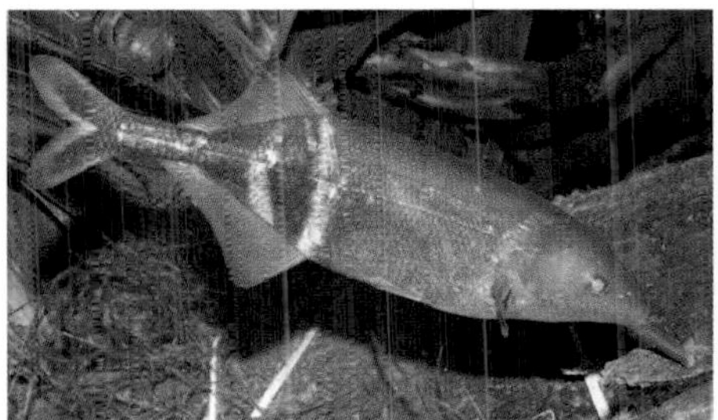

Elephantnose fish are a curious-looking freshwater species native to western and central Africa. They are found in slow-moving rivers and muddy pools.

DEEPEST FISH

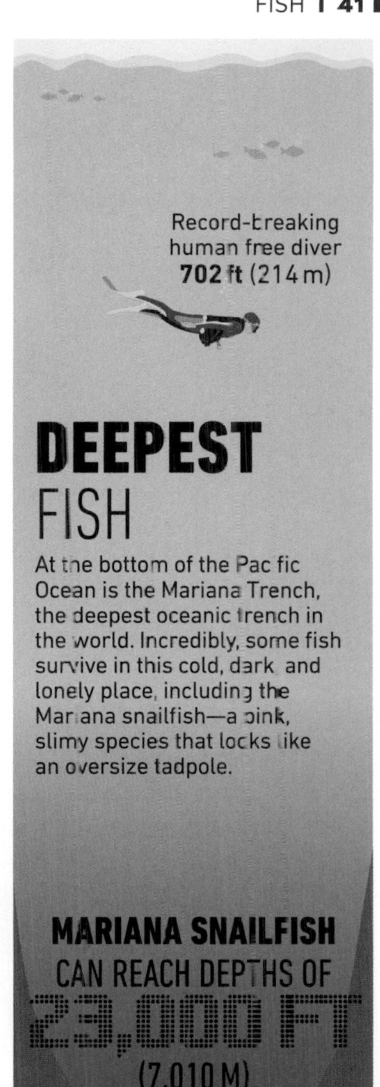

Record-breaking human free diver
702 ft (214 m)

At the bottom of the Pacific Ocean is the Mariana Trench, the deepest oceanic trench in the world. Incredibly, some fish survive in this cold, dark, and lonely place, including the Mariana snailfish—a pink, slimy species that looks like an oversize tadpole.

BIGGEST FISH

WHALE SHARKS GROW 40 FT (12 M) LONG—ABOUT THE SAME LENGTH AS A BUS.

SMART FISH

Found in the Indian and Pacific oceans, the reef-dwelling tuskfish can use a rock to smash open shellfish, making it the first wild fish observed using tools.

FASTEST FISH

Named for their spectacular dorsal fin, sailfish would easily win a race against the fastest human swimmer. They live in the warm Atlantic and Indo-Pacific waters.

MICHAEL PHELPS **OLYMPIC SWIMMER** AT **4.7 MPH** (7.6 KPH)

SAILFISH AT **70 MPH** (113 KPH)

Sea lamprey

The sea lamprey is a jawless fish—instead of jaws it has a sucker filled with teeth, which it uses to feed on the blood of other fishes. It grows up as a larva in the rivers and lakes of North America and Europe, then lives its adult life in the salty North Atlantic Ocean, before returning to freshwater habitats to breed and die.

Northern waters
Sea lampreys can be found all across the North Atlantic, from the frigid waters of Greenland to the balmy latitudes of Spain and Florida, USA. While most adults live in the ocean, some make the Great Lakes of North America their home all year round.

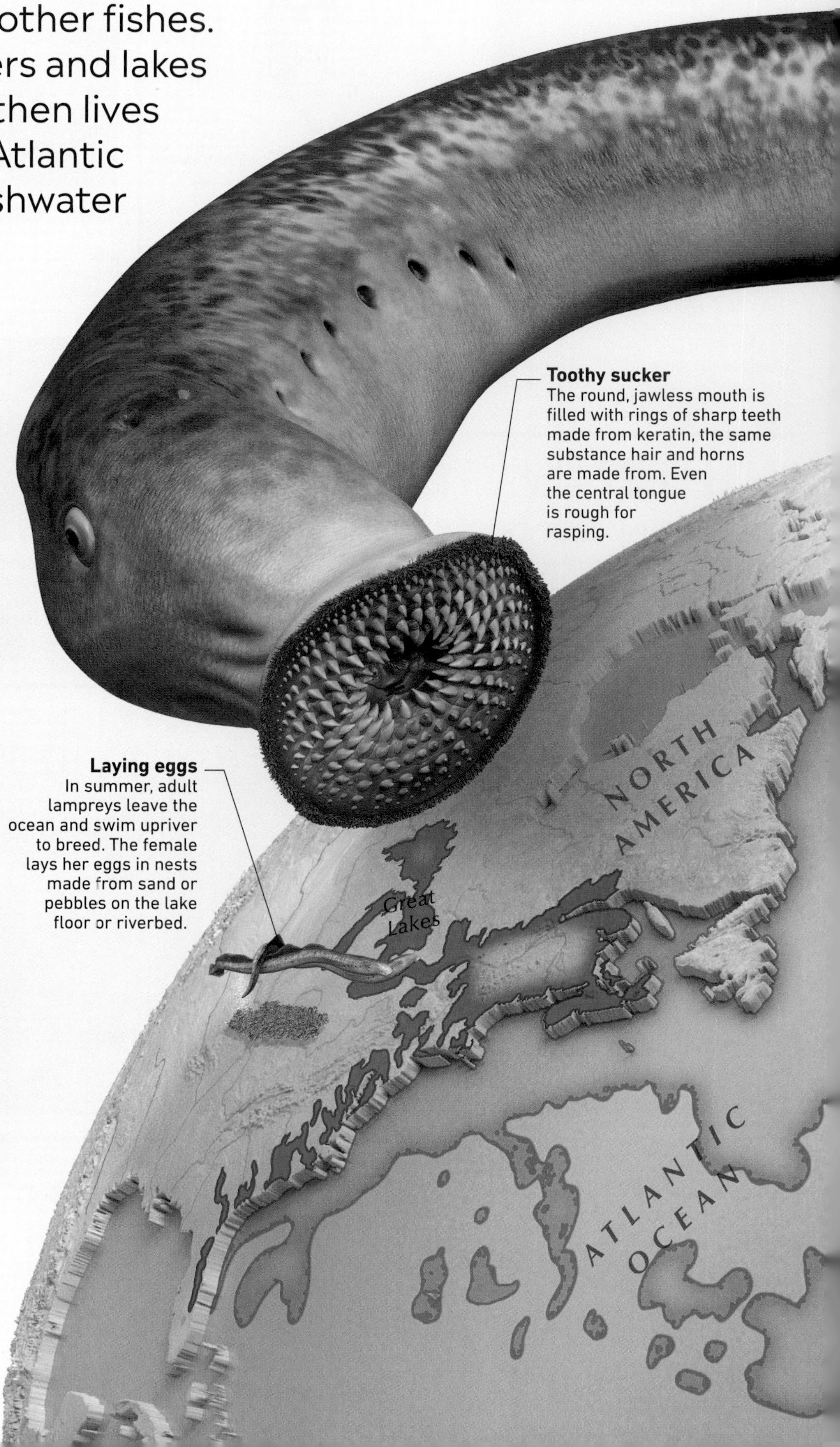

Toothy sucker
The round, jawless mouth is filled with rings of sharp teeth made from keratin, the same substance hair and horns are made from. Even the central tongue is rough for rasping.

Lamprey larvae
Sea lamprey eggs hatch into young called larvae. The larvae burrow into gravel on the riverbed, leaving their heads exposed. They filter feed on tiny particles swept into their mouth by tiny microscopic hairs called cilia. This larval phase can last for up to three years.

Laying eggs
In summer, adult lampreys leave the ocean and swim upriver to breed. The female lays her eggs in nests made from sand or pebbles on the lake floor or riverbed.

NORTH AMERICA

Great Lakes

ATLANTIC OCEAN

Feeding on blood
Adult lampreys clamp onto other fish with their sucker-like mouths to feed. They use their horny teeth and tongue to cut a hole in the prey's skin, swallowing its blood as food. The lamprey's saliva stops the blood clotting so it keeps flowing, often until the victim dies.

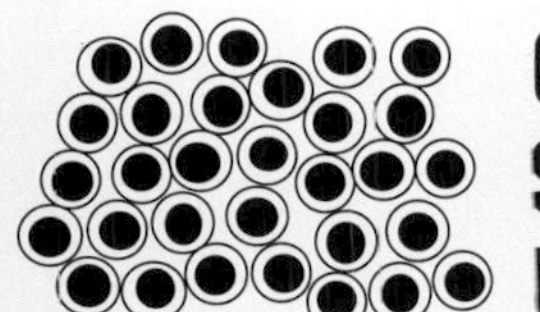

ONE **SPAWNING** FEMALE **SEA LAMPREY** MAY LAY UP TO **300,000 EGGS**

THE **LENGTH** OF A **SEA LAMPREY** CAN BE UP TO

(1.2 M)

KEY

Sea lamprey marine range

Sea lamprey freshwater range

Tail fin
A tail fin and two dorsal fins running along the back help stabilize the body when swimming. Unlike most jawed fishes, lampreys have a skeleton made of cartilage, not bone, and no paired fins.

Greenland

North Sea

Baltic Sea

EUROPE

Adriatic Sea

Mediterranean Sea

Feeding at sea
Most mature adult sea lampreys feed at sea, where they consume the blood of other fishes, such as cod and herring, or even marine mammals, such as dolphins.

Freshwater larvae
The larvae of sea lampreys spend their time in freshwater rivers and lakes. When they reach maturity they swim down river and out toward the open ocean.

Long-distance swimmers
Sea lampreys can travel long distances into the open ocean in search of food, and may descend to depths of 2½ miles (4 km).

Mediterranean lampreys
Lampreys in the Mediterranean Sea spawn in the rivers of southern Europe.

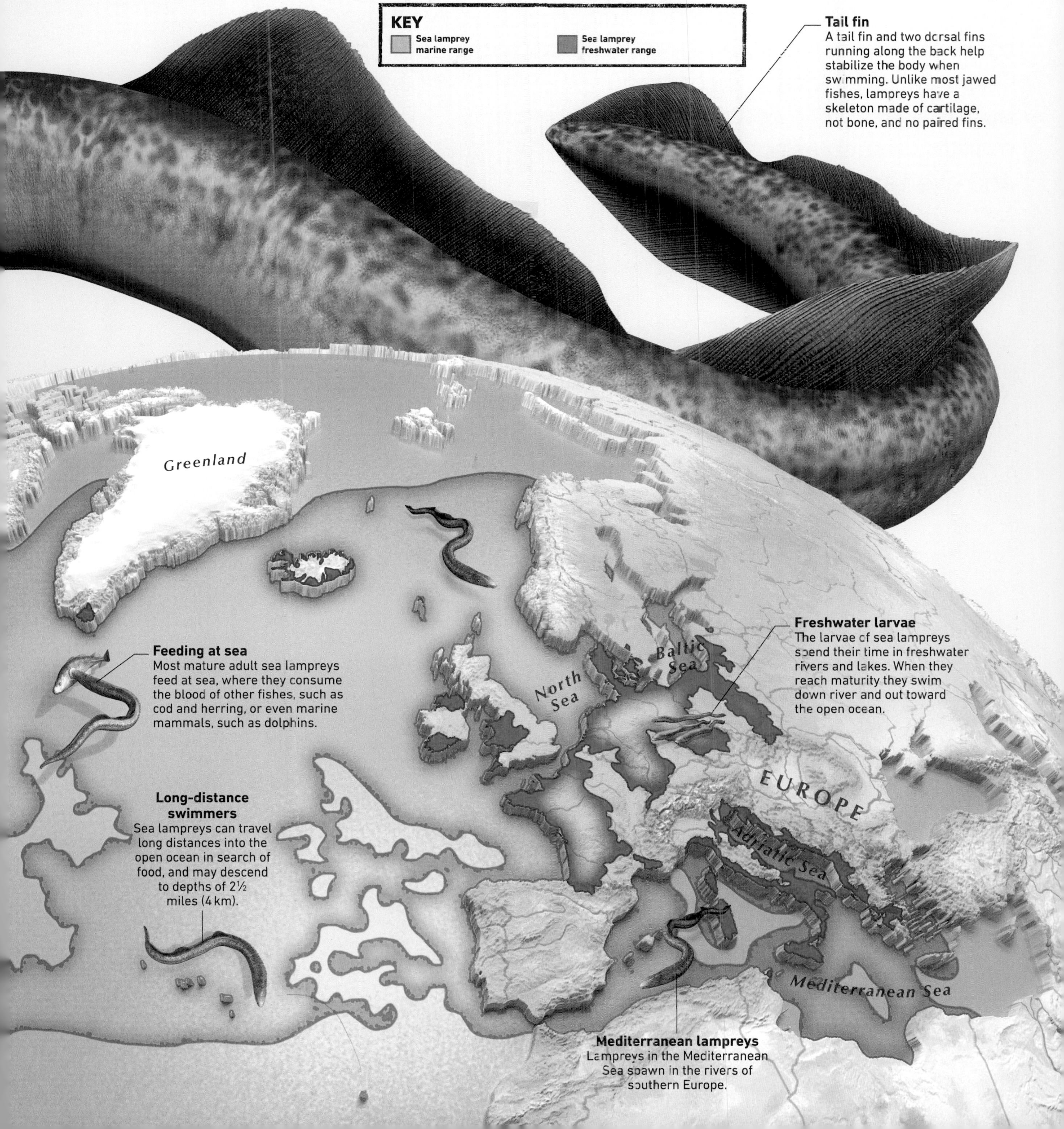

Great white shark

Armed with razor-sharp teeth and a sleek body shaped like a torpedo, the great white shark is a fast, formidable predator. This wanderer roams throughout the world's oceans, but returns to the coast to hunt marine mammals such as seals, dolphins, and even small whales.

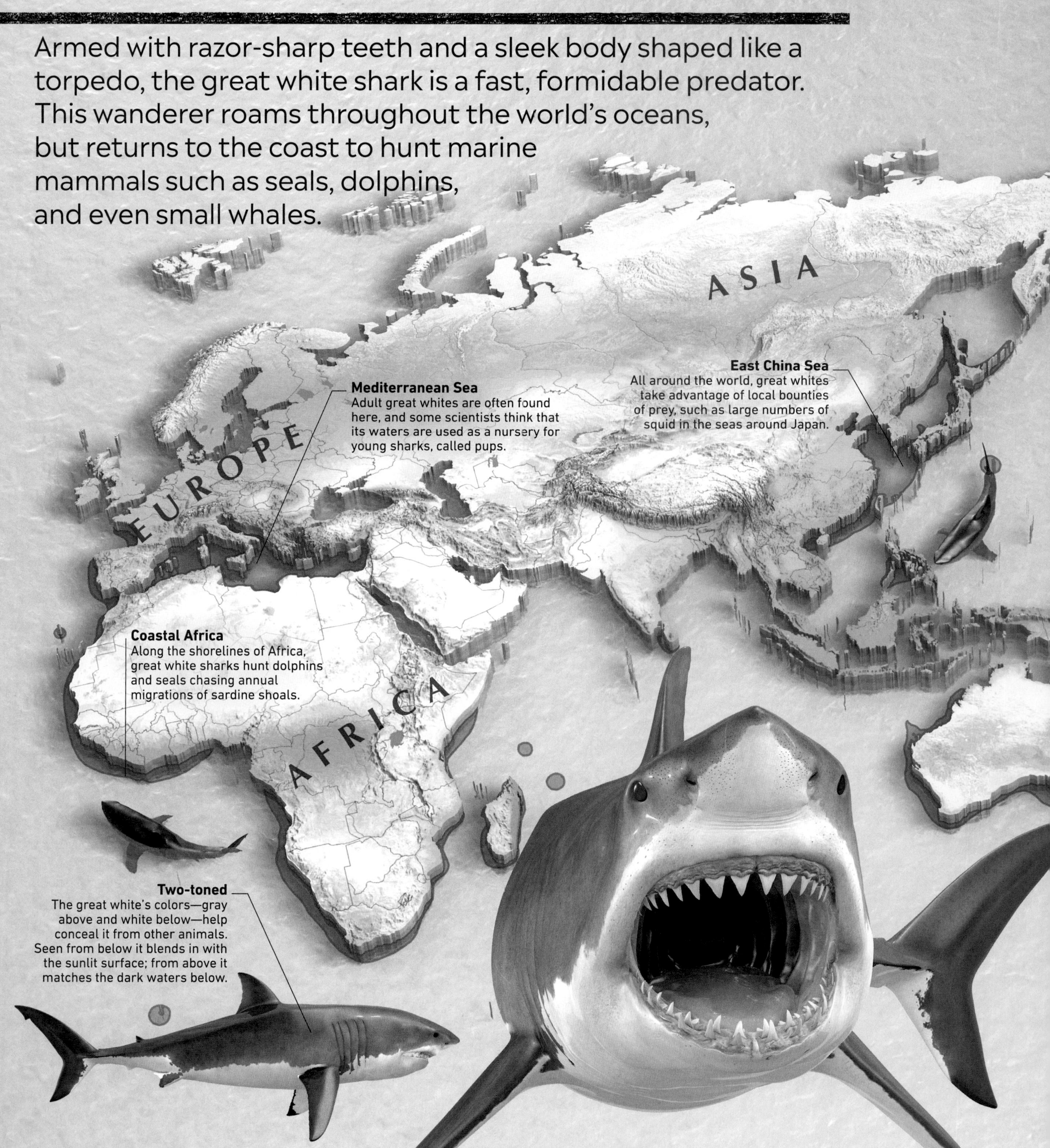

East China Sea
All around the world, great whites take advantage of local bounties of prey, such as large numbers of squid in the seas around Japan.

Mediterranean Sea
Adult great whites are often found here, and some scientists think that its waters are used as a nursery for young sharks, called pups.

Coastal Africa
Along the shorelines of Africa, great white sharks hunt dolphins and seals chasing annual migrations of sardine shoals.

Two-toned
The great white's colors—gray above and white below—help conceal it from other animals. Seen from below it blends in with the sunlit surface; from above it matches the dark waters below.

ANIMALS IN DANGER

Great white shark
- **IUCN status:** vulnerable
- **Population estimate:** unknown

KEY

Great white shark range

Tracking sharks

Little is known about the exact movements of great whites, but they can be followed by fitting them with tracking devices. These transmit signals to satellites, which send information back to Earth about the animal's location. Such studies show they travel thousands of miles across the oceans.

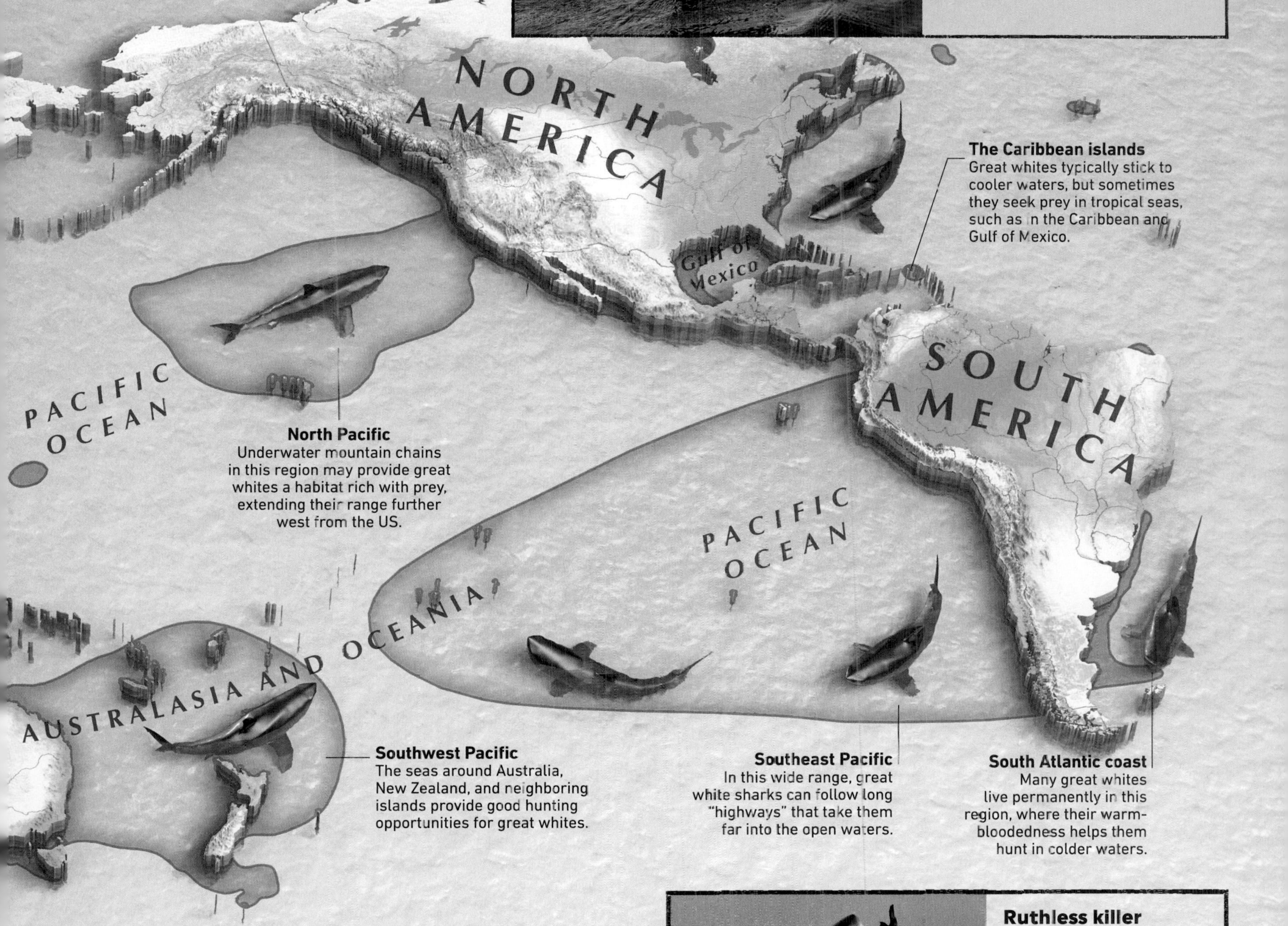

NORTH AMERICA

SOUTH AMERICA

PACIFIC OCEAN

AUSTRALASIA AND OCEANIA

Gulf of Mexico

The Caribbean islands
Great whites typically stick to cooler waters, but sometimes they seek prey in tropical seas, such as in the Caribbean and Gulf of Mexico.

North Pacific
Underwater mountain chains in this region may provide great whites a habitat rich with prey, extending their range further west from the US.

Southwest Pacific
The seas around Australia, New Zealand, and neighboring islands provide good hunting opportunities for great whites.

Southeast Pacific
In this wide range, great white sharks can follow long "highways" that take them far into the open waters.

South Atlantic coast
Many great whites live permanently in this region, where their warm-bloodedness helps them hunt in colder waters.

Long-distance wanderer

The great white shark is the world's widest-ranging fish and can be found in most oceans, but is found most often in the ranges shown on this map. Unusually for a fish, it maintains a high body temperature, helping it survive in colder waters and chase down warm-blooded mammals.

A **GREAT WHITE SHARK** CAN HAVE UP TO **300 TEETH**

Ruthless killer

Once a great white shark sights a target near the water's surface, it moves in quickly for the kill. It attacks its prey, such as this sea lion, with a single ferocious bite—and in the process can breach the surface in spectacular fashion. It then lets the victim bleed to death before starting to feed.

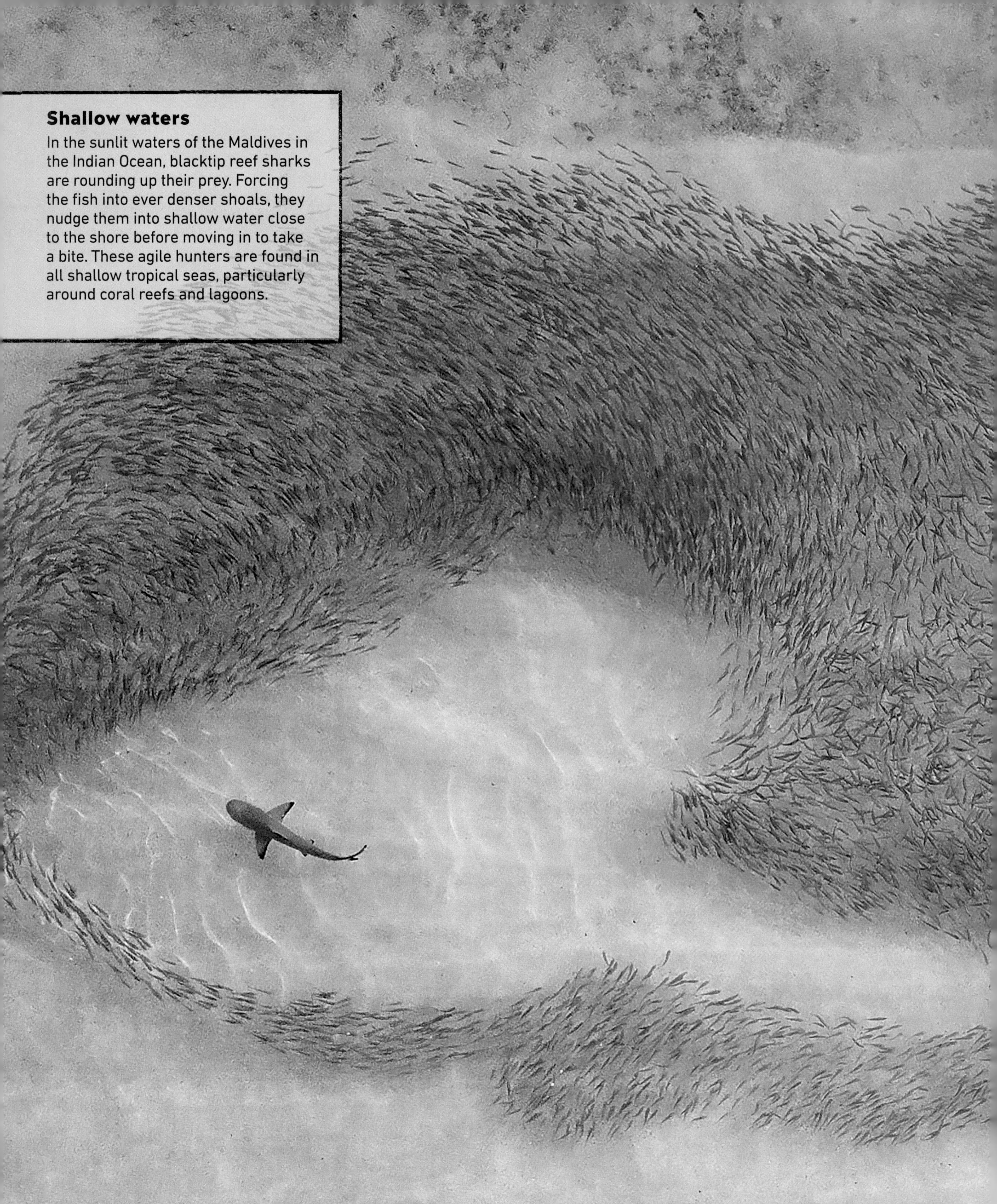

Shallow waters

In the sunlit waters of the Maldives in the Indian Ocean, blacktip reef sharks are rounding up their prey. Forcing the fish into ever denser shoals, they nudge them into shallow water close to the shore before moving in to take a bite. These agile hunters are found in all shallow tropical seas, particularly around coral reefs and lagoons.

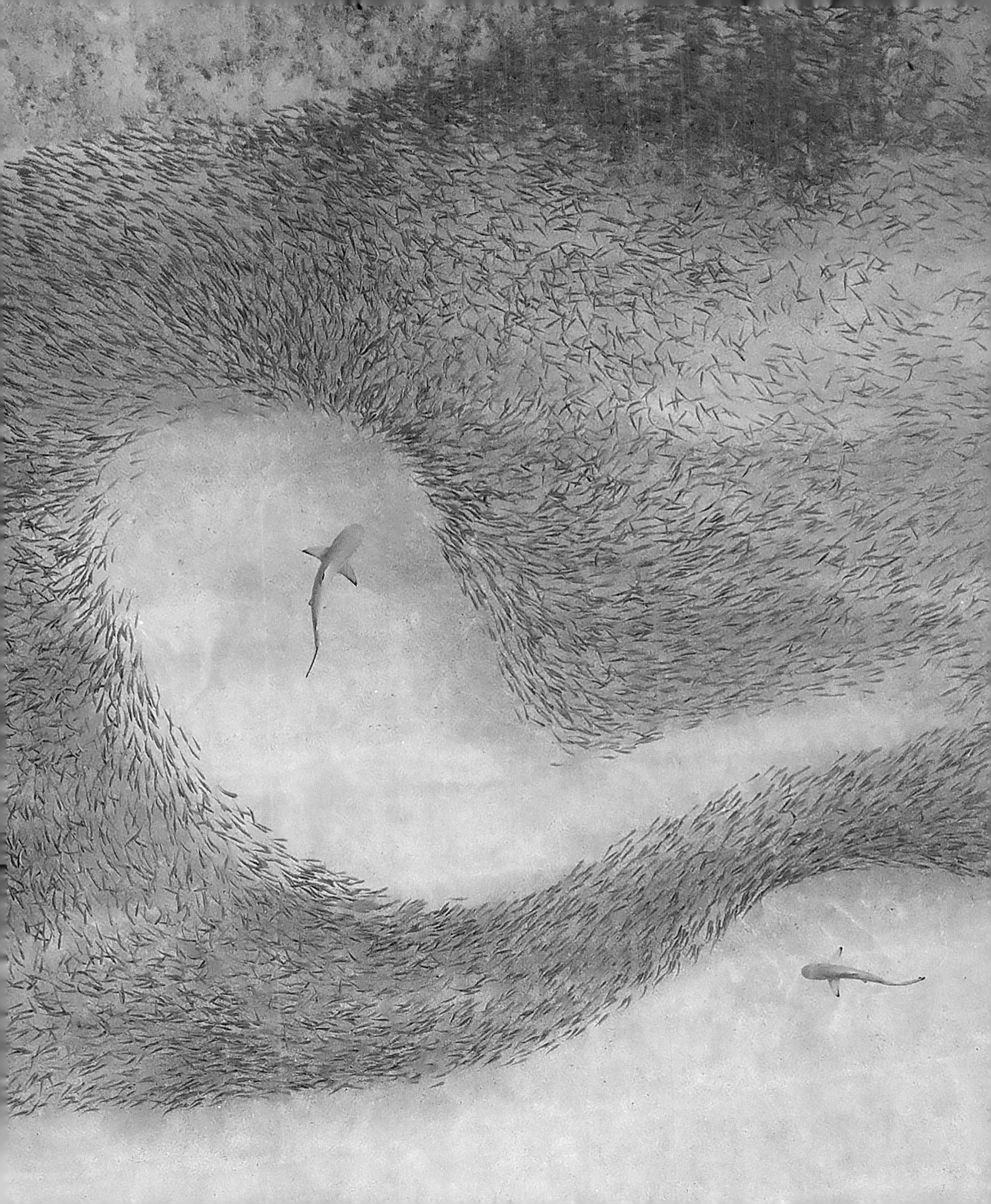

Slimy blanket

While it sleeps, a steephead parrotfish produces slime from its skin to build up a cocoon around it. This shield takes around an hour to make, and protects the fish from predators and also serves as a barrier to infectious parasites.

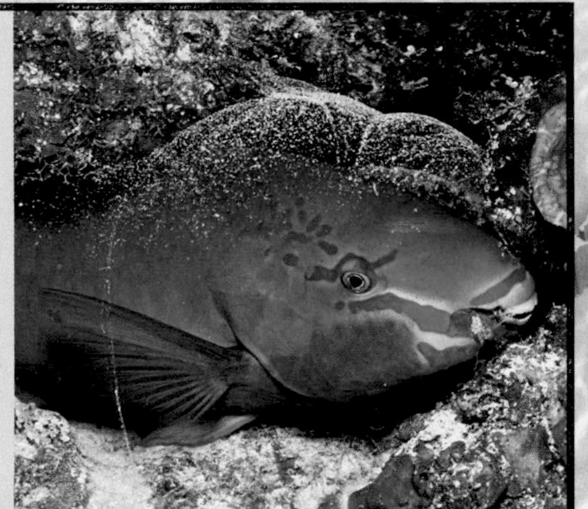

Diversity hot spot

The stunning coral reefs between the Philippines and Papua New Guinea have the highest diversity of marine animals in the world. Known as the Coral Triangle, this region covers 2¼ million sq miles (6 million sq km) and is also home to 75 percent of all coral species.

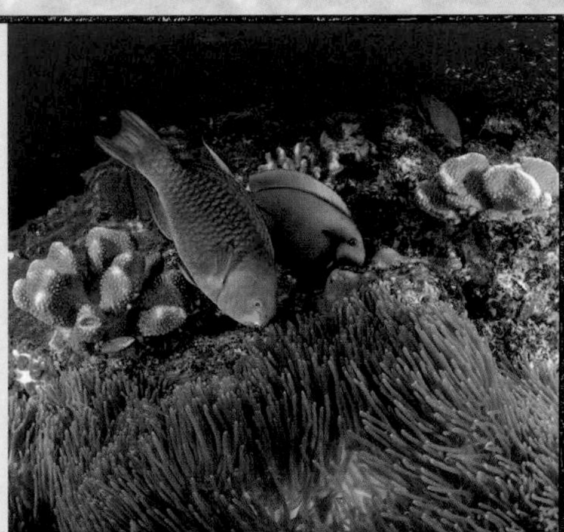

The Philippines
The warm, shallow waters around the Philippines represent the northernmost reach of the Coral Triangle, a region known for its diverse coral reefs and fish species.

White-sand islands
Many tiny islands in the western Pacific are surrounded by white beaches made of sand produced by the poop of thousands of coral-eating parrotfish.

Papua New Guinea
Islands off the coast of this country have some of the richest reefs anywhere on Earth.

AUSTRALASIA

SOLOMON ISLANDS

Indo-Pacific beauty

The steephead parrotfish is scattered throughout parts of the Indian Ocean to the Pacific islands of Polynesia. This species' showy colors help them recognize their own kind in crowded, reef-dwelling communities. It also uses its beak to break the rocky coral, digesting its softer flesh and pooping the rocky parts as white sand.

PARROTFISH HAVE A SET OF **TEETH IN THEIR THROAT** TO GRIND DOWN **ROCKY CORAL**

Northwest Australia
Coral reefs on the narrow continental shelf around this region extend the range of Indo-Pacific fish, such as the steephead parrotfish, into the fringes of the Indian Ocean.

Head hump
Only males of the steephead parrotfish develop a head hump, but all youngsters have the potential to do so. This is because younger females can change their sex and turn into males.

INDIAN OCEAN

Steephead parrotfish

Around one-fifth of the world's fish live on tropical coral reefs. Many of these beautiful species, including the steephead parrotfish, are dependent upon coral for their survival, finding shelter in their nooks and crannies. This parrotfish, however, is also known for its unique ability to eat the tough coral using its strong, parrotlike beak.

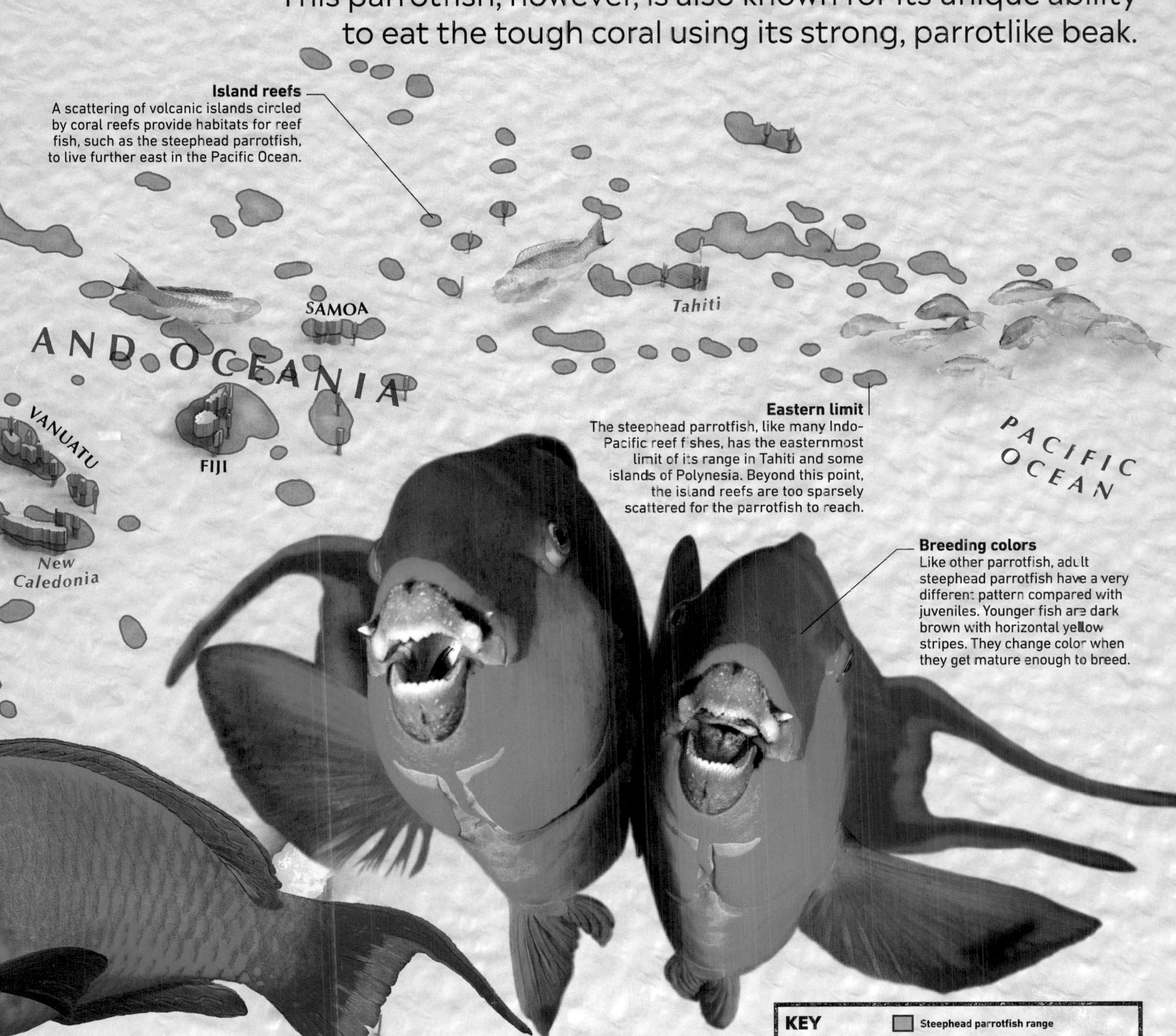

Island reefs
A scattering of volcanic islands circled by coral reefs provide habitats for reef fish, such as the steephead parrotfish, to live further east in the Pacific Ocean.

Eastern limit
The steephead parrotfish, like many Indo-Pacific reef fishes, has the easternmost limit of its range in Tahiti and some islands of Polynesia. Beyond this point, the island reefs are too sparsely scattered for the parrotfish to reach.

Breeding colors
Like other parrotfish, adult steephead parrotfish have a very different pattern compared with juveniles. Younger fish are dark brown with horizontal yellow stripes. They change color when they get mature enough to breed.

RED-BELLIED PIRANHAS **"BARK" TO WARN OFF OTHER FISH**

KEY

Red-bellied piranha range

White waters
Most red-bellied piranhas live in the cloudier, sediment-heavy "white waters" closer to the Amazon's mouth, where the river drains into the Atlantic.

Steady waters
Red-bellied piranhas prefer the lower section of rivers, which are wider, deeper, and move more slowly. They are less likely to be found in the narrower and faster-flowing sections nearer the river's source.

Shoaling

Piranhas are often feared as blood-thirsty fish that attack big prey in frenzied shoals. But studies have shown that shoaling, as with other fish species, is more a way of protecting themselves from predators. Plenty of Amazon animals, such as giant otters, eat piranhas as prey.

Carnivorous fish

Found in rivers, streams, lakes, and flooded forests, the red-bellied piranha is known for its vicious appetite. In reality it usually hunts fish and other small aquatic animals, and avoids anything bigger. Only in the dry season, when pools run low and hungry piranhas are forced together, may piranhas attack bigger land animals that stumble into the waters.

Red-bellied piranha

The rivers running through the Amazon Basin in northern South America are home to the biggest diversity of freshwater fish in the world, including 38 species of piranha. Among them is the red-bellied piranha—a fish with a fearsome reputation.

Red bellies
This species is recognizable for its red belly and silvery body.

Tocantins
Many of the rivers that are home to the red-bellied piranha empty into the Amazon. But the Tocantins River empties directly into the Atlantic, so populations of piranhas are cut off from those of the Amazon.
Brazilian Highlands
São Francisco
Tocantins
Araguaia
Xingu
Flowing south
In the southernmost part of their range, red-bellied piranhas live in the Paraná and Paraguay rivers, which flow through South America's open grasslands and drain into the Atlantic Ocean.
Paraguay
Paraná
Pampas
SOUTH AMERICA
SOME PIRANHAS HAVE A BITE FORCE EQUAL TO 30 TIMES THEIR OWN BODY WEIGHT
Sharp teeth
The teeth are arranged in a single row in the upper and lower jaws, and have sharp, bladelike edges for puncturing and cutting through the flesh of animal prey.
PIRANHA RELATIVES
Pacu
A giant relative of the piranhas, the pacu has strong jaws for cracking seeds and nuts that fall into the waters when the Amazon is flooded during the rainy season.
Neon tetra
Tetras are tiny relatives of the piranhas that eat small invertebrates. Many, such as the neon tetra, are brightly colored—making them popular in aquariums.
Freshwater hatchetfish
Small piranha relatives called hatchetfishes swim near the surface and prey on insects. Their muscular bodies help them jump from the water to escape danger.
African tiger fish
Close cousins of the piranhas live across the Atlantic in African rivers. Some, such as the African tiger fish, are also sharp-toothed meat-eaters.
Congo tetra
The brightly colored Congo tetra lives in Africa. These ancestors of piranha relatives first evolved when South America and Africa were joined.

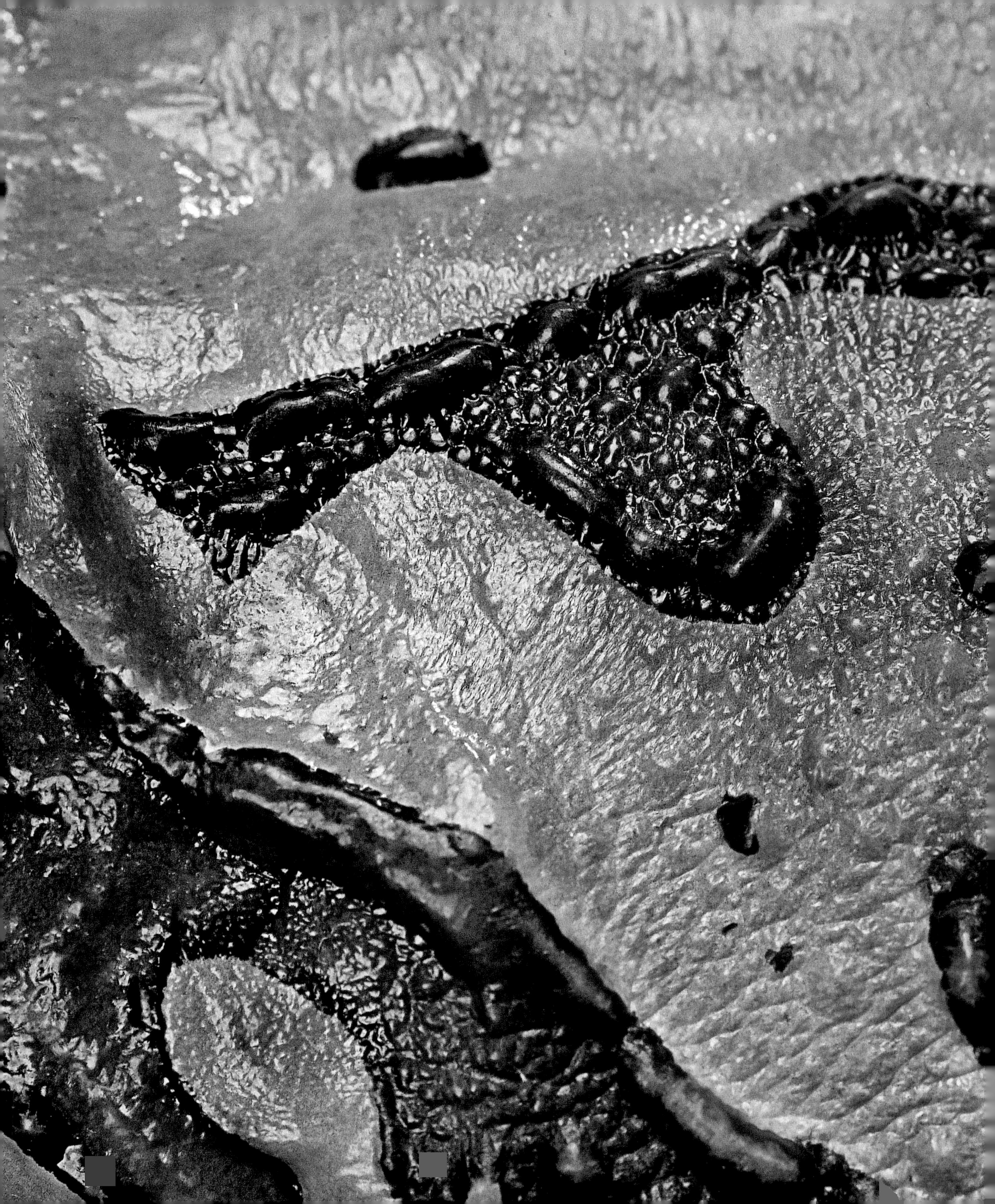

AMPHIBIANS

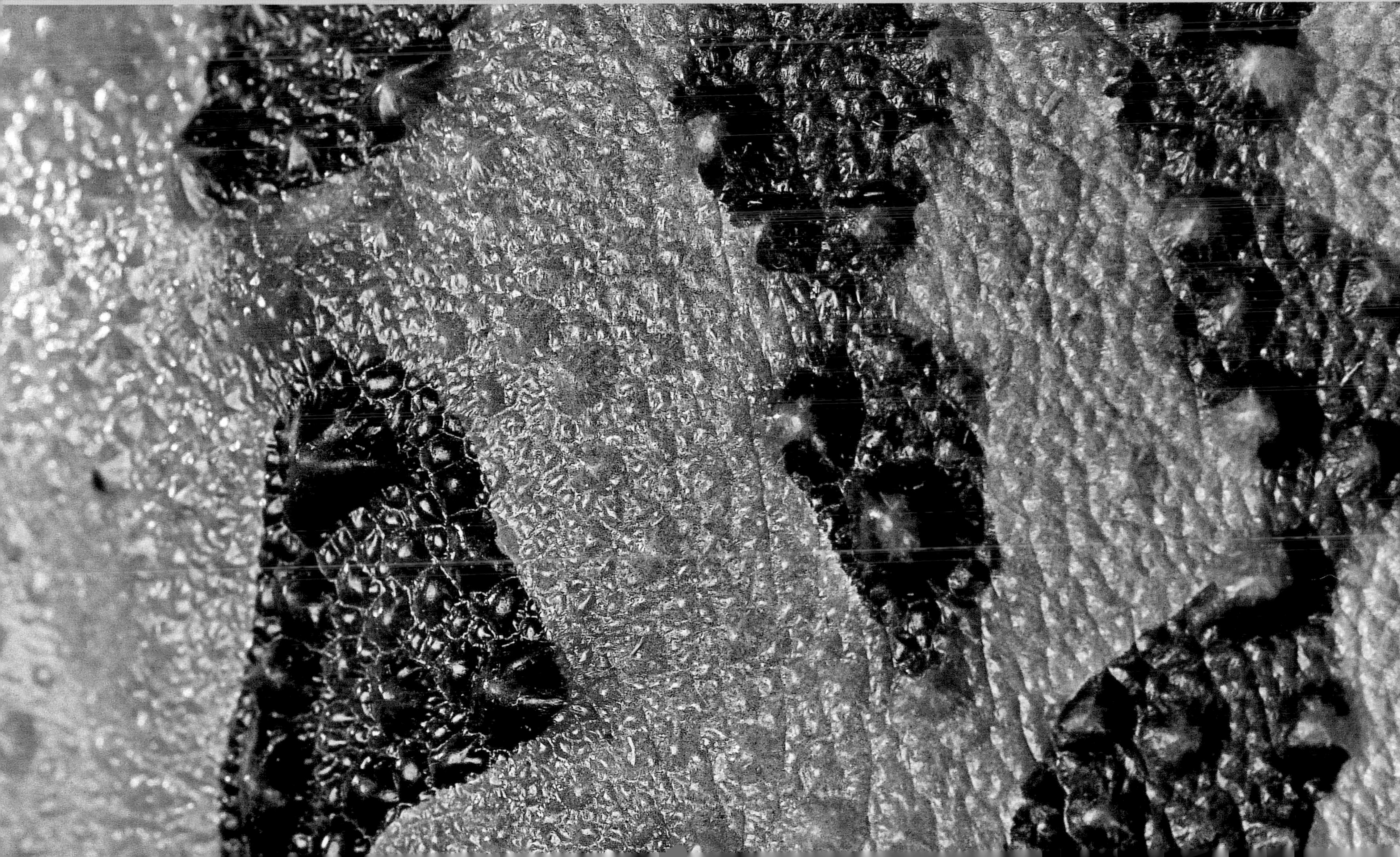

Amphibian facts

The first amphibians evolved from fish and moved on to land amore than 300 million years ago. Today, most amphibians move between land and water. They are found throughout the world, and most commonly in moist, freshwater habitats like woodlands and rainforests.

WHAT IS AN AMPHIBIAN?

Vertebrates
Like their fish ancestors, all amphibians have an internal skeleton made of bone.

Cold-blooded
The body temperature of amphibians fluctuates with that of the air and water around them.

Lay eggs
Most amphibians lay soft eggs, but some give birth to live young.

Aquatic young
The young hatch and stay for a time as tadpoles in water, eventually turning into amphibious adults.

Moist skin
Water passes through an amphibian's thin, moist skin, allowing it to breathe under water.

AMPHIBIAN **TYPES**

ESTIMATED NUMBER OF AMPHIBIAN SPECIES:

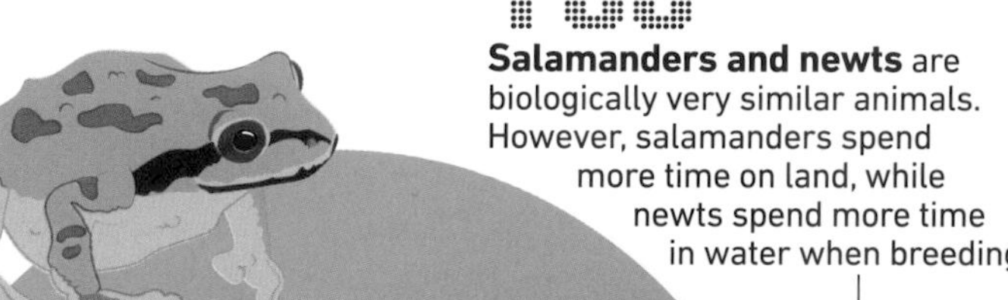

760

Salamanders and newts are biologically very similar animals. However, salamanders spend more time on land, while newts spend more time in water when breeding

7,280

Frogs and toads are the largest group of amphibians. Scientifically, frogs and toads belong to the same animal group, but frogs typically have smoother skin.

210

Caecilians are small, snakelike amphibians with no limbs and tentacles on their heads. They spend most of their lives underground, eating insects and worms. Some species live in water and have a tail fin for swimming.

EXTREME HABITATS

These unique amphibians can withstand the toughest conditions, from icy winters to the darkest caves.

Water-holding frogs have adapted to harsh Australian deserts. They burrow underground and form a waxy cocoon from layers of skin, which retains moisture necessary for survival.

Olms are blind, aquatic salamanders that live in the caves of Slovenia and Croatia. They have excellent smell and hearing, which is helpful when foraging for food, such as snails.

Crab-eating frogs are able to tolerate saltier habitats than other amphibians. Native to Southeast Asia, this frog mainly eats insects, but it also preys on crabs, hence its name.

NEARLY 50% OF ALL **AMPHIBIANS** ARE **THREATENED**, DUE TO WATER **POLLUTION**, HABITAT **DESTRUCTION**, AND THE INTRODUCTION OF **INVASIVE** SPECIES.

FROG **LIFE CYCLE**

Most frogs undergo a dramatic physical change from a newborn to an adult through several distinct stages—a process known as metamorphosis.

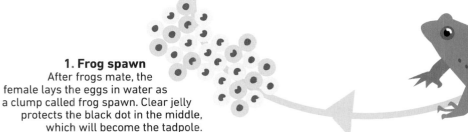

2. Tadpoles
After about 10 days, tadpoles begin to move inside the eggs, before hatching. Over the next nine weeks, they will develop the ability to swim and eat.

3. Froglet
After about nine weeks, the tadpole starts to resemble a frog, with hind and front legs and a pointed head. The long tail will also shorten to a mere stub.

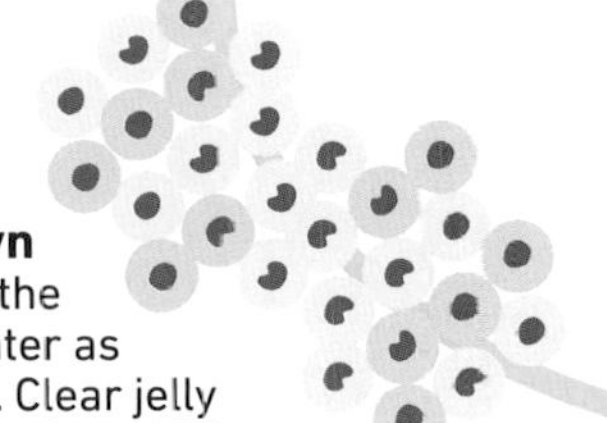

1. Frog spawn
After frogs mate, the female lays the eggs in water as a clump called frog spawn. Clear jelly protects the black dot in the middle, which will become the tadpole.

4. Frog
At 12 weeks, it is almost a fully formed frog and can leave the water. When it is an adult, it can mate and have young of its own.

BIGGEST AMPHIBIAN

THE **SOUTH CHINA GIANT SALAMANDER** CAN GROW

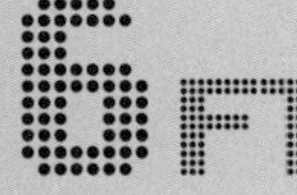

6 FT (1.8 M) LONG—ABOUT THE LENGTH OF **FOUR DOMESTIC CATS.**

SMALLEST AMPHIBIAN

PAEDOPHRYNE AMAUENSIS, A FROG FROM PAPUA NEW GUINEA, IS NO BIGGER THAN A FLY, UP TO 5/16 IN (7.7 MM) LONG.

ISLAND FROGS

Some frogs live on only one island, where the conditions—from the weather and habitat to food—are just right.

Solomon Island leaf frogs resemble the color and shape of leaves on the Solomon Islands in the South Pacific. Curiously, they hatch from eggs as fully developed frogs.

Gardiner's Seychelles frogs are one of the tiniest frogs in the world, growing to just ⅜ in (1 cm). Living in the Seychelles, off the eastern edge of Africa, their habitat is threatened by wildfires.

VENOMOUS AMPHIBIANS

Of all the amphibians, caecilians are probably the most mysterious because they are hard to find in their burrows. However, some experts think these curious creatures, such as the giant caecilian, could have venomous saliva. There are only very few known venomous amphibians, such as Brazil's Greening's frog.

Giant caecilian

HIGHEST AMPHIBIAN

BOULENGER'S LAZY TOADS LIVE 17,290 FT (5,270 M) HIGH, IN **GURUDONGMAR LAKE**, INDIA.

ONE **GIANT LEAP**

Growing up to 6 in (15 cm), American bullfrogs can leap 20 times their own body length, often pouncing on prey such as insects, fish, and even snakes. They live in freshwater ponds, lakes, and marshes in parts of North America.

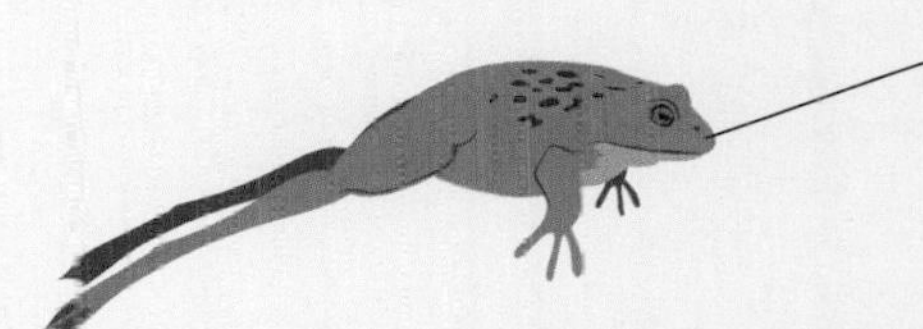

The American bullfrog is the largest frog in North America.

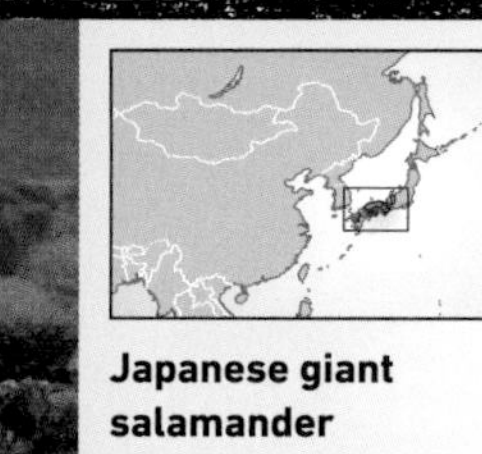

Japanese giant salamander
This is one of the biggest amphibians—up to 4½ ft (1.4 m) long. It lives in cold mountain streams and gets almost all its oxygen directly through its wrinkled skin.

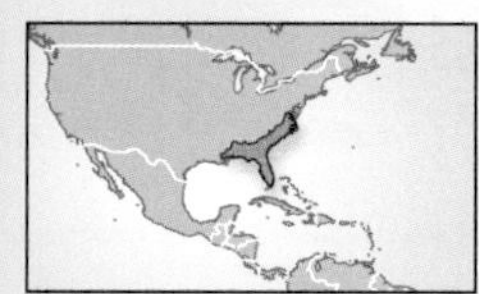

Amphiuma
Only found in North America, this aquatic salamander, with its tiny limbs and eel-like body, has both gills and lungs, but the gills are hidden under flaps of skin.

Mushroom-tongued salamander
This tiny salamander is one of nearly 500 species from the Central American tropics that lack lungs and breathe only through their skin.

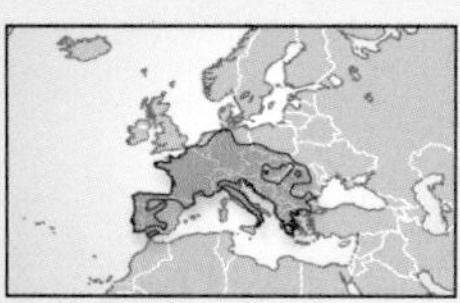

Fire salamander
This air-breathing salamander from European forests is unusual in giving birth to live young—as aquatic larvae—rather than laying eggs.

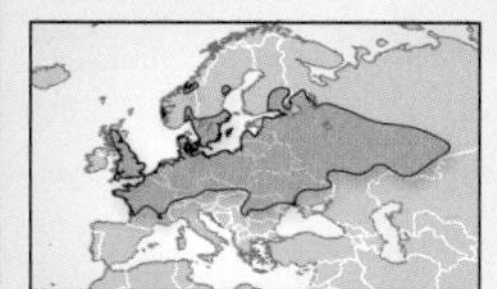

Great crested newt
Newts are land salamanders that return to water to breed, changing their appearance by developing smoother skin and tail fins.

Mudpuppy

Salamanders are amphibians shaped like lizards, with long tails and short legs. The mudpuppy is a salamander that lives on river- and lake beds in North America. They get their unusual name because it was once thought they barked like a dog, but in fact their sound is more like a squeak.

Lake living

The common mudpuppy is one of eight species of mudpuppies found in the wettest parts of the United States and Canada—mainly in the Great Lakes and the rivers that flow from them. It lurks among the mud and silt, hiding during the day and emerging at night to feed.

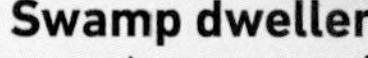

Swamp dweller
In the warm, wet swamps of southern Louisiana, many mudpuppies are yellower than elsewhere in the US and youngsters often venture out of water into woodland leaf litter.

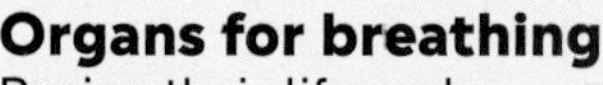

Organs for breathing

During their life cycle, most amphibians go through a big change called metamorphosis, where their aquatic larva turns into an air-breathing adult. But in some salamanders, such as the mudpuppy, this process is incomplete. The adults keep their gills, allowing them to continue breathing underwater.

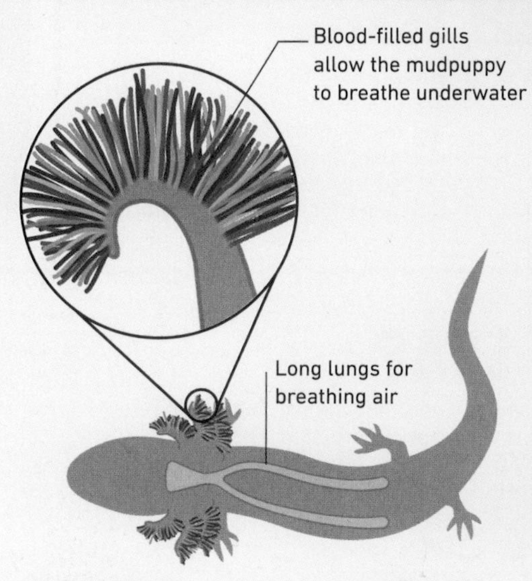

THERE ARE **MORE THAN** 760 **SALAMANDER SPECIES** IN THE WORLD

LIKE ALL OTHER AMPHIBIANS, **MUDPUPPIES** TAKE IN SOME **OXYGEN** DIRECTLY **THROUGH THEIR SKIN**

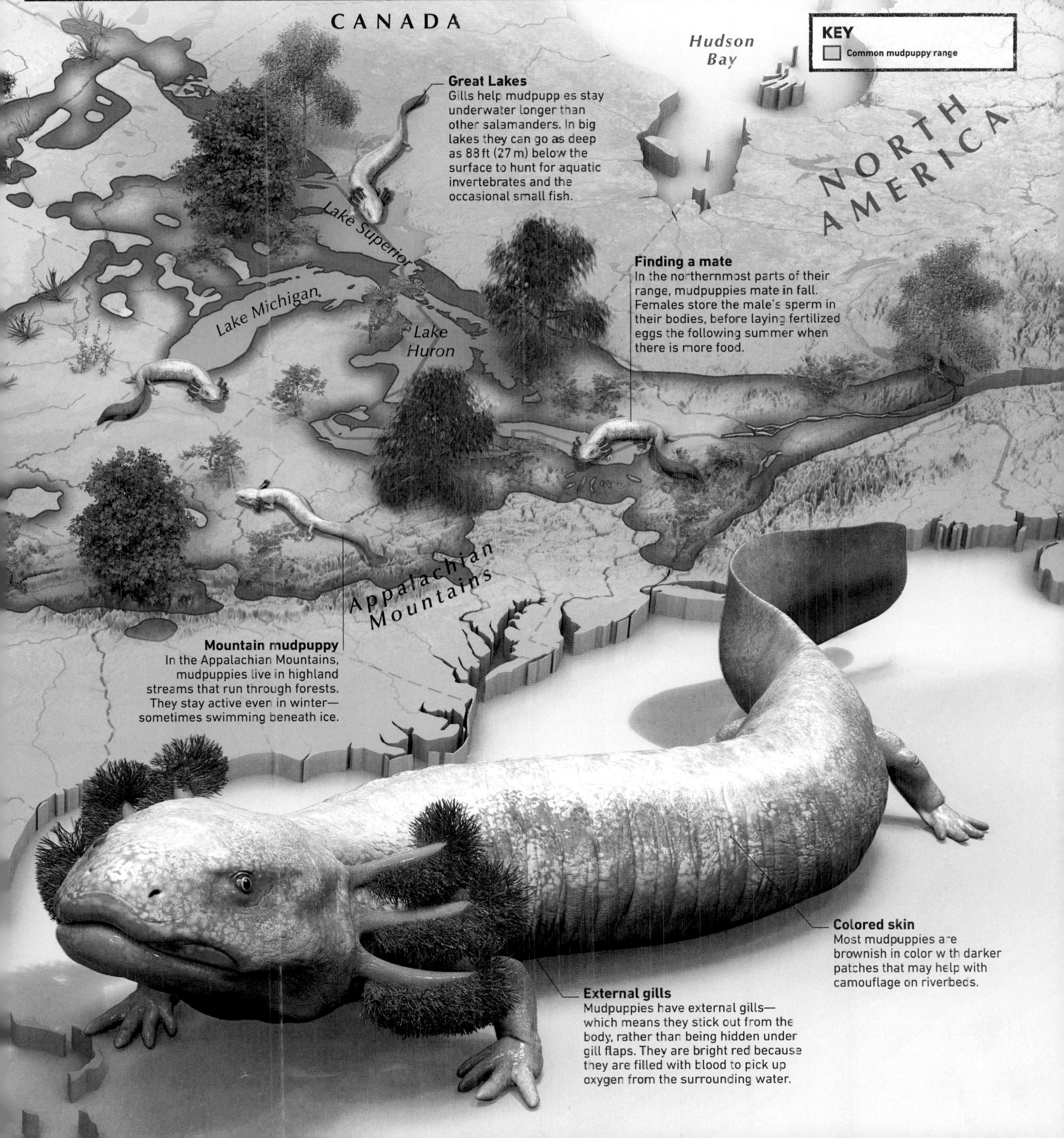

Great Lakes
Gills help mudpuppies stay underwater longer than other salamanders. In big lakes they can go as deep as 88 ft (27 m) below the surface to hunt for aquatic invertebrates and the occasional small fish.

Finding a mate
In the northernmost parts of their range, mudpuppies mate in fall. Females store the male's sperm in their bodies, before laying fertilized eggs the following summer when there is more food.

Mountain mudpuppy
In the Appalachian Mountains, mudpuppies live in highland streams that run through forests. They stay active even in winter—sometimes swimming beneath ice.

Colored skin
Most mudpuppies are brownish in color with darker patches that may help with camouflage on riverbeds.

External gills
Mudpuppies have external gills—which means they stick out from the body, rather than being hidden under gill flaps. They are bright red because they are filled with blood to pick up oxygen from the surrounding water.

Mossy frog

The Vietnamese mossy frog lives in the rainforest-covered mountains of northern Vietnam. Its mottled green skin, covered in bumps and ridges, blends in with the wet moss that lines the river banks and caves of the frog's forest habitat. It breeds in water-filled tree holes, laying its eggs above the waterline, safe from predators below.

Northern range
The strawberry poison frog reaches as far north as southeastern Nicaragua. The frogs here may have more purplish-colored legs and a few black spots on their back.

Coastal frogs
The densest populations of frogs occur in the wet lowland rainforest that hugs the Caribbean coasts. Frogs here hop along the ground and occasionally climb into low vegetation.

NICARAGUA

Lake Nicaragua

COSTA RICA

KEY

Strawberry poison frog range

Rainforest frog

Mountains running through Central America keep many different lowland animal species apart on either side. The strawberry poison frog lives in the eastern forest along the Caribbean coast. These frogs are small: adults are only about ¾ in (2 cm) long. Most are bright red with blue or black legs—but in some places colors vary.

Calling out
Strawberry frogs live on plants near the forest floor. The males use their low, buzzing call to defend their tiny territories and attract females.

Blue jeans
Most strawberry poison frogs have red bodies and blue legs, earning them the nickname "blue jeans" frogs. In the south of their range some mainland frogs are grayish or yellow.

Plant pool

Strawberry poison frogs are careful parents. They lay their eggs on forest leaves. When they hatch, the tadpoles are carried on the mother's back to a pool of water in a bromeliad plant, where they turn into frogs.

Color varieties

The strawberry poison frog comes in more than 100 different colored varieties called morphs. Most of these varieties occur on tiny islands off the Central American coast, where frogs are cut off from those on the mainland. They have different colors because their populations have been separated for thousands of years and have evolved to look different.

Color morphs of the strawberry poison frog

Strawberry poison frog

Most amphibians rely on poisons to defend themselves. Glands in their skin ooze chemicals that can be irritating or even deadly. The strawberry poison frog from Central America excels at defending itself in this way—and warns off enemies with its bright colors.

THIS FROG GETS ITS **POISON** FROM THE **ANTS IT EATS**

THERE ARE 200 **SPECIES** OF **POISON FROGS** IN THE AMERICAS

Island frogs
The tiny islands of Bocas del Toro off the Caribbean coast of Panama are home to many different colors of strawberry poison frogs (see panel below).

Poison skin
The skin is moistened by secretions from two types of gland: one produces mucus and makes it slimy, the other oozes poison that tastes repulsive to predators.

Common toad

Amphibians need moisture to survive, but some are tolerant of a range of different habitats. The common toad, one of more than 600 toad species across the world, is the most widespread in Europe. It lives equally well in forests, alpine meadows, and dry sand dunes.

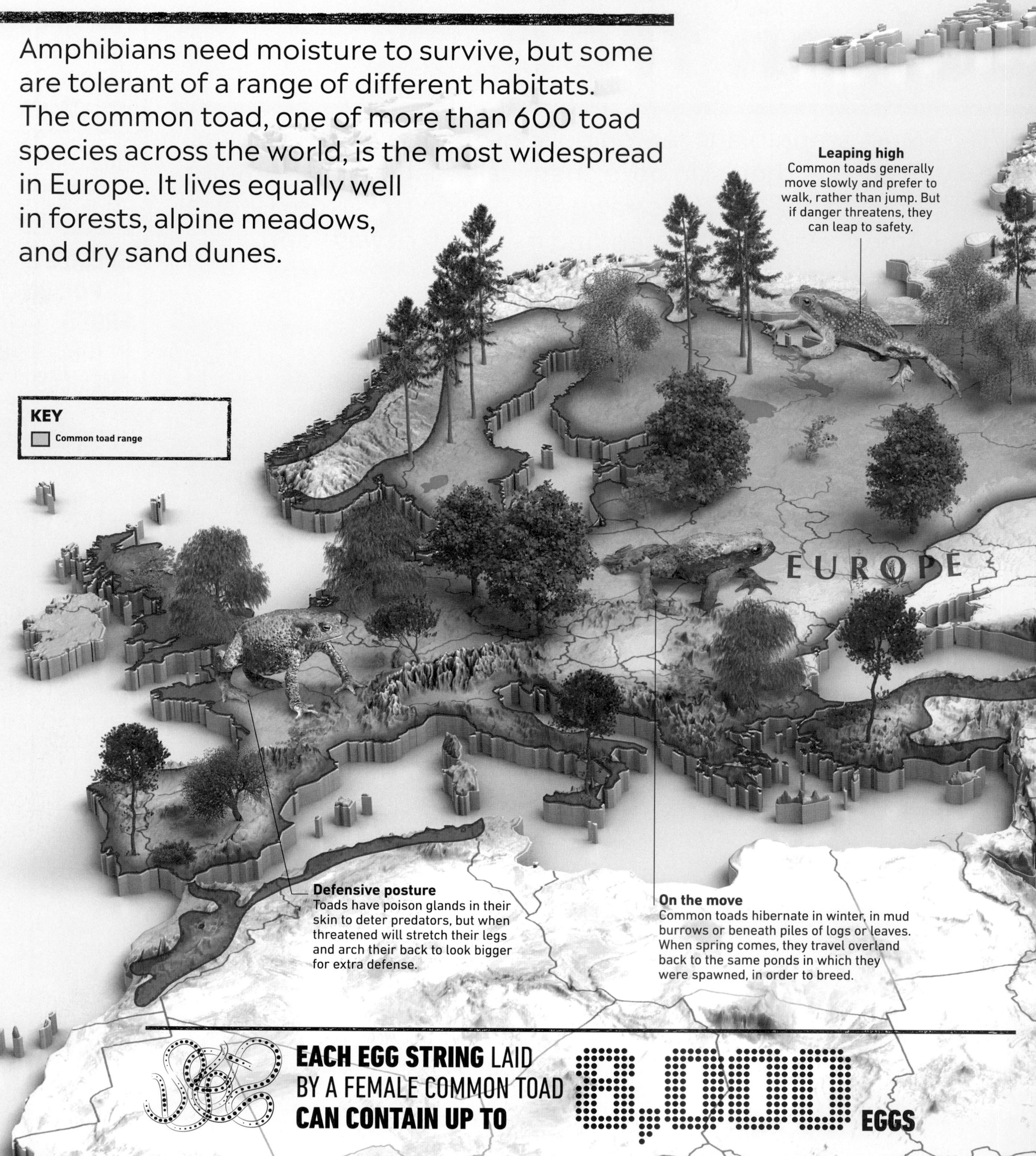

Leaping high
Common toads generally move slowly and prefer to walk, rather than jump. But if danger threatens, they can leap to safety.

Defensive posture
Toads have poison glands in their skin to deter predators, but when threatened will stretch their legs and arch their back to look bigger for extra defense.

On the move
Common toads hibernate in winter, in mud burrows or beneath piles of logs or leaves. When spring comes, they travel overland back to the same ponds in which they were spawned, in order to breed.

EACH EGG STRING LAID BY A FEMALE COMMON TOAD **CAN CONTAIN UP TO** 8,000 **EGGS**

Breeding pools
Like most amphibians, toads lay their eggs in pools of water. The female common toad lays her eggs in two long strings, each up to 16 ft (5 m) long. The eggs will hatch into aquatic larvae, or tadpoles.

Mass migration
Each springtime, large numbers of common toads emerge from hibernation and travel to their breeding pools. In some places, special toad-crossing tunnels have been built to help them cross roads safely.

Mating toads
When mating in ponds, the male toad grabs the larger female around the waist just behind her front legs and then fertilizes the strings of eggs as they are released into the water.

ASIA

Temperate belt
The common toad is found throughout much of Europe—in the temperate belt south of the cold polar regions and north of hotter Africa and Asia. It lives most of its life away from water, hiding in damp, shady places, returning to the water only to breed.

Bulging eyes
The large eyes of a common toad give it good night vision. Common toads are most active at night, using the cover of darkness to hunt for prey.

Tongue attack
The toad catches invertebrate prey, such as slugs, snails, and spiders, with a long, sticky-tipped tongue that shoots out of its mouth at lightning speed.

REPTILES

Reptile facts

Scaly and cold-blooded, reptiles first appeared around 310 million years ago and were the first backboned animals that could live entirely on land. From desert snakes to migrating sea turtles, reptiles today are scattered throughout the world, except the very coldest habitats.

WHAT IS A REPTILE?

Vertebrates
From slithery snakes to giant tortoises, all reptiles are supported by a bony skeleton.

Cold-blooded
The body temperature of all reptiles changes depending on their environment.

Lay eggs
Most reptiles, from crocodiles to lizards, lay soft, leathery, and waterproof eggs.

Live young
Some snakes and lizards do not lay eggs like most other reptiles, but instead give birth to live young.

Scaly skin
Reptilian skin is covered in protective scales, or in some cases, horny plates.

REPTILE TYPES

ESTIMATED NUMBER OF REPTILE SPECIES: 11,340

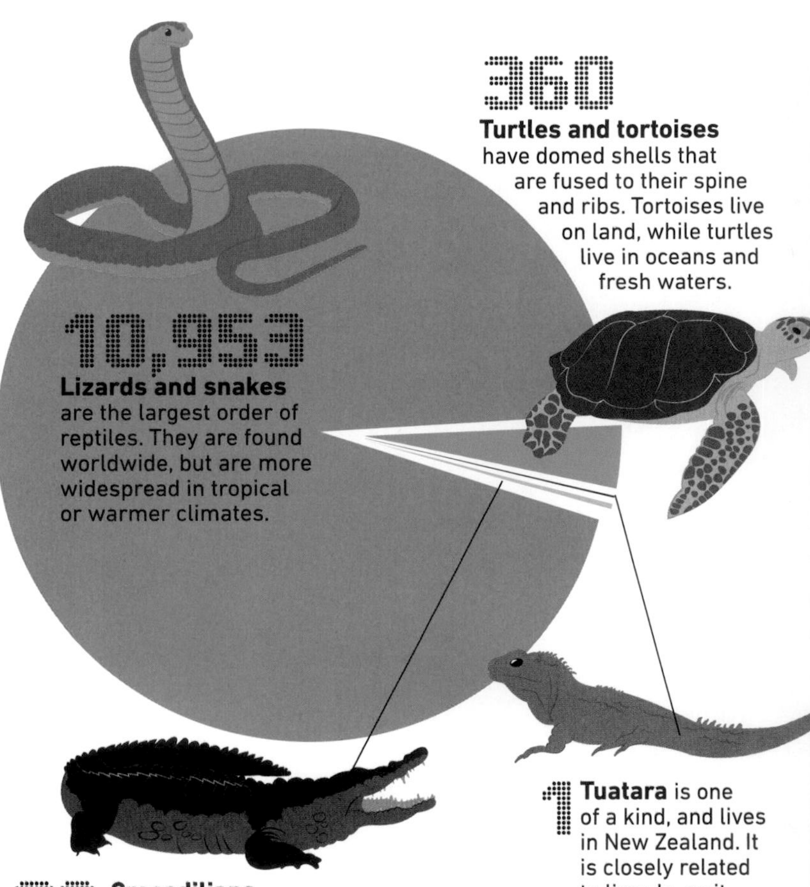

10,953
Lizards and snakes
are the largest order of reptiles. They are found worldwide, but are more widespread in tropical or warmer climates.
360
Turtles and tortoises
have domed shells that are fused to their spine and ribs. Tortoises live on land, while turtles live in oceans and fresh waters.
1
Tuatara is one of a kind, and lives in New Zealand. It is closely related to lizards, as it has small scales on its skin.
26
Crocodilians
include crocodiles, alligators, and their relatives. They are the biggest and most formidable of all reptiles. They spend most of their time in water, although some hunt on land.

EXTREME HABITATS

From the freezing Arctic to underground burrows in the desert, some reptiles survive and thrive in the most incredible ways.

Common European adders are the only snake species found within the Arctic Circle. Its huge range also extends from temperate woodlands to the European Alps 9,840 ft (3,000 m) high.

Gopher tortoises survive the intense heat and cold of the American Mojave Desert by burrowing underground with their sharp claws. They spend up to 95 percent of their lives in these burrows.

Sea snakes are the best-adapted reptile for life in water. All true sea snakes give birth to live young, without ever coming ashore to lay eggs. They live mainly in tropical oceans.

LONGEST MIGRATION

LEATHERBACK TURTLES CAN TRAVEL **12,750 MILES** (20,500 KM) FROM THEIR **INDONESIAN** BREEDING GROUND TO FEED OFF THE PACIFIC COAST OF **THE USA.**

BIGGEST **GATHERING**

EACH **SPRING** INSIDE THE SNAKE DENS OF NARCISSE, **MANITOBA, CANADA, 75,000 RED-SIDED GARTER SNAKES** CONGREGATE IN A MATING FRENZY, WITH UP TO **100 MALES** VYING FOR **EVERY FEMALE.**

SMALLEST REPTILE

THE **VIRGIN ISLANDS DWARF SPHAERO** IS ONLY 5/8 IN (1.6 CM) LONG.

OLDEST REPTILE

BORN IN 1832, THE **OLDEST-LIVING** LAND ANIMAL IS A **SEYCHELLES GIANT TORTOISE** CALLED **JONATHAN**.

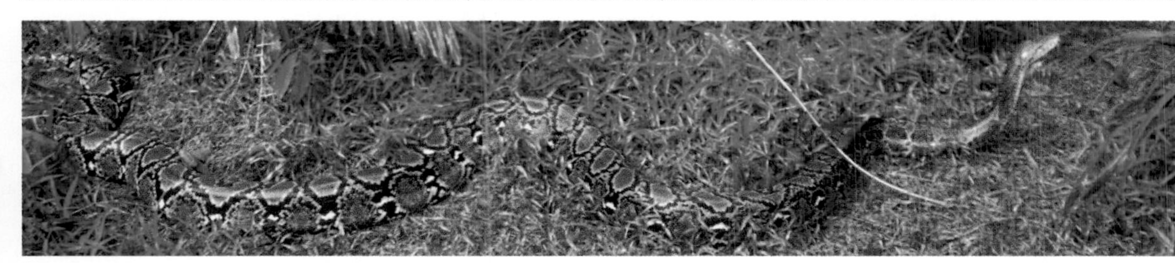

LONGEST REPTILE

THE **RETICULATED PYTHON** OF SOUTHEAST ASIA HAS SET THE RECORD-BREAKING LENGTH OF 33 FT (10 M).

FASTEST **REPTILE**

In a reptilian race between the fastest snake and swiftest lizard, the lizard would easily cross the finish line first.

FASTEST SNAKE: SIDEWINDER AT **18 MPH** (28 KPH)

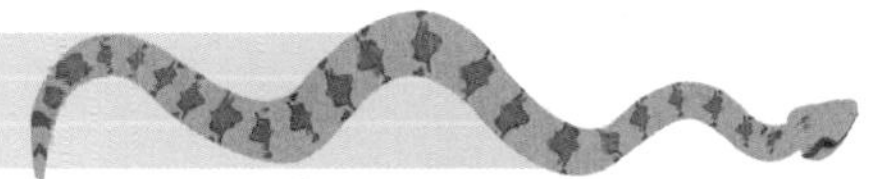

FASTEST LIZARD: BEARDED DRAGON AT **25 MPH** (40 KPH)

SNAKE **MOTION**

A snake can move in four main ways. Some species can switch between styles of moving, depending on the surface.

Straight
Scales along a snake's belly provide traction on the ground for it to propel itself in a line, using the muscles around its long ribcage.

Sidewinding
In open spaces such as sandy deserts, some snakes fling their head sideways through the air, with the rest of the body following.

Tail is pressed to the ground as snake bunches up

Snake launches, then bunches up again

Concertina
To get a good grip on a smooth surface, a snake can bunch up before pulling its back end up and launching itself forward.

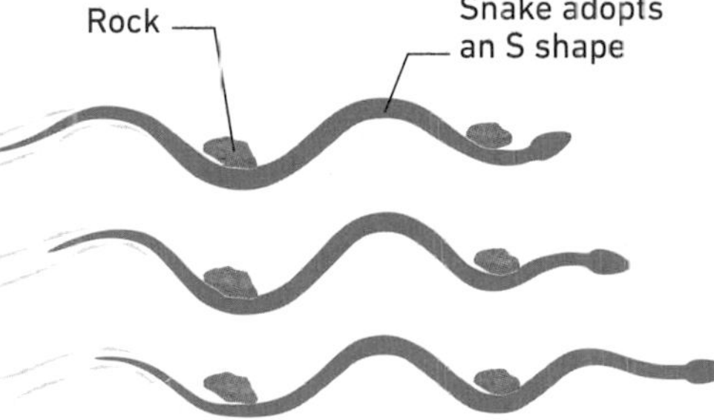

Serpentine
This common style involves a snake pushing itself off a bump on a surface or an object, and continuing forward in a wavy motion.

HIGHEST-LIVING REPTILE

THE **RED TAIL TOAD-HEADED LIZARD** HAS BEEN SEEN AT 17,390 FT (5,300 M). IT LIVES IN THE QIANGTANG PLATEAU IN NORTHERN TIBET.

SMART REPTILE

The mugger crocodile in India has been observed using sticks to lure birds, such as egrets or herons, who may be looking to build a nest. It waits motionless and partially submerged, then snaps up its unsuspecting prey when it is close enough.

KEY
Volcán Wolf giant tortoise
Fernandina giant tortoise
Volcán Alcedo giant tortoise
Santiago giant tortoise
Santa Cruz giant tortoise
San Cristóbal giant tortoise
Española giant tortoise
ANIMALS IN DANGER
Of the 14 species of Galápagos giant tortoise listed by the IUCN, six are regarded as critically endangered, three as endangered, two as extinct, and the rest as vulnerable. Hunting and habitat destruction have been threats in the past, but now conservation measures are slowly making progress.
Isla Pinta
Isla Marchena
PACIFIC OCEAN
Santiago giant tortoise
Giant tortoises on Santiago have been hunted extensively in the past, but protection is now helping to restore the species. Their shells are intermediate, between dome-shaped and saddleback-shaped.
Volcán Wolf giant tortoise
Volcán Wolf, the highest volcano in the Galápagos, on the island of Isabela, is home to a species of giant tortoises that have either domed shells or saddleback shells, like the one shown here.
Isla Santiago
Volcán Alcedo giant tortoise
The different habitats on Isabela has meant that different species of giant tortoise have evolved there. Those on the volcano of Alcedo have a black, domed shell.
Isla Pinzón
Isla Fernandina
Isla Isabela
Fernandina giant tortoise
For more than 100 years, the saddleback-shelled tortoises from the island of Fernandina were thought to be extinct, until a century-old female was discovered in 2019, raising hopes that others have survived too.
Horny beak
Tortoises lack teeth, but instead have a sharp-edged beak that is used to crop vegetation – mostly in the form of grass, shrubs, cactuses, and the occasional fruit.
Bony shell
Like other tortoises, giant tortoises have a hard, protective shell made from bony plates that are fused to the reptile's backbone and ribs.
THE ESTIMATED LIFESPAN OF A GALÁPAGOS GIANT TORTOISE IS 170 YEARS
Santa Cruz giant tortoise

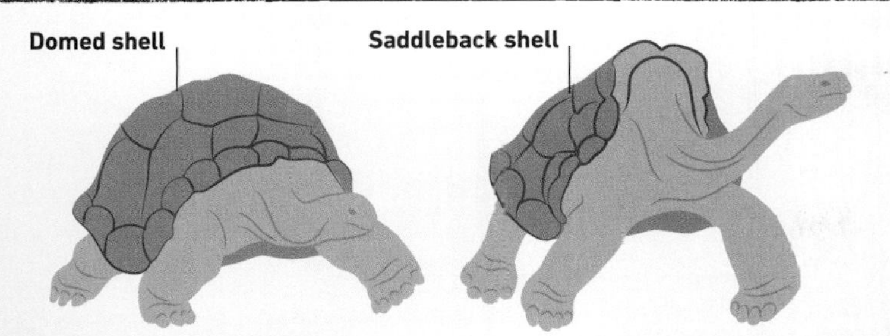

Shell shape and diet
On wetter islands with plenty of ground plants to graze, the shells of Galápagos giant tortoises are dome-shaped. But on drier islands, tortoises have evolved raised shells – called saddlebacks – and long necks. This helps them reach tall cactuses that grow higher from the ground.

Lonesome George
In 1971, scientists found the only surviving Pinta Island giant tortoise. The rest of its kind had died out, due to the overgrazing by goats introduced to the island. Named Lonesome George, this tortoise became a symbol of conservation, living out his life in captivity. He died in 2012.

Santa Cruz giant tortoise
The dome-shelled giant tortoises of Santa Cruz live in separate populations on this island, and studies suggest that they might be different species.

Isla Santa Fe

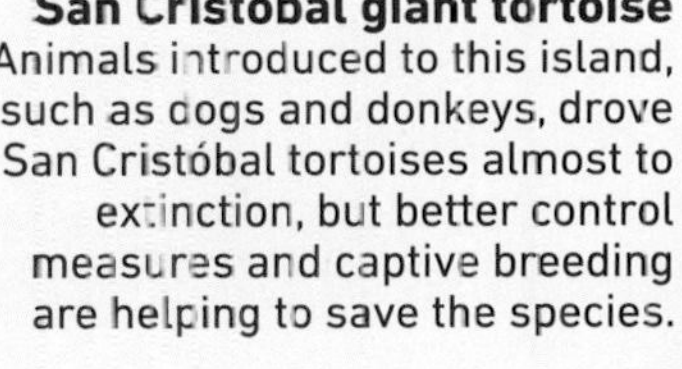

San Cristóbal giant tortoise
Animals introduced to this island, such as dogs and donkeys, drove San Cristóbal tortoises almost to extinction, but better control measures and captive breeding are helping to save the species.

Island giants

The Galápagos Islands erupted from the ocean more than three million years ago. Tortoises landed on their shores after floating across the waters from South America. With no natural predators, they evolved into giants and, as they adapted to the different conditions and food sources on each island, into separate species. Seven of these are shown on this map.

Española giant tortoise
On one of the oldest and most barren of the Galápagos Islands, Española tortoises have especially high-saddled shells to help them reach up to nibble on the scarce food growing here, such as cactuses.

Isla Española

Galápagos Islands

Isla Santa Maria

Galápagos giant tortoises

Tortoises are slow-moving reptiles with a heavy, protective shell. Some of the biggest tortoises on Earth live on the rugged, volcanic Galápagos Islands far out in the Pacific Ocean. Each island is home to its own species.

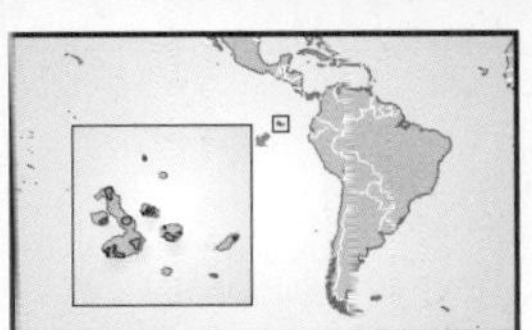

Who lives where?

The crocodiles are the largest group and the most wide ranging—16 species live in either Africa, Asia, or the Americas. Alligators and caimans, of which there are eight species in total, only occur in the Americas and China. Two species of gharials live in Southeast Asia.

American alligator
The American alligator is the northernmost crocodilian in the Americas. During the coolest months, it basks in the sun to keep warm.

Spectacled caiman
Caimans, found in tropical parts of the Americas, are smaller relatives of alligators. The spectacled caiman is one of the most common, found in slow-moving rivers, ponds, and lakes across its range.

Nile crocodile
The most widespread crocodilian on the African continent, the Nile crocodile is also its biggest freshwater predator. Adults prey on antelope coming to drink at waterholes.

Crocodile teeth
Crocodilians are the only reptiles that grow teeth from sockets in the jaws—more like those of mammals. Teeth are replaced as they wear down or fall out.

Saltwater crocodile

Boy or girl?

Crocodilian eggs get incubated in a nest, wrapped in warm soil or vegetation, before hatching like this little Nile crocodile. There can be up to 80 eggs in a nest, and the sex of each depends on its temperature. The warmer eggs turn male and the cooler ones female.

Crocodilians

The world's biggest reptiles live wherever it is warm enough for them to hunt and raise a family—by rivers and lakes in tropical regions on both sides of the equator. They are divided into three groups: alligators and caimans, crocodiles, and gharials.

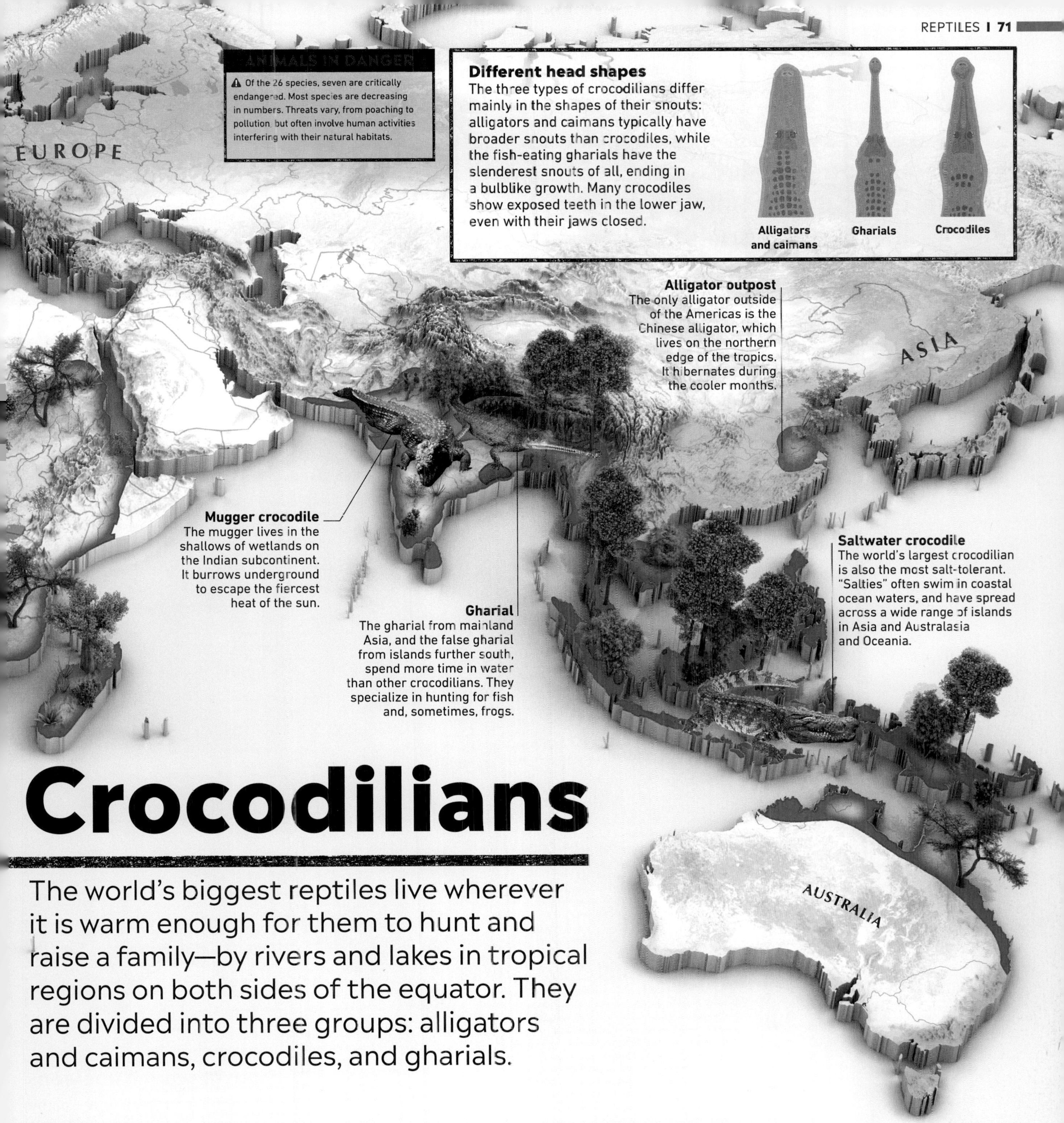

ANIMALS IN DANGER

⚠ Of the 26 species, seven are critically endangered. Most species are decreasing in numbers. Threats vary, from poaching to pollution, but often involve human activities interfering with their natural habitats.

Different head shapes

The three types of crocodilians differ mainly in the shapes of their snouts: alligators and caimans typically have broader snouts than crocodiles, while the fish-eating gharials have the slenderest snouts of all, ending in a bulblike growth. Many crocodiles show exposed teeth in the lower jaw, even with their jaws closed.

Alligators and caimans | Gharials | Crocodiles

Alligator outpost

The only alligator outside of the Americas is the Chinese alligator, which lives on the northern edge of the tropics. It hibernates during the cooler months.

Mugger crocodile

The mugger lives in the shallows of wetlands on the Indian subcontinent. It burrows underground to escape the fiercest heat of the sun.

Gharial

The gharial from mainland Asia, and the false gharial from islands further south, spend more time in water than other crocodilians. They specialize in hunting for fish and, sometimes, frogs.

Saltwater crocodile

The world's largest crocodilian is also the most salt-tolerant. "Salties" often swim in coastal ocean waters, and have spread across a wide range of islands in Asia and Australasia and Oceania.

THE **NUMBER OF TEETH** OF A **GHARIAL—MORE** THAN **ANY OTHER CROCODILIAN**

THERE ARE **FEWER THAN 80** ADULT **CHINESE ALLIGATORS** LEFT IN THE WILD

Chameleons

KEY
Madagascan giant chameleon
Labord's chameleon
Elongate leaf chameleon
Panther chameleon
Parson's chameleon

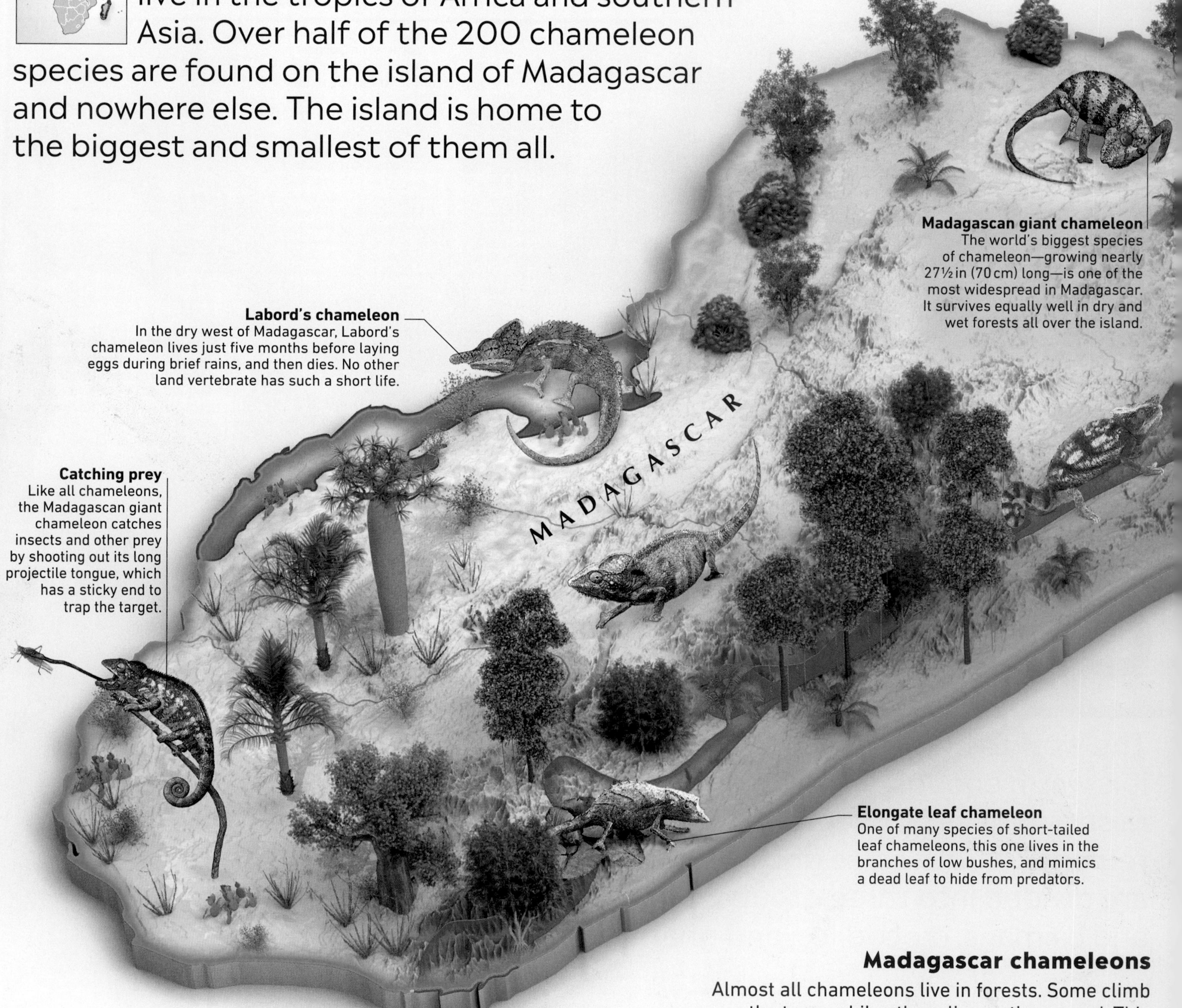

Strange-looking, slow-moving lizards with conical eyes and grasping tails, chameleons live in the tropics of Africa and southern Asia. Over half of the 200 chameleon species are found on the island of Madagascar and nowhere else. The island is home to the biggest and smallest of them all.

MADAGASCAR

Madagascan giant chameleon The world's biggest species of chameleon—growing nearly 27½ in (70 cm) long—is one of the most widespread in Madagascar. It survives equally well in dry and wet forests all over the island.

Labord's chameleon In the dry west of Madagascar, Labord's chameleon lives just five months before laying eggs during brief rains, and then dies. No other land vertebrate has such a short life.

Catching prey Like all chameleons, the Madagascan giant chameleon catches insects and other prey by shooting out its long projectile tongue, which has a sticky end to trap the target.

Elongate leaf chameleon One of many species of short-tailed leaf chameleons, this one lives in the branches of low bushes, and mimics a dead leaf to hide from predators.

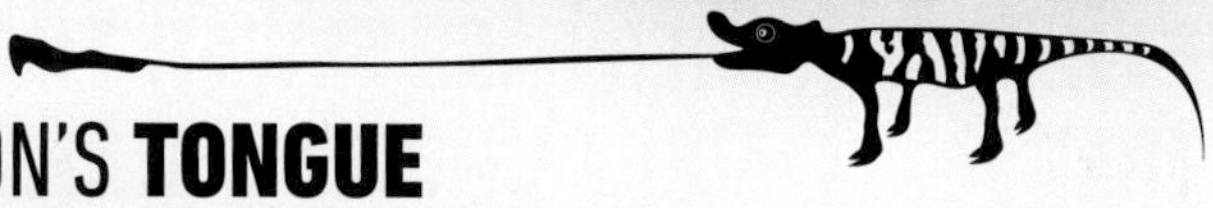

Madagascar chameleons

Almost all chameleons live in forests. Some climb the trees while others live on the ground. This map shows five of the chameleon species that live on Madagascar. The island is drier in the west and wetter in the east, and it is in the rich rainforests of eastern Madagascar that most species occur, but many are now threatened by deforestation.

A CHAMELEON'S **TONGUE** CAN EXTEND **TWICE THE LENGTH** OF ITS **BODY**

ANIMALS IN DANGER

Labord's chameleon
IUCN status: vulnerable
Population estimate: unknown

Elongate leaf chameleon
IUCN status: vulnerable
Population estimate: unknown

Parson's chameleon
IUCN status: near threatened
Population estimate: unknown

Panther chameleon
Male panther chameleons vary a great deal in color depending on where they live. Some are red, green, and yellow, others are turquoise-green or grayish. Most females are pinkish-brown.

Chameleon colors

Chameleons have a famous ability to change color, usually according to their mood. A male panther chameleon switches to an especially bright pattern when showing off to potential mates or competing males. The color change comes from tiny crystals in the skin that reflect light in different ways.

Parson's chameleon
In some chameleons, such as the Parson's chameleon, the males have prominent horns on their nose, which they use in "jousting" contests when defending territory.

Body shape
A chameleon's body has flat sides, making its high-arched back look like a crest running from head to tail. Green or brown colors help hide chameleons among leaves.

Feet for gripping
The five toes of a chameleon foot are fused together into two mitten-like pads. This unique arrangement helps them hold on tightly to any branch.

Parson's chameleon

Prehensile tail
Chameleons are among the very few lizards with completely prehensile tails. This means they can use their tail like a fifth limb to grip branches as they climb through trees.

Mini chameleon

The world's smallest chameleon, known only by its scientific name of *Brookesia micra*, is also one of the smallest reptiles in the world. It can grow to just 1⅛ in (3 cm) long, tail included, and spends its life among leaf litter. It was discovered on the tiny islet of Nosy Hara off the north coast of Madagascar.

Armored lizard

The dragon-like armadillo girdled lizard is covered by protective spiny plates—except on its underside. To shield its soft belly from predator attacks, it grabs hold of its tail and curls up in a ball, like an armadillo (see p.109). This lizard lives in large family groups inside rock crevices in South Africa's western deserts.

Green anaconda

All snakes prey on other animals, but the biggest kill by constriction, rather than venom. The green anaconda, at home in South America, is the heaviest of all constrictors, and can tackle animals the size of small deer.

River snake
More than 1,000 rivers run through the Amazon Basin, making it the perfect habitat for the green anaconda, which can swim faster than it crawls on land.

Big meal
Loosely connected jaw bones and a stretchy body help an anaconda swallow prey whole. Large prey, such as deer or caimans, can take weeks to digest.

ANACONDAS **GIVE BIRTH** TO UP TO **50** **YOUNG AT A TIME**

Squeezed prey
Constrictors such as anacondas kill not by crushing, but by suffocation. The snake squeezes tighter each time its victim exhales, so breathing becomes impossible, and the heart stops.

Wetland giant

The green anaconda grows so heavy that adult snakes tend to stick to rivers and wetlands, where their bodies are supported by water. The river-filled Amazon Basin merges with grasslands in the south, where much of the land is flooded during the rainy season, making a large part of South America prime anaconda habitat.

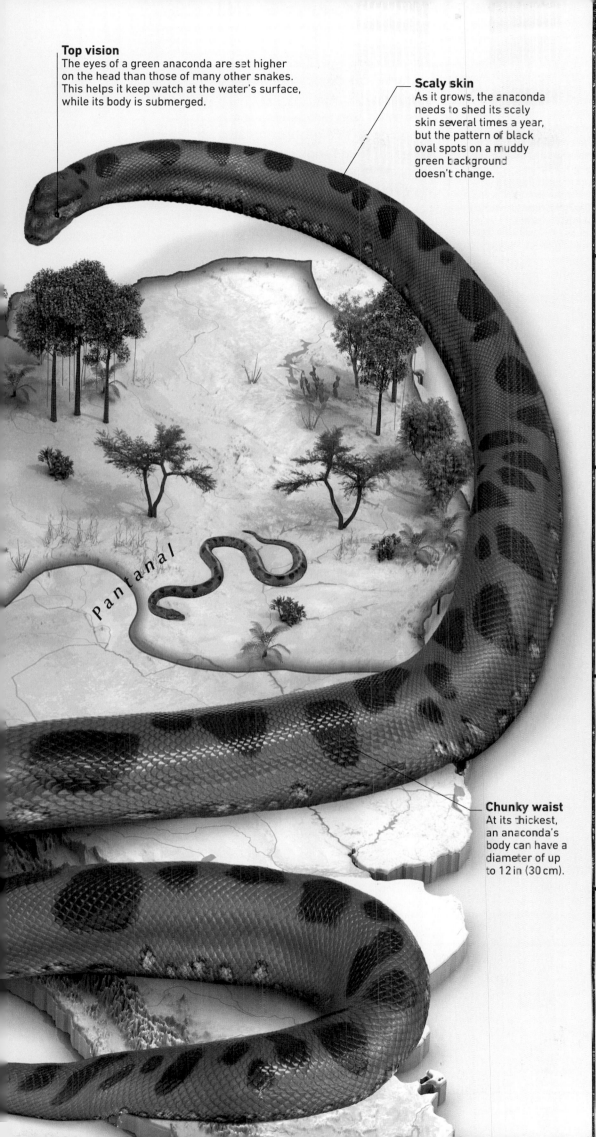

Top vision
The eyes of a green anaconda are set higher on the head than those of many other snakes. This helps it keep watch at the water's surface, while its body is submerged.

Scaly skin
As it grows, the anaconda needs to shed its scaly skin several times a year, but the pattern of black oval spots on a muddy green background doesn't change.

Chunky waist
At its thickest, an anaconda's body can have a diameter of up to 12 in (30 cm).

OTHER LARGE CONSTRICTORS

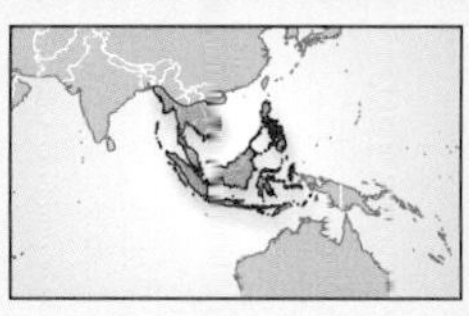

Reticulated python
The green anaconda is the heaviest, but the longest snake is likely to be the reticulated python from Southeast Asia, with recorded lengths of more than 23 ft (7 m).

African rock python
The biggest snake in Africa, growing to 20 ft (6 m) long, the African rock python has the strength to prey on large crocodiles.

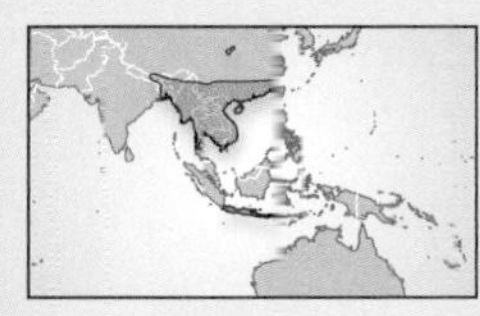

Burmese python
Weighing around 400 lb (180 kg), the Burmese python from Southeast Asia is the heaviest recorded snake after the green anaconda.

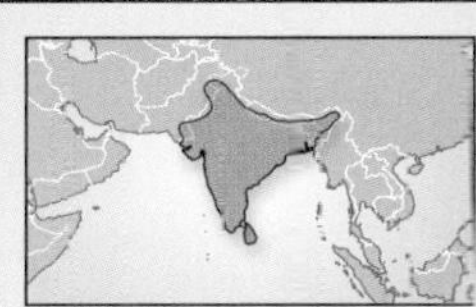

Indian rock python
Only slightly smaller than the Burmese and African rock pythons, this snake swims well and is common in wetlands and forests of India and Sri Lanka.

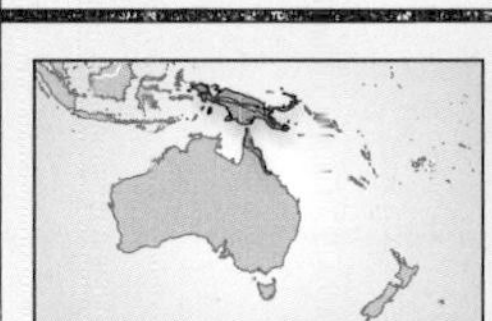

Amethystine python
Australia's largest snake hunts possums and wallabies, and sometimes slides into human homes. It is also widespread in New Guinea and nearby islands.

NORTH AMERICA
SOUTH AMERICA
AFRICA
Deadly snakes
The warm tropics are home to the greatest number of snake species. The most dangerous venomous types belong to two groups: vipers, with large, hinged fangs, and elapids, with shorter fangs that are always raised. This map shows seven of the world's deadliest snakes.
Western diamondback rattlesnake
One of the largest venomous snakes found in North America, this rattlesnake hunts desert rodents, but is also responsible for many human injuries in the US.
Common lance head
A relative of the rattlesnakes, the common lance head moves about at night, and is one of the most dangerous vipers found in the tropical forests of South America.
Fangs
Rattlesnakes are vipers, and have some of the biggest fangs of any snake. The largest rattlesnakes can have fangs more than 2 in (5 cm) long.
Warning rattle
The tail tip rattle is made up of special scales that produce a warning sound when shaken if predators come too close.
Black mamba
Named for the black lining of its mouth, this elapid is one of the longest and fastest of the venomous snakes in Africa and quickly inflicts multiple dangerous bites.
Western diamondback rattlesnake
Snake venom
Venom is a poisonous fluid that flows from glands in the snake's upper jaw. When the snake bites, a muscle squeezes venom out through the fangs. Viper fangs reach further forward than those of elapids.
Elapid
Elapids have small, fixed fangs at the back of the jaw
Viper
Viper fangs swing forward as the jaw opens
KEY
Western diamondback rattlesnake
Common lance head
Black mamba
Saw-scaled viper
Indian cobra
Many-banded krait
Tiger snake

Venomous snakes

There are around 3,850 species of snakes around the world, and about 20 percent of these are venomous. They use their venom to kill their prey—but some also strike in self-defense and, when they do so, some species can be dangerous to humans, such as the ones shown here.

Arabian Peninsula

INDIA

ASIA

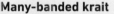

AUSTRALIA

Saw-scaled viper
With a dangerous bite, and often found living close to humans, this snake is probably responsible for more human deaths than any other. Similar saw-scaled vipers occur elsewhere on the Arabian Peninsula and in parts of Africa.

Indian cobra
The Indian cobra is an elapid that warns anyone approaching that it will strike in self-defense. It extends ribs close to its neck to produce a flat hood, while rising up to appear bigger.

Many-banded krait
Kraits are boldly patterned elapid snakes found across Asia. Living near water, the many-banded krait hides during the day and hunts at night, preying on fish. If surprised, it uses its deadly bite in self-defense.

Tiger snake
The tiger snake is one of many highly venomous elapid snakes found in Australia. Individuals vary in color and not all have the stripes that give the species its name.

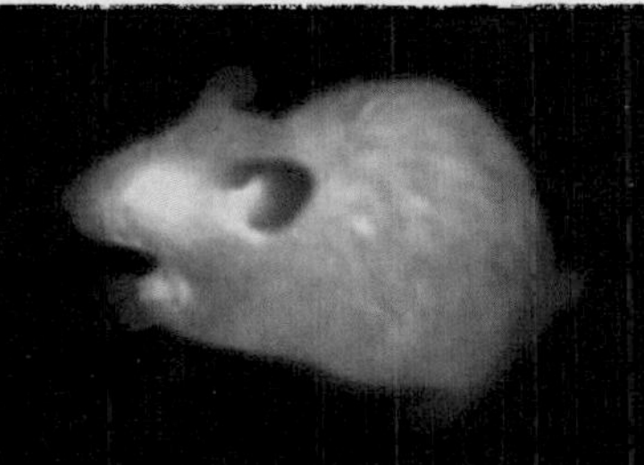

Hunting by heat
Vipers have an extra sense that helps them locate prey. Heat-sensitive pits on their head allow them to "see" the body heat of warm-blooded animals, in the same way that the mouse shows up against a cold background in this thermal image.

ABOUT 200 **SNAKE SPECIES** HAVE **VENOM** THAT IS HARMFUL TO **HUMANS**

AROUND 138,000 **PEOPLE DIE** FROM A SNAKE **BITE** EVERY **YEAR**

BIRDS

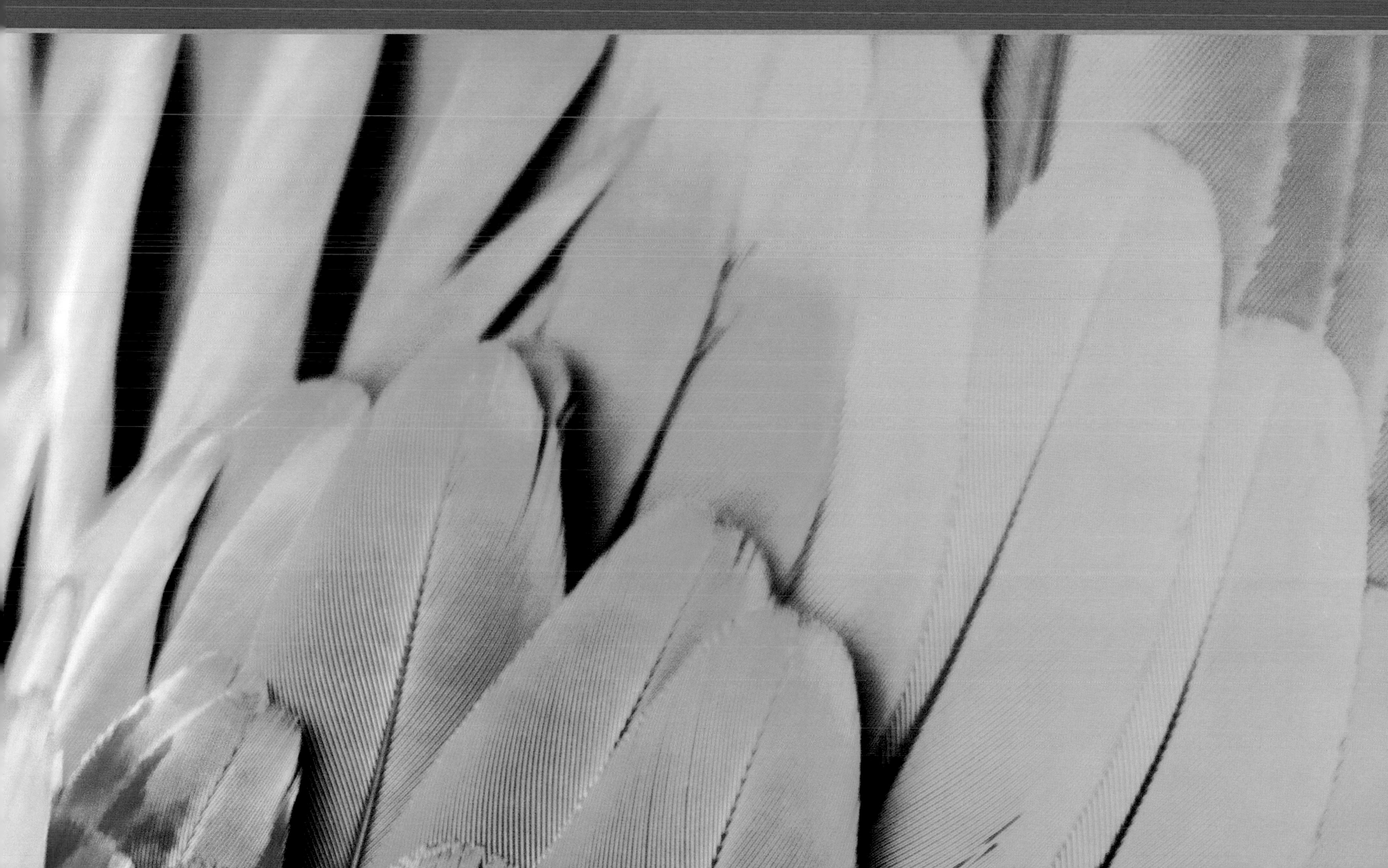

Bird facts

Evolving from two-legged dinosaurs, the first birds took flight about 140 million years ago. Today, birds are found on every continent and in a diverse range of habitats, from grasslands to deserts. Many birds migrate incredibly long distances to breed or find food.

WHAT IS A BIRD?

Vertebrates
Birds have thin and lightweight, yet strong, internal skeletons made of bone.

Warm-blooded
From humid rainforests to chilly mountaintops, birds generate and maintain a stable body temperature.

Lay eggs
Birds breed by laying hard eggs, which chicks crack open when ready to hatch.

Most fly
Using their wings, most birds can take to the skies, however some birds are flightless.

Feathered
Feathers are important for retaining body heat and helping birds fly.

BIRD **TYPES**

ESTIMATED NUMBER OF BIRD SPECIES: 11,500

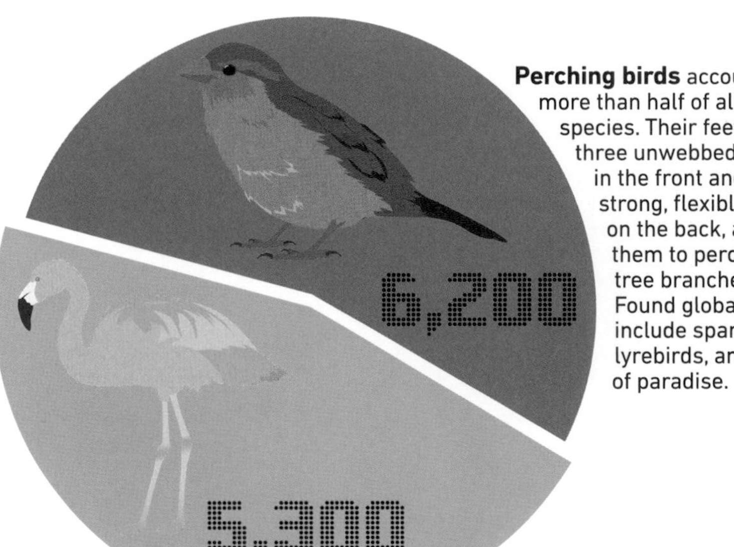

Perching birds account for more than half of all bird species. Their feet have three unwebbed toes in the front and one strong, flexible toe on the back, allowing them to perch on tree branches. Found globally, they include sparrows, lyrebirds, and birds of paradise.

Non-perching birds account for all other species. They include a wide range of birds located across the world including parrots, owls, flamingos, and birds of prey, as well as flightless birds, such as ostriches, emus, and penguins.

COLOMBIA HAS OVER 1,850 BIRD SPECIES—**MORE THAN ANY OTHER COUNTRY** IN THE WORLD.

HIBERNATING BIRD

The common poorwill, seen here on a roof, is the only bird species known to hibernate. Its diet of insects rapidly declines during winter, so it goes into a state of hibernation for weeks or even months. This bird is found in the grassy areas of North America.

LONGEST **MIGRATION**

ARCTIC TERNS FLY AN AMAZING 59,650 MILES (96,000 KM) FROM THEIR BREEDING GROUND IN THE **NORTH ATLANTIC** TO **ANTARCTICA** AND BACK AGAIN.

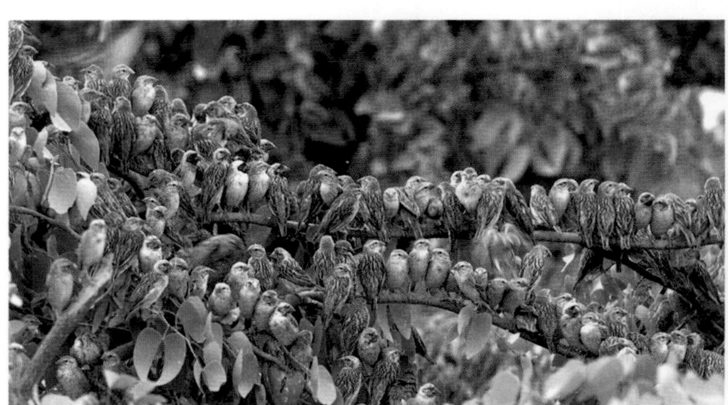

BIGGEST **GATHERING**

Flocks of more than 1.5 billion red-billed quelea have been witnessed flying over the African savanna. In such great numbers, this small bird is a constant threat to crop farmers. In fact, it is such a pest, it is often called the "feathered locust."

BILL SHAPES

Over millions of years, birds have evolved many different bill shapes. Here are five of them, each designed to help the bird eat or catch its prey.

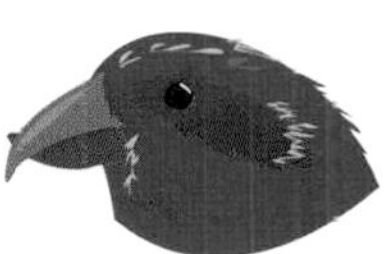

Seed-eater
Birds such as crossbills have strong bills for eating seeds. The crossbill can extract seeds from pine cones with its overlapping bill.

Water-sifter
Flamingos have long, wide bills that they sweep from side to side in shallow waters, sifting out animals to eat.

Nectar-gatherer
The pointed bills are designed for precision. Sunbirds' bills also curve downward, which is ideal for extracting flower nectar.

Mud probe
Birds with long, sensitive bills can explore soft mud in search of prey. The snipe looks for snails and small crustaceans.

Butchery tool
This hooked bill, as seen on a golden eagle, is perfect for stripping meat from the bones of fish, birds, or mammals.

THE **LARGEST FLYING BIRD** IS THE **WANDERING ALBATROSS,** WITH A WINGSPAN OF **12 FT** (3.6 M).

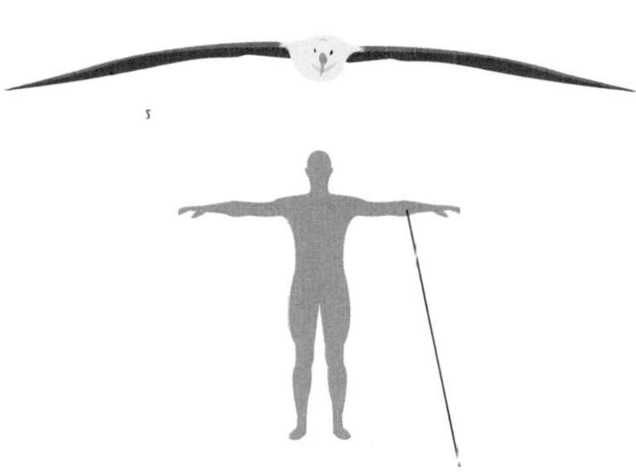

The average female arm span is about 5.2 ft (1.6 m).

BIGGEST BIRD AND EGGS

THE OSTRICH, A FLIGHTLESS BIRD FROM SUB-SAHARAN AFRICA, IS THE WORLD'S TALLEST BIRD.

IT ALSO BEARS THE LARGEST EGGS, UP TO **6 IN** (15 CM) LONG—NEARLY THREE TIMES LONGER THAN A HEN'S EGG.

SMALLEST BIRD

THE **BEE HUMMINGBIRD** IS JUST **2.4 IN** (6 CM) LONG. THIS TINY BIRD IS NATIVE TO **CUBA.**

FASTEST BIRD

Found throughout the world, peregrine falcons are formidable hunters. They swoop in on prey, such as other birds and bats, at a record-breaking speed.

SWOOPING SPEED = **200 MPH** (320 KPH)

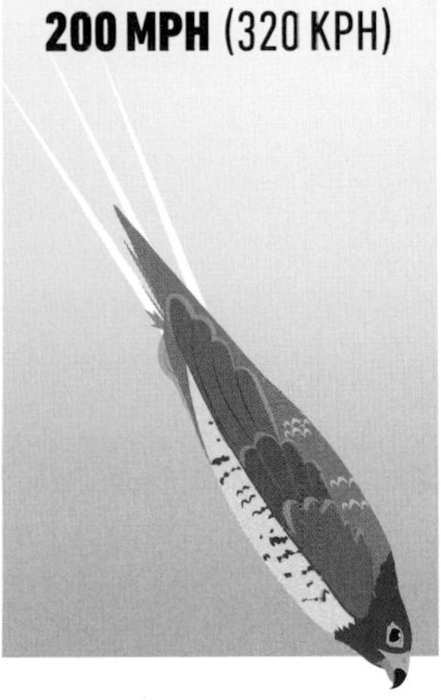

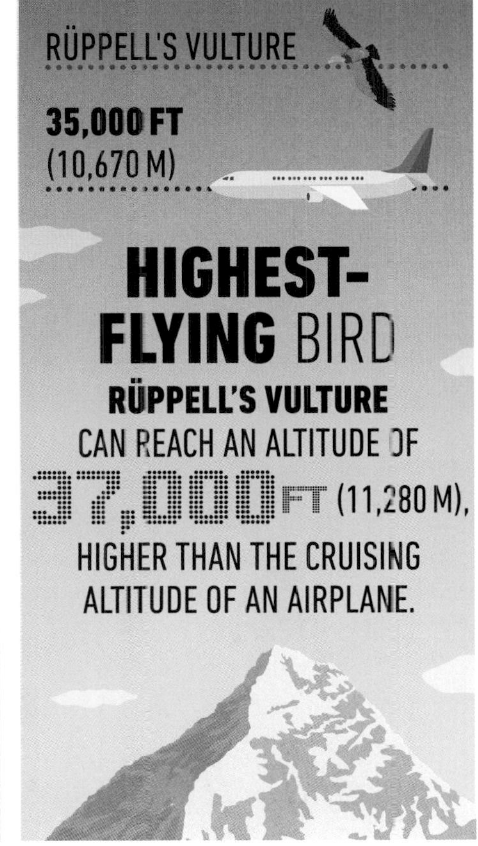

HIGHEST-FLYING BIRD

RÜPPELL'S VULTURE CAN REACH AN ALTITUDE OF **37,000 FT** (11,280 M), HIGHER THAN THE CRUISING ALTITUDE OF AN AIRPLANE.

BIGGEST NEST

SOCIABLE WEAVERS MAKE AND MAINTAIN NESTS THAT CAN HOUSE UP TO **500** BIRDS.

SMART BIRD

Found in the remote Pacific islands after which it is named, the New Caledonian crow can manipulate and use twigs to dig out prey, such as grubs, from trees. These intelligent forest-dwelling birds are the first to be observed making and using tools in this way.

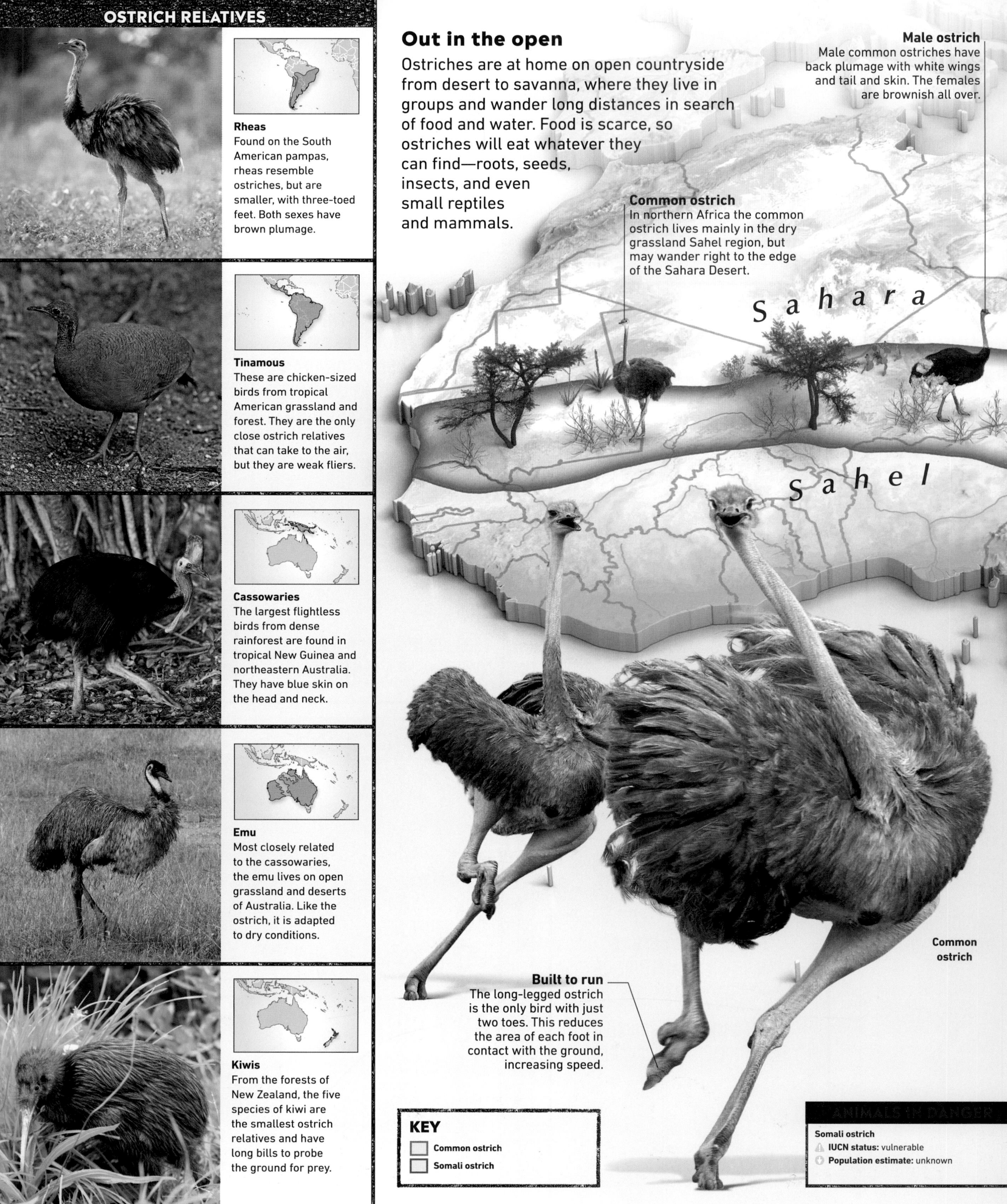
OSTRICH RELATIVES
Rheas
Found on the South American pampas, rheas resemble ostriches, but are smaller, with three-toed feet. Both sexes have brown plumage.
Tinamous
These are chicken-sized birds from tropical American grassland and forest. They are the only close ostrich relatives that can take to the air, but they are weak fliers.
Cassowaries
The largest flightless birds from dense rainforest are found in tropical New Guinea and northeastern Australia. They have blue skin on the head and neck.
Emu
Most closely related to the cassowaries, the emu lives on open grassland and deserts of Australia. Like the ostrich, it is adapted to dry conditions.
Kiwis
From the forests of New Zealand, the five species of kiwi are the smallest ostrich relatives and have long bills to probe the ground for prey.
Out in the open
Ostriches are at home on open countryside from desert to savanna, where they live in groups and wander long distances in search of food and water. Food is scarce, so ostriches will eat whatever they can find—roots, seeds, insects, and even small reptiles and mammals.
Male ostrich
Male common ostriches have back plumage with white wings and tail and skin. The females are brownish all over.
Common ostrich
In northern Africa the common ostrich lives mainly in the dry grassland Sahel region, but may wander right to the edge of the Sahara Desert.
Sahara
Sahel
Common ostrich
Built to run
The long-legged ostrich is the only bird with just two toes. This reduces the area of each foot in contact with the ground, increasing speed.
KEY
Common ostrich
Somali ostrich
ANIMALS IN DANGER
Somali ostrich
IUCN status: vulnerable
Population estimate: unknown

Ostriches

A bird that can't fly, and roams where there is very little cover, has to run fast to escape predators. The flightless ostrich does just that. As well as being the world's biggest bird it is the fastest animal on two legs. There are two species and both live in open habitats in Africa.

Ostrich chicks
All female ostriches in the group lay their eggs in a communal nest, so adults may end up guarding large crèches of chicks.

Somali ostrich
This species lives in the eastern horn of Africa—in Somalia, Ethiopia, and Kenya. Males have a gray head, neck, legs, and feet, and a deeper black plumage than the common ostrich.

Masai region
In the Masai region of east Africa, common ostriches have a reddish-tinge to their neck but are more closely related to the gray-necked ostriches further south.

Desert dweller
In the southernmost part of their range, common ostriches live in hot, dry desert.

Rift Valley
The two species of ostrich are separated by the Great Rift Valley (pictured below). On the eastern side, the Somali ostrich has split away from common ostriches and evolved into a separate species.

MALE OSTRICHES STAND UP TO **9 FT** (2.7 M) **TALL**

AT TOP SPEED AN OSTRICH CAN RUN ABOUT 43 MPH (70 KPH)—THAT'S **FASTER THAN A RACEHORSE**

Changing colors

Each year, thousands of Caribbean flamingos are born in one of the world's largest flamingo colonies, Mexico's Ría Lagartos Biosphere Reserve. The chicks' gray feathers turn pink when they eat shrimp and other invertebrates containing a dye. This bird's population is rising, from the Caribbean to South America.

ON **ANTARCTIC COASTS** THE **WINTER WINDS** CAN BLOW UP TO **200 MPH** (320 KPH)

EMPEROR PENGUINS ARE **UNDER THREAT FROM CLIMATE CHANGE**, AS RISING TEMPERATURES **MELT THE WINTER SEA ICE**

KEY

Breeding site

Swimming range

SOUTHERN OCEAN

Weddell Sea

Ronne Ice Shelf

ANTARCTICA

South Pole

Ross Ice Shelf

Ross Sea

Sleek swimmer
The streamlined body of a penguin is superbly adapted for swimming. Underwater, these birds flap their paddle-like wings for propulsion.

Contact call
The call of an emperor penguin can be heard more than half a mile (1 km) away. Each bird recognizes the call of its mate, which helps them locate one another in the crowded colony.

Feeding time
Males feed their chick with a special curd produced from their food-pipe, until the mother arrives with fish and krill caught at sea.

Breeding site
At colonies around the coast, emperors gather to find a mate. The female lays a single egg then returns to the sea, leaving the male to incubate the egg alone.

Standing tall
Penguins stand very upright because their feet are set far back on the body. The emperor is the tallest of all—up to 4¼ ft (1.3 m).

Polar penguin

Emperor penguins feed in the icy waters of the Southern Ocean around Antarctica. They can dive deeper than any other seabird to catch fish and krill. Each year, emperors gather in their thousands at breeding sites around the coast to mate and raise their single chicks.

Emperor penguin

The life of the world's biggest penguin is a story of surviving extremes. It is one of the very few animals to live and breed on the Antarctic continent—the coldest place on Earth. Emperor penguins raise their chicks in the dark, bitter Antarctic winter, when the temperature can drop to -76°F (-60°C).

Fluffy chicks
Emperor penguin chicks have downy gray feathers. They stay on the ice, dependent on their parents, until they molt into their adult plumage and set off to sea to fish for themselves.

Speedy sliders
Penguins waddle around slowly on land, but they have a way of speeding up—"tobogganing" over snow and ice on their bellies.

SOUTHERN OCEAN

ANIMALS IN DANGER

Emperor penguin
IUCN status: near threatened
Population estimate: 595,000 in 2009

Keeping warm

Thousands of males huddle together to stay warm in the harsh Antarctic winter. Each is incubating a single egg under his belly, on top of his feet. The males stay on the ice with their egg all winter, until the females return.

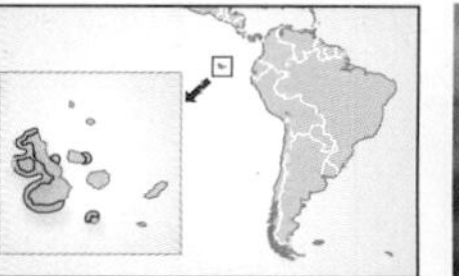

Galapágos penguin
All 18 species of penguin live in the southern hemisphere. The most northerly one lives on the Galápagos Islands at the equator, nesting in crevices in the volcanic rock.

Jackass penguin
The only African penguin nests and feeds mainly on and around offshore islands, but is also sometimes found on the coasts of Namibia and South Africa.

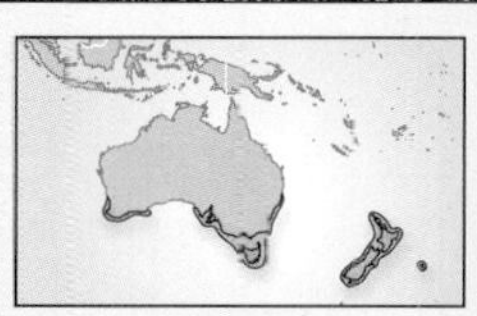

Little penguin
This is the world's smallest penguin, at only 16 in (40 cm) tall. It lives on southern Australian, Tasmanian, and New Zealand coasts, nesting on the dunes.

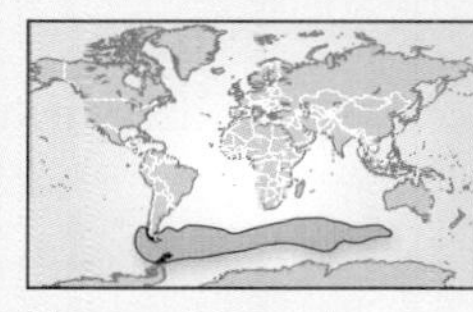

Macaroni penguin
Like most penguin species, the macaroni penguin lives on islands in the Southern Ocean, between Antarctica and warmer waters further north.

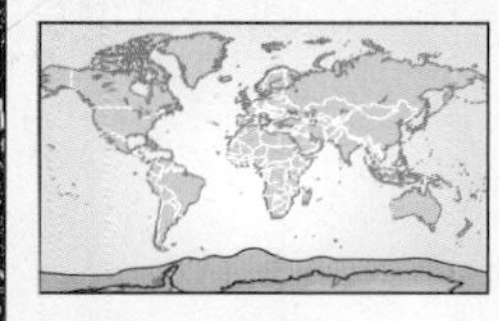

Adélie penguin
The Adélie penguin is the only other penguin species restricted to Antarctica. Unlike the emperor, it breeds on ice-free shores during the summer months.

Snowy owl

Few predatory birds are found as far north as the snowy owl. Many other owl species live in cold northern forests, but only the snowy can survive on the treeless tundra, where the ground is frozen solid and covered in snow for much of the year.

Ground nester
Unlike other owls, the snowy owl must nest on the ground in its open tundra habitat. It chooses an elevated site to give it a view of approaching danger.

Variable clutch
The number of eggs a snowy owl lays depends upon how much food is available. When there are plenty of prey animals to hunt, the owl may lay eight or more.

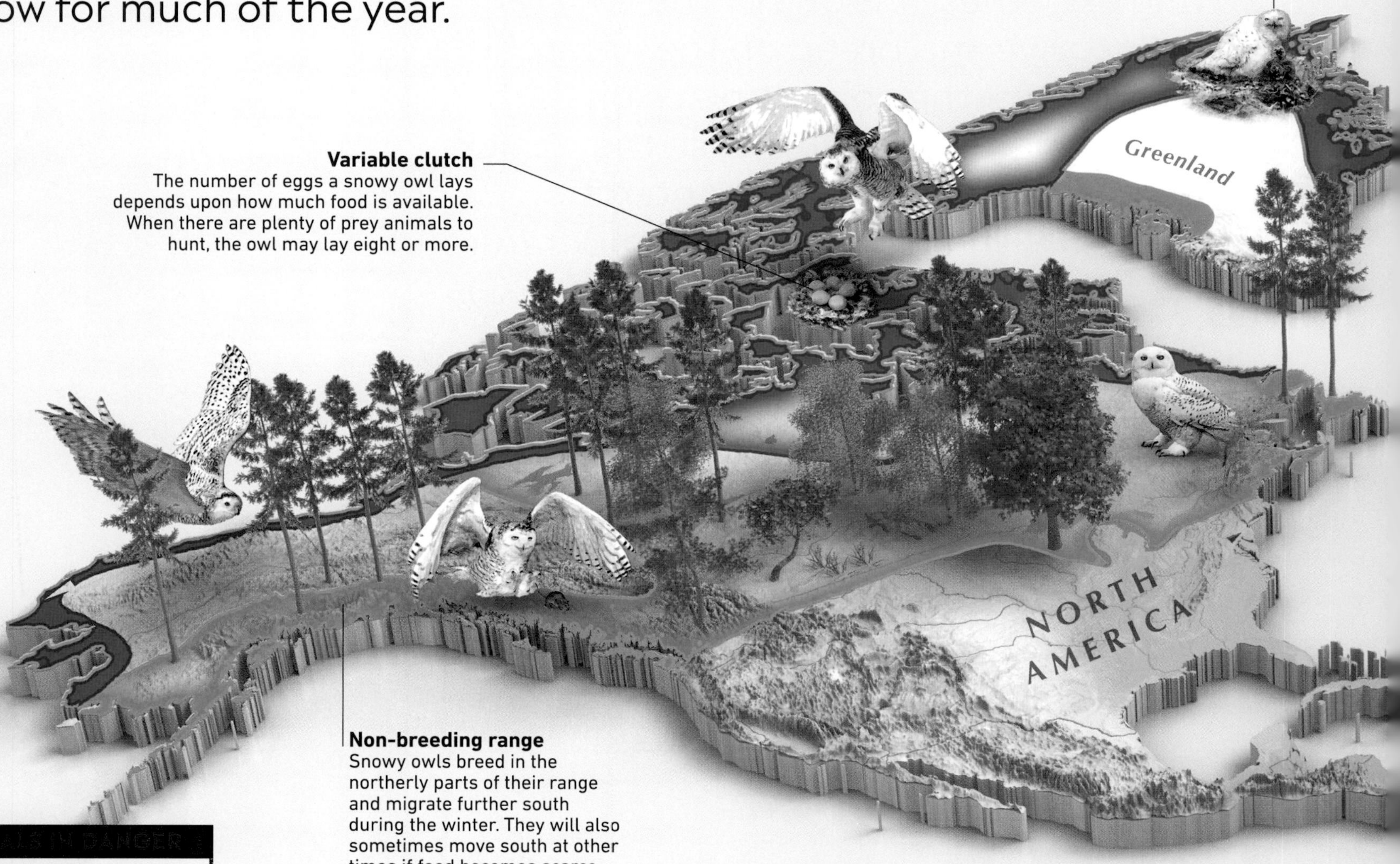

Greenland

NORTH AMERICA

Non-breeding range
Snowy owls breed in the northerly parts of their range and migrate further south during the winter. They will also sometimes move south at other times if food becomes scarce.

ANIMALS IN DANGER

Snowy owl
IUCN status: vulnerable
Population estimate: 28,000

Blending in

The snowy owl is the only owl with an all-white plumage. This helps disguise it against the snowy ground, especially during the Arctic summer when there is almost continuous daylight and the bird is breeding and hunts at all hours.

Hunting

The snowy owl has such good hearing it can detect the position of prey burrowing beneath a blanket of snow. It swallows small rodents whole, but will tear larger animals, such as hares and rabbits, to pieces first.

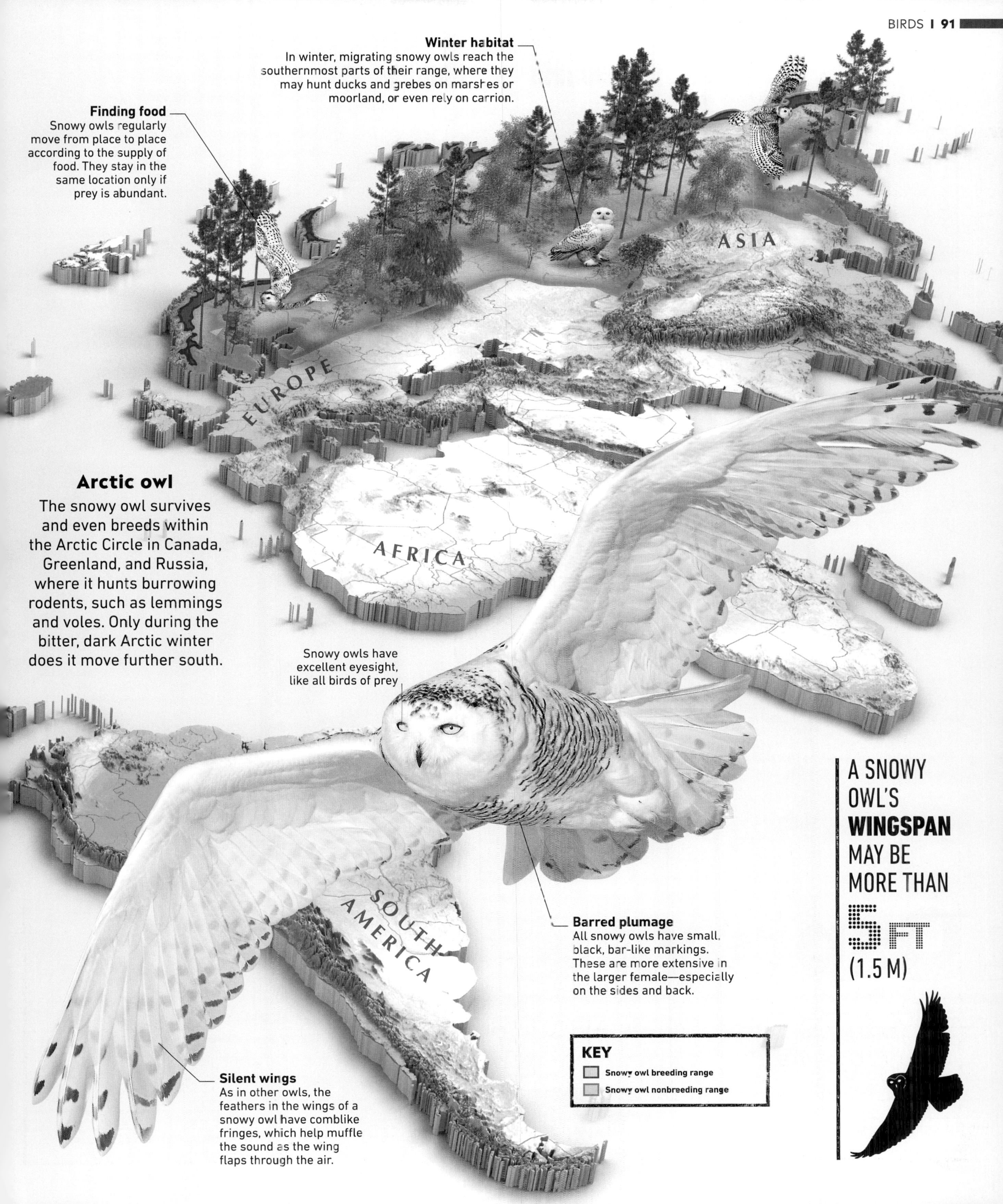

Winter habitat
In winter, migrating snowy owls reach the southernmost parts of their range, where they may hunt ducks and grebes on marshes or moorland, or even rely on carrion.
Finding food
Snowy owls regularly move from place to place according to the supply of food. They stay in the same location only if prey is abundant.
ASIA
EUROPE
AFRICA
SOUTH AMERICA
Snowy owls have excellent eyesight, like all birds of prey
Barred plumage
All snowy owls have small, black, bar-like markings. These are more extensive in the larger female—especially on the sides and back.
Silent wings
As in other owls, the feathers in the wings of a snowy owl have comblike fringes, which help muffle the sound as the wing flaps through the air.
KEY
Snowy owl breeding range
Snowy owl nonbreeding range
A SNOWY OWL'S WINGSPAN MAY BE MORE THAN 5 FT (1.5 M)

Arctic owl

The snowy owl survives and even breeds within the Arctic Circle in Canada, Greenland, and Russia, where it hunts burrowing rodents, such as lemmings and voles. Only during the bitter, dark Arctic winter does it move further south.

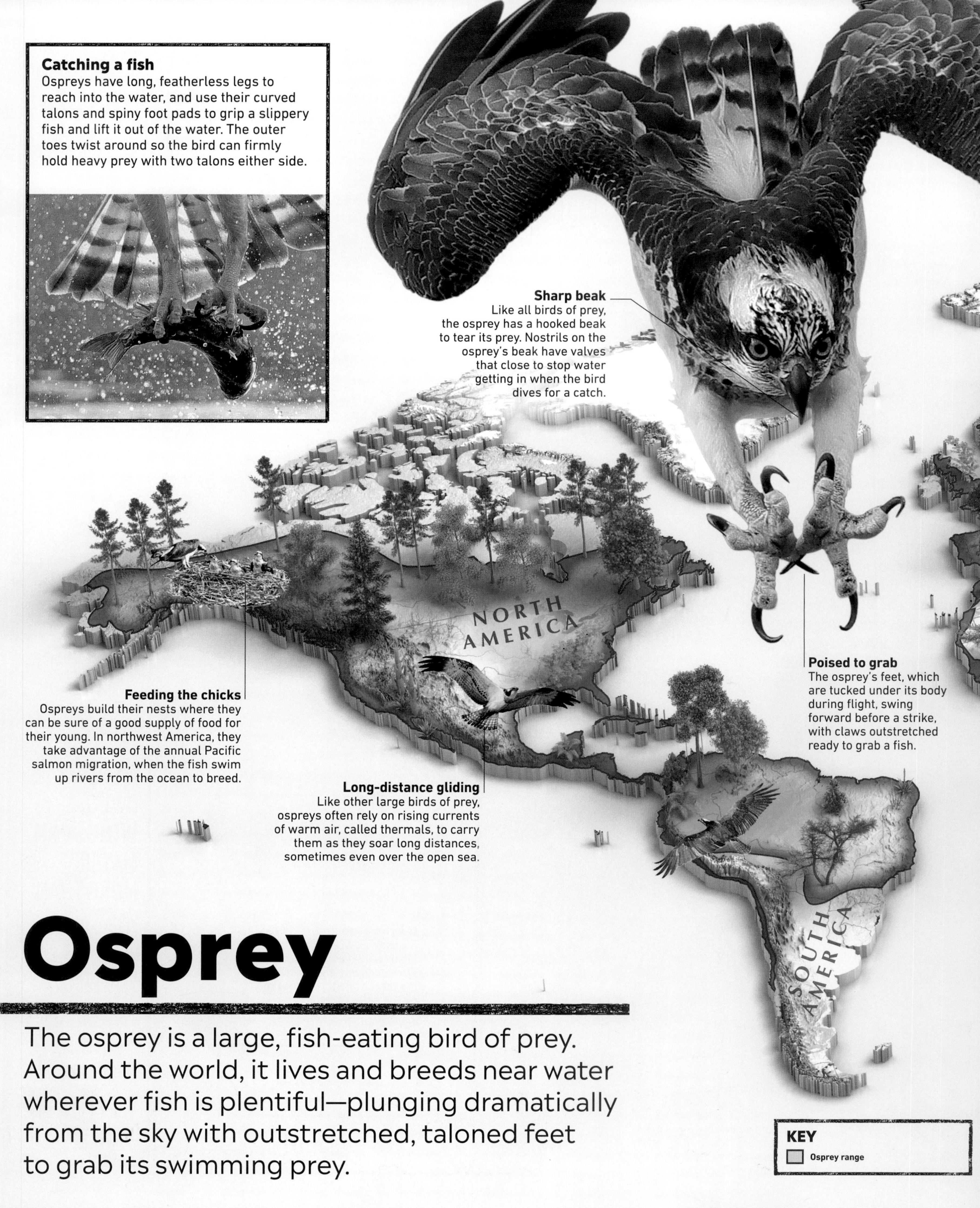

Osprey

The osprey is a large, fish-eating bird of prey. Around the world, it lives and breeds near water wherever fish is plentiful—plunging dramatically from the sky with outstretched, taloned feet to grab its swimming prey.

Catching a fish
Ospreys have long, featherless legs to reach into the water, and use their curved talons and spiny foot pads to grip a slippery fish and lift it out of the water. The outer toes twist around so the bird can firmly hold heavy prey with two talons either side.

Sharp beak
Like all birds of prey, the osprey has a hooked beak to tear its prey. Nostrils on the osprey's beak have valves that close to stop water getting in when the bird dives for a catch.

Feeding the chicks
Ospreys build their nests where they can be sure of a good supply of food for their young. In northwest America, they take advantage of the annual Pacific salmon migration, when the fish swim up rivers from the ocean to breed.

Long-distance gliding
Like other large birds of prey, ospreys often rely on rising currents of warm air, called thermals, to carry them as they soar long distances, sometimes even over the open sea.

Poised to grab
The osprey's feet, which are tucked under its body during flight, swing forward before a strike, with claws outstretched ready to grab a fish.

Passing through
In the northern parts of their range, ospreys are seasonal visitors, arriving to hunt and breed in spring and summer, before migrating south to avoid the bitter winters.
Breeding pair
Ospreys start breeding at around three years old. Typically, a male mates with a single female, but if he can defend two nests, he might have a second partner.
ASIA
EUROPE
AFRICA
AUSTRALIA
Year-round residents
In warmer parts of the world, such as southern Asia, some populations of osprey are resident throughout the year and do not migrate.
Smaller birds
The ospreys in Southeast Asia, New Guinea, and Australia are slightly smaller than those in the rest of the world. Some scientists think that they belong to a different species.
Winter visitors
Across sub-Saharan Africa, ospreys are winter visitors, traveling from Europe at the end of the northern summer. Only in Egypt and other parts of northeastern Africa are they resident all year.

AN OSPREY CAN **CARRY PREY** WEIGHING AROUND **2 LB** (1 KG)—HALF ITS OWN BODY WEIGHT

AN OSPREY'S **WINGSPAN** MAY BE UP TO **6 FT** (2 M) WIDE

Waterside nests
Ospreys nest along the shores of lakes and rivers or by marshes, typically choosing an exposed tree in which to build a platform of sticks before laying a clutch of three eggs. The first-born chicks are the strongest—younger ones may be left to starve if food is scarce.

OSPREYS **MIGRATING** FROM **AFRICA** TO **EUROPE** IN SUMMER TRAVEL UP TO **5,000 MILES** (8,000 KM)

Worldwide raptor

The osprey is one of the world's most wide-ranging birds. It lives almost everywhere there is water to fish, except for the cold polar regions and the remotest islands. Birds in the northern hemisphere migrate south for the winter, but ospreys around the equator tend to stay in the same place all year round.

A committee of vultures

From a rocky peak in the Eastern Rhodope Mountains, Bulgaria, a group of griffon vultures survey their surroundings for food. These large birds of prey are scavengers—they feed on carrion (dead animals). Using their huge wings, they soar on thermal air currents while scanning the ground for fresh carcasses.

Blue-and-yellow macaw

This spectacular bird is one of the biggest of the world's 405 parrot species. The blue-and-yellow macaw flies in noisy flocks over the canopy of the world's largest forest, the Amazon, which covers much of northern South America.

Colorful plumage
Like other species of macaw, this parrot has bright colors—blue above and yellow below—but it is surprisingly difficult to spot it when foraging high in the forest canopy.

Amazonian parrot
The blue-and-yellow macaw is found throughout the Amazon forest. Here, tall trees provide fruit and nuts for feeding, while the trunks of dead palms offer comfortable holes to nest. This parrot is still common throughout much of the region, but it is becoming threatened by deforestation and the pet trade.

Long tail
As well as their large size, reaching up to 34 in (86 cm) in length, macaws are also distinguished from other parrots by their long, tapering tail.

Tools for dining
Like all parrots, the blue-and-yellow macaw is equipped to pick up and crack open hard-shelled nuts. It uses its clawed feet and a very powerful, but sensitive, beak to grasp and break open nuts. Sometimes, one macaw may try to steal the seed from another.

BLUE-AND-YELLOW MACAWS ARE NOT ENDANGERED, BUT THEIR NUMBERS ARE DECLINING DUE TO SHRINKING HABITATS

MACAWS ARE HIGHLY PRIZED AS PETS, LEADING POACHERS TO TARGET THESE BIRDS AND SELL THEM ILLEGALLY

Flooded forests
In the central Amazon, the blue-and-yellow macaw lives in a type of forest called várzea. This region gets flooded during the rainy season, but the birds can stay feeding in the canopy high above the rising waters.

Dry forests
In some parts of its range, the blue-and-yellow macaw lives in woodlands very different from the wet rainforest. Here, the trees are deciduous and lose their leaves during the dry season.

KEY
Blue-and-yellow macaw range

Savanna
In the driest seasons, macaws in the southern part of their range wander further into open country in search of food—taking them over tropical grassland as far south as Paraguay and Argentina.

Highlands
Over much of its range, the blue-and-yellow macaw is a bird of the Amazon lowlands, but in the Andean foothills of Peru it lives in forests at an altitude of 4,920 ft (1,500 m).

Salt lick
Salt is scarce in the rainy Amazon rainforest, so macaws and other animals are attracted to exposed mineral-rich mud banks. Here they nibble the clay, which supplies much of the salt and other nutrients that keep them healthy. Macaws and other parrots are among the few kinds of birds to participate in this unusual feeding behavior.

Crossing the globe
Barn swallows are found across much of the world, and each year most cross the equator in their migrations—between North and South America or the wildest stretches of Asia. Swallows from Europe even travel across Africa's Sahara Desert to reach their wintering grounds.
NORTH AMERICA
North America
Barn swallows in North America breed from May to August. The swallows here—like those in far eastern Siberia—have reddish-brown, rather than pure white, underparts.
Europe
Throughout summer, barn swallows breed across Europe, and as far south as northern Africa. Most of those from northern and central Europe start their migration south in September or October.
EUROPE
Caribbean passage
Swallows migrating south from North America either island-hop through the Caribbean, or follow the path of land through Central America.
South America
Barn swallows arriving in South America reach Colombia and the Guianas by late August, and Brazil, Paraguay, and Argentina by September.
AFRICA
SOUTH AMERICA
Africa
Barn swallows overwinter across vast regions of Africa: birds arriving from western Europe tend to head to the west, and those from eastern Europe to the east. The longest distance traveled between Europe and Africa is an incredible 7,245 miles (11,660 km).

Barn swallow

More than half of all bird species are small perching birds, or passerines. Many are expert at hunting insects on the wing. Barn swallows nest and raise their young in the northern summers, when the skies are buzzing with life. But they must migrate to the warmer tropics before winter comes and insect numbers fall.

KEY
- Barn swallow range (breeding and resident)
- Barn swallow range (nonbreeding)
- North American migration
- European and Western Asian migration
- Central and East Asian migration

Wide bill
The bill is short and flat, but can open wide to scoop up insects in flight, or collect mud to make nests.

Western Asia
To the east, the barn swallow's range extends across Central Asia and Russia. Most of these birds will overwinter in southern Asia.

Forked tail
For controlled flight, the long tail spreads wide to help the barn swallow slow down.

Nesting
Many barn swallows attach their mud nests to the walls of buildings such as houses or barns, hence their name. They often line their nests with grasses or feathers, the whole construction taking about ten days to complete.

ASIA

India
Most barn swallows seen in India are winter visitors only, but further north of this country—and in a few other warmer parts of the world—they may be resident all year.

Eastern Asia
In this part of the world, swallows breed from the Himalayas to Japan. The birds here have creamy-white underparts, but those in far-eastern Siberia have reddish underparts, like those in the Americas.

Hunting for flies
Barn swallows use their long, pointed wings to maneuver themselves in flight. Flying up to 25 mph (40 kph), these acrobatic birds can turn quickly to snap up insects with a wide open beak.

Australia
Barn swallows breeding in eastern Asia typically overwinter in Southeast Asia, but during the twentieth century started migrating further into Australia.

AUSTRALIA

THESE EXPERT NAVIGATORS CAN COVER MORE THAN **200 MILES** (320 KM) **IN A SINGLE DAY**

MAMMALS

Mammal facts

The first mammals evolved 220 million years ago, when dinosaurs dominated the Earth. Today, mammals have adapted to live almost everywhere and are spread all over the world, from grasslands and rainforests to icy poles and deep oceans.

WHAT IS A MAMMAL?

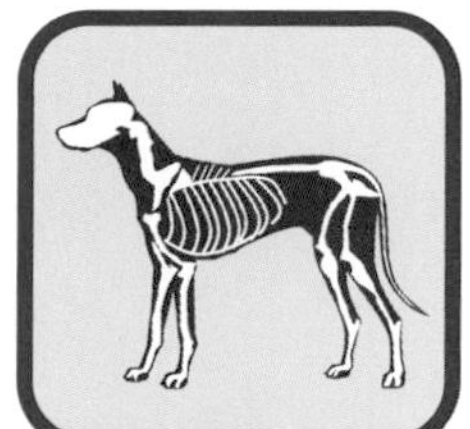

Vertebrates
Although they may look different, all mammals have an internal skeleton that is made of bone.

Warm-blooded
Mammals maintain a stable body temperature, whether they are in a hot or cold environment.

Live young
Most mammals give birth to live young, rather than hatching from eggs like birds.

Drink milk
Young mammals feed on milk from their mother, which provides vital nutrients for their growth.

Hair
Mammals have fur, spines, or scales to trap heat. Marine mammals have insulating blubber.

MAMMAL **TYPES**

ESTIMATED NUMBER OF MAMMAL SPECIES: 6,550

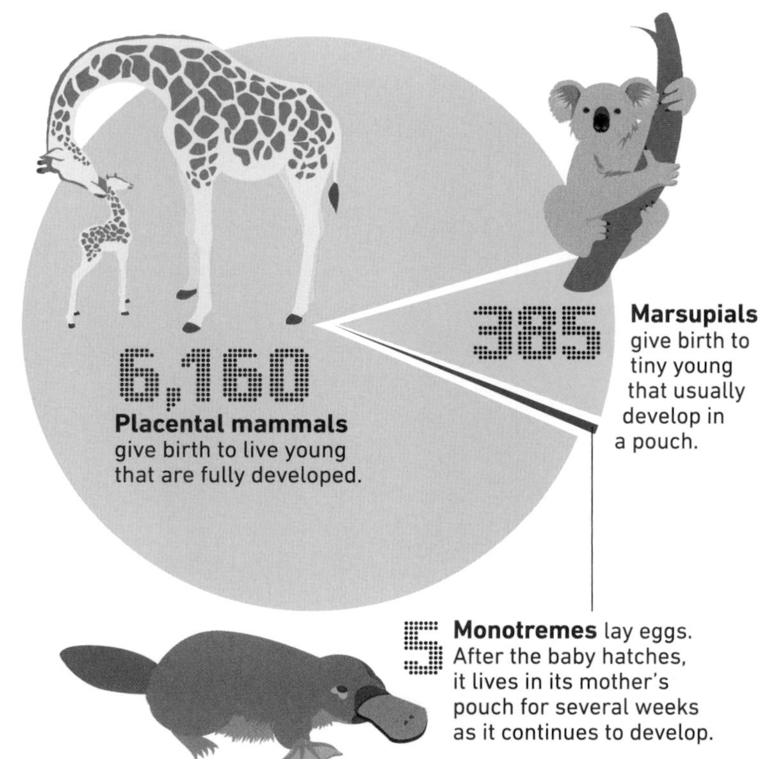

6,160
Placental mammals give birth to live young that are fully developed.

385
Marsupials give birth to tiny young that usually develop in a pouch.

5
Monotremes lay eggs. After the baby hatches, it lives in its mother's pouch for several weeks as it continues to develop.

THE **TAILLESS TENREC** OF **MADAGASCAR** CAN HAVE UP TO 32 **BABIES** IN ONE LITTER.

EXTREME HABITATS

Some hardy mammals have adapted to survive in extremely hot, cold, or rather odd places.

Musk oxen use their hooves to dig through snow and find edible plants in temperatures below freezing. They live mainly in the tundra regions of Greenland and Arctic North America.

Kangaroo rats have adapted to live in the extreme heat of the deserts in the western US and Mexico. This rodent does not drink water, instead getting moisture from desert grass seeds.

Goats can grip tiny crevices with their hooves, allowing them to ascend a vertical cliff safely. These rock-climbing goats are in Greece, but this mammal can be found all over the world.

INDONESIA IS HOME TO

291 MAMMAL SPECIES

MORE THAN ANY OTHER **COUNTRY.**

BIGGEST MAMMAL

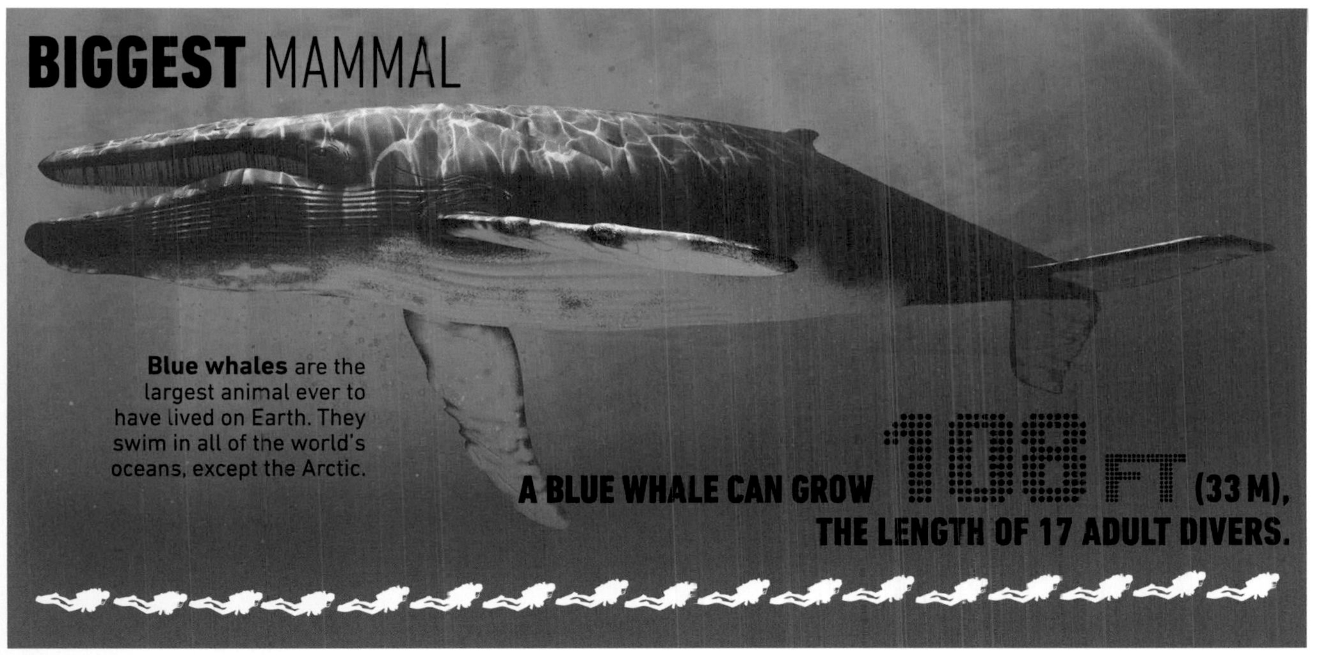

Blue whales are the largest animal ever to have lived on Earth. They swim in all of the world's oceans, except the Arctic.

A BLUE WHALE CAN GROW 108 FT (33 M), THE LENGTH OF 17 ADULT DIVERS.

SMALLEST MAMMAL

The **Kitti's hog-nosed bat** lives in limestone caves near rivers in parts of Thailand and Myanmar.

ITS HEAD-BODY LENGTH IS UP TO 1 3/8 IN (34 MM)—TWICE AS LONG AS A BUMBLEBEE.

FASTEST MAMMALS

Whether on water, land, or in the air, these mammals are some of the fastest in the animal kingdom.

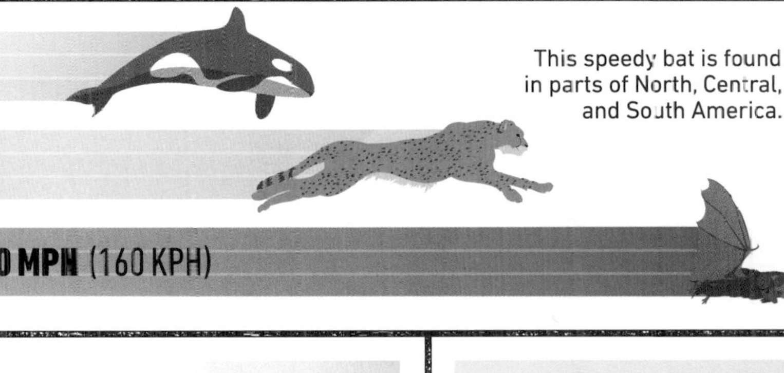

IN WATER: ORCA AT **55 MPH** (88 KPH)

ON LAND: CHEETAH AT **70 MPH** (113 KPH)

IN THE AIR: BRAZILIAN FREE-TAILED BAT AT **100 MPH** (160 KPH)

This speedy bat is found in parts of North, Central, and South America.

LONGEST OVERLAND MIGRATION

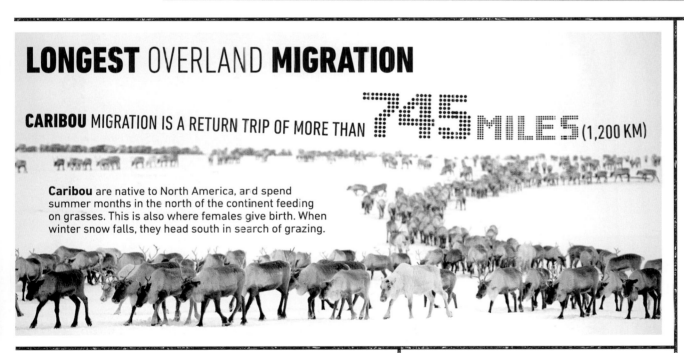

CARIBOU MIGRATION IS A RETURN TRIP OF MORE THAN 745 MILES (1,200 KM)

Caribou are native to North America, and spend summer months in the north of the continent feeding on grasses. This is also where females give birth. When winter snow falls, they head south in search of grazing.

DEEPEST DIVE

Cuvier's beaked whales are found worldwide. The record-breaking dive of this mammal reached a depth equal to the height of **3.5 Burj Khalifa** buildings.

The **Burj Khalifa** in Dubai, UAE, is the world's tallest building, at a height of **2,720 ft** (830 m).

CUVIER'S BEAKED WHALE 9,816 FT (2,992 M)

SMART MAMMALS

Bottlenose dolphins in Shark Bay, Australia, use protective marine sponges (an invertebrate) to disturb sandy seafloors filled with potential prey, such as spothead grubfish. It is thought that only females do this, and they pass on this useful fishing skill to their daughters.

LONG JUMPER

WHITE-HANDED GIBBONS OF **SOUTHEAST ASIA** CAN JUMP 40 FT (12 M) FROM BRANCH TO BRANCH.

Egg-laying mammals

Some mammals lay eggs instead of giving birth to live young. These are the monotremes, found only in Australia and the island of New Guinea. They include the duck-billed platypus and four species of spiny-coated echidnas.

Sir David's long-beaked echidna
This species lives in a tiny area of a mountain range in Indonesia. Only one specimen has ever been found in the wild.

INDONESIA

Western long-beaked echidna
Long-beaked echidnas from hotter lowlands look spinier because they have less insulating fur than those that live in cooler highlands.

Highly adaptable

Monotremes inhabit a wide variety of habitats, from Australia's arid deserts to the snow-covered mountains of Papua New Guinea. Short-beaked echidnas are the most adaptable and have the largest range, while the other monotremes are limited to smaller areas.

Arnhem Land

Tanami Desert

Eastern long-beaked echidna

Spiny coat
An echidna's coat is made up of protective spines interspersed with fur. If threatened, the echidna can roll into a spiky ball.

Short-beaked echidna
This adaptable monotreme is the only species that lives in the dry, arid interior of Australia, known as the "outback."

Gibson Desert

Great Victoria Desert

Toothless feeding

All monotremes lack teeth, and instead have sensitive beaks for catching invertebrate prey. Echidnas dig through soil with sharp claws to expose prey and use their long, sticky tongue to trap them. The platypus uses its sensitive bill to find shellfish buried in the mud, then crushes them with horny plates inside its bill.

Forest dwellers
In the forests of western Australia, short-beaked echidnas make their homes among rocks, in the spaces between tree roots, and inside hollow logs.

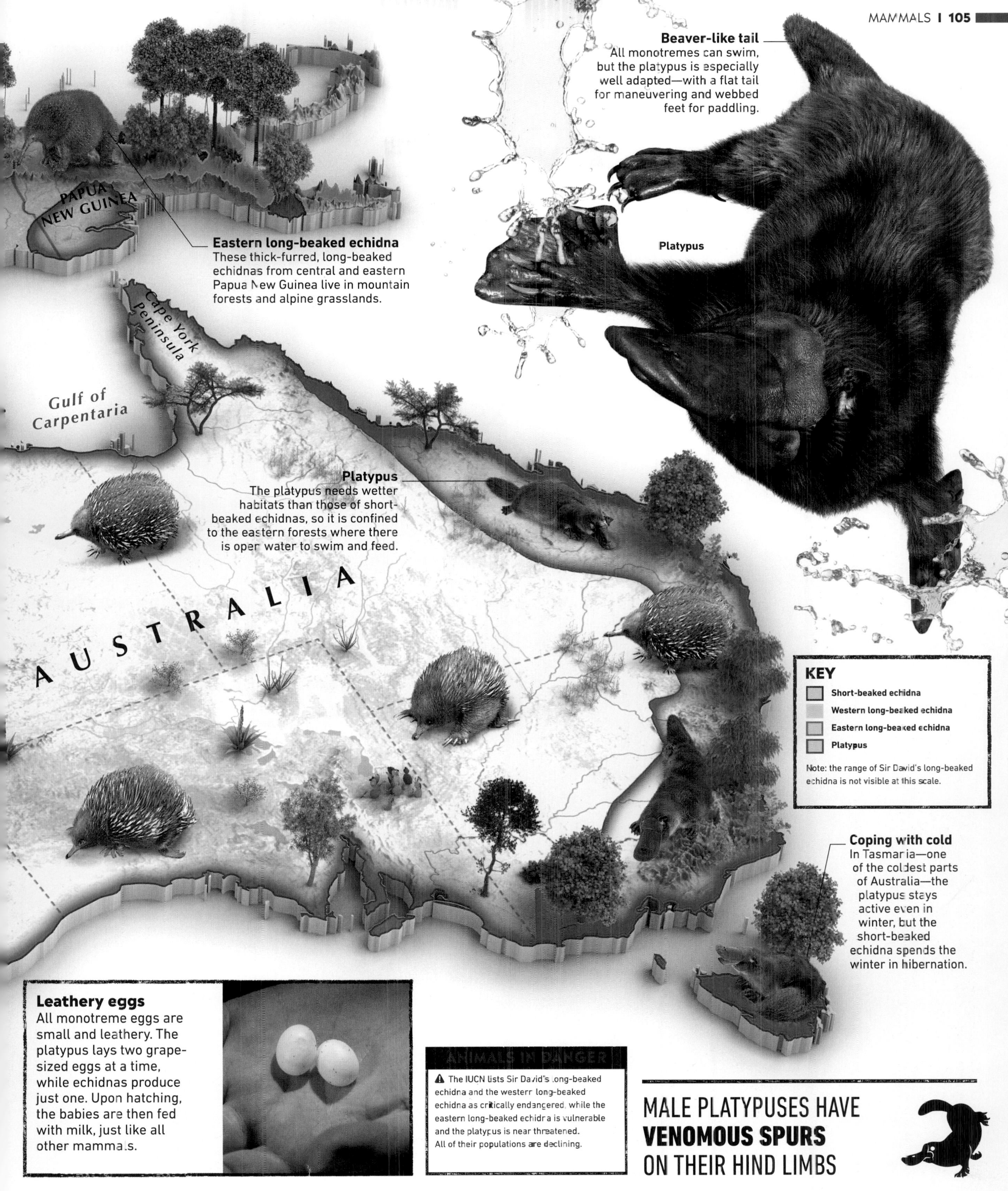

Beaver-like tail
All monotremes can swim, but the platypus is especially well adapted—with a flat tail for maneuvering and webbed feet for paddling.

Eastern long-beaked echidna
These thick-furred, long-beaked echidnas from central and eastern Papua New Guinea live in mountain forests and alpine grasslands.

Platypus
The platypus needs wetter habitats than those of short-beaked echidnas, so it is confined to the eastern forests where there is open water to swim and feed.

Coping with cold
In Tasmania—one of the coldest parts of Australia—the platypus stays active even in winter, but the short-beaked echidna spends the winter in hibernation.

Leathery eggs
All monotreme eggs are small and leathery. The platypus lays two grape-sized eggs at a time, while echidnas produce just one. Upon hatching, the babies are then fed with milk, just like all other mammals.

ANIMALS IN DANGER

⚠ The IUCN lists Sir David's long-beaked echidna and the western long-beaked echidna as critically endangered, while the eastern long-beaked echidna is vulnerable and the platypus is near threatened. All of their populations are declining.

MALE PLATYPUSES HAVE **VENOMOUS SPURS** ON THEIR HIND LIMBS

18-20 HRS
KOALAS SLEEP UP TO 20 HOURS EACH DAY
KEY
Koala range
Keeping cool
In northeastern Australia, where the climate is very hot, koalas have shorter, paler, fur to help keep them cool.
ANIMALS IN DANGER
Koala
IUCN status: vulnerable
Population estimate: 100,000–500,000
Cape York Peninsula
Gulf of Carpentaria
Facing forward
The koala is the only marsupial with forward-facing eyes. This makes it a better judge of distance, which is important for clambering through branches without falling.
AUSTRALIA
Following eucalyptus
Though koalas are found in a range of habitats, from subtropical forests to grasslands and savannas, their range is dependent on the presence of eucalyptus trees, the leaves of which make up the large majority of their diet. Much of their habitat has been lost due to logging, forest clearing, and bushfires, putting many koala populations at risk of extinction.
Tough digestion
The leaves of eucalyptus are hard and fibrous, making them very difficult to digest. They quickly fill the stomach of a browsing koala, but provide little nutrition, meaning that when they are not eating or sleeping, koalas spend their time resting to conserve energy.

Koala

Found only in the eucalyptus forests of Australia, koalas belong to a group of mammals called marsupials. Unlike most other mammals, marsupials give birth to tiny young that do most of their growing outside their mother's body—usually in a pouch.

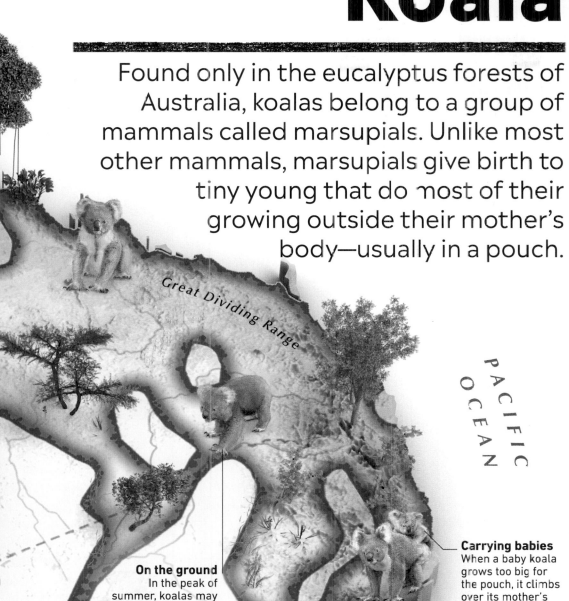

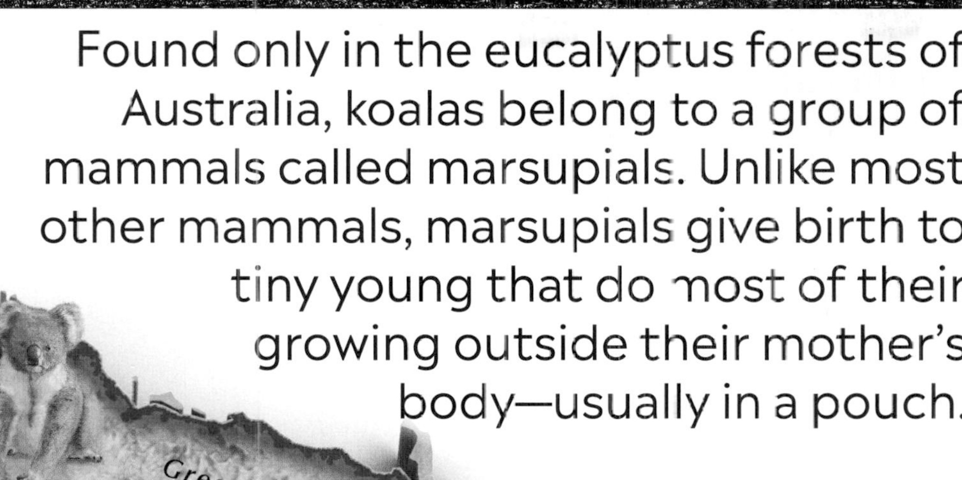

PACIFIC OCEAN

On the ground
In the peak of summer, koalas may come down to the ground to seek better shade. They can bound quickly across the ground to escape predators, such as dingoes.

Carrying babies
When a baby koala grows too big for the pouch, it climbs over its mother's shoulder or head and clings to her back. It only returns to the pouch to feed.

Climbing trees
Long forelimbs and a muscular upper body help make the koala an effective climber in eucalyptus trees. Its feet have padded palms and soles for traction and claws for gripping.

OTHER MARSUPIALS

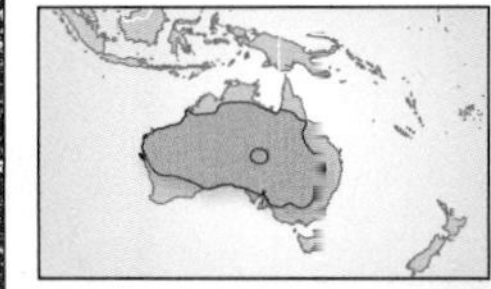

Red kangaroo
The largest species of kangaroo is well adapted to cope with Australia's dry interior, and ranges widely over the semi-deserts of the country.

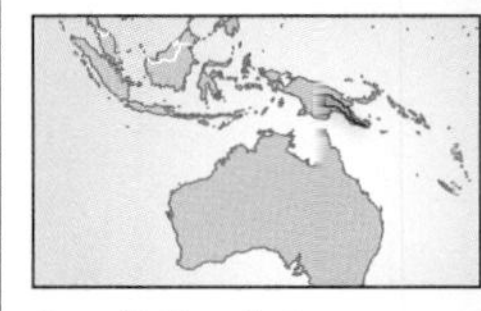

Goodfellow's tree kangaroo
In the tropical rainforests of New Guinea, Goodfellow's tree kangaroos have evolved to climb through the branches.

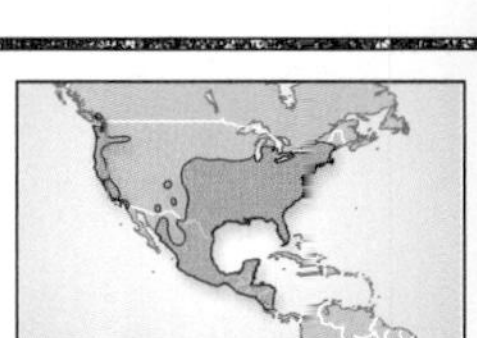

Virginia opossum
There are 120 species of opossums, mostly found in tropical South and Central America. Only the Virginia opossum ranges into temperate North America.

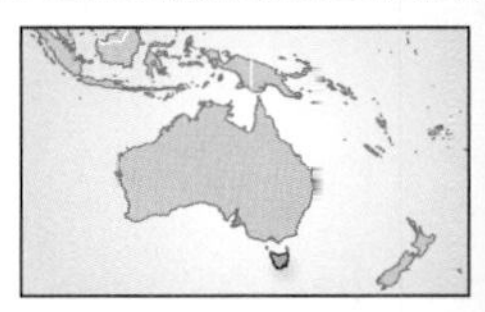

Tasmanian devil
The carnivorous Tasmanian devil used to be widespread across all of Australia, but is now restricted to the southern island of Tasmania.

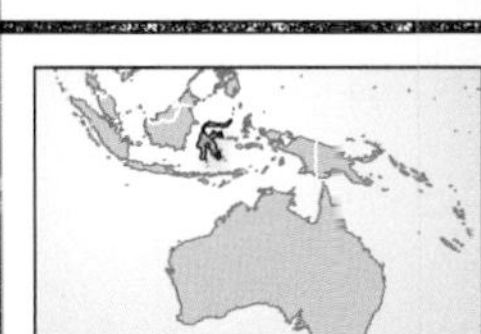

Bear cuscus
Living in tropical lowland forests on the Indonesian island of Sulawesi, the bear cuscus is the most western-dwelling marsupial in Australasia and Oceania.

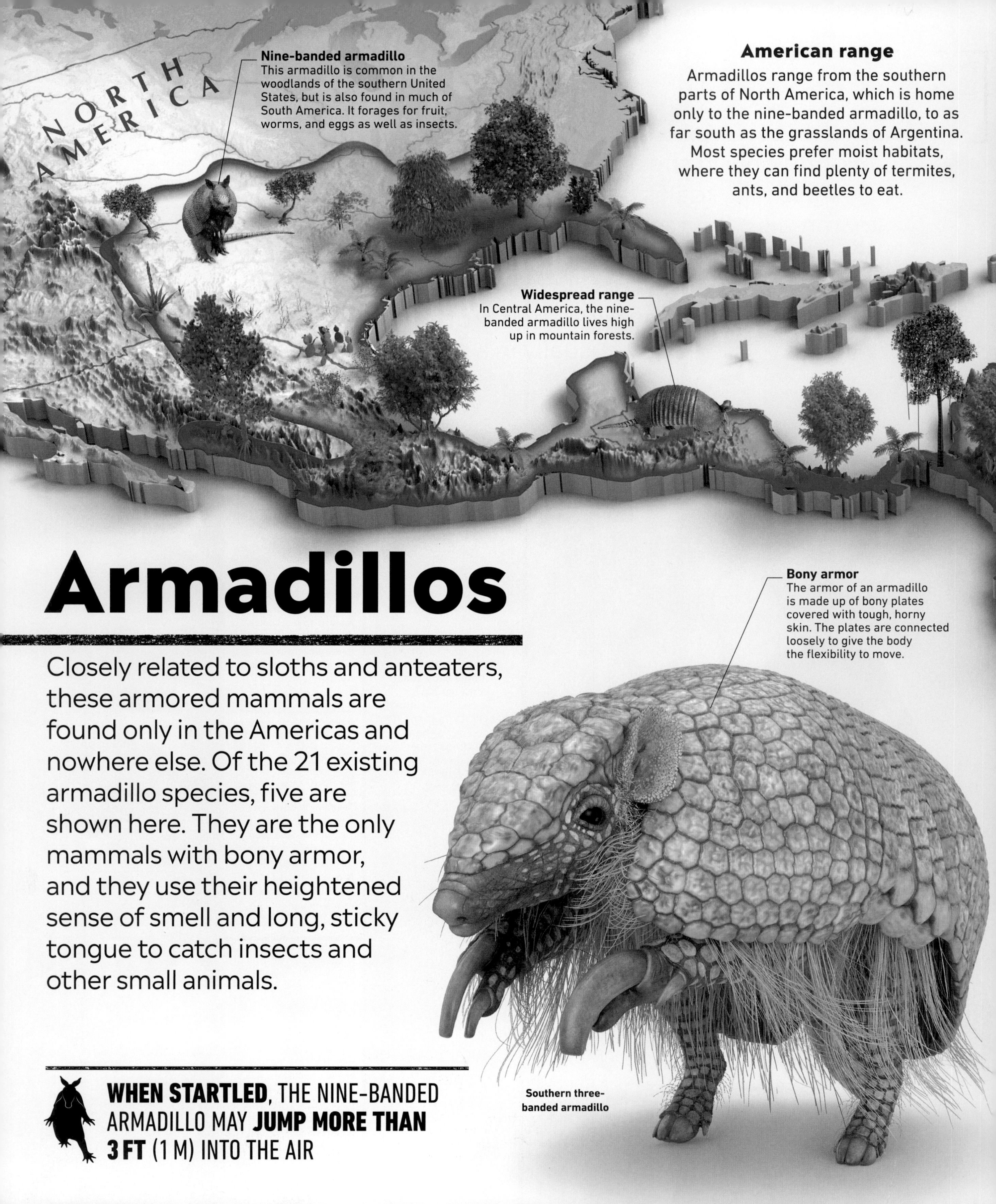

NORTH AMERICA
Nine-banded armadillo
This armadillo is common in the woodlands of the southern United States, but is also found in much of South America. It forages for fruit, worms, and eggs as well as insects.
Widespread range
In Central America, the nine-banded armadillo lives high up in mountain forests.
Bony armor
The armor of an armadillo is made up of bony plates covered with tough, horny skin. The plates are connected loosely to give the body the flexibility to move.
Southern three-banded armadillo

American range

Armadillos range from the southern parts of North America, which is home only to the nine-banded armadillo, to as far south as the grasslands of Argentina. Most species prefer moist habitats, where they can find plenty of termites, ants, and beetles to eat.

Armadillos

Closely related to sloths and anteaters, these armored mammals are found only in the Americas and nowhere else. Of the 21 existing armadillo species, five are shown here. They are the only mammals with bony armor, and they use their heightened sense of smell and long, sticky tongue to catch insects and other small animals.

WHEN STARTLED, THE NINE-BANDED ARMADILLO MAY **JUMP MORE THAN 3 FT** (1 M) INTO THE AIR

MAMMALS I 109
KEY
Nine-banded armadillo
Giant armadillo
Hairy long-nosed armadillo
Southern three-banded armadillo
Pink fairy armadillo
ANIMALS IN DANGER
Southern three-banded armadillo
IUCN status: near threatened
Population estimate: unknown
Giant armadillo
IUCN status: vulnerable
Population estimate: unknown
Burrowing down
All armadillos are burrowers, and use their strong clawed feet to dig tunnels with sleeping chambers. Most species spend much of the day in their burrows to avoid the heat of the sun or to hide from large predators, such as pumas.
Giant armadillo
The Amazon Basin is home to the biggest species of armadillo. The 130-lb (60-kg) giant armadillo lives in undisturbed tropical forests. It is hunted for its meat and threatened by deforestation.
ATLANTIC OCEAN
Amazon
SOUTH AMERICA
Andes
Gran Chaco
Hairy long-nosed armadillo
This armadillo's armor is covered with hair. It lives in the remote cloud forests of the Andes Mountains.
Rolled up
Only three-banded armadillos can roll into a ball and pull their limbs inside when threatened.
Southern three-banded armadillo
This species is found in drier habitats than most other armadillos. It lives in the thorny forest, scrub, and savanna of the Gran Chaco—a wide grassy area in central South America.
Pink fairy armadillo
The mole-like pink fairy armadillo is the smallest armadillo species. Its body ends with a vertical rump plate, which it uses to compact sand in burrows or even seal their entrance when danger threatens.

Brown-throated sloth

Few animals are so tied to life in trees as the sloth. These plant-eaters climb the branches with slow, deliberate movements and have long arms and claws that act as grappling hooks. There are six species of sloths living in tropical forests of the Americas, but the brown-throated sloth is the most common.

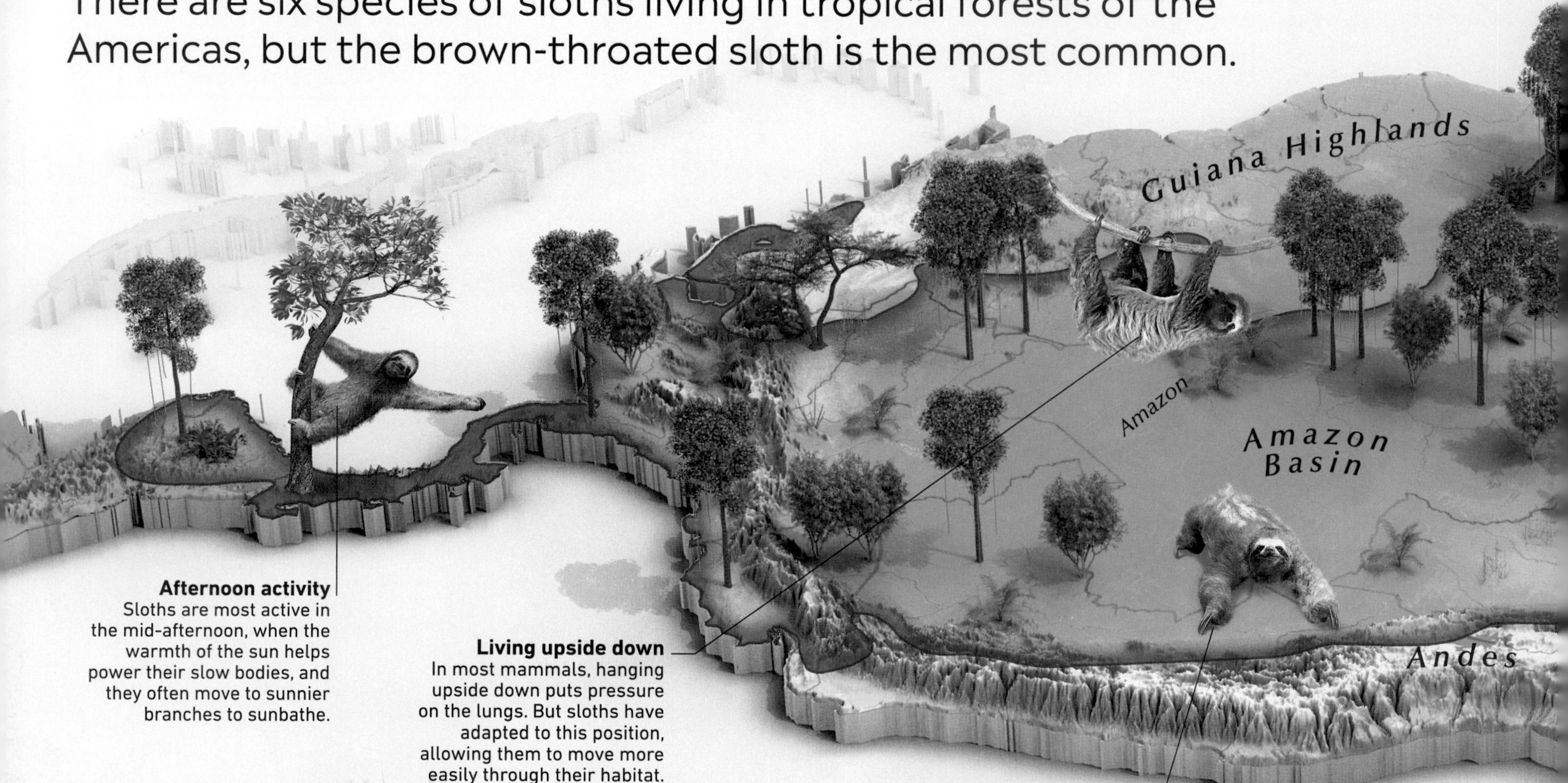

Guiana Highlands

Amazon

Amazon Basin

Andes

Afternoon activity
Sloths are most active in the mid-afternoon, when the warmth of the sun helps power their slow bodies, and they often move to sunnier branches to sunbathe.

Living upside down
In most mammals, hanging upside down puts pressure on the lungs. But sloths have adapted to this position, allowing them to move more easily through their habitat. They have fibers that attach their inner organs to their lower ribs, holding the organs in place so they don't crush the lungs.

Ground crawler
On the rare occasions when the brown-throated sloth leaves the safe haven of the trees, it is able to crawl across the ground by pulling forward with one forearm and the opposite hind foot at the same time.

KEY

Brown-throated sloth range

Trips to the toilet

The brown-throated sloth descends from the trees for just one reason: to poo. Once a week, it makes its way down to the forest floor, digs a small depression with its short tail, and defecates. It then covers the dung with leaf litter and climbs back up. If forced to do so, a sloth can crawl along the ground using the soles of its front and back feet, but will soon make for the nearest tree to return to the safety of the canopy.

Living together

Algae that grow on the fur of the brown-throated sloth tinge its fur green, helping disguise it among the leaves. The algae are fertilized by the droppings of a species of moth that lives only in the sloth's fur. When the sloth descends to the ground to poo, the moths briefly leave the sloth's fur to lay their eggs, and their larvae feed on the dung.

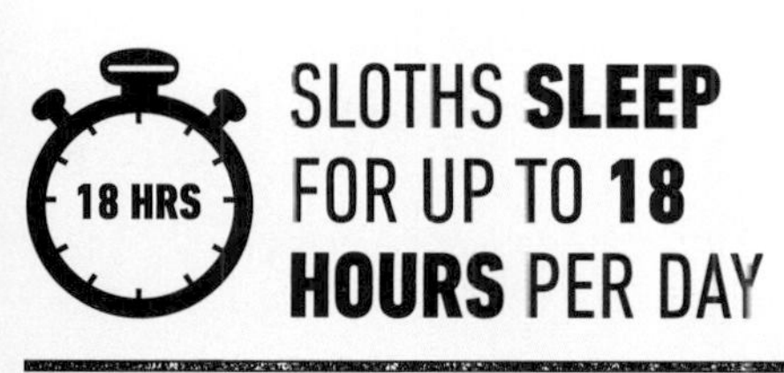

SLOTHS **SLEEP** FOR UP TO **18 HOURS** PER DAY

IT CAN TAKE AS MANY AS **50 DAYS** FOR A SLOTH TO **DIGEST EACH MEAL**

THE **BROWN-THROATED SLOTH** MOVES ONLY AROUND **130 FT** (40 M) **IN A DAY**

Climbing trees
Sloths climb up and down trees by hugging the tree trunk. When moving horizontally, they hang upside down from the branches.

Leafy diet
Sloths move slowly because the rainforest leaves of their diet don't contain many nutrients. The little energy they gain from their diet is needed for both getting around and digestion.

Brazilian Highlands

Paraguay

Paraná

Water absorbent
The dense fur of a sloth absorbs a lot of water when it rains. It is thought that a water-soaked coat helps protect it from extreme temperatures.

Atacama Desert

SOUTH AMERICA

Life in trees

These slow-moving tree dwellers live in the dense tropical rainforest canopies of Central and South America. They are able to eat the leaves of around 50 species of rainforest tree, but individuals tend to spend most of their time in a single tree that contains their favorite leaves.

AFRICA
Western ranges
African savanna elephants in western grasslands are widely scattered and isolated from other savanna elephants.
Sharing habitats
In open woodland and forest edges of parts of Central Africa, it is likely that African forest and African savanna elephants live together in similar habitats.
Red Sea
Gulf of Guinea
African forest elephant
These elephants are smaller than African savanna elephants. The largest groups occur where the forest is broken up with patches of savanna.
Horn of Africa
African savanna elephant
African savanna elephant
Most African savanna elephants live in dry woodland and shrubland, but in more arid parts of the continent they reach into deserts—as long as they have access to pools of water.
Large ears
Both species of African elephants have much bigger ears than those of Asian elephants. Blood circulating through them is cooled as the ears are waved back and forth.

Elephants

These giants are the world's heaviest land animal. They are well known for their long trunks and mighty tusks. Two of the three existing species can be found in fragmented ranges around Africa, while their smaller cousins inhabit the tropical forests of Southeast Asia.

20,000 AFRICAN ELEPHANTS ARE KILLED EACH YEAR FOR THE **ILLEGAL IVORY TRADE**

THE AFRICAN ELEPHANT POPULATION HAS DROPPED BY **90%** OVER THE LAST **100 YEARS**

ANIMALS IN DANGER

African forest elephant
IUCN status: endangered
Population estimate: 100,000

African savanna elephant
IUCN status: vulnerable
Population estimate: 315,000

Asian elephant
IUCN status: endangered
Population estimate: 20,000–40,000

Habitats at risk

From the savannas, open woodlands, and shrublands of Africa to the grasslands and humid forests of Asia, elephants are a key part of their ecosystems. But human intervention is leading to the destruction of their natural habitats, putting them at risk of extinction.

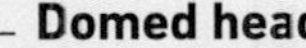

Asian elephant
In mainland Asia—including India—elephants live in grassland or forest. Their natural ranges are shrinking, leaving them access to only 15 percent of their original range.

Domed head
Asian elephants are smaller than their African cousins and have a two-domed, rather than single-domed, forehead. Their skin is also smoother and hairier than the rough skin of African elephants.

KEY
- African forest elephant
- African savanna elephant
- Asian elephant

Smaller sizes
Asian elephants living in forests in Borneo are shorter than those on the mainland. They are sometimes called Bornean pygmy elephants.

Asian elephant

Spreading seeds
Elephant herds can flatten foliage and tear down trees, but they also help scatter seeds. They eat ripe fruit from their favorite trees, and the seeds pass out in piles of fertilizing dung.

Tree browsers
Elephants are not picky eaters—they browse on leaves, seeds, fruit, flowers, grass, and tree bark. They will even push over trees to get to the nutritious roots deep underground.

Eurasian red squirrel

Around 90 species of tree squirrel live in forests around the world. Among them is the Eurasian red squirrel, which dwells in cool northern forests. Unlike most rodents, bushy-tailed squirrels are active during the day and they can often be spotted climbing trees.

Competing squirrels
In Britain, the introduced eastern gray squirrel has displaced the red squirrel from most of its original range (see panel below). It now survives only in places where gray squirrel numbers are controlled.

Raising babies
In spring, female squirrels give birth to litters of up to six kits in tree holes or dreys (nests) made from twigs and leaves in the forest canopy.

Expansive forests
Red squirrels survive best in big expanses of forest. In places where forests are fragmented, their numbers drop.

Outcompeted
In parts of Europe, such as the UK and Italy, the eastern gray squirrel, introduced from North America, has driven out the native red squirrel because it is stronger and spreads a virus that can be lethal to its red cousins.

Squirreling nuts away
In fall, the red squirrel stores pine cones, acorns, nuts, and seeds by burying them. It uses memory and a good sense of smell to find them, even under snow in winter, helping it stay active and keep feeding.

Bushy-tailed rodent

The Eurasian red squirrel has a wide range, from western Europe to Siberia. It feeds on tree seeds, especially pine nuts. Its long, bushy tail can be used as a windbreak when the squirrel is feeding, or as shelter from rain or hot sun.

A RED SQUIRREL CAN JUMP UP TO 6½ FT (2 M) BETWEEN TREES—10 TIMES ITS OWN BODY LENGTH

IN BRITAIN, THERE ARE AN ESTIMATED 140,000 RED SQUIRRELS, COMPARED TO 2.5 MILLION GRAY SQUIRRELS

Social dynamics
Red squirrels spend most of their time alone, but will huddle in groups in nests on cold nights, or gather together when food is plentiful.

Cold taiga habitat
Across Siberia, the red squirrel lives in the great taiga forest: a vast expanse of pine and spruce trees on the edge of the cold Arctic region.

ASIA

Tufted ears
Red squirrels have distinctive tufts of fur on their ears, which grow longer in winter months.

Staying active
Even in the coldest winters, red squirrels do not hibernate for long periods, as many small mammals do. Instead, they may stay snug in their nests in bitter weather.

Coniferous habitats
Pine seeds are a favorite of red squirrels, so they are especially abundant in pine forests. They hoard pine cones, seeds, and nuts as a winter store—particularly when food crops are low during the coldest months.

Chisel-like teeth
Like other rodents, red squirrels have chisel-like front incisor teeth. They use these to bite into the woody shells of nuts to reach the nutritious seed inside.

Colorful fur
Most red squirrels have reddish-brown fur with a white underside, but some individuals are black, brown, gray, or even blueish.

KEY
Eurasian red squirrel range

Desert rodent

The elusive long-eared jerboa inhabits the deserts and shrublands that stretch between southern Mongolia and northern China. Its elongated feet help it hop around the desert sand and leap into the air to catch insects. The large surface area of the jerboa's ears helps keep it cool by radiating heat from its body.

Star-nosed mole

With its hyper-sensitive nose and lightning fast reflexes, this unique North American mole is a highly successful hunter of small invertebrates such as worms, insects, and spiders. It spends most of its life in its intricate system of burrows, where it rests, builds nests for rearing young, stores food, and traps prey.

Western barrier
The star-nosed mole relies on wet habitats to feed and survive, so the western border of its range ends where the drier central prairies of North America begin.

Lake Superior

NORTH AMERICA

Wet habitats
The star-nosed mole lives in a range of habitats across eastern North America, including coniferous and deciduous forests, swamps, peat bogs, and along the banks of streams, lakes, and ponds. It prefers to build its burrows in water-logged ground, and relies on its sense of smell to detect prey underground.

KEY
Star-nosed mole range

Mole hill
Most of its life is spent in underground burrows, but occasionally the star-nosed mole heads to the surface through mole hills in order to hunt prey at night.

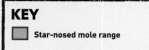

Semi-aquatic mammals
Star-nosed moles are excellent swimmers, and many of their burrows open underwater. They use their highly sensitive nose to hunt for prey—such as aquatic insect larvae, snails, and shrimp—in the waterbed. The rest of their burrow system is built above the water level to prevent flooding.

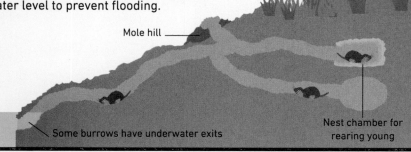

Mole hill

Nest chamber for rearing young

Some burrows have underwater exits

THERE ARE **25,000 TOUCH SENSORS** ON THE **TENTACLES** OF A STAR-NOSED MOLE

STAR-NOSED MOLES EAT **50% OF THEIR BODY WEIGHT** IN PREY ANIMALS **EACH DAY**

Sociable moles
Star-nosed moles are probably more sociable than other species of moles, and occasionally form loose colonies. They mate in the fall and live together until the babies are born in the spring.
Northern mole
At the northernmost reaches of its range, the star-nosed mole lives in the coniferous forests of Canada's cold taiga.
Lake Huron
Lake Erie
Appalachian Mountains
Up high
In the Appalachian Mountains, the star-nosed mole is found at altitudes of more than 5,250 ft (1,600 m).
Nose tentacles
The nostrils of most star-nosed moles are surrounded by 22 little tentacles—each measuring up to 5⁄32 in (4 mm) long.

Catching prey

With the help of its super sensitive nose, the star-nosed mole is perfectly adapted for finding tiny prey in the water-soaked ground. The fleshy tentacles around the mole's nose are packed with thousands of touch sensors, and it can take less than a fifth of a second for the mole to detect and grab each morsel.

Lemurs

There are more than 100 species of lemur, and all of them are found only on the island of Madagascar and nowhere else. The five ranges on this map represent a small sample of these isolated primates, and they all heavily depend on their forest habitats for survival.

50 SILKY SIFAKAS ARE LEFT IN THE **WILD**—THEY ARE ONE OF THE **RAREST PRIMATES IN THE WORLD**

Spiny tree habitat
Thorny forests in the dry south of Madagascar—where spiny trees grow like giant cacti—are home to particular kinds of lemurs, such as Verreaux's sifaka. They have padded palms and soles on their hands and feet, allowing them to leap from trunk to trunk without injury.

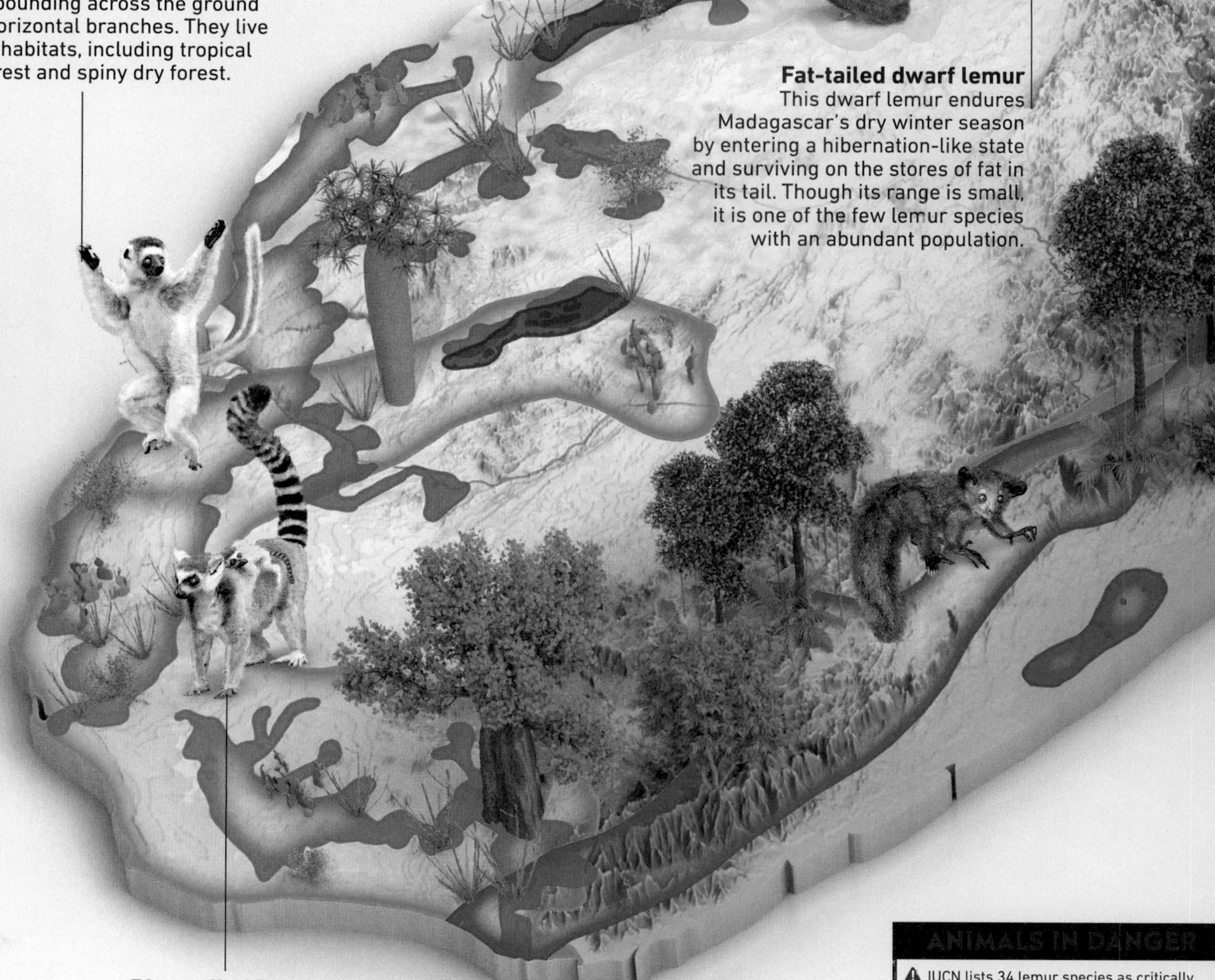

Red-tailed sportive lemur
Despite its name, this species is not very active. Restricted to a tiny area of dry deciduous forest between two rivers, individuals rarely travel more than ⅗ mile (1 km) from their home range. When their habitats are deforested, they are unlikely to move to distant trees.

Verreaux's sifaka
The powerful thighs of a sifaka—good for leaping from tree to tree—are also used for bounding across the ground or along horizontal branches. They live in forest habitats, including tropical rainforest and spiny dry forest.

Fat-tailed dwarf lemur
This dwarf lemur endures Madagascar's dry winter season by entering a hibernation-like state and surviving on the stores of fat in its tail. Though its range is small, it is one of the few lemur species with an abundant population.

Ring-tailed lemur
The ring-tailed lemur is found only in Madagascar's dry southern forests and arid open areas. It spends 70 percent of its time on the ground, more than any other lemur species.

ANIMALS IN DANGER

⚠ IUCN lists 34 lemur species as critically endangered, including the red-tailed sportive lemur and Verreaux's sifaka, and 45 as endangered, including the ring-tailed lemur and aye-aye. Most others are vulnerable.

Lemurs in danger

Each species of lemur is adapted to live in a different type of forest habitat, from the ring-tailed lemur in the dry forests of the south to the rainforest-dependent aye-aye. Because many lemurs are restricted to tiny areas of habitat, they are increasingly vulnerable to threats such as deforestation.

Aye-aye
This nocturnal lemur can be found in the rainforests of eastern Madagascar. Despite being rare wherever it occurs, the aye-aye could be one of the widest-ranging lemur species.

Wet nose
Lemurs have forward-facing eyes like related monkeys, but differ from monkeys in having a more pointed, wet nose—good for sniffing scents, especially at night.

WEIGHING ONLY **1 OZ** (31 G), **MADAME BERTHE'S MOUSE LEMUR** IS THE **SMALLEST PRIMATE IN THE WORLD**

Tail flag
The long, striped tail of a ring-tailed lemur is a visual signal. When traveling in their group, lemurs wave their tails like a flag to help keep members together.

Ring-tailed lemur

Hunting for woodworm

The aye-aye is a highly specialized feeder. It preys on invertebrates, such as fleshy wood-boring grubs, which live inside tree branches. By tapping a branch and listening to the echo, it can detect if a grub is inside. It gnaws a hole in the wood and hooks the grub out with a specially adapted spindly finger.

Japanese macaque

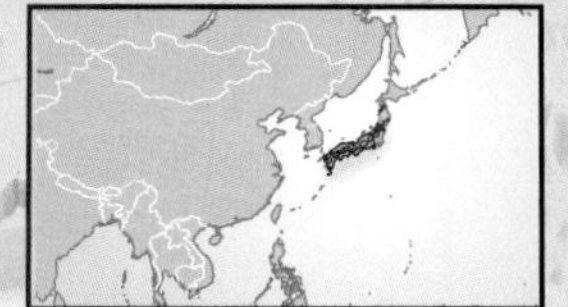

Most of the more than 330 species of monkeys around the world live in the hot tropics, but the Japanese macaque tolerates the cold. In Japanese forests, it lives further north than any other nonhuman primate, sometimes ranging high up into cold mountains with heavy winter snowfall.

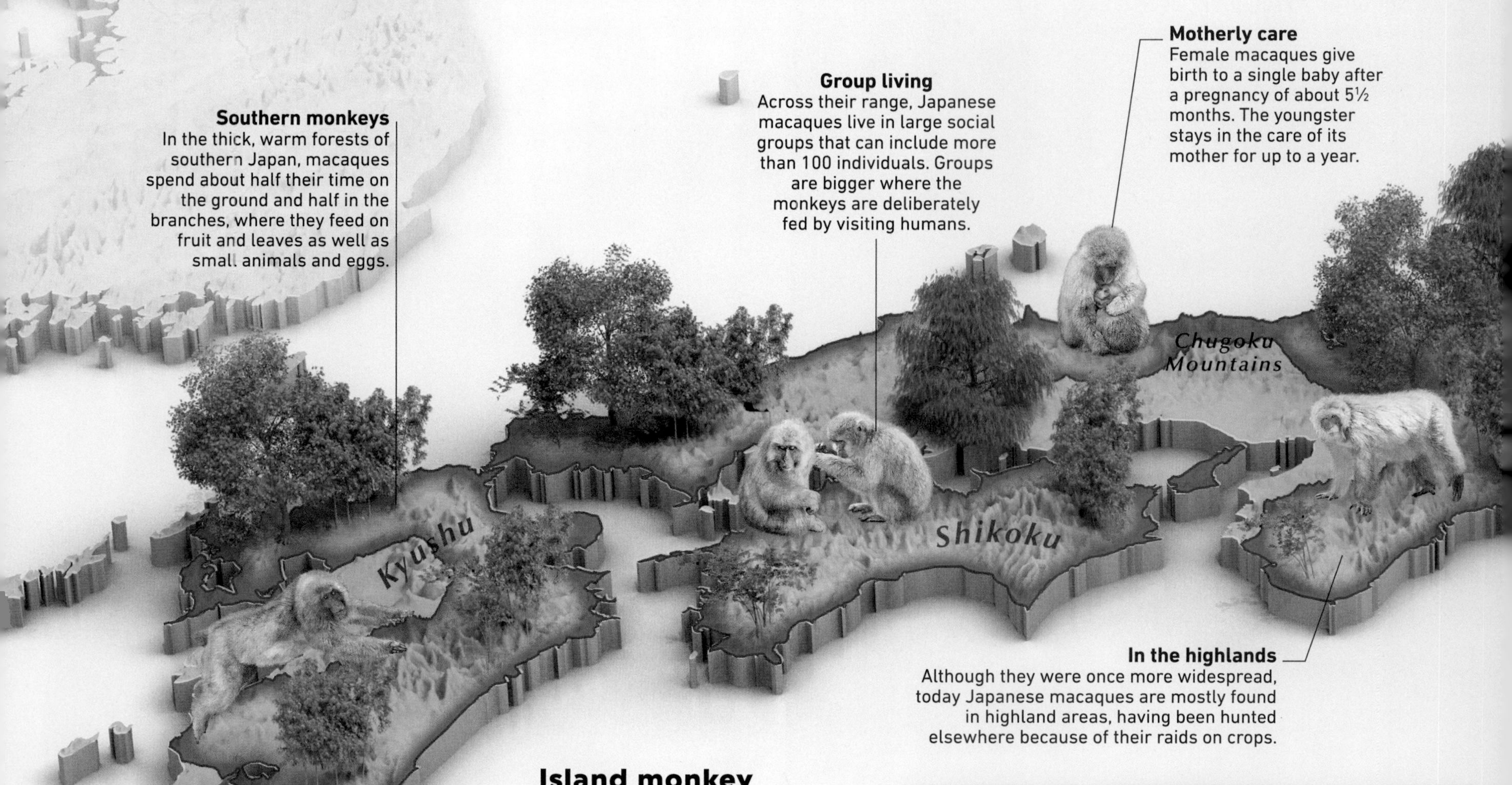

Motherly care
Female macaques give birth to a single baby after a pregnancy of about 5½ months. The youngster stays in the care of its mother for up to a year.

Group living
Across their range, Japanese macaques live in large social groups that can include more than 100 individuals. Groups are bigger where the monkeys are deliberately fed by visiting humans.

Southern monkeys
In the thick, warm forests of southern Japan, macaques spend about half their time on the ground and half in the branches, where they feed on fruit and leaves as well as small animals and eggs.

Chugoku Mountains

Kyushu

Shikoku

In the highlands
Although they were once more widespread, today Japanese macaques are mostly found in highland areas, having been hunted elsewhere because of their raids on crops.

Island monkey

The Japanese macaque lives on the main Japanese islands of Honshu, Shikoku, and Kyushu. In the southern parts of its range this monkey lives in warm, temperate evergreen forest, but it also inhabits temperate deciduous forest further north.

Beach monkeys
On the tiny Japanese island of Koshima, off the coast of Kyushu, Japanese macaques have learned skills that get passed down as youngsters copy adults. On beaches, the monkeys wash food such as sweet potatoes in the sea, and separate lighter grains of wheat from heavier sand by letting the grains float upward in the water.

THE JAPANESE MACAQUE **CAN SURVIVE** IN TEMPERATURES **AS LOW AS 5°F** (-15°C)

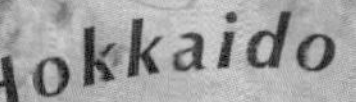

Northernmost range
No wild monkey in the world lives further north than the Japanese macaque. Like macaques in the central mountains, they keep warm by bathing in hot springs.

Snow monkey
Japanese macaques living in the snowy mountains of central Honshu—close to ski resorts—have become a popular tourist attraction.

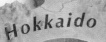

Hot springs
In the mountains of central Honshu, temperatures plunge below freezing in the winter. Here, Japanese macaques survive the cold by regularly bathing in thermal pools that are common in this volcanic region.

Naked face
Pink skin shows through a very fine coating of fur on the face of an adult macaque, encircled by long, pale whiskers.

Deciduous forests
In the northern parts of their range, Japanese macaques range into mountainous areas with deciduous trees—trees that lose their leaves during the winter. At this time of year, macaques move to lower elevations, where there is more food.

Thick fur
The grayish fur grows especially long and thick on its back and sides, which helps trap body heat. The monkey molts its coat in late spring so its fur is shorter in the summertime.

KEY

☐ Japanese macaque range

BETWEEN 1995 AND 2000, THE **EBOLA VIRUS KILLED THREE-QUARTERS** OF THE WESTERN GORILLA POPULATION

GREAT APES LIVE IN **LARGE FAMILY GROUPS**—ONE EASTERN GORILLA GROUP HAD A RECORD **65 MEMBERS**

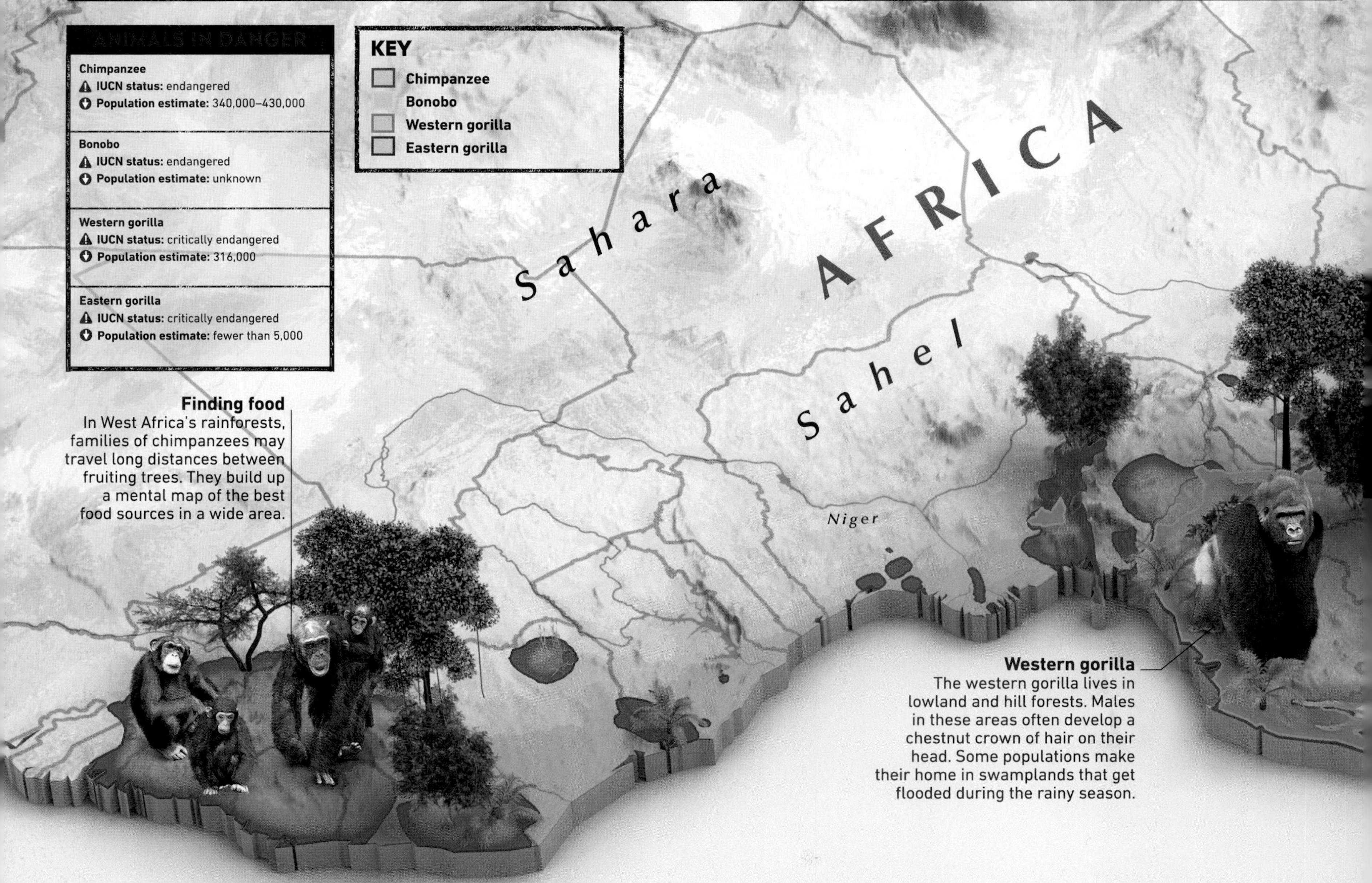

ANIMALS IN DANGER

Chimpanzee
IUCN status: endangered
Population estimate: 340,000–430,000

Bonobo
IUCN status: endangered
Population estimate: unknown

Western gorilla
IUCN status: critically endangered
Population estimate: 316,000

Eastern gorilla
IUCN status: critically endangered
Population estimate: fewer than 5,000

KEY
- Chimpanzee
- Bonobo
- Western gorilla
- Eastern gorilla

Sahara

AFRICA

Sahel

Niger

Finding food
In West Africa's rainforests, families of chimpanzees may travel long distances between fruiting trees. They build up a mental map of the best food sources in a wide area.

Western gorilla
The western gorilla lives in lowland and hill forests. Males in these areas often develop a chestnut crown of hair on their head. Some populations make their home in swamplands that get flooded during the rainy season.

Green living
Great apes use branches and foliage to build nests for sleeping at night, and sometimes for resting during the day. Chimpanzee and bonobo nests are built high in trees but gorillas, who are heavier, often nest on the ground, like the one seen here.

Great apes

The great apes are our closest animal relatives. All great ape species, except the orangutans (see pp.126–127), are found on the continent of Africa. Living in sociable groups in forests around the equator, chimpanzees and bonobos spend more time in trees, while gorillas stay mainly on the ground.

Horn of Africa

White Nile

Chimpanzee
Like other great apes, the chimpanzee walks on its knuckles when on all fours. In the eastern part of its range, it roams central highland forests as high up as 9,155 ft (2,790 m).

Eastern gorilla
Eastern gorillas have thicker, blacker fur than western gorillas. Some live in lowland habitats, but eastern mountain gorillas live at heights of up to 12,470 ft (3,800 m); they are the stockiest, furriest gorillas.

Using tools

Gorillas and bonobos mainly eat plants and fruit, but chimpanzees are more carnivorous, and even use tools to help catch prey or collect food. They use twigs to pull termites from holes, sharpened sticks to spear tiny primates, and stones or clubs to crack nuts. Young chimpanzees watch older ones to learn how it is done.

Threat display
Adult male gorillas intimidate rivals by standing upright to look bigger, while rhythmically beating their chest with cupped hands and hooting or roaring loudly. Older males are known as silverbacks.

Congo

Great Rift Valley

Male eastern mountain gorilla

Bonobo
Also called the pygmy chimpanzee, the bonobo is more lightly built than the chimpanzee. Its range is separated from that of its bigger cousins, who live on the other side of the great Congo River.

Congo

Shrinking habitats

The chimpanzee has the widest range of any great ape and can survive in drier, more open woodland than bonobos and gorillas. But all great ape species are threatened with extinction as the cutting down of rainforest continues to shrink their natural habitats, while poaching kills large numbers every year.

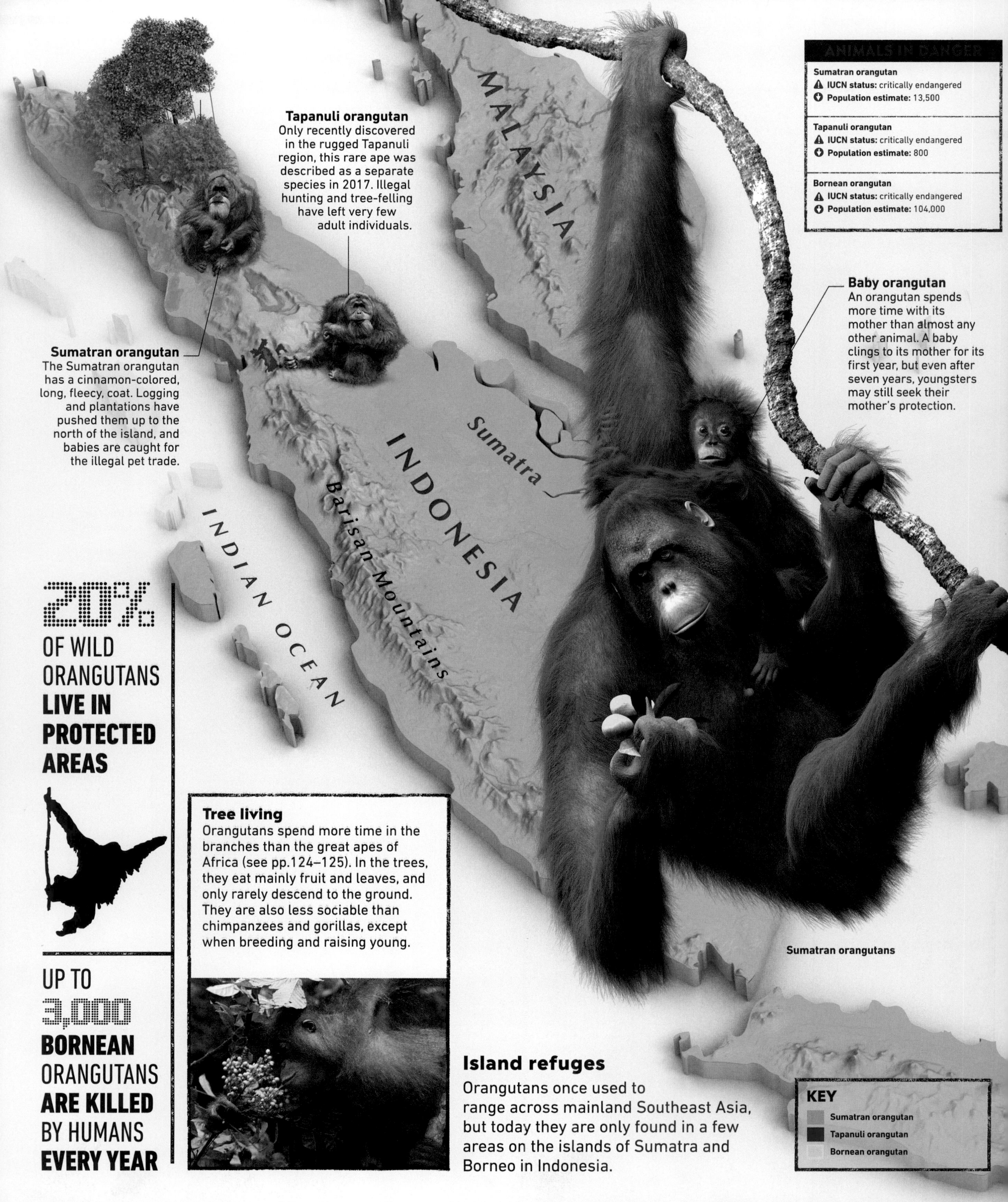

ANIMALS IN DANGER
Sumatran orangutan
IUCN status: critically endangered
Population estimate: 13,500
Tapanuli orangutan
IUCN status: critically endangered
Population estimate: 800
Bornean orangutan
IUCN status: critically endangered
Population estimate: 104,000
Tapanuli orangutan
Only recently discovered in the rugged Tapanuli region, this rare ape was described as a separate species in 2017. Illegal hunting and tree-felling have left very few adult individuals.
MALAYSIA
Sumatran orangutan
The Sumatran orangutan has a cinnamon-colored, long, fleecy, coat. Logging and plantations have pushed them up to the north of the island, and babies are caught for the illegal pet trade.
Baby orangutan
An orangutan spends more time with its mother than almost any other animal. A baby clings to its mother for its first year, but even after seven years, youngsters may still seek their mother's protection.
Sumatra
INDONESIA
Barisan Mountains
INDIAN OCEAN
20% OF WILD ORANGUTANS LIVE IN PROTECTED AREAS
UP TO 3,000 BORNEAN ORANGUTANS ARE KILLED BY HUMANS EVERY YEAR
Tree living
Orangutans spend more time in the branches than the great apes of Africa (see pp.124–125). In the trees, they eat mainly fruit and leaves, and only rarely descend to the ground. They are also less sociable than chimpanzees and gorillas, except when breeding and raising young.
Sumatran orangutans
Island refuges
Orangutans once used to range across mainland Southeast Asia, but today they are only found in a few areas on the islands of Sumatra and Borneo in Indonesia.
KEY
Sumatran orangutan
Tapanuli orangutan
Bornean orangutan

Orangutans

Three species of orangutan represent the great apes of tropical Asia. They depend on their wild rainforest habitats, so are now endangered as deforestation breaks up their home ranges into ever smaller patches.

Far from their kind
Shrinking habitats, separated by barriers such as rivers or roads, make it harder for adult orangutans to meet and breed. This means fewer babies are born, and populations shrink.

Bornean orangutan
Mature male orangutans look very different from smaller females: males have fleshy cheek pads that stick out from the face, especially in the Bornean species.

Fur color
Adult Bornean orangutans have orange-brown or maroon fur.

Under threat
Sumatra and Borneo have lost more than half of their rainforests in the past century—mainly as trees are cleared for plantations that produce crops such as palm oil. If current trends continue, all orangutans could be extinct within decades.

Indian flying fox

With more than 1,400 species, bats make up the second-biggest order of mammals after the rodents, and live in most parts of the world except the poles and remote islands. The Indian flying fox is one of the world's largest bats, and is found in tropical forests and swamps across the Indian subcontinent.

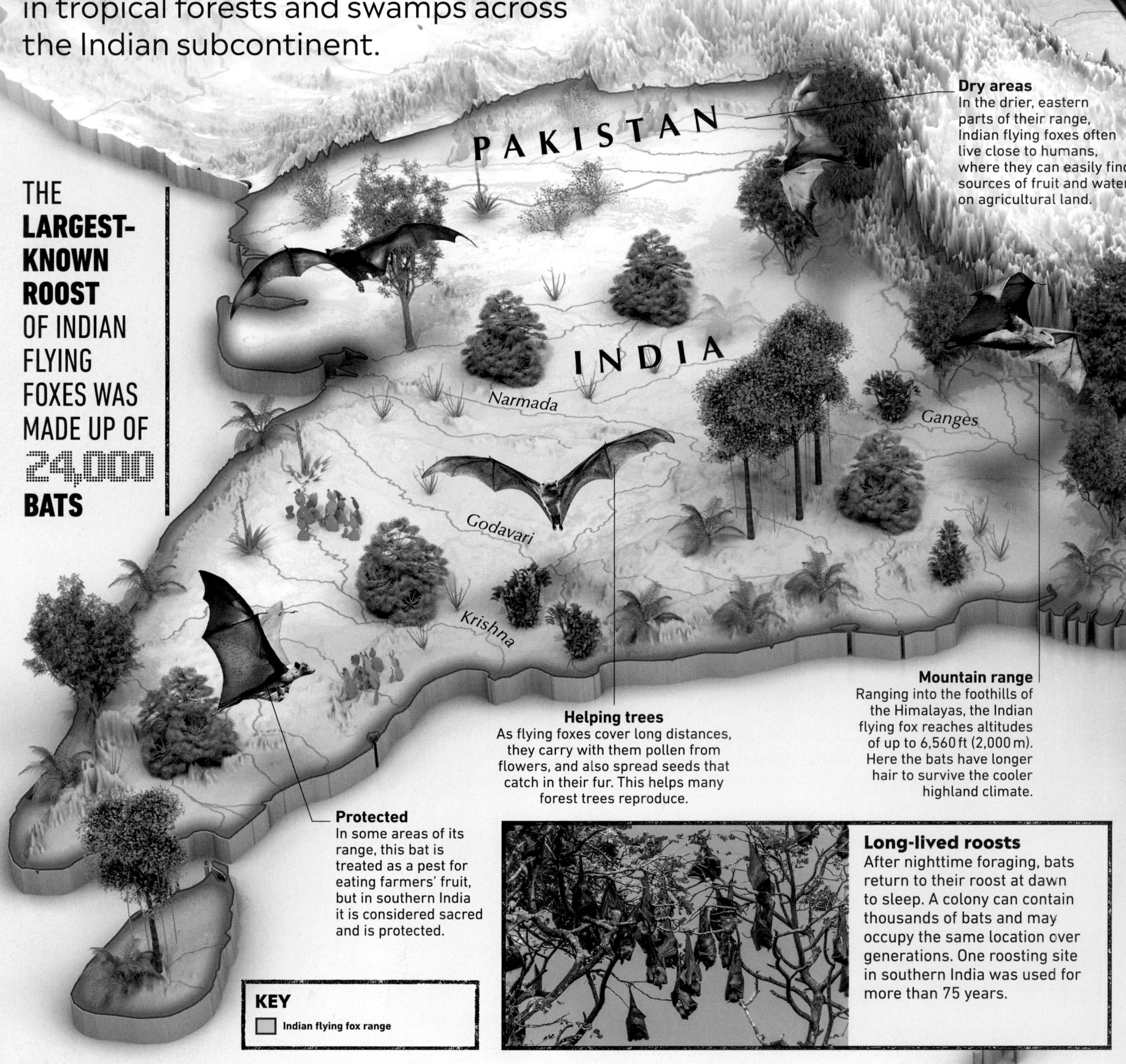

THE **LARGEST-KNOWN ROOST** OF INDIAN FLYING FOXES WAS MADE UP OF 24,000 **BATS**

Dry areas
In the drier, eastern parts of their range, Indian flying foxes often live close to humans, where they can easily find sources of fruit and water on agricultural land.

Mountain range
Ranging into the foothills of the Himalayas, the Indian flying fox reaches altitudes of up to 6,560 ft (2,000 m). Here the bats have longer hair to survive the cooler highland climate.

Helping trees
As flying foxes cover long distances, they carry with them pollen from flowers, and also spread seeds that catch in their fur. This helps many forest trees reproduce.

Protected
In some areas of its range, this bat is treated as a pest for eating farmers' fruit, but in southern India it is considered sacred and is protected.

Long-lived roosts
After nighttime foraging, bats return to their roost at dawn to sleep. A colony can contain thousands of bats and may occupy the same location over generations. One roosting site in southern India was used for more than 75 years.

Forest colonies
In Bangladesh, the biggest colonies of Indian flying foxes live in the densest forest—where there is a richer supply of fruiting trees and less disturbance from humans.

Himalayas

Handy wing
The wings of all bats are made of thin sheets of skin that extend out from the sides of the body and stretch between the long finger bones of their hands.

Finding fruit

The Indian flying fox lives across India, Pakistan, Bangladesh, and Sri Lanka. These large, fruit-eating bats sleep through the day and wake at dusk to seek out food. They are known to fly up to 90 miles (150 km) in search of the best sources of food—especially fig trees that are heavy with fruit—which they locate with their highly sophisticated senses of sight and smell.

THE **WINGSPANS** OF INDIAN FLYING FOXES CAN REACH **UP TO 6 FT** (2 M)

OTHER BATS

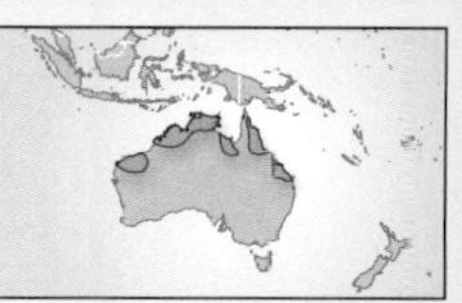
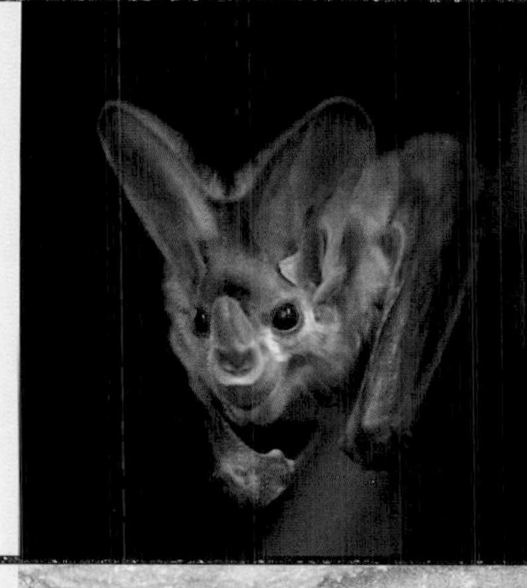

Ghost bat
Northern Australia is home to one of the world's biggest predatory bats. The ghost bat hunts mice, lizards, birds, and other bats.

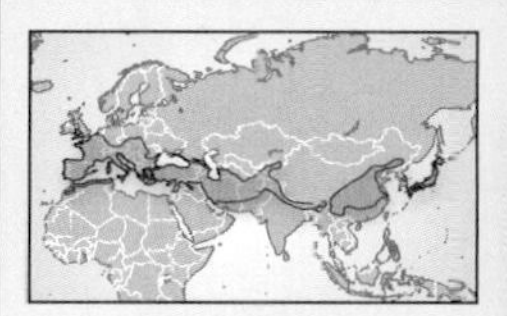

Greater horseshoe bat
Like many other bats, this species tracks insects in flight by homing in on the sound of echoed clicks. This is called echolocation.

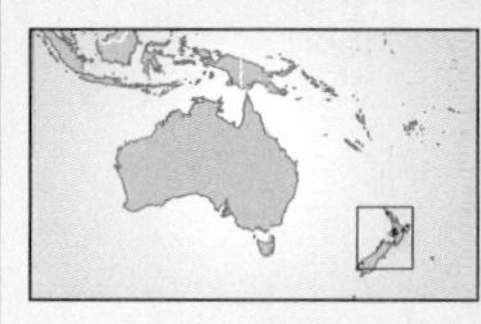

New Zealand lesser short-tailed bat
Having evolved on islands originally free of predators, this bat crawls along the ground more than any other species.

Madagascar sucker-footed bat
This bat clings to the smooth surfaces in between folds of palm leaves using tiny suckers on its wrists and ankles.

White-winged vampire bat
This tropical South American bat mainly targets birds—biting and lapping the blood of a sleeping victim.

TIGERS HAVE DISAPPEARED FROM MORE THAN 90% OF THEIR ORIGINAL HABITAT RANGE, MAINLY DUE TO ILLEGAL POACHING
KEY
Tiger range
ANIMALS IN DANGER
Tiger
IUCN status: endangered
Population estimate: 2,150–3,160
ASIA
Himalayas
Bengal tigers
On India's central plateau, below the Himalayas, Bengal tigers live in floodplains with marshes and oxbow lakes, as well as in the drier deciduous forest further south.
INDIA
Mangrove habitat
In far eastern India and Bangladesh, Bengal tigers cope with the changes of the coastal Sundarbans—the world's biggest area of mangrove forest, a place that is flooded daily by the tides.
Dry and wet forests
In southern India, Bengal tigers are found in the wet evergreen and dry deciduous forests in the hills that line the foothills of the Western Ghats.
INDIAN OCEAN
Indochinese tigers
Tigers from the tropical rainforests and dry forests of mainland Southeast Asia are smaller than those of India but larger than the ones in Sumatra. Only a few hundred remain.
INDONESIA
Sumatran tigers
The smallest tigers—nearly half the size of those from Siberia—live in the remaining rainforests of Sumatra in Indonesia. Their thinner coats are darker orange and have more stripes.
Vanishing tigers
A century ago, tigers lived from the Caspian Sea in the west to Java and Bali in the east. Today no tigers survive in these places, and throughout the rest of their range they exist in ever smaller patches. Poaching, often for the illegal trade in body parts which are used in traditional medicine, poses the biggest threat to remaining tigers.
Caspian Sea
RUSSIA
KAZAKHSTAN
CHINA
INDIA
INDONESIA
Java
Bali
Historic range

THERE ARE **MORE** TIGERS KEPT **IN CAPTIVITY** THAN THERE ARE IN THE **WILD**

A TIGER CAN **EAT** MORE THAN **80 LB (35 KG)** OF MEAT IN **ONE MEAL**

CHINA

Siberian tigers
Tigers of Russia's Siberian pine forests are among the largest of all cats, with paler coloring, fewer stripes, and thick fur that keeps out the bitter cold of winter.

Tiger territories
There are local populations of tigers in different regions of Asia, but they all belong to the same species. Adult tigers only come together to mate and otherwise live alone, patrolling territories to protect their own supply of prey. Since prey is scarcer for Siberian tigers, they need to roam territories four times bigger than those of the Bengal tigers on the Indian subcontinent.

Top cat
A tiger has massive forelimbs, needed to strike with enough strength to bring down large prey. Its fiery-colored coat helps conceal it in sun-dappled forests.

Tiger

The tiger is the world's biggest cat. But this formidable hunter is also hunted: across Asia, tiger numbers are falling as more become victim to poachers, or lose their habitat to farming, logging, and ever greater numbers of humans needing space.

Lone hunter
Adult tigers hunt alone, stalking their prey from the cover of vegetation. Blending in, a tiger can sneak close to its prey before ambushing it. Grabbing the prey with its broad forepaws, and with its long claws extended, the tiger kills its victim by a bite to the neck.

ANIMALS IN DANGER

Lion

IUCN status: vulnerable

Population estimate: 20,000–32,000

KEY

Lion range

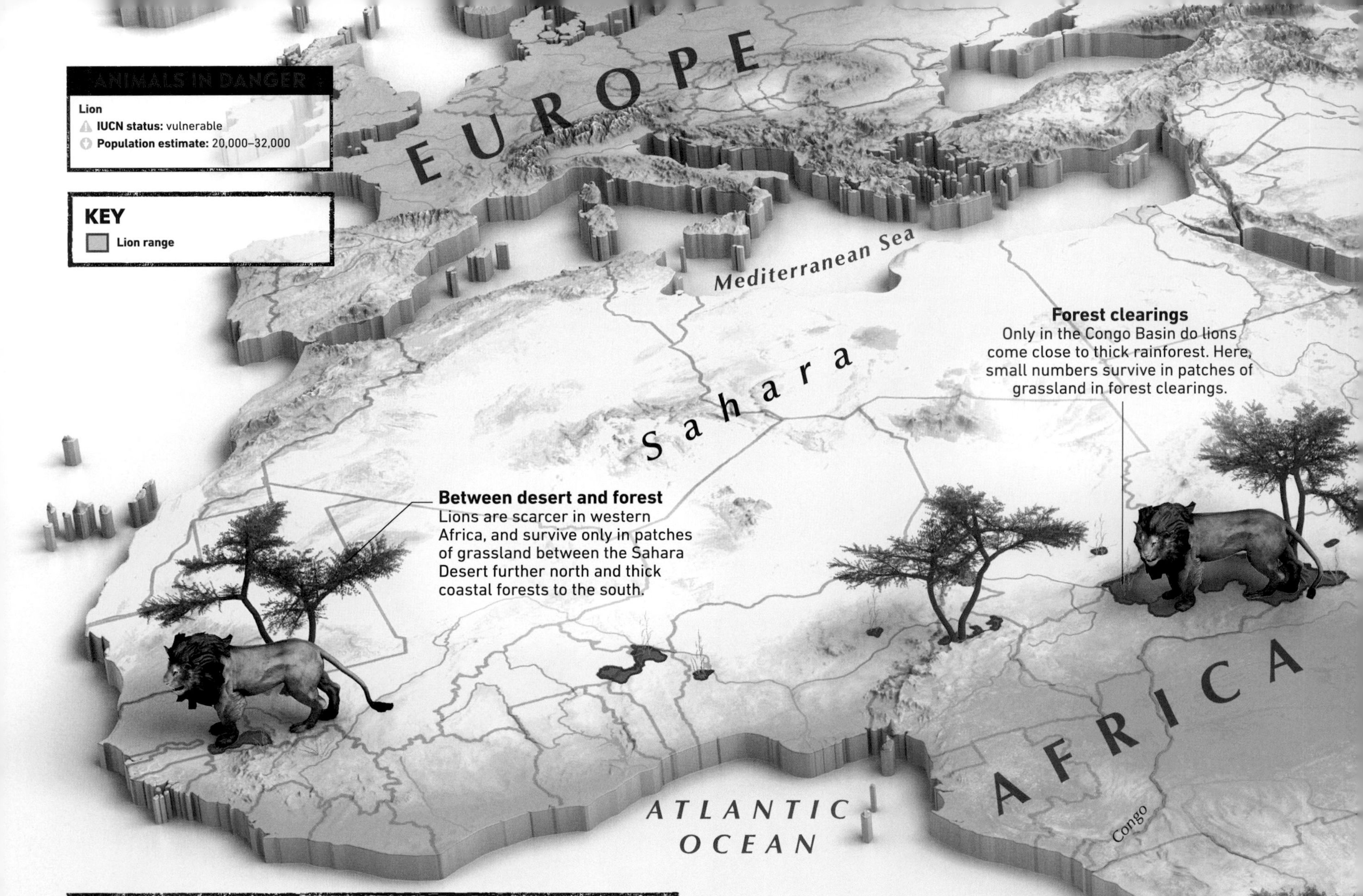

EUROPE

Mediterranean Sea

Sahara

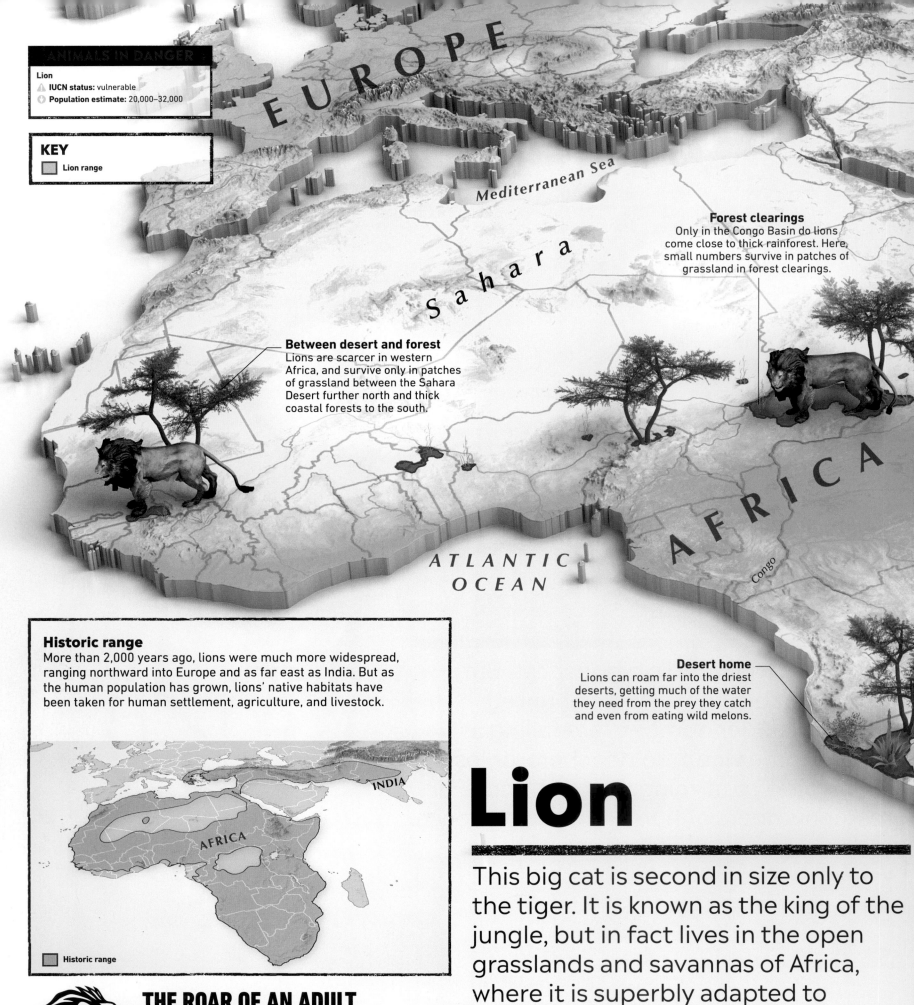

Forest clearings
Only in the Congo Basin do lions come close to thick rainforest. Here, small numbers survive in patches of grassland in forest clearings.

Between desert and forest
Lions are scarcer in western Africa, and survive only in patches of grassland between the Sahara Desert further north and thick coastal forests to the south.

AFRICA

ATLANTIC OCEAN

Congo

Historic range
More than 2,000 years ago, lions were much more widespread, ranging northward into Europe and as far east as India. But as the human population has grown, lions' native habitats have been taken for human settlement, agriculture, and livestock.

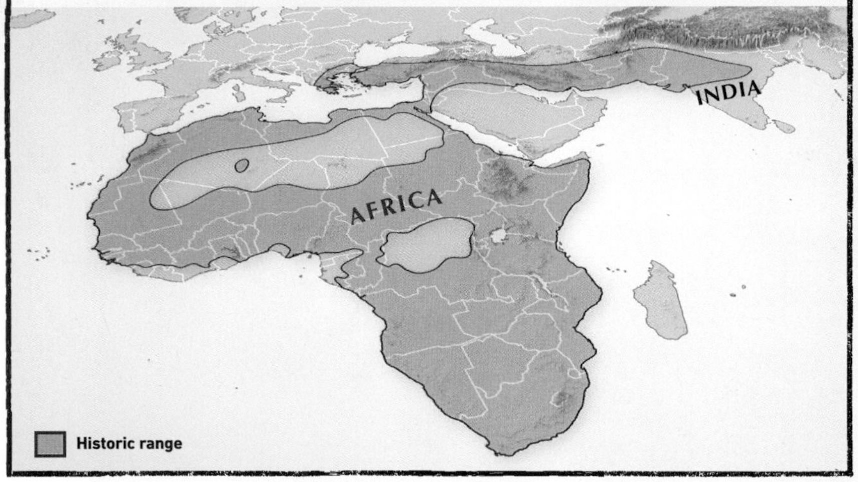

INDIA

AFRICA

Historic range

Desert home
Lions can roam far into the driest deserts, getting much of the water they need from the prey they catch and even from eating wild melons.

Lion

This big cat is second in size only to the tiger. It is known as the king of the jungle, but in fact lives in the open grasslands and savannas of Africa, where it is superbly adapted to hunting. Unlike most cats, which are solitary hunters, lions work together as a group, or pride, to bring down prey.

THE ROAR OF AN ADULT MALE LION IS SO LOUD THAT IT CAN BE HEARD CLEARLY UP TO **5 MILES** (8 KM) **AWAY**

Asiatic lions
The only wild lions left outside of Africa live in the dry scrublands and deciduous forests of India's Gir National Park.

Savanna trees
Although lions hunt in open grassland, a pride often gathers under shady trees during the heat of the day and climbs into branches to reach cool breezes. This vantage point also helps them spot prey animals traveling through the grasslands.

Fragmented habitats

Lions once freely roamed the savannas, grasslands, scrub, and open woodlands of the African continent, but much of their natural habitat has been lost. They are now largely limited to game reserves and national parks.

Mane
The thicker and darker a male lion's mane is, the more attractive he is to females.

Male lion

Camouflage
By matching the color of the surrounding grassland of the African savanna, females can get close to prey—including targets as big as buffalo and giraffe—before giving chase.

Female lion

Retractable claws
Like those of all cats, the long claws of a lion are pulled back when not in use. They are only extended when needed—such as for attacking prey.

Stealthy lynx

Recognizable by the pointy tufts of hair on their ears, these Iberian lynxes are hunting European rabbit—their favorite prey. Once common across the Iberian Peninsula, these cats are now found in only two small areas in southern Spain. A drop in rabbit populations and the spread of human settlements have led to their decline.

Finding prey
Wolves from North America live in plains and forests where there is plenty of prey, including beavers, white-tailed deer, and moose. Packs work as a team when hunting big prey, but they hunt alone for smaller meals.

Arctic tundra
Arctic wolves are especially adapted to survive in the far-north regions of Greenland and North America.

Local populations

In different parts of the wolf's huge range, local populations have habitat-specific adaptations and even look different, from the northern Arctic wolf to the southern dingo. But they all belong to the same species—gray wolf. Packs control and hunt in vast territories, and they communicate with each other by howling and scent-marking.

Padded feet
The feet of wolves and dogs have soles with protective pads and clawed toes. Unlike those of cats, their claws are blunt and not retractable.

Fur
In most wolves the fur is mottled gray, but some wolves are born white or black. Wolves living in the coldest climates grow thicker fur.

Gray wolf

This wide-ranging canine is a highly social animal, living and hunting in family groups, known as packs. It is found across vast areas of the globe in many different habitats, from the frozen Arctic to hot, dry deserts.

Eurasian wolf
Wolves that live in the forests of Scandinavia and Russia prey on anything from red deer and wild boar to hares and voles. They may also attack livestock and raid human garbage.

ASIA

Himalayan habitat
Found in a variety of alpine habitats, from high-altitude mountains to temperate forests, wolves living here hunt yaks and goats and shelter in alpine caves.

Siberian tundra
Living on the open frozen ground across northern Siberia, the large tundra wolf develops a thicker, darker coat in winter and hunts some of the largest prey, including caribou and musk ox.

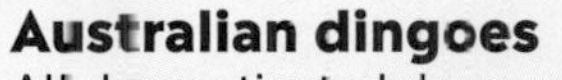

KEY

 Wolf range

Dingo
Dingoes are highly adaptable and can be found in every habitat in Australia, even deserts—as long as they have access to drinking water.

AUSTRALIA

Australian dingoes
All domesticated dogs, which we keep as pets, are descended from the gray wolf and belong to the same species. Dingoes originated from domesticated dogs that were brought to Australia from Asia by humans 4,000 years ago and then returned to the wild.

Arctic wolves
Found in the Arctic tundras of Greenland and North America, the Arctic wolf is one of the biggest types of wolf. It survives freezing conditions by having long, thick fur and a thick layer of body fat, and stays white throughout the year as effective camouflage against the snow.

SOME WOLF **TERRITORIES** EXTEND UP TO **1,000 SQ MILES** (2,600 SQ KM)

THE **LARGEST-KNOWN PACK** WAS MADE UP OF **36** WOLVES

WOLVES CAN **ROAM** UP TO **12 MILES** (30 KM) IN A **SINGLE DAY**

Range of habitats

Bears are found across Europe, Asia, North America, and in parts of South America. The largest bear species—polar and brown bears—live in the cold north. Further south, smaller bears with smaller ranges live in the tropics.

Brown bear
Spanning the Northern Hemisphere, brown bears have the widest range of any bear species. On the Pacific coast of North America, they fish for salmon.

American black bear
The most populous bear species is an excellent opportunist, eating seasonal nuts and berries, scavenging carrion, and even raiding human garbage or stores of food.

Polar bear
This bear eats meat and little else. It specializes in hunting for Arctic seals, and regularly swims more than 30 miles (50 km) in search of food.

Andean bear
This shy bear is mainly a plant-eater. It prefers the remote rainforests of the Andes Mountains, though it will descend in search of food and has been found in many different habitats, including thorny, dry forests and even coastal deserts.

Grizzly bear
The fur of brown bears varies in color across their range. Some regional populations in North America have silver-tipped, or grizzly, hair.

Brown bear

ANIMALS IN DANGER

Andean bear
IUCN status: vulnerable
Population estimate: 2,500–10,000

Polar bear
IUCN status: vulnerable
Population estimate: 22,000–31,000

Sloth bear
IUCN status: vulnerable
Population estimate: unknown

Adapting to climate

Polar bears are perfectly adapted to life in their Arctic habitat. Their thick fur is made of hollow hairs that trap warmth close to the body. Even their paw pads are furry, with tiny bumps to help grip slippery ice. Their small ears and tail minimize heat loss. Loss of their unique habitat is putting these bears at risk, as climate change reduces the sea ice on which they depend.

Bears

There are eight different species of bear across the world. They include the largest land carnivores with the power to bring down the biggest prey. But not all bears are ferocious hunters—some eat mainly insects, while others prefer plants and berries.

ANIMALS IN DANGER

Sun bear
IUCN status: vulnerable
Population estimate: unknown

Giant panda
IUCN status: vulnerable
Population estimate: 1,800

Asiatic black bear
IUCN status: vulnerable
Population estimate: unknown

ASIA

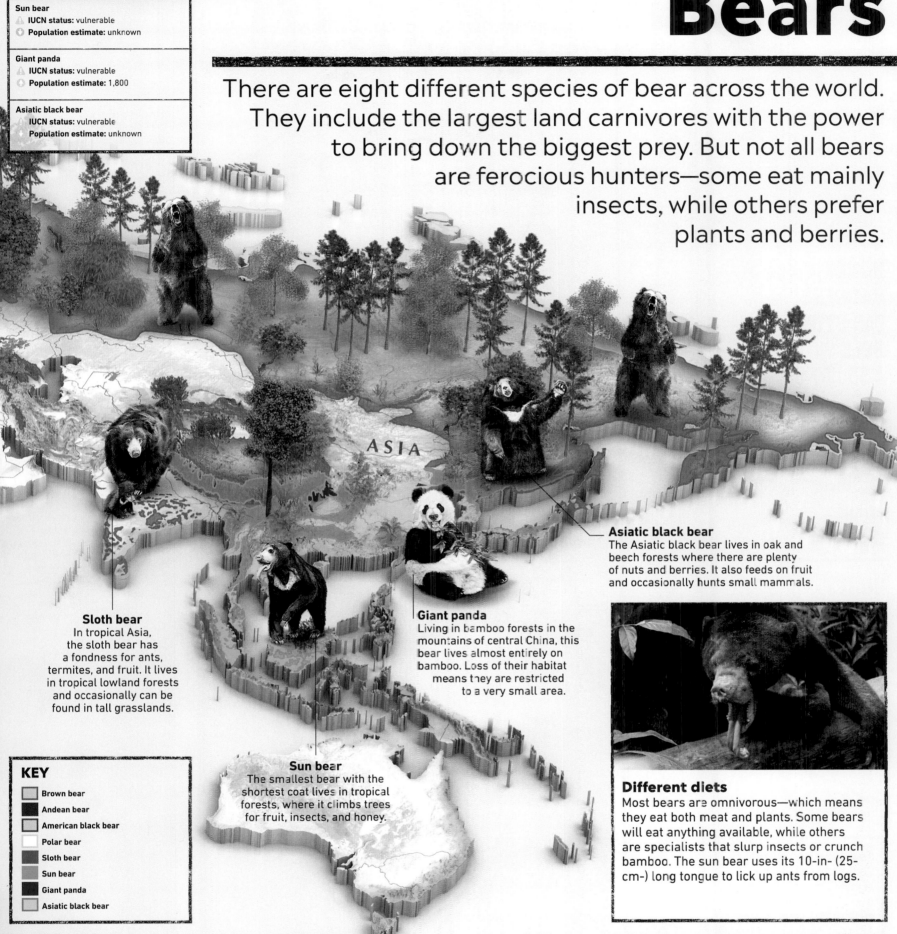

Asiatic black bear
The Asiatic black bear lives in oak and beech forests where there are plenty of nuts and berries. It also feeds on fruit and occasionally hunts small mammals.

Sloth bear
In tropical Asia, the sloth bear has a fondness for ants, termites, and fruit. It lives in tropical lowland forests and occasionally can be found in tall grasslands.

Giant panda
Living in bamboo forests in the mountains of central China, this bear lives almost entirely on bamboo. Loss of their habitat means they are restricted to a very small area.

Sun bear
The smallest bear with the shortest coat lives in tropical forests, where it climbs trees for fruit, insects, and honey.

KEY
- Brown bear
- Andean bear
- American black bear
- Polar bear
- Sloth bear
- Sun bear
- Giant panda
- Asiatic black bear

Different diets
Most bears are omnivorous—which means they eat both meat and plants. Some bears will eat anything available, while others are specialists that slurp insects or crunch bamboo. The sun bear uses its 10-in- (25-cm-) long tongue to lick up ants from logs.

POLAR BEARS ARE THE **BIGGEST SPECIES** AND CAN WEIGH **UP TO 1,760 LB** (800 KG)

Sahara
Desert scavengers
Along the fringes of the Sahara Desert, honey badgers are expert at digging out spiny-tailed lizards and gerbils from burrows, or grubbing for roots and insects, but they also scavenge on carrion (the flesh of dead animals).
Helpful hunters
In the grasslands of East Africa, other predators, such as goshawks and jackals, have learned to follow digging honey badgers, and catch small animals that escape their notice.
HONEY BADGERS CAN STUN BEES WITH A SQUIRT OF REPELLENT SPRAY FROM GLANDS AROUND THEIR BOTTOM
Finding honey
In central Africa, honey badgers roam in lush tropical rainforests, raiding wild beehives to steal the honey, as well as to eat the bee larvae.
Congo Basin
AFRICA
Thick-skinned badger
The honey badger's thick skin is loose, especially around the neck, enabling it to twist around to bite when grabbed by an attacker. A thick skin also protects it from snake bites and bee stings.
HONEY BADGERS ARE RESISTANT TO SNAKE VENOM
Badger baby
Honey badger mothers bring up their babies alone, moving them from den to den in their mouth every few days.
Fearless badgers
Sometimes honey badgers see off threats from predators much larger than themselves, such as this pack of wild dogs. Although they will rarely pick a fight, if attacked they rush at the assailants, hissing, raising their hackles, and releasing a stench from their anal glands.

KEY
Honey badger range
Caspian Sea
ASIA
Arabian Peninsula
INDIA
Caspian badgers
On the dry, grassy plains of southwest Asia, the honey badger reaches the northernmost limits of its range around the Caspian Sea.
Arabian badgers
Honey badgers survive the dry deserts of the Arabian Peninsula by catching venomous prey, including scorpions and snakes. They shelter under rocks during the hottest part of the day.
Indian badgers
The honey badger is widespread across the Indian subcontinent, but is most common in forests and grasslands, where it may share its territory with tigers and sloth bears.

Opportunistic living

Few animals can survive such a wide range of habitats as the honey badger. Across Africa, India, and the Arabian Peninsula, it lives in forests, savanna, marshes, and deserts—wherever this nocturnal animal can dig a burrow. It is not found in the very driest parts of the Sahara.

Honey badger

Six species of badgers live across North America, Africa, and Eurasia—and all are stocky, strong-bodied animals. The honey badger has a particular reputation for toughness. With a strong bite, thick skin, and sharp claws, it is a fierce hunter that braves stinging bees to satisfy its taste for honey.

Digging for prey
As well as excavating burrows, the strong front paws with their long claws can rip open bee hives and dig out animal prey such as rodents from underground. Food is found by smell and sound.

Zebras

Zebras are the most distinctive members of the horse family. Three species live on the grassy savannas in the eastern and southern parts of Africa, each with their own species-specific pattern of stripes.

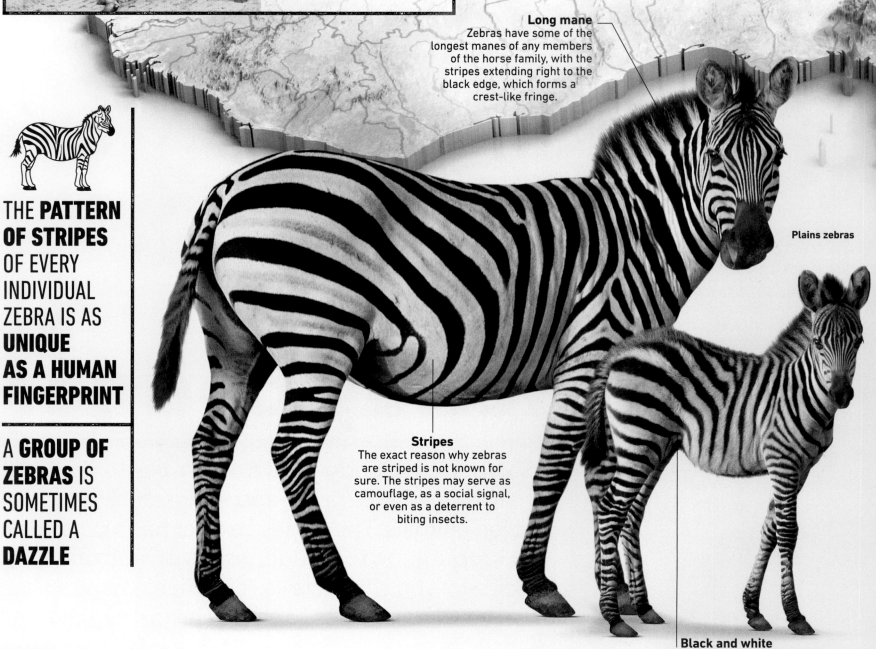

Quagga
A subspecies of the plains zebra with fewer stripes, called the quagga, was once common in southern Africa, but was hunted to extinction by about 1883. Today scientists are breeding zebra with quagga-like characteristics to try to bring the animal back.

African grazers

Zebras graze on the grasses of a variety of habitats, from the plains zebra in open grasslands and savannas, to the Grevy's zebra in semi-arid scrub, and the mountain zebra on mountainous slopes and plateaus. During the dry season, the Grevy's and mountain zebras spread out further in their range to find better sources of food and water, but the plains zebra follows seasonal rains—to wherever the grass is greener—in large migrations.

Long mane
Zebras have some of the longest manes of any members of the horse family, with the stripes extending right to the black edge, which forms a crest-like fringe.

Stripes
The exact reason why zebras are striped is not known for sure. The stripes may serve as camouflage, as a social signal, or even as a deterrent to biting insects.

Black and white
Underneath their fur, zebras actually have dark skin. Their stripes develop as white over black rather than vice versa.

Plains zebras

THE **PATTERN OF STRIPES** OF EVERY INDIVIDUAL ZEBRA IS AS **UNIQUE AS A HUMAN FINGERPRINT**

A **GROUP OF ZEBRAS** IS SOMETIMES CALLED A **DAZZLE**

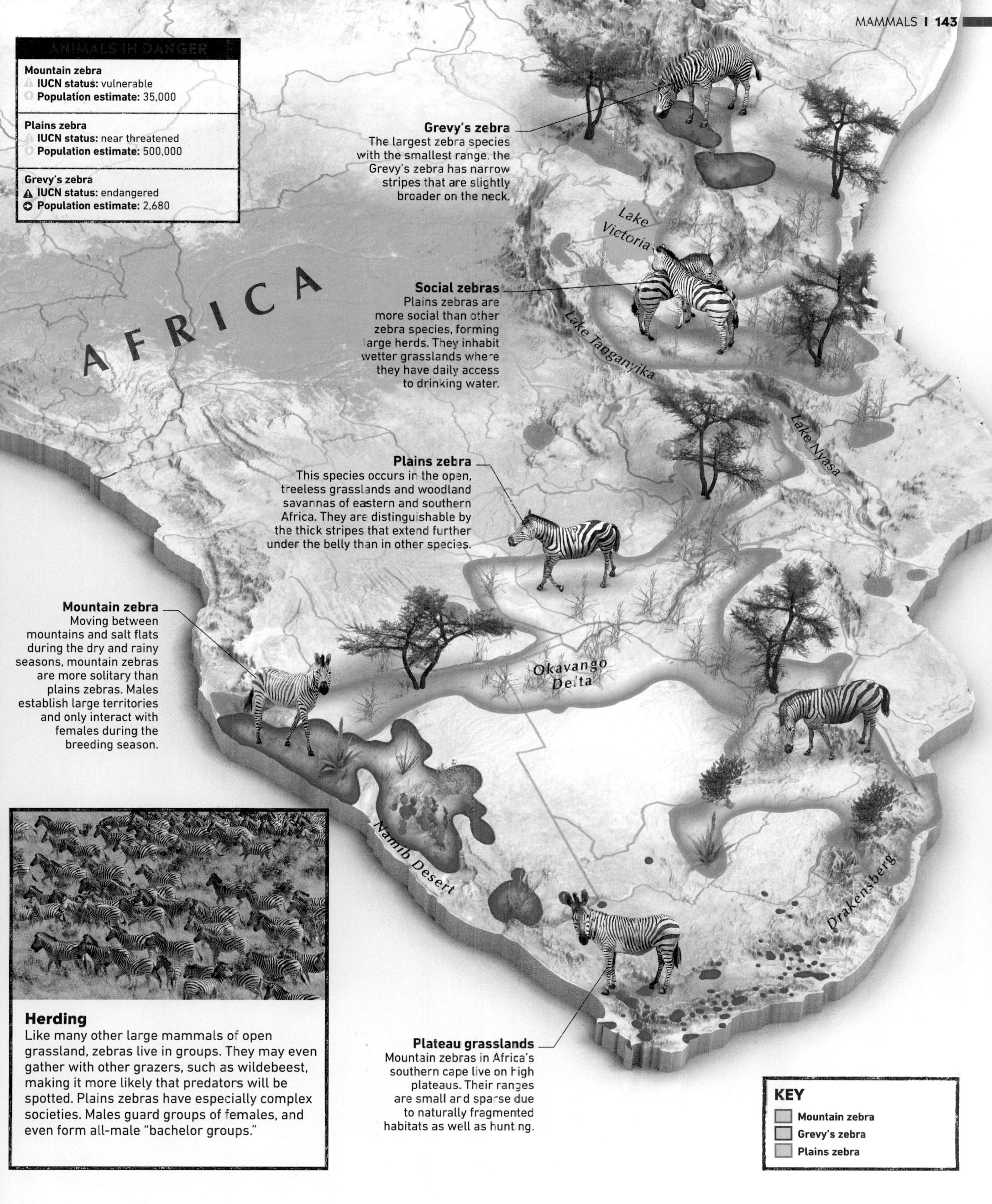

ANIMALS IN DANGER

Mountain zebra
IUCN status: vulnerable
Population estimate: 35,000

Plains zebra
IUCN status: near threatened
Population estimate: 500,000

Grevy's zebra
IUCN status: endangered
Population estimate: 2,680

Grevy's zebra
The largest zebra species with the smallest range, the Grevy's zebra has narrow stripes that are slightly broader on the neck.

Social zebras
Plains zebras are more social than other zebra species, forming large herds. They inhabit wetter grasslands where they have daily access to drinking water.

Plains zebra
This species occurs in the open, treeless grasslands and woodland savannas of eastern and southern Africa. They are distinguishable by the thick stripes that extend further under the belly than in other species.

Mountain zebra
Moving between mountains and salt flats during the dry and rainy seasons, mountain zebras are more solitary than plains zebras. Males establish large territories and only interact with females during the breeding season.

Plateau grasslands
Mountain zebras in Africa's southern cape live on high plateaus. Their ranges are small and sparse due to naturally fragmented habitats as well as hunting.

Herding

Like many other large mammals of open grassland, zebras live in groups. They may even gather with other grazers, such as wildebeest, making it more likely that predators will be spotted. Plains zebras have especially complex societies. Males guard groups of females, and even form all-male "bachelor groups."

THE ESTIMATED NUMBER LEFT OF ADULT BREEDING JAVAN RHINOS IS ONLY
18
RHINOS ARE HUNTED FOR THEIR HORNS, WHICH ARE WORTH MORE THAN THEIR WEIGHT IN GOLD
Black rhinoceros
Just four countries—Kenya, Zimbabwe, Namibia, and South Africa—protect more than 95 percent of all surviving black rhinoceroses. Protection means that numbers are rising in these nations.
ATLANTIC OCEAN
AFRICA
White rhinoceros
Most remaining white rhinos are found in the grasslands of southern Africa; a few have been reintroduced to eastern parts of the continent.
KENYA
TANZANIA
ANGOLA
ZAMBIA
NAMIBIA
BOTSWANA
ZIMBABWE
MOZAMBIQUE
SOUTH AFRICA
Black and white
Despite their names, both kinds of African rhinoceroses are in fact grayish-brown. These symbols are black or white to distinguish the two species on the map.
Thick-skinned
The black rhino has coarse skin, in places up to 1½ in (4 cm) thick. This protects it from being scratched by thorny shrubs as it eats.
Mud bath
All rhinoceroses, including this female black rhino and her calf, like to wallow in mud pools. It helps cool the body and protect it from biting insects.
Grasping lip
The fingerlike upper lip of the black rhino helps grasp foliage. White rhinos have a flat, wide upper lip for grazing grass.
Black rhinoceros

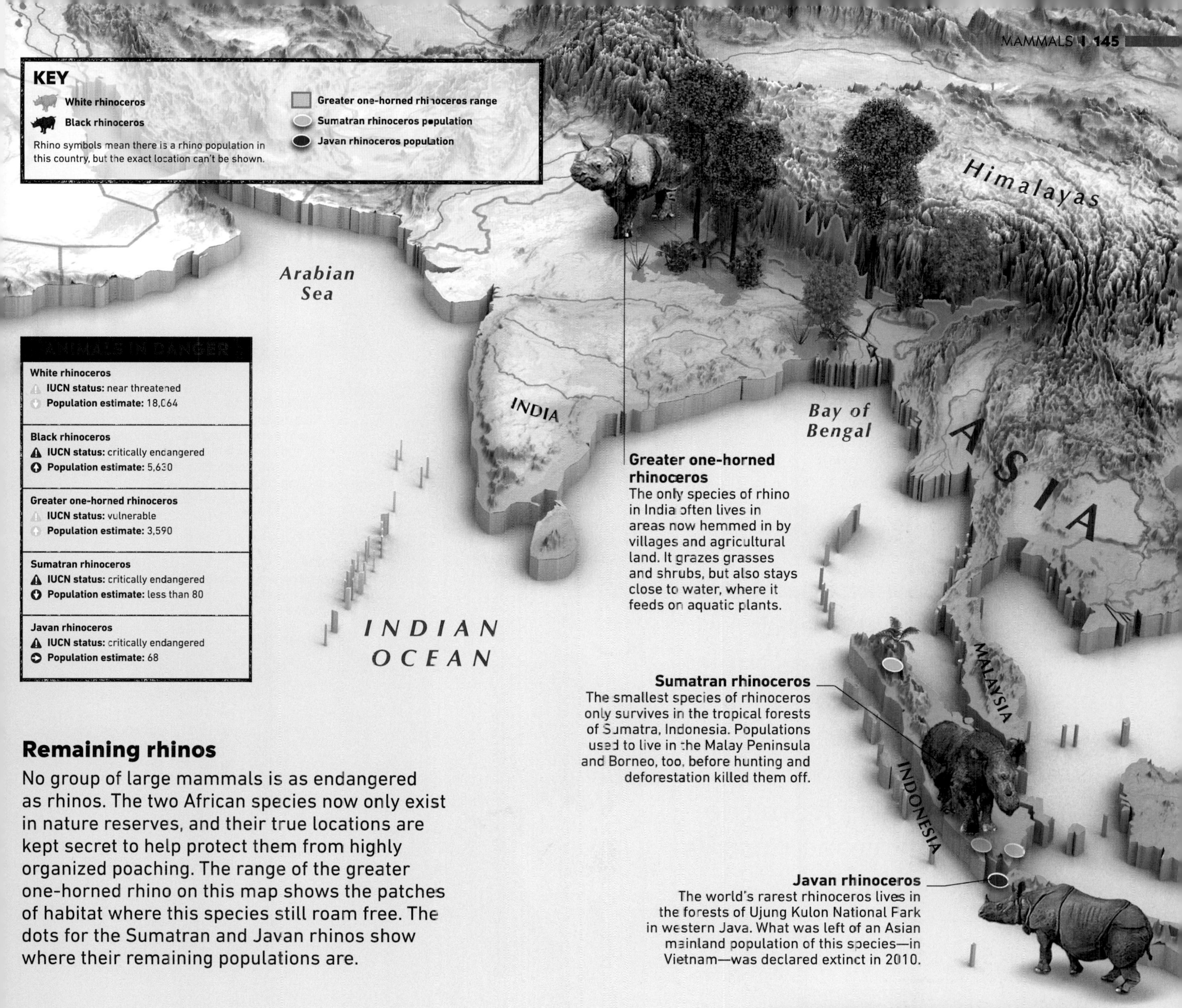

Rhinos

In prehistoric times, rhinoceroses ranged across large areas of the globe. Today, five species survive on savannas in Africa and in forests and grassland in Asia, but poaching and habitat destruction have edged these unique creatures to the brink of extinction.

Remaining rhinos

No group of large mammals is as endangered as rhinos. The two African species now only exist in nature reserves, and their true locations are kept secret to help protect them from highly organized poaching. The range of the greater one-horned rhino on this map shows the patches of habitat where this species still roam free. The dots for the Sumatran and Javan rhinos show where their remaining populations are.

KEY

- White rhinoceros
- Black rhinoceros
- Rhino symbols mean there is a rhino population in this country, but the exact location can't be shown.
- Greater one-horned rhinoceros range
- Sumatran rhinoceros population
- Javan rhinoceros population

Arabian Sea

INDIA

Bay of Bengal

Himalayas

ASIA

MALAYSIA

INDONESIA

INDIAN OCEAN

ANIMALS IN DANGER

White rhinoceros
IUCN status: near threatened
Population estimate: 18,064

Black rhinoceros
IUCN status: critically endangered
Population estimate: 5,630

Greater one-horned rhinoceros
IUCN status: vulnerable
Population estimate: 3,590

Sumatran rhinoceros
IUCN status: critically endangered
Population estimate: less than 80

Javan rhinoceros
IUCN status: critically endangered
Population estimate: 68

Greater one-horned rhinoceros
The only species of rhino in India often lives in areas now hemmed in by villages and agricultural land. It grazes grasses and shrubs, but also stays close to water, where it feeds on aquatic plants.

Sumatran rhinoceros
The smallest species of rhinoceros only survives in the tropical forests of Sumatra, Indonesia. Populations used to live in the Malay Peninsula and Borneo, too, before hunting and deforestation killed them off.

Javan rhinoceros
The world's rarest rhinoceros lives in the forests of Ujung Kulon National Park in western Java. What was left of an Asian mainland population of this species—in Vietnam—was declared extinct in 2010.

Guarded treasure
Rhinos are poached for their horns, which some people wrongly believe have medicinal qualities. Armed guards help protect some rhinos, including this white rhino in Kenya.

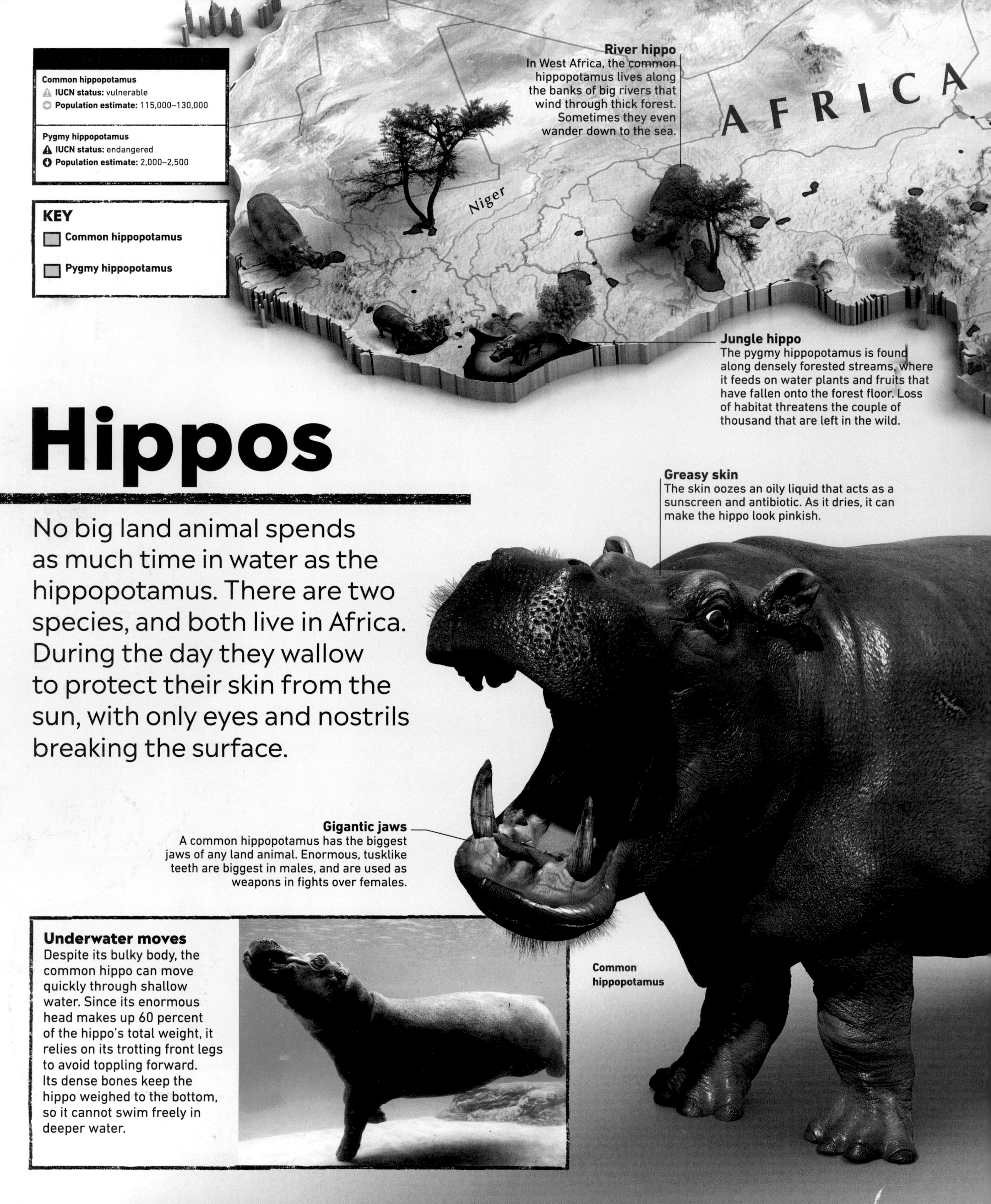

Common hippopotamus
IUCN status: vulnerable
Population estimate: 115,000–130,000

Pygmy hippopotamus
IUCN status: endangered
Population estimate: 2,000–2,500

KEY
Common hippopotamus
Pygmy hippopotamus

River hippo
In West Africa, the common hippopotamus lives along the banks of big rivers that wind through thick forest. Sometimes they even wander down to the sea.

Jungle hippo
The pygmy hippopotamus is found along densely forested streams, where it feeds on water plants and fruits that have fallen onto the forest floor. Loss of habitat threatens the couple of thousand that are left in the wild.

Hippos

No big land animal spends as much time in water as the hippopotamus. There are two species, and both live in Africa. During the day they wallow to protect their skin from the sun, with only eyes and nostrils breaking the surface.

Greasy skin
The skin oozes an oily liquid that acts as a sunscreen and antibiotic. As it dries, it can make the hippo look pinkish.

Gigantic jaws
A common hippopotamus has the biggest jaws of any land animal. Enormous, tusklike teeth are biggest in males, and are used as weapons in fights over females.

Common hippopotamus

Underwater moves

Despite its bulky body, the common hippo can move quickly through shallow water. Since its enormous head makes up 60 percent of the hippo's total weight, it relies on its trotting front legs to avoid toppling forward. Its dense bones keep the hippo weighed to the bottom, so it cannot swim freely in deeper water.

A HIPPO CAN **OPEN ITS** ENORMOUS MOUTH UP TO AN ANGLE OF 180 **DEGREES**— WIDER THAN ANY OTHER **LARGE MAMMAL**

ADULT MALE COMMON HIPPOS CAN WEIGH UP TO **4,400 LB** (2,000 KG)

Fertile lakes
Dung produced by hundreds of pooping hippos helps enrich lakes, fertilizing the water with nutrients that can support food chains with big shoals of fishes.

Coastal hippos
The coast of the Namib Desert is the only place where hippos can be seen cooling off in shallow seawater.

Nocturnal grazer
The common hippo gets most of its food on land. It grazes on grass at night, using its fleshy lips to pluck the blades.

Hippo havens

The common hippopotamus, the larger of the two species, lives in patches of woodland and grassland around rivers across sub-Saharan Africa. The pygmy hippopotamus only survives in a few fragments of rainforest in West Africa.

HIPPOS CAN **HOLD THEIR BREATH** FOR

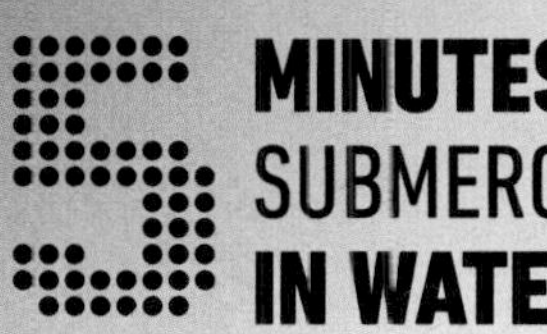

MINUTES SUBMERGED **IN WATER**

Mini hippo
The forest-dwelling pygmy hippopotamus is about half as tall as its bigger cousin. Shaded by over-hanging trees, it probably spends more time out of water during the day than the common hippo, but its habits are little known.

1,700 LB (770 KG) IS THE **HEAVIEST RECORDED WEIGHT** OF AN ADULT MALE MOOSE

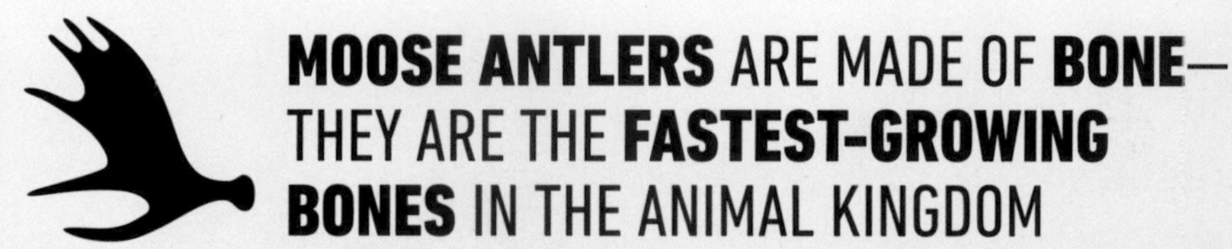

MOOSE ANTLERS ARE MADE OF **BONE**—THEY ARE THE **FASTEST-GROWING BONES** IN THE ANIMAL KINGDOM

NORTH AMERICA

AFRICA

Alaskan giants
The biggest moose occur in Alaska and Siberia. Calves born in Alaska can weigh nearly twice as much as those born in Europe.

Migration
In the parts of their range with the coldest winters—in North America and Siberia—moose migrate south during the bitter months in search of better food. North American moose may travel up to 125 miles (200 km).

KEY
Moose range

Antler
A male's antlers start growing in April and are fully formed by summer. Antlers are covered in a nourishing layer of skin, called velvet, that gets rubbed off before the antler is shed in December.

Marshes and wetlands

Moose favor the damp, boreal forests that stretch across North America, Europe, and northern Asia, where the snow does not get too deep in winter and temperatures remain cool in summer. They stick to wetland areas, where their favorite food plants—birch, alder, and willow trees—grow in abundance.

Moose

The world's biggest species of deer also has one of the widest ranges. The moose is an animal of marshy forests and is found across temperate regions of the northern hemisphere—where there is plenty of vegetation to browse and cover for females to raise their calves.

Motherly care
A female moose gives birth to one or two calves and feeds them with milk for up to five months. The thick cover of the northern forests helps protect them from predatory gray wolves and brown bears.

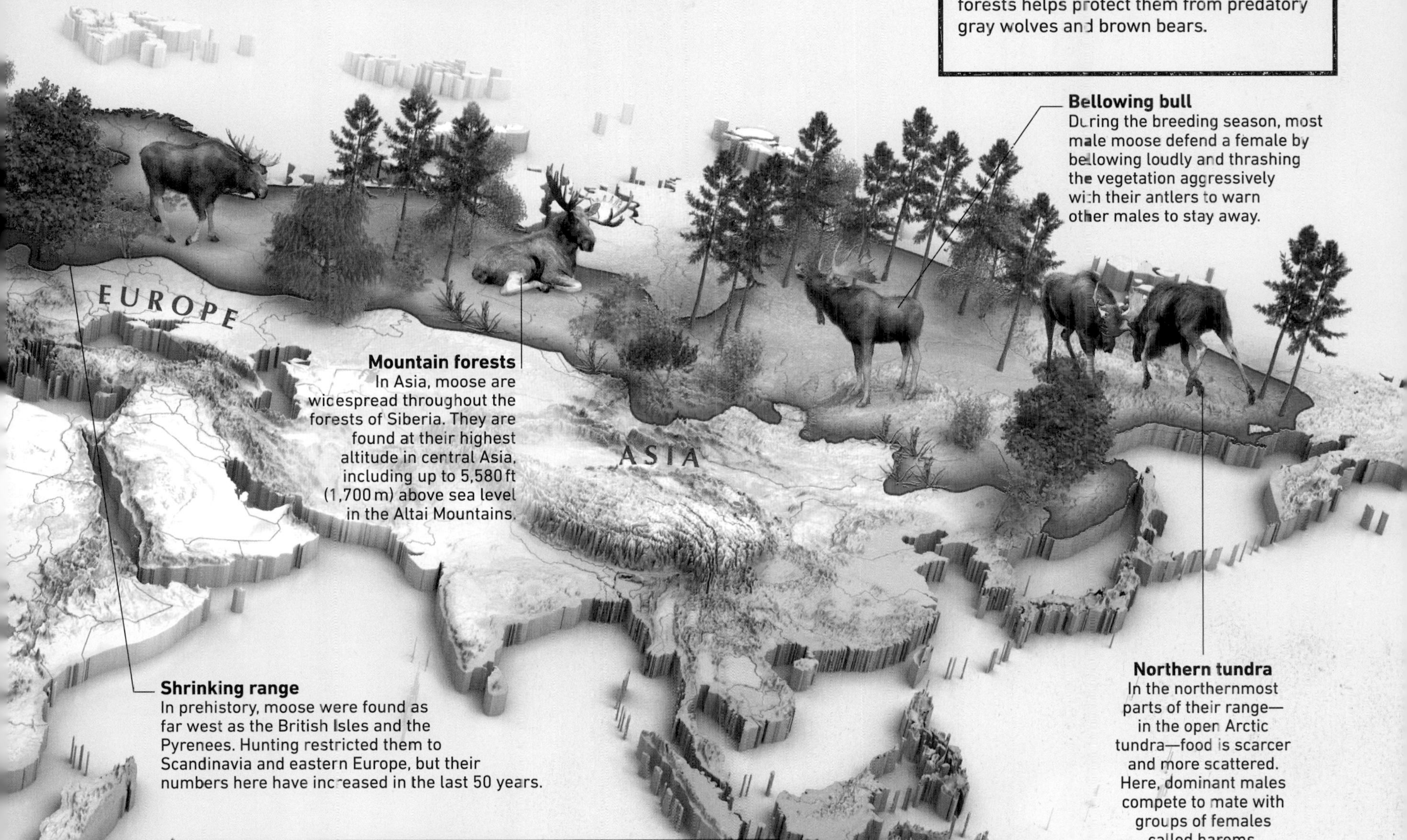

Bellowing bull
During the breeding season, most male moose defend a female by bellowing loudly and thrashing the vegetation aggressively with their antlers to warn other males to stay away.

EUROPE

ASIA

Mountain forests
In Asia, moose are widespread throughout the forests of Siberia. They are found at their highest altitude in central Asia, including up to 5,580 ft (1,700 m) above sea level in the Altai Mountains.

Shrinking range
In prehistory, moose were found as far west as the British Isles and the Pyrenees. Hunting restricted them to Scandinavia and eastern Europe, but their numbers here have increased in the last 50 years.

Northern tundra
In the northernmost parts of their range—in the open Arctic tundra—food is scarcer and more scattered. Here, dominant males compete to mate with groups of females called harems.

Giant antlers
Like almost all other deer, only male moose grow antlers. These enormous bony weapons—each more than 3 ft (1 m) long—grow new each year as males defend their mates and territories, before being shed at the end of each breeding season.

AUSTRALIA

A **HUMPBACK WHALE** CAN SWALLOW **UP TO 4 TONS OF PREY** EACH DAY

WHALE SONGS CAN BE HEARD UP TO **20 MILES** (30 KM) **AWAY**

Icy feeding grounds
In the cold waters around the Arctic, humpback whales feed on a mixture of small animals—including fishes such as herring and pollack, and shrimplike crustaceans such as krill.

Pacific routes
Whales that feed in the waters around Alaska follow two migration routes—either across the Pacific to breed in Hawaii or along the US coast to California.

Farthest travelers
Whales migrating up the west coast of South America travel a record-breaking distance for this species—crossing up to 5,160 miles (8,300 km) between Central America and Antarctica.

ATLANTIC OCEAN

PACIFIC OCEAN

Northern Indian Ocean
Whales only migrate within one hemisphere. In the northern Indian Ocean—which is north of the equator—whales can't migrate further north, so they live here year round.

Heading north
Whales in the Southern Ocean begin their northward migration around May to breeding grounds in the tropics, such as around the coast of eastern Africa and Madagascar.

SOUTHERN OCEAN

Antarctic waters
The cold Southern Ocean around Antarctica teems with krill—a shrimplike crustacean that drifts in enormous swarms. Krill supplies almost all the food of whales feeding here.

ANTARCTICA

Raising young
After a pregnancy lasting nearly a year, a humpback whale gives birth to a single calf that already weighs almost a ton. The baby grows quickly on more than 90 lb (40 kg) of milk every day, and stays with its mother for up to a year.

KEY
- Feeding grounds
- Breeding grounds
- Year-round population
- Migration routes

Ivory
The hard substance from which elephant tusks are made.

Jet propulsion
The act of pushing forward by jetting out water, used by squids and octopuses.

Keratin
A tough material that makes up body parts such as hair, feathers, scales, and claws.

Krill
Tiny marine crustaceans that many animals, such as fish, whales, and seabirds, depend on for food.

Larva
The immature stage of animals that hatch from eggs and undergo metamorphosis (complete change) to become adults.

Mangrove
Trees that grow along muddy shores and river banks, often in salty water, and with many of their roots exposed.

Marine
Relating to the ocean or sea.

Metamorphosis
When an animal goes through a major change in body shape during its life cycle, such as when a caterpillar turns into a butterfly.

Microscopic
Something that is very small and can be seen only through a microscope.

Migration
The regular movement of animals from one place to another, often to find food or breed.

Mimicry
When an animal has evolved to look or act like another animal, in order to attract prey, or avoid getting eaten.

Mollusk
One of a group of invertebrates that includes snails, clams, and octopuses.

Monotreme
A group of mammals that lay eggs.

Molt
The way an animal sheds part of its outer skin, coat, or exoskeleton. In crustaceans, the regular shedding of the hard outer skeleton (exoskeleton) to allow the animal to grow.

Nectar
A sugar solution produced by flowers to attract pollinating animals such as bees and butterflies.

Nocturnal
When an animal is active at night.

Nutrition
The process of eating and processing food to absorb substances necessary for life.

Omnivorous
Refers to an animal that eats plants and meat.

Oxbow lake
A U-shaped lake formed from a river bend cut off from a river that over time has changed its course.

Pampas
Wide-stretching, grass-covered plains in temperate parts of South America.

Parasite
An organism that feeds on another, called the host, weakening it, and sometimes eventually killing it.

Pesticide
Chemicals used to kill insects and other pests that eat or damage crops.

Pigment
A substance that gives something color.

Plankton
Small organisms that drift in water.

Poaching
Illegal hunting and killing of wild animals.

Pollination
When insects and other animals carry pollen from one flower to another so that fertilization takes place and new plants can grow.

Prairie
Large, flat grasslands, with very few trees, in North America.

Prehensile
Able to coil around an object and grip it, like the tail of a monkey or chameleon.

Primate
One of a group of animals that includes lemurs, monkeys, apes, and humans.

Proboscis
A long snout, or similar organ.

Protein
A type of complex chemical found in all living things.

Range
Referring to the territory, or area, within which an animal lives.

River basin
The land in which water gathers from one or more rivers.

Roost
To settle for the night, or a place where birds, bats, and butterflies do this.

Savanna
Open grasslands in tropical regions, with only a few trees.

Scavenger
An animal that feeds on the remains of dead animals or other organic waste from living organisms.

Spawning
Releasing eggs and sperm into water so that fertilization can take place.

Species
A group of similar organisms than can interbreed and produce fertile offspring.

Subcontinent
A large landmass that is part of a bigger continent.

Subspecies
A variant of a species, usually only found in one particular area.

Subtropical
An area or climate that is nearly tropical, located at the northern or southern edge of the tropics.

Taiga
The vast coniferous forests covering the northern parts of Eurasia and North America.

Talons
The large, hooked claws of a bird of prey.

Temperate
The mild, variable climate found in areas between the tropics and the cold polar regions.

Thermals
Currents of rising warm air.

Tropical
Referring to the climate or habitats in the region around the equator, known as the tropics.

Tundra
A treeless habitat in the cold, northernmost parts of North America, Europe, and Asia, in which the ground is frozen for much of the year.

Index

Page numbers in **bold** refer to a main topic

Acknowledgments

Dorling Kindersley would like to thank: Sheila Collins for design assistance; Georgina Palffy for editorial assistance; Hazel Beynon for proofreading; Elizabeth Wise for indexing.

The publisher would like to thank the following for their kind permission to reproduce their photographs:

(Key: a-above; b-below/bottom; c-center; f-far; l-left; r-right; t-top)

2 FLPA: Greg Basco, BIA / Minden Pictures. **4 Alamy Stock Photo:** Narint Asawaphisith (crb). **Getty Images:** Martin Harvey / The Image Bank (tr); James L. Amos / Corbis Documentary (cr). **5 Alamy Stock Photo:** David Carillet (tr). **Dreamstime.com:** Toldiu74 (cl). **Getty Images:** jopstock (clb); Paul Starosta (tl). **6-7 FLPA:** Ralph Pace / Minden Pictures (b). **8-9 Getty Images:** Martin Harvey / The Image Bank. **10-11 Alamy Stock Photo:** National Geographic Image Collection (c). **12 Alamy Stock Photo:** Jelger Herder / Buiten-Beeld (tr); Val Duncan / Kenebec Images (cr); franzfoto.com (cb); Sheila Haddad / Danita Delimont (br); National Geographic Image Collection (tc). **naturepl.com:** Matthias Breiter (cla). **13 Alamy Stock Photo:** John Bennet (bc); Anatoliy Lastovetskiy (bl); Michal Sikorski (crb); Eric Dragesco / Nature Picture Library (cr). **14 Alamy Stock Photo:** Urbach, James / Superstock (c). **Dreamstime.com:** Svetlana Foote (crb). **naturepl.com:** Jane Burton (br). **15 Alamy Stock Photo:** Nobuo Matsumura (cr). **Getty Images:** uzairabdrahim (cra). **naturepl.com:** Cyril Ruoso (clb). **16 Dreamstime.com:** Sandamali Fernando (cra). **17 Alamy Stock Photo:** Ryhor Bruyeu (cl); Allen Galiza (tr). **Getty Images / iStock:** DaveThomasNZ (cr). **Getty Images:** Caroline Pang (bl); UniversalImagesGroup (tl). **18-19 Getty Images:** Ralph Lee Hopkins. **20 Getty Images:** Picture by Tambako the Jaguar. **21 Alamy Stock Photo:** Kevin Elsby (clb); Alex Mustard / Nature Picture Library (cla). **Getty Images:** Arterra (cr); Don Smith (tr); Michael Mike L. Baird flickr.bairdphotos.com (bl); Sandra Standbridge (br). **22-23 Getty Images:** James L. Amos / Corbis Documentary. **24 123RF.com:** Igor Serdiuk (bc); Anna Zakharchenko (c). **Richard E. Lee:** (crb). **Science Photo Library:** Woods Hole Oceanographic Institution, Visuals Unlimited (br). **25 Alamy Stock Photo:** Philip Dalton (br); Fiedler, W. / juniors@wildlife / Juniors Bildarchiv GmbH (tr). **naturepl.com:** Gavin Maxwell (cb). **26 naturepl.com:** Fred Bavendam (clb). **27 naturepl.com:** Fred Bavendam (tr). **28 naturepl.com:** Doug Perrine (bc). **29 Alamy Stock Photo:** Marevision / agefotostock (tr). **30 Dreamstime.com:** Cosmin Manci (tl). **30-31 Dreamstime.com:** Lee Amery (cb). **31 Dreamstime.com:** Maria Shchipakina (br). **Getty Images / iStock:** Merrimon (tr). **32-33 naturepl.com:** Phil Savoie. **34-35 Natural History Museum Bern,. 34 Alamy Stock Photo:** Razvan Cornel Constantin (br). **35 Alamy Stock Photo:** FLPA (bl). **36 Alamy Stock Photo:** FLPA (bl). **37 Alamy Stock Photo:** blickwinkel / H. Baesemann (br). **38-39 Alamy Stock Photo:** Narint Asawaphisith. **40 Alamy Stock Photo:** Jezper (bl). **naturepl.com:** Piotr Naskrecki (bc/ Lungfish). **Shutterstock.com:** Rachasie (bc). **41 Alamy Stock Photo:** blickwinkel / F. Teigler (c); WaterFrame_sta / :WaterFrame (ca); Paulo Oliveira (crb). **Getty Images:** torstenvelden (clb). **42 Alamy Stock Photo:** Marevision / agefotostock (cl); Paulo Oliveira (bl). **45 123RF.com:** Sergei Uriadnikov (br). **Alamy Stock Photo:** Nature Picture Library (tc). **46-47 Getty Images / iStock:** E+ / FilippoBacci. **48 123RF.com:** Richard Whitcombe (tr). **Alamy Stock Photo:** Stephen Frink Collection (tl). **48-49 Shutterstock.com:** Rich Carey (bc). **49 Alamy Stock Photo:** Adam Butler (b). **50 Dreamstime.com:** Chee-Onn-Leong (c). **51 Dreamstime.com:** Tatiana Belova (tr, crb); Slowmotiongli (cra); Gorodok495 (cr); Valeronia (br). **52-53 Getty Images:** Paul Starosta. **54 Alamy Stock Photo:** Pablo Méndez / agefotostock (bc/Frog); Wild Wonders of Europe / Hodalic / / Nature Picture Library (bc). **naturepl.com:** D. Parer & E. Parer-Cook (bl). **55 Alamy Stock Photo:** Odilon Dimier / PhotoAlto (clb); Anton Sorokin (cb). **Getty Images / iStock:** AdrianHillman (c). **naturepl.com:** Fred Olivier (fclb). **Shutterstock.com:** Arun Kumar Anantha Kumar (crb). **56 Alamy Stock Photo:** blickwinkel / W. Pattyn (bl). **Ardea:** Phil A. Dotson / Science Source / ardea.com (cla). **Dreamstime.com:** Slowmotiongli (clb); Martin Voeller (tl); Kevin Wells (cl). **58-59 Alamy Stock Photo:** Chris Mattison / Nature Picture Library. **60 123RF.com:** Dirk Ercken (cb, bc/below). **Alamy Stock Photo:** MYN / JP Lawrence / Nature Picture Library (crb). **Dreamstime.com:** Dirk Ercken (br); Dirk Ercken / Kikkerdirk (fbr). **naturepl.com:** Paul Bertner (fcrb); Michael & Patricia Fogden (clb). **61 naturepl.com:** Lucas Bustamante (b). **63 Alamy Stock Photo:** Rich Bunce (tc). **naturepl.com:** Cyril Ruoso (tr). **64-65 Dreamstime.com:** Toldiu74. **66 123RF.com:** Shakeel SM (bc). **Getty Images:** imageBROKER / Michael Weberberger (bc/Sea snake). **Shutterstock.com:** Grzegorz Lukacijewski (bl). **67 Alamy Stock Photo:** A & J Visage (cla); Mike Robinson (cra); Ken Gillespie Photography (tl); Rweisswald (crb). **Vladimir Dinets:** (br). **69 Alamy Stock Photo:** Krystyna Szulecka Photography (tc). **70 Alamy Stock Photo:** Anthony Pierce (bl). **Getty Images:** Mark Deeble and Victoria Stone (br). **73 Alamy Stock Photo:** Claude Thouvenin / Biosphoto (cra); imageBroker / Thorsten Negro (bl). **Science Photo Library:** Frans Lanting, Mint Images (c). **74-75 Shutterstock.com:** NickEvansKZN. **76 Avalon:** Tony Crocetta (bc). **77 Alamy Stock Photo:** Horizon / Horizon International Images Limited (tr); Arco / G. Lacz / Imagebroker (crb); Sibons photography (br). **naturepl.com:** Jen Guyton (cra); Barry Mansell (cr). **79 Dorling Kindersley:** Daniel Long (bl). **Science Photo Library:** Edward Kinsman (clb). **80-81 Getty Images:** jopstock. **82 Alamy Stock Photo:** blickwinkel / McPHOTO / PUM (crb). **Shutterstock.com:** Rachel Portwood (clb). **83 Alamy Stock Photo:** Christine Cuthbertson (crb); Kike Calvo / Alamy Stock Photo (cr); Bob Gibbons (c). **SuperStock:** Jean Paul Ferrero / Pantheon (br). **84 Alamy Stock Photo:** Neil Bowman (cla); imageBROKER / Konrad Wothe (cl). **Dreamstime.com:** Gerfriedscholz (clb). **Getty Images:** Its About Light / Design Pics (tl); Oliver Strewe (bl). **85 Getty Images:** Lisa Mckelvie (br). **86-87 naturepl.com:** Claudio Contreras. **89 Alamy Stock Photo:** Auscape International Pty Ltd / Ian Beattie (cr); Stefano Paterna (tr); NSP-RF (cra); David South (crb). **Dreamstime.com:** Willtu (br). **naturepl.com:** Stefan Christmann (bc). **90 Alamy Stock Photo:** Nature Picture Library / Markus Varesvuo (bl); Prisma by Dukas Presseagentur GmbH / Bernhardt Reiner (br). **91 Getty Images:** DanielBehmPhotography.Com (cb). **92 Taiwanese Photographer Wilson Chen:** (cla, tr). **93 Getty Images:** 500px / David Gruskin (bc). **94-95 Shutterstock.com:** Ondrej Prosicky. **96 Alamy Stock Photo:** Ger Bosma (tl). **Getty Images / iStock:** RNMitra (bl). **97 Alamy Stock Photo:** Blue Planet Archive AAF (bc). **98 Alamy Stock Photo:** Tierfotoagentur / T. Harbig (bl). **99 Alamy Stock Photo:** blickwinkel / H. Kuczka (cra); VWPics / Mario Cea Sanchez (tc). **naturepl.com:** Phil Savoie (br). **100-101 Alamy Stock Photo:** David Carillet. **102 Alamy Stock Photo:** Arco / C. Hütter (bc); Peter M. Wilson (bc/Goats); Robert Haasmann / imageBROKER (bl); Zoonar / Artush Foto (crb). **Dreamstime.com:** Godruma (cra). **103 Alamy Stock Photo:** Sciepro / Science Photo Library (tl); Nature Picture Library (clb). **Shutterstock.com:** Yann hubert (bl); Lab Photo (cb). **104 Ardea:** D. Parer & E. Parer-Cook (clb). **105 Dreamstime.com:** Valentyna Chukhlyebova (tr). **naturepl.com:** Doug Gimesy (bl). **106 Alamy Stock Photo:** Rawy van den Beucken (br). **Dreamstime.com:** Zcello (bl). **107 Alamy Stock Photo:** National Geographic Image Collection (cra). **Dreamstime.com:** Carolina Garcia Aranda (tr); Holly Kuchera (cr); Hotshotsworldwide (crb). **naturepl.com:** Nick Garbutt (br). **109 naturepl.com:** Gabriel Rojo (cra). **110 naturepl.com:** Suzi Eszterhas (bc, br). **111 123RF.com:** vilainecrevette (r). **112 Alamy Stock Photo:** Cathy Withers-Clarke (br). **TurboSquid:** mohannadhisham / Dorling Kindersley (elephant models). **113 Alamy Stock Photo:** AfriPics.com (br); Friedrich von Hörsten (bc). **TurboSquid:** Skazok / Dorling Kindersley (elephant models). **114 123RF.com:** Dmitry Potashkin (bc). **Alamy Stock Photo:** Giedrius Stakauskas (bl). **115 Dreamstime.com:** Isselee (br). **116-117 naturepl.com:** Klein & Hubert. **119 Science Photo Library:** Ken Catania / Visuals Unlimited, Inc (crb). **120 Alamy Stock Photo:** Michele Burgess (clb). **121 Alamy Stock Photo:** Life on white (crb); Nick Garbutt / RGB Ventures / SuperStock (bl). **Dorling Kindersley:** Jerry Young (br). **122 naturepl.com:** Hiroya Minakuchi (br). **123 Alamy Stock Photo:** Diane McAllister / naturepl.com (tr). **naturepl.com:** Konrad Wothe (b). **124 Alamy Stock Photo:** Arco Images / Vnoucek, F / Imagebroker (bl). **125 Dreamstime.com:** Daniel Bellhouse / Danox (tr). **126 naturepl.com:** Thomas Marent (bc). **127 Alamy Stock Photo:** RDW Environmental (clb). **Dreamstime.com:** Sergey Uryadnikov (br). **128 Alamy Stock Photo:** Marius Dobilas (bc). **129 Alamy Stock Photo:** FLPA (cr); Daniel Romero / VWPics (br). **Dreamstime.com:** Kyslynskyy (tl); Slowmotiongli (cra). **131 Alamy Stock Photo:** Andy Rouse / Nature Picture Library (bc). **133 Dorling Kindersley:** Roman Gorielov (bl). **Getty Images:** David Chen / EyeEm (tc). **134-135 naturepl.com:** Laurent Geslin. **136 Getty Images:** Jim Cumming (b). **137 Alamy Stock Photo:** Arco / TUNS / Imagebroker (cb); Werner Layer / mauritius images GmbH (bc). **138 Dreamstime.com:** Outdoorsman (bc). **139 Alamy Stock Photo:** Genevieve Vallee (crb). **140-141 Dreamstime.com:** Matthijs Kuijpers (bc). **140 naturepl.com:** Suzi Eszterhas (bc). **141 FLPA:** Vincent Grafhorst / Minden Pictures (br). **142 Alamy Stock Photo:** Steve Bloom / Steve Bloom Images (c); Photo Researchers / Science History Images (tl). **143 Alamy Stock Photo:** Mint Images / Mint Images Limited (clb). **144 Alamy Stock Photo:** Denis-Huot / Nature Picture Library (bl). **145 Alamy Stock Photo:** Ann & Steve Toon / Nature Picture Library (br). **146 Alamy Stock Photo:** Lena Ivanova (bc). **147 Alamy Stock Photo:** Juniors Bildarchiv / F300 / Juniors Bildarchiv GmbH (bc). **148 Alamy Stock Photo:** Doug Lindstrand / Alaska Stock RF / Design Pics Inc (bl). **149 Getty Images:** Doug Lindstrand / Alaska Stock RF / Design Pics Inc (bc). **Paul Williams:** Paul Williams (tr). **150 Dreamstime.com:** Seanothon (bl). **151 Alamy Stock Photo:** blickwinkel / AGAMI / M. van Duijn (br). **152-153 naturepl.com:** Flip Nicklin.

All other images © Dorling Kindersley
For further information see: www.dkimages.com

Map data sources:

IUCN 2020. The IUCN Red List of Threatened Species. Version 2020-2. https://www.iucnredlist.org:

28–29 Butler, M., Cockcroft, A., MacDiarmid, A. & Wahle, R. 2011. *Homarus gammarus*. The IUCN Red List of Threatened Species 2011: e.T169955A69905303. https://dx.doi.org/10.2305/IUCN.UK.2011-1.RLTS.T169955A69905303.en (Common lobster). **42–43** NatureServe. 2013. *Petromyzon marinus*. The IUCN Red List of Threatened Species 2013: e.T16781A18229984. https://dx.doi.org/10.2305/IUCN.UK.2013-1.RLTS.T16781A18229984.en (Sea lamprey). **44–45** Rigby, C.L., Barreto, R., Carlson, J., Fernando, D., Fordham, S., Francis, M.P., Herman, K., Jabado, R.W., Liu, K.M., Lowe, C.G, Marshall, A., Pacoureau, N., Romanov, E., Sherley, R.B. & Winker, H. 2019. *Carcharodon carcharias*. The IUCN Red List of Threatened Species 2019: e.T3855A2878674. https://dx.doi.org/10.2305/IUCN.UK.2019-3.RLTS.T3855A2878674.en (Great white shark). **56–57** IUCN SSC Amphibian Specialist Group. 2015. *Necturus maculosus*. The IUCN Red List of Threatened Species 2015: e.T59433A64731610. https://dx.doi.org/10.2305/IUCN.UK.2015-4.RLTS.T59433A64731610.en (Mudpuppy). **56** Geoffrey Hammerson. 2004. *Amphiuma means*. The IUCN Red List of Threatened Species 2004: e.T59074A11879454. https://dx.doi.org/10.2305/IUCN.UK.2004.RLTS.T59074A11879454.en (Amphiuma); IUCN SSC Amphibian Specialist Group. 2020. *Bolitoglossa mexicana*. The IUCN Red List of Threatened Species 2020: e.T59180A53976360. https://dx.doi.org/10.2305/IUCN.UK.2020-1.RLTS.T59180A53976360.en (Mushroom-tongued salamander); Sergius Kuzmin, Theodore Papenfuss, Max Sparreboom, Ismail H. Ugurtas, Steven Anderson, Trevor Beebee, Mathieu Denoël, Franco Andreone, Brandon Anthony, Benedikt Schmidt, Agnieszka Ogrodowczyk, Maria Ogielska, Jaime Bosch, David Tarkhnishvili, Vladimir Ishchenko. 2009. *Salamandra salamandra*. The IUCN Red List of Threatened Species 2009: e.T59467A11928351. https://dx.doi.org/10.2305/IUCN.UK.2009.RLTS.T59467A11928351.en (Fire salamander); Yoshio Kaneko, Masafumi Matsui. 2004. Andrias japonicus. The IUCN Red List of Threatened Species 2004: e.T1273A3376261. https://dx.doi.

org/10.2305/IUCN.UK.2004.RLTS.T1273A3376261.en (Japanese giant salamander); Jan Willem Arntzen, Sergius Kuzmin, Robert Jehle, Trevor Beebee, David Tarkhnishvili, Vladimir Ishchenko, Natalia Ananjeva, Nikolai Orlov, Boris Tuniyev, Mathieu Denoël, Per Nyström, Brandon Anthony, Benedikt Schmidt, Agnieszka Ogrodowczyk. 2009. *Triturus cristatus*. The IUCN Red List of Threatened Species 2009: e.T22212A9365894. https://dx.doi.org/10.2305/IUCN.UK.2009.RLTS.T22212A9365894.en (Great crested newt). **60–61** IUCN SSC Amphibian Specialist Group. 2015. *Oophaga pumilio*. The IUCN Red List of Threatened Species 2015: e.T55196A3025630. https://dx.doi.org/10.2305/IUCN.UK.2015-4.RLTS.T55196A3025630.en (Strawberry poison dart frog). **62–63** Aram Agasyan, Aziz Avisi, Boris Tuniyev, Jelka Crnobrnja Isailovic, Petros Lymberakis, Claes Andrén, Dan Cogalniceanu, John Wilkinson, Natalia Ananjeva, Nazan Üzüm, Nikolai Orlov, Richard Podloucky, Sako Tuniyev, Uğur Kaya. 2009. *Bufo bufo*. The IUCN Red List of Threatened Species 2009: e.T54596A11159939. https://dx.doi.org/10.2305/IUCN.UK.2009.RLTS.T54596A11159939.en (Common toad). **68–69** Cayot, L.J., Gibbs, J.P., Tapia, W. & Caccone, A. 2017. *Chelonoidis donfaustoi*. The IUCN Red List of Threatened Species 2017: e.T90377132A90377135. https://dx.doi.org/10.2305/IUCN.UK.2017-3.RLTS.T90377132A90377135.en (Eastern Santa Cruz Giant Tortoise); Rhodin, A.G.J., Gibbs, J.P., Cayot, L.J., Kiester, A.R. & Tapia, W. 2017. *Chelonoidis phantasticus* (errata version published in 2018). The IUCN Red List of Threatened Species 2017: e.T170517A128969920. https://dx.doi.org/10.2305/IUCN.UK.2017-3.RLTS.T170517A1315907.en (Fernandina giant tortoise); Caccone, A., Cayot, L.J., Gibbs, J.P. & Tapia, W. 2017. *Chelonoidis becki*. The IUCN Red List of Threatened Species 2017: e.T9018A82426296. https://dx.doi.org/10.2305/IUCN.UK.2017-3.RLTS.T9018A82426296.en (Wolf Volcano giant tortoise); Cayot, L.J., Gibbs, J.P., Tapia, W. & Caccone, A. 2018. *Chelonoidis vandenburghi* (errata version published in 2019). The IUCN Red List of Threatened Species 2018: e.T9027A144766471. https://dx.doi.org/10.2305/IUCN.UK.2018-2.RLTS.T9027A144766471.en (Volcán Alcedo giant tortoise); Cayot, L.J., Gibbs, J.P., Tapia, W. & Caccone, A. 2017. *Chelonoidis porteri*. The IUCN Red List of Threatened Species 2017: e.T9026A82777132. https://dx.doi.org/10.2305/IUCN.UK.2017-3.RLTS.T9026A82777132.en (Western Santa Cruz giant tortoise); Caccone, A., Cayot, L.J., Gibbs, J.P. & Tapia, W. 2017. *Chelonoidis chathamensis*. The IUCN Red List of Threatened Species 2017: e.T9019A82688009. https://dx.doi.org/10.2305/IUCN.UK.2017-3.RLTS.T9019A82688009.en (San Cristóbal giant tortoise); Cayot, L.J., Gibbs, J.P., Tapia, W. & Caccone, A. 2017. *Chelonoidis hoodensis*. The IUCN Red List of Threatened Species 2017: e.T9024A82777079. https://dx.doi.org/10.2305/IUCN.UK.2017-3.RLTS.T9024A82777079.en (Española giant tortoise). **72–73** Jenkins, R.K.B., Andreone, F., Andriamazava, A., Anjeriniaina, M., Brady, L., Glaw, F., Griffiths, R.A., Rabibisoa, N., Rakotomalala, D., Randrianantoandro, J.C., Randrianiriana, J., Randrianizahana, H., Ratsoavina, F. & Robsomanitrandrasana, E. 2011. *Furcifer oustaleti*. The IUCN Red List of Threatened Species 2011: e.T172866A6932058. https://dx.doi.org/10.2305/IUCN.UK.2011-2.RLTS.T172866A6932058.en (Oustalet's chameleon); Jenkins, R.K.B., Andreone, F., Andriamazava, A., Anjeriniaina, M., Brady, L., Glaw, F., Griffiths, R.A., Rabibisoa, N., Rakotomalala, D., Randrianantoandro, J.C., Randrianiriana, J., Randrianizahana, H., Ratsoavina, F. & Robsomanitrandrasana, E. 2011. *Calumma parsonii*. The IUCN Red List of Threatened Species 2011: e.T172896A6937628. https://dx.doi.org/10.2305/IUCN.UK.2011-2.RLTS.T172896A6937628.en (Parson's chameleon); Jenkins, R.K.B., Andreone, F., Andriamazava, A., Anjeriniaina, M., Brady, L., Glaw, F., Griffiths, R.A., Rabibisoa, N. Rakotomalala, D., Randrianantoandro, J.C., Randrianiriana, J., Randrianizahana H., Ratsoavina, F. & Robsomanitrandrasana, E. 2011. *Furcifer pardalis*. The IUCN Red List of Threatened Species 2011: e.T172955A6947909. https://dx.doi.org/10.2305/IUCN.UK.2011-2.RLTS.T172955A6947909.en (Panther chameleon). **72** Jenkins, R.K.B., Andreone, F., Andriamazava, A., Anjeriniaina, M., Brady, L., Glaw, F., Griffiths, R.A., Rabibisoa, N., Rakotomalala, D., Randrianantoandro, J.C., Randrianiriana, J., Randrianizahana, H., Ratsoavina, F. & Robsomanitrandrasana, E. 2011. *Palleon nasus*. The IUCN Red List of Threatened Species 2011: e.T172773A6915062. https://dx.doi.org/10.2305/IUCN.UK.2011-2.RLTS.T172773A6915062.en (Elongated leaf chameleon); Jenkins, R.K.B., Andreone, F., Andriamazava, A., Anjeriniaina, M., Brady, L., Glaw, F., Griffiths, R.A., Rabibisoa, N., Rakotomalala, D., Randrianantoandro, J.C., Randrianiriana, J., Randrianizahana, H., Ratsoavina, F. & Robsomanitrandrasana, E. 2011. *Furcifer labordi*. The IUCN Red List of Threatened Species 2011: e.T8765A12929754. https://dx.doi.org/10.2305/IUCN.UK.2011-2.RLTS.T8765A12929754.en (Laborde's chameleon). **77** Stuart, B., Nguyen, T.Q., Thy, N., Grismer, L. Chan-Ard, T., Iskandar, D., Golynsky, E. & Lau, M.W.N. 2012. *Python bivittatus* (errata version published in 2019). The IUCN Red List of Threatened Species 2012: e.T193451A151341916. https://dx.doi.org/10.2305/IUCN.UK.2012-1.RLTS.T193451A151341916.en (Burmese python); Stuart, B., Thy, N., Chan-Ard, T., Nguyen, T.Q., Grismer, L., Auliya, M., Das, I. & Wogan, G. 2018. *Python reticulatus*. The IUCN Red List of Threatened Species 2018: e.T183151A1730027. https://dx.doi.org/10.2305/IUCN.UK.2018-2.RLTS.T183151A1730027.en (Reticulated python); Tallowin, O., Allison, A., Parker, F. & O'Shea, M. 2017. *Morelia amethistina*. The IUCN Red List of Threatened Species 2017: e.T177501A1489667. https://dx.doi.org/10.2305/IUCN.UK.2017-3.RLTS.T177501A1489667.en (Amethystine python). **78–79** Spawls, S. 2010. *Dendroaspis polylepis*. The IUCN Red List of Threatened Species 2010: e.T177584A7461853. https://dx.doi.org/10.2305/IUCN.UK.2010-4.RLTS.T177584A7461853.en (Black mamba); Frost, D.R., Hammerson, G.A. & Santos-Barrera, G. 2007. *Crotalus atrox*. The IUCN Red List of Threatened Species 2007: e.T64311A12763519. https://dx.doi.org/10.2305/IUCN.UK.2007.RLTS.T64311A12763519.en (Diamond-backed rattlesnake); Ji, X., Rao, D.-q. & Wang, Y. 2012. *Bungarus multicinctus*. The IUCN Red List of Threatened Species 2012: e.T191957A2020937. https://dx.doi.org/10.2305/IUCN.UK.2012-1.RLTS.T191957A2020937.en (Many-banded krait); Michael, D., Clemann, N. & Robertson, P. 2018. *Notechis scutatus*. The IUCN Red List of Threatened Species 2018: e.T169687A83767147. https://dx.doi.org/10.2305/IUCN.UK.2018-1.RLTS.T169687A83767147.en (Tiger snake). **84–85** BirdLife International. 2018. *Struthio camelus*. The IUCN Red List of Threatened Species 2018: e.T45020636A132189458. https://dx.doi.org/10.2305/IUCN.UK.2018-2.RLTS.T45020636A132189458.en (Common Ostrich, Somali ostrich); BirdLife International. 2016. *Struthio molybdophanes*. The IUCN Red List of Threatened Species 2016: e.T22732795A95049558. https://dx.doi.org/10.2305/IUCN.UK.2016-3.RLTS.T22732795A95049558.en (Common Ostrich, Somali ostrich). **86** BirdLife International. 2020. *Rhea tarapacensis*. The IUCN Red List of Threatened Species 2020: e.T22723206A177987446 (Puna rhea); BirdLife International. 2017. *Casuarius unappendiculatus*. The IUCN Red List of Threatened Species 2017: e.T22678114A118134784. https://dx.doi.org/10.2305/IUCN.UK.2017-3.RLTS.T22678114A118134784.en (Northern cassowary); BirdLife International. 2018. *Dromaius novaehollandiae*. The IUCN Red List of Threatened Species 2018: e.T22678117A131902466. https://dx.doi.org/10.2305/IUCN.UK.2018-2.RLTS.T22678117A131902466.en (Common emu). **88–89** BirdLife International. 2018. *Aptenodytes forsteri*. The IUCN Red List of Threatened Species 2018: e.T22697752A132600320. https://dx.doi.org/10.2305/IUCN.UK.2018-2.RLTS.T22697752A132600320.en (Emperor Penguin). **89** BirdLife International. 2018. *Pygoscelis adeliae*. The IUCN Red List of Threatened Species 2018: e.T22697758A132601165. https://dx.doi.org/10.2305/IUCN.UK.2018-2.RLTS.T22697758A132601165.en (Adelie penguin); BirdLife International. 2018. *Spheniscus mendiculus*. The IUCN Red List of Threatened Species 2018: e.T22697825A132606008. https://dx.doi.org/10.2305/IUCN.UK.2018-2.RLTS.T22697825A132606008.en (Galapagos penguin); BirdLife International. 2018. *Spheniscus demersus*. The IUCN Red List of Threatened Species 2018: e.T22697810A132604504. https://dx.doi.org/10.2305/IUCN.UK.2018-2.RLTS.T22697810A132604504.en (Jackass penguin); BirdLife International. 2018. *Eudyptula minor*. The IUCN Red List of Threatened Species 2018: e.T22697805A132603951. https://dx.doi.org/10.2305/IUCN.UK.2018-2.RLTS.T22697805A132603951.en (Little penguin); BirdLife International. 2018. *Eudyptes chrysolophus*. The IUCN Red List of Threatened Species 2018: e.T22697793A132602631. https://dx.doi.org/10.2305/IUCN.UK.2018-2.RLTS.T22697793A132602631.en (Macaroni penguin). **90–91** BirdLife International. 2017. *Bubo scandiacus* (errata version published in 2018). The IUCN Red List of Threatened Species 2017: e.T22689055A127837214. https://dx.doi.org/10.2305/IUCN.UK.2017-3.RLTS.T22689055A119342767.en (Snowy owl). **92–93** BirdLife International. 2019. *Pandion haliaetus* (amended version of 2016 assessment). The IUCN Red List of Threatened Species 2019: e.T22694938A155519951. https://dx.doi.org/10.2305/IUCN.UK.2019-3.RLTS.T22694938A155519951.en (Osprey). **96–97** BirdLife International. 2018. *Ara ararauna*. The IUCN Red List of Threatened Species 2018: e.T22685539A131917270. https://dx.doi.org/10.2305/IUCN.UK.2018-2.RLTS.T22685539A131917270.en (Blue-and-yellow macaw). **98–99** BirdLife International. 2019. *Hirundo rustica*. The IUCN Red List of Threatened Species 2019: e.T22712252A137668645. https://dx.doi.org/10.2305/IUCN.UK.2019-3.RLTS.T22712252A137668645.en (Barn swallow). **104–105** Leary, T., Seri, L., Flannery, T., Wright, D., Hamilton, S., Helgen, K., Singadan, R., Menzies, J., Allison, A., James, R., Aplin, K., Salas, L. & Dickman, C. 2016. *Zaglossus bartoni*. The IUCN Red List of Threatened Species 2016: e.T136552A21964496. https://dx.doi.org/10.2305/IUCN.UK.2016-2.RLTS.T136552A21964496.en (Eastern long-beaked echidna): Leary, T., Seri, L., Flannery, T., Wright, D., Hamilton, S., Helgen, K., Singadan, R., Menzies, J., Allison, A., James, R., Aplin, K., Salas, L. & Dickman, C. 2016. *Zaglossus bruijnii*. The IUCN Red List of Threatened Species 2016: e.T23179A21964204. https://dx.doi.org/10.2305/IUCN.UK.2016-2.RLTS.T23179A21964204.en (Western long-beaked echidna); Aplin, K., Dickman, C., Salas, L. & Helgen, K. 2016. *Tachyglossus aculeatus*. The IUCN Red List of Threatened Species 2016: e.T41312A21964662. https://dx.doi.org/10.2305/IUCN.UK.2016-2.RLTS.T41312A21964662.en (Short-beaked echidna); Woinarski, J. & Burbidge, A.A. 2016. *Ornithorhynchus anatinus*. The IUCN Red List of Threatened Species 2016: e.T40488A21964009. https://dx.doi.org/10.2305/IUCN.UK.2016-1.RLTS.T40488A21964009.en (Platypus). **106–107** Woinarski, J. & Burbidge, A.A. 2020. *Phascolarctos cinereus* (amended version of 2016 assessment). The IUCN Red List of Threatened Species 2020: e.T16892A166496779. https://dx.doi.org/10.2305/IUCN.UK.2020-1.RLTS.T16892A166496779.en (Koala). **107** Salas, L., Dickman, C., Helgen, K. & Flannery, T. 2019. *Ailurops ursinus*. The IUCN Red List of Threatened Species 2019: e.T40637A21949654. https://dx.doi.org/10.2305/IUCN.UK.2019-1.RLTS.T40637A21949654.en (Bear cuscus); Ellis, M., van Weenen, J., Copley, P., Dickman, C., Mawson, P. & Woinarski, J. 2016. *Macropus rufus*. The IUCN Red List of Threatened Species 2016: e.T40567A21953534. https://dx.doi.org/10.2305/IUCN.UK.2016-2.RLTS.T40567A21953534.en (Red kangaroo); Pérez-Hernandez, R., Lew, D. & Solari, S. 2016. *Didelphis virginiana*. The IUCN Red List of Threatened Species 2016: e.T40502A22176259. https://dx.doi.org/10.2305/IUCN.UK.2016-1.RLTS.T40502A22176259.en (Virginia opossum); Hawkins, C.E., McCallum, H., Mooney, N., Jones, M. & Holdsworth, M. 2008. *Sarcophilus harrisii*. The IUCN Red List of Threatened Species 2008: e.T40540A10331066. https://dx.doi.org/10.2305/IUCN.UK.2008.RLTS.T40540A10331066.en (Tasmanian devil); Leary, T., Seri, L., Wright, D., Hamilton, S., Helgen, K., Singadan, R., Menzies, J., Allison, A., James, R., Dickman, C., Aplin, K., Flannery, T., Martin, R. & Salas, L. 2016. *Dendrolagus goodfellowi*. The IUCN Red List of Threatened Species 2016: e.T6429A21957524. https://dx.doi.org/10.2305/IUCN.UK.2016-2.RLTS.T6429A21957524.en (Tree kangaroo). **108–109** Anacleto, T.C.S., Miranda, F., Medri, I., Cuellar, E., Abba, A.M. & Superina, M. 2014. *Priodontes maximus*. The IUCN Red List of Threatened Species 2014: e.T18144A47442343. https://dx.doi.org/10.2305/IUCN.UK.2014-1.RLTS.T18144A47442343.en (Giant armadillo); Loughry, J., McDonough, C. & Abba, A.M. 2014. *Dasypus novemcinctus*. The IUCN Red List of Threatened Species 2014: e.T6290A47440785. https://dx.doi.org/10.2305/IUCN.UK.2014-1.RLTS.T6290A47440785.en (Nine-banded armadillo); Superina, M. & Abba, A.M. 2014. *Dasypus pilosus*. The IUCN Red List of Threatened Species 2014: e.T6291A47441122. https://dx.doi.org/10.2305/IUCN.UK.2014-1.RLTS.T6291A47441122.en (Hairy long-nosed armadillo); Superina, M., Abba, A.M. & Roig, V.G. 2014. *Chlamyphorus truncatus*. The IUCN Red List of Threatened Species 2014: e.T4704A47439264. https://dx.doi.org/10.2305/IUCN.UK.2014-1.RLTS.T4704A47439264.en (Pink fairy armadillo); Noss, A., Superina, M. & Abba, A.M. 2014. *Tolypeutes matacus*. The IUCN Red List of Threatened Species 2014: e.T21974A47443233. https://dx.doi.org/10.2305/IUCN.UK.2014-1.RLTS.T21974A47443233.en (Southern three-banded armadillo).

110–111 Moraes-Barros, N., Chiarello, A. & Plese, T. 2014. *Bradypus variegatus*. The IUCN Red List of Threatened Species 2014: e. T3038A47437046. https://dx.doi.org/10.2305/IUCN.UK.2014-1.RLTS.T3038A47437046.en (Brown-throated sloth). **112–113** Blanc, J. 2008. *Loxodonta africana*. The IUCN Red List of Threatened Species 2008: e.T12392A3339343. https://dx.doi.org/10.2305/IUCN.UK.2008.RLTS.T12392A3339343.en (African forest elephant & African savannah elephant); Choudhury, A., Lahiri Choudhury, D.K., Desai, A., Duckworth, J.W., Easa, P.S., Johnsingh, A.J.T., Fernando, P., Hedges, S., Gunawardena, M., Kurt, F., Karanth, U., Lister, A., Menon, V., Riddle, H., Rübel, A. & Wikramanayake, E. (IUCN SSC Asian Elephant Specialist Group). 2008. *Elephas maximus*. The IUCN Red List of Threatened Species 2008: e.T7140A12828813. https://dx.doi.org/10.2305/IUCN.UK.2008.RLTS.T7140A12828813.en (Asian elephant). **114–115** Shar, S., Lkhagvasuren, D., Bertolino, S., Henttonen, H., Kryštufek, B. & Meinig, H. 2016. *Sciurus vulgaris* (errata version published in 2017). The IUCN Red List of Threatened Species 2016: e. T20025A115155900. https://dx.doi.org/10.2305/IUCN.UK.2016-3.RLTS.T20025A22245887.en (Eurasian red squirrel). **118–119** Cassola, F. 2016. *Condylura cristata* (errata version published in 2017). The IUCN Red List of Threatened Species 2016: e. T41458A115187740. https://dx.doi.org/10.2305/IUCN.UK.2016-3.RLTS.T41458A22322697.en (Star-nosed mole). **120–121** Louis, E.E., Sefczek, T.M., Randimbiharinirina, D.R., Raharivololona, B., Rakotondrazandry, J.N., Manjary, D., Aylward, M. & Ravelomandrato, F. 2020. *Daubentonia madagascariensis*. The IUCN Red List of Threatened Species 2020: e.T6302A115560793. https://dx.doi.org/10.2305/IUCN.UK.2020-2.RLTS.T6302A115560793.en (Aye-aye); LaFleur, M. & Gould, L. 2020. *Lemur catta*. The IUCN Red List of Threatened Species 2020: e. T11496A115565760. https://dx.doi.org/10.2305/IUCN.UK.2020-2.RLTS.T11496A115565760.en (Ring-tailed lemur); Louis, E.E., Sefczek, T.M., Bailey, C.A., Raharivololona, B., Lewis, R. & Rakotomalala, E.J. 2020. *Propithecus verreauxi*. The IUCN Red List of Threatened Species 2020: e.T18354A115572044. https://dx.doi.org/10.2305/IUCN.UK.2020-2.RLTS.T18354A115572044.en (Verreaux's sifaka); Louis, E.E., Bailey, C.A., Frasier, C.L., Raharivololona, B., Schwitzer, C., Ratsimbazafy, J., Wilmet, L., Lewis, R. & Rakotomalala, D. 2020. *Lepilemur ruficaudatus*. The IUCN Red List of Threatened Species 2020: e. T11621A115566869. https://dx.doi.org/10.2305/IUCN.UK.2020-2.RLTS.T11621A115566869.en (Ring-tailed lemur); Blanco, M., Dolch, R., Ganzhorn, J., Greene, L.K., Le Pors, B., Lewis, R., Louis, E.E., Rafalinirina, H.A., Raharivololona, B., Rakotoarisoa, G., Ralison, J., Randriahaingo, H.N.T., Rasoloarison, R.M., Razafindrasolo, M., Sgarlata, G.M., Wright, P. & Zaonarivelo, J. 2020. *Cheirogaleus medius*. The IUCN Red List of Threatened Species 2020: e. T163023599A115588562. https://dx.doi.org/10.2305/IUCN.UK.2020-2.RLTS.T163023599A115588562.en (Fat-tailed dwarf lemur). **122–123** Watanabe, K. & Tokita, K. 2020. *Macaca fuscata*. The IUCN Red List of Threatened Species 2020: e.T12552A17949359. https://dx.doi.org/10.2305/IUCN.UK.2020-2.RLTS.T12552A17949359.en (Japanese macaque). **124–125** Fruth, B., Hickey, J.R., André, C., Furuichi, T., Hart, J., Hart, T., Kuehl, H., Maisels, F., Nackoney, J., Reinartz, G., Sop, T., Thompson, J. & Williamson, E.A. 2016. *Pan paniscus* (errata version published in 2016). The IUCN Red List of Threatened Species 2016: e. T15932A102331567. https://dx.doi.org/10.2305/IUCN.UK.2016-2.RLTS.T15932A17964305.en (Bonobo); Maisels, F., Bergl, R.A. & Williamson, E.A. 2018. *Gorilla gorilla* (amended version of 2016 assessment). The IUCN Red List of Threatened Species 2018: e.T9404A136250858. https://dx.doi.org/10.2305/IUCN.UK.2018-2.RLTS.T9404A136250858.en (Western gorilla); Plumptre, A., Robbins, M.M. & Williamson, E.A. 2019. *Gorilla beringei*. The IUCN Red List of Threatened Species 2019: e. T39994A115576640. https://dx.doi.org/10.2305/IUCN.UK.2019-1.RLTS.T39994A115576640.en (Eastern gorilla); Humle, T., Maisels, F., Oates, J.F., Plumptre, A. & Williamson, E.A. 2016. *Pan troglodytes* (errata version published in 2018). The IUCN Red List of Threatened Species 2016: e.T15933A129038584. https://dx.doi.org/10.2305/IUCN.UK.2016-2.RLTS.T15933A17964454.en (Chimpanzee). **126–127** Ancrenaz, M., Gumal, M., Marshall, A.J., Meijaard, E., Wich, S.A. & Husson, S. 2016. *Pongo pygmaeus* (errata version published in 2018). The IUCN Red List of Threatened Species 2016: e.T17975A123809220. https://dx.doi.org/10.2305/IUCN.UK.2016-1.RLTS.T17975A17966347.en (Bornean orangutan); Singleton, I., Wich, S.A., Nowak, M., Usher, G. & Utami-Atmoko, S.S. 2017. *Pongo abelii* (errata version published in 2018). The IUCN Red List of Threatened Species 2017: e. T121097935A123797627. https://dx.doi.org/10.2305/IUCN.UK.2017-3.RLTS.T121097935A115575085.en (Sumatran orangutan); Nowak, M.G., Rianti, P., Wich, S.A., Meijaard, E. & Fredriksson, G. 2017. *Pongo tapanuliensis*. The IUCN Red List of Threatened Species 2017: e.T120588639A120588662. https://dx.doi.org/10.2305/IUCN.UK.2017-3.RLTS.T120588639A120588662.en (Tapanuli orangutan). **128–129** Molur, S., Srinivasulu, C., Bates, P. & Francis, C. 2008. *Pteropus giganteus*. The IUCN Red List of Threatened Species 2008: e.T18725A8511108. https://dx.doi.org/10.2305/IUCN.UK.2008.RLTS.T18725A8511108.en (Indian flying fox). **129** Armstrong, K.D., Woinarski, J.C.Z., Hanrahan, N.M. & Burbidge, A.A. 2019. *Macroderma gigas*. The IUCN Red List of Threatened Species 2019: e.T12590A22027714. https://dx.doi.org/10.2305/IUCN.UK.2019-3.RLTS.T12590A22027714.en (Ghost false vampire bat); Bates, P., Bumrungsri, S. & Francis, C. 2019. *Craseonycteris thonglongyai*. The IUCN Red List of Threatened Species 2019: e. T5481A22072935. https://dx.doi.org/10.2305/IUCN.UK.2019-3.RLTS.T5481A22072935.en (Hog-nosed bat); Piraccini, R. 2016. *Rhinolophus ferrumequinum*. The IUCN Red List of Threatened Species 2016: e.T19517A21973253. https://dx.doi.org/10.2305/IUCN.UK.2016-2.RLTS.T19517A21973253.en (Greater horseshoe bat); O'Donnell, C. 2008. *Mystacina tuberculata*. The IUCN Red List of Threatened Species 2008: e. T14261A4427784. https://dx.doi.org/10.2305/IUCN.UK.2008.RLTS.T14261A4427784.en (New Zealand (lesser) short-tailed bat); O'Donnell, C. 2008. *Mystacina robusta*. The IUCN Red List of Threatened Species 2008: e.T14260A4427606. https://dx.doi.org/10.2305/IUCN.UK.2008.RLTS.T14260A4427606.en (New Zealand (greater) short-tailed bat); Monadjem, A., Cardiff, S.G., Rakotoarivelo, A.R., Jenkins, R.K.B. & Ratrimomanarivo, F.H. 2017. *Myzopoda aurita*. The IUCN Red List of Threatened Species 2017: e.T14288A22073303. https://dx.doi.org/10.2305/IUCN.UK.2017-2.RLTS.T14288A22073303.en (Madagascar sucker-footed bat); Barquez, R., Perez, S., Miller, B. & Diaz, M. 2015. *Diaemus youngi*. The IUCN Red List of Threatened Species 2015: e. T6520A21982777. https://dx.doi.org/10.2305/IUCN.UK.2015-4.RLTS.T6520A21982777.en (White-winged vampire bat). **130–131** Goodrich, J., Lynam, A., Miquelle, D., Wibisono, H., Kawanishi, K., Pattanavibool, A., Htun, S., Tempa, T., Karki, J., Jhala, Y. & Karanth, U. 2015. *Panthera tigris*. The IUCN Red List of Threatened Species 2015: e.T15955A50659951. https://dx.doi.org/10.2305/IUCN.UK.2015-2.RLTS.T15955A50659951.en (Tiger). **132–133** Bauer, H., Packer, C., Funston, P.F., Henschel, P. & Nowell, K. 2016. *Panthera leo* (errata version published in 2017). The IUCN Red List of Threatened Species 2016: e.T15951A115130419. https://dx.doi.org/10.2305/IUCN.UK.2016-3.RLTS.T15951A107265605.en (Lion). **136–137** Boitani, L., Phillips, M. & Jhala, Y. 2018. *Canis lupus* (errata version published in 2020). The IUCN Red List of Threatened Species 2018: e. T3746A163508960. https://dx.doi.org/10.2305/IUCN.UK.2018-2.RLTS.T3746A163508960.en (Grey wolf). **138–139** Garshelis, D.L., Scheick, B.K., Doan-Crider, D.L., Beecham, J.J. & Obbard, M.E. 2016. *Ursus americanus* (errata version published in 2017). The IUCN Red List of Threatened Species 2016: e. T41687A114251609. https://dx.doi.org/10.2305/IUCN.UK.2016-3.RLTS.T41687A45034604.en (American black bear); Wiig, Ø., Amstrup, S., Atwood, T., Laidre, K., Lunn, N., Obbard, M., Regehr, E. & Thiemann, G. 2015. *Ursus maritimus*. The IUCN Red List of Threatened Species 2015: e.T22823A14871490. https://dx.doi.org/10.2305/IUCN.UK.2015-4.RLTS.T22823A14871490.en (Polar bear); Swaisgood, R., Wang, D. & Wei, F. 2016. *Ailuropoda melanoleuca* (errata version published in 2017). The IUCN Red List of Threatened Species 2016: e.T712A121745669. https://dx.doi.org/10.2305/IUCN.UK.2016-2.RLTS.T712A45033386.en (Giant panda); McLellan, B.N., Proctor, M.F., Huber, D. & Michel, S. 2017. *Ursus arctos* (amended version of 2017 assessment). The IUCN Red List of Threatened Species 2017: e. T41688A121229971. https://dx.doi.org/10.2305/IUCN.UK.2017-3.RLTS.T41688A121229971.en (Brown bear); Garshelis, D. & Steinmetz, R. 2016. *Ursus thibetanus* (errata version published in 2017). The IUCN Red List of Threatened Species 2016: e.T22824A114252336. https://dx.doi.org/10.2305/IUCN.UK.2016-3.RLTS.T22824A45034242.en (Asiatic black bear); Scotson, L., Fredriksson, G., Augeri, D., Cheah, C., Ngoprasert, D. & Wai-Ming, W. 2017. *Helarctos malayanus* (errata version published in 2018). The IUCN Red List of Threatened Species 2017: e.T9760A123798233. https://dx.doi.org/10.2305/IUCN.UK.2017-3.RLTS.T9760A45033547.en (Sun bear); Dharaiya, N., Bargali, H.S. & Sharp, T. 2020. *Melursus ursinus* (amended version of 2016 assessment). The IUCN Red List of Threatened Species 2020: e. T13143A166519315. https://dx.doi.org/10.2305/IUCN.UK.2020-1.RLTS.T13143A166519315.en (Sloth bear); Velez-Liendo, X. & García-Rangel, S. 2017. *Tremarctos ornatus* (errata version published in 2018). The IUCN Red List of Threatened Species 2017: e. T22066A123792952. https://dx.doi.org/10.2305/IUCN.UK.2017-3.RLTS.T22066A45034047.en (Spectacled bear). **140–141** Do Linh San, E., Begg, C., Begg, K. & Abramov, A.V. 2016. *Mellivora capensis*. The IUCN Red List of Threatened Species 2016: e.T41629A45210107. https://dx.doi.org/10.2305/IUCN.UK.2016-1.RLTS.T41629A45210107.en (Honey badger). **142–143** Rubenstein, D., Low Mackey, B., Davidson, ZD, Kebede, F. & King, S.R.B. 2016. *Equus grevyi*. The IUCN Red List of Threatened Species 2016: e.T7950A89624491. https://dx.doi.org/10.2305/IUCN.UK.2016-3.RLTS.T7950A89624491.en (Grevy's zebra); King, S.R.B. & Moehlman, P.D. 2016. *Equus quagga*. The IUCN Red List of Threatened Species 2016: e. T41013A45172424. https://dx.doi.org/10.2305/IUCN.UK.2016-2.RLTS.T41013A45172424.en (Plains zebra); Gosling, L.M., Muntifering, J., Kolberg, H., Uiseb, K. & King, S.R.B. 2019. *Equus zebra* (amended version of 2019 assessment). The IUCN Red List of Threatened Species 2019: e.T7960A160755590. https://dx.doi.org/10.2305/IUCN.UK.2019-1.RLTS.T7960A160755590.en (Mountain zebra). **144–145** Emslie, R. 2020. *Diceros bicornis*. The IUCN Red List of Threatened Species 2020: e. T6557A152728945. https://dx.doi.org/10.2305/IUCN.UK.2020-1.RLTS.T6557A152728945.en (Black rhino); Emslie, R. 2020. *Ceratotherium simum*. The IUCN Red List of Threatened Species 2020: e.T4185A45813880. https://dx.doi.org/10.2305/IUCN.UK.2020-1.RLTS.T4185A45813880.en (White rhino); Ellis, S. & Talukdar, B. 2019. *Rhinoceros unicornis*. The IUCN Red List of Threatened Species 2019: e. T19496A18494149. https://dx.doi.org/10.2305/IUCN.UK.2019-3.RLTS.T19496A18494149.en (One-horned rhino). **146–147** Lewison, R. & Pluháček, J. 2017. *Hippopotamus amphibius*. The IUCN Red List of Threatened Species 2017: e. T10103A18567364. https://dx.doi.org/10.2305/IUCN.UK.2017-2.RLTS.T10103A18567364.en (Hippopotamus); Ransom, C, Robinson, P.T. & Collen, B. 2015. *Choeropsis liberiensis*. The IUCN Red List of Threatened Species 2015: e. T10032A18567171. https://dx.doi.org/10.2305/IUCN.UK.2015-2.RLTS.T10032A18567171.en (Pygmy hippo). **148–149** Hundertmark, K. 2016. *Alces alces*. The IUCN Red List of Threatened Species 2016: e.T56003281A22157381. https://dx.doi.org/10.2305/IUCN.UK.2016-1.RLTS.T56003281A22157381.en (Moose). **150–151** Cooke, J.G. 2018. *Megaptera novaeangliae*. The IUCN Red List of Threatened Species 2018: e. T13006A50362794. https://dx.doi.org/10.2305/IUCN.UK.2018-2.RLTS.T13006A50362794.en (Humpback whale).

Other Data Credits:

26–27 Food and Agriculture Organization of the United Nations.

30–31 The Genetics Society of America (GSA): The Functional Basis of Wing Patterning in Heliconius Butterflies: The Molecules Behind Mimicry, Marcus R. Kronforst and Riccardo Papa, GENETICS May 1, 2015 vol. 200 no. 1 1-19; https://doi.org/10.1534/genetics.114.172387 / Copyright Clearance Center - Rightslink.

34–35 World Spider Catalog (2020). World Spider Catalog. Version 21.5.

36–37 Aquamaps: Computer generated distribution maps for Asterias rubens (common starfish), with mode lled year 2050 native range map based on IPCC RCP8.5 emissions scenario. www.aquamaps.org, version 10 / 2019. Accessed 12 Oct. 2020.

42–43 This map was retrieved, with permission, from www.fishbase.org/summary/Petromyzon-marinus.html.

48–49 Aquamaps: Scarponi, P., G. Coro, and P. Pagano. A collection of Aquamaps native layers in NetCDF format. Data in brief 17 (2018): 292-296.

50–51 Multidisciplinary Digital Publishing Institute.

68 Rune Midtgaard, RepFocus (www.repfocus.dk)

70–71 Rune Midtgaard, RepFocus (www.repfocus.dk).

76–77 Rune Midtgaard, RepFocus (www.repfocus.dk).

79 Rune Midtgaard, RepFocus (www.repfocus.dk).

88–89 Elsevier.

132–133 PLOS Genetics.

137 Wikipedia: (Dingo).

150–151 NOAA.

ARCTIC OCEAN
Ellesmere Island
Greenland
Greenland Sea
Queen Elizabeth Islands
Beaufort Sea
Baffin Bay
Victoria Island
Baffin Island
Chukchi Sea
Brooks Range
Yukon
Mackenzie
Great Bear Lake
Denmark Strait
Iceland
Norwegian Sea
Bering Strait
Denali (Mount McKinley) 6,194 m (20,320 ft)
Great Slave Lake
Davis Strait
Hudson Bay
Rocky Mountains
Coast Mountains
Canadian Shield
Bering Sea
Aleutian Basin
Aleutian Islands
Aleutian Trench
Gulf of Alaska
Laurentian Mountains
Labrador Sea
British Isles
North Sea
NORTH AMERICA
Vancouver Island
Missouri
Great Lakes
Great Plains
Appalachian Mts
Mendocino Fracture Zone
Iberian Peninsula
Azores
Murray Fracture Zone
Sierra Madre Occidental
Sierra Madre Oriental
Mississippi
North American Basin
Mid-Atlantic Ridge
Madeira
Atlas Mountains
Canary Islands
Ahaggar
Hawaiian Islands
Gulf of Mexico
West Indies
Greater Antilles
Hawaii
Yucatán Peninsula
Cape Verde Islands
Clarion Fracture Zone
Caribbean Sea
Lesser Antilles
Line Islands
Middle America Trench
Niger
ATLANTIC
Clipperton Fracture Zone
Orinoco
Guiana Highlands
PACIFIC
Galápagos Islands
OCEAN
Kiritimati
Polynesia
Amazon
Gulf of Guinea
Amazon Basin
OCEAN
SOUTH AMERICA
Marquesas Islands
Peru-Chile Trench
Andes
Brazil Basin
Angola Basin
Planalto de Mato Grosso
Tuamotu Islands
Peru Basin
Brazilian Highlands
Nazca Ridge
Pitcairn Island
Gran Chaco
Sala y Gomez Ridge
Paraná
Rio Grande Rise
Tubuai Islands
Easter Island
Aconcagua 6,959 m (22,837 ft)
Roggeveen Basin
Pampas
Cape Basin
Southwest Pacific Basin
East Pacific Rise
Argentine Basin
Patagonia
Eltanin Fracture Zone
Falkland Islands
Tierra del Fuego
South Georgia
America-Antarctic Ridge
Cape Horn
Scotia Sea
Drake Passage
KEY
mountain
river
Southeast Pacific Basin
Antarctic Peninsula
Weddell Plain
Bellinghausen Sea
Weddell Sea